Current Biography Yearbook
1999

EDITOR
Clifford Thompson

PRODUCTION STAFF
Gray Young (Manager)
Jacquelene Latif
Beth Levy
Sandra Watson

SENIOR EDITOR
Miriam Helbok

ASSOCIATE EDITOR
Josh Robertson

ASSISTANT EDITORS
Willie Gin
Katrin Sjursen
Olivia Jane Smith

STAFF WRITERS
Mike Batistick
Matthew Creamer
Terence J. Fitzgerald
Yongsoo Park
Constantina Petropoulos

GUEST WRITERS
Edward Moran
Brian Solomon
Selma Yampolsky

RESEARCHER
Tia Brown

EDITORIAL ASSISTANT
Carolyn Ellis

CONTRIBUTING EDITOR
Kieran Dugan

THE H. W. WILSON COMPANY
NEW YORK   DUBLIN

SIXTIETH ANNUAL CUMULATION—1999

PRINTED IN THE UNITED STATES OF AMERICA

International Standard Serial No. (0084-9499)

International Standard Book No. (8242-0988-5)

Library of Congress Catalog Card No. (40-27432)

Table of Contents

PREFACE

The aim of *Current Biography Yearbook 1999*, like that of the preceding volumes in this series of annual dictionaries of contemporary biography, now in its seventh decade of publication, is to provide reference librarians, students, and researchers with objective, accurate, and well-documented biographical articles about living leaders in all fields of human accomplishment the world over. Whenever feasible, obituary notices appear for persons whose biographies have been published in *Current Biography*.

Current Biography Yearbook 1999 carries on the policy of including new and updated biographical profiles that supersede earlier articles. Profiles have been made as accurate and objective as possible through careful researching of newspapers, magazines, the World Wide Web, authoritative reference books, and news releases of both government and private agencies. Immediately after they are published in the 11 monthly issues, articles are submitted to biographees to give them an opportunity to suggest additions and corrections in time for publication of the *Current Biography Yearbook*. To take account of major changes in the careers of biographees, articles are revised before they are included in the yearbook.

Classification by Profession and *Cumulated Index 1991–1999* are at the end of this volume. *Current Biography Cumulated Index 1940–1995* cumulates and supersedes all previous indexes.

For their assistance in preparing *Current Biography Yearbook 1999*, I thank the staff of *Current Biography* and other members of The H. W. Wilson Company's General Reference Department, and also the staffs of the company's Art, Computer, and Manufacturing departments. In addition, I thank Michael Schulze, former vice president in charge of General Reference.

Current Biography welcomes comments and suggestions. Please send your comments to: The Editor, *Current Biography*, The H. W. Wilson Company, 950 University Ave., Bronx, NY 10452; fax: 718-590-4566; email: cthompson@hwwilson.com.

Clifford Thompson

List of Biographical Sketches

xi

Current Biography Yearbook
1999

Current Biography Yearbook 1999

Abbas, Mahmoud

*1935– Palestine Liberation Organization official
and chairman of Fatah. Address: c/o Palestinian
National Authority, Jericho Area, West Bank*

Mahmoud Abbas is the secretary general of the Palestine Liberation Organization (PLO) and the
PLO's chief negotiator. He played an integral role
in the forging of the Declaration of Principles, the
historic peace accord signed in 1993 by PLO chairman Yasir Arafat and Prime Minister Yitzhak Rabin of Israel. The accord led to limited autonomy
for Palestinians in two Israeli-occupied territories—the Gaza Strip and the West Bank town of Jericho—and set a deadline of May 1999 for a final
agreement on the status of all territories seized by
Israel from its Arab neighbors in the wake of the
1967 Arab-Israeli War. The Declaration of Principles also boosted hopes that a lasting peace might
truly be possible among Jews and Arabs in the
strife-torn region once called Palestine.

Known also as the Holy Land, Palestine once encompassed what is now Israel, Jordan, and parts of
Egypt. The history of the Jews in Palestine dates
back to biblical times. By the 19th century Jews
were clustered in urban centers, such as Jerusalem,
Jericho, and Hebron; in rural areas, the population
was made up almost entirely of Arabs. Arabs had
begun to enter Palestine in significant numbers after about 640 A.D., by which time Muslim Arabs
from other Middle Eastern lands had captured the
territory from Byzantium Romans. In the late
1800s, partly to escape violent outbreaks of anti-
Semitism, Jews from Eastern Europe began settling
in Palestine, which was then under the control of
the Ottoman Turks. With the assistance of area
Arabs, Great Britain gained control of Palestine
during World War I. In 1917, in a letter that came
to be called the Balfour Declaration, the British
government promised leaders of the Zionist movement that Britain would help to establish a homeland for Jews in Palestine while recognizing the
rights of non-Jewish Palestinians. Great Britain
also promised Arab leaders that it would support
the founding of independent Arab states in the
Middle East. The declaration contained some
vague wording, and Arab leaders' interpretations
of parts of it differed from those of British officials
and Jewish settlers.

Ahmed Jadallah/Archive Photos

For much of the 20th century, bitter conflict between Jews and Palestinians has plagued the Middle East, first over the land of Palestine and then,
after Israel was proclaimed an independent country, on May 14, 1948, over the 7,992 square miles
that constitute Israel. (For comparison, New Jersey,
which is the fourth smallest among the 50 states in
the U.S., covers 8,722 square miles.) The conflict
erupted into full-scale armed combat on the day
that Israel was proclaimed a state and again in
1956, 1967, and 1973. Almost continuously since
the founding of the PLO, in 1964, the organization
has waged military, guerrilla, and political war
against Israel, with the goal of forming a Palestinian state. Israel, in turn, has repeatedly denounced
the PLO as a terrorist organization, and for many
years, unlike many other countries, refused to recognize it as the official government in exile of Palestinians living under Israeli occupation.

Given this tumultuous history, it came as a great
surprise to countless people in the Middle East and
elsewhere when, on September 13, 1993, Yasir Arafat and Yitzhak Rabin, two former sworn enemies,
stood together on the White House lawn, in Washington, D.C., and—with gentle prodding from Pres-

ident Bill Clinton—shook hands. Their handshake signaled their signing of the Declaration of Principles (a pact also known as the Oslo Accords). In recognition of their contributions as negotiators for the agreement, Arafat, Rabin, and Israeli foreign minister Shimon Peres were jointly awarded the Nobel Peace Prize in 1994.

Although the Nobel Committee did not honor him, Abbas played a role almost as crucial as those of the three prizewinners. In the more than five and a half years since the signing of the Declaration of Principles, he has remained prominent in the effort to gain greater autonomy for Palestinians in the Gaza Strip and the West Bank—a formidable task in the face of the considerable strain between Israel and the Palestinian National Authority (PNA), the governing body formed in May 1994, in accordance with the terms of the Declaration of Principles, to represent Palestinians in the occupied territories. In addition to serving as the chief negotiator for Arafat, who is currently president of the PNA, Abbas heads Fatah, the most influential faction in the PLO and the source of much of Arafat's political support.

Mahmoud Abbas was born in 1935 in the Palestinian town of Safad. He was not yet a teenager when, in 1947, the United Nations General Assembly adopted a resolution calling for the partitioning of Palestine into Arab and Jewish states as a means of easing the sectarian conflict between native Palestinians, who made up the majority of the populace, and the increasingly numerous Jewish settlers. The proposal's implementation was thwarted by opposition from Palestinians and their sympathizers among neighboring Arab nations. In May 1948 British forces withdrew from Palestine, and Israel declared its independence. This turn of events prompted Arab forces from Egypt, Syria, Lebanon, Jordan, and Iraq to attack the fledgling nation. Israel proved surprisingly resilient and actually gained more territory by the time an armistice was reached, in 1949. At about this time Mahmoud Abbas was forced to flee to Syria, where he began living in a refugee camp, along with thousands of other displaced Palestinians. Abbas succeeded in improving his situation: he later studied law at the University of Damascus, in Syria, and then worked in the Persian Gulf during the oil boom there.

Abbas eventually settled in the United Arab Emirates and found work as a civil servant. He cultivated ties with other displaced Palestinians and became a member of Fatah, a group founded in 1959, mostly by Persian Gulf–based Palestinians, with the goal of liberating Palestine. In 1967 Abbas was appointed to Fatah's central committee. That year Fatah and other groups committed to working abroad for Palestinian liberation were further galvanized by Israel's capture of the Golan Heights from Syria, the West Bank from Jordan, and a smaller parcel of land, the Gaza Strip, from Egypt, during the Arab-Israeli War. Through Fatah, Abbas became an associate and supporter of Yasir Arafat,

who was molding Fatah into one of the most prominent and best-organized groups dedicated to the formation of a Palestinian state. Eventually Fatah became the backbone of the PLO, which was created by the coming together of disparate groups. In 1969 Arafat was named chairman of the PLO's executive committee.

In 1980 Abbas was elected to that committee. Four years later he served as head of the PLO's pan-Arab and international-affairs department. Often using the alias Abu Mazen, he came to represent a less militant faction of the PLO, one that was ideologically aligned with Arafat. (Arafat's controversial denunciation of terrorism as the PLO's official tactic, which became public knowledge in 1985, met with disapproval from more-militant factions within the PLO.) Meanwhile, Abbas completed a doctorate on the subject of Zionism at Moscow University, in the Soviet Union, and came to be regarded in the Arab world as an expert on Israeli affairs.

During the late 1980s Abbas emerged as one of the most influential of Arafat's aides. He began serving as Arafat's spokesperson in missions to Eastern Europe and the Gulf states. He also cultivated ties to Europeans sympathetic to the cause of greater autonomy for Palestinians. In 1988 Arafat appointed him the PLO's political directorate chief (a post comparable to that of national security adviser or foreign relations chief in the U.S.), to replace Khalil al-Wazir (also known as Abu Jihad), who had been assassinated by an Israeli commando force. At around that time, the PLO initiated tentative negotiations with Israel, employing King Hussein of Jordan as an intermediary, but little of substance resulted from those forays into diplomacy. In December 1987 talks were put on hold indefinitely after demonstrations and rioting by impoverished Palestinians broke out in Israeli-occupied slums on the West Bank and in the Gaza Strip. This uprising, which came to be known as the intifada, significantly boosted international sympathy for the plight of the Palestinians in the Israeli-occupied territories.

In November 1988 the Palestine National Council, the PLO's parliament in exile, adopted the Algiers Declaration, which proclaimed an independent Palestinian state on the West Bank and the Gaza Strip. In addition, it implicitly recognized Israel's right to exist. That and other signs of decreasing hostility prompted the U.S. to intervene in the peace process and begin a diplomatic dialogue with the PLO. By the end of 1988 some 70 countries had recognized the PLO. However, these developments turned out to be premature harbingers of peace, and the talks among Israel, the PLO, and the United States broke off in 1990, after the PLO refused to condemn a raid into Israel by one of its factions. The PLO further compromised its position by its support of Iraq's invasion of Kuwait, which precipitated the six-week, 1991 Persian Gulf War. Toward the end of 1991, peace talks between representatives of Israel and the PLO started up again. Over the next two years the talks continued with little progress. Because Israel refused to recognize the PLO, the Palestinian delegation at these talks, which were held mostly in Madrid, Spain, consisted of non-PLO Palestinians.

Meanwhile, additional negotiations, between members of Israel's ruling Labor Party and the PLO, were carried out in secret, with Norway serving as host. Abbas met periodically with Israeli foreign minister Shimon Peres in Oslo, Norway, over the course of some eight months beginning in early 1993. Unbeknownst to most of the world, the two diplomats and their delegates succeeded in opening the way for mutual recognition of their respective governments, for the negotiation of a peace settlement, and for a shared commitment to tackle the difficult task of initiating Palestinian self-rule in the occupied territories. "The mood and atmosphere in the entire region will change," Abbas said soon after the talks became known publicly, as quoted by William Drozdiak in the *Washington Post* (September 8, 1993). "We are counting on mutual goodwill to resolve the more difficult problems as we move from the interim to the final stage. The nature of the situation will change all the facts on the ground." Abbas later documented the negotiations in his book, *Through Secret Channels: The Road to Oslo, Senior PLO Leader Abu Mazen's Revealing Story of the Negotiations with Israel* (1995).

Thanks to a significant degree to Abbas's efforts, on September 10, 1993 Arafat and Israeli prime minister Yitzhak Rabin exchanged letters of mutual recognition of their respective governments. For the first time in history, the PLO explicitly recognized Israel's right to exist, and Israel recognized the PLO as the official representative of the Palestinian people. Three days later Rabin and Arafat signed the Declaration of Principles, with the U.S. and Russia serving as co-sponsors of the accord. According to the agreement, an interim Palestinian government was to be established, initially in the Gaza Strip and Jericho and later in the rest of the West Bank. It was the first agreement reached between Israel and Palestinians and Israel's first with an Arab enemy since the peace treaty it forged with Egypt in 1979.

Although the accord was widely hailed as a breakthrough in diplomacy, it met with resistance from both Israeli and Palestinian right-wing groups. In Israel, Rabin and the accord faced opposition from an increasingly powerful conservative element led by the Likud bloc, headed by Benjamin Netanyahu. These groups stressed security concerns and took issue with the accord for recognizing the PLO and conceding power and land to the Palestinians. Some Palestinian groups and more-militant factions of the PLO opposed the accord because it incorporated what they perceived to be too many concessions to Israel.

As stipulated in the accord, mechanisms to facilitate Palestinian self-rule were discussed at a series of meetings held in Egypt, but the talks failed to clear the way for Israeli withdrawal from the Gaza Strip and Jericho on the agreed date—December 13, 1993. Disputes surrounding the terms of the withdrawal as well as disagreement about the precise size of the territory to be handed back to the Palestinians led to additional talks later that same month. Subsequent disagreements concerning security provisions for Israeli settlers in the Gaza Strip and disputes over limitations on the passage of Palestinians from Egypt into the Gaza Strip and from Jordan into Jericho contributed to the delays. The differences narrowed during meetings held in February 1994. Then, that month, the peace process was halted, after an Israeli gunman killed 29 Muslims who were worshiping at a mosque in the West Bank town of Hebron, the long-time base of a small group of staunch right-wing Israeli settlers. The killer, Baruch Goldstein, who was slain at the scene by surviving worshipers, had been a follower of the extreme-right-wing Israeli politician and rabbi Meir Kahane (who was killed in New York in 1991 by an Egyptian-American Muslim). A definitive agreement implementing the Oslo Accords was eventually signed by Rabin and Arafat in Cairo in May 1994. Subsequently, on May 10, 1994, Palestinian officials assumed responsibility for maintaining security in the Gaza Strip, and three days later Israeli troops withdrew from Jericho, thereby ending 27 years of Israeli occupation of the town.

In accordance with the 1993 peace accord, increasing numbers of West Bank towns came under PLO control throughout 1994 and 1995. Concurrently, the debate among Israelis over the concessions grew increasingly heated. On November 4, 1995, in the midst of this controversy, Rabin was assassinated by Yigal Amir, a right-wing Israeli zealot who regarded an expansion of Palestinian autonomy as a virtual death warrant for Israel. Although it was feared that Rabin's murder would further jeopardize the peace process, Shimon Peres, who took over as prime minister without a challenge from the Likud Party, continued to implement the measures to which Israel had previously agreed.

On May 29, 1996, ahead of schedule, Israelis went to the polls in the nation's first direct election for prime minister. Peres's decision to hold early elections was widely perceived as an effort to take advantage of the wave of popular support that he and the Labor Party had enjoyed in the wake of Rabin's murder. But by the day of the election, that advantage had evaporated, and in a surprising turn of events, Netanyahu beat Peres, with a margin of 50.4 percent of the vote to Peres's 49.5 percent, a difference of about 29,000 votes out of approximately three million cast. The prevailing opinion was that the many civilian fatalities that had resulted from four Arab suicide attacks against Israelis between February 28 and March 4, 1996 had spurred many voters to reevaluate the 1993 peace accord and the leadership of the Labor Party.

The installation of the Likud government ushered in a new era in the peace process. Netanyahu, who enjoyed support from less moderate Israelis as well as those who had settled in what was now Palestinian territory, held fast to his party's campaign pledges and pursued a more hard-line stance toward Palestinian self-rule. The government stressed Israeli security concerns and categorically ruled out the eventual creation of an independent Palestinian state. Moreover, it pledged additional financial and other support for Israeli settlers in the West Bank and also slowed the proposed withdrawal of Israeli residents and troops from most of Hebron. In effect, he reneged on the concessions that had been agreed upon in the 1993 peace accord.

Meanwhile, in a popular election held in the West Bank and the Gaza Strip in January 1996 for the presidency of the Palestinian National Authority (PNA), Arafat had won solidly, gaining 88 percent of the vote. Arafat's mandate as president of the PNA, which serves as the governing body of the Palestinian people in those territories, was also bolstered by the success of Fatah: 50 Fatah members were elected to the 88-member Palestinian Council, the PNA's legislature, in the January plebiscite.

During much of 1996 the Likud government and the PNA made little headway toward peace. In August of that year, in another move that amounted to a reversal of the peace process, Netanyahu's government lifted a four-year-old freeze on the expansion of Israeli settlements in the West Bank and the Gaza Strip. Denouncing the new policy as a flagrant violation of the 1993 Oslo agreement, Arafat called for Palestinians and other Arabs to participate in a general strike in the occupied territories on August 29. Additional hostility erupted at the end of September in response to the opening of a new entrance to an ancient tunnel located near Muslim holy sites in Jerusalem. The Labor government had delayed opening the entrance indefinitely, in deference to Palestinians' feelings about a place they considered holy. But Netanyahu approved the opening, citing reports that the site would suffer no physical damage. In light of the heightened tension sparked by these events, U.S. president Bill Clinton arranged an emergency summit at the White House. Held on October 2 and attended by Netanyahu, Arafat, and King Hussein of Jordan, the meeting led to high-level negotiations between Netanyahu and Arafat. Thanks in part to increasing pressure on Netanyahu from the U.S., in January 1997 an agreement was reached that resolved the Hebron impasse and provided for the gradual withdrawal of Israeli troops from more of the West Bank by mid-1998.

In spite of the January 1997 agreement, there was little progress toward Palestinian self-rule, in part because of the Likud government's insistence on measures to ensure the security of Israeli citizens and its refusal to implement troop withdrawals in the West Bank, as had been agreed upon in the 1993 accord. As the chief negotiator for the PLO, Abbas continued to meet with his Israeli and U.S. counterparts. However, the meetings often resulted only in agreements to hold more meetings. In March 1997 Abbas resigned as the PLO's chief negotiator, as a way of protesting Israel's withdrawal of only 9 percent of the Israeli troops stationed in the West Bank. (Palestinians had expected that about 30 percent of the soldiers would leave.) Abbas later returned to his post, but much of 1997 saw Israel and Palestinians mired in a stalemate; the PNA demanded that Israel live up to the terms of the 1993 peace agreement, and the Likud government insisted that they would not do so without additional safety guarantees from the PNA. To support their position, the Israeli government cited the increasing influence of militant factions within the PLO and semimilitary Palestinian groups such as Hamas and Islamic Holy War.

A freeze on negotiations ended contact between the Israeli government and the PNA for much of 1998. During that time the U.S. attempted to serve as a mediator to forge a compromise position that would entail an Israeli withdrawal from an additional 13 percent of the West Bank. In return, the Palestinian government would commit to implementing additional antiterrorism measures, including the extradition or imprisonment of suspected terrorists sought by Israel and the revising of the Palestinian National Covenant, the PNA's de-facto charter, to exclude any call for the destruction of Israel. The American plan was accepted by the PNA but met with resistance from Israel. Netanyahu's government has insisted that it would concede 13 percent of its territory in the West Bank on the condition that 3 percent be set aside as a national preserve, in which Israel would hold veto power over construction projects. By mid-1998 negotiations had once again stalled; Netanyahu had not proceeded with the unconditional withdrawal of Israeli troops from the disputed territory in the West Bank, a step that the Palestinians and the U.S. had sought as a condition for resuming negotiations. In October 1998, in another blueprint for peace, Netanyahu, Arafat, Clinton, and the ailing King Hussein of Jordan signed what is known as the Wye River Memorandum, commonly referred to as the Wye River Accords. Subsequently, Israel completed the first of three planned withdrawals from the West Bank and released 250 Palestinian prisoners. Nevertheless, the agreement soon began to unravel. Violence erupted in the West Bank and the Gaza Strip, and, with each side blaming the other for the trouble, Netanyahu halted further withdrawals.

The impasse has continued into 1999. At one point Arafat announced that, with or without the acquiescence of Israel, he would declare a Palestinian state on May 4, 1999, the deadline stipulated by the Oslo accord for a final peace settlement. But in late April he canceled that plan, and May 4, a "sacred date," as he had referred to it, passed as a normal workday for Palestinians, with only a few inconsequential marches held to protest Arafat's backing away from his unilateral declaration.

On May 18, 1999 the people of Israel voted Prime Minister Netanyahu out of office and chose Ehud Barak, the chairman of the Labor Party and a former chief of staff of the Israeli army, to succeed him. With Barak in the prime minister's post, hopes arose throughout the world that the Middle East peace process, which had remained at a standstill during much of Netanyahu's time in office, would be reinvigorated. Such hopes were soon realized. On September 9, 1999 Barak and Arafat signed the Sharm el Sheikh Memorandum, which established a five-month timetable for the implementation of measures that had been agreed upon in the Wye River Memorandum. According to the memorandum, by January 20, 2000 Palestinians will control 41 percent of the West Bank. The agreement also set September 13, 2000 as the target date for the creation of a final peace settlement between Israel and the PNA.

Many Israelis and Palestinians already consider the existence of a Palestinian state a reality. "Whether [the Netanyahu government] like[s] it or not, our state is already established," Arafat told members of the media on May 3, as reported by

Deborah Sontag in the New York Times (May 5, 1999, on-line). And Sontag quoted Yossi Sarid, the leader of Meretz, an Israeli political party, as saying, "The Palestinian state doesn't already exist? Then I don't know what a state is. They have territory, an elected president and an elected parliament. They have an anthem, a flag, a symbol and relations with more than 100 countries. High-ranking visitors come and go. They have an army that is called a police force."

Mahmoud Abbas has been described as having a "Western presence" and a good command of English. According to various sources, Arafat regards Abbas as his likely successor. — Y.P.

Suggested Reading: New York Times A p1+ Aug. 30, 1993, with photos, A p12 Sep. 14, 1993, with photos, A p3 Dec. 28, 1993, with photo, I p1 Sep. 13, 1997, with photo, A p6 July 23, 1998, A p5 July 25, 1998; Washington Post A p21+ Sep. 8, 1993, with photos

Selected Books: Through Secret Channels: The Road to Oslo, Senior PLO Leader Abu Mazen's Revealing Story of the Negotiations with Israel, 1995

Abrams, Floyd

July 9, 1936– Lawyer; First Amendment advocate. Address: c/o Cahill Gordon & Reindel, 80 Pine St., New York, NY 10005-1702

Hanging on a wall in Floyd Abrams's office at the New York City law firm Cahill Gordon & Reindel is a page from the January 13, 1898 edition of the French newspaper L'Aurore. A birthday present from his wife, Efrat, the century-old page contains what is considered by Abrams and many other people to be the finest piece of journalism ever published: the article "J'accuse" ("I accuse"), by the great French novelist and social reformer Emile Zola. In "J'accuse," which took the form of an open letter to the president of France, Zola denounced as an instance of widespread anti-Semitism in the French military the court-martial of Captain Alfred Dreyfuss, a wealthy Alsatian Jew who had been convicted of treason on the basis of fabricated evidence and sentenced to solitary confinement. Zola, in turn, was tried for and found guilty of libel and escaped imprisonment only by going into temporary exile in England. Thanks to a significant extent to "J'accuse," Dreyfuss's plight was not forgotten, and he was eventually exonerated. Upon noticing in early 1998 that the hundredth anniversary of the publication of Zola's article was just days away, Abrams assembled a gaggle of media luminaries and clients—among them the 60 Minutes journalist Morley Safer, the writer Dominick Dunne, and the media watchdog Steve Brill—to

Courtesy of Cahill, Gordon & Reindel

toast Zola's achievement. In the New Yorker (January 26, 1998), Jeffrey Toobin reported that Abrams told his guests that "J'accuse" remained an example of how "good speech triumphed over bad speech."

Although Abrams was celebrating the triumph of "good" speech, he firmly believes that society must accept the dissemination of "bad" speech, too. Freedom of expression—a right preserved for Americans in the First Amendment to the United States Constitution—is a principle Floyd Abrams holds dear; in his opinion, the nation's preservation of freedom of speech and of the press is what makes the U.S. the envy of the world. But those freedoms, he feels, cannot be taken for granted. The question of whether limits should ever be imposed on forms of expression, and if so, how far those limits should extend, has been a matter of endless debate; during the last three decades of that debate, Floyd Abrams has become the nation's premier advocate of the First Amendment. He has led the struggle to define and expand the parameters of what the media can report and the individual can say. His work has led him to argue more than a dozen cases before the Supreme Court of the United States, including the groundbreaking Pentagon Papers case, and he has served as the legal representative of many of the nation's leading print and broadcast news organizations. Commenting on Floyd Abrams and his body of work, William J. Brennan, who served on the Supreme Court from 1956 to 1990, once said, as quoted by Jeanie Kasindorf in New York (December 21, 1992), "The First Amendment has no better friend."

The son of Isidore Abrams, a successful businessman, and his wife, Rae (Eberlin) Abrams, Floyd Abrams was born on July 9, 1936 in New York City. He grew up in the upper-middle-class section of Forest Hills, in the borough of Queens. A gifted student, he graduated from high school at the age of 15 and then entered Cornell University, in Ithaca, New York, where he studied government. As a college senior Abrams wrote a paper that argued for more judicial control over the press. "My views then were quite a bit different than they later became," he told Kenneth P. Nolan in an interview for the American Bar Association's quarterly publication Litigation (Fall 1996). "I basically advocated . . . that we come closer to the English system of punishing the press more often for what it published rather than freeing it still more to publish potentially harmful materials." His thesis, he explained to Jeanie Kasindorf, was "a very appreciative look at the English system, where, after someone's arrested, all you're allowed to report on is what happens in court, period. . . . I wouldn't have gone all the way to the English system, but I would have increased the judges' power to hold journalists in contempt for out-of-court commentary during a trial."

After graduating from Cornell, with a B.A. degree, in 1956, Abrams enrolled at the Yale University Law School, in New Haven, Connecticut, where he completed a law degree in 1960. He was admitted to the New York State bar in 1961. From 1961 to 1963 he served as a clerk for a U.S. District Court judge in Delaware. Later in 1963 he joined Cahill Gordon & Reindel, and in December of that year, he married the Israeli-born Efrat Surasky. He has been a partner in Cahill Gordon & Reindel since 1970.

Abrams's first years with Cahill were spent pursuing corporate law, but he was destined to do greater things—at least, that's what a soothsayer told him in 1967. During a visit to New Delhi, India, that year, he accompanied a law-school classmate of his to her fortune-teller, who at one time had predicted the future for Jawaharlal Nehru, India's first prime minister. The fortune-teller "was in a storefront with mice running around, sitting in a white sheet," Abrams recalled to Kasindorf. "He spoke only Hindi. He knew I was an American lawyer; that's all. I was 31, and I had not yet done any First Amendment work. And he told [Abrams's friend], 'Before he is 35, he will go to his country's capital and do something very famous.' . . . The Pentagon-papers case ended 10 days before my 35th birthday."

Whether or not Abrams's success was written in the stars, his introduction to First Amendment law was serendipitous. It occurred in the late 1960s, when his law firm took on a number of cases involving what Abrams described to Kenneth P. Nolan as "the creation of a First Amendment privilege for confidential sources for journalists." "There was very little law on that topic and very little press law in general at that time," he explained to Nolan. "Most of the law established by the Supreme Court under the First Amendment really started in the 1960s, with very few exceptions." Abrams was assigned to the case of Paul Pappas, a reporter for the NBC television network, who refused to name his sources—specifically, people at an office of the Black Panthers—before a Massachusetts grand jury. The U.S. Supreme Court agreed to issue a decision on his case conjointly with two other, similar cases, one involving a New York Times journalist, Earl Caldwell, and the other a Kentucky reporter, Paul M. Branzburg, each of whom had refused to testify before grand juries about certain events they had witnessed. While working on the Pappas case, Abrams began to work closely with the Times in-house general counsel, Jim Goodale.

While the Pappas et al. case was moving forward, the Times came into possession of a government study of U.S. involvement in Southeast Asia from about 1948 through 1968. The study was essentially an in-depth history of the U.S.'s role in the Vietnam War and the events that led up to it. Commissioned by Secretary of Defense Robert McNamara in 1967, during the administration of President Lyndon B. Johnson, and completed in 1969, soon after President Richard Nixon took office, the document consisted of 3,000 pages of analysis and 4,000 pages of official documents, most of which spelled out various policy decisions. The document, which came to be known as the Pentagon Papers, chronicled numerous embarrassing foreign-policy miscues on the part of the U.S. government that had never been disclosed. Filling 40 book-length volumes, the study was considered so top secret that according to rumor even Presidents Johnson and Nixon did not know of its existence. A disenchanted former government official, Daniel Ellsberg, who had drafted part of the document, had leaked it to the *Times*, which on June 13, 1971 began to reprint sections of the papers and publish articles based on them.

When federal government officials learned of the leak, the Department of Justice petitioned for an injunction barring publication of the information contained in the papers, arguing that publicly revealing such material posed a threat to national security and thus was prohibited by the Espionage Statute of 1917. A temporary restraining order was granted on June 15, marking the first time in American history that a gag was placed on the press. When Jim Goodale called the *Times*'s lawyers at the firm Lord Day & Lord to represent the newspaper in court, they refused, contending that publishing the Pentagon Papers was illegal and unpatriotic. Goodale then turned to Floyd Abrams and Abrams's former law professor Alexander Bickel, who had helped Abrams draft briefs for his defense of Pappas. Though they had little prior practical experience in that area of the law, Abrams and Bickel agreed to take the case.

"Bickel and I came into my office . . . in the middle of the night, and we were alone in the library fishing out the Espionage Act and reading it to see what it said," Abrams recalled to Kenneth P. Nolan. "Neither of us knew. Nor did Attorney General [John] Mitchell. He even cited the wrong section of the act in his telegram to the *Times*." The Espionage Statute, which Congress passed during World War I, ruled illegal actions that "willfully obstruct the recruiting or enlistment service of the United States" or promote disloyalty within the ranks of the armed services. Discovering no judicial precedent for restraint of the press, Abrams and Bickel petitioned the Supreme Court of the United States to hear the case. The petition was granted.

The Pentagon Papers case, officially known as *New York Times v. the United States* and involving the *Washington Post* as well as the *Times*, came before the Supreme Court that same month. "The assistant attorney general in charge of internal security was Robert Mardian, and he was in court staring at us malevolently," Abrams has recalled. "Bickel [who had immigrated to the U.S. from Europe at age 12] turned to me and said, 'Every time he looks at me, I think he wants to deport me back to Romania.' There was that feeling in the air." In arguing their case, representatives of the executive branch of the government maintained that the executive branch was the sole judge of national security and as such should be allowed to stop the press from publishing any document whose dissemination would, in its view, threaten that security. Abrams and Bickel, on behalf of the *Times*, countered that the freedoms granted under the First Amendment override the powers of the executive branch, par-

ticularly in this case, where, according to the newspaper, the government was motivated by the desire to censor rather than protect.

On June 30, 1971, by a vote of six to three, the Supreme Court ruled in favor of the *Times*. While leaving open the possibility that in future situations, the probability of demonstrable dire and immediate consequences might justify restricting the publication of government documents, the court weighed heavily in favor of freedom of the press and expanded the power of the media. The subsequent publication of the remainder of the Pentagon Papers aroused widespread disillusionment about U.S. military involvement in Vietnam. Moreover, many historians cite the appearance of the papers and events connected with their publication as factors that led President Richard Nixon to authorize illegal methods to discredit Ellsberg and others whom the president had placed on his notorious "enemies list." Among the many petty burglaries carried out by White House operatives was the break-in of the Democratic Party's Watergate offices, an action that led to Nixon's downfall.

As for Abrams, his views about freedom of the press had begun to change with his involvement in the Pappas case, and by the time the Supreme Court had handed down its decision in *New York Times v. the United States*, he stood firmly in favor of a strict reading of the First Amendment. "If you were involved in [the Pentagon Papers] case, you don't need hypothetical cases to teach you the potential harm of government control over the press," he told Jeanie Kasindorf. "Here you had a president in power, supported by the people around him, who quite literally wanted to suppress speech, and to suppress it not because it would do any immediate harm to the country but because it just wasn't viewed as a good idea to let these revelations about how we became involved in the war in Vietnam be made public."

The Pappas case was decided almost one year to the day after the *Times*'s Pentagon Papers victory. In a five-to-four ruling dated June 29, 1972, the Supreme Court declined to extend special privilege to the relationship between a reporter and his or her sources. The majority (Justice Byron R. White, who was appointed to the court by President John F. Kennedy, and four justices appointed by President Nixon) ruled that "the public interest in pursuing and prosecuting those crimes reported to the press" had greater importance than its interest in future news that might be withheld from reporters because of the possibility that confidentiality would not be maintained. One of the dissenting justices, Potter Stewart, warned that public officials might try "to annex the journalistic profession as an investigative arm of government"—in other words, allow public officials to call on journalists and their sources at will to aid government probes. But Justice Lewis F. Powell Jr., who voted with the majority, contended that "the solicitude repeatedly shown by this court for First Amendment freedoms" made it unlikely that such attempts would succeed.

The preparation Abrams has habitually undertaken prior to arguing before the Supreme Court is a lesson in legal practice. Noting how grueling and incisive the questions posed by the justices can be, Abrams commits himself to "start fresh" on a case days before the opening of argument. "I start fresh in the sense of rereading all the [relevant] cases," he told Kenneth P. Nolan. "I certainly start fresh in the sense of rereading the entire record and annotating it. If I am asked by some member of the Court where something is that is relevant, I can find it." Abrams has also developed some unorthodox methods for preparation. "I used to make great use of my daughter when she was about 11, 12, 13 because she had just about the right attention span, three or four minutes, like a lot of judges," he explained to Nolan. Abrams's daughter, Ronnie, and his son, Daniel, have followed in his footsteps: both are attorneys.

Though Abrams continues to handle cases involving several different fields of law, it is his representation of media clients that has kept him in the public eye. Recently and most notably, Abrams provided legal support for National Public Radio's legal-affairs correspondent Nina Totenberg and for CNN. The former case dates to October 1991, when Totenberg broke the story of Anita Hill's allegations of sexual harassment at the hands of then–Supreme Court nominee Clarence Thomas. In response to Totenberg's account, the Senate special counsel tried unsuccessfully to force her to reveal her sources. As Totenberg told Jeanie Kasindorf, Abrams's help went beyond legal advice. "He was brilliant, supportive, patient. He was my lawyer, my advisor, my psychiatrist, my friend." The CNN case involved a news story that aired in June 1998 on the premiere of *NewsStand*, a feature produced by CNN in collaboration with *Time* magazine. Titled "Valley of Death," it focused on the claim that in 1970, during a mission called Operation Tailwind, U.S. military forces used nerve gas in Laos while pursuing defectors from the Vietnam War. *Time* magazine later picked up the story and published an article about it. After the Defense Department labeled the story untrue, CNN hired Abrams to investigate independently the validity of the account. In a report filed on July 2, 1998 and reprinted on CNN's Web site, Abrams wrote, "A decision was made by CNN to broadcast accusations of the gravest sort without sufficient justification and in the face of substantial persuasive information to the contrary. CNN should retract the broadcast and apologize to the public and, in particular, the participants in Operation Tailwind." CNN subsequently retracted the story and apologized for airing it (and also fired its two producers).

In addition to his continuing advocacy of the First Amendment in court, Floyd Abrams is a champion for the press beyond the bar. As a sought-after public speaker, he strives to present the press in a positive light. "It is a constant teaching process," he told Jeanie Kasindorf. "Journalists are a hard group of people to love, but they're an easy group to defend. Even though there are abuses, what they do matters." Abrams taught as a visiting lecturer at Yale in 1974–80 and 1986–89 and at Columbia University, in New York City, from 1981 to 1985. Since 1994 he has served as the first William J. Brennan Jr. visiting professor on First Amendment issues at the Columbia University Graduate School of Journalism. "I have spent a lot of years teaching law students what to do after journalists are in trouble," Floyd Abrams has said, as quoted by Nadine Brolan in the *New York Times* (March 2, 1994). "I thought I could make a little more of a contribution keeping the journalists out of trouble." — T.J.F.

Suggested Reading: *CNN.com* (on-line); *Litigation* p28+ Fall 1998; *New York* p114+ Dec. 21, 1992, with photo; *New Yorker* p28+ Jan. 26, 1998; *Who's Who in America, 1999*

Kim Kulish/Archive Photos

Abramson, Leslie

Oct. 1943– *Criminal defense lawyer. Address: c/o Simon and Schuster, 1230 Ave. of the Americas, New York, NY 10020*

According to the criminal lawyer Leslie Abramson, her job is not to defend the innocent—a description that, she has acknowledged, applies to few of her clients. Rather, she believes her responsibility is to defend people who are "less culpable than charged and in peril of unjust punishment," as she explained to Curt Schleier for *Biography* (September 1997). Abramson is resolutely opposed to capital punishment, and since its reinstatement in California in 1977, she has helped many of her clients avoid the death penalty. "I'm drawn to cases where very nice people and very good people are accused of crimes because the law lags behind psychology, like people who have been abused and battered," she told Seth Mydans for the *New York Times* (December 20, 1993). "I don't like to see people suffer, and I don't like the hard-heartedness of other people towards them. . . . I'm very drawn to these people because they are delightful clients and they are decent human beings and they need me." Abramson is best known for defending Erik Menendez, who, with his brother, Lyle, shot and killed his parents in 1989 while the couple were watching television. "Fired with moral indignation, rolling her eyes, tossing her wild yellow hair, shrugging, scribbling, whispering, raising objections," Mydans reported during one of the two Menendez trials, Abramson "dominates a courtroom." "Admired or detested," he wrote, "Leslie Abramson is a lawyer who is always noticed."

The second of three children, Leslie Abramson was born in October 1943 in the Bronx, a borough of New York City, and she spent most of her childhood in the neighboring borough of Queens. When she was six years old, her parents divorced. About eight years later, after her mother remarried, Leslie's father disappeared, presumably because he did not want to continue to pay child support. Leslie received a postcard from him saying goodbye. The sadness she felt over the loss of her father was not mitigated by the new home she moved into with her mother and stepfather. Her stepfather, she told Schleier, "was a yeller and a screamer and he controlled us with the anger in his voice." While describing the possible effects of child abuse to the court during the Menendez trials, Abramson revealed that her mother, too, had been abusive. "My mother was a very good person," she told the jury. "She had a very bad temper, and she used her hands a lot; she was a hitter." Once, when Abramson was about 12, her mother struck her with a wooden coat hanger—"something she had never done before," Abramson said. According to Mydans's retelling of the story, Leslie was so upset that she grabbed the hanger from her mother and hit her back. After that her mother never hit her again. "No one would have accused me of being a happy child," Abramson once said, as quoted by Mydans.

When she was very young, Abramson was disturbed by accounts of World War II, and particularly of the Holocaust, that she heard from adults in her family, which is Jewish. "I remember being three years old and hearing about it," she told Schleier. "I saw pictures. The idea that someone in the world would have killed me just for being born who I was never left me. That's an overwhelming idea for a child, that someone out there wants to kill me, kill all of us." She believes that her childhood fear of the Holocaust contributed to her eventual decision to become a lawyer. "What victims— or people who feel like victims—tend to do is . . .

go out to rescue people," she told Schleier. "In that way they sort of rescue themselves. It certainly influenced a desire [in me] to help the oppressed or the enemies of the government or who the government declared was its enemies. Governments have always made me nervous."

One of her grandmothers, Fanny Kaprow, would probably have agreed with that last remark. Kaprow was an organizer for the International Ladies Garment Workers Union and, according to Schleier, a Communist. "She believed in women making their own way. She was willful and stubborn," Abramson told David Ellis for *People* (October 11, 1993). Like her grandmother, who, she has said, was a major influence in her life, Abramson is a staunch liberal, and she has devoted much of her energy to fighting for the rights of those who she believes are treated unjustly. "Because I was raised to have empathy for ground-down people, it was easy to become their lawyer," Abramson told Ellis.

As a youngster Abramson tried to forget her feelings of unhappiness by reading comic books; in college she turned to what she has described as "obsessive" cheerleading . "I was not popular," she told Schleier. "I don't know why. You have to ask all the guys who ignored me. I was four feet, 11 inches. I was skinny. I was flat-chested. I had frizzy hair. Looking back at pictures, I still think I was quite cute. But I also had a motor mouth. I was very tough, very defensive, not willing to play dumb girl. So I wasn't the flavor of the month."

After graduating from a local four-year college, in about 1964, Abramson married a pharmacist and moved to California. Almost immediately after the birth of her daughter, Laine, in about 1965, she enrolled in the law program at the University of California in Los Angeles. Balancing the commitments of motherhood with her studies, she completed her law degree in 1969 and then took a job in the Los Angeles public defender's office. That same year she and her husband divorced. "My real childhood was after the divorce," she told Schleier. "It was the first time I had a dating life."

Abramson worked in the Los Angeles public defender's office for seven years. During that time she became known for her relentlessness in defending her clients, and she was eventually assigned to the city's toughest cases. She left that position and joined a private practice in 1977—the same year that capital punishment was legalized in California. The possibility of a client of hers receiving a death sentence profoundly affected Abramson's approach to her work. "If someone is going to die it's serious business," she told Ellis. "I guess the peril brings out the rescuer impulse in me." In cases in which Abramson felt that obtaining an acquittal was virtually impossible, she focused on getting a reduced sentence. As an example, Schleier cited the case of a man who had participated in an armed robbery that went awry, resulting in the deaths of a police officer and several other people. Because Abramson's client was "on the lookout" rather than at the immediate scene of the murders, she succeeded in saving him from the death penalty. Another client—a contract killer—is quoted in Abramson's memoir, *The Defense Is Ready* (1997), as saying, "Leslie was so good. For a while there she even had me believing I didn't do it." Prior to the Menendez trials, in Abramson's 14 capital murder cases (cases in which, if found guilty, the accused may be sentenced to death), only one of her clients received a death sentence. "Maybe [judges and prosecutors] are used to people rolling over and putting their feet up in the air and playing dead. But I don't think that's representing my client," Abramson told Ellis.

Abramson has said that she has constantly struggled against judges who hold what she described to Schleier as a conservative, "let's-lock-'em-up" attitude toward all defendants. "There's nothing wrong with locking people up who commit crimes. But there's something wrong when the judge's mindset becomes focused on punishing everybody," she said. "He's supposed to be fair. He's supposed to be evenhanded. He's supposed to be concerned with the issues of guilt or innocence. Half of them behave as if they're still in the prosecutor's office, which is where most of them came from." Abramson has also expressed disapproval of the way that facts are sometimes miscommunicated to the public by the media. "It's pretty obvious that the media has had a negative effect on the judicial system," she told Schleier. "It's always important to [be sure the press has access] to courts, so we can watch that the courts don't go kaflooey. But they're not watching it from the sense of being fair to people. They are more unfair than the system ever could be. They try, they convict, before there's even a trial. They make snap judgments. It's all sensationalistic."

The first of the two trials of Erik and Lyle Menendez began in 1993, four years after the brothers shot and killed their wealthy parents, Jose and Kitty Menendez, in their Beverly Hills home. Abramson represented Erik, the younger brother, who was 22 years old at the outset of the first trial; Jill Lansing headed the defense team for Lyle, and two separate juries were sworn in. Erik and Lyle admitted killing their parents; they rested their case on a plea of self-defense: they contended that their father, Jose Menendez, a successful entertainment executive, had regularly sodomized them for many years while their mother stood watch. Sometime before the murders, according to their courtroom testimonies, the brothers, then 18 and 20 years old, threatened to report their father's abuse; Jose, in turn, threatened to kill them. At that point, the defense claimed, the brothers—fearing that their father really would kill them—purchased the two 12-gauge shotguns with which they committed the murders. The prosecution claimed that Erik and Lyle had cold-bloodedly murdered their parents so that they could get their hands on their inheritance, about $14 million. They pointed to the spending spree on which Erik and Lyle had em-

barked right after the slayings as proof of the brothers' mercenary motive.

In defending Erik Menendez, Abramson used what in legal jargon is called the "abuse excuse." Usually employed in the defense of battered wives, the abuse excuse is a way of exculpating defendants who have been psychologically damaged by their abusers and have lashed out violently, often at a time when—like Lyle and Erik Menendez—they are not in an immediately threatening situation. "These boys were not responsible for who they turned out to be," Abramson told the jurors, as quoted by Mydans. "They were just little children being molded. They were never free of the clutches of their parents. When you terrorize people and they react from terror, you pretty much get what you sowed. It's not an issue of individual responsibility. It's an issue of people getting caught in events, and they act precisely as you would expect them to."

Abramson, who aimed for prison sentences of four years each for Erik and his brother instead of the death sentence, called the case "*the* most interesting and most important" of her career, according to Mydans. Not surprisingly, her tactics were aggressive, and the testimonies that she included in the defense, Mydans reported, "had most of the courtroom in tears along with [the brothers]." The writer Dominick Dunne, who covered the trial for *Vanity Fair* and who became one of Abramson's most vociferous critics, described the jury as being "in the thrall of a tiny, mesmerizing, brilliant, overpowering 50-year-old woman who dominated the proceedings from the beginning to the end, leaving everyone in the dust behind her. She was impassioned. She was moving. . . . She was possessed with fervor. She was often enraged. She was also mean, harsh, crude, and gutter-mouthed." Several times during the trial, the judge, Stanley Weisberg, threatened to find Abramson in contempt of court. After one such warning from Weisberg, she explained to him, "I'm only saying there's only so much unfairness one can bear." On another occasion the judge criticized her for shaking her head defiantly each time he made a ruling. Yet another time he called her "unprofessional" for comforting Erik Menendez during breaks after emotional testimonies. "That's one of the myths, one of the vast piles of B.S., that if you're a woman, you get emotionally attached to your clients, but if you're a man, you don't," Abramson told Ellis.

The first trial of Erik and Lyle Menendez, which lasted for more than six months, resulted in hung juries and was therefore declared a mistrial. Each of the six women on the jury deliberating the case against Erik voted to acquit him of the murder charges, while the six men voted to convict him. As she had done many times before in her career, after the trial was over, Abramson invited "her jurors," as she referred to the women on the panel, to her home for dinner, and asked them to explain to reporters the reasoning behind their decision to acquit Menendez. Abramson also attempted, albeit unsuccessfully, to plea bargain to avoid a retrial. "We are willing to plead to something," she told Mydans for the *New York Times* (February 1, 1994). "We think that they will never get a unanimous verdict, and we're just going to be wasting a tremendous amount of time and money and emotion on a retrial. I think a reasonable plea bargain that gives both sides something can be worked out."

A plea bargain was not granted, however, and in April 1994 Abramson agreed to represent Erik Menendez again. Because the Menendez estate, from which her fees for the first trial had been paid, was depleted, the state of California hired Abramson as a court-appointed lawyer for the case, for $125,000 per year. According to an Associated Press article in the *New York Times* (April 6, 1994), the judge believed that the taxpayer expense was justified because Abramson's familiarity with the case would allow the trial to proceed much more quickly than it would if a new public defender took over. During the second trial of the brothers, which began in March 1995 before a single jury, Abramson was accused of editing the notes of the psychiatrist William Vicary, who had treated Erik prior to the murders. This accusation complicated but did not halt the trial, and on March 20, 1996 the Menendez brothers were convicted of first-degree murder; later, they were sentenced to life in prison with no possibility of parole. In 1997 the California Bar Association dropped the investigation of Abramson's alleged tampering with evidence.

In 1996 Abramson signed a contract with the Twentieth Television production company to host her own daytime talk show, to be called *Exclusive with Leslie Abramson*. The show was slated for broadcast on the Fox television network, and although Abramson is opposed to the presence of television cameras in the courtroom, she told Sue Karlin for *Working Woman* (March 1996) that she would use video clips from trials on her show. "Why shouldn't I have access to the same advantages as all the other journalists?" she asked.

Abramson's book, *The Defense Is Ready: Life in the Trenches of Criminal Law*, was published in 1997. In her review of the book, Judith Newman wrote, "What's really scary is that Ms. Abramson's account is so persuasive, so seductive that by the end of *The Defense Is Ready*, a fascinating and infuriating chronicle of her most notorious murder trials, you'll like her felons too. . . . She makes us understand the horrors of young lives thrown away because of power, drugs, and violence." Abramson has made many guest appearances on Court TV, and she was a commentator on ABC's *Nightline* during the murder trial of O. J. Simpson. In her most recent court case, she represented Jeremy Strohmeyer, a 19-year-old who was charged with the sexual assault and murder of a seven-year-old girl in Nevada. In a plea bargain agreed to in the fall of 1998, just before his trial was to begin, Strohmeyer was sentenced to life in prison without the possibility of parole.

Leslie Abramson has been married to the *Los Angeles Times* writer Tim Rutten since 1977. In addition to Abramson's daughter, the couple have an adopted son, Aidan. — C.P.

Suggested Reading: *ABCnews.com* May 30, 1998; *Biography* p50+ Sep. 1997, with photos; *CourtTV.com*; *New York Times* A p30 Nov. 19, 1993, with photo, D p9 Dec. 20, 1993, with photo, A p10 Feb. 1, 1994, with photo, Apr. 6, 1994, with photo, VII p20 Mar. 16, 1997, I p24 Oct. 12, 1997; *People* p52+ Oct. 11, 1993, with photos; *Working Woman* p15 Mar. 1996, with photo

Eric Draper/Associated Press

Akebono
(ah-kay-boh-noh)

May 8, 1969– Sumo wrestler. Address: c/o Japan Sumo Association, 1-3-28 Yokozuna Sumidaku, Tokyo 130, Japan

In 1993, after a string of tournament victories, the sumo wrestler Akebono was elevated to the rank of *yokozuna* and thus became, in his words, "something like a god" in sumo-crazy Japan. During the approximately 300 years since the designation "*yokozuna*" originated, only 67 wrestlers have reached this exalted status, which brings with it much honor, moderate fortune, and—in recent years, at least—the adulation of young fans. What made Akebono's promotion even more significant is that he is Hawaiian, not Japanese, and he was the first (and up until a short time ago, the only) foreigner to become a *yokozuna*. Many traditionalists view sumo wrestling as half sport, half religion; indeed, to those who consider a *yokozuna* an acolyte of the guardian spirits of Shintoism, Akebono's ascension might be said to be comparable to the selection of a non-Catholic as pope.

At six feet eight inches, Akebono is one of the tallest sumos ever to don a silk loincloth and wrestle in Japan's tournaments. Currently weighing around 500 pounds, he is also among the heaviest. The heavyweight boxer Lennox Lewis, by contrast, is only 245 pounds, while Gilbert Brown, the formidable defensive tackle for the Green Bay Packers, tips the scales at about 350 pounds; thus, in terms of weight, it would take about two Lewises or a little less than one and a half Browns to equal one Akebono. The few sumo wrestlers who are larger than Akebono include the retired Hawaiian sumo Konishiki (born Salevaa Atisanoe), who weighed about 570 pounds when he was active in the sport. Emmanuel Yarbrough, a 700-pound behemoth, wrestles in the international sumo federation but not in Japan. Size is not the crucial factor in sumo, but it certainly makes a difference. Akebono has won nine tournaments, mostly in 1993 and 1994, the years in which he dominated the sport. Since 1994, however, he has been plagued by injuries and has won only two tournaments; for the most part, he has been overshadowed by the smaller, more agile Takanohana, who became a *yokozuna* in 1994 and has racked up an impressive 20 tournament victories. Although the 30-year-old Akebono is probably past his prime as a sumo wrestler, he has continued to perform respectably in the ring, occasionally upsetting Takanohana as well as some younger contenders.

The eldest of three children, Akebono was named Chad Rowan when he was born, on May 8, 1969, in Hawaii. His mother, Jan Rowan, is Hawaiian-Cuban; the ancestry of his father, Randy Rowan, is Irish, Portuguese, Chinese, and Hawaiian. With his two brothers, Randy Jr. and George, Chad grew up in the Lamanauwa area of the island of Oahu. As a high school student, when he weighed about 270 pounds, he aimed to play basketball professionally. He was an all-state player and won a basketball scholarship to Hawaii Pacific College. But after redshirting his freshman year at Hawaii Pacific, he quit basketball and soon afterward dropped out of college.

Rowan was earning the minimum wage pulling weeds for a nursery when he met Jesse Kuhaulua, an American who had wrestled in Japan for 20 years under the name Takamiyama and had become the first American to win a grand sumo tournament. Kuhaulua later became a Japanese citizen and opened a wrestling stable under the name Azumazeki Oyakata. Frequently traveling back to the United States in search of talent, he had scouted the famous 570-pound Hawaiian sumo wrestler Konishiki. In 1988 Kuhaulua offered to train Rowan and his brother George.

After overcoming the resistance of their mother, Chad and George Rowan moved to Japan to undertake the traditional, monastic discipline of sumo wrestling. Japanese sumo wrestlers typically live in communal, unheated dorms called *beyas*, in which a hierarchical culture prevails. A stable's top wrestler is virtually a lord. His room is apart from the others, and he eats and bathes before his stablemates. Junior wrestlers are expected to act deferentially toward him and others above them in the hierarchy—even if their "superiors" are younger than they are—and they must clean rooms, scrub toilets, launder clothes, help prepare meals, fetch drinks, and wipe the sweat from their seniors' faces.

The Rowan brothers found it extremely difficult to adjust to their new circumstances. "For the first half a year I cried every night," Chad Rowan told David Sanger for the *New York Times* (February 17, 1993). "I thought that I was a man but I found out that I was a baby." George eventually left Japan, but Chad stuck with the training. "When I first got here I hated doing all that stuff: taking out the trash and cooking and cleaning," he recalled to Karl Taro Greenfeld and Christopher Seymour for the *Village Voice* (March 31, 1992). "I used to lie awake at night or during those long, boring afternoons and think about running away. But I didn't know how to get around Tokyo and I couldn't speak Japanese. I was scared and alone. But I also wanted to prove to everybody that I was tough, that I could take it." Much later he came to appreciate the psychological benefits of the training; as he told Greenfeld and Seymour, he realized that "sumo teaches you discipline and respect and hard work."

Like the other wrestlers in the stable, Rowan gorged himself to increase his weight greatly. Sumo wrestlers usually skip breakfast, work out in the morning, then have their first meal around noon, by which time they have developed an enormous appetite. They eat a dish called *chanko nabe*, a high-calorie, high-protein stew of fish, meat, and vegetables. (During his early days in Japan, Rowan added ketchup to his portion to make it taste more familiar.) "I often eat four bowls of it at a sitting, and also chow down a couple of dozen chicken nuggets, four or five eggs (both raw and fried), and lots of pickled vegetables, fried noodles, and grilled fish," he wrote of his eating habits for *Life* (May 1995). "I eat rice, of course (about three pounds a day), and I drink a gallon of iced tea with my meal. Then I take a three-hour nap. That's important for my training too. Dinner is the same as lunch, but I sometimes ask the kitchen to cook up a package or three of hot dogs—they're very good with rice." Within just a few years, Akebono had increased his weight by over 50 percent.

Adopting the professional name Akebono, which means "sunrise," Rowan quickly distinguished himself as a wrestler. Sumo wrestlers battle in a ring, called a *dohyo*, that is about 14 feet in diameter. Matches tend to be short, lasting from a few seconds to a minute. The object is to drive one's opponent out of the ring or to make him touch the floor with any part of his body besides the soles of his feet. Striking with closed fists, grabbing hair, gouging eyes, biting, kicking, and using choke holds are illegal moves. Virtually every other move is legal. The 70 recognized techniques for winning include various combinations of slapping, pushing, dodging, tripping, grabbing, and throwing. Akebono's relatively high center of gravity was thought to be a disadvantage, but he soon realized that he could use his height and his long arms to grab an opponent around the shoulders and face and shove him out of the ring.

Six sumo grand tournaments are held in Japan each year. Each tournament lasts 15 days, with wrestlers facing a different opponent each day. The wrestler with the best record wins the tournament. At the lower levels, having a winning record in a tournament—eight wins to seven losses or better— is often enough to move up the ranks; in the higher ranks, winning tournaments is necessary for promotion. There are 10 ranks, divided into two divisions of five ranks each. Of the 800 professional sumo wrestlers in Japan, only about 40 are in the upper division, consisting of the top five ranks. Akebono debuted in March 1988, and in his first 18 tournaments, he compiled winning records. In 1991, at the age of only 21, he achieved the ranking of *sekiwake*, which is sumo's third-highest rank.

Akebono wasn't the only non-Japanese sumo wrestler enjoying great success at that time. Konishiki was the first foreigner to reach the rank of *ozeki*, which is sumo's second-highest rank. The rules of promotion to *yokozuna* are unspecific and highly subjective. Some judges consider two consecutive tournament victories the benchmark for promotion; other judges emphasize the wrestler's *hinkaku*, which translates roughly as "dignity" or "grace." Although Konishiki had never won two consecutive tournaments, some observers thought that he stood a good chance of being promoted to *yokozuna* by about 1992. That possibility sparked anguished debate in the country and even led to death threats against Konishiki. The debate, in which some Japanese traditionalists insisted that foreigners should not be promoted to *yokozuna*, prompted international criticism and accusations that the sport was racist.

It is possible that the international outcry over the question of Konishiki's potential promotion made it easier for Akebono to be promoted to the highest rank after he began dominating the sport. He won his first tournament in July 1992, followed by consecutive victories in November 1992 and January 1993. Unlike Konishiki (who as of mid-1999 remained an *ozeki*), Akebono was always a humble winner and never ruffled any feathers in his public statements; thus he could not be accused of lacking *hinkaku*. After his victory in January 1993, sumo traditionalists could produce no good arguments for denying him a promotion to the top rank. In January 1993 he officially became Japan's 64th *yokozuna*. Having participated in just 30 tournaments, Akebono became a *yokozuna* faster than any other sumo wrestler in history. Demonstrating his *hinkaku* at the promotion ceremony, he stated, as quoted in the *Washington Post* (January 30, 1993), "I humbly accept this honor. I will devote myself to the utmost in my practice so as not to disgrace the position of [*yokozuna*]." Following his promotion Akebono won tournaments in July, September, and November 1993 and March 1994.

Akebono, who has said that he feels more Japanese than American, became a Japanese citizen in 1996. That move ensures that if he chooses, he will be able to open his own wrestling stable and become a trainer when he retires. A *yokozuna* is expected to retire if he starts losing at tournaments. He cannot be demoted, though; the title *yokozuna* is permanent.

Although not nearly as lavishly compensated as a star athlete in the U.S., Akebono has led a comfortable life since becoming a *yokozuna*. His salary is about $200,000 a year, and he earns more from endorsements. His perks include servants. Star sumo wrestlers are considered sex symbols in Japan, and it is not uncommon for them to date waif-like models. The position also entails a busy schedule of charity, benefit, and ceremonial appearances; in "autograph" sessions, Akebono inks his hand and stamps prints of it for his fans. At the opening ceremonies of the 1998 Winter Olympics, in Nagano, Japan, he performed the ancient rite of purification.

In 1994 Akebono underwent surgery on both his knees, and he has never recaptured his previous dominance in sumo wrestling. Since the operations he has had only two tournament victories, in March 1995 and May 1997—though he has had winning records. His main rival has been Takanohana, the 65th *yokozuna*, who dominated the tournaments between 1994 and 1997 and, with 20 tournament victories, is one of the greatest *yokozuna* of all time. More recently, Akebono has faced stiff competition from Takanohana's brother, Wakanohana, who, in 1998, became the 66th *yokozuna*, and Musashimaru (born Fiamalu Penitani), a Hawaiian who, in May 1999, became the 67th (and the second non-Japanese) *yokozuna*.

In October 1998, after years of announcing himself in love with various women, Akebono married the former Christine Kalina. A slender, five-foot four-inch American, she is the first non-Japanese woman to wed a sumo star. Should Akebono become a stable master, she would be expected to cook food for the young wrestlers in his group and to work with sponsors and fan clubs. He and his wife have one child. — W.G.

Suggested Reading: *Chicago Tribune* V p1+ Feb. 21, 1993, with photos; *Japan Quarterly* p193+ Apr.–June 1993; *Life* p102 May 1995, with photo; *New York Times* A p4 Jan. 26, 1993, with photo, B p15 Feb. 17, 1993, with photo; *People* p87 Feb. 2, 1993, with photo; *Sports Illustrated* p12 Jan. 10, 1994; *Village Voice* p156+ Mar. 31, 1992, with photo; *Washington Post* A p22 Mar. 18, 1991, with photo, A p1 Jan. 25, 1993, with photos, D p1 Jan. 30, 1993, with photos, B p1 May 28, 1996, with photo, D p8 Feb. 11, 1998, with photo

Courtesy of the Embassy of the Republic of Azerbaijan

Aliyev, Heydar

May 10, 1923– President of the Republic of Azerbaijan. Address: Office of President Aliyev, Baku, Azerbaijan

President Heydar Aliyev of Azerbaijan, one of the world's most oil-rich countries, has ruled his native land for nearly six years through authoritarian means. A leader of Azerbaijan in its days as a Soviet republic, he rose to power again after the threat of a civil war forced the duly elected president, Abulfez Elchibey, to flee Baku, the nation's capital. Aliyev—who had been drifting in political obscurity since 1987, when then–USSR general secretary Mikhail Gorbachev forced him from his position as deputy chairman of the Soviet Council of Ministers—held a questionable election in late 1993, in which he garnered nearly 99 percent of the vote. Supporters point out that the president, who won another dubious election in October 1998, has played an integral part in maintaining peace in a region plagued by instability and ethnic conflict. Having watched Aliyev enforce the Armenian-Azeri cease-fire of 1993 and keep domestic bloodshed at a minimum, Western nations have come to recognize him as the rightful Azeri head of state. Many outsiders, however, question the motives behind the international community's support of Ali-

yev; since the fall of the Soviet Union, Azerbaijan's territory has been reopened to Western investors, and given the country's vast oil reserves, many feel that Aliyev's stamp of legitimacy as a leader is based primarily on his willingness to share Azerbaijan's one important natural resource. Now 76 years of age, Aliyev has turned his nation's dilapidated capital into a cosmopolitan mix of venture capitalists, international crime lords, and global diplomats while transforming his once economically ailing nation into a financial and political force in the Caucasus region.

Heydar Alirza oglu Aliyev was born on May 10, 1923 in the ancient Azerbaijan city of Nakhichevan, capital of the Azeri region of the same name, which is separated geographically from the rest of Azerbaijan by Armenia. His mother, Izzet-khanum, raised Aliyev and his four brothers and three sisters while his father, Alirza, worked for the railroad. An excellent student, Aliyev studied at the M. Azizbeyov Industrial Institute before entering Baku State University, where he studied history. Upon graduation he went to work for the government of the Nakhichevan Autonomous Soviet Socialist Republic, as the region had become known in 1924. Displaying leadership potential, Aliyev advanced quickly within the Communist Party, working his way up the ranks of the State Security Committee of Azerbaijan. In 1967 he became chairman of that powerful organization, and he developed a reputation as a sycophantic lieutenant of then–Soviet general secretary Leonid I. Brezhnev. By the time Aliyev was granted leadership of the Azeri republic, in 1969, he had become known as one of the most corrupt politicians in all of the Soviet Union. His alliance with Brezhnev served Aliyev so well—he showered the general secretary with lavish gifts in order to remain in the leader's good graces—that in the early 1980s Aliyev became a full member of the Soviet Politburo, the most powerful inner body of the USSR.

When Mikhail Gorbachev became the Soviet general secretary, in the mid-1980s, it appeared at first that Aliyev's star would continue to rise. Aliyev aimed his campaign of flattery and bribery at the new Soviet leader, and for a time it seemed to be working; in 1986 Aliyev became deputy chairman of the USSR Council of Ministers. But soon Gorbachev's sweeping reforms brought attention to Aliyev's alleged corruption. The Azeri leader was removed from power in 1987.

By the time the Soviet Union began to crumble, in the early 1990s, Aliyev was a disgraced, out-of-work politician living in relative obscurity in his native Nakhichevan. He held several positions within the government there, but these posts were primarily decorative and carried little power. Aliyev's official Web site, *president.az*, states that he officially left the Communist Party in 1991, around the time that bloody skirmishes broke out between Armenians and Azeris, rekindling ethnic animosity between the two nations that can be traced back to the Middle Ages. The Soviet Union, then in the last throes of disintegration, was powerless to stop the fighting, and upon the USSR's official demise, in late 1991, Armenians mounted an all-out offensive on Nagorno-Karabakh, a long-disputed territory within Azerbaijan that has a majority population of ethnic Armenians. To this day, the Armenians, although not officially in control of Nagorno-Karabakh, hold the substantial areas of land they gained during the conflict.

In 1992 Azerbaijan held its first free elections as a sovereign nation, voting in as president Abulfez Elchibey, a scholar and former dissident who headed a broad coalition called the Popular Front. Carrying a landslide 60 percent of the vote, Elchibey enjoyed enormous popularity in his first few months as president, but in the long term he proved unable to put an end to rampant governmental corruption, restore the economy to health, or regain the land in Nagorno-Karabakh lost to the Armenians. By 1993 Elchibey was under intense pressure to resign—primarily from his prime minister, Surat Husseinov, a millionaire wool processor and provincial warlord. Husseinov, who maintained an army of his own and also served as defense minister, security minister, and interior minister in the coalition government, finally marched on Baku in an attempt to take control of the government.

It was then that Elchibey turned for help to Aliyev, who had been serving for the previous year as the leader of the still-autonomous state of Nakhichevan; in the New York Times (July 4, 1993), Serge Schmemann compared this move to "calling in the fox to restore order among the chickens." Indeed, within a short time Elchibey was in exile and Aliyev had named Husseinov his prime minister and head of all security forces in return for the post of acting president. In the election held on October 3 of that year, Aliyev won close to 99 percent of the vote.

In order to stabilize his position, Aliyev brought international attention to Azerbaijan by inviting several Western oil companies to join his government in a deal to tap the country's vast oil supply, much of which lies off Azerbaijan's Caspian Sea coast. The plan worked: American oil companies, most notably Penzoil, saw huge potential profits while the United States government saw a chance to wean itself from Middle Eastern oil. "Oil is our strategy, it is our defense, it is our independence," Aliyev's foreign-policy adviser Vasa Gilizade told Jeffrey Goldberg for the New York Times Magazine (October 4, 1998). "Iran is dreaming dreams of Azerbaijan and if the Russians were strong, they would colonize Azerbaijan. But they can't because Aliyev invited the whole world in to watch." With so many international representatives in the country, fighting between Azeri and Armenian forces was soon quelled, and a cease-fire was signed. Although relations between the two sides remain tense, the cease-fire is still in effect.

With the fighting at an end, the economy of the region healthier, and international interest in the country's oil reserves at peak levels, Azerbaijan, in 1995, found itself at peace for the first time in half a decade. The United States—which for a time had officially recognized the exiled Elchibey as president—soon recognized Aliyev's administration in return for rights to exploit the oil reserves. In mid-1998 Aliyev announced that new elections would be held; as expected, despite the presence of several fervent opposition parties, Aliyev won handily.

Although often referred to as a warlord in the Western press—deposed president Elchibey, who remains critical of the Azeri government, told the New York Times (October 11, 1998) that Aliyev is an "autocrat who toys with democracy"—Aliyev is at the same time considered one of the few people with the influence and political know-how to maintain peace in the volatile region. "You may laugh, but [Azerbaijan is] the most democratic country in the Caucasus region," Alexie Malashenko of the Carnegie Endowment in Moscow told a New York Times (October 11, 1998) reporter. In response to critics who disagree with that assessment, Aliyev told Jeffrey Goldberg, "No one was born a democrat in this country, including myself. This is not your country. Maybe if we establish conditions of democracy, my grandson will have democracy." Aliyev accepted an invitation to the White House in 1997, and his visit greatly enhanced his regional prestige. With the support of the United States, lucrative oil deals with Western companies, and a treaty with Georgian president Eduard Shevardnadze to transport Azeri oil, Aliyev appears to have a firm hold on the leadership of his country's 7.5 million people.

A widower, Aliyev has a son, a daughter, and six grandchildren. — M.B.

Suggested Reading: National Review p22+ Dec. 27, 1993; New York Times A p3 June 23, 1993, with photo, A p2 July 1, 1993, with photo, D p4 July 4, 1993, with photos, I p16 Sep. 21, 1997; New York Times (on-line) Mar. 24, 1999, with photos, Apr. 22, 1999, with photos; New York Times Magazine p50+ Oct. 4, 1998, with photos; Newsweek p30 July 9, 1984; Washington Post C p2+ Feb. 1, 1998

Alou, Felipe
(ah-LOO, fay-LEE-pay)

May 12, 1935– Manager of the Montreal Expos. Address: c/o Montreal Expos, P.O. Box 500, Station M, Montreal, Quebec H1V 3P2, Canada

"We are not American, we are different, maybe that is why we are able to survive," the Dominican-born Felipe Alou, manager of the Montreal Expos, told Steve Marantz for the Sporting News (June 21,

Felipe Alou

Courtesy of the Montreal Expos

1993). "When I came over here I didn't know English. I was supposed to be a darkie. I had no baseball teaching. I didn't know about the racial encounters that I was going to endure. I didn't know about winter or snow. I survived that. Hundreds of Latins will tell you the same thing. The only reason we survived is because we are different. We are survivors. We never give up; we never quit. We quit when we die. This is the spirit of the Latin. We are a hard people to put away."

Alou entered American baseball in 1955, when he signed with the New York (later San Francisco) Giants. After three years in the minor leagues, he joined the Giants' major-league club, becoming only the second Latino ever to play in the majors. Upon retiring, in 1974, he returned to the Dominican Republic for two years, then took a job with the Expos-affiliated minor-league team in West Palm Beach, Florida. In 1992 he took over as the Expos' major-league manager. Since that time Alou has become one of the most respected managers in the game, keeping a team with one of the lowest payrolls in baseball in play-off contention almost every year. With more than 500 wins in his six full years as manager of the Expos, Alou has proven himself to be one the greatest motivators of players the game has ever known. In 1994 he was named the National League manager of the year.

Many feared that the 1999 season would find Alou, the Expos' all-time winningest manager, in a Los Angeles Dodgers uniform; indeed, the Dodgers pursued him vigorously, hoping to have him fill their vacant managerial position, but at the last minute Alou signed a three-year, nearly $6 million contract with the Expos. Discussing Alou, the Chicago Cubs manager, Jim Riggleman,

told Joseph A. Reaves for the *Chicago Tribune* (July 21, 1995), "I think one of his biggest strengths is that he is a very nice man, a very compassionate man who understands how the moves you make in this game can affect a person. . . . He does everything based on what is good for the ball club, but Felipe has a knack for doing that and still having the respect and understanding for his players."

Felipe Rojas Alou was born on May 12, 1935 in the small town of Haina, in the Dominican Republic. His father, Jose Rojas, a poor blacksmith and carpenter, had had two children with a woman who died young; one of the grandsons of that union is New York Mets relief pitcher Mel Rojas, Felipe Alou's half-nephew. Felipe's mother was Donã Virginia, whose father was a gardener for Dominican dictator Rafael Trujillo Molina. She and Jose had two other boys: Matty, born in 1939, and Jesus, born in 1942. All three sons would eventually play in the major leagues. "My father did three things for me," Alou told Michael Farber for *Sports Illustrated* (June 19, 1995). "He bought me a pair of spikes when I was 14, though later he cut off the cleats and wore those shoes to work in his shop because he didn't have any other shoes. He gave me permission to sign my contract. And he was behind me till the day he died." Although the boys played baseball often when they were kids, fishing was the activity that their father encouraged. "It's just the way we are in the part of the world where I grew up," Alou told Stephen Brunt for the *Toronto Globe and Mail* (July 23, 1994). "That's what we did when we were kids. The days when we got up and we knew that there was nothing to eat. Go fishing and try to catch something. And if you don't catch something, well you don't catch something. There's nothing you can do about that. It's the same in baseball. My feeling is this. I've never been afraid to lose my job. I believe the players benefit from the fact that they don't see panic from the manager during the games."

As a boy Felipe talked about wanting to become a surgeon, and his family enrolled him at the University of Santo Domingo, where the state paid for his tuition. After a time, however, it became clear the family could not afford to pay for necessities, such as books, clothes, and food, that were not covered by the state, and his university career came to an end. Felipe's physical abilities had been known to the government, apparently through word of mouth, since he was a teenager, and partly as a result he participated in the 1955 Pan American Games, as a sprinter and javelin thrower. In the following year he nearly made the Dominican Olympic track team. "But economic necessity steered him towards baseball," Brunt wrote. Under the Trujillo regime, Dominicans were not normally allowed to play professional baseball until after they had represented the country in three international competitions. But as it happened, during the 1955 games one of the national baseball team's players was suspended for assaulting a member of Trujillo's security staff, and at the last minute Alou was recruited to play. Alou was the first baseman and cleanup hitter for the Dominican team, which defeated the U.S. for the gold medal in Mexico City that year. A scout for the then–New York Giants was at the final game, watching as Alou got four hits in five at-bats. Within months, Alou had signed with the team.

Alou was sent first to the minors—as a player with the Evangeline league—but a problem arose when that segregated organization questioned his heritage. "Was I black?" Alou said to Marantz. "I didn't know. The Alous are white. The Rojases are black. We didn't know. And when we came over here that was a little difficult." Unsure about his racial classification, the league allowed Alou to play for a time while "Jim Crow's finest minds debated," as Marantz put it. When it was decided that Felipe was indeed black, the Giants sent him to Cocoa Beach, Florida, to compete in the Florida State league, where, Marantz wrote, "blacks were allowed to play so long as after the games they stayed on their side of the railroad tracks." Alou arrived in Cocoa Beach with a limited English vocabulary and only $12 in his pocket. In 1956 he led the league in hitting, with a .380 batting average and 99 RBIs. When he returned to the Dominican Republic that winter, he was given his old bed and told to observe the family's longstanding 9 p.m. curfew. "Here I was 21 years old and I have been on my own for six months, and now I've got to be in bed by nine o'clock," Alou told Marantz. "It is no wonder that the Alou brothers got to be baseball players for a long, long time, because of the training and discipline we got in the home. I thank my father and mother every time I can for preparing us for anything in life. When we left the house, we were ready for anything."

During the 1958 season Felipe was called up to play his first major-league game for the Giants (who had moved to San Francisco that year); he thus became the first native-trained Dominican to play in the big leagues and the second Dominican of any description to do so. (Ozzie Virgil, who grew up in New York, was the first.) Alou batted .275 in his first full year with the team. Two years later his brother Matty joined the Giants, and in 1963 Jesus followed suit. On September 10 of that year, in a game against the New York Mets, Felipe, Matty, and Jesus Alou became the first trio of brothers ever to play in the same major-league game.

Felipe Alou's first wife, Maria Beltre, was 15 years old when she met the future baseball star, and she dropped out of high school to marry him two years later, in a civil ceremony that took place on February 2, 1959. Felipe II was born nine months later, followed by Maria, Lois, and finally Moises, who would grow up to play for the Expos under his father. In 1968, two years after Moises's birth, the couple divorced. "To tell you the truth," Maria told Marantz, "the divorce was a relief. A baseball wife, you live and die with your husband's performance. You watch the TV and read the papers to see if things go well for him. Things

go bad, you've got to keep up his spirits. It's not easy." Alou later married the American Beverly Martin, with whom he had three daughters—Christina, Cheri, and Jennifer. After he and Martin divorced, he married Elsa Brens, a Dominican, and fathered Felipe Jose Rojas and Luis Emilio Rojas, both of whom are now considered excellent baseball prospects. Alou and Brens divorced in 1985. His current wife, Lucie Gagnon, is French-Canadian; their children are Valerie and Felipe Jr. "I joke that I like marriage so much that I got married four times," he told Stephen Brunt for the *Toronto Globe and Mail*. He later told Farber, "People ask me how a man who likes to be home with his family gets married four times. All of the evils that go on in life, the evils of the life of a traveling ballplayer, I wasn't immune to that. But I loved all my wives and children. And all my children were by my wives. . . . I wasn't there all the time, but I knew their shoe sizes. There are 10 kids now, and they've never been at the same place at the same time. But they're all friends. They all visit each other. They all went to school. In this time of drugs and alcohol and corruption and lies and so on, I haven't seen any of that from them." One of Alou's children, Felipe II, died in 1976, in a swimming accident.

Alou spent his first six years in the majors with the Giants, playing in all seven games of the 1962 World Series (the Giants lost to the Yankees). He went on to play with five other clubs: the Atlanta Braves (1964), the Oakland Athletics (1970), the Yankees (1971), the Expos (1973), and, finally, the Milwaukee Brewers (1974). By the time he retired, in 1974, he had become only the 31st player in major-league history to amass 2,000 hits and 200 home runs. He ended his playing career with 852 RBIs, three All-Star Game appearances (1962, 1966, and 1968), and a lifetime .286 batting average. Upon his retirement, Alou returned to the Dominican Republic. "I really didn't want to stay in baseball," Alou told Brunt. "I had all kind of misleading hopes that I was going to go back home to my country and make money there." He showed up with $11,000 worth of video equipment, wanting to produce television programs about sports in the Dominican Republic. He later became involved in a venture to establish pro baseball on the island. Both efforts failed, and by 1977 his prospects had begun to look bleak. Later that year, he accepted a job managing the Expos' Class A affiliate in West Palm Beach. According to Brunt, when asked about his hopes upon returning to baseball, Alou replied, "To stay alive."

As his managerial career progressed, it became clear that Alou had a flair for leadership. But "like so many Latins before him, he wasn't ever going to be given a chance to manage in the bigs," as Brunt put it. He coached all over the nation with various minor-league teams, including those in Denver, Wichita, Indianapolis, and Memphis. The year 1986 found him back at the affiliate where he began his coaching career, in West Palm Beach. By this point he had resigned himself to being a career A-ball coach. Then, in 1991, a call came from the Montreal Expos, who wanted him to bench-coach the team for the 1992 season. Thirty-seven games into that season, interim coach Tom Runnells was fired, and Alou was appointed manager.

In his first year on the job, he steered the team to second place in the National League East, and he repeated that feat in the next season. (At the time Alou was hired, his son Moises was already playing for the Expos; the elder Alou took pains to ensure that no one would accuse him of nepotism, once punishing Moises severely for violating a team rule that involved beer.) The 1994 season saw Alou's team on top of the National League East and poised for their first play-off berth in years—only to have the season cut short by a players' strike, resulting in the cancellation of the World Series. Nevertheless, Alou was named manager of the year, and in 1995 he was elected to coach the National League All-Star team.

A major problem for the Expos during the 1990s has been the loss of young talent to free agency. Such star players as closing pitcher John Wetteland, slugger Larry Walker, and All-Star outfielder Marquis Grissom were all swiped by wealthier teams in the off-season free-agency deal agreed upon by players and owners to end the 1994 strike. In 1996 Alou lost his nephew, Mel Rojas, to the Chicago Cubs. Then, in 1997, Moises Alou left for the Florida Marlins, who would go on to win the World Series that year. All the while, Felipe coached to the best of his ability. "I'm no fool," he told Michael Kinsley for the Sporting News (March 3, 1997). "I know this business. In most instances, what you see out there is money. And the bottom line is that I don't want to leave because of money." The latest free-agent calamity came after the 1997 season, when the Expos lost their starting pitching ace, Pedro Martinez—who won the Cy Young Award that year—to the Boston Red Sox, who made him, at the time, the highest-paid baseball player ever. Like the 1997 season, 1998 was a bit of a disappointment—the Expos finished well under .500 both years, and in 1998 they also lost longtime outfielder Henry Rodriguez to the Chicago Cubs. On a positive note, on August 19, 1998, Alou surpassed Buck Rogers as the winningest manager in Expos history.

By the end of 1998, Alou's contract with Montreal was up, and both the Colorado Rockies and the Los Angeles Dodgers began courting him to fill their recently vacated managerial positions. The Rockies exited the bidding when they hired Jim Leyland, the former coach of the Florida Marlins, in early October. The Dodgers, who had also been courting Leyland, intensified their pursuit of Alou, who had stated publicly that he felt the Expos no longer wanted him. In an 11th-hour deal, the Expos' general manager, Jim Beattie, offered Alou a package worth a reported $2 million a year—making him one of the highest-paid managers in baseball. Alou told Jason Read for the Los Angeles

Times, according to the Sporting News (October 11, 1998, on-line), "I have to be honest about this: I was on my way out to Los Angeles. I accepted a plane ticket to go to Los Angeles to have a press conference." Dodgers general manager Kevin Malone, according to ESPN Sportszone (October 12, 1998, on-line), suggested that Alou's choice to stay in Montreal was an example of why the Dodgers coveted him: "Character and his loyalty. I'm happy for Felipe. I just wish him the best." The terms of the contract keep Alou in Montreal, where he lives with his fourth wife and their two children, for another three years. If the team is sold or leaves Montreal, Alou will be released from his contract. "I'm a very happy man now," Alou told Marantz. "I thank God for two kids given me when I was 50 years old. And I got one boy who loves baseball even though he's not two years old."

The Montreal Expos, since their inception in the 1970s, have been one of the lowest-paid teams in all of baseball. In part because of the economic hardships the city has experienced in the past two decades, the Expos have not been able to build a substantial treasury to keep the talented young players they develop in their farm system. The Expos also play in one of the more decrepit parks in the league, the structurally flawed Olympic Stadium (built in 1976), and lobbied for a long time to get a new structure financed and built by the city. At the time of the efforts to keep Alou in Montreal, those with a stake in the team felt that his presence was essential if the team were to bid successfully for a new stadium. During the summer of 1999, Montreal businessman Jeffrey Loria purchased a majority of shares in the Expos and subsequently secured a stadium deal for the franchise as well, thus ensuring that the team will remain in Montreal for the foreseeable future.

Although the Expos ended the 1999 season 35 games behind the National League Eastern Division champions, the Atlanta Braves, five Expo players—slugger Vladimir Guerrero, outfielder Rondell White, closing pitcher Ugueth Urbina, catcher Chris Widger, and utility man Mike Mordecai—had the best season of their careers. All five players are under contract until 2001.

Most experts believe that Felipe Alou will be elected to the Baseball Hall of Fame, in recognition of his accomplishments as a manager. — M.B.

Suggested Reading: Sporting News p10+ June 21, 1993, with photos; Sporting News (on-line) Oct. 11, 1998; Sports Illustrated p88+ June 19, 1995, with photos, p26 Mar. 3, 1997, with photos; Toronto Globe and Mail A p18+ July 23, 1994, with photos

Courtesy of Houston Astros

Alou, Moises
(ah-LOO, MOY-ses)

*July 3, 1966– Baseball player. Address: c/o
Houston Astros, P.O. Box 288, Houston, TX
77001*

Now wearing the uniform of the Houston Astros, outfielder Moises Alou is one of the most well-rounded players in baseball. An able fielder with a remarkable eye both in position and at the plate, he had one of his best seasons in 1998, hitting a solid .312 with a career-high 38 home runs. Son of Montreal Expos manager Felipe Alou, cousin of Los Angeles Dodgers relief pitcher Mel Rojas, and nephew of ex–major leaguers Matty Alou and Jesus Alou, he is a member of perhaps the most famous Dominican family ever to play the game. Considered a top prospect when he was drafted, in 1986, Alou entered the majors in 1990 with the Pittsburgh Pirates. He was traded to the Montreal Expos later in the season and expected to see more playing time on the younger team, but he was often kept off the field by a recurring shoulder injury, which plagued him for nearly three years. He did not play his first injury-free season until 1994, when he went on to have his finest season to date, batting an extraordinary .339. Managed by Alou's father, Felipe, at the time, the Expos seemed poised to go to the World Series that year, but their dreams were dashed when the players went on strike, canceling the Series for the first time in 91 years. In 1997, after two more respectable seasons, Alou signed with the Florida Marlins, who went on to defeat the Cleveland Indians in that year's World Series, becoming the youngest team (the club was five years old) ever to win a championship. Alou was traded

in the off-season to the Houston Astros. Now entering his 10th major-league season, Moises Alou is in the prime of his career.

Moises Rojas Alou was born on July 3, 1966 in Atlanta, Georgia. His father, Felipe Alou, was the first native-born Dominican to play in the majors and has since become one of the game's premier managers. When Moises's mother, Maria Beltre, was 17, she dropped out of high school in the Dominican Republic to marry Felipe, and only days after the wedding ceremony, on February 2, 1959, the newlyweds left for Phoenix, Arizona, where Felipe began spring training with the San Francisco Giants. That winter, the couple returned to the Dominican Republic, and nine months after their wedding, Maria gave birth to their oldest son, Felipe II. Daughter Maria and son Luis followed, and in 1966, while the family was in Atlanta (Felipe was now playing for the Braves), Maria gave birth to Moises. By the time Moises was born, however, his parents' marriage was in disrepair, and a divorce followed two years later. "I'm not angry with [Felipe Alou] because I understand," Moises Alou told Steve Marantz for the *Sporting News* (June 21, 1993). "Things didn't work out with my mother, and he had to do what he had to do. Even though he was divorced and he was on the road, he always kept in touch and he always supported us. Even though he wasn't there for much of my childhood, I appreciate that he took care of us. The one thing that bothered me a little was that most of my friends' parents were together. I used to see them with both of their parents, and I felt kind of bad. I wish I would have lived with both of my parents."

Felipe never made very much money as a baseball player, so Moises, his mother, and his siblings had to stretch every penny. "But I was [the] happiest kid in the world," he told Michael Farber for *Sports Illustrated* (June 19, 1995). "My dad would pick me up sometimes when he was home, and we'd go to a beach house in Salinas [in the Dominican Republic] and go fishing. We'd drive around, and people would stare at us. People would come up and want to shake his hand. You know how good that makes a kid feel? Maybe afterward it was, 'O.K., see you in a couple of months,' but I felt proud when I was with him. He was the most famous player, maybe the most famous person, on the island, *and he was my father.*"

Although Felipe was around as much as he could be, he spent most of every year in the United States, playing professional baseball with, successively, the Giants, the Braves, the Athletics, the Yankees, the Expos, and, finally, the Brewers. His playing career ended in 1974, and in the following season, Felipe took a job coaching a Montreal Expos minor-league team in Florida. Occasionally Moises Alou visited his father and saw him at work. At home in the Dominican Republic, it was Felipe II who took on the role of Moises's surrogate father. "We would play a lot," Moises told Marantz, "Felipe and me and my sister and brother

Luis. In games, it was me and Felipe." One day when Moises was 10, Felipe II, a confident and athletically gifted 16-year-old, dove into the shallow, murky waters of a newly constructed swimming pool, breaking his neck and dying instantly. "It killed me," Moises told Marantz. "He treated me like his son. He had the attitude of a 25- or 30-year-old man. He took me fishing and to play basketball. He was a great kid. He wouldn't let me get up from the table until I ate my meal. When it happened . . . that was the worst feeling I ever had in my life. I didn't want to believe it."

Although Moises showed unusual skills as an athlete and performed well in school, Felipe's death affected him deeply, and by the time he graduated from high school, his mother had noticed that he seemed to lack direction. Perhaps to counteract this, in June 1984 Maria Alou prompted Moises to attend a baseball camp in San Jose, California. Within a few days, counselors took notice of the young man's raw ability, and with the encouragement of coaches, Moises stayed in U.S. and entered Canada College, in Redwood City, California. He promptly joined the baseball team and hit .340 in his first season. In his second he batted a remarkable .447. When he entered the major-league free-agent draft, in 1986, the Pittsburgh Pirates selected him as the second player overall. His mother, worried that Moises was entering professional baseball too soon, persuaded the Pirates to agree to pay for her son's college education should he not make the team. The Pirates never had to make good on that promise, however: in 1990 Moises played his first game in a big-league uniform. (For four years beginning in 1986, he had played in the minor leagues.) A few months before he was called up to play for the Pirates, on May 15, 1990, Moises married his longtime girlfriend, Austria.

The Pirates were a mature and powerful team in 1990, but they needed a strong starting pitcher in order to contend for the National League Pennant. Therefore, shortly into the season, Pirate brass sent Alou—along with Scott Ruskin and Willie Greene—to Montreal in exchange for pitching ace Zane Smith. In his first year Alou saw little playing time with the Expos, and he was periodically shipped down to the team's Triple A affiliate. Late in the year, Alou hurt his shoulder, which caused him to miss the entire 1991 season. While Moises was rehabilitating his shoulder, his father was working his way up the Expos' managerial ranks. Just before the beginning of the 1992 season, Felipe was promoted to bench coach for the Expos; just 37 games into the season, he became the manager, after interim coach Tom Runnells was fired. Moises, healthy, ready to play, and with a newborn son in tow, was inspired by the support of his father, and the 26-year-old batted .282 in 115 games. Moises claimed that the birth of his son was the reason for his remarkable season. "If I had known how nice it would be, I would have had him earlier," Moises told Marantz in 1993. "It helps me a lot in my mar-

riage. I've got something to look forward to when I go home. I'm not saying I'm bored with my wife, but it's great having a kid. I play with him as much as I can. He's throwing a baseball now."

The year 1993 proved to be even more productive: Moises Alou hit .286 with 85 RBIs. But that season had its rocky moments. Felipe, worried that other players might suspect him of nepotism, benched Moises periodically when he went into a slump. In *Sports Illustrated* (June 19, 1995), Michael Farber wrote that Moises "had at least three closed-door meetings with his father to find out why he wasn't playing more." Lou Brock, a base-running coach for the Expos at the time, told Marantz that nepotism was not an issue, adding, "You have to play somebody when they're hitting .340." "I think [Felipe Alou] sometimes worries too much of what people might think or write about me," Moises told Marantz. "He shouldn't because I am one of the 25 players on this team. . . . He should treat me the same as everybody else." Once, Felipe punished Moises severely for taking beer with him when he left the clubhouse, despite the fact that most team members knew the rule against such behavior was rarely enforced. "I have to be really tough on Moises, and I am," Felipe told Marantz. "This is not a regular relationship. It is being watched by a lot of TV, newspapers, fans, the rest of my family, my other children. So I have to be careful that as long as I am the manager and he is with the team, that we have a healthy relationship based upon me treating him as other players, with the exception that I can't let anything pass by that he does wrong." The season, for Moises, ended on a bad note, when he twisted his ankle, with less than a month left in the season and with the team only five games behind the division-leading Philadelphia Phillies.

In 1994 the Expos at last enjoyed a combination of fine leadership and talented young players. Felipe, in only a few years, had come to be respected as one of the game's finest managers, and a number of the team's young stars, brought up by the farm system, were coming to maturity. In addition to Moises, who hit a career-high .339 that year, pitcher John Wetteland, slugger Larry Walker, and outfielder Marquis Grissom all had stellar seasons. That year also found Moises's cousin, Mel Rojas, a gifted relief pitcher, contributing significantly to the team. For the first time in his pro career, Moises played an entire season without sustaining a serious injury, and by August the Expos had secured first place in the National League East and boasted the best record in baseball.

Then, just when the team was poised to clinch the division title, disaster struck. The Players Union, which had allowed the players to suit up that season without a new contract agreement with the owners, decided—with less than two months left in the season—to walk out. For the first time since 1904, the World Series would be canceled. Three years later Moises would tell Bill Koenig for *USA Today* (October 22, 1997), "I still feel we had a very good chance of going to the World Series in 1994. We had the best record in baseball. It wasn't guaranteed that we were going to go to the World Series, but I really felt, and the rest of my ex-teammates felt, that we were going to make it there."

Coming off the disappointment of 1994, Moises entered the next season with high hopes—only to find more roadblocks waiting. The Expos, who have traditionally been a small-market team, did not have the budget to hang on to their young talent. By the start of the 1995 season, Walker, Grissom, and Wetteland had all been swiped up by wealthier teams. Moises initially played up to expectations, but toward the middle of the season, his numbers began to dip significantly. It was discovered in August that he had reaggravated his shoulder injury, and on August 18 he went on the disabled list—in the thick of the pennant race that saw Montreal only a few games in back of division-leading Atlanta. Moises came back to the Expos for a six-day spell in September but was forced to return to the disabled list, now with pain in both shoulders.

During that season he spent a significant amount of time with his two children, his wife, and his younger half-brothers in the Dominican Republic, Felipe III and Luis—both of whom have been considered excellent baseball prospects. "I try not be a dad [to Luis and Felipe III, whose mother Felipe had divorced], but I know what they're going through because I went through it," Alou told Marantz. "It helped that I had my brother who died. It's always nice to have an older brother to take care of you." In the off-season his cousin Mel Rojas signed a lucrative contract with the Chicago Cubs, but Moises returned to the Expos lineup and had one of his best seasons ever, hitting .286 with a career-tying 28 home runs and a career-high 96 RBIs and making the All-Star list. For the team as a whole, however, the 1996 season was one of the Expos' most disappointing under the leadership of Felipe, and it looked as though Moises, with his contract expiring at season's end, would go the route of most of the Expos' young talent: free agency. Moises's fantastic season now put him out of the Expos' price range, and his father advised him to go to the team that stood the best chance of winning a World Series.

The Florida Marlins, who had recently been purchased by the wealthy businessman H. Wayne Huizenga, began an "$89 million Marlins shopping spree during the [1996] off-season that procured a few things you can't find at Wal-Mart," as Koenig wrote. Aggressively courting Alou, the Marlins enticed the outfielder with the signing of respected manager Jim Leyland, formerly of the Pittsburgh Pirates. Within days Moises was a Florida Marlin. "I had no choice," Alou told Koenig after signing a five-year, $25 million contract. "Montreal never offered me a contract when I became a free agent. It wasn't that hard because I was prepared for it. I knew that moment was coming. I miss my [father]

because he really helped me a lot. My ex-teammates, the coaching staff really helped me a lot. But I made the right choice to come here. Like I say all the time, I came here to be on a winning team and everything is turning out the way I expected it to." Alou's 1997 season, his first with the Marlins, proved to be stellar. He hit .292 with 23 home runs and 115 RBIs, and the Miami press voted him the Marlins' most valuable player.

In October the Marlins went to the World Series, against the overachieving Cleveland Indians. In the first game Alou hit the game-winning, three-run homer. (A week before, during the National League Championship Series against the Atlanta Braves, Alou's wife had given birth to their third son, Kirby. "I named him Kirby because Mr. Kirby Puckett was one of my idols in baseball," Alou told Koenig. Puckett, one of the game's premier hitters during the 1980s and 1990s, officially retired in 1996 after being diagnosed with a severe case of glaucoma.) The World Series would prove to be a topsy-turvy event, with the teams going tit for tat until the seventh, and final, game. Although the Marlins were a new franchise, only five years old at the time, the team was full of seasoned veterans, many of whom were hungry for their first World Series title. The Indians, on the other hand, had not won a championship since 1948 and had narrowly lost the Series in 1995 to the Atlanta Braves. Now, in the final game of the baseball season, each team needed just one victory to become baseball's world champions.

The contest saw 22-year-old Indian pitcher Jaret Wright hurl an impressive eight innings, and in the bottom of the ninth, the Indians were up 2–1—and a mere three outs away from victory. Tribe manager Mike Hargrove brought in closing pitcher Jose Mesa to finish the job. Moises Alou came to bat and, after a hard-fought showdown with Mesa, blooped a light single into the outfield. With one out, thanks to a sacrifice fly, Alou was able to get to third base. Next at bat was second baseman Craig Counsell, whose high pop fly into the outfield allowed Alou to score, and the game went into extra innings. The game remained tied until the bottom of the 11th inning, when Indian second baseman Tony Fernandez missed a routine ground ball, allowing the Marlins' Craig Counsell and Greg Zaun to reach first and second base, respectively. The Indians' pitcher Charles Nagy intentionally walked Jim Eisenreich, which loaded the bases and brought up to bat Colombian-born shortstop Edgar Renteria. After fouling off numerous pitches, Renteria slapped the game-winning single into center field. Moises Alou, who just a week before had become the fourth Alou to play in a World Series, was now a member of the world-championship team.

Late in 1997 the Marlins' owner, Huizenga, announced that, despite his team's having won the championship, he had lost millions of dollars during the season. He gave the Marlins' front office specific instructions to let loose much of its high-priced talent. By opening day the Marlins had cut their payroll, which had been fourth highest in the majors at the start of the previous season, in half. Alou was one of the first players to go, and before the new year, he was a Houston Astro. For some time, the Astros had been a competitive team, and Houston's brass felt that Alou was a perfect fit for their already-impressive lineup. Within the clubhouse Alou became a team leader and went on to his best season ever, hitting .312 with a career-high 124 RBIs. He missed only three games the entire season—a far cry from the 60 he missed in 1992 with the Expos—and he became an integral run-scoring component of the Astros' offense, belting an astounding 38 home runs. His bat helped propel the Astros to the play-offs. (The team went on to lose to the San Diego Padres.) At the season's conclusion, Astro general manager Gerry Hunsicker lobbied hard to keep Alou in Houston. On November 6, 1998 the Astros agreed to give Alou $3 million in January 2000 in addition to the $10.5 million he would make over the next two years. "This is an extremely important player to this franchise," Hunsicker told *ESPN Sportszone.* "It would have been devastating to lose him." Alou

himself said, "I feel I have some unfinished business here. I didn't come here to have a good season. I came here to win a championship with these guys."

Shortly before the start of spring training in 1999, Alou fell in his home in the Dominican Republic (reportedly while adjusting the speed of his treadmill) and tore the anterior cruciate ligament in his left knee. He did not play at all that season. Despite his absence, the Astros did very well, winning the National League Central Division in the final week of the season over the surprisingly strong Cincinnati Reds. Then, in the National League Division Series, Houston fell to the Atlanta Braves, three games to one. It is expected that Alou will join the Astros' camp for spring training in March 2000. — M.B.

Suggested Reading: *ESPN Sportszone* (on-line) Nov. 6, 1998; *Sporting News* p10+ June 21, 1993, with photos; *Sports Illustrated* p88+ June 19, 1995, with photos; *Toronto Globe and Mail* A p18+ July 23, 1994, with photos

---

Alvarez Bravo, Manuel

Feb. 4, 1902– Photographer. Address: c/o Mexican Cultural Institute of New York, 27 E. 39th St., New York, NY 10016

In the first half of the 20th century, the celebrated Mexican photographer Manuel Alvarez Bravo spent a great deal of time with many of the artists, photographers, and filmmakers who established the surrealist movement in visual arts. But Alvarez Bravo feels that his love for his country, rather than any specific school of artistic thought, is at the heart of his work. "A photograph's style has more to do with the state of emotion you're in the moment you click the shutter," he told Tim Padgett for *Time* (February 24, 1997, on-line). "My officio— my calling—is with Mexico's exterior, or rather with capturing that exterior to explore all the complicated layers beneath it." It was, however, the complex essence of Mexico, the mixture of Spanish and Meso-American cultures, that attracted the surrealist artists—who brought elements of the subconscious to otherwise realistic-looking works of art—to Alvarez Bravo's homeland. What is inspired by his feelings about Mexico and what is an outgrowth of the surrealist influences, therefore, are often difficult to distinguish in his work. Writing in *Americas* (November 1991), David Lyon quoted the Mexican artist Diego Rivera, who was a friend Alvarez Bravo's, as saying that Alvarez Bravo's work is "Mexican by cause, form, and content. Anguish is omnipresent and atmosphere is supersaturated with irony."

Manuel Alvarez Bravo was born on February 4, 1902 in Mexico City, in a location he described to David Lyon as "behind the cathedral, in the place where the temples of ancient Mexican gods must have been." When he completed his schooling, he worked for a few years as a clerk in the treasury department of the state of Oaxaca, in southern Mexico. In 1924 he bought his first camera, a Century Master 25, and he trained himself to be a photographer by learning techniques from books and magazines and studying photos in them. In the following year he won first prize in a local photography contest.

During the 1920s Mexico enjoyed a cultural renaissance and received attention from American and European visual artists who were involved in the surrealist movement. An international publication entitled *Mexican Folkways* documented the country's exciting mural movement, in which artists such as Diego Rivera, José Orozco, and David Alfaro Siqueiros painted enormous, brightly colored murals in public spaces. The Italian-born actress and photographer Tina Modotti, who was the in-house photographer for the publication, helped to get Alvarez Bravo some of his first photography assignments. She also taught him some sophisticated new methods, for processing film and printing black and white photos, that were beginning to be used in Europe. (Throughout his career Alvarez Bravo has worked predominantly in black and white, and various methods of processing and printing, which create greater clarity through distinct shades of gray, have proved to be very important to the overall quality of his work.) Modotti also sent some prints of Alvarez Bravo's work to her boyfriend, the American photographer Edward

David Scheinbaum, © 1988/Courtesy Scheinbaum & Russek Ltd.

Manuel Alvarez Bravo

Weston, who was duly impressed with what he saw. By 1929 Alvarez Bravo was doing enough professional photography to quit his job at the Oaxaca treasury. In 1930, when Modotti was deported from Mexico on account of her alleged Communist activities, Alvarez Bravo bought most of her equipment, and on her recommendation he took over her position at *Mexican Folkways.*

After proving himself adept at that job, Alvarez Bravo was hired by the surrealist filmmaker Sergei Eisenstein as the camera operator for his film *Que Viva Mexico!* (1932). Other prestigious jobs included commissioned portraits of the artists Diego Rivera and Frida Kahlo and the Soviet Communist leader Leon Trotsky. In 1932 Alvarez Bravo's first solo exhibit was mounted in Mexico City's Galeria Posada. In 1935, at his first exhibit in New York, at the Julien Levy Gallery, his works were hung alongside those of the French photographer Henri Cartier-Bresson, who was a good friend of his. In subsequent years Alvarez Bravo was credited with having influenced Cartier-Bresson. In the *New York Times* (March 23, 1997), Vicki Goldberg wrote, "The question of influence in either direction has never been resolved, but the two men proceeded along parallel lines, and their work was shown together several times in the 1930s."

By the mid-1930s Alvarez Bravo's preoccupation with the dramatic Mexican landscape, his country's poor and working-class citizens, and the folklore and religiosity that permeated Mexican culture was apparent in his work. Some of his favorite subjects were eerily realistic religious statues, ruins of the indigenous people of Mexico, and rural grave sites decorated with flowers, all lit dramatically by the strong Mexican sunlight. When asked why the theme of death has been so important to his work, Alvarez Bravo explained to Tim Golden for the *New York Times* (December 16, 1993) that in Mexican culture, the subject of death is usually approached with less fear and sadness than it is elsewhere. "From the time I was a boy we have played with death. You see all those little skeleton toys we have; it is a custom we have always had. Maybe because of that, one does not insist much in thinking about it."

Describing the air of mystery that many of Alvarez Bravo's photographs share with the works of his surrealist contemporaries, Lyon wrote, "The most significant part of an Alvarez Bravo photograph is often what is missing from the frame and, therefore, must be imagined by the viewer." Lyon cited as one example the 1932 photo *Washerwoman Implied,* which featured freshly washed laundry carefully laid out on a Mauguey cactus to dry in the sun. Another photo, *The Mother of the Shoeshine Boy and the Shoeshine Boy*, shows a small boy and his mother sitting casually on a ledge, eating with their hands, and talking. A dark shadow shrouds their heads, as if they are sharing a secret. "[Alvarez Bravo] makes pictures to be looked at rather than seen," Peter Schjeldahl wrote in the *Village Voice* (March 11, 1997). "You absorb their content as thought and feeling before your eye can digest their form. (You are always about to see them and you never do.)" Alvarez Bravo told Lyon that the poignant titles he gives his photographs "are not guides to seeing the photograph. They are juxtapositions."

One photograph that Alvarez Bravo will readily classify as surrealistic is *La buena fama durmiendo*, or "The Good Reputation Sleeping." The photograph was commissioned by the French poet and art critic André Breton for a surrealist exhibition in Mexico City, in 1939, and has since become one of Alvarez Bravo's most famous pictures. The print features a Mexican woman lying on her back, presumably sleeping, on a thick woolen blanket strewn with cactus flowers. The woman's body is partially wrapped in bandages, but her most vulnerable parts are exposed to sun, which pales her olive-toned skin. "I did it in a surrealist manner, suddenly, and automatically," the photographer told Juan Garcia de Oteyza for *On the Arts* (online). "A model that worked in [a class that I was teaching at San Carlos Academy of Arts] was in the same line waiting for her paycheck and I asked her on the spot to climb to the rooftop, telling her I would join her shortly. Then, I still don't know why, I asked some students to bring me . . . a bunch of abrojos (thorny cactus flowers). I then called [a doctor] . . . who was a good friend of mine. I told him to come to the academy with bandages. . . . We all went to the rooftop and I took the picture." Alvarez Bravo said that the idea of bandages occurred to him probably because he had previously photographed some dancers who had bandaged their feet during rehearsals.

By the 1930s most photographers had begun working with 35-millimeter cameras, which allowed them to shoot much more quickly and to shoot more film per session than ever before. One of the ways in which Alvarez Bravo's work differs from that of other photographers of that era is that, instead of working with a 35-millimeter camera, he preferred using a Graflex, a camera that accommodates larger film and that requires a little more time between exposures. The result, according to Vicki Goldberg in the *New York Times* (March 23, 1997), is that "[Alvarez Bravo's] work generally seems more studied, less intuitive, less captured on the fly than much of its kind." "When you work with a 35 millimeter, of course you have to finish the roll," the photographer explained to Tim Golden of his preference for the slower method of shooting film. "There are 36 exposures. As much as you convince yourself when you go to the countryside—

'I'm going to take very little'—what you shoot is not the same. [Thirty-five millimeter] is not something that brings you closer, but a mechanicalness. You can move yourself aside; there is not that same relationship with the model."

With his reputation as an art photographer growing in the 1940s, Alvarez Bravo began selling many of his prints to New York galleries and museums. "I remember that a gentleman used to visit me in Mexico and he would pay me $3 per photo," Alvarez Bravo told Garcia de Oteyza. "I thought it was a little more, but recently, my friends at the Museum [of Modern Art in New York City] confirmed that it was indeed $3." In 1955 he founded and served as the chief photographer of La Fonda Editorial de la Plastica Mexicana, which published books about Mexican art. In the same year, a group photography exhibit featuring Alvarez Bravo, Walker Evans, August Sander, and Paul Strand began a tour of the U.S. and Europe, receiving acclaim that was unprecedented for a show of its kind.

With the decline of surrealism in the 1960s and 1970s, Alvarez Bravo's work, and that of his contemporaries Evans, Sander, Strand, Cartier-Bresson, and others, receded from the limelight. The next important showing of Alvarez Bravo's work was not until 1991, when the exhibit "Revelaciones: The Art of Manuel Alvarez Bravo" toured the U.S. and Canada. Charles Hagen of the *New York Times* (March 22, 1992), sharing the opinion of others, felt that the exhibit did not do justice to Alvarez Bravo's work. "In many ways this is a frustrating show, with simplistic text panels and a disjointed sequencing in which the works are hung in no apparent order," he wrote. "Further hampering efforts to understand the work is the reverential tone of the wall labels and catalogue essay, which seem aimed at ratifying Mr. Alvarez Bravo's status as a great master without giving sufficient critical attention to the nature or quality of his photographs."

The 1991 show nevertheless generated a renewed interest in Alvarez Bravo, and in 1997 the Museum of Modern Art in New York City mounted a major retrospective that included many photographs that had not previously been exhibited in a formal setting. Reviewing this exhibit, Schjeldahl wrote, "There isn't a bad picture among the 175 here, and only a few are merely good. The rest flirt with badness, among other disasters, in the hair-raising way of only the largest creative spirits." At about the same time, the Witkin Gallery, a private gallery in New York City, mounted a show of Alvarez Bravo's work called "Ninety-five Images for a 95th Birthday," and the Mexican Cultural Institute, also located in New York City, created an exhibit of the photography of Alvarez Bravo and Mexican artists whom he had influenced. In Mexico City, in the same year, the Centro de la Imagen exhibited some of Alvarez Bravo's most recent work.

Manuel Alvarez Bravo lives in Coyoacán, a bohemian district in the southern part of Mexico City, with his third wife, Collette Urbajtel de Alvarez. Although he enjoys working both on location and in the studio, he finds himself, at 96, shooting most often in his high-ceilinged work building—"The Blue House"—located just across the street from his home. When asked if he had any plans to retire, he told Golden, "I could sit around here and take the sun. That would be terrible! I mean, I couldn't. In the mornings, I read the newspaper headlines—not the articles—and then to work. But not exactly to 'work' as you put it, but to do things. Because I cannot say that I work, exactly. It is part of my life to take photographs, to develop. It is like eating. It is a spontaneous thing." According to Golden, above some developing trays in the photographer's darkroom is a sign that reads "Hay tiempo," or "There is time." Alvarez Bravo seldom gives interviews because, as he told Lyon, he feels that people who are interested in his work should "have discourse with the photographs, not the photographer."

Among Alvarez Bravo's many awards and honors are the Sourasky Art Prize, in 1974; the Mexican National Art Prize, in 1975; a John Simon Guggenheim Memorial Fellowship, in 1975; an induction into the French Order of Arts and Letters, in 1981; the Victor and Edna Hasselblad Prize, in 1984; and the International Center of Photography's Master of Photography Award, in 1987. — C.P.

Suggested Reading: *Americas* p28+ Nov. 1991, with photos; *New York Times* II p37 Mar. 22, 1992, with photo, C p1 Dec. 16, 1993, with photos, II p39 Mar. 23, 1997, with photo; *On the Arts* (on-line); *Time* (on-line) Feb. 24, 1997; *Village Voice* p83 Mar. 11, 1997, with photo

---

Michael Williamson/Courtesy of Houghton Mifflin

Angier, Natalie

Feb. 16, 1958– Science writer for the New York Times. *Address: c/o* New York Times, *229 W. 43d St., New York, NY 10036*

"Every single story that nature tells is gorgeous," Natalie Angier wrote in her second book, *The Beauty of the Beastly*. "She is the original Scheherazade, always with one more surprise to shake from her sleeve." In a rave write-up of *The Beauty of the Beastly* for the *New York Times Book Review* (June 18, 1995), F. Gonzalez-Crussi declared,

"More than ever, we need good interpreters [of science], and Natalie Angier is one who is constitutionally incapable of writing a boring sentence." That is high praise indeed, considering that Angier's sentences are peppered with such terms as "apoptosis," "oxytocin," and "Caenorhabditis elegans," that her beat encompasses such realms as molecular biology, gynecology, and genetics, and that her interests extend into bizarre crannies of nature—the fecundity of cockroaches or the genetic mutations of roundworms, for example—usually consigned to scientific journals or droning nature documentaries. In her two decades as a science writer, most prominently for the *New York Times*, Angier has displayed an erudition, wit, and clarity that have helped to make science comprehensible to countless readers and placed her, along with such masters of the genre as Lewis Thomas and Loren Eiseley, in that small pantheon of highly successful popularizers of science. "What I try to do," she has said, "is to humanize everything, to give the reader the feeling that they are right there in the middle of the scientific process."

Natalie Marie Angier was born on February 16, 1958 in New York City, where her father, Keith, was a machinist, and her mother, Adele, worked as an indexer in the library of Time Warner. Angier spent two years at the University of Michigan before transferring to Barnard College, in New York City. She studied English, physics, and astronomy and, as she wrote in an on-line autobiographical sketch for the Santa Fe Institute, "dreamed of starting a popular magazine about science for intelligent lay readers who wanted to know more about what's going on across the great divide of C. P. Snow's two cultures." The "great divide" that Snow, a British physicist and writer, discussed in his widely read book *The Two Cultures and the Scientific Revolution* (1960) stemmed from the general lack of communication between people working in the arts and humanities, on one side, and those devoted to science and technology, on the other.

Upon graduating from Barnard, magna cum laude, in 1978, Angier went to work as a staff writer for *Discover* magazine, the first issue of which was published in 1980. She remained with *Discover* for four years, mostly covering biology. Next she worked as an editor at the now-defunct woman's magazine *Savvy*, taught in New York University's Graduate Program in Scientific and Environmental Reporting, and, for *Time*, reported on scientific and environmental subjects—among them the space shuttle, genetically altered mice, superstring theory, inherited disorders, theories about mass extinctions of species, and the preservation of the Great Salt Lake. In the 1980s and early 1990s, articles by Angier appeared in such periodicals as *Sea Frontiers*, *Seventeen*, *Atlantic*, *Parade*, *Washington Monthly*, *Reader's Digest*, *American Health*, and *Mademoiselle*.

In March 1990 Angier joined the staff of the *New York Times* as a science reporter. Just one year later she won a Pulitzer Prize for beat reporting, for what the Pulitzer committee described as her "compelling and illuminating" pieces on scientific topics. The 10 feature stories that the *Times* had sent to the committee demonstrated her range; they included articles about scorpions, sexual infidelity among animals, and the Human Genome Project.

Angier's first book, *Natural Obsessions: The Search for the Oncogene* (1988), recounts the efforts of scientists at the Whitehead Institute, a research center affiliated with the Massachusetts Institute of Technology (MIT), in Cambridge, Massachusetts, to isolate oncogenes, which are genes that can trigger changes that cause a normal cell to become cancerous. Off and on for a year and a half, Angier kept track of the advances of the head of the Institute, Robert Weinberg (who discovered the first oncogene) and his 15 assistants as they sought to gain not only knowledge but renown, prestige, and, perhaps, the Nobel Prize. She also reported on a group of Weinberg's rivals: Michael Wigler's team, based at the Cold Springs Harbor Laboratory on Long Island, New York. *Natural Obsessions*, which shed light on the oft-ignored human elements behind the long hours of sometimes tedious, sometimes invigorating research, was hailed as an excellent depiction of the focused, if not obsessive, professional lives of many scientists. "Angier admirably dispels any thought that the ivory tower of research is a haven for selfless nerds and drudges," Eric Lax wrote for the *New York Times Book Review* (July 10, 1988). "The people in her book are as attractive and as complex and even as quirky as their subjects. They of course do brilliant and painstaking research, but they also gossip about one another and fight over experimental turf and authorship of results." Angier also captured the "fun" of science, Lax reported: "[The researchers] keep a pink Cadillac with no roof and go to the dog races in gold lamé and top hats (after a 'prerace seminar' in which they 'learn the history of dog racing and the proper way to place a bet')." "One does not have to be a molecular biologist or follow every step to enjoy the fun and appreciate the beauty, or to share in the frustration of a promising hypothesis that hits a dead end after months of work and hope," Lax wrote. Reviewers also marveled at Angier's ability to explain, in words that nonscientists could understand, complicated theories and processes being developed by some of the best, most highly trained scientists in the world. Described as "a work of grand adventure, beauty, and literature" by Peter Gomer in the *Chicago Tribune* (June 15, 1988), *Natural Obsessions* earned Angier the Lewis Thomas Award for writing about the life sciences.

Angier's next book, *The Beauty of the Beastly: New Views on the Nature of Life* (1995), consists of more than 40 essays, each about five to eight pages in length and most of which originally appeared in the *New York Times*. The book ranges widely across the plant and animal kingdoms, as Derek Bickerton reported in the *New York Times* (June 14, 1995), and offers insights into how "the behavior of all species, including our own, can be explained in terms of biochemistry and the imperatives of genetics (looking out for one's kin, maximizing the fitness of one's offspring and so forth)." Many of the species Angier chose to illustrate her thesis are short on popularity among Homo sapiens. "I have made it a kind of hobby, almost a mission, to write about organisms that many people find repugnant," Angier explained: "spiders, scorpions, parasites, worms, rattlesnakes, dung beetles, hyenas. I have done so out of a perverse preference for subjects that other writers generally have ignored, and because I hope to inspire in readers an appreciation for diversity, for imagination, for the twisted, webbed, infinite possibility of the natural world." According to Bickerton, "the only serious flaw" in Angier's book can be traced to the author's "uncritical acceptance of socio-biological theory, which insists on adaptive explanations for the most negative of human behaviors. Such acceptance makes her treat suicide as perhaps 'self-sacrifice for the good of surviving relatives' and state that would-be suicides 'often give an altruistic explanation' of their action as 'the wise, clever, and thoughtful thing to do.' Reading this made me want to sentence Ms. Angier to 21 days on a suicide hot line, an experience that would surely disabuse her of such notions." Nevertheless, Bickerton concluded, "No brief review can do justice to the richness and variety of these essays, which entertain as thoroughly as they instruct, and leave the reader wishing there were more."

For her most recent book, *Woman: An Intimate Geography* (1999), Angier turned her attention to a subject that has generated an enormous amount of misinformation: the biology of the human female. As the subtitle suggests, she regarded no bodily function, organ, or process as too private to be discussed and nothing as taboo. Her "geographical tour," as Abraham Verghese described it in the *New York Times* (May 23, 1999, on-line), "begins at the primordial level with the egg, chromosomes, sex differentiation and then ascends to the clitoris, . . . uterus, ovary, breast, hormones, and muscle before moving to the high elevations: love, aggression, and evolutionary psychology." *Woman: An Intimate Geography* has been favorably compared with the 1970s classic *Our Bodies, Ourselves*. Indeed, according to some reviewers, many women may find it even more inspirational than that earlier work, not least because Angier not only debunked many myths about women's bodies but also celebrated female anatomy and physiology and offered evidence to show that in some ways women's bodies are superior to those of men. (For example, she pointed out that the clitoris has about 8,000 nerve endings, twice the number present in the head of the penis, and unlike the penis, which serves an excretory as well as a sexual function, it is purely a sexual organ.) Angier also rejected the theory, propounded by such evolutionary psychologists as Robert Wright and David M. Buss, that women are less interested in sex than men and seek sexual liaisons less aggressively than men. With rare exceptions throughout recorded history, she noted, cultures (virtually all of which have been dominated by men) have punished sexually promiscuous women. In a review for *Salon* (April 5, 1999), Maggie Jones complained that Angier "has a propensity to engage in cheerleading about everything female." "The result can be sisterhood mush," Jones declared. "Still, this is a minor quibble about a meaty book," she continued. "Angier challenges readers to question assumptions about women's bodies and minds. She prods us to understand biology as a feminist tool. And her book provides the analysis and the ammunition with which to do just that." In October 1999 *Woman: An Intimate Geography* was nominated for a National Book Award for nonfiction.

In September 1990 Angier married Rick Weiss, a science reporter for the *Washington Post*. The two live with their daughter, Katherine Weiss Angier, in Takoma Park, Maryland, a suburb of Washington, D.C. In the *New York Times* (November 26, 1996), Angier described the ordeal she experienced when, after undergoing ultrasound while pregnant with her daughter, she was told, erroneously, that the fetus had a clubfoot.

In addition to the Pulitzer Prize and the Lewis Thomas Award, Angier's honors include the American Association for the Advancement of Science Award for excellence in journalism, the General Motors International Award for her writings about cancer, and the Barnard Distinguished Alumna Award. In the *1995 Forbes MediaGuide*, she was given four stars—Forbes's top rating for journalists. — M.C.

Suggested Reading: *Chicago Tribune* V p3 June 15, 1988; *New York Times* C p19 June 14, 1995, with photo; *New York Times Book Review* p7+ July 10, 1988, p10 June 18, 1995; *Salon* (on-line) Apr. 5, 1999

Selected Books: *Natural Obsessions: The Search for the Oncogene*, 1988; *The Beauty of the Beastly*, 1995; *Woman: An Intimate Geography*, 1999

Suesch Bayat/Courtesy of Philips Classics

Argerich, Martha

(AR-ger-itch)

June 5, 1941– Classical pianist. Address: c/o Philips Classics, 825 Eighth Ave., New York, NY 10019; c/o Richard Paulsen, Goette Konnzert Direktion, Colonnaden 70, 2000 Hamburg 36, Germany

"I love to play the piano but I don't want to be a pianist. I have a conflict." The Argentine-born Martha Argerich, who made that revelation to Fred Hauptfuhrer and Mary Vespa for *People* (April 7, 1980), nevertheless has made her career as a classical pianist, and many of her admirers rank her among the world's greatest masters of the keyboard. "Martha has one of the most astounding techniques that I have ever heard," the pianist, conductor, and composer André Previn told the *People* interviewers, "and that includes Vladimir Horowitz. She has a total grasp of what she's playing and she's phenomenally exciting to hear." "Argerich has no limits," Richard Dyer, a music critic for the *Boston Globe* (August 24, 1998, on-line), declared in a review of her rendition of Serge Prokofiev's Third Piano Concerto at Tanglewood, in Lenox, Massachusetts. Calling her pianistic gifts "astounding," he wrote that "she pounces on the keyboard like a cat—she is blindingly quick, unerring in aim and leap. Her playing has dynamism, precision, variety of articulation, and mordancy; musically speaking, it is straightforward but never mechanical."

Reviewers have often tried to convey the feverish, explosive power of Argerich's performances, by using such adjectives as "fiery," "incendiary," "electrifying," and even "crazed" and such phrases as "blow-torch incandescence," "leonine energy," "hellbent fervor," "feral intensity," "vertiginous, fire-spitting bravura," and "raw passion." But, as many have noted, her playing can also be supremely delicate and restrained, and critics have chosen such words as "poetic," "lyrical," "graceful," "elegant," and "supple" to characterize it. Argerich herself has often been described as eccentric and also, Anthony Tommasini reported in the *New York Times* (October 29, 1995), as "undisciplined, flighty, chaotic, hyperkinetic, [and] unstable." She is viewed that way for various reasons: for example, she is notorious for frequently canceling scheduled appearances; she has turned in many over-the-top performances, some marked by such breakneck tempos that orchestras can barely keep pace; she has made relatively few solo recordings and given unusually few solo concerts, confining herself mostly to chamber music and concertos (nearly all from the romantic canon); she almost never sits for interviews; and she has defied convention in her personal life. When, during one of her rare interviews, conducted for the Call Project in April 1997 and transcribed on-line by Johns Hopkins University's Peabody Institute, Jura Margulis asked her what she believed was the "most important thing for an artist," Argerich responded, "Freedom."

The daughter of two foreign-service professionals, Martha Argerich was born on June 5, 1941 in Buenos Aires, Argentina. She began studying the piano at the age of about three. Her first teacher was Ernestine C. de Kussrow, "who taught small children to play by ear," John Gillespie and Anna Gillespie reported in their book *Notable Twentieth-Century Pianists* (1995). When she was five her mother engaged the internationally esteemed Italian maestro Vicenzo Scaramuzza to give her lessons. Her mother "always wanted the best . . . ," Argerich told Jura Margulis. "She was not herself a musician, but she knew what was the best thing to do." In her early years of teaching, Argerich said, Scaramuzza had behaved like "a despot with sadistic tendencies"; by the time she met him, when he was in his mid-50s, he still used fear as a pedagogic device, albeit a little less brutally. "Let's just say I was very shy and intimidated by him," Argerich told Margulis. "When he would say mean, caustic things, he would do it very calmly, very coolly, such things as one was an idiot, and one shouldn't come to the lesson, and I had to concentrate on the mole next to his nose in order not to cry. He told my father I squeezed him like a lemon, took everything, but didn't give anything back." Scaramuzza's "teaching style," she told Margulis, "was very Italian, very much oriented towards cantabile, breathing, of course weight, and also anatomical things. When the sound was empty, he would say it sounded like pants walking into a room with nobody inside them."

Argerich made her professional debut in 1949, at the age of eight, in a Buenos Aires concert hall, where she played Mozart's Piano Concerto in D Minor and Beethoven's Piano Concerto in C Major. "Before the concert I went to the bathroom, knelt down, and told myself that if I missed a single note, I would explode," she recalled to Margulis. "I don't know why I believed that, but I didn't miss a single note. It's terrible for a young person, and that explains something about me today, I think." One thing that young Martha found "terrible" was the stress she felt when she played in public. "I hated coming out for bows and would rather have just run off the stage," she told the *People* reporters. She did not like to practice, either. According to John and Anna Gillespie, as an eight-year-old, Martha played for the great German pianist Walter Gieseking, who, "perhaps realizing how much [she] disliked performing, advised her parents to leave her in peace." But her parents continued to push her, while Martha continued to resent their insistence on disciplined practice.

Between the ages of 10 and 12, Argerich studied with Scaramuzza's assistant, with whom she learned to sight-read music. Each week she had to prepare two études by Chopin and two preludes and fugues by Bach. "It was very good for me," she told Margulis. After that she lived for two years in Geneva, Switzerland, where she studied with Madeleine Lipatti, the widow of the celebrated Romanian pianist and teacher Dinu Lipatti. Argerich told Margulis that she felt irritated with Madame Lipatti's attempts to rein in her tempestuousness, with such remarks as, "You don't want people to love you, you play like you're on a drowning boat in the midst of a terrible storm." Argerich said she "just loved" a remark that Nikita Magaloff, another well-known teacher (with whom she later studied briefly) made to Lipatti: "Madeleine, you can't make a race horse trot."

In 1955 Juan Perón, the dictatorial president of Argentina, arranged to have Argerich's parents work in the Argentine embassy in Vienna, Austria, so that Argerich could study with top-flight instructors—specifically, Friedrich Gulda, a classical virtuoso and jazz pianist who was then 25 and whom Argerich had met earlier, in Argentina. She has described the year and a half that she spent under Gulda's tutelage as "a fantastic experience." "Gulda gave me incredible impulses," she recalled to Margulis. "We didn't have a language in common, he spoke a little bit of Spanish, I spoke a little German, he called the language we used together 'pan-Romanic.' I remember in the beginning he tried to transmit a certain emotion in the music to me, and since he couldn't find words, he grabbed me and pulled me to the bathroom, picked up a wet sponge, and dampened his face. Pointing to his soaked face, he said, 'Like that! Like that!'"

In 1957 the 16-year-old Argerich made a huge splash in the world of classical music by earning first prize at the Ferruccio Busoni International Competition in Bolzano, Italy, and then, just three weeks later, winning the International Music Competition in Geneva. She spent the next four years giving concerts in Europe and making recordings. At 17 she performed with the legendary violinist Joseph Szigeti, an experience that is said to have cemented her passion for chamber music.

Lacking companionship during her concert tours, Argerich grew increasingly lonely. She also began to feel "empty," she told the *People* reporters. "I wasn't enjoying [my career] either as an artist or a person." At age 20 Argerich all but abandoned the piano; during the next few years, she devoted her time to socializing, seeing movies, eating out, watching television, listening to records, and playing Ping-Pong. Her only reported music-related activities were a handful of widely spaced lessons in Italy with the reclusive pianist Arturo Benedetti Michelangeli, with whom she worked on a single piece. She also lived in New York City for a while during this period. At one point, according to the *People* profile, she toyed with the idea of earning her living as a secretary.

Meanwhile, at age 22, Argerich had married the violinist Robert Chen. (A conductor and composer as well, he is currently the concertmaster of the Chicago Symphony Orchestra.) Shortly before their daughter, Lyda, was born, in 1964, the couple separated; they later divorced. When Lyda was about a month old, Argerich's mother entered Argerich in the Queen Elisabeth of Belgium Piano Competition, in Brussels. Despite her almost total lack of preparation, Argerich traveled to Brussels, where by chance she met the pianist Stefan Askenase, one of the contest's jurors. She wound up living in the residence that Askenase shared with his wife and taking piano lessons from him. But it was Askenase's wife, who Arterich has said "had something very special, like a sun," who restored her confidence in herself as a pianist and performer.

In the autumn of 1964, Argerich resumed concertizing, with engagements in Zurich, Switzerland, and London. Then, in early 1965, in a stunning coup for an artist from the Western Hemisphere, she won first prize at the Chopin Piano Competition in Warsaw, Poland. Despite media reports of insomnia and exhaustion so severe that she required the attention of a physician, she also captured the Polish Radio Prize for her interpretation of Chopin mazurkas. "Though a slight, delicate girl, she played with an almost masculine power and assertiveness," a reporter wrote for *Time* (March 26, 1965). "For more introspective passages, she tempered her mercurial attack with

a limpid, poetic tone and subtlety of phrasing." The Chopin specialist James Methuen-Campbell has noted, as paraphrased by John and Anna Gillespie, that "one of the most telling features of an Argerich performance is that she always manages to preserve her musical taste and judgment even when playing fiendishly difficult music."

On January 16, 1966 the 24-year-old pianist made her United States debut, with a recital at Lincoln Center as a featured performer in the Great Performers Series. On February 19, 1970, in her New York City orchestral debut, she played Prokofiev's Piano Concerto no. 3 with the New York Philharmonic conducted by Claudio Abbado. The previous year she had married the well-known Swiss conductor Charles Dutoit, with whom she had her second daughter, Anne. Five years later she and Dutoit divorced. The father of Argerich's youngest daughter, Stephanie, who is now almost 30, is the pianist Stephen Kovacevich (once known as Stephen Bishop and later as Stephen Bishop-Kovacevich). Argerich and Kovacevich "were twice about to marry but never did," Argerich told the *People* interviewers in 1980. "I've not been lucky in these matters. I don't have a very mature attitude about marriage. It never was a great goal or conviction of mine."

In addition to performing at live concerts with Dutoit, who conducts the Montreal Symphony Orchestra and the NHK Symphony Orchestra, in Tokyo, Argerich has made several albums with him. They include, among others, recordings of Béla Bartók's Piano Concerto no. 3; Chopin's Piano Concertos nos. 1 and 2 (the most recent renditions of which are on an EMI disk released in May 1999); Prokofiev's Piano Concerto nos. 1 and. 3; and Tchaikovsky's Piano Concerto no. 1. With Kovacevich, Argerich has recorded Bartók's Sonata for Two Pianos & Percussion; Claude Debussy's *En blanc et noir* (*In Black and White*); and Mozart's Andante and Variations for Piano Four Hands in G Major, K. 501.

Argerich has also performed with such conductors as Daniel Barenboim, Riccardo Chailly, Christoph von Dohnanyi, Nikolaus Harnoncourt, James Levine, Zubin Mehta, Seiji Ozawa, Mstislav Rostropovich, Giusepe Sinopoli, and Michael Tilson Thomas. Her orchestral repertoire includes Bartók's Concerto for Two Pianos, Percussion, and Orchestra; Beethoven's Piano Concertos nos. 1 and 2; Manuel de Falla's *Nights in the Gardens of Spain*; Haydn's Piano Concerto in D Major; Ravel's Piano Concerto in G Major; Saint-Saëns's *Carnival of the Animals*; Schumann's Piano Concerto in A Minor; Shostakovich's Concerto for Piano and String Orchestra; Richard Strauss's Burleske in D Minor for Piano and Orchestra; and Stravinsky's *Les Noces*. Notable among her albums is a recording of the live 1982 radio broadcast during which Argerich played Rachmaninoff's Piano Concerto in D Minor, under Riccardo Chailly. In the New York *Daily News* (October 24, 1995), Terry Teachout declared that Argerich's rendition "definitely ranks right up there" with those of Vladimir Horowitz and Van Cliburn; in *Stereo Review* (February 1996), Richard Freed wrote, "How the sparks fly here! How those big tunes sing! No speed is excessive for Argerich, no storm of musical passion an excuse for less than flawless finger work—or less than total accord between soloists and conductor. . . . At the end, the grateful listener is not exhausted but amazed and enriched by the brilliance, the involvement, the intimacy and exhilaration and genuineness of it all."

In an assessment of her work for *PCPlus* (online) in 1995, Jeremy Siepmann wrote, "Like all the greatest performers, she's not just a player but a listener, and her collaboration with others is invariably an exercise in musical conversation as its most involving." Argerich has performed and recorded with such artists as the pianists Nelson Freire and Alexandre Rabinovitch, the cellist Mischa Maisky, the flutist James Galway, and the violinists Gidon Kremer and Ivry Gitlis. In his 1995 *New York Times* article, Anthony Tommasini wrote that Argerich "has done some of her most solidly impressive work with Mr. Kremer." In his view, their recording of Beethoven's Sonatas for Violin and Piano nos. 6, 7, and 8 is "exquisite" and shows "the depth of the pianist's gifts." "In the first movement of the Sixth Sonata," Tommasini wrote, "Ms. Argerich's playing is positively elegant. She shapes the genial theme with grace and suppleness. This is a stylistically informed and handsome performance. Yet you always sense that just below the surface is a volcanic force waiting to erupt. Striking details—16th-note outbursts, syncopations, melodic leaps, rumbling base lines—emerge with arresting energy. . . . The Eighth Sonata is vibrant, charged by Ms. Argerich's barely contained wildness no matter how genial the music. Traveling with Ms. Argerich to where the wild things are is always an adventure. But when she is reined in by a sympathetic colleague like Mr. Kremer, the results are ultimately more rewarding."

For her solo albums, Argerich has recorded such works as Bach's English Suite no. 2, Partita for Piano no. 2, and Toccata in C Minor; Bartók's Sonata for Piano; Beethoven's Piano Sonata no. 28; Brahms's Rhapsodies, opus 79; many compositions by Chopin; Debussy's Preludes; and Schumann's Fantasia in C Major, *Fantasiestücke*, *Kinderszenen*, and *Kreisleriana*. Argerich is one of 80 artists chosen for inclusion in *Great Pianists of the 20th Century*, a 200-CD set compiled by Philips in collaboration with many other record producers and the Steinway piano company. The Argerich disk contains mazurkas, preludes, scherzos, and sonatas by Chopin, Liszt's Hungarian Rhapsodies and Sonata in B Minor, and Schumann's Sonata no. 2 in G Minor.

"A highly nervous performer, [Argerich] always looks as if she'd rather be anywhere in the world than where she is, at least until she's finished, when she's all smiles," Richard Dyer wrote in his 1998 *Boston Globe* profile of her. "She hides her face from the audience behind a curtain of hair, which serves as a kind of shield." "To the outsider," Jeremy Siepmann observed, "Argerich would appear to have everything: genius, fame, wealth, beauty, but her manner, in the face of the most tumultuous ovation, is unfailingly modest and reserved." Diffident in public, she is a nonstop talker when she is with her friends or family; indeed, she has referred to talking as one of her "vices." According to John and Anna Gillespie, she has "a wonderful gift for musical parody that enables her to create devastating takeoffs on many of the great pianists." — M.B.

Suggested Reading: *Boston Globe* (on-line) Aug. 24, 1998; New York *Daily News* p20 Oct. 24, 1995, with photo; *New York Times* II p33 Oct. 29, 1995, with photo; Peabody Institute (on-line); *People* p67+ Apr. 7, 1980, with photos; Gillespie, John, and Anna Gillespie. *Notable Twentieth-Century Pianists*, 1995

Selected Recordings: Bach: Cello Sonatas nos. 1 and 2, English Suite no. 2, Partita no. 2, Toccata in C Minor; Bartók: Concerto for Two Pianos, Piano Concerto no. 3, Sonata for Piano, Sonata for Two Pianos and Percussion, Violin and Piano Sonata no. 1; Beethoven: Cello Sonatas nos. 1–5, Piano Concertos nos. 1 and 2, Piano Sonata no. 28, Violin Sonatas nos. 1–9; Brahms: Rhapsodies op. 79, Sonata for Two Pianos in F Minor, Variations on a Theme by Haydn for Two Pianos, Waltzes for Two Pianos, Chopin: Ballade no. 3, Barcarolle in F-sharp Major, Etudes op. 4, Fantasie in F Minor, Impromptu no. 4, Mazurkas op. 24 no. 2, op. 59 nos. 1–3, Nocturne no. 16 in E-flat, Piano Concertos nos. 1 and 2, Polonaise no. 6, Preludes op. 28; Scherzos nos. 2 and 3; Sonatas no. 2 and 3; Debussy: *En blanc et noir*, *Estampes*, Sonata for Cello and Piano, Sonata for Violin and Piano in G Minor; Dvořák: Piano Quintet; de Falla: *Nights in the Gardens of Spain*; Haydn: Concerto for Piano and Orchestra in D Major; Liszt: Piano Concerto no. 1; Mendelsohn: Concerto for Violin, Piano and Strings in D Minor; Mozart: Andante and Variations for Piano Four Hands in G Major, Sonata for Two Pianos in D Major, Sonatas for Piano Four Hands in C Major and D Major; Prokofiev: Piano Concertos no. 1 and 3; Ravel: *Gaspard de la Nuit, Jeux d'eau, La Valse*, Piano Concerto in G Major, *Rhapsodie espagnole*, *Le Tombeau de Couperin*, *Valse nobles et sentimentales*; Saints-Saëns: *Carnival of the Animals*

Jeff Christensen/Archive Photos

Armstrong, C. Michael

Oct. 18, 1938– CEO of AT&T. Address: c/o AT&T Corp., 295 Maple Ave., Basking Ridge, NJ 07929

C. Michael Armstrong is one of the most powerful CEOs in the world. When he took over as the chief executive officer at AT&T, in November 1997, he brought with him a reputation for being as decisive as he was unorthodox: in addition to rejuvenating his former company, the Hughes Electronics Corp., he often refused to wear a suit to work and insisted on driving his Harley-Davidson motorcycle to the office. During his five years as head of Hughes, formerly the Hughes Aircraft Co., he slashed the company's costs by 30 percent, sold off their costly weapons business and auto-parts division, and began focusing the company's attention on its vast satellite communications network. Under his guidance, Hughes developed DirecTV, now the most popular home-satellite television hook-up in the United States. Since he joined AT&T, Armstrong has pushed through three megadeals—with TCI in June 1998, with British Telecom a month later, and with Mediaone in May 1999—as well as several other big transactions, for a total commitment of more than $90 billion.

With those deals, coupled with AT&T's booming stock, Armstrong has performed a feat many pundits would have thought impossible two years ago: he has infused life into the seemingly outdated, stock market–stagnated, traditionally conservative corporate dinosaur that was AT&T. "Armstrong is even tearing AT&T from its roots as the provider of closed-circuit telephone connections," Fred Vogelstein wrote for *U.S. News & World Report* (August 10, 1998, on-line). "He wants all

AT&T calls eventually to travel only over the Internet, rather than being routed by switches over dedicated wires, as they have been since the first exchange was installed [by Alexander Graham Bell] in New Haven, Connecticut, in 1878." An example of his slash-and-burn, fat-cutting style was his decision to make AT&T executives' bonuses correspond to company profits (for decades, top brass received hefty bonuses no matter how the company performed). After having spent the first 31 years of his working life as an employee of IBM, Armstrong has established himself as one of the boldest and most innovative chief executives of the 1990s.

The oldest of the three sons of Charles H. and Zora Jean (Brooks) Armstrong, C. Michael Armstrong was born on October 18, 1938 in Detroit, Michigan. A gifted athlete, Armstrong was awarded a scholarship in 1957 to play football at Miami University, in Ohio. His days on the gridiron were cut short, however, when he suffered a shoulder injury that required extensive surgery. The operation rendered his right arm shorter than his left, and he was never again able to play football, but this setback only led him to focus more of his attention on his studies and other areas. No longer eligible for an athletic scholarship, he began working odd jobs to pay tuition; he also became heavily involved in his fraternity, Sigma Nu, in which he was so popular that he was elected fraternity president. His frat brother Richard R. Lamb, a businessman in Sacramento, told a reporter for *Business Week* (June 20, 1988) about Armstrong's qualities as both a leader and a friend, "You could almost quote the Boy Scout motto: loyal, friendly, trustworthy." In addition to his duties as fraternity president, Armstrong was a member of the Interfraternity Council, the publications board, and the honorary business society. In 1961 he graduated with a B.S. degree in business and economics, married his longtime girlfriend, Anne Gossett, and promptly moved to Indianapolis, having been hired soon after graduation as a service engineer for IBM.

Within his first few years at "Big Blue," as the company is nicknamed, Armstrong was able to maneuver his way into a marketing and sales position. It was largely because of this that his star began to rise, as IBM's computer business mushroomed in the 1970s. By late 1978 Armstrong had worked his way up the ranks to become the president of IBM's most important marketing arm, the Data Processing Division. His success with the division resulted in his promotion, in March 1987, to the head of all IBM operations in Europe; after 26 years with the company, Armstrong was the heir apparent to the CEO of IBM.

Because he was the first American to lead the IBM World Trade Europe/Middle East/Africa division, Armstrong's appointment was met with as much skepticism as applause; many had expected a European to be appointed to the position. Armstrong's predecessors, Jacques G. Masionroughe of France and Kaspar V. Cassani of Switzerland, were both well-versed in European business and politics and able to converse in several languages. Armstrong, on the other hand, spoke only a little Spanish at the time of his appointment and had to begin French lessons as soon as he moved to the company's European headquarters, in Paris. On the other hand, IBM's European sales had fallen off substantially in the late 1980s, and Armstrong's appointment represented an attempt on the part of top brass to shake things up. The strategy worked—within his first few months on the job, Armstrong began to turn things around in Europe. Most notably, he changed some longstanding pricing policies, implemented sweeping deregulatory measures that gave more autonomy to IBM subsidiaries in European countries, and improved corporate relations with large European companies. By the beginning of 1992, due to his impressive success abroad, industry analysts had come to assume that Armstrong would replace CEO John Akers upon Akers's retirement in 1994.

In February 1992, however, Armstrong shocked the business world by leaving the only company for which he had ever worked to become the CEO at Hughes. Although many theories were put forth to explain why he left IBM, the most commonly accepted one was that by the time Armstrong was due to inherit the reins, he would have been 56—four years short of IBM's mandatory retirement age. At Hughes, Armstrong had the option to serve as company head until the age of 65. By signing on as CEO of the Los Angeles–based Hughes, a weapons-technology firm started by the legendary Howard Hughes in 1932, Armstrong was able to show off his skills as an executive. Hughes, when Armstrong took the helm, was in serious financial trouble. The country's defense budget was being trimmed, and Hughes—owned by General Motors—"was starting to show its own battle scars," as Debra Sparks wrote for *FinancialWorld* (April 22, 1996). In 1991 Hughes, with regard to profits, ranked 22d out of 22 aerospace companies. "And that was the good news," Sparks wrote. "'The bad news was how far we were from being 21st,' admits Armstrong."

One of Armstrong's first acts at Hughes was to cut costs by 30 percent by eliminating unnecessary expenditures and releasing 12,000 people (15 percent of all employees) from their jobs. Next, Armstrong ordered the sale of some of the numerous buildings the company owned in downtown Los Angeles. Then, in the company's riskiest endeavor in decades, he set about consolidating Hughes's telecommunications and space divisions by launching DirecTV—a satellite broadcast system that offered 175 channels and round-the-clock, pay-per-view movies—in 1995. Available at stores that sell electronic products, the DirecTV dish has since become the best-selling satellite television system. With revenues beginning to come in as a result of Hughes's DirecTV venture, Armstrong began to sell off the company's cumbersome auto-parts and missile-producing divisions, shedding large, nagging debt that had plagued the company

since the recession of the late 1980s. By 1996 DirecTV had close to two million subscribers, and in that year AT&T paid Hughes $137 million for a 2.5 percent share of the profits. During this miraculous financial turnaround, Armstrong also served as chairman of the President's Export Council (PEC), a position to which he was appointed in 1995. The council, a public-private partnership begun in 1973, was set up to advise the president of the U.S. on important export trends and strategies.

With Hughes continuing to soar toward even greater profitability in 1997, Armstrong announced his plans to leave the company and to take over as CEO at AT&T, the country's largest communications corporation, whose legacy dates back to Alexander Graham Bell's first telephone, built in 1876. On the day of the announcement—October 20, 1997—AT&T's stock rose 5 percent, adding $3 billion to the company's overall worth. It had been rumored for some time that Armstrong was being considered for the post, and he had reportedly been offered the position in 1996, only to have the offer rescinded when then-CEO Robert E. Allen decided to remain at the helm. "It's been an exciting and thrilling day," Armstrong told Seth Schiesel for the *New York Times* (July 27, 1998). "I've got a lot of adrenaline flowing. I don't think I'm going to let that adrenaline stop for the rest of my career." At the time of Armstrong's appointment, AT&T was suffering greatly. Part of the reason was that the firm did not have a cost-efficient business infrastructure. Armstrong told Peter Elstrom for *Businessweek.com* (May 1998), "I have not seen a cost structure like this since IBM in the days of the mainframe. It has to change. We don't have a strategy if we don't have a cost-competitive company. It's just the underpinning of everything we go out and do."

In late January 1998 Armstrong announced his first wave of drastic changes at AT&T. In addition to cutting some 18,000 jobs nationwide, he unveiled plans to exploiting the vast resources of AT&T by expanding aggressively into digital cable and wireless networks, which the company had been developing for some time. As a result of these developments, AT&T stock, after years of going virtually nowhere, began to soar.

On June 17, 1998 Armstrong hit his first bump in the road as chief executive, when America Online (AOL), the nation's largest on-line service, rejected a takeover bid by AT&T. At the time AOL had nearly 12 million subscribers worldwide, while 1.1 million were using AT&T's on-line service, AT&T Worldnet. Armstrong, undeterred, announced only a week later AT&T's acquisition of Tele-Communications Inc. (TCI). According to the terms of the all-stock deal, which was worth an estimated $48 billion, AT&T would merge its long-distance, wireless, and Internet services with TCI's cable, telecommunications, and high-speed Internet business to form a new subsidiary, AT&T Consumer Services. The deal, according to TCI's CEO, John Malone, was put together staggeringly quickly—in just eight days. The most important aspect of the deal was that TCI's extensive local phone service, with nearly 13 million customers nationwide (including such major markets as Denver, Chicago, Portland, Pittsburgh, Dallas, San Francisco, Salt Lake City, St. Louis, and Seattle), gave AT&T direct telephone connections to individual homes, which it had lost when it was split up by the government in a 1984 antitrust suit. For over a decade AT&T's telephone services had been solely long-distance based, after it had been forced to let its local providers become autonomous companies. Armstrong told Jeff Pelline for *News.com* (June 24, 1998, on-line), "Today we are beginning to answer a big part of the question about how we will provide local service to U.S. consumers. Through its own systems and in partnership with affiliates, AT&T Consumer Services will bring to people's homes the first fully integrated package of communications, electronic commerce, and video entertainment services."

Just over a month later, on July 27, AT&T announced plans to merge its international operations with British Telecom, the United Kingdom's largest telecommunications company. "The alliance between AT&T, the United States' largest communications company, and British Telecom, Britain's largest leading communications provider, is a stark demonstration that even the brawniest communications giants no longer feel big enough to take on the global marketplace on their own . . . ," Seth Schiesel observed. "Both AT&T and British Telecom have . . . stumbled in creating strong partnerships overseas. But in agreeing to actually transfer assets and customers to the new company instead of signing a vague marketing pact, AT&T . . . made its biggest commitment yet to a comprehensive global strategy." The deal was so large that Federal Communications Commission officers were said to be considering whether to examine the merger on the grounds that it might create a monopoly in the industry. "This is about following our customers into a world that is opening markets," Armstrong told Schiesel. "This puts meat underneath the concept that we would be doing everything that we could to enable a global universal service." In early October 1999 British Telecom and AT&T announced that the new company would be called Concert (the same moniker chosen by British Telecom and MCI Communications for a joint venture that ended in 1997, when MCI agreed to be bought by Worldcom Inc.). Meanwhile, in September 1999 MCI Worldcom Inc. acquired the Sprint Corp., and it will thus present even more formidable competition for Concert, which cannot begin operating in the U.S. until the U.S. Justice Department gives its approval.

Earlier, Armstrong and AT&T had announced two additional developments. The first, launched in mid-1998, was the Digital One Rate Plan, which made phone calls within certain geographic areas far less expensive than before. By early 1999 the lower rates offered by the plan had lured thou-

sands of cell-phone customers to AT&T. Then, on January 27, 1999, Armstrong unveiled the Personal Network package, providing users with one flat rate on long-distance calls made with either a calling card, cell phone, or home phone.

By the beginning of 1999, it was clear that AT&T's hiring of Armstrong had truly paid off. In February AT&T shares, at the time the most widely held in the United States, had grown in value by 65 percent, and analysts predicted that the company's stock would rise another 20 percent over the course of the year. Later that month AT&T announced that it had rewarded Armstrong with lucrative bonus payments, following his highly successful year and a half at the helm. According to *Yahoo!News* (March 22, 1999, on-line), AT&T paid Armstrong a $1.9 million bonus—$800,000 more than they had paid former CEO Robert Allen in 1997—in addition to his $1.4 million salary and a prorated $291,667 for his services in 1997. AT&T stated that Armstrong was also given the option to acquire 300,000 shares in the company and that he was receiving $3 million for miscellaneous expenses, including $32,785 for use of the corporate jet and $2.3 million to purchase an insurance policy.

AT&T made front-page news again in early May 1999, when it agreed to buy the Mediaone Group, which provides local and long-distance telephone connections, digital television, and access to the Internet to 8.5 million homes. Earlier, the company had arranged partnerships with Time Warner and the Comcast Corp. that will enable AT&T to offer telephone service to millions of additional customers using those companies' cable systems. With those latest deals, AT&T committed a total of more than $90 billion to create a network capable of delivering not only local phone service to more than 56 million homes but also, as Seth Schiesel reported in the *New York Times* (May 7, 1999), "high-speed Internet access and television programming to more than 28 million homes." Making this plan a reality will require transforming cable into a medium that transmits information not only one way, from a company to a user, as cable systems do now, but also back and forth, as telephone systems do. And making the cable system capable of routing "millions, even billions of bits of digital information from one point to another every second," in Schiesel's words, and able to perform other complicated tasks will require the development of still untested, extremely complex, and exceedingly expensive technology. "We need to figure out how to build it, how to deploy it, how to support it, how to maintain it," Armstrong told Schiesel. "The stakes are especially high for AT&T because its reputation with consumers, built over decades, will be on the line," Schiesel wrote. "When a telephone cuts off for no apparent reason, when an Internet connection drops in the middle of a big download, when the television shuts off during the big game, customers rarely forget."

On May 6, 1999 Armstrong announced that the software giant Microsoft Corp. will be investing $5 billion in AT&T, with the understanding that AT&T will increase its purchases of Microsoft products.

C. Michael Armstrong, who has been a supporter of higher education for most of his career, has been awarded honorary doctor of law degrees from Pepperdine University (1997) and Loyola Marymount (1988). He is currently a trustee at Johns Hopkins University and a member of the Yale School of Management advisory board. Armstrong is also on the board of directors at Travelers Corp. and on the supervisory board of the Thyssen-

Bornemisza Group. He and his wife have three daughters—Linda, Julie, and Kristy. — M.B.

Suggested Reading: *Aviation Week & Space Technology* p55+ Apr. 26, 1993, with photos; *Business America* p4+ Apr. 1995, with photos; *Business Week* p96+ June 20, 1988, with photos; *FinancialWorld* p28+ Apr. 22, 1996, with photos; *New York Times* D p1 Feb. 20, 1992, with photo, D p1 Oct. 11, 1996, D p4 Oct. 21, 1997, p1 June 29, 1998, with photo; *New York Times* (on-line) Feb. 1, 1998, July 27, 1998; *News.com* (on-line) June 24, 1998, with photo; *U.S. News & World Report* (on-line) Aug. 10, 1998

Courtesy of the U.S. Senate

Ashcroft, John

May 9, 1942– U.S. Senator from Missouri.
Address: 705 Hart Bldg., Washington, DC 20510

John Ashcroft, a former governor of Missouri and currently its junior senator, is one of the most influential politicians in the state's history. Ashcroft became Missouri's 50th governor in 1984, after two terms as the state's attorney general. Upon his election, he and Missouri's two other high-ranking GOP officials—Senators John C. Danforth and Kit Bond—ushered in an era of Republican dominance in a state that had traditionally been controlled by Democrats. As governor, Ashcroft imposed strict limits on welfare and tough standards for student advancement. Highly popular after two terms but barred by state law from running for a third, Ashcroft ran in 1994 for the seat being vacated by

Senator Danforth, winning an impressive victory. Many of his legislative proposals in the Senate have met with resistance; his staunchly conservative stances on such issues as welfare reform have at times alienated even his Republican colleagues. His popularity at home remains high, however, bolstered in part by his reputation as a gospel singer in churches all over Missouri. Ashcroft is seeking reelection to the Senate in 2000; his announced challenger is the state's governor, Mel Carnahan, a moderate Democrat.

John Ashcroft was born on May 9, 1942 in Chicago. Early in his childhood, Ashcroft's family moved to Springfield, Missouri, in order to be closer to the world headquarters of the Assembly of God church, in which his father was a minister; at the time of the family's relocation, Springfield was becoming a center for adherents of conservative Protestant theology. As a high school student, Ashcroft, who had played the guitar since childhood, made a name for himself throughout the state as a talented gospel singer. Exceptionally bright, he enrolled as a history major at Yale University, in New Haven, Connecticut, graduating in 1964. He met his wife, Janet, while attending the University of Chicago Law School, where they both obtained degrees in 1967. Married soon afterward, the couple began practicing law together and were both subsequently hired by Southwest Missouri State University to teach business. During their time as faculty members, the couple coauthored two textbooks, *Law for Business* and *It's the Law.*

Preaching fiscal conservatism, Ashcroft mounted an ill-fated campaign for the United States House of Representatives in 1972. His efforts were noted by then-governor Kit Bond, who a year later appointed him to the vacant position of state auditor. Ashcroft sought election to the post in 1974, but lost. Not easily discouraged, in 1976 he launched another political campaign, this time for state attorney general, and won handily, replacing Republican mainstay John C. Danforth, who had recently vacated the position to run for the U.S. Senate. With his reelection in 1980, Ashcroft was seen as a rising star within the Missouri Republican Party, his image inseparable from his deeply held religious convictions and his gospel-music pursuits. By the end of his second term as attorney general, GOP brass considered him a front-runner for governor in 1984. Accepting the challenge, Ashcroft won his party's nomination, and in the general election, he triumphed over his Democratic opponent, Lieutenant Governor Kenneth J. Rottman, a moderate-to-liberal political veteran from St. Louis. Ashcroft succeeded his political mentor, Kit Bond, who would later run for Senate.

According to *Politics in America 1998*, "the best-known event of Ashcroft's governorship" was *Webster v. Reproductive Health Services*, a lawsuit handled by Ashcroft's attorney general. The case concerned Missouri statutes that asserted that life began at conception; prohibited the use of public funds or facilities for abortions; and required physicians to perform "fetal liability" tests on women 20 weeks pregnant or beyond who were seeking abortions, to determine whether their fetuses could live outside the womb. In a 5–4 vote, the Supreme Court upheld the Missouri statutes, thus reinforcing the rights of the states to restrict abortion.

In a contest against Betty Cooper Hearnes, a Democratic state representative and the wife of former Missouri governor Warren E. Hearnes, Ashcroft won reelection in 1988 with 65 percent of the vote, the widest margin of victory in a Missouri gubernatorial race since the Civil War. During his tenure as governor, he initiated strong welfare and educational reform that fell firmly along conservative guidelines; they included reducing the amount of state aid to those on government subsidies and implementing stringent testing requirements for grade-school students.

In 1993, when John Danforth announced that he was retiring from the Senate, state GOP officials looked to Ashcroft to run for the open seat. Ashcroft's opponent in the general election was the longtime U.S. House of Representatives member Alan Wheat, the first African-American in Missouri history to become a statewide candidate. Wheat spent much of his campaign money during the grueling battle for the Democratic nomination, and as a result he found his resources dwarfed by Ashcroft's deep campaign war chest. Wheat ran a number of TV ads that accused the former governor of having made regular use of a state airplane at taxpayer expense; Ashcroft denied the allegations and launched a counter-assault, portraying Wheat as a liberal who was soft on murderers and other criminals. Wheat did not have the money to rebut the commercials, and Ashcroft won easily, garnering 60 percent of the vote. His first, and arguably most visible, act as junior senator was his involvement in the formation of a barber-shop quartet with three other Republican senators—Larry E. Craig of Idaho, James M. Jeffords of Vermont, and Trent Lott of Mississippi. They dubbed themselves the "Singing Senators."

Most of Ashcroft's proposed legislation has not seen the light of day. In the debate over the dismantling of welfare, he was among many Republicans in both the Senate and the House who wanted to place limits on aid to people having children out of wedlock, impose strict work requirements on welfare recipients, and cut off aid completely to noncitizens. Some of the proposals made by him and other Senate Republicans provided the basis for the welfare legislation that President Bill Clinton signed in 1996, but as *Politics in America 1998* stated, "Ashcroft would have liked to have taken it further"—with a 20 percent reduction in benefits for parents who did not have their children properly immunized and a plan to turn over the food-stamp program to state control. Ashcroft has also advocated term limits for the Senate and House, once commenting, "Term limits would end congressional stagnation and careerism and bring a healthy infusion of new ideas and new people." The term-limit legislation, introduced with the help of the first-term Tennessee senator Fred Thompson, has proven highly unpopular among his colleagues, as have Ashcroft's efforts to require applicants for all federally funded job-training programs to take randomly applied drug tests. Additionally, his bid to reduce funding for the National Endowments for the Arts and the Humanities by half has also garnered little support. His only major legislative contribution has been a measure allocating federal funds to hire religious groups to provide services for the needy.

His spotless personal record and deep Protestant convictions, however, have made the senator highly popular among the nation's religious right, particularly the Christian Coalition and its founder, the preacher Pat Robertson, who is a former presidential candidate. A favorite slogan of Ashcroft's, as he told Jessica Lee for *USA Today* (November 10, 1994), is "The only government handout I want is the government's hand out of my pocket." This attitude has endeared him to the politically and theologically conservative, and in a straw poll taken by the Christian Coalition in February 1998, 65 percent of respondents named Ashcroft the most popular government official from Missouri. Only a few months later, however, a meeting of the coalition—which was supposed to be a "coming-out" party of sorts for the senator as a viable presidential candidate—ended on an unfortunate note for Ashcroft: Malcolm S. "Steve" Forbes, the publishing magnate and Oval Office hopeful, delivered a rousing speech that made the senator's seem dull by comparison. Earlier in 1998 Ashcroft had told John J. Miller for the *National Review* (March 23, 1998) that mounting a campaign for the presidency is "like running the mile. You have to run the first few laps, and run them hard, before you know if you're really even in the race." By early 1999 George W. Bush, the governor of Texas and a son of former president George Bush, had emerged as a favorite to win the Republican nomination for president. Bush's entry into the race virtually nullified Ashcroft's chances of gaining the nomination.

Later in 1999 Ashcroft announced his bid for a second term in the U.S. Senate. Considered a shoo-in just a few months ago, he faces a strong opponent in Mel Carnahan, the popular two-term Democratic governor of Missouri. One campaign issue concerns Carnahan's decision, in January 1999, to bow to Pope John Paul II's request that he spare the life of Darrell Mease, who had been sentenced to death for the murder of three people. Carnahan, who supports the death penalty and has approved more than two dozen executions by the state, commuted Mease's sentence to life in prison without the possibility of parole after a prayer service held during the pope's one-day visit to St. Louis. Ashcroft has condemned Carnahan's action in the Mease case, and in May he held a hearing on victims' rights to which he invited relatives of one of the people Mease was convicted of killing. In the *New York Times* (April 28, 1999, on-line), B. Drummond Ayres Jr. reported that Governor Carnahan denounced the hearing as "shameless political exploitation," while Ashcroft defended it as an effort to ensure that victims' rights are "taken more seriously than they are at present."

Ashcroft and his wife, Janet, live near St. Louis, in the town of Ballwin, Missouri, where they raised their three children—Martha, Jay, and Andrew. Janet Ashcroft currently teaches business law at Howard University. Senator Ashcroft is an avid fan of baseball. When, in 1985, Missouri's two baseball teams battled each other in the World Series, Ashcroft—not wanting to offend hometown fans of either team—commissioned a special hat, with one side displaying the logo of the St. Louis Cardinals and the other that of the Kansas City Royals; the then-governor flipped the cap around between innings so that he could root for the team at bat. — M.B.

Suggested Reading: *New Republic* p18+ Dec. 22, 1997, with photo; *New York Times* (on-line) Jan. 31, 1998, with photo; *USA Today* A p11 Nov. 10, 1994, with photo, A p6 Feb. 18, 1998, with photo; *Washington Post* A p7 Dec. 31, 1992, with photos, A p15 May 29, 1995, A p1 Apr. 14, 1998, with photos; *Politics in America 1998*

Brian Killigrew/Courtesy of U.S. Chess Federation

Ashley, Maurice

Mar. 1966– Grandmaster chess player. Address: c/o United States Chess Federation, 3054 Route 9W, New Windsor, NY 12553

Bishop to King seven! With that move at a tournament sponsored by the Manhattan Chess Club on March 14, 1999, Maurice Ashley made history by becoming the first African-American to gain the ranking of grandmaster (GM), the highest level in professional chess. He thus joined the approximately 700 chess grandmasters in the world and fulfilled a dream that had driven him since he had fallen in love with the game, at age 14. "The stereotype in this country is that African-Americans don't do well at things like chess," he noted after the March tournament, as quoted by the Associated Press (March 26, 1999, on-line). "We're understood as physically gifted and great entertainers, but when it comes to something intellectual, that lags behind." In an interview with Barbara Stewart for *Sam Sloan's Chess Page* (March 17, 1999, on-line), he said, "It's not significant to me to be the best black chess player in the world. But it is sweet to be the first [black grandmaster]."

Almost from the beginning, chess has been much more than just a form of recreation for Ashley. "I play because this game forces me to go to the limit," he told Brian Killigrew for *Chess Life* (May 1999). "In this case, my intellectual limit, but also my personal limit as a being, as a fighter. It forces me to expend everything that I am in order to play well. It's not often in life that you get situations like that, where it's such a joy that you can extend yourself and work really hard at some truly complicated issue. . . . You've got to work with every bit of your spirit and soul to play this game and yet you can still be creative, you can still have fun, and you can actually do something wonderful on the board. I think that whole creative process that extends everything we are, that requires every bit of our attention, is what wraps us up in this game." In establishing himself among the game's elite, Ashley has set many records and blazed trails for other African-American players. By coaching young players and working to attract new participants and audiences, he has helped to increase the game's following.

Born in March 1966 in Kingston, Jamaica, Maurice Ashley moved to the United States with his family some years later and settled in the New York City borough of Brooklyn. Games, including dominoes and cards, were a favorite pastime in his family. Ashley learned the rules of chess when he was eight years old, by watching his brother play. In contrast to such grandmasters as Gary Kasparov, whose prodigious talents at chess became obvious when he was six, and Bobby Fischer, who attracted the attention of an international master at eight, Ashley did not attach any particular importance to chess until one day when he was 14—an advanced age in competitive circles. On that day a Brooklyn Technical High School classmate of his challenged him to a match. "He just demolished me completely," Ashley recalled to the television talk-show host Charlie Rose in an interview broadcast on April 7, 1999. "And we don't take losing lightly in my family." Stung by his defeat, he got hold of a book about the Louisianan Paul Morphy (1837–84), considered the first American master of chess, who at age nine defeated the great American general and self-styled chess expert Winfield Scott. "I opened the book up, and it was like . . . a fairy tale," Ashley told Charlie Rose. "I couldn't believe it. It was kings and queens and knights and the pageantry of the game, really. It just had such a majesty to it. And it was fascinating—strategy and tactics and ideas and attacks and defense. And it was like—it was football, really. I mean, it was, like, amazing, all the action in the game. And so I just . . . fell in love."

Back at Brooklyn Tech, Ashley linked up with a group of young African-American chess fanatics, who played every day after school in a classroom. "We would stay there from three o'clock until 6:52," Ashley told Charlie Rose. "And the reason 6:52 is 'cause we had a train pass where you could get on the subway system for free coming out of high school, and, if you got there at seven o'clock—you're too late. So, at 6:52, it's 'Go ahead, make your move. . . . All right, we gotta go.' . . . And we were out." The students often gathered on Friday nights for marathon sessions of chess. "We were fighters, gladiators," Ashley told Barbara Stewart. "You couldn't enter this group without being ready to go to war. Nobody would leave until Sunday. They'd shower, sleep a little, and get up and play. Many a girlfriend was lost over weekend chess rumbles." Ashley soon began playing competitively in tournaments, and while still in high school, he earned an 1800 rating from the United States Chess Federation (USCF). (The rating is determined by means of computations that involve a logarithmic function and is based in part on the ratings of a player's opponents. For example, winning or losing to a player rated higher results in a differ-

ent number of points added or subtracted than does winning or losing to one with a lower rating. The rating system is described on the USCF's Web site and in its rule book.) According to the March 26, 1999 Associated Press dispatch, during his youth Ashley spent a lot of time in Brooklyn's Prospect Park, learning from and competing with a group that called themselves the Black Bear School of Chess.

After graduating from high school, in about 1984, Ashley entered the City College of New York. His mother repeatedly urged him to get his degree; she did not play chess and, as he told Charlie Rose, "knew nothing" about the world of chess, and she could not envision anyone deriving a livelihood from it. Nevertheless, he focused most of his energy on chess rather than his course work, and he eventually dropped out of college.

Meanwhile, Ashley had begun pitting himself against stronger competitors. While expanding his skills, he developed a penchant for playing aggressively. "I'm never interested in the easy game," he told Killigrew. "I want to play the guy that totally crushes me, who makes me sit and fight to my last breath trying to beat this guy or woman." In 1986 he gained the rank of national master, and in 1993 he became the first African-American to become an international master.

Earlier, in 1989, he had started coaching public-school chess teams under the aegis of the Manhattan Chess Club School, which sponsored chess teachers in more than 100 schools in the New York City area. From 1991 to 1997 he served as the chess director of the Harlem Educational Activities Fund. In total, he coached three players to individual U.S. championships in their age groups and school teams to three U.S. championships, in 1991, 1994, and 1995. One of the teams he led to a national title—specifically, the 1991 national junior-high chess championship—was the Raging Rooks, from the Adam Clayton Powell Jr. Junior High School in the Harlem section of New York City. The Rooks triumphed over 60 other teams—including the defending champions, from the prestigious Dalton School, a private school in New York City—to tie for first place. Another of Ashley's winning teams was the Dark Knights, from Mott Hall, a specialized intermediate school, also located in Harlem. Speaking of his work with inner-city youths shortly after leading the Raging Rooks to victory, Ashley told John Tierney for the New York Times (April 26, 1991), "When I started, there weren't a lot of good black chess players, so there wasn't a high ceiling for me to shoot for. Now I'm the ceiling for these kids, and I'm hoping they'll surpass me. I want them to become role models. [The Rooks'] victory already makes a major statement about the potential of kids in the inner city—and about the lost potential of those adults you see on street corners."

At around that time, Ashley recalled to Charlie Rose, a friend of his who worked in finance offered him a job with a six-figure salary. "Banks were coming to chess players because they knew that chess players were calculators, were also intuitive, made decisions very quickly with lots of facts in front of us," Ashley explained to Rose. Although he was earning less than $20,000 a year then, he turned down the offer outright. "I said, 'What, are you kidding? Why would I do that? What kind of job is that?' . . . Working for the money was out of the question 'cause . . . you're in love with something. This is your passion."

In the mid-1990s Ashley found himself playing less well. In 1997, after a particularly disappointing performance at a competition in Bermuda, he stopped coaching, with the goal of focusing on his dream of becoming a grandmaster. "The 1997 tournament in Bermuda was the most pivotal tournament in my life," he told Killigrew. "The players . . . were really focused on chess. They were young players that were really hungry for chess, they knew about the chess world and were interested in staying on top of chess. I wasn't at that stage; I was heavily into teaching, I was always distracted by other things, and I wasn't doing what I needed to do to become a really strong player, to become a GM."

With the financial backing of an unidentified sponsor, Ashley began a rigorous training regimen. It included intensive study of previous games and chess theory; workouts at a gym three times a week; and, starting in 1998, individual instruction from Gregory Kaidanov, a premier U.S. player. His work with Kaidanov, with whom he spends several days each month, entails more than chess strategies; much of their time together is devoted to "the competitive issues that face a player and the psychological issues that can hamstring you," as Ashley explained to Killigrew. He added, "When I compete, I see the same problems over and over again. The same personal foibles, the same personal limitations that kill me again and again when I'm playing. . . . I realize that in the bigger picture, the same things where I fall short in play, I fall short in life."

At the international tournament held in Bermuda in 1998, it was plain that he had profited greatly from his efforts. Although he "just missed" achieving grandmaster status, as he recalled to Killigrew, he "finished well in the top of the pack . . . a great result." The outcome was outstanding not least because he defeated the winner of the 1997 tournament, Julian Hodgson. "After the game, [Hodgson] said, 'Wow, Maurice, I see a difference in your games. I think you're getting good.' And that made me feel really good because I respect his words." During his conversation with Barbara Stewart, Ashley said, "I'm still a beginner, as far as I'm concerned. There's so much to learn. The game is still fresh for me."

Ashley attained the ranking of grandmaster on March 14, 1999 at a tournament at the Manhattan Chess Club, by fulfilling the requirements established by the Fédération Internationale des Échecs (International Chess Federation), which is known in chess circles by the acronym FIDE (pronounced FEE-day). Typically, acquiring the title involves competing in at least three tournaments in which the participants include other very strong FIDE-rated players (at least three of whom are grandmasters and at least one-third of whom are from countries other than the candidate's) and winning a specified number of games in each event, the number being based on the average rating of all the players in each tournament. In the decisive match, Ashley capitalized on his opponent's mistake and finished the tournament in second place. He joined 49 other grandmasters in the United States and some 700 worldwide. As of May 1999 his USCF rating was 2515.

In addition to playing competitive chess, Ashley is a popular chess commentator and master of ceremonies at chess functions. He was the play-by-play commentator for the matches between Garry Kasparov, the reigning world champion, and Deep Blue, the computer developed by IBM specifically to challenge Kasparov. (Kasparov beat Deep Blue in 1996, four games to two, and lost in 1997, winning just one game and drawing three in a best-of-six-game series.) Ashley has also helped design a popular CD-ROM chess tutorial, *Maurice Ashley Teaches Chess*, which is geared to people as young as seven years old and to people at various levels of skill. He serves as the "dean of chess" at Chess-Wise University, which offers instruction on-line.

Ashley and his wife, Michele, live in the Park Slope section of Brooklyn. The couple have a four-year-old daughter, Nia, who also plays chess. Ashley is an avid sports fan, and he enjoys aikido and reading. Among the books that he regards as particularly inspirational for him are *Mastery: The Keys to Success and Long-Term Fulfillment* (1992), by George Leonard, and *I Never Had It Made* (1972), the autobiography of Jackie Robinson. "I live everyday trying to be inspired by something," he said to Brian Killigrew. "It may be my daughter's smile. I look for inspiration in life because I think there is inspiration in everything, everywhere." — Y.P.

Suggested Reading: *Chess Life* p28+ May 1999, with photos; *New York Times* A p1 Apr. 26, 1991, with photo

---

Aulenti, Gae

(ow-LEN-tee, gay)

Dec. 4, 1927– Architect. Address: 4 Piazzo S. Marco, 20121 Milano, Italy

"It's not possible to define a style in my work," the architect Gae Aulenti told Carol Vogel for the *New York Times Magazine* (November 22, 1987). Best known for her conversion of the Orsay railway station, a Beaux-Arts landmark built in Paris in 1900, into a museum for Impressionist art, Aulenti spe-

Gae Aulenti

cializes in redesigning the interiors of historic buildings so as to turn them into museums. Her job involves preserving preexisting architectural features while transforming or updating the inside space. While Aulenti considers her designs to be in the "modernist vein," as Vogel put it, she works to find a thread connecting a building's original design, the new spaces she creates within the structure, and the artwork the building will house. Aulenti's main goal is, in Vogel's words, "the marriage of a given design with the art work it must accommodate. Ideally, this union . . . juxtaposes elements of the past with the present." "If you're designing an airport, then airplanes are important," Aulenti told Vogel. "It's no more complicated designing a museum. I prefer museums for my own personal passion—the art."

Gaetana Aulenti was born on December 4, 1927 in the town of Palazzolo dello Stella, in the Udine region of Italy. Her father worked in the nearby city of Trieste as an economist. "My parents really wanted me to be a dilettante, a nice society girl," the architect told Vogel about her upbringing. "But I was rebellious. I enrolled in architecture school in opposition to their wishes." Aulenti was one of only two women in a class of 20 students at the Milan Polytechnic School of Architecture, from which she graduated in 1954.

After completing her studies Aulenti was hired as an art director at *Casabella*, a magazine that Vogel described as having been run at that time by "a small group of avant-garde architects who explored architecture and design from a broad, philosophical point of view." Aulenti and her cohorts called their movement "Neo–art nouveau," or "Neo liberty," Vogel reported; the design style they

promoted could be described as a reaction to both the Bauhaus movement and the fascistic style in architecture that came into fashion around the time of World War II. "We had endless discussions about the future of architecture," Aulenti told Vogel. She explained that "a confrontation with the modern movement was necessary to us. More than anything, we were trying to recognize our own identity." During the 10 years that she worked for *Casabella*, Aulenti's diverse social circle grew to include the architect Alto Rossi, the furniture designer Mario Bellini, the writer Umberto Eco, and the pianist Maurizio Pollini. "In Italy, theory and practice go hand in hand," she told Vogel. "We are taught to learn about all facets of design—as well as philosophy, history, art, and music. A cross pollination of disciplines has always been important."

Aulenti taught at the Venice School of Architecture, from 1960 until 1962, and then at the Milan School of Architecture, from 1964 until 1967. During the mid-1960s Italy (Milan in particular) was known for its innovative furniture and product designers. At around this time Aulenti began designing furniture in the pop-art style for such manufacturing companies as Knoll, Zanotta, Poltronova, and Kartell, and creating lamps for Artemide, Stilnovo, and Martinelli-Luce; some of her designs for those companies are now considered masterpieces, and items produced from her blueprints are still being sold. She also designed a variety of products and store interiors for an appliance company.

According to Vogel, when Aulenti started out as an architect, it was difficult to get work in her field. Thus many of her early commissions were from personal acquaintances who were designing or redesigning their homes. Her first commission, in 1956, involved designing a two-story brick complex that included stables and a living area for Elena Cumari, who was the architect's office manager when Vogel wrote her profile of Aulenti, in 1987. Working out of her Milan apartment, Aulenti won commissions with increasing frequency during the 1960s; her first nonresidential architectural jobs came in 1962, when she designed an elementary school in Monza, Italy, a hotel in the small town of Trento, and a historical center in Milan. Later in the 1960s the clothing manufacturer Max Mara and the auto company Fiat both hired her to create office and showroom spaces. Fiat chair Giovanni Agnelli, who has become a close friend of Aulenti's, told Vogel, "Even then, it was evident she was destined to be a major figure, a great talent." Aulenti took on increasing numbers of corporate and commercial projects in Italy and abroad during the 1970s, including housing developments in Milan, Rome, and Caracas, Venezuela.

In about 1976 Aulenti began collaborating on set designs with the renowned Italian theater director Luca Ronconi at the Prato Theater Design Workshop. Aulenti told Vogel that working in the theater was "a rich experience because designing for the theater forces me to confront many complexities of architecture in a different way." Among her notable designs were sets she created for productions of Henrik Ibsen's play *The Wild Duck* and Alban Berg's opera *Wozzeck*, in 1977; the Rossini operas *Il Barbiere di Seviglia* (*The Barber of Seville*) and *La Donna del Lago* (*The Lady of the Lake*), in 1975 and 1981, respectively; and the Verdi opera *Rigoletto*, in 1985.

In 1978 the government of France decided that the Gare d'Orsay, designed by Victor Laloux and known for its impressive 450-foot-long central hall enclosed by a vaulted ceiling of steel and glass, would be transformed into an art museum for Impressionist works from the Louvre, the Musée Luxembourg, and the Galerie Nationale du Jeu de Paume. The government sponsored a design competition to solicit plans for the conversion; six French architectural firms were invited to participate. Although the design submitted by the Paris-based firm A.C.T. Architecture won, Valéry Giscard d'Estaing, France's president at that time, was not satisfied with the firm's plans for the interior of the museum. Therefore, a second competition was announced, and five architects with international reputations, including Aulenti, were asked to participate. Michel Laclotte, who was then the inspector general of the national museums of France, told Vogel that Aulenti's design was chosen because "she understood art as well as architecture." A.C.T. was hired for the exterior renovations required to convert the railway station into a museum, and Aulenti was commissioned to design the interior. According to Vogel, the criticisms voiced in the French press in response to the selection of Aulenti revealed the perceptions that with the exception of private homes, she had never designed a new building, and that she came from "an eclectic, small-scale, and uniquely Milanese background."

The Musée d'Orsay was an arduous project that took more than seven years to complete and involved an intense collaboration between Aulenti and a team of curators. Aulenti helped to decide on the placement of 2,300 paintings, 250 pastels, 1,500 sculptures, 13,000 photographs, and 1,100 other art objects. "We built a program determining where each piece of art should go," Michel Laclotte told Vogel. "We talked our plans through with Gae nearly every day for two years. It was a constant dialogue of ideas about location and presentation." He added, "Certainly there were many heated discussions, many arguments, but Gae is a genius as a mediator. I remember at the end of one particularly long day she threw down her glasses, looked at me and said, 'It's tiring having always to be so strong.'" Aulenti told Vogel that working on the Musée d'Orsay helped her to develop a method that she could apply to future museum projects: "We first take each period separately, figure out how much space is needed, then design that portion of the museum around each piece of art. This is the only way the art and the architecture can become one."

Critical responses to Aulenti's design for the Musée d'Orsay, which opened in December 1986, tended to be extreme. "Some critics had lavish praise for the project," Vogel reported, "but others used words like 'tomb' and 'prison' to describe architectural elements and 'fascistic' to describe the overall design." Many labeled the museum's style "postmodern," a term viewed as derogatory in some circles. As Vogel put it, at that time "most European architects, and indeed Aulenti herself, look[ed] down upon [postmodernism] as pointlessly imitative," because of its incorporation of historical references into contemporary designs. The architecture critic Bruno Zevi described the new museum to Vogel as "not frankly modern." "There are too many hints of historicism," he explained. For example, Aulenti had designed stone walls in the Musée d'Orsay with holes drilled along the top near the ceiling, a gesture Vogel described as "a sort of modernist reinterpretation of a traditional wall's cornice." The holes serve as both openings for picture hangers and sound absorbers; for the latter purpose, other holes are located along the bases of the walls.

Aulenti's defense of her work is based on her belief that the architecture of a museum must suit the art that it contains; thus, in her view, it is appropriate for a museum housing art from the past to contain historical references in its design. In support of Aulenti's design for the Musée d'Orsay, the architect Renzo Piano, who co-designed the Centre Georges Pompidou in Paris, told Vogel that "[Aulenti's] competence comes from the years of day-by-day work on everything. She knows art, and she has developed a style that works." The American architect Philip Johnson, an admirer of Aulenti's work, said, as quoted by Vogel, "Anyone who makes as strong a statement as Gae did is going to run into a buzz saw." In response to vehement criticisms of the museum in the French press, Aulenti said, "As a culture the French are opposed to change. They are also not very progressive in their thinking about architecture, so that when new buildings are designed they are usually opposed to them." In 1987 Aulenti was awarded the Chevalier de la Légion d'Honneur by President François Mitterrand, and the title Commander of Arts and Letters by the French Ministry of Culture.

In 1982, while she was working on the Musée d'Orsay, Aulenti was contracted to redesign a portion of another museum—the permanent galleries of the Centre Georges Pompidou, the French national museum of modern and contemporary art. According to Vogel, for this project Aulenti "employed a straightforward modern style—a series of simple, clean-lined rooms with stark cutouts that create passageways and alcoves." This commission was followed by a third museum project, the restoration of the Palazzo Grassi in Venice, which Aulenti completed in about 1985. While it is unusual for an architect to be awarded several museum commissions in less than a decade, in 1987 Aulenti was chosen to redesign the neoclassical

Palacio Nacional de Montjuic, in Barcelona, Spain, which had been built for an international exposition in 1929 and was being converted into an art museum. Although it was originally intended as a temporary structure to be torn down following the exposition, as Vogel wrote, the building's four towers and large cupola had become as "important to the skyline of Barcelona as the Empire State building is to New York or the Eiffel Tower to Paris." The building had housed the Museum of Catalan Art, and the restoration was undertaken to provide space for the display of more works, including art and decorative objects from the 12th century to the present, as well as to improve the structure's framework, which needed repair. "Structurally, the problems were similar to those at the Musée d'Orsay," John Sureda, who directs the museum, told Vogel. "Therefore, Gae was a natural choice as the architect. She understands old buildings." One of the most notable changes Aulenti made was the sectioning off of the building's large domed arena, originally used as a grand ballroom, into several levels of smaller gallery spaces. "Life is different now than it was in 1929," she told Vogel.

Some of Aulenti's recent works include the Feshane Museum of Modern and Contemporary Art in Istanbul, Turkey, in the early 1990s, and a number of boutiques for the fashion designer Adrienne Vittadini. In 1994 her design for the ground floor galleries of the Palazzo Della Trienalle, in Milan, was highly praised. In the *New York Times* (December 18, 1994), Herbert Muschamp wrote, "As someone who has often felt that Aulenti's work, while always intelligent, shows a weak command of space, I am happy to report that her design for Milan is first-rate." According to Muschamp, it "continues [the] synthesis of modern and classical forms" that is present in the rest of the building, which was designed in 1931. Aulenti's galleries, he continued, are "simple, spare . . . [and] based on an ingenious system of partitions. . . . Though classically simple, the walls are modern in their geometric clarity as well as in their function, for each partition is also a mechanical device that houses equipment for lighting, security, and air conditioning. Set parallel to form corridors, or rotated to enclose a gallery, the convex partitions create spaces at once intimate and ample."

In late 1996 Aulenti was chosen to create the conceptual design for the Asian Art Museum of San Francisco, California, her first major commission in the United States. Housing one of the largest collections in the Western world devoted exclusively to Asian art, the museum originally occupied a building in San Francisco's Golden Gate Park, where it opened in 1966. Aulenti is part of a team of architects charged with converting the city's former main public library—a 1917 building in the classic Beaux Arts style, located prominently in the city's Civic Center district—into a new, larger home for the museum. Aulenti told *Inland Architect* (No. 4, 1998) that her design for the new museum building "recognizes the fundamental

difference in the uses and expectations of libraries and museums. Libraries serve the focused, concentrated interaction between the individual and the written word. On the other hand, museums serve the energetic interaction between the individual and the panorama of art and culture represented in each collection. That requires space, light, and the best possible perception and orientation for museum visitors." While preserving the building's exterior and its prominent interior features, which include a grand staircase, Aulenti's design features a large central interior courtyard with natural light from skylights. The new museum is slated for completion in 2001.

Gae Aulenti lives and works in a multilevel apartment of her own design on the Piazza San Marco in Milan. Twice divorced, the architect was formerly married to Franco Buzzi, an architect, and later to Carlo Ripa di Meana, a former minister of the environment in the Italian government and at one time the European Community's cultural-affairs commissioner. Aulenti's daughter, Giovanna Buzzi, a costume designer, and two grandchildren also live in Milan. When questioned about the dearth of prominent female architects, Aulenti told Vogel, "There are plenty of other talented women architects, but most of them seem to link up with men. I've always worked for myself, and it's been quite an education. Women in architecture must not think of themselves as a minority, because the minute you do, you become paralyzed. It is most important to never create the problem."

Aulenti was the recipient of the 1964 Grand International Prize at the Milan Trienalle, the 1978 Ubu Prize for the best Italian stage design, the 1983 Medal for Architecture from the Academy of Architecture of France, the 1984 Josef Hoffman Prize for Architecture and Design in Austria, and the Special Prize for Culture from the Italian Ministry of Culture in 1989. She is an honorary member of the Italian National Society of Interior Designers, the American Society of Interior Designers, the Bund Deutscher Architecten of Germany, the American Institute of Architects, the Movimento Studi per l'Architettura of Italy, and the Italian National Academy of Architecture. She is a member of the boards of directors of the Milan Trienalle and the publication *Lotus*. Among the many books about her work is *Gae Aulenti* (1997), which includes photos, drawings, and blueprints of her designs and is the first book about her to be published in English. She has lectured extensively in Europe and the United States. — C.P.

Suggested Reading: *Blueprint* p36+ June 1998, with photos; *New York Times* II p48 Dec. 18, 1994, with photos; *New York Times Magazine* p26+ Nov. 22, 1987, with photos; Emanuel, Muriel, ed. *Contemporary Architects*, 1994

Courtesy of Henri Bollinger Associates

Barker, Bob

Dec. 12, 1923– Television game-show host; animal-rights activist. Address: c/o The Price Is Right, CBS-TV, 7800 Beverly Blvd., Los Angeles, CA 90036-2112

If there were an iron-man award for game-show hosts, Bob Barker would surely win it. The white-haired Barker has hosted game shows for 43 years—*Truth or Consequences* for 18 years and *The Price Is Right* for 27. (For about two years he hosted them concurrently.) When one considers that he could be seen shepherding contestants five days a week, 52 weeks a year for all that time, his longevity on television seems even more remarkable. In two past editions *The Guinness Book of World Records* named him most durable performer, for chalking up more consecutive appearances than any other game-show emcee, and most generous host in television history, for doling out the most money and merchandise to contestants. Currently, the cash prizes and the cash value of the dishwashers, cars, and other items that he has given out are estimated to total about $200 million. "I'm the last of the dying breed," Barker told Ron Miller for the New York *Daily News* (January 1, 1991). "There's no place where you can go and learn what I do anymore."

Although, in the past few decades, television game shows have become an endangered species, *The Price Is Right* remains a highly rated daytime program and an icon of popular culture. Since the 1981–82 television season, Barker has won nine Emmy Awards for best audience participation host, and he earned a Daytime Emmy for lifetime achievement in 1999. According to Barker, the

show's success is partly due to the fact that his fans regard him as a friend. "That's because I've never played a role on television," he explained to a reporter for *People* (April 27, 1998). "I've never been a cowboy, a detective, or a doctor. I've just been Bob Barker. When my wife was alive, she used to come on the show occasionally. I used to bring my dogs and cats. People who watch know me better than the people I socialize with."

Barker is also a prominent animal-rights activist. In 1995, as a means of ending overpopulation among domestic animals, he set up the DJ&T Foundation, which subsidizes clinics that offer free or low-cost spaying and neutering of dogs and cats. For years he has ended each edition of *The Price Is Right* with a plea to viewers to have their pets sterilized.

One-eighth Sioux Indian—his paternal grandmother was half Sioux—Robert William Barker was born on December 12, 1923 in Darrington, Washington. His father, Byron John Barker, died when he was very young. When Robert was in the second grade, he and his mother, the former Matilda Tarleton, moved to Mission, South Dakota, where his mother became a teacher at the Rosebud Indian Reservation; she was later appointed county superintendent of schools. Mother and son lived on the reservation until Robert was in eighth grade, when Matilda remarried (her new surname became Valandra) and the family moved to Springfield, Missouri. "The reservation was an ideal place for boys and girls to grow up," Barker recalled to a *National Enquirer* (February 17, 1974) interviewer. "It was a happy kind of free life that kids in the big city don't get to experience." He added, "Indian boys are supposed to be great horse riders, but I was an exception. I'm afraid I embarrassed my forefathers by falling off almost every horse that I ever got on."

After graduating from Springfield Central High School, in about 1941, Barker won a basketball scholarship to attend Drury College, in Springfield. In 1943, two years after the United States entered World War II, he left school to train as a fighter pilot with the U.S. Naval Reserve; he was awaiting an assignment when the war ended. After his military discharge, as a lieutenant (junior grade), in 1945, he returned to Drury College, where he was elected president of his class and earned a B.A. degree in economics, summa cum laude, in 1947. He planned to pursue a master's degree in business administration, but after working at a radio station to earn money for tuition, he became interested in a career in radio. Barker tried a variety of radio jobs—reading the news, delivering sports scores, and spinning records—before he found what he was really good at: audience-participation programs and man-in-the-street interviews. In 1950, after working at a Florida radio station for a while, he moved to California, where he got his own program, *The Bob Barker Show*, an audience-participation show broadcast from a Burbank radio station. He hosted it for the next six years.

By chance, Ralph Edwards, who created *Truth or Consequences* as a radio game show in 1940 (and launched its long run on TV in 1950), came upon Barker's program while fiddling with his car radio. "It was at the height of our search for an MC for the daytime [televised *Truth or Consequences*]," Edwards recalled to Leslie Raddatz for *TV Guide* (January 3, 1976). "I suddenly heard this voice. It sounded like a young Jack Benny—the same timing. We tracked him down and asked him to come in for an interview. We were making bets on what he'd look like. Then in walks this handsome guy." Greatly impressed by Barker, Edwards hired him to succeed Jack Bailey as the host of *Truth or Consequences*. "I remember the headline in the *L.A. Times*: 'Unknown to Host *Truth or Consequences*,'" Barker told Jeanne Wolfe for the New York *Daily News* (February 18, 1996). "NBC didn't want to take a chance on me, but Ralph insisted, so they gave me a four-week contract. We did the show at the El Capitan Theater in Hollywood, and when I went there for my first show [on December 31, 1956] I looked at the marquee and it said, 'FREE DOUGHNUTS and Bob Barker.' When they extended my contract, the first thing I made them do was change the sign to read, 'BOB BARKER and free doughnuts.'"

Truth or Consequences was a half-hour show in which contestants had to answer a question before a buzzer sounded—usually in less than a second; as punishment if they failed, they had to perform bizarre stunts. The series was broadcast during the day on NBC until 1966, when it became syndicated. Barker remained with it until it went off the air, in 1974. (It was resurrected in 1977, with a different host, as *The New Truth or Consequences* and aired sporadically until 1989.)

Before that, on September 4, 1972, Barker had started hosting a second game show, *The Price Is Right*. Produced by Mark Goodson and Bill Todman, *The Price Is Right* debuted on NBC in 1956 and switched to ABC in 1963; it has aired on CBS since Barker's arrival as host. It features about 60 different types of games, among them "Plinko," "Golden Road," "Hole in One," and "Safe Cracker," all of which require contestants to guess the prices of various goods—everything from toasters and automobiles to weird, impractical items, such as a hamburger-shaped couch. To find unusual merchandise, a team of *Price Is Right* staffers visit trade shows throughout the United States. The program's cast includes female models who exhibit each prize. Among the longest-serving of "Barker's Beauties," as they became known, were Holly Hallstrom, Dian Parkinson, and Janice Pennington. Another long-time fixture was the announcer Johnny Olson, whose cry to those in the studio audience whom Barker selected as contestants—"Come on down!"—became a catchphrase. (Olson died in 1985.)

In November 1975 *The Price Is Right* became the first daytime game show to run for an hour, and in 1990 it eclipsed *Truth or Consequences* as the longest-running daytime game show. (*What's My Line* is television's longest-running prime-time show in that genre.) In explaining the success of *The Price Is Right*, Barker told Ron Miller, "The concept is so powerful: prices. Everyone can identify with prices." He has also attributed the show's longevity to the spontaneity of his repartee with contestants. "I think viewers enjoy seeing people in unrehearsed conversations," he told Alan Flippen for the *New York Times* (August 23, 1996). More recently, though, he admitted to David Daley for the *Hartford (Connecticut) Courant* (June 3, 1999, on-line), "We don't know what we did right." He also told Daley that *The Price Is Right* has become "a cult show for college kids." "College students from all over the country—from Harvard and Yale, I might add—come out here on their spring break and get tickets for *The Price Is Right*," he said. "They tell us that they rearrange their class schedule so as not to miss the show. I can't understand why some programmer at a network doesn't point to the success of *The Price Is Right* and think about new game shows, even in prime time."

Barker has often been asked whether being a game-show host requires any talent, and according to him, the answer is yes. "It takes an experienced MC to make a contestant funny, and most important, to do it without hurting him or exposing him to ridicule," he told Leslie Raddatz. Barker believes that over the years he also developed a knack for sensing which members of the studio audience will make the best competitors. "The worst possible contestant is the parlor comic," he told Raddatz. "A person can be frightened, quiet, or straight-faced and still be a good contestant."

For 22 years beginning in 1966, Barker hosted the Miss U.S.A. and Miss Universe beauty pageants, both of which are televised annually. In 1987, spurred by his growing concern for the humane treatment of animals, he protested the use of fur coats in the Miss U.S.A. pageant and persuaded the organizers of the event to substitute synthetic furs. The following year the producers of the contests refused to acquiesce to his request that they remove fur coats from the winners' prize packages, and he declined to host either pageant. Barker has also turned down appearances in commercials for fast-food chains and other companies that he believes have acted cruelly toward animals or profited from such cruelty.

For two weeks in 1980 and two months in 1981, Barker hosted the short-lived hour-long CBS variety show *That's My Line*. Produced by Mark Goodson and Bill Todman, the creators of *What's My Line?*, *That's My Line* spotlighted people with highly unusual jobs—a man who gave other men lessons in "how to pick up girls" for one-night stands, for example, and strippers in a clothing store who sold apparel right off their bodies.

Barker hosted the Pillsbury Bake-Off contest from 1969 to 1985 and the Tournament of Roses Parade, in Pasadena, California, from 1969 to 1988; he has also hosted the Thanksgiving Day parade held in New York City. On the big screen, Barker played himself in Adam Sandler's *Happy Gilmore* (1996). In a scene that won the MTV Film Award for best fight sequence that year, Barker and the character portrayed by Sandler attack each other at a celebrity golf tournament, and Barker prevails. "It was all in fun, but I think I could have taken him out for real," Barker told Jeanne Wolfe. "Adam may be young, athletic, and in good shape, but I'm tough and tricky, even if I'm old. I think this could open up a whole new career for me. I'd love to be an action hero." Barker has trained in the martial arts with Jackie Chan, Chuck Norris, and Pat Johnson, the last of whom choreographed the 1984 film *The Karate Kid*.

In 1994 Barker was charged with sexual harassment in a lawsuit filed by Dian Parkinson, who left *The Price Is Right* in 1993, after 18 years with the show. Parkinson charged that Barker had forced her to have sex with him under the threat of losing her job. Barker admitted publicly that he and Parkinson had had intimate relations during a year-and-a-half period that ended in 1991, but he maintained that their "fling," as he called it, had been consensual. Eventually, Parkinson dropped the suit. Barker recalled to Jeanne Wolf, "No one can imagine what I went through. . . . The most heartening thing was how my fans stood by me. I got tons of letters, and complete strangers would come up to me on the street and say, 'Bob, we don't believe a word that woman is saying.' But it does make you a bit leery about becoming involved with a woman the next time around."

Barker married his high-school girlfriend, Dorothy Jo Gideon, on January 12, 1945. His wife produced his game shows until she died of cancer, in 1981. Barker named the DJ&T Foundation for his wife and his mother, who was known as Tilly. The goal of the foundation, which is based in Beverly Hills, is to decrease the number of cats and dogs born in the U.S. and thus to end the destruction of thousands of unwanted animals.

Barker, who will celebrate his 76th birthday in 1999, has no plans to retire. In 1998, shortly after his 5,000th appearance on *The Price Is Right*, Barker told an interviewer for *People* (April 27, 1998), "I enjoy going to that studio. Many, many days, that's the happiest two hours I have, doing that show." — W.G.

Suggested Reading: *Coronet* p105+ Oct. 1964, with photos; *Entertainment Weekly* p30+ June 17, 1994, with photo; *Esquire* p152 Mar. 1998, with photo; *National Enquirer* p19 Feb. 17, 1974, with photo; New York *Daily News* p53 Jan. 1, 1991, with photo, p12 Feb. 18, 1996, with photo; *People* p14 Apr. 27, 1998, with photos; *TV Guide* p24+ Jan. 3, 1976, with photo; *Washington Post* B p1 Feb. 3, 1981

Selected Television Shows: *Truth or Consequences*, 1956–74; *The Price Is Right*, 1972– ; *That's My Line*, 1980, 1981

Nathaniel Welch/Outline Press

Barrett, Craig

Aug. 29, 1939– President and CEO of Intel Corp. Address: c/o Intel Corp., 2200 Mission College Blvd., Santa Clara, CA 95052-8119

Craig Barrett was appointed CEO of the Intel Corp. on March 26, 1998, when his legendary predecessor, Andrew Grove, stepped down. For more than 20 years, Barrett has been a key player in Intel's rise to the top of the microchip industry. A former materials-science professor at Stanford University, he is well known not only for his scientific expertise but also for his tough managerial style, which has helped Intel, which earned $6.9 billion in profits and held 88 percent of the international microprocessor market in 1997, to maintain its edge in the relentlessly competitive technology market. As Barrett told Dean Takahashi for the *Wall Street Journal* (May 22, 1997), one of his famous mottos is, "Put the capacity in place, and don't blink." "We accept that people are coming after us," he explained to Laurent Belsie for the *Christian Science Monitor* (August 3, 1994). "That just permeates our entire management style. If you stop and take three breaths and smell the roses . . . what will happen to you?"

Craig Barrett was born in San Francisco, California, on August 29, 1939. From 1957 until 1964 he studied at Stanford University, also in California, where he earned his bachelor's, master's, and doctoral degrees in materials science. In 1965 he received a NATO postdoctoral fellowship and continued his work in materials science at the National Physical Laboratory in England. At the age of 25, he became a professor at Stanford; he remained at that institution for nine years, except for a period in 1972, when a Fulbright fellowship took him to the Technical University of Denmark, in Copenhagen. While teaching at Stanford, Barrett wrote more than 40 technical papers about the influence of the microstructure of materials on the properties of those materials. According to several sources, his colleagues at Intel still call Barrett "the professor."

In 1974 a friend of Barrett's who was working for Intel, then a small, new technology company that specialized in the development of semiconductors for the emerging personal-computer market, approached Barrett in search of bright students to recruit into the company. Barrett, who had become bored with teaching, went to work for Intel himself, in his first nonacademic position. "I wanted to make some use of all that high-falutin technology that I was teaching students and doing research on," he told Sam Whitmore for the *Ziff-Davis Network* (May 24, 1997, on-line). "The semiconductor industry seemed like a great place to go." After a short time, perhaps because he was unaccustomed to the world outside academia, Barrett returned to teaching. Then, having taught for just one more semester, he returned to Intel as a technology development manager.

During the early 1970s, when the computer industry was in its formative years, Japanese manufacturers invented dynamic random-access memory chips (called DRAMS), which at that time were far more efficient than any of the computer memory devices being produced in the U.S. As a result Japanese companies such as Hitachi, NEC, and Toshiba maintained a formidable advantage over their competitors in the computer industry, and they pushed companies like Intel almost entirely out of the burgeoning market. According to Brent Schlender in *Fortune* (May 11, 1998), at one point during the 1970s, Intel nearly went out of business and had to fire almost one-third of its employees in order to stay afloat. "The DRAM was a call to arms," Barrett told Belsie. "It woke us up to the realities of the competition. You couldn't just do high-tech for high-tech's sake. You had to watch out for people who wanted to buy their way into the market."

In the early 1980s Barrett helped to form a computer industry organization called Sematech, which aimed to boost the quality of U.S. computer products through the cooperation of the leading technology companies. He was also a driving force behind the annual *Technology Roadmap*, an industry publication that, according to Leslie Helm of the *Los Angeles Times* (March 27, 1998, on-line), helped corporations to coordinate their efforts in tackling common technical obstacles.

Barrett spent many years helping to forge a place for Intel products, and for U.S.-made semiconductors in general, in the microprocessor industry. The early 1980s saw the invention of Intel's high-speed memory chips, which were used in virtually all personal computers following the mid-1980s boom in that market. Intel secured its lead in the

market by carefully guarding its rights to its chip against companies who attempted to copy it. According to Schlender, Barrett "studied every scrap of public and academic information about how competitors designed and managed their operations" and then, based on what he had learned, restructured the company's operations. "If there is a key to how we changed," Barrett told Schlender, "it was that we outlawed one excuse from our vocabulary—complexity. By refusing to hide behind the fact that each generation of chip was more complex, we were able to set expectations throughout the company to get better by every measure, each turn of the screw." Barrett was promoted to vice president in 1984 and executive vice president in 1987. In 1993 he was named chief operating officer of the company. Several smaller microprocessor companies offered CEO positions to Barrett, but he always refused.

By the mid-1990s Intel was the well-established leader in the microprocessor industry, with yearly profits of more than $8.87 billion. Then, in 1994, the company experienced a large-scale manufacturing problem that caused Intel's newest Pentium processor to make errors when performing extremely complex mathematical calculations. Andrew Grove, Intel's CEO, insisted that only computer users performing certain high-level math and physics calculations would be affected. However, the problems led many of Intel's most important clients, including IBM, to withdraw their orders from the company. Although Grove was still the undisputed leader of the company, it was Barrett who, after several disastrous attempts, was finally able to broker an agreement whereby all of Intel's affected customers were given replacement chips. In the following year, Barrett was able to put an end to a lawsuit that Advanced Micro Devices Inc., one of the small competitors who sought to produce similar, lower-priced memory processors, had launched against Intel several years earlier. After these incidents Barrett and Grove came to be seen as a management pair. "We're kind of a 'Mr. Outside, Mr. Inside' team," Barrett explained to Whitmore. "I worry about all of the stuff that goes on in terms of designing, manufacturing, creating products; I work with our design engineering teams, our manufacturing teams, our process technologists. And then all of the background work that makes Intel run smoothly . . . on a daily basis." For his part, Grove told Helm, "[Barrett's] personal style is more organized, more steady. I tend to be a bit more random and volatile."

In addition to serving as the company's chief negotiator, Barrett took on the job of overseeing Intel's overseas manufacturing operations. According to Mark Leibovich of the *Washington Post* (March 27, 1998), once a year Barrett conducts what has come to be called his "death march"—a tour of each of the company's plants around the world. Leibovich wrote that Barrett is known for "quizzing low-level employees on the arcana of their jobs and admonishing plant managers over scraps of trash on the floor." Barrett's trips abroad usually include meetings with government officials about tariffs and import and export laws. He also spends time visiting electronics stores around the world in order to keep track of the availability of new products and their price ranges. "The whole point is to keep the machine running," he told Takahashi of his business trips.

Barrett was named president of Intel on May 21, 1997 and CEO on May 20, 1998, when Grove stepped down and took the title of chair of the board of directors. This shift happened during a period when, for the first time in 10 years, Intel's profits were declining, mainly because of the ability of competitors such as Cyrix and Advanced Micro Devices Inc. to make cheaper microprocessors for personal computers. Following a 1997 contract made between Compaq, one of Intel's major clients, and Cyrix, a company that makes less expensive microchips, Intel drastically lowered the prices of some of their Pentium processors. Barrett explained to Kelly Spang of *Computer Reseller News* (April 1, 1998, on-line) that accommodating the under-$1,000 computer market would be one major shift in manufacturing that the company would make over the next few years. "It was really more of a matter of recognizing that [the] sub-$1,000 category was going to be appreciable and then modifying our product plans to create products specifically designed for that segment," he said. "We're obviously not just taking the standard high-performance desktop processor and just lowering the ASP [average selling price] to stick it in that category, but we're doing some special things to the [chips'] architecture to make products specifically for [the sub-$1,000] category. We think it will be business as usual."

Other plans that Barrett has for Intel include the development of new chips that expand the ability of personal computers to accommodate images and video. He also intends to move Intel into the arena of electronic commerce, by providing services to other companies; specifically, Intel would help companies process transactions made via the Internet, thus improving their management of supplies and inventory. "We're pretty good at planning and logistics, so why not try to sell what we know," Barrett told Schlender. Regarding what many believe to be a trend toward computers that are less expensive because they are linked to a network and use shared systems and memories, Barrett told Lisa DiCarlo of the *Ziff-Davis Network* (May 21, 1997), "Rather than go off and create servers in the sky here or an entirely new architecture there, what we're looking for is taking the basic, powerful, flexible personal computer and keep[ing it] as a personal—and I stress personal—computer." Barrett also stressed to Leibovich that he did not think Intel's overall business strategy would change very much in the next five years and that its major product would still be microprocessors. "Why leave something that is growing at 18 percent a year?" he asked rhetorically.

In June 1998, shortly after Barrett had taken up the reins at Intel, the Federal Trade Commission (FTC) filed an antitrust suit against the company. The FTC suit alleged that Intel had withheld technical information about its chips to three computer manufacturers—Intergraph Corp., Digital Equipment Corp., and Compaq Computer Corp.—to coerce the companies into providing Intel with patented technology. (In order to design computers, manufacturers must know a chip's technical specifications; since Intel produces the vast majority of chips used in computers, Intel's refusal to release technical information about its chips can effectively halt a computer manufacturer's production.) Intel admitted to withholding the data but claimed that doing so was a legitimate response to patent infringement cases filed by the three companies against Intel. In March 1999 Intel reached a settlement with the FTC that clarified the specific conditions under which Intel could refuse to release technical data pertaining to its chips. The settlement prevented Intel from withholding the crucial chip data as a response to patent infringement disputes but allowed Intel to withhold the information from computer makers who have not paid their bills; who have embarked on their own chip-development programs; or who have violated non-disclosure agreements by leaking chip information to third parties. Commenting on the agreement, Barrett told the *New York Times* (March 9, 1999), "We view this compromise agreement as a win-win for both parties, and we are satisfied that the agreement gives us value for our intellectual property rights."

Craig Barrett is in the habit of waking up at 4:00 a.m. and working until well after 6:00 p.m., mostly at Intel's offices in Santa Clara, California. He reserves his weekends for his family—he lives in Paradise Valley, Arizona—and he vacations at his 333-acre ranch near Darby, Montana. His wife, Barbara Barrett, is a lawyer, pilot, and politician; in 1994 she ran unsuccessfully for the governorship of Arizona. The couple have two grown children, Scott and Dawn.

A muscular six-foot-two, Barrett is widely admired for his stamina. He routinely climbs the stairs to get to his fifth-floor office. "I don't think he's ever been on an elevator here," an unnamed Intel manager told Cooper. "He's the most physical guy I've ever seen. You just don't want to mess with him." A close friend with whom Barrett has often hiked told Leibovich, "In all the time I've known him, I've never seen him flag." An avid sportsman, Barrett enjoys, in addition to hiking, skiing, golfing, snowmobiling, golfing, horseback riding, fly fishing, and bicycling; on one vacation, in 1992, he cycled 575 miles, from Utah to Mexico.

In 1969 Barrett earned the Hardy Gold Medal from the American Institute of Mining and Metallurgical Engineers. His textbook, *Principles of Engineering Materials*, which was published in the 1970s, is still in use in American universities. Barrett is a member of the National Academy of Engineering, and he has led the Semiconductor Council of the U.S. Department of Commerce. — C.P.

Suggested Reading: *Christian Science Monitor* p9 Aug. 3, 1994, with photo; *Fortune* p161+ May 11, 1998, with photos; *Los Angeles Times* (on-line) Mar. 27, 1998, with photo; *Technology Network* (on-line) Apr. 1, 1998; *Wall Street Journal* B p1 Jan. 14, 1997; *Washington Post* E p1+ Mar. 27, 1998, with photo; *Ziff-Davis Network* (on-line) May 21, 1997, May 24, 1997, with photo, Mar. 26, 1998, with photo

Courtesy of Autodesk, Inc.

Bartz, Carol

Aug. 28, 1948– Software-industry executive. Address: c/o Autodesk Inc., 111 McInnis Pkwy., San Rafael, CA 94903

One of the few female chief executive officers (CEOs) in the computer-technology industry, Carol Bartz is chairman and CEO of Autodesk Inc., a San Rafael, California–based company that creates computer-aided design (CAD) software programs, such as AutoCAD. These programs have allowed designers and engineers to create electronic blueprints for everything from buildings to cars to the animated dancing baby on the popular television show *Ally McBeal*. In the seven years since Bartz joined Autodesk, in 1992, the once struggling company has gotten back on its feet, and its revenues have more than doubled. Currently, Bartz is overseeing the company's efforts to diversify into new areas and to expand into CAD markets for more-powerful computer workstations.

In addition to her business accomplishments, Bartz is known for being a prominent advocate of women's issues. At her company, she has pushed for more internships and other learning projects for teenage girls. Such programs have helped many young women become more interested in science and technology, which still tend to be seen as "male" fields. Bartz knows firsthand how such stereotypes can hold one back. Despite being a very successful vice president with Sun Microsystems in the 1980s and 1990s, Bartz felt for a long time that she "lacked that male-dominant gene, the one that says you have to be a CEO, like that one that says you don't ask for directions," as she told Lawrence Fisher for the *New York Times* (November 29, 1992). Once she became the head of Autodesk, however, she found being a CEO thrilling. "Now that I'm a CEO, it is wonderful," she told Fisher. "I can't imagine doing anything else."

Carol Bartz was born on August 28, 1948 in Winona, Minnesota. From early on she showed unusual aptitude in math and science; her third-grade report card, for instance, noted that she was the best math student in her class. Bartz believes she flourished in these subjects partly because in the rural schools she attended, the classes were very small, and thus there were more opportunities for girls to participate in all subjects. Bartz has also credited her family for encouraging her and never presuming that women were not meant to study science or math.

After graduating from Alma High School, Bartz entered William Woods College for Women, in Fulton, Missouri. She initially planned to major in math, but in her sophomore year, she took a computer-programming course and became fascinated with the machines. After two years at Woods, she transferred to the University of Wisconsin at Madison, where she earned a bachelor's degree in computer science, in 1971.

Prior to her position at Autodesk, Bartz held product-line and sales management jobs at 3M Corp. and Digital Equipment Corp. In 1983 she joined the computer workstation manufacturer Sun Microsystems as a customer marketing manager. Within a year she became marketing vice president. In 1987 she was promoted to head of Sun's Federal Systems Division. At first U.S. military procurers didn't take her seriously; often they assumed upon meeting her that she was the secretary of "Mr. Bartz." Those misconceptions were quickly dispelled, and within a year, Bartz helped triple the division's sales. She then served as vice president of customer service until mid-1990, when she was promoted to vice president of worldwide field operations. As the company's number-two executive, she was in charge of half of Sun's 12,000-person workforce. The company did very well during her tenure in that position. In fiscal year 1992, for instance, Sun's worldwide revenues increased from $2.6 billion to $3.6 billion.

With her stellar track record at Sun, Bartz was easily a top candidate to succeed Alvar J. Green, the president, chairman, and CEO of Autodesk Inc., when he left the company, in 1992. At that time Autodesk was growing little, if at all, and profits were falling. Part of the problem may have been an extremely loose management structure. Typically, for example, design and marketing decisions were made through a time-consuming process of consensus-building among managers and programmers. The company's founder, John Walker, blamed the company's problems on the executives, whom he himself had selected.

Despite the company's problems, Autodesk was still a big name in the CAD software industry. In 1991 the company pulled in about $275 million in revenues and was among the top five or six CAD software companies, with about 10 percent of the CAD market overall and 70 percent of the market for personal computers specifically. Bartz, who optimistically envisioned boosting the company's revenues to $1 billion within five years, officially succeeded Green in April 1992 and promptly introduced a more rigid management hierarchy. At least initially, this caused a lot of friction and led to meetings in which Bartz was bombarded with complaints. "All that breathing stuff you learn when you have a baby is useless for giving birth," she told Lawrence Fisher for the *New York Times*, "but great for keeping your cool."

In the seven or so years since Bartz took over the reins, Autodesk has gotten back on track. Revenues have grown to about $740 million annually, and the company has diversified into broader markets. In 1996 the company created an animation division, called Kinetix, and is currently developing programs that will allow designers to work in three dimensions, not just two. "I've had people say to me, 'Gee, isn't design automation kind of boring, Carol?'" she recalled to the *New York Times* (November 7, 1993). Her response to that question was that "everything that is going to be created starts with someone's imagination, and we've got the tools that let them turn imagination into products. . . . What more exciting business can you be in?"

Bartz's accomplishments at Autodesk are even more impressive in light of the fact that on the second day at her job, she was diagnosed with breast cancer. She subsequently underwent a mastectomy and then seven months of chemotherapy. During the first month she kept her illness a secret while she put in place her new management structure. After the mastectomy she returned to work in four weeks, at least two weeks before the date recommended by her physicians. She did this to stave off any potential criticism of female CEOs. "I didn't want people to make too big a deal of it," she told Lawrence Fisher. "I didn't want people saying, 'There—women finally get to be CEOs and look what happens.'"

Bartz's experience with breast cancer led her to commit more of her free time to advocating for women's health issues. She has served on the board of the National Breast Cancer Research Foundation, for example. An advocate of separate classes or schools for boys and girls, she has also been active in female education issues. Her commitment to this facet of education comes not only from her own experiences but also from watching her daughter, Layne, grow up with gender stereotypes. By the time Layne was in third grade, for instance, Bartz noticed that her daughter had concluded that boys were smarter than girls because they answered more questions in class. Layne had also developed the notion that girls just didn't have to know math or science.

To help overcome some of the negative attitudes widely held among girls, Bartz has brainstormed with the women in her staff about how to get more young women in Autodesk's internship programs. She has also promoted such programs as "Design Your Future" to get female teens to work with employees on actual programming projects. "We have girls coming in in the morning saying this is stupid and you can't kick them out at 5 o'clock," Bartz told a reporter for the *Washington Post* (November 18, 1998).

While Bartz has been particularly mindful of helping young women, she has striven to improve education for both genders. One program at Autodesk, for instance, encourages employees to volunteer in area schools on company time. In recognition of her efforts to improve student achievement, Bartz won the National Alliance of Business Founders Award. She has also earned the Donald C. Burnham Manufacturing Management Award from the Society of Manufacturing Engineers.

An extremely busy woman, Bartz currently serves on the boards of AirTouch Communications, BEA Systems, Cadence Design Systems, Cisco Systems, Network Appliances, and the Foundation for the National Medals of Science and Technology. She is also a member of President Bill Clinton's Export Council, the California Business Roundtable, and the Business School Advisory Council of Stanford University.

Bartz and her husband, William Marr, a vice president for Sun Microsystems, live in Atherton, California. Her hobbies include tennis and gardening. She has also taken a race-car driving course. — W.G.

Suggested Reading: *New York Times* D p5 Apr. 15, 1992, III p4 Nov. 19, 1992, with photo, III p10 Nov. 7, 1993; *San Jose Mercury News* (online), with photo; *Washington Post* C p26 Nov. 18, 1998

Courtesy of Family Research Council

Bauer, Gary L.

*1956– President of the Family Research Council;
chairman of the Campaign for Working Families;
social activist. Address: c/o Family Research
Council, 801 G St. N.W., Washington, DC 20001-
3729*

Gary L. Bauer, the president of the Family Research
Council and chairman of the Campaign for Working Families, has become one of the most influential crusaders for what he refers to as the "pro-
family, pro-life, pro–free-enterprise" agenda of the
Christian right. Bauer collaborates closely with
James C. Dobson, who founded both the conservative Christian organization Focus on the Family (of
which he is president) and the Family Research
Council. In his daily minute-and-a-half radio message, Bauer has repeatedly called for laws to ban
abortion, same-sex marriage, and assisted suicide,
and he advocates legislation that would permit
prayer and the teaching of religion in public
schools. "There is no way that the American people would vote to do many of the things that the
courts have forced upon us," he declared in his October 2, 1998 radio broadcast, as transcribed on his
Web site. "Americans would never have voted for
abortion on demand. We would have never tried to
sanitize the public square from any religious influence. No state would ever vote to change the definition of marriage so that men could marry men
and women marry women. All of this is happening
because of out-of-control judges." In the opinion of
many Republicans, Bauer's uncompromising
stance cannot be reconciled with their attempt to
re-create their party as a "big tent" that would encompass not only far-right social conservatives but

moderate Republicans as well. Bauer's rejection of
the "big tent" approach notwithstanding, he has
been mentioned as a dark-horse candidate for president of the United States in the year 2000.

Gary Lee Bauer was born in 1956 in Covington,
Kentucky, and grew up in Newport, Kentucky, a
working-class town that he once described as being
overrun by organized crime. His father, Spike Bauer, an ex-marine, held a variety of jobs while Gary
was growing up. Despite being a high-school dropout and binge drinker, Spike Bauer instilled values
in his son that Gary Bauer still holds dear: pride in
one's country and a respect for education. "I can remember, my father would come home after a bad
day at work covered with grime," Gary Bauer recalled to Thomas B. Edsall for the *Washington Post*
(January 20, 1998). "He would say, 'Look at me.
Study, so you don't have to do this.'" Bauer heeded
his father's advice: he earned a B.A. degree from
Georgetown College, in Georgetown, Kentucky, in
1968, and a doctorate in law from Georgetown University, in Washington, D.C., in 1973.

Bauer entered the large-scale political arena in
1980, as a senior policy analyst for the Reagan–
Bush presidential campaign. According to a biographical sketch of him posted on the World Wide
Web, he worked in the office of the president-elect
as "assistant director for policy/Community Services Administration." In October 1982 he joined
the U.S. Department of Education as the deputy
undersecretary for planning, budget, and evaluation. Believing it his duty to ensure that the administration's agenda became perfectly clear to people
in his department, he made it a habit to distribute
to his staff drafts of speeches and transcripts of testimony given before congressional committees.
"The professional career employees here now understand that the president is serious," he told Robert Pear for the *New York Times* (December 4,
1984), "even if they don't share our agenda in their
personal beliefs." Reportedly, even those on Bauer's staff who disagreed with his views respected
his abilities and noted his influence.

As the Education Department's representative
on the White House Cabinet Council for Human
Resources and as the chair of the Working Group
on School Discipline, Bauer continued to voice his
strong opinions on schooling. He condemned what
he regarded as academia's contempt for the U.S.
political system. "Nowhere," he declared to Pear,
"is one more likely to hear the words 'imperialist,
oppressive, militaristic, and warmongering' applied to one's own nation and leaders than within
the ivy-covered walls of some of the finest schools
in America."

In July 1985 the Senate unanimously approved
Bauer's appointment as undersecretary of education. In that position, he spoke out forcefully
against "value-free" curriculums that purportedly
placed equal weight on all ideas and standards. As
a key speaker at the Christian Congress for Excellence in Public Education, held in Kansas City,
Missouri, in August 1985, he declared that by sup-

porting "moral equivalency," school systems made it impossible to emphasize such values as self-discipline, kindness, fidelity, and diligence, and he blamed schools' "value-free" approach to education for the breakdown in morality in American society. In September 1985, in a speech delivered at an anti-pornography conference, he charged that publishers of pornography enjoyed complete freedom of speech, while the same freedom was denied those who—like himself—advocated prayer in public schools. "When pornography is protected in the name of 'freedom,' our children receive a very disturbing message—since pornography is allowed, it is all right," he warned during the conference.

In 1986 Bauer was appointed chair of the Special Working Group on the Family, a White House task force whose mission was to evaluate the effects of various federal programs on families. After seven months of research, the 22-member, interdepartmental committee presented to President Reagan its report—written mostly by Bauer—entitled "The Family: Preserving America's Future." The report claimed that there had been a halt in the two-decade-long increase in crime, drug use, out-of-wedlock and teen pregnancy, divorce, sexually transmitted disease, and poverty in the U.S., and that the Reagan administration was responsible for that halt. The report recommended, among other things, an increase in tax exemptions for families with children; that all government agencies and departments be required to include a "family fairness statement" in proposed legislation; and the denial of subsidized housing for single mothers under the age of 21 who did not live with their parents. "As a study, the report is not objective or dispassionate," Robert Greenstein, who was then the director of the Center on Budget and Policy Priorities (a nonprofit research organization), told Leslie Maitland Werner for the New York Times (November 14, 1986). "But some of the recommendations are worthy of consideration."

In 1987 Bauer was named President Reagan's chief adviser on domestic policy. At that time, the administration had increasingly come under scrutiny because of the Iran-contra scandal (an illegal operation in which the Reagan administration had agreed to sell arms to Iran in exchange for Iran's cooperation in arranging the release of American hostages in Lebanon and had then used the money from those sales to fund the contras—counterrevolutionary guerrillas—in Nicaragua). While Bauer's staff apparently felt that, under the circumstances, it was best to keep a low profile, Bauer did not curb his outspokenness; rather, he "kept talking about divisive social issues," Dinesh D'Souza, a former aide of Bauer's, recalled to Michelle Cottle for the Washington Monthly (April 1998). "Gary was seen as this nerdy little fellow, . . . quixotic, extreme, dogmatic," D'Souza said; according to D'Souza, those characteristics had led colleagues and co-workers of Bauer's to ostracize him.

In 1988 Bauer stirred a national controversy, when he released his draft of an executive order to ban the use of fetal tissue (obtained during voluntary abortions) in medical research. Many people were upset not only about the ban but about the fact that Bauer had issued his draft before the government advisory panel appointed to study the issue had even met. (The panel eventually recommended approval of scientists' use of such tissue.)

Bauer's bold pursuit of his agenda attracted the attention of James Dobson, the president of Focus on the Family (which, with over 2 million followers, is currently larger than the Christian Coalition). In 1982 Dobson had created the political advocacy group Family Research Council (FRC), to gather the results of others' research on social issues of concern to him and his followers and to promote their own views in Washington, D.C. In October 1988 Bauer accepted the positions of president of the FRC and of senior vice president of Focus on the Family. With Bauer at the helm, the FRC increased its influence significantly. The council, when he arrived, had a budget of $200,000, 3,000 members, and a staff of three. By 1998 the council's budget had increased to $14 million, the membership rolls had risen to over 450,000, and its workforce had expanded to 93 paid employees.

Meanwhile, in 1992, the FRC had legally split from Focus on the Family, and Bauer had stepped down as the latter group's senior vice president. But the two organizations have remained connected, albeit informally. For example, Dobson, as the host of Focus on the Family's nationally syndicated radio show, read in his broadcasts portions of Bauer's daily news briefs, known as "Washington Updates." Also, Dobson included bulletins prepared by Bauer in his frequent mailings to members of Focus on the Family. By 1995 Bauer had become a key source for Republicans and others seeking insights into the concerns of "pro-family" conservatives.

The presidential election campaign of 1996 marked a turning point in Bauer's career as a Republican spokesperson. At first, Bauer leaned toward the candidacy of the conservative commentator Patrick J. Buchanan, but the primary campaign ended without his official endorsement of any presidential aspirant. Late in the primary race, Bauer engaged in a heated conflict with Senator Bob Dole of Kansas, the eventual Republican candidate, over Dole's effort to include expressions of tolerance for pro-choice Republicans in the party's platform. In the National Review (December 22, 1997), Kate O'Beirne reported that Bauer declared even before the day of the election, "This is the second failed [Republican presidential] campaign in a row. I'm sick and tired of the political party that stands for death [i.e., the Democratic Party] being bold and outspoken, while my party appears to be afraid. If we can't find someone . . . to stand up for the sanctity of life, in four more years I'll do it myself."

To that end, Bauer founded his own political action committee (PAC), to help fund candidates who he felt could be counted on to support the position of the Christian right on "pro-family" issues. The Campaign for Working Families (CWF), as the PAC came to be called, raised $2.6 million in 1997, one of the highest totals for any PAC in the nation. That year, the CWF actively supported two conservative "pro-family" candidates, one in a special congressional election in New Mexico and the other in the race for attorney general in Virginia.

When, in July 1997, Ralph Reed resigned as head of the Christian Coalition, he left a gap in the leadership of the religious right into which Bauer easily slid. Further cementing his new prominence, Bauer openly and forcefully opposed the Republican Party's support of maintaining China's most-favored-nation trade status, because of the Chinese government's continuing persecution of Christians and other religious groups. He rejected the position of many mainstream GOP politicians, who contended that unfettered trade was the best way to influence the Chinese government because, they said, it made possible the exchange of cultural ideas. As a guest on the PBS talk show *Firing Line* in October 1997, Bauer declared, "It wasn't *Dallas* that brought the Soviet Union down, it was Ronald Reagan being willing to speak the truth to evil." To advance his stand, Bauer forged alliances with liberal Democrats who, like him, called for "moral economics."

Bauer played an important role in the National Republican Committee's January 1998 resolution to deny funding to any Republican candidate who refused to support a ban on late-term abortions (usually called "partial-birth" abortions by those who oppose such procedures). The resolution met with strong opposition from pro-choice members of the party and the Republican Leadership Council (an organization of economically conservative donors), and it failed to pass. Also in January 1998, in a special primary election held in California's 22nd Congressional District, Bauer and his organizations threw their weight behind the Republican Tom Bordonaro, who favored a ban on late-term abortions. Bordonaro's opponent was the candidate backed by the then-Speaker of the House, Newt Gingrich—the moderate Republican Brooks Firestone, who did not support such a ban. Thanks in part to Firestone's stand on the issue and to an expensive TV advertisement campaign that Bauer's PAC, the CWF, directed against late-term abortions, Bordonaro won the Republican primary. But in the special general election, held in March, Bordonaro lost to Lois Capps, a liberal Democrat, who captured the votes of many former Firestone supporters. According to various political analysts, most voters were more interested in education, health care, and other matters emphasized by Capps than they were in the issues stressed by Bauer and his PAC.

In a public-opinion poll conducted in February 1998, Bauer emerged with flying colors. The poll elicited the reactions of television viewers to various commentators who had discussed the scandal involving President Bill Clinton and the former White House intern Monica Lewinsky. Bauer received the most favorable response by far, from Republicans, Democrats, and independent voters alike. When talking before lay audiences about other matters as well, Bauer is said to communicate better than many Republican politicians. "Talking in concrete and vivid terms and connecting with people's actual experiences [make Bauer] unlike 99 percent of other Republicans, who get up there and show bar charts about the balanced budget," Tony Snow, the host of *Fox News Sunday*, once said, according to the *Washington Monthly* (April 1998).

Bauer has continued his crusade to bring specific social issues to the forefront of Republican politics. In the spring of 1998, he and James Dobson teamed up to warn Republican Party officials that they would withdraw their support (and, by extension, that of their followers) if the party did not set a higher priority on legislation that would ban late-term abortions, abolish the National Endowment for the Arts, stop government support for programs that provided clean needles for drug addicts, and eliminate the "marriage penalty" from the tax code. Bauer is also in favor of a flat tax that treats child-rearing as an investment and that continues Social Security as a government-run program rather than a private enterprise (so that mothers who never worked will continue to receive their husbands' benefits even after their spouses' deaths). At the request of Bauer and Dobson, Republican Party officials recently formed what they dubbed the Values Action Team to work on legislation that supports the positions of the two men.

Apparently convinced that more must be done, Bauer started to consider a bid for the Oval Office, although he acknowledged that his election to the presidency would be a long shot. In the nation's capital, he is treated as an outsider; reportedly, neither the former Speaker of the House nor the majority leader of the Senate (former representative Newt Gingrich and Senator Trent Lott, respectively) is known to have consulted him. Moreover, Washington insiders who support his agenda were said to fear that in running for president, he would deflect attention from more "marketable" candidates. In June 1998 Bauer took part in a gathering held in Cedar Rapids, Iowa, that featured prospective Republican presidential candidates. Those attending, all of whom delivered speeches on social and moral themes, included Reggie White, a defensive lineman for the Green Bay Packers. Several months before, White had aroused controversy by making negative comments about homosexuals and certain racial and ethnic groups in a speech before the Wisconsin State Assembly. At the Cedar Rapids meeting, Bauer publicly defended White's denunciation of homosexuality as a sin.

The Cedar Rapids gathering was the first step in Bauer's bid for the White House. In January 1999 Bauer announced that he was taking a leave of absence from the FRC, so that he could devote himself full-time to his campaign. Soon afterward he formed an exploratory committee that examined his prospects. By April he felt ready to formally announce his candidacy, and he did so in his hometown, Newport, Kentucky. As a presidential candidate Bauer has stressed his traditional convictions on issues pertaining to the family and abortion. Nevertheless, he is wary of being dismissed as a "religious candidate" with no mainstream appeal. To avoid such brush-offs, he has attempted to move beyond religious issues to focus attention on his stances on pressing international matters and tax reform. Above all, he is trying to fashion himself as the candidate who best espouses the ideals of former president Ronald Reagan. "What I speak for is Reagan conservatism," he told Hannah Rosin for the *Washington Post* (April 21, 1999). "And most Republicans have forgotten his message."

Gary Bauer lives in Virginia with his wife, the former Carol Hoke, and their three children— Elyse, Sara, and Zachary. He has written articles for such magazines as the *National Review, Governing,* the *Saturday Evening Post,* and *Education Digest.* He is also the author of three books: *Our Journey Home: What Parents Are Doing to Preserve Family Values* (1992); *Children at Risk: The Battle for the Hearts and Minds of Our Kids* (1994), which he wrote with James Dobson; and *Our Hopes, Our Dreams: A Vision for America* (1996). — K.S.

Suggested Reading: *Washington Monthly* p9+ Apr. 1998, with photo; *Washington Post* A p3 Feb. 14, 1987, A p9 Jan. 20, 1998, with photo

Selected Books: *Our Journey Home: What Parents Are Doing to Preserve Family Values,* 1992; with James Dobson—*Children at Risk: The Battle for the Hearts and Minds of Our Kids,* 1994; *Our Hopes, Our Dreams: A Vision for America,* 1996

Courtesy of UNICEF

Bellamy, Carol

Jan. 14, 1942– Executive director of UNICEF. Address: c/o UNICEF, 3 United Nations Plaza, New York, NY 10017-4486

Carol Bellamy is the executive director of UNICEF, the United Nations Children's Fund, an international humanitarian organization familiar to millions of Americans who, as youngsters, collected money for it as Halloween trick-or-treaters. For two

years before taking the top job at UNICEF, in 1995, Bellamy headed another humanitarian group—the United States Peace Corps, which is associated with the burst of idealism ushered in by the administration of President John F. Kennedy in 1961. Bellamy herself served in the Peace Corps, as a volunteer in Guatemala, for two years in the 1960s. Her résumé also includes jobs in the private sector, as a corporate lawyer and investment banker, and in the political arena, as a Democratic member of the New York state Senate and president of the New York City Council. With her corporate savvy and passionate altruism, she resists easy pigeonholing. As she remarked to Malcolm Gladwell for the *Washington Post* (September 29, 1993), "I have always been too conservative for my liberal friends, and too liberal for my conservative friends." In September 1999 Bellamy was appointed to another five-year term as the head of UNICEF.

The first of two children, Carol Bellamy was born on January 14, 1942 in Plainfield, New Jersey, and grew up in nearby Scotch Plains. Her brother, Robert Bellamy, became a high-school principal. Her father was a telephone installer who voted Republican; her mother, a nurse, switched her party affiliation from Republican to Democrat after Bellamy entered politics. Discussing her lifelong refusal to dwell on failures or disappointments, Bellamy told Joyce Purnick for the *New York Times* (December 29, 1985), "As a kid, if I did badly on a test, I just truly wanted to repress that and go on to the next one, I just kept moving forward. I was a pretty independent kid. My parents have always been wonderful and supportive. But I always went out and did something, and then I'd tell them what I did. . . . I never really discussed things with anybody. I just made up my own mind."

Bellamy acted in student productions of musicals at Scotch Plains-Fanwood High School, from which she graduated in 1959. At Gettysburg College, in Pennsylvania, she studied sociology and psychology and earned a B.A. degree, in 1963, thus becoming the first member of her family to graduate from college. Citing "the need to set off on her own," as Francis X. Clines reported in the *New York Times Magazine* (February 25, 1979), she joined the Peace Corps. Assigned to serve in Guatemala, she helped raise chickens, ran a lunch program for underprivileged children, and hosted a Spanish-language health and nutrition series, *The Housewife's Hour*, that aired daily on local radio. "The weather was hot and hotter, and nobody ever came to see us except Ford and Fulbright types who seemed to be drinking their way through Latin America," she told Clines, in a reference to the Ford and Fulbright fellowship programs. Nevertheless, she regarded her experience in the Peace Corps as "magnificent," as Don Singleton quoted her as saying in the New York *Daily News* (September 11, 1977).

In 1965, after completing her obligatory two years with the corps, Bellamy moved to New York City and enrolled at the New York University School of Law, having concluded that if she ever wanted to pursue a career in politics or international relations, she would need the credentials provided by a law degree. To pay her tuition, she worked as both a waitress and a switchboard operator. Upon earning a J.D. degree, in 1968, she was hired as an associate by Cravath, Swaine & Moore, then one of the most prestigious law firms in the United States.

In the late 1960s, with the anti–Vietnam War movement in full swing, Bellamy began to develop a public identity as a tough-minded liberal thinker. She founded, and became the first president of, the Lawyers Committee to End the War, the primary objective of which was to offer pro bono representation for peace activists. A few years later she helped found the Council of New York Law Associates, a group that, in the early to mid-1970s, became a popular training ground for young lawyer-activists, who offered their skills free of charge to civic and antipoverty coalitions.

Bellamy's impressive résumé attracted the attention of New York City's mayor, John V. Lindsay, who in 1971 made her an assistant commissioner in the Department of Mental Health. After a year with that department, Bellamy, who had earlier moved to the New York City borough of Brooklyn, quit her job to mount a bid for state senator from a Brooklyn district. She won the Democratic primary by a mere 323 votes and the 1972 general election by another slim margin. Before her first term was up, reapportionment "carved her out of her district," Don Singleton wrote, pointing out that "it was no accident": she had irritated Senate Republicans, who were in the majority, by such actions as questioning the purpose of "sleeper" legislation and refusing to participate in the pervasive

senatorial deal-making. In 1974 she ran for reelection in a different Brooklyn district against a long-time incumbent, and much to the surprise of political veterans, she emerged victorious. By all accounts an effective legislator, she expended her greatest energies on matters involving New York City.

During her second term in the state Senate, Bellamy "made a decision not to run again and to join a commercial law firm," she recalled to Jack Newfield for the *Village Voice* (September 25, 1978). "Then I started to think about running for some higher office. I considered running for Congress, and [state] attorney-general, and then, in the fall of 1976, I decided to run for City Council president." By the time Bellamy had announced her bid for the Democratic nomination, four men had already thrown their hats into ring. The early front-runner was Paul O'Dwyer, the incumbent City Council president, an iconoclastic Democrat who, in Bellamy's view, had only weak support among many liberal voters, a group that made up a significant portion of the city's electorate. Buoyed by the endorsements of the city's three major newspapers and the Citizens Union, Bellamy came in first, and O'Dwyer second, in a four-way race that necessitated a run-off election between the two top vote-getters. In an unanticipated reversal for O'Dwyer, Bellamy received 60 percent of the vote in the run-off election; on November 8, 1977, in a contest with the openly reluctant Republican candidate, state assemblyman John Esposito, she captured 83 percent of the ballots cast and thus became the first woman in the Big Apple's history to be elected to citywide office.

With her unexpected victory, Bellamy emerged as a high-profile office holder in the nation's largest city and so immediately became one of the hottest politicians in New York State. By 1979 she was considered a Democratic favorite to win any of several statewide offices. "Carol Bellamy is dynamite," the campaign consultant David Garth told Clines a year after Bellamy took office. "I don't know anybody in politics like her where people, within three minutes of meeting her, trust her. It's unbelievable. Sooner or later, she is going to be the highest woman executive in the state. She can be governor. She can be mayor. Her potential is limitless."

Earlier, on the day that Bellamy won the City Council presidency, Edward I. Koch was elected to his first term as the city's mayor. Their simultaneous victories marked the start of a rivalry that would dominate the political scene in New York City for the next seven years. In early 1982, after a series of well-publicized clashes between Bellamy and Koch over such issues as foster care, police protection, sanitation, and tax abatements for real-estate developers, the mayor announced that he was going to seek the Democratic nomination for governor. According to the city charter, if Koch were to win the governorship and thus leave the mayor's office vacant, Bellamy, as City Council president, would succeed him. In the Democratic primary, Koch, whom Bellamy supported, faced Mario Cuomo, who was still smarting from his loss to Koch in the 1978 Democratic mayoral primary. This time Cuomo got the better of his rival, and Koch kept his job.

In February 1985, with less than a year left in Koch's second term, Bellamy announced that she intended to try to unseat the very popular mayor. By April, however, Bellamy's bid seemed doomed, primarily because her vigorous campaigning had generated little press. Part of the problem stemmed from the candidacy of Denny Farrell, a prominent black city leader, which had drained away much of Bellamy's support among African-Americans. Koch, meanwhile, in a deliberate attempt to diminish his opponents' campaigns, had laid low and refused to acknowledge any of their criticisms. "Ed Koch is acting as though he were not up for reelection," Michael Kramer wrote for New York (April 1, 1985). "He hasn't even officially announced for a third term, and according to the current game plan, he won't do so until June. 'If we had our druthers,' says a Koch adviser, 'we wouldn't announce till a week before the primary, in September.'" Koch's strategy worked, and despite some mudslinging by Bellamy—during the race she called Koch a "fraud," a "Scrooge," and a "phony"—she lost the primary by a wide margin. "Am I going to have a bruise on my ego? Probably . . . ," Bellamy, who was the first woman to run for the New York mayoralty, said to Joyce Purnick. "Not only didn't I make it, I really lost big. But I'm not a person who harbors a grudge. I ran against him and I lost. I'm not going to be nasty. And the fact is, I'm glad I did it. I'd like to believe some people are a little better off because I did it, a few issues probably moved faster because we did it."

A month after her electoral defeat, Bellamy announced that when her term as City Council president ended, on January 1, 1986, she would be taking a job with Morgan Stanley & Co. as an investment banker. "I'm going to roll up my sleeves and get out there and put together some deals," she told the New York Times (December 4, 1985). "It's dealmaking in the best sense. You've got to be smart, you've got to be creative, you have to have the best product."

The public sector did not hear from Bellamy again until 1990, when she ran for New York State comptroller, a job that entails supervising all state borrowing and overseeing the public-employee pension fund, which then totalled $156 billion. On Election Day she won several counties but lost the race narrowly to Edward V. Regan, the Republican incumbent. Forced to leave her position at Morgan Stanley when she had begun her campaign, Bellamy soon found employment at Bear Stearns Co. Inc., another investment firm, as the managing director of the public-finance department. In February 1993 Comptroller Regan resigned, and the state legislature had to find someone to fill his position until the next election. In April Bellamy made a case for herself at a legislative hearing in Albany, the state capital, where she distributed a graph detailing the demographics of the 49 percent of the vote she had won in the 1990 general election. "I am the only candidate who has demonstrated public support for the office of state comptroller," she told legislators, as reported by Kevin Sack in the New York Times (April 26, 1993). "In 1990, running against a three-term incumbent, almost 2 million voters, or 49 percent of the electorate, voted for me. From Niagara Falls to Montauk, those votes were cast by tens of thousands of your constituents in every single Senate and Assembly district across the state." Many observers considered Bellamy the overwhelming favorite to take over as interim comptroller. Nevertheless, in an 11th-hour deal, Democratic brass threw their weight behind the younger, up-and-coming Democrat H. Carl McCall, an African-American. "The fact of the matter is, it never went to a vote and if it had, she would have won it," Karen S. Burstein, a state legislator and close friend of Bellamy's who later became a judge, told Malcolm Gladwell for the Washington Post. "She ran a brilliant campaign. She didn't make any errors. If there is a rule in politics, it is that if you pay your dues you get repaid. She paid her dues and when the opportunity arose, it was snatched from her." "It left the worst taste of any campaign I've been involved in," Bellamy told Gladwell. "[But] it's time to let the new blood come in. I don't want to be the stopper in the bottle."

In November 1992 Bill Clinton won election to the U.S. presidency. He subsequently offered Bellamy a choice of two positions—deputy secretary of transportation or director of the Peace Corps—and she eagerly accepted the latter. Reflecting on the timing of Clinton's move, which came soon after her chance for the comptroller's office evaporated, Bellamy told Gladwell, "It's like someone [once] said to me. . . . 'Sometimes when windows close, doors open.'" Karen Burstein told Gladwell, "Carol has had a growing sense of frustration at her inability to do at heart what she cares about, which is to be involved with the people's good. I know that sounds sappy. But all the time she has been an investment banker and has been sitting on boards and running around doing things, she has said it's not meaningful enough. Making money is not enough."

The Peace Corps was launched by President John F. Kennedy in March 1961, just two months after he entered the White House. Its founding has been linked with words that Kennedy uttered during his inaugural address: "And so, my fellow Americans: ask not what your country can do for you—ask what you can do for your country. My fellow citizens of the world: ask not what America will do for you, but what together we can do for the freedom of man." The first director of the Peace Corps was R. Sargent Shriver, one of Kennedy's brothers-in-law and later a vice-presidential candidate. In October 1993 Bellamy became the first former Peace Corps volunteer to head the organization.

When Bellamy came on board, the Peace Corps badly needed redefinition, first because the Reagan and Bush administrations had tried unsuccessfully throughout the 1980s and early 1990s to cut its funding, and second because within the States, Clinton's new national service program, America Corps, threatened to siphon interest away from it. Bellamy relished this challenge, and she succeeded in increasing both the number of beneficiary countries (in part through the addition of several newly formed Eastern European republics) and the number of volunteers. In June 1993 the first Peace Corps volunteers to serve in China began working there as English teachers. After a year on the job, Bellamy told Lynne Marek for the *Chicago Tribune* (March 27, 1994), "We've opened up so many countries so quickly that one of the things I want to do is stabilize the programs in those countries and make sure what we're doing makes sense." (To date, Peace Corps workers have served in more than 130 nations; currently, some 6,700 volunteers are on assignment in more than 90 countries. President Clinton has signed legislation aimed at increasing the number of workers to 10,000 by the year 2003.)

In January 1995 the executive director of UNICEF, James P. Grant, who was fatally ill, resigned after 14 years of service. He and his two predecessors were all Americans, and soon after Grant's death, reports began circulating that the United States was pushing Boutros Boutros-Ghali, the secretary general of the U.N. at that time, to appoint another American to head UNICEF—in particular, Carol Bellamy, who had become popular in Washington, D.C., since taking over the Peace Corps. Supplying 25 percent of the organization's $1 billion annual budget, the U.S. was UNICEF's largest single contributor. But about 50 percent of the funding came from the 15-member European Union, and most of its members favored a Finnish candidate. On April 10, 1995, after much wrangling between representatives of the U.S. and the European Union, Boutros-Ghali named Bellamy as UNICEF's next executive director. She took office on May 1, 1995, with the rank of U.N. undersecretary-general. "UNICEF has had three wonderful male directors before me—the children of the world couldn't have been better served, so I'm a little reluctant to say, 'Thank God they have finally got a woman,'" Bellamy told an interviewer for *Oneworld.com* (on-line). "But I do hope that, as a woman, I bring a perspective, an understanding of the interrelation between the status of women and the quality of life that children have in this world today."

The United Nations Children's Fund was created in 1946, the first year that the U.N. General Assembly convened; the acronym UNICEF comes from the organization's original name, United Nations International Children's Emergency Fund. Its mission is to improve the health, nutrition, and general well-being of mothers and children throughout the world and to expand children's op-

portunities so that they can "reach their full potential," as the official UNICEF Web site put it. In the two years that preceded Bellamy's appointment, UNICEF was beset by unfavorable audits and management reviews and a financial scandal in its Nairobi, Kenya, affiliate. High on Bellamy's agenda from day one, therefore, was a large-scale restructuring of UNICEF, to increase efficiency and lower costs. "There's no reason a 'do-gooder' organization should be any less well run or well managed than any other," Bellamy observed to Lucia Mouat for the *Christian Science Monitor* (November 29, 1995).

The places in which UNICEF strives to "do good" are the native countries of billions of children, huge numbers of whom face problems ranging from serious to dire. In many countries, such as Balkan nations and the Sudan, ongoing warfare has left countless children physically and emotionally damaged, orphaned, and homeless. In a speech to the U.N.'s Humanitarian Issues Working Group in April 1999, Bellamy said, "Flagrant violations of human rights and humanitarian law—whether by direct attack, silent starvation, or forcible displacement—are not experiences that children easily grow out of. We know from long experience that the trauma of war causes wounds in children that fester for generations. That is why . . . it is folly to think that any sustained, long-term effort to promote peace and resolve conflict can possibly succeed unless children are recognized as a distinct and priority concern."

Many other acute problems have drawn Bellamy's attention in the past four years. In North Korea, massive crop failures that followed floods and then drought have caused the deaths of thousands of children and adults and severe malnutrition in untold numbers of others. In large parts of sub-Saharan Africa, thousands of children have been stricken with the AIDS virus. In many developing countries, many children—a disproportionate number of them female—grow up illiterate. Child labor and other forms of child abuse are widespread. Millions of children have not been immunized against such diseases as polio and tetanus, and millions live in areas that lack sanitary water supplies. Bellamy has pointed out that reacting to crises is not UNICEF's primary goal; rather, as she said to Lucia Mouat, "we are trying to provide some consistent normality for children, so development can continue." In an on-line interview with Angela Neustatter for the OneWorld News Service, which provides daily reports on human rights and environmental issues, Bellamy said, "We have to consider what kind of a world we are bringing . . . children into. That is a challenge for me."

Although Bellamy's term as executive director of UNICEF is not scheduled to end until May 2000, in September 1999 Kofi Annan, the secretary general of the U.N., announced that Bellamy had been appointed to a second five-year term. Bellamy, Annan said, as reported by Barbara Crossette in the

New York Times (September 14, 1999), had carried out her job "with distinction and devotion."

A confirmed workaholic who has never married, Bellamy is noted for her seemingly boundless energy and for talking "in a rapid, enthusiastic rush," as Neustatter reported. "Carol is one of the few people I know whose inner life is her outer life," Karen Burstein told Clines. "She is not reflective. She is action-oriented. She's not a big small-talker—no personal stuff." On one of the rare occasions when Bellamy has indulged her love for hiking, she joined an all-women's trek in the Himalayas. A fellow trekker, the educator and former federal official Diane Ravitch, told Karen De Witt for the *New York Times* (October 15, 1993) that Bellamy, whom she described as having a "Girl Scout" persona, "was in charge of the first-aid kit on that trip because she likes taking care of people. She has this real earnest interest in public service." Bellamy's close friends also include Donna Shalala, the secretary of the U.S. Department of Health and Human Services, who organized the Himalaya trip.

In a 1996 article for the Children's Express News Agency, reproduced on-line by OneWorld, Natasha Asare, age 13, and Martin Webb, 11, wrote that when they interviewed Bellamy, she "was open and friendly. She treated us not like children, not like adults, but like people. By the way she responded to our questions, Ms. Bellamy seems to take us seriously as young people—and bridged the gap between us and people of our generation in other parts of the world by telling us about their problems." "At the Peace Corps I used to say that I had the best job in Washington," Bellamy told Neustatter. "Now I think I have the best job in the world." — M.B.

Suggested Reading: *Christian Science Monitor* p13 Nov. 29, 1995, with photo; *New York* p25+ Mar. 8, 1982, with photos; New York *Daily News* p4+ Sep. 11, 1977, with photo; *New York Times* p20 Dec. 29, 1985, with photo, A p26 Oct. 15, 1993, with photo, p1+ Sep. 20, 1997, with photo; *New York Times Magazine* p18+ Feb. 25, 1979, with photos; *Village Voice* p1+ Sep. 25, 1978, with photo; *Washington Post* p21 Sep. 29, 1993, with photo

---

Benigni, Roberto

(beh-NEE-nee)

Oct. 27, 1952– Filmmaker and actor. Address: Via S. Anselmo #29, 00153 Rome, Italy

With thinning hair that looks as if it is statically charged, and a knack for playing bumbling but good-hearted characters who get into unfortunate but very funny situations, Roberto Benigni has been one of Italy's most beloved slapstick comics since the late 1980s. His humor is said to have helped turn public opinion against the former Italian prime minister Silvio Berlusconi, and he was once banned from television for a year for making fun of the Pope. The director Jim Jarmusch, who has worked with him on two American films, compared the manically energetic Benigni to one of the Marx brothers. "Like Harpo he does have an amazing anarchistic quality," Jarmusch told Alan Cowell for the *New York Times* (July 19, 1992). "He can walk into a room and turn it upside down or make it explode. His true gift is improvisation and, I would add, disruption. Working with him is really a riot because you don't know what to expect from him."

Because Benigni is associated so closely with puerile humor and gags, his most famous film to date, the Holocaust fable *La Vita è bella* (*Life Is Beautiful*), initially struck many people as incongruous. Before the release of the film—in which a Jewish father desperately tries to protect his son by pretending that the concentration camp in which they are imprisoned is merely the setting for an

Fred Prouser/Archive Photos

elaborate game—there were fears that the story would offend some viewers with its partly comic treatment of so grave a theme. After *La Vita è bella* premiered, in 1998, some critics did indeed blast the movie for trivializing the genocide of Jews. Many others, however, found the film to be a strange but affecting tragedy. Benigni, who wrote, directed, and starred in the film, won the 1999

Academy Award for best actor, and *La Vita è bella* captured the Oscar for best foreign film.

In what was by far the liveliest acceptance speech at the Oscars ceremony, Benigni climbed over the heads and seats of Hollywood moguls, hopped up the stairs like a frenetic bunny, and expressed his joy at receiving his two awards by holding them up to his ears like antennae and announcing, in garbled English, that he wanted to be like the god Jupiter—so that he could "kidnap everybody and lie down in the firmament making love to everybody." "He doesn't remotely seem or look like a movie star," Blake Edwards, who directed Benigni in *Son of the Pink Panther* (1993), told a reporter for the *Washington Post* (August 31, 1993). "He's more like an Italian waiter—balding, painfully thin, strangely angular. . . . And yet there's a romanticism in him that's unusual, unexpected."

The only son of Luigi and Isolina Benigni, Roberto Benigni was born on October 27, 1952 in Italy. His mother worked with textiles, while his father worked odd jobs connected with farming, carpentry, and bricklaying. The family's first home was in a rural community near Arezzo (where the first half of *La Vita è bella* takes place). The post–World War II years were lean for many Italians, and the Benignis were no exception. Their house had no running water or electricity. Later, when they moved to Vergaio, another small farming town, their situation improved slightly, but they still had few amenities. Until he was 12, for example, Benigni shared a bed with his mother and his three older sisters (Bruna, Albertina, and Anna). The Benignis did not own a television, and while their town did have an outdoor movie facility, they were unable to afford the price of admission. Roberto often watched the movies from behind the screen, seeing the images in reverse.

Benigni was a clever, irrepressible boy. As a youth he could recite whole passages from Dante's *Divine Comedy*, and when he had an audience, he liked to tell jokes. He also excelled in ottava rima competitions, a popular Tuscan pastime dating back to the 13th century, in which two people debate while improvising eight-line rhyming verses. When he was about 12, a local priest who had recognized his intellectual gifts took him to Florence and enrolled him at a seminary. Were it not for a flood of the Arno River in 1966 that shut the school down, Benigni might have become a priest. Sometime later he left home again to work as a magician's apprentice in a circus, a job that ended after three months, when "my hand got burnt because a joke didn't work so good," as he told an interviewer for the *San Francisco Chronicle* (October 25, 1998, on-line). "So I was saved from one profession by the water and from another by the fire."

Benigni's formal education ended at a mostly female secretarial school. His rise to stardom began during one election year, when he jumped on a platform meant for a candidate and pretended to represent a new party that advocated free love and sex. That caught the notice of the director of an avant-garde, experimental theater, who in 1972 recruited Benigni to join his group in Rome. Giuseppe Bertolucci, the younger brother of the filmmaker Bernardo Bertolucci, befriended Benigni in Rome and helped him develop a monologue in which he presented himself as a native of Tuscany and talked about his unusual sex life. Exposure on the stage led to a gig on the Italian television show *The Other Sunday*, in which Benigni played a movie critic who pronounced judgment on films that he didn't understand and often hadn't seen. The lewdness and irreverence of Benigni's routines often provoked the police into threatening him with obscenity charges. In 1980, after poking fun at Pope John Paul II, he was banned from television for one year.

Meanwhile, at about the same time that his television career was taking off, Benigni had written and starred in a film by Giuseppe Bertolucci called *Berlinguer, ti voglio bene* (*Berlinguer, I Like You*, 1976). The title refers to Enrico Berlinguer, the head of the Italian Communist Party from 1972 to 1984. Explaining his sympathies for the Communist Party, Benigni told the *New York Times* reporter Alan Cowell, "I was Communist because being Communist was something very romantic. In my little village, 90 percent of the people were Communists. . . . All my family tradition was Communist. I didn't ask why I was Communist."

Benigni appeared in six more films—*I Giorni cantati* (1979), *Chiedo asilo* (1979), *Clair de femme* (1979), *La Luna* (1979), *Il Pap'occhio* (1981), and *Il Minestrone* (1981)—before he directed his first film. Benigni wrote the screenplay for that movie, called *Tu mi turbi* ("You Move Me," 1983), and he starred in it as well. Nicoletta Braschi, whom he cast as the Virgin Mary in that film, has since appeared in most of Benigni's films, and the two married in 1991. "What I love best about her is that she is a woman who really knows how to laugh," Benigni told Alessandra Stanley for the *New York Times Magazine* (October 11, 1998).

Benigni appeared in two more Italian films—*F.F.S.S. cioè che mi hai portato a fare sopra Posillipo se non mi vuoi più bene* (1983) and *Non ci resta che piangere* (1984)—before he appeared in his first American film, *Down By Law* (1986), directed by the independent filmmaker Jim Jarmusch. Benigni played an Italian tourist who lands in jail and proposes to two cellmates (played by John Lurie and Tom Waits) that they break out "just like they do in American movies." Benigni proved to be well-suited for the role. He had never been to the United States before and his command of English was minimal. While assisting Benigni with his English, Lurie, feeling mischievous, taught the Italian actor some fake English words. As a result Benigni thought "frump" meant "glass," "clamp" meant "cup," "wuzbee" meant "angry," and "I have to flame" meant "I have to urinate." "All the set started to use my fake words," Benigni recalled to a *New York Times* (October 19, 1988) interviewer.

"Even Jim would sometimes have to use them because they were all I understood. He'd say 'Stay in the boat' and I wouldn't understand. He'd repeat stay in the boat. Then he'd say 'Oh the gramp—stay in the gramp.' Then I understood." Benigni added, "Now I am waiting for John Lurie to come to Italy to work. I want to teach him Italian."

Benigni's appearance in *Down By Law* brought him offers from Disney, Warner Bros., and other American studios. Supposedly he was offered a part in the picture *Beetlejuice*, but the title turned him off. "Look what that film did for Michael Keaton [who accepted the part]," Benigni joked to Alessandra Stanley. "I could have been Batman. Well, maybe Robin." Six years passed before Benigni appeared in another American picture. That film, *Night on Earth* (1992), also directed by Jarmusch, is about the adventures of five cab drivers and their passengers on a single night. Benigni played a cabbie who confesses the sordid details of his strange sex life to a passenger who is a priest. Benigni's third American movie was *Son of the Pink Panther* (1993), the eighth sequel in the Pink Panther series made famous by Peter Sellers, who played the original Inspector Clouseau. Benigni played Jacques Gambrelli, Clouseau's illegitimate, bumbling son.

Benigni's first three American films did not turn him into a household name in the U.S. In Italy, by contrast, he was rapidly becoming the best-known star in the country. He wrote the screenplay for, directed, and starred in *Il Piccolo diavolo* ("The Little Devil") in 1988 and appeared in the director Federico Fellini's film *La Voce della luna* (*The Voice of the Moon*) in 1990. In the latter, he played Ivo Salvini, a deranged innocent who concocts a plan to capture the moon with a machine. In *Johnny Stecchino* ("Johnny Toothpick," 1991) Benigni played both the title role—a Mafia boss who has squealed on his associates—and a school-bus driver who resembles the hunted Mafia boss. Braschi played the mob boss's wife, who comes up with a plan to kill the bus driver so that she can escape to another country with her husband. The film, directed by Benigni and co-written by Benigni and Vincenzo Cerami, broke all previous Italian box-office records and even earned more in Italy than such American imports as *Robin Hood*, *Hook*, and *Terminator II*. Another highly successful Benigni film was *Il Mostro* ("The Monster," 1994), which again smashed Italian box-office records. Benigni assumed the role of a mannequin transporter who, in a comedy of misidentification, is accused of being a serial rapist and killer. Braschi appeared as a police detective out to seduce and trap Benigni's clumsy character.

Had it not been for the astounding financial success of *Titanic* (1997), Benigni might have broken the Italian box-office record for a third straight time with *La Vita è bella* (*Life Is Beautiful*, 1998), which currently stands as the second-highest-grossing film in Italian history. The film revolves around Guido, a goofball Italian-Jewish waiter. In the first half of the film, he wins the heart of Dora (Braschi), who happens to be dating a local Fascist leader. In the second half, which takes place several years later, Guido and his son, who is about five, are abruptly taken away to a German concentration camp, where Dora, who is not Jewish, insists on joining them. Guido attempts to shield his son from the horror of the situation by pretending that everything happening is just part of a game. He tells his son that by following the rules of the Germans in charge of the camp, they can earn enough points to win a real-life tank.

The inspiration for the film came during a brainstorming session Benigni held with his co-writer Cerami. "I had this strong desire to put myself, my comic persona, in an extreme situation," Benigni told Alessandra Stanley. The most extreme situation he could think of was the Holocaust, and the two writers then came up with the basic plot of *La Vita è bella*. Benigni realized that this was a risky project. He knew, for example, of a previous attempt by the comedian Jerry Lewis to make a film, *The Day the Clown Cried*, in which the Nazis hire a German clown to distract children headed to the gas chamber. That picture was never released. Despite this disheartening precedent, and despite the advice of many people who warned him that his film would turn audiences off, Benigni, after thinking about the idea for a year, decided to proceed. "What is more simple or more beautiful than to protect innocence, and to have the right to say life is beautiful until the very last moment?" he explained to a writer for *Interview* (November 1998). "Historically, the movie may have its inaccuracies. But it's a story about love, not a documentary."

Another part of Benigni's motivation was personal. His father had served in the Italian cavalry in Albania during World War II. When Italy dropped out of the Axis coalition, in 1943, and became an Allied partner, Benigni's father was captured by the Germans and spent the next two years in a German labor camp. By the time he was released, many of his friends had been killed, and he had shrunk to a mere 80 pounds. Years later, wanting to tell his son and daughters about the experience without frightening them, he followed his wife's suggestion and described what had happened to him in a humorous manner. "Like in my movie, my father was telling us like it was a fable," Benigni explained to *Salon* (October 20, 1998, online). "He was afraid to make us fearful. He was protecting us, like I am protecting the son in the movie, because this is the first instinct."

When *La Vita è bella* premiered, in 1998, many critics accused Benigni of trivializing or otherwise misrepresenting the Holocaust experience; many others, though, found the film very moving. "The notion of making a game out of a death camp is, of course, absurd, but it mirrors the absurdity of Nazi ideology and the evil that flowed from it," Sharon Waxman wrote for the *Washington Post* (November 1, 1998). Benigni and Cerami had written the script with advice from Marcello Peetti, of the Center for Documentation of Contemporary Judaism in Milan, and two Auschwitz survivors, among others. In addition, prior to its release, the film had been screened for various Jewish groups, and though some of them pointed out a few historical errors, these viewers generally liked the story. One group recommended that the film be called a fable, and that is how Benigni has been describing his movie to the media.

Life Is Beautiful was later screened at the Jerusalem Film Festival, where it was well received. Jerusalem's mayor subsequently gave Benigni an award for furthering the understanding of Jewish history. At the Cannes Film Festival, the film won the Prix du Jury, and Benigni, in a preview of his highly energetic display at the Oscar ceremony, kissed the feet of the director Martin Scorsese. "It's a sign of mediocrity when you demonstrate gratitude with moderation," Benigni told *Newsweek* (February 8, 1999). *Life Is Beautiful* received seven Academy Award nominations and won the honors for best actor, best foreign film, and best musical score. (Nicola Piovani composed the music.) Benigni became the first filmmaker in 50 years (since Laurence Olivier) to win an Oscar as an actor under his own direction; the first Italian to be named best actor (two Italian women have won the award for best actress); and the 12th Italian director to win for best foreign film.

In August 1999 Miramax released to American theaters a version of *La Vita è bella* that had been dubbed into English. Benigni approved of the change. "If you are reading subtitles, you cannot see the whole picture," he explained to Leonard Klady for the *New York Times* (August 29, 1999), "and you miss the eye contact with the actors that is the soul of the picture."

Benigni is slated to appear in *Astérix et Obélix contre César* (*Asterix and Obelix versus Caesar*), a French film based on the European comic book. He and his wife currently live in Aventino, a posh neighborhood in Rome. For fun he likes to play cards; he also exchanges riddles and linguistic games with the Italian semiotician Umberto Eco. — W.G.

Suggested Reading: *Entertainment Weekly* p51+ Dec. 4, 1998, with photos; *Interview* p123+ Apr. 1990, with photos; *New York Times* II p1+ Oct. 19, 1986, with photos, II p9+ July 19, 1992, with photos; *New York Times Magazine* p42+ Oct. 11, 1998; *San Francisco Chronicle* (on-line) Oct. 25, 1998; *Washington Post* D p1+ Aug. 31, 1993, with photo

Selected Films: as writer, director, and actor—*Tu mi turbi*, 1983; *Non ci rest che piangere* ("Nothing Left to Do But Cry"), 1984; *Il Piccolo diavola* ("The Little Devil"), 1988; *Johnny Stecchino* ("Johnny Toothpick"), 1991; *Il Mostro* ("The Monster"), 1994; *La Vita è bella* (*Life Is Beautiful*), 1998; as actor and writer—*Berlinguer ti voglio bene*, 1977; *Chiedo asilo*, 1979; as

actor—*La Luna*, 1979; *Clair de femme* ("Womanlight"), 1979; *I Giorni cantati*, 1979; *Il Minestrone*, 1981; *Il Pap'occhio* ("In the Pope's Eye"), 1981; *F.F.S.S. cioè che mi hai portato a fare sopra Posillipo se non mi vuoi più bene*, 1983; *Down by Law*, 1986; *La Voce della luna* ("The Voice of the Moon"), 1989; *Son of the Pink Panther*, 1993

Joyce Ravid/Courtesy of Random House

Berg, Elizabeth

Dec. 2, 1948– Writer. Address: c/o Random House, 201 E. 50th St., New York, NY 10022

In her novels, *Durable Goods* (1993), *Talk Before Sleep* (1994), *Range of Motion* (1995), *The Pull of the Moon* (1996), *Joy School* (1997), *What We Keep* (1998), and *Until the Real Thing Comes Along* (1999), Elizabeth Berg has limned the stages of modern American women's lives, from the beginnings of adolescence to middle age, encompassing the turmoil of a parentless childhood; the claiming of a friend by a fatal disease in midlife; obsession with impossible love; the joys and tribulations of marriage and child raising; and the ending of marriage. "I wanted to write about my experience in a fictional way, to create characters and events that, although imagined, would testify to the emotional truth of what happened," Berg wrote in the prefatory note to *Talk Before Sleep*, as quoted by Nicholas A. Basbanes in *Publishers Weekly* (August 21, 1995). Reviewers have praised her "luminous" prose and her avoidance of mawkishness in writing about emotionally charged subjects.

Elizabeth Berg was born on December 2, 1948 in St. Paul, Minnesota, to Jeanne and Arthur Hoff. Because her father was a career army officer, she lived in many places in the United States during her childhood. She returned to her native city to attend the University of Minnesota before earning an A.A.S. degree from St. Mary's Junior College in Minneapolis, which enabled her to become a critical-care nurse. In 1974 she married Howard Berg, with whom she had two daughters and settled in Massachusetts, near Boston.

In about 1985 Berg decided to quit nursing to stay home with her children. She submitted an essay about that decision to *Parents* magazine. Weeks later, having gotten no response from *Parents* and having concluded that her piece had been rejected, she received a letter informing her that she had won the magazine's "Parentwise" contest. "I couldn't *believe* it," she told Nicholas Basbanes. "Five hundred dollars! And they were going to publish my story! I just went berserk." From then on she dedicated herself to writing, producing a large number of articles for *Parents* and other magazines, among them *Family Circle*, *Redbook*, and *Ladies' Home Journal*.

At about the same time that she began her life as a writer, Berg received a diagnosis of mycosis fungoides, a T-cell lymphoma. Her decision to become a writer was reinforced by the knowledge that she had a potentially fatal disease. In addition, she was determined to continue her normal life as a homemaker and mother. "I have always appreciated the small, quiet things in life, and what I learned right away is how important to me they are, and how important to me they will always be."

Berg's first book was *Family Traditions* (1992), a nonfiction volume about ways in which families can celebrate holidays and other special occasions. The book was done on a work-for-hire basis, and the writing of it, as she told Basbanes, was a chore. "No matter what I am doing, I want to have fun, and I wasn't having any fun with that book. It just wasn't freeing enough, and what I wanted most of all was to pull at the most creative part of myself." She reached into that creative part to produce stories that she read to her writers' group every Wednesday. After six months she was able to combine the stories into *Durable Goods*, her first novel.

Durable Goods is set during a summer on an army base. The narrator is 12-year-old Katie, whose widowed father treats his two daughters "like boot-camp recruits," even to the point of physically abusing them. After running away with her older sister and her sister's boyfriend, Katie returns, hoping for a renewed understanding with her father. Berg has emphasized that although there are autobiographical elements in *Durable Goods*, the father in the story is entirely fictional. The work won great praise from reviewers. Regina Weinreich wrote in the *New York Times Book Review* (October 24, 1993) that the protagonist's "fresh yet wise voice evokes that tender passage from being a girl to being a grown-up." Weinreich added that the title "seems off, a bit mercantile for such a luminous work." Donna Seaman in *Booklist* (April 15, 1993) termed *Durable Goods* "a tender, smart, and perfectly constructed little novel, suffused with humor and admiration for youth's great capacity for love and instinct for truth," and *Kirkus Reviews* (February 15, 1993) called it a "finely observed, compassionate book" in which "hope and sorrow mingle."

Berg used her own life as a basis for her next novel, *Talk Before Sleep*, as well. This time it was the experience of a friend with cancer that inspired her. *Talk Before Sleep*, the story of beautiful, extroverted Ruth's losing battle with breast cancer, is narrated by the quiet, more ordinary Ann. While Ruth is surrounded by a circle of loving friends, Ann's relationship with Ruth is her first deep friendship with another woman. Although Berg herself lost a close friend to breast cancer, she said—as paraphrased by Basbanes—that "this book, like all of her fiction, embodies a good deal of invention." She admitted that the "talk between Ruth and Ann about cancer is my dialogue with myself. I did not have talks as soulful and searching as that with my friend. It is one of my regrets, in fact, because my friend did not accept that she was going to die."

Reviewers responded to *Talk Before Sleep* as positively as they had to *Durable Goods*. Donna Seaman in *Booklist* (April 15, 1994) lauded "another perfectly constructed and tender novel" and "a particularly sensitive coming-to-terms-with-death tale." She concluded, "Life surely goes on, Berg seems to say, but we do miss our dead." Brigitte Frase, who reviewed *Talk Before Sleep* for the *Washington Post Book World* (June 5, 1994), deemed Berg successful in avoiding the traps of "a medical soap opera or an earnest polemic about the disease of the month." She found that without "losing the grieving heart of the book, Berg sidesteps weepy swamps with admirable poise. . . . Far from being depressing, this is an unexpectedly lively book. Tender and irreverent by turns, it offers mature intelligence and a buoyant spirit, like a very good friend."

Some reviewers, however, had complaints. Richard M. Ratzan, for instance, in his assessment for the *Literature, Arts & Medicine Database* (July 24, 1997, on-line), a Web site sponsored by the New York University School of Medicine, found that Berg "missteps into the territory of bathos" and portrays men almost entirely as "unfeeling" and "laughable caricatures who do nothing to lend a sense of balance and fairness to this author's otherwise obvious talent for narrative." Although Lauren Belfer, in the *New York Times Book Review* (May 22, 1994), found *Talk Before Sleep* "otherwise haunting and sensitive," with "interludes when the novel soars," she felt that it was marred by "anti-man chatter" and by Berg's glorification of a dying person, "as though the prospect of death absolves a person of moral responsibility."

Nicholas Basbanes noted that the narrative voice Berg employs "is always one and the same." "I write about people that I wish I were like, but it's always me talking," Berg conceded. "It's always the same motivation, whatever theme it takes. For me, there will always be life-affirming stuff. I'm a rank sentimentalist, and I make no apologies at all for it."

Range of Motion, her 1995 novel, focuses on Lainey, a wife and mother whose husband, Jay, has been struck by a piece of falling ice that has left him in a coma. (The title refers to exercises care givers perform with helpless patients.) Lainey copes with the misfortune, comforted by her neighbor Alice and strengthened by her faith that her husband will recover. After several months Jay emerges from his coma with a new ability to listen to "the telling songs of the wider life." Marilyn Chandler McEntire, the reviewer for the *Literature, Arts & Medicine Database* (April 16, 1998, online), called *Range of Motion* "a thoughtful meditation on what it takes to live with ongoing uncertainty, loss, fear, and responsibility, and still sustain hope" and described it as "exceptional in its delicate handling of inner life with its strands of memory, imagination, desire, grief, frustration, rage, and hope. Even the intercalary passages that offer a speculative representation of the comatose state avoid the kind of fancifulness that would invalidate them as invitations to empathy." In *Booklist* (August 19, 1995), Donna Seaman wrote that "Berg's impeccable prose gives voice to that element in our psyche that enables us to cope with the impossible."

Berg continued her explorations of issues in women's lives with *The Pull of the Moon*, a novel in which a 50-year-old woman leaves her husband and college-bound daughter to embark on a journey—both physical and emotional—to find herself. Some reviewers, such as Rebecca A. Stuhr-Rommereim in *Library Journal* (April 1, 1996), were disappointed with the novel. "Conveniently, Nan is a woman of privilege, traveling in relative comfort. . . . She has little or no anxiety about how her husband might react to her flight, and there seems to be nothing in her life beyond her relationship with him and with her . . . daughter," she wrote, terming Berg's "treatment of an individual in transition" to be "not altogether satisfactory." Joan Mooney, in the *New York Times Book Review* (May 26, 1996), agreed that while "Nan's story is presented engagingly with chapters alternating between letters and journal entries, she never probes very deeply and only occasionally expresses herself in a distinctive way." *Booklist* (April 1, 1996) reviewer Joanne Wilkinson, however, felt that Berg drove "her narrative home with direct heartfelt language" and displayed "a real gift for imbuing ordinary lives with emotional weight and heft."

In 1997 Berg produced a sequel to *Durable Goods*—*Joy School*, which continues the story of Katie, now 13 years old, after she has returned to

her father. Katie finds that she has to adjust to a great deal; her sister has eloped and is living in Mexico, and Katie, after moving with her father to Missouri, misses her best friend, whom she left behind in Texas. The title refers to what a priest tells Katie about sorrow: "It could teach you about joy." Claire Messud wrote in the *Washington Post Book World* (April 13, 1997) that the "pleasures, like the homilies, to be found in *Joy School* are sweet but artificially flavored." Most reviewers disagreed with her negative assessment. Polly Morrice, in the *New York Times Book Review* (June 15, 1997), observed that "Katie's lively narrative voice provides the novel's greatest pleasure. . . . *Joy School* need not be read as a sequel. It stands successfully on its own, treating a venerable theme with freshness." For Barbara Maslekoff, the *Library Journal* (March 1, 1997) reviewer, the characters "are so real, so perfectly drawn, that readers will become 13 again, if only for a short while."

Berg has described to interviewers her practice of selecting details from her own life and transmuting them into fiction. In the story "The Getaway," published in *Good Housekeeping* (May 1996), Berg wrote of a middle-aged couple on a trip without their daughter, Rachel. "You know," Phyllis, the wife, says, "Rachel told me about this one kind of star, a white dwarf. It collapses inward." She tells her husband, George, "I feel like that star. . . . I feel like I'm collapsing inward. Like the star." Attracted to a man who has made romantic overtures to her, Phyllis nevertheless decides to stay with George, so that their daughter's life will remain on a steady course. The story drew from Berg's personal experience; in an article in *Good Housekeeping* (March 1998), Berg mentioned a dramatic change in "the cycle of my own life. . . . I got divorced, left a 23-year marriage to start a new and truer—if harder—life." That ending differed from the one Berg gave her protagonist in *The Pull of the Moon*, in which the character Nan returns to her husband. Berg's 1998 novel, *What We Keep*, a story of the repercussions of a woman's having left a marriage, is narrated from the perspective of Ginny, a 47-year-old woman who was 12 when her mother left. For most of the novel, Ginny is en route to California from the East Coast to reunite with the mother she hasn't seen in 35 years. She spends that time remembering the past, and her memories prove less than accurate when she meets her mother.

What We Keep garnered mixed reviews. Caroline M. Hallsworth, writing in *Library Journal* (May 1, 1998), thought that the novel was among Berg's best: "Berg's precise, evocative descriptions create vivid images of Ginny's physical world, while Berg's understanding and perception are an eloquent testimony to Ginny's emotional turmoil." She felt that Berg's examination of "the roles and relationships of mothers and daughters" revealed "how truth, forgiveness, and understanding are possible in healing intergenerational rifts between women." Janet Kaye, the critic for the *New York*

Times Book Review (June 7, 1998), on the other hand, felt that although *What We Keep* was "highly readable," it was "sketchy" and "perfunctory" overall. The *Booklist* (May 15, 1998) reviewer termed it "plodding and predictable."

Berg's 1999 novel, *Until the Real Thing Comes Along*, drew similar responses. The story of a single woman who is prevented from having normal relationships with men because of her obsessive love for a man who is gay, it was called "50's women's fiction grafted onto the 90's dreary obsession with women's ticking biological clocks" by Dana Kennedy, whose notice appeared in the *New York Times Book Review* (July 25, 1999).

Berg's nonfiction work *Escaping Into the Open: The Art of Writing True* (1999) is an examination of the art of writing both fiction and nonfiction; it offers exercises, discussions of workshops and other writers' aids, and interviews with writing teachers, editors, and agents. GraceAnne A. DeCandido, who reviewed the volume for *Booklist* (June 1, 1999), professed herself charmed by it. "Anyone who ever needs to write anything will find bright shards of useful stuff here, like the box of many textured scraps a friend gave Berg labeled 'touch,'" DeCandido concluded. — S.Y.

Suggested Reading: *Booklist* p1491 Apr. 15, 1993, p1514 Apr. 15, 1994, p1342 Apr. 1, 1996, p1593 May 15, 1998; *Good Housekeeping* p104+ Mar. 1998; *Library Journal* p114 Apr. 1, 1996, p1108 Mar. 1, 1997, p135 May 1, 1998; *New York Times Book Review* p22 Oct. 24, 1993, p35 May 22, 1994, p15 May 26, 1996, p22 June 15, 1997, p22 June 7, 1998; *Publishers Weekly* p40+ Aug. 21, 1995, with photo; *Washington Post Book World* p4 June 5, 1994, p6 Apr. 13, 1997

Selected Books: *Family Traditions*, 1992; *Durable Goods*, 1993; *Talk Before Sleep*, 19934; *Range of Motion*, 1995; *The Pull of the Moon*, 1996; *Joy School*, 1997; *What We Keep*, 1998; *Until the Real Thing Comes Along*, 1999; *Escaping into the Open: The Art of Writing True*, 1999

Bumper Inc.

Berry, Halle
(HAL-lee)

Aug. 14, 1968– Actress. Address: c/o William Morris Agency, 1325 Ave. of the Americas, 15th Fl., New York, NY 10019

Ask the actress Halle Berry what effect race has had on her career and you're more than likely to receive a conflicted response. While Berry, the daughter of a black father and a white mother, often expresses a wariness about dwelling too much on her biracial heritage, she has at the same time exhibited a professional commitment to confounding stereotypes, having played a wide variety of roles in movies and on television. A former model, she has also struggled to overcome attitudes that equate beauty with a lack of acting ability. Her filmography runs the gamut from testosterone-juiced action movies like *The Last Boy Scout* (1991) to such idiosyncratic comedies as *B.A.P.S.* (1997) and *Why Do Fools Fall in Love?* (1998) to socially engaged films like *Jungle Fever* (1991) and *Bulworth* (1998). Over her decade-long career, Berry has acquitted herself as a versatile and at times daring actress willing to play down her movie-star aura in gritty and unflattering roles.

Halle Berry was born on August 14, 1968 in Cleveland, Ohio. Her first name, which rhymes with "Sally," was chosen by her mother, Judith, after she visited a Halle Brothers department store. Judith, a nurse, had been disowned by her white, middle-class family when she married Jerome Berry, an African-American. After fathering two children, Halle and her older sister, Heidi, Jerome abandoned the family, leaving them to subsist on Judith's salary. When Halle was in the fourth grade, the Berrys moved to a suburb of Cleveland, where her skin color led to a less than warm reception. While Berry maintains that her childhood wasn't as difficult as the lives of many of the characters she has portrayed, she has recalled annoying episodes—such as an Oreo cookie placed in her mailbox and name-calling at school—that arose because of her racial status. At the largely white Bedford High School, Berry felt compelled to succeed, to convince her peers that she was as smart and industrious as they were. She became a cheerleader, editor of the school newspaper, and president of the honor society. Her classmates did not seem to resent her extracurricular achievements until she was almost elected prom queen, whereupon she was promptly accused of stuffing the ballot box. "That's when it hit me," she told *Premiere* (April 1995). "They like me until I'm representing a symbol of beauty in our school."

At Cuyahoga Community College, in Cleveland, Berry initially channeled her ambition for success into the area of broadcast journalism. During her internship at a local radio station, however, she discovered that she had little in the way of journalistic instincts, and she dropped out of school. Next, with connections she had formed on the beauty-contest circuit—she had won the 1986 Miss Teen Ohio pageant and finished second and third in the Miss U.S.A. and Miss World competitions, respectively—she pursued a modeling career in Chicago. (At five-foot-six, she was too short for the runways of New York or Europe.) At first, life in that city was tough for Berry, but she eventually got offers to do lingerie and catalog shoots. Berry's career received a boost in 1989, when she was referred to a New York talent manager by a friend from her pageant days. Berry sent the manager a videotaped monologue and soon received an offer of representation on the condition that she give up modeling and move to New York City.

Berry's first weeks in New York were less than auspicious: she slept in a homeless shelter and then in a YWCA. Soon, however, she obtained her first acting job, a role as a brainy model in the short-lived television sitcom *Living Dolls*. After the show's cancellation, Berry moved to Los Angeles, where she won a recurring part on the prime-time soap opera *Knots Landing*. Her first big break came in 1991, when she was cast in Spike Lee's film *Jungle Fever*, a story of an interracial romance. To prepare for her part, as Vivian, a crack addict, Berry toured a Washington, D.C., crack house, escorted by an undercover police officer. This was an eye-opening experience for the young actress, as she told the New York *Daily News* (February 13, 1993). "I saw 12- and 13-year-old girls perform oral sex on men for a hit," Berry recalled. "There were automatic weapons and knives everywhere." To immerse herself further in her role, Berry went without showers for the 10 days prior to shooting. Critics generally appreciated her efforts, and this success led to her next film, *The Last Boy Scout* (1991). For her small but pivotal part as a stripper in this action film, which was co-produced by Joel Silver of *Lethal Weapon* (1987) fame, Berry again sought out a real-life experience to inform her performance—this time visiting a strip club and even trying her hand at exotic dancing. The following year Berry won a substantial role, as the object of Eddie Murphy's affection in the romantic comedy *Boomerang* (1992). Meanwhile, she was receiving an increasing amount of media attention; both *Us* and *People* magazines named her one of the World's Most Beautiful People.

In 1993 Berry shot the television miniseries *Queen*, based on Alex Haley's book of the same name, which was a continuation of his *Roots* saga. (Incomplete at the time of his death, the book was published as a novel.) The six-hour movie detailed the life of Haley's biracial paternal grandmother, a subject very close to Berry's heart. "Being [from] an interracial [background] myself, I felt if I had lived back then, then some of those things could have happened to me," she told the New York *Daily News*. "I read the script the night I learned Alex Haley was dead, and I couldn't put it down. I knew I had to play this part." The producers, however, were less sure, fearing that Berry was too young and beautiful to be convincing as an elderly woman. But in the end Berry's persistence—she had interrupted the shooting of *Boomerang* to audition a second time—won out. *Queen*, which also starred Danny Glover, Ruby Dee, Ossie Davis, Ann-Margret, and Martin Sheen, got a rather cool critical reception—a *Washington Post* (February 14, 1993) reviewer, for example, called it "criminally slow and riddled with showboat melodrama." Berry's performance fared a little better. In the *New York Times* (February 12, 1993), John J. O'Connor wrote that Berry, "although a touch weak in some of the more emotional scenes, maintains a steady flow of lovely persuasion."

Berry next landed roles as a co-ed in the film *The Program* (1993), a drama about a college football team, and a vixen in *The Flintstones* (1994), a live-action rendition of the 1960s cartoon. Berry's performance in the latter consisted largely of slithering across Fred Flintstone's desk, in what *Jet* (June 6, 1994) called "a hot, sexy manner," to distract him from his work. The next year Berry took part in another epic saga, playing the Queen of Sheba to Jimmy Smits's King of Israel in the made-for-cable movie *Solomon and Sheba* (1995). This was followed by the feature film *Losing Isaiah* (1995), which paired Berry, again playing a crack addict, and Jessica Lange, as a social worker, in the story of a custody battle over the Berry character's baby. Both the movie and Berry's performance took hits. "As Khaila, Halle Berry is in over her head, or she would be if the script gave her anything real to do. Mostly she just looks good in the manner of a high-fashion model displaying the latest street styles," Andy Pawelczak wrote for *Films in Review* (July 1995).

Such comments—whether the fault of Berry or of critics who refuse to see past the actress's physical appearance—have plagued Berry's career. The situation did not improve with her role in the high-altitude action flick *Executive Action* (1996), which features Kurt Russell, Joe Morton, Steven Seagal, and B. D. Wong. Dismissed as "window dressing" by Janet Maslin of the *New York Times* (March 15, 1996), Berry played a flight attendant alongside Marla Maples Trump in what was deemed an effective if by-the-numbers genre film.

Berry gained a measure of respect from critics with her first leading role in a feature film, the neo-noir *The Rich Man's Wife* (1996). The movie was by no means a box-office smash, but Berry's portrayal of a blackmail victim, murder suspect, and adulteress garnered some decent reviews. In the *New York Times* (September 13, 1996), Lawrence Van Gelder wrote, "After a slow start, Ms. Berry becomes a plucky protagonist."

Berry next took parts in two comedies: *B.A.P.S* (1997) and *Why Do Fools Fall in Love?* (1998). *B.A.P.S*, a Robert Townsend effort, is a culture-clash story in which two gaudily attired black waitresses from Georgia move to Los Angeles to start a combination restaurant/beauty salon. In L.A., the women set up housekeeping with a rich old man (Martin Landau), who, falling under their spell, soon starts listening to rap and eating soul food. The film's humor was lost on most critics. Riffing on the titular acronym, which stands for "Black American Princesses," Mike Clark of *USA Today* (March 8, 1997) quipped, "Anyone who sees this movie will sink almost immediately into a deep N.A.P." Janet Maslin of the *New York Times* (March 28, 1997) agreed, calling the film "weak and condescending," but she praised Berry for being "as funny as she is gorgeous (very)."

Why Do Fools Fall in Love? depicted the professional and married lives of the 1950s teenage singing star and bigamist Frankie Lymon. Berry played Zola Taylor, lead singer of the Platters and one of three wives all vying for the singer's unpaid royalties after his death. The film received mixed reviews, but the scenes involving the trio of angry wives—the other two were played by Vivica A. Fox and Lela Rochon—were called "particularly vivid" by *People* (September 7, 1998). Berry followed this with *The Wedding* (1998), a television movie based on the Dorothy West novel about an impending interracial marriage in the early 1950s. In Warren Beatty's satire *Bulworth* (1998), which starred Beatty as a sell-out politician who metamorphoses into a rapping visionary, Berry took on the role of Nina, a young leftist and would-be assassin who gives the title character a political lesson.

In 1999 Berry starred in and served as executive producer of *Introducing Dorothy Dandridge*, a made-for-television movie that chronicles the tragic life of that 1950s African-American screen icon. The film was a personal victory for Berry, who for years had tried without success to interest producers in making it. "The answer was no, no, no," Berry told Bernard Weinraub for the *New York Times* (August 15, 1999), "and the very reason I wanted to make the movie was the very reason they didn't want to make it—and that's because nobody knew who [Dandridge] was." Finally, HBO gave the project a green light. "Halle's passion for it, her commitment, was extraordinary from the outset," Jeff Bewkes, the chairman of HBO, told Weinraub. Written by Shonda Rhimes and Scott Abott and directed by Martha Coolidge, *Introducing Dorothy Dandridge* earned some of the highest ratings in HBO's history as well as plaudits from critics. In the *New York Times* (August 20, 1999), for example, Caryn James described the film as an "engaging, socially aware look at an accomplished yet tortured life," and she reported that Berry "gives a shining, controlled performance throughout."

Most recently, Berry has appeared in makeup commercials as a Revlon spokesmodel, and she was cast in *Ringside*, a film about boxing directed by the writer Norman Mailer, which was scheduled for release in late 1999.

Jill Gerston, writing about Berry in the *New York Times* (March 12, 1995), mentioned her "exquisite cheekbones, . . . flawless cafe au lait skin, . . . eyes like two huge dark caramels, and . . . wrists so narrow they look as if they could almost fit through the hole of a doughnut." Late in 1992, after a six-month courtship, the actress married the Atlanta Braves outfielder David Justice; the couple divorced in 1996. Berry, who is diabetic and maintains a low-sugar diet, lives in Los Angeles with her dogs. — M.C.

Suggested Reading: *Ebony* p118+ Apr. 1993, with photos, p114+ Dec. 1994, with photos, p22+ Mar. 1997, with photos; *Essence* p60+ June 1994, with photos; *New York Times* II p15+ Mar. 12, 1995, with photo; *People* p34+ Feb. 22, 1993, with photos, p102+ May 13, 1996, with photo; *Premiere* p78+ Apr. 1995, with photos; *Redbook* p46+ July 1994, with photo

Selected Films: *Strictly Business*, 1991; *Jungle Fever*, 1991; *The Last Boy Scout*, 1991; *Boomerang*, 1992; *The Program*, 1993; *The Flintstones*, 1994; *Losing Isaiah*, 1995; *The Rich Man's Wife*, 1996; *B.A.P.S.*, 1997; *Why Do Fools Fall In Love*, 1998; *Bulworth*, 1998; for television—*Queen*, 1993; *Solomon and Sheba*, 1995; *The Wedding*, 1998; *Introducing Dorothy Dandridge*, 1999

Selected Television Shows: *Living Dolls*, 1989; *Knots Landing*, 1991–92

Berry, Mary Frances

Feb. 17, 1938– Chair of the United States Commission on Civil Rights; historian; lawyer. Address: c/o Commission on Civil Rights, Office of the Chairman, 624 Ninth St. N.W., Washington, DC 20425

"I don't know anybody who can do as many things at the same time and do all of them well," the Yale University historian John Blassingame said of his colleague and friend Mary Frances Berry during an interview with Alex Poinsett for *Ebony* (January 1977). Berry, who has won accolades as an equal-rights activist, educator, historian, legal scholar,

Courtesy of Mary Frances Berry

Mary Frances Berry

and author of eight books, is currently chair of the United States Commission on Civil Rights and the Geraldine R. Segal professor of American thought at the University of Pennsylvania. Though she prefers the quieter life of scholarship and writing, Berry has developed a reputation as a tireless and vocal champion for equal rights for women and minorities.

"I never had any childhood really," Berry was quoted as saying in Brian Lanker's book *I Dream a World* (1989). "I read my first fairy tales about three years ago." Born on February 17, 1938 in a rural area on the outskirts of Nashville, Tennessee, Mary Frances Berry was raised by her mother, Frances Wiggins Berry, and her older brother, George. Her father, George Ford Berry, deserted his wife and children sometime in the 1940s. "He was a laborer," Mary Berry explained to a reporter for *USA Today* in the 1980s. "It's one of those cases of a poor black family with a man who couldn't find a job after he came back from [World War II]. He had great difficulty finding employment and became very depressed. He went on the road and never came back."

Supporting a young family was an unending struggle for Berry's mother. Since she was a black woman living in the 1940s and 1950s South, her native intelligence and voracious reading of books did not help her in her search for jobs; indeed, her employment options were even more limited than her husband's had been. Eventually, Berry's mother was pushed to desperate measures to ensure that her children would be fed. "My mother made so little money around the time I was four years old that we stayed at an orphanage funded in part by a local charity," Berry recalled to the *USA Today* reporter.

Unbeknownst to Frances, the orphanage was anything but charitable. Mary Berry's memories of the place are reminiscent of Charles Dickens's descriptions, in his novel *Oliver Twist*, of the deplorable conditions in 19th-century British orphanages. Berry reported that the children in the orphanage were perpetually hungry; they were fed such things as milk diluted with water and meatless bones, for which they were charged a nickel apiece. The administrators "would go to the store and get food that was being thrown out by the supermarket, like chicken necks and wings," she told *USA Today*. "They cooked it with lots of black pepper to cover the fact that it was almost spoiled. They would make the kids stand up—holding this little diluted glass of milk with this little plate of this rotten food on the table—and sing, 'Thank you Lord for this food.'"

While her children were in the orphanage, Frances attended classes at a beauty school. Her new trade enabled her to earn enough to provide for her children at home. It is from her mother's example that Berry absorbed the tireless work ethic for which she has become well known. Her mother demanded hard work and diligent study from her children, and at age 10, while attending grammar school, Mary began working full time, doing domestic chores for white people. She has said that she has never gone jobless since.

At Pearl High School, in Nashville, Berry came under the influence of another strong female role model—Minerva Hawkins, a history teacher whom she has described as "kind" and "supportive." In *I Dream a World*, Berry was quoted as saying that Hawkins "took me under her wing and said, 'We're going to get these rough edges off. You are a diamond in the rough. You're smart, but you've led a rather crude, backward kind of life. We're going to polish you up a bit.'" Hawkins was aware that Berry's classmates sometimes taunted her because of her poverty. "I think she was shy because she didn't have the clothes or the money to cope with some of her peers," she told Poinsett. "I think her shyness is one of the drives that made her excel in other areas." Hawkins also noticed that Berry "always finished everything before anybody," as Berry told Poinsett, "and that I was always bored because I didn't have anything else to do." Hawkins "used to always give me other things to do and things to read."

Berry's subsequent academic career reflects the influences of both her mother and Hawkins. "My mother always told me to be overqualified for everything," Berry recalled, as quoted in *I Dream a World*. "She said, 'Always have more qualifications than anybody else you're sitting in the room with. If there are people there who have one degree, you get two. If they got two, you get three.'" Berry got four. She spent her first year in college at Fisk University, in Nashville, with a scholarship that she had won with the help of Hawkins, a Fisk alumna. After a year Berry transferred to Howard University, in Washington, D.C., from which she earned a B.A. degree, in 1961, and a master's degree, in 1962. She then entered the University of Michigan, from which she received a Ph.D. in 1966. According to one source, Berry spent time in Vietnam in 1967 with a Marine combat battalion as a civilian journalist and then returned to Michigan to study law. In 1970 she earned a J.D. degree from the University of Michigan Law School.

All through her student years, Berry continued to work to support herself and to help her mother financially. "The entire time I went to Howard and the whole time I was in graduate school at Michigan, I worked in hospital labs," Berry was quoted as saying in *I Dream a World*. "Went to school full time and worked on the 3:00-to-11:30 shift full time until the day I got my Ph.D. They were very stressful conditions, going to school all day long, then staying up half the night to write papers while other people were going out on dates and hanging out." "If I could change something [in my life], I might change that," Berry told *USA Today*. "Most of the things that happen to students when they are in college didn't happen to me."

The next decade was a period of remarkable career advancement for Berry. She first taught history at two relatively small state universities—Central Michigan University, in Mount Pleasant (1966–68), and Eastern Michigan University, in Ypsilanti (1968–69)—and then moved on to the University of Maryland, in College Park, where she served as the acting director (1970–72) and then director (1972–74) of the school's Afro-American studies program and as provost of the division of behavioral and social sciences (1973–76). Berry, who prior to her arrival at Maryland had no experience as an academic administrator, was put in charge of a relatively inactive group of professors, most of whom were contributing only sporadically, if at all, to the scholarship in their respective fields. By refusing to solicit grants or other research funding for her charges until they began producing meaningful work, she inspired a spurt in productivity. Within a year, faculty members were publishing papers and developing book-length studies. Based on her successes as provost at Maryland, the University of Colorado, which is widely regarded as the foremost intellectual link between the universities surrounding Chicago and brain trusts in California, offered Berry their chancellorship. Upon accepting that post, in 1976, she became the first black woman—and only the second woman—to be named the head of a major American university.

In 1977, only six months into her tenure as the University of Colorado's chancellor, President Jimmy Carter appointed Berry assistant secretary for education in the United States Department of Health, Education, and Welfare (HEW). As assistant secretary, Berry was responsible for guiding the education division of HEW, identifying the major national issues involving education, and advising the president and the HEW secretary as to the appropriate federal response to these issues. During her four-year term, Berry fought for the reorganization of HEW—specifically, its division into two entities, the Department of Health and Human Services and the Department of Education. A bill calling for the change passed in the Senate, by a vote of 69 to 22, on September 24, 1979, but almost died in the House of Representatives, where it was opposed by some conservative members of Congress, who feared that an autonomous department of education would take control away from local school boards; in addition, some liberal members feared that an independent department would have difficulty extracting funding from Congress. On September 27, the bill squeaked through the House, by a vote of 215 to 205, and it was signed into law by President Carter on October 17.

Drained by her fight for the Department of Education bill, Berry had thoughts of taking some time off, for perhaps the first time in her life, before returning to the familiar quiet of an academic post. But succumbing to persuasion by her mother and President Carter, Berry took on a new responsibility after completing her term with HEW, in 1980: she was named by Carter to the U.S. Commission on Civil Rights, an independent bipartisan agency of six members—half of whom are appointed by Congress, the other half by the president—established in 1957 by Congress. (Since 1983, by an act of Congress, the commission has comprised eight members.) The commission investigates complaints by citizens who allege they have been deprived of their right to vote; monitors adherence to federal laws and equal-opportunity programs; and serves as a national clearinghouse for information on civil rights. "I took the appointment because I thought it was going to continue to be this quiet little agency where we did some things on civil rights that might be helpful. It wouldn't take up a whole lot of time," Berry, who concurrently accepted a teaching post at Howard University, explained to *USA Today*. "I could basically be out of the public eye, and still be making a contribution."

As it turned out, the commission was entering perhaps its most turbulent period to date. President Ronald Reagan, whose first term in office began in 1981, was opposed to such programs as affirmative action and school busing, whose goals were to achieve greater racial integration in the workplace and schools. Berry publicly voiced her criticisms of the policies of Reagan and his administration. In an effort to reshape the agency to more closely reflect his politics, the president dismissed Berry from the commission before her six-year term expired. Berry fought the dismissal and was reinstated to her post by a federal district court. Following the expansion of the commission, Congress reappointed Berry, thus removing her from the reach of the president. Since its reconfiguration, which was followed by an audit of the agency's finances conducted by the federal General Accounting Office amid never-confirmed allegations of improprieties in spending, the commission has reestablished its place as governmental watchdog.

Beginning in 1984, acting on her commitment to civil rights, Berry helped lead the Free South Africa movement. Before apartheid ended in South Africa, in 1994, she could be found several days a week outside the South African Embassy in Washington, organizing demonstrations and even getting arrested while protesting. Meanwhile, in 1987 Berry was named the Geraldine R. Segal professor of American thought at the University of Pennsylvania, where she has continued to teach history and law while maintaining her post on the Civil Rights Commission.

Berry was a leading critic of President Bill Clinton's 1993 decision to rescind his nomination of Lani Guinier as the head of the Justice Department's civil rights division. Supposedly, after further reviewing Guinier's stand on civil rights, Clinton had determined that the views of Guinier, a professor of law, were not in line with his own. Guinier had long been a proponent of changing the electoral system to guarantee that members of minorities were elected to a certain number of seats in Congress, so as to at least approach equal representation; Clinton, by contrast, threw his support behind social programs that would aid the disenfranchised—indigent children, for example, and people who can't afford health insurance—regardless of race. Despite Berry's criticism of him in the Guinier case, in 1993 President Clinton appointed her to lead the U.S. Commission on Civil Rights. She thus became the first woman to head that agency.

Currently, the Commission on Civil Rights is looking into issues surrounding the 2000 national census. It is generally accepted that the traditional method of taking the census, via a head count, misses a significant portion of the minority population. Since, as stipulated in the Constitution, the apportionment of representatives in Congress in the following decade depends solely on census numbers, minorities are usually underrepresented. Some policymakers, therefore, have proposed using statistical sampling methods, wherein only a portion of a population is counted and then statistics are used to project the total, as a way of increasing accuracy. Critics of that method, however, fear that sampling would be less accurate, because it would create "virtual Americans," and would thus weaken the intent of the Constitution, which embraces the principle of "one man, one vote." Because of its constitutional and civil-rights implications, the census has become one of the most controversial and hotly contested issues in current American politics.

In another matter that is at the top of its agenda, on May 26, 1999 the Commission on Civil Rights held a public hearing on charges of misconduct by the New York (City) Police Department (NYPD) as part of a larger probe into the management of the department and the effects of possible mismanagement on the greater community. This investigation came in the wake of the shooting by four NYPD officers of Amadou Diallo, an unarmed man with no criminal record. Diallo's killing has raised concerns about the violation of civil rights by police.

A prolific writer in spite of her numerous responsibilities outside academia, Mary Berry has published eight history books. Eschewing the tradition according to which historical accounts describe events chronologically, Berry prefers to write about history thematically, showing the sociological impact of a series of documented events. All of her works have been received well, and some have been described as "groundbreaking." Her latest work, *The Pig Farmer's Daughter and Other Tales of American Justice: Episodes of Racism and Sexism in the Courts from 1865 to the Present* (1999), describes court cases in which judicial decision making has been clearly affected by questions of race, class, and gender. In other words, it is a history of stereotyping within the American legal system. In light of the volatility of the subject, one reviewer for *Kirkus Reviews* (March 15, 1999) noted that Berry "is such a gentle writer that the material has a way of not calling undue attention to itself. Certainly, no one could accuse her of exploiting her subject matter. She is, in fact, so subdued, so understated, in approach that it is part of the volume's strength. Although the collection could be used as propaganda against the American judicial system, Berry resists the temptation to gloat in hindsight at her findings."

Berry has received the NAACP's Roy Wilkins and Image Awards, the Southern Christian Leadership Conference's Rosa Parks Award, and *Ebony's* Black Achievement Award. She has also been named one of the American Women of the Century by the Women's Hall of Fame. "My life illustrates that solving the problems of poor people or black people by a one-dimensional approach isn't going to work," Berry told *USA Today*. "I was lucky enough that all the pieces came together." — T.J.F.

Suggested Reading: *Ebony* p58+ Jan. 1977, with photos; *USA Today* June 1, 1984, Sep. 15, 1987; Lanker, Brian. *I Dream a World*, 1989; *Who's Who in America 1999*

Selected Books: *Black Resistance/White Law: A History of Constitutional Racism in Amercica*, 1971; *Military Necessity and Civil Rights Policy: Black Citizenship and the Constitution, 1861–1868*, 1977; *Stability, Security, and Continuity: Mr. Justice Burton and Decision-Making in the Supreme Court*, 1978; *Why ERA Failed: Politics, Women's Rights, and the Amending Process of the Constitution*, 1986; *The Politics of Parenthood: Child Care, Women's Rights, and the Myth of the Good Mother*, 1993; with John Blassingame—*Long Memory: The Black Experience in America*, 1982; with V. P. Franklin—*Black Self-Determination: A Cultural History of African American Resistance*, 1993

Courtesy of National Hockey League

Bettman, Gary B.

June 2, 1952– Sports executive; attorney.
Address: c/o National Hockey League, 1251 Ave.
of the Americas, New York, NY 10020

For the first 75 years of its existence, the National Hockey League (NHL) did not have a commissioner. The league created the post in 1992 and recruited Gary B. Bettman to fill it. The sports entertainment industry was then experiencing a tremendous boom, led by the National Basketball Association (NBA), but the NHL was not caught up in it. Mired in tradition and lacking significant television exposure, it was deeply in the red. Bettman, the NHL hoped, would stop the bleeding. Regarded as the quintessential sports executive, he had ended a dozen-year career at the NBA as its senior vice president and general counsel. Since taking the helm at the NHL, he has concentrated on attracting new fans, expanding the league, cracking down on violence on the ice, and controlling the rate at which players' salaries have been increasing.

Gary Bruce Bettman was born in New York City on June 2, 1952, the son of Howard G. and Gretel J. (Pollack) Bettman. A native of the New York City borough of Queens, he graduated in 1974 from Cornell University, in Ithaca, New York, where he studied labor relations. In 1977 he earned a J.D. degree from New York University Law School. He then went to work for the prestigious New York City law firm of Proskauer, Rose, Goetz and Mendelson. There he met David Stern, from whom, as he tells it (his impressive academic credentials notwithstanding), he got his best education. He spent 12 years under the tutelage of Stern, learning, he has said, at "the feet of a master."

In 1978 Stern left the law firm to accept the job of general counsel for the NBA, and three years later Bettman joined him there, as assistant general counsel. Stern proceeded to rise through the NBA's ranks, ultimately assuming control of the league and guiding it through what has proved to be its greatest period of growth to date. Bettman's duties, too, steadily increased. His last promotion at the NBA made him senior vice president and general counsel and third in the NBA's chain of command. Bettman was the chief labor negotiator for the league. His work led to the NBA's 1988 collective-bargaining agreement with the players' union. Furthermore, as watchdog of the league's salary-cap system, he policed the teams' expenditures on talent. His experience in labor relations with a proven, well-marketed sports-entertainment commodity led the NHL's board of governors to turn to him in 1992. The board unanimously elected him commissioner on December 11, 1992.

When Bettman arrived at the NHL—he officially assumed the newly created post of commissioner on February 1, 1993—the league was awash in difficulties. One huge problem was that the NHL did not have a deal with an over-the-air television network (that is, channels other than cable); it was the only major professional sports league without one. In large measure because of the absence of such a deal, several teams were operating in the red, and markets in traditional hockey strongholds, including Hartford, Connecticut, and the Canadian cities of Winnipeg and Quebec, were no longer able to support professional sports franchises. In addition, the relationship between owners and players was distrustful at best, and the league was governed by owner committees that appeared to be less unified than the NHL Players Association, which was guided by Bob Goodenow, its executive director. Another serious problem was the excessive fighting that went on among players during games. All of those difficulties fueled a bad public image, one that discouraged potential fans and kept sponsors away. Bettman, however, professed to see the NHL's troubles in a different light. "I don't think the NHL has a tarnished image," he told Larry Wigge for the *Sporting News* (January 11, 1993). "I think that is a bad characterization. This is a sport that hasn't fully exploited its assets, that hasn't fully exploited its potential fan base."

A major challenge Bettman has faced in marketing hockey has been reaching new spectators, particularly in warmer climates, without alienating core fans. Hockey always has had difficulty taking root throughout the United States, where it competes for attention with baseball, American football, and basketball, all of which were invented and developed in the U.S. Though the origin of hockey is debatable, Canada can make the strongest claim to inventing the sport. In the second half of the 19th century, hockey grew in popularity as a pastime so rapidly in Canada that by the 1890s leagues had sprung up across the nation. Today, the majority of NHL franchises are located in the

U.S., but Canada remains a strong presence: approximately 60 percent of NHL players are from Canada, with half of the remaining 40 percent from the U.S. and the other half from Europe.

Throughout most of its 81-year history, the National Hockey League has relied heavily on the devotion of its traditional core audiences in Canada and the northeastern United States. However, tradition is no longer enough to maintain a stable professional sports league. As the business of sports entertainment has grown increasingly competitive, many sports vie for the attention of fans. Usually, the sport that is packaged best wins the largest audience, which translates into the largest profits for team owners. The 1980s and early 1990s saw an extraordinary expansion in the sports-entertainment industry, most remarkably in the NBA. Under the leadership of David Stern, the NBA executed a stunning turnaround, primarily through marketing, from a strife-torn league to the second-most-recognizable sports property in the world (after the Olympics). The NHL, by contrast, had begun a disastrous decline: whereas, in 1989, the league as a whole earned a profit of $50.3 million, in 1994 it *lost* $37.6 million.

While the NHL's attendance at games was impressive—on average league-wide, arenas would fill to 90 percent of capacity—Bettman was convinced that to prosper, the NHL needed to attract audiences beyond arena walls. Sometimes, even obvious means of gaining attention had been ignored. For example, Bettman was distressed by the scanty media coverage of the Pittsburgh Penguin star Mario Lemieux, who had captured his fourth league scoring title despite missing 23 games out of 84 in the 1992–93 season for medical reasons: he was being treated for Hodgkin's disease. "That's the best sports story of the year, and no one knows about it," Bettman complained to Terry Lefton for *Brandweek* (April 26, 1993).

To get NHL events and personalities into the evening news and other popular media, Bettman staffed his office with veteran marketing and television sports executives and charged them with the task of making the game accessible to a wider audience. In addition, Bettman directed the league to realign its teams into a more straightforward regional format; the names of the divisions were changed from Adams, Patrick, Norris, and Smythe to Northeast, Atlantic, Central, and Pacific, respectively. Also, Bettman and his staff took advantage of advances in technology to improve viewing for television audiences. They experimented with camera angles and computer enhancements to make the puck more visible on television screens. Such tactics "[do] not mean gutting the game," Bettman told Robert Lipsyte for the *New York Times* (November 10, 1995). "We need to market around the edges, teach it to Americans, add music, video boards, promotions between periods, push it into the conscious[ness] of the country."

In 1993, with the aim of devoting most of his time to the current state of the sport, Bettman set up in the NHL offices a department for fan development that would focus on future fans. In an interview with *USA Today* (October 6, 1995), Bettman talked about the power of the younger market. "There is a huge crossover between roller blading, roller hockey, street hockey, and hockey interest. All this means down the road there are going to be generations of kids who may be deciding we are their sport of choice." He explained to Robert Lipsyte, "The interest level is huge among kids, it's unchanneled and untapped, but we won't really see it for five or 10 years, until they get out of college, buy their own tickets and take control of their TV remotes." NHL Fan Development has focused its efforts primarily on grassroots programs. Two of the more successful organizations have been NHL Breakout, touted as "the world's premier street and in-line hockey league" for young adults, and Nike/NHL Street, a street-hockey league for boys and girls ages six to 16 that boasts 295,000 participants in more than 1,300 community centers across North America. Both programs take advantage of the recent popularity of in-line skating and the existence of suitable playing surfaces in virtually all climates.

While experimenting with ways to reach untapped markets, Bettman established himself as an aggressive administrator and effective leader. He ushered in two expansion franchises—the Florida Panthers, owned by the former Blockbuster Entertainment Group chair Wayne Huizenga, and the Anaheim Mighty Ducks, owned by the Walt Disney Co.; engineered an expansion draft; and successfully relocated the Minnesota North Stars to Dallas. (All three transactions had been announced publicly prior to Bettman's arrival at the NHL, but no plans existed for their execution.) He set rules for the expansion draft and stricter guidelines for franchise relocation. Bettman told James Deacon for *Maclean's* (April 26, 1993), "I'd like to know, going in, before the moving vans are unloaded, that there are 10,000 season tickets, that there is a good media contract, that there is a great lease."

Bettman has made headway controlling renegades on the ice and in franchise front offices. Enforcing his plan to reduce the rough play that often leads to fighting, he suspended the Washington Capitals' player Dale Hunter for a record 21 games after Hunter hit the New York Islanders' Pierre Turgeon in the 1993 play-offs. The next season he settled a 16-day strike by game officials without interrupting the schedule. And in July 1994 Bettman fined coach Mike Keenan $100,000 and suspended him for 60 days for breaking his contract with the New York Rangers to accept a job as coach and general manager of the St. Louis Blues. The Blues were also fined a league-maximum $250,000 for entering talks with Keenan while he was under contract to another team. By the end of his first 18 months in office, Bettman had advanced NHL policy through precedent, won a five-year, $155 million network deal with Fox Sports, and attracted Nike and Anheuser-Busch as sponsors.

By the start of the 1994–95 season, however, the NHL was no longer moving forward rapidly. For an entire year, the league had operated without a labor agreement between the team owners and players. If another season were to begin without a contract, there was a distinct possibility that the players would go on strike before the play-offs and place the owners in a weak bargaining position. In 1992 a 10-day players' strike had exposed some of the owners' weaknesses, not least of which was that a committee negotiated for them. The owners recognized the danger and, with Bettman's help, formed a united front. They preempted a players' strike by postponing the season and refusing to pay the players until a new collective-bargaining agreement was signed. The owners' chief concern was the rapid escalation of player salaries: between 1989 and 1994 the salary average had increased 140 percent, while league revenues had increased only 80 percent. The players, on the other hand, wanted to avoid a salary cap.

Bettman represented the owners' interests. He recalled to Dave Sell for the *Washington Post* (April 20, 1995), "I told the owners—and ultimately it's the owners' decision—before the lockout began that 'you must understand that if you're going down this route, you must be prepared to lose the season. It could happen. And you can't come to me in six weeks and say we have to play, so just take any deal. That's worse. If you're going to [cave in], do it now before we start.'" In January 1995 a labor contract was signed; the lockout had ended and an abbreviated, 48-game season followed. The players had staved off a league-wide salary cap, making the NHL the only professional sports league to have unrestricted free agency without such a limit, but they also made many concessions, including the inclusion of a salary cap for rookies. As of early 1999, the agreement had succeeded in slowing, on average, the rate of salary increase.

Bettman received a lot of criticism over the lockout. Many observers contended that, from a business standpoint, the NHL had lost a golden opportunity to attract fans, since the league had just completed a good season that had been capped by the New York Rangers' Stanley Cup win, the first in 54 years for the Rangers, which is the oldest team in the league's largest market. Furthermore, professional baseball was suffering from a players' strike that ended their season prematurely and forced the cancellation of the play-offs and the 1994 World Series. Many thought that, deprived of baseball, disgusted sports fans might have turned to hockey for consolation.

The criticism of Bettman did not stop there; indeed, it grew more personal. Some Canadian hockey fans, who even before the lockout had characterized Bettman as a slick New York lawyer who knew nothing about the sport, reportedly made negative references to his height (five feet, five inches) and his Jewish heritage. Even more disturbing was an utterance by the Chicago Blackhawks' player Chris Chelios; two months into the three-and-a-half-month lockout, Chelios said publicly, "If I was Gary Bettman, I'd be worried about my family. I'd be worried about my well-being now. Some crazed fans, or even a player—who knows?—they might take matters into their own hands and figure if they can get him out of the way, things might get settled." Recognizing the highly emotional circumstances under which Chelios had spoken, Bettman accepted a personal apology from the player in his office. No disciplinary action was taken against Chelios.

As the decade of the NHL's most rapid expansion (by the 2000–01 season, there will be 30 teams) draws to a close, the league is experiencing growing pains. Of continuing concern are the problems that arise when franchises must relocate because of failing markets. (In one case with a happy ending, a group of local investors saved the Edmonton Oilers, one of the most successful teams in the league during the 1980s, from having to move to Houston, Texas.) Even when relocation is not an issue, changes in team ownership can lead to difficulties for the league office. The case of Joseph Spano illustrates that. In 1996 the NHL approved Spano as a suitable buyer for the New York Islanders. To obtain loans from various financial institutions, Spano admitted to lying about his net worth and pled guilty to fraud in three states. The NHL thereupon became the target of critics who questioned the stringency of its criteria for approving potential franchise owners.

Other problems stem from Canada's high taxes, which, on average, cost each Canadian team about $8 million more than what each U.S. team pays annually. In April 1998, making a foray into lobbying, Bettman and several other NHL executives testified before a subcommittee of Canada's Parliament in Ottawa on behalf of the six remaining teams based in Canada. They contended that unless the Canadian government offered tax breaks and other government assistance, those teams might no longer be able to compete with U.S. franchises and might be forced to move to U.S. markets.

The issue of hockey hooliganism reared its head again in the aftermath of the 1998 Winter Olympics, in Nagano, Japan. Earlier, in March 1995, Bettman and Goodenow had met with Juan Antonio Samaranch, the president of the International Olympic Committee, to request that NHL players be allowed to represent their countries in the Olympics, as NBA stars had in the summer Games. Bettman's intent was to expand the international exposure of the league; in the best possible scenario, teams from Canada and the U.S., both comprised entirely of NHL players, would compete in the gold-medal game, thus showcasing hockey's elite. The plan backfired, in part because neither team won a medal (the Czech Republic, which had the fewest NHL players on their squad, won the gold, benefiting from the presence of the NHL's leading scorer, Jaromir Jagr, and the NHL's MVP, goalie Dominik Hasek). Perhaps more damaging to the league was the scandalous behavior by the U.S. team, which caused $3,000 worth of damage to their living suites in Nagano. The vandalism jeopordized the chances that U.S. all-star hockey teams would be allowed to play in future Olympics.

It has been noted frequently that Bettman does not take criticism well, whether it is directed at him or at the NHL. Recent attacks by sportswriters and analysts on both sides of the Canadian border, however, do not appear to have shaken his focus. In August 1998 the NHL signed a deal with the Walt Disney Co. to televise league games on the ABC, ESPN, and ESPN2 networks, all of which Disney owns. The deal will bring $600 million to the NHL over five years, starting in 1999, and ensures that more than 200 games plus the Stanley Cup series will be televised each year.

Gary Bettman and the former Michelle Weiner, who have been married since 1975, have three children—Lauren, Jordan, and Brittany. According to David Stern, Bettman is "a peripatetic workaholic." On the rare occasions when he is not immersed in his job, he enjoys skiing, sailing, and tennis. — T.J.F.

Suggested Reading: *Brandweek* p36+ Apr. 26, 1993, with photo; *Business Week* p108 Apr. 26, 1993, with photo; *Maclean's* p36 Apr. 26, 1993, with photo; *New York Times* B p12 Nov. 10, 1995, with photo; *Sporting News* p7 Jan. 11, 1993, with photo; *Sports Illustrated* p48 Feb. 15, 1993, with photo; *USA Today* E p2 Oct. 6, 1995; *Washington Post* B p5 Apr. 20, 1995, with photo; *Who's Who in America, 1999*

Courtesy of Lincoln Center Theater

Bishop, André

Nov. 9, 1948– Artistic director of Lincoln Center Theater. Address: c/o Lincoln Center Theater, 150 W. 65th St., New York, NY 10023

"My whole life has been enriched and informed by working in the theater, and it was all I could do to muster the courage to knock at the theater's door," André Bishop told David Richards for the *New York Times Magazine* (September 13, 1992). "I look at myself . . . and I think, 'My God, there's hope for everyone.' I really mean that." Bishop is currently the artistic director of Lincoln Center

Theater, in New York City—one of the most prestigious theaters in the United States. Previously, Bishop served as artistic director of Playwrights Horizons, a not-for-profit theater that is known for giving new playwrights a chance to show their work to audiences and critics. Among the shows that Bishop produced at Playwrights Horizons were the Stephen Sondheim and James Lapine musical *Sunday in the Park with George* (1983), Alfred Uhry's *Driving Miss Daisy* (1987), and Wendy Wasserstein's *The Heidi Chronicles* (1989), each of which went on to win a Pulitzer Prize for drama. Although his work at Lincoln Center entails producing fresh stagings of classics as well as new plays and musicals, Bishop remains dedicated to nurturing new theater. With this goal in mind, he founded the Lincoln Center Playwrights and Directors Program, which organizes readings, workshops, and symposia aimed at developing the works of new artists. "If you remain clear about what you do, you keep your sense of purpose," he told Wilborn Hampton for the *New York Times* (April 10, 1988), explaining how he has maintained his passion for his work in the theater for more than 20 years. "When that clarity goes, it discourages creativity. You lose optimism when you lose your sense of purpose. And one needs an undimmed optimism to keep going."

André Bishop was born André Bishop Smelianinoff ("Smolianinoff," according to several sources) on November 9, 1948 in New York City. His father, André Smelianinoff, immigrated to New York from Belarus and eventually became an investment banker. His mother, Felice, for whom this was a second marriage, was distantly related to the prominent Harriman family of New York. Bishop's parents separated when André was five. His father died of a coronary occlusion about a year later, and shortly thereafter, Felice changed her son's name to André S. Bishop, because, as she explained to Richards, his original surname was "impossible to pronounce." "André senior always used to say to people, 'Just think of smiling on and off,'" she said. "After he died, I didn't think Bishy [André's childhood nickname] should have to carry the name the rest of his days and be forced to explain it. So we just switched it around." In 1956 Bishop's mother married Dwight Francis, an independently wealthy New Englander, and Bishop was sent to La Claireire, a boarding school in Switzerland. He later attended the Fay School in Massachusetts and St. Paul's in New Hampshire. "I discovered how to be a survivor at a very young age in this jungle of schools," Bishop told Terri Jentz for the *West Side TV Shopper* (September 24–30, 1983). He told Richards, "The thing that was weird about me was that even though I grew up at a time when the hockey players were the heroes and the guys who did [the Gilbert and Sullivan operetta] *The Gondoliers* were suspect, I was always very popular. I guess I thought that's how I'll get through this. I am not strong physically and I'm terrible at hockey and football. So the thing you do is make people like you. And they always did."

As a child Bishop had a special interest in theater. "The first stage show I ever saw was the Mary Martin *Peter Pan*," he told Richards. "My aunt had gotten tickets in the front row. What was unbelievable about it, as I remember, was that I was totally taken in by the magic of it. But I was also sitting close enough so that I could see how it worked. And there was one moment when I saw a light glinting on the wires. Maybe this is ludicrously, ridiculously Freudian, but I've always chosen to think that that moment informed what happened to me in the theater. I both believed in the illusion and I saw it for what it was. That just made it all the more wonderful." Bishop's personal involvement with theater began with his putting on puppet shows and reading *Theater Arts Magazine*. During one summer that he spent with his family on the island of Martha's Vineyard, in Massachusetts, he met the actress Katherine Cornell and often took long walks on the beach with her. "She took a bizarre shine to me," Bishop recalled to Richards. "Well, why shouldn't she? I was this stage-struck kid, somewhat plump, I'm sure, and something of a sissy."

After graduating from Harvard University, in Cambridge, Massachusetts, with honors, in 1970, Bishop moved to New York City, where he took various odd jobs associated with the theater. One of the most memorable was in the box office of the Delacorte Theater in New York's Central Park. Tickets to the Delacorte, home of the New York Shakespeare Festival, are free, and seats for successful productions are in great demand. Shortly after Bishop started working there, a rock-'n'-roll version of Shakespeare's *The Two Gentlemen of Verona* became an enormous hit, and some theatergoers, angry that they could not get tickets, threw chicken bones at him. Bishop quit that job soon afterward. He spent some time taking acting classes

with Wynn Handman, the artistic director of the American Place Theater. "I was the star of the class because I could cry more easily than the girls," Bishop told Richards. "I kept a diary that year. It was all about how I wanted to devote myself to Art. Every entry ended plaintively with 'My God!'" Richards quoted Handman as saying that Bishop had done "satisfactory work" but that he did not have a large range as an actor. Handman cast Bishop in several bit parts in a production of Robert Lowell's *Old Glory* at the American Place in 1976, but it was obvious that acting was not chief among his talents. Bishop believes that his training in acting served mainly to develop a solid understanding of dramatic writing. "I came to love well-written plays that had highly performable bravura roles in the center," he told Richards. He explained to Douglas C. McGill for the *New York Times* (January 3, 1982) what he meant by "bravura roles": "I don't like acting that is just like life because I think that's where you start, and theater has to go beyond that. Otherwise, why not just turn on the TV?"

In 1975 Bishop began volunteering at Playwrights Horizons, a nonprofit organization that produced new plays in a rundown theater on West 42d Street. He has described the Off-Broadway theater scene at that time as "struggling and totally impoverished. There were a lot of little places doing a lot of work. And we were all the beneficiaries of that. If you wanted to work and didn't need money, you could do what you wanted." At Playwrights Horizons, Bishop assisted the organization's founder, Robert Moss, by running errands and standing in for absent actors at rehearsals. "I . . . helped in any way I could," he told Louis Botto for *Playbill* (February 1992). "I admired what Bob was doing—building a home for American writers— and I wanted to be a part of that."

At Moss's request, Bishop began reading plays that were submitted to Playwrights Horizons and writing short reports about them. He demonstrated such a knack for finding suitable plays for the theater that Moss soon hired him as literary manager. In 1981, when Moss left the organization, Bishop became artistic director. "Suddenly I was the head of Playwrights Horizons, and I felt amazed," Bishop recalled to Botto. "I had a lot of learning to do and a lot of growing up to do in order to shoulder this great responsibility." In spite of the pressures he felt, Bishop's first season as artistic director was a success; it included debuts of A. R. Gurney's *The Dining Room*; Christopher Durang's *Sister Mary Ignatius Explains It All for You*, a musical satire of Catholic-school education in the United States; *The Geniuses*, a Hollywood satire by Jonathan Reynolds; the librettist William Finn's musical about gay men, *The March of the Falsettos*; and *Herringbone*, a one-man murder mystery performed by David Rounds. In the following years, Bishop produced *Sunday in the Park with George*, which was co-written by Stephen Sondheim and James Lapine and based on George Seurat's painting *Sunday Afternoon on the Ilse of La Grande*

Jatte; Driving Miss Daisy, by Alfred Uhry; and *The Heidi Chronicles*, by Wendy Wasserstein. Besides winning Pulitzer Prizes, all three shows moved from Playwrights Horizons to Broadway, where they had commercially successful runs. *The Heidi Chronicles* won the 1989 Tony Award for best play, and the film adaptation of *Driving Miss Daisy* won the 1989 Academy Award for best picture. "It was a very emotionally gripping time when I realized that my instincts had been right," Bishop told Jentz. "Suddenly everything made sense."

Bishop attributes his accomplishments as a producer of new theater to his ability to improve plays after their initial staging by directors. After matching a new play with a director, Bishop told Richards, he does not attend rehearsals until the show is in previews. He then acts as a "fresh pair of eyes" and makes adjustments. His suggestions, unlike those of many other producers, are not dreaded by those involved with the play. Just before the opening of Wasserstein's *The Heidi Chronicles*, for instance, Bishop detected serious problems with one long monologue spoken by the actress Joan Allen, who played Heidi in the original run of the show and on Broadway. According to Richards, Bishop not only identified what was wrong, but also found a diplomatic way of communicating to Allen his ideas for improvement, so as not to cause a panic in the cast shortly before the play's opening. Heidi is an art historian, and Bishop told Allen to think about, as Richards put it, "envisioning the monologue as a large canvas and its sundry details as so many brush strokes. What if she 'painted' the speech for the audience?"

A member of Playwrights Horizons recalled to McGill an occasion when he overheard Bishop "yelling at a playwright, 'This rewrite is hackwork! Don't ever do that! Take it back and do it again!' Well I saw the playwright later and he wasn't insulted or embarrassed. I know that the only thing he wanted to do was go home and rewrite that script." Regarding his rare ability to critique without offending, Bishop told Laurie Winer for the *New York Times* (August 19, 1990), "While a lot of good work in theater does come out of fear, I like working with people who need positive energy. Artists are very vulnerable. You have to create an atmosphere where they can listen and hear the criticisms that you do have, where they don't feel threatened constantly. They need to know that you're on their side." But in Bishop's case, being supportive does not mean being easy to please. For example, he fired one actor just before the opening of *Sister Mary Ignatius Explains It All for You*. "People think because I'm pleasant and nice that I'm a pushover," he told McGill. "But I have an iron will."

Another important element in Bishop's success is his uncanny discernment in choosing projects: at Playwrights Horizons, he picked the gems from among more than 2,000 plays submitted annually to the organization. "I tend to like writers who express themselves in comedy, but behind the come-dy is a real, real anger," Bishop told McGill. "Anger at the world around them, anger at their lives, at the lives of others. Anger at certain kinds of American establishments—the Catholic Church, the media, even the family." He also said, "I'm often drawn to work that is not all neatly tied up and beautifully structured. I like plays that are lucidly framed, but within that frame, I'm drawn to writing that is unpredictable, that comes to you in strange ways, that astonishes you verbally by expressing strange thoughts."

To make it possible to produce a larger percentage of the scripts submitted to Playwrights Horizons, in 1988 Bishop expanded the organization by converting some extra space into the New Theater Wing—a smaller stage where plays by unknown writers were assigned to directors with little professional experience. Tickets for shows at the New Theater Wing initially cost only $5, and budgets were kept to around $30,000 per production. "I always wanted to do theater that was cheaper than the movies," Bishop told Hampton. "Everybody cries, 'The theater is too expensive; there are no directors; the critics are killing the theater.' A lot of people are sitting around moaning and I hate that. There are always answers to problems." To help recoup the losses that resulted from this critically successful but financially unprofitable endeavor, Bishop initiated a program of classes in acting, directing, writing, dramaturgy, and theater management, in conjunction with New York University. Most of the classes were taught by Playwrights Horizons' nine resident playwrights, who included Wasserstein, Durang, and Reynolds. Bishop also established a set workshop, Scenic Central, which was made available to other nonprofit groups, and Ticket Central, a box office that sold tickets for productions at more than 15 Off-Broadway theaters.

With three Pulitzer Prize–winning plays under its belt, Playwrights Horizons grew to be one of the most respected theaters in New York, and many of the plays it produced moved on to Broadway. "The years went by, and we became legitimate," Bishop said during his 1988 interview with Hampton. "Because we did a lot of shows that had a longer life, everybody thought, 'Oh, that must be good.' The economic stakes got higher. When the price of tickets goes up, expectations go up." Bishop felt that the success of Playwrights Horizons hampered his ability to produce "risky" or experimental plays. "It's odd that more money creates less freedom, opens fewer doors," he said. "Now I find the doors that used to be open aren't any more."

Bishop was appointed artistic director of Lincoln Center Theater in January 1992, following the departure of the previous artistic director, Gregory Mosher. Lincoln Center's two theaters have, in total, five times the seating capacity of Playwrights Horizons, as well as a much bigger annual budget and a huge list of subscribers—48,000 as of 1999. Bishop's salary, which had hardly grown over the past 10 years, more than doubled. His feelings about money's "closing doors" on risk-taking theater notwithstanding, Bishop told Richards of his new job, "For all I'm giving up at Playwrights Horizons—the flawed, but interesting play; the ability to fail less publicly—I'm also getting a lot. Working on a bigger scale is a great challenge. I've sort of never been happier."

While Playwrights Horizons is devoted exclusively to new plays, at Lincoln Center, Bishop has the entire theatrical canon available to him (subject to the agreement of the board of directors and Bernard Gersten, the executive producer), and each year he has generally chosen a mix of classics and contemporary plays and musicals, including some by writers he worked with at his former post. Gersten, with whom Bishop works very closely, told Richards, "What André is bringing here more than anything else is an openness to a larger group of playwrights than has been manifest up to now." Among Bishop's first productions at Lincoln Center Theater were Wendy Wasserstein's *The Sisters Rosensweig*; a revival of Frank Loesser's musical comedy *The Most Happy Fella*; John Guare's *Four Baboons Adoring the Sun*; Jon Robin Baitz's *The Substance of Fire*; the new musical *My Favorite Year*, a collaboration of Joseph Dougherty, Stephen Flaherty, and Lynn Arens; and the Rodgers and Hammerstein classic *Carousel*. Bishop shares with Gersten and Lincoln Center Theater the Tony Awards for best revival of a musical for *Carousel* (1994) and best revival of a play for both Ruth and Augustus Goetz's *The Heiress* (1995) and Edward Albee's *A Delicate Balance* (1996). Their recent offerings have included the new musical *Parade* (1998), by playwright Alfred Uhry and composer-lyricist Jason Robert Brown, and Shakespeare's *Twelfth Night*, starring Helen Hunt as Viola; the former won 1999 Tony Awards for best book of a musical and best original score, and the latter was nominated for a Tony for best revival of a play. Lincoln Center Theater's productions, including the shows that the organization produces at Broadway theaters, were nominated for a total of 16 Tonys in 1999. In October of that year, Lincoln Center Theater's new musical *Contact*, billed as a "dance play," became one of the first hits of the fall season after receiving rave reviews; Ben Brantley, writing in the *New York Times* (October 8, 1999), called the show "the most powerful antidepressant available in New York at the moment." Bishop has also initiated Lincoln Center's Playwrights and Directors Program, which organizes readings, workshops, and symposia and aims at developing the work of new playwrights and directors in cooperation with several Off-Broadway theaters.

Looking back on his long career in the theater, Bishop told Richards, "I've never been able to understand how someone like me—shy, very impressed with other people, nervous—did what I did. . . . I'm very at home in the shadows. My favorite moments are either getting in bed or sitting on my sofa and reading and having no responsibilities whatsoever. I'm also very at home getting up and talking, making decisions, trying to figure out

what to do. But for some reason, my life has no meaning in between. . . . The problems I have are all in the twilight zone between utter solitude and passivity and utter take-chargeness." Richards quoted the playwright A. R. Gurney as saying that he didn't know "anybody who's ever said an unkind word" about Bishop. Upon hearing about that remark, Bishop responded, "I wish somebody would say, 'He's nice, yes, but he's also smart.' It's not just that I'm this nice guy who's wafting through his life on a tide of good will. A, I work like a dog, and B, I can fix Act II." In the *Village Voice* (May 17, 1983), Don Shewey described Bishop as "the epitome of urban articulate. . . . He has the resonant voice and the preternaturally clean-shaven good looks of an actor (which he used to be), as well as the soft-spoken demeanor of someone who gets along with everybody. You would never guess that such a mild-mannered person would have the power to single-handedly shape a theater to his personal taste and vision the way Bishop has."

Under Bishop's direction Playwrights Horizons won the 1983 Margo Jones Award for contributions to the American theater and the 1989 Lucille Lortel Award for Outstanding Achievement for a Body of Work, for the theater's development of new plays. In 1992 Bishop won a special Drama Desk Award in recognition of his work at Playwrights Horizons. He serves on the Theater, Opera, and Musical Theater adjudicating panels for the National Endowment for the Arts, and he has taught classes at New York University and Hunter College, in New York City.

Bishop lives in the Greenwich Village neighborhood of New York City with his cat, Squeaky, named after a character in the Stephen Sondheim musical *Assassins*, which Bishop produced in 1991. He owns a Greek revival–style vacation home on Vinalhaven, an island off the coast of Maine, where he has been known to sequester himself for days at a time. — C.P.

Suggested Reading: *New York Times* II p4 Jan. 3, 1982, with photo, II p22 Apr. 10, 1988, with photo, II p5 Aug. 19, 1990, with photo; *New York Times* (on-line) Aug. 23, 1999, with photo; *New York Times Magazine* p53+ Sep. 13, 1992, with photo; *Playbill* p40+ Feb. 6, 1992, with photos; *Village Voice* p94+ May 17, 1993, with photo; *West Side TV Shopper* p21 Sep. 24–30, 1983, with photo

Selected Theater Productions: *March of the Falsettos*, 1981; *Herringbone*, 1982; *Sister Mary Ignatius Explains It All for You*, 1981; *The Dining Room*, 1982; *Sunday in the Park with George*, 1983; *Driving Miss Daisy*, 1987; *The Heidi Chronicles*, 1989; *Once on This Island*, 1990; *Falsettoland*, 1990; *Assassins*, 1990, *The Substance of Fire*, 1991; *Carousel*, 1994; *The Heiress*, 1995; *A Delicate Balance*, 1996; *Parade*, 1998; *Twelfth Night*, 1998

Kosta Alexander/Archive Photos

Blanchett, Cate

Jan. 1, 1969– Actress. Address: c/o Robyn Gardiner, P.O. Box 128, Surry Hill, 2010 NSW, Australia

An Australian by birth, Cate Blanchett worked as a stage actress in Sydney before achieving international fame by way of her two breakthrough films, *Oscar and Lucinda* (1997), in which she starred alongside two-time Oscar nominee Ralph Fiennes, and *Elizabeth* (1998), her best-known film to date, for which she won a Golden Globe Award and received an Oscar nomination. "There's a duality to Cate. She's got a very cheeky sense of humor, a very galumphing kind of down-to-earth personality," Oscar winner Geoffrey Rush, who starred with her in an Australian stage production of *Oleanna*, told Laura Jacobs for *Vanity Fair* (March 1999). "And then suddenly you look at her and go, 'My God, you're so strikingly beautiful.' She seems to flicker between the two." In *Elizabeth*, directed by Shekhar Kapur, Blanchett portrayed the young Queen Elizabeth I of England. Blanchett has said that she is drawn to such larger-than-life female characters, another being Lucinda Leplastrier, of *Oscar and Lucinda*, "a woman not afraid to risk the disdain of polite society by frequenting illicit Sydney card rooms," as York Membory wrote for *Associated Newspapers Limited* (on-line). Blanchett told Laura Winters for the *New York Times* (December 28, 1997), "I like to take on things that I think I can't do. If you're always trying to play things close to yourself, you're not extending your knowledge or being stretched." Kapur told Winters, "Cate has a combination of strength and vulnerability, which, for me, is what Elizabeth is all about. She attacks

a role with ferocious intellectuality. You can't pass anything by her, and you can't sweet-talk her into anything. But inside, she is all emotion."

A middle child, Cate Blanchett was born on January 1, 1969 and grew up in Melbourne, Australia. Her American-born father, who worked in advertising, died when Cate was 10 years old. Cate, her older brother, Bob, and her younger sister, Genevieve, were close, and they had a "very low and very squat and very fast" dog named Snoopy, according to Laura Jacobs. As Blanchett told Michael Fitzgerald for *Time.com* (January 24, 1998), one day following their father's death, she and her siblings were "left in a room with one of [their father's] managers from work, and he sat us down and said, 'This is gonna be a very, very hard time for your mother. You have to be very, very good.' And it kind of framed my whole relationship with the family."

When asked if she had wanted to be an actress while growing up, Blanchett told Jacobs, "No. I think any child that is not comatose and shows off a little bit, people say that she's bound to be an actor. I was much more bossy than that, and by the age of seven I thought, I'll direct—though I don't know enough to direct traffic yet." She attended a high school of about 2,000 students, where her friends referred to her simply as "Blanche." There, she acted in theater and played tennis. At Melbourne University she studied economics and fine arts. She told Jacobs, "I really wanted to get to international relations, which was in fourth year, so I guess you could say it was sort of restlessness that led me to acting, because I couldn't stand sitting through four years" of the prerequisite courses. During the run of one play, someone suggested to her that she try out for the National Institute of Dramatic Art; she auditioned and won admission.

Blanchett was still not sure that she wanted to commit her life to acting when, in her third year at the school, she was cast in the title role of the Greek tragedy *Electra*. "It was pretty awful, pretty chaotic . . . ," she told Jacobs. "It was this messy situation where another girl was supposed to play it—I still feel bad about it—and I ended up playing it. I didn't have long to rehearse. . . . It was one of those situations where, because I had to assume the role, I didn't realize how much ill feeling there was till afterwards. For me there was no time to fear." Geoffrey Rush, who was living at the time with Lindy Davies, the director of this modernized version of the classic play, told Jacobs that Blanchett's performance was "amazing. The assurance. You're seeing somebody who's already, even in drama school, having a kind of consummate facility to actually be able *to do it*. Not only to bring great imaginative resources to it, but to define it with such emotional clarity and to etch it with such classical dimensions." The experience of playing Electra apparently solidified Blanchett's desire to perform professionally. She told Membory, "It was only when I realized how actors have the power to move people that I decided to pursue acting as a career."

Not long after she graduated, in 1992, Blanchett joined the Sydney Theatre Company's production of the British playwright Caryl Churchill's *Top Girls*. Following that success, she was promptly cast in the role of Felice Bauer in Timothy Daly's *Kafka Dances*. For her work in that play, she won the 1993 New Comer Award, given out by the Sydney Theatre Critics Circle. With her star on the rise, Blanchett was cast alongside Geoffrey Rush in the Australian production of the American playwright David Mamet's controversial, politically charged play *Oleanna*. "I thought, I can't do this play, it's a misogynist piece of crap," she told Jacobs. "But it angered me so much that I *had* to do it." The play, staged at the Sydney Theatre Company, was a box-office hit, and its run was extended. Blanchett won the Rosemont Best Actress Award for her performance. Soon afterward she went to the U.S., where she signed on for the role of Beth in the ABC television miniseries *Heartland* (1994), and in that same year she made guest appearances on the television programs *G.P.* and *Police Rescue*.

In 1995 Blanchett returned to Australia, where she received critical acclaim for her performance as Ophelia in the Belvoir Theatre Company's production of *Hamlet*. A year later she worked with the director and writer Kathryn Millard on the Australian film *Parklands*. Her international film debut was in Bruce Beresford's *Paradise Road* (1997), in which she played an imprisoned Australian nurse in a Japanese POW camp during World War II. Others in the cast included Glenn Close and Frances McDormand. Blanchett next appeared in the title role in *Thank God He Met Lizzie* (1997), for which she won that year's Australian Film Institute Award for best supporting actress.

Despite those accomplishments, Fox Searchlight Pictures, which was producing Gillian Armstrong's adaptation of Peter Carey's picaresque, Booker Prize–winning novel *Oscar and Lucinda*, was wary of casting the relatively unknown Blanchett in the big-budgeted film drama of the same name. The company's executives finally gave Blanchett the nod after viewing her work in *Paradise Road*, another Fox Searchlight film. The role of Lucinda, an Australian businesswoman who shares with a British missionary (Ralph Fiennes) a love of gambling, brought Blanchett major press attention. Armstrong told Jacobs, "There are many wonderful actresses and many really beautiful actresses, but I always felt Lucinda couldn't be just beautiful, she had to have a little something that was off. When I saw Cate's auditions, the thing I realized she had—and I hadn't even articulated that we were looking for—was this ability to go into other worlds. . . . Cate has a slightly magical quality. There's something extraordinary about her."

Shekhar Kapur, acclaimed director of such international hits as *Mr. India* (1987) and *Bandit Queen* (1994), first saw Blanchett while watching a promo reel for *Oscar and Lucinda*. Looking for an actress to play Queen Elizabeth I of England in his upcoming epic, *Elizabeth*, he was taken aback by the scene in which Blanchett's pale face rises to the surface of a pool. "You're looking for a face," he told Jacobs. "It's very difficult to describe what you are looking for until you see it. In that shot, there was a certain ethereal quality. I was totally fascinated because that's how I saw Elizabeth at the end, very ethereal. And there was a certain fire in her eyes. . . . I was so shocked that I called my casting director up and said, 'Why have you not told me about this girl?' And she said, 'Well, who do you think I was asking you to go see on the Sydney stage?'" Blanchett soon signed on to play the role.

Elizabeth focuses on the early life of Queen Elizabeth, who held the throne of England for 44 years in the 16th and early 17th centuries. "Confronting the much debated issue of Elizabeth's virginity is central to Blanchett's interpretation," Kitty Bowe Hearty wrote for *Harper's Bazaar* (December 1998). With her romantic feelings for Robert Dudley, Earl of Leicester (played by Joseph Fiennes), unfulfilled, Elizabeth dedicates herself to her country. "It is only at the end of the movie that the Virgin Queen declares that she is married to England," as Hearty reported. She quoted Blanchett as saying about Queen Elizabeth, "She was an astonishing politician and cultural ambassador . . . and the fact that her virginity is the one thing that is remembered about her I think is abhorrent."

Elizabeth, released in late 1998 mostly in art-house theaters, received splendid reviews from American critics, and the film gradually returned higher and higher box-office receipts, largely thanks to word of mouth. "We all discussed the fact that this would not be a totally accurate historical portrait of Elizabeth," Blanchett told *Mrshowbiz* (on-line). "That was never the intention. What I did go back to, out of frustration, particularly at male historians who dwelled on her so-called virginity, were the letters she wrote. It was there I could see the mechanics of her brain and her thought processes and the way she was able to play people off against each other, as well as her extraordinary intelligence."

At the Golden Globe Awards ceremony, Blanchett got the nod for best actress in a drama; with the award in tow, she was considered a strong candidate for an Oscar nomination, which she received in early 1999. This series of events helped to turn Blanchett into one of the hottest actresses in the movie business, and she soon began appearing on the covers of major magazines, most notably the March 1999 cover of *Vanity Fair*, a publication considered to be a major voice in pop-culture circles. In response to all the hoopla over her performance in *Elizabeth*, she told Fitzgerald, "I hate seeing acting as a business. And I feel at times that the way people talk to me about work, I should be carrying a briefcase and have a laptop. It actually kills the intangible, inexplicable reasons for why you do something."

Blanchett returned to the big screen for the first time since her Oscar nomination in *Pushing Tin* (1999), a film about air-traffic controllers, carousing husbands, and jealous wives that also starred John Cusack and Billy Bob Thornton. Of her performance, Janet Maslin of the *New York Times* (April 23, 1999) wrote, "Whatever possessed Ms. Blanchett to play . . . a jaunty Long Island housewife with a strong local accent has stood her in good stead. She fits in so well here that it may be a while before you wonder why Elizabeth I is talking about tuna casseroles." In 1999 Blanchett appeared, in positive notices, in a movie version of Oscar Wilde's play *An Ideal Husband*. Later that year she agreed to take on the role of Galadriel in an adaptation for the screen of J. R .R. Tolkien's classic trilogy *Lord of the Rings*, a fantasy about Middle-earth, an imaginary land that is inhabited by creatures called hobbits. She will appear in all three films in the trilogy: *The Return of the King*, *The Two Towers*, and *The Fellowship of the Ring*. Blanchett co-produced the film *Dreamtime Alice*, a project in which she also acted; it is set for release in 2000. Although she has enjoyed considerable success in films, she told York Membory, "My heart's still in the theater. . . . I hope to return to the stage soon. I'm quite fluid about my career. I might even end up directing. I don't plan ahead and have no idea where I'll be in a few years' time."

Blanchett is an avid reader who particularly likes the works of Marcel Proust and cites *Hamlet* as her favorite Shakespeare play. "I love what it wrestles with," she told Jacobs. "A lot of productions fail because they try to stamp a decision on the play rather than letting the complexities breathe." Blanchett is married to the Australian screenwriter Andrew Upton, who has helped to edit such films as *Babe: Pig in the City* (1998) and *A Little Bit of Soul* (1998). The two met while she was performing the role of Nina in Chekhov's *The Seagull*. She told Jacobs, "He thought I was aloof and I thought he was arrogant. And it just shows how wrong you can be. But once he kissed me, that was that." They share an apartment in Sydney, near the ocean. — M.B.

Suggested Reading: *Associated Newspapers Limited* (on-line) Mar. 18, 1998; *Mrshowbiz* (on-line); *New York Times* p22+ Dec. 28, 1997, with photo; *New York Times* (on-line) Apr. 23, 1999, with photo; *Time.com* (on-line) Jan. 26, 1998; *Vanity Fair* p216+ Mar. 1999, with photos

Selected Films: *Parklands*, 1996; *Paradise Road*, 1997; *Thank God He Met Lizzie*, 1997; *Oscar and Lucinda*, 1997; *Elizabeth*, 1998; *The Talented Mr. Ripley*, 1999; *An Ideal Husband*, 1999; *Pushing Tin*, 1999

Bogart, Anne

1953– Theatrical director and teacher. Address: 507 W. 113th St., #82, New York, NY 10025

"Anne Bogart is one of the most compelling and controversial theater artists today." This is according to Mel Gussow, a theater critic for the *New York Times*, as quoted on the Web site of Smith and Kraus, the publisher of *Ann Bogart—Viewpoints* (1995), a book about Bogart's theories and techniques. "As a director," Gussow continued, "she is renowned for her intense collaborative approach; as an instructor she has developed training techniques derived from sources as varied as the postmodern dance field and American vaudeville. . . . Depending on the point of view, Anne Bogart is either an innovator or a provocateur assaulting a script."

As Gussow noted in an essay that appears in *Anne Bogart—Viewpoints*, the theater pieces Bogart has created fall into roughly four categories: first productions of new plays, such as Paula Vogel's *The Baltimore Waltz* and Eduardo Machado's *In the Eye of the Hurricane*; theatrical portraits of well-known and influential cultural figures, such as Bertolt Brecht (*No Plays, No Poetry* . . .), Marshall McLuhan (*The Medium*), and Robert Wilson (*Bob*); new and sometimes iconoclastic interpretations of classic and popular plays, such as *Picnic*,

Jim Block/Courtesy of Saratoga International Theatre Institute

by William Inge, *Miss Julie*, by August Strindberg, and the Rodgers and Hammerstein musical *South Pacific*; and original "performance art" pieces, in

Gussow's words. Developed in collaboration with actors, Bogart's works in the last category often examine the cultural history of the United States, as is the case with her trilogy comprising *American Vaudeville* (1992), *Marathon Dancing* (1994), and *American Silents* (1997), the last of which is about the birth of the film industry.

Bogart counts postmodern dance and the European tradition of expressionist theater among her chief influences, and all of her work incorporates a wider palette of movement than does naturalistic theater. As Gussow wrote in the *New York Times* (March 12, 1994), "Her principal concern is with [in her words] 'the relationship between choreography and psychology.'" Since early in her career, Bogart has been developing a movement technique she calls Viewpoints, which teaches actors to have greater awareness of their environment and enables them to express their impulses spontaneously through movement. "In a culture where the best acting is done from the neck up," Jon Jory wrote in *Anne Bogart—Viewpoints*, "Anne's work is an obvious antidote. . . . It's rife with visual composition. It's dance done by actors in the service of dramaturgy." Yet, while her methods and aesthetic break with modern American and British theater, Bogart uses the forms she has developed to explore concerns that have been the traditional domain of theater throughout much of history. "To me the theater is about memory, about remembering the big questions pertaining to being human," Bogart wrote for the Web site of the SITI company, a troupe she co-founded with the Japanese stage director Tadashi Suzuki in 1992. "A great play lasts because it asks us to remember some important human issues."

Anne Bogart was born in 1953 in Newport, Rhode Island, the only child of a career naval officer and his wife. When she was in high school, she saw a Kabuki-style production of Shakespeare's *Macbeth* at the Trinity Repertory Theater in nearby Providence, and the experience inspired her to direct her first play, Eugene Ionesco's *Bald Soprano*. Bogart attended Bard College, in Annandale-on-Hudson, New York, and graduated in 1974. Soon afterward she began a master's program at the Tisch School of the Arts at New York University (NYU). While at NYU she produced her own version of *Macbeth* (1976); *Two Portraits* (1976), by Dee Dee O'Connel, which was performed in both Manhattan and San Francisco; and an adaptation of Virginia Woolf's *The Waves* entitled *RD1, The Waves* (1977). After finishing her course work, in 1977, Bogart went on to produce independently several of her own theater works, including an adaptation of Anton Chekhov's *The Seagull* entitled *Out of Sync* (1980). Returning to NYU-Tisch, Bogart directed an original dance theater work at the school's undergraduate Experimental Theater Wing (ETW). Entitled *Artourist* (1980), it was a collaboration with the influential postmodern dance choreographer Mary Overlie. Although this was Bogart's first and only noted collaboration with the choreographer, Overlie's theories about movement have had a profound influence on Bogart throughout her career; it was from Overlie's ideas that Bogart developed the Viewpoints. The following year Bogart created, among other pieces, *Exposed!*, an original theater piece, based the work of Alfred Hitchcock, that was also performed at ETW. "After that she studied and taught extensively in Europe and spent some time at the Max Reinhardt Schule in Berlin, Germany, where she began to explore on stage the differences between German and American theatrical traditions," Hilary De Vries reported in the *New York Times* (October 8, 1989). "It was also in Europe that she first began to earn a reputation as an avant-garde theater artist of note." One of Bogart's better-known pieces from this period was an interpretation of the classic Tennessee Williams play *A Streetcar Named Desire*, which Bogart staged with eight Stanleys (that is, the character Stanley) and 12 Blanches, one of whom was a man. The work was performed at the Abia Theater in Northampton, Massachusetts.

In 1984 Bogart directed an experimental version of *South Pacific*, which was developed at NYU-Tisch. Set on a sunny tropical island, the musical as originally staged "may be the ultimate romanticization of World War II," Gussow wrote in *Anne Bogart—Viewpoints*. To comment on the musical's political context, Bogart, in her version, changed the setting to a home for mentally disturbed war veterans. "In this context," Gussow wrote in the *New York Times* (March 12, 1994), "'There Is Nothin' Like a Dame' became a shell-shocked battlefront song about male bonding. Naturally, the Hammerstein estate raised objections." The controversy over the piece and acclaim from critics brought Bogart to prominence within the theater world and earned her a Bessie Award for performance art. In 1985 Bogart created a dramatic piece based on the Gertrude Stein novel *The Making of Americans*. The piece, which shared the novel's title, was performed at the Music-Theatre Group in Stockbridge, Massachusetts, and at St. Clement's Church in New York City. Later that year, at Bennington College, in Vermont, Bogart premiered her interpretation of Claire Booth Luce's 1930s comedy *The Women*.

Over the next two years, several of Bogart's theater works were produced in the New York City borough of Brooklyn. She directed *Cleveland*, by Mac Wellman, which played at BACA Downtown in 1986, and *In His Eighteenth Year*, by Gillian Richards, which was presented there and at the Clement Theater in 1987. Also in 1986 Bogart went on tour with the piece *1951*, which she co-wrote with Mac Wellman and which she directed. Originally produced at the New York Theatre Workshop, *1951* toured at the University of California at San Diego, in La Jolla, and the American Center in Paris, France.

In 1988 Bogart directed what is widely considered to be her finest work: *No Plays, No Poetry, but Philosophical Reflections, Practical Instructions,*

Provocative Prescriptions, Opinions, and Pointers from a Noted Critic and Playwright. According to Gussow, writing in the *New York Times* (March 12, 1994), the piece "staged the theories and criticisms of [the early 20th-century German playwright] Bertolt Brecht, turning them into a playful, walk-through environment of ideas." The play debuted at the Ohio Theater, in downtown New York, and it cemented Bogart's reputation among the elite of the American avant-garde. She won a 1988 Obie Award for best direction for the production.

Later that year, in the wake of that project's success, Bogart accepted the job of artistic director of the Trinity Repertory Company, a highly respected but artistically troubled regional theater. The position marked a major career shift for Bogart, who until that time was known mainly in avant-garde circles and in New York. Bogart had worked at a regional theater only once before; in 1989, she had directed a production of Calderon de la Barca's 17th-century Spanish drama *Life Is a Dream* at the American Repertory Theatre, in Cambridge, Massachusetts, one of the more forward-thinking regional theaters, and the production had met with mixed reviews. Bogart, however, pursued the Trinity appointment because of the affection she had had for that theater while she was growing up in Newport. After she took over, in the 1989–90 season, Hilary De Vries wrote, "Among the current ranks of young regional theater heads . . . none is considered by many theater people to be more of a harbinger of the future than Ms. Bogart."

Bogart brought *No Plays, No Poetry* to the Trinity as her first show of the 1989–90 season, and on opening night she held an audience discussion after the performance. "This piece is a way for us to collectively examine why we go to the theater at all," she told the audience, as quoted by De Vries. After a few moments, De Vries recalled, a longtime subscription ticket-holder stood up and said, "This isn't my kind of theater at all," as she headed up the aisle. "I miss my company. When my company comes back, then I'll come back." Bogart's season of plays at Trinity Rep also included Maxim Gorky's *Summerfolk*, a nontraditional version of *A Christmas Carol*, Brecht's *Baal*, which was directed by Robert Woodruff, and the musical comedy *On the Town*.

When she had arrived at the Trinity, the theater was in the midst of a financial crisis stemming from a large budget deficit, and the deficit worsened during her tenure. Subscription ticket sales, which had fallen during the two seasons prior to her appointment, did not improve, a situation that many observers attributed to her choice of plays and style of directing. Bogart's reputation within the company was hurt by several unpopular administrative decisions, most notably the dropping of 10 actors, including several longtime and well-liked company members, from the Trinity's 30-person troupe. Because of the theater's precarious finances, the Trinity's board asked Bogart to accept a 25 percent budget cut for her second season as ar-

tistic director. "Anne's season was artistically acclaimed, but not a box-office bonanza," John Howland, the chairman of the Trinity's board, explained to De Vries for the *New York Times* (July 15, 1990). Having already planned the 1990–91 season with the original, larger budget in mind, Bogart refused to accept the cuts, and the board took her refusal as a de facto resignation. "If they had come to me at the beginning of the year and said, 'Look, this is the way it is,' I would have done things differently," Bogart told De Vries for the *New York Times* (July 15, 1990). "Instead, they wanted me to be the hatchet woman and I wouldn't. At the time I didn't know I was resigning."

In 1991 Bogart directed Brecht's *In the Jungle of Cities* at the Joseph Papp Public Theater in New York City. Frank Rich, then a drama critic for the *New York Times* (November 6, 1991), wrote that "the director almost seems to be discoursing on the play for a graduate-school seminar rather than staging it afresh for new audiences." Rich gave a more positive assessment of Bogart's 1992 production of Paula Vogel's *The Baltimore Waltz* at Circle Repertory Company in New York. (The production later appeared at the Alley Theater in Houston, Texas.) "[The production] finds the director Anne Bogart treating a new script with a becoming delicacy and polish she does not always lavish upon the classics," Rich wrote for the *New York Times* (February 12, 1992). Bogart won her second Obie for her direction of *The Baltimore Waltz*.

In 1992 Bogart and Tadashi Suzuki founded a theater company that they named the Saratoga International Theater Institute (SITI), after the company's original home base, in Saratoga, New York. Their intention was to put into practice the artistic theories of both Bogart and Suzuki and create a haven for innovative theater. Over the course of her career, Bogart has been refining a technique she calls Viewpoints, based on theories developed by Mary Overlie. Tina Landau described the method in *Anne Bogart—Viewpoints*: "The Viewpoints are a philosophy of movement translated into a technique for 1) training performers and 2) creating movement on stage. The Viewpoints are the set of names given to certain basic principles of movement; these names constitute a language for talking about what happens or works on stage. The Viewpoints are points of awareness that a performer or creator has while working." The SITI company members combine Bogart's Viewpoint theories with a movement technique created by Suzuki, dubbed the Suzuki Method. According to the *siti.org* Web site, "The Suzuki Method is a rigorous physical and vocal discipline for actors. . . . The method is designed to regain the perceptive abilities and powers of the human body. Drawing on a unique combination of traditional and innovative forms, the training strives to restore the wholeness of the body as a tool of theatrical expression." The group originally worked together only during the summers; while SITI still holds an annual summer training program for actors in Saratoga, they eventually established a year-round base in New York City. Since the company's inception, SITI has performed throughout the world. The first piece Bogart directed with the group, *Orestes*, by Charles L. Mee Jr., toured to Toga-mura, Japan.

In April 1993 Bogart presented a short work entitled *Behavior in Public Places* at St. Mark's Theater in New York. Bogart and the actors created the piece by drawing text and ideas from two influential books by the sociologist Erving Goffman (the play takes its title from one of the books). "[The performance] begins with a woman who is seated on a park bench and muttering to herself," D.J.R. Bruckner wrote for the *New York Times* (April 29, 1993). "Eventually two groups of three people each appear on the fringes of her space and begin to move through it in choreographed steps that variously suggest excitement, astonishment, fright, flight, and menace. . . . This little play is a nifty comment on what theater is." Also in 1993 Bogart restaged her version of *The Women* at Hartford Stage in Connecticut. David Richards wrote for the *New York Times* (January 13, 1994), "The unorthodox production . . . is frequently surprising, occasionally illuminating and almost never funny. . . . The director has such an idiosyncratic vision of the script that Luce's contribution seems altogether secondary."

During her tenure at the Trinity Repertory Company, Bogart told De Vries, "I think [Americans] as a culture pretend we are literary when we are really visual and aural. We pretend we're European, but actually we are much more comfortable with evangelical ministers than, say, James Joyce, [but] we have never established in this country why we need theater." With that in mind, 1992 Bogart began developing a trilogy that would take her three years to complete and that, as Gussow wrote in the *New York Times* (March 12, 1994), attempted "to set the American oral and visual tradition against the European literary tradition." The first installment, *American Vaudeville*, premiered at the Alley Theater in 1992, and in 1994 the second production, entitled *Marathon Dancing*, premiered in New York. "If you're in the mood to consider alternative theater, you couldn't do much better than to check out *Marathon Dancing*, the vivid new site-specific performance piece now being performed by En Garde Arts at the Masonic Hall . . . ," Vincent Canby wrote for the *New York Times* (March 20, 1994). "*Marathon Dancing* is a musical and a melodrama as well as a very entertaining slice of American social and architectural history. It's not your average theater experience." Set in 1932, at the height of the Great Depression, the entire piece takes place at a dance marathon in which the participants have been competing for several hundred hours. "For more than four weeks, they have been dancing 45 minutes out of each hour, using their 15 minute breaks to sleep, eat, brawl, and take care of bodily functions and consider man's fate as America confronts collective despair," Canby

wrote. The piece included 16 period songs by Richard Rodgers, Lorenz Hart, and Oscar Hammerstein II, among other composers.

The final piece in the trilogy, *American Silents*, debuted in 1997 at the Raw Space in New York City. In a promotional statement on the Columbia University Web site, Bogart wrote, "*American Silents* traces the birth of the film industry in the United States. . . . During this time an unprecedented atmosphere of innovation and invention drew artists from theater and vaudeville and business into the creation of a new art form. Every move they made was new because they were acting, writing, directing, and producing a new entity that was to become a cultural phenomenon around the world. They were inventing a whole new deal." Each of the actors in *American Silents* portrayed a real-life figure who was instrumental in the development of film, including Claire Booth Luce, Mary Pickford, and D. W. Griffith. The script was compiled using excerpts from the interviews and memoirs of the people being portrayed, so that each actor spoke the words of his or her real-life character.

Conceived and first produced in 1993 with the SITI Company, in Saratoga, Bogart's work *The Medium* is based on the theories and philosophy of Marshall McLuhan, who died in 1980. "McLuhan argued that people are more influenced by how messages are conveyed than by the content of messages themselves," Kim McDaniel explained in the *Salt Lake Tribune* (May 13, 1996). "He discussed the impact of technology on our daily lives and said the electronic age promised to bring the people together in a global village. He was largely dismissed as a crackpot." Bogart brought *The Medium* to New York in 1994, and Ben Brantley wrote in his review for the *New York Times* (May 17, 1994), "Ms. Bogart, seldom one to accentuate the positive . . . demonstrate[s] the ways in which we have become technology's slaves. . . . The director and her ensemble and technical team have created a vivid, surprisingly diverting piece of expressionist theater." *The Medium* traveled to San Francisco, Pittsburgh, Louisville, Columbus, and Dublin, Ireland, where it won an award for best foreign production.

Bogart also directed another Paula Vogel play, *Hot n' Throbbing*, in 1994, at American Repertory Theater, and a few months later, she opened yet another piece, at P.S. 122, in Manhattan, based on the work of Anton Chekhov. "Ms. Bogart, who has never wanted for ambition, is taking on all five of Chekhov's major plays in a theatrical collage called *Small Lives, Big Dreams*," Ben Brantley wrote for the *New York Times* (February 7, 1995). "[The production] certainly brings out the texts' darkly farcical elements, which the playwright insisted were too often overlooked. But the approach is, finally, reductionist, turning all dialogue into a homogenized series of epitaphs for an age." The play went on to visit Louisville, the 1996 Summer Olympics in Atlanta, and Japan.

Going, Going, Gone, another project developed with SITI, was performed in San Francisco in 1997. According to Steven Winn, writing for the *San Francisco Chronicle* (May 13, 1997), the play "translates relativity theory, the Heisenberg uncertainty principle, and other notions of reality into the sight and sound of people moving about the stage." Bogart created the piece by first rehearsing the play *Who's Afraid of Virginia Woolf*, by Edward Albee. Once the actors' movements were set, Bogart replaced Albee's dialogue with quotes from famous scientists and philosophers regarding theoretical physics. The one-upmanship and mind games practiced by Albee's married couples, evident in the staging, match up in surprising ways with the debate on physics superimposed by Bogart. The piece "succeeds on a visceral, intuitive level," Winn wrote. "Brainy as it sounds . . . the show turns ideas into a caustic, funny, and finally moving human event."

In 1998 Bogart developed a piece called *Bob*, based on the life of the experimental theater director Robert Wilson, who had staged visually stunning productions of original operas such as *Einstein on the Beach*. "A strikingly composed 90-minute rumination . . . *Bob* may seem like a tribute to a like-minded artist," Peter Marks wrote for the *New York Times* (May 8, 1998) of the production at New York Theater Workshop. "But it is also Ms. Bogart's clever use of biography to make the case for her own art." In September 1998 *Culture of Desire*, a play combining events in the lives of Andy Warhol and the band he discovered, the Velvet Underground, with events portrayed in Dante's *Inferno*, was performed at the same venue. "When Warhol, played as a sniveling supernerd by the actress Kelly Maurer, takes his Dante-esque journey below, he finds people looking vaguely like underground superstars pushing shopping carts and chanting commercial slogans and brand names," Ben Brantley wrote for the *New York Times* (September 17, 1998).

"As a director, Anne Bogart resolutely probes behind the words, searching for fabric and context," Gussow wrote in the *New York Times* (March 12, 1994). "If the play is a classic, she says, she wants to rediscover its 'original energy' and learn 'what we can see in it as people in the 90s.' Each time out, she asks herself, 'Who needs to see this, and also who needs to perform it?' In her process, she pans her eye 360 degrees around a play or a playwright." Bogart is an associate professor at the Graduate School of the Arts at Columbia University, in New York City, and her Viewpoints technique is now taught at many drama schools around the country. In 1997 she made her New York City Opera directing debut with a production of *The Seven Deadly Sins,* by Kurt Weill and Bertolt Brecht. In November 1998 her production of *Alice's Adventures* opened at the Wexner Center in Columbus, Ohio.

Bogart worked on several notable projects in 1999. *Cabin Pressure*, for which she collaborated with actors from SITI, was included in the 23d annual Humana Festival of New American Plays (March 31–April 6, 1999) at the Actors Theatre of Louisville, Kentucky. That summer she directed *Gertrude and Alice: A Likeness to Loving*, a play based on the writings of Gertrude Stein and her companion, Alice B. Toklas. Co-starring Lola Pashalinski as Stein and Linda Chapman as Toklas, *Gertrude and Alice* opened on May 29 at the Signature Theatre, in New York City. Bogart's most recent production, which she co-directed with the acclaimed performance artist Laurie Anderson, was *Moby Dick*. Bogart and Anderson's reimagining of Herman Melville's classic novel as a postmodern musical, *Moby Dick* played to sold-out audiences at the Brooklyn Academy of Music, in New York City, in October 1999.

Anne Bogart—Viewpoints (1995), edited by Michael Bigelow Dixon and Joel A. Smith, outlines Bogart's theory of the Viewpoints. It contains essays on Bogart's work written by fellow theater artists and critics and includes Bogart's essay "Terror, Disorientation and Difficulty."

Bogart is a warm, soft-spoken woman who is known for fostering a spirit of community among those with whom she works. Her intensely collaborative approach to creating theater has won ardent praise from many of the actors involved in her productions. — M.B.

Suggested Reading: *New York Times* B p5 Oct. 8, 1989, with photos, H p20 July 15, 1990, with photos, C p19 Nov. 6, 1991, with photos, C p15 Feb. 12, 1992, with photo, C p21 Apr. 29, 1993, C p13 Jan. 13, 1994, with photo, C p12 Mar. 14, 1994, with photo, A p11 Mar. 12, 1994, with photo, C p20 May 17, 1994, with photo, C p14 Feb. 7, 1995; *New York Times* (on-line) May 8, 1998, Sep. 17, 1998; *Salt Lake Tribune* B p1 May 13, 1996, with photo; *San Francisco Chronicle* D p1 May 13, 1997; Dixon, Michael Bigelow, and Joel A. Smith, eds. *Anne Bogart—Viewpoints*, 1995

Selected Theater Works: *Artourist*, 1980; *Sehnsucht* (an adaptation of *A Streetcar Named Desire*), 1982; *South Pacific*, 1984; *The Women*, 1985; *The Making of Americans*, 1985; *1951*, 1986; *Cleveland*, 1986; *The Dispute*, 1987; *In His Eightieth Year*, 1987; *Cinderella/Cendrillon*, 1988; *No Plays, No Poetry*, 1988; *Once in a Lifetime*, 1988; *Strindberg Sonata*, 1989; *Life is a Dream*, 1989; *Summerfolk*, 1989; *On the Town*, 1990; *In The Eye of the Hurricane*, 1991; *Another Person is a Foreign Country*, 1991; *In the Jungle of Cities*, 1991; *The Baltimore Waltz*, 1992; *American Vaudeville*, 1992; *Orestes*, 1992; *Picnic*, 1992; *The Medium*, 1993; *Marathon Dancing*, 1994; *Hot n' Throbbing*, 1994; *Small Lives/Big Dreams*, 1994; *The Adding Machine*, 1995; *Going, Going Gone*, 1996; *American*

Silents, 1997; *Miss Julie*, 1997; *Culture of Desire*, 1997; *Private Lives*, 1998; *Bob*, 1998; *Alice's Adventures*, 1998; *Cabin Pressure*, 1999; *Gertrude and Alice: A Likeness to Loving*, 1999; with Laurie Anderson—*Moby Dick*, 1999

Courtesy of University of California at Berkeley

Borcherds, Richard

Nov. 29, 1959– British mathematician. Address: c/o Dept. of Pure Mathematics and Mathematical Statistics, Trinity College, Cambridge University, Cambridge CB2 1TQ, England

There is no Nobel Prize for achievements in mathematics. For mathematicians, the most prestigious prize is the Fields Medal, which is awarded to four individuals every four years at the International Congress of Mathematicians. Recipients of the solid-gold medallion, which bears a Latin inscription that challenges the winner "to transcend human limitations and grasp the universe," must be younger than 40. In 1998 Richard Borcherds won the medal for his work in algebra and geometry—specifically, for his proof of the so-called Monstrous Moonshine Conjecture, which had defied verification since its formulation in the late 1970s and which Borcherds had struggled to prove for about eight years. Currently on leave from his job as full professor at the University of California at Berkeley, Borcherds has held the post of Royal Society research professor in the Department of Pure Mathematics and Mathematical Statistics at the University of Cambridge, in England, since 1996. In the London *Guardian* (August 31, 1998, online), Simon Singh reported that Borcherds's proof

of the Monstrous Moonshine Conjecture is so abstruse that of the dozens of mathematicians and scientists at Cambridge, only one (besides Borcherds) really understands it.

Richard Ewen Borcherds was born on November 29, 1959 in South Africa. His family moved when he was six months old, and he grew up in the city of Birmingham, England. Throughout his schooling, he ranked at the top of his classes, but math was the only academic subject that ever interested him; he also had a passion for chess in his youth. In 1985 he earned a Ph.D. in math at Trinity College, and subsequently he began his academic career as a researcher there.

Borcherds realized early on that although many mathematicians are capable of comprehending the existing tenets of higher math, only a handful have the ability to come up with original ideas. The chances that he was among that handful, he suspected, were not good. "I wasn't getting very far," he told Simon Singh. "Most of the time I was struggling to keep my job. I'd see other people my age, such as Simon Donaldson [a 1986 Fields medalist], being considerably more successful, and I thought I'm obviously not all that good. There were times when I thought of dropping out."

His worries notwithstanding, at around this time Borcherds produced his first notable work. While reading some physics papers whose authors had used a vertex of intersecting lines to represent interacting particles, Borcherds became interested in new calculations the physicists had used to predict what would occur at a specific vertex (the point at which two or more lines intersect). It struck him, though, that they had performed the math carelessly. By approaching their ideas with his own, meticulous methods, he opened up a fertile new branch of mathematical research, which he labeled vertex algebras. Because he was young and had not established a reputation, for several years no one but Borcherds himself valued his discovery. "I was pretty pleased with it at the time," he told Singh. "But after a few years, I got a bit disillusioned, because it was obvious that nobody else was really interested in it. There is no point in having an idea that is so complicated that nobody can understand it."

While he was waiting for the rest of the mathematical community to catch on to vertex algebras, Borcherds began grappling with a problem that many mathematicians thought would never be solved. In 1978 the mathematician John McKay of Concordia University, in River Forest, Illinois, had discovered a seemingly inexplicable link between two disparate mathematical structures. The idea that they were somehow related was dubbed the Monstrous Moonshine Conjecture. "Monstrous" refers to one of the structures, the Monster group, so-named for its unimaginably large size; "moonshine" is a term scientists use to describe outlandish scientific ideas.

The Monster group is what is known as a purely mathematical entity; it exists only in the abstract and is impossible to picture. In math, a group is a set of elements for which certain arithmetic rules apply; for example, all whole numbers and their sums make up a group. The symmetries of geometric structures (that is, the properties that do not change when the structures undergo certain changes) also make up a group. A cube, for instance, has 24 symmetries, meaning that there are 24 ways in which it can be twisted and rotated and still look exactly the same. Those 24 symmetries make up a finite group containing 24 elements. The Monster group, which is, in math terminology, the "largest sporadic, finite, simple group" identified by mathematicians, exists in 196,883 dimensions and has approximately $8 \times 10 \times 10 \times \ldots \times 10$ symmetries (where 10 is multiplied by itself 52 times): that is, 808,017,424,794,512,875,886,459,904,-961,710,757,005,754,368,000,000,000 symmetries. (That number is greater than the number of elementary particles—the particles in atoms—believed to exist in the universe.)

What McKay noticed is that 196,884, the sum of the first two elements (1 and 196,883) in the Monster group, is equal to the one of the coefficients (specifically, the third coefficient) of the j function. The j function is known as an elliptic modular function; such functions are used in modeling structures in two dimensions. Unlike the Monster group, elliptic functions are of practical value; they are sometimes used in chemistry to describe molecular structures. The j function enables scientists and mathematicians to convert a doughnut shape into a corresponding complex number. The connection between the Monster group and the j function seemed virtually certain to be mere coincidence. As Borcherds told W. Wayt Gibbs for *Scientific American* (November 1998), "When John McKay told people about his observation that the third coefficient of the j function matched the smallest dimension of the Monster, they told him that he was completely crazy. There was no connection that anyone could imagine." Improbable as the idea was, it merited a closer look, and eventually other mathematicians found that the connections went even further. "It turned out that every coefficient of the modular function is a simple sum of the numbers in this list of dimensions in which the Monster lives," Borcherds told Gibbs. The British mathematician John Conway, a Cambridge professor who is Borcherds's mentor, theorized that the Monster group and the j function were related in some significant way, and he named his conjecture Monstrous Moonshine. The conjecture spawned a new specialization within higher math, which entailed the attempt to prove the theory correct.

Although many people imagine that higher math is extremely logical, solving a problem such as the Monstrous Moonshine Conjecture requires a creative leap. Speaking of his work in general, Borcherds told Gibbs, "The logical progression comes only right at the end, and it is in fact quite tiresome to check that all the details really work. Before that, you have to fit everything together by a lot of experimentation, guesswork, and intuition." Borcherds spent about eight years working on the Monstrous Moonshine problem without any breakthroughs. Then, in 1989, he had a sudden flash. "I was in Kashmir," Borcherds told Singh. "I had been travelling around northern India, and there was one really long, tiresome bus journey, which lasted about 24 hours. Then the bus had to stop because there was a landslide and we couldn't go any further. It was all pretty darn unpleasant. Anyway, I was toying with some calculations on this bus journey and I finally found an idea which made everything work."

The solution to the conjecture lies in string theory, an area of physics that posits that elementary particles are not elementary at all, but are made up of loops of one-dimensional strings. String theory was developed as part of the search for what is referred to in physics as the grand unified theory, which scientists hope will unite theories involving the so-called weak forces, strong forces, and gravity—the basic forces that exist in the universe. The math used in string theory describes what happens when the strings intersect; in other words, it uses vertex algebras, the area in which Borcherds did pioneering work early in his career. Borcherds invented a specific vertex algebra—the rules in a particular string theory—that describe a 26-dimensional space, with all 26 dimensions curled so as to form a doughnut shape that folds in on itself; hence, the connection with the j function. The Monster group, then, is the group of all the symmetries of the complex folded doughnut shape defined by this particular string theory.

Borcherds's solution to the Monstrous Moonshine Conjecture has no practical application whatsoever and bears no relation to any object that could exist in the universe. Very few people in the world can truly understand or appreciate it. Borcherds could not share his stunning insight with his companion on the bus trip, for example, because his travel mate was not a mathematician. Nor can Borcherds's wife, Ursula Gritsch, a mathematician who specializes in topology, understand his proof fully. Because of the highly specialized nature of modern mathematics, Borcherds, in turn, is incapable of comprehending the intricacies of Gritsch's research.

Borcherds accepts, and perhaps even welcomes, the isolation that comes with his elite place in an elite profession. (That isolation is so nearly complete that he and the person at Cambridge who understands his solution to the Monsterous Moonshine Conjecture almost never see each other, according to Singh.) Borcherds blames his slow climb to recognition in the math community partly on his inability to communicate his ideas. "I'm not very good at expressing feelings and things like that," he told Gibbs. "I read once somewhere that the left side of the brain handles mathematics and the right side handles emotions and expression.

And I've often had the feeling that there really is a disconnect of some sort between the two." Borcherds's wife suspects that he may have a very mild form of autism called Asperger's Syndrome, which causes those afflicted to be introverted and unemotional.

Borcherds no longer teaches or gives tutorials, and he does not enjoy collaborating with others. He spends most of his time working at his desk in a spare office at Cambridge. Although at times during the 1980s, Borcherds felt keenly the desire to be recognized by his peers, after getting the Fields Medal, he realized he prefers the satisfaction of solving a difficult problem, even if no one else appreciates what he has accomplished. "I didn't really feel anything," he told Singh of his reaction to the news that he had won the medal. "Before the award, I used to think it was terribly important, but now I realize that it's meaningless. However, I was over the moon when I proved the moonshine conjecture. If I get a good result, I spend several days feeling really happy about it." In 1992 Borcherds won both the Junior Whitehead Prize from the London Mathematical Society and the Prize of the City of Paris, and in 1994 he was made a fellow of the British Royal Society.

While Borcherds has virtually no hobbies or interests outside his work, he does enjoy an occasional movie. *Godzilla* and the *Star Wars* trilogy rank among his favorites. — O.J.S.

Suggested Reading: *American Mathematical Society* (on-line), with photo; (London) *Guardian* (on-line), Aug. 31, 1998; *Scientific American* p40+ Nov. 1998, with photo; *University of California News Release* (on-line) Aug. 19, 1998

Jacques Boissinot/CP Picture Archive

Bouchard, Lucien

(boo-SHARD, loo-see-EN)

Dec. 22, 1938– Premier of Quebec. Address: 885 Grande-Allée est, 3e étage, Québec, Canada

Ever since 1867, when Canada gained dominion status within the British Empire and became, in effect, an independent nation, the predominantly francophone citizens of Quebec have clamored to distinguish themselves from the rest of the country, whose predominantly anglophone citizens enjoy cultural and historical ties to England. Some of the nearly 7.3 million citizens of Quebec— Canada's largest province in area and second largest in population—have even gone so far as to advocate secession from Canada and the establishment of Quebec as an independent nation. Indeed, Quebecers have voted on the issue of secession in two referendums, in 1980 and 1995, respectively. The issue calls into question the very definition of a nation and has great resonance not only for the future of Quebec but for all of Canada. Thus it is not surprising that Quebec's premier since 1996, Lucien Bouchard, who is arguably the most prominent champion of Quebec's sovereignty, has often been hailed as a hero by those who favor secession and denounced as a villain by many who do not.

A former lawyer and ambassador to France who entered electoral politics in 1988, Lucien Bouchard emerged as a leading proponent of an independent Quebec in 1990, when he left the conservative, pro-federalist government of Prime Minister Brian Mulroney to form a bloc of pro-Quebec members of the House of Commons, the Canadian Parliament's lower house. As premier of Quebec, he has implemented measures to try to improve Quebec's economy and sought to win greater sovereignty for Quebec from Canada's federal government.

The oldest of the five children of Philippe Bouchard, a truck driver, and Alice Bouchard, Lucien Bouchard was born on December 22, 1938 in Saint-Coeur-de-Marie, a town in the district of Lac-Saint-Jean, in the Canadian province of Quebec. He grew up in a francophone, working-class, Catholic home in the rural northern Quebec town of Jonquière, near the family farm, which had been homesteaded by Bouchard's grandfather around the end of the 19th century. As a boy Bouchard read widely, devouring accounts of such famous historical figures as Alexander the Great, Julius Caesar, Hannibal, and Napoleon. In 1959 he graduated from Jonquière Classical College, where he had studied French and Latin. He considered entering the priesthood, but instead obtained a bachelor's degree in social science and a law degree from Laval University, in Quebec City, the capital of Quebec, in 1964. He was admitted to the Quebec bar in the same year and practiced law in Chicoutimi, a city in south-central Quebec, until 1985.

As a student Bouchard was sympathetic to the New Democratic Party, a socialist group. He later became a devotee of the Liberal Party, which championed free trade and gradual social reform and which governed Canada from 1963 to 1984, with a brief lapse from late 1979 to early 1980. Next, around 1972, he joined the Quebec Party (Parti Québécois), which sought greater sovereignty for Quebec. Despite his Quebec Party membership, he served as counsel for the 1974 Cliche Commission, which, under the aegis of Quebec's Liberal Party government, investigated reports of violence in the Quebec construction industry. He worked for the Quebec Party after it won control of Quebec's provincial assembly in 1976 and formed a government under the leadership of René Lévesque. He campaigned for the sovereignty-association option in the 1980 referendum, which separatists lost by a wide margin, and in the early 1980s he served as Quebec premier Lévesque's chief negotiator in talks with unionized public workers in the province. In that capacity he faced down disgruntled union members to impose wage cuts.

Bouchard changed his political affiliation yet again in 1984, leaving the Quebec Party to help the Progressive Conservative Party (PCP)—a pro-federalist party that had long been resistant to Quebec separatism—in the September 1984 federal election. He helped craft speeches and campaign strategy for Brian Mulroney, the leader of the PCP and a friend from his days at Laval University. With Bouchard's help the PCP won 58 of Quebec's 75 seats in Canada's federal House of Commons, and Mulroney became Canada's prime minister.

In July 1985 Mulroney appointed Bouchard Canada's ambassador to France. He held that post until March 1988, when he relinquished it to join Mulroney's cabinet as Canada's secretary of state. But in order to become a member of Mulroney's government, he first had to win a seat in the House of Commons, which met in Ottawa, the capital of Canada. He did just that as a PCP candidate in a by-election (a special election held between regular elections) called in June 1988. With the help of Mulroney, who campaigned for him, Bouchard took a seat in the House of Commons as the representative of his rural home district, Lac-Saint-Jean. Commenting on his transition from ambassadorship to electoral politics, Bouchard told Lisa Van Dusen for *Maclean's* (June 20, 1988), "In Paris, it was 'Would his excellency like more soup?,' 'Would his excellency like his limousine now?' Here, it's 'Yeah, you seem like a nice guy, but what are you going to do about unemployment?' It has been a very useful exercise in modesty." He won reelection to his Commons seat in the federal election of November 1988, in which Mulroney's Conservatives again emerged victorious. In January

1989 Mulroney appointed Bouchard acting minister of the environment. Bouchard also served on the priorities and planning committee of the cabinet, the influential committee that sets the government's legislative agenda.

Then, in May 1990, Bouchard resigned from that post and from the government, thereby ending his 30-year relationship with Mulroney. The break followed disputes between Bouchard and Mulroney over the government's handling of the Meech Lake constitutional accords, which sought to help resolve the issue of sovereignty for Quebec and other Canadian provinces. At the time of Bouchard's resignation, the accords were, by most accounts, on the verge of failure. In his five-page resignation letter, Bouchard wrote, as quoted by E. Kaye Fulton for *Maclean's* (June 4, 1990), "I deeply believe that we have to rethink this country. We must stop trying to fit Quebec into the mold of a province like the others."

Bouchard kept his Commons seat and continued to represent Lac-Saint-Jean as an independent. Meanwhile, in June 1990, the Meech Lake negotiations collapsed. Bouchard confirmed his break from Mulroney and the PCP that July, when he led eight other members of the House of Commons in forming the Quebec Bloc (Bloc Québécois), which functioned, in effect, as a political party and supported pro-Quebec issues in the House of Commons. In June 1991 the Quebec Bloc held its founding meeting, and Bouchard was elected chairman and leader of the party.

During this time Bouchard captured much attention as a fiery politician with a gift for oratory, arousing crowds with exhortations embellished with references to Quebec's cultural and historic traditions. "If we are all together here today, it is, above all, because we are Quebecers," he said in a speech given in Tracy, Quebec, as quoted by Nancy Wood for *Maclean's* (July 22, 1991). "And we wish to remind the Canadians that we are proud of this difference and wish to celebrate it by taking complete charge of our destiny. Destiny. Yes, destiny."

Bouchard's rise was not without detractors. Some took issue with his political meanderings and questioned his dedication and commitment to Quebec sovereignty. In response to such charges, others suggested that Bouchard's circuitous political journey reflected similar shifts in the positions held by his constituency in Quebec. Another criticism of the political viewpoint Bouchard espoused came from those who had long been committed to the establishment of Canada as a bilingual country of provinces that stand on equal footing. To those holding this view, Bouchard's proposals threatened to tear the country apart. Moreover, Bouchard and Quebec separatists who were perhaps even more hard-line were criticized for fueling xenophobic nationalist sentiments. In the *Washington Post* (October 18, 1995), Charles Trueheart offered a quote in which Prime Minister Jean Chrétien, who is critical of Quebec nationalists, pointed out malevolent aspects of Quebec nationalism: "In order to be a good Quebecer, you have to be white rather than colored, you certainly have to speak French rather than English, and you definitely have to be a separatist."

Federalism versus sovereignty soon emerged as Canada's most hotly debated political issue. Meanwhile, although the Quebec Bloc's mandate was officially limited to matters affecting Quebec, the group quickly became a political force whose influence spread beyond the province. In the October 1993 federal election, the PCP lost public support and watched helplessly as its parliamentary representation fell from 153 to two. In its place the Liberal Party formed a government with Chrétien as prime minister. Bouchard's Quebec Bloc, which finished with 54 candidates elected to the House of Commons, emerged as the official opposition party. Bouchard's bloc captured 49.5 percent of the popular vote in Quebec. In his new capacity as leader of the opposition, Bouchard lobbied for pro-Quebec issues on the federal level and, in Quebec's assembly elections, campaigned for the Quebec Party, a provincial political party seeking sovereignty for Quebec.

In December 1994 Bouchard suffered a personal tragedy: he lost his left leg to necrotizing myositis, a rare flesh-destroying disease. Oddly enough, his bout with the debilitating disease, which left him with a prosthetic leg and forced him to use a cane, endowed him with even greater political currency for his separatist cause; in some circles he came to be viewed almost as a martyr.

Bouchard nearly led Quebec separatists to victory in the province's October 1995 referendum on secession, which proposed an independent Quebec with close economic ties to Canada. In an election in which 94 percent of voters went to the polls, the margin of victory for those who voted to remain a part of Canada was just over 50,000 votes out of nearly five million cast—a mere 1 percent of the ballots. Bouchard was credited with having mobilized Quebec separatists and having wrested control of the campaign in early October from Jacques Parizeau, the leader of the Quebec Party and premier of Quebec. Asked why he sought sovereignty for Quebec, Bouchard told *Time* (March 17, 1997, on-line), "Because we will make our own decisions. We will keep our own taxes here. We will shape our policies in our own specific interest. That's the bottom line. We feel that we are a people. We like to be what we are."

Bouchard quickly eclipsed Parizeau as the beacon for the cause of Quebec sovereignty and won the support of the Quebec Party. Partly for this reason, in December 1995 Parizeau resigned under pressure as premier of Quebec and leader of the Quebec Party. (Another factor that led to his resignation was the controversy surrounding statements in which he had blamed the loss of the referendum on nonwhites in Quebec.) Bouchard's rise to the peak of Quebec politics was cemented in January 1996, when he resigned from the Quebec Bloc, gave up his seat in the House of Commons,

left federal politics, and became leader of the Quebec Party and premier of Quebec. "Unconsciously, all my career has prepared me for this," he had declared upon launching his bid to succeed Parizeau in November 1995, as quoted by Barry Came for *Maclean's* (December 4, 1995). "I can do something for Quebec," he added. "I'm almost obliged to plunge in and take up the challenge."

The Quebec Party chose Bouchard to succeed Parizeau; he was sworn in as Quebec's premier on January 27, 1996. Although the issue of sovereignty had long monopolized political debate in Quebec, during his first term Bouchard concentrated largely on economic matters. According to figures supplied by Barry Came, Bouchard inherited a province with a $78 billion debt (in Canadian dollars)—the highest per-capita debt of any of Canada's 10 provinces. Moreover, Quebec was burdened by an unemployment rate of nearly 11 percent (the Canadian average was 9.4 percent).

A fiscal conservative, Bouchard implemented a series of budget cuts, many of them in the areas of public health-care programs and education, with the goal of eliminating Quebec's budget deficit. In *Time* (March 17, 1997, on-line), Andrew Purvis reported that Bouchard cut spending on social programs by $1.85 billion in 1996. Such measures, as well as Bouchard's fostering of stronger ties with big business, reduced the support for his party traditionally given by Quebec's strong labor unions. Indeed, many people, including some in his own party, took issue with Bouchard's budget cuts. Prior to Bouchard's installation as premier, the Quebec Party, which had left-of-center roots, had advocated a prominent governmental role in providing social services and establishing public safety nets.

Although the focus of his administration was on economic recovery, Bouchard had not forgotten his pledge to win greater sovereignty for Quebec from the federal government. He kept the cause alive by advocating another referendum on Quebec secession before the year 2000. Meanwhile, he lobbied Prime Minister Chrétien and Canada's federal government to allow for constitutional changes to give Quebec more sovereignty.

Despite the backlash sparked by his fiscal policies, Bouchard has enjoyed relatively strong support from Quebec's francophones. He was reelected premier on November 30, 1998, when he narrowly beat Jean Charest, the provincial leader of the Liberal Party. Bouchard's party won 75 seats, two fewer than in 1994, out of a total of 125 in the provincial assembly, while the Liberal Party captured 48 seats, one more than it had taken in 1994. By contrast, Bouchard's party won only 42.7 percent of the popular vote, while the Liberal Party, led by Charest and seeking to maintain Quebec's relationship with the rest of Canada, won 43.7 percent. (In Quebec's election system, a greater share of popular votes doesn't necessarily translate into a greater number of seats in the provincial assembly.) Bouchard's small margin of victory precluded the likelihood of a referendum on Quebec's secession from Canada. "Quebecers have said that the time is not propitious for a referendum, at least not immediately," Bouchard said following his victory, as quoted by Anthony DePalma for the *New York Times* (December 2, 1998, on-line).

Bouchard retains the right to hold a referendum at any time during his term, which lasts five years. Quebec's elections, though regional, have been widely perceived to have important and lasting repercussions for Canada as a whole, in that they reflect the level of popular support for holding referendums on sovereignty. After his election victory, Bouchard declared that a new referendum on Quebec's sovereignty would be held only if public sentiment seemed to favor secession. He then continued to lobby for more provincial control over health care and other social programs from the federal government.

Bouchard's marriage of 20 years to Jocelyne Cote ended in divorce in 1986. He and his second wife, Audrey Best, who is American, have two sons, Al-

exandre and Simon. The family lives in Montreal. Bouchard's autobiography, *On the Record*, was published in 1992. He is also the author of various articles on law and labor relations. In addition to French, Bouchard speaks English, which he learned at age 40. — Y.P.

Suggested Reading: *Business Week* p60 Feb. 5, 1996, with photos; *Maclean's* p24+ June 4, 1990, with photos, p14+ Nov. 29, 1993, with photo, p20+ June 13, 1994, with photos, p18+ Dec. 12, 1994, with photos, p36+ Oct. 19, 1998, with photos; *New York Times* I p22 Oct. 29, 1995, A p9 Apr. 8, 1996, with photo; *Time* (on-line) Mar. 17, 1997; *Washington Post* A p14 Oct. 12, 1995, with photo, A p19 Sep. 28, 1998, with photos

Selected Books: *On the Record*, 1992

Courtesy of Detroit Red Wings

Bowman, Scotty

Sep. 18, 1933– Coach of the Detroit Red Wings. Address: c/o Detroit Red Wings, 600 Civic Center Dr., Joe Louis Arena, Detroit, MI 48226

Scotty Bowman, the head coach of the Detroit Red Wings, has already earned his place in history as one of the best coaches ever, in any sport. Now in his 27th season as a head coach in the National Hockey League (NHL), he has racked up achievements that speak for themselves. He is a member

of the NHL Hall of Fame and the winningest coach in NHL history. He has recorded more than 1,000 regular-season victories. He is the only coach ever to have led teams to 60 wins in a single season, and he accomplished that feat twice. He has the best winning percentage (.658) among those who have coached more than 600 games. He is one of the two head coaches who hold the record of eight Stanley Cup championships. And he is the only coach ever to win the Stanley Cup with three different teams (the Montreal Canadiens, the Pittsburgh Penguins, and the Red Wings).

According to those who know him, Bowman's success stems from his obsession with winning. Writing for *Sports Illustrated* (May 10, 1993), E. M. Swift described Bowman as "a bottom-line guy. . . . At the end of the day he's interested in two things: Did we win? and, What can I do to help us win tomorrow?" Doug Risebrough, who played for Bowman in Montreal and later became an NHL general manager, told Swift that Bowman "was an intense, intense individual. He treated every game as if it was the most important game of the year, and he expected everyone to treat it the same way." Bowman pushes his players to perform at the peak of their abilities every day. Early in his career, he showed little regard for his players' feelings when he selected tactics designed to spur the team to success. For example, he frequently benched players without explanation. Known for being taciturn and unpredictable, Bowman is respected and feared as a coach, but he is not always well liked. Steve Shutt, another of Bowman's Montreal players, once remarked that players hated Bowman every day of the year except one: the day they put on their Stanley Cup championship rings.

A key factor in Bowman's longevity, according to many, has been his ability and willingness to change his approach to adapt to changes in his sport. Bowman has attributed his flexibility to his desire to win games. "If you don't adapt, you are not going to win, it's that simple," Bowman told *Sports Illustrated* (December 12, 1994). "And you won't survive. I've changed my style many times; you have to." One of the most visible changes Bowman has made is his way of interacting with his players. "I have more experience, more patience [now]," Bowman told Swift. "Players are much more sensitive today. It used to be, if a guy's unhappy, so what? Now it might disturb the chemistry of the team. You take players off the ice, and you see they have the big lip on. So you have to explain they missed a few shifts because we needed more offense. You hope they accept it. Ten years ago I wouldn't have bothered. That's the reality of team sports today. In many ways, it's more intriguing now."

The second of four children of Scottish emigrants to Canada, William Scott Bowman was born on September 18, 1933 in Montreal, Quebec. He grew up in Verdun, a working-class suburb of Montreal, where the Bowmans lived in a six-family tenement. His father worked as a blacksmith for a railway company for 31 years and never took a sick day. Bowman is said to have inherited his competitive drive from his mother, Jean, who throughout her adult life would throw her cards into the fire if she lost at euchre. "If you like the game, Scott, why lose at it?" she once said, as quoted by Swift.

During winters when he was a child, Bowman skated down ice-covered streets to city rinks, where he learned the game of hockey. In 1951, at age 17, he began playing for the Junior Canadiens, the youth team of the NHL's Montreal Canadiens. He was a small, speedy, hard-working player who was very knowledgeable about the game. As a Junior Canadien, he participated in the Junior A play-offs held in 1952. At one point during the play-offs, his team was on the brink of winning a game and thus eliminating their opponent, Trois-Rivières, from contention. Feeling angry and frustrated, Jean-Guy Talbot, an opposing defenseman, struck Bowman's shoulder and head with his stick. In that era, hockey players did not wear helmets, and the effect of the blow to Bowman's head "was like being scalped," as he recalled to Swift. After he recovered sufficiently, he played two more seasons of junior hockey, with the Montreal Royals as well as with the Canadiens. But he never returned to his pre-injury form, and he realized he had no hope of entering the NHL. "All I ever wanted to be was a player," Bowman told the *Toronto Star* (June 13, 1998, on-line). "But that was it for me. I was never the same player afterward. I just didn't have the confidence. I had a lot of headaches and blurred vision and things like that in the off-season and the club recommended that I quit as an active player." Bowman never held a grudge against Talbot, and Talbot later spent three seasons playing under Bowman for the St. Louis Blues.

The Canadiens' management paid Bowman's tuition for classes in business at Sir George Williams University in Montreal. Bowman also began coaching hockey, initially with 12- and 13-year-olds and then with 14- and 15-year-olds. In 1954 he got his first semi-pro coaching job, with the Park Extension Junior B team, near Montreal, whose players were only a few years younger than he was. He earned only $250 a season, and to help support himself, he took on a second job, at a paint company a short walk from the Forum, the Canadiens' stadium in Montreal. He spent his lunch hours watching the Canadiens practice under their head coach, Dick Irvin.

Bowman's ability to lead players so close to him in age impressed coaches around Montreal, and in 1956, after the Junior Canadiens were relocated from Montreal to Ottawa, Sam Pollock, their coach and general manager, hired Bowman as his assistant. Bowman worked with that team until they won the Memorial Cup, junior hockey's top honor, in 1958. Then he became the head coach of another Junior A team, in Peterborough, Ontario. After three seasons there, Bowman was hired by the Montreal Canadiens as their head scout for eastern Canada.

Bowman eventually realized he preferred working with a team to scouting, and in 1963 he debuted as an NHL coach. After coaching nine games with the Omaha Knights, he quit, because of conflicts with the team's owners. In particular, he felt their cost-cutting measures—for example, forcing the team to take long trips by bus and skimping on money for their meals—were compromising the players' well-being. Some observers also suspected that although Bowman had guided the Knights to second place, he was not ready for the pressure of the NHL.

Whatever the reason for his departure, Bowman rejoined the Junior Canadiens as their head coach. The move helped him immeasurably, because while in that position, he was mentored by Toe Blake, who coached the Montreal Canadiens and is the only coach besides Bowman to win eight Stanley Cups. From Blake, Bowman learned several techniques that later became his hallmarks. One was to place the right players on the ice at the right time. "I used to go into [Blake's] office a lot," Bowman told Swift. "And he might say something like, 'I'll let you in on a tip. Your friend Terry Harper's not going to play much tonight.' He knew how each of his players did against everyone else. Certain guys do well against one team but not another. He was a good strategist and a good matchup man and wasn't afraid to sit guys out to change his ammunition." Bowman also learned from Blake the importance of changing strategy in mid-game. One season Bowman led the Junior Canadiens to the play-offs, where they faced a more talented team. Blake showed him three different forechecking plans to try in the game, and Bowman discovered that all three worked. He thus learned that, as Swift wrote, "if you threw something different at a team, almost anything, it got the players out of rhythm, slowed them down, kept them off-balance. No matter how clever the opposing coach was, it took his team some time to react to the changes. And by that time, Bowman, always a step ahead, might have altered his strategy again." Among Bowman's many strong points, those two—knowing which team members to have in play and keeping several steps ahead of the opponent—are mentioned most frequently.

In 1967 the NHL expanded from six teams to 12, and Lynn Patrick, the head coach of one of the new franchises, the St. Louis Blues, took Bowman on as assistant coach. During the 16th game of the season, Bowman advised Patrick to remove a certain player for one shift. Patrick didn't do so, and the opposing team scored and went on to win the game. Patrick's error in judgment was enough to convince him that coaching was not the right job for him, and at the next game, Bowman took over as head coach. The Blues had won only four of their first 16 games; under Bowman they posted a 23–21–14 win–loss–tie record, and they finished third in the Western division. In the play-offs, they upset two favored opponents and thereby advanced to the Stanley Cup finals. In that series the Blues lost each of their four games against the Montreal Canadiens (coached by Blake) by only one goal. The next two seasons (1968–69 and 1969–70), Bowman led the Blues to a first-place finish in the Western division, and the team again advanced to the Stanley Cup finals, where they lost. In 1968–69, the Blues had a goals-against average of 2.07, which, after the league's expansion, remained a record low until 1993.

During Bowman's years with the Blues, the league was arranged so that one of the six expansion teams was guaranteed to make the Stanley Cup finals. The new teams started off on equal footing, but Bowman quickly led the Blues to dominate the other five. One step that contributed to his success was his use of videotapes of games to assess the opposition and prepare for upcoming matches—a technique reportedly never before used by an NHL coach. "He knew more about the other team than the guy coaching them," Dan Kelly, a broadcaster for the Blues, told Swift.

In 1969–70, Bowman became general manager of the Blues as well as coach. For a short time in 1970–71, Al Arbour took over as coach; when Arbour resumed his career as a player, in February 1970, Bowman began coaching again. In the first round of the play-offs in the spring of 1971, the Blues were eliminated by the Minnesota North Stars, and the son of the Blues' owner promptly fired Arbour and another player, Cliff Fletcher. In protest, Bowman resigned as head coach.

Sam Pollock had by then become the general manager of the Montreal Canadiens, and in June 1971 he hired the 37-year-old Bowman as their head coach. In his eight years with Montreal, Bowman led the Canadiens to five Stanley Cup titles, one in 1972–73 and then, from 1975–76 to 1978–79, four in a row. Bowman's Canadiens rank among the dynasties in sports history, having posted a win–loss–tie record of 419–110–105, for a winning percentage of .742. In 1976–77, the team scored 132 goals, which is still the NHL season record. Among those Bowman coached in Montreal were the All-Star Guy Lafleur, Larry Robinson, Guy Lapointe, and Ken Dryden. "I have always appreciated ability, but I don't think you [should] throw out a lot of compliments," Bowman told Sports Illustrated (December 12, 1994). "And that might be one regret I have, not telling those players in Montreal how good they were."

In 1979 Bowman was passed over for the position of Canadiens general manager, and he left the team to become coach and general manager of the Buffalo Sabres. Bowman never intended to keep both jobs; once the team was on solid footing, he planned to have someone else take over as coach. He head coached during the 1979–80 season with two assistants and is credited with being among those who introduced team coaching to the NHL. Over the years, he hired three replacement coaches: Roger Neilson, in 1980–81; Jimmy Roberts, in 1982; and Jim Schoenfeld, in 1986. None lasted more than a season, and in each case, Bowman appointed himself as the replacement; he coached the Sabres himself from 1982 to 1985.

In December 1984 Bowman became the winningest coach in NHL history, with his 691 career victories surpassing Dick Irvin's total. The Sabres' win–loss–tie record with Bowman as coach was 210–134–60, but the team never made it past the conference finals in the play-offs. Bowman has said that, pressed to serve as both coach and general manager when he could not find a coach of sufficient ability to replace him, he had been "spread too thin." Many observers suspected that the problem was Bowman's intimidating demeanor as a coach; while it had produced stellar results in St. Louis and Montreal, where many of the players were veterans, it was evidently ineffective with the younger players in Buffalo. At the beginning of the 1986–87 season, Bowman stopped coaching once again to focus on the job of general manager. The team got off to a shaky start, and less than a month later, Bowman was fired.

From 1987 to 1990, Bowman worked as a television analyst for the CBS program Hockey Night in Canada. The job gave him a new perspective on hockey. "Working in TV gives you the position of the media," Bowman told the New York Times (October 21, 1991). "It's the 1990s now. The game is different. Who would have expected the big-name trades, the higher salaries? It's two different eras."

In June 1990, having lost interest in coaching but longing to work for a team, Bowman joined the Pittsburgh Penguins as their director of player personnel. He worked closely with their head coach, Bob Johnson, and although the coaching styles of the two men have been described as polar opposites—Johnson was as open, upbeat, and positive as Bowman was inscrutable, uncommunicative, and hard-nosed—they respected each other highly.

Bowman even gave advice about coaching occasionally, and with support from the general manager, Craig Patrick, the collaboration made for an excellent club. In 1991 the Penguins, led by their star player Mario Lemieux, won their first Stanley Cup. Also that year, Bowman was inducted into the NHL Hall of Fame.

During the off-season in 1991, Johnson was diagnosed with two brain tumors. At that point Bowman had no intention of coaching again, but Patrick asked him to step in until Johnson recovered, and Bowman agreed. After Johnson died, that November, Patrick asked Bowman to continue as coach. Bowman realized he would have to alter his methods, both because times had changed and because the players had been accustomed to Johnson's way of coaching. Bowman told Swift, "I was aware that if I coached the way I did in the past, it wouldn't have brought the same results. I knew I had to be different. If you're critical of a player today, especially openly, it's perceived as being negative. Bob Johnson was so positive. You have to stroke them more." According to one player, it took several months for Bowman and the Penguins to adjust to each other.

At a crucial point in the season, with the Penguins down three games to one against the Washington Capitals in the first round of the play-offs, Bowman rallied the team around a forechecking system suggested by Lemieux. The Penguins came back to win the next three games; then they advanced to the next round, where, after trailing two games to one, they eliminated the New York Rangers, who held the league's best record that season. The Penguins then swept the Boston Bruins in the semifinals and the Chicago Blackhawks in the finals—recording 11 play-off victories in a row, a league record—and won the Stanley Cup. It was Bowman's sixth as a coach.

Bowman continued to coach the Penguins in 1992–93, leading the team to the best record in the NHL before their elimination in the play-offs. In June 1993 he accepted a lucrative offer from the Detroit Red Wings to become their head coach. From 1994 to 1997 he also acted as their head of player personnel. Bowman led the Red Wings to the best record overall in the NHL during the 1995 season (which was shortened by a players' strike) and repeated this accomplishment during the 1995–96 season. In December 1995, Bowman surpassed Al Arbour and set a new record for number of NHL games coached—1,607. By the 1996–97 season, Bowman had put together a team led by captain Steve Yzerman, Brendan Shanahan, goalie Mike Vernon, and the Russian players known as "the Russian five," whom Bowman mixed and matched with others on his lineup, sometimes having them play out of their usual positions. In February 1997, in overtime against the Penguins, Bowman recorded the 1,000th regular-season victory of his career, and during the play-offs that year, he coached his 2,000th NHL game. By keeping the Philadelphia Flyers off-kilter, the Red Wings,

thanks largely to Bowman's coaching tactics, won their first Stanley Cup since 1955. It was Bowman's seventh. After the victory Bowman donned skates and became the first NHL coach to circle the rink holding the Stanley Cup—a moment he had dreamed of since his youth.

In 1997–98 the Red Wings were a very different team. Their best defensive player, Vladimir Konstantinov, had suffered brain damage in a limousine accident six days after the team had won the Stanley Cup. A top forward, Sergei Fedorov, had become a free agent and was unsigned halfway into the season. (Eventually, before the 1998 play-offs, he rejoined the Red Wings.) And Vernon, the most valuable player of the 1997 play-offs, had been traded for two draft choices. Yet, under Bowman's guidance, other players stepped in to fill the gaps. In the first three games of the 1998 Stanley Cup finals, according to the *New York Times* (June 15, 1998), the Red Wings "dominated virtually every facet of play and . . . demonstrated a team game that [was] remarkable for its depth and versatility." The Red Wings swept the Washington Capitals, and Konstantinov was handed the Stanley Cup as his teammates escorted him onto the ice in his wheelchair.

Six days after Bowman guided the Red Wings to win their second straight Stanley Cup—and his eighth—his brother Jack died after having heart surgery. The next month, Bowman was diagnosed with a blockage in one of his arteries. In light of those events, many people hazarded the guess that Bowman would retire from coaching. But he did not, and he has remained head coach of the Red Wings.

During the 1998–99 NHL season, the Red Wings led the Western Conference's Central Division, finishing the year with a 43–32–7 win–loss–tie record after being eliminated from the play-offs by the Colorado Avalanche in the Western Conference Semifinals. Early in the 1999–2000 season, the Red Wings are off to a good start, leading their division with a 7–1–1 record thus far, and the team is expected to make the play-offs in the spring of 2000.

After his tenure with the Buffalo Sabres, Bowman decided it was unfair to his family to uproot them each time he began working for a new team. After the Penguins hired him, he commuted for a while between his home in a suburb of Buffalo and Pittsburgh. Upon resuming coaching, he began staying in hotels or renting places to live during the hockey season, visiting his family when his schedule permitted. Although his job demands that Bowman spend time away from his wife and children, he is, according to those who know him, extremely devoted to them. He has been married for over 30 years to Suella; their five children—Alicia, David, Stanley, and the twins Nancy and Bob, who are the youngest—are all in their 20s. — O.J.S.

Suggested Reading: *Chicago Tribune* Sports p12 June 2, 1997, with photos; *Los Angeles Times* C p1+ May 12, 1996, with photo; *New York Times*

VIII p4 Oct. 20, 1991, B p12 June 2, 1992, B p11 June 6, 1995, C p5 June 9, 1997; *New York Times* (on-line) June 15, 1998, June 17, 1998, June 18, 1998; *Sporting News* p50 Oct. 20, 1979, with photo, p31 Feb. 3, 1986, with photos; *Sports Illustrated* p80 Apr. 21, 1980, with photos, p58+ May 10, 1993, with photos, p12+ Dec. 12, 1994, with photos, p98+ Feb. 2, 1998, with photo; *Village Voice* p125 June 17, 1997; *Washington Post* B p1+ June 15, 1998, with photos

Lee Breuer/Courtesy of Mabou Mines Theater Company

Breuer, Lee

(BROO-er)

1937(?)– Theater director and playwright.
Address: c/o Mabou Mines Theater Company,
150 First Ave., New York, NY 10009

He depicted a torrential storm and a shipwreck by having a toy helicopter crash on stage in a 1979 production of *The Tempest* for the New York Shakespeare Festival. He reconfigured Shakespeare's *King Lear* by reversing the genders of the characters and setting the action in the American South of the 1950s, with scenes unfolding in a rustic kitchen and at a backyard barbecue. In *The Warrior Ant* (1988), he used music from cultures around the globe, more than 100 performers, and traditional Japanese puppetry techniques rarely seen in the West to tell an epic story about an insect. The avant-garde playwright and director whose imagination spawned these innovations is Lee Breuer, whom Ross Wetzsteon described in the *Village Voice* (May 19, 1987) as "pure artist/hustler, pure director/writer, pure

pop/classicist, pure guru/charlatan, pure New York/California—a one-man avant-garde—jive theoretician, auteur-terrible, funky shaman—the bad boy of Mabou Mines—the Jerzy Grotowski/Busby Berkeley, Antonin Artaud/Cecil B. De Mille of the American theater."

Breuer, who began working in theater in the late 1950s, is a living institution of the American avant-garde, having amassed a highly original body of work that explores the essence of theater as a form of expression. He has won many grants, fellowships, and awards from philanthropic organizations and universities, including, in 1997, a so-called genius grant from the John D. and Catherine T. MacArthur Foundation. He and Mabou Mines, the troupe he co-founded in 1970, have also received numerous Obie Awards, which recognize excellence in Off-Broadway theater. Despite critical acclaim, however, Breuer—like many artists whose work is considered experimental—has spent much of his career working in relative obscurity, without much financial success or mainstream recognition.

Lee Breuer was born Asher Leopold in about 1937 in Philadelphia, Pennsylvania, and spent his first years in Wilmington, Delaware. His father was drafted into the marines during World War II, and during that period the family moved from one military base to another along the eastern seaboard and in the American South, living briefly in such places as Camp Lejune, in North Carolina; Long Island, New York; and Virginia. The Leopolds eventually settled in Portland, Oregon, when Breuer was about 10, and for several years afterward they enjoyed some stability, thanks to his father's budding career as an architect. According to Breuer, his father would have preferred a career as a painter, and his mother, a homemaker, wanted to be a writer. "She was a flamboyant literary type who projected her dreams onto me," Breuer told Wetzsteon, "so the message I was getting from her when I was being programmed was—become an artist." Several years after the family moved to Portland, Breuer's father designed a department store. Against his advice, the owners eliminated a number of safety features to cut costs, and as a result, a child was killed in the store when an elevator door did not close properly. According to Breuer, his father felt responsible for the child's death. Shortly thereafter, the family moved to Venice, California, where Breuer's father grew ill and died, when Breuer was 16. After his father's death his mother suffered an emotional breakdown; for three months she felt too depressed to get out of bed. As Breuer recalled to Wetzsteon, "She'd gotten married when she was 17, she knows it's too late to start another life without my father, and this doctor—I'm 16 years old, my father's died practically yesterday—and this doctor, he shoves a paper at me and asks me to sign it. It's to commit my own mother. Sixteen years old, man. I've had two lives—before 16 and after 16. Sometimes I think I'm so hooked into 16 I'll never get past it."

Left on his own, Breuer attended the University of California at Los Angeles (UCLA) and supported himself by working as a parking attendant. At first, Breuer told Wetzsteon, he was interested only in UCLA's film department and the beaches near the school. Then he took a course that examined works by the French existentialists Albert Camus and Jean Paul Sartre, the playwrights Jean Anouilh and Jean Genet, the radical theater theorist Antonin Artaud, and the Irish playwright Samuel Beckett. That course, in his words, "totally changed" his life. Breuer began writing plays, winning some acclaim at and around UCLA; he earned a campus award for best playwright two years in succession.

Meanwhile, Breuer, who never completed his degree, met Ruth Maleczech, whom he would later marry. The two drifted around California, thinking that they would eventually make their way to Paris, where Breuer hoped to follow in the footsteps of Camus. Instead, the couple settled in San Francisco and began working with the San Francisco Mime Troupe and the San Francisco Actors' Workshop. The latter soon hired Breuer as a director and Maleczech as an actress. During the rest of the late 1950s and the early 1960s, Breuer directed several productions for the Actors' Workshop, including plays by Bertolt Brecht, Genet, and Harold Pinter.

In 1965 Breuer and Maleczech went to Europe, where they traveled extensively and worked with the Berliner Ensemble, in Germany, and the Polish Laboratory Theater, an acclaimed institution headed at that time by the director and theoretician Jerzy Grotowski. The couple then settled in Paris, where, in about 1968, Breuer and a group of expatriate American artists began toying with the idea of forming a theater collective.

After returning to the U.S., in 1970, and settling in New York City, Breuer and his circle—which included Maleczech, the actress and director JoAnne Akalaitis, the composer Philip Glass, and the actor David Warrilow—followed through on that idea and founded Mabou Mines Theater Company, naming it for a mining town in Nova Scotia near where they had worked on a theater piece. For the rest of the 1970s, the company's de facto home base was the Joseph Papp Public Theater; they later relocated to the New Victory Theater. Breuer was the dominant creative force behind the troupe for much of this period; he served as its primary writer, director, and producer, while the other members served as actors and in supporting capacities.

The company's productions from this time tended to be small in scale and visually minimal. They included, most notably, a trilogy consisting of *The Red Horse Animation* (1970), *The B. Beaver Animation* (1975), and *The Shaggy Dog Animation* (1978). All three works were written and directed by Breuer and developed over years of rehearsals and workshop performances, and thus their dates are approximate. They combine to form an epic about the adventures of a female dog who is an aspiring filmmaker. In an article for the *Village Voice* (August 2, 1976), Terry Curtis Fox described the

plays as "investigations into the basic problems of theatrical perception." He continued, "*The Red Horse* describes the coming to consciousness of the beast; *The B-Beaver*, an attempt to organize experience. *The Shaggy Dog* . . . is about an effort to alter a given reality." *The Shaggy Dog Animation*, which was also about feminism and rock-'n'-roll, earned an Obie Award for best new American play for the 1977–78 season. (The Obies are awarded by their founder, the *Village Voice*.) With a portion of the $1,000 prize money, Breuer created an emergency fund for indigent Off-Broadway actors. Thanks to the trilogy, Breuer developed a reputation as an enfant terrible of the avant-garde theater.

By the late 1970s Breuer's role in Mabou Mines had begun to change. Due to fissures in the group that arose, in large part, from the emergence of other members as creative forces in their own right, Breuer had to relinquish some of his power to determine the troupe's agenda. Concurrently, Akalaitis and Maleczech began creating and directing their own works, and Warrilow and Glass left the company to focus on their own pursuits. Daunted by the new dynamics of the troupe, Breuer left the company briefly and began taking on other work.

In 1979 Breuer directed a production of *The Tempest* (1979) for the New York Shakespeare Festival, which is produced in Central Park by the Public Theater. The production was widely panned, and many critics took particular issue with Breuer's decision to have Raul Julia, who was playing Prospero, simulate a shipwreck by crashing a toy helicopter. "At first I thought it was terrible," Joseph Papp, the founder and director of the Public Theater, told Wetzsteon, speaking of the production as a whole. "It was too far away from Shakespeare, too contemporary—something else entirely. But over the course of the run I began to see what Lee was driving at. By the fourth week Shakespeare even began to poke his nose out. If he'd had another couple of weeks it would've turned out okay. Lee's the kind of genius who has to mull over a piece, work on it, let it grow."

Breuer wrote and directed *Prelude to a Death in Venice* (1980), which was performed at the Public Theater. The work, which drew partly on Breuer's relationship to his father and his feelings about his identity as a Jew, won him an Obie Award for playwriting for the 1979–80 season. Breuer has repeatedly culled material from his life for use in his plays. "I call it autography rather than autobiography," he told Mel Gussow for the *New York Times* (February 10, 1997). "It's my autograph. My modus operandi is to make metaphors and fantasize over psychological events in my own life."

Breuer also wrote and directed *Sister Suzie Cinema* (1980), a 30-minute doo-wop opera, on which he collaborated with the composer Bob Telson and a group of African-American actors. In the early 1980s Breuer and Telson collaborated again, on what became perhaps Breuer's best-known work. Inspired by one of his fundamental beliefs—that society needs theater—and based on Sophocles' tragedy *Oedipus at Colonus*, Breuer's show, entitled *The Gospel at Colonus*, is a musical in which the story of the classical play is set during a contemporary African-American Pentecostal church service, complete with gospel choirs. "All of us who are really involved with theater on a spiritual basis are in it for catharsis, but where is it [in theater today]?" Breuer told Wendy Smith for the *New York Times* (March 20, 1988). "The more I understood Greek theater, the more I began to feel . . . that the important element in it for me was its spirituality. I lived in Greece for a year, and it was hard to walk around those theaters, with the altar in the center, and not know that they were basically churches. So I began trying to find a language for this feeling. I think all theater is finding the right translation for your audience, and I wanted to translate Greek tragedy into an American language for American viewers. I wanted to show them: This is the cathartic experience, this is what Aristotle was talking about, this is what Greek tragedy is, this is what our entire Western dramatic culture is based on. You begin to understand catharsis by experiencing it." Breuer continued, "What I found was that the Pentecostal, Afro-American church, which is part of the American language, gives you a living experience of catharsis in the world today. I wasn't trying to say anything about gospel, because I don't want to presume that I know anything about it. I was trying to say something about classical theater. Gospel was a metaphor, gospel was an inspiration, gospel was the living repository of an emotion and a spirituality that had become academic and archeological in our theater."

The show, which grew out of Telson's score and rehearsals with a group of African-American actors and gospel singers, began as a 30-minute work with two songs, one actor, and five singers, and it was produced in this form at P.S. 122, a venue for experimental performance on Manhattan's Lower East Side. Breuer and Telson continued to develop the script and the score, respectively, during workshops and small regional productions, and both the length and the cast of the piece grew. Through those engagements, Breuer discovered that there were structural parallels as well between Greek tragedy and African-American Pentecostal church services. "The Greek chorus became a choir. The first actor in Greek tragedy was a preacher-style narrator. Little by little the whole concept came," he recalled to Peter Cieply for *Stagebill* (on-line). The work eventually became a full-length musical featuring a dozen songs and a cast of 60, among them the actor Morgan Freeman.

The Gospel at Colonus became something of a sensation; it opened at the Brooklyn Academy of Music's Next Wave Festival in 1983 to much fanfare and won an Obie Award for best musical in the 1983–84 season. It toured the country before playing on Broadway at the Lunt-Fontanne Theater, in 1988. The work was a departure of sorts for Breuer in that it was highly accessible and appeared to be populist entertainment. It was also the first large-scale production in which Breuer worked with an African-American cast. With *Gospel*, Breuer said, as quoted by William Harris in the *New York Times* (January 21, 1990), "I wanted to make a statement that a white man can work not just with a bunch of black intellectuals who have gone to Yale, but with the real performers—that I could respect their art and they could respect mine, and that we would not rip each other off, thus disproving the idea that never the twain shall meet. In other words, that I could make an integration statement in terms of this country by making it happen on stage."

Breuer again collaborated with Telson on *The Warrior Ant* (1988), a visually spectacular musical produced by and performed at the Brooklyn Academy of Music. The play, which Breuer wrote and directed, told the story of an ant who goes on a quest to find the meaning of his existence. "*Warrior Ant*'s my attempt to write a large epic work that'll hold up as literature as well as theater," he told Ross Wetzsteon. "It's patterned after *The Aeneid* and *The Inferno*, but yeah, I guess the ant is me. I wanna know more about why I wanna stay alive." Although Breuer also compared the play's narrative to that of the classic Chinese text *Journey to the West*, the production was most noted for its fusion of cultural elements from the world over and its large cast, which consisted of more than 100 singers, dancers, puppeteers, and musicians. The stage action was accompanied by a score drawn from an eclectic array of sources, among them traditional African, Caribbean, Brazilian, Japanese, Native American, and Middle Eastern music. Although the show incorporated live belly dancers, its characters were portrayed chiefly by various types of puppets. The lead performer was the Japanese Bunraku puppet master Tamamatsu Yoshida, who operated a puppet designed as an 18th-century human character. Breuer had first encountered Bunraku puppetry in Paris in 1968. "I was completely totaled, instantly," he recalled to Eileen Blumenthal for the *New York Times* (October 16, 1988). "It was the most brilliant theater I'd ever seen—and still is."

In the 1990s Breuer continued to work sporadically with Mabou Mines. To the distaste of some purists, he directed the company in a production of *Lear* (1990) that transformed Shakespeare's *King Lear* into a drama revolving around a southern matriarch, played by Maleczech. While using Shakespeare's original text, Breuer reversed the gender of every character in the play except the fool—a man in Shakespeare's version, the character dressed in women's clothes in Breuer's adaptation. "The key issue in *Lear* is the relationship between love and power," Breuer told Harris. "I feel the essential question confronting women in America today is can they have love and power at the same time." "I'm doing a work about an aging matriarch," Breuer added, "a classic mother figure in a country where the mother is an essential archetype. The women's movement has been the most important political event in my life. I can see how it has changed my mother, age 86, Ruth, age 51, and my daughter, age 20. Most of my large work has a political intent, but I don't mount works with leftist dialogue and fist-shaking. I try to mount the work *as* a political statement, not that *says* the political statement." *Lear* collected four Obie Awards for its performers.

By this time many critics had noted changes in Breuer's aesthetic since Mabou Mines' founding. Whereas he had created minimalist productions in the 1970s, during the 1980s and with *Lear*, his works were more elaborate and featured elements culled from international sources and popular culture. "In the '70s I felt in the middle of the minimalist-conceptualist tradition," he told Ross Wetzsteon for the *Village Voice* (May 26, 1987). "But I never rode it very far. I jumped ship. I don't even pay lip service anymore. I've made a 180 degree turn." With regard to drawing inspiration from an array of cultures, Breuer told Allan Wallach for New York *Newsday* (October 16, 1988), "I think that I have a little bit of a bone to pick with American theater in that I don't think it reflects American culture." He continued, "What I really feel is that we have a kind of theater that reflects only a small part of American culture; it doesn't reflect the African-based American culture and it doesn't reflect the Asian-based culture, and it *certainly* doesn't reflect the South American culture."

Despite his critical successes, Breuer, like other members of Mabou Mines, still struggled financially. By the late 1980s he had begun to express increasing frustration with the state of American theater and his own place in relation to the mainstream. "You don't get established in the avant garde. If you're established it means that you're no longer part of the avant garde," he told Wallach. In 1990, at about the time that *Lear* was being performed, he said that the show would be his last major one with the company. "This 20th anniversary is an enormous turning point," he said, as quoted by Harris. "I'm not saying I'm leaving the theater, but I am taking a back seat. I would like to continue to produce with Mabou Mines, but I have to pull back. I can do tiny, little stuff like I did in the 1970's, or commercial work that I can be proud of. As we go into the era of Helms"—the conservative North Carolina Republican senator Jesse A. Helms, who has long opposed funding for the arts— "radical work becomes more useless: less funded, less received, less listened to."

Breuer wrote and directed *The Quantum* (1991), and *The MahabharANTa* (1992), which saw the courageous warrior ant battle the Republican White House. In 1995 he wrote and directed *An Epidog*, a play that returned to the dog character from his early trilogy. That work won a Fund for New American Plays Award, and Julie Archer and Barbara Pollitt earned Obie Awards for their performances in the show in the 1995–96 season. In 1996 Breuer directed an adaptation by Liza Lorwin of J. M. Barrie's *Peter Pan*, based on Barrie's 1911 novelization of his 1904 play. The resulting production, *Peter and Wendy*, featured Karen Kandel as the narrator and Wendy, and she also performed the voices of Peter Pan, Tinker Bell, Captain Hook, Mrs. Darling, and the Lost Boys, all of whom were represented by puppets, many of them in the Bunraku style. In a review for the *New York Times* (February 7, 1997), Peter Marks praised the production: "Breuer's highly theatrical flourishes turn out to be ideally suited to a children's story." Kandel won an Obie Award for her performance in the 1996–97 season.

In an ongoing project, Breuer has recently reorganized his plays into three books, and he repeatedly revises all of them. Several of Breuer's works were published years ago. *The Red Horse Animation*, *The B. Beaver Animation*, and *Shaggy Dog Animation* were published together in 1979 as *Animations: A Trilogy for Mabou Mines*. A second collection, *Sister Suzie Cinema, Collected Poems and Performances, 1976–1986*, came out in 1986. Breuer has often maintained that he is first and foremost a writer. "I've been using theater to hide that I'm really a writer," he told Wetzsteon for the *Village Voice* (May 19, 1987). "I wanna confront the literary world as well as the theater world. I wanna stand defenseless as a writer." Breuer has also maintained that his most recent productions have been attempts to create a new kind of theater. "The theater I've created is both Eastern and Western because Western theater alone is too psychologically based," he told Rachel Shteir for the *Village Voice* (January 30, 1996).

In addition to his MacArthur grant, Breuer is the recipient of awards, grants, or other honors from the National Endowment for the Arts, the Guggenheim Foundation, and the Rockefeller Foundation, among many other sources. He has taught theater and directing at Harvard University, in Cambridge, Massachusetts, and Yale University, in New Haven, Connecticut. He lives in New York City with Ruth Maleczech, who is the mother of two of his five children. — Y.P.

Suggested Reading: *New York Times* II p5+ Oct. 16, 1988, with photo, II p5+ Jan. 21, 1990, with photos, C p3 Feb. 7, 1997, with photo; *Village Voice* p19+ May 19, 1987, with photos, p33+ May 26, 1987, with photos, p68 Jan. 30, 1996, with photo

Selected Plays: as writer and director—*The Red Horse Animation*, 1970; *The B. Beaver Animation*, 1975; *The Shaggy Dog Animation*, 1978; *Prelude to a Death in Venice*, 1980; *Sister Suzie Cinema*, 1980; *The Gospel at Colonus*, 1983; *The Warrior Ant*, 1988; *The Quantum*, 1991; *The MahabharANTa*, 1992; *Epidog*, 1995; as director—*The Tempest*, 1979; *Lear*, 1990; *Peter and Wendy*, 1996

Selected Books: *Animations: A Trilogy for Mabou Mines*, 1979; *Sister Suzie Cinema, Collected Poems and Performances, 1976–1986*, 1986

Courtesy of Rogers & Cowan

Bruckheimer, Jerry

1945– Film producer. Address: c/o Jerry Bruckheimer Films Inc., 1631 10th St., Santa Monica, CA 90404

During his 13-year partnership with Don Simpson, Jerry Bruckheimer produced some of the highest-grossing action films of the past two decades, and he has continued to do so since 1996, when his collaboration with Simpson ended. As of mid-1999, Jennifer Wilson reported in *Los Angeles Magazine* (July 1999), his films had grossed more than $3 billion worldwide. Bruckheimer's first major hit was *Flashdance* (1983), whose earnings far surpassed the expectations of its parent company, Paramount Pictures. Bruckheimer and Simpson followed that success with two megahits—*Beverly Hills Cop* (1984) and *Top Gun* (1986), the latter of which ranks as one of most profitable pictures in Paramount's history. In the mid-1990s, after the somewhat disappointing *Days of Thunder* (1990), Simpson and Bruckheimer bounced back with such action films as *Bad Boys* (1995) and *Crimson Tide* (1995) and with the drama *Dangerous Minds* (1995). When Bruckheimer and Simpson ended their partnership, amid rumors about Simpson's serious personal problems, many Hollywood insiders expressed misgivings about how Bruckheimer would fare without his partner. The success of Bruckheimer's 1997 blockbuster *Con Air* dispelled such doubts.

The son of German immigrants, Jerry Bruckheimer was born in about 1945 in Detroit, Michigan. As a youngster he enjoyed watching motion pictures at Detroit's Motor City theater. "I started dreaming about Hollywood when I was a child," he

told a staff writer for *Mirabella* (February 1990). "L.A. seemed like somewhere I thought I'd never get to, a place of golden sunshine with movie stars and palm trees." Bruckheimer also became interested in photography at an early age, and he won some local prizes for his work. By his own account, he was "always an organizer." "I put hockey teams together when I was a kid," he recalled to Lea Russo for *boxoffice magazine* (on-line). "I could always get people motivated and team them up and organize them."

After receiving a bachelor's degree from the University of Arizona, Bruckheimer took a job in the mail room of an advertising agency. He eventually worked his way up in that company and began producing television commercials. Those efforts led him to venture into full-length film production. Among the films in which he had a hand are *Farewell My Lovely* (1975), *March or Die* (1977), and *Defiance* (1980). Earlier, at a screening of the film *The Harder They Come*, in 1973, Bruckheimer had met Don Simpson, who was then a studio publicist. Soon afterward Bruckheimer and his first wife, Bonnie, divorced, and he and Simpson, who grew up in Alaska, moved into a house together in Laurel Canyon, California.

In 1979 Paramount Pictures hired Bruckheimer on a freelance basis to produce the film *American Gigolo* (1980). Despite its dismal critical reception, *American Gigolo*, written and directed by Paul Schrader, attracted a large audience, undoubtedly because of its frank treatment of a formerly taboo subject—male prostitution—and because its young star, Richard Gere, performed one scene in the nude. Simpson had been hired by Paramount in about 1976 as a writer, and he had risen quickly up the company's ranks, eventually securing the title of president of Worldwide Production. In 1982 Paramount's chairpersons, Barry Diller and Michael Eisner, removed Simpson from his executive position because of his alleged drug problems. Because of his rare talent, however, Diller and Eisner allowed him to continue producing films for Paramount.

The first film that Simpson produced after his removal from Paramount's staff was *Flashdance*, on which he collaborated with Bruckheimer. The story of a beautiful, lithe, female construction worker (played by Jennifer Beals) who becomes a dancer through self-discipline and determination, *Flashdance* cost only $7.5 million to make, and Paramount did not expect it to become a hit. Nevertheless, it earned $95 million at U.S. box offices—an enormous profit. In addition, the *Flashdance* soundtrack became a best-seller, and the clothing that the Beals character wore sparked a major fashion trend. "It was all by accident," Bruckheimer told Russo. "[The clothing and music] weren't designed. What's interesting is that you think we're so smart. We were way behind the eight ball. As an example, the record company shipped only 60,000 albums to the entire country. They were gone within one hour of the picture opening. Nobody had the foresight to see that [it] was going to be a success—including us."

Flashdance was followed by the even more popular action-comedy *Beverly Hills Cop* (1984), which stars the comedian Eddie Murphy. Bruckheimer and Simpson produced its sequel, *Beverly Hills Cop II* (1987), too. In between those films, Bruckheimer and Simpson produced *Top Gun* (1986), a story about a top U.S. Navy fighter pilot who falls in love with one of his instructors. In addition to establishing the young actor Tom Cruise as a major star, *Top Gun* grossed more than $300 million in worldwide ticket sales, thus becoming one of Paramount's most successful films ever.

Together, Bruckheimer and Simpson were named producers of the year by the National Association of Theater Owners in 1985 and 1988. In 1988 they were also named motion-picture showmen of the year by the Publicists Guild of America. Speculating in the *Wall Street Journal* (January 26, 1996) about the reasons for Bruckheimer and Simpson's success, Thomas R. King and John Lippman noted that "while the typical movie producer puts together a film's creative team, they did much more: They got involved at the ground level, coming up with ideas and hunkering down over scripts, music, and other creative details." Simpson's specialty was the fine-tuning of scripts; Bruckheimer, according to King and Lippman, is "adept at pulling all of a film's elements together and polishing the all-important 'look' and the music for their movies." Early in 1990 the partners signed a contract with Paramount that allocated several hundred million dollars for their next five films and guaranteed Bruckheimer and Simpson an unusually high percentage of the net profits of those movies. The contract was touted as the one of the most lucrative in the history of Hollywood filmmaking.

Bruckheimer and Simpson's next film, *Days of Thunder*, which starred the now immensely popular Tom Cruise, was released later in 1990. Described as a variation on *Top Gun*, featuring race-car drivers rather than pilots, *Days of Thunder* pulled in over $200 million in box-office receipts around the world. Nevertheless, Paramount regarded the film as a disappointment because U.S. audiences had been relatively small. Moreover, rumors of extravagant spending on the set of *Days of Thunder* circulated throughout the film industry, and several articles and a BBC documentary that were highly critical of Bruckheimer and Simpson appeared. "We opened ourselves up to a lot of articles that had an agenda," Bruckheimer explained to Rick Lyman for the *New York Times* (June 25, 1997), referring to several interviews that they had given willingly. "We didn't suspect a thing. We believed what they told us about what kind of articles they wanted to do." He and Simpson became, in Lyman's words, "symbols of Hollywood's bloated budgets and creative torpor."

Bruckheimer and Simpson's damaged reputation, coupled with *Days of Thunder's* comparatively small audiences, led Paramount to attempt renegotiating the duo's contract. The new contract was significantly less favorable to Bruckheimer and Simpson than their original agreement, and the men rejected it. After leaving Paramount, they joined the Walt Disney Co., where two of their former Paramount associates, Michael Eisner and Jeffrey Katzenberg, were then in charge. According to Lyman, Disney offered the partners a contract that was "potentially as lucrative [as their original Paramount contract], but left the studio final word on which movies would actually be made." "It took us a while to regenerate our development," Bruckheimer told Russo. "Once we moved studios, a lot of the projects we had got stalled. . . . When we came to Disney, they were making a different type of movie than we had developed. They were making soft comedies . . . [not] the kind of pictures we were good at."

One of the projects that Bruckheimer and Simpson had been working on for some time was *The Ref*, about a kidnapper and his two insufferable hostages. Lyman described the film as "a small dark comedy . . . completely unlike [the partners'] usual big, star-driven movies." "We'd gotten trapped into this situation where we were expected to make these huge, event movies," Bruckheimer told Lyman. "We decided to go back to making the kind of movies we wanted to make." A Bruckheimer/Simpson production, *The Ref* (1994) was co-produced by Ron Bozman, Richard LaGravenese, and Jeff Weiss and executive-produced by Bruckheimer and Simpson. The film cost relatively little to produce, and while it didn't gross nearly as much the partners' blockbusters, it placed fourth in American box-office receipts in March 1994.

Bruckheimer and Simpson released three successful films in 1995: *Crimson Tide*, a story of conflict between a submarine captain (Gene Hackman) and his second-in-command (Denzel Washington); *Dangerous Minds*, which stars Michelle Pfeiffer as a novice schoolteacher in a tough, urban school; and *Bad Boys*, a comical story about two Miami cops who must contend with the theft of drugs confiscated in their precinct.

Meanwhile, Bruckheimer and Simpson had begun having problems as partners. Simpson's weight, alcohol, and drug problems had become well known in the film industry, and he was often away, receiving treatment at a rehabilitation center. Rumors about his involvements with prostitutes had also surfaced. In 1995 an associate of Simpson's, Stephen W. Ammerman, was found dead of a drug overdose near the swimming pool at Simpson's home. Shortly after that incident, Bruckheimer announced that he would end his partnership with Simpson and continue working on his own. "It was coming for a long time," Amy Wallace quoted him as saying in the *Los Angeles Times* (May 11, 1998, on-line). "Don's interests lay elsewhere. And I loved what I was doing. And he drifted from it."

On January 19, 1996, during the shooting of *The Rock*, starring Sean Connery, Simpson was found dead in his home. According to the autopsy report, he had died of heart failure caused at least in part by his use of both legal and illegal drugs. Bruckheimer dedicated *The Rock* (1996) to Simpson; a popular film that received mixed reviews, it is the last picture that he and Simpson completed together. Bruckheimer has said that if he develops any of the ideas that he and Simpson discussed, he will produce them under both their names. Simpson, he told Wallace, "transferred an enormous amount of knowledge to me during our partnership from 1982 to 1996. I have a lot of him in me that he taught me." "I miss him," he said to Wallace. "I think about him all the time."

The first film that Bruckheimer made after Simpson's death was *Con Air*, which Lyman described as "another multimillion-dollar action extravaganza, loud, clever, and violent." Starring Nicolas Cage, John Malkovich, John Cusack, and Steve Buscemi, the film focuses on a prison transport plane that is hijacked by the convicts. "I wanted to make a film that was really an odyssey," Bruckheimer told Russo. "All [Nicolas] Cage's character wants to do is go home to his wife and child, and he's caught in this horrendous situation. To me it's like classic Greek tragedy . . . and I love that." The film earned $50 million in its first two weeks and, eventually, $300 million worldwide.

Bruckheimer's most recent films are *Enemy of the State*, a techno-thriller directed by Tony Scott and starring Will Smith, and *Armageddon*, in which the character played by Bruce Willis saves the Earth from destruction by a Texas-size meteor. Both were released in 1998 and were commercially successful. *Armageddon* was Bruckheimer's third collaboration with the director Michael Bay, who also directed *Bad Boys* and *The Rock*.

When asked where he gets the ideas for his films, Bruckheimer told Amy Wallace that they come from "everywhere." "They come from what [journalists] write about, from novels, writers' heads, our heads," he said. "Being able to recognize a good idea—that's the hard part. Or what we're really good at here is taking an idea that maybe you've seen before and putting a new spin on it." His knack for creating extremely popular action films notwithstanding, Bruckheimer told Wallace that his job can be difficult. "When you do it right, it looks really easy, seamless. But it takes a lot of pain and a lot of brain cells to get it there, even if the subject matter isn't what you'd consider something brilliant. A picture that you might not think is a great movie . . . [might entertain] millions and millions of people. A lot of people try to get into this genre. . . . They get in and say, 'My God, this is really hard.'" Regarding the changes he has seen in the film industry in the past two decades and what is still to come, he told Lyman, "It's absolutely frightening what you can do now. The

envelope has been pushed so far. . . . Anything you can see or imagine, you can put on film in a cost-effective manner these days. Technically, there are very few barriers." According to Lyman, the producer usually has approximately 40 film projects in the making, but very few of them reach fruition. "I try not to ever give up on any of them, but that's the reality," Bruckheimer said.

Jerry Bruckheimer lives in an elegant home in West Los Angeles with his wife, Linda Balahoutis, a magazine editor, and a daughter from her previous marriage. In his free time he enjoys running and playing pick-up games of ice hockey at a local rink. Rick Lyman described the producer as "exud[ing] calm, health, and thoughtfulness, a far cry from the wild days when he and Mr. Simpson whizzed around Southern California in black Porsches, helping make superstars of Tom Cruise and Eddie Murphy." — C.P.

Suggested Reading: *Boxoffice* (on-line) May 1997, with photo; *Los Angeles Times* (on-line) May 11, 1998; *New York Times* III p1+ Apr. 14, 1991 with photos, C p11+ Mar. 14, 1994, with photo, C p1+ June 25, 1997, with photo; *Time* p78 June 9, 1997, with photo; *Wall Street Journal* A p1+ Jan. 26, 1996, with photo

Selected Films: *Con Air*, 1997; *Enemy of the State*, 1998; *Armageddon*, 1998; with Don Simpson—*Flashdance*, 1983; *Beverly Hills Cop*, 1984; *Top Gun*, 1986; *Beverly Hills Cop II*, 1987; *Days of Thunder*, 1990; *The Ref*, 1994; *Dangerous Minds*, 1995; *Bad Boys*, 1995; *Crimson Tide*, 1995; *Dangerous Minds*, 1995; *The Rock*, 1996

Buffett, Jimmy

Dec. 25, 1946– Musician; writer; entrepreneur. Address: c/o Margaritaville Records, 54 Music Sq. E., Nashville, TN 37203-4315

Perhaps for lack of a better way of characterizing his unique combination of country and western, calypso, conga, and Cuban music, Jimmy Buffett's musical style has been named for Key West, the famous south Florida town where it originated. "People began to call it the Key West Sound" after Buffett's third album came out, in 1974, Gordon Chaplin wrote for the *Washington Post* (March 20, 1977)—even though, as Chaplin pointed out, "there was no one else in Key West that could play it." Buffett's career as a recording artist peaked with his sixth album, *Changes in Latitudes, Changes in Attitudes* (1977), which includes his perenially popular song "Margaritaville." While his subsequent albums have not been nearly as successful, Buffett has remained remarkably popular as a concert artist, and he has attracted a huge fol-

Frank Capri/Archive Photos

Jimmy Buffett

After earning a B.S. degree, in 1969, Buffett lived for a short time in New Orleans, Louisiana. "My age of innocence ended when I moved into the [city's] French Quarter," he told Harrington. "I came from a very Catholic background, and I had been pretty sheltered." Buffett began playing guitar and singing with a band, but he was unable to make ends meet. Often, he would steal food from supermarkets. "I was a good shoplifter," he acknowledged to *Time* (April 18, 1977). Although, he told Harrington, he found musical inspiration in what he called the "melting pot of musical talent" in New Orleans, he eventually "had to face the facts": he would have to live in New York, Los Angeles, or Nashville to make it in the music business. "I had an offer to go to L.A. but I only had enough gas money to go to Nashville," he said.

Once settled in Nashville, Buffett began performing with a group called the Now Generation. Thanks to his having studied journalism in college, he also landed work as a Nashville correspondent for *Billboard* magazine, and that job helped him form a network of contacts in the recording industry. Buffett eventually established himself as a solo country-and-western act, and he got a contract with a small company called Barnaby Records. His first album, *Down to Earth* (1970), reportedly sold only a few hundred copies, and Barnaby did not release his second album, *High Cumberland Jubilee*, until 1976—after he had become famous. "The problem with those albums was they didn't fit the mold of country," Buffett told Harrington. "So I was already off on my own path then."

In the early 1970s Buffett moved to Florida and played regularly at a club called Bubba's in the Coconut Grove section of Miami. One day he drove down to Key West with a friend, and he became infatuated with the town's local color and the carefree attitude of its residents. Key West struck him as "completely virgin territory," he recalled to Chaplin. "[It was] completely different than what I'd left behind. Incredible characters, great bars. A different form of life, almost."

One of the first people with whom Buffett became acquainted in Key West was the writer Thomas McGuane, who offered Buffett a room in his guest house. (Later, in 1977, McGuane married Buffett's sister, Laurie.) Within a few weeks, the young musician gave up his regular job in Miami. Partly because he was under the influence of McGuane and McGuane's writer friends, and partly because he was enchanted by the atmosphere of Key West, Buffett began writing narrative songs about love, the sea, and his bohemian lifestyle. He soon became a favorite in several Key West clubs and coffeehouses. "When I found Key West . . . I wasn't really successful yet," he told Harrington. "But I found a lifestyle and I knew that whatever I did I would have to work around my lifestyle. . . . I'm really glad I found what made me happy first."

lowing of fans, dubbed "parrot heads," for the bright, tropical garb they don for his concerts. In addition, he has ventured into other businesses: he owns restaurants, clubs, and gift shops. He is also a writer; his work includes children's books, a collection of autobiographical sketches and short stories, a novel, and a memoir.

Jimmy Buffett was born on December 25, 1946 in Pascagoula, Mississippi. His father, James Delaney Buffett, was a shipwright (one source described him as a naval architect); his mother, Lorraine (Peets) Buffett, was a writer who, in Buffett's words, "had been off to school and all." When Jimmy was two, his parents relocated to Mobile, Alabama. "Mobile was a very southern provincial town, but the great thing about my background was that my grandfather was a sea captain," Buffett told Michelle Genz for the *Miami Herald* (March 28, 1997), as reported on the *Parrot(t)Head* Web site. "My whole family had very Caribbean roots. . . . I would hear those stories about the Caribbean since I was a kid." His grandfather is the subject of Buffett's popular ballad "Son of a Son of a Sailor."

After graduating from St. Ignatius Catholic High School in Spring Hill, Alabama, Buffett enrolled at the Montgomery, Alabama, campus of Auburn University. At some point he transferred to the University of Southern Mississippi, in Hattiesburg, where he studied history and journalism. "I started thinking about writing before I thought about music," he told Richard Harrington for the *Washington Post* (December 17, 1989). "Journalism was the only curriculum that was any fun to study when I went to school." During his college years, Buffett took private guitar lessons and sang at a local pizza place on weekends.

In addition to writers, the people with whom Buffett began to associate in Key West included fishermen, sailors, and other, rather unsavory characters who, it has been inferred, led a "wild" lifestyle and indulged regularly in alcohol and drugs. In some of Buffett's songs, among them "The Great Filling Station Holdup" and "Peanut Butter Conspiracy," both cuts from his album *A White Sports Coat and a Pink Crustacean*, he sings of Key West's purported criminal underlife as if he himself were a part of it. Many of his fans assume that he actually was deeply involved with drugs and that he committed crimes, but Buffett has rejected such notions as gross distortions of reality. "If I had drunk as much and taken as much dope as everybody thinks I have, I would have been dead 10 years ago," he told Lynn Van Matre for the *Chicago Tribune* (October 30, 1983).

Meanwhile, Buffett's fusion of his new, narrative style and the tropical styles of music to which he had been exposed in Key West had been attracting increasing notice throughout the South. By the mid-1970s he was touring extensively. He eventually landed a contract worth $25,000 to make a new album with ABC records in Nashville. That album was *A White Sports Coat and a Pink Crustacean*, which ABC released in 1973. The notable songs from the disc include "He Went to Paris," in which Buffett imagines himself in his old age, and two songs that have become parrot-head favorites: "Rail Road Lady" and "Why Don't We Get Drunk."

Buffett's next album, *Living and Dying in 3/4 Time* (1974), spawned his first single to make the U.S. pop charts—his ballad "Come Monday." Next came *A-1-A* (1974); named for the highway that runs down the east coast of Florida, it contains many lyrical descriptions of Key West. In the title song Buffett says that he lives "three blocks away from highway A-1-A," and that clue to his address led many fans to go to Key West in hopes of finding him. "People came and waited in the trees to see me," the singer told Van Matre. "They even stole the hammock out of my yard. I relish my privacy, and when that stuff started happening, I started thinking maybe it was a mistake to put that in. But it was a genuine feeling at the time." Buffett is sometimes blamed for what many consider to be the overdevelopment of Key West, but the singer has maintained that his presence there was only one of several reasons for the construction and tourism booms that began in the 1980s. He told Van Matre, "People who think that [I am responsible] don't know anything about the history of the town."

In the mid-1970s Thomas McGuane launched his career in film, by writing the screenplay for Frank Perry's *Rancho Deluxe* (1975). Buffett wrote the score for the film, a comedy about two drifters that stars Sam Waterston, Jeff Bridges, and Elizabeth Ashley. Also in 1975 Buffett formed his Coral Reefer Band, with whom he is still performing and recording. Their first album together was *Havana Daydreaming* (1975). It was during Buffett's tour to promote this album that his fans began wearing Hawaiian shirts and brightly colored beachwear to his concerts. During his performances the parrot heads, as they came to be called, gesticulated and danced in ways that they developed specifically for such occasions.

After the release of his 1977 album, *Changes in Latitudes, Changes in Attitudes*, and the resounding success of the single "Margaritaville," which has been described as "a humorous song about alcohol-inspired melancholy and lost love," Buffett signed a four-year contract with ABC records. Then he went on tour as the opening act for the famous rock-'n'-roll band the Eagles. The following year he released two albums, *Son of a Son of a Sailor* and the concert album *Jimmy Buffett Live: You Had to Be There*, both of which went gold. Recalling how he felt about his newfound success, Buffett observed to Harrington, "I didn't know how long I was going to be around. So the first time I ever made any money I went out and paid off all my debts, bought my parents a house, and bought myself a boat. If it all fell apart tomorrow, I could live on that boat and be happy and nobody could take it away from me." Buffett named his boat *Euphoria*.

In 1986, capitalizing on the huge popularity of "Margaritaville," Buffett opened his own club, Jimmy Buffett's Margaritaville, on Duval Street in Key West. The establishment includes a restaurant, a bar, and a souvenir shop that sells the line of casual clothing, labeled Caribbean Soul, that Buffett launched in the mid-1980s. He opened a second Margaritaville club, in New Orleans, a few years later, and a chain of smaller establishments sprang up on several Caribbean islands, including St. Barthélemey, in the French West Indies, where he had been spending a great deal of time. Many people have asked Buffett to reveal the location of the real Margaritaville. *That* Margaritaville is "mostly in people's minds," he told Vernon Silver for the *New York Times* (May 16, 1993). "I wrote [the song] in about seven minutes. I haven't got a clue." Corporations such as Disney and MCA have made attractive offers to buy Buffett's Margaritaville businesses from him, but he has repeatedly refused. "I didn't get this way to be bought up," he told Harrington. "[Corporations] have their fantasy world and I've got mine and they're not the same."

Buffett launched his literary career with *The Jolly Mon* (1988), a children's book about a fisherman who finds a magic guitar floating in the Caribbean Sea. His daughter Savannah Jane was his co-author. He followed *The Jolly Mon* with *Tales from Margaritaville* (1989), a collection of nonfictional anecdotes and fictional stories, some of which correspond loosely with songs on Buffett's 1989 album *Off to See the Lizard*. Most reviewers liked aspects of *Tales from Margaritaville*, and the public—including, undoubtedly, a large number of parrot heads—greeted it enthusiastically as well. It remained on the *New York Times* best-seller list for seven months, and according to Michelle Genz, more than a million and a quarter copies have been sold, half a million of them in hardcover.

Buffett's next collaboration with his daughter Savannah Jane was *Trouble Dolls* (1991), a second book for children. He produced another best-seller with his first novel, *Where Is Joe Merchant?* (1992), a mystery about a famous rock singer, and yet another with his memoir, *A Pirate Looks at Fifty* (1998). In an interview with Beth Levine for *Publishers Weekly* (October 12, 1990), Buffett noted that in some ways, writing lyrics is more difficult for him than writing prose. "I was so used to having to compress thoughts to fit into three verses and a chorus," he explained. "In short stories and novels, I have so much more room to expand and say things that I really can't get into a song."

His ventures outside the music business notwithstanding, Buffett has continued to be active as a musician. In the 1980s he launched his own record label, Margaritaville, which has produced two successful albums of his greatest hits—*Songs You Know by Heart* (1985) and *Boats, Beaches, Bars, and Ballads* (1992)—as well as several less-popular albums of his more recent music. Works by new bands that Buffett has discovered have also been released on the Margaritaville label. In 1987 Buffett signed a lucrative contract with Corona, a Mexican beer company; he sang on their radio commercials, and they promoted his concerts, which continued to sell out in the U.S. "We're selling more tickets than we ever had," Buffett told Vernon Silver in 1993. "If you look at the figures, us and the Grateful Dead will be the biggest-grossing acts on the road."

One of Buffett's recent projects is a musical based on *Don't Stop the Carnival*, a 1965 story by Herman Wouk, the author of the Pulitzer Prize–winning novel *The Caine Mutiny*. Buffett wrote the music and lyrics and Wouk wrote the libretto for the musical, which focuses on a New Yorker who makes a new life for himself on a tropical island. The musical ran for six weeks in Miami in 1997; the album *Don't Stop the Carnival* was released on the Margaritaville label in 1998.

Buffett, who owns homes in Key West and on the islands of St. Barthélemey and Martinique, currently resides in Palm Beach, Florida, with his second wife, Jane, with whom he reunited several years ago after a separation of about seven years. The couple have three children—Savannah Jane, Sarah Delaney, and Cameron—who in 1998 were about 18, five, and four years old, respectively. "I didn't want to raise my children in Key West," Buffett told Michelle Genz. "My wife wouldn't live there. Besides, I spend more time in the islands than I do in Key West these days, and it's easier to get there in my airplane. Palm Beach is closer to the Bahamas. And it has good schools." In his spare time Buffett enjoys sailing and flying seaplanes. An active environmentalist, he is a founding member of the conservation groups Friends of Florida and Save the Manatee. According to Genz, Buffett's name regularly appears on the *Forbes* list of the world's wealthiest entertainers. — C.P.

Suggested Reading: *Chicago Tribune* XIII p5 Oct. 30, 1983, with photo; *New York Times* IX p3 May 16, 1993, with photos; *Parrot(t)Head* Web page; *Publishers Weekly* p39 Oct. 12, 1990; *Washington Post* G p1 Dec. 17, 1989, with photos; *Washington Post Magazine* p14 Mar. 20, 1977, with photos; Buffett, Jimmy. *A Pirate Looks at Fifty*, 1998; Eng, Steve. *Jimmy Buffett: The Man from Margaritaville Revealed*, 1996; Humphrey, Mark and Harris Levine. *The Jimmy Buffett Scrapbook*, 1993; Ryan, Thomas. *The Jimmy Buffett Trivia Book: 501 Questions and Answers for Parrot Heads*, 1998

Selected Recordings: *A White Sport Coat and a Pink Crustacean*, 1973; *Living and Dying in 3/4 Time*, 1974; *A-1-A*, 1974; *Havana Daydreamin'*, 1975; *High Cumberland Jubilee*, 1976; *Changes in Latitudes, Changes in Attitudes*, 1977; *Son of a Son of a Sailor*, 1978; *Jimmy Buffett Live: You Had to Be There*, 1978; *Volcano*, 1979; *Somewhere Over China*, 1981; *Coconut Telegraph*, 1981; *One Particular Harbour*, 1983; *Riddles in the Sand*, 1984; *Songs You Know by Heart*, 1985; *Floridays*, 1986; *Hot Water*, 1988; *Off to See the Lizard*, 1989; *Live-Feeding Frenzy*, 1991; *Boats, Beaches, Bars, and Ballads*, 1992; *Fruitcakes*, 1994; *Barometer Soup*, 1995; *Banana Wind*, 1996; *Christmas Island*, 1996; *Don't Stop the Carnival*, 1998

Selected Books: *The Jolly Mon*, 1988; *Tales from Margaritaville*, 1989; *Trouble Dolls*, 1991; *Where Is Joe Merchant?*, 1992; *A Pirate Looks at Fifty*, 1998

Buscemi, Steve

(boo-SHEH-mee)

Dec. 13, 1957– Actor; director; screenwriter. Address: c/o William Morris Agency, 151 El Camino Dr., Beverly Hills, CA 90212

With his bulging blue eyes, less-than-perfect teeth, wiry build, and jittery screen persona, the actor Steve Buscemi has most often been cast as a crook, a con, or a psychopath. "These characters are so far from the image I have of myself, and yet I always find something within the character to hook into, so I can put in some of myself," the actor told Matthew Gilbert for the *Chicago Tribune* (March 15, 1996). "It's great to have a vehicle to explore the darker side. Everybody has a dark side; they just don't get to express it very much." Buscemi's resumé includes more than 50 films, many of them made by such popular independent filmmakers as the brothers Joel and Ethan Coen, Quentin Tarantino, Jim Jarmusch, and Alexandre Rockwell. In 1996 Buscemi made his debut as a screenwriter and director with his own independent feature,

Victor Malafronte/Archive Photos

Steve Buscemi

Trees Lounge, a story about the kinds of people who frequented a bar in the actor's suburban hometown.

Of Italian and Irish descent, Steve Buscemi was born in the New York City borough of Brooklyn on December 13, 1957. When he was very young, his family moved to the Long Island, New York, town of Valley Stream. With the exception of his role as the Lion in his school's production of *The Wizard of Oz* when he was in the fourth grade, Buscemi did no acting as a child. In fact, throughout his youth he was considered a jock.

At 16 Buscemi obtained a false form of identification and began drinking at Trees Lounge, supporting his habit by working a variety of odd jobs. "I was a real barfly," he told Louis B. Hobson for the *Calgary Sun* (June 1, 1997). "From 16 to 20 . . . I had periods in my life when I hung out at the bar all night, every night. I never saw it as a problem. I had my fake [identification] to protect the bar owners, but everyone knew I was a kid."

In his senior year of high school, Buscemi took his first acting class, and while he enjoyed acting and theater greatly, he doubted that he would ever be able find paying work in the field. His father, a sanitation worker, encouraged him to take a civil-service exam for the job of firefighter. But there were no openings on any nearby fire squads at that time, so Buscemi sold ice cream out of a truck and continued to spend a lot of time at Trees Lounge. He took one semester of liberal-arts classes at a nearby community college but decided that school was not for him.

When he was about 20, Buscemi received $6,000—the result of a suit filed by his family following a traffic accident in which he was involved

at the age of four. He used the small fortune to study acting at the Lee Strasberg school, in New York City, to which he commuted from his parents' home. He took classes with John Strasberg, the son of the school's renowned founder. "I did this scene in class and [John Strasberg] said, 'Wow, you really enjoy this,'" he recalled to Eyal Goldshmid for the *Slant* Web site. "I said, 'Yeah.' And he said, 'Then you should do it.' That really inspired me a lot." Determined to apply himself more seriously to his new pursuit, he moved to New York City. But he did not indulge in too much fantasizing about becoming a movie star. "When I used to allow myself to dream, I'd see myself exactly where I am today, getting great character parts in big movies and small movies," he told Louis Hobson. "On a more realistic level, I hoped I would get a small recurring role in a TV series."

Buscemi did not find work as an actor immediately after completing his courses at the Strasberg school. Having already passed the firefighter's examination, he took a job on the fire squad at Engine Company No. 55, on Broome Street in Manhattan. "[Firefighting] was a great job because it was more than just a way to pay the rent," Buscemi told Gilbert. "It was very fulfilling, as far as work goes. If acting hadn't taken up so much of my time, I'm sure I'd still be on the job, because I liked it a lot."

When asked how he made the transition from firefighting to acting, Buscemi told Goldshmid, "I didn't know how to break into acting, so I did stand-up comedy, because the clubs were there, and you only needed yourself and you could write it." Buscemi was moderately successful at New York clubs such as the Improv, and he used comedy as a springboard for more theatrical work. "I learned that comedy wasn't for me," he told Goldshmid. "The stand-up [work] I found really hard. I realized I liked working with other people. I think I do my best work when I'm with people who are really, really good."

Buscemi teamed up with Mark Boone Jr., a friend from acting school, to develop a comedy revue called *Pawns of Love*. The positive response they received encouraged them to continue working together, and they produced several comic plays at small, hip theaters, such as New York's La Mama. According to Henri Behar on the *Filmscouts* Web site, a *Village Voice* journalist once wrote of them, "Cynical, detached, and yes, cool, Boone-and-Buscemi became the Laurel and Hardy of the 1980s."

Through his theatrical work, Buscemi was recognized by several New York City casting directors, and it was thus that he got his first film role, in the director Bill Sherwood's *Parting Glances*. Buscemi played a rock musician who has been identified as a carrier of the HIV virus, and although his was not one of the lead roles, his performance was said to be the strongest in the film. On the strength of his work in *Parting Glances*, he was cast in several other small, independent films as well as in television shows, among them *Miami*

Vice. Buscemi next won major roles in Martin Scorsese's *New York Stories* (1989), in which he played a performance artist, and Jim Jarmusch's *Mystery Train* (1989), for which he was cast as a hapless barber.

In 1990 Buscemi, beginning what was to be one of the most important collaborations of his career, accepted one of the smaller gangster roles in Joel and Ethan Coen's film *Miller's Crossing.* That highly praised picture was followed by the Coens' *Barton Fink* (1991), in which Buscemi played a chatty bellhop in an eerie Los Angeles hotel. In 1994 Buscemi made an appearance as a beatnik bartender in the Coen brothers' *The Hudsucker Proxy.* He had larger parts in two of the Coens' more recent films, *Fargo* (1996) and *The Big Lebowski* (1998). Speaking of his work with the renowned independent-filmmaker duo, Buscemi told Goldshmid, "If you're going to die [on-screen] for somebody, it may as well be the Coens. In . . . *The Big Lebowski,* I was grateful that I just had a heart attack. In *Fargo,* they not only killed me, but they beat me up and shot me in the face and had an axe."

The role for which Buscemi is perhaps most famous is that of Mr. Pink in Quentin Tarantino's debut film, *Reservoir Dogs* (1992). Tarantino himself originally intended to play the part of Mr. Pink, who is one of a group of men involved in a diamond heist that goes horribly wrong. He changed his mind after seeing a videotape of Buscemi in which the actor, he told Goldshmid, "looked like a criminal." "I auditioned twice [for *Reservoir Dogs*], and I didn't do that great," Buscemi told Goldshmid. "I'm just not a good auditioner. But Quentin saw me, another video of me [at] an audition for a Neil Simon film, . . . and the woman casting that film was also casting *Reservoir Dogs.* . . . So the lesson here to actors is: Go on any audition, even if you feel you're not right or you don't like the film. Just go." Buscemi's performance as Mr. Pink brought a great deal of energy to *Reservoir Dogs.* In the *Washington Post* (October 24, 1992), Hal Hinson wrote, "As Mr. Pink, Buscemi . . . is like an anxiety-seeking missile; the man is wired so tight that his flesh has been burned away, leaving only a set of bones and a pair of pinned eyeballs." After the enormous success of *Reservoir Dogs,* Buscemi was cast in similarly outlandish roles in other independent films, among them the director Robert Rodriguez's *Desperado* (1995) and Gary Fleder's *Things to Do in Denver When You're Dead* (1995). Although these crime films were only moderately successful, they served to display Buscemi's skill at playing slimy underworld types.

Throughout the 1990s Buscemi played other types of roles as well, including one in Alexandre Rockwell's *In the Soup* (1992) and another in Tom DiCillo's *Living in Oblivion* (1995), which satirizes the difficulty that unknown filmmakers experience in trying to produce their first films. "As a shlemiel, Buscemi is perfection," Joseph Gelmis wrote in a *Newsday* (October 2, 1992) review of *In*

the Soup, in which the actor played Nick Reve, a nerdy screenwriter who finds a benefactor from the world of organized crime. Assessing his performance as Reve, Janet Maslin of the *New York Times* (March 17, 1995) described Buscemi as "an actor who ordinarily plays wide-eyed lunatics and whose edginess proves just right for this situation." In the comedy *Living in Oblivion,* Buscemi was cast as a director trying—with limited success—to maintain order during a film shoot.

After working on his own script for more than five years, Buscemi made his screenwriting and directorial debut with *Trees Lounge* (1996), in which he also starred, as an unemployed mechanic whose life is in a downward spiral and who spends much of his time in a Long Island bar. Buscemi told Hobson that of all the films in which he has performed, the largely autobiographical *Trees Lounge* distressed his mother the most. "Because of the nature of most of the films I've been in, she's had to watch me die some pretty excruciating deaths," the actor said. "Yet she wept watching all the tragic things that happen to me in *Trees Lounge.* I think she realizes if I hadn't become an actor, she'd be watching all those things for real." In *Maclean's* (November 11, 1996), Brian D. Johnson wrote, "With an eye reminiscent of [John] Cassavetes or [Robert] Altman, [Buscemi] has cut a diamond-in-the-rough faceted with strong, true performances from a large ensemble cast. And in carving out his own character with transparent honesty, Buscemi reveals the human frailty at the heart of those nasty pulp roles."

Since directing *Trees Lounge,* Buscemi has been commissioned to direct a series of television commercials for the Nike athletic-wear company. He plans to direct more feature films as well. "What I really want to do is direct, because you are involved in every aspect of [the making of a film]. And then seeing the final product on-screen, it is a sense of accomplishment," he told David Fenigsohn for the MSNBC Web site in 1998. Buscemi also said that he felt that his wealth of experience as an actor will help him in his future directing endeavors. "Being an actor doesn't necessarily make you a better director. But it helps to understand what actors go through. Whenever you have a director who understands what actors need, then I think it makes the work go a little more smoothly."

In addition to acting in independent films, Buscemi has worked on much larger-budgeted studio films, such as *Con Air* (1997) and *Armageddon* (1998), both produced by the action-film specialist Jerry Bruckheimer. Although such jobs are lucrative for actors, Buscemi told Fenigsohn that he wasn't "specifically looking to do big action films. . . . It is not like I want to move in that direction. Doing *Armageddon* helps me . . . take the time off and put a lot of care into [my next project], which is not going to be a big money maker for me." The directing project to which Buscemi referred is a film version of Edward Bunker's novel *The Animal Factory* (1977), which is set in the San Quentin prison, in California.

Steve Buscemi lives in New York with his wife, Jo Andres, a performance artist with whom he sometimes collaborates. The couple have a seven-year-old son, Lucian. According to Matthew Gilbert, the real-life Buscemi is "remarkably low-key and modest, without a hint of his frazzled screen persona." — C.P.

Suggested Reading: *Chicago Tribune* L p1 Mar. 15, 1996; *Maclean's* p76 Nov. 11, 1996; MSNBC Web site; *Slant* (on-line)

Selected Films: as actor—*Parting Glances*, 1986; *New York Stories*, 1989; *Mystery Train*, 1989; *Miller's Crossing*, 1990; *Barton Fink*, 1991; *In the Soup*, 1992; *Reservoir Dogs*, 1992; *The Hudsucker Proxy*, 1994; *Pulp Fiction*, 1994; *Things to Do in Denver When You're Dead*, 1995; *Living in Oblivion*, 1995; *Desperado*, 1995; *Fargo*, 1996; *Con Air*, 1997; *The Big Lebowski*, 1998; *The Wedding Singer*, 1998; *Armageddon*, 1998; as screenwriter and director—*Trees Lounge*, 1996

John Gillan/Courtesy of Governor's Office

Bush, Jeb

Feb. 11, 1953– Governor of Florida. Address: c/o Office of the Governor, Tallahassee, FL 32300-0001

In his first, unsuccessful run for the governorship of Florida, in 1994, Jeb Bush called himself a "head-banging conservative"—that is, a conservative who unwaveringly and unapologetically championed positions resting on the far right of the political spectrum. He placed at the top of his pro-posed agenda such measures as drastically shrinking welfare, replacing the public-school system with a school-voucher program, and building more prisons, and he went on record as opposing abortion and gun control. Once, when asked what he might do to ease the problems of black Floridians, he answered, "Probably nothing." In what proved to be an exceedingly close race against the popular incumbent governor, Lawton Chiles, Bush earned only 4 percent of the votes cast by black Floridians.

In his second, successful run for governor, in 1998, Bush adopted a strikingly different approach. "We need to embrace diversity . . . ," he told one gathering of African-Americans, as reported in *Tampa Bay Online* (April 8, 1998). "Through unity there's a chance to improve the lot of people in this state." While asserting that he remained a conservative and still believed firmly in "limited government," he also strived to persuade voters that he could no longer be counted among the "head bangers." As various observers noted, he presented himself as a "kinder, gentler" candidate—adjectives that his father, George Bush, had used a decade earlier during his first presidential campaign, when he had talked about his vision for the United States. The "new" Jeb Bush promised to work to develop better schools for *all* children, to subsidize new businesses as a means of creating jobs and renewing run-down urban areas, and to protect Florida's environment by expanding the state's land-acquisition program, and he vigorously reached out to groups that had been traditionally Democratic or otherwise disconnected from the Republican Party.

"We have compassion fatigue because we've defined compassion by how much money we've been willing to send to Tallahassee [the capital of Florida] and Washington," Bush told Christopher Rapp for the *National Review* (October 26, 1998) a week before the election. True compassion, he went on, "is defined as 'suffering with,' acting on a sense of consciousness when you've seen the hurting and the misery around you." On November 3, 1998 nearly 30 percent of the African-Americans who went to the polls cast their ballots for him, and thanks largely to their support and that of others who usually vote Democratic, Bush easily captured the governorship.

John Ellis Bush was born on February 11, 1953 in Houston, Texas. Called Jeb all his life (a nickname derived from his initials), he is the second of the six children—four sons and two daughters—of former president George Bush and Barbara Pierce Bush. (One of his sisters died at the age of three.) Unlike his father and his older brother, George W. Bush (who was reelected to his second term as governor of Texas in 1998), both of whom attended Yale University, Jeb Bush earned his bachelor's degree from the University of Texas, where he majored in Latin American studies. Earlier, while on a student-exchange program in Mexico, he had met Columba Garnica; the two married in 1974. In the 1970s Bush worked in banking, mainly in Houston. Early in the next decade, he and his wife settled in Miami, Florida. "I thought it would be difficult pursuing my dreams in Houston, where my Dad's long shadow would fall over us," Bush told J. D. Podolsky for *People* (November 8, 1993).

In Miami, Bush established a real-estate company, and in about 1982 he formed a partnership with the well-known Cuban-American developer Armando Codina. (Bush served until recently as president and CEO of the Codina Group, which develops both commercial and residential real estate.) Eventually, according to various sources, Bush became a millionaire.

In 1985 Bush and Codina bought a downtown-Miami high-rise office building. Their purchase was financed by the Broward Federal Savings and Loan Association, a Florida bank. As Jeff Gerth reported in the *New York Times* (April 19, 1992), Bush and Codina defaulted on the $4.6 million loan, and that loss, along with others, led to the bank's collapse. Bush and his partner eventually repaid about one-eighth of their debt; the rest came out of the coffers of the federal government. After an investigation of the matter, federal regulators accused Broward of approving the loan to Bush and Codina without first determining whether their company was creditworthy. Also in the 1980s, Curtis Lang reported in the *Village Voice* (June 23, 1992), Bush had real-estate dealings with Alberto Duque, a Colombian national who gained control of the City National Bank of Miami. Duque, who had received backing from the government of Libya (which the U.S. government has designated as a terrorist state), was eventually sentenced to 15 years in prison for fraud. In addition, throughout the 1980s Bush supplied what Jeff Gerth described as "nonlethal support" to the counterrevolutionary guerrillas (better known as the Contra rebels) in Nicaragua.

Meanwhile, Bush had become active in Florida politics. From 1984 through 1987 he served as the chairman of the Dade County Republican Party. The biggest city in the county is Miami, and Miami's large, politically powerful Cuban population is predominantly Republican. Bush, who is fluent in Spanish, proved to be an effective leader for Miami's Spanish-speaking Republicans as well as the English-speaking members of the party. In 1986 he considered running for Congress, but his father discouraged him, reminding him that, since he had three young children at home, his main responsibilities were with his family. The following year Bush took the job of secretary of commerce for Florida; an appointee of then-Governor Bob Martinez, he remained in that position until 1988. In 1990 he chaired Martinez's unsuccessful reelection campaign.

In 1994, with his father's encouragement, Bush made his first run for the governorship of Florida. Throughout his campaign he emphasized his steadfast support of ultraconservative values. Decrying the failures of the welfare system, he emphasized "the virtue of work," Richard L. Berke reported in the *New York Times* (September 2, 1994); he repeatedly said that single mothers who were on welfare "should be able to get their life together and find a husband," and he proposed strictly limiting aid to welfare recipients to no more than two years. He also urged abolishing Florida's education department and replacing public schools with charter schools, which would be publicly funded but privately run. He called for the building of new, work-oriented prisons and, as that increase in cell space would make possible, requiring inmates to serve a much larger portion of their sentences before becoming eligible for parole—specifically, 85 percent of their sentences, rather than the 37 percent that the average prisoner then served. He also expressed his opposition to homosexual rights and abortion and his strong support for corporal punishment and prayer in public schools. In light of President Bush's politically fatal failure to keep his promise about not raising taxes in 1988, many interviewers asked Jeb Bush whether, as governor, he would ever raise taxes. "I am a student of history," he said, as quoted by Berke. "I am not going to make any no new taxes pledges."

The two other Republicans who were vying for the Republican nomination, Tom Gallagher and Jim Smith, teamed up and made a commercial contending that Bush had "made a fortune with a partner who is now an international felon," as Richard Berke reported in the *New York Times* (August 2, 1994). Smith subsequently withdrew from the race, and Bush won the Republican nomination. He lost the general election to the Democratic incumbent, Lawton Chiles, by approximately 64,000 votes, or less than 2 percent of the vote—the slimmest margin ever in a Florida gubernatorial contest. After the election it was discovered that, under the guise of a senior citizens' group, people working for Chiles's campaign had made thousands of phone calls falsely telling people that Bush intended to do away with Social Security benefits for the elderly. In his 1998 article for the *National Review*, Rapp quoted Richard Scher, a University of Florida political scientist, as saying, "A lot of people felt that Jeb Bush was actually elected but for a minor technicality. And since then he's acted as if he's the rightful heir."

After his electoral defeat, Bush attended adult-education classes at the Catholic church to which his wife had belonged for several years (and which he had attended sporadically), and in 1995 he converted to Catholicism. "I vowed to myself after the election that I would convert," he recalled to S. C. Gwynne for *Time* (June 8, 1998). "It turned out to be a pretty therapeutic thing. . . . Had I won, I would have been up in a cocoon in Tallahassee and protected. . . . I'm convinced that I'm better off for not having won." Bush had also become somewhat alienated from his family during his months of 16-hour-a-day campaigning, and he felt that he needed to spend more time with them. "I had got so immersed that while I was still connected to my family on one level, I left them behind," he told

Gwynne. "So when I came back to the real world, there were some problems I began to see. . . . That hardship was devastating."

In a process of change that Bush has called his "journey," he "became determined to give his conservatism a human, caring face," Michael J. Gerson wrote in *U.S. News & World Report* (November 16, 1998). In 1995 Bush established the Foundation for Florida's Future, a conservative organization that, according to its home page, "strives to involve individuals in public policy and reconnect state and local government with the citizens it serves." In collaboration with T. Willard Fair, the president of the Urban League of Greater Miami, and with funding from the foundation, Bush established the Liberty City Charter School, in a poverty-stricken, predominantly African-American section of Miami. Bush remains a staunch supporter of charter schools, which are designed to offer both the benefits of public schools (they cannot charge fees and must accept anyone who wants to attend, for example) and certain features of private schools (they govern themselves and are free from most state and local education-department regulations, so that they can establish their own curricula, set class sizes, and hire as teachers whomever they want). To get their charters renewed, the schools must demonstrate that their students have performed well, and in that way the schools are accountable to the state.

In the process of establishing the Liberty City school, Bush visited various public schools to educate himself about day-to-day life in the classroom, and what he saw profoundly affected him. "I would walk into the class, and a kid would come up to me and touch my skin or feel my hair, and it happened every day I was there," he recalled to S. C. Gwynne. "This just blew me away. What kind of a place do we live in where a six-year-old child hasn't touched a white person before?" At a fundraising event for the Liberty City school, as Mireya Navarro reported in the *New York Times* (May 12, 1998), Bush declared, "I'm here to tell you that unless we figure out a way to transfer the power of knowledge not just to a third of our children but to every child who has the God-given ability to learn, then we will move to a thing that I believe will be defined as economic apartheid. Now that's not the America that I want. That's not the Florida that we want."

To reinforce his commitment to creating better schools for all children, Bush chose Frank Brogan, Florida's education commissioner, as his running mate—that is, his candidate for lieutenant governor—in the 1998 race for the governorship. Building on his growing popularity among African-Americans, he included on his campaign trail many stops in what is generally considered to be Democratic terrain: African-American churches, housing projects for the elderly, camps for migrant workers, shelters for victims of domestic violence, and one-street towns in some of Florida's poorest and most rural counties. "Seldom has a political campaign more closely resembled the Peace Corps," Michael J. Gerson observed. When Navarro asked him why the tone of his 1998 campaign differed so dramatically from that of 1994, Bush said, "The ideological battle is not as important as it once was." Indeed, his Democratic opponent in the election, Florida's then–Lieutenant Governor Kenneth "Buddy" MacKay, told Navarro, "The issues [Bush] took in 1994 were way to the right. Now he's moved way to the left, and in some cases is further to the left than me."

The lack of focus in McKay's campaign in the early weeks of the race helped Bush's candidacy. Having raised $6.7 million in campaign funds—some of it from out-of-state former members of President George Bush's administration—Jeb Bush had another great advantage over McKay, whose war chest amounted to only about $2.2 million. Bush also benefited immeasurably from an incident in early 1998 that involved Democratic legislators in Florida: namely, their rejection of state representative Willie Logan, an African-American, as the next speaker of the Florida House of Representatives. Logan would have been the first African-American to hold that position. The Democratic lawmakers' action angered many blacks and helped to push into the Republicans' camp significant numbers of people who had already been leaning toward Bush. On November 3, 1998, in a resounding victory, Bush captured 55 percent of the vote for governor.

Bush has worked as a volunteer with the Miami Children's Hospital, the United Way of Dade County, and the Dade County Homeless Trust. Recently he helped organize a series of conferences in which law-enforcement professionals learned ways to deal with abuse and neglect of the elderly, a problem that has been increasing in Florida. In 1995 he co-authored the book *Profiles in Character*, which is about 14 of Florida's civic heroes.

Jeb Bush and his wife have three children—George P., Noelle, and Jeb Jr. (In his campaign speeches Bush often mentioned that his children are Hispanic.) In January 1999 the family took up residence in the governor's mansion in Tallahassee. — C.P.

Suggested Reading: *Miami Herald* (on-line) July 31, 1998; *Naplesnews.com* Aug. 9, 1998, with photo; *National Review* p38+ Oct. 26, 1998; *New York Times* I p14 Apr. 19, 1992, with photo, A p1 Nov. 30, 1993, with photos, A p1 Sep. 2, 1994, with photos, A p1 May 12, 1998, with photo, A p20 Nov. 19, 1998, with photo; *Time* p54+ June 8, 1998, with photos; *Village Voice* p35+ June 23, 1992, with photo

Bebeto Matthews/AP/Wide World Photos

Butts, Calvin O.

July 19, 1949– Pastor; college president. Address: c/o Abyssinian Baptist Church, 132 W. 138th St., New York, NY 10030

Abyssinian Baptist Church—on West 138th Street between Malcolm X and Adam Clayton Powell Jr. Boulevards in the Harlem neighborhood of New York City—is one of the most famous African-American churches in the United States. It has existed almost as long as the country, and from its white Italian marble pulpit, some of the most prominent African-American ministers have spoken—most notably its former pastor Adam Clayton Powell Jr., who served in the U.S. House of Representatives for over two decades. Abyssinian's current pastor is Calvin O. Butts III, who some think will follow in the footsteps of Powell. Many are predicting that sometime in the next decade, Butts will run either for the New York City mayor's post or for the congressional seat that includes Harlem.

Should Butts's candidacy become a reality, the election would implicitly serve as a referendum on different strategies for achieving social change. Unlike other African-American political aspirants who have built their reputations by leading mass demonstrations in the streets, Butts has pursued a quieter politics of backdoor deal-making and economic development. This was not always Butts's style. In the early 1980s he openly criticized mainstream politicians, both white and black, for being too timid in addressing New York City's racial problems. But in the past decade, Butts's rhetoric has cooled substantially. Instead of continuing to criticize politics from the outside, Butts has become a consummate insider and has used his base

of support to win millions of dollars' worth of development deals for Harlem.

The questions and concerns surrounding Butts's program of social change echo an earlier debate within the African-American community—that between W. E. B. DuBois and Booker T. Washington. Does one remain an outside critic, at the risk of being ineffective, or does one try to work on the inside, forming alliances that may compromise one's principles in one area in order to realize a gain in another? Butts is well aware that his younger self might have criticized the things he is doing now. Especially with his endorsement of New York's Republican governor George Pataki, he may come off looking to some like an Uncle Tom. To others, however—especially those who appreciate the new multimillion-dollar shopping and entertainment centers being built in Harlem—Butts is helping his community achieve real economic, as opposed to symbolic, gains.

Calvin O. Butts III was born on July 19, 1949 in New York City. His father was a chef at the Black Angus steakhouse; his mother was an administrator in a city human-resource-administration office. The family lived in the Lillian Wald Houses, a public housing project on the Lower East Side of the borough of Manhattan, until Butts was eight, when they moved to Corona–East Elmhurst, then a primarily African-American neighborhood in the borough of Queens. Amidst protests over school desegregation efforts, Butts was bused to a junior-high school in Forest Hills, another section of Queens. Then, in 1964, he started attending the predominantly white Flushing High School. A popular student who could work across racial lines, he was elected class president in his senior year.

In 1967 Butts began attending Morehouse College, in Atlanta, Georgia. He initially planned to study industrial psychology but became interested in religious studies after talking to a few seminary recruiters. The fact that some of the most inspiring African-American figures were ministers also helped push Butts toward a religious vocation. One of those figures was Adam Clayton Powell Jr., whom Butts heard preach when he was 13 years old; Butts remembered the Abyssinian pastor as "a man bigger than life" and as being "like a god," as he told Eric Pooley for *New York* (June 26, 1989). There were also the towering examples of Martin Luther King Jr. and Malcolm X. Butts eventually decided to major in philosophy and minor in religion.

Although he liked to wear a suit and carry a briefcase while walking around campus, Butts was not as straitlaced as he might have appeared. "They say all good preachers have a season of sin," he told Eric Pooley, "and I had mine. We danced and—what is the word?—*partied*." The young Butts also experienced moments of rage. Butts has admitted that when King was assassinated, in 1968, and more than 100 cities exploded into rioting, he participated in the riots. Later, he came to believe that violence was not a solution and recommitted himself to his religious studies. After he graduated from Morehouse, Butts began attending Union Theological Seminary, in New York, in 1972. At the beginning of his studies in New York, an opportunity to become associated with Abyssinian Baptist Church presented itself.

Abyssinian was established in 1808, when 13 Ethiopian merchants and African-Americans attending a primarily white Baptist church in the downtown area of New York City were told that they had to sit in a segregated balcony. In protest the Ethiopians and the African-Americans started their own church a few blocks away, naming it for Abyssinia, which is the former name of Ethiopia. In about 1923 the church was moved to its current location, in Harlem. Adam Clayton Powell Sr. served as pastor from 1908 to 1937. His son, Powell Jr., served from 1937 to 1972. Known for his outspoken civil-rights activism, Powell Jr. was elected to the House of Representatives in 1944. He served for about 23 years before accusations of misuse of congressional funds hurt his political prospects. Charles Rangel defeated him in the 1970 elections.

Following Powell Jr.'s death, in 1972, the Reverend Dr. Samuel D. Proctor took over as pastor of Abyssinian. Some had felt that because of Powell Jr.'s political activities, the church's membership—which is composed of African-Americans from throughout the city—had been neglected. Proctor devoted much more attention than his predecessor to the church's activities, and as a result membership and church revenues slowly began to increase. To help him carry out these changes, Proctor hired Butts, then about 22 years old, as a junior minister. Butts served under Proctor for 17 years, at the same time earning his master's degree, in 1975, from Union Theological Seminary and his doctorate in church and public policy, in 1982, from Drew Theological School, in Madison, New Jersey.

While Proctor quietly refocused the mission of the church, his protégé, Butts, established himself as more outspoken. He led mass protests (one involved painting over liquor billboard ads that targeted the African-American community) and grabbed headlines with his inflammatory remarks about the racial situation in New York. In an interview with Bob Herbert for the New York *Daily News* (June 18, 1987), he claimed that the racism in the city was "worse than it was in Alabama and Mississippi 35 or 40 years ago." Butts called then–New York City mayor Ed Koch an unprincipled opportunist who had "polariz[ed] the city"; Butts also excoriated such black political figures as David Dinkins and Congressman Rangel for being too timid. "Stop being so damned cautious," he admonished black leaders, as quoted by Bob Herbert, "because we are living in critical times and caution will result in all of us being literally wiped out."

It was a sign of Butts's growing prominence in the Harlem community that Jewish leaders approached him in 1986 to condemn the Nation of Is-

lam leader, Louis Farrakhan, who had called Judaism a "gutter religion." Butts, however, refused to condemn Farrakhan, drawing a distinction between the latter's ideas about Jews—with which Butts disagreed—and his ideas about black empowerment in general. "Don't dictate to me," Butts, as quoted by Eric Pooley, told the Jewish community. "I don't hate Jewish people. . . . But don't make me a boy and tell me what to do."

Butts's agitation was sometimes effective. In 1983, for instance, he and a fellow Morehouse alumnus, C. Vernon Mason, successfully lobbied Congress for hearings on police brutality. The hearings were held in New York, and some believe that they led to the appointment of the city's first black police commissioner, Ben Ward. However, even Proctor occasionally took issue with Butts's comments. "It wasn't so much telling him to cool the rhetoric, it was a question of being more *factual*," Proctor told Eric Pooley. "He'd say, 'We don't have a single responsible black official,' then Charlie Rangel's office would call *me* up and say, 'What does he *mean* by that?' I'd say, '*Butts*, you have an obligation to demonstrate the weight of your charges. These labels are the kind of thing you'd say at a heated-up rally. Ministers are supposed to be conciliatory. Someone a long time ago said, "Love your enemies."'" Still, if Proctor had complaints about some of Butts's public remarks, he had no doubts about his ability to lead Abyssinian. When Proctor retired, in 1989, he did not hesitate to recommend that Butts take over.

It is not entirely clear what caused Butts to move away from mass-protest politics and turn to political deal-making. What is clear is that even with his previous agitation, the economic and social situation in Harlem wasn't improving substantially. Even some of the buildings on the same block as the church had been abandoned and taken over by crack addicts and drug dealers. Such vivid reminders of the lack of concrete economic change in Harlem may have eventually led Butts to change his philosophy. "There is room for the uncompromising, belligerent, nasty, guerrilla activist," he told the *New York Times* (December 3, 1995). "But you change when you are responsible for an institution. I got folks I got to pay. I got families."

Butts's earlier style of activism didn't disappear altogether. In 1993, for instance, he led a protest against negative rap lyrics. More of his attention, however, was focused on winning economic development deals for the community. By the end of 1998, the Abyssinian Development Corp., in operation since 1989, had investments of about $65 million in the neighborhood. Two buildings across the street from the church have been transformed: one is a transitional housing center for homeless people, and the other is home to the development corporation, a child-care center, and low- to moderate-income housing. Butts has also played a role in the renovation of the historic Renaissance Ballroom and in commercial development on 125th Street. The latter includes a Pathmark supermarket, the Harlem Center (a shopping and entertainment complex), and Harlem USA (a shopping center). The three projects on 125th Street alone have been funded by $13.6 million in state loans. Another project—the East River Plaza, a shopping complex on 116th Street—is being developed with $3 million in state loans. Abyssinian Development Corp. is a co-developer of the Pathmark store and the Harlem Center. Butts also helped establish the Thurgood Marshall Academy for Learning and Social Change, a public intermediate school for approximately 300 students.

These development deals, however, have come at the price—some might say the very high price—of supporting Republican political leaders. Butts, frustrated with Democratic Party leaders and the way they had, in his opinion, unfairly relegated Jesse Jackson to the political sidelines, initially tried to explore third-party alternatives. In 1992 Butts endorsed the presidential campaign of Ross Perot and served as one of his senior New York State campaign officials. Later—after Perot had offended many by referring to African-Americans as "you people," and after the Democrat Bill Clinton won the presidency—Butts told the *New York Times* (June 5, 1993) that his support of Perot was "the biggest mistake I probably ever made."

With support for Perot obviously a political nonstarter, Butts turned to George Pataki. Ever since Pataki won his first term as New York's governor, in 1994, Butts has nurtured a relationship with him. He served as a member of Pataki's transition team and was appointed by Pataki to the Empire State Development Corp. Butts, in turn, endorsed Pataki over the Democratic candidate, Peter F. Vallone, the speaker of the New York City Council, in the 1998 gubernatorial election. While the relationship has helped Butts win key development projects in Harlem, some African-American community leaders have been outraged by what they regard as Butts's betrayal—arguing that despite Pataki's patronage, his policies have hurt African-Americans in other ways, particularly by bringing the death penalty back to the state (African-Americans are heavily represented on death row) and slashing social-welfare programs.

How the African-American community at large will react to the path that Butts has chosen will become apparent if and when Butts decides to seek political office. According to Butts, he has not yet sought political office because of his church duties. "I've wanted to be a mayor of New York since the third grade," he told Craig Horowitz for *New York* (January 26, 1998). "And I'd like to be a U.S. senator at some point. That's very clear to me. But what you wanna be and what you *need* to be are two different things." Many political commentators expect that Butts will make a move soon. He could challenge Rangel for his congressional seat or run for the mayoral office in 2000 should the current mayor, Rudolph Giuliani, choose to seek a higher office.

One possible political opponent is the Reverend Al Sharpton, whose political strategy is more dependent on leading mass social protest in the streets. "Social movements are what excite people," Sharpton told Craig Horowitz. "You cannot show me any city where a guy building supermarkets was elected mayor. . . . I think I could beat Calvin in his own church." Referring to two highly publicized incidents of racial violence against blacks, Sharpton continued, "From Bensonhurst to Abner Louima, Butts has not been involved. He's chosen the inside path, and that's fine—it's worked for his church. But that's not the same thing as running for office." In defense of the insider approach he has taken, Butts told Horowitz, "I think marching and demonstrating is very, very important. . . . But you have to build alliances. You have to build coalitions. You have to raise substantial amounts of money in order to really bring about the kind of change that is needed."

It is widely thought that Butts would be more acceptable to white voters than Sharpton—a view seemingly embraced by a recent *New York* magazine cover, which asks, "Which would you choose, Dr. King?" and displays a noticeably bigger image of Butts than of Sharpton. Early tests of Butts's appeal among African-Americans are ambiguous. For example, Butts recently questioned Henry Lyons's leadership of the National Baptist Convention, the nation's largest black organization. Despite Butts's charges of fiscal improprieties on Lyons's part, Lyons was reelected. "They say Calvin will attack a black guy—whether it's Mike Tyson or Lyons or the rappers—'cause he knows the white media will give him coverage," Sharpton told Horowitz. "But where's Calvin on racial incidents? Where's Calvin when white cops shoot us? They felt Calvin knew Lyons was an easy shot." (Sharpton, however, is not without his own political baggage. He endorsed the Republican senator Alfonse D'Amato in 1986, and he drew considerable fire for his advocacy of Tawana Brawley, the black teenager who in 1987 claimed to have been raped by several white men, including Steven Pagones. Pagones later won a defamation-of-character suit against Sharpton. Butts, by contrast, managed largely to avoid association with the Brawley case, even though his friend C. Vernon Mason was involved.)

There are signs that Butts still has some of the "guerrilla activist" in him. For instance, in 1998, on the New York One cable-television program *Inside City Hall*, he accused Mayor Giuliani of being a racist. Butts criticized several of Giuliani's policies that he felt had had a particularly negative impact on the black community. These included the firing of 600 employees, many of them African-American, at Harlem Hospital, and police procedures that Butts felt verged on fascism. While many black leaders agreed with Butts's criticisms—though they did not go so far as to call Giuliani a racist—some wondered why Butts had not leveled similar criticisms at Governor Pataki.

Later, on April 20, 1999, Butts sparked more debate, when he publicly embraced Giuliani during a service at New York's St. Patrick's Cathedral. During the time that he made the controversial gesture, the city's police force was being subjected to much scrutiny for the killing by police officers of Amadou Diallo, an unarmed West African immigrant, three months earlier. "I didn't embrace [Giuliani] as an acknowledgement of his policies," Butts told the *New York Times* (May 3, 1999). "I embraced him to say that this may be an opportunity to begin a process of reconciliation—to at least take the conversation above my calling him a racist and his responding in some harsh tone."

On September 22, 1999 Butts was named president of the State University of New York College at Old Westbury, a campus with about 3,700 students, roughly half of whom are members of minority groups. His acceptance of this academic appointment indicates that he has put a career in politics on hold. His previous academic positions include serving as an adjunct professor at the City College of New York (1976–80) and at Fordham University (1977–79). Butts has said that he will continue his duties as pastor of Abyssinian.

Butts is director and vice chair of the United Way in New York City. He is also the director of the C. T. Walker Housing Corp., the Central Park Conservancy board, and the New York City Partnership. He is a member of the Advisory Committee on National Black Initiatives on Cancer. Butts's Sunday sermons are regularly broadcast on a local New York City radio station.

Butts and his wife, Patricia, have been married for more than 20 years. They have three children and live in Harlem. — W.G.

Suggested Reading: *New York* p42+ June 26, 1989, with photos, p20+ Jan. 26, 1998, with photos; *New York Newsday* p9 Nov. 27, 1983, with photo, p89 June 18, 1987, p83 July 17, 1991, with photo; *New York Times* I p28 Aug. 9, 1987, with photo, p23+ June 5, 1993, with photo, XIII p4 Dec. 3, 1995, with photo; *New York Times Magazine* p19+ Jan. 20, 1991; *Village Voice* Metro p11+ June 12, 1990, with photos, p54+ June 2, 1998, with photo; *Village Voice* (on-line) Oct. 21–27, 1998

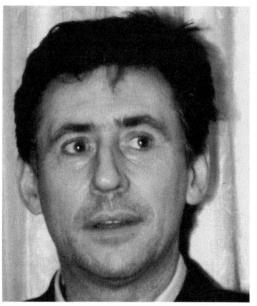

Kosta Alexander/Archive Photos

Byrne, Gabriel

May 12, 1950– Actor; director; producer; writer.
Address: c/o International Creative Management, 8942 Wilshire Blvd., Beverly Hills, CA 90211

The career of the Irish actor Gabriel Byrne has followed anything but the typical path to fame in Hollywood. Byrne was almost 30 before he ventured into acting, and even then, it was several years before he starred in a successful film. And now that he has achieved a level of popularity as a performer, with roles in the films *Miller's Crossing* (1990), *Little Women* (1994), *The Usual Suspects* (1995), and other projects, Byrne has begun to feel that he prefers producing, writing, and directing to acting. "I've gotten great satisfaction out of the . . . films I've produced because they've enabled me to express things I'm passionate about," Byrne told Kristine McKenna for the *Chicago Tribune* (April 23, 1995). "As an actor, I don't have that opportunity because I'm not a No. 1 box office star. I don't see myself as a successful actor, and though I admire great actors, I've never been obsessed with acting."

Gabriel Byrne was born on May 12, 1950 in Dublin, Ireland, and was raised in the more rural outskirts of the city. "We grew up on a little road that led to a larger road that led to the mountains," Byrne told Phoebe Hoban for *New York* (September 17, 1990). "There were hay carts and farms all over the place." Byrne's father was a cooper; when many of the local beer companies began storing beer in metal, rather than wooden, casks, he ran out of work. Byrne's mother then took a job in a hospital, while his father stayed home to care for Gabriel and his five siblings. Byrne told Hoban that he believes that growing up in Ireland gave him his deep appreciation for literature. "My mother could quote reams of poetry. She would always have a line from Robbie Burns to cover any situation," he said. His grandmother greatly admired the work of the English poet Alfred, Lord Tennyson and the Irish writer Oscar Wilde. "I remember growing up thinking that [my grandmother] knew [Wilde] because she used to say, 'Poor old Oscar, what they did to him.'"

Although as a child he never thought about acting, Byrne remembers that once, when his mother read to him from Charles Dickens's *The Old Curiosity Shop*, he went around for several weeks pretending to be a hunchback. "One day the men came to deliver coal," he recalled to Hoban. "I was sitting at the kitchen table with this big hump. And the coal men turned to my mother in horror and said, 'It don't matter about the money, ma'am. You have your own cross to bear.'"

Early in his life Byrne expressed a desire to become a priest. "I went to a school that was run by Irish Christian Brothers who wore long, black soutanes and if you didn't know your algebra would lift you up by the hair," he recalled to Hoban. "One day, a guy came in with a slide projector and he showed us photographs of these guys in white shorts with little black people smiling. And he said, 'How many of you boys feel that you would have a vocation to save souls?' About 15 of us put up our hands. I went away to England to this seminary in the heart of the countryside." While he was at that school, one of his male teachers attempted to seduce him. Soon after that incident, Byrne, who played on the soccer team and did well in Latin, was expelled for smoking in a nearby graveyard.

Upon his return to Ireland, Byrne worked at a wide variety of odd jobs. He eventually won a scholarship to Ireland's University College, where he took up the studies of phonetics, languages, and archaeology. "I don't know why I did that combination, but I had this image of being a swashbuckling scholar," he told Hoban. After graduating, he worked briefly as an archaeologist. Recalling that experience, he told Nancy Bilyeau for *Rolling Stone* (November 1, 1990), "I found that my romantic expectations as an archaeologist and the reality clashed greatly. It was rain, mud, and scraping things with little brushes and being shouted at and bumping into people in confined spaces and not finding the lost city." After that, Byrne went to Spain, where he trained to be a bullfighter. Bullfighting, he told Chris Chase for *Cosmopolitan* (September 1993), is "very beautiful until you remember that it ends in death. It's the ritual of life and death lived out in the space of 10 or 15 minutes. I can understand why people find it exciting, but the thing of it is, I don't anymore. It's just when you're 20, and you've been feasting on novels, you expect to get off the plane and be met by Papa Hemingway saying, 'Come on, I'll show you the real Spain.'"

Byrne next went back to Ireland and took a job as a Spanish teacher, which he described to Bilyeau as "teaching the present tense and past tense and *Don Quixote* to totally uninterested 17-year-old girls." He also took up writing, producing a column for *Magill*, an Irish political magazine, as well as several short stories, one of which was recently published in an anthology called *Ireland's Best Contemporary Short Stories*. During this time

Byrne also began acting at small theater companies. He eventually earned a name for himself in Dublin's theater scene and was invited to join the well-known Abbey Theater Company.

Byrne's appearances at the Abbey led to his being cast in the wildly popular television show *The Riordans*, which ran for a total of 18 years on Irish television. That program "was my father's absolute favorite thing," the actor told Hoban. "I think that one of the biggest thrills of my entire life was to see my father sitting there for the first episode and me walk onto the television screen. And he said, 'I never thought I'd see the day when a son of mine would walk onto the Riordans' farm, but there you are.'" When that series ended, Byrne's character became the subject of a new series called *Bracken*. "Bracken was a farmer who was living by himself and cheating on about six women," Byrne explained to Hoban. "He was a real lovable liar—there's a kind of sneaking respect for a character like that in Ireland. He's up to every roguish thing with a wink and a smile. So there's lots of shots of me looking meaningful in flocks of sheep." *Bracken* made Byrne a star in Ireland.

Byrne's first films were, for the most part, unsuccessful. "I've always tried to pick films that are interesting and offbeat," he told Nancy Bilyeau, in discussing the several box-office flops in which he starred during the 1980s. His early roles included Uther, the father of King Arthur, in *Excalibur* (1981), the district attorney Joshua Herzog in *Hanna K.* (1983), a journalist named Nick Mullen in *Defense of the Realm* (1985), and the poet Lord Byron in *Gothic* (1986). He also had a small part in the 1985 television miniseries *Mussolini: The Untold Story*. During the shooting of *Mussolini*, Byrne saved the actor Robert Downey Jr. from being seriously injured by an airplane propeller on the set.

Another commercially unsuccessful film for Byrne was *Siesta* (1987), in which he portrayed a Spanish trapeze instructor opposite Ellen Barkin, whom the actor married the following year. Byrne first met Barkin while she and the director Mary Lambert were finalizing the casting for the film. "Ellen came to London with Mary to make sure they more or less agreed on the same cast," Byrne told Hoban. "Little did I realize how fatal that meeting was going to be. I had never heard of her and she had never heard of me, but my agent said, 'She's a really up-and-coming American actress, and I think you should meet her.' I told her some ridiculous story about some cardinal I knew who had died in flagrante delicto, so to speak. . . . I don't know why I told her that, but I think she responded to it." In *Siesta*, Barkin's character, a dying stuntwoman, relives the most passionate moments of her life. Although the film was generally deemed forgettable, Byrne told Hoban that he didn't regret making it. "All the reasons that I did that movie are still things that really interest me," he said. "Obsession. Sex. Death. Spain. The idea that somebody can rewind their lives."

It wasn't until he was cast in the brothers Joel and Ethan Coen's stylish *Miller's Crossing* (1990) that Byrne found his niche as an actor. In that film, set in the 1920s in an unnamed U.S. city, Byrne played Tom, an Irish immigrant and the right-hand man of a mob boss named Leo (Albert Finney); estranged from the older man after his affair with Leo's lover (Marcia Gay Harden) comes to light, the tough, quiet, stoical Tom appears to switch allegiance, consorting with a rival mob faction. According to Bilyeau, Byrne "turns in a subtle yet forceful performance as an impassive man concealing deep pain." To prepare for the role, Byrne watched gangster movies from the 1930s and 1940s, "to see if there was anything I could maybe subconsciously absorb," he told Hoban. "There was one scene in [the 1932 film] *Scarface* where Paul Muni lights his cigarette off a policeman's badge, so I stuck that in." As he explained to Bilyeau, his preparation also involved watching chess matches in the SoHo section of New York City. "The intensity with which these guys play was interesting because it's about working from in here," he said, indicating his head. He continued, "I've known people like Tom—totally in charge and totally unhappy. He was a difficult character to play, because he's enigmatic, mysterious. How do you know how much to give and how much to leave to the imagination? I used to say to Joel [Coen], 'Is the audience going to buy this? Are they not just going to say, "Oh, we don't care what he does."' And Joel said, 'No, this guy is a thinker, a plotter and a man who knows how to use power.'" Indeed, the complexity of this role seemed to allow Byrne to utilize his talents more fully than he had in the past. Until *Miller's Crossing*, "I don't think [filmmakers] knew what to do with me," he told Hoban. "Is he a character actor, is he a leading guy? And I think that in *Miller's Crossing*, they finally figured it out."

Not long after achieving fame for his work in *Miller's Crossing*, Byrne began producing films. The first was *Into the West* (1992), a fable about the strength of a mother's love. "It began with friends of mine walking through the projects in Dublin," Byrne told Chris Chase. "And seven floors up, they saw a white horse on a balcony. One of them sat down and wrote a short story on it, and later we got Jim Sheridan, who wrote *My Left Foot*, to do a script, but it took us a long time to convince anyone that two kids and a white horse was something people wanted to see. . . . We cobbled the money together from various places, and we still didn't have enough, so then I went to Harvey and Bob Weinstein at Miramax, who are sympathetic toward small independent movies, and we sat in this restaurant in Tribeca [a New York City neighborhood], and I told them the story, and when I was done, they just said, 'Okay, we'll make it.'"

In *Into the West*, Byrne played an Irish gypsy who, after his wife dies in childbirth, moves into a Dublin housing project with his two sons. "The movie says the mother comes back to ensure that

the kids are really okay," Byrne explained to Chase. "It says that the love of a mother for her children is stronger than death." *Into the West* became the number-one film in Ireland that year and also won acclaim at the Sundance Film Festival. Although it was not a huge success at U.S. box offices at the time of its release, it has since become popular on home video.

In 1993 Byrne produced the Academy Award–nominated film *In the Name of the Father*. Starring Daniel Day Lewis, that film tells the story of an innocent man forced into "confessing" his role in a bombing arranged by the Irish Republican Army. Byrne also continued acting, appearing in less-noticed films such as *Point of No Return* and *A Dangerous Woman*, both released in 1993, as well as playing opposite Winona Ryder in *Little Women* (1994). During the same period he produced his first documentary film, *A Road to Remember*, which addresses the U.S. involvement in the Irish potato famine of the mid–19th century. He also made his screenwriting and directorial debut, with *Lark in the Clean Air*, a made-for-television movie.

In 1995 Byrne again garnered a great deal of attention as an actor, with his role in Bryan Singer's *The Usual Suspects*. He played the volcanic Dean Keaton, a criminal—and former cop—who tries to go straight but is forced into a heist by an unseen, mythic underworld figure. *The Usual Suspects* became that summer's sleeper hit. "He's very modest," Singer told Jan Hoffman for the *New York Times* (September 24, 1995) about Byrne, "but he does things effortlessly. Only when you're looking at the screen do you notice that Gabriel does all these subtle things with his hands, and especially his eyes." The success of *The Usual Suspects* prompted Harvey Weinstein, one of the co-chairs of Miramax (with whom Byrne had worked on *Into the West*), to give Byrne free rein to produce *The Last of the High Kings*, based on Byrne's own screenplay about an Irish boy's coming-of-age. Byrne also acted in the film. "When it comes out, people are finally going to see Gabriel not just as a handsome leading guy, but as a triple threat," Weinstein told Hoffman. By this time Byrne was in high demand, but this fact did not seem to affect his approach to his work. "While Steven Spielberg bites his nail waiting for my answer and Clint [Eastwood] wonders if I'm going to pass on the next one, I work on my producing thing, and I work on my writing," Byrne told Hoffman. "I basically live life the way she should be lived: with plenty of time to enjoy it."

Since the release of *The Last of the High Kings*, in 1996, Byrne has continued to act, in such movies as *Mag Dog Time* (1996), the made-for-TV *Weapons of Mass Destruction* (1997), *Enemy of the State* (1998), and *An Ideal Husband* (1999); he has also served as producer for films including *Mad About Mambo* (1999). His memoir, *Pictures in My Head*, was published in 1995.

Byrne and Ellen Barkin divorced in 1993; the couple share custody of their son, Jack, born in 1989, and daughter, Romey Marion, born in 1992. Byrne now spends time in both Ireland and Los Angeles. In an interview with Hoban in 1990, Barkin described her then-husband as "a bit hard to place in Hollywood. . . . Most stars are not threatening. They have nice, sweet faces. . . . And Gabriel is definitely not that. He looks like he could hurt you. He has that edge." Regarding his considerable sexual appeal, the actor and director John Turturro, one of Byrne's co-stars in *Miller's Crossing*, told Hoban, "I'm not a woman, but if I was one, I probably would go for him. . . . If you look into his face, there's an empathy there." — C.P.

Suggested Reading: *Chicago Tribune* XIII p28 Apr. 23, 1995, with photos; *Cosmopolitan* p178+ Sep. 1993, with photos; *New York* p46+ Sep. 17, 1990, with photos; *Premiere* p78+ Sep. 1993, with photo; *Rolling Stone* p75+ Nov. 1, 1990, with photo

Selected Films: as actor—*Excalibur*, 1981; *Hanna K.*, 1983; *Defense of the Realm*, 1985; *Mussolini: The Untold Story*, 1985; *Gothic*, 1986; *Siesta*, 1987; *Miller's Crossing*, 1990; *Into the West*, 1992; *A Dangerous Woman*, 1993; *Point of no Return*, 1993; *In the Name of the Father*, 1993; *Little Women*, 1994; *The Usual Suspects*, 1995; *Mad Dog Time*, 1996; as director—*Lark in the Clean Air*, 1996; as screenwriter—*The Last of the High Kings*, 1996; as producer—*Mad About Mambo*, 1999

Courtesy of Badgley, Connor, King

Casey, Bernie

June 8, 1939– Actor; painter; poet; director; screenwriter; former football player. Address: c/o Badgley, Connor, King, 9229 Sunset Blvd., #311, Los Angeles, CA 90069

Bernie Casey, a former professional football player, is a 30-year veteran of both television and film acting. Yet even before he began his acting career, Casey was by no means a typical National Football League (NFL) player. "Football is my hobby," he told Larry Merchant for the *New York Post* (December 15, 1967), "painting is my profession." In addition to painting, he was also writing poetry. When asked about the part pro football played in the creative aspects of his life, he told Merchant, "My growth as an artist is correlated only to my growth as a man. I never painted or wrote one thing about football. Football doesn't interest me creatively. I play, I practice, I play as well as I can, and I forget about it. . . . To me football isn't life and death. There are more important issues that confront us— poverty, the racial crisis, war, things like that. I like the game, I like the money because it will give me an independence as a man and as an artist, but it's a game." When he retired from professional football, in 1970, Casey had already appeared in two films—*Tick, Tick, Tick* (1970), with ex–football-great-turned-action-star Jim Brown, and *Guns of the Magnificent Seven* (1969), a low-budget western. Within a few years he had become a superstar of "blaxploitation" films, a controversial genre of movies made in the 1970s. *Black Chariot*, *Hit Man*, and others among them are now considered cult classics. By the end of the 1970s, Casey had established himself as a movie star; a respected American poet, with five books of poetry to his name; and a painter, with numerous one-man exhibitions in galleries throughout the world. Casey has continued his film career with memorable supporting roles, and he has appeared in such TV dramas as *Star Trek*, *Hunter*, *L.A. Law*, and *Murder, She Wrote*. In 1997 he made his debut as a screenwriter, producer, and director, with his critically acclaimed film *The Dinner*.

Bernie Casey was born on June 8, 1939 in Wyco, West Virginia. When he was very young, his parents divorced, and Bernie moved with his mother to Columbus, Ohio, where he spent most of his childhood. As a grade-school student, he became interested in painting, writing poetry, and acting. At some point he entered and won a citywide contest in which students were asked to paint a picture of their school buildings. "[Our school] had been built in 1882. It was quaint looking, and I won,"

Casey told William Gildea for the *Washington Post* (December 8, 1967). "The prize was a trip of about 25 miles to Chillicothe, Ohio. It was the biggest thing in my life. But I got sick and blew my chance." While he was in high school some of his poems were published in the school newspaper, and he performed in school plays. "I was always a movie fan," he told Hollie I. West for the *Washington Post* (May 7, 1977). "You go see a film and you think, 'I could do better than that.'" He also began to show promise as a wide receiver on the school football team. Casey had tried out for football because many of his friends had, but after he made the team, and despite his success on the field, he found that the sport was not entirely to his taste. "I was timid," he told Martin Kasindorf for *Newsweek* (September 30, 1968). "I didn't like all that *team* junk. Basically, I'm afraid of people." He also turned into a talented baseball player and track star, and in his senior year colleges wooed him with scholarships; some 20 of them offered to cover his expenses completely. Casey chose Bowling Green University, in Ohio, because of its arts program. "[I] decided to go to college one week before I graduated high school," he told Gildea for the *Washington Post.* "It dawned on me I didn't want to go to work in a filling station. I had a chance for an athletic scholarship. But I had played high-school football only because everyone else was going out. Pro football is the result of happenstance. I have a more sustained interest in painting."

At first Casey struggled to establish his dual identity as a serious artist and a scholarship athlete. Casey told Kasindorf that he felt Bowling Green's attitude was, "We got you here for football, get back to the Phys Ed department." "But . . . I decided this is me, my bag, man, sink or swim," he recalled to Kasindorf. "Painting was a new romance, and I knew it was a love affair that would never stop." His prowess with the pigskin, however, was undeniable, and by the end of his stay at Bowling Green—where he earned a master's degree in fine arts—Casey clearly had the makings of a professional football player. In 1961 he played his first NFL game, as a flanker (a combination running back and receiver) for the San Francisco 49ers.

As Casey's athletic career took off, so did his artistic career: the first exhibition of his paintings was held at the John Bolles Gallery, in San Francisco, in 1963. "That first show drew because it was a phenomenon," Casey told Kasindorf. "But once the freak thing wore off, the openings were like normal openings, with mainly art patrons and very few sports fans." Soon Casey's paintings were commanding respectable prices. "Casey is no curiosity, however rare a black, football-star painter may be," Kasindorf wrote. "His work is an effective fusion of warm, rich colors, glowing suns and floating crosses, primitive patterns and poetry." Kasindorf reported that the *Los Angeles Times* art critic Henry Seldis had praised him as "a serious young painter with good potential," and that as of 1968,

galleries in San Francisco and Los Angeles had sold more than 100 Casey paintings. Casey's patrons included the renowned collector Joseph Hirshhorn, the Beverly Hills Public Library, a congressman, and such entertainment-industry figures as Barbara McNair and Hope Lange. The Los Angeles gallery owner Joan Ankrum told Gildea, "Some of [Casey's] earlier works were angry, which is very understandable. He has a smoldering emotion—and a lyrical side. He paints semi-abstract, and has a great deal of communication on many levels." Meanwhile, he continued to excel on the playing field, and by 1967, when the six-foot, four-inch Casey, who then weighed 212 pounds, was acquired by the Los Angeles Rams, he had established himself as a dangerous offensive weapon.

In the late 1960s Casey, like many other prominent African-Americans, was publicly expressing his views on civil-rights issues. And, like those of many others, his words had taken on a militant and defiant—even ominous—tone. "You have intellectual involvement when a white man says, 'The Negro needs help. Let's get some more money for him,'" Casey told Gildea. "But does he want equality for the Negro on, say, only the west side of town? It is emotional involvement when you live next to a Negro and see him cutting his grass and your kids playing together. There are very few whites who would, if emotionally involved, want equality for the Negro. . . . Caucasians are just beginning to realize how long Negroes have hated them. Negroes don't want their love. We want the whites to get off our backs. Our antennae are up because of the problem. It is a lot for a man to be troubled by. . . . There's going to be blood in the streets. It's going to be worse." Casey also told Gildea that he supported the boxer Muhammad Ali, who had been stripped of his heavyweight-title belt and spent time in jail for his refusal to serve in the military in Vietnam. "He stood strong in the face of adversity," Casey told Gildea. "Whether it is right or wrong is his decision to make."

Before football camp began in 1968, Casey acted in his first feature film, *Guns of the Magnificent Seven* (1969), in which he played the supporting role of Cassie. In 1969 he published his first book of poetry, *Look at the People.* A year later, at age 30, Casey retired from football to pursue his painting, writing, and acting careers. To an extent, he was following in the footsteps of the successful African-American running back Jim Brown, who had left the game a few years earlier to pursue a career in film. One of Casey's first films after quitting football was *Tick, Tick, Tick* (1970), in which he co-starred with Brown. "I play a very militant rabble-rousing baddie, and Jim plays the sheriff who has come to get me . . . ," Casey told Bob Rubin for *Sport* (January 1970). "The reason why I think it's going to be good is that it portrays real human beings. The whites are good and bad and the blacks are good and bad. And Jimmy is not some super nigger but just a guy who has all the vulnerabilities and anxieties of any other human being." According to Rubin, Casey's paintings were then selling for as much as $1,000 apiece (about $4,200 in 1999 dollars), and he had been given seven one-man exhibitions.

As the 1970s wore on, Casey became a superstar of so-called black exploitation or "blaxploitation" cinema, starring in such films as *Black Chariot* (1971), *Hit Man* (1972), *Black Gunn* (1972), and *Dr. Black, Mr. Hyde* (1976), in the last of which—the director William Crain's follow-up to *Blacula*—he played a Dr. Jekyll/Mr. Hyde–like character. Perhaps his most memorable action flick of the decade was *Cleopatra Jones* (1973), which starred Tamara Dobson. More than two decades later, Casey told Prairie Miller for *Allmovie.com*, "I take exception to that phrase 'blaxploitation,' and always did. . . . [I prefer] just 'action films.' At the time that it happened in the '70s there were a few but not a great many of them. It seemed so, because there had been none. But there were some films made with Black people in the 'hood,' and it was a usual bill of fare about dope smuggling, hustling, and those things. Some of the films I like, and some I didn't. But it was our first time really, in a collective way in front of the screen."

Casey starred in some well-received mainstream dramas as well, most notably the Martin Scorsese–directed Bonnie-and-Clyde–type adventure *Boxcar Bertha* (1972), in which Casey was cast in the supporting role of Von Morton; *Cornbread, Earl and Me* (1975), in which he played Officer Atkins; and the highly acclaimed film *The Man Who Fell to Earth* (1976), which starred David Bowie. *Brothers* (1977) proved to be Casey's most provocative and critically acclaimed acting effort of the decade. The film is a barely fictionalized account of the real-life felon George Jackson, a prison inmate whose published revelations about the penal system and sudden, violent death drew attention to the need for prison reform. To prepare for the role of Jackson, Casey visited penitentiaries around the nation. "Folsom [State Penitentiary in northern California] was very depressing," he told the *New York Times* (March 25, 1977). "The guards walk the tiers in the mess halls with their rifles ready, and there is an oppression that weighs heavily on you every second you're there. The overcrowding is shocking, and you know how psychologically devastating that can be; just look at New York. I don't say that prisons should be eliminated, but I do say that the penal system is particularly abusive to minority prisoners." In 1979 Casey starred in the television miniseries *Roots: The Next Generations* and the sitcom *Harris and Company*. He played Major Jeff Spender in the TV miniseries *The Martian Chronicles* (1980), based on a Ray Bradbury story, and was a supporting character in the action movie *Sharky's Machine* (1981), directed by and starring Burt Reynolds.

Although his hope of becoming a mainstream acting presence had not been realized, by the late 1970s Casey's other artistic pursuits were flourishing: he had already published five books of poetry and had 15 exhibitions of his paintings. In an interview with a reporter for the *New York Times* (March 25, 1977), he said, "Years ago, my painting was very abstract, but lately it has gotten much more lyrical. Some of it contains social comment, but not a lot. And my poetry has gone from dealing with universal themes—the strife and stress between people, races, and nations—to a much more personalized point of view."

By the mid-1980s Casey's star in the TV and film firmament appeared to be dimming; parts were not coming as frequently as they had in the 1970s, and the roles that were offered to him were mostly peripheral. He made brief but memorable appearances in the James Bond film *Never Say Never Again* (1983), the Dan Aykroyd/Chevy Chase vehicle *Spies Like Us* (1985), and the surprise hit comedy *Revenge of the Nerds* (1984), but not until Keenen Ivory Wayans's film *I'm Gonna Git You Sucka* (1988) did Casey once again appear in a resounding critical and commercial hit. In that parody of blaxploitation films, Casey teamed up with such prominent 1970s stars as the musician Isaac Hayes and the actors Jim Brown, Steve James, and Antonio Fargas. The movie instantly became a cult favorite.

In the 1990s Casey has done his most notable television work, appearing in various popular science-fiction dramas, including *Star Trek: Deep Space Nine*, *Babylon 5*, and *Time Trax*. Casey also wrote, directed, produced, and starred in the 1997 film *The Dinner*. "A bit of Louis Malle's *My Dinner with Andre* stirred up with a touch of Baraka's *Dutchman*, *The Dinner* eavesdrops on the table conversations of three prosperous Black men in an elite white Southern restaurant," Prairie Miller wrote. "Though the friends have clearly achieved affluence and economic security in their lives, racial issues continue to gnaw away at their confidence." *The Dinner*, helped by a buzz within independent film circles, was shown at the prestigious Montreal Film Festival. When asked what inspired him to make the film, Casey told Miller, "I felt a need to bring forth another voice and a different vision, both of which we need desperately. There's been in the continuum a plethora of films that I think need to be reviewed and reconsidered because of their pejorative posture about African Americans. . . . Most of the films I see deal with urban dysfunctional, mean-spirited aberrations of what is misperceived to be Black people and Black culture. Obviously, there's a much larger vision and picture than we have been allowed to see. So I was inspired to bring forth a different voice."

Recalling his work in films, Casey told Miller, "I've enjoyed doing those big-budget things. They're a lot of fun, like *Never Say Never Again*, and *Sharky's Machine*. But I've also enjoyed some small, really wonderful films, like Tim Reid's *Once Upon a Time . . . When We Were Colored* [1996]. It's an extraordinary, insightful, warm film about family and community substantiation in the South back when cotton was king. . . . [And] I liked

Charles Burnett's *The Glass Shield* [1994], where I played an attorney that defends a character played by Ice Cube in a wrongful death shooting. So I've had a chance to make some decisions about different points of view. I've been blessed because I've had a long career." Despite his gratitude about his long life in film, Casey has remained outspoken about the position of African-Americans in the industry and in American society as a whole. "I think [black people in films] are primarily peripheral. We still don't have a lot of things to do, or much to say," he told Miller. "There are a few actors who are blessed with having careers of some impact. But primarily we are still an addendum. We are just sort of an afterthought." — M.B.

Suggested Reading: *Allmovie.com* (on-line); *Chicago Tribune* VII p63 Apr. 22, 1994, with photo; *New York Post* p107 Dec. 15, 1967, with photo; *New York Times* C p6 Mar. 25, 1977, E p1+ Nov. 27, 1997, with photo; *Newsweek* p94+

Sep. 20, 1968, with photo; *Sport* p8 Jan. 1970, with photo; *Washington Post* D p1+ Dec. 8, 1967, C p5 May 7, 1977, with photo

Selected Films: as actor—*Guns of the Magnificent Seven*, 1969; *Tick, Tick, Tick*, 1970; *Black Chariot*, 1971; *Hit Man*, 1972; *Boxcar Bertha*, 1972; *Black Gunn*, 1972; *Maurie*, 1973; *Cleopatra Jones*, 1973; *Cornbread, Earl and Me*, 1975; *The Man Who Fell to Earth*, 1976; *Brothers*, 1977; *Sharky's Machine*, 1981; *Never Say Never Again*, 1983; *Revenge of the Nerds*, 1984; *Spies Like Us*, 1985; *Steele Justice*, 1987; *Backfire*, 1987; *I'm Gonna Get You Sucka*, 1988; *Rent-a-Cop*, 1988; *Bill and Ted's Excellent Adventure*, 1989; *Another 48 Hours*, 1990; *Under Siege*, 1992; *Street Knight*, 1993; *The Cemetery Club*, 1993; *The Glass Shield*, 1994; *In the Mouth of Madness*, 1995; *Once Upon a Time . . . When We Were Colored*, 1996; as screenwriter, producer, and director—*The Dinner*, 1997

Jed Jacobson/Allsport USA

Chaney, John

Jan. 21, 1932– Head basketball coach at Temple University. Address: c/o Temple University, Vivacqua Hall, 4th Fl., P.O. Box 2842, Philadelphia, PA 19122-0842

John Chaney, the head coach of the Owls, Temple University's men's basketball team, has established a reputation as both a successful coach and a caring mentor who demands discipline and prepares his players for success off the court. Despite

the Owls' relatively sparse facilities, its small budget, and its cast of unheralded players, the team has consistently led the Atlantic Ten Conference and has regularly been selected as one of the 64 teams to compete in the NCAA's postseason tournament—commonly referred to as March Madness. As of the end of the 1998–99 season, Chaney's 17th season at the helm of the Owls, he had compiled a career record at Temple of 380 wins and 159 losses, and the Owls had played in the postseason NCAA tournament 15 times. Prior to Chaney's arrival, they hadn't played in the tournament since 1972.

Serving as a testament to Chaney's insistence on discipline, the Owls' success on the court has come about in a seemingly anachronistic fashion. In an era in which fast-paced play dominates much of college basketball and players routinely take the first shot available, Chaney's teams consistently maintain a controlled pace and employ a judicious style of play. They concentrate on playing an aggressive defense and usually commit fewer turnovers than their opponents.

Many have suggested that such discipline and success stem from the close relationships Chaney cultivates with his players. Although he does not refrain from barking at his players on occasion, he clearly cares about them, and he has taken steps to ensure that they will succeed after their college basketball careers end. He has long preached the importance of a college education, and he holds practices at 5:30 in the morning, in part to encourage his players to attend their morning classes. He also requires his players to attend tutoring sessions. "The coach, he taught me more than the game," Mark Macon, who played under Chaney from 1987 to 1991, before turning pro, told B. G. Kelley for *Inside Sports* (January 1994). "He taught me how to put balance in my life in order to make wise decisions. He taught me how to deal with critical situations so there would be a positive outcome. He taught me not to be a failure. Our relationship was and is multi-dimensional: father to son, friend to friend, brother to brother."

Chaney, who is a member of the executive committee of the Black Coaches Association, has also been a vocal critic of the controversial measures implemented by the National Collegiate Athletic Association (NCAA) to bar academically at-risk students from gaining athletic scholarships and participating in college athletics. The NCAA's Proposition 48 rule, put in place in 1986, made players ineligible for play as freshmen if they had not maintained at least a 2.0 grade-point average on core subjects in high school and failed to score a total of 700 or more on the Scholastic Aptitude Test (SAT). In August 1996 the NCAA instituted the more stringent Proposition 16, which stipulated that in order for a prospective college freshman to be eligible for an athletic scholarship, he must have maintained a 2.5 grade-point average in core subjects and achieved a total score of at least 820 on the SAT. Although some have questioned Chaney's motives for protesting such rules, he has long held that it and other, similar regulations ultimately and unfairly deprive many young African-Americans of a college education. "The NCAA says it's concerned about the integrity of education. Hell, image is what it's concerned about," he declared to Kelley. "If you're a school like Temple, which is not afraid to take a chance on a kid, give him an opportunity to get an education—and that's what I'm all about, opportunity—[the NCAA] begins to look at you with its nose turned up, saying, 'Well, Temple is not as academic as others. They're taking in the sick and the poor.' It's like the Statue of Liberty turning her ass and saying to the sick, the poor, the tired, 'Get the hell out.'"

Indeed, Chaney has routinely recruited players who have failed to meet the requirements of Proposition 48, knowing full well that they would miss at least one season of play. Several of those recruits, including Eddie Jones, now a professional with the Los Angeles Lakers, and Aaron McKie, a 1993 Owls star, have proved themselves to be exemplary athletes and students. "My degree [in social work] means a lot," McKie told Michael Bradley for the Sporting News (January 17, 1994). "Maybe it helps the next guy, who can say, 'Aaron McKie was a Prop. 48, and he made it through college.' Maybe that guy does, too."

Chaney's impressive work has often been overshadowed by his violent outbursts. He has shoved opposing coaches on several occasions, and following a 56–55 loss to the University of Massachusetts Minutemen in February 1994, he charged John Calipari, the Minutemen's coach, during a press conference, screaming, "I'll kill you!" Chaney, who received a one-game suspension after that episode, explained that he had lashed out at Calipari because he thought Calipari had verbally

intimidated the referees after the tense game. Regardless of the motivation behind these highly publicized incidents, his fits of anger have been met with severe criticism from sportswriters, fans, and other coaches. Commenting on those outbursts, Chaney told Kelley, "I can be an ass at times," then added, "but I don't want my kids to be one."

John Chaney was born into poverty on January 21, 1932 in Jacksonville, Florida. His father abandoned the family when John was young, and he was raised by his mother, Earley, and his stepfather, Sylvester Chaney, a carpenter. In 1945 the Chaney family moved to Philadelphia, where they settled in a cramped apartment above a garage.

Basketball offered Chaney solace from his tough home life. "I found mistrust when I came north. I found evil. But then I found basketball, and all the fear and evil didn't matter, because I was going past them to play basketball," he told Gary Smith for Sports Illustrated (February 28, 1994). He played point guard for Ben Franklin High School in Philadelphia, and in 1951 he was named most valuable player of Philadelphia's public-school league. Despite this recognition, he was not recruited by colleges in and around Philadelphia. "MVP of the city, and nobody called," he told Smith. He has cited two reasons for the lack of offers. "First of all," he told Kelley, "I didn't have the necessary college preparatory courses. Second, it was a time when there wasn't much sympathy for blacks. There were only a couple of blacks playing for colleges in Philadelphia then."

The only college that expressed interest in Chaney was Bethune-Cookman College, a small, predominantly African-American college run by the legendary educator Mary McLeod Bethune, in Daytona Beach, Florida. Chaney attended Bethune-Cookman on an athletic scholarship and became a standout in the National Association of Intercollegiate Athletics (NAIA), a smaller governing body for college athletics than the more prominent NCAA. He was named MVP of the NAIA playoffs in 1953, and in 1955 he graduated from Bethune-Cookman with a degree in health and physical education.

After college Chaney returned to Philadelphia. The National Basketball Association (NBA) did not express an interest in him, but he had a short stint with the Harlem Globetrotters. He reportedly quit after two months because he did not enjoy playing games whose outcomes were prearranged. He spent the next few years teaching physical education at a Philadelphia junior high school, waiting tables, and playing in the semiprofessional Eastern Basketball League, which paid him $60 to $70 per game. He was MVP of that league in the 1959–60 season. In 1966, injuries that he sustained in a car accident ended his playing career. For the next decade he coached at public schools in Philadelphia. After leading Sayre Junior High School to 59 wins and nine losses over several seasons, he coached at Simon Gratz High School and turned that school's basketball team into perennial contenders.

Chaney made the leap to coaching in the college ranks in 1972, at Cheyney State University (now called Cheyney University of Pennsylvania), a predominantly African-American university that competes in the NCAA's Division II bracket (less competitive than Division I but more so than Division III). He led Cheyney State to a Division II national championship title in 1978. By the time he left the school, in 1982, he had compiled a record there of 228 wins and 59 losses.

Chaney took over as the head coach of the Owls starting with the 1982–83 season. As he had always done, he stressed discipline and hard work. Although the Owls finished with 14 wins and 15 losses in that first season, they quickly improved under Chaney's leadership, and a winning tradition was established. Chaney's teams, often made up of talented but not highly prized high-school recruits, became known for guarding the ball carefully and committing few turnovers. They also employed an aggressive half-court zone defense when most teams were utilizing defensive schemes like the man-to-man and the full-court press. "The thing that carries us is our defense—and the mystique other teams have about our defense," Chaney told Mike DeCourcy for the *Sporting News* (January 8, 1996). "If you're in a conference where they just run up and down and shoot and gun . . . a lot of leagues just play man-to-man. They don't play zone. It's not something teams are accustomed to." Chaney has also insisted that the Owls play top-ranked teams. Their tough schedule has consistently placed them in a strong position at the end of the season, when sportswriters use a team's schedule as one criterion in selecting the 64 teams for the NCAA postseason tournament.

Of the Owls' many winning seasons, the 1986–87 and 1987–88 seasons stand out as two of the most memorable. The team finished the 1986–87 season with 32 wins and four losses, and Chaney was named coach of the year by the U.S. Basketball Writers Association. The following year the Owls enjoyed the number-one ranking in the nation for a time and finished the regular season with 29 wins and one loss. That season marked the emergence of freshman sensation Mark Macon, a six-foot-five-inch guard who provided key scoring and leadership and was named freshman of the year by the U.S. Basketball Writers Association. Chaney was named coach of the year by the U.S. Basketball Writers Association for the second time.

In December 1997 Temple opened a new, 10,000-seat arena called the Apollo of Temple. (The Owls had previously played at McGonigle Hall, a modest arena with 3,900 seats.) The Owls finished the 1997–98 season with 21 wins and eight losses, then were eliminated by West Virginia University in the first round of the NCAA postseason tournament. At the end of the 1998–99 season, the Owls had 24 wins and 11 losses; they lost to Duke University 85–64 in the Elite Eight round of the NCAA postseason tournament.

Meanwhile, Chaney was at least partially vindicated in his efforts to end the NCAA's use of standardized-test scores in choosing athletic-scholarship candidates. In early March 1999, just prior to the start of March Madness, U.S. federal district court judge Ronald Buckwalter ruled that Proposition 16 was racially discriminatory and that the NCAA could not use standardized-test scores to bar students from receiving athletic scholarships. The NCAA appealed the decision and was granted a stay, permitting it to operate for the time being without having to implement new measures.

John Chaney and his wife, Jeanne, live in Philadelphia. They have three children. — Y.P.

Suggested Reading: *New York Times* C p1+ Mar. 12, 1998, with photos; *Sporting News* p64+ Dec. 15, 1997, with photos; *Sports Illustrated* p72+ Feb. 28, 1994, with photos

Allsport U.S.A.

Chávez, Julio César

July 12, 1962– Boxer. Address: c/o International Boxing Hall of Fame Museum, P.O. Box 425, Canastota, NY 13032

The historical comparisons flew like confections from a broken piñata on September 11, 1993 at the aptly named Alamodome, in San Antonio, Texas, where the Mexican champion Julio César Chávez was set to take on the American fighter Pernell Whitaker for the World Boxing Council (WBC) welterweight championship. The fight was being touted as a rematch of the 1836 battle of the Alamo, in which Mexican general Antonio López de Santa Anna and his army routed a small American force that included the likes of Davy Crockett and James Bowie. Specters of this historic episode haunted the arena, as boxing pundits and promoters invoked the bloody battle in their discussions of the physical combat about to be waged. The boxing promoter Don King weighed in with the majestic—if uninformed—proclamation, "This time the Mexicans will win."

The fight was to a great degree a clash between cultures: specifically, between a fabled Mexican fighter and an American boxing establishment that he both disdained and dominated. The outcome would determine whether a Latino puncher who refused to slough off his heritage in submission to American commercialism, who refused, even, to learn English or to move to the United States, would rise to the top of a sport where stature is a function of popularity—and popularity, in turn, a function of a fighter's appeal to the U.S. boxing community. Having eschewed an assimilation that would have led to big purses while forcing him to abandon his own culture, Chávez seemed to many the embodiment of resistance to the omnivorous hegemony of the United States. None of this was lost on Chávez. "When I fight, all of the eyes in Mexico are upon me," Chávez said through a translater, as quoted by the *Chicago Tribune* (September 12, 1993). "It's a big responsibility. Sometimes it seems I am defending the nation." Some have speculated that these priorities stunted his popularity and relegated him to the undercard for longer than was necessary, but all signs pointed to the contrary, as the San Antonio crowd of 65,000, many of them waving Mexican flags and chanting the name of the fighter and his country, made their loyalty to Chávez indistinguishable from their national pride. They cheered a boxer who had associated Mexico not with drugs, poverty, and governmental corruption but with strength and cultural sovereignty.

Although Chávez could fight Whitaker only to a draw, his boxing legend had long been established. A veteran of more than 100 fights, nearly all of them victories, Chávez, at five-foot-seven and about 140 pounds, has overcome the lack of attention paid to smaller boxers by a public enamored with heavyweights like Mike Tyson, Evander Holyfield, and George Foreman. His combination of technical perfection and sheer power and tenacity has garnered him the worship of tens of thousands of fans; his fight against Whitaker had the largest paid attendance of any boxing match up to that time, with a pay-per-view audience of over one million.

Julio César Chávez was born on July 12, 1962 to Rodolfo Chávez, a railroad engineer, and Isabel Chávez, in Culiacán, Mexico, the capital of the northwestern state of Sinaloa, now notorious as a hotbed of narcotic trafficking. The Chávezes, a poor family, lived in a converted railway car rented to them by the government. One of 10 children,

Chávez sold newspapers, washed cars, and painted houses to help his family make ends meet. Stories abound of the family's having to sell medicine for food or boil down a green weed called *quelite* for sustenance. Following in the footsteps of his older brothers, Rodolfo and Rafael, Chávez took up boxing at an early age. He would often fight a teenage girl named Pilly, whose left hook tamed most of the neighborhood boys. "She was tough. Very tough. Not a dainty girl," Chávez told Phil Berger for the *New York Times* (September 10, 1992). "She looked like a little bull and was the same age as me. We would put the gloves on. Crowds would gather around, some of them making wagers." Pilly's brother described to Gary Smith of *Sports Illustrated* (February 22, 1993) how he saw in those fights intimations of Chávez's later style. "He threw punches at her body, the way he does now. She was just growing breasts then, and he hurt them so much that she quit boxing. I could see then how great he would be."

Sensing his potential, Chávez quit school at the age of 16 to devote all of his time to training. In his first professional fight, two years later, he crushed a boxer named Andres Feliz, knocking him out in the sixth round. Fighting at the 130-pound level, Chávez defeated 32 more opponents in Mexico before traveling to California to defeat Jerry Lewis. In 1984, in his first title shot, he took the WBC superfeatherweight championship from Mario Martinez with an eighth-round knockout. He quickly picked up his second title, the World Boxing Association (WBA) lightweight championship, by defeating his toughest opponent up to that time, the Puerto Rican legend Edwin Rosario. Vacating these belts, Chávez moved up to 140-pound competitions in 1989 and quickly captured the WBC juniorwelterweight belt from Roger Mayweather, who had provoked Chávez with racial epithets before the bout.

In the following year Chávez attempted to unify his title by taking on Meldrick Taylor for the International Boxing Federation (IBF) juniorwelterweight championship. Taylor, a Philadelphia native and Olympic gold medalist, was widely expected to break Chávez's undefeated streak. This was nearly the case, as Taylor controlled the action for the first 11 rounds. In the 12th and final round, however, when Taylor let up for a moment, Chávez let fly two rights, a hook, and another right, which sent Taylor stumbling into a neutral corner. Getting no coherent response from Taylor, the referee stopped the fight, awarding Chávez a technical knockout. Pandemonium broke out as Taylor's manager stormed into the ring and security guards were called upon to protect the fighters.

Chávez coasted through more than 15 fights in the next three years, defeating such prominent opponents as Hector Camacho and Greg Haugen. He brutalized the flamboyant Camacho not long after the latter strutted into the ring, wearing a cape patterned after the Puerto Rican flag. As usual, Chávez started slow, but then exploded with a series of hooks to the body. After watching their fighter take a very thorough beating for 10 rounds, Camacho's corner asked the boxer if he had had enough. But Camacho persisted, though to no avail, as Chávez took the decision. "It was like watching a jackhammer rip up a sidewalk," Pat Putnam of *Sports Illustrated* (September 21, 1992) wrote, describing Chávez's body-punishing style.

Vindication of his career as well as a title defense was on Chávez's mind during his February 1993 fight against the American Greg Haugen. Before the fight Haugen accused Chávez of padding his record by fighting weak opponents—"a bunch of Tijuana taxi drivers," as Haugen called them. In a brief but brutal bout that testified either to the inaccuracy of his challenger's remarks or to the surprising pugilistic proficiency of Tijuana cab drivers, Chávez sent Haugen to the canvas for good in the fifth round, in front of 150,000 spectators in Mexico City.

By this time Chávez had become, without a doubt, Mexico's greatest fighter, and some boxing aficionados were beginning to bestow upon him the unofficial yet coveted and controversial title of "best boxer in the world, pound for pound." He had developed a reputation as a powerful body puncher whose mantra was, "I hate boxers who dance." His orthopedist liked to joke that Chávez knew more about vital organs and nervous systems than he did. And no less an authority than Ferdie Pacheco, Muhammad Ali's legendary fight doctor, told the *New York Times Magazine* (August 29, 1993) that Chávez was "a lot like Ali in terms of sheer presence. Only he comes to do life-and-death battle, not to put on a boxing exhibition." By 1993 Chávez had amassed 87 wins, 75 of which were knockouts, and no losses.

The first stain on Chávez's record came seven months after his disposal of Haugen, in a bout against Pernell Whitaker. Chávez could not crack the defenses of his younger and faster opponent, and the two pounded each other to a draw, although most ringside reporters thought Whitaker had won by at least three rounds. Uncharacteristically, after the fight Chávez carped that his opponent had grabbed his left arm and repeatedly hit him below the belt. But more disinterested observers maintained that Whitaker outwitted and outboxed Chávez, by allowing him to advance and then shifting sideways to deflect Chávez's trademark body-blows off his shoulders and elbows. Such desperation signaled to some that Chávez's best days lay behind him, in the late 1980s, with his stunning victories over Edwin Rosario and Jose Ramirez.

Suspicions that Chávez was slipping as he approached his mid-30s were confirmed by his January 1994 loss to Frankie "The Surgeon" Randall, in yet another controversial match. Although Randall, a 32-year-old Tennessean, was a 16–1 underdog going into the bout, he fought Chávez closely, warding off his body blows and using an effective counterpunching strategy. But once again, the outcome was determined ultimately not by boxing acumen but by a controversial call from the official. In the 11th round, the referee penalized Chávez for the second time for throwing low blows, removing two points from his score. When the judges' scores were tallied at the conclusion of the 12th round, the penalties proved to be the deciding factor in Chávez's loss. Unwilling to admit defeat, Chávez took his case to the media after the fight. But his complaints fell on deaf ears, as more and more boxing writers were concluding that Chávez's game was diminished. Chávez responded to such pronouncements by hiring Emmanuel Steward, a trainer who had previously worked with heavyweight champion Evander Holyfield.

Despite a win in the rematch against Randall four months later, Chávez did little to bolster his faltering reputation, largely because this victory was also tainted by controversy. The rematch was stopped in the eighth round, after referee Mills Lane saw Randall unintentionally head-butt Chávez, whose right eye then began to spout blood. Chávez gave the impression to the examining ringside doctor that he could not continue the fight. Under WBC rules, the decision then went to the judges, two of whom had Chávez ahead in scoring at the time of the head-butt. The outcome was decided by a penalty point, this one subtracted from Randall's score after the head-butt. It put Chávez over the top, but not without the complaints of many boxing fans who saw a certain lack of logic in a ruling that allowed a fighter to quit and still win. Following that controversial bout, however, Chávez won decisive victories later in 1994 and in 1995, defeating Meldrick Taylor in a rematch as well as Tony Lopez and David Kamau. During this time Chávez discontinued his association with Don King, whom he accused of not paying enough attention to his career, and took up with Bob Arum's Top Rank Boxing.

In June 1996 Chávez ran into what has proven to be an unmovable roadblock—the undefeated Oscar De La Hoya. In his 99th career fight, in an atmosphere of great hype, Chávez faced off against the 22-year-old Olympic medalist and fashion-magazine cover boy. The fight, however, did not live up to media expectations—it was stopped in the fifth round because of excess bleeding from a cut opened above Chávez's left eye in the first 30 seconds of the match. Chávez later claimed that he had cut the eye while sparring in preparation for the fight, but to many, this statement had the same whiny tone of many of his other recent post-fight reactions.

Bouncing back from the De La Hoya loss, Chávez celebrated his 100th career victory on June 28, 1997, in a 10-round decision over Larry Lacoursiere. In a March 1998 attempt for the WBC super-lightweight championship, Chávez fought Miguel Angel Gonzalez to a draw in a tough fight. But his next big bout, a rematch against De La Hoya in September 1998, would not prove to be as successful. Wanting not only a victory but Chávez's respect,

De La Hoya, rather than trying to finesse his opponent as his corner advised, stood toe-to-toe and slugged it out with his idol for eight rounds, after which Chávez's corner had to throw in the towel because of profuse bleeding from the fighter's cut lower lip. This most recent loss, with all its symbolism as a changing of the guard, has fueled much speculation as to when Chávez will retire. Whenever he chooses to do so, Chávez will be assured a reputation as one of boxing's all-time best, a place in the Hall of Fame, and, perhaps most important to him, a legacy as a Mexican hero.

Julio César Chávez lives in Culiacán, Mexico, with his three sons. His wife, Amalia, recently filed for divorce. Chávez's collection of cars includes a white Mercedes limousine, three Corvettes, and two antique Fords. His professional record is 101–3–2. — M.C.

Suggested Reading: *New York Times* B p15 Sep. 10, 1992, with photo; *New York Times Magazine* p28+ Aug. 29, 1993, with photos; *Sporting News* p62 Oct. 31, 1988, with photo; *Sports Illustrated* p28+ Sep. 21, 1992, with photo, p50+ Feb. 22, 1993, with photos, p28+ Mar. 1, 1993, with photos, p70+ June 17, 1996

Courtesy of Center for Equal Opportunity

Chavez, Linda

1947– Founder and president of the Center for Equal Opportunity. Address: c/o Center for Equal Opportunity, 815 15th St. N.W., Suite 928, Washington, DC 20005

"I have had more difficulty with what I consider discriminatory and prejudiced behavior from liberals who thought they were doing me a favor than I have ever experienced from bigots," Linda Chavez, the founder and president of the Center for Equal Opportunity, told Phil McCombs for the *Washington Post* (January 30, 1984). "Maybe it shaped some of my attitudes on the whole affirmative action and quota business." This statement goes a long way toward explaining how Chavez turned from liberal Democrat into conservative Republican and became a staunch opponent of race-

and gender-based preferences in the workplace and schools and a champion of cultural assimilation.

Chavez began her career in politics as an aide for the Democratic National Committee. By the mid-1980s she had become a high-ranking official in President Ronald Reagan's administration. Her recent work as a policy analyst has placed her on the front lines of the battle between liberals and conservatives over affirmative action and bilingual education in the United States. Preaching the value of individual accomplishment, Chavez believes that merit and hard work should take precedence over racial quotas. Though her critics have labeled her a political opportunist and poor representative for the Hispanic community, Chavez dismisses the notion that any ethnic group needs representation. "I don't speak for anyone but Linda Chavez," she asserted to Macarena Hernandez for the *New York Times* (August 19, 1998).

The daughter of a working-class couple, Linda Chavez was born in 1947 in Albuquerque, New Mexico. Her father, Rudy Chavez, earned a living primarily as a house painter. Her mother, Velma (McKenna) Chavez, worked in restaurants during Linda's early childhood and later got jobs in clothing stores. According to Phil McCombs, Chavez has said that her parents had "a lot of kids," but she was "the only one who survived to adulthood."

Chavez's father traced his ancestry in New Mexico to the 1600s. One of his forebears was General Manuel Armijo, a governor of the Mexican territory of Nuevo Mexico. Armijo's failure to confront United States Army troops near Santa Fe in 1847, during the Mexican War (1846–48), resulted in the American annexation of the territory, part of which became New Mexico. Chavez's paternal grandfather, Ambrosio Chavez, was an accountant who turned to bootlegging during the Prohibition era (1919–33) and landed in jail. After his incarceration, his son Rudy, Chavez's father, had to drop out of high school to help support the family. Although Rudy Chavez's formal education ended in ninth grade, he was well-read, and he engendered in his daughter a lifelong love of books. From the age of four or five, Linda would accompany her father to the library. Chavez has said that her father had a profound influence on her.

When Linda was nine, the Chavezes moved to Denver, Colorado. In the building where they lived, they shared a bathroom with the residents of four other apartments. Linda attended a local Catholic high school, where she did well. Though she never seriously thought that college was an option for her, on a whim she applied to the University of Colorado and was accepted. During her freshman year, her dance teacher got her involved in working with disadvantaged children. The teacher also introduced Chavez to her son, Christopher Gersten. Chavez and Gersten were married soon after, in 1967.

Meanwhile, Chavez had become increasingly busy with social activism. She took part in campus rallies for affirmative action and remedial academic programs for minorities. Though at the time she supported affirmative-action programs, she also felt strongly that minority students should be assimilated into the general student population. In her experience, though, members of minorities tended to separate themselves from other students, and for that reason she gradually grew disenchanted with the aims of the public protests and rallies she had been supporting.

In 1970, after she graduated from the University of Colorado, with a bachelor's degree in English literature, Chavez entered the Ph.D. program in literature at the University of California at Los Angeles (UCLA). Earlier, she had applied for a Ford Foundation grant that was designed to enable minority students to pursue advanced studies, and she traveled to New York City for an interview with foundation representatives. "There were these two Anglo men and this one Puerto Rican woman and they asked me to talk about myself a little bit, and I did, and the next thing I knew, one of the men said to me, 'You speak English so *well*, Miss Chavez,'" she recalled to Phil McCombs. "And I was stunned. I mean, here I am applying for a PhD in English literature, I've got a 3.85 grade average in English, and they're telling me I speak English well. It was really unbelievable, and it went down hill from there." (The interviewer mistakenly assumed that Chavez's native language was Spanish; actually, her parents did not speak Spanish, and she grew up speaking only English at home.)

Chavez's dismay at the interview notwithstanding, she accepted an assistantship at UCLA. She was assigned to teach a course in Mexican-American literature that had been set up for Hispanic students in UCLA's open-admissions program. "It was a disaster," she told Phil McCombs. "[The students] were not terribly interested in reading books. They wanted to come in and rap about their experiences." According to Chavez, when she tried to enforce her reading requirements, a group of students walked out of the class. After she gave the worst students failing grades, she began to be harassed, reportedly suffering such indignities as disturbances at her home in the middle of the night and deposits of excrement on the front seat of her car. The harassment did not stop until the university's Mexican-American student association intervened. "As one would imagine, that really soured me on teaching and soured me on what the open admissions program was supposed to be about," she told McCombs. Fernando Chavez, a son of the civil-rights activist Cesar Chavez (and no relation to Linda Chavez) and a student in one of Linda Chavez's classes, observed to Macarena Hernandez, "There were a lot of students who were hard on her because they didn't feel she was, quote, 'Chicano enough.'"

Chavez left UCLA without completing her doctoral degree. She relocated to Washington, D.C., where her husband was working with the AFL-CIO's Committee on Political Education project, and embarked on a career in public service. For two years beginning in 1972 she worked for the Democratic National Committee, and then, for a year, with a U.S. House of Representatives subcommittee—specifically, the Judiciary Committee's Subcommittee on Civil and Constitutional Rights, which was headed by Democratic representative Don Edwards of California. Next, Chavez became a lobbyist for the National Education Association, and after that, in 1977, the editor of American Federation of Teachers (AFT) publications, among them the award-winning quarterly journal *American Educator*. Under the influence of the AFT's president, Albert Shanker, Chavez grew increasingly conservative in her views on such issues as affirmative action, racial quotas, and bilingual education. "I really love this country and what it stands for, and the way in which it allows people like me to make it on their own, on their own initiative, on hard work," she told Phil McCombs. "I think I still have that sense that if you work hard enough, you'll make it, and I don't think it does a service to people when you say, 'Well, you don't have to work very hard because we'll give you a preference.'" Her ideas were reinforced by the views of noted conservatives whose articles she edited for the AFT journals. Among them were Jeane Kirkpatrick, the U.S. ambassador to the United Nations from 1981 to 1985; Robert Bork, a U.S. Court of Appeals judge, whose nomination to the Supreme Court by President Ronald Reagan in 1987 was defeated after a bitter confirmation battle between liberals and conservatives on the Senate Judiciary Committee; and William J. Bennett, who served as the U.S. secretary of education during part of the Reagan presidency. Chavez's contact with Bennett proved particularly fruitful. He helped her compile for publication a series of articles she had written, and the views on education she expressed in them attracted the attention of Reagan administration officials. In 1983, after Bennett made a few well-placed introductions and recommendations, Chavez was appointed staff director of the U.S. Commission on Civil Rights.

An independent, bipartisan agency that was formed by an act of Congress in 1957 and reconstituted in 1983, the Civil Rights Commission was established to investigate complaints by citizens who claim they have been deprived of their right to vote; to act as a watchdog over equal-opportunity programs; and to serve as a clearinghouse for information on civil rights in the U.S. The agency is comprised of eight commissioners—four of whom are appointed by the president and the others by Congress—and an administrative staff. Chavez has said that, despite her connection to William Bennett, she was not a shoo-in for the job. "I don't know that they really, at first, knew what to make of me," she told McCombs. "Here I was, a Democrat out of a labor union. They weren't quite sure whether I was for real." Chavez revealed herself to be a champion of the Reagan administration's stance against affirmative action. During her stormy two years with the commission, she spearheaded studies showing the ill effects of affirmative action in schools and the workplace. According to Chavez, giving preferences based on race and gender fosters the perception that minorities and women are hired or admitted into universities only because of their ethnicity or gender and not because of their qualifications. Her frequent, public denunciations of quotas were seen by some as inappropriate, because Chavez was not a commissioner but an administrator, and as threatening to the independent status of the commission. Her detractors labeled her an apparatchik of the Reagan administration and pointed out what they saw as the irony of her criticizing programs identical to one from which she herself had benefitted.

Chavez left the commission in April 1985, when President Reagan named her chief of the White House office of public liaison, in which capacity she served as one of his deputy assistants. Commenting obliquely on the appointment, commission member Mary Frances Berry told Marilyn Milloy for *Newsday* (April 10, 1985), "It's the first time in the history of the civil rights commission that someone has so ingratiated themselves to the administration that they are given a plum job." Suspicions about Chavez's biases were reinforced when, at the time of her appointment, she announced that she planned to change her party affiliation from Democrat to Republican, to reflect her gradual alienation from the principles of the Democratic Party. She claimed to have long avidly supported an aggressive foreign policy and an expanded military, to the extent that she abstained from voting in 1972 and 1976 because she thought the Democrats weak on these issues. In 1980, she said, she had cast her first vote for a Republican, when she pulled the voting-booth lever for Reagan, with whose foreign policy and military platform she agreed. "I came from a family where my father was a Purple Heart winner in the Second World War, and a lot of my views about defense issues and foreign policy issues were very firmly held before I would have ever thought of myself as a Republi-

can," she told Gerald Boyd for the *New York Times* (June 3, 1985).

In her new post Chavez reported directly to the White House communications director, Patrick Buchanan, who was so impressed with her that he urged her to pursue elective office. A new resident of Maryland, Chavez set her sights on the Senate seat being vacated in 1986 by the three-term Republican incumbent Charles Mathias. In Maryland, where Democrats outnumbered Republicans by a ratio of about three to one, Mathias had been a GOP stalwart. Although his moderate views on issues had attracted a sufficient number of Maryland Democrats to keep him in office, the Republican Party saw his retirement as an opportunity to nominate someone more conservative. They were drawn to Chavez, who, as a member of an ethnic minority and as someone who had turned from liberalism to conservatism, attracted a lot of attention from the media, which seldom failed to mention the difficulty of categorizing her career in conventional political terms. The focus on Chavez's ethnicity vexed her mother, who is of Anglo-Irish extraction. "Sometimes it annoys me because she's just as much Anglo as I am and she's just as much mine as she is her father's," Velma Chavez told Michael McQueen for the *Washington Post* (August 17, 1986). "It annoys me because they always write about her as if she's just Hispanic, and she's not. She's a mixture just like everybody else in the United States."

After easily securing the GOP nomination, Chavez faced off against Democrat Barbara Mikulski, a 10-year veteran of the House of Representatives. A native of Baltimore, Mikulski grew up in the city's eastern, industrial section, where her parents had managed a small store. Short and stocky, the gritty Mikulski contrasted sharply with the slender and more polished Chavez. Though known for her fiery temperament—frequently displayed during debates on social issues—Mikulski kept her temper in check during the campaign, and that proved to be an excellent strategy against Chavez's assault. Despite repeated challenges from Chavez, Mikulski closed off most opportunities for confrontation and debate (a strategy common among frontrunners), and she responded to Chavez's salvos with reserve. Chavez could not overcome her image as a carpetbagger (she had lived in Maryland for less than two years) and political opportunist (she had registered as a Republican even more recently). She lost the race with 39 percent of the vote to Mikulski's 61 percent.

Linda Chavez has remained active in politics as a policy analyst. From 1987 to 1988 she served as president of U.S. English, a group that lobbies for legislation on the local, state, and federal levels that would declare English the nation's official language. In 1989, having found the scope of U.S. English too narrow for her taste, she became a senior fellow of the Manhattan Institute, a conservative political think-tank based in New York City that funds research on such issues as welfare, crime, education, and taxes. Chavez's research resulted in her first book, *Out of the Barrio: Toward a New Politics of Hispanic Assimilation* (1991), in which she presented arguments for assimilation and against ethnocentricity while dealing with such topics as immigration, voting rights, affirmative action, and bilingual education. The book was well-received among conservative critics and panned by liberal reviewers.

In 1995 Chavez founded the Center for Equal Opportunity, a project of the Equal Opportunity Foundation. The center is a research group that studies issues of race, multiculturalism, and assimilation; through the organization, after years of behind-the-scenes analysis, Chavez's public-policy work began to gain a much wider audience. In 1996, at the behest of California conservatives, Chavez, who is president of the center, exhorted voters to approve the passage of Proposition 209, which barred state and local governments from using race- and gender-based preferences in school admissions, public hiring, or government contracting. Constitutional challenges to Proposition 209 by civil-liberties organizations ended in failure: in April 1997 the U.S. Ninth Circuit Court of Appeals in San Francisco upheld the measure, and it went into effect in August of the same year. Based on Chavez's accomplishment in connection with Proposition 209, California millionaire Ron K. Unz enlisted her aid in the passage of Proposition 227, which ended bilingual education in the state. Proposition 227, too, was challenged by civil-liberties groups and followed a similar path through the court system: in July 1998 the U.S. Ninth Circuit Court of Appeals refused to block the measure, and it became law the following month.

Linda Chavez's second book, *From Sugar Daddies to Uncle Sam*, which is about feminism, is scheduled to be published in the fall of 1999. Chavez is also the author of a weekly syndicated column carried in more than 50 periodicals nationwide, among them the *Philadelphia Inquirer* and the *Chicago Tribune*. A frequent contributor to the *New York Times*, the *Wall Street Journal*, the *Washington Post*, the *New Republic*, and *Fortune*, she has appeared regularly as a guest analyst on such television programs as *CNN & Co.*, the *McLaughlin Group*, and *NewsHour with Jim Lehrer*. She served as the U.S. expert on the United Nations Subcommission on Human Rights (1992–96). Currently, she sits on the board of directors of several nonprofit organizations and is a director of Greyhound Lines, Inc. and ABM Industries, Inc. She lives in Purcellville, Virginia, with her husband, Chris Gersten, currently the political director of the American Israel Public Affairs Committee, a pro-Israel lobbying group. The couple have three grown sons: David, Pablo, and Rudy. Outside of politics, literature remains Chavez's primary interest. — T.J.F.

Suggested Reading: *New York Times* A p28 Aug. 19, 1998, with photo; *Washington Post* B p1+ Jan. 30, 1984, with photos, D p1+ Aug. 17, 1986, with photo

Selected Books: *Out of the Barrio: Toward a New Politics of Hispanic Assimilation*, 1991; *From Sugar Daddies to Uncle Sam*, 1999

Bob Greene/Courtesy of HBO

Cheadle, Don

Nov. 29, 1964– Actor; playwright; screenwriter.
Address: c/o Liberman-Zerman Management, 252 N. Larchmont Blvd., Suite 200, Los Angeles, CA 90004

Don Cheadle, who has appeared in more than a dozen feature-length films, is a rising star in Hollywood as well as on the independent film scene. Best known for his roles in *Devil in a Blue Dress* (as the trigger-happy Mouse), for which he was named best supporting actor by the Los Angeles Film Critics, and *Boogie Nights* (in which he played the discontented adult-film star Buck Swope), Cheadle, who is black, feels that it is important to take race into account when making a film. He told Justine Elias for *Interview* (August 1997), "Color blindness [in casting films] is ridiculous. Even dogs or a person with color blindness can differentiate shades—nobody is shade-blind. You don't need to ignore your race. . . . I'm glad that people try to write roles that anyone can do, but I also don't ever want to end up in movies where the fact that I'm a black man is a nonissue. In America, it's always an issue." A screenwriter and playwright in addition to being an actor, Cheadle has enjoyed success on both sides of the camera and has flirted several times in his 10-year career with Academy Award nominations. Among his other film credits are Dennis Hopper's *Colors* (1988), John Singleton's *Rosewood* (1997), and Warren Beatty's *Bulworth* (1998). He earned a Global Globe Award for his portrayal of Sammy Davis Jr. in the 1998 HBO movie *The Rat Pack*, and Emmy nominations for both his *Rat Pack* role and his work in another HBO film, *A Lesson Before Dying*.

Don Cheadle was born on November 29, 1964 in Kansas City, Missouri. His father is a psychologist; his mother is a teacher. Cheadle's first acting role came while he was in elementary school. "I was Templeton the rat in *Charlotte's Web* in fifth grade; that's when I got the acting bug," Cheadle told Elias. "I'd always been creative, and I sang with the band at my elementary school in Kansas City where the music teacher really helped me focus." He has also cited his father—particularly his father's profession—with influencing his own career choice. "Getting into different characters and playing so many people and figuring out their psychology and their motivation," he told Ed Leibowitz for the *Los Angeles Times* (May 24, 1998, on-line), "I probably got a lot of that just by osmosis."

Having acted in plays and musicals in high school, he enrolled at the California Institute of the Arts (Cal Arts), in Valencia. The school's audition required him to read from a classical play; Cheadle chose a passage from Molière's *Tartuffe*. "I picked the first monologue that had archaic language in meter and said, OK, I'll learn this," he told Elias. "But what did I know about Molière? I didn't know this [expletive] was supposed to be funny." As the interviewers sat dumbfounded by how badly he had misinterpreted the meaning of the passage, Cheadle pleaded, "'Wait! I have another piece!' I did something from *The Shadow Box* which I knew well and understood. The dean took me aside later and said, 'Do me a favor. Don't try Molière again until you know what you're doing.'"

Cheadle recalls his four years at Cal Arts fondly. During his tima there, he performed in numerous stock plays and various student-written dramas. Upon graduating, in 1986, Cheadle received $500 from his parents; the money "lasted me a month," he told Elias. "Right before I ran out of money, I got *Hamburger Hill*." In that 1987 Vietnam War drama, directed by John Irvin, the still-green actor played the role of Washburn. Cheadle and the rest of the cast spent a good part of 1986 in the Philippines, where the filmmakers re-created a Vietnamese jungle. After he returned to the States, in 1987, he was unemployed for a mere three weeks before the renowned stage director JoAnn Akalaitis cast him in a show at the prestigious Guthrie Theater in Minneapolis, Minnesota. Not long after appearing in the Dennis Hopper police drama *Colors* (1988) alongside Robert Duvall and Sean Penn, Cheadle found steady television work, on such programs as *The Fresh Prince of Bel-Air* (1990), *Picket Fences*

(1992), and the short-lived series *The Golden Palace* (1992). Cheadle's other notable television appearances include guest spots on *Fame* (1986), *Hill Street Blues* (1987), *Night Court* (1988), and *China Beach* (1988).

After he had given supporting performances in such films as *Roadside Prophets* (1992), *The Meteor Man* (1993), and *Things to Do in Denver When You're Dead* (1995), Cheadle's breakthrough role came in Carl Franklin's *Devil in a Blue Dress* (1995), based on the novel by Walter Mosley and starring Denzel Washington. Although the film was a box-office disappointment, it brought Cheadle a great deal of attention in film-industry circles, and his portrayal of Mouse—the fast-talking, foul-mouthed, homicidal sidekick of Washington's detective, Easy Rawlins—even created a buzz about an Oscar nomination. While that nomination didn't pan out, Cheadle did secure awards for best supporting actor from the National Board of Review and the Los Angeles Film Critics.

Between acting projects, Cheadle wrote his first play, *Groomed*. A drama about four black men who attend the wedding of a friend in Lincoln, Nebraska, it premiered at the Mark Taper Forum in Los Angeles in late 1995. A few months later the play saw a limited run at the Hartford Stage, in Connecticut. Cheadle then returned to acting, landing the lead role in the 1996 HBO original film *Rebound: The Legend of Earl "The Goat" Manigault*, in which he played a basketball prodigy who falls prey to drug addiction.

In the same year Cheadle received a call from the acclaimed director John Singleton, who enlisted Cheadle's services for his project *Rosewood*. Singleton asked Cheadle to portray Sylvester Carrier, a mild-mannered piano teacher in 1920s Florida who tries to defend his family against a horde of racists. Appearing in the film with Ving Rhames and John Voight, Cheadle again generated an Oscar buzz.

Cheadle's next big film was the sleeper hit *Boogie Nights*, the sophomore effort from critically acclaimed director/screenwriter Paul Thomas Anderson. A fictionalized account of the adult-entertainment industry in the late 1970s and early 1980s, starring Burt Reynolds and Mark Wahlberg, the film earned several Academy Award nominations for both acting and writing. "When I read the script, I didn't really dig it," Cheadle told *Roughcut* (October 30, 1997, on-line). "I didn't really understand it. It was like the first time I read Chekhov. I had no context for it." Cheadle played Buck Swope, a porn actor who engages in several business ventures in an attempt to leave the adult-film world behind. With his name recognition increased as a result of that film's success, Cheadle appeared in the big-budget *Volcano* (1997) with Tommy Lee Jones and Anne Heche. Describing the experience of acting in a special-effects-driven film, Cheadle told Ed Leibowitz, "Once I got on the set I realized, 'It ain't about you. The movie's called *Volcano*. . . . You're going to say what you're going to say, and then they're going to look at the lava.'. . . [The Hollywood blockbuster] is a weird beast. It resembles acting enough to confuse you, but this business is about making money. You know, they'd put a shoe up there on screen for two hours if people would pay to see it."

In 1998 Cheadle played a supporting part in the Warren Beatty film *Bulworth* and a feature role, as Maurice "Snoopy" Miller, the violent friend of a bank robber, in Steven Soderbergh's critically acclaimed action film *Out of Sight*. Based on a book by the best-selling crime novelist Elmore Leonard, *Out of Sight* is about an FBI agent (played by Jennifer Lopez) who becomes enamored of the robber (George Clooney) in the course of attempting to capture him after his escape from prison. The film, which reunited Cheadle with Ving Rhames, did not perform as well in theaters as many had expected, but it was well reviewed and has become something of a cult classic on video. Soon afterward, Cheadle portrayed the legendary Sammy Davis Jr. in the HBO movie *The Rat Pack*, also starring Ray Liotta, as head Rat-Packer Frank Sinatra. Of Davis's private life—which disintegrated behind the glamorous public façade of the Rat Pack's hard-living entertainers—Cheadle told Leibowitz, "[Davis] created this gilded cage he could not get out of. He was trying to be a dad and be home and do the right things, but he realized he was cutting into 'Sammy' time. And he realized that his whole life up to that point had been about creating this character, this fabulous thing. And he realized he couldn't drop it even for his family."

In his interview with Ed Leibowitz for the *Los Angeles Times*, Cheadle discussed the separation between work and family in his own life. Leibowitz reported that the actor "sometimes creates elaborate unwritten histories for his characters distinct from his own," as much to "prevent himself from becoming ensnared" as to enhance his performances. "It's a self-defense mechanism against getting lost," Cheadle explained. "I don't want to come home damaged and depressed and wanting to shoot heroin. I have two kids and a family that I care about. I've got to create strong characters so that I'm not taking too much of me."

In 1999 Cheadle starred in the critically acclaimed movie *A Lesson Before Dying* (1999), a stark depiction of racial conflict that aired on HBO. Set in 1948 and based on the best-selling Ernest Gaines novel with the same title, *A Lesson Before Dying* is about Grant Wiggins (Cheadle), a teacher who returns to the small Louisiana town where he was raised to counsel a young black man wrongfully accused of the murder of a white man. Cheadle's current projects include a remake of the 1973 "blaxploitation" hit *Cleopatra Jones*, for which he is writing the screenplay, and a starring role in Brian De Palma's film *Mission to Mars*, which is set for release in 2000.

Cheadle lives in Los Angeles with the actress Bridgid Coulter, who portrayed Sylvester Carrier's wife, Gertie, in *Rosewood*. He and Coulter are the

parents of two children, and that made the filming of *Rosewood* "kind of difficult," he told Henri Behar for *Filmscouts* (on-line). "Our daughter was with us on location. We had three weeks of night shoot in a row! So just as I would be getting home, she'd be waking up. And we'd be too tired to play with her. Then she'd be taking her nap and we'd have to go to work. That, really, is the difficult part of working as much as that. You miss a day in a one-year-old's life, or two days, you've missed something. Something they weren't doing two days ago. And suddenly they're in Harvard." Cheadle was recently elected a member of the Academy of Motion Picture Arts and Sciences. — M.B.

Suggested Reading: *Filmscouts* (on-line); *Interview* p82+ Aug. 1997, with photos; *Metahollywood* (on-line) May 24, 1998; *New York Times* B p18 Oct. 22, 1995, with photos; *Roughcut* (on-line) Oct. 30, 1997, with photo

Selected Films: *Hamburger Hill*, 1987; *Colors*, 1988; *Roadside Prophets*, 1992; *The Meteor Man*, 1993; *Things to Do in Denver When You're Dead*, 1995; *Devil in a Blue Dress*, 1995; *Boogie Nights*, 1997; *Rosewood*, 1997; *Volcano*, 1997; *Bulworth*, 1998; *Out of Sight*, 1998; *Wings Against the Wind*, 1999; *Mission to Mars*, 2000; for television—*Rebound: The Legend of Earl 'The Goat' Manigault*, 1996; *The Rat Pack*, 1998; *A Lesson Before Dying*, 1999

Selected Television Shows: *China Beach*, 1988; *The Fresh Prince of Bel Air*, 1990; *The Golden Palace*, 1992; *Hangin' with Mr. Cooper*, 1992; *Picket Fences*, 1993; *Lush Life*, 1996

Chen, Joan

Apr. 26, 1961– Film actress; director. Address: c/o Rigbert-Roberts Co., 1180 S. Beverly Dr., Suite 608, Los Angeles, CA 90035; c/o Innovative Artists, 1999 Ave. of the Stars, Suite 2850, Los Angeles, CA 90067

"The only thing I achieved going to the States was that I became an exotic beauty," the Chinese-born actress and director Joan Chen once said, as quoted by Richard Corliss for *Time* (April 5, 1999). "I did my best to give a version of Chinese-ness that the West was looking for. But I also understood that that version of me was worthless. I wanted to do something more serious." Chen began acting in films at age 14 in China, where she became a major star. After she settled in the United States, in 1981, she struggled to get satisfying work, hampered by both cultural and language barriers and the film industry's notorious lack of substantial roles for actors of Asian ancestry. In overcoming those obsta-

Armando Gallo/Retna Ltd.

Joan Chen

cles, she has forged an impressive career in her adopted country. Probably best known in the West for her portrayal of the disenchanted empress in Bernardo Bertolucci's *The Last Emperor*, she has also appeared in the movies *Tai Pan* and *Golden Gate*, among other pictures, and in the television series *Twin Peaks*. In 1998 she made her directorial debut, with *Xiu Xiu: The Sent-Down Girl*, a feature film about the effect of the Cultural Revolution in China on a naïve teenage girl.

When, in an interview for the *New York Times Magazine* (May 23, 1999), Melanie Rehak asked her what lessons "the more ideological aspects of [her] Chinese upbringing" had given her for her "current life in America," Chen answered, "It instilled in me an appetite for something intangible, spiritual and grander outside of the practical pursuit of self-interest. That's what drives me to make films. I'm actually extremely comfortable materially. I feel very rich; I don't need any more. It's the other side of me that's hungry." She added, in a reference to *Xiu Xiu: The Sent-Down Girl*, "From getting an idea to completing this film to talking with you was obstacle after obstacle after obstacle. I think without that drive, that spiritual need to tell a meaningful story, I would not have been able to do it."

The second of the two children of prominent physicians, Joan Chen was born Chong Chen on April 26, 1961 in Shanghai, China. Beginning when she was five, China underwent a period of enormous social and political upheaval—the decade dominated by the Great Proletarian Cultural Revolution, which Mao Zedong, the chairman of the Chinese Communist Party, and radical leftist factions implemented with the goal of rooting out

"bourgeois" and moderate values. Chen's parents were among the millions of professionals who were sent to the countryside to be "reeducated"— that is, indoctrinated with Communist Party dogma—among peasants. "Because my parents were intellectuals, they suffered during the Cultural Revolution . . . ," Chen recalled to Bob Thomas for the New York *Daily News* (September 4, 1988). "My grandparents took care of my brother and me. Actually, it was a lot of fun being away from our parents for a while." Millions of other children were forced from their homes "to help build socialism," often in remote areas, Chen explained to Melanie Rehak, and their experiences were usually anything but fun. "Stories came out about how horrible it was," Chen told Rehak.

Serendipitously, when Chen was 14 and in her first year of high school, employees in the state-run film industry selected her to appear in a film being produced in Shanghai. Being picked in this way was "very, very rare," Chen told Rehak. "Mao's wife planned to do three movies about the Long March"—the 6,000-mile trek (1934–35) in which Chinese Communist forces fled from their enemies and relocated to the remote northwestern part of China—"and she had to personally approve all the cast. I was proud to be doing propaganda, to be of use to the Communist cause." According to one source, Chen was trained in acting in a program run by the Shanghai Film Studio. Earning the equivalent of about $18 a month, she appeared in five films within the next six years, among them *Youth* (1977), *The Little Flower* (1980), and *Awakening* (1981), in all of which she portrayed virtuous young women. She soon became one of China's most popular film stars.

"I was very young and pure, and I didn't enjoy fame," Chen told Melanie Rehak. "I would be on a street in any city, and there would be thousands of people falling down hurting themselves, crowding me, their bicycles all trampled, and I wouldn't be able to get out. That scared me." She has recalled wishing she could become a parachuter rather than an actress, because the parachuters' uniforms "looked so handsome, and the female uniform actually had a waistline. . . . In school, our outfits didn't show our shapes." (The idea behind the uniforms, as Chen observed to Rehak, was that "when you have no physical appearance of being a woman, you seem to have less vulnerability. And we were taught that we shouldn't behave any differently than the boys.") Her feelings about stardom notwithstanding, Chen received many honors for her acting work. At age 18 she received a Golden Rooster Award, the Chinese equivalent of an Oscar, and the Hundred Flowers Award, which honored the country's most beloved actor or actress, as determined by a nationwide poll.

In the late 1970s the Chinese government sent Chen's mother and other scientists to the United States to do research; for a time her mother worked at the Sloan Kettering Institute, in New York City. Her father, too, did scientific research in the U.S.

"Sometimes [my mother] sent me materials from America—pages from magazines she thought I should read," Chen recalled to Michael J. Bandler for the *Chicago Tribune* (February 20, 1994). "I was studying English. She would underline certain things. For instance, she taught me that when you say 'Forget it,' it doesn't really mean you forget it. It just means, 'Don't mention it anymore.'" The contents of her mother's parcels whetted her appetite for American culture, and she began to dream of emigrating to the U.S. She did so in 1981, at the age of 20.

Adjusting to a new way of life in a foreign land proved difficult for Chen. "I was clueless when I arrived," she recalled to Richard Corliss. "The cultural shock—even the toothpaste tasted different! My desire to go to the States was so vague, yet so strong. It's like going to heaven: you don't plan what happens after you enter." She briefly attended the State University of New York at New Paltz, where she considered following in her parents' footsteps and preparing for a career in medicine. Then she transferred to California State University at Northridge, after attending, at the invitation of that school, a screening there of one of her Chinese-made films. At Northridge she studied film production. "My mother was astonished. 'Can filmmaking be a major?' she asked," Chen recalled to Kirk Honeycutt for the *Chicago Tribune* (November 20, 1986).

While working as a waitress to help support herself as an undergraduate, she began auditioning for acting roles; during that period she adopted the name Joan. "I started part-time during my summer vacations," she told Honeycutt. "But a very surprising thing happened to me. I got rejections. I was highly in demand in China. If I wanted to act [in China], of course people wanted me. I had to realize that [in the U.S.] nobody had seen Chinese movies. . . . I learned that what [American casting directors] wanted was different. So I changed myself. I felt it was a challenge." Of the meager number of parts offered to actors or actresses of Asian ancestry, the majority were those of prostitutes or gangsters. Chen's jobs were mainly bit roles on television shows.

Her big career break came when the Italian producer and director Dino De Laurentiis spotted her in a Metro-Goldwyn-Mayer parking lot. "Did you know that Lana Turner was discovered in a drug store?" he said to her—a remark that caught her off-guard, partly because at that time she didn't know who Lana Turner was. Thanks to that chance encounter, she won a prominent role, as the concubine May-May, in *Tai-Pan* (1986), an adaptation of the same-named, best-selling novel by James Clavell about the founding of Hong Kong as a British colony in the mid-19th century. Directed by Daryl Duke and produced by De Laurentiis's daughter Raffaella, *Tai-Pan* was resoundingly panned by virtually all critics, and Chen, who disrobed in several sex scenes, did not escape their barbs. Moreover, her appearance in *Tai-Pan* did not endear her

to her fans back in China; indeed, it was a "shock" to them, she told Jamie Portman for the *Chicago Tribune* (December 20, 1987). "It hasn't been shown in China yet, but they've all heard about it. To them I have always been the nice young girl—clean and sweet and lovely. There was never anything in those early characters I played that would arouse desires in men. And now I play somebody's mistress! I don't regret shocking them. I have to go on with what I want to do. You see, I was 14 when I started—and they expect me to be 14 all my life."

Despite the negative reactions to *Tai-Pan* in China and the United States, the film significantly boosted Chen's career. In the next year she co-starred in Bernardo Bertolucci's epic *The Last Emperor* (1987), which—notwithstanding its extremely limited distribution in the U.S., to only 100 theaters—won nine Academy Awards, including that for best picture. The film chronicles the life of Pu Yi, who was crowned emperor of China at age three, in 1908, was deposed in 1912 but remained in the imperial palace until 1924, had an arranged marriage, became a playboy and nightclub singer, was made the puppet emperor of Manchuria during the 1930s by the Japanese, was imprisoned for 10 years by the Chinese Communists as a war criminal, was "reeducated" after his release, and, at his death in 1967, was working as a gardener—an ordinary citizen of the People's Republic of China. Chen received critical acclaim and an Oscar nomination for her portrayal of Pu Yi's wife, Wan Yung, who became dependent on opium and died as a result of her addiction. The director's cut of *The Last Emperor*, containing 60 minutes of film deleted from the 1987 release, became available in 1998.

From 1988 through 1996 Chen appeared in 13 films. They include *The Blood of Heroes* (1989), *Where Sleeping Dogs Lie* (1991), *Steel Justice* (1992), *Shadow of a Stranger* (1992), and *Killing Beach* (1993), in all of which Chen was relegated to playing stereotypical exotic Asian beauties; none of those movies fared well critically or commercially. In meatier roles, in other 1990s films, she turned in a series of strong performances. Heavily made up to look much older, she played the mother of the heroine in *Heaven and Earth* (1993); the last in Oliver Stone's trilogy of Vietnam War films, *Heaven and Earth* depicts the harrowing experiences of a Vietnamese woman (played by Hiep Thi Le in her cinematic debut) who lives through three decades of war. In *Golden Gate* (1993), a story by David Henry Hwang about 1950s anti-Communist witch hunts that is set in San Francisco's Chinatown, Chen starred opposite Matt Dillon. In another feature role, she played an Inuit environmental activist in *On Deadly Ground* (1994), a high-minded adventure tale, starring and directed by Steven Seagal, that critics labeled an egregious failure. As the wife of an underworld figure in the steamy thriller *Wild Side* (1995), she appeared in a love scene with Anne Heche, who was cast as a banker cum high-priced prostitute. Chen's 1990s credits also include roles in such forgettable films as *Judge Dredd* (1995), *The Hunted* (1995), and *Precious Find* (1996) and in several Chinese-language films made in Hong Kong, among them *The Temptation of a Monk* (1994), in which she played the dual roles of princess and assassin, and *Red Rose, White Rose* (1994), which was directed by Stanley Kwan and co-starred Winston Chao.

Earlier, in 1990, Chen appeared as Jocelyn Packard in the critically acclaimed television series *Twin Peaks*, which was created by David Lynch. Chen relished the part of Jocelyn, a mysterious woman who lives on the fringe of a strange town, because it gave her the opportunity to portray traits associated with villainy. "For once I could look into myself and recall there were times when I wanted to be jealous, when I wanted to do revenge, and I never gave myself the chance because I was always proper," she told Michael J. Bandler.

Chen made her directing debut with *Xiu Xiu: The Sent-Down Girl* (1998), about a 15-year-old girl (played by Lu Lu) who is sent far from her home in the city of Chengdu to be reeducated during the Cultural Revolution. "From the time I was nine or 10, it was what we all talked about, how to keep out of getting 'sent down,'" Chen told Seth Faison for the *New York Times* (April 29, 1999). "My parents talked about it all the time. We were obsessed by it. I always heard stories, with horror but also with some fascination, about people who went to the countryside." Xiu Xiu (pronounced "Show Show") winds up in a remote rural area near where Tibet borders the province of Sichuan. She learns to herd horses from her only companion—her tentmate (played by Lopsang), an elderly nomad who grows to love her; castrated during an earlier uprising, he presents no sexual threat to her. The official papers required for her return to Chengdu never arrive, and in a vain effort to get them, she has sex with a series of soldiers and petty bureaucrats who pretend to have clout. By the end of the film, Xiu Xiu's innocence, trust, and gung-ho enthusiasm for what she believes is a coming Communist utopia have vanished, and she is overwhelmed by despair.

In addition to directing the film, Chen served as executive producer and co-wrote the screenplay with Yan Gelin. The film is based on a novella by Yan, who, like Chen, emigrated from China to the U.S. Determined to shoot on location, Chen applied for a permit from China's Film Bureau, a government body that monitors and controls film production in the country. "But they wanted me to make revisions to the script and I didn't want to," she recalled to Faison. "If they had revisions that would make it a better movie, fine. But I wasn't going to make revisions that made it worse." Armed with a counterfeit permit, Chen proceeded to make her movie without informing the government. To prevent confiscation of the film, much of it was smuggled out of the country at the end of each day. Thus Chen could not view the daily shoots, as is the practice of most directors. Adding to the difficulties of shooting was the ruggedness of the barren, isolated locale, 13,000 feet above sea level. "It

was hard to breathe," Chen told Corliss. "We didn't take showers for a month. We were all sniffing each other. Lunch on the set was always late and cold. Or it wouldn't arrive. So we ate yak meat, yak meat, yak meat." While on the set, Chen told Melanie Rehak, she made use of what Rehak labeled her "screen-siren femininity" and "the androgeny [she was] taught" in China. "I've learned that I could combine these two things," Chen said. "When I was directing this movie, I had to command a crew of 60 that consisted mostly of men. So I tried to see what was most effective: should I be straightforward or should I be coy? Sometimes batting your lashes works. I had to recognize feminine power; now it's good because I have both faces." When, later, the Chinese government learned that Chen had made a film without proper authorization, it fined her $50,000 and forbade her to work in the country again.

Elsewhere, *Xiu Xiu* was greeted warmly. It was screened at the 1998 Berlin Film Festival, and in Taiwan it won seven Golden Horse Awards, the equivalent of the Academy Awards in the U.S. Although to G. Allen Johnson, in a review for the *San Francisco Examiner* (July 9, 1999, on-line), the film was both "simplistic and emotionally draining," he judged the story to be "riveting despite its aura of doom. We've seen enough of these movies to know things aren't going to end well. But the narrative's skilled juxtaposition between the herdsman's honest love and Xiu Xiu's unraveling is properly devastating, a tone of emotional detachment heightening the drama." "There's real urgency and lyricism in *Xiu Xiu*," Hannah Brown reported in an undated on-line review for the *New York Post*; in showing "the gradual corruption and victimization of a docile young woman," Brown wrote, the film "has the power and sweep of a Chinese 'Tess'"—a reference to *Tess of the D'Urbervilles*, by the 19th-century British novelist Thomas Hardy. The film is "also clearly a metaphor for the [Chinese] government's betrayal and manipulation of its own people," she continued, "but the characters are so compelling, it doesn't feel heavy-handed." In the *Village Voice* (May 5–11, 1999, on-line), Dennis Lim offered a dissenting view. "*Xiu Xiu* plays like an exploitative melodrama," he complained. "The movie is competently filmed (the steppe landscapes and night skies are in fact gorgeous), but it's fundamentally misconceived. . . . Methodically devastating and yet barely cognizant of the complicated psychology of the situations it hurls its characters into, [it] has one main point to make—'this is tragic'—and knows precisely one way of making it: rub the viewer's face in the tragedy."

Joan Chen's first marriage, to the film producer Jimmy Lau, ended in divorce in the late 1980s. She and her second husband, Peter Hui, a cardiologist, have been married since 1992. The couple live in the Russian Hills district of San Francisco. Her glamorous image notwithstanding, Chen has often been described as modest. At some point in her early years, Chen became a skilled markswoman. — Y.P.

Suggested Reading: *Chicago Tribune* V p13 Nov. 20, 1986, with photo, XIII p8+ Dec. 20, 1987, with photos, VI p10 Feb. 20, 1994, with photo; *New York Times* E p1 Apr. 29, 1999, with photos; *New York Times Magazine* p17 May 23, 1999, with photo; *Time* p60+ Apr. 5, 1999, with photos

Selected Films: as actress—*Youth*, 1977; *The Little Flower*, 1980; *Awakening*, 1981; *Tai-Pan*, 1986; *The Last Emperor*, 1987; *The Blood of Heroes*, 1989; *Where Sleeping Dogs Lie*, 1991; *Steel Justice*, 1992; *Shadow of a Stranger*, 1992; *Killing Beach*, 1993; *Heaven and Earth*, 1993; *Golden Gate*, 1993; *On Deadly Ground*, 1994; *Wild Side*, 1995; *Judge Dredd*, 1995; *The Hunted*, 1995; *Precious Find*, 1996; as director and writer—*Xiu Xiu: The Sent-Down Girl*, 1998

Selected Television Shows: *Twin Peaks*, 1990

Corky Lee/Courtesy of Coffee House Press

Chin, Frank

Feb. 25, 1940– Writer. Address: c/o Coffee House Press, 27 N. Fourth St., Suite 400, Minneapolis, MN 55401

Designated by a *Village Voice* reviewer as the "loudmouth godfather to the 1970s Asian American literary movement" and as a "cranky Chinatown Cowboy," Frank Chin at 59 remains one of multicultural America's most provocative and opinionated authors. A novelist, essayist, dramatist, and cultural critic, Chin vents his spleen with equal vigor against "righteous whites" and pusillanimous, politically correct Asian-Americans at risk of bargaining away their birth-rights for a mess of melting-pottage. As a self-avowing "Chinaman," Frank Chin helped galvanize a generation of colleagues with Asian roots as they were negotiating a perilous course through the American cultural landscape just after the Vietnam War. Hollywood's stereotypical portrayal of Asians as either sinister or passive has always been an object of Chin's ire. In his essay "The Three-Legged Toad," published in *Bulletproof Buddhists* (1998), he wrote, "Several generations of American-born Chinese Americans huffing hyphens sponged up Charlie Chan–Fu Manchu at the Bijou, never heard of the mandate of heaven, and don't want to now because it's Chinese and sounds icky. I belong to one of those generations of the American Cultural Revolution born and raised in the United States between 1925 and 1966."

Among Chin's first literary projects was his co-editorship of *Aiiieeeee!* (1974), a landmark anthology of works by American authors of Asian heritage; its original editors revised it in 1991, to mark the emergence of a younger generation of writers. Chin also claims to be "the first Chinese-American to have a play produced on a New York stage"— *The Chickencoop Chinaman* and *The Year of the Dragon* were first performed at the American Place Theatre in New York during the early 1970s. A number of short stories Chin published over the years were included in the Coffee House Press collection *The Chinaman Pacific & Frisco R.R. Co.* (1988). In his novels Chin routinely makes use of epic Chinese mythology and imagery, as in *Donald Duk* (1991), about a Chinese-American youngster in San Francisco coming to terms with his ancestral heritage, and *Gunga Din Highway* (1994), a satirical critique of how Asians are imagined in Hollywood films. His most recent book, *Bulletproof Buddhists*, includes several first-person essays written over a quarter-century, including an account of a visit to Cuba just after Fidel Castro took power, a commentary on a visit to contemporary Singapore, and reflections on Asian gangs in multicultural Los Angeles in the wake of the 1992 riots.

Chin is especially disdainful of the "model minority" status of Asian-Americans, by which members of that group are elevated to a pinnacle against which other people of color can be invidiously compared by the majority culture. As he wrote in one of the essays in *Bulletproof Buddhists*, "White America is as securely indifferent about us as men as plantation owners were about their loyal house niggers. House niggers is what America has made of us, admiring us for being patient, submissive, aesthetic, passive, accommodating, essentially feminine in character—what whites call 'Confuciusist,' dreaming us up a goofy version of Chinese culture to preserve in becoming the white man's dream minority." But Chin remains a person of nuance and tries not to be guilty of the monoculturalism he inveighs against; for example, he told an interviewer for the *New York Times* (March 31, 1991) that he had firmly established a practice of reading Shakespeare to his son, then six years old.

Frank Chew Chin Jr. was born in Berkeley, California, on February 25, 1940, the son of Frank Chew Chin and Lile Bowe Yoke (Quan) Chin. As a youngster he attended "American school"; in addition, for two hours every afternoon, he studied Chinese and participated in athletics at the Wah Kue Chinese School in a building the school shared with the Chinese Nationalist Party headquarters in Oakland. Chin credits a teacher at Wah Kue school, an idealistic college professor he knew as Mr. Mah, with awakening his sense of pride in his heritage by challenging the "myth of timid, meek, passive Chinamen."

Chin attended the University of California at Berkeley from 1958 to 1961. In 1961, in the early days of the Castro regime, Chin visited Cuba for two weeks, staying at the American mobster Meyer Lansky's old Riviera Hotel, which had been appropriated in the cause of the revolution. In Cuba, which then had the second-largest Chinatown outside of Asia and San Francisco, Chin was frequently mistaken for an intellectual from mainland China or even for an "existentialist," though he claims the trip's primary purpose was to enable him to go to flamenco clubs and buy a decent guitar or two. A narrative of this trip, interspersed with anecdotes about forays to New Orleans and Iowa City, is included in Chin's essay "I Am Talking to the Strategist Sun Tzu About Life When the Subject of War Comes Up," published in *Amerasia Journal* in 1991 and reprinted in *Bulletproof Buddhas and Other Essays*.

Chin spent two years at the University of Iowa before receiving his bachelor's degree from the State University of California at Santa Barbara, in 1965. (Some published sources differ on the details regarding his undergraduate education.) In California he helped pay his way through college by working as a clerk and brakeman for two railroad companies, the Western Pacific and the Southern Pacific. That experience inspired the settings for a number of short stories he later wrote for small literary magazines; eight of them were reprinted in *The Chinaman Pacific & Frisco R.R. Co.*

Chin's first writing positions, in the late 1960s, were with King Broadcasting in Seattle, where he worked as a story editor and writer. In 1969 he became a part-time lecturer in Asian-American studies at the University of California at Davis and at San Francisco State College, then a hotbed of radical student activity on the West Coast. In 1971 he married Kathleen Chang, the daughter of a prominent family of Chinese emigré intellectuals in the United States. The marriage ended after five years. Beset by messianic visions involving her role in a utopian world order, Chang died by self-immolation in 1996, on the campus of the University of Pennsylvania.

It was in the early 1970s that Chin came to prominence as an interpreter of the Asian-American experience in contemporary culture, as an editor and as a playwright. He was a founder of the Asian American Theater Workshop in 1972; over the next several years, two of his plays, *The Chickencoop Chinaman* and *The Year of the Dragon*, would be produced at the American Place Theatre, in New York. In 1974 he received a Rockefeller Playwrights grant and a National Endowment for the Arts creative writing grant; in the same year he served as an editor, with Jeffrey Chan, Lawson Inada, and Shawn Wong, of the groundbreaking book *Aiiieeeee! an Anthology of Asian American Writers*, published by Howard University Press.

In their introduction to *Aiiieeeee!*, Chin and his colleagues wrote, "Before we can talk about our literature, we have to explain the sensibility. Before we can explain our sensibility we have to outline our histories. Before we can outline our history, we have to dispel the stereotypes." The editors based the book's title on the fact that its contributors were "American born and raised" and "got their China and Japan from the radio, off the silver screen, from television, out of comic books, from the pushers of white American culture that pictured the yellow man as something that when wounded, sad, or angry, or swearing, or wondering whined, shouted, or screamed 'aiiieeeee!'"

A sequel to this book, *The Big Aiiieeeee! The History of Chinese America and Japanese America in Literature*, edited by the same team, was published in 1991. In this work Chin and his colleagues criticized an American monocultural educational system that demeaned as primitive and alien any who deviated from the majoritarian norm, as when immigrants were told that "to be foreign was to be stupid, backward, sexually unattractive, impotent in modern society."

Published in 1988, *The Chinaman Pacific & Frisco R.R. Co.* includes eight of Chin's short stories that had appeared in various forms in literary magazines during the 1970s. The first of them, the autobiographical "Railroad Standard Time," originally published in *City Lights Journal* in 1978, describes the meditations of a Chinese-American writer-cum-railroad brakeman who, as a "twelve, maybe fourteen" year old, was initiated into his family heritage when he received his grandfather's railroad watch as a gift. Chin, as narrator, makes use of the story to reminisce about his early identity struggles, such as his frustrating quest to find himself in a "MOVIE ABOUT ME" by going to Peter Lorre films at "a matinee in a white neighborhood . . . the only Chinaman in the house," or, "full of ghostpiss," driving "right past what's left of Oakland's dark wooden Chinatown and dark streets full of dead lettuce and trampled carrot tops, parallel all the time in line with the tracks of the Western Pacific and Southern Pacific railroads." Most of the stories in this collection, such as "The Chinatown Kid" and "The Sons of Chan," alternate between acerbity and nostalgia in describing the psychic landscape of the Chinatowns remembered by their author. In his afterword to *The Chinaman Pacific & Frisco R.R. Co.*, however, Chin launched a no-holds-barred volley against Western hegemony in a magical-realist fairy tale that imagines the psychic fate of an alien French girl in Canton dreaming about an ancestral past in which a gender-bent Joan of Arc is burned by her barbaric ancestors only to reemerge as a Nazi despot in a Christian Dark Age armageddon of militant lesbians and debauched ecclesiastics. A quote from Jack Kroll of *Newsweek* on the book's jacket reads, "A gifted writer and electric sensibility, Frank Chin is part Chinese Lenny Bruce, spritzing a comedy of bitter alienation, and part Number One Son, drawn to the traditional Chinese values—family, duty—which have been diluted by American culture."

In 1991 Coffee House Press published Chin's novel *Donald Duk*, a broadly satirical look at life on the periphery of both China and America as seen through the eyes of the precocious 12-year-old title character. The son of a restaurant owner named King Duk, the boy is forced to straddle the two cultures in San Francisco's Chinatown. Chin's choice of his hero's name, an ancestral moniker that sounds like that of a comic-book character, accentuates the identity conflicts of young Donald, who revolts against his parents' traditional Chinese New Year celebrations. The novel is structured as a series of dreams the boy has during the 15-day celebration. In the dreams young Donald is transported back to the 1860s, when his Chinese ancestors worked as coolie labor on the Central Pacific Railroad. The dream sequences allow Chin, qua Duk, to explore issues of ethnic identity and self-consciousness. The sequences are sometimes related in a dizzying cascade of surrealistic images, as in this passage from the beginning of Chapter 14: "Donald Duk dreams he's sleeping at night and wakes up dreaming, and wakes up from that dream into another, and wakes up into the real." Or: "The dream comes in like a movie all over his eyes." Chin uses the dream sequences as a vehicle for Donald Duk to discover that his ancestors were not the passive, nonassertive characters he sees in American portrayals, but a hard-working group of people who demanded fair treatment from their employers. Duk tells his father: "Everything I dream is true, and nobody knows what we did. Nobody, just me. And I don't want to be the only one who knows, and it makes me mad to be the only one who knows, and everything I dream makes me mad at white people and hate them." Thus is born a sense of community solidarity, in which Duk claims his mission in life is to set the record straight in his junior-high-school history class.

In 1992, along with five other emerging writers "of distinctive literary merit who demonstrate potential for outstanding future work," Chin was awarded a Lannan Fellowship. Two years later Coffee House Press published his *Gunga Din Highway*, a satirical novel lampooning the stereotyped images of Asians in Hollywood films, while also exposing a serious generation gap between older and younger Chinese Americans, a point made by the Tokyo-born author Kenneth LaMott and expanded upon by Chin in "Confessions of a Chinatown Cowboy." The novel's title is derived from the low-caste Hindu water-boy character in Rudyard Kipling's century-old poem "Gunga Din," now widely regarded as a symbol of Asian colonial subservience. *Gunga Din Highway* tells the story of members of two generations of the Kwan family: the elder, Longman, described as "The Chinaman Who Dies" in minor screen epics, and his son, Ulysses, who believes that his father's dream of playing Charlie Chan is a sellout to contemporary identity politics. Although the name Ulysses alludes to Homeric legend, Chin, in an author's note, took pains to explain that his book is divided into four parts (The Creation, The World, The Underworld, and Home) according to "the world of Chinese myth." In this worldview, "the world, the giant, and the Mother of Humanity create a world where every hero is an orphan, a failed scholar, an outlaw, an outcast, an exile on the road of life through danger, ignorance, deception, and enlightenment." The novel consists of alternating first-person passages in which Longman and his son Ulysses unburden their memories. Longman talks about long-ago struggles for a foothold in a recalcitrant white America. Ulysses represents Frank Chin himself, with his narratives of 1960s protest movements and of working on the railroad. The two worlds collide time and time again as young Ulysses seeks to find his own way in life.

In 1998 the University of Hawai'i Press published Chin's *Bulletproof Buddhists and Other Essays*, a collection of six pieces that had earlier appeared in several Asian-American and West Coast publications. The name of the title essay, about Asian-immigrant gang members in Los Angeles, is a reference to their belief that they are protected from violence by Buddha and martial-arts traditions. Most of the selections date from the 1990s; the earliest, "Confessions of a Chinaman Cowboy," was published in the *Bulletin of Concerned Asian Scholars* in 1972. It is primarily in this essay that Chin set forth his critique of identity politics, as when he declared, "America doesn't want [Asians] as a visible native minority. They want us to keep our place as Americanized foreigners ruled by immigrant loyalty. But never having been anything else but born here, I've never been foreign and resent having foreigners telling me my place in America and America telling me I'm foreign." The opening essay, "I Am Talking to the Strategist Sun Tzu about Life When the Subject of War Comes Up," an account of Chin's 1961 trip to Cuba, was published in *Amerasia Journal* in 1991. In the final essay, "A Chinaman in Singapore," the only one that had not previously appeared in a periodical, Chin recounted his brief visit to Singapore, where he had been invited by the National Arts Council to give a reading of his work. In addition to describing his experiences there, Chin digressed to express his rage at the political stance of some other prominent Asian-American authors, further underscoring his reputation for outspokenness in his own community. "The proof that Chinese are despised," he writes, "is the popularity of the patently white racist rabidly Christian writing of Maxine Hong Kingston, David Henry Hwang, Amy Tan, which are taught in the public schools as the real thing while the Chinese fairy tales they fake are banned. Not one of the champions of Kingston and Tan have done step one of literary criticism."

Mainstream reviewers were not kind to *Bulletproof Buddhists*. Kitty Chen Dean warned in *Library Journal* (June 1, 1998) about "rantings . . . [that] often seem mean-spirited and incomplete," while a reviewer for *Publishers Weekly* (June 13, 1998) found fault with Chin's "emotional . . . bitterly accusatory" tone. A somewhat more positive view was published in the *Village Voice* (September 8, 1998), where Vince Shettweiler pointed out that "Chin's famous faults remain on display—his martial philosophy idealizes a hetero-macho 'manliness,' and his grouchy defense of cultural authenticity is too tactless for current intellectual debates"; but, he concluded, these "famous faults" are redeemed by the book's "streetwise sensibility that, Chin reminds us, is the only hope for our cultural survival."

In the world outside his novels, Chin has been a vocal social critic of the media, which, he believes, portray Asian images in stereotypical fashion. He was quoted in a profile of him in the *New York Times* (March 31, 1991) as saying, "The Jeffersonian ideal that public education would create generations of informed, morally conscious citizens has failed." As a result, children like his fictional Donald Duk struggle to resolve their ethnic self-images within the larger American environment. Particularly incensed at Wayne Wang's film adaptation of Amy Tan's novel *The Joy Luck Club*, he once said, as reported in the *Washington Post* (September 27, 1993), that the film was "not Chinese but white racist." But he reserved his bitterest venom for Miramax's plans to revive the old Charlie Chan series, even though this time the character was to be portrayed by Russell Wong, a Chinese-American, not a Caucasian actor in yellowface, as in the classic films of the 1930s and 1940s. Chin has pointed out, as quoted in the *New York Times* (January 5, 1997), that "Charlie Chan will always be a symbol of white racism, no matter who plays him. If you put a black man in a hood, does that make the Ku Klux Klan a civil rights organization?"

Chin has also been a harsh critic of the "model minority" paradigm by which white Americans are prompted to express their admiration of Asians for maintaining a standard of excellence against which other races are negatively compared. He wrote in "Confessions of a Chinatown Cowboy," "The myth of the Chinese Sojourner, the stereotype of the gutless, passive, effeminate Chinaman has become too precious a part of the American white

male legend for America to give it up easily. Virtually everything being written about us today reveals our true racist value to America as a race of white right hands to hit the blacks and 'less assimilated' races in the head with. We're numerous enough to showcase as a minority but don't count enough to take up America's media time and space speaking for ourselves." — E.M.

Suggested Reading: *Amerasia Journal* p175+ 1993, p158+ 1996, p85+ 1997; *Booklist* p111 Sep. 15, 1994; *Library Journal* p220 Feb. 15, 1991, p111+ Oct. 1, 1994; *New York Times* C p17 Oct. 14, 1992, D p7 Oct. 14, 1996, B p1 Nov. 27, 1996, II p20 Jan. 5, 1997; *New York Times Book Review* p22 Jan. 15, 1989, p9 Mar. 31, 1991, p16 Jan. 29, 1995; *Parnassus: Poetry in Review* p88+ 1992; *Publishers Weekly* p99 Sep. 2, 1988, p25+ Feb. 8, 1991, p52 and p67 May 31, 1991, p41+ Aug. 22, 1994; *Village Voice Literary Supplement* pSS23+ Feb. 8, 1994, pSS26+ Mar. 7, 1995; *Washington Post* B p1 Sep. 27, 1993; *Washington Post Book World* R p13 Apr. 7, 1991, p4 Jan. 30, 1994; *World Literature Today* p487+ Summer 1989, p715 Autumn 1991, p360+ Spring 1995

Selected Works: *Charlie Chan on Maui*; *The Chickencoop Chinaman*, 1972; *The Year of the Dragon*, 1974; *The Chinaman Pacific & Frisco RR Co.*, 1988; *Donald Duk*, 1991; *Gunga Din Highway*, 1994; *Bulletproof Buddhists and Other Essays*, 1998; as co-editor—*Aiiieeeee!: An Anthology of Asian-American Writers*, 1974; *The Big Aiiieeeee!: An Anthology of Chinese American and Japanese American Literature*, 1991

Chrebet, Wayne

(kreh-BET)

Aug. 14, 1973– Football player. Address: c/o New York Jets, 1000 Fulton Ave., Hempstead, NY 11550-1099

At only five feet, 10 inches and 185 pounds, Wayne Chrebet isn't the biggest or tallest receiver in the National Football League (NFL). He's not even the fastest: his ability to run 40 yards in 4.4 seconds is good but not outstanding. For the most part he has been overshadowed by his much bigger and more outspoken teammate on the New York Jets, Keyshawn Johnson. In *Just Give Me the Damn Ball! The Fast Times and Hard Knocks of an NFL Rookie* (1997), the memoir that Johnson wrote with Shelley Smith, Johnson even questioned the team's choice of Chrebet as a starting receiver. Both Johnson and opposing defenders have found, however, that to dismiss Chrebet because of his unimposing physical presence is a mistake. What Chrebet lacks in height and sheer mass, he makes up in gritty de-

Courtesy of New York Jets Football Club, Inc.
Wayne Chrebet

termination, a three-foot vertical jump, and that most important quality of a wide receiver, good hands. His quarterbacks in college and now with the Jets have turned to him for his sure-handedness, particularly in crucial third-down plays. The facts speak for themselves: he currently holds the record (150) for receptions hauled in during a player's first two years in the NFL.

Wayne Chrebet Jr. was born on August 14, 1973 in Garfield, New Jersey. His father, Wayne Chrebet Sr., was a former bodybuilder who had been crowned Mr. New Jersey and Mr. East Coast. Wayne Sr. and his wife, Paulette, currently run a collection agency. They have one other child, Jennifer, who is a reporter.

When Wayne Jr. was seven, he started working out with his father. This helps explain why today he has a lean, muscular body, only 3 percent of which is fat. At Garfield High School, Chrebet played football, baseball, and basketball. After graduating from Garfield he attended Hofstra University, in Hempstead, New York. He majored in criminal justice and played football for Hofstra's Division I-AA team. As a receiver he broke many of Hofstra's receiving records, including touchdowns in a game (five, which ties the National College Athletic Association record held by Jerry Rice); touchdowns in a season (16); touchdowns in a college career (31); and yardage in a single game (245). Both George Beisel, Chrebet's quarterback in 1992 and 1993, and Carlos Garay, his quarterback in 1994, were astounded by his ability to catch ball after ball. "My motto was just to put it in an area where he could make a play," Garay told Harvey Araton for the *New York Times* (November 7, 1998, on-line). "Make it humanly catchable, and he'll

catch it." In Chrebet's senior year he had 57 receptions, 1,200 yards, and 16 touchdowns, and he was named most valuable player.

Despite his achievements in college, no NFL team approached Chrebet, because of his size and small-time college background. Even Canadian and Arena League teams showed no interest in him. During the draft that year, Chrebet went unpicked. Two hours after the draft, however, he got a call from John Griffin, the coordinator of college scouting for the Jets. Griffin had seen a videotape of the highlights of Chrebet's college career, and he suggested that Chrebet come to the Jets' training facility to try out for the team. During what amounted to a do-or-die audition, Chrebet proceeded to win Griffin over. "If I had to use one word to describe Wayne's workout, it would be *spectacular*," Griffin told John Ed Bradley for *Sports Illustrated* (May 12, 1997). "Richard Mann, our receivers coach, threw him about 50 balls, and Wayne didn't drop one. Obviously the object of the game is to throw balls that are either very hard or impossible to catch, but Rich couldn't get any past him."

When Chrebet arrived at the Jets' camp, the security guard, thinking he was just another autograph seeker, wouldn't let him in at first. Chrebet was the 10th on the Jets' list of 10 possible receivers, but his fears that he might be cut at any moment proved unwarranted: he out-played every defender put in front of him. "The first time Wayne beats [cornerback] Aaron [Glenn], you think, Well, the grass is wet," Griffin told John Ed Bradley. "But then Wayne goes up against a few other quick defensive backs and beats them, too, and you think, Well maybe they're not in shape. But then after he's gone up against everybody and beaten them all, you go, Hey, wait a minute here." Chrebet made the team and signed the standard rookie contract, for a salary of $119,000 a year.

During the 1995 regular season, Chrebet started in all 16 Jets games. He was particularly effective when he was lined up in the slot position and ran short patterns in the middle of the field, where wide receivers tend to be more vulnerable to getting drilled by defensive backs. With Boomer Esiason as the Jets' primary quarterback, Chrebet caught 66 passes for 726 yards, an average of 11 yards per reception, and made four touchdowns. He made more receptions in 1995 than any other rookie in the team's history and was surpassed only by the Seattle Seahawks' Joey Galloway among NFL rookies that year. Chrebet's efforts alone couldn't turn things around for the Jets, who finished the season with a 3–13 win–loss record. Still, the Jets' coach, Rich Kotite, showered praise on him. Kotite later predicted, as quoted by John Ed Bradley, that Chrebet was "going to become one of the best players this league has seen in many, many years. . . . He's incredible."

At the end of the 1995 season, Chrebet accepted a three-year, $2 million contract. However, his position as a starter was by no means assured. During the off-season the free-agent wide receivers Jeff

Graham and Webster Slaughter were brought in from other teams, and the Jets used their number-one pick in the draft to take the outstanding college wide receiver Keyshawn Johnson, who subsequently signed a six-year, $15 million deal. In the second round, the Jets drafted yet another receiver, Alex Van Dyke. At the beginning of the 1996 season, Chrebet was a starter, but he was later relegated to the bench. Even though he wasn't playing every down, Chrebet distinguished himself. In the nine games he started, he caught 84 passes for 909 yards, an average of 10.8 yards per catch, and made three touchdowns. Among all NFL players, he was 13th in receptions, 28th in yardage, and first in third-down receptions (31). His 150 receptions in two seasons in the NFL set a record; the total racked up by the previous record-holder, Gary Clark, who played his first two pro-football years for the Washington Redskins, in 1985 and 1986, was 146.

Though 1996 was a season of personal accomplishment for Chrebet, it was disastrous for the team: the Jets won only one game. In his book, *Just Give Me the Damn Ball!*, a disgruntled Johnson cited Chrebet as one of the problems. Referring to Chrebet on some 25 pages, he accused the coaches and the new quarterback, Neil O'Donnell, of favoritism towards Chrebet. "Chrebet wouldn't even make anybody else's team," Johnson wrote. "It was time to stop this love affair with the little dude from Hofstra." Johnson speculated that the coaching staff and the quarterback favored Chrebet in the passing game because he was white, and Johnson argued that instead of dumping off short passes to Chrebet, the quarterback should have thrown the ball to Johnson or the other black receivers on the team. Johnson's accusations were widely reported in the media. When asked to respond to them, Chrebet, displaying his typical reserve, shrugged them off. "To be honest it makes me kind of nervous that a grown man thinks about me so much," John Ed Bradley quoted him as saying. "Between you and me, I think Keyshawn has a crush on me."

In 1997 Bill Parcells became the Jets' coach. Downplaying Johnson's controversial remarks, he insisted that there were no problems between Johnson and Chrebet. Sparked by Parcells's coaching, the Jets had their first winning season since 1988; they finished third in their division, with a 9–7 win–loss record. With Neil O'Donnell and Glenn Foley alternating at the quarterback position, Chrebet was again very productive. Although he started only one game, he made 58 receptions for 799 yards—an average of 13.8 yards per reception—and made three touchdowns. As usual, he was used primarily in third-down situations, though Parcells also had him run deep patterns down the sidelines, which accounts for his higher yards-per-catch average. Playing against Seattle in September, Chrebet made two touchdowns in a single game for the first time in his NFL career.

With the Jets' startling transformation into a division contender, expectations soared for the 1998 season. The running back Curtis Martin was brought in to improve the Jets' ground attack; in the passing game, the burden placed on Chrebet was increased. No longer simply a third-down receiver, he was elevated to starter opposite Johnson. In a further sign of their faith in Chrebet's ability, the Jets extended his contract four more years, for a total of $11.5 million. So far Chrebet has shouldered the burden well. In the 1998 regular season, with Vinny Testaverde firmly established as the Jets' quarterback, Chrebet made 75 receptions for 1,083 yards (increasing his average to 14.4 yards per catch) and eight touchdowns. The Jets won their division, the American Football Conference (AFC) East, finishing the regular season with a 12–4 win–loss record, and they advanced in the play-offs to face the Denver Broncos in the AFC championship game, the Jets' first appearance in that match since 1983.

Johnson's and Chrebet's lockers are next to each other, but the two men reportedly don't talk or hang out much. Still, they have managed to work together, despite Johnson's earlier criticisms of Chrebet. Their relationship has inspired one local tabloid to dub the receiving duo the "odd couple." Chrebet believes that he and Johnson complement each other very well. "We have two different styles of play," he was quoted as saying by Leonard Shapiro in the *Washington Post* (September 29, 1998). "But that's good as long as we're on the same page. He's more of a downfield guy. He'll stretch the defense. They'll pull back on him, and that gives me more room to maneuver inside. If they try sinking on me, we'll just go over the top to him." For his part, Johnson seems to have moderated his opinion of Chrebet. "I've always had respect for him," he told Leonard Shapiro. "I've never really had a personal issue with the young man. I probably said [in the book] some things I shouldn't have, but that was just my own frustration with what was happening here. It was not really about him, as I've said time and time again. I like the way he plays the game. I never really had a problem with him. I only had a problem with the guy [Kotite] who is not here anymore."

At the start of the 1999 football season, many sports commentators considered the Jets a team that could go all the way to the Super Bowl. Injuries, however, have almost certainly ruined the Jets' season. On September 3 Chrebet broke his foot, while trying to make a cut on artificial turf in the Jets' final preseason game. Further misfortune followed when Testaverde and several other starters were sidelined because of freak injuries. In mid-October, when Chrebet was ready to return to the field, the Jets had a disappointing 1–4 record and slim chance of making the play-offs.

With his consistently good performance, Chrebet is fast becoming a popular player among fans. Jerseys bearing his number, 80, are selling well, and people are beginning to recognize him in public. "People like to root for me as the underdog," he told the *New York Times* (August 7, 1997). "I'll accept that." — W.G.

Suggested Reading: *New York Times* B p12 Aug. 13, 1996, with photo, VIII p2 Oct. 6, 1996, with photo, B p15 Aug. 7, 1997, with photo, B p13 Sep. 4, 1997; *New York Times* (on-line) Nov. 7, 1998; *Sports Illustrated* p76+ May 12, 1997, with photos; *Washington Post* B p4 Sep. 29, 1998; Johnson, Keyshawn with Shelley Smith. *Just Give Me the Damn Ball! The Fast Times and Hard Knocks of an NFL Rookie*, 1997

Benoit Doppagne/Archive Photos

Clark, Wesley K.

Dec. 23, 1944– Supreme Allied commander in Europe; commander in chief of United States armed forces in Europe. Address: c/o HQ USEUCOM (ECPA), Unit 30400, Box 1000, APO AE 09128, USA

General Wesley K. Clark, the supreme Allied commander in Europe, is the head of all military forces in the North Atlantic Treaty Organization (NATO) and commander in chief of all United States forces in Europe. A 1966 graduate of the United States Military Academy at West Point and a former Rhodes scholar, Clark rose rapidly through the ranks of the United States Army. Working closely with the American diplomat Richard C. Holbrooke in 1995, he was instrumental in fashioning the Dayton peace accords, which put an end to ethnic conflict in the former Yugoslav republic of Bosnia-Herzegovina. Head of all military negotiations

while in Dayton, the general wrote the crucial section of the agreement that gave the military commander in Bosnia-Herzegovina "authority, without interference or permission of any party, to do all that the commander judges necessary and proper, including use of military force," as Craig R. Whitney reported in the *New York Times* (February 23, 1999). Three years later, Holbrooke wrote in his book, *To End a War* (1998), "Clark's boyish demeanor and charm masked, but only slightly, his extraordinary intensity." On March 24, 1999 NATO launched an Allied air assault on the former Yugoslav republic of Serbia, one of the Balkan states involved in the 1995 Dayton peace accords, whose leaders had for months been attempting to rid their neighbor to the south, the republic of Kosovo, of ethnic Albanians. On April 13, 1999 Clark, in control of all NATO forces in Europe, gave an address to the media explaining the specifics of the air raids. As Michael R. Gordon reported in the *New York Times* (April 14, 1999), "General Clark gave a smooth performance. His methodical, technocratic style contrasted with the blustery manner of some of his predecessors, like General H. Norman Schwarzkopf in the Persian Gulf War in 1991." After leading the Allies to a fragile victory in the Balkans and playing an instrumental role in implementing provisions designed to maintain peace there, Clark announced that he would be stepping down from his position as supreme Allied commander in Europe sometime in 2000.

An only child, Clark was born Wesley Kanne on December 23, 1944 in Chicago. In the *New York Times* (May 3, 1999, on-line), Elizabeth Becker reported that Clark's paternal grandfather, Jacob Nemerovsky, emigrated from Russia during the 1890s to escape recurring pogroms against Jews and gained entrance to the United States with a false passport that gave his surname as Kanne. Clark's father, Benjamin Jacob ("B.J.") Kanne, a veteran of World War I, was a lawyer who worked as an assistant prosecuting attorney in Chicago and then in the office of the city's corporation counsel; later, he served as a city alderman before launching a private law practice. When Wesley was five, his father died, and his mother, Veneta, settled with her son in Little Rock, Arkansas, her hometown, where she raised Wesley as a Southern Baptist. Veneta later remarried, and her second husband, Victor Clark, adopted the boy. To avoid disrupting her new life, B.J.'s relatives kept in touch with Veneta only through correspondence. Wesley Kanne Clark, as he was officially renamed, remained completely unaware of his Jewish ancestry until the age of about 23; since then he has maintained contact with his father's relatives.

As a youth Clark excelled at athletics, particularly swimming. He ranked first in his class when he graduated from high school. He then entered the United States Military Academy at West Point, where he spent four stellar years, again graduating at the top of his class, in 1966. Earlier, in 1965, he had met fellow Arkansan Bill Clinton during a student conference at Georgetown University, and like the future president, he became a Rhodes scholar. At Oxford University, in England, Clark earned a master's degree in philosophy, politics, and economics in 1968. From there, he began his quick ascent in the military chain of command, attending the National War College, armor officer advanced and basic courses, and, finally, ranger and airborne schools. In the early 1970s he held a combat command in Vietnam, where he was in charge of three companies (among them a highly mechanized infantry group). While in Vietnam he converted to Roman Catholicism; he was also wounded four times and received the silver and bronze stars for valor.

Upon his return to the U.S., he served stints as an instructor at West Point and a member of the army chief's staff (helping with plans for the all-volunteer army) before enrolling in the Command and Staff College at Fort Leavenworth, Kansas, where he finished first in his class. Clark then served as a White House Fellow, from 1975 to 1976, was soon promoted to the rank of major—at the uncommonly young age of 31—and subsequently served a tour of duty as an operations officer in a brigade in Germany. In the late 1970s Major Clark worked for a year and a half as the assistant executive officer to General Alexander Haig Jr., who then headed NATO. Shortly thereafter he was promoted to the rank of lieutenant colonel and, as the first member of his graduating class at West Point to command a battalion, led the 1st Battalion, 77th Armor, 4th Infantry Division from 1980 to 1982 at Fort Carson, Colorado.

"In 1981, a *Washington Post Magazine* piece that profiled the intense, soft-spoken Clark as the ideal modern Army officer threatened to set him up for a fall by overexposure," Bradley Graham wrote for the *Washington Post* (March 31, 1997). But his star continued to rise, and in July 1983 Clark took a job in Washington, D.C., at the office of the deputy chief of staff for operations and plans, receiving the title of plans integration division chief. After leaving that office, in September 1983, he assumed a post under the chief of staff of the army. From April 1986 to March 1988, at the height of the nuclear arms race, Clark commanded the 3rd Brigade, 4th Infantry Division, and for five years beginning in the late 1980s, he was commander of the National Training Center in Fort Irwin, California, under an outfit known as the Battle Command Training Operation (BCTP). In that capacity, Clark helped to train many soldiers who saw combat in the Persian Gulf War; he also developed new training methods. By the time Clark was promoted to commander of the 1st Cavalry Division at Ford Hood, Texas, in August 1992, he had commanded almost every possible type of military unit in the United States Army, beginning with the command of a company (as a captain), then leadership of a battalion (as a lieutenant colonel) and a brigade (as a full colonel), and, finally, control of the 1st Cavalry Division (as a major general). Before

leaving his post with the 1st Cavalry, in April 1994, he "transformed the Division into a rapidly deployable force and conducted three emergency deployments to Kuwait," according to *eucom.mil* (on-line).

In the latter half of 1994, Clark took the position of director of strategic plans and policy at the Joint Chiefs of Staff, where he was the staff officer in charge of U.S. military strategic planning for matters that involved far-reaching political issues. It was in this post that Clark worked closely with U.S. envoy Richard Holbrooke, as the two brokered the peace accords between the former Yugoslav republics—most notably Serbia and Croatia—in the wake of ethnic conflicts in that region. Now known as the Dayton peace accords, after the town in Ohio where talks took place among representatives of the Croatian, Serbian, and Muslim populations of the former Yugoslavia, the negotiations successfully halted the bloody war that erupted in the Balkans following the fall of the Soviet Union. Clark, who was in charge of the military aspects of the negotiations, made additions to the treaty that have been hailed as the foundation of the peace that has been maintained in Bosnia. Subsequently, Clark was promoted to commander in chief of the United States Southern Command, which had its headquarters in Panama. From June 1996 to July 1997, he commanded all United States forces in the region and was responsible for U.S. military action throughout the Caribbean and Latin America. Then, in early 1997, it was announced that Clark would become head of all NATO forces in addition to taking command of all U.S. forces in Europe later in the year. He assumed his NATO post on July 11.

"[Clark's] selection is arguably the second most significant military appointment Clinton will have to make this year, after naming a new chairman of the Joint Chiefs of Staff, given the controversial issues of NATO expansion, relations with Russia, and operations in Bosnia confronting the United States and its European Allies," Graham wrote. A Pentagon official explained to Graham the reasons for Clark's appointment: "We wanted somebody who's both a soldier and statesman, someone with diplomatic and policy experience." Indeed, Clark, then 52, brought to his assignment a grasp of the complexity of the situation in Bosnia and a knowledge of Russian as well as his military credentials. It was not long after he took over the reins at NATO that trouble in the Balkans erupted once again: in the final months of 1998, Serbians began attacking ethnic Albanians in the Yugoslav Republic of Kosovo. Considered a holy land, Kosovo is thought by Serbians to be the place in which the modern state of Serbia was born. Within a few days, reports of "ethnic cleansing" of Kosovar Albanians—that is, their murder or forced emigration to neighboring nations—began to reach international news organizations; these events were similar to those that had occurred in Bosnia just a few years earlier. Clark and other U.S. diplomats immediately began attempting to broker a peace agreement.

On February 23, 1999 Clark flew to an air base near Rambouillet, France, to begin negotiations on a settlement. Having explained several weeks earlier to Serbian president Slobodan Milosevic that NATO aircraft could wreak havoc on his military installations if he failed to participate in the peace process, Clark informed the Kosovo Albanian representatives that if they accepted autonomy in place of independence, NATO peacekeepers would help ensure that the Serbs would not threaten stability. Despite the return of Richard Holbrooke to the negotiating table in late February, the deal did not pan out, as Serbian representatives refused to sign the deal. For the next month, attacks against Albanian Kosovars continued, and reports of Serbian atrocities flooded Western news sources on almost a daily basis. During a press conference, Clark described his meeting with a top Serbian general in October 1998. When that general "insisted that the Yugoslav military could have finished off the Kosovo Liberation Army in two more weeks if it had been allowed to continue sweeping villages and towns," as Michael R. Gordon wrote, Clark responded, "Yes, and you created about 400,000 homeless people in this process." Clark stated at the press conference, "That's when I realized that there was still this very strong proclivity to believe that this problem was a problem which was appropriate to be solved by military force." On March 24, 1999 NATO began air strikes against military targets in Yugoslavia.

On the first day of the offensive, NATO stated that it had shot down at least three Serb warplanes and hit more than 40 important military sites, including an airport and an airplane plant near Belgrade, Serbia's capital. Yugoslavia reported that 10 civilians had been killed and 60 more injured. "We have tried to ensure that we get a peaceful settlement to this . . . ," British prime minister Tony Blair told cnn.com (on-line). "This is a difficult decision, but it's the right decision and we have to see it through all the way." Only hours after the strike began, both China and Russia spoke out against the military effort—the first NATO had carried out since its formation in 1949. "Russia is deeply upset by NATO's military action against sovereign Yugoslavia, which is nothing more than open aggression," Russian president Boris Yeltsin said, as quoted by cnn.com (on-line). On day four of the bombing, Serbs shot down a Stealth bomber—a multimillion-dollar plane designed to be capable of avoiding radar detection. The pilot survived and was rescued by Allied forces soon after the crash. A few days later three American servicemen were captured while patrolling a disputed border in southern Yugoslavia. (After several weeks in captivity, they were returned to the U.S., thanks to unofficial diplomatic efforts by the Reverend Jesse Jackson.)

On April 13 Clark held an hour-long press conference to discuss recent developments in the NATO operation. "General Clark stopped short of declaring that the alliance would win with a victory from the air . . . ," Gordon wrote. "Asked at one point whether NATO's political leaders had been too slow to act against Mr. Milosevic this year, General Clark said, 'You're asking judgments about political leadership, which it's not appropriate for me to give.'"

In late May the Kosovo Liberation Army succeeded in flushing out Serb troops hiding in southern parts of Kosovo. Forced into the open, Yugoslav soldiers became easy targets for Allied war planes. With the continuing bombing of Belgrade, Serb casualties became increasingly severe in the final days of May and beginning of June, and on June 3, Milosevic agreed in broad terms to NATO's demands for peace. Negotiations in the following days did not go smoothly, however, and the NATO bombings continued. On June 10, Serb and NATO representatives agreed to a peace plan, which, as Steven Lee Myers reported in the New York Times (June 10, 1999, on-line), "included the withdrawal of all Serbian forces [from Kosovo], the intervention of a NATO-led peacekeeping force, and the return of the Kosovo Albanians who fled their homes." In what NATO called "the first stage" of the plan, Clark was directed to make sure that Yugoslav forces withdrew from Kosovo during the next 24 hours. A day later, on June 11, the general gave the nod for NATO secretary general Javier Solona to stop the bombings. American troops—led by Clark until he leaves his post, in 2000—will remain in the region to oversee the peace, which will entail rebuilding the battered sections of Kosovo and Serbia, a task certain to take many years. The ultimate aim, Craig R. Whitney wrote for the New York Times (June 11, 1999, on-line), is to "rais[e] all the Balkans to the economic and social level of the rest of Europe, in an effort to make another war there after a decade of ethnic conflict as unthinkable as it is now in France, Britain, or Germany."

Among his many military honors, Clark—a four-star general—has been awarded two Defense Distinguished Medals, four Legion of Merit Awards, two Meritorious Service Medals, and a Purple Heart. He is married to the former Gertrude Kingston of Brooklyn, New York. The couple have one son, Wesley. — M.B.

Suggested Reading: cnn.com (on-line); eucom.mil (on-line); New York Times A p1+ June 10, 1995, A p10 Feb. 23, 1999, A p1+ Apr. 14, 1999, with photos, A p1+ Apr. 15, 1999, with photos; us.net (on-line) Apr. 19–25, 1997; Washington Post A p6 Mar. 31, 1997, with photo

Archive Photos

Coburn, James

Aug. 31, 1928– Film and television actor.
Address: c/o Elkins Entertainment, 8306 Wilshire Blvd., Beverly Hills, CA 90211

Armed with a six-shooter and a few days' worth of stubble, James Coburn was, in his younger days, one of the most leathery-faced actors portraying gruff cowboy-types on the big screen. "When his face is relaxed it looks as if he's about to spit," one film critic wrote in the mid-1960s of the fledgling star, who had appeared on such television shows as *Bonanza* and *Gunsmoke* and in films including *The Magnificent Seven* (1960). The film critic added, "This is a man who was born to wind up with the hero's bullet smearing him across the screen." Because of his rough exterior, some casting directors predicted that he could never move beyond playing the "heavy"—that somewhat dated term for the hero's nemesis. He just wasn't handsome enough, nor his grim face sexy enough, according to the conventional Hollywood wisdom.

Defying that forecast, Coburn became an omnipresent figure on the big screen and proved himself one of the most versatile of lead actors of the late 1960s and 1970s. Working with some of the most hard-boiled directors (John Sturges, Sergio Leone, and Sam Peckinpah) and actors (Steve McQueen and Charles Bronson), Coburn continued to take on macho roles that capitalized on his stark visage. At the same time, a substantial portion of his work was in comedy. In his first starring movie role, *Our Man Flint* (1966), for instance, Coburn was one of the first actors to spoof the James Bond spy genre— predating the comic actor Mike Myers's *Austin Powers* films by over three decades. Other roles included a crime-solving doctor, hustling gamblers, and a psychoanalyst to the U.S. president.

After he had made numerous films in the 1970s, Coburn's work was severely curtailed in the 1980s by a crippling bout of arthritis. Since his near recovery, he has remained productive in the industry. Though not usually a lead actor in film or television anymore, he continues to work as a character actor in at least one project a year. A typical supporting role for the 70-year-old Coburn these days is as a white-maned patriarchal figure—a wealthy industrialist, a city elder, or a senior mob figure, for example. With a charged performance as an abusive, alcoholic father in *Affliction* (1998), Coburn won an Oscar—his first—for best supporting actor. That role was the first for which he was nominated for an Academy Award.

An only child, of Swedish, Irish, and Scottish descent, James Coburn was born on August 31, 1928 in Laurel, Nebraska, where the Coburns had lived for several generations. His great-grandfather was a successful cattle rancher who acquired a great deal of land in western Nebraska and in Laurel. Coburn's grandfather inherited the property in Laurel but lost much of it during the Great Depression. As a result, Coburn's father was forced to work as an auto mechanic; he later acquired a Ford dealership that never made very much money. When James was five, the family, in search of better opportunities, packed up their belongings in their Model A Ford and drove to Compton, California, where two of James's uncles lived.

As the family put down new roots in Compton, Coburn led what Dick Kleiner described in *Coronet* (May 1966) as a "very normal childhood." He sang bass in choirs, played drums in the school band, and at one point aspired to become a jazz drummer. After briefly attending Compton Junior College, he ended up joining the army. His musical background and "a few lies," as he admitted to Kleiner, managed to land him a job in the Army Public Information office, where he subsequently became a disc jockey on army-sponsored radio in Texas. Later, when his unit—the 42d Armored Field Artillery of the 2d Armored Division—was shipped out to Mainz, Germany, Coburn got an assignment narrating army films. This gave him the idea of a career in cinema.

After his discharge from the army, Coburn signed up for classes at Los Angeles City College (LACC), supported by the generous financing provided to veterans under the GI Bill. He originally intended to transfer to the filmmaking department at the University of Southern California as soon as he had amassed enough credits, but after taking one acting class, Coburn caught the acting bug and decided to stay with LACC's drama department. He studied there for about two and a half years, while also taking extra lessons from the well-regarded acting coach Jeff Corey. Coburn appeared in several college productions, as well as a La Jolla Playhouse staging of *Billy Budd* with the actors Vincent Price, Sean McClory, and Richard Lupino.

Emboldened by the La Jolla production, Coburn and three of his friends pooled their resources and, in around 1954, drove to New York City. One of his first gigs was swinging a golf club in a television commercial for U.S. Rubber. He also took more acting classes—this time with the famed East Coast teacher Stella Adler, whose other students at the time included Warren Beatty and Gene Saks. Coburn might have become just another aspiring actor struggling to make a living had he not caught a lucky break in an audition for the electric-razor company Remington. He was ordered, along with other auditioning actors, to let his facial hair grow for three days, and his hirsuteness proved to be the most telegenic. For the actual commercial, he let his beard grow out for 11 days, then shaved it on a live, 53-second commercial spot. He appeared in several more commercials and became television's unofficial "shaving man." The income from this job allowed Coburn the freedom to explore other interests—such as meditation and various esoteric pursuits—rather than having to scramble for jobs.

From electric-shaver pitchman Coburn eventually moved on to roles on live television shows. Also during this period, he and some of his fellow actors started an Off-Broadway theater company, which managed to stage only three or four plays. In about 1959, after noticing that the television industry was shifting from New York to Hollywood, Coburn decided to move back to California. He landed some work for General Electric Theater, then hosted by Ronald Reagan. He also got his first film role—a small part in a western entitled Ride Lonesome (1959). A bit part in the western melodrama Face of the Fugitive (1959) followed, as did appearances on TV westerns such as Bonanza, Gunsmoke, and Wanted: Dead or Alive. On November 12, 1959 Coburn married Beverly Kelly, who had a daughter, Lisa, from a previous marriage. The couple's son, James, was born a few years later.

Coburn's breakthrough role—which certainly stands as one of his most remembered today—was in the western The Magnificent Seven (1960), directed by John Sturges and based on director Akira Kurosawa's popular film The Seven Samurai. Coburn, a fan of the Japanese film, lobbied hard for a particular character in Sturges's film—Britt, a knife-toting cowboy who can sling a blade faster than the ordinary man can fire a bullet. Coburn got the part, and along with several of his co-stars—Robert Vaughan and Steve McQueen, among others—was launched into prominence. "That role elevated me," he told Kristin McMurran for People (May 29, 1978). "I started playing featured heavies. [My characters] died a lot. It was marvelous." As Kleiner put it in Coronet, "From then on, Hollywood was Coburn-conscious."

One person who had noticed Coburn was the actress Audrey Hepburn, whom Coburn has credited with getting him a part in Charade (1963). In that film he played one of four thugs terrorizing Hepburn's character, who the thugs believe has knowl-

edge of the whereabouts of $250,000 in hidden gold. Other supporting roles for Coburn included military men in the World War II dramas Hell Is for Heroes (1962), The Great Escape (1963), and The Americanization of Emily (1964); an Indian scout in Sam Peckinpah's cowboy-Indian shoot-'em-up, Major Dundee (1965); and a Caribbean pirate in A High Wind in Jamaica (1965). On television Coburn appeared as an adventurer in the Alaskan gold-rush drama series Klondike (October 1960–February 1961). In mid-season the show was drastically reworked into Acapulco (February–April 1961), starring Coburn as a thrill-seeking beach bum cavorting in contemporary Mexico.

The first film in which Coburn got top billing was the spy spoof Our Man Flint (1966). In the film Coburn played a suave, uncomplicated hero, Derek Flint—the most complicated thing about him is the fact that his lighter has 82 different espionage uses, 83 if one counts lighting cigarettes. Seemingly surrounded by seductive nymphets at all times, Flint is assigned by his employers, the Zonal Organization World Intelligence Espionage (ZOWIE), to foil a dastardly plot by the GALAXY organization to disrupt world weather patterns.

Following Our Man Flint Coburn appeared in several comedies. He had a small part in The Loved One (1965), adapted from the novelist Evelyn Waugh's satire of the mortuary business. In What Did You Do in the War, Daddy? (1966), Coburn played a lieutenant in an American unit ordered to take an Italian town. After the Americans find the war-weary Italian troops eager to surrender, a bacchanalian carnival ensues, with Coburn helping to stage mock battles so that neither side's superiors catch on to the unauthorized peace. In Dead Heat on a Merry-Go-Round (1966), Coburn appeared as a prisoner who finagles a parole by seducing a psychologist; this was among the first of several films in which he would play a charming criminal. In Like Flint (1967), the sequel to Our Man Flint, pitted Coburn against three females with an insidious plot to install a substitute president. Water Hole Number 3 (1967) is a western comedy, in which Coburn played an itinerant gambler antihero looking for stolen gold. In Avec, Avec (a.k.a. Duffy, 1968), he had a starring role as a hippie drifter hired by two brothers to steal money from their wealthy father.

The popular tag line about Coburn during this period was that if he accepted all the movie parts offered to him, he would be busy until the year 1990. Projects were lining up at the door, and he certainly had all the accoutrements of success, including two Ferraris and a 22-room house designed in Egyptian, French, and Italian decor. Yet, as many journalists noted at the time, Coburn appeared not to let fame and its trappings affect him. "To me the ideal is to be an egoless actor—to become so lost in art that you become selfless," he told the New York Post (August 15, 1966). In the same interview, he also explained that what mattered to him was not material wealth but self-evolvement: "The important thing is to find out what kind of a human being you are, and whether you are growing—and if not, why not." Statements like those struck many as vaguely hippie-ish, and indeed, Coburn sympathized with the countercultural movements going on at the time. He railed against the Vietnam War and experimented with Sufi meditation, fasting, Chinese gongs, vegetarianism, and psychotropic drugs including LSD (as far back as 1959) and peyote. Quite unlike a preening star, he had his wife cut his hair. ("I just trim it short for sophisticated parts, let it grow a little longer for funky, western parts," he told Dick Kleiner. "It's very easy to manage.") On the other hand, he did not consider himself part of any organized movement, countercultural or otherwise. "I'm an absolute nongroupist," he told Elizabeth Weiner for *Coronet* (January 1970). "Everybody wants to say, 'Come with us and we'll do this and do that.' Well, I'm on my own trip."

Typical of Coburn's desire for independence was his formation of his own production company, Panpiper Productions, in the mid-1960s. One of the few productions of the company was the satire *The President's Analyst* (1967). Coburn starred as a New York psychiatrist called upon to relieve the anxieties of the president of the United States. The secrets he learns in the process turn him into a target for abduction by foreign governments and into a target for assassination by security-conscious U.S. intelligence agencies.

In the 1970s Coburn continued to appear in films at a hectic pace. Noting the virtual ubiquity of Coburn, one critic for the *Toronto Globe and Mail* (September 1972) wrote, "Not since the early Michael Caine gobbled up films like they were going out of style, has one man so dominated the marquee." Coburn's prominence was in part fueled by archetypical virile cowboy roles. In *A Fistful of Dynamite*, a.k.a. *Duck You Suckers* (1972), directed by Sergio Leone, Coburn played a walking explosives storehouse who becomes involved in the Mexican revolution. Coburn also appeared in *Honkers* (1972), the title of which is derived from rodeo slang for either a dangerous bull or an easy woman. He starred as a rodeo rider whose philandering ways destroy his marriage and family. In *Pat Garrett and Billy the Kid* (1973), directed by Sam Peckinpah, Coburn was Pat Garrett, the gunman-turned-sheriff chasing the outlaw of the title. In *A Reason to Live, A Reason to Die* (1974), he played a Yankee colonel who surrenders Fort Holman, in the Santa Fe area, to the Confederates; facing court martial, he sets off with seven condemned men to recapture the fort. For *Bite the Bullet* (1975) Coburn appeared as an ex–Rough Rider who enters an endurance horse race. *The Last Hard Men* (1976) features Coburn as a half-Indian seeking revenge against a retired lawman. World War II films provided Coburn with yet more grist for the macho mill. In *Midway* (1976) he played a captain in the famous naval battle. *Cross of Iron* (1977), directed by Sam Peckinpah, found Coburn in the role of a war-weary German platoon sergeant on the Russian front. More-contemporary action roles came in the film *Skyriders* (1976), in which he was a hang-glider pilot who rescues a woman and her children from terrorists, and in *Firepower* (1979), in which he took the part of a retired hitman pressured by the FBI into abducting a wealthy industrialist hiding out in the Caribbean. Yet another typical role for Coburn and his grizzled features was that of an urban hustler. In *Harry in Your Pocket* (1973), Coburn played a "cannon," an expert pickpocket teaching apprentices the art of "dip tricks." *Hard Times* (1975), which takes place during the Depression, featured Coburn as Speed, a small-time gambler who manages a down-on-his-luck pugilist (Charles Bronson). *The Baltimore Bullet* (1980) starred Coburn and Bruce Boxleitner as a father-and-son pool-hustling team.

Cutting his hair and trimming his beard, Coburn showed that he was capable of portraying patrician and bourgeois roles as well. In *The Carey Treatment* (1972) he was an urbane pathologist who must solve a crime in order to clear the name of a colleague. For *The Last of Sheila* (1973), he portrayed a Hollywood producer whose wife has been killed by a hit-and-run driver; he subsequently arranges a cruise on which the killer will be revealed. *The Internecine Project* (1974) featured Coburn as a criminally connected economics professor who, in order to win a high position in the government, has to cover up his past and eliminate four people who pose potential problems. *The Last of the Mobile Hot-Shots*, a.k.a. *Blood Kin* (1975), is an adaption of Tennessee Williams's play *The Seven Descents of Myrtle*. In the film Coburn played the part of the childless southern plantation owner who doesn't want his land to be inherited by his black half-brother. The sex comedy *Loving Couples* (1980) starred Coburn as a workaholic doctor who reacts to his wife's affair by having one of his own. In *Looker* (1981), directed by the writer Michael Crichton, Coburn is the head of a conglomerate out to take over the world via powerful subliminal messages in ads.

Meanwhile, in television Coburn appeared in the movies *The Dain Curse* (1978), *Malibu* (1983), and *Sins of the Father* (1985). He also appeared in the television miniseries *Jacqueline Susann's Valley of the Dolls* (1981), hosted the suspense series *Darkroom* (1981), and directed a segment of the *Rockford Files*.

Early in 1980 Coburn and his wife divorced. At around the same time, he began to suffer from agonizing jolts of arthritis. At times he could barely move at all, and he was forced to curtail drastically the number of films in which he appeared. Coburn blamed the stress of the divorce for aggravating his arthritis. To deal with the problem, he turned to both holistic and Western medicine. He changed his diet, began a swimming regimen, and explored treatments like deep-tissue massage and electromagnetic therapy. He also believed that his physical well-being depended on emotional healing.

"What I had to do was forgive the thing that had caused me the pain," he told Mark Goodman and Craig Tomashoff for *People* (June 17, 1991). "With me, it was the divorce."

Once he had gotten his arthritis under control, Coburn worked on more commercials and returned to the big screen, more often as a supporting actor than as a leading man. In the 1990s the films in which he has appeared include *Young Guns II* (1990), *Hudson Hawk* (1991), *The Player* (1992), *Sister Act 2: Back in the Habit* (1993), *Deadfall* (1993), *Maverick* (1994), *The Set Up* (1995), *Eraser* (1996), *The Nutty Professor* (1996), *The Disappearance of Kevin Johnson* (1996), *Keys to Tulsa* (1997), *Affliction* (1998), and *Payback* (1999). His role in *Affliction* has probably been his most acclaimed in recent times, if not in his entire career. Janet Maslin, writing for the *New York Times* (December 30, 1998), called Coburn's acting a "shockingly savage performance." For his work in the film, in which he played opposite Nick Nolte, Sissy Spacek, and Willem Dafoe, Coburn won the Academy Award for best supporting actor, the first Oscar for which he has been nominated.

On television Coburn hosted the short-lived series *Hollywood Stuntmakers* (1991) and appeared in the movies *Mastergate* (1992), *Crash Landing: The Rescue of Flight 232* (1992), *The Hit List* (1993), *Ray Alexander: A Taste for Justice* (1994), *Greyhounds* (1994), *Ray Alexander: A Menu for Murder* (1995), *The Avenging Angel* (1995), *The Cherokee Kid* (1996), *The Second Civil War* (1997), and *Noah's Ark* (1999). With his distinctive, resonant voice, he has narrated several documentaries, including *Hugh Hefner: Once Upon a Time* (1992) and *Palau: Paradise of the Pacific* (1998).

Coburn currently lives in Sherman Oaks, California. In October 1993 he married Paula Murad, a former television newswoman. — W.G.

Suggested Reading: *Chicago Tribune* III p17 Nov. 11, 1981, with photo; *Christian Science Monitor* V p4 May 28, 1968, with photo; *Coronet* p18+ May 1966, with photos, p105+ Jan. 1970, with photos; *Details* p93 Mar. 1999, with photo; *New York Daily News* p32 Jan. 24, 1966, with photo; *New York Newsday* C p2 Nov. 16, 1964, with photo; *New York Sunday News* p6+ July 20, 1969, with photos; *Parade* p15 Aug. 19, 1990, with photo; *People* p75+ May 29, 1978, with photos, p67+ June 17, 1991, with photo; *Toronto Globe and Mail* p25 Sep. 2, 1972, with photo, E p17 Sep. 5, 1980; *Variety* p7 Jan. 24, 1968; *Washington Post* TV p3 Dec. 13, 1981, with photo

Selected Films: *Ride Lonesome*, 1959; *Face of the Fugitive*, 1959; *Magnificent Seven*, 1960; *Charade*, 1963; *Hell is for Heroes*, 1962; *The Great Escape*, 1963; *The Americanization of Emily*, 1964; *Major Dundee*, 1965; *A High Wind in Jamaica*, 1965; *Our Man Flint*, 1966; *The Loved One*, 1965; *What Did You Do in the War,*

Daddy?, 1966; *Dead Heat on a Merry-Go-Round*, 1966; *In Like Flint*, 1967; *Water Hole Number 3*, 1967; *Avec, Avec* a.k.a. *Duffy*, 1968; *The President's Analyst*, 1967; *A Fistful of Dynamite* a.k.a. *Duck You Suckers*, 1972; *Honkers*, 1972; *The Carey Treatment*, 1972; *The Last of Sheila*, 1973; *Pat Garrett and Billy the Kid*, 1973; *Harry in Your Pocket*, 1973; *A Reason to Live, A Reason to Die*, 1974; *The Internecine Project*, 1974; *Last of the Mobile Hot-Shots* a.k.a. *Blood Kin*, 1975; *Bite the Bullet*, 1975; *Hard Times*, 1975; *The Last Hard Men*, 1976; *Skyriders*, 1976; *Midway*, 1976; *Cross of Iron*, 1977; *Firepower*, 1979; *The Baltimore Bullet*, 1980; *Loving Couples*, 1980; *Looker*, 1981; *Young Guns II*, 1990; *Hudson Hawk*, 1991; *The Player*, 1992; *Sister Act 2: Back in the Habit*, 1993; *Deadfall*, 1993; *Maverick*, 1994; *The Set Up*, 1995; *Eraser*, 1996; *The Nutty Professor*, 1996; *The Disappearance of Kevin Johnson*, 1996; *Keys To Tulsa*, 1997; *Affliction*, 1998; *Payback*, 1999

Selected Television Shows: *Klondike*, Oct. 1960–Feb. 1961; *Acapulco* Feb.–Apr. 1961; *The Dain Curse*, 1978; *Malibu*, 1983; *Sins of the Father*, 1985; *Jacqueline Susann's Valley of the Dolls*, 1981; *Darkroom*, 1981; *Hollywood Stuntmakers*, 1991; *Mastergate*, 1992; *Crash Landing: The Rescue of Flight 232*, 1992; *The Hit List*, 1993; *Ray Alexander: A Taste for Justice*, 1994; *Greyhounds*, 1994; *Ray Alexander: A Menu for Murder*, 1995; *The Avenging Angel*, 1995; *The Cherokee Kid*, 1996; *The Second Civil War*, 1997; *Noah's Ark*, 1999

Cochran, Johnnie L. Jr.

(KOK-ran)

Oct. 2, 1937– Lawyer. Address: 4929 Wilshire Blvd., Suite 1010, Los Angeles, CA 90010-3824

Johnnie L. Cochran Jr. received a call from former National Football League (NFL) running back O. J. Simpson in June 1994. The call was somewhat unexpected, since Cochran and Simpson were little more than casual acquaintances. Cochran soon learned that Simpson was calling from jail, having been charged with murdering his ex-wife, Nicole Brown, and her friend Ronald Goldman. Simpson pleaded with Cochran for legal support. In hindsight, it is not surprising that Simpson called Cochran. Over the previous 10 years, numerous celebrities in trouble with the law had made similar calls. In 1985 another former NFL great, Jim Brown, had contacted Cochran after being charged with attempted rape. Cochran found evidence that shed significant doubt on the accuser's account and persuaded prosecutors to drop all charges. Five years later Todd Bridges, star of the television show *Diff'rent Strokes*, sought help from Cochran after

Courtesy of Court TV

Johnnie L. Cochran Jr.

he was jailed for shooting a man in what was thought to be a drug deal gone bad. Cochran's defense of Bridges led to an acquittal. And just six months prior to Simpson's call, the pop superstar Michael Jackson had turned to Cochran. Jackson stood accused of child molestation, and in a textbook example of damage control, Cochran helped negotiate a settlement with the child's parents for a reported $20 million. The settlement kept the civil suit out of the courts and, in turn, out of the public eye, and it averted a criminal investigation. In each case Cochran's client came away relatively unscathed.

O. J. Simpson's case would prove no different. On October 3, 1995—one day after Cochran's 58th birthday—the Los Angeles Superior Court jury hearing the case returned a highly controversial verdict of "not guilty," marking the end of the racially divisive case that had riveted the nation's attention for over a year. The Simpson verdict made Cochran a household name throughout the nation and ensured that he will go down as one of the most famous trial lawyers in history.

Despite that stunning victory and many others like it, Cochran's career has been defined as much by his defeats as his victories. In May 1966 a young black man, Leonard Deadwyler, was rushing his pregnant wife to the hospital when the couple were pulled over by the Los Angeles police for speeding. According to police reports, as the officer approached the vehicle, Deadwyler made a sudden move, prompting the officer to open fire on him. Deadwyler, who was unarmed, was killed. Just four years out of law school and in the first year of his private practice, Cochran was hired by the family to sue the city of Los Angeles for wrongful

death. The atmosphere in Los Angeles at the time—less than 12 months after riots had blighted the Watts section of the city—was charged with racial tension, and the trial generated a great deal of publicity. Fearful that the trial would aggravate lingering unrest, Los Angeles decided to televise the coroner's inquest, and the 28-year-old Johnnie Cochran gained immediate notoriety. Unfortunately for Cochran, the jury decided that the shooting was justified.

On the heels of Cochran's first major defeat, he was retained as the lead counsel for the defense of Elmer "Geronimo" Pratt. Pratt, a Vietnam veteran and high-ranking official of the Black Panthers, was accused in 1970 of the 1968 murder of a young schoolteacher in Santa Monica, California. To this day Pratt maintains that he was attending a Black Panther meeting in Oakland, almost 400 miles away, when the shooting occurred, but he could not corroborate his testimony. Pratt was embroiled in a dispute at the time with the leader of the Black Panthers, Huey Newton, who reportedly instructed members not to step forward on Pratt's behalf. Despite the fact that the victim's husband, who was also injured in the shooting, identified another person as the assailant, Pratt was convicted and sentenced to life behind bars.

While those losses, particularly the Pratt case, were painful to Cochran, both taught him valuable lessons that he would carry with him to later successes. "[The Pratt trial] taught me that you can work within the system and believe in it, but if the government wants to get you, they can certainly go out and get you," Cochran told *Vibe* magazine (December/January 1994, on-line). "It also taught me that you never stop fighting." Indeed, Cochran continued to visit Pratt and kept fighting to overturn the conviction for more than 27 years. Cochran also learned two other things from his early setbacks: to question the "official version" of crime, by which he means the government's version, and to effect change by hitting the legal system where it hurts most: the pocketbook.

Johnnie L. Cochran Jr. was born in Shreveport, Louisiana, on October 2, 1937 to Johnnie L. Cochran Sr. and Hattie Cochran. He moved with his family to California when he was six years old. The family eventually settled in Los Angeles, where Johnnie Sr. became a top salesman for Golden State Mutual Life Insurance. Hattie harbored hopes that her bright son would become a doctor, but he had other plans. "I wanted to persuade people," Cochran told Tamara Jones for the *Washington Post* (October 3, 1994). "I like to talk." Armed with confidence in his verbal abilities and inspired by Thurgood Marshall's landmark argument in *Brown v. Board of Education*, which persuaded the United States Supreme Court to end school segregation, he set out to become a lawyer.

Cochran graduated from the University of California at Los Angeles in 1959 and received a degree in law from Loyola University in 1962. He served a three-year stint with the criminal division of the

Los Angeles city attorney's office before striking out on his own. He then proceeded to build a lucrative and well-regarded practice by defending clients who claimed they had been mistreated by the police. Eventually, however, Cochran concluded that he was not doing his best to bring about social change. So it was that in 1978, he accepted a post as assistant district attorney and number-three prosecutor in the Los Angeles DA's office, the largest in the country. "I took a five-fold pay cut, but I was able to make changes from the inside," Cochran told *People* (June 13, 1994). "I created a special 'roll-out' unit of deputy DAs to investigate police shootings."

While working for the DA's office, Cochran was himself involved in a situation similar to the one that resulted in Leonard Deadwyler's death. In 1979, as he was driving down Sunset Boulevard in his Rolls-Royce, he was pulled over by the police. Using a bullhorn, the officers demanded that he get out of the vehicle. "They had their guns drawn," Cochran recollected for Tamara Jones. "The kids were in the back—my baby Tiffany would have been about 10, and Jonathan was six. They both started crying." "It was dehumanizing," he said. During an ensuing search of the car, the police found his badge from the DA's office. After a brief, embarrassed apology, the cops drove away. Though Cochran has recounted the story numerous times in interviews, he never filed a formal complaint or brought charges against the police for illegal search. By his own account, he has chosen instead to harvest the indignation he suffered as fuel in the courtroom.

In 1981 Cochran returned to private practice. Again he built a reputation as a first-rate cop-buster and a lucrative practice that, prior to the O. J. Simpson trial, had won over $45 million in judgments against the Los Angeles police department. Though he was sought-after by celebrities, Cochran has asserted that the vast majority of his clients were not O.J.s but "no-Js." In other words, most of his clients were people of limited means who had been mistreated and had no other way of fighting back. For example, in 1981 Cochran was hired by the family of Ron Settles, a student and football player at California State University at Long Beach, who had been pulled over and arrested for speeding in Signal Hill, a suburb of Los Angeles. After Settles was found hanging in his cell, the death was ruled a suicide, but his family doubted that he had taken his own life. Cochran persuaded the family to exhume the body for an autopsy, which showed that Settles had been choked to death. The family won a judgment of $760,000. Cochran told *People*, "What was really important about the case was that the Signal Hill police chief resigned and the department had to change its way of doing things." In another case, which took place a decade later in Los Angeles, Cochran represented the families of 18 black third-grade girls who claimed they were being molested by their teacher. Cochran was able to show that the teacher had a past record of

pedophilia, and, moreover, that the school knew about it. He negotiated the most costly settlement in the history of the school district. "Not only does the settlement ensure none of the girls will ever have to work," Cochran told Laura Randolph for *Ebony* (April 1994), "I made sure a major fund was established should any of them ever suffer psychological problems."

Cochran's public persona is defined in part by his smooth manner and eye-catching wardrobe. He does not often dress in the usual lawyerly, power-broking gray or blue suits; he prefers colorful pastels with bold, geometrically patterned ties. His courtroom style is equally flashy. He possesses a prodigious memory for details; his ability to call to mind facts and statements from the record, instantly and often verbatim, gives him an air of extreme competence. While delivering rhetoric he exudes charm, which has proved to be an important asset in winning over juries. Another formidable weapon in Cochran's arsenal is his network of connections. Having worked in Los Angeles for his entire career, Cochran has developed an intimate knowledge of the legal workings of the city and accumulated a cadre of influential friends, including community leaders, judges, and even Gilbert Garcetti, the city DA who prosecuted O. J. Simpson and once worked under Cochran in the DA's office. "On one level, Johnnie benefits from having been raised, gone to school, and spent his entire professional life in the same city," Carl Douglas, managing attorney in Cochran's firm, told *Vibe*. "And that, in conjunction with his very engaging personality and obvious intelligence and wit, has endeared him to a wide spectrum of people over the years."

For all his style and connections, however, most of Cochran's success can be traced to his performance in court. His closing argument before the jury in the Simpson case, considered by many to be a masterpiece of legal rhetoric, is a good example of his persuasive skills. The prosecution's case was founded in large part on a time line, established through testimony, with which the prosecution attempted to reconstruct the sequence of events leading up to the murders of Nicole Brown and Ron Goldman. By recalling exact testimony from 11 different witnesses, some of whom had testified for the prosecution over the course of the nine-month trial, Cochran dismantled the time line by exposing its inaccuracies. He then mocked the prosecution's assertion that Simpson had worn a knit cap as a disguise. Donning a cap similar to the one entered as evidence, he said to the jurors, as quoted in the *New York Times* (September 28, 1995), "You have been seeing me for a year. If I put this cap on, who am I? I am still Johnnie Cochran with a knit cap." He also attacked the prosecution's contention that a pair of blood-stained gloves found at the scene had been worn by Simpson; he recalled for the jury that the gloves did not fit Simpson when he was asked to put them on in front of the court. And repeatedly throughout the closing statement, referring to both the gloves and the overall evidence, Cochran intoned the now-famous phrase, "If it doesn't fit, you must acquit." Los Angeles lawyer John Burris explained to Richard Price and Sally Ann Stewart for *USA Today* (September 28, 1995) that the prosecution in a criminal trial usually uses logic and facts in its final argument while the defense usually relies heavily on emotion. "Cochran essentially switched the roles," said Burris. "By relying on logic, he seized the high ground back."

In Chris Darden's closing argument for the prosecution, by contrast, Darden appealed to the emotions of the jury. He reminded the jurors that Nicole Brown had been a battered wife, and he played audio recordings of her calls to the police on occasions when Simpson had struck her. Many legal analysts have contended that given the way Darden and the principal prosecutor, Marcia Clark, built their case against Simpson, and in light of Darden's summation, Darden had no choice but to present his closing argument as he did.

After his victory in the Simpson trial, Cochran hosted his own nightly talk show, *Cochran and Company* (later renamed *Johnnie Cochran Tonight*), on the cable channel Court TV. He took up part-time residence in New York City, where the show was broadcast, and became involved in widely publicized cases there involving police brutality. Within the past year, he was part of the legal teams representing Abner Louima, who was beaten and sodomized while in custody of the police, and the family of Amadou Diallo, an unarmed man who died in a hail of 41 bullets fired by police officers.

On June 10, 1997 a ghost that had haunted Cochran for 27 years was exorcized. Determining that the chief witness testifying on behalf of the Los Angeles police and Federal Bureau of Investigation had lied under oath, a California Superior Court judge overturned the conviction of Geronimo Pratt and set him free. A lawsuit, filed by Cochran and Pratt against the police and the FBI in May 1998, is pending.

Though he has expressed great satisfaction with his work, Cochran has also said that he looks forward to retiring in the not-too-distant future. He told Aldore Collier for *Ebony* (November 1996), "I want my legacy to be leaving a first-class law firm, a firm of first-class lawyers. . . . If the Lord blesses me, on December 31, 1999, I'll retire." The likelihood that he will do so seems remote: In September 1999 he announced that his Los Angeles–based firm was joining forces with the Manhattan personal-injury law firm Schneider, Kleinick, Weitz, Damashek & Shoot. The new concern, named the Cochran Firm, Schneider, Kleinick, Weitz, Damashek & Shoot, combined Cochran's stable of 33 lawyers and unparalleled police-misconduct expertise with the Schneider firm's infrastructure and impressive personal-injury track record. (In several cases Schneider clients were awarded more than $100 million in damages.) To focus on his

new venture, Cochran gave up his nightly talk show.

Cochran and his second wife, Dale, live with his widowed father. — T.J.F.

Suggested Reading: *Ebony* p112+ Apr. 1994, with photos, p92+ Nov. 1996, with photos; *Essence* p86+ Nov. 1995, with photos; *New York Times* A p27 Jan. 20, 1995, with photo, A p1+ Sep. 28, 1995, with photos; *People* p97+ June 13, 1994, with photos; *Time* p102+ Dec. 25, 1995–Jan. 1, 1996, with photo; *USA Today* A p3 Sep. 28, 1995; *U.S. News & World Report* p32+ Jan. 23, 1995, with photos; *Vibe* (on-line) Dec.–Jan. 1994, with photos; *Washington Post* B p1 Oct. 3, 1994, with photos

Courtesy of William Morrow & Co.

Collins, Gail

Nov. 25, 1945– Newspaper columnist; journalist; nonfiction writer. Address: c/o New York Times, 229 W. 43d St., New York, NY 10036

Gail Collins is one of America's premier editorial and opinion writers. Her columns and articles, which often focus on political subjects, combine unsparing analysis with sometimes understated, sometimes guffaw-producing humor. Her latest book, *Scorpion Tongues: Gossip, Celebrity, and American Politics* (1998), a well-received history of political gossip in the United States, has made Collins—who has spent most of her journalistic career working in Connecticut and the New York metropolitan area—a name known throughout the country. Collins joined the *New York Times* editorial board in 1995, after having worked for the New York *Daily News*, the now-defunct *New York Newsday*, and United Press International, and she has since become a regular contributor to the *Times*'s daily edition as well as an occasional writer for the *New York Times Book Review* and the *New York Times Magazine*. Of her new book, Collins told *Amazon.com* (on-line), "After years of writing about scandal and rumors about politicians in the present tense, it was fun looking at what had gone before, and discovering how much of what seems new now had actually happened in the past."

Gail Collins was born Gail Gleason on November 25, 1945 in Cincinnati, Ohio. Her mother, Rita, was a homemaker, and her father, LeRoy, was an executive in the area of fuel procurement at Cincinnati Gas and Electric Co. Collins attended Marquette University, in Milwaukee, Wisconsin, where she received a B.A. degree in journalism in 1969. Shortly thereafter she enrolled at the University of Massachusetts at Amherst, where she obtained her master's degree in government.

Upon her graduation, in the early 1970s, Collins moved to Connecticut and began working as a writer for the *Fairpress in Westport*; soon afterward she became a contributing editor at *Connecticut Magazine*. As the decade progressed, Collins began covering politics from the state capital, Hartford. She also founded the Connecticut State News Bureau. At its height the bureau provided political coverage of the state capital for 35 syndicated newspapers. "[While] running the news service, I wrote an average of 100 stories a week, trying to tell the various [Connecticut] towns what the developments in Hartford meant to them . . . ," Collins told *Current Biography*. "My most definitive memory of that period was hosting a public TV program in Fairfield County, where my first guest was a local planning official who seemed to be either frightened or drunk, and where the last page of the script they handed me stopped mid-sentence. The sentence was, 'There will be only one bias on this show, and that will be' . . . "

Collins operated the bureau until the early 1980s, when she left to work as a columnist for United Press International (UPI) in New York City. During this time she wrote numerous business pieces for both *Venture* and *Institutional Investor*, her subjects ranging from the financial prosperity of the Burger King Corp. to up-and-coming executives in the personal-computer industry. From 1981 to 1982 she was a Bagehot Fellow in economic journalism at Columbia University, in New York City. She left UPI in 1985.

"[For the rest of] the 1980s, I was mainly a columnist for the New York *Daily News*," Collins told *Current Biography*. "I wrote a lot about election fraud, unrepresentative government, and social services that I thought were important and interesting. But the stories I got the most response from were: 1) The revelation that the city Department of Transportation, in its eagerness to complete a side-

walk repair project, had inadvertently killed all the maple trees that lined the streets in one Bronx neighborhood. It became known as the Massacre of Mosholu Parkway. 2) A story about the Statue of Liberty's birthday party which revealed that the crews doing restoration work on the crown, having been required to go all the way back to the ground when they wanted to use the bathroom, were answering the call of nature instead from the side of the statue. As a result, a patch of the base had eroded away before the restoration was done. This story did not have a cute name." In addition to her work at the New York *Daily News*, Collins continued to contribute to *Venture*, and she also broadened her journalistic horizons by writing for the computer magazine *Datamation* and *Working Woman*. In 1989, for *Ms.*, Collins wrote "Rap as a Second Language," which told the story of the Mother Fussin' Rappers, a group composed of three Brooklyn-area mothers who defeated more than 100 rap groups to win first prize in Rapsearch 1988. As Collins reported, the group had learned to rap from the son of a member, and Mother Fussin' Rappers attempted to send positive messages to black youth. In 1987 Columbia University honored Collins with the Meyer Berger Award (named for a renowned *New York Times* reporter). In 1989 she received the Matrix Award for Women in Communications.

Over the next few years, Collins's pieces began increasingly to address the situation of professional women in America. Over the course of several articles published in *Working Woman* in the early 1990s, Collins's subjects ran the gamut of female occupational concerns. She wrote, for example, of high-profile women (such as Marilyn Quayle, the wife of former vice president Dan Quayle) who had given up successful careers for the sake of their families, and of the often discriminatory practices of big businesses toward career-minded women. In its April 1991 issue, *Working Woman* published a Collins piece concerning a new Parker Brothers' board game, "Careers for Girls!," which was aimed at eight- to 12-year-olds. The only options presented in the game were college graduate, fashion designer, rock star, schoolteacher, animal doctor, and "super mom." Collins, in her customary eloquent-yet-blunt prose, voiced her dismay at the astonishingly meager choices.

In 1991 Collins left her post at the New York *Daily News* to write for the paper's crosstown rival, *New York Newsday*. The same year saw the publication of *The Millennium Book*, which she wrote with her husband, Dan Collins. *The Millennium Book* is "a general guide to thinking about the year 2000, with chapters on calendars, what life was like in the year 1000, how writers in the past envisioned the year 2000, forecasts for the future, and millennial list making," Collins told *Current Biography*. Using information she had gathered in the course of writing the book, Collins wrote a humorous New Year's piece for the January 1992 issue of *Women's World*. Consoling women who did not keep their New Year's resolutions, Collins compared the hardships of the modern woman to those of women alive in the year 1000. The article was titled, "New Year's Blues? It Could Be Worse." In 1994 Collins was awarded the coveted Associated Press Award for commentary.

In the summer of 1995, *New York Newsday* ceased production. Collins had left the paper shortly before. On September 5 the *New York Times*'s editorial-page editor, Howell Raines, announced that Collins would join the *Times*'s prestigious editorial board. Since then, her editorials—with byline—have appeared regularly in the *Times*'s daily edition, covering topics that have ranged from Bob Dole's unsuccessful 1996 presidential campaign and Geraldine Ferraro's ill-fated 1998 run for the Senate to the hazards of jury duty. Collins has also written feature articles for the *New York Times*, about such political figures as former presidential aide George Stephanopoulos, then–New York senator Al D'Amato, and New York City mayor Rudolf Giuliani. In addition, she has penned occasional critiques for the *New York Times Book Review*.

In the summer of 1998, William Morrow published Collins's second book, *Scorpion Tongues: Gossip, Celebrity, and American Politics*, to a mostly warm critical response. "From Civil War rumors that President Lincoln had 'Negro blood' and was nicknamed 'Abraham Africanus the First,' to stories of Prohibitionist Americans angrily pointing fingers at Teddy Roosevelt's drinking habits, Collins' book traces the history of American gossip through the eyes of the public . . . ," Eliot Sloan wrote for the *Washington Monthly* (June 1998). "The real essence of the book, however, lies not in the titillating tales about what happened to whom in what room, but in Collins' discussion of the social context that allows rumors to run wild. Collins argues that gossip 'really does need some kind of context to give it meaning.' Take, for example, the current allegations of presidential philandering. Collins attributes gossip's ability to spread so quickly and so out of control to the speed of our high-technology era."

"When I was out publicizing *Scorpion Tongues* I was actually pleasantly surprised by how much background in history and politics many of the people who interviewed me had," Collins told *Current Biography*. "But . . . one young man from a radio station in Georgia did keep asking me to compare Bill Clinton's sexual escapades with Richard Nixon's. I couldn't figure out what he was getting at until I realized that he thought Watergate was about sex, and that when Clinton defenders said Watergate was much worse than anything the president had done, he interpreted that to mean that Richard Nixon had more affairs."

Collins has served as a host of the *New York Times*'s cable-TV news program, *This Week Close-Up*, since 1997. In 1999 the *Times* assigned her to write a twice-a-week column for the op-ed page about the current presidential campaign. She is scheduled to return to the paper's editorial board in late 2000.

Gail Collins lives with her husband, Dan, in Manhattan. Her articles appear regularly not only in the *New York Times* but in many nationally circulated magazines, including *Redbook*, *McCall's*, and *Ladies' Home Journal*. — M.B.

Suggested Reading: *Amazon.com* (on-line); *Nation* p44+ May 11, 1998; *New York Times* C p15 Sep. 5, 1995; *New York Times* (on-line) Nov. 10, 1996; *Salonmagazine.com* (on-line) Apr. 8, 1998; *Washington Monthly* p48 June 1998

Selected Books: *The Millennium Book*, 1991; *Scorpion Tongues: Gossip, Celebrity, and American Politics*, 1998

Gary Gershoff/Retna Ltd.

Colvin, Shawn

Jan. 10, 1956– Singer; songwriter. Address: c/o Columbia Records, 550 Madison Ave., 26th Fl., New York, NY 10022

Shawn Colvin's hard-won success has come relatively late in her career. After spending over a decade plying her craft in bars and coffeehouses across the country, Colvin released her debut album, *Steady On*, in 1990, at the ripe age of 33—making her a rarity in the contemporary-music industry, which is dominated by 20-something performers like Jewel and Alanis Morrisette. But Colvin has turned age and experience to her advantage, winning five Grammy nominations and three Grammy Awards and earning praise from Bonnie Raitt and other musicians and from such reviewers as Richard Corliss, who declared in *Time* (November 11, 1996) that Colvin is "close to the best there is in today's bounty of singer-songwriters."

Shawn Colvin was born on January 10, 1956 in Vermillion, South Dakota, the home of the University of South Dakota. At the time of her birth, her parents, Bob and Barbara Colvin, were in effect academic gypsies (her father was pursuing advanced degrees in behavioral psychology, her mother in law). Their scholastic pursuits led the family to Carbondale, Illinois, in 1967, where Shawn's father entered a Ph.D. program at Southern Illinois University. Relocating proved painful for the 11-year-old Shawn. "Whatever instability I had, the move sent me into—I don't know—a dark part of myself," Colvin explained in an interview with Helen Thorpe for *Texas Monthly* (April 1995). "It probably would have happened one way or another, but it took me 15 years to recover." Colvin took solace in music. Her parents were musically gifted, though music was for them a hobby, and her father introduced Shawn to the guitar when she was 10. "His love for music was maybe one of the most sincere things that I got from him," *Rolling Stone* (February 4, 1993) quoted Colvin as saying. "He was a typical dad of that era. He went to work, Mother did the emotional caretaking, Dad did the disciplining. That was the side of my father that I will always treasure, watching him play music with his pals."

In the fall of 1973, Shawn Colvin enrolled at Southern Illinois University. A year and a half later, she dropped out. "I started getting work singing [at Carbondale bars], and it was just too alluring," she told Steven Lang for *People* (June 9, 1997). In 1976 she joined a western swing band called the Dixie Diesels and moved to Austin, Texas. While she was there, various insecurities began to haunt her. "I was plagued by severe depression and anxiety attacks, and nobody really knew how to help me," she explained to Helen Thorpe. "I had the idea that I was going to stop breathing." Colvin eventually quit the band and performed solo back in Illinois and then in San Francisco.

In 1980, at the invitation of Buddy Miller, a friend of hers from Texas, Colvin went to New York City to join his band. Nine months after she arrived there, Buddy Miller quit the group, which was then renamed the Shawn Colvin Band. To replace Miller, the band hired the guitarist John Leventhal. Leventhal awakened the songwriter in Colvin; previously, she had felt most comfortable interpreting songs written by other performers. "He was writing more sophisticated music than I thought I was capable of and I liked it; was inspired by it," she said in an interview for *Playback* (January/February/March 1998). "He needed lyricists. I would write lyrics for these songs of his. It was four or five years before the best of what we both could do came together—it took a long time for us to find the right way to work."

Colvin underwent a personal transformation during this period. She sought professional help for her depression, conquered a drinking habit she

had developed while touring the country, and started to gain control of her life. "The idea that I had choice in my life was this novel thing," she told Helen Thorpe. "It started by learning I had a choice about some very basic addictive behaviors, and once I got those out of the way, the idea transferred into my lifestyle. Learning that was like the key to the universe."

In 1988 Colvin and Leventhal secured a contract with Columbia Records, and two years later their album *Steady On* was released. Although it won critical acclaim and a Grammy Award for best folk recording, it was not a commercial success. Meanwhile, Colvin and Leventhal had became romantically involved; after the release of *Steady On* they broke up and ended their collaboration (temporarily, as it turned out).

Colvin's second album, *Fat City* (1993), was recorded in the home studio of Joni Mitchell (one of Colvin's early influences), with Mitchell's husband, Larry Klein, handling production. This joint effort spawned another critical success: the National Academy of Recording Arts and Sciences nominated *Fat City* for Grammy Awards in two areas. The following year Colvin released her third album, *Cover Girl*, a compilation of cover tunes she had performed solo in clubs before her recording career began. As a nod to her roots as a performer, Colvin's decision to record *Cover Girl* was understandable, but many observers felt that the album had stalled her career. Colvin disagreed, noting that she had developed by performing other people's music, not her own; songwriting was relatively new for her, and she found it difficult. "Whatever momentum [*Cover Girl*] cost me was not apparent to me," she told Chuck Taylor for *Billboard* (May 3, 1997). "I think radio and retail wondered what was happening. I'm glad I didn't have their perspective. . . . The break in writing was good for me."

Judging from record sales, Colvin was building an extremely loyal fan base of between 300,000 and 400,000. Positive industry attention was coming her way, and Columbia Records wanted to expand her reach beyond her traditional audience of triple-A radio format listeners. ("Triple-A" is a radio-industry term meaning "album adult alternative.") In an effort to reach people who listened to adult contemporary, alternative, Top 40, and rock music, Colvin began appearing on the TV talk-show circuit. To shed any residual "folkie" image, she was shown fronting a band rather than performing solo. Though she had been heralded as a forerunner of the "New Folk" movement, with a style reminiscent of those of Bob Dylan and Mitchell, Colvin rejected such labels. She told Vince Winkel for the *Christian Science Monitor* (February 23, 1993), "It's not that I don't like folk music, it's just that I don't really know what that's supposed to mean. It's all too easy to dismiss a supposed folk musician as someone without an edge."

Another failed romance—she divorced her first husband, Simon Tassano, whom she had met in 1991 and married in 1993—inspired Colvin's most successful album to date: *A Few Small Repairs*. Released in the fall of 1996, it marked the renewal of Colvin's collaborative relationship with John Leventhal, and was hailed uniformly by critics for its thematically unified lyrics and rich sound. In *Stereo Review* (January 1997), Alanna Nash wrote that Colvin's "instrumentation seems to grow organically from the songs, rather than being hung onto their skeletons." And Stephen Holden, writing for the *New York Times* (March 1, 1997), set Colvin apart from Sheryl Crow and other performers, whose work he tagged "the angry-young-women school of rock." "Ms. Colvin's voice isn't the harsh nagging whine of a sexual warrior, but the sweet edged-with-a-sob cry of a toughened up folk singer who has been dealt some hard knocks but is still in thrall to the old romantic myths." Best of all for Colvin, *A Few Small Repairs* attained commercial success, by going platinum and tying the record—11 weeks, attained by Celine Dion—as the number-one record on *Gavin*'s adult-contemporary chart. The album's long-charting hit, "Sunny Came Home," won two Grammys, for record of the year and song of the year.

Throughout her career, Shawn Colvin's most enthusiastic fans have been musicians and live audiences. David Crosby, for one, introduced her as his "favorite new singer-songwriter of the last five years" when she opened for Crosby, Stills, and Nash in the early 1990s. Mary Chapin Carpenter told Steven Lang, "I love the lyrics [and] that voice—I'm transported." And Indigo Girl Emily Saliers told Doug Hamilton for the *Atlanta Journal-Constitution* (December 11, 1995), "She's one of my favorite contemporary songwriters. I've been a major fan ever since her first record came out. Her writing is intellectual and honest. It appeals to my mind and my heart and my musical sensibilities." Prior to her recording career, Colvin's live performances were legendary for her energy and stage presence. "If you are one of those lucky hipsters who saw any of Colvin's solo gigs at LaVal's in Berkeley during the early 80s, you know how talented and ingratiating a performer she was back then," Michael Snyder wrote for the *San Francisco Chronicle* (December 1, 1994). According to Hamilton, her ability to develop a rapport with her audiences has grown with experience. "Those acquainted with Colvin only through her albums should know that, live, she's a cutup. At times during the set, it seemed like two Joans—Baez and Rivers—were at war over the singer's soul."

Shawn Colvin currently lives in Austin with her second husband, Mario Erwin, an advertising photographer, and their daughter, Caledonia Jean-Marie. Colvin recorded a fifth album, *Holiday Songs & Lullabies*, in June 1998, while eight-and-a-half months pregnant with Caledonia. The record, released in time for the Christmas season, was inspired by one of Colvin's favorite children's books,

Lullabies & Night Songs, illustrated by Maurice Sendak. A selection of Sendak's original artwork adorns Colvin's holiday album.

Some observers question how long an over-40 singer-songwriter can compete in a business that stresses youth, but those who have seen Colvin perform live maintain that her talent is timeless. "The essence of Ms. Colvin remains her solitary performance, as she strums and croons her way into new insights," Ann Powers wrote in the *New York Times* (November 17, 1992). "The image of a woman thinking for herself never grows outdated." — T.J.F.

Suggested Reading: *Atlanta Journal-Constitution* (on-line) Dec. 11, 1995; *Billboard* p3 Oct. 10, 1992, p75 May 3, 1997; *Christian Science Monitor* p14 Feb. 23, 1993, with photo; *New York Times* C p14 Nov. 17, 1992, with photo, I p16 Mar. 1, 1997, with photo; *People* p97+ June 9, 1997, with photos; *Playback* p4 Jan./Feb./Mar. 1998, with photo; *Rolling Stone* p58+ Feb. 4, 1993, with photo; *San Francisco Chronicle* (on-line) Dec. 1, 1994; *Stereo Review* p93 Jan. 1997; *Time* p93 Nov. 11, 1996, with photo; *Texas Monthly* p42+ Apr. 1995, with photo

Selected Recordings: *Steady On*, 1990; *Fat City*, 1993; *Cover Girl*, 1994; *A Few Small Repairs*, 1996; *Holiday Songs & Lullabies*, 1998

Colwell, Rita R.

Nov. 23, 1934– Director of the National Science Foundation. Address: c/o National Science Foundation, 4201 Wilson Blvd., Arlington, VA 22230

"I've always had a holistic view of research," Rita R. Colwell, a microbiologist and the director of the National Science Foundation (NSF), told *Science* (January 28, 1994). "I don't see departments and the disciplinary separations." Throughout a career during which she has emerged as a leading expert on marine biotechnology and cholera bacteria, Colwell has been noted for her ability to see "the big picture," drawing connections between disparate areas of scientific inquiry. In her research on how the disease cholera is spread, for example, she studied weather patterns and proposed a link between warmer ocean-water temperatures and cholera outbreaks. Colwell is a builder of bridges in other ways as well; she is a longtime advocate of increased transnational cooperation among scientists, the merging of pure and applied scientific research, and interactions between scientists and the public. She is also, according to her peers, a talented advocate, adept at winning support, financial and otherwise, for scientific causes. As Jay Grimes, a colleague of Colwell's, told Jeffrey Mervis for *Sci-*

Courtesy of the National Science Foundation

Rita R. Colwell

ence (March 13, 1998), "She's aggressive in a nice way. She's convincing and articulate. And she's very hard to say no to."

Colwell's multifaceted approach to furthering science serves her well as the director of the NSF, the government agency responsible for funding basic scientific and engineering research. President Bill Clinton nominated Colwell for the position, one of the top science-related jobs in the federal government, in February 1998, and she took office as the 11th director of the NSF in August of that year. In doing so she became the first woman, and the first biologist since the advent of modern biotechnology, to head the NSF, which will celebrate its 50th anniversary in the year 2000. Prior to assuming her post, Colwell had been the president of the University of Maryland Biotechnology Institute since 1991, as well as a professor of microbiology at the University of Maryland since 1972.

Colwell was born Rita Rossi on November 23, 1934 in Beverly, Massachusetts, the seventh of the eight children of Louis and Louise (Di Palma) Rossi. Her father had immigrated from Italy to the United States, where he ran his own construction company. Rita's mother, who died when Rita was 13, expressed pride in her daughter's academic accomplishments and passed on to her children her belief in the importance of education. In the sixth grade, Rita scored higher on an IQ test than any student in her school's history. This prompted her principal, a woman, to tell Rita that she had a responsibility to go to college. Rita received less encouragement, however, from high-school science teachers. As she recounted in a speech to the Alaska chapter of the Association for Women in Science, given on October 26, 1998 and transcribed on

the NSF Web site, "I could say that I got my start in science out of sheer stubbornness. When I went to high school, girls were simply not allowed to take physics. What's more, my high school chemistry teacher told me I'd never make it in chemistry— because women couldn't. That angered but also galvanized me. I had begun to see science as a way to understand the world and make my way in the world."

Colwell received a scholarship to attend Purdue University, in Indiana, where she began as a chemistry major but was quickly put off by the large classes and the dry manner in which introductory courses were taught. As a senior, she took a class in bacteriology (the term microbiology had yet to be coined) taught by Dorothy Powelson. As Colwell told Claudia Dreifus for the *New York Times* (February 16, 1999), "A woman bacteriologist in those days was unbelievably rare. [Powelson's] approach was, 'Look under the microscope and what do you see?' She got me hooked." In her speech, Colwell pointed out that all six female students in Powelson's class went on to earn M.D. or Ph.D. degrees. Colwell herself was accepted at medical school, but in the last semester of her senior year at Purdue, she met Jack Colwell, whom she has described as a "handsome, six-foot-two" graduate student in physical chemistry; during their first date they decided to get married, and on May 31, 1956, after a short courtship, they wed. "The marriage, incidentally, has lasted 40-plus years," Colwell told Dreifus. "So I think it was a good decision. But once I made it, medical school was out," since, as she explained to *Current Biography*, she "would be staying at Purdue, which at that time did not have a medical school or medical school affiliation." The same year she got married, Colwell graduated from Purdue with distinction, with a B.S. degree in bacteriology.

After deciding to forgo medical school, Colwell started looking for fellowships to attend graduate school in bacteriology. When she approached the head of Purdue's department, however, he informed her, "We don't waste fellowships on women," as Colwell told Dreifus. When Colwell's undergraduate adviser, Alan Burdick, a geneticist, offered her a fellowship to earn a master's degree in genetics at Purdue, she accepted. Her research entailed the counting of gene lineages in 186,000 fruit flies, work that she has cited as instrumental in preparing her for a career in microbiology. Colwell finished her M.A. in 1958. She and her husband then relocated to Seattle to earn their Ph.D. degrees from the University of Washington. There, Colwell studied bacteria commensal to marine animals, meaning bacteria that obtain food or otherwise benefit from the animals without causing them harm or doing them good. Colwell's research helped lay the groundwork for the scientific classification of marine bacteria. She received her Ph.D. in 1961.

That same year Jack Colwell received a fellowship to conduct research in Ottawa, at the Canadian National Research Council. Endeavoring to remain with her husband and conduct her own research as well, Colwell also applied to the council for a fellowship. Her proposal, however, was rejected, due to an antinepotism rule that prevented the council from providing funding to both members of a married couple. The council would give her lab space but no money. Colwell then applied jointly, with her thesis adviser, John Liston, to the NSF to fund her research, and the result was the first of many grants she has received from the agency. In 1963 Colwell was hired as an associate professor at Georgetown University, in Washington, D.C. She was the first female faculty member in science at Georgetown, where she received tenure in 1966 and taught until 1972. Colwell and her research team at Georgetown became the first to discover that cholera bacteria are native to estuaries, after isolating the bacterium in Chesapeake Bay, off the coast of Maryland.

In March 1963 Colwell gave birth to the first of her two daughters. Her husband's friends were shocked when, several months after giving birth, Colwell left Jack at home with the baby while she presented an invited paper at a scientific conference. Jack's colleagues were openly critical of his decision to let his wife work, and one of their wives went so far as to suggest that the Colwells' children would not succeed in life because of their mother's career. Later, when it was time for their daughters to attend college, Colwell and her husband encouraged each to major in whatever she wished, with the stipulation that they both take math up through the level of calculus and two years of chemistry, including basic and organic. Their daughter Alison, now age 36, has a Ph.D. in population biology and works for the U.S. Geological Survey, and their daughter Stacie, 33, is an M.D. and Ph.D. postdoctoral fellow at Harvard University, in Cambridge, Massachusetts. Stacie's Ph.D. is in women's studies and African history. Jack Colwell is currently a physicist at the National Institute of Standards and Technology.

According to the Institute for Scientific Information, Colwell's most frequently cited research, begun while she was at Georgetown, examined how pathogens can exist for long stretches of time in "a nonculturable but viable state," as Jeffrey Mervis wrote. Scientists had long been mystified by the question of what happens to cholera and other types of bacteria between outbreaks of disease. When Colwell embarked on her research, it was widely assumed that cholera was spread from person to person and lived in humans, perhaps in a dormant state, between epidemics. During the 1960s, Colwell became the first U.S. scientist to create a computer program that analyzed data related to the taxonomic classification of different strains of bacteria. This led to her revolutionary discovery that the strain of cholera bacteria that had been linked to the disease belonged to the

same species as benign strains of cholera. She and her team of researchers later found that both the harmless and the disease-causing (toxin-producing) strains were found commonly in estuaries and coastal waters. The disease-causing strain, Colwell discovered, was found on the surface and in the intestines of common zooplankton called copepods, and it goes through a dormant phase in the cold months of the year, during which it is difficult to detect. Copepods feed on phytoplankton, which bloom at certain times of year in correspondence with a rise in sea-water temperatures. Blooms may also occur due to warm water temperatures caused by weather conditions such as El Niño. An increase in phytoplankton in turn causes an increase in the numbers of copepods feeding on them, and thus an increase in the presence of harmful cholera bacteria in the water. Since humans contract cholera by drinking water in which a million or more bacteria per teaspoonful are present, they are at greater risk, Colwell theorizes, whenever sea temperatures rise.

Colwell has been able to use satellite data to draw a connection between phytoplankton blooms and outbreaks of cholera in Bangladesh, and she speculates that there was a link between El Niño and an outbreak in Peru in 1991. In a related effort, through experimentation Colwell and her researchers developed a simple, household method for filtering cholera bacteria out of drinking water, to be used in countries such as Bangladesh, which cannot afford sophisticated filtering systems such as those used in the United States, and where flood conditions and lack of fuel wood regularly make it impossible to boil drinking water. Colwell found that sari cloth, an inexpensive material found in virtually all homes, was effective in straining water, filtering out plankton and thus cholera bacteria attached to the particulate matter, including plankton, as well.

Colwell's findings could have major implications for predicting outbreaks and preventing cholera, which has killed thousands of people worldwide. She hopes that her research will pave the way for scientists to be able to predict the various conditions which set the stage for cholera outbreaks and thus enable people at risk to take preventive measures. Colwell presented an overview of her research in a paper entitled "Global Climate and Infectious Disease: The Cholera Paradigm," which was published in the December 20, 1996 issue of *Science*. In it, Colwell pointed more generally to climate and the environment as underexplored factors in the study of infectious diseases. The implications of Colwell's findings on cholera and climate with respect to the effects of global warming have aroused controversy in scientific circles. Many scientists agree that her theory demonstrates the need for further research on the subject.

In 1972 Colwell accepted a tenured position as a professor of microbiology at the University of Maryland at College Park. There, she expanded her research in the area of marine biotechnology, a field in which she is considered a trailblazer. Biotechnology refers to applied biological science and includes fields such as genetic engineering, and marine biotechnology applies its methods and goals to ocean life. In 1983 Colwell noticed that *Science* had devoted a special issue to biotechnology that failed to even mention marine applications, an oversight that had also occurred at conferences and discussions in which she had participated. This glaring omission inspired Colwell to write a paper entitled "Biotechnology in the Marine Sciences," which was published in the October 7, 1983 issue of *Science*. According to a later article in *Science* (January 28, 1994), Colwell's paper "laid out directions for using the techniques of genetic engineering to study and harvest the rich genetic resources of the oceans. . . . It essentially defined the field of marine biotechnology." Colwell particularly advocated the use of genetic engineering to develop medicines from marine sources. Colwell's research has generally focused on the ecology and genetics of marine bacteria and viruses. She has also conducted tests using bacteria that break down oil, to determine if the bacteria were effective in cleaning up oil spills, and she discovered a bacterial film that, when found on underwater surfaces, encourages oyster colonies to develop and grow.

Colwell has supported the growth of marine biotechnology not only through her own research, but also through the roles she has taken on at the University of Maryland. She helped expand the university's marine research program into the Sea Grant College, of which she served as the director from 1977 to 1983. In 1985 Colwell was a key force in the creation of the University of Maryland Biotechnology Institute (UMBI), an independent research branch of the University of Maryland system, which comprises 13 institutions of higher learning throughout the state. As of 1998 UMBI was made up of five main components: the Medical Biotechnology Center, located in Baltimore; the Center of Marine Biotechnology, located in Baltimore's Inner Harbor; the Center for Advanced Research in Biotechnology, in Shady Grove; the Center for Agricultural Biotechnology; and a "program without walls," the Center for Public Issues in Biotechnology—the latter two of which are located in College Park. Colwell was the president of UMBI from 1991 until 1998, when she left to take her post as director of the NSF. While at the UMBI, she oversaw 125 faculty members and 43 graduate students and an annual budget of $36 million. Colwell also served as vice president for academic affairs for the University of Maryland system from 1983 until 1987.

Colwell is also one of the four collaborators responsible for the creation of the Columbus Center, located in Baltimore's Inner Harbor. The Center was conceived in 1987 and envisioned as a world-class research center for marine biotechnology. It provided a new and larger home for the UMBI's Center of Marine Biotechnology (COMB). Colwell founded COMB, served as its director from 1987 to 1991, and maintained her 25-person lab there. The Columbus Center also provided space for a public exhibition hall intended to draw visitors and teach the public about marine research. The Hall of Exploration, as the exhibition wing is called, allows the public to watch COMB scientists at work and has created the opportunity for informal dialogue between the researchers and visitors. Colwell's active role in getting the Columbus Center built was seen by many as an example of her skill as an administrator, a fund-raiser, and an advocate for research as well as for science education for general audiences. The facility cost $160 million to build. In 1990 Colwell was given Maryland's highest award for economic development for her role in planning the center. Seven years later the private company that ran the exhibition center defaulted on $6 million in loans due to high costs and low attendance, and the Hall of Exploration has been temporarily shut down; the University of Maryland has taken over the Hall of Exploration and will reopen it in partnership with the Baltimore Aquarium. COMB itself, the part of the Columbus Center for which Colwell was responsible, has proven to be highly successful.

In addition to the prominent administrative roles she took on at the University of Maryland, several other posts helped prepare Colwell for her job as head of the NSF. From 1984 until 1990 she sat on the National Science Board, whose members are appointed by the president and which oversees the NSF. In 1994–95 she served a one-year term as the president-elect of the American Association for the Advancement of Science (AAAS), and subsequently she spent a year as chair of the AAAS board, during which she emphasized the association's role in promoting basic research and science education. Colwell has also served as the president of Sigma Xi and of the American Society for Microbiology. She has impressed many of her peers with her ability to conduct copious research while also serving in high-level administrative posts. She is author or co-author of around 500 scientific papers and 16 books, with an average of 18 papers per year since 1981, and she is considered an expert on marine biotechnology, cholera bacteria, the molecular genetics of marine and estuarine bacteria, and the microbiology of Chesapeake Bay. She has also produced an award-winning film, entitled *Invisible Seas*, and advised more than 50 Ph.D. candidates, all of whom graduated and many of whom continue to regard her as a key mentor. Thus, when she was nominated to head the NSF, Colwell already enjoyed a high profile in scientific circles; as she was well-respected as a researcher, an administrator, and a teacher, her nomination received widespread support among her peers. In coming to the NSF, Colwell took responsibility for a 1,250-person organization with an annual budget of about $3.8 billion, headquartered in a five-year-old, 12-story building in Arlington, Virginia. The organization funds research in all 50 states through grants and contracts to more than 2,000 universities and other nonprofit organizations.

Colwell began her six-year appointment as NSF director with clearly stated priorities for scientific research. Of these, Colwell's true brainchild is the study of a field that she terms biocomplexity. As she described it in an address given before a House Appropriations subcommittee on March 4, 1999, "Biocomplexity is a multidisciplinary approach to understanding our world's environment. For generations, scientists have studied parts of our environmental system—individual species and habitats—in isolation. Now it is time for a better understanding of how those parts function together as a whole. . . . Biocomplexity is about looking at phenomena, whether they be weather or proteins or human society, at many scales. Such a viewpoint will let us identify the principles and patterns that operate at multiple levels of organization in the earth's systems, across time and space." As a writer for *Scientific American* (December 1998) put it, Colwell "declares that her goal is to build up from the ecological interactions in a crumb of soil 'to see how the planetary system works.'" As part of this effort, Colwell calls for methods by which scientists working independently around the world may better share their findings in order to create a more comprehensive base of scientific data, which would aid the international community in its decision-making on environmental issues. To stress the need for such coordinated efforts, she points to the fact that, for example, forest fires in one part of the world have an effect on the environment of areas across the globe. Sharing information will create better "ecological forecasting," as Colwell calls it, with practical benefits for agriculture and environmentally related industries worldwide.

Colwell and the NSF will also spearhead a major government initiative to increase funding of research in information technology. The Internet has grown at a remarkable rate, and estimates show, Colwell has stated, that information technology has accounted for one-third of the country's recent economic growth. An independent government panel recently reported, however, that the U.S. is severely underinvesting in the computer-related research that is necessary to stay ahead of the curve in this field. In addition to supporting information technology research on its own merit, Colwell also sees its importance for other scientific disciplines. "It will deliver tools and capabilities that will benefit every field, every discipline, and every level of education," she said in her March 4, 1999 speech before a House Appropriations subcommittee. For example, central to Colwell's biocomplexity initiative is use of computers to perform tasks ranging from genetic sequencing, to the study of weather patterns, to the sharing of data among scientists on a transnational basis.

Colwell's third major goal is that of improving education in science and math, particularly at the elementary- and secondary-school levels. She feels

that part of the task entails changing the attitudes of professional scientists, who generally feel that educating the public is not part of their jobs. "There is no group of people who should feel more responsible for science and math education than our scientists and scientists-to-be," Colwell said at an AAAS seminar, as quoted by the *Chronicle of Higher Education* (November 20, 1998). While it is common for graduate students in science to instruct undergraduates, Colwell has created a new graduate teaching-fellows program that provides financial support for graduate students to teach in classrooms from kindergarten through 12th grade, under the guidance of trained teachers. Colwell is also exploring ways to increase the salaries of, or otherwise reward, those who are considered the best teachers, regardless of their prominence in research. A few of Colwell's other responsibilities at the NSF include modernizing the South Pole Station, the location of which makes it an ideal place to conduct research in a great number of fields; increasing funding for the Plant Genome Research Program; and creating a new Network for Earthquake Engineering Simulation, which will lead to "a national, fully-interconnected network of major earthquake research facilities," as Colwell said in her March 4, 1999 speech.

While Colwell's track record as a researcher, administrator, and teacher speaks for itself, perhaps just as impressive is the admiration she garners from her peers. Al Chiscon, a newly retired Purdue professor of biology, was Colwell's labmate and fellow graduate student in bacteriology there. He told Jeffrey Mervis of Colwell, "She knew a lot more than I did, she could see meaningful relationships among things that didn't seem connected, she worked incredibly hard, and she could explain what she was doing both to other scientists and to a general audience. . . . She's so much more than a good scientist. I don't know how she does everything." In July 1999 Colwell accepted an appointment to the National Commission on Mathematics and Science Education for the 21st Century, which was set up by the U.S. Department of Eduation a few months earlier; chaired by former senator and astronaut John H. Glenn Jr., the commission aims to recruit, train, and retain high-quality math and science teachers for kindergarten through 12th grade. Of her many awards, she takes particular pride in the honorary doctor of science degree she received from Purdue in 1993. As for her hobbies, besides jogging daily and racing sailboats with her husband, she has a longstanding interest in creative writing and is working on a novel about a female scientist. — O.J.S.

Suggested Reading: *Chronicle of Higher Education* A p34 Nov. 20, 1998, with photo; *New York Times* F p3 Feb. 16, 1999, with photo; *NSF.gov* (on-line); *Science* p549 Jan. 28, 1994, p1047+ Aug. 19, 1994, p2025+ Dec. 20, 1996, p1122+ Feb. 20, 1998, p1622+ Mar. 13, 1998, p1944+ Sep. 25, 1998; *Scientific American* (on-line) Dec. 1998; *Washington Post* B p1+ Oct. 11, 1992, with photo, A p6 Feb. 14, 1998, with photo

David Calle/Courtesy of American Ballet Theatre

Corella, Angel

(kor-AY-ah, AN-hel)

Nov. 8, 1975– Spanish ballet dancer. Address: c/o American Ballet Theatre, 890 Broadway, New York, NY 10003-1278

When he dances, Angel Corella told Elizabeth Kaye for *Dance* (November 1995), the feeling he experiences "is like being in love for the first time, and being loved back." Now a principal dancer with American Ballet Theatre (ABT), one of the world's preeminent troupes, the Spanish-born Corella languished for years in a ballet company in his native land. His superiors there assigned him to dance in the back row of the corps de ballet and led him to believe he had little talent. He was on the verge of giving up dance when Ricardo Cue, a former director of the National Ballet of Spain, took up his cause and became his manager. Months later, in December 1994, Corella won first place in an international dance competition in Paris. After seeing him dance, Kaye reported, Natalia Makarova, a former prima ballerina with the Kirov Ballet and ABT and a judge of the contest, described Corella as "an angel who has been sent to us."

Less than six months later, at the age of 19, Corella made his debut with ABT, at the Metropolitan Opera House in New York City. His arrival had been preceded by unprecedented fanfare for a dancer so young and professionally untested;

dancing on the stage of the Met, he proved that the rumors of his talent had not been exaggerations. Since then, Corella has won an ardent following among ballet fans and has demonstrated both surpassing technical virtuosity and an impressive subtlety of expression in such roles as Romeo in *Romeo and Juliet* and Albrecht in *Giselle*. "Sometimes I feel like it's sad to say this," Corella told Robert Sandla for *Stagebill* (on-line), "but dance is my life. I don't think I could live without dance. I express myself dancing. That's just the way I am. I wish everybody could dance. When you worry about something or there's something you don't like, you dance and everything goes away. It's a way to explode."

Angel Corella was born on November 8, 1975 in Madrid, Spain. The only son in a middle-class family, he has two older sisters. Their mother, a homemaker, would listen to classical music while she performed household chores. His sisters attended ballet classes, and at age seven, Corella began studying judo. In class one day, he witnessed as a man's nose was broken and bloodied. Young Angel was appalled. "This is not for me," he thought, as Kaye reported. He persuaded his mother to allow him to join his sisters and take ballet instead. He began studying in Colmenar Viejo, a city near Madrid, and later studied in Madrid with Karemia Moreno.

At age 14 Corella became a member of a minor Spanish ballet company. In 1991, when he was 16, he won first prize in the National Ballet Competition of Spain, but even this seeming confirmation of his talent did not improve his standing within the troupe. He received little encouragement from the company's management and did not advance through the ranks. (The reasons for the management's behavior toward him, Corella has come to believe, were purely personal.) Although he still loved to dance, Corella felt so discouraged about his prospects that he thought seriously of quitting. Concerned about her son's future, his mother sought the advice of a retired dancer, who, in turn, approached Ricardo Cue. As Kaye reported, when Cue asked Corella what he wanted to do, the young dancer responded, "I want to get out of here."

Cue immediately thought that Corella should become a member of ABT, the favorite company of both men. But first, Cue wanted him to enter a major dance competition. He felt confident that Corella would win first place, which would help in getting the working papers—and the clout—necessary to expedite Corella's dance career in the United States. The application period for the next important contest—the Concours International de Danse de Paris—had ended, however, and the next competition after that was six months away. Corella felt incapable of waiting half a year for his fate to be decided. "If I have to wait that long, I'll quit dancing," he told Cue, as Kaye reported. Cue flew to Paris and managed to persuade the officials of the Concours International de Danse de Paris to accept Corella as a late entrant. Cue told Kaye, "Taking Angel from his company was like taking a tiger from a cage." Corella practiced with passionate dedication, and in a field of 94 contestants, he won first prize.

Almost overnight Corella's life changed. After winning the contest he was chauffeured by limousine to a dinner attended by Madame Jacques Chirac, the wife of the then–mayor of Paris, and Madame Georges Pompidou, the widow of the former French president. It took some time, however, for his newfound success to erase the effects of years of reproach. Cue recalled to Kaye that when Cue would assert that Corella would soon be making a splash, dancing with one of the world's top companies, the younger man would respond, "That is ridiculous. That is crazy." Shortly after the French contest, Corella and Cue traveled to New York, where Natalia Makarova's glowing recommendation helped Corella gain an audience with Kevin McKenzie, the artistic director of ABT. McKenzie was so impressed by Corella's audition that he not only asked Corella to join the company, but also hired the young dancer as a soloist—an unusual move that made it clear to the world that Corella was an exceptional talent. "I can't wait for people to see him," McKenzie said at the time, as quoted by Kaye. Corella was promoted to principal dancer in 1996.

Although becoming a member of ABT was a dream come true for him, Corella (who did not speak English when he arrived in New York) felt misgivings about his new situation at first. After signing his contract with ABT and thus committing himself to dancing with them for the near future, he worried that his ambitions might be thwarted once again. However, he soon found out that he would perform with the company during the 1995 season, which was to begin in a few weeks, in two small, stand-out roles: the Bronze Idol in La Bayadère and the male part in the Peasant Pas de Deux in Giselle. He danced the latter role with such abundant joy that his partner, Shawn Black, was moved to say, "He made me remember why I became a dancer," as Kaye reported. Describing Corella's performance, Kaye wrote that his "typically musical reading of the Bronze Idol, one of ballet's most stylized and virtuosic solos, . . . revealed his capacity to forge a connection with the audience even in a role so narrowly confined." In fact, at Corella's first performances with ABT, audiences greeted him like a star, shouting "Bravo!" and throwing roses at his feet, despite the brevity of his roles. The other ABT dancers were taken with Corella as well; as Kaye reported, they gathered around him during classes, applauding his remarkable pirouettes, executed one after another, faster and faster, until he seemed to spin like a top.

After Corella's third performance as the Idol, McKenzie assigned him a role that would require him to live up to the most lofty expectations of him: that of the lead dancer in George Balanchine's Theme and Variations. In Dance, Kaye reported that Mikhail Baryshnikov, one of the most famous ballet dancers of all time, once told Julio Bocca, a

fellow virtuoso, "If you can do a good Theme and Variations, you can do a good anything." In the opinion of Erik Bruhn, another exceptional male dancer, it is the most technically difficult male role in the ballet canon. Thus, when McKenzie gave Corella the part—what would be his first major role at ABT—"it would be difficult not to read that gesture as both an accolade and a trial," in Kaye's words. Furthermore, Corella had only a few weeks to rehearse the role, which he had performed only once before, in Spain, at age 15. Despite the pressure, when McKenzie gave him the news, "Corella's face broke into his lustrous, contagious smile, and his dark eyes beamed," as Kaye wrote. "He had no fear of dancing Theme and Variations. . . . He knew only that he wanted every opportunity, every possibility, every challenge."

About an hour before Corella was to perform Theme and Variations, Cue asked him what he was thinking about. Corella replied, as Cue recalled to Kaye, "I'm thinking of every day I had to get up at seven in the morning and go two hours to class. And I feel that in this moment I am receiving the reward." The news of an exceptional new male dancer had spread quickly, and Corella's debut in Theme and Variations, part of a mixed bill on a Monday night, attracted an unusual amount of attention. "I knew a lot of people were coming," Amanda McKerrow, Corella's partner for the performance, told Kaye for Dance, "and I knew they were coming to see him." When it came time for Corella and McKerrow to go onstage, company members crowded the backstage wings to watch, and when the dancers made their entrance, the audience broke into applause, just as they might have for a major star. Corella's performance was hailed as "astonishingly polished" by the dance critic Anna Kisselgoff; in the New York Times (June 7, 1995), Kisselgoff wrote of his solos, "The first showed off his pure classical line and his easy pirouettes. The second began with a soaring diagonal of perfectly shaped steps and included a superbly executed series of alternating double turns in the air and pirouettes." The single small flaw Kisselgoff noted in the performance was the absence of a leg swing to the back to finish off some of the turns. "Yet Mr. Corella came amazingly close to a definitive performance," she wrote. "The precision of his form is filled out with an engaging lilt that gives his dancing its joyful glow. . . . In the right place at all times, Mr. Corella simply danced for the sheer pleasure of dancing and his smile proved contagious to Ms. McKerrow."

During his first season, Corella was also seen as the lead dancer in the Mandolin dance in Romeo and Juliet, and as the lead gypsy in Don Quixote. In McKenzie's staging of that ballet, the lead gypsy performs a virtuosic solo that McKenzie created on Corella (meaning that, while choreographing the solo, McKenzie had Corella dance the steps so that McKenzie could see what the solo looked like and could then make adjustments). More recently, during ABT's 1998 season, Corella debuted in four roles (that is, he danced them for the first time with ABT): that of James, the male lead, in the second act of *La Sylphide*; the title role of Conrad, the pirate, in *Le Corsaire*; the Boy in Blue in *Les Patineurs*; and the leading role of Albrecht, in *Giselle*. In the *New York Times* (June 19, 1998), Jennifer Dunning called his performance in the last-named role "a major breakthrough for Mr. Corella, a bravura whiz kid of a dancer who has with touching humility continued to perfect his art. He was almost unrecognizable as Albrecht, looking older and more rooted than ever before and hinting at new facets to the character." She continued, "[His] mime was full and bold from the first, in finely nuanced acting that illuminated the lyrical flow, clarity, and virtuosity of his dancing. . . . [He] shaded technical feats by adapting his body line and impetus to suggest sadness and panic with the subtlety of a much older and more experienced performer than he." Among Corella's other notable roles at ABT are Romeo, in *Romeo and Juliet*; Franz, the male lead in *Coppelia*; Basil, the male lead in *Don Quixote*; and Ali, the slave, in *Le Corsaire*. As the slave, a role that was made famous by Rudolf Nureyev, Corella "brought down the house," according to Kisselgoff in the *New York Times* (July 7, 1998). Corella has also danced in Twyla Tharp's *Known by Heart*, in a role that he helped the choreographer to create and that he was the first to perform. In a statement that might summarize the critical response to Corella's dancing, Kisselgoff wrote in the *New York Times* (October 29, 1998): "Happiness is a performance by Angel Corella. . . . At the ripe old age of 23, he has also grown . . . to combine an astonishing technique with artistic depth."

Corella is obviously a preternaturally gifted dancer. He once commented to Cue, as quoted by Kaye, "When I dance, I feel as if I am being moved by something outside myself. It is the feeling of being a puppet." But despite the seeming ease with which he performs the most technically challenging feats—his multiple pirouettes and light, lofty jumps chief among them—he also works exceedingly hard in the dance studio, often practicing alone for hours at a time after his rehearsals are finished. In the small apartment in which he lived in Spain, he would view videos of entire ballets and then dance all the parts himself, humming the music. "Onstage I never worry about technique or if I have to do one pirouette or one jump that has to be correct," Corella told Robert Sandla. "It's the whole movement and the whole piece together. I never think about steps. I always think about the whole variation. It's a different concept." As he warms up backstage before a performance, Corella usually listens to music on a Walkman to energize him, often choosing recordings by alternative bands such as Rage Against the Machine.

According to Elizabeth Kaye, Corella has a kindly exterior, underneath which lies the determined constitution of "a rock," as he describes himself. After his first New York season with ABT, he said of his success, as quoted by Kaye, "When you want

something very badly and you don't have it, you forget about it, and then it comes to you. That always happens to me." — O.J.S.

Suggested Reading: *Dance* p52+ Nov. 1995, with photos; *New York Times* II p26 May 21, 1995, with photo, C p14 June 7, 1995, with photo, E p27 June 19, 1998, with photo; *Stagebill* (on-line)

Selected Ballets: *Americans We* (featured role); *Ballet Imperial* (featured role); *La Bayadère* (Solor); *Cinderella* (Jester); *Coppélia* (Franz); *Le Corsaire* (Conrad and Ali); *Don Quixote* (Basil and lead gypsy); *Fancy Free* (leading role); *Giselle* (Albrecht and Peasant Pas de Deux); *Les Patineurs* (the Boy in Blue); *Romeo and Juliet* (lead Mandolin dancer, Benvolio, and Romeo); *The Sleeping Beauty* (the Bluebird and Gold); *Swan Lake* (Benno); *Stepping Stones* (leading role); *Tchaikovsky Pas de Deux* (leading role); *Theme and Variations* (leading role)

Courtesy of Congressman Cox's office

Cox, Christopher

Oct. 16, 1952– U.S. Representative from California. Address: 2402 Rayburn House Office Bldg., Washington, DC 20515

Since he became a member of the House of Representatives, in 1988, Christopher Cox, the Republican chairman of the House Policy Committee and the fourth-ranking member of the Republican House leadership, has emerged as one of Congress's strongest supporters of business. Often described as a pragmatic conservative, Cox has served as a spokesperson for the effort to reduce the size of the federal government and ease the tax burden on U.S. citizens. In 1998 he came to prominence when he headed a select committee to probe allegations that some prominent U.S. companies, one with ties to President Clinton's administration, may have given China illegal access to military technology, thereby jeopardizing national security.

Christopher Cox was born on October 16, 1952 in St. Paul, Minnesota, to Charles C. Cox, a publisher, and Marilyn A. Cox. He left Minnesota in 1970 to attend the University of Southern California (USC), in Los Angeles, from which he graduated in 1973 after participating in an accelerated program. Even when he was a college student, his views leaned toward those of the Republican Party. Unlike many of his generation, who rebelled against the conservatism of their parents, he did not protest the U.S.'s involvement in the Vietnam War. Neither did he enlist in the military: he held a student deferment until 1971, then drew a high number in the lottery that decided the order of draftee enlistment.

After USC Cox attended both business school and law school at Harvard University, in Cambridge, Massachusetts, where he served as an editor of the *Harvard Law Review*. In 1976 he received a J.D. degree and an M.B.A. degree. During that time he joined other Republicans in support of Ronald Reagan's ultimately unsuccessful bid for the Republican presidential nomination.

From 1977 to 1978 Cox served as a law clerk for U.S. Court of Appeals judge Herbert Choy. Next, from 1978 to 1986, he worked at the law firm of Latham & Watkins, in Newport Beach, California, specializing in corporate finance and venture capital law. He became a partner in the firm in 1984.

Meanwhile, for the 1982–83 academic year, Cox had returned to Harvard Business School to lecture on business administration. Then, in 1984, he and his father founded Context Corp., through which they created and marketed English translations of *Pravda*, the daily newspaper controlled by the government of what was then the Soviet Union. Their publication lasted until 1988 and served as a valuable resource for colleges and universities as well as government intelligence and military agencies.

In 1986 Cox took a leave of absence from his law firm to serve as President Reagan's senior associate counsel. In that position, which he held until 1988, his main task was to help draft measures to streamline the complicated process of establishing the federal budget. He also found time to pen several speeches for the president. "It was a wonderful place to work," Cox told Weston Kosova for the *New Republic* (February 20, 1995). "As the ultimate boss, President Reagan was an outstanding person for whom to work. Among other things, there was never a story of Ronald Reagan picking up a book and throwing it across the room or anything like that."

When Cox left the White House, he sought the House seat that had been vacated by Robert Badham, who had represented California's 47th Congressional District, in Orange County—long a Republican stronghold. He entered the race late, and some people, citing his East Coast affiliations, questioned the extent of his conservatism. But he campaigned strongly, and with the help of the Republican icons Oliver North and Robert Bork, both of whom made campaign appearances for him, he beat out 10 candidates in the Republican primary, then won 67 percent of the vote in the general election to become a member of the 101st Congress.

In his first term Cox won a seat on the House Budget Committee and worked to cut federal spending. He was credited with actively taking part in the legislative process, helping, for example, to introduce the Budget Process Reform Act. Although the bill did not become a law, Cox emerged as a champion of that issue.

Cox handily won reelection to his seat in subsequent elections, and he has served his constituents by voting with his party on key issues regarding finance. For example, in 1996 he voted to limit the compensation awarded to litigants in product-liability cases and voted against increasing the minimum wage. He has served on nearly a dozen House committees, including the Joint Economic Committee, the Government Operations Committee, and the Government Reform and Oversight Committee, of which he is currently a vice chairman. He gained his current post of chairman of the Policy Committee in 1995, following the elections of 1994, in which Republicans gained a majority in the House for the first time in four decades.

Throughout his career Cox has consistently sought to promote the interests of the business community. He has worked to establish the Internet as a business-friendly entity, free from government regulation and taxation. Moreover, he authored the 1995 Securities Litigation Reform Act, which earned the distinction of being the only legislation for which Congress has overridden a veto by President Clinton. This legislation increased protection for executives and their advisers in litigation brought against them by disgruntled investors, by requiring investors to prove recklessness on the part of executives. Part of Cox's impetus to work on the legislation stemmed from his own experiences as a corporate investment lawyer, which convinced him that executives and their advisers were often harmed by frivolous and baseless litigation. Cox had been the subject of such a suit in the mid-1990s and was later found to be guiltless.

In addition to his legislative work, Cox made headlines in May 1998 when he was named head of a select committee investigating China's acquisition of high-security U.S. technology. Cox's committee—the Select Committee on U.S. National Security and Military/Commercial Concerns with the People's Republic of China—sought to determine the extent to which U.S. foreign policy and national security had been compromised by domestic technology companies that had done business with China. It was alleged that Loral Space & Communications Ltd. and Hughes Electronics Corp., which had been connected with a failed 1996 satellite launch in China, had allowed that nation to gain valuable information that led to the improvement of its missile guidance systems. The inquiry followed President Clinton's February 1998 decision to allow Loral, a satellite manufacturer, to work in conjunction with the Chinese government, despite resistance from the U.S. Department of Justice. There were allegations that President Clinton's decision may have been influenced by political contributions made to the Democratic Party by Bernard Schwartz, Loral's chairman and CEO.

The inquiry led by Cox was one of several that took place that year and, like the others, was widely perceived to be fueled by partisan interests. Cox acknowledged such views upon starting the inquiry. "There is a well-worn rut into which anything labeled 'investigation' has fallen," he was quoted as saying by Francis X. Clines for the *New York Times* (May 21, 1998). "In order to stay clear of that well-worn partisan rut, the focus of this select committee should be and will remain national security." To help keep partisanship from tainting the inquiry, the committee was made up of four Democrats and five Republicans. Cox also limited press and public access to the inquiry and imposed a deadline of January 1999, in order to limit the length and cost of the investigation.

The select committee completed its investigation on December 30, 1998, after interviewing 150 witnesses and examining 500,000 pages of documents. A declassified report containing an estimated 70 percent of the committee's findings was released on May 25, 1999. According to the abbreviated account, systematic Chinese espionage, which began 20 years ago and continues today, enabled China to obtain design secrets for key U.S. nuclear warheads. The report included 38 recommendations; among other measures, it called for implementation of tighter security measures, enhanced intelligence efforts, and controls on the export of U.S. technology.

Cox and his wife, Rebecca, have three children. When not in Washington, D.C., he lives with his family in Newport Beach, California. — Y.P.

Suggested Reading: *New York Times* A p19 May 26, 1995, with photo, I p20 June 18, 1995, A p26 May 21, 1998, with photo, A p1+ May 26, 1999, with photo; *New Republic* p22+ Feb. 20, 1995

Cunningham, Michael

1952– Writer. Address: c/o Farrar Straus & Giroux, 19 Union Sq. W., New York, NY 10003

In his novels, *Golden States* (1984), *A Home at the End of the World* (1990), *Flesh and Blood* (1995), and *The Hours* (1998), Michael Cunningham has explored the changing nature of the concept of family. For *The Hours*, the winner of a Pulitzer Prize and the PEN/Faulkner Award for Fiction, Cunningham turned for inspiration to a great English novelist of the 20th century, Virginia Woolf, and especially to her novel *Mrs. Dalloway*. Discussing Woolf—who committed suicide in 1941—during an interview with David Streitfeld for the *Washington Post Book World* (January 24, 1999), Cunningham explained that he found fascinating "the notion that somebody like Virginia Woolf, who could see the world as deeply and fully and completely as she did, who had as deep a sense of the joy of being alive as anyone, could still ultimately decide not to live." In *The Hours*, Cunningham has succeeded in capturing that "joy of being alive," the profundity to be found in the ordinary moments of everyday life.

Michael Cunningham was born in 1952 in Ohio. His father, who worked in advertising, moved the family shortly after Michael's birth, first to Europe and then to California. Cunningham attended Stanford University, in California, and then, after a period of wandering around the West and supporting

Courtesy of Columbia University/The Pulitzer Prizes

himself as a bartender, received an offer to join the prestigious University of Iowa Writers Workshop in 1978. While at the university—where he received a master of fine arts degree—he had a story published in the *Atlantic Monthly* and another in the *Paris Review* and also acquired a literary agent.

That early success and the encouragement of his teachers, especially Hilma Wolitzer, bolstered him greatly but led him "to the entirely false conclusion that if writing wasn't exactly easy, well it was going to be easy for me. I would just write things and publish them," he told Michael Coffey in an interview for *Publishers Weekly* (November 2, 1998). "Boy was I mistaken!" he added. After leaving the university he went to work for the Carnegie Corp., a philanthropic foundation, where he wrote public-relations pieces; he stayed there until 1990, when his second novel was published.

Cunningham's first novel, *Golden States*, is the story of a boy's journey toward maturity in southern California. Although reviewers praised the novel as a good first effort, Cunningham himself told Mel Gussow, in an interview for the *New York Times* (April 20, 1999), that he considered *Golden States* "a journeyman effort." For the next 10 years, Cunningham traveled, picking up jobs as a waiter or bartender. At one point, wanting to impress upon his companion, Ken Corbett, the difficulty of a writer's life, he sent a chapter from a work in progress to the *New Yorker*—to see how fast it would be rejected. Although Daniel Menaker, the editor who read the story, had previously been unresponsive to Cunningham's work, he loved the new submission. Published as "The White Angel" in the *New Yorker* in 1988, the story became the nucleus of *A Home at the End of the World*.

In that novel, Cunningham placed characters from traditional families in new kinds of familial relationships. Three friends, Clare, Jonathan, and Bobby, live together; Bobby comes from a terrible family situation—his mother has committed suicide—and moves in with Alice and Ned, Jonathan's parents, when Jonathan leaves for college. Later Bobby and Jonathan share quarters in New York, joined by Clare, who wants to have a child with Jonathan but winds up having one with Bobby. Eventually, Erich, Jonathan's former lover, dying of AIDS, comes to live with the three friends. The writer David Leavitt, quoted by Danny Karlin in the *London Review of Books* (May 23, 1991), praised the novel for telling "the story . . . of the unmaking of the traditional family, with its gender and generational roles, its economic and psychic hierarchies, its unquestioned power to shape moral and sexual choices." Leavitt expressed skepticism over the likelihood of the creation of new types of families, which he termed "wish-fulfilment," and he found Cunningham's characters to be "not as typical" as he would have liked. Still, he praised *A Home at the End of the World* for "its imaginative design and the beauty of its writing."

By contrast, the *New York Times Book Review* (November 11, 1990) critic, Joyce Reiser Kornblatt, cited "the power of the book's vision and the depth of its concerns." She observed that this "is not the story of gay culture in America or the AIDS tragedy or the yearning for family even as families entrap and wound their members—or the story of the

presence of death in life. All of these dramas work themselves out in convincing detail as the book progresses, but only as they emerge out of the daily realities of the characters' lives." The novel was nominated for the Irish Times-Aer Lingus International Fiction Prize.

Flesh and Blood, Cunningham's 1995 novel about several generations of the family of Constantine Stassos, a Greek immigrant to America, drew the same sort of language from reviewers as did *A Home at the End of the World*. "Cunningham evokes the unanticipated moments of 'clear vaulting happiness' and everyday grace that sustain these characters. In the process, gratefully, he passes some of that grace along to us," Dwight Garner wrote in his review for *Harper's Bazaar* (April 1995). In the novel, Stassos, a child of poverty and neglect, acquires a beautiful wife and makes a great deal of money by building shoddy houses in America. He becomes a patriarch, a man who dominates his wife, approaches his daughter Susan sexually, beats and denigrates his gay son, and drives his younger daughter, Zoe, to run away to the East Village in New York—where drugs and, ultimately, AIDS take possession of her. Zoe has a son, but her main relationship is with a nurturing transvestite, who later becomes a friend of her mother's. Susan marries unhappily to escape from her father; her son grows up tragically unable to deal with his homosexuality. Zoe's son, meanwhile, is tormented by his mother's death. Only Constantine's son, called Billy in childhood and Will as an adult, succeeds in accepting himself and finding true companionship—with another man.

Reviewers generally deemed *Flesh and Blood* an enlargement of Cunningham's artistic reach. Garner observed that "this elegiac meditation on anger, mistrust, and loneliness has a ferocious perceptiveness that puts Cunningham on another level as an artist." Meg Wolitzer, in the *New York Times Book Review* (April 16, 1995), found in the novel "a certain cinema vérité quality" with an "added layer of lyricism and mystery that is found in the best fiction." Michiko Kakutani of the *New York Times* (April 7, 1995) and Jonathan Yardley of the *Washington Post Book World* (April 2, 1995) dissented from the praise heaped on *Flesh and Blood*. Both deemed it less effective than *A Home at the End of the World*, Kakutani for what she saw as "a patronizing tone" toward the characters, and Yardley for what he felt was the novel's mixed bag of "all the fashionable preoccupations of the campuses and the literary precincts." Yardley called *Flesh and Blood* "an up-to-date version of those World War II movies in which every foxhole had its Yankee, its cracker, and its representatives of the appropriate (white) ethnic groups. . . . Now . . . membership in the foxhole is determined not by regional or national origin but by sexual preference . . ."

In 1995, after the publication of *Flesh and Blood*, Cunningham received a Whiting Writers' Award, an honor created to recognize "outstanding talent and promise." Cunningham's promise was deemed by many critics to be fulfilled with *The Hours* (1998). The title stems from Virginia Woolf's working title for her 1923 novel, *Mrs. Dalloway*. As a high-school student in Pasadena, California, Cunningham told Mel Gussow during the *New York Times* interview, his cultural interests centered on the lyrics of Bob Dylan and Leonard Cohen. One day, wanting to impress an older, more sophisticated student, he mentioned the latter's poetry. She, in turn, asked him if he had ever heard of T. S. Eliot or Virginia Woolf. Cunningham found, when he went in search of books by those two authors, that the only one on the school library's shelves was *Mrs. Dalloway*. Although he did not fully understand the novel at first, *Mrs. Dalloway* "overwhelmed" him: "Something about what she was doing in terms of trying to find the profundity in the most outwardly ordinary experience registered with me even as a not especially precocious 15-year-old, and it has stayed with me ever since," he said. When Cunningham set out to write *The Hours*, he first attempted a version of Woolf's book with a gay man as the protagonist and the AIDS epidemic as the background. The result did not satisfy him, because, he realized, his approach "was just a parlor trick and not a sufficient idea for a novel. . . . The world didn't need my take on a great book, it already had the original," he told Gussow. Cunningham explained to Michael Coffey for *Publishers Weekly* that Woolf was "interested in using the most idiosyncratic, poetic language possible to get to the heart of human experience, which, by Woolf's lights, was contained in every atom of human experience. One of the great accomplishments of *Mrs. Dalloway* was Woolf's insistence that everything you need to know about human life can be contained in two people having coffee together."

Whereas *Mrs. Dalloway* focuses on one character, Clarissa Dalloway, as she goes through one ordinary day, and counterpoints her story with that of Septimus Warren Smith's dissolution into madness in the aftermath of World War I, *The Hours* intertwines stories of three characters at three different times in history. Cunningham included in the novel's prologue a description of Woolf's suicide, to evoke "the shadow cast by Woolf's death, because it represents the condition under which we find whatever light there is," according to Michael Wood, writing in the *New York Times Book Review* (November 22, 1998). The suicide, which occurred in 1941, "haunts every mental image in the rest of the novel, keeping the mundane trivia of these characters' lives from seeming tedious or overwhelming," Jameson Currier wrote in the *Washington Post Book World* (November 22, 1998). "Cunningham's emulation of such a revered writer as Woolf is courageous, and this is his most mature and masterful work." Cunningham explained to David Streitfeld in an interview for the *Washington Post Book World* (January 24, 1999) that the choice of life or death hinges on one's response to the fact

of temporality: "The fact that the world's just disappearing, and that I'm disappearing in the face of it, shoots me through the hours of the day. It's invigorating, the notion of Here it goes, grab it."

The characters in *The Hours* are each "grabbed" on one day. Their stories alternate fugally in the text. One of the characters is Virginia Woolf, "snapped" in 1923 as she is writing *Mrs. Dalloway*. She has lost her way in the novel, and tired and annoyed by a visit from her sister Vanessa Bell and Bell's children, she escapes for a while. During this respite she arrives at the conclusion that it should not be Clarissa Dalloway who dies in the novel. "Cunningham's insightful use of the historical record concerning Woolf in her household outside London in the 1920s is matched by his audacious imagining of her inner life," the *Publishers Weekly* (August 31, 1998) reviewer wrote.

Another character is Laura Brown, spotlighted in Los Angeles in 1949, four years after the end of World War II and eight years after Woolf's suicide. Laura runs away briefly from her marriage, her child, and her neighbor, Kate, with whom she has exchanged what may be a significant kiss and who may have a fatal disease. She rents a room in a hotel, where she contemplates and discards the idea of suicide and reads *Mrs. Dalloway*. "Cunningham acknowledged the possibility that Laura's reading of *Mrs. Dalloway* has a subtle but considerable effect on her life, both in terms of the comfort she receives in reading it, and something darker, a certain sense of Virginia Woolf as a dark angel who has walked into death ahead of her," Gussow wrote.

The contemporary protagonist is Clarissa Vaughan, called Mrs. Dalloway by her friend Richard, a writer, who is dying of AIDS and for whom Clarissa is planning a party. Clarissa, a lesbian, is a book editor living in Greenwich Village, New York, and her day consists—partly like Clarissa Dalloway's—of thinking about her life while walking around the city. Michael Coffey observed in *Publishers Weekly* that "readers mesmerized by Cunningham's attention to quotidian detail [in *The Hours*] will gasp when, out of the blue, the stories cohere in a moving final tableau that evokes a familiar Cunningham theme: family." The author himself had felt that he was finished with that theme, remarking, "Finally I'm not writing about families anymore. . . . And guess what? As it turns out, here, once again, is the specter of the queer, extended post-nuclear family." For *The Hours*, Cunningham was awarded the Pulitzer Prize (which is administered by Columbia University's Graduate School of Journalism) in the category of fiction and the PEN/Faulkner Award for Fiction (which is administered by the Folger Shakespeare Library) in 1999.

Michael Cunningham lives in New York City and teaches at Columbia University. — S.Y.

DAVIS

Suggested Reading: *Booklist* p868 Jan. 15, 1995; *Harper's Bazaar* p108 Apr. 1995; *London Review of Books* p22 May 23, 1991; *Nation* p21 July 1, 1991; *New York Times* C p31 Apr. 7, 1995, with photo, B p1 Apr. 20, 1999, with photo; *New York Times Book Review* p12 Nov. 11, 1990, p13 Apr. 16, 1995, p6 Nov. 22, 1998; *Publishers Weekly* p53+ Nov. 2, 1998, with photo, p46 Aug. 31, 1998; *Voice Literary Supplement* p28 Apr. 1995; *Washington Post Book World* p3 Apr. 2, 1995, p4 Nov. 22, 1998, p15 Jan. 24, 1999; Nelson, Emmanuel S., ed. *Contemporary Gay American Novelists*, 1993

Selected Books: *Golden States*, 1984; *A Home at the End of the World* , 1990; *Flesh and Blood*, 1995; *The Hours*, 1998

Courtesy of Governor Davis's Office

Davis, Gray

Dec. 26, 1942– Governor of California. Address: Capitol Building #1114, Sacramento, CA 95814

For many years the joke about Gray Davis was that most of his political career was spent trying to move just 15 steps—the approximate distance from his former office, as chief of staff to former California governor Jerry Brown, to the governor's office. In November 1998 Davis got the last laugh. With an impressive victory over his Republican opponent, Dan Lungren, Davis was elected California's 37th governor, becoming the first Democrat to hold the position in 16 years.

Davis's triumph disproved many pundits' pronouncements that he had little chance to make it past even the primary. In what turned out to be the most expensive primary campaign ever for an office other than the presidency—more than $67 million was spent by the Democratic candidates alone—most political commentators had thought that Davis's wealthier opponents, Al Checchi and Jane Harman, would fare better. Davis was also considered to be a bland politician whose first name more or less summed up his demeanor.

Davis, a political moderate, doesn't deny that he projects an uncharismatic image. "You read all these commentaries about me, and they're always saying how dull and stodgy and predictable, but that's just the way I am," he was quoted as saying by Todd S. Purdum for the *New York Times* (January 5, 1999). "Happily, the people were in the mood for the kind of person that I am." At his inauguration, in 1999, Davis promised incremental, pragmatic improvements and no radical changes during his tenure. He is a supporter of the death penalty, abortion rights, a less lenient parole system, affirmative action, more rigorous standards for teachers and students, and bans on offshore oil rigging.

The oldest of the five children of Joseph Graham Davis and Doris Meyer Davis, the governor was born Joseph Graham Davis Jr. on December 26, 1942 in the New York City borough of the Bronx. He lived in Connecticut until he was 11, when his father, an advertising executive for Time Inc., was relocated to California. Davis attended public, private, and Catholic schools and was active in sports. He played baseball, football, and tennis and won two Junior Cup championships in golf.

Davis graduated from Harvard School (now Harvard Westlake), in the North Hollywood neighborhood of Los Angeles, and then attended Stanford University, in California. During his sophomore year, his parents divorced. To help pay his way through school, he joined the Reserve Officer Training Corps in 1961. After graduating from Stanford, in 1964, he enrolled at the Columbia University Law School, in New York, from which he earned a J.D. degree in 1967. Immediately afterward he served in the U.S. Army (1967–69) and rose to the rank of captain while on tour in Vietnam, where he received a Bronze Star for meritorious service. He has said that his military experience—particularly, seeing firsthand the disproportionate number of racial minorities in the military—fueled his sense of injustice and played a part in his decision to enter politics.

Davis started his political career as a financial director for Tom Bradley's Los Angeles mayoral campaign in 1973. In the following year Davis ran against Jesse M. Unruh for state treasurer, but lost. He became chief of staff to California governor Edmund G. "Jerry" Brown Jr. in 1975; he was credited with the idea of having Brown ride in a blue Plymouth as a symbol of the governor's fiscal austerity. He also ran the state government while Brown campaigned for president in 1976 and 1980. Even back then Davis expressed moderate political beliefs that fell to the right of Brown's positions.

Davis won his first election in 1982, becoming a California State Assembly representative from the west side of Los Angeles. He served for two assembly terms, during which, among other things, he successfully campaigned to put pictures of missing children on milk cartons, shopping bags, and billboards. In 1986 Davis was elected the state's controller (the chief fiscal officer) and served two terms, from 1987 to 1995. He campaigned against Democrat Dianne Feinstein for a U.S. Senate seat in 1992, but was trounced. (An ad in which he compared Feinstein to Leona Helmsley, the hotelier convicted of tax evasion, backfired because it was seen by many voters as too negative.)

In November 1994, bouncing back from his Senate defeat, Davis was elected California's lieutenant governor, serving under Governor Pete Wilson, a Republican. He had beaten his opponent, Cathie Wright, a state senator, by more than one million votes, and his victory was one of the few bright spots for Democrats in an election year dominated by Republicans. While serving as lieutenant governor, Davis chaired the Commission for Economic Development and the State Lands Commission and served as a regent of the University of California and a trustee of California State University.

Davis's relationship with Governor Wilson was initially tense. Wilson tried to evict Davis from his office in the capitol building, proposed cutting five of his 19 staff members, and tried, unsuccessfully, to pass an initiative to gut the powers of the lieutenant governor. Eventually, however, the two men managed to co-exist amicably. Davis served as acting governor while Wilson campaigned for the presidency from the spring of 1995 to September of that year. Many politicians and journalists remembered the example of the former lieutenant governor Mike Curb, who served as acting governor in 1979, when Brown was out of the state, and who, during that period, appointed a controversial judge whose selection Brown had opposed; as acting governor, Davis launched no such "Pearl Harbors," as he put it.

Under California's term-limits law, Wilson could not run for a third term as governor in 1998, so the field was wide open. In California's first open gubernatorial primary (in which voters could cast ballots for any candidate, regardless of party affiliation), Davis faced the Republican Dan Lungren, then the state's attorney general, and two Democrats: Al Checchi, the Northwest Airlines tycoon, and Jane Harman, a U.S. representative from Los Angeles and wife of Sidney Harman, a millionaire audio-component businessman. Many political commentators did not think Davis had a chance in the election. Both of his Democratic opponents could rely on their private wealth to finance their campaigns; moreover, it was thought that Harman's gender was a plus in a state where over 50

percent of registered Democrats are women. Davis, however, remained confident. "I don't relish running against the 313th richest man in America, but when I look at what I could be against [i.e., Senator Dianne Feinstein, Los Angeles mayor Richard Riordan, or former congressman and Cabinet officer Leon Panetta] I feel fortunate to have drawn the opponents I did," he told Eric Pooley for Time (May 18, 1998). Moreover, he did not regard his upright, uncharismatic manner as a mark against him, since previous California governors George Deukmejian Jr. and Wilson had not been regarded as firebrands either. He joked to Pooley, "Given the history I've decided to hold my charisma in reserve."

Early in the campaign, both Checchi and Harman polled well, while Davis lagged behind. Checchi spent approximately $40 million of his individual wealth, while Harman shelled out about $15 million, and Davis, relying on more traditional means of fundraising, had a war chest of about $12 million. As Checchi and Harman hurt each other with attack ads, Davis quietly overtook both of them in May, running television ads that announced that he was a man with "experience money can't buy." Davis's ploy seemed to work: in the June 3 primary election, he received about 35 percent of the vote, Lungren got 34 percent, and Checchi and Harman each ended up with about 12 percent.

Free to concentrate on Lungren, Davis attempted to exploit the differences between himself and his opponent, although, in many respects, the candidates were quite similar. Both are white, middle-aged Catholics with moderate, centrist views. Davis alluded to the fact that Lungren did not serve in Vietnam (a sports-related knee injury had kept him out of the war) and also drew a lot of attention to Lungren's anti-abortion stance. In the November elections, Davis proved more popular than Lungren among both sexes and virtually every ethnic, racial, and age group. Latino voters were particularly influential in the election, with four out of five of them supporting Davis.

The 1998 election marks the first time since the late 1950s that residents of California chose only Democrats to serve as their governor, lieutenant governor, attorney general, and two U.S. senators; Democrats also hold majorities in both houses of the state legislature. The partisan imbalance has thus left the Democratic Party well positioned to take advantage of congressional redistricting after the 2000 census is conducted. This could cement Democratic power in the state for the first decade of the next millennium. Yet there is immense pressure that goes with the power imbalance: should a crisis arise during Davis's tenure, it would be hard to blame recalcitrant Republicans. At his inauguration, Davis promised that he would make no drastic changes. "I will govern neither from the right nor the left, but from the center, propelled not by ideology, but by common sense that seeks better results," he was quoted as saying by Todd S. Purdum for the New York Times.

DeLAY

According to polls, education is the number-one issue on California voters' minds. Davis has promised to toughen standards for hiring and evaluating teachers, even though teachers' unions heavily supported him in the elections. Davis also wants to end "social promotion" of failing students and increase funding for textbooks and other classroom necessities.

One issue that Davis faced soon after he took office was Proposition 187. Passed in a statewide referendum in 1994 with 60 percent of the vote, that measure called for the discontinuation of services to illegal immigrants residing in California. Opponents of Proposition 187 sued to have it overturned as soon as it was passed; when Davis was sworn in as governor, the legal fight had been going on for five years. Davis, caught between the wishes of immigrant advocacy groups and those of the majority who voted in favor of Proposition 187, took what

some called "the easy way out" by leaving the decision with a federal appeals court—which killed the measure.

On another controversial front, in July 1999 Davis signed into California law the nation's toughest ban on assault weapons.

Davis met his wife, the former Sharon Ryer, in 1978, when she worked as a flight attendant. Davis had arrived late for a plane, and Ryer lectured him. Five years later, on February 20, 1983, they married. — W.G.

Suggested Reading: *Los Angeles Times* (on-line) Jan.1, 1995, Mar. 24, 1995, Sep. 17, 1995; *New York Times* A p12 June 1, 1998, with photo, A p10 Jan. 5, 1999; *San Francisco Chronicle* (on-line) Dec. 11, 1998; *Time* p52+ May 18, 1998, with photo; *Washington Post* A p3 July 7, 1998, with photo, A p40 Nov. 5, 1998

Shepard Sherbell/Saba

DeLay, Tom

Apr. 8, 1947– U.S. Representative from Texas; House majority whip. Address: 341 Cannon House Office Bldg., Washington, DC 20515; 12603 Southwest Freeway, Suite 285, Stafford, Texas 77477

Theoretically, Tom DeLay, the U.S. House of Representatives majority whip, is the third most powerful Republican legislator in the House, after the Speaker and the majority leader of the House. But in reality, according to many political observers, DeLay, an eight-term member of Congress from the

22d District of Texas, is probably the most powerful person in the House, and perhaps the most feared as well. DeLay was first elected House majority whip during the 104th Congress; a strong supporter of deregulation, small government, and fiscal conservatism, he is considered a great friend to the business lobby in Washington. "Once a small-business owner, Mr. DeLay came to detest government regulations, and as the head of a pest control company, he developed a special hatred for the Environmental Protection Agency," Lizette Alvarez wrote for the *New York Times* (November 18, 1998). DeLay's party underwent a leadership overhaul in the wake of the Democrats' five-seat gain in the 1998 mid-term elections, which prompted Speaker of the House Newt Gingrich to resign. At the 11th hour, however, through deft maneuvering that has come to typify his political style, DeLay refortified his coveted position as majority whip and eventually ran for the post unopposed. On a table off to the side in his Washington office, DeLay keeps a bull whip as a symbol of his position and authority. "Once he digs his teeth into something, he's a pit bull on issues and on winning," retired congressman Bill Paxon told Alvarez shortly after DeLay was reelected majority whip. "But that is not why he [ran] unopposed in this maelstrom. It's because of the personal relationships. It's important to be respected in this town. But the real reason for his personal success has nothing to do with people fearing him. It's because they love him."

Tom DeLay was born into a deeply religious Baptist family in the Texas border town of Laredo on April 8, 1947. His father was a successful oil-rigging contractor, and Tom, as a child, spent much of his free time traveling with his dad to oil rigs in both the Texas prairies and Venezuela. One day a crane operator amused himself by swinging the machine's wrecking ball dangerously close to the youth's head as Tom was working in the field.

Scared, Tom marched to his father's office and told him he wanted to quit. According to Jeffery L. Katz for *Congressional Quarterly* (July 4, 1998), Tom DeLay recalls his father saying, "Son, you're going back. And you're going to take care of this problem. You ain't going to quit on me. Nobody quits on me." Tom then returned to the field and picked a fight with the crane operator, earning the man's "respect," as he told Katz.

Because his father wanted him to become a doctor, Tom majored in biology at the University of Houston, from which he graduated in 1970. Shortly thereafter he began working for a small pesticide company. After he had put in three years of service and failed to advance to his satisfaction, he went into business for himself, founding Albo Pest Control. "I bought me a truck, started killing bugs," DeLay told Katz. "That's all I knew how to make money." According to Michael Weisskopf and David Maraniss of the *Washington Post* (March 12, 1995), DeLay "hated" the name of the company but kept it anyway because "a marketing study noted it reminded consumers of a well-known brand of dog food." DeLay claims to have built Albo into "the Cadillac" of Houston exterminators. "But his frustration with government rules increased in tandem with his financial success," according to Weisskopf and Maraniss. The ever-increasing, difficult-to-follow, fiscally constricting regulations placed on his company by the government eventually led him into politics. He told Weisskopf and Maraniss, "I found out government was a cost of doing business, and I better get involved in it."

In 1978 DeLay was elected to the Texas legislature, representing his home county of Fort Bend. By his own account, he became the first Fort Bend County Republican ever elected to the Texas House of Representatives. By the time DeLay first ran for the U.S. Congress, in 1984, his county—and his future district, which also included parts of Brazoria and Harris Counties, both of which had been historically Democratic—had become overwhelmingly Republican. DeLay had come to be known as "Mr. DeReg" while in the Texas House, and the nickname followed him to the nation's capital. In Congress he gave out "Red Tape Awards" for regulations he found to be particularly trivial. His attempts to advance the cause of deregulation, however, gained little notice in the Democrat-controlled House, where industry regulation was used as a bulwark against exploitative and ecologically hazardous practices on the part of big business. Still, despite the Democratic majority, DeLay was awarded a choice seat on the House Appropriations Committee during his second term.

During the 1994 election campaign, DeLay raised the second-largest amount of funds for the candidates of the Republican party, finishing just behind Newt Gingrich. "We'd rustle up checks for [a candidate] and make sure Tom got the credit," David Rehr, a beer lobbyist closely allied to DeLay, told Weisskopf and Maraniss. "So when new members voted for majority whip, they'd say, 'I wouldn't be here if it wasn't for Tom DeLay.'" In 1995, on the day before the vote for majority whip, DeLay had commitments from 52 of the 72 House freshman and easily won the election. As majority whip, DeLay was determined to ensure that Republicans upheld the party platform when they voted.

By this time DeLay had organized a group of business lobbies, which, collectively, he dubbed Project Relief. The coalition was designed to stall some impending environmentally friendly regulations that would, among other things, allow the EPA to impose a strict air-pollution ordinance in California, which in turn would force many shipping companies, including UPS, to replace their trucking fleets. After the White House denied his original request—which asked for a 100-day waiting period on the vote—DeLay had legislation drafted that mandated a 13-month moratorium on the environmental rules. The new whip wanted to ensure enough votes for the bill to override a presidential veto, but DeLay and his allies, after a flurry of last-minute negotiating, fell just 14 votes short of the necessary number. He had lost the day but gained much respect in the House—not only from Republicans, but also from Democrats, 51 of whom had crossed party lines to support the bill

DeLay soon attracted increased public attention because of his staunch deregulation stances and his strong support of the Christian right and their socially conservative causes. Since arriving in Congress, he has stated, he has grown more dedicated to Christ and to Baptist beliefs—but he admitted, as he told Katz, "I've never been able to understand that turn-the-other-cheek stuff." As Jan Reid of *Mother Jones* (September–October 1996, on-line) reported, in his first two weeks in his new post, DeLay tried to repeal the 1990 amendments to the Clean Air Act, which were "widely seen as one of President Bush's most significant accomplishments." DeLay's fund-raising methods and his success at keeping fellow House Republicans in line earned him the nickname "The Hammer." Reid pointed out DeLay's close ties to his brother, Randy, who, since Tom came to power within GOP ranks, has developed into a powerful corporate lobbyist. Randy DeLay, working closely with the Union Pacific and Southern Pacific Railroads in their merger attempt in 1996, "was lobbying his own brother on behalf of the rail merger—apparently with considerable success." The merger passed, perhaps due to the support of DeLay's allies in Congress and despite pressure from Democrats and local Houston politicians (and DeLay's constituents). The episode demonstrated that the whip was not afraid to use whatever allies he deemed necessary to achieve political ends—no matter how it might appear to outsiders.

In January 1996 DeLay took a firm stand on an issue that went against his usual philosophy. The Houston Oilers of the National Football League announced their intention to move to Tennessee the following season. DeLay opposed the move, stating, according to Reid, that he felt professional sports teams had "special responsibilities" to their hometowns. In other words, DeLay placed professional sports among the few businesses the government should be allowed to regulate.

DeLay is perhaps best known for his part in the July 1997 coup against House Speaker Newt Gingrich. In a late-night meeting, DeLay told a group of GOP rebels that he would vote with them to oust Gingrich, who had recently been censured by Congress for ethics violations. The coup failed—and greatly harmed DeLay's relationship with both the Speaker and the majority leader, Dick Armey. "The biggest thing I learned is you don't meet with a bunch of members after 12:30 at night," DeLay told Katz. After opposing Republicans had thwarted the attempted coup—and after DeLay had apologized and admitted that his tactics were wrong—the whip attempted to mount support for New York congressman Bill Paxon's run for Armey's position. The escapade, which failed to produce the desired result, eventually led to Paxon's decision to retire from Congress at the end of his term, because he felt he was no longer an ascending member of the House elite.

The Republicans lost five seats in the House as a result of the 1998 midterm elections. Pundits theorized that the American public's distaste for the Republican zest to impeach President Bill Clinton over testimony related to his affair with former White House intern Monica S. Lewinsky caused the overturn. In the aftermath of the election, Gingrich resigned, and Dick Armey was seriously challenged by Representative Steve Largent of Oklahoma. Despite grumblings of discontent and threats of upheaval from ambitious House Republicans, DeLay retained his post. Conventional wisdom held that he succeeded because, with the diminished Republican majority, nobody wanted the job. "As majority whip, he is responsible for counting heads and delivering votes. His job is as basic as it gets—to use whatever combination of bullying and begging it takes to pass legislation that leadership cares about. He is painfully aware of the difficulties in managing the slimmest House majority either party has held in 44 [now 45] years," Jeffrey L. Katz wrote.

Contrary to widespread expectations, the results of the 1998 election did not deter Republican desires to impeach the president. DeLay continued regular meetings of his "war room," a group of Republican representatives dedicated to ousting Clinton. On December 19, 1998 the House approved two articles of impeachment, charging the president with perjury before a federal grand jury and obstruction of justice in his efforts to conceal his affair. When the debate moved on to the Senate (where the president was eventually acquitted), DeLay urged senators to avoid making a deal for censure. "The reason the House adopted articles of impeachment was due to the overwhelming evidence against the president," DeLay said, as quoted by Larry Margasak of the Associated Press, according to *Yahoo!.News* (December 23, 1998, online). "Before people look to cut a deal with the White House or their surrogates who will seek to influence the process, it is my hope that one would spend plenty of time in the evidence room."

Although House Republicans' hopes for the president's removal from office were dashed, DeLay has managed to keep his star high in Washington. Since Gingrich's departure, following the 1998 mid-term elections, and the subsequent resignation (because of a past sexual indiscretion) of Congressman Bob Livingston, who many assumed would succeed Gingrich as Speaker, DeLay has become perhaps the most powerful member of the House. The current House Speaker, Dennis Hastert, whom most Capitol Hill insiders describe as nonconfrontational, was elected to the post largely because of DeLay's deft political wrangling. According to most sources, DeLay's opinion holds tremendous sway with Hastert. "I think [DeLay]'s never been more influential than he is right now," Representative John T. Doolittle, a Republican from California, told Alison Mitchell and Marc Lacey for the *New York Times* (October 16, 1999). Marshall Wittmann, a congressional analyst at the conservative Heritage Foundation, told Mitchell and Lacey that DeLay is "the most powerful majority whip in the history of the House of Representatives." DeLay does not demand from House Republicans complete support on every legislative goal set forth by party leaders, but he does expect each Republican representative to tell him which way he or she will vote. "There are members who on any given issue, because of their districts or their own particular circumstances, can't vote for a particular thing," Representative Doolittle told Mitchell and Lacey. "[DeLay] knows who they are." DeLay is currently the chief fund-raiser for the National Republican Congressional Committee; he has helped to raise $11 million—half of the committee's kitty for the first half of 1999.

DeLay's most ambitious project in 1999 has been the formation of a nonprofit corporation whose aim is to raise anonymous campaign dollars. Created in response to organized labor's centralized plan to provide Democratic congressional hopefuls and incumbents with a generous supply of campaign funds, DeLay's organization is unusual, in that he and his associates are trying to register with the Internal Revenue Service (IRS) as a nonprofit political corporation. If the IRS approves that label, the group would not be required to release donors' identities—a distinct enticement for would-be contributors who might wish to remain in the shadows. The IRS's code specifies that a nonprofit political corporation may not be affiliated with any candidates. Thus, while DeLay is the group's primary fund-raiser, its head is a former DeLay aide, Karl Gallant. "We are separate from the DeLay operation," Gallant told Mitchell and Lacey. "I have had to leave the nest [of the House] to get this started."

Tom DeLay lives with his wife, Christine Ann Furrh, in Houston. The couple have one daughter, who is currently attending college. — M.B.

Suggested Reading: *Congressional Quarterly* p827+ July 4, 1998, with photos; *Mother Jones* (on-line) Sep.–Oct. 1996, with photo; *New York Times* A p1+ Nov. 12, 1998, A p26+ Nov. 18, 1998, with photos, A p1+ Nov. 19, 1998, with photos; *Texas Monthly* (on-line) 1996; *Washington Post* A p1+ Mar. 12, 1995, with photo; *Yahoo!.News* (on-line) Dec. 23, 1998

Courtesy of Julian Belfrage Associates

Dench, Judi

Dec. 9, 1934– Actress. Address: c/o Julian Belfrage Associates, 46 Albemarle St., London W1X 4PP, England

"I don't like making films," the British actress Judi Dench told Alan Riding for the *New York Times* (July 13, 1997). "I never have liked making films. I like doing a play because you go on and on and it gets better. I don't like doing one take, or four takes, because I'm not sure of myself." Dench had expressed much the same sentiment in an interview with Matt Wolf for the *New York Times* (January 28, 1990) more than seven years earlier, when she was starring in a London production of Anton Chekhov's drama *The Cherry Orchard*. "Film somehow crystallizes a performance, and then it doesn't get any better," she said then. "It's like a fossil for me; you have no control over it, whereas tonight may be the best performance of *The Cherry Orchard* we've ever done."

Despite her preference for theater over film, Dench has appeared in many motion pictures. But in nearly all of them, she was cast in a supporting role—for example, that of Miss Lavish in *A Room with a View* (1986), Mrs. Beaver in *A Handful of Dust* (1988), the barmaid Quickly in Kenneth Branagh's *Henry V* (1989), and M in the James Bond films *Goldeneye* (1995) and *Tomorrow Never Dies*. That is probably why—although she has performed since the late 1950s with the most renowned theatrical companies in Great Britain, has won many of Britain's most prestigious acting awards, and has starred in popular British television shows (among them *A Fine Romance, Behaving Badly*, and *As Time Goes By*)—she remained largely unknown in the United States until 1997. That year, she played the lead in the movie *Mrs. Brown*, which is about Queen Victoria of Great Britain, and she was nominated for an Academy Award as best actress. She won the Oscar for best supporting actress in 1999, for a far smaller role—that of another British monarch, Queen Elizabeth I, in *Shakespeare in Love*. Also in 1999 she won a Tony Award for her performance in the Broadway production of David Hare's drama *Amy's View*.

Since those triumphs the media have often referred to Dench as an international treasure, and by virtually universal agreement, she has joined the ranks of the world's greatest actresses. In the opinion of Billy Connolly, her co-star in *Mrs. Brown*, Dench is "far and away the best" actress he ever worked with. "I didn't care if she was a stage actress or a film actress," Connolly told Alan Riding. "I just knew I was being dragged along in the slipstream of this extraordinary performer. She has that ability to switch it on immediately. She can be telling you a little joke, and they'll say, 'Action,' and she instantly becomes the other person. It's terrifying to watch."

Judi Dench was born on December 9, 1934 in York, England. As a youngster, she attended the Mount School, in York. When she was a teenager, her brother, Jeffrey, was in acting school, and he encouraged her to take up acting. She took his advice, and after completing high school, she enrolled at the Central School of Speech and Drama, in London. In 1957, shortly after her graduation from that school, she landed her first important role—that of Ophelia in Shakespeare's tragedy *Hamlet*—in a production mounted at the Bristol Old Vic Theatre. Speaking of her portrayal of the brokenhearted, unhinged Ophelia with a reporter for *Hollywood Online* in 1997, Dench said, "I must have been the maddest girl known to man. I mean, I must have done everything I could think of to be mad, to show that she was mad. In actual fact, what I should have done is just choose one thing. . . . I've only just, in the past five years, learnt that [in the art of acting] less is more."

During the next 10 years, Dench "won half a dozen major awards and played many of the parts everyone wants to play," as Georgina Howell wrote for the (London) *Observer* (September 29, 1968). In

1961 Dench joined the Royal Shakespeare Company (RSC) and gave highly praised performances as Isabella in *Measure for Measure* and Titania in *A Midsummer Night's Dream*. In 1968 she appeared in a musical for the first time, in the role of Sally Bowles in a production of *Cabaret* directed by Hal Prince in London. "I approached *Cabaret* with terror," Dench recalled to Catherine Stott for the London *Guardian* (November 14, 1968). "I was aghast, but I love to do the thing that is so difficult." Dench explained to Matt Wolf, "I'm not a singer; I sing the way I speak. But I had the most wonderful time doing it. I used to read [Christopher] Isherwood's book *Berlin Stories*, a source for [*Cabaret*], every night before going on."

After a nine-month run of that show, Dench turned down many offers to star in other musicals and dramas in London theaters. Instead, in what was considered an unusual move for an up-and-coming thespian, she returned to the RSC—where she had already become a favorite with audiences—and went on what was described as a lecture and recital tour of Africa. "I don't want to be in the West End any more," she explained to Stott. "I don't want to be in London, although I've just bought a lovely house in Hampstead. It isn't that there's someone I don't want to meet or anything; I just have always found time to expand and breathe out of London. Here, I'm always in a hurry, and somehow a lot of things get pushed out. In Stratford [the home base of the RSC], one notices the actual moment. This may sound corny, but one is aware of the day the house martins go and come back, and of the sunset." When asked if she considered herself ambitious, she replied, "An ambitious person wouldn't be going 'backwards' again, would she? I'm not ambitious in that I don't want to go on acting. It is not a 'not-put-outable light.' What I want from life is my own family that is as close as my own family was: extremely close."

In 1970 Dench toured Japan and Australia with the RSC. Once, in Japan, she performed for people who, with few exceptions, did not understand English and did not use translation devices. "It's extraordinary, the sense of communicating with people who don't speak your language," she told John Hall for the London *Guardian* (June 24, 1970). "They roared at *The Merry Wives [of Windsor]*, which is a very visual play anyway, and we, in turn, were fascinated by their theater. At the Kabuki theater, one sat open-mouthed at this extraordinary style of acting, and the Noh plays were like nothing you've ever seen before—something like Chaucer, . . . where it takes three-quarters of an hour to walk one step. It's quite riveting." After seeing Dench in *Cymbeline* at Stratford in 1970, the critic Michael Billington wrote, as quoted in Malcolm Hay's profile of Dench in *Plays and Players* (November 1984), that she was "right up there with [Dame Peggy] Ashcroft and [Vanessa] Redgrave."

In the early 1980s Dench played a wide variety of roles on stage and in television and film. For her portrayal of a very suburban Englishwoman on the

British television series *A Fine Romance*, readers of the British publication *TV Times* voted her the funniest female on TV in 1982. During the same year, Dench played Lady Bracknell in a production of Oscar Wilde's comedy *The Importance of Being Earnest* that Peter Hall directed at the National Theatre, and although she was considered exceedingly young for that role, she was a success (as was the play). Next came *A Kind of Alaska*, a trio of plays by Harold Pinter that debuted at the National Theatre in 1982. In one of the three—Pinter's dramatization of an account in the book *Awakenings*, by the neurologist Oliver Sacks—Dench played a middle-aged woman who emerges from a 29-year-long "waking" coma and then reverts to a comatose state. In the *New York Times* (November 21, 1982), Benedict Nightingale quoted part of an enthusiastic review of the triple bill for the London *Sunday Telegraph*, in which Francis King wrote that with "extraordinary virtuosity, [Dench] becomes now the young girl stirring to life in an aging body, now the even younger girl struggling against her imminent entombment, now the middle-aged woman painfully attempting to adapt to a world in which so many people are dead and so many things altered." In 1983 she played a middle-class woman who becomes involved in espionage, in Hugh Whitmore's drama *Pack of Lies*. Describing her performance, Malcolm Hay wrote, "The strength . . . lay in the way that depths of anguish were so effectively explored within such an ordinary setting." In *Pack of Lies*, Dench starred opposite her husband, the actor Michael Williams. "It was interesting and amusing to see how we would make room for the other, rather like competing to give the other center stage," she told Hay.

In 1984, after seeing her husband star in Howard Davies's production of *Schweyk in the Second World War*, by Bertolt Brecht, Dench accepted the role of Mother Courage in Davies's production of another Brecht drama, *Mother Courage and Her Children*. "When [Davies] approached me about *Mother Courage*, I was very interested," she told Hay. "But I had never seen it on stage, . . . and I dislike reading a play . . . until just before the start of rehearsals. So Howard came round to see me, and we sat down and he took me through what happens and told me the story. . . . I didn't read *Mother Courage* until the day before rehearsals. Otherwise, I would have been sure that I couldn't do it." Benedict Nightingale, who saw the production in England, wrote for the *New York Times* (December 9, 1984) that Dench had "somehow managed to transform her face to gray dough and knead that dough into a combative pout. Her voice, normally to be heard huskily frisking up and down the musical scale, has become flat, cynical, and grating, a blend of Cockney salesgirl and sandpapering machine. . . . Altogether, it's a remarkable, blunt, and candid picture of someone emotionally and spiritually shaped by years spent scavenging in and around the battlegrounds of 17th-century Europe."

Dench scored another victory in 1987, in Peter Hall's production of Shakespeare's *Antony and Cleopatra* at the Olivier Theatre, in London, in which she starred opposite Anthony Hopkins. Unlike most of the actresses who have portrayed Cleopatra, Dench is far from glamorous. "When [people] heard about [my playing] Cleopatra . . . they just roared," Dench told Matt Wolf. "I like it best when people say, 'Judi Dench as Cleopatra? That's a bit daft.' I like to take a big jump." Reviewing her performance for the London *Guardian* (April 26, 1987), John Hall wrote, "No one could be more real than Judi Dench's breathtaking Cleopatra. She is capricious, volatile, the mistress of all moods, who in the course of a single scene can switch easily from breathy languor . . . to cutting humor . . . to a pensive melancholy. . . . Ms. Dench ensures that Cleopatra's sexual magnetism lies not in any centerfold posturing but in emotional extremism."

In 1989, at the Aldwych Theatre, in London, Dench gave a tour-de-force performance as Ranyevskaya, in Anton Chekhov's *The Cherry Orchard*. "Dench fuses absurdity and sorrow in a reinterpretation of the part which redeems the production," Kate Kellaway wrote in a review for the London *Observer* (October 22, 1989). "She shows Ranyevskaya as both a coquette and a casualty, a woman pampered and misused, with more experience than wisdom." Dench had appeared in previous productions of *The Cherry Orchard* as well: In the late 1950s, she gave a well-received performance as the character Anya, and in 1981, in a made-for-television version of the play, she was cast as Ranyevskaya.

Later in the 1980s Dench took on jobs on the other side of the footlights. In 1988 she directed a Renaissance Theater Company production of Shakespeare's *Much Ado About Nothing*, starring Kenneth Branagh. Two years later she directed Branagh again, in a revival of the John Osborne play *Look Back in Anger*. Also in 1990 Dench returned to her alma mater, the Central School of Speech and Drama, to direct a student production of Shakespeare's *Macbeth*. In the summer of 1991, Dench directed a production of the Rogers and Hart musical *The Boys from Syracuse* mounted at the Open Air Theatre, in Regents Park, in London. "I'm enjoying every minute," she told Michael Coveney for the London *Observer* (July 21, 1991) during the run of the musical. "But I keep thinking it will be lovely to get back to the acting."

Dench displayed her extraordinary talents as an actress for an international audience in 1997, when she appeared in the film *Mrs. Brown*. Directed by John Madden and based on various accounts of the widowhood of Queen Victoria of Great Britain (which lasted for 40 of the 64 years she sat on the throne), the film shows how John Brown (Billy Connolly), a Scottish servant, helped Victoria overcome the consuming sadness she felt after the death of her husband. (The unusual relationship between Brown and the queen led the British press to nickname her Mrs. Brown.) Reviewing the film

for the *Washington Post* (July 25, 1997), Rita Kempley wrote, "Judi Dench, a British theater legend, brings enormous dignity as well as a wealth of insecurities to the title role. Connolly, a stand-up comic, and Dench, a grand dame, are as odd a coupling as were the robust Brown and the stuffy Victoria, but they are wholly believable. And although she is plain as a scone without clotted cream and jam, she manages to become both radiant and feminine in his company." For her performance in *Mrs. Brown*, Dench won a Golden Globe Award and a Golden Satellite Award, and she was nominated for an Academy Award and a Screen Actors Guild Award.

Dench captured the Oscar for best supporting actress for her portrayal of the shrewd, flinty, and fiercely imperial Queen Elizabeth I in the hugely successful 1998 romantic comedy *Shakespeare in Love*, which won the 1999 Academy Award for best picture. Directed by John Madden and written by Marc Norman and Tom Stoppard, *Shakespeare in Love* imagines that the young Shakespeare (played by Ralph Fiennes) is suffering from writer's block; after falling madly in love with a young noblewoman (the fictional Lady Viola, played by Gwyneth Paltrow, who won the Academy Award for best actress), his problem vanishes, and he completes the script for *Romeo and Juliet*. A reviewer for *Entertainment Weekly* (March 1, 1999) called Dench's performance "a definitive example of 'presence.' . . . Though on screen for only a handful of minutes, the longtime English stage actress manages to dominate every scene she's in."

Also in 1999, in her first appearance on the New York stage in nearly four decades, Dench gave a reprisal of her starring role in *Amy's View*, a drama by David Hare that came to Broadway some two years after its opening in London. Directed by Richard Eyre, *Amy's View* focuses on Esme Allen, a grande dame of the theater who is reduced to accepting a part in a television soap opera. The play examines Esme's anguished relationship with her beloved daughter, Amy, whose husband's views are anathema to Esme and the values that define her, prominent among them her love of the theater. *Amy's View* earned decidedly mixed reviews in the U.S., but critics lavished praise on Dench for her highly nuanced performance. Ben Brantley wrote in the *New York Times* (April 16, 1999), "Those who have seen Ms. Dench only in movies will discover qualities that a camera can't capture: a force of willpower, concentration, technique, and sheer radiance that brands her presence into your memory." Dench won a 1999 Tony Award for best actress in a play for her work in *Amy's View*.

Also in 1999 Dame Judi appeared on the big screen in *Tea with Mussolini*, in which she played Arabella Delancey, a fluttery British expatriate in Italy who fancies herself a painter. The film, which also stars the British actresses Dame Maggie Smith and Joan Plowright and the American performers Cher and Lily Tomlin, was directed by Franco Zeffirelli, who co-wrote the screenplay with John

DePAOLA

Mortimer. The story, which is set just before and during World War II and is about a group of women and a young Italian boy entrusted to their care, is borrowed from a chapter in the director's autobiography. The film was popular with audiences and enjoyed successful runs at independent cinemas. Dench will appear as M in the James Bond film *The World Is Not Enough*, due in theaters in late 1999.

Richard Eyre, the former director of the National Theatre, told Alan Riding for the *New York Times* in 1997, "When you talk about Judi, you unpack a suitcase full of superlatives. She's sort of diffident. There's not a trace of self-advertisement about her. She's genuinely modest. But in my view, she is our greatest actress." Dench observed to Kate Kellaway, "I think people are used to seeing me [on television] sitting in the corner of their rooms. When people see me on the train, they'll say, 'Hello Jude, how are you?' I don't think I'm a very frightening person. I don't think I'm a very grand person." Dench also said that even after more than 40 years in the theater, she still gets nervous before performances. But nerves are necessary, she added; "like deep sorrow or great love, [they] produce a huge quantity of adrenalin, which is what you have to use." Dench practices Quakerism, because, she has said, she feels it helps her to remain calm and focused in the tense world of theater.

Among Dench's many awards and honors are two 1995 Oliviers (the British equivalent of Tonys), one for her performance in Anthony Page's play *Absolute Hell* and the other for her work in Stephen Sondheim's *A Little Night Music*. In 1985 she won the British ACE Award for her acting in the TV program *Mr. and Mrs. Edgehill*. Dench has also won British Association of Film and Television Arts (BAFTA) Awards for best actress in a comedy series, for her work in *A Fine Romance* (1982); best supporting actress in a motion picture, for *A Room with a View* (1986) and *A Handful of Dust* (1988); and best actress for her work in *Mrs. Brown* (1997). Judi Dench was awarded the Order of the British Empire in 1970, and she became a Dame of the British Empire (the female equivalent of being knighted) in 1988. She has received honorary doctorates from the Universities of Birmingham, Loughborough, Warwick, and York and the Open University (all in Great Britain).

Judi Dench is five foot one and wears her hair very short. She and her husband, Michael Williams, have one daughter, Tara, who is an actress (and is better known as Finty in the theater world). *With a Crack in Her Voice*, a biography of Dench by John Miller, was published in 1999. Dench is a patron of more than 200 charities. — C.P.

Suggested Reading: (London) *Guardian* p9 Nov. 14, 1968, with photo, p9 June 24, 1970, with photo, p20 Apr. 26, 1987, with photo; (London) *Observer* p29 Sep. 29, 1968, with photo, p43 Oct. 22, 1989, with photo; *New York Times* H p5 Dec. 9, 1984, with photo, I p5 Jan. 28, 1990, with photo, II p10 July 13, 1997, with photo; *New York Times* (on-line) Feb. 21, 1999, with photo; *Newsweek* p68 Apr. 26, 1999, with photo; *Plays and Players* p18+ Nov. 1984, with photos; *Time* p70+ Jan. 25, 1999, with photo; *Vogue* p288+ Mar. 1999; *Washington Post* D p6 July 25, 1997, with photo

Selected Plays: as actress—*Hamlet* (Ophelia), 1957; *Twelfth Night*, 1959; *Henry V*, 1959; *Romeo and Juliet*, 1960; *Measure for Measure*, 1961; *A Midsummer Night's Dream*, 1961; *Cabaret*, 1968; *The Merry Wives of Windsor*, 1970; *Cymbeline*, 1970; *Macbeth*, 1976; *Much Ado About Nothing*, 1976; *The Importance of Being Earnest*, 1982; *A Kind of Alaska*, 1982; *Pack of Lies*, 1983; *Mother Courage and Her Children*, 1984; *Antony and Cleopatra*, 1987; *Hamlet* (Gertrude), 1989; *The Cherry Orchard*, 1989; *The Seagull*, 1994; *Little Night Music*, 1995; *Absolute Hell*, 1995; *Filumena*, 1998; *Amy's View*, 1999; as director—*Much Ado About Nothing*, 1988; *Look Back in Anger*, 1990; *Macbeth*, 1990; *The Boys from Syracuse*, 1991

Selected Films: *A Study in Terror*, 1965; *A Room with a View*, 1986; *A Handful of Dust*, 1988; *Henry V*, 1989; *Golden Eye*, 1995; *Hamlet*, 1996; *Mrs. Brown*, 1997; *Tomorrow Never Dies*, 1997; *Shakespeare in Love*, 1998; *Tea With Mussolini*, 1999; *The World Is Not Enough*, 1999

Selected Television Shows: *Talking to a Stranger*, 1966; *A Fine Romance*, 1981; *Mr. and Mrs Edgehill*, 1985; *Behaving Badly*, 1988; *As Time Goes By*, 1992

---

dePaola, Tomie
(de-POW-luh, TOM-ee)

Sep. 15, 1934– Author and illustrator of children's books. Address: c/o Putnam and Grosset Book Group, 200 Madison Ave., New York, NY 10016-3903

When asked why his books are so popular among children, Tomie dePaola said to Anne Marie Gravel for the *Childsplay* Web site, "I remember what it was like being a kid, and I think that helps. I'm an optimist, and I don't think that hurts either." Many book critics, teachers, and librarians—and parents and young readers, too—would probably attribute dePaola's success to his distinctive illustrations and delightful stories, many of which are humorous retellings of age-old European tales. DePaola's illustrations are imbued with childlike innocence and rendered in a style reminiscent of Christian art of the Middle Ages, Romanesque art and architecture, and folk art. An artist by training, he has written and illustrated more than 100 children's books and has collaborated as illustrator on

168   CURRENT BIOGRAPHY YEARBOOK 1999

Suki Coughlin/Courtesy of G. P. Putnam's Sons
Tomie dePaola

at least 100 more. "It's a dream of mine that one of my books, any book, any picture, will touch the heart of some individual child and change that child's life for the better," he told Dieter Miller for *Something About the Author* (1990). "I don't even have to know about it. I hope it's not a far-fetched dream. Meanwhile, I'll keep working, doing the best I'm capable of."

Of Italian and Irish descent, Thomas Anthony dePaola was born on September 15, 1934 in Meriden, Connecticut, where he and his three siblings grew up. DePaola has described his mother, Florence (Downey) dePaola, as "an avid, read-aloud mother"; the time she spent reading to him, he believes, significantly influenced his choice of vocation. "I was always drawing and doodling . . . complementing the stories she would read," he recalled to Gravel. He told Dieter Miller that his father, Joseph N. dePaola, whose jobs included union official, barber, and liquor salesman, was "a quiet and thoughtful man who was loads of fun and loved to cook," adding that he himself "grew up not knowing that men didn't cook." As a child dePaola was also very close to his paternal and maternal grandparents, and his affection for them inspired several of his books. "Our family was the kind to always tell stories about each other as they sat around the kitchen table," he told Gravel. "I would sit there and absorb every bit of gossip I could. I just look at it as my job." One of dePaola's goals in writing is, in his words, to "encourage [kids] to gravitate toward the older generation."

DePaola has expressed his doubts about the often-made suggestion that his approach to illustration can be traced to his exposure to the art in the Roman Catholic church he and his family attend-

ed. "The stained glass and the statues in the church where I was brought up were really awful," he told Richard Harrington for the *Washington Post* (December 21, 1985); in his view, he said, they were "not even medium high art, but real schlock." He added, however, that "going into church and sitting in that space and being surrounded with color probably did affect me a lot more than I'll ever know."

DePaola was just four years old when he decided that he wanted to be an artist. From that point on, thanks to his parents' provision of generous quantities of art supplies, he drew and painted whenever he could, and he won many art contests at his school and in his town. He also studied tap dance and sang in school concerts and plays. As a 10th-grader, he wrote to the Pratt Institute, a renowned college of art in the New York City borough of Brooklyn, to find out what courses he should take to prepare himself for entrance to the school. He apparently followed the advice he received, and in the fall of 1952, supported by a Maloney scholarship, he began his studies there.

Pratt, dePaola told Miller, "prescribed a very strict course of studies. . . . It wasn't four courses a semester; it was nine to five, five days a week." He soon developed a great admiration for some modern artists to whom he had not been exposed previously. "I went off to art school thinking that Norman Rockwell and Jon Whitcomb, famous illustrators at the time, were the zenith," he recalled to Miller. "But I learned to keep my mind open and not make any judgments about things until I knew more about them. I was like a vacuum cleaner, devouring everything. It didn't take more than a couple of months before I suddenly discovered [Pablo] Picasso, George Rowe, and [Henri] Matisse." While living in New York, dePaola enjoyed riding the subway into Manhattan to visit the Museum of Modern Art and the city's many art galleries. In Greenwich Village, which became his favorite neighborhood, he often spent as many as nine hours at a stretch sipping cappuccino in Italian cafés.

DePaola spent the summer before his senior year studying at the Skowhegan School of Painting and Illustration, in Maine, under the direction of the celebrated painter Ben Shahn. Shahn "probably had the most impact on me of any of the teachers I had," dePaola told Miller. "He told me that being an artist was more than the kind of things you do. 'It's the way you live your life,' he said. I've never forgotten that."

After graduating from Pratt, with a bachelor's degree in fine arts, in 1956, dePaola stayed in a Benedictine monastery in Vermont for six months. The monastic life "solidified . . . some deep spiritual values that I have," he told Miller. Benedictines have long regarded the arts as an expression of their spirituality, and while at the monastery, dePaola devoted part of his time to studying art and developing his artistic style. "The 'candy box' religious art from my Catholic boyhood was replaced by Cimabue, Giotto, Botticelli, and all those unknown sculptors and fresco painters of the Romanesque period," dePaola wrote in the *Horn Book* (October 1993). DePaola has described his style as "simple and direct." In the *Horn Book*, he wrote that it "hasn't really changed in over 35 years. The roots are there in my early drawings and paintings. . . . There are white birds, pink tiled roofs, arched doors and windows. . . . My work is recognizable. I've chosen to follow my own vision rather than switch around and try what is fashionable or au courant. It thrills and pleases me when teachers, parents, and librarians tell me that young children can tell when they are looking at one of my books or pieces of art." Chronic headaches eventually led to dePaola's departure from the monastery, but he remained on good terms with the monks and later helped them establish their own Christmas-card business.

In 1961 dePaola had a one-man show of his paintings and drawings in Boston, and he soon began to make what he has described as a "fairly nice living" from sales of his art work. In 1962, after a stint as an art teacher at the College of the Sacred Heart, in Newton, Massachusetts, he moved into a loft in what is now the Soho district of New York City. Thanks to the intervention of a friend, he secured an agent, Florence Alexander, and through Alexander, got his first illustration assignment for a book: *Sound* (1965), by Lisa Miller, a science book for children. On the jacket of the first edition of *Sound*, his name was misspelled, and although this upset him, he thought it best not to complain lest the entire project be canceled. *Sound* was the first of the more than 60 books on which dePaola would collaborate with the editor Margaret Frith, who is now the president of the Putnam and Grosset Book Group, one of dePaola's publishers. *The Wonderful Dragon of Timlin*, the first book that dePaola both wrote and illustrated, was published in 1966.

In 1967, after his marriage of a year and a half ended and after another, shorter stint at the monastery, dePaola landed a job as an art teacher at the San Francisco College for Women (later renamed Lone Mountain College). "San Francisco . . . helped me to raise my consciousness—about women's issues especially—and to realign my thinking about antiwar and peace organizations," he told Lisa Lane for the *Christian Science Monitor* (December 15, 1988). In 1969 he earned a master's degree in fine arts from the California College of Arts and Crafts, in Oakland.

Meanwhile, dePaola had started an intensive program of psychotherapy, with a practitioner who requested payment in drawings rather than money. "After six months she put all the drawings out on the floor and there it was," he recalled to Harrington. "What was going on inside me unconsciously was right out there on the floor. I didn't realize that I was already expressing what was inside through my pictures. I started to pay attention to that." He had also begun working with children as a volunteer at San Francisco's Sacred Heart Parish. During this period, he told Harrington, he was able to get "back in touch with the child that I had succeeded in locking up in a closet. You're told to grow up, to stop acting like a child. But in a field like mine, if I don't have direct access to that child, I don't have access to what I really need."

In 1971, after earning a doctoral equivalency degree in art from Lone Mountain College, dePaola moved back to the East Coast. He took up residence in Boston and taught at both Chamberlayne Junior College, in Boston, and Colby-Sawyer College, in New London, New Hampshire. He also became involved in theater, taking jobs in technical direction and set design in and around Boston.

Although he had already had some success as an author-illustrator of children's books, it wasn't until 1973 that dePaola made his mark, with the publication of three books that he both wrote and illustrated—*Charlie Needs a Cloak*; *Andy, That's My Name*; and *Nana Upstairs, Nana Downstairs*—all of which became children's best-sellers and have enjoyed several reprintings. *Nana Upstairs, Nana Downstairs*, which is based on the death of one of his grandmothers, is one of dePaola's most famous books; when it appeared, a quarter-century ago, it was one of the few children's books that dealt with the subject of death. "My grandmother's death made a large impression on me as a child," dePaola told Lisa Lane. "It was scary to write about." A commemorative, full-color edition of this perennially popular book was published in 1998.

One of the first folktales that dePaola retold in book form is about a lovable old Italian witch named Strega Nona. Published in 1975, *Strega Nona* describes how a comical character named Big Anthony attempts to discover the secret of Strega Nona's magic pasta pot while she is away. The book spawned four sequels—*Strega Nona's Magic Lessons* (1982), *Merry Christmas Strega Nona* (1986), *Strega Nona Meets Her Match* (1993), and *Strega Nona: Her Story* (1996). Big Anthony became the hero of two of dePaola's books—*Big Anthony and the Magic Ring* (1979) and *Big Anthony: His Story* (1998). Among other dePaola works that are based on folktales are *Helga's Diary: A Troll Love Story* (1977); *The Legend of Old Befana* (1980); *The Mysterious Giant of Barletta* (1984); and *Tony's Bread* (1989), which is a playful take on how the sweet Milanese Christmas bread called *pannetonne* originated. Published in 1985, *Tomie dePaola's Mother Goose*, which contains 204 well-known rhymes, was praised for the multiracial content of its illustrations; in *Horn Book* (January–February 1985), Ann A. Flowers wrote that it was "destined to become a classic."

Although he is known best as a storyteller, dePaola has also produced nonfiction books for children. *The Cloud Book* (1975), for example, aims to teach children about, and foster their appreciation of, clouds. *The Popcorn Book* (1978) explains the scientific principles behind the phenomenon of popping corn and offers a few recipes for children to try at home. Several other, holiday-themed books present crafts and art projects for kids.

DePaola, who is a devout Catholic, has also produced many religious books for children. Some are Bible stories: *Francis the Poor Man of Assisi* (1982), *The Parables of Jesus* (1987), *The Miracles of Jesus* (1987), *Noah and the Ark* (1983), *The Story of the Three Wise Kings* (1983), *Tomie dePaola's Book of Bible Stories* (1990), *Tomie dePaola's Book of the Old Testament* (1995), and *Mary, the Mother of Jesus* (1995). Other dePaola books have Christian but nonbiblical themes. *The Clown of God: An Old Story* (1978), for example, is about a poor old juggler who brings about a miracle by offering his talent as a gift to Christ. DePaola has also written several Christmas books and two books about Jewish celebrations—*My First Chanukah* (1989) and *My First Passover* (1991).

Others among dePaola's books tell stories that are entirely original. His well-known *Now One Foot, Now the Other* (1981) is about a boy named Bobby who helps his grandfather relearn how to walk after he has a debilitating stroke. For *Watch Out for the Chicken Feet in Your Soup* (1974), dePaola drew on his childhood memories of watching his Italian grandmother as she put some seemingly unusual ingredients in her pot of chicken soup. Another of dePaola's semiautobiographical works is *The Art Lesson* (1989), in which a boy named Tommie learns to express his creativity.

Fostering creativity in children is one of dePaola's major concerns as an artist. He believes that by about the time they reach the third or fourth grade, children generally lose interest in illustration, because, he explained to Harrington, they "become too self-conscious about the *written* word." "You get lots of teachers who are trained in teaching reading systems, but it's trickier teaching young people how to *look*," he said. "The very young do look, they spend a *lot* of time [with illustrations], they are absorbed in it."

To encourage children to respond more actively to his artwork, dePaola has created some books that tell stories without words. He told Harrington, "It's terrific because the children get out of the pictures what they want to, and not necessarily what I put into them. It's wild what they come up with, it's like Rorschach tests." One of his best-known pictures-without-words books is *Sing, Pierrot, Sing* (1983), which depicts the tale of Harlequin and Columbine. Reviewing this book in the *School Library Journal* (December 1983), Helen Gregory wrote, "This silent paean to mime is one of dePaola's best, obviously a labor a love, profuse with rich double-page spreads." Another, more humorous example of dePaola's wordless books is *Pancakes for Breakfast* (1978), in which an old woman who wants pancakes for breakfast has a very difficult time making them.

DePaola's huge body of work includes murals, greeting cards, posters, magazine and catalog covers, record-album covers, theater sets, and costumes, most often created for Roman Catholic organizations. He is a member of the advisory council of the Children's Theater Company of Minneapolis, Minnesota, and sits on the board of directors of the Ballet of the Dolls Dance Company, which is also based in Minneapolis. DePaola has written several plays for radio, and he serves on the board of directors of the Children's Radio Theater. Recently, he resumed exhibiting paintings and drawings in fine-art galleries around the U.S. "I would like to see where that is going to go," he told Gravel. "I do it for the sake of doing it, and I don't know yet who that audience is so that makes it harder than illustrating. I'm also thinking of more children's books, so I have no plans for retirement."

Described by Gravel as having "a zest for life" and "bubbl[ing] with exuberance," dePaola has said that his main character flaw is "thinking so much that I sometimes forget to listen." He spends a great deal of his free time reading his books to children at libraries, schools, and bookstores.

Among the many awards that dePaola has won are the Kerlan Award for singular attainment in children's literature, from the University of Minnesota, in 1981; the Regina Medal, from the Catholic Library Association, in 1983; a Smithsonian Medal, in 1990; and the Milner Award, in 1996. DePaola also received a 1976 Caldecott Honor Book Award, from the American Library Association, for *Strega Nona*, and he has earned several honorary doctoral degrees. — C.P.

Suggested Reading: *Childsplay* (on-line); *Christian Science Monitor* p30 Dec. 15, 1988, with photos; *Horn Book* vol. 69, Oct. 1993; *Washington Post* E p1 Dec. 21, 1985; *Something About the Author* vol. 59, 1990

Selected Books: *The Wonderful Dragon of Timlin*, 1966; *Andy, That's My Name*, 1973; *Charlie Needs a Cloak*, 1973; *Nana Upstairs & Nana Downstairs*, 1973; *The Cloud Book*, 1975; *Strega Nona*, 1975; *Helga's Dowry: A Troll Love Story*, 1977; *The Christmas Pageant*, 1978; *The Clown of God*, 1978; *Pancakes for Breakfast*, 1978; *The Popcorn Book*, 1978; *Big Anthony and the Magic Ring*, 1979; *The Legend of Old Befana*, 1980; *Now One Foot, Now the Other*, 1981; *Francis, the Poor Man of Assisi*, 1982; *Strega Nona's Magic Lessons*, 1982; *Noah and the Ark*, 1983; *Sing, Pierrot, Sing*, 1983; *The Story of the Three Wise Kings*, 1983; *The Mysterious Giant of Barletta*, 1984; *Tomie dePaola's Mother Goose*, 1985; *Merry Christmas Strega Nona*, 1986; *The Parables of Jesus*, 1987; *The Miracles of Jesus*, 1987; *The Art Lesson*, 1989; *Tony's Bread*, 1989; *My First Chanukah*, 1989; *Tomie dePaola's Book of Bible Stories*, 1990; *My First Easter*, 1991; *My First Passover*, 1991; *Strega Nona Meets Her Match*, 1993; *Tomie DePaola's Book of the Old Testament*, 1995; *Strega Nona: Her Story*, 1996; *Big Anthony: His Story*, 1998

George Lange/Corbis Outline

Donovan, Carrie

1928– Spokeswoman for Old Navy; former fashion critic and editor. Address: c/o New York Times, 228 W. 43d St., New York, NY 10036-3913

To many Americans, the name Carrie Donovan evokes images of the woman, clad in head-to-toe black and wearing gargantuan pearls and enormous black-rimmed eyeglasses, who cavorts on beaches, airplanes, and elsewhere with Morgan Fairchild and a dog named Magic in TV commercials for the retail clothing chain Old Navy. With her distinctive features—prominent jaw, narrow eyes—she might impress viewers as a striking character actress. While her role in the popular, campy ad campaign for Old Navy, an offshoot of the higher-priced chain the Gap, has won Donovan greater face recognition, most people know little about the woman behind the glasses and are unaware that for four decades she worked as a fashion writer and editor—and was, in fact, "the most powerful and influential newspaper fashion editor in America, perhaps in the world," according to a 1990 *Vogue* profile. A 26-year veteran of the *New York Times*, Donovan is an all-around fashion insider who has counted the designers Bill Blass, Calvin Klein, and Oscar de la Renta as both friends and foes during her long career of monitoring the catwalks. As the style editor of the *New York Times Magazine* from 1977 to 1993, Donovan brought its readers the latest news about fashion, beauty, home design, and food. In addition, Donovan served as the editor of the twice-yearly *Fashions of the Times* (printed as Part 2 of the magazine), which brought in millions of dollars in advertising

revenue and was thus a key contributor to the financial renaissance of the paper in the late 1970s and early 1980s. A note published in the *New York Times Magazine* (October 24, 1993) on the occasion of Donovan's retirement as style editor said that during her years there, she "achieved international stature for the way she has changed fashion journalism and even fashion, bringing to the subject a sure eye for excellence and an invariable touch of wit."

Born in 1928, Carolyn Gertrude Amelia Donovan grew up on a farm in Lake Placid, New York. She has had an interest in fashion since at least 1937, when, at the age of nine, she became fascinated by Wallis Simpson's wedding to the Duke of Windsor and made a paper trousseau for the bride. Donovan graduated from Parson's School of Design, in New York City, in 1950 and worked as a designer on Seventh Avenue before starting at the *New York Times*, in 1955. At that time there were very few women working as writers or editors at the paper, and most of those, including Donovan, were relegated to the women's department, a space with pink walls located six floors above the *Times* newsroom. There, the women reported mainly on the topics deemed appropriate for female writers—fashion, food, furnishings, and family, "the famous four Fs," as a later *Times* article referred to them. Donovan spent eight years at the women's desk, first as a fashion reporter and then as associate fashion editor, before moving on in 1963 to become an editor at *Vogue*, where she was mentored by the legendary Diana Vreeland. Following this, Donovan served as a senior fashion editor at *Harper's Bazaar* and as a vice president at Bloomingdale's before returning to the *Times*, in 1977, as the style editor of the Sunday magazine.

At that time the paper was in a state of flux, as it tried to maintain its prominence in a rapidly changing world. The women's department and its pink walls were gone, and female journalists had begun to occupy important editorial and writing positions at other desks. Moreover, television and radio were increasingly cutting into newspapers' traditional audience, and in its effort to compete, the *Times* underwent a makeover, giving an increasing amount of attention to soft news items and running more consumer-oriented articles. Part of this transformation involved the proliferation of magazine inserts—special editions of the magazine section, among them *The Sophisticated Traveler*, *Good Health*, and *Business World*, that appeared several times a year in addition to the regular weekly *Times Magazine*. The most profitable of these was *Fashions of the Times*, which under Donovan's editorship generated enormous advertising revenue for the paper. By 1990 eight supplements on fashion and related subjects—including women's, men's, and children's editions of *Fashions of the Times*—were appearing each year, all edited by Donovan.

Opinions of Donovan's work at the *Times* vary greatly. In the *New York Times Magazine* (January 17, 1999), in the same pages Donovan once edited, Amy M. Spindler wrote an appreciation of the now-retired doyenne: "There was never the stench of pretension in anything Carrie did when she was the style editor of *The New York Times Magazine*. She often dug her elbows into the skinny ribs of fashion—like when she had the model Wallis Franken play Wallis Simpson, with the sly joke of the Duke of Windsor coming out of the bedroom closet. Or when she made a grand statement about 'fashions in the '90's' by putting the trendiest designer clothes on men and women in their 90's. These shoots are memorable almost 10 years later, while most of today's fashion shoots are forgettable 10 minutes later. Carrie's fashion pages were about the three L's: laughing, learning, and leaving the store carrying the bag." The same article hails Donovan for being first and foremost a journalist rather than a creator of thinly veiled advertisements, as many current fashion editors are regarded. "Her first shoot for the magazine," Spindler recounted, "happened when she grabbed a photographer and went down Seventh Avenue visiting designers' showrooms for the latest news. Her pages weren't just pictures selling clothes posturing as art." As to how she selected content for her fashion spreads and editorials, Donovan told Spindler, "If something interested me, I figured it would interest the reader. That's it! That's all it was! I know it sounds awfully frivolous but that's how I did it! But because I'd been trained at *The Times*, I understood you don't just throw it at people. You say, 'Here it is, and this is why we've done it,' more or less. That's what people appreciated! They got the raison d'être behind it."

In his book *Behind the Times* (1993), the journalist and media critic Edwin Diamond offered a different perspective on Donovan's tenure at the magazine. According to Diamond, tensions existed between Donovan and the *Times*'s advertising sales staff, who disapproved of the clothes Donovan featured, calling them "'elitist,' 'fantasy,' [and] 'impractical for ordinary people.'" The sales staff contended that *Fashions of the Times* repeatedly showcased the work of the same high-end design houses—mainly Yves St. Laurent, Karl Lagerfeld, Calvin Klein, Chanel, and Norma Kamali. "In the advertising department's view," Diamond wrote, "the editors were 'ignoring major societal changes such as the professional working woman.'" Most of the designs appearing in *Fashions of the Times* were prohibitively expensive for the typical *Times* reader. For example, one *Times* advertising salesperson calculated that in the summer 1984 edition of the children's fashion supplement, the average cost of the outfits displayed in the editorial pages was $125.25. In her own defense, Donovan told Pamela Kruger for *New York Woman* (April 1988), "My first job is to report the news. Most of the time that translates into expensive fashion."

By the 1990s there were also complaints that Donovan's taste had, to some degree, failed to keep pace with fashion's constant changes. Pamela Kruger quoted an anonymous former employee of Donovan's, who griped, "Carrie is far more personality than substance. She is definitely not on the cutting edge." In one example of her failure to keep in sync, Donovan wrote in the *New York Times Magazine* (October 24, 1993), "I try, but cannot understand, the appeal of big, clunky men's shoes on women or of skin pierced with safety pins." On the other hand, Donovan is often credited with drawing attention to little-known designers; she was the first American journalist to write about French designer Christian LaCroix, who became a major fashion figure during the 1980s. "I get a chill of excitement when I spot a really good new talent," she wrote in the *Times Magazine* (October 24, 1993). "And I get a rush from seeing a truly beautiful piece of clothing. It can be in the process of creation, or finished, polished, and ready to fly. Then I want to soar, too."

According to Jack Rosenthal, who as editor in chief of the *New York Times Magazine* was Donovan's boss, her work habits were beyond reproach. While some might assume that an editor of her stature would be little more than a figurehead, Rosenthal wrote in the magazine (February 26, 1995) that Donovan "stands for energy. No one here works longer hours and, as habitués of *The Times* cafeteria know, goes out to lunch less. She is the first to arrive at a fashion show, insuring unhurried access, and, efficiently agile, the first to exit when the show's over." As for that part of her job, Donovan wrote in the magazine (October 24, 1993), "Attending fashion shows sounds glamourous. Actually, it's more like combat duty." Offering tips on how to fight the hordes of journalists, photographers, celebrities, and hangers-on at such events, Donovan quipped, "Elbows, firm footwork, a sharp-edged tote, and a properly aimed umbrella are useful tools." Donovan retired as style editor of the magazine in 1993 (Holly Brubach succeeded her) and as editor of the women's *Fashions of the Times* in 1995, after editing 36 issues of that supplement.

Charges of elitism are not likely to be made in connection with Donovan's post-retirement career as a spokeswoman for Old Navy, which sells fashion basics at affordable prices. Her relationship with the company originated when Old Navy approached her to write an ad that would appear weekly in the *Times* in the form of a fashion memo and would be signed by Donovan and accompanied by caricatures of her, drawn by Al Hirschfeld. Soon after the drawings began appearing around New York on taxicabs, Old Navy kicked off its television ad campaign, which starred Morgan Fairchild, an actress who made a name for herself in the 1980s on such programs as *Dallas* and *Falcon Crest*. Donovan told Degen Pener for *Entertainment Weekly* (June 5, 1998), "I jokingly said [to the ads' creators], 'Oh, I'd be awfully good on TV. If something happens with Morgan, let me know.'"

DUNCAN

Old Navy's ad department may have seen the comic potential in Donovan's larger-than-life persona. As Jack Rosenthal described her in the *New York Times Magazine* (February 26, 1995), "To know Carrie is to know a pronounced presence. . . . Her look is pronounced, individual: huge glasses, black bows, leopard-print skirts, colossal fake pearls. Her sound is even more pronounced: crisp diction, animated in-to-NA-tion, a singular vocabulary drawing loosely from the French. Sometimes, her most captivating vocabulary consists not of words at all but of sounds, like a long, loud '*whoo-ooo*.'" Donovan soon joined Fairchild and a dog named Magic in the TV ads, which have often presented her in situations that seem incongruous with her persona. Recent commercials, for example, have shown her hula-hooping and singing. In the commercials, Donovan wears tailored black clothes from her own closet that contrast with the splashy sets. She also wears her own jewelry—a string of big, fake pearls and large, lacquer, Chanel bangle bracelets that were a gift from the designer Karl Lagerfeld. She had her famous oversized glasses, the frames of which are handmade in England, fitted with nonreflective lenses for television. Many fans of her television work know nothing about her prestigious former career, but this does not bother Donovan. "The thing that I do love most is that the commercials seem to give people pleasure," she told George Wayne for *Vanity Fair* (August 1998). "They stop me on the street, and they will say, 'Are you the lady in the Old Navy commercials?' The delivery boy from Food Emporium doubles over in laughter at the idea of me trying to do the hula."

In the *New York Times Magazine* (October 24, 1993), Donovan identified what she regarded as one of the most significant changes to take place in the fashion business during her years as an editor: "After dallying for two decades, women have finally reached the point where they dress as they damn please." She continued, "Lots of women—I'm one of them—have evolved their own style and stick with it. In my case, it's simple, well-cut jackets, pullovers, slim skirts or pants. I love the luxurious feel of fabrics like velvet and cashmere, and I love almost anything printed with a leopard's pattern. To function, I must have the color red nearby, but I prefer to wear black. It's declarative. It's slimming. It's dramatic." According to the 1990 profile of her in *Vogue*, Donovan, who has never married, lived at that time in a small one-bedroom apartment on 65th Street in Manhattan. In 1981 she was named a Fellow of the Rhode Island School of Design. She is the editor of *Living Well: The New York Times Book of Home Design and Decoration* (1981). — M.C.

Suggested Reading: *Entertainment Weekly* p22 June 5, 1998, with photo; *New York Times* D p7 Oct. 4, 1993, with photo; *New York Times Magazine* p8, p206 Oct. 24, 1993, with photo, p4 Feb. 26, 1995, p43+ Jan. 17, 1999, with photos; *New York Woman* p34 Apr. 1988, with photo; *Vanity Fair* p106 Aug. 1998, with photo

Selected Books: as editor—*Living Well: The New York Times Book of Home Design and Decoration*, 1981

Duncan, Tim

Apr. 25, 1976– Power forward for the San Antonio Spurs. Address: c/o San Antonio Spurs, Alamodome, 100 Montana, San Antonio, TX 78203-1031

Had it not been for an ill-timed hurricane and shark-infested seas, it is conceivable that Tim Duncan—the seven-foot-tall power forward for the San Antonio Spurs and arguably the top player in the National Basketball Association (NBA)—might never have seriously pursued the game of basketball. He might never have enjoyed a stellar career as a college player at Wake Forest University. And the New York Knicks, whom Duncan destroyed—nearly singlehandedly, in the opinion of some—in the 1999 NBA finals, might have earned the championship title the team has sought for so long.

But all that is conjecture. As things are, Duncan dominated the NBA for much of the 1998–99 season, his second one as a pro, and convincingly led the Spurs through the play-offs against teams whose ranks included such formidable opponents as Kevin Garnett, Shaquille O'Neal, Rasheed Wallace, and Marcus Camby. Armed with a powerful and graceful post-up game and a nearly complete package of basketball skills, Duncan has appeared unstoppable, befuddling one opponent after another with a flurry of seemingly effortless moves. In so doing he has become a superstar whom many consider to be the premier big man in the game. Moreover, with his calm demeanor and reliance on solid technique rather than flashy showmanship, he has emerged as a role model and a sportsman at a time when trash-talking and theatrical outbursts have become commonplace in the NBA.

Tim Duncan was born on April 25, 1976 in St. Croix, the largest of the U.S. Virgin Islands, to William Duncan, a mason and hotel employee, and Ione Duncan, a midwife. He grew up on the island in a middle-class environment with his older sisters, Cheryl and Tricia, and a brother, Scott. As a child he excelled in swimming, and he worked to follow in the footsteps of Tricia, who competed for the Virgin Islands national team in the 100-meter and 200-meter backstroke competitions at the 1988 Olympic Games in Seoul, South Korea. Duncan was encouraged in that pursuit by his mother, who often volunteered as a timer at his swim meets.

Mike Segar/Archive Photos

Tim Duncan

"She was my biggest fan," Duncan told Tim Crothers for *Sports Illustrated* (November 27, 1995). "Every meet she was the loudest parent there. Somehow I could always pick out her voice yelling over everybody else."

Fueled by her encouragement, by the time Duncan was 13, he had become a top swimmer for his age group in the 400-meter freestyle competition. "Timmy was even better than me," Tricia Duncan told Crothers. "There is no doubt in my mind that he would have gone to the 1992 Olympics and held his own against the world." However, Duncan's swimming career ended abruptly, in September 1989, when Hurricane Hugo swept through the Caribbean. The swimming complex where he trained, the sole facility of its kind in St. Croix, was destroyed overnight. Duncan's only option was to train in the ocean, but he chose not to do so, partly out of fear of the sharks that lurk in the waters around St. Croix. Meanwhile, his mother had been diagnosed with breast cancer. The hurricane had damaged the closest hospital, making it difficult for her to get treatment, and in April 1990 she died.

Deprived of a place to swim and his most ardent fan, Duncan turned his attention to basketball, a sport that his sister Cheryl's husband, Ricky Lowery, a former member of a Division III college basketball team in the U.S., had encouraged him to try. At Lowery's urging, Duncan, who was then in ninth grade and about six feet tall, began playing basketball for St. Dunstan's Episcopal High School in Christiansted, St. Croix. Duncan quickly became one of the top young players on the island. He also grew 10 inches. "I remember thinking that after basketball season ended, I'd go back to swimming," Duncan told Crothers, "but then basketball season never ended."

As a high-school senior, Duncan averaged 25 points, 12 rebounds, and five blocks per game. Despite those impressive figures, he did not attract the attention of many U.S. colleges, which have tended to overlook the Virgin Islands as a source of potential recruits. One of the few schools with a top-caliber basketball team that sought Duncan was Wake Forest University, in Winston-Salem, North Carolina. Dave Odom, the head coach of the Wake Forest Demon Deacons, had learned about Duncan from Chris King, a former player for Wake Forest and a 1992 NBA draftee who had spotted Duncan while on a trip to promote the NBA in the Caribbean. In exhibition games in St. Croix, Duncan had played against King and other recent pro-draft picks, including Alonzo Mourning. At King's urging, Odom visited St. Croix and made one of the biggest recruiting coups in National Collegiate Athletic Association (NCAA) history, when he signed up the little-known but enormously talented Duncan, who had been approached by only three other NCAA Division I schools: Georgetown University, Providence College, and Delaware State University.

In the autumn of 1993, Duncan began his college career at Wake Forest. Despite playing against top-caliber competition for the first time, he developed his skills quickly and became invaluable as the starting center for the Demon Deacons. He finished his freshman season with averages of 9.8 points and 9.6 rebounds per game. In July of the following summer, he played on a team of college all-stars in an exhibition game against Dream Team II, the squad made up of NBA superstars who represented the U.S. in international competition. In that contest Duncan held his own playing opposite the towering NBA center Shaquille O'Neal. In July 1996 Duncan played against Dream Team III, which represented the U.S. at the Olympic Games in Atlanta, Georgia, later that summer.

Meanwhile, Duncan had finished his sophomore season with averages of 16.8 points and 12.53 rebounds per game and led his team to an Atlantic Coast Conference (ACC) championship title. He also helped the Demon Deacons reach the "Sweet 16" round of the NCAA Division I postseason tournament; in what is often referred to as "March Madness," 64 teams compete in the tournament for the national title each year. At the end of the season, Duncan was named national defensive player of the year by the National Association of Basketball Coaches (NABC), an honor he earned in the next two years as well.

By this point Duncan was considered a promising prospect for the NBA, and there was speculation that he would leave the college ranks and enter the 1995 pro draft. Because centers are generally the most prized draftees in the NBA, such a move on Duncan's part would have secured him a highly lucrative contract. Indeed, the 1995 NBA draft featured several young players who were widely viewed as Duncan's rivals: they included Rasheed Wallace, a sophomore at the University of

North Carolina, who was drafted fourth overall by the Washington Bullets, and Joe Smith, a sophomore at the University of Maryland, who was drafted first overall by the Golden State Warriors. Duncan, however, chose to remain in school, and while his peers were playing under the spotlight in the NBA, Duncan finished his junior year averaging 19.1 points and 12.34 rebounds per game and led his team to a 26–6 win–loss record and their second consecutive ACC championship title. Duncan then helped the Demon Deacons advance to the "Elite-Eight" round of the NCAA tournament, where they lost, 83–63, to the University of Kentucky, the eventual tournament champions. Duncan was named player of the year by numerous basketball and press associations, and he was again pegged as a top NBA-draft prospect. Duncan, who had promised his mother that he would earn a college degree, chose to remain at Wake Forest for his senior year. His decision quickly earned him praise from those who lamented what they viewed to be the premature mass exodus of promising high-school and college players to the ranks of the NBA. "I think I see life differently than most basketball players . . . whose lives have been focused on basketball all the way through, whereas mine has been up and down," Duncan told David Nakamura for the *Washington Post* (February 1, 1997). "I've had much more important things that have happened than basketball." Wake Forest coach Dave Odom had a different explanation for Duncan's decision. "He truly enjoys being 20 years old," Odom said, as quoted by Nakamura. "And, as an NBA player, you can't be 20. You're stuck in a hotel 50 nights a year with 30- to 35-year-old men."

Duncan, like other top NBA prospects who choose to stay in college, faced the small risk that he might suffer a serious injury during his final year at Wake Forest and thus lose out on the chance for a pro career and a multimillion-dollar contract. However, his senior year also afforded him opportunities to continue developing his skills. He improved his strength and his passing and developed offensive moves that he could perform with either hand. In his last season of college play, he led the NCAA's Division I in rebounding, with an average of 14.7 rebounds per game, and he also averaged 20.8 points per game, emerging as the undisputed top player in college basketball. "[Duncan's] learned the little nuances and subtle things that guys who come out early are deprived of," Chuck Douglas, the assistant general manager of the Washington Bullets (now the Wizards), commented to Nakamura. "What you do with a lot of guys who come out early is give them the benefit of the doubt. In this case, you have a guy who not only has legitimate size for his position, which is rare, but you have a player who can step right in and compete at a high level. His staying in school made our job easier. It takes away the guess-work. He's not a project."

Buoyed by Duncan's phenomenal play, in February 1997 the Demon Deacons were ranked as high as number two in the nation according to various polls, and they were expected to do well in the postseason. However, the team failed to capture the ACC championship title, and then they experienced a disappointing upset loss to Stanford in the second round of the NCAA tournament, finishing the year with a win–loss record of 24–7. Despite this somewhat lackluster end to an otherwise spectacular college career, Duncan was selected as college basketball's player of the year by the Associated Press, the U.S. Basketball Writers Association, the National Association of Basketball Coaches, the *Sporting News*, and the *Basketball Times*. He also won the James A. Naismith Award and the John R. Wooden Award, both of which honor the nation's top collegiate basketball player. He finished his career at Wake Forest as the all-time leading shot-blocker in ACC history, with 481 blocked shots, and he became only the 10th player in NCAA Division I history to both score at least 2,000 points and get at least 1,500 rebounds.

In June 1997 Duncan earned a B.A. degree in psychology. After he graduated he made his long-awaited entrance into the NBA draft, and on June 25, 1997 he was selected first overall by the San Antonio Spurs. A once formidable team that had experienced a slump as a result of injuries to their star center, David Robinson, the Spurs had finished the 1996–97 season with the worst record in their history, with 20 wins and 62 losses. Soon after Duncan was chosen, he signed a three-year deal with the Spurs that was reportedly worth a little more than $10 million. Duncan made a smooth transition to the professional level. He worked out with his new teammates over the summer and quickly proved to be a fine complement to Robinson, who had made a full recovery. As the 1997–98 season progressed, the media dubbed Duncan, who started for the team at power forward, and Robinson, the starter at center, the "Twin Towers." The two demoralized opposing teams with their combination of size, speed, and power, Duncan crushing opponents with an arsenal of unspectacular but effective post-up moves. Bolstered by their two alpine stars, the Spurs finished the regular season with 56 wins and 26 losses—36 more victories than they had notched the previous season. Much of that turnaround was attributed to Duncan, who started in all 82 regular-season games and whose season averages ranked among those of the league leaders in several key categories: he was 13th in the NBA in scoring, with an average of 21.1 points per game; third in rebounding, with 11.9 rebounds per game; sixth in shot-blocking, with 2.51 blocks per game; and fourth in field-goal percentage, with 54.9 percent. Duncan was named rookie of the month for all six months of the NBA regular season, becoming only the third player, after Ralph Sampson in 1983–84 and Robinson in 1989–90, to sweep that honor. In addition, he was the only rookie selected to participate in the 1998 NBA All-

Star Game, and he won rookie-of-the-year honors almost unanimously, receiving 113 of 116 votes. In the first round of the 1998 NBA play-offs, he helped the Spurs beat the Phoenix Suns, three games to one, in a best-of-five-game series. San Antonio then lost to the Utah Jazz, four games to one, in a best-of-seven-game series. Duncan averaged 20.7 points, 9.0 rebounds, and 2.56 blocks per game in the postseason.

Duncan continued to be a dominant player in the 1998–99 season, which was abbreviated by a lockout of players by NBA team owners during contract disputes between the two sides; the regular season consisted of 50 games, less than two-thirds the normal number. Duncan helped the Spurs finish the shortened season with 37 wins and 13 losses, tying the Utah Jazz for best record in the NBA that year. Duncan was named to the 1998–99 All-NBA First Team and to the 1998–99 NBA All-Defensive First Team. He led the Spurs in scoring, with an average of 21.7 points per game; rebounding, with 11.4 rebounds per game; and blocked shots, with 2.52 blocks per game. In the NBA as a whole, Duncan ranked seventh in scoring, fifth in rebounding, seventh in shot-blocking, and eighth in field-goal percentage, hitting 49.5 percent of his shots.

Duncan was hailed as a hometown hero in the Virgin Islands and by basketball aficionados for possessing a game that was fundamentally sound. His mechanics are superb, his footwork is exemplary, and his arsenal of post-up moves is nearly flawless. He is able to catch even some errant passes, and his solid medium-range jump shot and soft shooting touch are rare in players of his size. Duncan's high skill level, which has been attributed to both hard work and to the quality coaching he received in college, stands in stark contrast to the general decrease in skill level among NBA rookies, which many observers attribute largely to the rush to recruit ever-younger talent. Many rookies, particularly forwards and centers, though often stronger and more athletic than their counterparts in earlier eras, lag behind their predecessors in fundamental basketball skills—shooting, passing, and playing defense, to name a few prime examples. This was far from the case with Duncan, who, in addition to his other formidable skills, became one of a handful of players—irrespective of size, position, or number of years as a pro—to successfully use the bank shot, in which the ball bounces off the backboard and into the basket. Although the high-percentage shot had nearly become extinct in the NBA, Duncan made it look easy and has used it regularly, to the dismay of his opponents.

However, Duncan has not entirely escaped criticism. Some basketball pundits took issue with his style of play, arguing that he is not physical enough and relies too much on finesse. They also complained about his seemingly emotionless demeanor during games. Unlike many players, who display their emotions by pumping their fists or thumping their chests, Duncan rarely so much as changes his facial expression, even during the most important or dramatic of contests. Duncan's placid appearance struck his detractors as evidence that he did not play with intensity and did not care about winning, charges that had plagued him since his days at Wake Forest.

Duncan convincingly put all such criticism to rest during the 1999 NBA play-offs. With the support of David Robinson and a cast of veteran starters, including small forward Sean Elliott, point guard Avery Johnson, and shooting guard Mario Elie, Duncan helped lead the Spurs to a remarkable postseason. In the first round of the play-offs, San Antonio won their series, three games to one, against the Minnesota Timberwolves, who were led by Kevin Garnett. Duncan and the Spurs then went on to sweep their next two opponents, winning the first four out of a possible seven games against the Los Angeles Lakers, who were led by the star players Shaquille O'Neal and Kobe Bryant, and the Portland Trailblazers, a team that featured Rasheed Wallace.

In the 1999 NBA finals, Duncan and the Spurs found themselves up against the New York Knicks, who had enjoyed a remarkable play-off run with upset victories over the Miami Heat, the Atlanta Hawks, and the Indiana Pacers; the Knicks were the first team to reach the finals after being seeded eighth in the Eastern Conference. (NBA teams are divided into the Eastern and Western Conferences.) As the series played out, it quickly became apparent that the Knicks were overmatched. With Duncan and Robinson, the Spurs featured two seven-foot-tall players in their front court; the Knicks, on the other hand, played without their injured center, Patrick Ewing, and relied on two relatively untested guards, Allan Houston and Latrell Sprewell, for the bulk of their offense. Not surprisingly, the Spurs prevailed, four games to one, and captured the franchise's first NBA championship title since the team had become part of the league, in 1976. Moreover, in the view of many basketball experts, Duncan's performance in the play-offs established him as the premier big man in the league. In four rounds of postseason play, Duncan averaged 23.2 points and 11.5 rebounds per game, and in the championship series alone, he averaged 27.4 points and 14 rebounds per game, stats that contributed to his being named most valuable player of the 1999 NBA finals. In just two seasons Duncan had reached the zenith of his profession and helped the veteran Robinson earn his first championship ring.

In the summer of 1999, Duncan joined other NBA stars on Team USA, which competed in the Tournament of the Americas, a warm-up for the Olympic Games that featured teams from Canada, Cuba, Brazil, Venezuela, and Puerto Rico, among other countries. Duncan contributed to the team's gold-medal victory against Canada, 92–66, in the championship game. Team USA's overall record in the tournament was 10 wins and no losses. Duncan is expected to be selected to represent the U.S. in the Olympic Games in Sydney, Australia, in the summer of 2000.

Duncan lives in San Antonio in a house with a swimming pool. In addition to basketball, he enjoys collecting knives, watching movies, and playing video games. — Y.P.

Suggested Reading: *New York Times* C p2 Mar. 31, 1998, with photo; *Sport* p34+ July 1997, with photos; *Sporting News* p11 Nov. 25, 1996, with photo, p52+ Dec. 15, 1997, with photos; *Sports Illustrated* p78+ Nov. 27, 1995, with photos, p29 Feb. 17, 1997, with photos; *Washington Post* H p3 Jan. 14, 1995, with photo, H p1 Feb. 1, 1997, with photo, D p1 Feb. 2, 1997, with photo

Courtesy of U.S. House of Representatives

Dunn, Jennifer

July 29, 1941– United States Representative from Washington State. Address: 432 Cannon House Bldg., Washington, DC 20515; 9 Lake Bellevue Dr., Suite 204, Bellevue, WA 98005

Although she does not agree with her party's stances on some women's issues, Congresswoman Jennifer Dunn, a Republican from the state of Washington, told Jerry Gray for the *New York Times* (February 3, 1996) that as a woman, she "not only has a place in the Republican Party, but in the leadership." In 1997, when she was elected vice chair of the House Republican Conference, Dunn became the highest-ranking woman in Congress. Although she resigned from that position in 1998 to make what was to be an unsuccessful run for House majority leader, she did not express disap-

pointment at having lost her leadership position. "We've broken another glass ceiling," she told a staff writer for *Spokane.net* (November 19, 1998, on-line). "This is the first time ever a woman has run for a top leadership position." Dunn believes that some of her most important qualifications for leadership involve her being a woman and her willingness to disagree with other Republicans. "I think I offer the opportunity to my party for greater success . . . [because I am] able to pull all those different people into the same room and get them working together," she stated on the CNN talk show *Evans, Novak, Hunt & Shields* (as transcribed on *CNN.com*, November 14, 1998, on-line). "We agree on 80 percent of things in our party. . . . We ought to be able to help come out with really good legislation by including everybody, their energy, their passions, their work."

Jennifer Dunn was born on July 29, 1941 in Seattle, Washington, and was raised in the nearby town of Bellevue. After graduating from Bellevue High School, she attended Stanford University, in California, graduating in 1959 with a B.A. degree in English literature. From 1964 to 1969 she worked as an IBM systems engineer, designing, programming, and teaching computer applications for small businesses. In about 1969 she and her husband became the parents of a son, Bryant, and a year or so later, their second son, Reagan, was born. She and her husband divorced when Bryant was eight. In 1978–80 she worked for the Kings County Department of Assessments, where her duties included public relations.

Dunn's experience in public relations eventually led her to become involved in politics. In 1980 she was elected chair of Washington's chapter of the Republican Party, and, reelected five times, she served in that position full-time until 1992, when she ran for Congress. During her first few years as chair, Dunn established a reputation as a "prodigious fund raiser." Karen Marchorio, who chaired Washington's Democratic Party then, told Robert T. Nelson of the *Seattle Times* (March 4, 1996, on-line), "She kept lists of contributors, preparing for the day when she would run for something herself. Even back then, you could tell she was just waiting to make her move."

According to *Congressional Quarterly* (January 16, 1993), under Dunn's direction Washington's Republican Party eventually secured the governorship, both Senate seats, and four of the state's nine congressional seats. Those successes led to Dunn's appointment to the executive committee of the Republican National Committee and to the position of chair of the National Organization of GOP State Chairs. In addition, Dunn served on a number of important committees and delegations during the administrations of Presidents Ronald Reagan and George Bush. She was appointed to President Reagan's advisory councils on volunteer service and historic preservation, and in 1982 she became part of a team representing the Republican National Committee in Taiwan. In 1984 she served as a U.S.

delegate to the 30th United Nations Commission on the Status of Women (UNCSW), and she attended that year's conference in Vienna, Austria, as well as the UNCSW's preparatory conference in Nairobi, Kenya, the following year. Dunn continued her involvement with that organization under President Bush.

In 1992 Dunn resigned from her position as chair of the Republican Party of Washington to campaign for the state's Eighth Congressional District seat, which would be vacated by Republican congressman Rod Chandler, who ran unsuccessfully for U.S. senator that year. One of Dunn's major opponents in the multi-candidate primary was Pam Roach, a staunchly conservative Republican state senator who was popular among Washington's many religious conservatives and antiabortion activists and who vehemently disagreed with Dunn's pro-choice stance on abortion. Though she captured only 32 percent of the votes in the primary, Dunn emerged triumphant, having won 2 percent more votes than Roach. In the state's general elections that year, she fared much better, beating the Democratic candidate, George Tamblyn, by more than 10 percent of the vote.

While Dunn was elated to win a seat in Congress, her party lost most of the other races in the state of Washington that year, leaving her the only Republican from Washington in the House for the 103d Congress. Thus, on her first day in Congress, Dunn had the special responsibility of escorting then–House Speaker Thomas S. Foley to his seat. (The senior member of Congress from the minority party who is also from the Speaker's home state is usually given this honor.)

During her freshman term Dunn became the only new member of Congress to hold a seat on the Joint Committee on the Organization of Congress. In accepting this important assignment, Dunn sacrificed her chance to serve on the Energy and Commerce panel, which had been her first choice. During the same term, she also served on the Public Works and Transportation Committee and the Science, Space, and Technology Committee. Her work on both of these panels was important to the thousands of employees of Boeing, a company, headquartered in her district, that makes airplanes and spacecraft. In 1994 Dunn participated in the creation of the Republican Party's "Contract with America" platform, which played a major role in the party's winning a majority of House seats for the first time in four decades. Among other items, the Contract with America sought a balanced-budget amendment, a reformed welfare system, and term limits for members of Congress.

During her second term in Congress, Dunn became the fifth woman in history to be elected to the House Ways and Means Committee, which deals with issues surrounding taxation, trade, health care, welfare, and Social Security. As a member of this committee, Dunn helped to initiate a bill that, if passed, would set a flat tax in place of the complex tax code currently used by the IRS. "I'm . . .

probably the greatest supporter of the flat tax," Dunn said on the *Evans, Novak, Hunt & Shields* program. "The reason that I am is because folks at home tell me all the time that if they could understand the code, if they believed businesses were paying their fair share, and if we are able to streamline or do away with the IRS, that's the way we should go." Many Republicans hope that the flat-tax bill will be signed into law after 2000 (an outcome probably contingent on the election of a Republican president). In 1998 Dunn worked with John Tanner, a Democratic representative from Tennessee, to introduce a bill that would put an end to estate taxes by the year 2009. Regarding her continual efforts to lower taxes, Dunn explained on *Evans, Novak, Hunt & Shields*, "I have learned a long time ago . . . that every time you get a chance to ratchet that tax burden which is up to 40 percent for a lot of folks down you should take it. . . . As we energize this economy and make [it] better for everybody, there's a larger pie and everybody has a bigger slice of it."

Meanwhile, two events in 1996 had caused Congresswoman Dunn to come to the attention of the media. First, in February, Dunn filed an ethics charge against the House minority leader, Richard Gephardt, believing he had lied to the ethics committee about some real-estate business that he had conducted and that he had violated some campaign-finance rules. According to Jerry Gray, this charge was widely viewed as the Republicans' way of retaliating for an action by the Democrats—specifically, the Democrats' accusation that then–House Speaker Newt Gingrich or his associates had illegally used tax-exempt money raised through GOPAC, Gingrich's political action committee, to underwrite a course that Gingrich had taught at Kennesaw State College, in Georgia, in 1993. And later in 1996, Dunn openly criticized two other Democratic representatives—Jim Moran of Virginia and Paul Kanjorski of Pennsylvania—for having made sexist comments during the so-called Travelgate hearings, in which President Clinton and his staff were accused of firing seven employees of the White House's travel office and replacing them with several of Clinton's friends. According to Hanna Rosin of the *New Republic* (June 24, 1996), Moran offended Virginia Thomas, the wife of Supreme Court Justice Clarence Thomas and aide to Majority Leader Dick Armey, by asking, "What is Mrs. Clarence Thomas doing here? I really smell a political witch-hunt." (The comment drew a connection between the Travelgate hearings and the hearings that preceded Clarence Thomas's confirmation as a Supreme Court justice, which were dominated by charges of sexual harassment brought against Thomas by Anita Hill, a former employee of his. Many observers considered both sets of hearings instances of "political witch hunts" in which the Republicans and Democrats, respectively, aimed to damage the opposing party.) Dunn objected to Moran's and Kanjorski's insinuation that Virginia Thomas's presence at the hearings was linked to her husband and his political past, when in fact she was there as a professional performing her job. In an indignant letter to the representatives that was signed by several of her female colleagues, Dunn wrote, "American women have struggled for decades to be seen as professional equals, and your remarks put these woman back in the category of chattel." According to Rosin, the letter also asked the two representatives to make an apology to "all working women."

When it was announced that at the end of 1996 Representative Susan Molinari of New York would be resigning from Congress to take a job with CBS News, Dunn made it clear that she was interested in filling Molinari's seat on the House Republican Conference. She informed many of her fellow Republican members of Congress that if she won the next congressional election she would not, as had been surmised, run for the Senate seat of Patty Murray, a Democrat from Washington State. James V. Grimaldi of the *Seattle Times* (May 29, 1997, on-line) quoted Dunn as saying, "It's a wonderful opportunity for me. If I win this slot that means there is potential to continue to move up in leadership. That's great for our district. This kind of clout could be great for Washington." Dunn was also House Speaker Newt Gingrich's choice for the Republican Conference, and her eventual election to its vice chairship was, to many House members, an affirmation of Gingrich's power in Congress.

In 1998, when Gingrich resigned as House Speaker, Dunn once again showed an interest in advancing her position in Congress—this time to that of majority leader. Although Dick Armey, the incumbent majority leader, had made no signs that he was stepping down, he was open to a challenge, since the majority leader is nominated by the incoming House Speaker. Dunn competed against both Armey and Congressman Steve Largent of Oklahoma in seeking the post. "What I bring to this table is a great opportunity for the Republican party to open up its leadership ranks, to put into leadership people who are capable, experienced, but also representative of people in America," Dunn told *Evans, Novak, Hunt & Shields* when Gingrich stepped down. "I'm a person who comes into this with great experience, having served as the Republican Party chairman [in Washington] for 11 years. Doing elections, hundreds of elections, pulling people with divergent points of view into the same room, when they really don't want to be there because they know each other." "I think I'm probably a better communicator than Dick Armey," she said. "I'm somebody who can relate what we're doing in the Congress to what folks are feeling out in the countryside." Armey was ultimately renominated.

Immediately after President Clinton gave the State of the Union address in January 1999, Dunn and her fellow congressman Steve Largent shared the job of delivering the Republican response. Dunn began her part of the presentation by stating that, in spite of the extreme tension on Capitol Hill caused by the Senate impeachment trial of the President, "life in America [would] go on." "Our lives will continue to be filled with practical matters, not constitutional ones," she said, according to a transcription of her speech on *CNN.com* (January 20, 1999, on-line). In response to the president's announced goal of redeeming the nation's ailing Social Security program by investing surplus government funds in the program, and by investing Social Security funds in private stock, Dunn said that Clinton's plan is not a real solution because it only "props [Social Security] up with extra cash." Dunn suggested that Americans be given the choice of placing their own Social Security money in individual retirement accounts. She also stressed the need for new, innovative means of addressing the Social Security issue, as well as other national problems, in the next century. "In spite of all the troubling things you hear about our nation's capital," she said, "I believe that good ideas can take root here, good things can grow here, and good things can blossom here."

Although Dunn's stance on abortion is officially pro-choice, her record of voting in support of abortion rights has dropped from 60 percent to 17 percent in the past five years. On *Evans, Novak, Hunt, and Shields*, Dunn attributed this to the fact that she does not support the federal funding of abortions. "I think those labels [i.e., 'pro-choice' and 'pro-life'] are half the problem in our discussion of a tough issue like this," Dunn explained on the talk show. "I'm a libertarian, and that just means government shouldn't get in on either side in this issue. I don't think we should spend people's taxpayer money to pay for abortions. You can leave that to . . . private groups."

Dunn's voting record on other women's issues varies as well: in 1992, for instance, she broke ranks with her party by supporting the Violence Against Women Act, which works toward increasing women's safety, but she voted against the Family and Medical Leave Act, which allows an employee to take unpaid leave in the event of a birth or an illness in his or her family. According to Robert T. Nelson, Dunn called the latter law "anti-business and anti-women." "The problem with that [bill] was that government was mandating on employers that they must give family and medical leave to employees," Dunn stated on *Evans, Novak, Hunt & Shields*. Dunn herself had worked on an alternate version of the bill in which family and medical leave was to be negotiated between employer and employee.

Describing Dunn's work in Congress, Dick Armey, the House majority leader, told Nelson, "She's been willing to put her shoulder to the wheel. Whatever's needed, you don't have to ask twice. She makes a good presentation, and she does it with style and grace. Her success doesn't have anything to do with her gender. It's the quality of her work."

Nelson reported that the petite, blond Jennifer Dunn often wears "stylish dresses often splashed with big, colorful flowers." Dunn is a certified scuba diver. — C.P.

Suggested Reading: *CNN.com* (on-line) Nov. 14, 1998; *New Republic* p6+ June 24, 1996; *New York Times* I p24 Feb. 3, 1996; *Seattle Times* (on-line) Mar. 4, 1996; *Spokane.net* (on-line) Nov. 19, 1998

Gaspar Tringale/Courtesy of Ballantine Publishing Group

Dunne, Dominick

1926– Writer. Address: c/o Crown Books, 201 E. 50th St., New York, NY 10022

The writings of the novelist and journalist Dominick Dunne stand among the foremost chronicles of the public and private lives of the rich and famous in the United States during the latter part of the 20th century. Dunne's familiarity with media-frenzied celebrity trials has led him to be dubbed the "preeminent novelist of scandal." In a half-dozen novels and many magazine articles, he has recounted the misadventures, criminal and otherwise, of such figures as Claus Von Bulow, William Kennedy Smith, and O. J. Simpson, as well as lesser-known society personages. The profiles he has penned for the glossy monthly *Vanity Fair* have confirmed his reputation as an insider whose connections have won him tough-to-get interviews with elusive celebrities, among them Diane Keaton, Elizabeth Taylor, Ava Gardner, and Princess Diana.

Dunne himself is a product of East Coast wealth. However, as an Irish-Catholic, he felt like an outsider in the predominantly Protestant circles in which he was raised. "We were like minor-league Kennedys," he told David H. Van Biema for *People* (August 12, 1985). "We belonged to the WASP clubs and schools but we were never a part of things. I felt I was always just looking in at the fancy life, an observer, not a participant." After a 20-year stint as a Hollywood producer, Dunne had already written his first novel when a tragic event—the murder of his daughter—inspired his first magazine story, a piece for *Vanity Fair* detailing the trial of her killer. In Dunne's second career, as a writer, he has earned derision from those who feel he is too close to the upper crust to be an effective critic of its members and mores. He has also achieved popular success, with several best-selling novels to his credit.

Dominick Dunne was born in 1926, the second of six children. His family lived in a large house in Hartford, Connecticut, and he and his siblings attended Catholic schools. Dunne has often credited his grandfather, an Irish immigrant who started out as a butcher and became a grocery tycoon, with influencing him in a very constructive way. "He was a simply remarkable man, my grandfather," Dunne said to Gerald Clarke for *Harper's Bazaar* (April 1993). "He was knighted by the Pope for his philanthropic work, but he never forgot he had been poor. Never!" Dunne's memories of his father, a heart surgeon whom Dunne has characterized as a hostile and domineering man, are not so fond. According to Dunne, his father often sneered at Dunne's artistic predilections, calling him a "sissy" for putting on little dramas and playing with sock puppets. This teasing sometimes escalated into beatings with wooden coat hangers. One thrashing was so severe that Dunne suffered partial hearing loss in one ear.

Dunne left home to attend the Canterbury School, in Connecticut, and then Williams College, in Williamstown, Massachusetts. His education was interrupted by World War II, during which Dunne gained some approval from his father when he won the Bronze Star for saving a wounded soldier at the Battle of the Bulge. After the war he returned to Williams College, graduating in 1949. He then settled in New York City, where he studied acting under Sanford Meisner at the Neighborhood Playhouse. Soon he moved behind the scenes, working as a television stage manager on *The Howdy Doody Show* and *Robert Montgomery Presents*. In 1954 he married Ellen "Lenny" Griffin, and they became the parents of three children—Griffin, Alex, and Dominique.

In the late 1950s the television business shifted its base to Los Angeles, and in 1957 Dunne and his family followed suit. Over the following decade, he gradually became involved in film. As a producer, Dunne was responsible for several successful films, among them *The Boys in the Band* (1970), a look at homosexuality; *The Panic in Needle Park* (1971), a love story set among drug addicts; and *Play It As It Lays* (1972), based on a book by Joan Didion, the wife of Dunne's brother John Gregory Dunne, also a writer. Both Didion and John Gregory Dunne were Dominick Dunne's partners in a production company called Dunne-Didion-Dunne.

Despite this provocative body of work, Dunne, who has described himself as a "B-level producer on an A-level social list," was better known for his social connections. Dominick and Lenny Dunne gave many parties, including a black-and-white ball that was attended by such celebrities as Warren Beatty, Paul Newman, Natalie Wood, Dennis Hopper, and Truman Capote and which has become part of Hollywood lore. The revelry took its toll on both Dunne and his marriage. "I was changed by Hollywood," he told Fionnuala McHugh for *Options* (May 1987). "I had success early, and I have to admit that it didn't bring out the best in me. My life began to fall apart. I began drinking heavily and I lost my goodness along the way." In 1972 Lenny and Dominick Dunne divorced. By the latter half of the decade, Dunne had developed a serious alcohol problem. In addition to his personal woes, his movie career stagnated. Following the failure of his feature film *Ash Wednesday* (1973), he was forced to pursue work that he found unsatisfying, in television. There is much debate over what ultimately caused Dunne's departure from Hollywood. He maintains that he left because he had insulted a very important agent, Sue Mengers, who retaliated by blackballing him, thus doing further damage to his career. Mengers disputes this, arguing that Dunne's lack of success as a producer, as opposed to her ill-will, put him out of favor in Hollywood.

Whatever the reason, Dunne left Los Angeles in 1979 with the intention of taking a short vacation. When his car broke down in the Cascade Mountains of Oregon, he took a cabin there and worked on a novel he had contracted to write. Dunne ended up staying in Oregon for six months, during which he was able to quit alcohol. By the time Dunne emerged from this period of relative seclusion, after receiving word that his brother Stephen, an artist, had committed suicide, he had decided to move back to the East Coast and become a full-time writer. Bringing just a few bags and a typewriter, Dunne stayed at his son Griffin's apartment in New York City before finding a small apartment on the Upper East Side of Manhattan. It was there that he finished his first book, *The Winners: Part II of Joyce Haber's The Users*, a sequel to Haber's 1976 novel. The book was panned, but Dunne was encouraged by the amount of attention it received.

On October 31, 1982, Dunne received the news that his daughter, Dominique, an actress who appeared in the hit horror film *Poltergeist* (1982), had been strangled to death by an ex-boyfriend. Dunne returned to California where the boyfriend, John Sweeney, a chef at a famous French restaurant in Los Angeles, stood trial for murder. Before Dunne left New York, Tina Brown, who was then poised to take over as editor in chief of *Vanity Fair*, encouraged him to keep a journal of the trial. Sweeney was convicted of voluntary manslaughter and was released from prison in 1986, after serving three and a half years of a six-and-a-half-year sentence. To Dunne, Sweeney's light sentence was a travesty, and it led to his profound mistrust of the justice system. Dunne's account of the trial appeared as an article entitled "Justice" in the March 1984 issue of *Vanity Fair*. This marked the beginning of his long tenure as a contributing editor to the magazine, in which capacity he has reported on high-profile murder cases and has written about numerous celebrities. His pieces for the magazine were collected in the book *Fatal Charms* (1986).

Meanwhile, Dunne worked on his second book, a barely fictionalized version of an actual murder case that took place on Long Island in the 1950s. *The Two Mrs. Grenvilles* (1985), which tells the story of a beautiful gold digger who marries the wealthy Billy Grenville and then kills him, was based on the true story of the socialite Ann Woodward, who killed her husband after she allegedly mistook him for a burglar. In the novel, Dunne introduced the theme that continues to occupy him—the dark underside of society life. The book was well-received by critics and quickly became a best-seller, going through four printings in two months.

Dunne's second best-seller, *People Like Us* (1988), explored the Wall Street of 1980s Manhattan, with its insider-trading schemes, corporate raiders, and society wives. The book received a strong prepublication buzz when *Woman's Wear Daily*, a bible of sorts to the chic and privileged, printed an excerpt from the first draft accompanied by an interpretive key which identified the real people on whom Dunne's characters were based. As a result, the author was shunned by certain social groups. Dunne, however, pointed out that he did not intend the book to be malicious. "This book is not about revealing secrets," he explained to Susan Mulcahy for *New York Newsday* (April 18, 1988). "I was out to show a segment of New York society in this extraordinarily affluent and superficial decade we are living in, and I think I've done that." Critics tended to agree, although they didn't necessarily see Dunne's moderation as commendable. "For all the talk in the tabloids, Dunne's view [of his characters] is not nearly so tough," Michael M. Thomas wrote for the *Spectator* (January 14, 1989). "His roughest punches are the literary equivalent of what is elsewhere known as 'beating up on the cripple.' With the big, juicy targets, he hedges his bets." Thomas, apparently unaware of *Women's Wear Daily*'s interpretive key, felt that Dunne's characters were composites—"diffuse walking mosaics of other people's attributes"—whose lack of correspondence to identifiable people diminished the efficacy of the book's social commentary. Among the novel's vignettes of excess and corruption, Dunne interwove his own life story, including the murder of his daughter, through an alter ego named Gus Bailey.

In his next novel, *An Inconvenient Woman* (1991), Dunne again chronicled a society murder. This time he shifted his locale to Los Angeles, the setting of the true story of the murder of Alfred Bloomingdale's mistress Vicki Morgan. Using fictitious names but a largely factual plotline, Dunne cast the story in terms of the struggle between a blue-collar mistress—Morgan's fictional counterpart—and a well-born wife for the affections of the character based on Bloomingdale. Jill Robinson, writing for the *New York Times Book Review* (June 10, 1990), praised the book: "This is a smart novel because Dominick Dunne understands the distance between Los Angeles society and the spicy bazaars of Hollywood." However, Bruce Cook of the *Chicago Tribune* (June 10, 1990) felt that the book was inconsistent, perhaps as a result of Dunne's attempt to create fictional characters who are slaves to real events. "It's as though Dominick Dunne decided to give the first part of the book to the characters and then was forced by the exigencies of the plot to twist them into strange shapes just so they would do what they had to do."

Dunne followed *An Inconvenient Woman* with two books published less than two years apart: a collection of his pieces for *Vanity Fair* entitled *Mansions of Limbo* (1991) and *A Season in Purgatory* (1993), a novel. The latter, following in the mode of Dunne's previous best-sellers, was a fictional recreation of real events, specifically both the rape trial of William Kennedy Smith, which Dunne had covered for *Vanity Fair*, and the less well-known story of the murder of Martha Moxley, a teenager in the wealthy community of Greenwich, Connecticut. Dunne created a Kennedy-like clan, the Bradleys, whose son is revealed early in the novel to be the murderer of a young woman. Most of the story concerns the murder's concealment, which occurs with the help of a family friend, Harrison Burns, a famous novelist and another of Dunne's fictional alter egos. With this, Dunne's fifth novel, it seemed that reviewers had become used to his subject matter and style and assumed that he had a built-in audience. Thus they did not give the book much criticism, either positive or negative. Maureen Dowd's appraisal in the *New York Times Book Review* (June 6, 1993) is representative: "If you can bear to read one more word, even with a gossamer veneer of fiction, about America's royal and sorrowful Irish Catholic clan, and if you like Mr. Dunne's dishy style of social vivisection, then you will probably enjoy his new tour of the toxic side of a golden American family."

The murders of Ronald Goldman and Nicole Brown Simpson on June 12, 1994, and the subsequent trial of the latter's husband, the football great O. J. Simpson, who was charged with the killings, occupied Dunne for the next few years and made him a nationally recognized media figure. Dunne, who had recently finished covering the murder trial of the Menendez brothers, wrote a monthly "Letter from Los Angeles" for *Vanity Fair* detailing Simpson's criminal trial, which lasted nine months. Because Dunne too had lost his child to a violent crime, the presiding judge, Lance Ito, gave him a prime courtroom seat near the Goldman family, from which Dunne viewed the proceedings first-hand. Dunne also appeared as a commentator

on the trial on national and local CBS television news broadcasts. He was much in demand on the Los Angeles dinner-party circuit, where fellow guests such as Nancy Reagan and members of the British and Jordanian royal families received his informal accounts of the courtroom drama. Dunne was certain of Simpson's guilt and frequented television talk shows hosted by Charles Grodin and Geraldo Rivera, on which verbal bashing of Simpson was de rigueur. Thus, on October 2, 1995, when Simpson was acquitted, Dunne was appalled and literally drop-jawed. In the *Memphis Flyer* (December 1, 1997, on-line), Leonard Gill wrote that Dunne's "courtroom reaction to the verdict appeared to be equal parts blow to the stomach and blow to the heart."

Dunne's *Another City, Not My Own* (1997) was the 63d book published about the O. J. Simpson trial. What sets his account apart from its predecessors is that Dunne's book emphasizes the rumors he picked up at social gatherings rather than the well-documented legal proceedings. As Dunne has pointed out, his book's subtitle, "A Novel in the Form of a Memoir," is crucial. "The book is not about O.J. The book is about me, in the guise of [the character] Gus Bailey, at the O.J. trial," Dunne told Alex Saville for *Packet Online* (April 14, 1998). "O.J. made me a star. And as a result of becoming a star—courtesy of Mr. Simpson—all these famous people pulled me into their lives. And I found that a very interesting thing." Hence, the novel's significance lies in its depiction of the trial's cultural milieu—that of Southern California's rich and famous—and its effects on the trial's participants, many of whom, like Dunne, became celebrities themselves as a result of their association with the case. For example, Lance Ito, according to Dunne's book, became a starstruck sycophant, sending fan letters to celebrities he barely knew and telling Dunne to "give his [Ito's] best" to Princess Diana when Dunne saw her next. The book also recounted the rumor that Simpson's friend Al Cowlings, who accompanied him during the televised 50-mile car chase by the Los Angeles police that ended with Simpson's arrest, had told his version of the full story to his idol, Keith Richards of the Rolling Stones, while backstage at a concert.

Some reviewers were put off by Dunne's inclusion of such information and by fictional flourishes such as the insertion of fashion designer Gianni Versace's murderer, Andrew Cunanan, who kills Gus Bailey at the end of the novel. "*Another City, Not My Own* strikes a tone of gossipy nattering from the start and maintains it, with numbing consistency, all the way to its preposterous finale," Laura Miller wrote in the *New York Times Book Review* (November 30, 1997). In *USA Today* (November 10, 1997), Deidre Donahue wrote, "*Another City, Not My Own* is not horrible to read. And eager fans will probably snatch it up. But to call this a novel when it's actually just Dunne reprinting his social engagements and story notes for the last few years is a cheap trick." Other critics found Dunne's assertion that the Simpson case "divided the races" lofty and misguided. Jonathan Veitch, writing for the *Boston Phoenix* (March 5-12 1998), countered that "Simpson didn't divide the races; nor did [his lawyer] Johnnie Cochran. The trial merely elicited divisions that have been an essential feature of American life since its birth." Veitch went on to call Dunne's novel a "big, empty book."

During the trial Dunne had a scare when his son Alex disappeared for a few days while on a hiking trip. Shortly after the trial, Dunne suffered the loss of both his ex-wife, Lenny, who had developed multiple sclerosis during the 1970s, and his nephew Richard, who died in a plane crash. Dunne has said repeatedly that he will not cover any more murder trials. However, he had stated his interest in reporting on Paula Jones's sexual-harassment lawsuit against President Clinton. (The suit was later settled out of court.) Dunne spent January and February of 1999 covering the impeachment trial of President Clinton. His next novel will be called *A Solo Act. The Way We Lived Then*, a coffee-table book consisting of his scrapbook from the 1950s and 1960s, was published in October 1999. The work contains snapshots from the Dunnes' parties and is also "an urbanely confessional memoir," according to *Booklist* (September 1, 1999). Dunne's books *Fatal Charms* and *The Mansions of Limbo* were recently reissued in a single volume, with added material. The writer lives in Connecticut and has a pied-à-terre in Manhattan. — M.C.

Suggested Reading: *Chicago Tribune* VII p25+ May 4, 1988, V p1+ May 21, 1993, with photo; *Cosmopolitan* p188+ Sep. 1988, with photo; *Harper's Bazaar* p250+ Apr. 1993, with photo; *New York Newsday* II p3 Apr. 18, 1988, with photo; *People* p77+ Aug. 12, 1985, with photos; *Time* p95+ Nov. 17, 1997, with photo

Selected Films: *The Boys in the Band*, 1970; *The Panic in Needle Park*, 1971; *Play It As It Lays*, 1972; *Ash Wednesday*, 1973

Selected Books: *The Winners: Part II of Joyce Haber's The Users*, 1982; *The Two Mrs. Grenvilles*, 1985; *Fatal Charms*, 1986; *People Like Us*, 1988; *An Inconvenient Woman*, 1991; *Mansions of Limbo*, 1991; *A Season in Purgatory*, 1993; *Another City, Not My Own*, 1997; *The Way We Lived Then*, 1999

Duval, David

Nov. 9, 1971– Professional golfer. Address: c/o Professional Golfers Association of America, 100 Ave. of the Champions, Palm Beach Gardens, FL 33410

With 11 victories on the Professional Golfers Association (PGA) Tour since October 1997, David Duval has emerged as one of the world's top golfers. Armed with an arsenal of skills and no apparent weaknesses, Duval is capable of driving the ball more than 300 yards, calmly sinking even the trickiest putts, and playing a game that has often been described as complete. Moreover, with concentration and composure that belie his youth, he appears to play with unshakable focus. Not surprisingly, along with Tiger Woods—the 1997 Masters tournament champion and perhaps the world's best-known golfer—Duval is generally credited with sparking new interest in golf among the general public. Many golf fans are eagerly anticipating years of competitive play and the development of a heated rivalry between Duval and Woods, who are both in their 20s. For a large part of 1998 and early 1999, Duval supplanted Woods, in the opinion of many aficionados, as the sport's premier competitor, and for a brief period in 1999 he overtook Woods as the world's top-ranked player. (Ranking is based on a golfer's overall performance during the two previous years.) However, despite Duval's impressive string of victories and record-breaking prize-money earnings, he has yet to win

Courtesy of PGA Tour

any of golf's four most illustrious tournaments, known collectively as the majors—the Masters, the U.S. Open, the British Open, and the PGA Championship—in which great golfers are expected to shine.

Born on November 9, 1971 in Jacksonville, Florida, David Robert Duval is from a family steeped in golf. His grandfather, Henry "Hap" Duval, was a skilled player and a lifetime member of the PGA of America. His father, Bob Duval, who is currently a successful player on the PGA Senior Tour, was a resident golf pro at Timuquana Country Club in Jacksonville when David was growing up, and. David took to the sport early on.

When David was nine years old, his 12-year-old brother, Brent, a victim of aplastic anemia, died as a result of complications arising from a bone-marrow transplant for which David had served as the donor. David found solace in golf, and many have attributed his reserved demeanor to the circumstances of Brent's death. "He watched his brother die," Bob Duval recalled to Clifton Brown for the New York Times (May 28, 1998, on-line). "It made him a more serious person. David knows what's important in life and what isn't. He's a very genuine person, a caring person. Around people he feels comfortable with, he has no trouble opening up."

Duval played baseball and displayed talent as a pitcher, but when he was in high school, golf clearly became his main interest. In 1989 he was named the American Junior Golf Association's player of the year and gained recognition as the U.S.'s top junior golfer. As a student at the Georgia Institute of Technology (Georgia Tech), from 1989 to 1993, he earned first-team All-American honors in National Collegiate Athletic Association (NCAA) Division I competition for four consecutive years, thereby becoming only the third person, after pro golfers Phil Mickelson and Gary Hallberg, to accomplish that feat. As a sophomore Duval finished second in the 1991 NCAA Tournament. Even then his intensity and focus on the golf course were apparent. Duval's college coach, Puggy Blackmon, recalled to Mark Starr for Newsweek (February 22, 1999), "He walked on a golf course like he was the only one there." During the summer following his junior year, Duval competed in several PGA Tour events. At the 1992 Bell South Atlanta Classic, he led through three rounds before finishing in a tie for 13th place, and he tied for 19th at the Centel Western Open. These forays into competition among the world's best confirmed that his goal of becoming a pro was well founded. "Once you've played in a PGA Tour event and felt you belonged out there, it's tough to play in college tournaments, even in some of the big amateur events," he said, as quoted by Tom McCollister for Golf (May 1993). Nonetheless, Duval returned to Georgia Tech for his senior year, and in 1993 he was named college player of the year.

In the latter half of 1993, after his graduation, Duval turned professional, but he did not earn a PGA Tour card (having failed to finish well in particular events) and thus did not qualify to play on the Tour in 1993 and 1994. Instead, he played on the Nike Tour, a less-competitive professional tour, consisting of some 30 events, that was started in 1990 as the Ben Hogan Tour and is run by the PGA Tour and Nike Inc. During Duval's abbreviated 1993 season he won twice, at the Nike Wichita Open and the Nike Tour Championship. He ended the following year with 15 top-10 finishes and acquired his PGA Tour card by finishing eighth in total earnings on the Nike Tour. (Top-season finishers on the Nike Tour ordinarily are permitted to play on the PGA Tour.)

In 1995, Duval's first season on the PGA Tour, he notched 15 top-10 finishes and 21 top-25 finishes. He also finished second in three tournaments—the AT&T Pebble Beach National Pro-Am, the Bob Hope Chrysler Classic, and the Memorial Tournament. With his strong performance overall, he finished 11th on the PGA money list that year; his prize money, $881,438, set a rookie record.

Despite those accomplishments, Duval did not quickly emerge as a genuine star. During this period he often performed poorly under pressure; for example, he failed to log a win in his first 86 PGA Tour events, leading many to question his mental toughness. Moreover, during the following season he was overshadowed by the emergence of Tiger Woods, who turned professional in August 1996 and notched six victories in his first 11 months on the PGA Tour. By contrast, Duval did not break through with a win until late 1997. Duval was further hampered by his public image. Many older players and people in the media regarded him as cocky and arrogant, a perception based in part on his appearance: while most pro golfers are clean-shaven and dress conservatively, Duval sported a goatee and often wore dark, wraparound sunglasses while playing in tournaments. (Some have suggested that his sunglasses are necessary because he suffers from a condition that makes his eyes extra sensitive to sunlight.) "People have made assumptions based on looks and appearances," Duval said, as quoted by Clifton Brown for the New York Times (May 28, 1998, on-line). "I'm starting to accept that's how it is, even though I don't like it. A guy asked me the other day if I was a rebel. Does wearing dark glasses and a goatee make you a rebel? That's not me. That's not what I'm about." Moreover, in contrast to Woods, who often displays enthusiasm and other emotions on the golf course, Duval comes across as cool and aloof, rarely showing any sign of his feelings.

After joining the PGA Tour, Duval finished second in tournaments seven times. Determined to notch his first victory and aware that he lacked stamina during the hot summer months, he implemented a rigorous fitness program and lost more than 30 pounds between 1996 and 1998. The hard work paid off. In October 1997 he won his first victory, at the Michelob Championship at Kingsmill in Williamsburg, Virginia. During a tight three-way play-off, which was made necessary because of a tie, Duval birdied the first hole to beat Grant Waite and Duffy Waldorf. A week later he won the Walt Disney World-Oldsmobile Classic after prevailing in a two-man play-off. Two weeks after that he won the Tour Championship, the last tournament of the season, for his third consecutive win, making him the first player since Nick Price in 1993 to win three consecutive tournaments and the first player in PGA history to achieve his first three victories in three consecutive tournaments. "Three victories in the year, no matter how they're spaced out, is a great year," he told Clifton Brown for the *New York Times* (November 3, 1997). "I don't think you ever can envision a streak of winning three starts in a row. But I've had enough patience and resolve to make the putts when I needed to. That adds up to wins." Woods, with four victories, was the only player to win more tournaments than Duval in 1997. Duval finished the season second behind Woods in earnings, with $1.8 million. (In addition, 1997 was Bob Duval's rookie season on the Senior PGA Tour, on which he has become a respected and successful player.)

In the 1998 season Duval picked up where he had left off, continuing to notch victories. He won the Tucson Classic, the Houston Open, the World Series of Golf, and the Michelob Championship. He also came within a stroke of winning his first majors event. At the Masters—a tournament held each year at the Augusta National Golf Club, in Georgia, and arguably the most illustrious event on the PGA Tour—Duval was in the lead until the very last stoke, when Mark O'Meara sank a highly improbable 20-foot putt in the final hole. Reflecting on the loss a year later, Duval said to Clifton Brown for the *New York Times* (April 6, 1999, on-line), "How did it feel? It was kind of like, ugh, what happened? It was a shock, but in a way, it wasn't a surprise, not with Mark putting. How could I be bitter? I shot five under par Sunday at the Masters. That's nothing to scoff at. And I proved to myself that I could handle that situation." Despite the disappointing loss, Duval finished the season strongly, with more than $2.59 million in tournament earnings, thereby topping Woods and setting a PGA Tour record for single-season earnings. Duval, who averaged 69.13 strokes per round that season, also won the Vardon Trophy, which is awarded to the player with the lowest strokes-per-round average on the PGA Tour.

With his solid string of victories, Duval earned the respect of other players, the press, and the public and cemented his reputation as one of the game's elite. Speaking of his earlier struggles, Duval explained to Clifton Brown for the *New York Times* (May 28, 1998, on-line), "I was trying too hard. You realize you don't have to hit incredible shots on every hole to win. Everyone wants to know the magic secret, why I'm winning now. But there is no magic, except that once you win that first one, you remember how to do it again." With long drives and precise putting, Duval's game blends power and finesse. Indeed, many golf aficionados have heralded him for displaying about as complete a game as any golfer in history. Fred Funk, a competitor on the PGA Tour, told Clifton Brown for the *New York Times* (January 11, 1999),

"If you look at his game, there's absolutely no weaknesses. He's tremendously long, he's tremendously straight, a great iron player, great wedge player, really good chipper, and a really good putter. He's in a different league." Moreover, Duval's uncanny concentration made his game extremely consistent, so much so that opponents "almost [expect] batteries to fall out of his back," Brown wrote for the *New York Times* (April 6, 1999, on-line).

Duval emerged as an especially suitable adversary for Woods, and many of the game's followers predicted and hoped for a rivalry in the tradition of those between Ben Hogan and Sam Snead, Arnold Palmer and Jack Nicklaus, and Nicklaus and Lee Trevino, all of which had fueled golf's popular appeal in the past. For his part, Duval has downplayed whatever competition exists between him and Woods. "From my point of view, it's flattering to be anointed the one who is going to challenge Tiger in the future years," Duval told Clifton Brown for the *New York Times* (February 3, 1999, on-line). "But I've played out here long enough to realize that there are many players who are just as able as Tiger or I am to win tournaments. For that reason, I don't put much focus on one-on-one rivalries, although I know people want to create one. I think the talk is good for the game. But I also think some people wish for stuff, not necessarily bad blood, but maybe a little jawing back and forth. That's just not me. And I like Tiger. I enjoy being around him and he's a really good guy." Nevertheless, fans and the press have repeatedly compared Duval and Woods, who is four years his junior. Indeed, their contrasting personalities and similar strengths on the course provide fodder for those who would pit them against each other. However, the two have yet to confront each other in the homestretch of a tournament competition.

Duval continued his streak of success into the 1999 season. He won the season's first tournament, the Mercedes Championship, and the second, the Bob Hope Classic. His victory at the latter was especially spectacular. Trailing by seven strokes before the final round, he shot a 59—13 under par—in the last round at the par-72 course to beat Steve Pate by one stroke. Duval thus became only the third player ever to shoot 59 in a PGA Tour event. (His two predecessors—Al Geiberger, in the 1977 Memphis Classic, and Chip Beck, in the 1991 Las Vegas Invitational—both did so on par-72 courses.) "It's not really something I expected to do in my career," Duval said to Clifton Brown for the *New York Times* (January 25, 1999, on-line). "In a sense, I feel bad for Steve, because I absolutely stole the golf tournament from him. Tell a guy starting the day that he'll shoot six under and get beat by a 59. He's going to tell you you're crazy. It's a tough situation." Brown pointed out that while shooting a 59 was in itself a spectacular feat, Duval shot a 28 on the back nine, playing his best when he was under the most intense pressure. Many commentators noted that Duval's expression of joy at the end of the round—he punched his fist in the air several times after his putt went in and again after he re-claimed his ball from the hole—seemed almost out of character, given his usual composure. "I know what it's like to win tournaments, and I know what it feels like to lose them," he commented after his nine-stroke victory at the Mercedes Champion-ship, as quoted by Clifton Brown for the *New York Times* (January 20, 1999, on-line). "That's why I don't get too high, or too low. On Sunday [at anoth-er tournament], there's probably going to be a spec-tacular chip or putt, but Jack Nicklaus was pretty famous for letting everybody beat themselves. That's the approach I try to take. I don't play spec-tacular golf."

Duval was officially ranked number three in the world, behind Tiger Woods and Mark O'Meara, on the occasion of his history-making round at the Bob Hope Chrysler Classic, but to his peers, Duval had long been performing at a level second to none. "He should have been number one a long time ago," Bob Tway, who was one of Duval's playing partners at the tournament, told Brown. Indeed, in March 1999, Duval did take over the number-one ranking, and as if to reinforce his new position, he continued his streak, winning back-to-back the Players Championship on March 25 and the Bell South Classic on April 1. Including his first win, in October 1997, Duval had notched 11 victories in 34 starts, a run that Clifton Brown ranked among the best in golf in the last 40 years. However, Du-val, who was then the undisputed favorite in near-ly every tournament he played in, had yet to win a majors event, and thus he aimed to capture the title at the Masters, which immediately followed the Bell South Classic in April 1999. "Golf can be a fickle game," he had commented earlier in regard to his lack of a majors title, as quoted by Starr. "To win a major, a lot of things have to go your way at exactly the right time." Those things didn't go Du-val's way at the Masters; he tied for sixth place, five shots behind the winner, Jose Maria Olazabal of Spain. (Woods came in 18th.)

After this relatively disappointing finish, Duval experienced a minor slump—he tied for 64th at the Shell Houston Open and failed to make the cut at the Compaq Classic in New Orleans. Then, after tying for third place at the Memorial Tournament in early June, Duval finished seven-over-par and tied for seventh at the U.S. Open at the Pinehurst Country Club in Pinehurst, North Carolina. (Woods finished one over par and tied for third.) Duval next tied for 10th place at the Buick Classic. In July 1999 he competed at the British Open at the Carnoustie Golf Club in Carnoustie, Scotland, where he finished 22-over-par and tied for 62nd. (Woods finished 10 over par and tied for 10th.) Soon afterward, after holding the number-one ranking for 14 weeks, Duval lost the position to Woods. However, Duval has continued to play strongly, tying for 11th at the Canon Greater Hart-ford Open and for 10th at the 1999 PGA Champion-ship, which Woods won, and finishing second at the Sprint International after stealing the lead late

in the tournament from David Toms, the eventual winner.

In the absence of a confrontation between Duval and Woods during a PGA tournament, golf promot-ers created a special event that would pit the two golf stars against each other. On August 2, 1999, in a rare two-person match-play exhibition, Duval faced Woods on an 18-hole course at the Sherwood Country Club in Thousand Oaks, California. The event was billed the "Showdown at Sherwood" and was broadcast live on ABC-TV during prime time, almost unheard-of in golf, in which tourna-ments, and thus live broadcasts, typically take place midday. "The only reservation I had, if you could call it that, was that it might focus too much attention on just two players," Duval commented to Clifton Brown for the *New York Times* (May 11, 1999, on-line). "But this will bring more attention to golf, and it's a great opportunity to play against the best match-play player in the world, if not the best player period." As anticipated, the event won a large television audience (its national Nielsen rating was 6.9), attracting viewers who normally do not tune in to golf. However, because the match was an exhibition, not much other than the prize money—$1.1 million for the winner and $400,000 for the loser, of which each would contribute $200,000 to charity—was at stake, and commenta-tors generally agreed that although it was an amus-ing novelty, the contest yielded little in the way of spectacular golf. After losing the first two holes, Woods came back to win four of the next six, and he led the match from that point on, despite Du-val's late rally, in which he won holes 13 and 14. The contest ended in a 2-and-1 victory for Woods. While after the event Duval admitted he did not play his best, both participants also told interview-ers that they had enjoyed themselves, that they hoped the exhibition had generated interest in their sport, and that they would consider partici-pating in similar events again.

In September 1999 in Brookline, Massachusetts, Duval and Woods joined 10 other American pro-fessional golfers to help the U.S. capture the Ryder Cup, in a competition that pits the best U.S. golfers against their European counterparts. After trailing badly in the early rounds, the U.S. team rallied to win the prestigious title. Their victory was tainted, however, by the unceremonious behavior of U.S. fans and players on the course. Meanwhile, in mid-August 1999, Duval had again replaced Woods as the world's top-ranked player. Woods quickly re-gained that position, and as of mid-October 1999, he still held it, while Duval was ranked number two.

Duval lives in Ponte Vedra Beach, Florida. In his free time he enjoys reading, fly fishing, surfing, and skiing. — Y.P.

Suggested Reading: *Golf* p106+ May 1993, with photo, p70+ July 1995, with photo, p126+ Mar. 1998, with photos; *Newsweek* p44+ Feb. 22, 1999, with photo; *New York Times* C p6 Oct. 31,

1997, with photo, C p6 Nov. 3, 1997, with photo; *New York Times* (on-line) May 28, 1998, Jan. 20, 1999, Jan. 25, 1999, Feb. 3, 1999, Apr. 6, 1999, May 11, 1999, Aug. 3, 1999; *Time* p85 Apr. 12, 1999, with photos

Patricia A. Orr/Courtesy of Main Events, Inc.

Duva, Lou

May 28, 1922– Boxing trainer and promoter.
Address: c/o Main Events, 811 Totowa Rd., #100, Totowa, NJ 07512

Lou Duva has done it all in boxing, first duking it out in the ring himself, then taking a backseat to become a promoter, manager, and trainer. For at least half of his career, it wasn't the money that motivated him—he barely cleared enough as a promoter to pay for a good dinner. It wasn't the fame, either; some people dubbed him the "Garbage Collector," because he was associated with second-rate boxers. Rather, it was simply his love of the sport, sweaty gyms and all, that carried him through his early days as a fight promoter in New Jersey.

Perseverance eventually paid off. In the 1970s Duva formed Main Events with his son, Dan Duva, and their operation expanded to a national scale. With Dan handling the business and legal aspects of Main Events, Duva trained and managed many of the boxers. Main Events has since become one of the most powerful outfits in the business, comparable to the operations of Don King and Bob Arum. The boxers currently in Duva's stable include Lennox Lewis, Pernell Whitaker, Ike Quartey, Andrew Golota, Michael Grant, Arturo Gatti, Junior Jones, Zabdiel Judah, Michael Moorer, David Tua, and Fernando Vargas.

Not all of those boxers are trained and managed by Duva. However, boxers who have been trained by him have won at least 13 world titles; according to the biography that appears on the Main Events Web site, he has also been the cornerman for boxers in over 70 title fights. When Evander Holyfield, a boxer he acquired after the 1984 Olympics, won the prestigious heavyweight title in 1990, Duva finally earned recognition among his peers as one of the sport's legendary managers and trainers. In 1998 he was inducted into the International Boxing Hall of Fame in Canastota, New York.

One of seven children of Italian immigrants who came to the United States in 1920, Duva was born on May 28, 1922 in the New York City borough of Manhattan. He lived there until the age of four, when the family moved to Paterson, New Jersey. In his early years, and especially when he was an adolescent and teenager, during the Depression, the Duvas lived in poverty. "We couldn't afford furniture, so we used to sit on crates," Duva was quoted as saying in the Main Events Web site biography. "I would have to stuff newspapers into my shoes to fill the holes because we couldn't afford to buy new ones."

When Duva was 10 his older brother Carl introduced him to boxing. Within a few years Duva began boxing at the amateur level, sometimes in the back of restaurants and bars. At the same time he took on odd jobs, such as delivering newspapers, shining shoes, and setting up pins in a bowling alley, to make extra money. Never a great boxer, in 1938 he joined the Civilian Conservation Corps (CCC), altering his birth certificate to meet the minimum age requirement of 18. While with the CCC he learned to drive a truck.

Soon after the U.S. entered World War II, Duva enlisted in the army and worked as a boxing instructor. He left the military in 1944 to help his parents manage their restaurant and to deliver pies for his cousin's baking business. Taking up boxing again, this time as a professional welterweight, he managed to accumulate a 15–7 record before he realized he was never going to be a serious contender, in part because he wasn't disciplined enough. "I would pour water all over my head, then lie to my brother that I was out running," he recalled for an Associated Press report (June 13, 1998). In 1947 he called his boxing career quits and went to New Jersey to start a trucking company, which he later sold to become a bail bondsman and a Teamsters Union organizer. At about this time he met his wife, Enes; they married in 1949 and had five children together.

Though his career as a boxer was over, Duva spent much of his free time hanging out at Stillman's Gym, in New York City, a boxing landmark that was frequented by celebrities and was often filled with cigar and cigarette smoke. "Fighters who asked that the window be opened were told, 'Find yourself another gym,'" Duva was quoted as saying in his Main Events Web site biography. Sensing an opportunity to become a trainer and manager himself, Duva observed carefully such trainers as Ray Arcel, Whitey Bimstein, Mannie Seamon, Chickie Ferrara, and Freddie Brown.

Duva eventually opened the Garden Gym in Totowa, New Jersey. Profits from his trucking business and some of his earnings as a bail bondsman were plowed into promoting local boxing events with relatively unknown fighters. Often he netted very little monetarily. "In spite of the financial ups and downs, Enes always encouraged me to stick with the boxing even when it was draining the family treasury," he has recalled. "She saw how much I loved it." He later became a partner with Rocky Marciano (who held the world heavyweight title from 1952 to 1956) in promoting fights and managing boxers. In 1963 he got his first taste of success, when one of the boxers he trained, Joey Giardello, defeated Dick Tiger to win the world middleweight title.

Duva recruited his family to help him with all aspects of the boxing business—everything from setting up the ring to distributing posters to working the box office. "My kids grew up speaking three languages: Italian, American, and boxing," Duva told the London *Guardian* (November 7, 1992). "After each promotion, we'd be in the back room, everybody yelling at each other," Duva's son Dan recalled to Phil Berger for the *New York Times* (August 11, 1991). "My brother Dino would pay the fighters. I'd do the box office. The money would never match the receipts. We'd have one of those bank bags and we'd throw it in the trunk and head for the diner." On a good night they cleared enough money to pay for their meal.

Once Dan received his law degree from Seton Hall University, in 1977, the Duva family boxing business took a leap forward. That same year Duva met Mitt Barnes, then a manager for Leon Spinks. At the time Spinks was under contract to the promoter Bob Arum, and Barnes was afraid of being ousted as Spinks's manager. He asked Duva if he knew any good lawyers, and Duva suggested his son. Dan made a lot of money representing Barnes, earning first a 10 percent, then a 30 percent cut of Barnes's share of Spinks's fight money. Spinks went on to beat Muhammad Ali for the heavyweight title in February 1978, then lost in the rematch in September of the same year; those two fights brought Dan a little over $300,000. That was when Dan realized that he and his father could earn a lot more money if they operated on a national scale. "I told my father, 'There's no magic to what Don King and Arum do. We can do this too,'" as he recalled to Phil Berger for the *New York Times*.

Main Events Inc. was formed in May 1978. While his son handled the legal and financial affairs, Duva took charge of managing and training the fighters. Shelly Finkel, a rock-concert promoter, was brought in to help recruit fighters and help manage the business end. Main Events eventually secured a deal to broadcast one fight a month from Ice World, in Totowa, New Jersey, through the fledgling sports cable channel ESPN.

In September 1979 Duva suffered a heart attack. That incident spurred him to give up his jobs as a bail bondsman and president of Teamster Local 286 to become a full-time trainer and manager. Still, it often seemed that boxing, rather than anything else, was going to be the end of Duva. He was an emotional trainer, known for yelling at referees and his fighters. He once even exchanged blows with Roger Mayweather, a boxer who had defeated one of Duva's fighters, Vinny Pazienza.

Main Events scored some coups, among them the 1981 welterweight unification bout between Sugar Ray Leonard and Thomas Hearns. (Leonard won.) Main Events's cut of the fight money amounted to about $1.5 million. Meanwhile, Main Events scooped up youthful talent. From the 1980 Olympics, Duva signed Tony Ayala, Tony Tucker, Mitch Green, Alex Ramos, and Johnny Bumphus. No longer was Duva the "Garbage Collector"; he was now assembling some of the best boxing prospects around.

In 1984 several Duva-trained boxers won world titles. On January 22, 1984 Bumphus won a decision against Lorenzo Garcia to acquire the World Boxing Association (WBA) junior welterweight crown. On February 26 that year, Rocky Lockridge knocked out Roger Mayweather in the first round to win the WBA junior lightweight title. Livingstone Bramble knocked out Ray Mancini in the 14th round on June 1 for the WBA lightweight championship, and on October 19 Mick McCallum won a decision against Sean Mannion to receive the WBA junior middleweight title. Duva's success inspired the Boxing Writers Association of America to name him manager of the year in 1985.

Duva has credited his success in managing and training fighters to his own abortive boxing career. Like a reformed con man, he knows all the tricks. "No fighter today can deceive me about his conditioning," he recalled for an Associated Press report (June 13, 1998). "I capitalized on everything I did wrong to make sure I did it right with my fighters."

Duva's success helped persuade many members of the 1984 U.S. Olympic boxing team to sign up with Main Events. Those boxers included Evander Holyfield, Pernell Whitaker, Mark Breland, Meldrick Taylor, and Tyrell Biggs; all except Biggs would go on to win world titles. Holyfield was the first to acquire one: in 1986 he won a decision against Dwight Muhammed Qawi to win the WBA cruiserweight crown. A year later Breland scored a technical knockout (TKO) in the seventh round against Harold Volbrecht to win the WBA welterweight title. Breland was followed by Vinny Pazienza, who won a decision against Greg Haugen to acquire the International Boxing Federation (IBF) lightweight crown. In 1987 Duva was named the trainer of the year by the WBA.

In 1988 Taylor scored a TKO in the 12th round against James McGirt to win the IBF lightweight championship. Duva had another good year in 1989. On February 5 Darrin Van Horne won the IBF middleweight crown by decision against Robert

Hines. Less than two weeks later, on February 18, Whitaker won a decision against Greg Haugen to win the IBF lightweight title. Later that year John-John Molina scored a TKO in the 10th round against Tony Lopez to win the IBF junior lightweight championship.

The year 1990 was especially gratifying for Duva; it was then that one of his boxers finally won the most coveted title in the boxing world, the heavyweight crown. On October 25 Holyfield managed a third-round knockout of James "Buster" Douglas, who had recently stunned the boxing world by beating the seemingly invincible Mike Tyson. Duva's name recognition skyrocketed. He made cameo appearances in TV sitcoms, acted as a cornerman for "Rowdy" Roddy Piper in a World Wrestling Federation bout, and appeared in the film *Blood Salvage* (1990) with Holyfield.

In 1995 Ed Hopson became Duva's 13th world champion, when he knocked out Moises Pedroza in the seventh round to win the IBF lightweight ti-tle. With the feat of training 13 world-title fighters under his belt, Duva was inducted into the International Boxing Hall of Fame, in 1998, though he chided the hall for selecting him in the non-participant category. "Can you imagine me in a fight, and I'm a non-participant," he was quoted as saying in an Associated Press report (June 15, 1998). "That's unbelievable. I'm looking to kick the hell out of somebody, and they're calling me a non-participant."

In 1981 Duva's wife developed multiple sclerosis; she died five years later. After Dan died from a brain tumor, in 1996, Duva's son Dino, who was serving as the company's comptroller, took over as president of Main Events. — W.G.

Suggested Reading: (London) *Guardian* p19 Nov. 7, 1992, with photo; *New York Times* VIII p1+ Aug. 11, 1991, with photo

---

Mike Marxer/Courtesy of Mary Engelbreit Studios

Engelbreit, Mary

June 5, 1952– Greeting-card and book illustrator.
Address: c/o Andrews McMeel Publishing, 4520
Main St., Kansas City, MO 64111

"Never heard of Mary Engelbreit?" read a headline from the *Seattle Times* (October 30, 1997, on-line). "Check your dish towel. And your coffee mug." Engelbreit began designing greeting cards in the late 1970s and established her own company, ME Ink., in 1983. Her highly detailed drawings, which also adorn such items as T-shirts and handbags, are evocative of the style of the 1920s and 1930s, and the characters and captions that Engelbreit has developed range from funny to inspiring. Reviewing the illustrated biography *Mary Engelbreit: The Art and the Artist* (1996) for *Book Page* (on-line), Ann Shayne wrote, "There's a little Maxfield Parrish in Engelbreit's work, some Joan Walsh Anglund, and a big dose of moppets in middy dresses. It's all beautifully rendered, clearly the work of a woman who has spent years perfecting her style." Today, Engelbreit's business has grown to include books, a variety of home-furnishing products, and a bi-monthly magazine, *Mary Engelbreit's Home Companion.* "I think the world could use a lot more cuteness," Engelbreit told Janet Chauncey for *Biography* (July 1999). "As the world gets more high-tech, it's nice to have old-fashioned stuff around. It's like comfort food." Her work, she said, "is comfort art."

Mary Engelbreit—who many people believe is a character made up for marketing purposes—was born on June 5, 1952 in St. Louis, Missouri. She is the eldest of the three daughters of Robert Engelbreit, a children's-clothing salesperson, and Mary Lois Engelbreit, a homemaker. According to Cheryl Jarvis in *Nation's Business* (April 1997), Mary "was drawing from the time she could hold a pencil." Among her first inspirations were drawings from children's storybooks from the 1920s and 1930s that her mother and grandmother used to read to her. She particularly admired the work of Johnny Gruelle, the creator of Raggedy Ann and Andy, and Jessie Wilcox Smith. Engelbreit has said that she taught herself to draw by copying book illustrations and cartoons. "If you do that long enough, you start drawing your own little people," she told Lynn Van Matre for the *Chicago Tribune*

(November 30, 1993). According to Chauncey, one day, while her mother was teaching her how to clean the bathroom, young Mary announced, "Mother, I don't have to know how to do that. I'm going to be an artist, and I'm going to have a maid." Engelbreit told Chauncey that when she became an adult, she would always "scrape some [money] together for a maid," even when she was struggling to support herself.

Engelbreit's parents encouraged her dream of becoming an artist, even emptying out an over-sized linen closet and making it into a small art studio for her. When she was a teenager, Engelbreit sold some original greeting cards to a local store for 25 cents apiece. Going against the advice of the nuns at her Catholic high school, Engelbreit decided not to attend college because, as she told Chauncey, she was "ready to start my life as an artist." Instead, she got a job at an art-supply store, where she met professional artists who helped strengthen her belief that she, too, could make a living in the field. Engelbreit left that job to work for a short time for a commercial design firm. After that she had another short-lived job, as a staff artist for the *St. Louis Post-Dispatch*. "I had a hard time taking orders from art directors who I thought liked to make changes just because they could," the artist was quoted as saying on the Mary Engelbreit Web site. "When I learned that my male peers with the same amount of experience were being paid more than I was, I objected and was fired. I was actually ecstatic because then I didn't have to get up and go to work at 8:30 in the morning since I worked on my drawings so late into the night. I was happier drawing what came out of my own head and from my own experiences and memories anyway."

In 1977 Engelbreit married Phil Delano, a St. Louis–based social worker. She has said that, especially in the early stages of her career, she probably would not have succeeded without her husband's support. "Even when we had no money, he never said, 'Go get a job,'" she told Chauncey. "I can't overemphasize how important this support was to me." On her Web site Engelbreit was quoted as saying that her husband "understood from the start that I could make a living at drawing if I got the right breaks, and he also saw that it was really the only thing I ever wanted to do." Shortly after she got married, the artist had a disheartening experience when she traveled to New York City to meet with some children's book publishers. "They all said they liked my work, but told me what I wanted to do was generally just not done," Engelbreit said, according to her Web site. "Their companies had in-house artists and they almost never hired free-lance or out-of-town book illustrators who didn't already have an established name." Not surprisingly, given that response to her work, one of the popular cards that Engelbreit's company later produced pictures a girl wearing long braids and overalls and sitting with her feet crossed on top of her desk, above a caption that reads, "We don't care how they do it in New York."

While she was in New York, someone advised Engelbreit to submit some of her work to greeting-card companies. Although she told Chauncey that she was initially "crushed" by the suggestion, shortly after returning to St. Louis, she sold three of her drawings to a local company for $50 each. Several months later, a San Francisco–based company, Portal Publications, offered her a contract according to which she would be paid royalties each time one of her cards was reissued. According to Cheryl Jarvis, this contract made her realize how naïve she had been in selling her first three cards for such a small sum. For the next several years, Engelbreit was able to make about $15,000 per year solely by selling her cards.

Engelbreit's first child, Evan, was born in 1980, and the artist says that having a child had a significant effect on her work, which, up until that time, could be described as evoking a fantasy world. "After I had children, the things happening in my day-to-day life were more interesting to me than unicorns and castles," the artist told Lynn Van Matre. "Since we lived a pretty ordinary life, I decided these things must be interesting to other people too." Engelbreit began drawing household scenes, often involving children, employing a highly detailed style reminiscent of 1920s and 1930s illustrations—the style for which she remains famous today. Describing for her Web site how she goes about creating her images, Engelbreit said, "I complete each drawing on a single piece of paper, first in pencil, then in pen and ink. I then color in with marker and shade with colored pencil. Each drawing takes me about two to three days to complete." Engelbreit culls the poignant and often humorous quotes that accompany the drawings on her cards from a number of sources, including, according to Lynn Van Matre, old books of quotations and the Bible. One of Engelbreit's all-time best-selling cards, however, uses a quote from real life: "Life is just a chair full of bowlies," uttered by the father of one of Engelbreit's ex-boyfriends. To accompany the words, the artist drew a picture of a large, old-fashioned armchair with many little bowls piled up on it. "He didn't even realize what he had said," Engelbreit told Chauncey. "It became a family joke. I remembered it and stole it. I still hear from the old boyfriend. The family keeps asking for their royalty checks and I keep telling them it's in the mail." Engelbreit's other popular cards include a picture of flowers with the legend "Bloom where you're planted," and a picture of a mother with two adolescent children who resemble aliens, whose caption reads, "This too shall pass."

It was also around the time of Evan's birth that Engelbreit began developing the character who would become the heroine of many of her works—Ann Estelle. Chauncey described the character, who was named after Engelbreit's maternal grandmother, as "a woman of varying ages with short, straight hair who usually sports big glasses and a hat (not to mention a frequently tart tongue)." "When I first started drawing her she didn't have a name. The name didn't evolve until much later," the artist told Elaine Markoutsas and Pamela Sherrod for the *Chicago Tribune* (February 26, 1995). "But Ann Estelle is really me. She gets to say and do all the things I want to." One of Engelbreit's best-selling cards features Ann Estelle in a suit; one index finger is touching the wide brim of her gray hat, and the caption reads, "Let's put the fun back into dysfunctional."

In 1983, while she was pregnant with her second son, Will, Engelbreit decided that producing and selling her cards on her own would be much more profitable than operating through other greeting-card companies. Although many women opt to wait until their children are grown to further their careers or start new business ventures, Engelbreit was quoted on her Web site as saying, "Proper timing is overrated. There's always a reason not to do things—it's too expensive, or it's not the best time, or this or that—but I believe there are wonderful opportunities sailing by, and you have to be ready to grab them." Engelbreit named her company ME Ink. Its first year was a particularly successful one for the artist; at a greeting-card trade show in New York City, she was contracted to create the first Mary Engelbreit calendar, and her first children's book—a rendition of the Hans Christian Andersen fairy tale *The Snow Queen*—spent several weeks on *Publishers Weekly*'s children's best-seller list. When asked if she was happy about finally having realized her dream of publishing a children's book, the artist told Chauncey, "It was fun, but oddly enough, I like doing cards best." She told Van Matre that she chose that particular fairy tale because "the little girl is the star of the show. In most fairy tales, the girl lies around waiting for her prince, but in this one, she goes out to rescue a little boy. I loved the way she just kept plowing ahead, having these adventures."

In 1986 Engelbreit licensed all of her existing greeting cards to Sunrise Publications so that she could focus on new projects. Some of her first products were T-shirts, mugs, journals, children's books, umbrellas, and tote bags. In the early 1990s she began working with the Andrews McMeel publishing company on a series of books about home decorating. The artist told Markoutsas and Sherrod that she took her cue from the many letters she received saying, "I wish my house could look like the rooms on your cards." The *Mary Engelbreit Home Companion* series of books was launched in 1994. In about 1995 Engelbreit licensed her name for a number of household-decor products such as wallpaper, fabric, dinnerware, clocks, tile, and bedding, and Mary Engelbreit shops opened in Chicago, St. Louis, Alpharetta, Georgia (near Atlanta), and Denver. The bimonthly magazine *Mary Engelbreit's Home Companion* began publication in 1996.

When asked if she feels there is competition between her own business and that of Martha Stewart, who also has a line of home-decor products and publishes a magazine, Engelbreit told Chauncey, "Our businesses are truly so different. First and foremost, I'm an artist and an illustrator. I do all the drawings. And I don't cook. I never want to cook. My full-time cook is my husband. I met Martha Stewart once at a showcase house in Connecticut, and she was perfectly cordial—but believe me, she doesn't think there's anything similar between us either." Engelbreit does, however, resent the recent tendency of other greeting-card publishers to produce cards that are unmistakably based on hers, and she has taken legal action against imitators more than once. "I know that imitation is the sincerest form of flattery, but I worked long and hard to develop a style and I think everybody else should do the same," she told Van Matre. Her company is said to gross more than $100 million each year, and she has well over 100 books to her name.

Mary Engelbreit continues to live and work in St. Louis. Her home is located less than 10 miles from the house where she was raised, and it is full of the art, furniture, toys, and other objects from the 1920s and 1930s that she collects. "My own house does look like my cards," she told Markoutsas and Sherrod. "I'm very visually oriented. . . . I like things where I can see them. Every room has some kind of collection." Her company, Mary Engelbreit Enterprises, is housed in a nearby converted Greek Orthodox church. Van Matre described Engelbreit as "a grown-up version of her characters with her bobbed hair, round-framed glasses, and baggy, vintage style frock." Chauncey wrote that she "maintains a sense of humor about practically everything—from people who seem shocked to find out she's real (not a made up character like Betty Crocker or Aunt Jemima) to her oft-mentioned penchant for cuteness." — C.P.

Suggested Reading: *Biography* p94+ July 1999, with photos; *Book Page* (on-line); *Chicago Tribune* V p1 Nov. 30, 1993, with photo, XV p1 Feb. 26, 1995, with photos; *Nation's Business* p16 Apr. 1997, with photo

Selected Books: *The Snow Queen*, 1983; *Don't Look Back*, 1994; *Everyone Needs Their Own Spot*, 1995; *Home Sweet Home: A Homeowner's Journal and Project Planner*, 1995; *Mary Engelbreit's Cross-Stitch*, 1996; *Time for Tea with Mary Engelbreit!*, 1997; *Believe: Christmas Treasury*, 1998; with Charlotte Lyons—*Mary Engelbreit's Home Companion: The Mary Engelbreit Look and How to Get It*, 1994; *Mary Engelbreit's Summer Craft Book*, 1997; *Mary Engelbreit's Spring Craft Book*, 1997; with Patrick Regan—*Mary Engelbreit: The Art and the Artist*, 1996

Ernie Paniccioli/Retna Ltd.

Evans, Faith

1973– R&B singer and songwriter. Address: c/o Bad Boy Entertainment, 8 W. 19th St., New York, NY 10011-4206

As the widow of the slain rap star Notorious B.I.G., the singer Faith Evans is probably best-known as the "Jackie O of rap." But before she ever met the rapper (also known as Biggie Smalls), Evans was a highly regarded songwriter and backup singer for artists like Mary J. Blige. She was also the first female to be signed to Sean "Puffy" Combs's Bad Boy Entertainment record label, on which she has recorded the albums *Faith* (1995) and *Keep the Faith* (1998). Having experienced fame, fortune, the death of a loved one, and motherhood all by the age of 25, Evans knows firsthand the pain and triumphs she often sings about in her soulful R&B songs, which to many listeners are comparable to the songs of such soul divas as Minnie Riperton, Ella Fitzgerald, Chaka Khan, and Mary J. Blige.

Faith Evans was born in about 1973 in Florida. Her mother, Helene Evans, was a Florida native who aspired to become a singer. It was while Helene was singing in a band that she met Faith's father, Richard Swain, a white musician. At the age of 18, Helene became pregnant with Faith, broke up with Swain, and faced the prospect of raising her daughter alone.

When Faith was six months old, her mother sent her to live in Newark, New Jersey, with Johnnie Mae Kennedy (Helene's cousin) and Johnnie Mae's husband, Orvelt Kennedy. Faith got along well with her new caretakers, and she affectionately referred to Johnnie Mae as "Ma" or "Grandma." When Helene later decided to move to Newark,

Faith found that she had two maternal figures in her life. "I used to tell her, you're blessed, having *two* Mas instead of one," Helene told Valerie Wilson Wesley for *Essence* (December 1997).

Evans's singing talent became evident early on. When she was less than five years old, she sang a version of "Let the Sunshine In" at her local church, Emanuel Baptist, and surprised everybody with the power of her voice. Her mother subsequently encouraged her to enter a variety of pageants, festivals, and contests. Later, at University High School, in Newark, Faith sang in the school's chorus and jazz band.

Faith graduated as an honor student and entered Fordham University, in the New York City borough of the Bronx. She initially planned to go into marketing, but after one year she dropped out to pursue a career in music. Despite having to deal with the burden of being a single mother—she gave birth to her first child, Chyna, at age 19—Faith managed to carve out a place for herself in the music industry. Within a short while she was writing and doing backup singing for such artists as Mary J. Blige, Pebbles, and Christopher Williams. Then, while working for Al B. Sure, Evans met Sean "Puffy" Combs, the president and CEO of Bad Boy Entertainment, and she became the first woman to be signed to the Bad Boy label.

Through Combs, Evans met another Bad Boy artist, Christopher Wallace, the drug dealer turned East Coast rapper who went by the nicknames "Notorious B.I.G." and "Biggie Smalls." Evans and Wallace quickly fell in love, and on August 4, 1994, just nine days after meeting, they married. Each was at the beginning of a promising solo career. Wallace's first album, *Ready to Die* (to which Evans contributed vocals on the song "One More Chance") was released in 1994; Evans's first album, *Faith*, a collection of romantic songs, was released in 1995. The latter, Dimitri Ehrlich wrote for *Interview* (December 1998), "wasn't the hip-hop-soul neutron bomb people had talked up. Instead of a booty-shaking style, Evans had a classic soul sensibility."

Difficulties soon emerged in their marriage, magnified by the attention they received as one of hip-hop's most famous couples. The press reported rumors of Wallace's affair with the rapper Lil' Kim. There were also rumors about Evans's affairs. The West Coast rapper Tupac Shakur, for instance, boasted of sleeping with Faith in retaliation for what he felt was Biggie Smalls's theft of his lyrics. Evans denied having an affair with Shakur, but the rumors wouldn't go away. When she had her second child—Christopher Jr.—scuttlebutt had it that the baby wasn't Wallace's. Whether or not these rumors were true, the problems in Evans and Wallace's relationship became too much for their marriage to bear. They separated in 1996, though they remained friends.

Then came the two murders that shocked the world of hip-hop. On September 7, 1996 Shakur was fatally injured by a bullet fired from a car in

Las Vegas. Approximately half a year later, on March 9, 1997, Wallace was killed in Los Angeles in a similar drive-by shooting. Many people wondered whether the much-hyped East vs. West Coast rivalry in rap had anything to do with the slayings, and whether Wallace had been killed in retribution for the death of Shakur. There was also speculation that Evans's supposed affair with Shakur was the root cause of the two men's deaths. "People said that I'm the reason they're dead," Evans told *People Online* (November 16, 1998). "If I wasn't as strong-minded as I am, I would probably have been somewhere trying to kill myself."

Dismissing the rumors, Evans has said that she has no idea who killed either Shakur or her husband. She has also said that the experience of her husband's death has profoundly changed her. According to her account, her last conversation with her husband had ended badly. "I had an attitude, he had an attitude," she told Valerie Wilson Wesley. They hung up on each other, and she never talked to him again. It is because of this that Evans, who now prays every day, says that she tries not to part with anyone, especially a person she loves, on a bad note.

After Wallace's death Evans took a break from the making of her second album to settle the complications of her husband's estate. She also contributed vocals to Combs's cover version of the Police song "I'll Be Missing You." Released in the summer of 1997 and dedicated to Wallace, the song was one of the biggest singles of that year.

Less than two years after Wallace's death, Evans seems to have regained some semblance of normality in her life. She released her second album, *Keep the Faith*, in October 1998. Though she doesn't mention Wallace explicitly in the album, some music reviewers believe that the sadder songs on it can be traced to Evans's feelings toward her ex-husband. There are also several upbeat songs. "*Keep the Faith* remains commercial R&B, all bedroom strings and Babyface-style acoustic accents," Matt Diehl wrote in *Entertainment Weekly* (October 30, 1998). He added: "We forget that Stevie [Wonder], Marvin [Gaye], and Aretha [Franklin]'s soul was considered too commercial, too. While Evans hasn't reached their heights, efforts like this give us faith that she might."

Evans is currently in a relationship with a music manager, with whom she has had her third child, Joshua. Her home is in Matawan, New Jersey.— W.G.

Suggested Reading: *Ebony* p96+ Mar. 1998, with photo; *Essence* p74+ Dec. 1997, with photo; *Interview* p112+ Dec. 1998, with photos; *People Online* Nov. 16, 1998, with photo

Selected Recordings: *Faith*, 1995; *Keep the Faith*, 1998

Fili-Krushel, Patricia

1954(?)– President of ABC Television Network. Address: c/o Capital Cities, ABC Inc., 77 W. 66th St., New York, NY 10023

When Patricia Fili-Krushel was appointed president of ABC Television Network, in August 1998, she became the first woman to head a major broadcast network. She took the reins at a critical time, when the network was grappling with one of the most serious challenges in its history: the continuing migration of viewers to cable television stations. "When you look at the 10 most profitable networks and see only one of them, NBC, is a broadcast network, you have to recognize the difficult time this is for broadcasters," she told Bill Carter for the *New York Times* (August 1, 1998). Among the people who are confident that Fili-Krushel can guide ABC to greater prosperity is her boss, Robert Iger, the president of the network's parent company, ABC Inc. "Pat has an extraordinarily diverse background in television programming and extensive business and operating experience," he was quoted as saying in an Associated Press (August 1, 1998) release. "Her background and experience are well suited for these new responsibilities and for the challenging times ahead."

Steve Fenn/Courtesy of ABC, Inc.

Fili-Krushel was born Patricia Fili in around 1954. She received a B.S. degree in communications arts from St. Johns University, in New York

City, in 1975. In 1982 she finished her MBA at Fordham University, in New York. Fili-Krushel started her career in television in 1975, as a secretary at ABC. Her talents soon became apparent, and before long she was made program controller of ABC Sports, working under Roone Arledge. In 1979 she joined Time Warner's Home Box Office (HBO) cable channel, where she eventually became vice president for business affairs and production. Her responsibilities included producing rock concerts, sports broadcasts, and films, and through her work, she developed relationships with Hollywood producers and agents.

After nine years with HBO, Fili-Krushel won the job of group vice president at the Lifetime cable channel, which was founded in 1984. As the person in charge of programming, she was expected to reverse Lifetime's sagging ratings as quickly as possible, but she did not rush to make changes. "There were so many needs at that point," she told Joshua Hammer for *Working Woman* (May 1991). "The network didn't have any projects in development. It didn't have a signature piece. My philosophy is that when you're in a new position, you need to take the time to watch and study." One of her first moves was to acquire 26 existing episodes of *The Life and Times of Molly Dodd* and commit to producing 39 new ones; by doing so, she calculated, she would both buy herself time and also motivate her staff. "It was something everyone could participate in and get excited about," she explained to Hammer. Written by the producer Jay Tarses with the actress Blair Brown in mind, the series was about an unhappy, divorced, 30-ish, 1980s career woman who refuses to measure success in conventional terms. Described as depicting "the darker side of yuppiedom," *Molly Dodd* offered no easy solutions or happy endings. Though the series was expensive and did not become profitable, it earned critical plaudits and brought some prestige to the channel.

Fili-Krushel later produced 15 made-for-television movies for Lifetime and acquired reruns of such series as *L.A. Law* and *Moonlighting*. Within her first three years at Lifetime, she changed about 60 percent of the channel's lineup, with the aim of gearing the channel solely to women. "It's important to us that women are not portrayed as victims, that they won't be saved by men at the end," she told Hammer. "We really program to who is home at that time. You can't talk down to women. It's not what women *need* to know, it's what they *want* to know."

Fili-Krushel's hopes of eventually heading Lifetime were dashed when, in 1993, Doug McCormick was named to succeed Thomas Burchill, who had stepped down as president. Later that year she left Lifetime and returned to ABC as president of the network's daytime division. For five years she helped maintain ABC's dominant ratings in daytime television among women viewers between the ages of 18 and 49. She was also instrumental in introducing, in 1998, the talk show *The View*, one of the few morning programs to become successful in recent years. Offering what Rachel X. Weissman, writing for *American Demographics* (January 1999), described as a "freewheeling mix of unscripted banter, celebrity interviews, and serious discussion of timely issues," *The View* is designed to appeal to women of all ages; its co-hosts—currently, Barbara Walters, Meredith Vieira, Star Jones, Joy Behar, and Lisa Ling—represent several generations. In its debut season *The View* was nominated for eight Emmy Awards.

In July 1998 Preston Padden, president of the ABC Television Network, left ABC to work as chief lobbyist for Disney, ABC's parent company, and Fili-Krushel was chosen to replace him. During Padden's tenure the president's duties had been limited to managing the network's sales and affiliate-relations divisions. With Fili-Krushel's appointment, the network president was once again given control over the news and entertainment divisions. "I was thrilled that [Robert Iger] chose to make this a bigger job," Fili-Krushel told Bill Carter for the *New York Times*. "Programming is what I've done the most and what excites me the most, but I feel I know both the programming and business sides and can handle them equally well. I like the combination in this new job." With regard to becoming the first female head of a major television network, she said, in a widely quoted remark, "I haven't run into a glass ceiling or had those kinds of issues. But I think I feel a certain responsibility as a role model for other women. I'm looking forward to meeting the challenge."

As head of ABC Fili-Krushel faces other challenges as well, foremost among them one that also confronts the other broadcast television networks: the steady loss of viewers to cable networks and the consequent, unavoidable drop in rates for commercial airtime. At the same time, the cost of acquiring popular programs has risen, because successful shows have sparked bidding wars among networks desperate to maintain ratings share. To cite one instance, ABC currently pays about $550 million a year for the broadcast rights to *Monday Night Football*.

To increase profits, Fili-Krushel is considering several options. For example, the networks can attempt to negotiate for longer licensing agreements for programs, so that shows are committed to stay with a network for a longer time. (Traditionally, shows have been committed for four years or less; Fili-Krushel intends to seek six- to seven-year agreements.) Alternatively, the networks can attempt to negotiate expanded rights to shows, to permit them to air the shows at additional times. ABC, for example, could then broadcast its soap operas during evenings or weekends on a cable channel. Another option is to persuade the network's local broadcast affiliates to pay more to help cover the increased cost of programming.

Within a year after Fili-Krushel's arrival, ABC reached a new accord with the board of ABC's affiliate television stations. On June 28, 1999 the board agreed to contribute $45 million a year to help the network pay for its *Monday Night Football* broadcasts and to give up ad spots on Saturday mornings. In exchange the affiliates will get more prime-time commercials to sell and a stake in ABC's soap-opera cable channel, which is scheduled to debut in 2000. Complex formulas according to which ABC might recycle programs were also negotiated. As of October 1999 the deal, which is to last three years, had yet to be approved by the individual affiliate stations.

Fili-Krushel is married to Kenneth B. Krushel, the senior vice president in charge of strategic development at NBC. "We've gotten used to not talking about [work-related] proprietary things at home," she remarked to Bill Carter. The couple have two children, Jacob and Kara. During her three-month leave of absence from Lifetime after the birth of her first child, in about 1990, she decided that she had carried her hands-on approach to management too far. "I realized that I didn't need to be involved with every detail [at work]," she told

Hammer. "I didn't need to read *every* draft of every script." By relying more on her staff, she was able to end her workday at 6:00 p.m. every night rather than 9:30. In addition, she told Dyan Machan for *Forbes* (November 30, 1998), motherhood had made her a better manager because it had perfected her "negotiating skills." She has set strict limits for her children regarding television—in 1998 they were permitted to watch only a half hour on weekdays (they saw only the Disney program *Bill Nye the Science Guy*) and only nonviolent cartoons, on ABC, Disney, or Nickelodeon, on Saturday mornings. Getting her daughter and son to obey her rules, she said, was "no problem. They listen." — W.G.

Suggested Reading: *Broadcasting & Cable* p18+ Dec. 21, 1998, with photos; *Forbes* p66 Nov. 30, 1998, with photo; *New York Times* D p1+ Aug. 1, 1998; *Washington Post* D p7 Aug. 1, 1998; *Working Woman* p79+ May 1991, with photo

Roll Call, Inc.

Finkelstein, Arthur J.

1945– Republican political consultant. Address: c/o Arthur J. Finkelstein & Associates, 16 N. Astor St., 3d Fl., Irvington, NY 10533

The Republican political consultant Arthur J. Finkelstein, known as the man who made "liberal" a four-letter word in American election campaigns and levied it against his clients' opponents at every opportunity, has earned both the derision and re-

spect of politicos in the United States and abroad. His trademark slash-and-burn campaign strategies, commonly referred to as "Finkel-think," have led some observers to describe him as Machiavellian and ingenious. Others, however, consider him a "one-trick pony": his tactics, they contend, boil down to a single set of principles that he recycles for each new campaign. A Republican New York state senator quoted by Joyce Purnick in the *New York Times* (November 14, 1994), for example, said that Finkelstein's advice to office seekers can be stated succinctly: "Set the agenda yourself, never respond to the other fellow's campaign, and just keep attacking." According to Finkelstein, however, his modus operandi cannot be described as "one size fits all"; rather, he told *Current Biography*, in the hundreds of political contests in which he has participated, he has used many approaches, because all campaigns are different. The one constant is his own political creed: Finkelstein is a libertarian, and as such, believes in limiting government to little beyond the preservation of personal freedoms of individuals (by maintaining the instruments of law enforcement and a judiciary to arbitrate disputes) and the protection of the country from attack by other nations (by maintaining the armed forces).

In the U.S. media, Finkelstein's political prowess and professional persona, as well as his extreme reclusivity in his personal life, have taken on mythic proportions. Finkelstein has built an impressive record: prior to 1996 he served as a consultant in 16 elections that were decided by less than 1 percent of the ballots cast, and in each of them, his client won. But sometimes he assists in races in which his candidates have little or no chance of victory. Even when such candidates lose, he told *Current Biography*, he judges their campaigns successful if, by Election Day, the public's opinion of the aspirants and their views have grown more positive or the candidates have otherwise strengthened their positions in the political arena. "I love my work," he told *Current Biography*, "and I feel just as passionately about what I do as I did when I started out, more than three decades ago."

One of the three sons of Jewish emigrants from Eastern Europe who became confirmed Democrats, Arthur J. Finkelstein was born in 1945 and grew up in the New York City borough of Brooklyn. He attended Queens College, a division of the City University of New York, and earned a bachelor's degree in 1967. As an undergraduate he worked as a radio interviewer for the libertarian ideologue and novelist Ayn Rand, whose ideas reinforced his own developing political philosophy. After he graduated from college, *NBC News* hired him to assist with its computer operations; he helped to write the programs that generated voting projections for the coming 1970 elections. Sometime after those elections he left NBC.

Meanwhile, Finkelstein had gotten involved in the New York senatorial campaign of the Conservative Party candidate James Buckley, who won election in 1970. In the following year he worked for the reelection of President Richard Nixon. In about 1974 he began extending his services to Joseph M. Margiotta, the chair of the Nassau County Republican Committee, on Long Island, New York, the state's wealthiest, most powerful political organization. In suburban Nassau County, he encountered the middle-class mores that, to a significant extent, would underlie his future campaign strategies. Settled by wealthy New York City socialites and populated after World War II primarily by veterans and participants in the middle-class exodus from the city, Nassau was a Republican stronghold in a predominantly Democratic state. When Finkelstein arrived on the scene, many of its voters were abandoning the Republican gentility associated with Nelson A. Rockefeller, a four-term governor of New York (1958–73) and vice president of the United States (1974–77), and embracing a grittier, ethnically based bourgeois conservatism.

In 1972 the staff of the conservative Republican Jesse Helms of North Carolina hired him as a pollster and political consultant during Helms's first, successful bid for a seat in the U.S. Senate. Four years later Finkelstein served in the same capacity during Ronald Reagan's attempt to defeat President Gerald Ford for the Republican presidential nomination. During early primaries Reagan had been soundly drubbed, and as the North Carolina primary approached, he was on the verge of dropping out of the presidential contest. Finkelstein suggested that Reagan take a more hawkish stance on national defense and strongly criticize the foreign policy of Ford and his secretary of state, Henry Kissinger. On Primary Day, March 23, 1976, Reagan walked away with a stunning come-from-behind victory.

Though Ford later secured the Republican nomination, many pundits consider the 1976 North Carolina primary a turning point in American politics, because if Reagan had withdrawn from the race, he might never have regained the momentum that carried him to the White House four years later. Reagan also won all 96 Republican delegates in the 1976 Texas presidential primary, held on May 1. In that campaign Finkelstein had advised Reagan to harp on Ford's proposal to turn over the Panama Canal to Panama, a prospect that was unpopular in Texas (as well as many other states). In what was described as "the worst defeat ever sustained by an incumbent in a presidential primary," Reagan beat Ford by more than two to one in nearly every district in the state.

Back on Long Island in the latter half of the 1970s, Arthur Finkelstein met the aggressive Alfonse D'Amato, a member of the Republican Party's new guard, who in 1977 had been elected presiding supervisor of the Town of Hempstead, the most populous community in Nassau County. D'Amato had designs on the U.S. Senate seat held by the four-term liberal Republican incumbent, Jacob K. Javits. "I trailed 67 [percent] to 4 [percent in opinion polls]," D'Amato recalled to Stephen Rodrick for *Boston Magazine* (October 1996). "[Finkelstein] said, 'That's the good news. The real truth is that only 1 percent really know you. You're terrible looking, you dress funny, and you have a terrible Brooklyn accent.'" Despite that harsh assessment, D'Amato hired Finkelstein as his strategist and would emerge as his most loyal client and supporter. The pair concocted a game plan that led to what has become notorious—among Democrats and Republicans alike—as one of the most brutal Senate campaigns ever. Having determined that Javits's voting record in the Senate was more moderate than those of many of his Republican colleagues and having discovered that few voters knew that Javits suffered from the degenerative nerve ailment known as Lou Gehrig's disease, Finkelstein scripted a television commercial that disdainfully labeled Javits a liberal and ended with the statement, "And now, at age 76 and in failing health, Jacob Javits wants six more years." Over the objections of many, D'Amato and Finkelstein ran the ad repeatedly, and D'Amato won the Republican nomination for the Senate seat, with 56.1 percent of the votes to Javits's 43.8 percent.

Finkelstein advised D'Amato to continue to attack Javits in his victory speech, rather than to focus on the winner of the Democratic primary, Elizabeth Holtzman, a four-term veteran of the U.S. House of Representatives. Finkelstein suspected that D'Amato's words would push the proud Javits to enter the race as a third-party candidate and thus draw votes away from Holtzman. "My natural inclination after primary victory was to go after Elizabeth Holtzman," D'Amato told Stephen Rodrick. "[Finkelstein] said, 'Absolutely not, don't do that, go after Javits.' That's Arthur, it's like illogical, but it's logical." D'Amato took Finkelstein's advice, and as Finkelstein had predicted, Javits joined the contest as the candidate of the Liberal Party. When the votes were counted on November 4, 1980, D'Amato had edged out Holtzman by only 80,000 votes, or just 1 percent of the 6,000,000 cast. Though exit polls reportedly showed that the 11 percent that went to Javits would have split in favor of D'Amato if Javits had not run, so that Finkelstein's ploy was actually unnecessary, Finkelstein demonstrated convincingly that he could manipulate voters, politicians, and the electoral process itself toward his own ends.

Finkelstein's technique of manipulation, as deconstructed by political analysts, is embodied in his principles for campaign success. Rule one is this: poll the public to pinpoint the social, economic, or other concerns of the electorate. Rule two: commit campaign resources to a detailed examination of the opponent's political record in search of liberal biases that may be used to play into those concerns. Rule three: using incendiary language, craft punchy slogans and televised messages that take advantage of the opponent's weaknesses, as indicated by the polling results. Rule four: repeat the slogans and commercials endlessly until Election Day. Finkelstein used this method time and again to great effect during the next 20 years. By repeating the word "liberal" to intimate the threats of excessive taxing and spending and the coddling of lawbreakers, and by cultivating an "us against them" atmosphere, Finkelstein's media-driven strategies have worked for an impressive number of Senate, House, and gubernatorial hopefuls.

With Finkelstein's help, D'Amato was reelected in 1986 and 1992. The senator's opponent in 1986, Mark Green, the New York City consumer advocate, went down without much of a fight, but for a while in 1992, D'Amato's rival, Robert Abrams, the New York State attorney general, led by a small margin in polls. Buoyed by Finkelstein's slogan "Bob Abrams. Hopelessly liberal," D'Amato succeeded in keeping the race close. The tide turned against Abrams after a campaign stop in upstate New York, when, unable to stop the heckling of D'Amato supporters, Abrams lashed out by calling his opponent a fascist. Finkelstein immediately turned Abrams's outburst to D'Amato's advantage by releasing a TV commercial in which the insult was interpreted as a reference to Benito Mussolini, Italy's fascist leader during World War II, and thus was presented as an ethnic slur.

Finkelstein again used "liberal" as a dirty word during Don Nickles's successful bid to represent Oklahoma in the Senate in 1986. The voting record in Congress of Nickles's opponent, the former Democratic representative Jim Jones, indicated that he was the most liberal member of the Oklahoma congressional delegation. To allude to his record, Finkelstein ran an ad that featured a farmer drawling, "If you act like a liberal, talk like a liberal, vote like a liberal, you're a liberal." In another case, the Finkelstein slogan "Hey Buddy, you're liberal" proved fatal to Democratic congressman

Kenneth H. "Buddy" MacKay in his 1988 battle with Republican congressman Connie Mack for a seat to represent Florida in the U.S. Senate. Although nearly every major newspaper in Florida had endorsed MacKay and independent analysts had rated him a moderate rather than a liberal, Mack—who spent an estimated $5.5 million in the campaign, about $2 million more than MacKay—captured just over 50 percent of the vote. In a third race—George Pataki's successful 1994 run for the governorship of New York against the three-term Democratic incumbent, Mario Cuomo—Finkelstein thought up another variation on the same theme: ads in which Pataki, a D'Amato protégé who was then an obscure state legislator and former mayor of the small industrial city of Peekskill, charged Cuomo with being "too liberal for too long."

Although Finkelstein has participated in some losing campaigns during his long career, the media have often portrayed him as nearly invincible. The widely publicized defeats of several of his candidates in recent years were thus seen as evidence of a chink in his armor. "The general feeling is that [Finkelstein's strategy] has sort of run its course," Charles Cook, editor of *Cook Political Report*, which tracks congressional campaigns, said to Adam Nagourney for the *New York Times* (September 27, 1998, on-line). In 1996, in one heavily covered contest, Minnesota Democratic senator Paul Wellstone successfully overcame the onslaught of a Finkelstein-led campaign and beat former Republican senator Rudy Boschwitz at the polls (though with a smaller percentage of the vote than any other incumbent Democratic senator). In 1998, in another blow for Finkelstein, Alfonse D'Amato, by then a three-term incumbent, lost his Senate seat to Charles Schumer, a liberal Democratic congressman from Brooklyn, after a long and bitter campaign—reportedly the most expensive in New York history and the second most expensive in Senate history—in which D'Amato tried to characterize Schumer as a tax-and-spend liberal and Schumer called D'Amato's ethics into question. Ironically, during the campaign D'Amato made a gaffe similar in kind to the one that had cost Robert Abrams the election six years earlier: D'Amato called Schumer, who is Jewish, a "putzhead." The word "putz" is a Yiddish vulgarism, and Schumer used the slur to undercut D'Amato's strong support in the Jewish community.

Finkelstein has also worked as a political consultant overseas. In 1996 Israel's right-wing Likud Party asked him to serve as an adviser in Benjamin Netanyahu's campaign for prime minister. Netanyahu's opponent, Shimon Peres, had been the country's foreign minister when, in November 1995, Prime Minister Yitzhak Rabin was murdered by a right-wing fanatic who opposed the Arab-Israeli peace negotiations brokered by Rabin and Peres. After Rabin's death, Peres had become prime minister. For Netanyahu's battle against the popular Peres, Finkelstein crafted a strategy that featured national security as a central issue. Netanyahu urged the adoption of a more hard-line stance in dealings with Israel's Arab neighbors, and he strenuously criticized the peace process. The slogan Finkelstein thought up for Netanyahu—"Making a secure peace"—reassured many Israelis, especially after four separate Arab suicide attacks in which dozens of Israelis were killed. On May 29, 1996, voting directly for their prime minister for the first time, Israelis chose Netanyahu by the razor-thin margin of 50.4 percent to 49.5 percent—less than 1 percent, or about 29,000 votes out of almost three million cast.

In 1999 the Likud Party called upon Finkelstein to manage Benjamin Netanyahu's push for reelection. Having apparently decided to fight fire with fire, the leftist Labor Party hired the American political consultant James Carville to mastermind the campaign of their candidate, Ehud Barak; a former chief of staff of the Israeli army, former minister of labor, and the most decorated soldier in the nation's history, Barak had been elected chairman of the Labor Party in 1997. Carville, like Finkelstein, is notorious for using extensive polling and opposition research and running bruising negative campaigns; in 1992 he helped steer Bill Clinton, then the governor of Arkansas, through a punishing Democratic presidential primary campaign and on to victory over George Bush, the incumbent Republican president, in the general election. Finkelstein, as he had three years earlier, presented Netanyahu as the best person to ensure the security of Israel, while Barak's camp focused on domestic and economic issues and questioned Netanyahu's ethics. On May 17, 1999 Ehud won by 12 percent, an unusually large margin of victory by Israel's standards.

Unlike his colleagues in political consultancy, who offer their opinions regularly on nationally televised news programs, Arthur Finkelstein guards his privacy assiduously, and his secrecy about his personal life has whet interest in him. According to various sources, before 1996 only one, outdated photograph of him was available through news services. Almost nothing was known about his personal life until October 1996, when *Boston Magazine*'s profile of him appeared. (Finkelstein has asserted that the piece grew out of an off-the-record meeting with its author.) In his article Stephen Rodrick reported that Finkelstein "has become a millionaire by working for politicians whose policies attack a very important and intimate part of his life. Specifically, four of Finkelstein's clients in the Senate—Jesse Helms of North Carolina, Bob Smith of New Hampshire, Don Nickles of Oklahoma, and North Carolina's Lauch Faircloth—form the core opposition to nearly all gay issues before Congress. . . . All of which is of interest because of one thing: Arthur Finkelstein is gay." Finkelstein responded to that disclosure by saying that he keeps his personal life separate from his professional life. Moreover, in his work, he told Adam Nagourney for the *New York Times* (April

25, 1999), "I think I'm the playwright or the director, and not the actor. And the actors need to be on-stage, not the director. And I think it's absurd that people who do what I do become as important, as celebrated, as the ones who are running."

Like people who run for office, some political consultants—Finkelstein among them—have found themselves the targets of harsh criticism as well. Finkelstein told *Current Biography* that some attacks on him are in the form of outright lies. In the *New Yorker* (September 11, 1995), for example, the political journalist Sidney Blumenthal (who has since become an aide to President Bill Clinton) reported that Finkelstein had masterminded an attempted drug bust in which D'Amato, Mayor Rudolph Giuliani of New York City, and Benjamin Baer, the chair of the Federal Parole Commission, went undercover as crack buyers. According to Blumenthal, the idea was to show the public that the three men were on the front line in the war against drugs. But the stunt was "widely ridiculed," he wrote, and it "took the three men years to live down." Finkelstein told *Current Biography* that, in fact, he had had nothing to do with the stunt and had known nothing about it until he heard about it on the news. In another case involving a complete fabrication, a number of newspapers reported that Finkelstein had been responsible for some racist attacks against Mayor Harvey Gantt of Charlotte during Gantt's 1996 race for the Senate seat held by Jesse Helms. In fact, Finkelstein told *Current Biography*, he has not worked for Helms since 1984.

Friends and clients of Finkelstein's have described him as warm and friendly. He maintains an office in Irvington, New York, and a home in Ipswich, Massachusetts, where he lives with his companion and the two children they are raising. — T.J.F.

Suggested Reading: *Boston Magazine* (on-line) Oct. 1996; *New York Times* VI p42 Apr. 25, 1999, with photo; *New Yorker* p36+ Sep. 11, 1995

Flynt, Larry

Nov. 1, 1942– Magazine publisher. Address: c/o Larry Flynt Publishing Inc., 8484 Wilshire Blvd., Suite 900, Beverly Hills, CA 90211

As the founder and publisher of *Hustler*, the porno magazine that has become synonymous with images of naked women being raped, mutilated, and fed into meat grinders, Larry Flynt is perhaps public enemy number one for antipornography groups from both the religious right and the feminist left. He has been called a "sultan of smut," and his rise from a poor Appalachian community to gaudy wealth has been labeled "a parody of the American

Jeff Christensen/Archive Photos

Larry Flynt

success story." Yet precisely because of the extreme nature of some of the images in his magazine, Flynt occupies a central place in debates over interpretation of the First Amendment. While very few people would defend his pornography as having any cultural, artistic, or intellectual value at all, many more have been willing to defend his freedom of speech. Flynt's pornography, along with Robert Mapplethorpe's controversial art and neo-Nazi hate speech, has become a test for the limits of tolerance in a liberal society.

Flynt—who once appeared in court wearing the U.S. flag as a diaper—likes to think of himself as a crusader for freedom, and to some degree he may have a claim to that title. Over the past three decades, he has been in and out of court, defending his magazine, and he has spent an estimated $40 million to $50 million in legal fees in these cases. For contemporary law students, suits involving Flynt often serve as exercises in understanding constitutional law. In his most significant victory, *Hustler v. Falwell* (1988), the Supreme Court ruled unanimously in favor of his freedom to publish a satirical cartoon featuring the televangelist Jerry Falwell committing incest with his mother. Flynt's thinking has often gone something like this: if freedom is assured to someone like Flynt himself, then freedom is definitely secure for the common person. While Flynt certainly has an economic interest in preserving his right to purvey pornography, the fact that he has often recklessly risked substantial fines and long prison terms seems to suggest at least some sincerity in his paeans to free speech.

A paraplegic since he was shot in the spine, in 1978, Flynt has often made national headlines for reasons other than his pornography. Most recently, while President Bill Clinton was facing impeachment for lying to a grand jury about an extramarital affair, Flynt turned the proceedings into more of a carnival than they already were, by setting out to expose the extramarital affairs of the same members of Congress who were most vociferously seeking Clinton's ouster. Flynt's muckraking eventually led to the downfall of one prominent Republican legislator, Robert L. Livinston, who had been set to become the 59th Speaker of the House of Representatives. Whether it is running for president or cursing out the justices of the Supreme Court, Flynt has shown time and time again that he can get under not only the clothes of the American public, but also its skin.

The son of Edith and Larry Claxton Flynt Sr., poor Appalachian sharecroppers, Larry Claxton Flynt Jr. was born on November 1, 1942 in Lakeville, Kentucky—a community where, as he has often said, the "biggest industry was jury duty." His parents divorced when he was a young boy, and he was shuffled among various relatives. He eventually dropped out of school, lied about his age, and joined the army, in 1958. Ousted from the army for insubordinate behavior within a year, he moved to another state, lied about his age again, and joined the navy, where he served from 1959 to 1964. He then started working on a General Motors assembly line. By the age of 21, he had already been married and divorced twice.

With his savings Flynt started a bar in Dayton, Ohio, originally called the Hillbilly Haven. He eventually opened seven more bars in Ohio, renamed the bars the Hustler Clubs, and added stripdancing to the bars' floor shows. To advertise his clubs Flynt began publishing a newsletter, which was gradually expanded into *Hustler*.

Flynt envisioned *Hustler* as a working-class version of such popular men's magazines as *Playboy* and *Penthouse*. His publication would not attempt to sandwich its nude photos between "literary essays," nor would it use airbrushing or be coy in displaying its models. It would not, in other words, pretend to be anything other than rude, lewd, and crude. With nothing barred from *Hustler's* editorial id, the magazine quickly became known for its explicitness and raunchy humor. The November 1974 issue, for instance, distinguished itself by featuring completely exposed female genitalia. That issue became the first *Hustler* to turn a profit.

Having crossed the boundaries of what was considered good taste, Flynt continued to provide his customers with increasingly outrageous pictorials. *Hustler* featured nude photos of pregnant women, 50-year-old women, and amputees, as well as photos with areas that could be scratched and sniffed. Popular icons were brought low. The magazine depicted Dorothy from *The Wizard of Oz* coupled with the Tin Man, and Santa Claus engaged in lascivious acts with Mrs. Claus. Flynt regularly offered famous women money to pose nude, and when they didn't take the bait, he found other ways to feature them with their clothes off—either by crude cutting and pasting or by acquiring pictures taken with telephoto lenses and without the subjects' consent. In August 1975, for instance, he published photos of Jacqueline Kennedy Onassis snapped while she had been sunbathing in the nude. The photos, which had earlier appeared in an Italian magazine called *Playmen*, had been offered to *Playboy* and *Penthouse*, both of which refused to print them. Flynt, on the other hand, showed no hesitation, and the issue dramatically boosted *Hustler*'s sales.

Encouraged by his magazine's success, Flynt grew even more inflammatory. Some photo spreads featured women copulating with knives or being raped, tortured, and dismembered. In one pictorial a nude woman was strapped like a dead deer on top of a car. A later cover showed a woman being fed into a meat grinder with the caption, "Grade A Pink." The cartoons in the magazine were just as offensive. *Hustler* regularly published "Chester the Molester," a cartoon strip featuring a character who stalks little girls. (The cartoonist, Dwaine Tinsley, was convicted in 1990 of sexually molesting his daughter, but the conviction was later overturned.) Other cartoons recalled the worst Sambo stereotypes of African-Americans. One featured a black man caught in a mousetrap baited with watermelon; another showed a black man shining a huge white penis.

Hustler quickly drew the fire of feminist, antipornography, and antiracist groups, who accused the magazine of deviancy and of encouraging hatred and violence against women and racial minorities. One of Flynt's responses was to take pictures of some of his feminist critics, among them Gloria Steinem and Andrea Dworkin, and cut and paste them onto mutilated bodies in his magazine. (Steinem and Dworkin later sued him, unsuccessfully, for damages.) To the public Flynt defended his magazine by stating that he was merely reflecting the private fantasies and attitudes of the larger society. Many critics, however, were quick to point to a 1983 *Hustler* pictorial entitled "Dirty Pool," which showed a woman being gang-raped on a pool table; two months later a woman was gang-raped in a similar fashion in New Bedford, Massachusetts. (Flynt later issued a postcard that read "Greetings from New Bedford, Massachusetts, the Portuguese Gang-Rape Capital of America.")

Sales of *Hustler* reached about two million copies a month in about 1976, thus making the publication the most popular skin magazine behind *Playboy* and *Penthouse*, both of which had circulations approximately double that of *Hustler*. "I had aimed at the 'Archie Bunkers' of America—the men who liked their beer, bourbon, sex, and humor straight—and hit the bull's eye," Flynt explained to a *Seattle Times* (December 13, 1996) reporter. "My hillbilly instincts had carried me through."

Flynt gradually branched out into other publications. In addition to creating *Chic* and other new sex magazines, he became involved in such mainstream publications as the *Plains (Georgia) Monitor*, the *Atlanta Gazette*, the *Los Angeles Free Press*, and *Ohio Magazine*. However, mainstream respectability eluded him. Embracing his image as a social outcast, Flynt attempted to be as provocative as possible. He offered $1 million for information about who carried out the Kennedy assassination, and also rewards to women who could prove that they were on congressmen's staffs for sexual purposes only. Later, he tried to sue the administration of President Ronald Reagan over restriction of journalistic access during the invasion of Grenada, and he put an ad in the *New York Times* speculating that the downing of Korean Air Lines Flight 007, in 1983, was part of a deliberate U.S. government plot to prolong the arms race.

Assisting Flynt in overseeing his publishing empire was his fourth wife, Althea Leasure, whom he married in 1976. Orphaned at the age of eight, when her father killed her mother, two others, and himself in a fit of jealousy, Leasure ran away from an orphanage at the age of 17, then worked as a dancer in one of Flynt's clubs in the 1970s. She later posed in *Hustler*, helped Flynt manage his bars, and grew close to him. Although it was well known that they did not have a monogamous relationship—Althea often helped Flynt find new sexual partners—Flynt declared Althea his one true love. The couple lived in a mansion in Bel Air that had formerly belonged to Sonny Bono and that was outfitted with a heart-shaped bathtub and the "Kentucky Room," where Flynt reconstructed the cabin he grew up in, to remind himself of his roots. Althea later became associate publisher of *Hustler*, and she claimed responsibility for some of the periodical's more extreme ideas. "I always liked the sick stuff," she was quoted as saying in *People* (July 20, 1987). "I'm the one who always wants to do it kinkier and kinkier."

Reviled by antipornography groups, Flynt became mired in legal battles. Charles Keating, the leader of Citizens for Decency and a member of Nixon's Commission on Obscenity and Pornography, led the opposition against Flynt in Cincinnati. In July 1976 Flynt, his brother Jimmy, Althea, and *Hustler* production manager Al Van Schaik were arrested and charged with several counts of pandering obscenity and engaging in organized crime. On February 8, 1977, in a Cincinnati court, Flynt alone was convicted and sentenced to seven to 25 years. Flynt appealed, and the case was dismissed on April 5, 1979 by the Ohio Supreme Court. He had no time to savor the victory, however: eight days earlier, on March 28, 1979, he had been convicted of 11 counts of violating Georgia's obscenity laws. The jail term was suspended on condition that he not violate the state obscenity laws again.

In one of the stranger events of his career, Flynt announced that he had become a born-again Christian after meeting and befriending, in the fall of

1977, the evangelist Ruth Carter Stapleton, who was the sister of President Jimmy Carter. "I owe every woman in America an apology," Flynt was quoted as saying by *Time* (December 5, 1977), and he promised changes in *Hustler*. "We will try to do what God would approve of in our stories and pictures," he told the *New York Times* (February 2, 1978). To Flynt, however, that did not mean getting rid of depictions of sex. There would still be nudity, but, as he put it in *Time* (December 5, 1977), "We will no longer treat women as pieces of meat." As examples of some of the changes he intended, he said that Chester the Molester would become Chester the Protector, and in the section where boyfriends were encouraged to send in nude photos of their girlfriends, nude photos of boyfriends would also be printed. He also considered including sexual scenes from the Bible. Many observers did not know what to make of Flynt's conversion; some speculated that it was a cynical ploy to help him in his court cases, while others wondered if he was merely drumming up publicity. His wife, Althea, who remained unconverted, complained to him that he was risking millions of dollars of the company's profits. The first issue of the new and improved *Hustler* came out in March 1978, absent the usual cover girl.

Shortly afterwards, on March 6, 1978, Flynt and his attorney, Gene Reeves, were shot outside Gwinnett County Court House, in Lawrenceville, Georgia. (Flynt was facing conviction on yet another charge of distributing obscene materials; the trial was declared a mistrial after the shooting.) Flynt initially contended that the shooting had taken place in order to silence his inquiry into the Kennedy assassination. Later, in 1984, Joseph Paul Franklin, a convicted murderer serving multiple life sentences in a federal prison for racially motivated murders, confessed to shooting Flynt, as well as the black civil rights leader Vernon Jordan (in a separate incident). Franklin asserted that he shot Flynt because he was upset about a pictorial of an interracial couple in the December 1975 issue of *Hustler*. Because of lack of evidence, Franklin was never brought to trial for the Flynt shooting.

Whether or not Flynt's born-again Christianity had been genuine, he renounced his Christian affiliation after the shooting. He had been shot twice in the abdomen; one bullet went through his spine, paralyzing him from mid-thigh down. Suddenly paraplegic and impotent, Flynt experienced severe, chronic pain from his spinal cord injury, and by his own admission, he became a drug addict in the course of easing his suffering. He overcame his drug addiction after surgery on his spine helped alleviate the pain, but Althea, who had contracted the AIDS virus and had joined him in his drug binges, had a harder time quitting. On June 27, 1987 she was found dead in the bath at the Flynt mansion, in Bel Air. The death was ruled accidental.

Getting around in a gold-plated wheelchair and with an entourage of bodyguards, Flynt refused to disappear from public controversy. If anything, his antics became even more outrageous, particularly during the period before his surgery. "I was in chronic, debilitating pain," he explained to William Booth for the *Washington Post* (February 10, 1997). "I'm paralyzed in a wheelchair. I didn't give a damn. I just took the attitude, What are you going to do to me? Kill me?" On October 16, 1983, for instance, Flynt announced his intention to run for the Republican nomination for president. As his advertisement in national papers put it, "I am running as a Republican rather than as a Democrat because I am wealthy, white, pornographic, and, like the nuclear-mad cowboy Ronnie Reagan, I have been shot for what I believe in." (He apparently did not believe John W. Hinckley Jr.'s assertion that he had shot Reagan to impress the actress Jodie Foster.) The advertisement further stated that his primary goals were "to eliminate ignorance and venereal disease." Regarding his brief presidential campaign, Flynt told *Hustler* (July 1996, on-line), "It was a funny way to make a statement and at the same time promote *Hustler*."

Meanwhile, in the courtroom, Flynt was at times uncontrollable and his behavior inexplicable. On November 8, 1983 he was present when the Supreme Court was hearing arguments in the case of *Keeton v. Hustler Magazine Inc.* At issue was whether Kathy Keeton, then the associate publisher of *Penthouse*, could sue Flynt for libel in any state. (*Hustler* had published a cartoon in the 1970s that suggested that Keeton had contracted venereal disease from Bob Guccione, the publisher of *Penthouse*. Keeton had initially sought to sue Flynt in Ohio, but the statute of limitations had run out there; she then attempted to sue him in New Hampshire.) After the justices refused to allow Flynt to represent himself, Flynt exploded into an expletive-laced tirade against them. He was charged with contempt, but the charges were later dismissed. Also in the fall of 1983, Flynt became involved in the trial of the automobile maker John DeLorean, who had been caught in an FBI cocaine sting operation. Somehow, Flynt acquired the FBI videotape of the sting, which he turned over to the TV news show *60 Minutes*. He also claimed to have an audiotape of the drug bust that revealed that DeLorean had been coerced by the FBI into the drug transaction. When Flynt was asked to produce the evidence, he appeared in court wearing an American flag as a diaper and yelled obscenities. It later turned out that the audiotape had been faked. Flynt was found in contempt and served six months in a federal prison, from February to the middle of July 1984.

Flynt's most famous court case was sparked in November 1983, when *Hustler* published a satirical cartoon about the televangelist Jerry Falwell. Done in the style of Campari's "The First Time" liquor advertisements, the cartoon depicted an alcoholic Falwell losing his virginity to his mother in an outhouse. Falwell sued for libel; in 1984 a jury in a Roanoke, Virginia, lower court ruled that Flynt had not committed libel, since it was clear that the cartoon was not meant to be factual. The jury did rule, however, that the cartoon intentionally caused Falwell emotional distress, and it awarded him $200,000 in damages. The amount, much less than the $45 million Falwell wanted, was easily payable by Flynt. But the battle between the two men did not end there. Flynt was infuriated by Falwell's statements that AIDS was God's punishment for sinners, perceiving these pronouncements as an attack against Althea. The publisher decided to appeal the Roanoke decision, though that meant spending more on legal fees and risking an even harsher judgment. The original decision was upheld in appeals court in 1986, then overturned by the Supreme Court in 1988 in a unanimous decision. As Chief Justice William Rehnquist put it in the decision, "Speech that is patently offensive and is intended to inflict emotional injury" on public figures was constitutionally protected so long as it did not purport to be fact. Flynt has boasted that through his role in this decision, he has obtained greater freedom for everyone from late-night talk-show hosts to editorial cartoonists. "Whether you agree with what I do or not, I paid a big price to be able to do it, and I played a part in advancing the cause of civil liberties," he said, as quoted in *Hustler* (July 1996, on-line).

After keeping a relatively low profile for much of the 1990s, Flynt was once again thrust into the national spotlight with the release of *The People vs. Larry Flynt* (1996). The film, directed by Milos Forman and produced by Oliver Stone, chronicles Flynt's career and sparked a new debate over his role in society. Some feminists ridiculed the idea of Flynt as a champion of the First Amendment and accused the film of "airbrushing" the offensiveness of *Hustler's* pornography, which could not be adequately represented in an R-rated film. Adding fire to the debate were the assertions of one of Flynt's daughters, Tonya Flynt-Vega, who stated at around the time of the film's release that she had been sexually molested by Flynt. (She elaborated on her charge in her book, *Hustled: My Journey from Fear to Faith* [1998].) Forman, who grew up in Czechoslovakia and witnessed the rule of the Nazis and the Soviets, called Flynt a "devil with wings," yet defended Flynt's right to produce pornography as integral to freedom for everybody. Forman told *Vanity Fair* (November 1996), "When people said [Flynt] was obscene I remembered something. Whether it was the Germans or the Russians, and I'd seen them both in my country, it always started with an attempt to 'clean things up.' Down with the perverts! Away with pornography!"

Hustler and Flynt's other sex magazines, including *Busty Beauties, Barely Legal, Leg World*, and *Taboo*, may soon face their greatest challenge—not from antipornography laws but from changes in technology. The newsstand sales of sex magazines have fallen off in the 1990s due to the availability of pornography through the Internet. The sales of *Hustler*, for instance, are far from the 1976 benchmark of two million copies a month; in 1996 the magazine was selling only about 500,000 copies a month. *Hustler Online* was created in 1995, to meet the challenge of the Internet. Perhaps a further sign of the shift toward on-line distribution was Flynt's sale of the Flynt Distribution Co., founded in 1976; the company handled newsstand distribution for Flynt magazines and other periodicals, among them the *New York Review of Books*.

Flynt's most recent legal battle occurred after he opened a Hustler store selling magazines, videos, and sex toys in Cincinnati, Ohio, in 1997. The city has one of the most stringent antipornography laws in the country, and *Hustler* had not been sold in Cincinnati since Flynt's 1977 conviction there. In response to Flynt's defiance of the law, a county prosecutor sent into the store a 14-year-old, who successfully purchased X-rated material. Flynt and his brother Jimmy were subsequently charged with several counts of pandering obscenity, disseminating material harmful to juveniles, and engaging in a pattern of corrupt activity; they faced a possible prison term of 24 years. While some accounts of the episode stated that Flynt intended to use the case to challenge laws that allow communities to restrict the availability of pornography, in May 1999 Flynt and his brother struck a plea deal. Hustler News and Gifts pleaded to two counts of pandering obscenity; the other 13 charges were dropped, with the understanding that Flynt would remove pornographic videos from the store, stop distribution of hard-core porn in all media, and pay a $10,000 fine.

Flynt grabbed national headlines once again in the fall of 1998, during the impeachment hearings of President Bill Clinton. With President Clinton facing impeachment for lying to a grand jury about an extramarital affair, Flynt set out to expose the extramarital affairs of the very same members of Congress who were most actively pursuing the matter. Flynt paid for a full-page ad in the *Washington Post* offering up to $1 million to any woman who could prove that she had had an adulterous sexual relationship with a member of Congress or another high-ranking government official. Flynt soon claimed to have uncovered four previous affairs of the designated Speaker of the House, Bob Livingston. Just days before Flynt was to publish his exposé, Livingston admitted to having had extramarital affairs and subsequently resigned from his congressional seat. Flynt later published his findings in the *Flynt Report*, which purported to uncover the affairs of several other Republican legislators. Coming on top of the impeachment hearings, as well as the attempts of other publications to uncover affairs, the report sparked concern about whether politicians' personal lives are being subjected to too much scrutiny. To some observers, Flynt's actions represented the height—or depths—of sleazy, invasive journalism; to others, Flynt had cleverly exposed the impeachment of President Clinton as a hypocritical sham.

Flynt was engaged for many years to his former nurse, Liz Berrios; they married on June 20, 1998. In addition to Tonya Flynt-Vega, his children are Lisa, Teresa, and Larry Claxton III. Flynt has been on lithium therapy for manic depression since 1987. In 1994 he had a third spinal operation, which eliminated almost all of the lingering pain associated with his shooting. He has sold his mansion in Bel Air and now lives in a more modest home outside Beverly Hills. The Larry Flynt Foundation for Human Development has donated money to the American Civil Liberties Union and to research on spinal-cord injuries, child abuse, and youth violence. — W.G.

Suggested Reading: *Hustler* (on-line) July 1996; *Interview* p86+ Dec. 1996, with photo; *Mother Jones* p12+ Feb./Mar. 1978; *New York Newsday* A p4+ Nov. 2, 1976, with photos; *New York Times* II p1+ Dec. 22, 1996, with photo, D p1 Apr. 7, 1997, with photo, B p3 Dec. 19, 1998, II p3 Jan. 17, 1999; *Newsweek* p69 Feb. 16, 1976, with photo; *People* p55+ Jan. 9, 1978, with photos, p31+ Aug. 1, 1983, with photos, p32+ July 20, 1987, with photos, p91+ Aug. 2, 1993, with photos; *Seattle Times* (on-line) Dec. 13, 1996; *Time* p64 Apr. 20, 1998, with photo; *Vanity Fair* p154+ Nov. 1996, with photos; *Washington Post* B p1+ Nov. 22, 1977, with photo, B p1+ Mar. 9, 1978, with photo, A p25 Sep. 9, 1983, with photo, D p1 Feb. 10, 1997, with photos, C p1 Jan. 11, 1999, C p11 Jan. 15, 1999; *Washington Post Magazine* p11+ Jan. 8, 1978, with photos

Selected Books: *An Unseemly Man: My Life as Pornographer, Pundit, and Social Outcast*, 1997

Associated Press

Ford, Harold E. Jr.

May 11, 1970– U.S. Representative from Tennessee. Address: 2111 Rayburn House Office Bldg., Washington, DC 20515

"My dad grew up without running water. If I grew up without a faucet, I'd be angry, too . . . but I'm fighting with a whole different set of tools," Representative Harold E. Ford Jr. of Tennessee told Dana Milbank for the *New York Times Magazine* (October 25, 1998). His father's generation of congressmen "had a hammer," he said, "but I have a screwdriver and a wrench." Ford's father, former representative Harold Ford Sr., was an 11-term, boisterously liberal congressman and visible member of the Congressional Black Caucus. By contrast, his son, who won his first congressional election in 1996—becoming the first African-American to succeed his or her parent in the House—has emerged as a centrist and as an outspoken critic of Democratic Party leadership, specifically House Minority Leader Dick Gephardt and other high-ranking officials. His stance is "a realistic assessment of where politics is going: toward a middle-class orientation as opposed to an exclusively poverty-oriented approach," Representative Albert R. Wynn, a black congressman from Philadelphia, told Milbank in support of Ford. But many Democrats feel that Ford—and the growing number of other young representatives who have joined the New Democrat Coalition in order to move the party closer to the center—are going against what their party is all about. As Milbank wrote, "the list of Ford's heresies is long": he has clashed with his Democratic elders on issues ranging from balanced-budget legislation to campaign-finance reform to proposed constitutional amendments designed to protect school prayer. "The party can't go on spewing the same old values," Ford told Milbank. "I want a new team. We've got to give serious thought to rearranging the leadership."

Harold Eugene Ford Jr. was born on May 11, 1970 in Memphis, Tennessee. According to his mother, Dorothy, now an employee of the U.S. Department of Agriculture in Washington, D.C., as a four-year-old Ford raised his hand as members of the 94th Congress were being sworn in, and he announced, "This is what I want to do when I grow up." During his father's first run for Congress—also when he was four—he cut a radio ad, used during the campaign, that contained a list of demands: better schools, a better house, and lower cookie prices. "While most young boys were out playing catch with their dads," as a writer for *Jet* (January 27, 1997) put it, Ford went with his father to meetings of the Congressional Black Caucus (CBC) and to the homes of such political luminaries as the Reverend Jesse Jackson.

At the University of Pennsylvania, from which he graduated with a bachelor's degree in history, in 1992, Ford co-founded Penn's longest-running black student newspaper, for which he also wrote a bimonthly column. Also during that time he ran his father's 1992 reelection campaign. After graduation he worked on the transition team of then-present-elect Bill Clinton, as a special assistant to the Justice and Civil Rights Cluster Group, and later as an aide to Tennessee senator Jim Sasser. Although he initially hoped to land a post in the White House, he deferred to his father, who advised him to attend law school so that he would be well positioned for a congressional campaign in 1996. Meanwhile, in 1993 Ford worked for a time with Ron Brown, the U.S. secretary of commerce, as a special assistant to the Economic Development Administration. During the next year he once again ran his father's campaign for reelection.

In 1996, after having served 22 years in the House—and having endured six years of intensive investigation of bank-fraud charges—Harold Ford Sr. announced that he was not going to run for another term. Harold Ford Jr., who had not yet completed his law degree, soon declared his candidacy for his father's seat. Only two months after he graduated from the University of Michigan Law School, he won the Democratic nomination, soundly defeating state representative Rufus Jones, the candidate backed by Memphis mayor W. W. Herenton. In the ensuing campaign against Republican Rod DeBerry—the same man his father had beaten two years earlier—Ford was ridiculed at first as "Junior." But he turned his youth into an advantage, finding support particularly among members of so-called Generation X. His platform called for greater spending on education; he cited the building of more prisons and the punishing of young offenders as inadequate, short-term solutions to longstanding problems rooted in a flawed system. On Election Day he trounced DeBerry with 62 percent of the vote, and two months later, on January 7, 1997, Harold E. Ford Jr. became the youngest member of the 105th Congress—and the first African-American in history to succeed his father in the House. "I have to think my learning curve will be less steep than others," Ford told the *New York Times*, according to *Jet*. "I've been training for this since I was a kid."

One day after being sworn in, Ford's freshmen colleagues in Congress voted him second vice president—a titular honor bestowed on first-termers who show particular promise—which effectively made him president of his freshmen class in the second term of the 105th Congress. "I am honored that my peers selected me to be one of their leaders," Ford told *Jet*. "I am optimistic that the 105th Congress will be able to forge a consensus on many important issues, including education, Medicare, campaign finance, and the budget. . . . We all know that the middle ground is not static. Finding it will require an enormous effort to make it happen. I am committed to making it happen." Within his first few months in office, Ford championed an income-based tax break for students pursuing higher education as well as a tax reduction for small businesses. Both proposals were attached to bills signed by President Clinton. Ford also became an advocate for the environment, supporting Democratic efforts to preserve endangered acreage and such wilderness areas as the Arctic National Wildlife Refuge, in Alaska. His biggest issue, though, was education. Ford campaigned for a plan to provide computers and Internet access to every classroom in the country. "Although America faces an array of challenges as we prepare to embark upon a new millennium, in my view, there is no single greater threat to our future economic prosperity, national security, and social stability than an uneducated workforce," Ford was quoted as saying on his *house.gov/ford* Web site. "In fact, if this nation is to compete and win in tomorrow's marketplace—driven and dominated by digitalization, deregulation, diversity, and globalization—then we must develop a workforce that is more highly skilled and computer literate than ever before." Ford is currently a member of the House Committee on Education and the Workforce.

Ford participated in heated debate as a member of the Committee on Government Reform and Oversight, chaired by the controversial Indiana representative Dan Burton. The committee was put in charge of investigating financial wrongdoing connected with the 1996 Clinton-Gore presidential election campaign. Burton, who was up-front and vocal about his dislike for the president, waged what many considered a partisan investigation into the affair. Although only a freshman member of Congress, Ford became one of the few representatives—led by California congressman Henry A. Waxman—to offer a dissenting voice on a committee overwhelmingly controlled by Republicans. In addition to his committee involvement, Ford was heavily involved in drafting legislation. He co-sponsored 20 bills in his first term and was the sole sponsor of three: one designed to raise Americans' awareness of school violence, another to prohibit the building and operation of solid and hazardous waste facilities near residential, school, church, and day-care areas, and a third to amend the Federal Election Campaign Act of 1971 to enforce campaign financing regulations more comprehensively. None of his three bills, however, has yet come to a vote. On the House floor Ford voted largely in favor of legislation that enforced penalties against those who committed hate crimes or were found guilty of racial, gender, or sexual-orientation discrimination.

Some of Ford's voting decisions, however, have departed from the party line, raising eyebrows among liberals in the House—such as Congressional Black Caucus member Barbara Lee of California, who registered surprise after Ford came out against funding a needle exchange for drug addicts. Ford again broke from his colleagues in the CBC when he supported President Clinton's national testing initiative, a measure many feared would reinforce the stigma of inferiority that burdens inner-city schools. "Don't tell me all these kids who memorize the words to Mase, Puff Daddy, Notorious B.I.G., Mary J. Blige and Kirk Franklin can't be taught to say 'I am' and 'he is' and 'we are,'" Ford told Milbank, in defense of the plan to set higher standards for students. He further angered many congressional liberals when he and 22 other House freshmen joined the New Democrat Coalition, an increasingly powerful group of moderate Democrats. At a lunch held by the Democratic Leadership Council (DLC), the parent organization of the New Democrats, Ford said, as quoted by Milbank, "I wouldn't have a white message and a black message. I'd have a message." House Minority Leader Gephardt has openly criticized the New Democrats, charging, Milbank reported, that its members "too often market a political strategy masquerading as policy."

As Election Day 1998 approached, partisan hostilities in the House escalated with the proposed impeachment of President Clinton on charges of perjury and obstruction of justice concerning his affair with one-time White House intern Monica Lewinsky. While the Democrats attempted in vain to prevent impeachment, many other political issues fell by the wayside. In an election largely viewed as a referendum to decide the fate of the president, Ford's Republican challenger, Claude Burdikoff, a Memphis real-estate agent, stood little chance of victory in the largely black and Democratic 9th District. Ford won easily, securing his second term in Washington. But the small increase in the number of House seats gained by Democrats did not stave off the crusade for impeachment. Although Ford—and most other Democrats—voted against the four articles proposed by the House for impeachment, Ford did at times openly criticize the president's behavior. In October 1998, according to Milbank, Ford "had to be gaveled to order twice for declaring on the House floor that the President had 'lied.'"

Since his reelection it has been rumored that Ford is considering a run for the Senate in the near future, and in various conversations he has all but confirmed such rumors. Recently he became one of only two African-American representatives to join the Blue Dog Coalition, a group of moderate-to-conservative Democrats, and he thus further cemented his reputation as a centrist. Observers have suggested that, if he chooses to seek a seat in the Senate, his conservative stances on some issues would help draw support throughout Tennessee, a state that currently has two Republican senators. "It's the absence of philosophy—it's whatever will get votes. It's between nihilism and pollsterism," Steve Cohen, a liberal Democratic Tennessee state senator, told Milbank, referring to Ford's middle-of-the-road views. In his defense, Ford said at a Sunday brunch in Memphis, according to Milbank, "If there's not a shake-up [in Democratic leadership in the House], we might as well get accustomed to being in the minority. We're still saying the same thing we were 24 years ago." When asked if there was a principle he would not compromise, Ford told Milbank, "What's right for my district." "I'm a Democrat—I like spending money," Ford has said, as quoted by Elizabeth Kolbert for the *New Yorker* (October 18 and 25, 1999). "But I like to be able to pay the bills. I don't think that's a black issue or a white issue. I think it's just common sense."

Harold Ford Jr. has been named by *Ebony* magazine as one of the nation's most eligible bachelors.
— M.B.

Suggested Reading: *Commercial Appeal* (on-line) Dec. 21, 1998, with photo; *Congressional Quarterly* p84+ Jan. 4, 1997, with photo; *house.gov/ford* (on-line); *Jet* p4+ Jan. 27, 1997, with photo; *New York Times Magazine* p40+ Oct. 25, 1998, with photos; *People* (on-line) Nov. 18, 1996, with photos; *Politics in America 1998*

Frakes, Jonathan

Aug. 19, 1952– Actor; director. Address: c/o Alder Green & Hasson, 10920 Wilshire Blvd. #1200, Los Angeles, CA 90024-6591

The actor and director Jonathan Frakes is best known for his involvement in the *Star Trek* television and movie series. He played the role of Commander William Riker in the highly successful TV show *Star Trek: The Next Generation* from 1987 to 1994, then made his feature-film debut with the same role in *Star Trek: Generations* (1994), a popular adaptation of the series. In the late 1970s and early 1980s, Frakes found steady work in television, making appearances in such long-running shows as *Barnaby Jones*, *Hart to Hart*, and *Falcon Crest*; his most notable work before *Star Trek: The Next Generation* was in the miniseries *North and South* (1985) and *North and South II* (1986), in which he played Stanley Hazard.

Not long after having secured the role of Riker, second-in-command of the *Starship Enterprise*, Frakes began working his way into the director's chair; to date, he is the only person to have directed episodes of all three spin-offs of the original *Star Trek* series (which aired on NBC from 1966 to 1969): *Star Trek: The Next Generation*, *Star Trek: Deep Space Nine*, and *Star Trek: Voyager*. Among the shows' fans, his directorial efforts have become cult favorites, and it wasn't long before the shows' producers called upon him to direct his first feature film, *Star Trek: First Contact*. Released in

Jonathan Frakes

Greg Lavy/Outline Press

decided to move to L.A. Steady television work on the West Coast soon followed, as he made appearances on long-running programs that included *Barnaby Jones*, *Quincy*, and *Eight Is Enough*. In the 1980s Frakes landed small parts on episodes of *Falcon Crest*, *The Dukes of Hazzard*, *Hill Street Blues*, and *The Fall Guy*. In 1984 he won his most important acting job up to that time—the role of Stanley Hazard, a member of a wealthy family in the years leading up to the Civil War, in the miniseries *North and South*, which was based on a best-selling novel by John Jakes. He reprised the role in the 1986 and 1994 sequels.

In 1987 Frakes auditioned for the role of William Riker on *Star Trek: The Next Generation*, developed by Gene Roddenberry, the creator of the original series. At first, Frakes felt that his chances of landing the part were slim, but Rick Berman, a producer and a longtime colleague of Roddenberry's, decided Frakes was right for the role. "He had a certain quality of charm to him," Berman told Marriott. The show, which premiered in the fall of 1987, went on to become one of the most successful syndicated programs in television history. Frakes and his fellow cast members, Patrick Stewart, Brent Spiner, Gates McFadden, Michael Dorn, LeVar Burton, Marina Sirtis, and Colm Meaney, became popular television successors of the aging original *Star Trek* series cast members William Shatner, Leonard Nimoy, and DeForest Kelley, who were then reprising their roles on the big screen.

Although Frakes's role as the rakish William Riker—second-in-command to Captain Jean-Luc Picard (Stewart)—was his most high-profile assignment to that date, he soon began to develop an interest in directing. With Rich Berman's blessing, Frakes underwent an apprenticeship, spending time in the cutting room and editor's booth and at casting sessions until, after about two years, he was ready to direct an episode himself. His first was "The Offspring," which finds the character Data (Spiner), an android who aspires to become more like a human, acting as a father to a female android he has created. "Jon just got better and better," Berman told Marriott. Of his training as a director, Frakes told *Sci-Fi Talk* (on-line): "Actors make good directors generally. . . . I spent my time at Paramount University doing the TV series and spending about 300 hours in the editing room. . . . I spent a lot of time on the set watching a lot of movies. I knew something about moving the camera, but the editing was a mystery to me. It was a training ground."

By the time *Star Trek: The Next Generation* ceased production, in 1994, Frakes had directed more than a half-dozen episodes. The show went off the air while it was still the number-one-rated syndicated program, and the cast soon capitalized on that popularity with a full-length motion picture, *Star Trek: Generations* (1994). Also featuring William Shatner—reprising his role as Captain James T. Kirk from the original *Star Trek* series—

1996—with a story line that included the *Enterprise* crew's arch-nemeses, the evil cyborg race known as the Borg—the film went on to earn $145 million worldwide. Frakes followed up this success with *Star Trek: Insurrection*, released in 1998. It, too, became a worldwide hit. Since then, the six-foot-plus, dark-haired actor/director has signed a deal with Miramax to direct the sequel to Arnold Schwarzenegger's 1990 mega-hit *Total Recall*, due for release in 2000. With Schwarzenegger now set to reprise his lead role in the film, many industry insiders have speculated that, if the film is a hit, Frakes may be able to pull off what other *Star Trek* stars have been unable to do—establish a legitimate movie career *outside* the sci-fi franchise.

Jonathan Frakes was born on August 19, 1952 in Bethlehem, Pennsylvania. As a psychology major at Pennsylvania State University, he discovered acting by accident, after wandering into the student-run college theater one day. He eventually changed his major, graduating in 1974 with a degree in theater arts, and went on to study drama for a time at Harvard University, in Cambridge, Massachusetts. He then moved to New York City and took up the life of a struggling actor—auditioning by day, waiting tables by night. His former boss, a restaurant owner, told Michel Marriott for the *New York Times* (December 18, 1996) that he "always charmed the customers." Frakes's first major job was in the chorus of the Broadway musical *Shenandoah* in 1976, and he was later hired to play a disturbed Vietnam vet in the short-lived soap opera *The Doctors*. In 1979, after his television career had begun to flower, with guest spots on such shows as *Charlie's Angels* and *The Waltons*, Frakes

the film, directed by David Carson, did not feature Frakes's character prominently. Despite tepid reviews, it performed respectably at the box office.

No longer constrained by the demands of a regular television series, Frakes, over the next few years, went on to direct various television programs, most notably several episodes of *Star Trek: Deep Space Nine*—the follow-up series to *Star Trek: The Next Generation*—and *Star Trek: Voyager*, the third and newest installment of the franchise. He did some work apart from *Star Trek* as well, directing episodes of *Diagnosis Murder* and *University Hospital*. In 1995 Frakes became embroiled in a minor controversy when he hosted a program for Fox television entitled *Alien Autopsy: Fact or Fiction?* The show included a film purportedly depicting a humanoid figure being operated on by a group of American physicians. The 17-minute, fuzzy, black-and-white tape—reportedly filmed in 1947—spurred *Alien Autopsy* to unexpectedly high ratings: so high, in fact, that Fox chose to run the program again a few weeks later. Richard Corliss, among others, questioned the film's authenticity, asking in *Time* (November 27, 1995), "Why does the film go so conveniently out of focus at crucial moments? Why is the camerawork so jumpy, in the modern *ER* fashion, instead of having the smoothness that even World War II combat cameramen aimed for? Why hasn't the original film stock been submitted to Eastman Kodak, which has a standing offer to do a chemical analysis that would verify if it was indeed manufactured in 1947?" Frakes, apparently not bothered by the controversy, would later host *Beyond Belief: Fact or Fiction?*, which focused on similar supernatural subject matter.

In 1996, when Berman was in need of a director for the upcoming film based on *Star Trek: The Next Generation*, he turned to Frakes. *Star Trek: First Contact* was released to positive reviews. "Under the suave direction of Jonathan Frakes, who also plays the Enterprise's second-in-command, the movie glides along with purpose and style," Richard Corliss wrote for *Time* (November 25, 1996). The film went on to earn well over $100 million worldwide, and Frakes suddenly became a hot directing commodity. As a result of the film's success, Frakes was able to ink a substantial deal with Paramount Pictures, according to which he would direct an unspecified number of movies through his own company, Goepp Circle Productions. In 1997 Frakes agreed to direct the next franchise film installment, *Star Trek: Insurrection*.

Initial buzz in the industry was that the film, with its familiar-sounding plot (involving a fountain of youth–type planet), was going to be a commercial disappointment. Gary Dauphin, in the *Village Voice* (December 22, 1998), reviewed the film upon its release: "Blame it on the aliens, but odd-numbered *Star Trek* movies tend to suck. The best flicks—from number two, *The Wrath of Khan* (probably the best in the series), to number eight, *First Contact*—are all even-numbered entries in the

franchise . . . ; the latest *Star Trek* flick, *Insurrection*, is the ninth, and although it doesn't suck as completely as some ignoble, odd-numbered low points, it doesn't exactly boldly go where no one has gone before." Fueled by heavy promotion and the presence of Academy Award–winning actor F. Murray Abraham as the diabolical alien villain Ru'afo, the film, despite the lukewarm reviews, went on to become Frakes's second box-office hit as a director.

In early 1999 Frakes announced that he had signed a contract with Miramax to direct the sequel to the 1990 Arnold Schwarzenegger vehicle *Total Recall*. A few weeks after Frakes signed on for the project, Schwarzenegger agreed to act in the film. Many industry insiders have predicted that if the film is a hit, Frakes may become an A-list director in Hollywood—not simply a "director of *Star Trek* films." He has hinted that he would like to direct a romantic comedy and, perhaps, do a bit more acting. "I would actually love to be on somebody else's movie for a while, and just be an actor," he told Christopher Brandon for *Roughcut.com* (January 11, 1999, on-line). Being an actor and director simultaneously, he continued, is "hard. It's exhausting. It's stressful. It's fabulous. It's exciting. It's satisfying." Recently, Frakes co-starred, along with Linda Cardellini, in the television miniseries *The Lot*. He also served as an executive producer on two projects for the small screen: the made-for-TV film *Dying to Live*, in which he also starred, and the WB Network series *Roswell*, a teen drama about a group of high-school students who are secretly aliens.

Frakes told *Sci-Fi Talk* (on-line) on the subject of his directorial technique, "My acting teacher taught me to steal from the good ones. [Before the filming of *Star Trek: Insurrection*,] I watched *Alien* and *Aliens*. Obviously Ridley Scott and James Cameron know [how] to shoot action. I watch[ed] *Jaws* a couple more times. We obviously pay homage to *Close Encounters* [*of the Third Kind*] at the end [of the film]. And Kubrick's *2001*[*: A Space Oddessey*] is paid homage to on the outside of the ship. So I try to steal from the good ones." He told Michelle Erica Green for *mania.com* (on-line), "People [in show business] always kid and say, 'God, I would hate to have to work for a living.' But it's a lot of work—it's work because it's demanding, and it takes a lot of preparation and concentration. But it's a wonderful place to be creative and to play, too."

Jonathan Frakes is married to the actress Genie Francis, best known for her role as Laura Spencer on the long-running soap opera *General Hospital*. The couple have two children. — M.B.

Suggested Reading: *Allmovie.com* (on-line); *IMDB.com* (on-line); *Mania.com* (on-line); *Mr.Showbiz.com* (on-line) June 11, 1997; *New York Times* C p12 Dec. 18, 1996, with photo; *New York Times* (on-line) Dec. 11, 1998, with photos; *Roughcut.com* (on-line), with photo; *Sci.-*

Fi Talk (on-line); *Time* p106 Nov. 25, 1996, with photo; *Time* (on-line) Nov. 27, 1995; *Village Voice* p138 Dec. 22, 1998, with photo

Selected Television Shows: as actor—*Bare Essence*, 1982; *Paper Dolls*, 1984; *North and South*, 1985, *North and South II*, 1986; *Star Trek: The Next Generation*, 1987; as director—*Star Trek: The Next Generation*, 1987–94; *Star Trek: Deep Space Nine*, 1993; *Diagnosis Murder*, 1993; *University Hospital*, 1994; *Star Trek: Voyager*, 1995

Selected Films: as actor—*Star Trek: First Contact*, 1996; *Star Trek: Insurrection*, 1998; as director—*Star Trek: First Contact*, 1996; *Star Trek: Insurrection*, 1998

Sigrid Estrada/Courtesy of Delacorte Press

Franken, Al

May 21, 1951– Comedian; writer; actor; political humorist. Address: c/o Leading Authorities, Inc., 919 18th St. N.W., Suite 500, Washington, DC 20006

In a 1996 interview for the *Chicago Tribune*, James Warren asked the comedian and political humorist Al Franken why he chose to title his second book *Rush Limbaugh Is a Big Fat Idiot and Other Observations.* "First of all [Limbaugh] is very, very fat. The guy is enormous. He is very, very, very fat," Franken answered, referring to the popular, politically conservative radio commentator. "I really should have called it *Rush Limbaugh Is a Big Fat Liar*, but I felt that was too confrontational." A

touch more seriously, Franken explained to Richard Blow for *Mother Jones* (November 1996) why he chose Limbaugh as the unifying target of his collection of satiric political essays. "Rush does a disservice to everybody. Anybody who deliberately propagandizes with lies should be held up to scorn and ridicule." With equal parts punch line–driven anecdote and statistical research, Franken's book assaults right-wing Republican ideology and leaves little doubt about which side of the political fence he occupies. The formula and choice of title worked: the book sold out its first printing—100,000 copies—in a matter of weeks, held the top spot on the *New York Times*'s best-seller list for over a month, and to date has sold nearly a million copies. In addition, Franken's recording of the book won him a Grammy for best comedy album. Al Franken has established himself as a political force—or farce—to be reckoned with.

A Harvard graduate who has always looked toward the Washington, D.C., beltway with a comedic eye, Franken first exposed his brand of political satire to a national audience as a member of the original writing staff for the television show *Saturday Night Live*. During his 15 years with the show, Franken became best known for his portrayal of the fictitious Stuart Smalley, who hosts a late-night cable self-help show. This character, whose treacly inspirational messages lampooned pop psychology, spawned a book (*I'm Good Enough, I'm Smart Enough, and Doggone It, People Like Me*), and a film, (*Stuart Saves His Family*). For his work on *Saturday Night Live*, which he left in 1995, Franken was awarded five Emmys, four for writing and one for producing. In March 1998 Franken debuted his sitcom, *Lateline*, a send-up of network news programs; for that show, which aired for a year, Franken wore three hats, as co-writer, producer, and star. More recently he published his third book, *Why Not Me?*, his account of his fictitious bid for the 2000 Democratic presidential nomination.

Born on May 21, 1951 in New York City and raised in St. Louis Park, Minnesota, a middle-class suburb of Minneapolis, Franken has traced his roots as a comedian and satirist back to elementary school. The girls in his second-grade class staged "this really insipid show, 'I'm a Little Teapot,'" Franken recalled for *People* (July 20, 1992). Franken countered the girls' performance with a parody of his own. "I got the other boys together, and we dressed in drag [and staged it]. The girls were in tears." Franken apparently got little encouragement to pursue a career as a performer. "My parents both did community theater," he told Lloyd Grove for the *Washington Post* (March 17, 1998). "But the idea of show business was really foreign [to them]." Franken's political interests, on the other hand, were piqued by his parents, Joe, a printing salesman, and Phoebe, a real-estate agent, during the 1960 Democratic and Republican national conventions. Now a longtime Democrat, Franken sided at the time with his father, a Richard

Nixon supporter, against his mother, who backed John F. Kennedy.

In high school Franken and a friend, Tom Davis, formed the comedy team Franken and Davis. The duo had moderate success doing stand-up routines in Minneapolis clubs, but they took a hiatus when Al enrolled at Harvard University, in Cambridge, Massachusetts, to study behavioral sciences. In 1973 Franken graduated and resumed his collaboration with Davis, this time in Los Angeles. Word of the pair's talent spread, and in the summer of 1975 Franken and Davis were hired by television producer Lorne Michaels to write for his newly created sketch-comedy show, *Saturday Night Live.* "We were the only people who Lorne Michaels hired but didn't meet," Franken said, as quoted in a profile of him on NBC's Web site. "I thought even then that it would be a huge hit. Before then, our generation had not been allowed to be on TV, even though we had grown up on it."

Saturday Night Live did indeed became a huge hit, and it is frequently cited as one of the most influential television shows of the 1970s. Franken and Davis's specialty was political satire. Among the more enduring sketches from their early work on the show was a parody of Richard Nixon's last days in the Oval Office and a series of skits making fun of Nixon's successor, Gerald Ford. Franken and Davis crafted a mock campaign slogan for Ford—"If he's so dumb, why is he President?"—and wrote the popular recurring bits in which Chevy Chase portrayed Ford as a klutz. "And arguably Gerald Ford was the best athlete who was ever in the White House," Franken noted to Richard Blow. "He tripped once coming off Air Force One. He fell once, and that was it." Franken and Davis themselves appeared on the show occasionally.

In 1980 Lorne Michaels left *Saturday Night Live.* His departure sparked a mass exodus of talent from the program, including Franken and Davis, who decided to make a joint foray into the movie business. Success in motion pictures proved elusive, however, and in 1985 the partners returned to *Saturday Night Live.* During his second run with the show, Franken's role expanded beyond writing to include frequent featured performances and producing. He created the narcissistic "Al Franken Decade" persona, who defined current events based on how they would "affect me, Al Franken." Like most of his characters, this persona became a vehicle for Franken's commentary on societal trends. The 1960s were commonly referred to as "The Us Decade"; accordingly, the 1970s were tagged "The Me Decade." "Our generation has defined its decades in terms of themselves," Franken observed to Phil Rosenthal for the *Chicago Tribune* (December 22, 1989). "And about this time 10 years ago, I noticed a lot of articles in which experts took to defining the upcoming '80s in terms of their own expertise. I remember there was a 'My Turn' column in *Newsweek* in which an energy expert predicted that the '80s would be 'the energy conservation decade,' that sort of thing, and I thought, it's just going to be 'The Me Decade' all over again."

Similarly, Franken created his most famous alter ego, the platitudinal 12-step-program addict Stuart Smalley, as his satiric nod to the growing popularity of New Age enlightenment, pop psychology, and self-help literature among Americans in the 1990s. The success of Stuart Smalley led Franken to collect Smalley's treacly aphorisms into his first best-selling book, *I'm Good Enough, I'm Smart Enough, and Doggone It, People Like Me* (1992), which in turn provided the basis for the film *Stuart Saves His Family* (1995). The movie, which Franken hoped would stand out among the many film adaptations of *Saturday Night Live* sketches, came at a critical juncture in Franken's career. "I've spent the last five years or so doing *Saturday Night Live* and doing outside stuff, on the theory that someday *Saturday Night Live* would end and I could move—laterally—into whatever career I was doing," he was quoted as saying by Scott Williams in the *Chicago Tribune* (April 10, 1995). "I actually think I've gotten to that point, now, where I can do that. And now that I've gotten to that point, I don't know what I'm doing. I have no clue." Despite generally positive reviews, *Stuart Saves His Family* was a commercial flop.

Earlier, Franken had found success as the executive producer of Luis Mandoki's film *When a Man Loves a Woman* (1994), which Franken also co-wrote, with veteran screenwriter Ron Bass (who had won an Oscar for his script for the film *Rain Man). When a Man Loves a Woman* is a love story about a young couple, played by Meg Ryan and Andy Garcia, struggling to maintain their marriage in the face of alcoholism. Franken had approached Bass years before with an idea for a comedy about alcoholism and co-dependency. As the two writers collaborated on the project, it evolved into a drama that focused less on the alcoholic's perspective and more on that of the person who has to live with the alcoholic. This ambitious project was well received critically and performed well at the box office, despite its limited release. "The strength of the screenplay by Ronald Bass and Al Franken is that it pays close attention to the feelings of both characters," Roger Ebert wrote for the *Chicago Sun-Times* (May 6, 1994, on-line). "Franken writes and plays the 12-step guru Stuart Smalley on *Saturday Night Live.* In the *SNL* bits, the jargon of 12-step groups is kidded. In the screenplay, the movie understands how AA helps alcoholics create a language to describe their feelings and deal with them." Franken, who has said he has had personal experiences similar to those portrayed in the film, furthered Ebert's point. "What people don't understand is that co-dependency is considered a disease by the rehab community," he told Bernard Weinraub for the *New York Times* (April 24, 1994). "People who are co-dependent do as much crazy stuff as alcoholics do."

Given the mixed success of his movie outings, when Franken finally chose to leave *Saturday Night Live* after the 1995 season, he did so with some trepidation. "*SNL* was not a place to get rich as a performer," Franken told Lloyd Grove. "But then if you're a writer, a valuable writer, you can get lots of money. When I was producer-writer, I was doing very well." In addition to the financial stability he was giving up, Franken was nervous about losing a vehicle for his comedy. "I felt a little less in sync with the show—which could have been as much my fault as the show's fault," he said to Richard Blow. "But I was still very happy if I wrote something good, and it went on, and it was really funny. So losing that forum was scary."

The risk paid off, however, as Franken came into his own as a political humorist the following year. He had begun building his reputation as a humorous political pundit in 1988, as a commentator for CNN's coverage of the Democratic National Convention. In 1992 he had anchored the cable channel Comedy Central's coverage of both parties' conventions and the presidential election, called *Indecision '92*, and was touted by media critics as the "Walter Cronkite of the '90s." Again in 1996 Franken was asked by Comedy Central to offer commentary on the national conventions. This time he was paired with Arianna Huffington, the outspoken, Greek-born conservative who first gained notice among Republicans through her husband, former California congressman Michael Huffington. The unlikely chemistry between Huffington and Franken resulted in spirited repartee and drew widespread praise from the media. In that same year Franken published *Rush Limbaugh Is a Big Fat Idiot and Other Observations*, which brought him national attention as a political satirist. Despite the repeated potshots Franken has taken at Limbaugh's girth—the book's index, for example, includes entries devoted to the talk-show host's size—he has noted that the book's true focus is not Limbaugh's eating habits. ("No one is more sensitive to the issue of overeating than the creator of Stuart Smalley," Franken told one reporter.) Rather, it was his status as the most vocal and popular of right-wing conservative commentators that made Limbaugh a natural target for Franken. "The reason I chose Limbaugh is first of all, when I made the decision, it was late '94, right before the congressional elections," he told Mark Schapiro in an interview for *Salon* (February 1996, on-line). "He was this huge power, he was being called the 'Majority Maker.' . . . And I listened to him, I just listened to him. And I thought, how does this guy get away with this? . . . Someone's got to do something that's funny. Someone's got to do something in his face." Despite Limbaugh's claim that his opinions reflect those of the majority, Franken saw his own views as more representative of those of his fellow citizens. "I'm part of the mushball middle," Franken told Marla Williams for the *Seattle Times* (March 11, 1996, on-line). "I consider 'confused' the majority position because, thankfully, most people would rather be uncertain some of the time than 100 percent positive all the time—even when they're wrong."

Rush Limbaugh Is a Big Fat Idiot received universally excellent critical notices. Commending, for instance, Franken's glib suggestion for cutting the budgets of Medicare and NASA by shooting the elderly into space, Susan Shapiro wrote for the *New York Times Book Review* (January 21, 1996), "Mr. Franken . . . is a surprisingly witty social commentator." Similarly, John D. Spalding described the book in *Christian Century* (March 20–27, 1996) as "a brilliant and wickedly funny satire of politics and public discourse." Spalding concluded, "Franken's blend of knowledge, appealing modesty (not unlike Stuart Smalley's), and hilarious zingers make this book a great read."

True to his statement, Franken and his book have remained in Rush Limbaugh's face. "My publisher sent the book to him . . . with a cover letter I wrote that said, 'Dear Rush: Al thinks it may help sales of the book if you mention it on your show,'" Franken told Mark Schapiro. According to various sources, Limbaugh has yet to mention the book publicly. Furthermore, Franken has quipped that he could write another book, based on Limbaugh's own *See, I Told You So*, the follow-up to his *The Way Things Ought to Be*. Franken threatened that the title for this volume would be *See, I Told You He Was a Big Fat Idiot*.

In the spring of 1998, Franken, a confessed news junkie, premiered his television sitcom *Lateline*. The series, starring and co-created by Franken, was a comedic behind-the-scenes look at a Washington, D.C.–based late-night network news program and the quirky relationships among its producers and on-air talent. To get a feel for the industry, Franken and his co-creator, John Markus, spent a lot of time backstage at their rival network's popular news magazine *Nightline*. "It's amazing how much access you can get when you bring a dozen cappuccinos and a box of muffins," Franken told Margaret Carlson for *Time* (March 23, 1998). With echoes of the popular sitcom *Murphy Brown*, which also parodied television news programs, *Lateline* booked various politicians and political celebrities to play themselves on the program; Dick Gephardt, the minority leader of the House of Representatives, once appeared as a guest. According to Lloyd Grove, a screening of that particular episode held at the National Press Club, in Washington, drew big laughs. This reaction among government insiders was exactly what Franken had hoped for. "I want a buzz in Washington that it's safe to be on our show. You know, that we're going to treat you well," Franken told Grove. "The message is: If we can make Gephardt look good, then we can make anyone look good."

Lateline premiered on NBC in mid-season, and the timing prevented Franken and Markus from offering their take on the sex scandal involving President Clinton, which would have played right into the show's premise. Instead, they took out a full-page ad in the *New York Times* in March 1998 to publish an open letter to Kenneth Starr, the independent counsel. The ad read, "Dear Ken: Please subpoena us. We know things." Despite positive reviews, *Lateline* never gathered popular momentum, perhaps because of its poorly timed, midseason debut, and in March 1999 it was cancelled.

Franken continued his political musings with the publication of his third book, *Why Not Me? The Inside Story of the Making and Unmaking of the Franken Presidency* (1999). This comic work tells of Franken's imaginary rise to the White House in the coming 2000 election; his successful campaign platform is founded on lowering ATM fees. Unlike Franken's previous work, which pointedly satirized specific conservative ideologies, *Why Not Me?* sends up the entire election-campaign process. "The idea was to create a scenario where I could win," Franken told David Postman for the *Seattle Times* (February 15, 1999, on-line). "And to me, that's the scathing part of the satire, that I could actually win." In his review of the book for the *New York Times Book Review* (February 14, 1999, on-line), the humorist P. J. O'Rourke, whose political views are diametrically opposite Franken's, questioned the necessity of such a work at this time in history. "Never has there been a moment when the American political system stood less in need of parody. Al Franken's *Why Not Me?* is the spoof for which these times do not call." Despite his reservations about the book, O'Rourke wrote, "Franken makes a manful attempt to lampoon a travesty, mock the behavior of zanies, and laugh in the face of jokes. And the results are, in part, very funny."

Al Franken lives in New York City with his wife, Franni, and their two teenage children. He is fond of pointing out that his marriage, which has endured since 1975, would make the staunchest socially conservative Republican proud. In addition to his work on television, Franken is highly sought after on the lecture circuit, which, as he told Richard Blow, is "a little bit more interesting [than stand-up]. Plus, the audience isn't drunk." Franken commands speaking fees in the tens of thousands of dollars for a single engagement. But, he confided to Blow, "I speak free to the Democrats and charge the Republicans."

Assessing his career, Franken explained to Mark Schapiro, "I consider myself foremost a comedian. I'm a comedian who pays a lot of attention to politics, because I'm a citizen. But I don't know if I want to commit my career to politics." Still, it would be hard to imagine Al Franken's comedy devoid of political commentary, since both are closely linked to the delight he clearly takes in observing people and society. — T.J.F.

Suggested Reading: *Chicago Tribune* II p3 Jan. 21, 1996, with photo; *Franken Web* (on-line); *Mother Jones* p22+ Nov. 1996, with photos; *Newsweek* p75 Feb. 19, 1996; *People* p100+ July 20, 1992, with photo; *Salon* (on-line) Feb. 1996; *Washington Post* D p1 Mar. 17, 1998, with photo

Selected Books: *I'm Good Enough, I'm Smart Enough, and Doggone It, People Like Me*, 1992; *Rush Limbaugh Is a Big Fat Idiot and Other Observations*, 1996; *Why Not Me? The Inside Story of the Making and Unmaking of the Franken Presidency*, 1999

Selected Films: as actor and screenwriter—*Stuart Saves His Family*, 1995; as executive producer and co-screenwriter—*When a Man Loves a Woman*, 1994

Selected Television Shows: *Saturday Night Live*, 1975–80, 1985–95; *Lateline*, 1998–99

Miriam Berkley/Courtesy of Farrar, Straus & Giroux

Galassi, Jonathan

Nov. 4, 1949– Editor in chief of Farrar, Straus & Giroux; translator; poet. Address: c/o Farrar, Straus & Giroux, 19 Union Sq. W., New York, NY 10003-3304

As editor in chief of Farrar, Straus & Giroux, one of New York City's eight major book publishers, Jonathan Galassi cannot avoid grappling with economic realities, but he does not allow his business concerns to taint his idealism, which he has retained since he entered his profession, in 1973, when he was in his early 20s. "A lot of publishing is about conveying the knowledge people have: not just today's insight, but also yesterday's, keeping those things in circulation," he told Craig A. Lambert for *Harvard Magazine* (November/December 1997, on-line). "There's a component of altruistic activity. Of course it's a business—it has to be—but it's also a cultural institution, contributing to the social weal." Renowned for his superlative editorial skills, Galassi has worked with three winners of the Nobel Prize for literature—Nadine Gordimer, Seamus Heaney, and Derek Walcott—and such other notable literary figures as Harold Brodkey, Alice McDermott, Luc Sante, Susan Sontag, John McPhee, Thomas L. Friedman, Ian Frazier, Jamaica Kincaid, Edna O'Brien, Oscar Hijuelos, Calvin Trillin, Scott Turow, Tom Wolfe, and Robert Pinsky, among many others. The announced heir apparent to Roger W. Straus Jr., the president, chief executive officer, and co-founder of Farrar, Straus & Giroux, Galassi is himself a published poet, and he has won universal praise for his translations from Italian into English of the poetry and prose of the Nobel laureate Eugenio Montale.

The eldest of three siblings, Jonathan White Galassi was born in Seattle, Washington, on November 4, 1949 to Gerard Goodwin Galassi, a lawyer for the United States Justice Department, and Dorothea Johnston (White) Galassi. His brother, Peter Galassi, is the curator of photography at the Museum of Modern Art, in New York. Galassi's paternal grandfather, a skilled craftsman, immigrated to the United States from Italy; though the terrazzo business that he built was only moderately lucrative, he made it possible for his children and grandchildren to gain Ivy-League credentials. When Jonathan Galassi was a child, his family moved from Seattle to Washington, D.C., then settled in the small Massachusetts town of Plympton. Socially awkward and bookish, young Jonathan relished visits from his grandmother, who would bring her grandchildren a fresh supply of reading material. As a teenager Galassi attended the prestigious private prep school Phillips Exeter Academy, in Exeter, New Hampshire. At Exeter, "I really got my education," he told Tom Prince for *New York* (December 21–28, 1992); while there, he developed his deep interest in and love for literature, and also, he recalled to Janny Scott for the *New York Times* (January 20, 1999), "the sense of a vocation in literature."

Like his father, Galassi attended Harvard University, in Cambridge, Massachusetts. As an undergraduate he was an editor of the *Harvard Lampoon*, the school's famous satiric magazine, and served as president of the *Harvard Advocate*, the campus literary magazine. His teachers at Harvard included two of the country's finest poets, Robert Lowell and Elizabeth Bishop. He remembers the latter as an especially fine teacher and an "example of greatness," in his words, thanks to what he described to Scott as Bishop's "combination of modesty, very high ambition and attainment." Another of his professors, the essayist Roger Rosenblatt, recalled to Prince that as an undergraduate Galassi had "a cheerful intelligence when everybody else thought it was fashionable to be despondent."

After graduating magna cum laude from Harvard, in 1971, with an A.B. degree, Galassi entered Christ's College, Cambridge University, in Eng-

land, on a Marshall scholarship. There, he continued to study literature. During his two years overseas, he traveled in Italy, where he learned Italian with the goal of reading the works of Dante as originally written. In thinking about his professional life, he ruled out an academic career, because, he told Lambert, he "didn't feel comfortable with the Yale approach [to studying literature] that was in vogue—semiotics, deconstruction. It just didn't feel congenial to me. I wanted to be more involved with the making of contemporary literature than with analyzing the literature of the past."

After returning to the United States, in 1973, Galassi accepted an editorial internship at the Boston-headquartered publishing firm Houghton Mifflin. Two years later he married Susan Grace, an art historian, and transferred to the New York City offices of Houghton Mifflin. In time he became one of the company's youngest senior editors. Among the writers with whom he worked was Pat Conroy, whose novels *The Great Santini* and *The Lords of Discipline* were published in 1976 and 1980, respectively. On his own time Galassi edited a collection of poems by John Cornford, a British volunteer in the Spanish Civil War who was killed in battle in 1936, at the age of 21. *Understand the Weapon, Understand the Wound: Selected Writings of John Cornford* was published by the Ecco Press in 1976. Also that year Cambridge University awarded Galassi a master's degree.

In 1981 Galassi left Houghton Mifflin to join the staff of Random House, in New York. "What I was most interested in, and probably best at, was working with new writers," he explained to Craig Lambert. "I thought Houghton Mifflin was too dowdy and not willing to take enough risks, and that this brash, highly successful company [Random House] would do that. It turned out that Houghton Mifflin was actually more willing to take chances on the kinds of authors I liked than Random House was." Shortly after Galassi's arrival, the owner of Random House, S. I. "Si" Newhouse, recruited Howard Kaminsky from Warner Books to become the company's next publisher, charging him with making Random House more profitable and more competitive with such publishing giants as Simon & Schuster. Galassi soon began to feel uncomfortable in his job. "It was never the right fit," he told Craig Lambert. He was especially disappointed when Random House turned down his recommendation to publish Pat Conroy's next book. "That was a very painful experience for Pat and me," Galassi told Prince. Shortly afterward, in 1986, Random House sent Galassi packing. "It was done in a collegial way," Galassi told Prince. "Basically, Howard [Kaminsky] said, 'You know, why don't you find another place to work?' So I did. At Farrar, Straus."

Despite ranking eighth among New York City's major publishing houses in total revenue, Farrar, Straus & Giroux (FSG) may be tops in prestige, rivaled only by Alfred A. Knopf in terms of the consistent high quality and artistic soundness of its titles. FSG's publishing philosophy proved congenial for Galassi. Within his first year there, in what an FSG Web page described as "practically his first acquisition," Galassi inked a deal with Scott Turow, to publish the lawyer turned writer's legal thriller *Presumed Innocent.* Turow accepted Galassi's offer even though it was far lower than the highest bid, because he considered FSG the most prestigious publisher in the United States and because years before, Galassi had spent an hour on the telephone with him critiquing one of Turow's early literary efforts. Turow hung on a wall of his study the letter in which Galassi had rejected the novel. "Every time Jonathan sees it, he's embarrassed all over again," Turow told Tom Prince. "He squirms like a boy. . . . It always seems like the joke is on him, probably because he's *always* too kind to say what we both know: The novel wasn't very good." Lauded by various reviewers as "packed with data, rich in incident, painstakingly imagined," "superbly crafted," and as "combining whodunit suspense with an elegant style and philosophical voice," *Presumed Innocent* became one of the major commercial and critical successes of 1986; it remained on the *New York Times* best-seller list for 44 consecutive weeks, sold over 700,000 hardback and four million paperback copies in the United States, and was translated into 18 languages. The story was optioned by Hollywood for a film of the same name; starring Harrison Ford, it was the 10th-highest-grossing film of 1990.

Described by authors he works with as part editor, part psychiatrist, and part friend, Galassi is said to possess a talent for drawing out a writer's best work without heavy-handed criticism. "He's a perfect sounding board," Alice McDermott, whose warmly received debut novel, *A Bigamist's Daughter*, came out in 1982, said to Tom Prince. "He asks you what *you* want the book to be—he doesn't start giving directions." In November 1995 another FSG novelist, Tom Wolfe, approached Galassi with a 1,000-page manuscript that had taken him eight years to write. While having lunch together, Wolfe and Galassi traded stories about their experiences in Atlanta, Georgia. After Wolfe remarked that he wished he had set his new novel in Atlanta rather than New York City, Galassi suggested that he change the setting. "The way he said it gave me the confidence to jettison literally hundreds of pages," Wolfe recalled to Janny Scott. "Jonathan has great aplomb and is tremendously courteous and not at all pushy. But he can make up his mind rapidly when it gets down to literary matters." Wolfe's book, *A Man in Full* (1998), went on to settle comfortably for weeks on best-seller lists across the country, and it was nominated for the 1999 National Book Award for fiction, losing out to another Galassi-edited work, Alice McDermott's *Charming Billy.*

During an on-line discussion sponsored by Barnes & Noble in April 1999, Galassi said, "I think that Farrar, Straus has tried to stay close to the mis-

sion that it developed over the years of publishing writers—of really being interested in the quality of the writing. Not just publishing ideas or books but trying to find real writers of all different kinds—poets, novelists, essayists, journalists. . . . First of all, we look for that intrinsic strength of the writing, the originality of the use of language, and we look for freshness—someone saying something that hasn't been said before. Someone who is writing with originality and genuineness. And we also of course look for things that are about issues that are of concern to people. But it starts with the writing itself."

Meanwhile, as Galassi was rising in the publishing world, he had also become immersed in another literary passion: translating works by the Italian poet, journalist, essayist, and short-story writer Eugenio Montale. In 1975 the poet Frank Bidart, knowing that Galassi had learned Italian, asked him to translate a poem by Montale for the journal *Ploughshares.* Later that year Montale won the Nobel Prize for literature, instantly making Galassi a translator of note in literary circles. In 1977 Galassi guest-edited a special issue—focusing on Montale—of the literary magazine *Pequod.* Upon completing that project he began delving more deeply into Montale's prose. *The Second Life of Art*, a collection of Galassi's translations into English of Montale's essays, was published in 1982, one year after the Nobel laureate's death. It contains pieces on art, music, cinema, social issues, and literature and includes the address, titled "Is Poetry Still Possible?," that Montale gave at the 1975 Nobel Prize ceremony. In the *Times Literary Supplement* (August 5, 1983), Judith Davies wrote, "Galassi improves on previous translations of Montale in preserving something of a style which is non-academic and conversational, yet urgent and precise too." "Galassi is at his best with the vivid, witty vignettes of personalities that Montale regularly turned out," Bernard McCabe declared in the *Nation* (April 30, 1983): "the poet meeting Italo Svevo for the first time, or edging around André Malraux, or on the track of Stravinsky in Venice, . . . or being insulted by the aged satyr Brancusi in his filthy Paris studio—the book is worth its price for such brilliant passages."

Galassi's next Montale collection was *Otherwise: Last and First Poems of Eugenio Montale* (1986). In 1984, in a project that occupied him part-time for 14 years, Galassi began translating Montale's early verse. The works appear in both English and Italian in *Collected Poems 1920–1954* (1998). Containing some 200 pages of Galassi's scholarly commentary, *Collected Poems 1920–1954* was widely praised as a model of Montale scholarship and artistic translation. In a "brilliant afterword," Tim Parks wrote for the *New York Review of Books* (February 4, 1999), Galassi "offers the best short account I have yet come across of the nature, import, and elusive content of Montale's work. . . . The voluminous notes Galassi provides, absolutely indispensable for a fruitful reading of Montale, the frequent quotations of critics and sources and letters, makes us aware of a huge joint effort in which the reader is invited to take part." During the on-line discussion sponsored by Barnes & Noble, Galassi told one questioner that he is "still obsessed" with Montale's work.

Galassi is also a poet in his own right. His first collection of original work, *Morning Run* (1988), impressed several critics. "While sophisticated in form," Janny Scott wrote, Galassi's poems are "intimate and revealing, infused with what the poet Frank Bidart called a 'vulnerability and poignancy about the inner life.'" Galassi's second volume of original verse, *North Street*, is scheduled for publication in the spring of 2000. Poetry rarely generates profits for publishers—and according to Galassi, that is precisely why it is valuable. "The role of poetry in the culture is stronger than it has been at other times," he noted to Craig Lambert in 1997. "A secret of the current success of poetry is that it's not commercial. It's one of the only things around that doesn't have dollar signs attached to it: it's authentic, priceless, hors de combat. That's a fundamental point of its attraction; it comes out of some necessity—people write poetry because they have to do it."

Galassi served as poetry editor for the *Paris Review* from 1978 to 1988. Since 1994 he has been president of the Academy of American Poets, a nonprofit organization that supports readers and writers of poetry. The academy sponsors contests and awards, coordinates public readings, and oversees the promotion of National Poetry Month (April). Galassi lives in the New York City borough of Brooklyn with his wife, Susan Grace Galassi, and their teenage daughters, Isabel and Beatrice. His wife is the assistant curator of the Frick museum (officially, the Frick Collection), a New York City mansionful of artworks acquired by the 19th–20th-century American industrialist Henry Clay Frick. An expanded version of Susan Grace Galassi's doctoral dissertation was published as *Picasso's Variations on the Masters*, in 1996. Jonathan Galassi's latest book is his translation from the Italian of Paolo Guarnieri's *A Boy Named Giotto*, a story for children ages four to eight about the early years of the pre-Renaissance Italian painter, sculptor, and architect Giotto di Bondone.

Galassi told Craig Lambert that he always attends the annual book sale held in the Connecticut town where he and his family spend weekends and vacations. "I give the book sale a lot of books," he said, "and also buy quite a few. From then on, that book has a potential life in our family—visitors, children, even grandchildren could read it. As a commercial object it has lost its connection to the publisher; it has only one chance to earn its author and publisher money. But as an object that can communicate, it could last a hundred years." — T.J.F.

Suggested Reading: *Harvard Magazine* (on-line) Nov./Dec. 1997, with photos; *New York* p88+ Dec. 21–28, 1992, with photo; *New York Times* E p1+ Jan. 20, 1999, with photos; *Who's Who in America, 1999*

Selected Books: as translator—*The Second Life of Art: Selected Essays of Eugenio Montale*, 1982; *Otherwise: Last and First Poems of Eugenio Montale*, 1984; *[Eugenio Montale] Collected Poems 1920–1954*, 1998; *A Boy Named Giotto*, 1999; as poet—*Morning Run*, 1988

Courtesy of Ballantine Books

Garcia, Cristina

July 4, 1959– Writer. Address: c/o Random House, Inc., 201 E. 50th St., New York, NY 10022

Cristina Garcia is one of the most prominent Cuban-American novelists of the 1990s. *Dreaming in Cuban* (1992), her first novel, received nearly universal critical praise and went on to be nominated for a National Book Award. The story of the del Pinos, a family whose members are widely scattered, the book explores the complexities that arise when one is displaced from one's native culture. "*Dreaming in Cuban* is beautifully written in language that is by turns languid and sensual, curt and surprising . . . ," Thulani Davis wrote in the *New York Times Book Review* (May 17, 1992). "I have no complaints to make. Cristina Garcia has written a jewel of a novel." Garcia's second novel, *The Aguero Sisters* (1997), cemented her reputation as one of the most innovative writers of fiction in the

United States. "There are definitely surrealistic elements to my books, and I'm definitely influenced by magical realism as it exists in contemporary Latin American fiction and elsewhere . . . ," she stated in an interview with *randomhouse.com* (on-line). "I like using different voices to tell a story because I find it creates a varying texture for narration that you don't get if you use a monolithic omniscient voice. A multiplicity of voices is also a more effective way to surround what I'm trying to get at in my stories."

The daughter of Frank M. Garcia and Hope Lois Garcia, Cristina Garcia was born in Havana, Cuba, on July 4, 1959, half a year after guerrilla forces led by Fidel Castro overthrew the government of General Fulgencio Batista. She and her family left the island nation when she was only two years of age, and Garcia spent most of her childhood living in predominately Jewish neighborhoods of New York City. She has said that when she was a child, her identification with her Cuban roots was "very private. It didn't have much to do with the rest of my life. The worlds didn't overlap till I started writing," as she told Florangela Davila for the *Seattle Times* (June 17, 1997, on-line). Early in her childhood Garcia became interested in poetry. She earned a B.A. degree from Barnard College, in New York City, in 1979 and an M.A. degree from Johns Hopkins University, in Baltimore, Maryland, in 1981. As a young adult, she had planned to become a diplomat, but instead she went to work, in 1983, as a researcher and reporter for *Time* magazine. In 1985 she was promoted to correspondent, and from 1987 to 1988, she served as the publication's Miami bureau chief. She left the magazine in 1990.

At the age of 30, Garcia visited her native country for the first time since her family's departure, and the experience proved to be a turning point in her life. "Going back to Cuba was instrumental in the resurgence of my own Cuban identity, which really didn't take hold until I began writing fiction," she said, as quoted on *randomhouse.com* (on-line). "There's something in the excavation process that one goes through in creating a book that allowed me to reach areas that I didn't even know existed within myself. The Cuban aspect of my identity has, to my surprise, become my wellspring. It is now an indelible, strong, and very visceral part of my identity." Garcia took a leave of absence from her job to begin work on her first novel. Published as *Dreaming in Cuban*, it was an immediate critical success. The story focuses on the del Pino family, a Cuban clan whose members are scattered from their native village of Santa Teresa del Mar to Havana to Brooklyn and Eastern Europe. Except for the matriarch, Celia—who still lives in Santa Teresa del Mar—the family members are in both geographical and spiritual exile. In her review Thulani Davis wrote, "Like Louise Erdrich, whose crystalline language is distilled of images new to our American literature but old to this land, Ms. Garcia has distilled a new tongue from scraps salvaged through upheaval. . . . Ms. Garcia also portrays . . . the fading of the light between mothers and daughters, between lovers, as communication fails. The language of such love songs as once were sung must be saved, Ms. Garcia seems to say, so that we may make songs in exile."

A Guggenheim Fellowship, a Cintas Fellowship, and a Princeton University Hodder Fellowship helped enable Garcia to work on her next book. With Joshua Greene, she put together a pictorial guide entitled *Cars of Cuba* (1995). The book emphasizes the effects of the United States' embargo against the island nation and the Cuban people's resulting need to preserve and drive automobiles that predate the Castro revolution. Photographs of 1950s Chevrolets, 1940s Fords, and even cars from the 1930s and 1920s provide a unique take on the indirect consequences of the embargo. In the book, Garcia pointed out that many antique cars in Cuba are among the best-kept specimens in existence.

Garcia published her much-anticipated second novel in 1997. Discussing *The Aguero Sisters*, Garcia told an interviewer for *randomhouse.com*, "I must admit that I did feel quite a bit of pressure to follow up with a strong second novel. My efforts in that direction became a struggle. In fact, *The Aguero Sisters* is my third book. I worked for two years on another novel that I eventually decided to shelve." The novel recounts the story of Reina and Constancia Aguero, two middle-aged sisters, and their life in the Cuban community of Miami in the 1990s. Like Garcia's previous novel, the book received positive reviews. "Ms. Garcia is a strikingly deft and supple writer, both in her sensibilities and her language," Deirdre McNamer wrote for the *New York Times Book Review* (June 15, 1997, on-line). "She has a talent for the oblique that allows her to write what amounts to a family saga by focusing not on the strict beat that constitutes conventional plot development but on seemingly offhand memories and exchanges. The large events in the book—a lightning strike, a patricide, a guerrilla attack on Cuba—occur in the wings, so to speak. They are not what Ms. Garcia's characters choose to tell us much about. The important stories occur in the interstices between these dramatic events."

Following the publication of *The Aguero Sisters*, Garcia embarked on a book tour that took her to numerous cities throughout the United States. Because she was expecting a child when *Dreaming in Cuban* went to press and gave birth shortly afterward, a tour for the first book had not been possible. "It wasn't until the *Aguero Sisters* came out that I did a real book tour, met a number of my readers, and began to fathom the impact of my work," she said, according to *randomhouse.com*. When asked if she had any advice for aspiring writers, Garcia replied, "You need to carve out, and protect, uninterrupted time for yourself on a daily basis. Getting in the habit of taking time seriously is important because the time is the ultimate factory for these novels. They don't get written without it. And you have to be comfortable with solitude because novel writing is not a collaborative process. Party animals need not apply when it comes to being a novelist."

Florangela Davila described Garcia as having "chestnut-colored hair and a smile that is slightly crooked, curling higher on the right side of her face. . . . She's gracious, warm, and funny." Garcia is a Whiting Writers Award recipient. She lives in California with her daughter, Pilar. Her avocational interests include music, contemporary dance, travel, and foreign languages. — M.B.

Suggested Reading: *New York Times* C p17 Feb. 25, 1992, with photos, C p14 May 17, 1992, with photo; *New York Times* (on-line) June 15, 1997; *randomhouse.com* (on-line); *Seattle Times* (on-line) June 17, 1997; *Time* p67 Mar. 3, 1992, with photo

Selected Books: *Dreaming in Cuban*, 1993; *Cars of Cuba*, 1995; *The Aguero Sisters*, 1997

Olan Mills/Courtesy of Martin Gardner

Gardner, Martin

Oct. 21, 1914– Writer specializing in mathematics, science, and pseudoscience. Address: 3001 Chestnut Rd., Hendersonville, NC 28792

"I think of myself as a journalist who writes mainly about math and science, and a few other fields of interest," Martin Gardner has said. Described as "one of the great intellects produced in this country in this century" by the Pulitzer Prize–winning computer scientist and writer Douglas Hofstadter, Gardner is the author of more than 60 books,

including some two dozen on recreational mathematics and others on science, pseudoscience, philosophy, and religion; he has also written fiction, poetry, literary criticism, and puzzle books for young people. He is probably best known as the creator of *Scientific American*'s "Mathematical Games" column, which he produced monthly for 25 years beginning in 1957, and as the author of *The Annotated Alice*, in which he revealed, alongside the texts of *Alice's Adventures in Wonderland* and *Through the Looking Glass*, the word games, parodies, and literary and other references that Lewis Carroll concealed within his classic fantasies. A co-founder of the Committee for the Scientific Evaluation of Claims of the Paranormal, he has spent much of his career "debunking bad science," in his words; according to another Pulitzer Prize winner, the paleontologist Stephen Jay Gould, he is "the single brightest beacon defending rationality and good science against the mysticism and anti-intellectualism that surround us."

Martin Gardner was born in Tulsa, Oklahoma, on October 21, 1914 to James Henry Gardner and Willie (Spiers) Gardner. His father, a petroleum geologist, started a small oil business and became a wildcatter, searching for oil on his own. In an autobiographical statement for *Something About the Author* (1979), Gardner said that his favorite pastimes during childhood were learning magic tricks and playing chess. He also got much pleasure from reading the Wizard of Oz series and others books among the dozens written by L. Frank Baum, whom Gardner has called the "greatest writer of juvenile fantasy" the United States has produced. In high school he was a member of the gymnastics team, "specializing in the horizontal bar," and he "played lots of tennis," as he told Kendrick Frazier for the *Skeptical Inquirer* (March/April 1998).

As a teenager Gardner looked forward to attending the California Institute of Technology (Caltech) and becoming a physicist. Caltech matriculated only those students who had had two years of study elsewhere, so after graduating from high school, in 1932, Gardner entered the University of Chicago. At that time the university was an especially exciting place for a budding intellectual. Its president, Robert Maynard Hutchins, in collaboration with the philosopher and educator Mortimer J. Adler, had introduced the so-called Great Books curriculum, the aim of which was to provide students with a broad liberal education and cultivate in them particular values—intellectual honesty, the ability to think clearly, a love of truth, and certain moral qualities. The curriculum was designed to bring students' minds in contact with those of people whom Hutchins and Adler considered to be the world's greatest thinkers, ranging from Aristotle and Plato to Immanuel Kant to Sigmund Freud. The course of study on which Gardner embarked included history, literature, the physical and biological sciences, and his major subject, philosophy. He wound up spending all four undergraduate years at the university.

When Gardner entered college, he considered himself a devout Methodist; his mother, he wrote in his book *The Whys of a Philosophical Scrivener* (1983; updated in 1999), had instilled in him what he described as "an ugly Protestant fundamentalism." He believed firmly in the divinity of Christ and Christ's Second Coming and "actually doubted the theory of evolution," he admitted to Kendrick Frazier. Because of the readings, course work, and lectures to which he was exposed at the University of Chicago, he told Frazier, "I quickly lost my entire faith in Christianity." "It was a painful transition that I tried to cover in my semiautobiographical novel *The Flight of Peter Fromm* [1973]," he said.

Gardner has said that religion and philosophy, particularly the philosophy of science, remain his primary intellectual interests, and that *The Whys of a Philosophical Scrivener* and *The Flight of Peter Fromm* are his favorites among the many books he has written. The introduction to the former consists of a single sentence: "This is a book of essays about what I believe and why." The chapter titles include "Truth: Why I Am Not a Pragmatist"; "Goodness: Why I Am Not an Ethical Relativist"; "Science: Why I Am Not a Paranormalist"; "Liberty: Why I Am Not a Marxist"; "Faith: Why I Am Not an Atheist"; "Prayer: Why I Do Not Think It Foolish"; "Immortality: Why I Do Not Think It Impossible"; "Evil: Why We Don't Know Why"; and "The Proofs: Why I Do Not Believe God's Existence Can Be Demonstrated."

The Flight of Peter Fromm is narrated by Homer Wilson, the fictional pastor of a Chicago church and a part-time teacher at the University of Chicago's Divinity School who is nevertheless an atheist. It spans the years from 1938, when Wilson meets Peter Fromm as a student in his class, to 1948, when Peter, while maintaining his belief in the existence of God, has an emotional breakdown and abandons his plan to become a clergyman. During the intervening decade Wilson and Fromm grapple with questions of faith, deepening their friendship as they wend their way on an intellectual and emotional journey that closely mirrors that taken by Gardner himself. In an assessment of *The Flight of Peter Fromm* for the *New York Times Book Review* (December 23, 1973), Martin Levin wrote, "This is a brilliantly illuminating metaphysical novel that employs ideas as adversaries and translates them into human dilemmas. It is not only the primal question of whether to believe or not to believe that is dealt with here. The question is in what to believe, and to find the answer (or nonanswer) to this question, Martin Gardner sends his hero searching the spectrum of Protestant doctrine from fundamentalism to humanism. . . . Can a novel whose action is essentially cerebral be exciting? Yes indeed—if the novelist is as engaged by the history of ideas as is Gardner." Speaking of his personal creed, Gardner told Kendrick Frazier, "I managed to retain my youthful theism in the form of what is called 'fideism'"—faith that is based on neither reason nor revelation and that in Gardner's case is, in his words, "independent of any religious movement."

After earning a B.A. degree, in 1936, Gardner remained at the University of Chicago for about a year, taking graduate courses although not pursuing a master's degree. He felt that he didn't need graduate credentials, because he knew he didn't want to teach; as an undergraduate he had decided that he wanted to be a writer. In about 1937 he returned to Oklahoma and took a job as a reporter for the *Tulsa Tribune*, and sometime later he returned to the University of Chicago, to work in the school's press-relations office. For four years beginning in 1942, soon after the United States entered World War II, he served in the U.S. Naval Reserve, as a yeoman on the destroyer escort U.S.S. *Pope.*

After completing his military service, Gardner embarked on a freelance writing career. It was launched when he sold to *Esquire* magazine a humorous story called "The Horse on the Escalator." Another among the dozen stories *Esquire* bought from him during the next few years was "The No-Sided Professor"; that one is based on topology, a branch of mathematics that deals with certain properties of geometric forms. "If you take a strip of paper and give it a half twist," Gardner explained to István Hargittai for the *Mathematical Intelligencer* (Fall 1997), "it becomes one-sided. My plot was about a professor of topology who discovered a way to fold a surface so it lost *both* sides, and just disappeared."

During this period, with funds provided under the G.I. Bill, Gardner enrolled in a seminar in the philosophy of science—what he has called "the most exciting course I ever took"—led by Rudolf Carnap. A member of a group known as the Vienna Circle, Carnap was a leading exponent of logical positivism, which is concerned mainly with the logical soundness of scientific language. "Carnap had a major influence on me," Gardner told Frazier. "He persuaded me that all metaphysical questions are 'meaningless' in the sense that they cannot be answered empirically or by reason. They can be defended only on emotive grounds." Years later, at Gardner's request, Carnap's wife recorded her husband's lectures, and Gardner reworded them to form the book *Philosophical Foundations of Physics* (1966; the title of the revised edition is *An Introduction to the Philosophy of Science*).

In the early 1950s Gardner moved to New York City, where he found steady employment with *Humpty Dumpty's Magazine*, a monthly periodical geared to children ages four through six. For each issue published during the eight or so years that he worked for the magazine, Gardner recalled for *Something About the Author*, he wrote "a short story (about Humpty Junior) [and] a poem of moral advice" and created puzzles and other "activity features." Some of his *Humpty Dumpty* poems were collected in *Never Make Fun of a Turtle, My Son* (1969).

Earlier, in 1956, Gardner had sold an article about mechanical logic machines to *Scientific American*. His byline next appeared in the magazine with an essay about hexaflexagons—hexagons, fashioned from strips of paper, that reveal different faces when flexed in different ways. Impressed by Gardner's illuminating discussion, *Scientific American*'s publisher asked Gardner if he could come up with enough material of a similar nature to fill a regular column. Though he didn't know for sure, Gardner said yes. He then promptly bought all the books about recreational mathematics that he could find in Manhattan bookstores.

Gardner's column, "Mathematical Games," debuted in the January 1957 issue of *Scientific American*. During the next 25 years, Gardner told István Hargittai, "it got steadily more and more sophisticated. This was because I was learning more and more mathematics." Gardner had not taken a single mathematics course after high school. To compensate for this gap in his learning, he now immersed himself in puzzle, logic, and math books. ("There is no better way to learn *anything* than to write about it!" he observed to Kendrick Frazier.) He also began receiving unsolicited, unpublished material from mathematicians. Many people have suggested that Gardner's lack of expertise and his consequent reliance not on academic jargon but on cross-cultural references, jokes, and anecdotes were precisely what made "Mathematical Games" so engaging and accessible to laypeople. The column also served to disseminate mathematical discoveries and innovations: although many recreational mathematicians were engaged in interesting and potentially valuable research, most of it received little attention from scholarly journals. *Scientific American*, by contrast, thanks to Gardner, provided a forum for such work. In 1981 Gardner gave up responsibility for his *Scientific American* column, having decided that its preparation took up time that he wanted to devote to other projects. (His successor was his friend Douglas Hofstadter, the author of the best-selling, 1979 Pulitzer Prize–winner *Gödel, Escher, Bach*.)

Gardner's nearly two dozen books on recreational mathematics include 15 assemblages of "Mathematical Games" columns. Among the titles are *The Scientific American Book of Mathematical Puzzles and Diversions* (1959); *Mathematical Carnival: From Penny Puzzles, Card Shuffles and Tricks of Lightning Calculators to Roller Coaster Rides into the Fourth Dimension* (1975); *Knotted Doughnuts and Other Mathematical Entertainments* (1986); *Time Travel and Other Mathematical Bewilderments (1988)*; *From Penrose Tiles to Trapdoor Ciphers: Essays on Recreational Mathematics* (1989), and *Fractal Music, Hypercards, and More*, 1992.

Gardner's first book, published in 1952, was *In the Name of Science*; entitled *Fads and Fallacies in the Name of Science* in subsequent editions, it exposes quackery in the guise of science, ranging from flat-earth cults to the French naturalist La-

marck's evolutionary theory of acquired characteristics to "evidence" of the existence of flying saucers. Among Gardner's next titles are *Relativity for the Millions* (1962; revised as *The Relativity Explosion*), a layperson's guide to Albert Einstein's famous theory regarding space, time, and motion, and *The Ambidextrous Universe* (1964; revised in 1990 as *The New Ambidextrous Universe*), in which Gardner discussed, among other subjects, symmetry in physical phenomena; the properties of mirrors; right-handedness and left-handedness in mollusks and crystals; such curiosities as the bathtub vortex (under carefully controlled laboratory conditions, water in a bathtub in the Northern Hemisphere drains in a counterclockwise direction, while in the Southern Hemisphere, the direction is clockwise); parity, which involves the behavior of subatomic particles and their mirror images; and the concept of God. *Visitors from Oz* (1999), a comic satire on L. Frank Baum's Oz books, is Gardner's most recent novel.

Gardner's most popular book by far is *The Annotated Alice: Alice's Adventures in Wonderland & Through the Looking Glass by Lewis Carroll* (1960). Containing in the margins notes about Lewis Carroll's hidden messages, subtle wordplay, and other literary tricks, it has never been out of print. *The Annotated Alice* and *More Annotated Alice* (1990) were published in one volume, with many new notes, in 1999. Others among Gardner's books of literary criticism or exegesis are *The Annotated Snark* (1962), which contains the full text of Lewis Carroll's nonsense epic poem "The Hunting of the Snark"; *The Annotated Ancient Mariner* (1965), which analyzes Samuel Taylor Coleridge's dreamlike ballad "The Rime of the Ancient Mariner"; *The Annotated Casey at the Bat* (1967), about E. L. Thayer's classic baseball poem; the *Annotated Innocence of Father Brown* (1987), about G. K. Chesterton's fictional detective, and *The Annotated Man Who Was Thursday* (1999), about Chesterton's philosophical comic fantasy; and *The Annotated Night Before Christmas* (1991).

The Numerology of Dr. Matrix (1967), revised as *The Incredible Dr. Matrix* (1975) and *The Magic Numbers of Dr. Matrix* (1985), is based on Gardner's once-a-year "conversations" with the fictional numerologist Dr. Matrix and his beautiful Asian assistant, recorded for his *Scientific American* column. Gardner told István Hargittai that he has "always been intrigued" by number mysticism—the seeming connections of numerals with the occult—but, he added, "of course, I don't take it seriously." The Dr. Matrix interviews, he explained, were his "way of getting into amusing numerology" and "spoofing" it. "It's amazing that some readers took these columns seriously," he said. "I got lots of letters from readers who wanted to get in touch with Dr. Matrix."

Gardner has felt not only amazement but uneasiness about people's seemingly increasing readiness to accept as real or useful such supernatural phenomena as faith healing, extrasensory perception, alien abduction, UFOs, psychic surgery, and astrology. "When I was a boy," he recalled to Frazier, "there were only one or two astrologers who wrote newspaper columns. Now almost every paper except the *New York Times*, not to mention dozens of magazines, features a horoscope column." In 1976, along with Carl Sagan, Isaac Asimov, and others, Gardner co-founded the Committee for the Scientific Evaluation of Claims of the Paranormal, which, according to its home page on the World Wide Web, "encourages the critical investigation of paranormal and fringe-science claims from a responsible, scientific point of view and disseminates factual information about the results of such inquiries to the scientific community and public." In 1983 Gardner began writing a column, "Notes of a Fringe Watcher," for the committee's bimonthly publication, the *Skeptical Inquirer*. "I like to think I am unduly harsh and dogmatic only when writing about a pseudoscience that is far out on the continuum that runs from good science to bad, and when I am expressing the views of all the experts in the relevant field," Gardner told Frazier. "When there are areas on the fringes of orthodoxy, supported by respected scientists, I try to be more agnostic. I am certain, for example, that astrology and homeopathy are totally worthless, but I have no strong opinions about, say, superstring theory [which was developed by theoretical physicists]. Superstrings are totally lacking in empirical support, yet they offer an elegant theory with great explanatory power." Gardner is also a member of the so-called mysterians, a group of intellectuals who reject the widely held assumption that computers will eventually become self-aware and even more intelligent and creative than the smartest and most imaginative humans. "I believe that the human mind, or even the mind of a cat, is more interesting in its complexity than an entire galaxy if it is devoid of life," he remarked to Frazier.

Martin Gardner and his wife, the former Charlotte Greenwald, have been married since 1952. The couple live in Hendersonville, North Carolina. Their son James is a psychology professor and the father of their three grandchildren; their younger son, Thomas, is an artist. Gardner's chief recreations are learning newly invented magic tricks and playing the musical saw. Cataract surgery performed on both eyes many years ago forced him to give up tennis. "Nothing pleases me more than to be alone in a room, reading a book or hitting typewriter keys," Gardner, who does not own a computer, told Frazier. "I consider myself lucky in being able to earn a living by doing what I like best. As my wife long ago realized, I really don't do any *work*. I just *play* all the time, and am fortunate enough to get paid for it." — M.C.

Suggested Reading: *Mathematical Intelligencer* p36+ Fall 1997, with photos; *Scientific American* p38+ Dec. 1995, with photo; *Skeptical Inquirer* p34+ Mar./Apr. 1998, with photo; *World Authors 1980–1985*

Selected Books: *In the Name of Science*, 1952 (revised as *Fads and Fallacies in the Name of Science*, 1957); *Mathematics, Magic and Mystery*, 1956; *Logic Machines and Diagrams*, 1958 (revised as *Logic Machines, Diagrams, and Boulean Algebra*, 1968); *The Scientific American Book of Mathematical Puzzles and Diversions*, 1959 (revised as *Hexaflexagons and Other Mathematical Diversions: The First Scientific American Book of Puzzles and Games*, 1988); *The Arrow Book of Brain Teasers*, 1959; *The Annotated Alice: Alice's Adventures in Wonderland & Through the Looking Glass by Lewis Carroll*, 1960; *The Annotated Snark*, 1962; *Relativity for the Millions*, 1962 (revised as *The Relativity Explosion*, 1976); *The Ambidextrous Universe*, 1964 (revised as *The New Ambidextrous Universe: Symmetry from Mirror Reflections to Superstrings*, 1990); *The Annotated Ancient Mariner*, 1965; *The Annotated Casey at the Bat*, 1967; *The Numerology of Dr. Matrix*, 1967 (revised as *The Incredible Dr. Matrix*, 1975); *Never Make Fun of a Turtle, My Son*, 1969; *The Flight of Peter Fromm*, 1973; *Mathematical Carnival: From Penny Puzzles, Card Shuffles and Tricks of Lightning Calculators to Roller Coaster Rides into the Fourth Dimension*, 1975; *Aha, Gotcha! Paradoxes to Puzzle and Delight*, 1982; *The Whys of a Philosophical Scrivener*, 1983, 1999; *The Magic Numbers of Dr. Matrix*, 1985; *Knotted Doughnuts and Other Mathematical Entertainments*, 1986; *The No-Sided Professor and Other Tales of Fantasy, Humor, Mystery, and Philosophy*, 1987; *The Annotated Innocence of Father Brown*, 1987; *Time Travel and Other Mathematical Bewilderments, 1988; The New Age: Notes of a Fringe-Watcher*, 1988; *From Penrose Tiles to Trapdoor Ciphers: Essays on Recreational Mathematics*; 1989; *Gardner's Whys and Wherefores*, 1989; *More Annotated Alice*, 1990; *The Annotated Night Before Christmas*, 1991; *Fractal Music, Hypercards, and More*, 1992; *The Annotated Man Who Was Thursday*, 1999; as editor—*The Wizard of Oz and Who He Was*, 1957; *Great Essays in Science*, 1957 (revised as *The Sacred Beetle and Other Great Essays in Science*, 1984); *Philosophical Foundations of Physics*, 1966 (revised as *An Introduction to the Philosophy of Science*, 1974); *The Wreck of the Titanic Foretold?*, 1986

Archive Photos

Gaultier, Jean-Paul

(goh-tee-AY, zhahn-pawl)

Apr. 24, 1952– Fashion designer. Address: 30 Rue Faubourg Saint Antoine, 750012 Paris, France

When asked how he comes up with innovative ideas for the clothing he creates, Jean-Paul Gaultier told Michael Gross for the *New York Times* (October 31, 1986), "I masticate. I am like a big stomach." Long considered the leading creator of avant-garde clothing, Gaultier takes inspiration from what may seem to be unlikely sources: television, garbage, Russian constructivism, the traditional dress of Hasidic Jews, and punk rock, to name just a few. "I love kitschy, trashy, tacky things," he told Peter Mikelbank for the *Washington Post* (July 17, 1993). "So I'm not insulted when people call me 'Trash.' I use a lot of trash, after all, for my inspiration. And, anyway, we are all trash to someone else." Gaultier's status as the enfant terrible of the Paris fashion scene has been repeatedly challenged by new designers. But according to Peter Stuart, the producer-director of the British comedy series *EuroTrash*, which Gaultier has hosted, none of his competitors "has been able to sustain a career out of it. What really goes unstated is how much [Gaultier has] contributed to [and] influenced fashion, how many of his ideas have been stolen and copied."

Jean-Paul Gaultier was born on April 24, 1952 in Arcueil, a middle-class suburb south of Paris, France. Because both his parents worked full-time when he was young, Gaultier spent a lot of time with his grandmother Marie Garrabe, a beautician who dabbled in faith healing and spiritual media-

tion. Gaultier has said that his grandmother was his "best friend and accomplice" and that he inherited from her his free-spiritedness and lack of inhibition. His grandmother taught him just about everything she knew about hairstyling and make-up. "I [would] hear her talking to her clients—'Oh, you should change your haircut'—and I realized that how you dress can say something," Gaultier recalled to Judy Rumbold for the London publication *Observer Life* (July 27, 1997). Once, Garrabe even allowed him to dye her hair; it came out pink, rather than the bluish grey she had wanted. "She was the first punk woman, I think," Gaultier told Gross.

Gaultier's parents, Jean Rene Gaultier and Solange Gaultier, did not indulge their son as Garrabe did. When, at a very young age, Jean-Paul asked them for a doll, they bought him a train and a teddy bear instead. The bear became the model for Gaultier's first fashions. By age 12, Gaultier was designing collections of clothes and writing his own press releases and reviews. When he was a teenager, his parents hoped, unrealistically, that he would become a Spanish teacher. "I always knew I wanted to be involved in fashion," he told Ashley Heath for the London *Observer* (April 3, 1994). "I read books about Christian Dior . . . and I wondered whether I would be like him when I grew up."

When Gaultier was 18, a family friend who was an editor at the French magazine *Jardin des Modes* suggested that he show his sketches to couturiers and ask for work. "I was too shy to take them to one designer, so I divided them up and sent one each to [Pierre] Cardin, [André] Courrèges, [Yves] Saint Laurent, and [Emanuel] Ungaro," Gaultier told Nina Hyde for the *Washington Post* (October 21, 1984). Pierre Cardin hired him. "Cardin was okay because there was a modern spirit in the house," Gaultier told Hyde. "It was not a bourgeois house like Dior. [Cardin] was always open to new ideas." After leaving Cardin, Gaultier did short stints with the designers Jacques Sterel, at Michel Goma, and Jean Patou. The house of Patou, he told Gross, "was very old fashioned. It made me grrrrrr."

In 1976, after again working briefly with Cardin, Gaultier established his own business. Joining forces with two of his oldest friends, Francis Menuge and Donald Portard, he created a moderately successful collection of glow-in-the-dark jewelry. Later that year he created his first collection of women's clothing, with Menuge and Portard as his business partners and advisers. "It was the beginning of big, loose, clothing," he told Gross. "Me, I said, 'Be contrary.'" The collection, shown at the Palais de la Decouverte in October 1976, consisted of short, sharply flared skirts paired with tight leather jackets—outfits startlingly different from the hippie-inspired look that was in vogue. The next season he showed a collection of Robin Hood–inspired designs.

Paris's demanding fashion critics admired both of Gaultier's first two collections, and the designer soon developed a strong local following. Nevertheless, neither of the two collections earned Gaultier any money. "The trouble was, we knew nothing about marketing clothes," he told Hyde. "All of us were working very hard, yet financially we seemed to be going nowhere." The enterprise survived thanks to friends who modeled or did hair and makeup for the Gaultier shows for free. Even most of the fabrics were donated.

In 1978 the Japanese company Kashimaya commissioned Gaultier to design clothing for their Paris boutique Bus Stop. "It was a fabulous moment for us," Gaultier told Hyde. "Everything was paid for. Whatever we needed we received. For the first time, I could create in a free atmosphere without spending my own money." Gaultier's next collection, produced for fall–winter 1979–80, had a James Bond air; it reintroduced the miniskirt, which had been absent from runways for several years, and also featured several variations of the belted trench-coat, much like those in which characters in Bond films conceal their weapons. On the strength of that collection, two Italian companies—Gibo and Equator—also invested in Gaultier's business and helped him to open his own boutiques throughout Europe.

While Gaultier became known early on as a zany, antiestablishment, avant-garde designer, Rumbold noted that much of his clothing sold better than is widely assumed. "Underneath the showbizery and the high camp," Hyde explained, "there was always a bedrock of the solid, commercial designs that were coveted not just by gay clubbers and awe-struck fashion students but by ordinary working women." "I start with classical, traditional clothes, like a blazer, a kilt, things like that," Gaultier told Hyde. "And I go on to destroy them. Not destroy, which is absolutely negative, but rather deliberately distort them. In reality, it is classical with new proportions . . . a new appearance." Gaultier's most popular early designs included a waisted, elongated denim jacket, pinstriped suits in unconventional and less-formal shapes, and generously curved skirts for both day and evening. The clothes were "a nod in the direction to power dressing without calling on the services of shoulder pads or nasty lapels," Rumbold wrote.

In the mid-1980s Gaultier used themes from films or historical dress in his seasonal shows. He held the shows in out-of-the-way places—which meant long rides on public transit for most of the people who wanted to see them—and often, near-riots occurred at the entrances to the shows. Gaultier's 1983 spring–summer collection was named "Le Dadaisme," which is the name of an early 20th-century movement in art and literature that discarded traditional, rational tenets of sensibility. For example, some of the clothes had seams and labels on the outside and looked as if they were being worn inside-out. The collection also contained items reminiscent of lingerie, such as dresses designed partly like corsets and pajama-like separates. Gaultier is credited with introducing the lingerie theme to fashion with his 1983 collection,

and 16 years later, the theme is still popular among designers and manufacturers of all types of clothing. At about the same time as "Le Dadaisme," Gaultier staged his first show in New York City, and he chose people off the street, rather than professional models, to wear his creations.

Gaultier's first collection for men came out in 1984. Surprisingly, it featured many of the same items as his women's lines. "There is no difference between my men's and women's clothes," the designer explained to Hyde. "A tailored jacket in a proportion that is not classical is not effeminate. Men buy it because they don't find it in a very classical men's shop." Gaultier's men's collections have almost always contained skirts, which, he has predicted, will eventually be a regular part of men's wardrobes. "Of course men will wear skirts," he declared to Hyde. "It is coming. Among more of the young generation the codification of what is masculinity has changed a lot. You don't wear your masculinity. You are masculine or you are not—it is not the clothes that make you masculine." He pointed out to Harriet Shapiro for *People* (May 6, 1985), "Look how men dress in Scotland and India. Putting a skirt on a man is not a travesty. Putting a bra on him is."

His reputation firmly established, in 1986 Gaultier was offered the job of artistic director at the house of Jean Patou, to succeed their former in-house designer, Christian Lacroix, who had found backing to start his own couture collection. He refused the offer, apparently because he had plans of his own: in 1987, he opened his own boutique in New York City, and he began work on his first Gaultier Junior line, which was to feature such easy-to-wear basics as jeans, logoed sweatshirts, and jackets. (Previously, Gaultier's designs had been sold in the United States only in a few high-end department stores.)

At the end of the economic boom of the 1980s, fashion turned toward more-somber designs, and while Gaultier was still a major force in the industry, he found himself increasingly at odds with fashion editors in both Europe and the U. S. When, in his spring–summer 1990 collection, he showed a variety of nun's habits—some of them transparent and revealing sexy undergarments—a fashion writer from the U.S. publication *Women's Wear Daily* described his work as being "like blue porn, sado-masochistic." According to Rumford, Gaultier shrugged off the criticism. "I sent Mr. Fairchild [the president of Fairchild Publications, which publishes *Women's Wear Daily*] a catalogue of real sadomasochism," he said. "I said, 'That is sado-masochistic.' What I presented was more [the sassy style of the Paris neighborhood] Pigalle." Gaultier also said that he took inspiration for the collection from the artist Richard Linder's brightly colored paintings of women wearing garter belts, suspenders, and thigh-high boots.

In 1990 Francis Menuge, Gaultier's longtime lover and business partner, died of AIDS. Gaultier has said that his sorrow had a sobering effect on his work, and indeed, his first few collections after Menuge's death were uncharacteristically simple, and he showed them in ordinary salons rather than at offbeat locations. "We're not in the mood for violence and tougher-looking styles, because there's so much aggression around us right now," he explained to Karen Schneider for *People* (December 10, 1990). "Not just the threat of international conflicts, but also threats to the environment and the threat of AIDS." While in mourning for Menuge, he "[tried] to decide if he still wanted to be doing all this," Ashley Heath reported, and he began thinking that his designs had "slipped into trying to be far too classic." So he resumed creating openly sexy clothes. "In present circumstances nothing could be worse than to cancel out desire," he told Heath in 1994. "Desire exists. It should be talked about and shown."

Meanwhile, toward the end of the 1980s, Gaultier had branched into different media. Commissioned to create costumes for Peter Greenaway's film *The Cook, the Thief, His Wife and Her Lover* (1989), he came up with outfits with both a 17th-century look and a bold, cowboyish flair. The styles he produced for the singer Madonna's *Blonde Ambition* tour, in 1990, included lingerie-like pieces, among them the single garment for which Gaultier perhaps remains most famous—the conical bra. "I love Madonna," he told Rumford. "That was one of the best times of my career." Later that same year Gaultier released his own album, entitled *How to Do That*. In following years, he created clothing for such films as Pedro Almodóvar's *Kika* (1993), Marc Caro and Jean Pierre Jeunet's *The City of Lost Children* (1995), and Luc Besson's *The Fifth Element* (1997).

Beginning in about 1990, Gaultier's popularity had begun to wane within the fashion industry. To rekindle interest in his work, he designed several collections based on the clothing of such groups as Eskimos and certain peoples in Siberia. The most controversial was his fall 1993 line, which contained adaptations of clothing traditionally worn by male Hasidic Jews. The many critics who assumed that the collection was merely a play for attention misunderstood his motives, Gaultier told Linda Doreska for the London *Guardian* (January 5, 1994). "It was not done to provoke . . . ," he told her. "In the first place, I find such clothes—the big fur hats, the long coats—simply beautiful. Secondly, I saw the collection as a homage to the Jewish culture which I find very interesting. And thirdly, this theme was dedicated to all the minorities at risk from the new waves of fanaticism, racism, and nationalism. We are experiencing the return of extreme movements, which we had considered dead a long time ago." The ethnically inspired collections marked another shift in Gaultier's career, in that they displayed the exuberant spirit for which he had originally become famous.

Gaultier's profits increased in 1992, when he launched the Gaultier Jeans collection, and again in 1993, when he introduced Gaultier, his fra-

grance for women; formulated to resemble the scents his grandmother preferred, the fragrance was sold in a bottle shaped like a woman's torso. "I don't want people telling me that my designs have to become more sedate now that we're a real business," he told Karen Schneider, noting that many other designers created much more conservative clothing after they became very successful.

Beginning in the mid-1980s, Gaultier had become a popular media personality. In 1993 he was chosen to host a new comedy series on British television called *EuroTrash*. "I will bring to my television show everything that is kind of tacky," he told Mikelbank shortly before the show premiered. "It will be fun for other people to laugh at Europeans, just as we've been laughing at them for years." His status as a celebrated designer notwithstanding, in several reviews of the show, he was said to come across as very down-to-earth and "normal." "Jean-Paul has adapted incredibly to the television medium," Peter Stuart, the producer of *EuroTrash*, told Heath. "By the end of the original six shows, he was already an old pro, delivering lines with the timing of Buster Keaton. He'll sometimes play the bimbo, but of course, he's an incredibly bright man."

Also in 1993 Gaultier, who for many years had designed furnishings for his showroom and for friends and clients, created his first line of furniture. It included a dresser made out of luggage, a full-length mirror mounted on a hand truck, and a chair on wheels that sat two.

Many fashion insiders thought that devoting so much time to his television and furniture projects would prevent Gaultier from producing noteworthy clothing designs. But they were mistaken. Indeed, the British magazine *Face* declared a "Gaultier renaissance" after the designer's spring 1994 women's show, in which the Icelandic singer Bjork, who had inspired the designs, served as a model. The inspiration for the designs in his successful 1994 fall collection were winter garments worn by natives of Mongolia. Yet another well-received Gaultier collection, for the spring of 1995, featured updated versions of dresses from the 1920s, 1930s, and 1940s. "A lot of young girls like old movies and dream to have old dresses that you can't find anymore," the designer explained to Amy M. Spindler for the *New York Times* (October 15, 1994). "I played with that. I tried to capture a synthesis of each period: the silhouette that was the most important, the print, the fabrics. It's a mix of the periods I love and admire, what I remember most about each of them. But it wasn't pretentious. I'm not trying to make it better than they did then, because it's impossible to make it better." Other Gaultier men's and women's shows in the mid-1990s featured tattoos and body piercings and paid homage to the punk subculture of London, which had intrigued the designer for many years. "I was always more British than French," he told Rumbold.

Gaultier designed his fall 1996 collection as a tribute to Pierre Cardin. Filled with stark, geometric shapes and colorful, spiral-printed fabrics, it was set to music from the soundtrack of the 1965 film *Who Are You Polly Maggoo?*, a satire about the world of high fashion. Reporting on the collection, Spindler wrote for the *New York Times* (March 18, 1996), "[Gaultier] has been passed over once too often for those job openings at establishment couture houses, and there was not a little bit of defiance in his work. This is what couture could look like done with a brain instead of pure politics, he seemed to be saying."

In 1997 Gaultier launched his own, long-awaited couture collection. He thus became only the second designer in 30 years to produce couture under his own name. These collections have provided Gaultier with a venue for his most extravagant creations, and they have generally won him praise in the fashion press for infusing the somewhat outdated tradition of made-to-order clothing with a modern spirit. Among his more remarkable recent couture designs are a strapless, denim ball gown trimmed with feathers, which appeared in his January 1999 show, and a dress whose skirt appears to be made entirely of guinea-hen and vulture feathers and whose bodice is encrusted with tiny seashells. The latter was shown in July 1999 and immediately became one of the most photographed couture dresses of the fall and winter season, despite the unlikelihood that it will ever be worn by anyone but a handful of models in fashion spreads. Gaultier's most recent ready-to-wear show, which unveiled clothing that will become available in the spring of 2000, had a *Love Boat* theme, inspired in part by the popular 1970s television series. The collection featured palazzo pants in tropical prints and tops with gathers around keyholes near the models' navels. Gaultier's business received a financial boost in mid-1999, when the French luxury-goods firm Hermès bought a stake in his company.

Discussing the long-term effect of Gaultier's work on the world of fashion, Rumbold wrote that while many designers have attempted to imitate the "enfant terrible," none has been able to "inspire the same sort of maternal zeal and goodwill that Gaultier does." The designer himself told Rumbold that he hesitates to take credit for putting "all the fun back into French fashion," because he believes that fashion has been and always will be fun.

In his spare time, Gaultier enjoys watching television; he has several sets stacked in the bedroom of his Paris home. "I'm completely neurotic about TV," he told Schneider. "I watch all the screens spurting out different programs at the same time." He also loves to roam London, where, he has said, he is most apt to be inspired. Gaultier is well known for his honesty in both personal and business matters. He is "lumberjack tall, with crystalline blue eyes," in Mikelbank's words, and he wears his hair in a bleached-blond crew cut. — C.P.

Suggested Reading: (London) *Guardian* p5 Jan. 5, 1994, with photo; (London) *Observer Life* p16 July 27, 1997, with photos; *New York Times* A p32 Oct. 31, 1986, with photos; *Newsday* p3 Sep. 27, 1984, with photos; *People* p88+ May 6, 1985, with photos, p123+ Dec. 10, 1990, with photos; *Washington Post* H p1 Oct. 21, 1984, with photos, F p1 July 17, 1993, with photos

Joseph Mehling/Courtesy of Center for Cognitive Neuroscience

Gazzaniga, Michael S.

(gah-ZAHN-ih-guh)

Dec. 12, 1939– Cognitive neuroscientist; teacher; writer. Address: c/o Center for Cognitive Neuroscience, Dartmouth College, 6162 Silsby Hall, Hanover, NH 03755-3547

W.J., as he is known in the scientific literature, was a victim of intractable epilepsy. By 1961 W.J., a veteran of World War II, had become virtually unable to function, and none of the available anticonvulsant medications helped him. That year, at the age of 48, he elected to have radical surgery to sever his corpus callosum, the large bundle of nerves that enables the left and right hemispheres of the brain to communicate with each other. Neurosurgeons had found that by severing the corpus callosum, they could greatly reduce the severity of, and in some cases eliminate, seizures in patients with untreatable epilepsy, apparently without affecting intelligence, behavior, or memory.

In 1961 Michael Gazzaniga was a 21-year-old psychobiology student studying for his Ph.D. at the California Institute of Technology (CalTech), in

Pasadena. As a member of a CalTech research team headed by the future Nobel laureate Roger Sperry (who died in 1994), Gazzaniga administered weekly tests to W.J. after the operation, to determine what, if anything, had resulted from the surgery. Most previous neurological studies had been conducted on humans with extreme brain damage or on animals—in Sperry's case, monkeys. Thus W.J., whose brain had appeared normal in spite of the epilepsy, presented scientists with what Gazzaniga characterized for Bruce Bower of *Science News* (February 24, 1996) as "one of those unforgettable moments in life": namely, the opportunity to study an otherwise normal, functioning brain in which the hemispheres were completely independent of each other.

Sperry and Gazzaniga's work, with W.J. and later subjects who underwent similar surgery, marks the beginning of what has become known as split-brain research, which has become central to cognitive neuroscience. Their work also marks the distinguished beginning of the career of Gazzaniga, one of the field's preeminent figures. Cognitive neuroscience is the study of how the brain enables humans to perform advanced mental functions—that is, the functions that are generally associated with what we call the mind. Split-brain research had the potential to advance scientists' understanding of how the brain works by revealing the separate functions and abilities of each hemisphere, if in fact they did function differently.

When Gazzaniga and Sperry embarked on their research, scientists already knew that information that is given to the left side of the body, through sight or touch, for example, is processed by the right side of the brain, and vice versa. Gazzaniga and Sperry tested their subjects, each of whom had a split brain, by giving information to only one side of the body, and thus one hemisphere of the brain, at a time, and then asking the people to perform tasks that used very specific cognitive skills. In one study, the scientists placed a spoon in each subject's left hand while preventing him or her from seeing the spoon. When asked to identify the object, none of the test subjects could name or describe the object in his or her hand, verbally or in writing. Four picture cards were then placed in front of each subject, only one of which showed a spoon, and the subjects were asked to select the card that depicted the object they were holding. All the subjects selected the correct card. This led Gazzaniga and Sperry to believe that even in the first part of the experiment, the right hemisphere had recognized the spoon but had been incapable of translating its perception into language.

Further tests showed that humans' language abilities are associated almost exclusively with the left side of the brain. In one test, for example, Sperry and Gazzaniga showed the subjects, first with one eye covered and then with the other covered, how to assemble simple three-dimensional puzzles. The subjects completed the puzzles rapidly after the method of assembly was demonstrated to their left eyes; after looking with only their right eyes at different puzzles being put together, however, the subjects could not complete the puzzles. Thus it seemed that the right side of the brain was more adept at perceiving spatial relationships. More generally, Sperry and Gazzaniga's research showed that each of the hemispheres of the brain appeared to have highly specialized functions. Gazzaniga recalled to Diane Connors and Kathleen Stein for *Omni* (October 1993) that this discovery prompted one psychologist to exclaim, "Now instead of one mind, you give me two! This is an advance?"

The son of Dante Achilles and Alice (Griffith) Gazzaniga, Michael Gazzaniga was born on December 12, 1939 in Los Angeles, California, into a large Italian-American family. (He now has six children of his own.) He earned an A.B. degree from Dartmouth College, in Hanover, New Hampshire, in 1961. In studying for a Ph.D. at CalTech, he rejected the advice of his father, a surgeon, that he get a degree in medicine. He received his Ph.D. from CalTech in 1964, and since then he has held prestigious teaching posts at a number of universities, among them New York University, from 1969 to 1973; Cornell University Medical College, also in New York, where he taught from 1977 to 1988 and founded the Cognitive Neuroscience Institute, in 1982; and the University of California at Davis, where, from 1992 to 1996, he headed the Center for Neuroscience, which was founded in 1990. In 1989 he became the founding editor of the *Journal of Cognitive Neuroscience*, and he was editor-in-chief of the book *The Cognitive Neurosciences* (1995), a 1,447-page synthesis of what was then known in the field. Since 1996 he has taught and conducted his research at Dartmouth, as director of the college's program in cognitive neuroscience. His title at Dartmouth is David T. McLaughlin distinguished professor.

In almost four decades of research, Gazzaniga has focused on how the brain facilitates such higher cognitive functions as remembering, speaking, interpreting, and making judgments. His recent research involves a method of mapping the brain's surface using three-dimensional computer models derived from magnetic resonance images (MRIs). The computer models allow scientists to measure the size of different regions in the cortex, or outer gray matter, of a subject's brain, and to compare normal brains with, for example, those of subjects with mental disorders such as schizophrenia. While Gazzaniga's research has shown that no two brains are physically identical, the brains of identical twins are more alike than are those of other people. Cases in which one identical twin suffers from a psychological disease and the other is mentally normal are of particular interest to scientists, because any physiological differences between the structures of their cortexes may offer clues to the disease or its absence.

A prolific writer whose list of scientific publications fills many pages, Gazzaniga has also published four books that draw on his research and that are intended for a general audience: *The Social Brain* (1985), *Mind Matters* (1988), *Nature's Mind* (1992), and *The Mind's Past* (1998). In his two most recent books, Gazzaniga stressed the political, philosophical, and educational implications of discoveries in cognitive neuroscience. In *Nature's Mind* he discussed human behavior and development and what influences them—environment, on one hand, and genetic factors, on the other—and thus thrust himself into the longstanding debate in psychology commonly referred to as nature (genetics) versus nurture (which includes such external factors as the circumstances of a child's upbringing). Recent research indicates, Gazzaniga argued, that environment serves mainly to lead humans to discover their innate abilities; thus, he concluded, genetic predisposition is ultimately of greater importance in determining how an individual will turn out. "While the environment may shape the way in which any given organism develops, it shapes it only as far as preexisting capacities in that organism allow," he explained in *Nature's Mind*. "Thus, the environment *selects* from the built-in options; it does not modify them."

This theory holds many implications for society. One example is the formulation of policy regarding drug use. Gazzaniga has contended that some individuals are genetically vulnerable to certain substances and predisposed to abuse. Others inherit character traits that lead them to seek relief through drug consumption. Therefore making the use of drugs illegal is useless, because despite a host of laws and law-enforcement initiatives, drugs are readily available to anyone who wishes to use them, and people with genetic predispositions will seek them out. Gazzaniga has concluded, as he wrote in *Nature's Mind*, that "it is far more reasonable to live with the dominant fact of drug use. Our species has mechanisms that allow us both to enjoy drugs and to regulate their moderate use." In an interview with a *National Review* (February 5, 1990) reporter, Gazzaniga further elaborated on his controversial stand: "I think illegality has little if anything to do with drug consumption. . . . Human beings in all cultures tend to seek out means of altering their mental state, and . . . although some will shop around and lose the powers of self-discipline, most will settle down to a base rate of use, and a much smaller rate of abuse, and those rates are pretty much what we have in the United States right now."

One of Gazzaniga's more disputed scientific theories, which he described in *The Mind's Past*, is the existence in the brain's left hemisphere of something that he has labeled the "interpreter." Humans perceive events and then sort and make sense of them; according to Gazzaniga, the interpreter is one of the more sophisticated cognitive mechanisms the brain uses to accomplish this. Gazzaniga told Diane Connors and Kathleen Stein about one of the tests that inspired the idea of the interpreter. "In a lab setting, you tell the right brain to go for a walk. As the split-brain patient gets up and starts walking, you say, 'Hey, where are you going?' Now you're talking to the left brain, and it says, 'I'm going to get a soda.' The left brain is looking at the fact that you're doing something and has got to come up with an explanation that makes sense. It does that routinely." In another example, the interpreter will attempt to explain a depression caused by a chemical imbalance in the brain by looking for an external cause, such as an event in the person's life. The interpreter is also responsible for relating causes and effects, "such as knowing that 'bleed' is an appropriate follow-up to 'pin' and 'finger,'" as Bower explained. To put it yet another way, as Gazzaniga told Bower, the interpreter is "constantly trying to find relationships between events that you encounter in the world and constantly assessing where you stand in relation to others."

As its name suggests, the conclusions that the interpreter draws are not always correct; research with split-brain subjects, Gazzaniga noted in *The Mind's Past*, shows that in "reconstruct[ing] the brain events" the interpreter "makes telling errors of perception, memory, and judgment." In one test, a picture of a chicken claw was shown exclusively to a patient's left hemisphere, and a snow scene was shown to the right hemisphere. Then the subject was shown two separate sets of pictures, each of which included one picture that correlated logically to the first images. The subject was asked to pick the pictures most closely connected to the first images. The patient correctly pointed to a snow shovel with his left hand and a chicken with his right. When Gazzaniga asked the patient why he chose those items, he responded, "Oh, that's simple. The chicken claw goes with the chicken, and you need a shovel to clean out the chicken shed." The left brain, the side that can communicate through language, was unaware that the right brain had seen the snow, and thus had no idea why the shovel was chosen. Gazzaniga concluded that when the left brain was forced to link two unrelated objects—the chicken and the shovel—it filled in the gaps in information to come up with a logical story. As Gazzaniga wrote in *The Mind's Past*, "The left hemisphere is perfectly capable of saying something like, 'Look, I have no idea why I picked the shovel.' . . . But it doesn't say this. The left brain weaves its story in order to convince itself and you that it is in full control."

While people with intact brains would have known why they selected the shovel, because the right brain would have alerted the left to the snow picture, this test and others led Gazzaniga to conclude that the human mind makes jumps in logic on a regular basis and often comes up with conclusions that have little connection with reality. Furthermore, Gazzaniga believes that the interpreter is even more prone to error when it reconstructs events more distant in time. "Our mind and brain accomplish the amazing feat of constructing our past and, in so doing, create the illusion of self," he wrote in *The Mind's Past*, but that reconstruction is far from the "truth." Thus, he declared, "biography is fiction" and "autobiography is hopelessly inventive." Gazzaniga believes that the interpreter is one of the few traits that, among all those in the animal kingdom, is uniquely human.

Michael Gazzaniga looks forward to seeing how work in his still-fledgling field will expand our understanding of one of the great mysteries of human existence: the workings of the human brain. "There have been incredible technological advances in brain imaging, but as yet we don't have a tool for understanding the basic principles of brain and cognitive function," he told Bruce Bower. Cognitive neuroscience is increasingly incorporating tactics from psychology and biology, and Gazzaniga feels the next major strides in cognitive neuroscience will inevitably emerge from a greater commitment to interdisciplinary research and greater cooperation among researchers. The current lack of sufficient collaboration, he has contended, is the biggest hindrance to our further understanding of the human mind: "A lot of what passes for cognitive neuroscience right now consists of brain researchers who stumble on a finding and immediately extrapolate it to some cognitive function without considering what cognitive scientists already know about that function." Gazzaniga favors a multidisciplinary approach in his own lab, and according to Connors and Stein, he is unusually cooperative and collaborative. As they reported, "Listening to colleagues, admiring other forms of intellectual energies, and sharing ideas (as well as restaurants) excites him."

Gazzaniga has served as a consultant on the PBS television series *The Brain and the Mind* (1988), the Time-Life series *The Brain* (1991), and the WGBH television series *History of Science* (since 1996). He organized and, since 1989, has directed the McDonnell Summer Institute in Cognitive Neuroscience, held variously at Dartmouth, Lake Tahoe, and the University of California at Davis. Gazzaniga lives in Sharon, Vermont, about 15 miles from Dartmouth. — T.J.F.

Suggested Reading: *National Review* p34+ Feb. 5, 1990; *Omni* p99+ Oct. 1993, with photos; *Science News* p124+ Feb. 24, 1996; *American Men and Women of Science, 1998–99*

Selected Books: *The Bisected Brain*, 1970; *Fundamentals of Psychology*, 1973; *Psychology*, 1980; *The Social Brain*, 1985; *Perspectives in Memory Research*, 1988; *Mind Matters*, 1988; *Nature's Mind*, 1992; *Conversations in Cognitive Neuroscience*, 1996; *The Mind's Past*, 1998; with J. E. LeDoux—*The Integrated Mind*, 1978; with D. Steen and B. T. Volpe—*Functional Neuroscience*, 1979; with R. Ivry and G. R. Mangun—*Fundamentals of Cognitive Neuroscience*, 1997

David James/Courtesy of Walt Disney Pictures

Gebrselassie, Haile
(GEB-rah-sel-lah-see, HI-lee)

Apr. 18, 1973– Distance runner. Address: c/o Walt Disney Pictures, 500 S. Buena Vista St., Burbank, CA 91521

Although in East Africa, which stretches from Sudan and Ethiopia to Tanzania, only a fraction of the land is arable and terrible droughts occur with dismaying frequency, most countries there base their economies on agriculture. Consequently, the per-capita incomes in those countries rank among the lowest in the world. In addition, political instability is the norm in East African nations, in each of which many different tribal groups and languages exist under a single flag. Despite such problems, the nations of East Africa—particularly Kenya and Ethiopia—have consistently produced the world's finest crops of long-distance runners. At the 1960 Olympic Games, held in Tokyo, the Ethiopian Abebe Bikila, running barefooted, took the gold medal in the marathon and thus became the first black African ever to win an Olympic medal. Ever since then, athletes from East Africa have dominated international distance-running competition. The Ethiopian runner Haile Gebrselassie has continued that tradition. Gebrselassie, whose career in international racing started in 1992, is regarded by many people as the greatest runner of all time. A versatile pacesetter who can compete at a world-class level over distances from 1,500 meters to 10,000 meters (a bit over 9/10 mile and slightly more than six miles, respectively), Gebrselassie first achieved international notice when he won the 5,000-meter and 10,000-meter World Junior Championships in 1992. He has since dominated international competitive track with many world championships, a gold medal at the 1996 Summer Olympics, in Atlanta, Georgia (in the 10,000-meter event), and a total of 15 indoor and outdoor world records. Despite competing against what many consider to be the finest pool of young distance-running talent ever—including the Kenyans Daniel Komen and Paul Tergat and the Moroccan Salah Hissou—Gebrselassie has remained virtually undefeated in international competition, due in large part to his legendary, overpowering closing sprint.

The eighth of 10 children, Haile Gebrselassie was born on April 18, 1973 on a farm in Asela, a village about 100 miles southeast of Ethiopia's capital, Addis Ababa, in a temperate, fertile region where most of the country's grain is grown. After his mother died (according to various sources, either from complications during childbirth or from uterine cancer), Gebrselassie and his siblings were raised by their eldest sister, Shawanness, and their father, Gebreselassie Bekele. (According to traditional Ethiopian naming practices, a father's first name becomes his sons' surname.) Along with his brothers and sisters, young Haile helped with the farm work. His dreams of becoming a runner kindled in 1980, when he was seven years old: listening to a radio broadcast of the Olympic Games, held that year in Moscow, he heard the excitement generated when an Ethiopian, Miruts Yifter, took the gold in both the 5,000- and 10,000-meter races. "I wanted to be famous," Gebrselassie recalled to Jere Longman for the *New York Times* (March 4, 1996). "I wanted people to talk about me."

Inspired by Yifter's achievement, Gebrselassie began running the six miles between his home and school, first imitating the styles of other athletes and then developing his own. His current form closely resembles that of a sprinter: he runs on the balls of his feet, heels never touching the ground, with his chest out and his head erect and motionless. His practice of running to and from school also explains the one flaw in his otherwise graceful and efficient stride. "Look at Haile's left arm," Gebrselassie's coach, Wolde Meskel Kostre, told John Brant for *Runner's World* (July 1996). "See the way it is crooked and rides up high? We tried and tried to get rid of that, but it stays with him. It is left over from his boyhood. It comes from when he carried his books to school as he ran."

Despite Gebrselassie's obvious commitment to the sport, his father did not approve of his son's passion. "I did not like all this running," Gebrselassie Bekele told John Brant. "My son is intelligent. He did well in his studies. I thought he could become a doctor or teacher, or work in an office for the government. I did not see what could be gained by all this running." Nevertheless, he bought a pair of running shoes (he could afford only one pair), which Haile shared with his older brother Tekeye (also spelled Tekeya) and his younger sister Yeshi (also spelled Yeshye).

As a member of his school track team, Gebrselassie entered student competitions. He showed promise in the 1,500-meter event, and at the age of 16, he entered the Abebe Bikila Marathon in Addis Ababa. With barely any prior formal training, Gebrselassie finished the race in an impressive two hours and 42 minutes. Over the next four years, he built a reputation on the junior level as one of the bright young stars in distance running. In 1992 he racked up dual wins, in the 5,000- and 10,000-meter competitions, at the World Junior Championships. Two years later, running in Hengelo, the Netherlands, he broke the world record for 5,000 meters with a time of 12 minutes and 56.96 seconds.

The year 1995 started on a sour note for Gebrselassie: because Ethiopia's track-and-field federation botched his team's travel arrangements, he and his fellow runners arrived late at their hotel the night before the World Cross Country Championships in England. An exhausted Gebrselassie finished fourth in his event. That defeat turned out to be his last in 1995. During the European track season that year, Gebrselassie—seemingly effortlessly—put away all challengers and walked away with three world records, in the two-mile, 5,000-meter, and 10,000-meter distances. At the conclusion of that season, a buzz started among distance runners and running aficionados that Gebrselassie could duplicate Miruts Yifter's feat and win the marathon at the 1996 Summer Olympic Games.

In the Amharic language, Haile means "my energy," making it a most appropriate given name for Gebrselassie, because his unusually high stores of energy give him his most tangible competitive edge. Most distance runners are trained to maintain a fast but steady pace throughout the duration of a race. The objective of this training philosophy is to evenly apportion the runner's energy (the extent of which has been gauged previously) from the start of a race to the finish, in the hope that the runner will outlast his competitors. During the closing meters of a race, however, long after his rivals have all but depleted their remaining stores of energy, Gebrselassie is capable of generating considerable power and speed from his five-foot three-inch, 130-pound frame. He spends most of any race behind the leader, who is also usually his strongest opponent, placing the onus on that runner to set the pace. As they approach the finish, Gebrselassie draws on his superior sprinting skills and passes the leader. Consequently, though a few other elite distance runners consistently post times that compare favorably with Gebrselassie's, they rarely fare well in head-to-head competition against him.

Gebrselassie used his tactics to win his first Olympic gold medal, in 1996. The 10,000-meter was scheduled before the 5,000, and in the final race, Gebrselassie faced Paul Tergat and Salah Hissou, both of whom would go on to set world records in the event in the following two years. Gebrselassie allowed Tergat to lead the entire race until the last lap, when he surged past the Kenyan to win the gold and set an Olympic record time of 27:07.34. But the race took its toll on him. Atlanta officials had had the Olympic track constructed with an especially hard surface, to provide optimum conditions for sprinters. The unyielding surface played havoc on Gebrselassie's feet, leaving them blistered, bloody, and bruised and thus making it impossible for him to compete for a second gold medal, in the 5,000-meter competition.

For the past two decades, human physiologists and sports kinesiologists have been arguing that runners are approaching the limits of human ability, and as a result, few, if any, world records will continue to be broken. However, since the 1996 Olympics Gebrselassie and his peers—in particular, Komen, Tergat, and Hissou—have led a remarkable assault on the record books that has stunned the experts. Furthermore, they have broken some records by four or more seconds—an astounding number in world-class distance-running competitions, where elapsed time is measured in hundredths of a second. As has happened with most leaps in human athletic achievement, the avalanche of falling records has led to questions about whether performance-enhancing drugs have played a role. Specifically, erythropoietin, commonly called EPO, has been named as a likely culprit. This substance increases the red blood cells' capacity to carry oxygen, thus increasing the body's capacity for work. No reliable test exists to detect the presence of EPO in the body, but naysayers have predicted that once one is developed, record breaking will cease. Gebrselassie and his co-competitors have maintained that they are clean and that further record-breaking will happen. Speaking of his most recent 10,000-meter record (26:22.75, set June 1, 1998), Gebrselassie told Tim Layden for *Sports Illustrated* (July 20, 1998), "It is not so fast. It was not so hard to run."

Some observers have suggested that what drives these runners to record-breaking speeds is not drugs but money. In much the same way that many inner-city American children dream of breaking their socioeconomic chains by earning millions as professional basketball, baseball, or football players, poor, rural East African children see running as their ticket out of poverty. Elite runners frequently receive upwards of $50,000 just for participating in a European race, and the winners come away with cars or other valuable prizes. Gebrselassie's annual income is reportedly close to $1 million per year, and he has won two Mercedes-Benz sedans.

In spite of his newfound wealth, Gebrselassie has maintained a modest lifestyle. He has never learned to drive, preferring to hitch a ride in his brother's car. He bought a house for his father (who now sees his son's passion for running as a good thing), has made substantial donations to his church, and routinely gives running shoes to friends and children who cannot afford them. "You must do as your people do," Gebrselassie told Jere Longman. "If my people are poor, I must be

poor. People ask me, 'Why don't you find a personal coach or a private car?' I can't. Then I won't be part of my people." Moreover, as he told John Brant, "If I have a good car, a good house, I worry I would lose my ability for athletics. You can't get sweaty and dirty as an athlete and then worry about messing up your nice car and house."

Adding to his already impressive string of wins, Gebrselassie captured the gold medal in the 10,000-meter contest at the 1999 World Track and Field Championships in Seville, Spain, defeating Kenya's Paul Tergat in a close race. He declined to compete in the 5,000-meter event because of adverse racing conditions—this time, excessive heat. Gebrselassie has expressed his intention to try again for gold medals, in both 5,000 meters and 10,000 meters, at the 2000 Summer Olympics, to be held in Sydney, Australia. After those Games he plans to begin training for the Olympic marathon, which Ethiopians consider the pinnacle of athletic achievement. "I would like to run the marathon tomorrow, but I will wait until after 2000," Gebrselassie was quoted as saying in *Runner's World* (November 1997). "Then I will run it in the 2004 [Summer] Olympics [in Athens, Greece]."

When not racing, Haile Gebrselassie divides his training time between his home in Ethiopia and his trainer's residence in Holland. The Walt Disney Productions docudrama *Endurance*, which is based on Gebrselassie's life, arrived in movie theaters in March 1999. Directed by Leslie Woodhead, with the Olympic sequences filmed by Bud Greenspan, *Endurance* features Gebrselassie and members of his family playing themselves and other relatives portraying him and his parents years ago. Several scenes re-create his courtship of Alem Tellahun, whom he married in the mid-1990s. — T.J.F.

Suggested Reading: *New York Times* A p1 Mar. 4, 1996, with photos; *Runner's World* p95+ July 1996, with photos; *Sports Illustrated* p34+ July 20, 1998, with photos

---

Gibbs, Lois

June 25, 1951– Environmental activist; organization official. Address: c/o Center for Health, Environment and Justice, P.O. Box 6806, Falls Church, VA 22040

Lois Gibbs once considered herself what she calls a "Dolly Domestic": an ordinary homemaker who devoted herself to making her house a haven from the outside world for her husband and two children. But when she learned that her house, in the Love Canal section of Niagara Falls, New York, stood near a toxic-waste site, and that chemicals emanating from the site might be damaging the health of her kids, she transformed herself into a

Courtesy of the Center for Health, Environment and Justice

Lois Gibbs

crusader against the dumping of hazardous chemicals. With only a high school education, the resources of the local library, and a tenacity that she herself hadn't known she possessed, she successfully organized her community and raised public awareness of toxic-waste dumping and the possibility that the poisonous substances in the ground in Love Canal may have damaged the health of area residents. Her efforts resulted in the evacuation of about 7,000 people from Love Canal in 1980 and passage by Congress that same year of the so-called Superfund law, the goal of which is the cleaning of toxic-waste disposal sites. In recognition of the role she played in the passage of the law, Gibbs is sometimes referred to as the "mother of the Superfund."

Gibbs's experience—which she described in her book *Love Canal: My Story* (1981) and which was the subject of a 1982 CBS television movie—led her to become a full-time environmental activist. To assist both budding and experienced grassroots environmental activists, in 1981 Gibbs founded the Citizens Clearinghouse for Hazardous Wastes, later renamed the Center for Health, Environment and Justice (CHEJ). By the end of 1999, the organization had worked with more than 10,000 community groups, whose members include many people who have been inspired by Gibbs's story. "I believe if there's enough people who understand how to participate in civic society, we can change the way this country is run," Gibbs told Libby Ingrid Copeland for the *Washington Post* (July 29, 1998).

Lois Gibbs was born on June 25, 1951 in Grand Island, New York, which lies between the cities of Buffalo and Niagara Falls. While she was growing up, her main ambition was to raise a family. "All

she ever wanted was a home and a husband and children," Gibbs's mother, Patricia Conn, told Libby Ingrid Copeland. Although Lois was somewhat shy—she intentionally skipped school on days when students had to deliver oral book reports—she had a streak of defiance, which, by her own account, stemmed from her relationship with her father. "I was one of six children in a family with a classic abusive father and my life was miserable," she told the journalist Adrienne Redd for an online article for the *Redd Pages*. "I am a very stubborn woman and I decided as a small child that nobody would ever hurt my children in the ways that I was hurt."

After graduating from high school, Lois married Harry Gibbs and moved to Niagara Falls, where her husband monitored a chemical vat at the local Goodyear plant. For years she was a contented homemaker, taking care of household tasks and raising her son, Michael, and daughter, Melissa, who were born in the early 1970s. "We had a white picket fence, we had a station wagon, we had a healthy child, we had a wood-burning stove, we had cable," she recalled to Copeland. "We had the whole American dream."

The family's domestic tranquility was shaken when five-year-old Michael was diagnosed with epilepsy and liver and urinary disorders soon after he started kindergarten. Gibbs began to suspect a connection between the boy's health problems and the presence of about 20,000 tons of toxic waste buried under the neighborhood school, which was just a few blocks from their house. A series of articles written by Michael Brown that had appeared in the local newspaper, the *Niagara Gazette*, in April 1978 had disclosed the history of the dumping ground. At some point Gibbs's daughter, too, developed an ailment—a blood disorder known by the acronym ITP—that Gibbs also linked to the presence of chemical wastes in the neighborhood.

Love Canal got its name from a project, begun at the end of the 19th century, to divert water from the Niagara River for hydroelectric power. The project, which involved the digging of a canal, was later abandoned. The Hooker Chemicals and Plastics Corp. bought the incomplete trench and between 1942 and 1953 disposed of waste products there. Then the company sold the land, for $1, to the Niagara Falls Board of Education, with a brief warning about the toxic waste and a disclaimer that absolved Hooker of any responsibility for the waste or anything connected with it. Ignoring the warning, or perhaps unaware of its full implications, the school board proceeded to construct an elementary school at the site, in 1955. About 900 families later settled in the area, unaware at first that their community had been established on top of toxic landfill. But it soon became apparent that something was amiss, because after heavy rains, foul-smelling substances would surface in backyards and basements.

Gibbs wanted to have her children transferred to another school, but school officials dismissed her fears as exaggerated. In trying to figure out her next step, she felt at a loss. "I waited at the house for somebody to knock on my door and tell me what to do at Love Canal," she told Copeland. Nobody ever came, so finally Gibbs decided that she had to take matters into her own hands. Going door to door, she exchanged with her neighbors stories of mysterious sicknesses, birth defects, miscarriages, and cancers among Love Canal residents, and she learned that many of her neighbors harbored exactly the same fears and suspicions that she did. Like her, they had been waiting for someone more knowledgeable to organize them.

Thus began a battle between the residents of Love Canal, on one side, and the New York State government and Hooker Chemical (by then renamed the Occidental Chemical Corp.), on the other. On August 2, 1978 Gibbs and her neighbors traveled to a New York State Health Department meeting in Albany, the state capital, and presented to government officials a petition, signed by 161 Love Canal residents, that called for the closing of the school. The officials agreed that the site was dangerous and recommended closing the school and evacuating pregnant women and children under the age of two from houses bordering what had been the canal. Five days later President Jimmy Carter declared the neighborhood a federal disaster area; this made funds available for the relocation of the 239 families who lived in the first two rows of houses abutting the canal. Gibbs and her fellow petitioners felt that such a measure did not go far enough; they objected especially to the arbitrary two-row radius, which didn't include Gibbs's home, just beyond the cutoff. They also opposed a later evacuation order, which stipulated that once the youngest child in a family passed his or her second birthday, families would have to move back to their Love Canal homes. Concerned residents thereupon formed the Love Canal Homeowners Association and elected Gibbs president.

Government agencies conducted studies of the toxic-waste site, but scientific certainty as to the connection between the poisons and human disorders eluded the researchers. (Certainty in such cases is usually elusive. The difficulty of establishing such cause-and-effect links was powerfully illustrated in the book *A Civil Action* [1995], by Jonathan Harr.) Some people believe that evidence of a link in the Love Canal situation remains weak. "Truth is, 20 years later, no long-term health effects on former residents have been proved," Copeland wrote for the *Washington Post*. "Many studies have been declared inconclusive, in part because of the small population of those affected and the intervening years." Residents of Love Canal who had to live directly in the presence of the chemicals were not as uncertain. They conducted their own surveys and found that 56 percent of children born within the area suffered from birth defects. Their claims were reinforced by an Environmental Pro-

tection Agency (EPA) report issued in May 1980, which, on the basis of blood tests, stated that the chromosomes of area residents showed signs of damage. Such damage has been associated with an increased risk of cancer and reproductive problems.

On May 19, 1980, angered by government delays and the EPA report, which had confirmed what they had been claiming for two years, Love Canal residents held two EPA officials hostage for five hours at the Homeowners Association headquarters. Gibbs called for the government to relocate additional families within a few days, threatening that if no such action were taken, "what we've done here today will look like a *Sesame Street* picnic [compared] to what we'll do then." On May 21 President Carter complied, ordering an emergency evacuation of all Love Canal residents. Later that year Congress allocated funds to purchase the homes of the approximately 7,000 people who had been relocated. (The Gibbses received $30,000 for theirs.) In December 1980, in direct response to the media coverage of events at Love Canal, Congress passed and President Carter signed into law the Comprehensive Environmental Response, Compensation and Liability Act—commonly known as the Superfund law—which established a $1.6 billion fund for cleanup of contaminated sites. (The law expired at the end of 1995.)

After her successful community-organizing experience, Gibbs's life changed. People who had seen her in the news, read her book, or watched *Lois Gibbs and the Love Canal*, the CBS movie adaptation of the story, contacted her for help in dealing with the problem of hazardous substances near their own homes. Gibbs felt that she could not turn them away. "My life was aimless before," she told Michael Weiss for *People* (February 22, 1982). "Now I have a goal, and it's my turn to help people."

Meanwhile, Gibbs's husband had grown uncomfortable with her transformation from full-time housewife to full-time activist firebrand, and he resented having to do domestic chores when she was away from home. The couple divorced, and in March 1981 Lois Gibbs moved to Falls Church, Virginia, where she started a new organization, called the Citizens Clearinghouse for Hazardous Wastes. Its primary mission was to help community groups prevent the dumping of toxic wastes near their homes. Over the next 16 years, the organization's scope expanded to include other grassroots environmental organizing efforts. To reflect that change, in 1997 the group was renamed the Center for Health, Environment and Justice (CHEJ). CHEJ, whose current annual operating funds of about $1 million come from membership dues and foundation grants, offers a broad array of scientific information, organizational training, small grants, and political advice to grassroots groups mobilizing against environmental degradation. The titles of its publications—among them the magazine *Everyone's Backyard*; such self-help guides as *How to*

Win in Public Hearings and *User's Guide to Lawyers*; and such exposés as *"Greening" Hospitals, Environmental Racism,* and *Center for Disease Control: Cover-up, Deceit and Confusion*—give some indication of CHEJ's reach. The organization even offers an "environmental justice" songbook.

By the end of 1999, CHEJ had provided assistance to some 10,000 community groups. Among other campaigns, the organization has assisted efforts to halt the creation of hazardous-waste landfills (only one new commercial hazardous-waste landfill has been built in the U.S. since that campaign started); prevent the deregulation of incinerator-ash emissions; close unsafe solid-waste-disposal facilities and encourage recycling; develop strategies for preventing waste removed from one site from being dumped at another; document the deliberate siting of unsafe waste-storage and -disposal facilities near rural communities or communities where most of the people are low-income, elderly, or members of minorities; and push fast-food chains to stop using Styrofoam. Stories abound about the influence and effectiveness of Gibbs, who is CHEJ's executive director. "What Lois did was show that an average person like me can prevail with enough tenacity and persistence," Joanne Muti, an activist who won a six-year fight involving a sewage landfill in Walpole, Massachusetts, told Scott Allen for the *Chicago Tribune* (August 30, 1998).

One of Gibbs's present campaigns is to increase awareness of the dangers of dioxin, a known carcinogen that has also been linked to reproductive problems and diabetes. The substance is produced when chlorine is burned (which occurs, for example, when paper is bleached during its manufacture and when hospital wastes are incinerated). Once released into the atmosphere, the toxin can travel thousands of miles before falling onto land or water, where it is ingested by animals and then travels up the food chain. To educate the public about dioxin, Gibbs and her co-workers wrote *Dying from Dioxin: A Citizen's Guide to Reclaiming Our Health and Rebuilding Democracy* (1995). Gibbs first learned about dioxin when she lived in Love Canal; it was one of the approximately 80 chemicals found at the site. "I thought my move to Virginia had protected my children from further damage from dioxin," she told Patrick Mazza for the on-line magazine *Cascadia Planet* (February 21, 1996). "I didn't know we were feeding our children dioxin every time they drank milk or ate fish or meat. I didn't realize that dioxin from a hazardous waste-burning aggregate kiln in Florida could end up in the milk of a cow or a new mother living in Michigan."

The struggle involving Love Canal has not ended. Occidental Chemical has paid more than $233 million in out-of-court settlements, though without admitting any wrongdoing or negligence. In September 1988 the New York State Department of Health declared parts of Love Canal "as habitable as other areas of Niagara Falls"—though these areas were never labeled "safe" by the department. Love Canal has been renamed Black Creek Village by the Love Canal revitalization agency, and homes there have been selling since August 1990. Although CHEJ and other organizations have protested, the resettlement has not stopped. Gibbs has described the ongoing struggle in *Love Canal: The Story Continues* (1998), the 20th-anniversary edition of her first book.

Gibbs typically works 60-hour weeks. One of her co-workers is her second husband, Stephen Lester, a toxicologist who leads CHEJ's science and technical-assistance programs. The two met after the state hired Lester to investigate conditions at Love Canal. Their household includes their two sons, and unlike what prevailed during Gibbs's previous marriage, she and Lester share domestic duties.

Gibbs's children from her first marriage have apparently recovered from their childhood illnesses. Her son Michael's hair has been gray since he was 17—a result, Gibbs believes, of his early exposure to contaminants. Gibbs has often been questioned about the seeming inconsistency between her concern about toxic pollutants and her cigarette habit; she has responded by saying that she does not smoke around her children.

Gibbs's many honors include the 1990 Goldman Environmental Prize and the 1998 Heinz Award for her work on the environment. She has been a board member of the Love Canal Medical Trust Fund since 1984 and of the Environmental Support Center since 1991. Since 1994 she has also sat on the advisory board of the Legal Environmental Assistance Foundation. — W.G.

Suggested Reading: *Chicago Tribune* Real Estate p7 Aug. 30, 1998; *People* p42+ Feb. 22, 1982, with photo; *Washington Post* D p1 July 29, 1998, with photos

Selected Books: *Love Canal: My Story*, 1981; *Dying from Dioxin: A Citizen's Guide to Reclaiming Our Health and Rebuilding Democracy*, 1995; *Love Canal: The Story Continues*, 1998

Gilchrist, Guy

Jan. 30, 1957– Cartoonist; children's writer. Address: c/o Gilchrist Publishing, P.O. Box 1194, Canton, CT 06019

Gilchrist, Brad

1959– Cartoonist; children's writer. Address: c/o Nancy, United Features Syndicate, 200 Madison Ave., New York, NY 10016

Brad (left) and Guy Gilchrist   Courtesy of Gilchrist Publishing

Guy Gilchrist is an award-winning author and illustrator of more than three dozen children's books, among them the *Mudpie* and *Tiny Dinos* series, which have been enormously successful not only in the United States and Canada but also in Japan and other countries overseas. A cartoonist and comic-strip artist as well, he collaborated with his brother, Brad Gilchrist, on the widely syndicated strip *The Muppets* in the 1980s. Brad Gilchrist has co-developed, with the Creative Learning Institute, a direct-mail product called Together Time!, the goal of which is to foster interaction between parents and their children. Working as a team again, the brothers have written and illustrated the comic-strip *Nancy* since 1995; a classic strip that Ernie Bushmiller began in the 1930s, it currently appears in nearly 400 newspapers worldwide.

Guy Gilchrist was born on January 30, 1957 in Winsted, Connecticut, and Brad was born in 1959 in Torrington, Connecticut. Their parents, Leonard Gilchrist and Louise Toth Gilchrist, raised them in central Connecticut. Guy has cited his mother as one of the people who most influenced him. She encouraged him to draw at an early age, showing him the rudiments; by his own account, he also taught himself to draw, by copying pictures from such children's books as the *Golden Books* series and stories by Theodore Seuss Geisel—the famous Dr. Seuss. On a class outing when he was eight, he heard a talk by Dr. Seuss, during which the author said, as paraphrased by Gilchrist in a bio of him on the *amazon.com* Web site, "Dreaming a dream is okay, but if you don't get up and do something about it, all you'll have is a pretty little dream. If you work hard at your dream, then you can be anything you want to be." "From that moment on, Guy knew he could be an artist," the *amazon.com* bio

went on. According to a biographical sketch of Gilchrist on his Web home page, he made his first sales during his youth, by pinning cartoons, drawn on cardboard, to a rope strung outside his father's store.

At age 16, Guy Gilchrist recalled on his home page, "I got a rejection letter from *Mad Magazine*. . . . It told me that 'cartoons were one step away from reality'. . . and I was 'too many steps away.' It told me to do life drawing, continuous-line drawing, gesture drawing . . . all real subjects. I was heartbroken over the rejection, but it was such a blessing to me. I started drawing *real*! And I've never stopped. Never stopped learning. Never stopped seeing . . . and getting my hand to draw what the eye sees . . . or . . . what my *imagination* sees." By his own account, in his teens he studied the work of a wide range of artists, among them the 15th-century Italian painter Botticelli, the 18th-century British architect Charles Bridgeman, the 19th–20th century British illustrator Arthur Rackham, and the 20th-century American painters and illustrators Maxfield Parrish and Norman Rockwell.

After graduating from high school, in about 1975, Gilchrist got a job with Weekly Reader Books. His illustrations and comic strips appeared in Weekly Reader's series *Superkernel Comics & Books* (1977–81); also for Weekly Reader, he wrote and illustrated *Ghoul and the Gang* (1979) and *Ghoul II* (1980).

In 1980, in what amounted to a veritable coup, Guy and Brad were commissioned to produce a comic strip based on Jim Henson's famous Muppets characters. Called *The Muppets*, the strip debuted in 1981, and for some of its six-year existence, it appeared in more than 660 newspapers worldwide. Guy's Muppet illustrations evidently struck curators at the Smithsonian Institution, in Washington, D.C., as particularly worthy of preservation: in the spring of 1984, some of them became part of the Smithsonian's permanent collection. Others among his Muppet pictures toured museums worldwide in an exhibit called *Art of the Muppets*. Guy Gilchrist's by-line appears on at least six Muppets paperbacks; all entitled *Jim Henson's Muppets*, they are subtitled, respectively, *Short, Green and Handsome, Light on Our Feet*, and *Moving Right Along* (all 1984); *Chickens Are People, Too!* (1985); *On the Town* (1986); and *Froggy Mountain Breakdown* (1988). According to *amazon.com* on December 7, 1998, he created the first four books along with Brad and wrote and illustrated the latter two himself.

In 1984 Guy, Brad, and the syndicated cartoonist Mort Walker, the creator of the *Beetle Bailey* comic strip, created *The Rock Channel* for the Cowles Syndicate, a comic-strip distributor. The strip, which lasted for a year, focused on the backstage antics of rock-'n'-roll video jockeys.

After *The Muppets* strip ceased publication, in 1986, Guy Gilchrist began concentrating on writing and illustrating children's books. By December 1998, according to *amazon.com*, some two dozen of the books in his *Tiny Dinos* series were available. On *amazon.com*'s list each of their titles bears his name, as in *Guy Gilchrist's Bronty and the Birdosaur: A Tiny Dinos Story About Love*. Three of the books—*Steggie Makes a Friend: A Tiny Dinos Story About Shyness, Plateo's Big Race: A Tiny Dinos Story About Learning*, and *Thanks a Lot, Triceratot: A Tiny Dinos Story About Helping Others*—won Children's Choice Awards, from the Children's Book Council and the International Reading Association, as best books of 1988. Gilchrist's *Mudpie Books* series includes *I Am Having an Excellent Day!, In My Own Backyard, My Dad's Okay*, and *My Mom's Okay* (all 1992).

Guy Gilchrist's other works for children include *Night Lights & Pillow Fights: A Trip to Storyland* (1990) and *Night Lights & Pillow Fights Two: The Box Set* (1997). "This delightful book is packed with original stories, rhymes, and limericks . . . [and] fanciful and enchanting illustrations," a reviewer for *American Bookseller* (April 1990) wrote of the former; a critic for the *Coast Book Review Service* (April 1990) described it as "a slightly off-center, definitely loony collection of stories, silly rhymes, and oddball limericks that offers something for everyone." Gilchrist's illustrations in *Night Lights . . . The Box Set* earned him a 1997 Reuben Award from the National Cartoonists Society. A 1997 reprinting of *Night Lights . . . Storyland* and the *Night Lights . . . Box Set* are sold by Gilchrist Publishing, which Guy and his wife founded in 1997. *Night Lights & Pillow Fights* also exists as a full-color page of illustrated verse, games, and comics for children that is carried by 50 newspapers and is distributed by Gilchrist/Voice Features Syndicate. Guy Gilchrist

told *Current Biography* that the series "gives me a chance to merge comics and children's books. I'm not sure people have done that since the turn of the century. It's really a joy."

In 1996 Guy launched two new projects—*Angelspeake* and *Screams. Angelspeake* is a limited edition of inspirational lithographs of angels; like T-shirts, original drawings, and many others among his works, the lithographs are available through the *Gilchrist Studios* Web site. *Screams* is a cartoon aimed at adults and teenagers that uses horror to add humor to everyday situations. In one *Screams* cartoon, for instance, Count Dracula has applied for a job, and the person interviewing him is reading from his résumé: "Hmmm . . . 'Schooling: MBA from Transylvania Community College . . . Previous job experience: 400 years as the prince of darkness . . .'" Guy also produces Positivenergy!, a line of inspirational gift items distributed by Russ Berrie, Inc. In addition, his body of work includes logos for several minor-league baseball teams, among them the Portland Sea Dogs (AA Florida Marlins affiliate), the Norwich Navigators (AA New York Yankees affiliate), the New Britain Rock Cats (AA Minnesota Twins affiliate), and the Binghamton Mets (AA New York Mets affiliate).

Like his brother, Brad Gilchrist has undertaken projects of his own. In 1991, in conjunction with the Creative Learning Institute in Portland, Connecticut, he began developing a direct-mail activity club called Together Time!, which suggests creative activities for parents to do with their children. Currently, it reaches some 40,000 families every month. In addition, for some time he has written and drawn a cartoon series called *CT Fan*. Originally, it appeared every game night in the magazine of the Hartford Whalers, a National Hockey League team; since the departure of the Whalers from Hartford, *CT Fan* has appeared in the *Hartford Courant*, a local newspaper.

In 1995 Guy and Brad teamed up to take over the comic strip *Nancy*. One of the longest-running comics of the 20th century, *Nancy* debuted in the early 1930s. After the death of its creator, Ernie Bushmiller, in 1982, a series of other cartoonists had continued it, but they apparently had lacked Bushmiller's wit and skill. Concerned about *Nancy*'s decreasing popularity, the distributor of the strip, United Features Syndicate, asked the Gilchrists, as Guy put it, to "audition" for the job. "I never expected to be involved with another daily strip after *The Muppets* . . . ," Guy told *Music City News* (December 1997). "I initially turned [United Features] down. But they persisted." Guy and Brad took the job after United Features agreed that they could reintroduce in the strip a character named Aunt Fritzi, who had been dropped at some point after Bushmiller's death. "When I asked the other [people who had worked on *Nancy*] why they had dropped her, they just said, 'Because we couldn't draw her,'" Guy recalled to *Music City News*.

"Growing up I read *Nancy* because it was easy to read," Guy told Janet Reynolds for the *New York Times* (September 28, 1997). "I would look at the art style and couldn't believe anyone could draw that precisely. When the opportunity came along, the only way I would do *Nancy* is to go back to Ernie's style and start from there." In the United Features (September 5, 1995) Web site *united-media.com*, Brad Gilchrist expressed a similar sentiment. "What Guy and I are attempting here is to bring the beauty, charm, and simple humor of the 1950s *Nancy* to a new generation of comic fans," he said. "*Nancy* strips were the most complicated, simple strips ever created and Bushmiller was a genius at turning a *Nancy* situation into a quirky, bizarre, and ultimately believable visual gag. *Nancy*'s charm flowed from every inch of the strip: the pacing and timing, the wonderful expressions, [and] the Zen-like quality of Nancy's simplistic world were perfect for kids."

According to various sources, the Gilchrists have succeeded in retaining the spirit of Bushmiller's *Nancy* while also putting their own stamp on it. "At first I tried to emulate Ernie. It was almost as if I didn't exist," Guy told Reynolds. "These days I don't look at Ernie's work anymore. It's become a combination of his work and mine." For example, in a touch that reflects one of his own fancies, Guy has included references to country music and has even inserted such popular country musi-

cians as Travis Tritt and Deana Carter as characters in some of the strips.

From his first marriage, Guy Gilchrist has a daughter, Lauren, and a son, Garrett. He has a step-daughter, Julia, from his marriage to Angie Brown, with whom he lives in Canton, Connecticut. Brad Gilchrist and his wife and their two daughters, Jayme and Carly, live in Avon, Connecticut. — Y.P.

Suggested Reading: *gilchriststudios.com* 1998; *New York Times* Connecticut edition XIII p15 Sep. 28, 1997, with photos; *unitedmedia.com* Sep. 5, 1995

Selected Books: Guy Gilchrist—*Ghoul and the Gang*, 1979; *Ghoul II*, 1980; *Sir Waldo's Island Adventure*, 1987; *Meet the Tiny Dinos*, 1987; *Tiny Dinos Silly Safari*, 1988; *Here Comes Mudpie*, 1988; *Mudpie's Island Adventure*, 1988; *Too Many Bunnies*, 1989; *Night Lights & Pillow Fights: A Trip to Storyland*, 1989; *My Dad's Okay*, 1991; *My Mom's Okay*, 1991; *Night Lights & Pillow Fights II: The Box Set*, 1997

Selected Comic Strips: Guy Gilchrist—*Screams*, 1996–; *Angelspeake*, 1996–; Guy and Brad Gilchrist—*The Muppets*, 1981–86; *Nancy*, 1995–; Guy and Brad Gilchrist and Grey Walker—*The Rock Channel*, 1984–85

Glenn, John H. Jr.

July 18, 1921– Former U.S. Senator from Ohio; astronaut. Address: c/o John H. Glenn Institute for Public Service and Public Policy, Ohio State University, 403 Fawcett Ctr., 2400 Olentangy River Rd., Columbus, OH 43210

Note: Earlier articles about John H. Glenn Jr. appeared in *Current Biography* in June 1962 and March 1976.

In 1962, when John Glenn became the first American to orbit Earth, the world was a much different place. Looking outside his space capsule, Glenn saw a planet in danger of nuclear destruction and divided ideologically between capitalists and communists. His very presence in space was a symbol of that conflict. Though the capsule he rode in was named *Friendship 7*, that benign appellation couldn't disguise the fact that his mission was meant to be an aggressive response—an "in your face"—to the Soviet Union, which had sent a man in orbit approximately 10 months earlier.

Thirty-six years later, the world is no longer driven by the division between capitalism and communism. Space flight has become routine—even boring, some might say. At least two things haven't changed, however. The first is the desire

Courtesy of NASA

on Glenn's part to "light the candle," as astronauts like to call blasting into space. And when Glenn did just that by stepping aboard the space shuttle

Discovery on October 29, 1998 and becoming, at the age of 77, the oldest person ever to be launched into the heavens, he demonstrated a second constant: his ability to capture the national imagination.

In a time when issues like Medicare and Social Security have taken the place of the Soviet threat in American political discourse, Glenn's second flight into space may be said to symbolize the change in the national mood. While some commentators have found plenty to laugh at in the launch—late-night talk-show hosts have had a field day with jokes about Tang mixed with Metamucil, or the necessity of shuttle pre-boarding for elderly passengers—for many others, Glenn's second flight has become a testament to the abilities of senior citizens to contribute to the national space program and other important areas of human endeavor. Glenn's shuttle ride seems the perfect ending to an already illustrious career devoted to service in the military, the space program, and the U.S. Senate, where Glenn served for 24 years.

The only son of John Herschel Glenn, a railroad conductor and the proprietor of a heating and plumbing business, and Clara (Sproat) Glenn, John Herschel Glenn Jr. was born on July 18, 1921 in Cambridge, Ohio. John and his sister, Jean, grew up in New Concord, Ohio, where the family moved in the 1920s. An honor student and a varsity letterman in three sports, he graduated in 1939 from a local high school, which has since been renamed for him. He then enrolled at Muskingum College, in New Concord, where he received a degree in engineering, and also began taking flying lessons.

Shortly after the United States entered World War II, Glenn decided to join the military. "My home town was a real-life version of *The Music Man*," he told Mark Goodman for the *New Times* (January 11, 1974). "Everyone, including my dad, took patriotism very seriously." In 1942 he volunteered for the Naval Aviation Cadet Program, and in 1943 he joined the Marine Corps. After marrying his high-school sweetheart, Anna Margaret Castor, in April of that year, Glenn was shipped off to the Pacific, where he flew 59 missions and earned two Distinguished Flying Crosses and 10 Air Medals. When the Korean War erupted, in 1950, Glenn—who had remained on active duty—once again entered battle, flying in 90 combat missions and winning two more Distinguished Flying Crosses and eight more Air Medals. In 1953, during the last nine days of the war, Glenn demonstrated why he was nicknamed the "MIG-mad Marine" by his cohorts in the Marine Fighter Squadron 311: he downed three enemy MIGs in combat over the Yalu River.

After the end of the Korean conflict, Glenn trained to become a military test pilot and flew some of the fastest jets then built. On July 16, 1957 he piloted an F8U-1 Crusader from Los Angeles to New York at a speed of 726 miles per hour, thus establishing a coast-to-coast travel record of three hours, 23 minutes, 8.4 seconds. Also that year, he had the distinction of winning $12,500 on the game show *Name That Tune*.

On October 4, 1957 the Soviet Union successfully launched the world's first artificial satellite, *Sputnik*, and the space race between the U.S. and the Soviet Union began. Determined not to let the Soviets claim superiority in that area, the U.S. government initiated an ambitious space program. A search was undertaken for potential astronauts with, as the writer Tom Wolfe famously put it, "the right stuff." In 1959 Glenn and six other military test pilots were selected to undergo rigorous training with the National Aeronautics and Space Administration (NASA).

The first phase of the American space program was Project Mercury, whose goal was to send a man into orbit around Earth. Once again, the Soviets humiliated Americans by beating the U.S. to the accomplishment: on April 12, 1961 the Soviet cosmonaut Yuri Gagarin became the first person to complete the orbit successfully. Glenn was scheduled to make the Americans' first orbital flight in December of that year.

After nearly a dozen delays due to technical difficulties and adverse weather, Glenn was given the go-ahead, on February 20, 1962 at 9:47 a.m. Eastern Standard Time. Crammed inside the nine-by-seven-foot capsule, *Friendship 7*, Glenn was propelled into space by an Atlas-D rocket. During the four-hour, 55-minute flight, he completed three orbits around Earth. There were a couple of harried moments: he had to take manual control of the capsule after the automatic control mechanism for the craft's stabilization jets failed during the first orbit. There were also uncertainties about whether the capsule's heat shield would withstand the high temperatures generated by reentry. In the end, however, *Friendship 7* splashed down intact in the Atlantic Ocean. National confidence in the space program was restored, and Glenn instantly became an American hero.

Although he was eager to go into space again and participate in NASA's future projects, including Project Apollo, the American effort to send a man to the moon, Glenn met with baffling resistance. Part of the reluctance of NASA officials may have been political. "It was only years later that I read in a book that Kennedy had passed the word that he didn't want me to go back up," Glenn told *Time.com* (August 17, 1998). "I don't know if he was afraid of the political fallout if I got killed, but by the time I found out, he had been dead for some time, so I never got to discuss it with him."

Frustrated by not being allowed to return to space, Glenn resigned from the space program in January 1964 to pursue a career in politics. That year he entered the Ohio Democratic primary to challenge the incumbent Democratic senator, Stephen M. Young. Two months into his campaign, after falling in a bathroom and injuring his inner ear, Glenn withdrew from the race. He subsequently turned to the private sector and became an executive for the soft-drink company Royal Crown Cola.

He also sat on the board of directors of the Questor Corp., invested in four Holiday Inn franchises, and hosted the *Great Explorations* documentaries on television.

After Senator Young announced his intention to retire from politics in 1970, Glenn made his second try for a Senate seat. His principal opponent in the Democratic primary was Howard M. Metzenbaum, the Cleveland lawyer and millionaire businessman who had managed Young's successful campaigns in 1958 and 1964. Glenn, who had greater name recognition and was initially favored to win the primary, carried 75 of Ohio's 88 counties, but he failed to win the major urban centers. The better-organized Metzenbaum, who outspent him by approximately five to one, beat him by 13,442 votes. Explaining the defeat, Glenn told Betty Carrott for *McCall's* (March 1975), "Rightly or wrongly, there was an air of the space program about me. I had studied the issues and prepared what I thought were good positions, but I'd walk into a meeting and the first question I'd hear would be 'Do astronauts really drink Tang?'" (In the general election, Metzenbaum lost to the Republican candidate, Robert A. Taft Jr.)

When Ohio's other Senate seat became vacant, in 1974, Glenn squared off against Metzenbaum yet again. This time the underdog, Glenn ran a much smarter campaign. He exploited the fact that Metzenbaum, who had a higher net worth than Glenn, had used legal shelters to pay less than Glenn had in taxes. In the May primary election, Glenn trounced Metzenbaum by more than 94,000 votes. That November, Glenn cruised to an easy victory over his Republican opponent, Ralph J. Perk, the former mayor of Cleveland, winning 64.6 percent of the vote.

In part due to his impressive victory and national name recognition, Glenn was selected as the co-keynote speaker for the 1976 Democratic National Convention. He was even considered a strong candidate to become the vice presidential running mate of Jimmy Carter, who had won the Democratic nomination and would go on to claim the presidency. However, according to some accounts, Glenn's less-than-stellar speaking style doomed him. "His chances for the vice presidential spot died as his listless address crashed into the restless crowd, which found no magic in him," Eugene Kennedy wrote in the *New York Times Magazine* (October 11, 1981).

In 1980 Glenn was reelected to the Senate in a landslide victory against his Republican opponent, James E. Betts. Glenn captured 69 percent of the vote, and that high margin, plus his status as a national hero, perhaps made people forget his lackluster speech at the 1976 convention. When Glenn declared his intention to seek the Democratic nomination for president in 1984—just one year after *The Right Stuff*, Tom Wolfe's highly acclaimed account of the first seven American astronauts, was made into a movie—many pundits initially considered Glenn the strongest challenger to the leading

candidate, Walter Mondale. Once again, however, Glenn's uninspiring public speaking and technocratic demeanor made it difficult for people to rally around him. After several disappointing finishes in the early state primaries, he dropped out of the campaign, $3 million in debt.

In his early years in the Senate, Glenn concentrated primarily on three committees—Foreign Relations, Governmental Affairs, and the Special Committee on Aging. *Politics in America: The 100th Congress* noted that he was "the polar opposite of the typically ambitious legislator struggling to get his finger into every pie." He became an expert on energy concerns, defense, and, particularly, nuclear-antiproliferation issues. He sponsored numerous pieces of legislation designed to prevent nuclear weapons technology from slipping into the hands of governments that did not already possess it. Those include amendments that prohibited U.S. aid to countries that exported or imported nuclear reprocessing equipment, and provisions that placed controls on the export of nuclear materials from the United States. His antiproliferation stance often put him into conflict with the Republican president Ronald Reagan. Glenn's military-like attention to detail and narrowness of concern did not always serve him well in the horse-trading environment of Congress. *Politics in America, 1984* described him as "a soporific speaker whose tendency to read speeches in full—even when no one is listening—often drives his colleagues to distraction." Still, Glenn's support in Ohio remained as strong as ever. In the 1986 election against Republican Thomas N. Kindness, Glenn won 62 percent of vote.

Following his 1980 reelection, Glenn left the Foreign Relations Committee and began serving on the Armed Services Committee. *Politics in America, 1992* stated that Glenn, coming from a military background, "tilted to the hawkish side," but added that his "overall record is that of a centrist who does not hesitate to oppose weapons systems." For instance, Glenn initially supported development of the B-1 bomber but later voted against it, arguing that it was too costly. Glenn served as chairman of the Governmental Affairs Committee from 1988 to 1994 and successfully sponsored the creation of the Cabinet-level Department of Veterans Affairs. On issues that he did not specialize in, he typically expressed moderate views.

In the late 1980s Glenn's political reputation suffered a blow through his association with Charles Keating Jr., a savings-and-loan-association operator who was later convicted of fraud. Glenn had met Keating in 1970, and Keating had raised for him over $200,000 in campaign funds by 1986. After an investigation of Keating was launched in the late 1980s, Glenn, along with four other senators—the Democrats Alan Cranston, Donald W. Riegle Jr., and Dennis DeConcini and the Republican John McCain— became known as "the Keating Five," as their ties with Keating were explored. In 1991 the Senate Ethics Committee found that

Glenn had not committed any crimes but had exercised bad judgment when he arranged a lunch meeting in January 1988 between Keating and the Speaker of the House, Jim Wright, just months after regulators had informed Glenn that prosecution against Keating was in progress.

Though Glenn had been found innocent of influence peddling, the political fallout from the "Keating Five" scandal became apparent in his reelection bid in 1992 against the Republican Mike DeWine, who was then the lieutenant governor of Ohio. DeWine hammered away at Glenn's Keating connection, as well as Glenn's failure to pay off the $3 million debt from his presidential campaign. A memorable ad that borrowed from Energizer's well-known battery commercials declared that Glenn "just keeps owing, and owing, and owing." Another negative ad suggested that Glenn was an out-of-touch astronaut: the ad asked, "After 18 years in the Senate, what on Earth has John Glenn done?" In the reelection fight of his life, Glenn countered with some negative ads of his own. He held on to his Senate seat by winning 51 percent of the vote to DeWine's 42 percent.

On February 20, 1997, the 35th anniversary of his orbit around Earth, Glenn announced that, because of his age, he would not be running for the Senate again in 1998. "There is still no cure for the common birthday," he quipped during the announcement. Glenn's decision meant the end, within two years, of a 24-year political career in which he had cast approximately 9,500 roll-call votes.

A year later, it became apparent that Glenn was planning to leave office with a bang. In January 1998, NASA announced that during his last year as a senator, Glenn would become the oldest human ever to be sent into space. (The previous record-holder was Dr. Story Musgrave, who was 61 when he made his last flight on the shuttle *Columbia*, in 1996.)

NASA's announcement came after two years of quiet lobbying on Glenn's part to win himself a place on the shuttle. He had long dreamed of going back into space, but he could not find an appropriate justification until 1995, when, as a member of the Senate Special Committee on Aging, he noticed that the physiological changes that occur in astronauts in space is similar to those that people on Earth experience as they get older. These changes include weakening of bones, deterioration of muscles, loss of coordination, greater susceptibility to infection, and disruption of sleep. "I figured we could learn a lot if we sent an older person up, studied what the effects of weightlessness were, and tried to learn what turns these body systems on and off," he told Jeffrey Kluger for *Time.com* (August 17, 1998).

After assembling some scientific data, Glenn pitched his case to NASA's administrator, Daniel Goldin, in the summer of 1996. After some consideration, Goldin agreed to let Glenn go up under two conditions: the study would have to pass scientific peer review, and Glenn's health would have to be acceptable. Both requirements were met. Glenn, who power-walked two miles every day and regularly flew his own plane between Ohio and Washington, D.C., was in excellent health.

The announcement of Glenn's impending shuttle ride made front-page news all across the country. Many people were moved by the sight of the elderly Glenn once again posing for the cameras in a spacesuit. Others questioned the validity of the study and the real motivations behind it. Some critics interpreted the Glenn venture as a ploy by NASA to attract publicity and funding. Others suspected that Glenn's shuttle ride was meant to reward him for protecting the Democrats during investigations of campaign finance abuses during the 1996 election campaigns. (The Republican Fred Thompson, who had taken over as chair of the Governmental Affairs Committee in 1994, had led the investigation. As the ranking Democrat on the committee, Glenn ran interference for his party, accusing Thompson of investigating only alleged abuses by Democrats. The resulting conflict in the committee prevented the investigation from accomplishing much.)

After undergoing extensive training and even more extensive media exposure, Glenn was launched back into space with six other scientists aboard the space shuttle *Discovery* on October 29, 1998. He noted that, in a weird bit of symmetry, his grandsons were the same ages, 16 and 14, that his daughter, Carolyn (called Lyn), and son, John (called Dave), were when they saw him go up in 1962. But there were also substantial differences in this space flight. Whereas Glenn's first trip into space could be compared to flying "coach" (he had had only 36 cubic feet of habitable space), his second flight was more like "first class." On the shuttle *Discovery*, there is over 332 cubic feet of room for each of the seven crew members, as well as tastier food than was provided for Glenn during his earlier orbit, such as smoked turkey, Kona coffee, and shrimp cocktail.

During the nine-day flight, Glenn was poked, prodded, and required to give samples of blood and urine to enable scientists to measure his muscle deterioration. During sleep, his breathing, brain activity, and eye movements were also closely monitored. Approximately 80 other experiments were conducted on the shuttle flight, in areas ranging from astronomy, to solar physics, to the design of drug-delivery systems. As a payload specialist, Glenn helped perform some of these tasks. Meanwhile, back on Earth, the two-term Republican governor of Ohio, George V. Voinovich, won Glenn's Senate seat in the November 3 elections.

After completing 134 orbits of Earth, the shuttle successfully landed at Kennedy Space Center, in Cape Canaveral, Florida, on November 7. Fears that, after the rigors of the flight, Glenn would have to be carried out of the shuttle on a stretcher proved to be unwarranted; he walked out under his own power and in good health. The mission was followed by 17 more days of monitoring to complete the geriatric experiments.

Glenn has said that he will undertake no more missions in space. His wife, he told the *New York Times* (November 9, 1998), has "been through enough. I owe her some consideration at this point in life." Glenn chairs the National Commission on Mathematics and Science Education for the 21st Century, which was set up by the U.S. Department of Education in March 1999; the goals of the commission are to recruit, train, and retain high-quality math and science teachers in kindergarten through 12th grade. Glenn's plans include working with students at the John H. Glenn Institute for Public Service and Public Policy, at Ohio State University, and at Muskingum College, in New Concord, Ohio, to combat political apathy and cynicism. — W.G.

Suggested Reading: *Life Online*; *New York Times* A p8 Jan. 17, 1998, A p7 June 13, 1998, with photos, A p1+ Nov. 8, 1998, with photo; *New York Times Magazine* p32+ Oct. 11, 1981, with photos; *Parade* p4+ July 11, 1976, with photos; *Time.com* Aug. 17, 1998, with photos; *Washington Post* C p1 Oct. 22, 1992, with photos, A p4 Feb. 21, 1997, with photos; *Politics in America 1998: The 105th Congress*, 1997

Robert Matthews/Courtesy of Princeton University

Gott, J. Richard III

Feb. 8, 1947– Astrophysicist. Address: c/o Princeton University, Dept. of Astrophysical Sciences, 118 Peyton Hall, Princeton, NJ 08544

In 1969, before pursuing a graduate degree in astrophysics at Princeton University, J. Richard Gott III—now a recognized authority in astrophysics—took some time to travel through Europe. In the course of his *wanderjahr*, he visited the Berlin Wall, which had been erected eight years earlier by the East German government to restrict free passage between its Communist-run segment of the city and democratic West Berlin. "People at that time wondered how long the Wall might last," Gott recalled to Timothy Ferris for the *New Yorker* (July 12, 1999). "Was it a temporary aberration, or a permanent fixture of modern Europe?" Gott made what might be called an extremely educated guess—of the sort that would eventually bring him a great deal of attention. Fresh from earning his undergraduate degree in physics from Harvard University, he considered the question in terms of probability theory and the Copernican principle. Named after the 16th-century Polish astronomer Nicholas Copernicus, who theorized that the sun, not Earth, was the center of our planetary system, the Copernican principle is the assumption that odds are against any specific time, place, or occurrence being special in the broad scheme. To calculate the probable life span of the Berlin Wall, Gott first determined that there was nothing special about his trip: it was completely random in time and circumstance. Then he envisioned the entire life span of the Berlin Wall divided into four quarters. Given the randomness of his visit, there was a 50 percent probability that his trip fell within the two middle quarters of the wall's life span; in other words, his visit was not made "special" by occurring in either the first or last quarter of the wall's existence. If his visit fell at the beginning of the wall's second quarter, Gott posited, then three-quarters of its life lay ahead, thus making the wall's potential future three times as long as its past. By multiplying the wall's age—eight—by the number of quarters it potentially had left to survive—three—Gott calculated that there was a 25 percent probability that the Berlin Wall would survive more than 24 years. If his visit fell at the end of the wall's third quarter, on the other hand, then only one-quarter of its life lay ahead, thus making the wall's future only one-third as long as its past. By dividing the wall's age by the number of quarters of its history that possibly had already passed—again, three—Gott determined that there was also a 25 percent probability that the Berlin Wall would survive fewer than two and two-thirds years. Gott surmised that there was therefore a 50 percent chance that the Berlin Wall would stand for a total of not less than two and two-thirds years and not more than 24 years. "Twenty years later, in 1989, the Wall came down, within those two limits that I had predicted," Gott told Timothy Ferris. "I thought, Well, you know, maybe I should write this up."

Gott published his findings, and explained his method, in 1993 in the scientific journal *Nature*. Afterward, he and some of his colleagues in the scientific community tested it in a variety of ways. The method was used to predict—with some degree of accuracy, as it turned out—the runs of various Broadway plays and the duration of the Conservative Party's control of the British government. Gott's prediction for the duration of the human race drew a great deal of scrutiny. Since scientists usually calculate predictions to a 95 percent level of confidence, Gott decided to conform to that standard when calculating how long humankind will survive. He based his calculations on the widely accepted estimate that Homo sapiens has existed as a species for 200,000 years. To begin, Gott assumed that all humans currently alive exist in the middle 95 percent of our species' total duration, because it is unlikely that we exist in either the first or last 2.5 percent of Homo sapiens' total existence. Since 2.5 percent is equal to one-40th of a whole, there is a 95 percent probability that our future as a species is no longer than 39 times but no less than one-39th our past. Using the same method as he had for the Berlin Wall, Gott multiplied 200,000 by 39, which equals 7.8 million, and divided 200,000 by 39, which equals a little more than 5,128. Therefore, Gott computed to a 95 percent confidence level that Homo sapiens will endure between 5,128 and 7.8 million more years. Because the average existence for mammalian species has been about two million years, this prediction seems to hold water. However, many have resisted Gott's prediction, choosing to believe either that the end of the world is approaching rapidly or that humankind will survive virtually forever. "That's because people like to think that they're living in special times," Gott noted to Timothy Ferris. "We like to think of ourselves as near the beginning of things, or in an apocalyptic situation near the end. It's more dramatic that way."

Citing such technological advancements as space exploration and genetic engineering to support their arguments, lay critics of Gott's method of predicting the duration of the human race have countered that, regardless of his assertion to the contrary, we are living in an exceptional era in which humans are exhibiting high cognitive powers and adaptability—a "special" time. Gott's response to those detractors has been that we live in an era in which Earth is more populated than it has ever been. (Statistically speaking, most people will be born in epochs of high population.) Since technological advancements are developed by humans, it stands to reason that a greater number of humans will result in a greater number of advancements. Furthermore, Gott has cautioned, higher intelligence does not guarantee survival. He observed to Timothy Ferris, "People think that, sure, other species go out of business every million or so years, but since we're smarter than they are we will last

longer. Unfortunately, the facts don't really bear this out. I mean, Einstein was very, very smart, but he didn't live longer than the rest of us. Smartness doesn't seem to be correlated very well with longevity in the animal kingdom, right up to and including very smart species, similar to us."

A second group of critics—scientists and others with a specialized knowledge of statistics—have found his ranges absurdly broad and therefore meaningless. In other words, they contend that there is virtually no difference between predicting that humans will exist as a species for between 5,128 and 7.8 million years and predicting that humankind will survive for a time between now and infinity. In a response to those critics, Gott told *Current Biography*, "I would say, of course, that understanding that there was a 95 percent chance that the future duration of the human race would lie between 5,128 years and 7.8 million years provides a lot more information than knowing that our future lies somewhere between zero and infinity. One is a finite range, the other is infinite! A finite range rules out many possibilities that are often discussed. It's important to know that the human race is not likely to go extinct in the next century, nor likely to last a trillion years!" Gott has used his rough estimates to get across his point that humans are a finite presence on the planet and to support his argument that further space exploration and colonization of other planets may ultimately offer our best chance of survival as a species. "A lot of people say there's no need for a manned space program, because we can learn just as much by sending out interstellar robots," Gott explained to Browne. "But this ignores the desire by the human race to survive. The earth is a pretty dangerous place. If we hope to survive in the long term, it would make sense to start colonizing other habitable planets." As Gott has pointed out, evolution has proven that those species that can successfully reproduce and spread out survive the longest. Therefore, he has concluded, by multiplying and spreading out through the colonization of other planets, we would increase our species' chances of overcoming extinction on Earth.

In the years between the summer of 1969 and the publication of his method of predicting life spans, Gott became one of the world's leading authorities on astrophysics and emerged as one of the most original thinkers in that specialty and mathematics. His groundbreaking work with Albert Einstein's equations of general relativity—which explain gravity as a curving of space and time—brought him to the vanguard of American scientific thought, while his extensive research in support of the theory that the universe is open, or forever expanding, has established him as a visionary in the area of abstract concepts. Gott's research frequently questions the basic theorems and assumptions with which physics has made sense of the known universe. Consequently, his theories have philosophical resonance, concerning as they do the very existence of humans and our environment—and they tend to unnerve scientists content to work solely with known quantities. His hypotheses, based on sound empirical mathematics, are difficult to dismiss, and they have held up well under the intense scrutiny to which they have often been subjected. In addition to winning attention for his research, Gott has been identified by students as one of their favorite professors at Princeton University, where he has taught since 1976. He has also been active in community education, conducting seminars and observations at Princeton's observatory that are open to the general public.

The only child of J. Richard and Marjorie (Crosby) Gott, J. Richard Gott III was born on February 8, 1947 in Louisville, Kentucky. His mother—a conservationist, landscape-design expert, and charter member of the Louisville Astronomical Society—engendered in her son a deep interest in science. By the time he had enrolled in Waggener High School, Gott was an active member of Louisville's Junior Astronomical Society. The organization, among the most sophisticated of its kind, offered students instruction in advanced astronomical concepts through more than 40 public programs each year, and access to such equipment as an observatory with a 21-inch reflector telescope. As Gott's interest in science grew, so did his role in the society: he acted as an editor for its publications, served as its vice president, and eventually was elected president. In the mid-1960s Gott had back-to-back first- and second-place finishes in the math divisions of the International Science and Engineering Fair and the Westinghouse Science Talent Search, respectively.

Upon graduating from high school, in 1965, Gott was accepted at Harvard University, in Cambridge, Masssachusetts, where he was awarded an undergraduate degree in physics in 1969. He then went on to receive a doctorate in astrophysics from Princeton University, in Princeton, New Jersey, in 1973, before accepting postdoctoral fellowships at the California Institute of Technology, in Pasadena, and Cambridge University, in England. He returned to Princeton in 1976 to begin his tenure as an assistant professor. In 1987 he obtained full professorship.

Gott's recent work with probability theory is not his first to be challenged by the scientific community. He has also faced controversy in connection with a theory, introduced in 1988 by Kip Thorne, a physicist from the California Institute of Technology, according to which time travel seemed possible. Thorne proposed that wormholes, which are theoretical channels that connect distant points in space and time and are thought to exist at the center of black holes, could offer a portal to the past. According to Einstein's theory of relativity, the speed of light is considered the threshold for time travel. As an object approaches the speed of light, time begins to slow for that object; if the object reaches the speed of light, time stops; therefore, if that object moves faster than the speed of light, it will travel backward in time. Since it is

universally accepted by physicists that it is physically impossible to exceed the speed of light, it has been assumed that time can move only forward. The notion of time travel is thus anathema to physicists' concept of the universe. Consequently, Kip Thorne's proposal for time travel through wormholes underwent an assault by such noted theorists as Cambridge University's Stephen Hawking, who wrote a treatise, titled "The Chronology Protection Conjecture," in which he argued the physical improbability of time travel and sarcastically cited, as part of his proof, the fact that "we have not been invaded by hordes of tourists from the future." Many have accepted Hawking's withering attack as the final word on time travel.

Meanwhile, Gott became the first scientist to solve the equations in Einstein's general theory of relativity specifically for cosmic strings. According to the big bang theory, all matter in the cosmos was once concentrated into an extremely small mass that exploded, approximately eight to 13 billion years ago, creating tremendous heat. The primeval fireball is thought to have lasted only a few hours as it expanded, but the energy released would have been great enough to induce atomic fusion. From there, according to the theory, matter would have cooled and condensed, forming galaxies, stars, solar systems, and other heavenly bodies. Cosmic strings are thought to be strands of vestigial energy from the big bang that have survived unaltered since creation. They are thought to be infinitesimally thin but extremely dense, containing trillions of tons of mass per inch. Because of their density and the tremendous gravitational pull that results, cosmic strings could warp all space and time surrounding them.

Thorne's proposal, despite the attacks mounted against it, intrigued Gott. He began to think of cosmic strings and his application of Einstein's equations—which allow scientists to compute the ways in which space and time can be distorted given a number of common variables—in terms of time travel. From his solutions to Einstein's equations, Gott calculated that if two parallel cosmic strings were to travel in opposite directions past each other near the speed of light, they would bend the surrounding area sufficiently to provide a shorter route between two points. Therefore, if a spaceship made a loop around both cosmic strings, effectively taking advantage of the shortcut formed by the cosmic strings, it could beat light to a given point without having to break the speed of light. According to the logic of relativity, even though the ship would not have traveled faster than the speed of light, by beating light to its destination the ship would arrive at its launching point before it had taken off.

Gott published the results of his calculations in the prestigious journal *Physical Review Letters* in 1991, and like Thorne he drew fire from all corners of the scientific community, most of which still considers time travel an impossibility even in the realm of theoretical physics. Many also had trouble accepting the philosophical implications of time travel. For instance, what would happen if a person traveled back in time and killed his or her grandparents? Would that person cease to exist? Gott has insisted that the debate should remain open, because even if time travel can be ruled out as a practical possibility, investigating it may lead to other discoveries. "Every time we find a new solution to Einstein's equations, we find out something new about physics," Gott said to David H. Freedman for *Discover* (April 1992). "That was the case with black holes, and now it's happening again with strings. This situation is trying to tell us something, and we should keep exploring it until we know what it is." Kip Thorne, concurring with Gott's assessment, told John Travis for *Science* (April 10, 1992), "If we can understand how nature protects herself from time travel, we would understand space and time more fully."

Described as a cheerful personality, a colorful dresser, and an avid punster, J. Richard Gott III lives in Princeton, New Jersey, with his wife, the

former Lucy Pollard, and their daughter, Elizabeth. In 1975 he received the Astronomical Society of the Pacific's R. J. Trumpler Award for his doctoral work at Princeton, and he was awarded an Alfred P. Sloan Research Fellowship that extended from 1977 to 1981, during which time he examined the theory that the universe is continuously expanding. Louisville's Waggener High School inducted Gott into its inaugural Hall of Fame class in 1996, and in 1998 Princeton honored him with a President's Award for Excellence in Teaching. — T.J.F.

Suggested Reading: *Discover* p54+ Apr. 1992, with photo; *New Scientist* (on-line) Dec. 6, 1997; *New York Times* C p1 June 1, 1993, with photo; *New Yorker* p35+ July 12, 1999; *Science* p179+ Apr. 10, 1992; *Science News* p202+ Mar. 28, 1992; *Time* p74 May 13, 1991, with photo; *Who's Who in America, 1999*

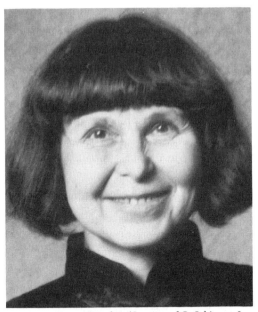

Monroe Warshaw/Courtesy of G. Schirmer, Inc.

Gubaidulina, Sofia

Oct. 27, 1931– Classical-music composer.
Address: c/o G. Schirmer Promotion Dept., 257 Park Ave. S., 20th Fl., New York, NY 10010

"A woman among composers; a freethinker among Soviet apparatchiks; a Christian among atheists; an Easterner, half Tatar, among Europeans; a modernist among reactionaries, and a reactionary among modernists: Sofia Gubaidulina has lived with

many conflicts both with the outside world and within herself," Paul Griffiths, a critic who specializes in avant-garde classical music, wrote for the *New York Times* (April 25, 1999). "Her arrival, in her 50s and 60s, at moments of extraordinary musical power has been a triumph of persistence and self-searching." During the 1960s and 1970s, Gubaidulina was forced to toil in relative obscurity, her career impeded by Soviet bureaucrats who frowned on her devotion to both Christianity and musical experimentation. Nevertheless, she held fast to her artistic vision, which is inextricably tied to her religious beliefs, as she made clear in a conversation with K. Robert Schwarz for the *New York Times* (February 13, 1994). "I can't think of any way to explain the existence of art other than as a means to express something greater than ourselves," she said. "I can't reach a single musical decision except with the goal of making a connection to God. If I separated the religious goal from the musical one, music would have no meaning for me."

Gubaidulina started to attract attention outside the Soviet Union during the 1980s, in large part as a result of Gidon Kremer's performances worldwide of *Offertorium*, for violin and orchestra, which is among her most highly regarded works. Since the last years of the 1980s, when profound changes in the political climate of her native land began to occur, she has emerged as one of Russia's most prominent composers—perhaps the most important one, in the opinion of many classical-music aficionados, since Dmitri Shostakovich, who died in 1975. She is ranked with such other leading Russian composers as Edison Denisov (1929–96) and Alfred Schnittke (1934–98).

Gubaidulina's dozens of compositions include symphonic, choral, and chamber music; concertos; works for piano, organ, flute, and other instruments, sometimes solo and sometimes in unusual combinations (tuba and piano, for example, or harp, double bass, and percussion); pieces for percussion instruments only; and music for folk and ritual instruments, such as the lute-like domra, from Russia, and the bayan, a drum from India. She has earned commissions from such patrons as the Chicago Symphony Orchestra, the New York Philharmonic, the Kronos Quartet, the Library of Congress, and the Berlin, Helsinki, and Holland music festivals.

More often than not, according to Paul Griffiths, a composition by Gubaidulina is "a journey through conflict toward new knowledge and illumination" that "uses a wide range of musical means" and "justifies that range as a crucial necessity to a composer intent on immediate expressive force." Gubaidulina, he wrote, "exhibits no commitment to fine style." "What makes Gubaidulina's music so special is its inherent spirituality, framed in an idiom both immediately accessible and rich in intellectual challenge," the musicologist Laurel E. Fay, who has served as the composer's English translator, once wrote, as quoted by Tim Page in New York Newsday (April 21, 1989). "On first acquaintance with almost any of her works, the extraordinary range of instrumental color is immediately apparent. The human qualities of her instrumental writing—the sounds of breathing, sighing, cries, screams—are especially haunting. . . . In what is clearly a highly personal expression of spiritual values, her music seems to tap the wellspring of a universal subconscious." "In her best works," Griffiths declared, Gubaidulina has "always delivered" the "same message": "a message of fierce struggles and ecstatic coming home."

Sofia Asgatovna Gubaidulina was born on October 27, 1931 in the city of Chistopol in the Tatar Autonomous Soviet Socialist Republic, a part of the former Soviet Union that is now called the Tatarstan Republic. She is the daughter of a Tatar father and a Russian mother; because of her Central Asian and European ancestry, Schwarz wrote, "she refers to herself as 'the place where East and West meet.'" Raised in Kazan, the capital of the Tatar Republic, she received instruction in piano and composition at the Kazan Conservatory, from which she graduated in 1954. For the next nine years, she continued her study of composition at the Moscow Conservatory. Her composition teachers there were Shostakovich's assistant Nikolai Peiko and Vissarion Shebalin. She also worked with Philipp Herschgowitz, a pupil of the avante-garde Austrian composer Anton von Webern (1883–1945), who had been strongly influenced by the Austrian-born musical innovator Arnold Schönberg (1874–1951), the developer of 12-tone, or serial, music. Gubaidulina's early years in Moscow coincided with the brief period of relative artistic freedom that followed the death, in 1953, of Joseph Stalin, the bru-

tal dictator who had ruled the Soviet Union since 1924, and she was able to embrace approaches to music, such as those of Webern, that had not been welcomed in Stalinist Russia. But before long the political winds reversed again, and the conservatory's old guard, who encouraged music that glorified the political regime, gained the upper hand. "The main demand the teachers made was that young composers be joyful and happy," Gubaidulina recalled to Schwarz. "And they were not pleased with someone who didn't want to uphold that idea."

Gubaidulina and her work were not without supporters, however. Prominent among them was Shostakovich, who, on the day of her graduation examination, said to her, "I want you to continue down your mistaken path." "I'll never forget those encouraging words," she told Karen Campbell for the Christian Science Monitor (August 27, 1997, on-line). "It is very difficult for a young person to hear only criticism. Shostakovich encouraged me to be myself, no matter what everybody else said, and I am very grateful for that." In a conversation with Bernard Holland for the New York Times (April 24, 1989), she said, "Dmitri Shostakovich and Anton Webern had the greatest influence on my work. Although their influence appears to have left no traces in my music, these two composers taught me the most important lesson of all: to be myself."

In contrast to most graduates of the Moscow Conservatory, Gubaidulina did not pursue a career as a music teacher. "It was impossible for me to teach composition then," she has explained, as quoted by Harlow Robinson for the Lincoln Center Stagebill (December 1984). "Maybe now I wouldn't be afraid of it, but then it was too early. You have to be so sure of your philosophical, mystical, and creative positions to teach composition. I think a composer's craft is his mystical understanding, which comes only with maturity. Modern culture is spiritual culture, not just intellectual. Only when you understand what you need and where you are going can you really teach others." Despite the Soviet establishment's disapproval of her work, she continued to compose, but few of her compositions were performed or recorded. "Up until about 1975, things were very negative," she recalled to John Rockwell for the New York Times (January 24, 1988). "I became depressed and disturbed. Finally I went to the Composers Union and explained my position. For some reason—I'm not sure why—things got a little better."

Meanwhile, Gubaidulina made a modest living by writing film scores. In total she composed the music for some 20 Soviet-made movies. As was customary, she received payment for each minute of music she wrote. By producing 50 minutes of music annually—a task that occupied her for about three months out of each year—she earned enough to cover her expenses. Although composing music for films was not her passion, she displayed both versatility and unusual skill in tackling her assignments. John Rockwell wrote that her works for cinema "encouraged what might be called a practical eclecticism (providing music to suit a dramatic situation), perhaps satisfied her theatrical inclinations (opera she rejects as involving too many collaborators), and even offered some personal satisfaction." "I've tried to choose films that allow me to be myself," she told Rockwell. Gubaidulina wrote the music for *Scarecrow*, the biggest box-office success in the Soviet Union in 1986. Directed by Rolan Bykov, who completed the movie in 1983, *Scarecrow* is about a schoolgirl who is ostracized by her peers. According to a review by Hal Hinson for the *Washington Post* (November 24, 1987), the School Teachers Union's disapproval of the story caused the three-year delay in the film's release. Gubaidulina's work for the movies also includes collaborations with Ida Garanina on animated films.

In 1975, along with the composer Viktor Suslin and the composer-ethnomusicologist Vyacheslav Artyomov, Gubaidulina co-founded the Astreya Ensemble (also spelled "Astrea," "Astreia," "Astraea," and "Astreja" in various sources), with the aim of improvising music using folk, ritual, and other nonorchestral instruments from the Caucasus region of southeastern Europe, Russia, and Central and East Asia. The ensemble performed publicly and also made studio recordings, some for movie soundtracks. "After an interval of several years," according to an undated on-line profile of Gubaidulina produced by the German record company Sikorski, she and Suslin "recently revived the idea" of the ensemble.

In a review of what Alex Ross, in the *New York Times* (July 6, 1995), described as an "extraordinary performance" by Astreya in Lockenhaus, Austria, at the 1995 Kremerata Musica Festival, founded by the Soviet-born violinist Gidon Kremer, Gubaidulina "demonstrated that a carefully controlled improvisation can have an electricity unmatched by printed music," as Ross wrote. After reporting that she "energetically whirled among an exotic array of Asian Russian folk instruments," he wrote that the two improvisational pieces Astreya presented "moved from . . . anarchic free-jazz-like textures to steady ostinato beats or widely spaced lyric solos. They seemed no less fully argued than the notated works heard later in the evening," he continued, among them Gubaidulina's "savagely concise 10 Preludes for cello. . . . At passing moments, her music alludes to Russian Orthodox chant, Russian and Tatar folk tradition, Bach, even Webern. But the associations are all part of a viscerally evolving fabric in which recognition of sources is secondary. She refuses the intellectualism common to 20th-century composers; her work is wholly devoted to fullness of sound and richness of story. Its deep intelligence becomes apparent only on later hearings."

Gidon Kremer has been one of Gubaidulina's staunchest supporters since the 1970s, when he repeatedly challenged what was, in effect, the Soviet government's ban on public performances of her music and that of other avante-garde Soviet composers. "I stumbled over profound resistance from Government officials, from concert organizers, who tried to convince me that I should not perform the music of Schnittke or [Arvo] Pärt or Gubaidulina," Kremer told Schwarz. "And every time I won a battle, I had my little satisfaction that another performance took place." Gubaidulina wrote *Offertorium* (1980), which she has called a "large symphonic piece with violin" rather than a violin concerto, for Kremer, who made it a staple of his repertoire. In January 1985 Kremer played it at its United States premiere, with the New York Philharmonic conducted by Zubin Mehta. Inspired by the theme from Johann Sebastian Bach's *Musical Offering* (composed in 1747 for Frederick the Great, the king of Prussia, who is said to have suggested the theme), *Offertorium* addresses the "task of formation, as in all my works," Gubaidulina told Harlow Robinson for the *Lincoln Center Stagebill*. After hearing the work, the critic John Rockwell wrote for the *New York Times* (January 5, 1985), "Gubaidulina is something of a mystical conceptualist, it seems. At times the central theme, at times the violin part, perhaps at times the violinist, become the participants in an artistic-religious rite. The precise rituals are unclear, but the intensity is overt, and affecting. . . . The varied idioms in *Offertorium* come together in an open, accessible yet unmistakably personal statement. . . . Not least of Miss Gubaidulina's achievements is the crafting of a solo part to which Mr. Kremer can address himself with full seriousness. It stretches his considerable technique, eliciting serene virtuosity."

Gubaidulina visited the U.S. for the first time in 1987, at the invitation of the University of Louisville School of Music in Louisville, Kentucky, to participate in its Sound Celebration. In 1988 her music was performed in Boston at the Making Music Together Festival, a collaborative effort that involved several hundred Soviet and American musicians and dancers. In April 1989 the new-music ensemble Continuum, under the direction of Joel Sachs and Cheryl Seltzer, presented a concert of Gubaidulina's music at Alice Tully Hall, in New York City. The program featured the U.S. premieres of *Perception* (1983), written for soprano, baritone, seven strings, and tape; *Quasi Hoquetus* (1984), for viola, bassoon, and piano; and *Quattro* (1974), for two trombones and two trumpets; as well as the New York premiere of *De Profundis* (1978), for solo accordion. Another among Gubaidulina's boosters is the Kronos Quartet, which the violinist David Harrington founded in 1973 with the goal of creating a wider forum for 20th-century music. The Kronos Quartet has performed her String Quartet no. 2 since 1987, the year she wrote it, and the group commissioned her String Quartet no. 4.

A notable feature of Gubaidulina's third quartet for strings is the total absence of bowing in its first half; instead, the musicians create sound by plucking and otherwise manipulating the strings with their fingers. "Every work needs a different technical method," Gubaidulina said to Harlow Robinson. "There is no one method." She has also said, "Serialism or any other techniques only fill in the background for me. The central idea is the most important thing."

"Gubaidulina isolates and reinvents the basic materials of music," Alex Ross wrote for the *New Yorker* (June 17, 1997). "She can take something as familiar as a major triad and send it spinning through all registers and tone colors until it becomes a new creature. When her players take moves from the avant-garde manual—cascades of overtones in the strings, raucous woodwind flutter-tonguing, tone-bending brass glissandos—the effects are controlled and developed until they become characters in a drama. . . . [Gubaidulina] is, most of all, a genius of narrative, marshalling sounds in a free, vital, and unstoppable procession."

Gubaidulina's orchestral works include *The Steps* (1971); Concerto for Symphony Orchestra and Jazz Band (1976); *Seven Words* (1982), for cello, bayan, and strings (the title refers to the seven last words of Christ); the 12-movement symphony *Stimmen . . . Verstummen . . .* (1986); *The Unasked Answer* (1989), for three orchestras; *Figures of Time* (1994); *In the Shadow of the Tree* (1998), which was commissioned by the NHK Symphony, a Japanese orchestra, and incorporates passages for solo koto (a long Japanese zither), bass koto, and zheng (a Chinese zither); and *Two Paths* (*Dedication to Mary and Martha*, 1999), for two violas and orchestra, which was commissioned by the soprano Tomoko Sakurai and had its world premiere in April 1999, with Kurt Masur (Sakurai's husband) conducting the New York Philharmonic. Gubaidulina's choral works include the cantatas *The Night in Memphis* (1968), *Rubaiyat* (1969), and *Perception* (1983); *Hour of the Soul* (1976), which is set to text by the Russian poet Marina Tsvetayeva; and *Alleluia* (1990), a work for large orchestra, organ, mixed chorus, and young male soloist. Her most recent compositions, dating from the late 1990s, include *And: The Festivities at Their Height*, for cello and orchestra, and a Viola Concerto, which was written for the violist Yuri Bashmet.

According to the 1984 profile of her by Harlow Robinson, Gubaidulina described herself as having "a lack of restraint, a stubbornness in dealing with authority, [and] a nomadic soul." When K. Robert Schwarz interviewed her, in 1994, Gubaidulina appeared "shy and reticent" at first. "But once the focus settled on music, she turned animated. Moving easily from the mundane to the spiritual, she seemed sincere and almost childlike in her exuberance. Although the life she recounted was one filled with pain, she showed no bitterness." Gubaidulina has maintained that the Soviet system was not without advantages for working composers. "It seems to me that we were luckier than wom-

en in [the United States]," she observed to Schwarz. "When I have spoken to women composers from the West, they have complained to me that they felt discrimination. In Russia, women composers never complained about discrimination. It was equally miserable for everyone." Gubaidulina won the Rome International Composer's Competition in 1974. Her many other honors include the Prix de Monaco (1987) and the Russian State Prize (1992). She earned the Koussevitzky International Record Award, bestowed annually by the Musicians Club of New York, in 1989 and 1994 for *Offertorium* and *Stimmen . . . Verstummen . . .*, respectively.

Gubaidulina has lived in Hamburg, Germany, since 1992; she also keeps an apartment in Moscow, where her husband lives. "I'm convinced that serious art can be distinguished from ephemeral art by whether it finds a form that connects to God," she told Schwarz. "Any convincing form is a path to the throne. The only difference between Bach and we simple people of the 20th century is that he had a stairway to the throne, and we only have an attempt." — Y.P.

Suggested Reading: *Christian Science Monitor* (on-line) Aug. 27, 1997, with photo; *Lincoln Center Stagebill* p33+ Dec. 1984, with photo; *New York Times* II p27 Feb. 13, 1994, with photo, C p13 Aug. 18, 1997, with photo, II p29 Apr. 25, 1999, with photos; *New Yorker* p109+ June 17, 1997

Selected Recordings: *Now Always Snow*, 1993; *And: The Feast Is In Full Progress*, 1993; *Offertorium/ Rejoice!*, 1993; *Concordanza*, 1994; *Seven Words*, 1996

Hamm, Mia

Mar. 17, 1972– Soccer player. Address: c/o U.S. Soccer Federation, 1801–1811 S. Prairie Ave., Chicago, IL 60616

Watching Mia Hamm speeding away from defenders on the soccer field, one might get a sense of the rocket-like trajectory of her career. She first played on the U.S. Women's National Soccer Team at the age of 15, making her the youngest player ever to do so. Twelve years later, the star forward has accumulated statistics that distinguish her from any other player, woman or man. She currently holds the record for most goals scored in international play, with 111 goals and nine "hat tricks" (three goals or more in a game) as of the end of the 1999 Women's World Cup. By comparison, Pelé—the Brazilian soccer star who played in the 1950s and 1960s and is widely considered the greatest player of all time—scored 77 goals in international play during his lifetime.

Gregory Foster/Corbis Outline

Mia Hamm

With many potential years of play ahead of her, Hamm has already been anointed by the media as the "best female soccer player in the world." Endorsement contracts from such companies as Nike, Gatorade, Fleet Bank, Power Bar, Earth Grain Bread, and Mattel (she is the spokesperson for a "Soccer Barbie" doll) have come easily to the telegenic star, who was voted one of the 50 most beautiful people in the world by *People* magazine in 1997. Comparisons to Michael Jordan, too, have flown fast and furious. "Mia is to terra firma what Michael Jordan is to the air," Erik Brady wrote in *USA Today* (July 15, 1996). She has even appeared with Jordan in a Gatorade commercial, in which each challenges the other in various sports while childlike male and female voices sing, "Anything you can do, I can do better."

Hamm, a consummate team player who is known for her humility, would be the first to admit that a bit of hype is helping to spur her current stardom. Sports, like films, need stars to draw mass audiences and money; the need is even greater for a relatively new sport like women's soccer, which is currently struggling to gain enough popularity to make possible the creation of a professional league in the U.S. Some people believe that the future of women's soccer depends on Hamm's ability to maintain her image as a superhuman player whom little girls can look up to and idolize. However, her performances during the most-watched women's soccer events did not strike observers as preternaturally spectacular. In each of the Women's World Cups—in 1991, 1995, and 1999—she has scored only two goals; at the 1996 Olympics she scored only one goal. That certainly doesn't mean she didn't have an impact in those games. To compare

her again to Michael Jordan, it was he who drew a double team from the opposing defense to allow his teammate Steve Kerr to get the winning shot in game six of the 1997 NBA finals. Similarly, Hamm usually draws the best defenders on opposing teams and thus opens up opportunities for her teammates.

Despite her failure to rack up dramatic scores in the World Cups, Hamm has generated plenty of excitement off the soccer field. When in public she is constantly besieged by autograph seekers and fans shrieking her name, and many small girls proudly wear replicas of her jersey. But Hamm prefers to share the spotlight, frequently telling interviewers, "The World Cup is not about me." Indeed, she has often pointed out that her teammates—Kristine Lilly, Michelle Akers, Julie Foudy, Tiffeny Milbrett, and Carla Overbeck, to name a few—have skills she doesn't possess. "I'm no better than a lot of people on this U.S. team," she told Mark Starr for *Newsweek* (June 21, 1999). Hamm's humble demeanor has given her a reputation as a reticent, even shy person. Her teammates, however, maintain that this is not the true Mia. "She cracks me up all the time," Foudy told Brady for *USA Today.* "Everyone thinks she's this quiet, reserved person because that's how she comes across in the media. But she is hilarious."

The fourth eldest in a family of four girls and two boys, she was born Mariel Margaret Hamm on March 17, 1972 in Selma, Alabama. Mia got her nickname from her mother, Stephanie, who had studied dance under a ballerina with the same name. Stephanie Hamm envisioned her daughter becoming a dancer, but Mia proved ill-suited for tutus and ballet slippers; enrolled by her mother in ballet classes when she was five, the reluctant Hamm made it through only one class. Hamm preferred sports, and she patterned herself after her older brother Garrett, an adopted Thai-American whom she has said was the real athlete of the family. "Garrett was an influence on me on any form of athletics," she told Jere Longman for the *New York Times* (June 11, 1999). "When he'd go play pickup football or baseball, I was always right behind him. He always picked me for his teams."

Hamm's father was a colonel in the United States Air Force, and her family moved from base to base, living in Italy, California, Texas, and Virginia. Though the frequent moves meant having to leave friends behind, Hamm made new friends easily through the various sports she played. Soccer in particular was a passion of her father's, and he watched, coached, and refereed the game. She started off in peewee leagues; by the time she was 10, she was the only girl on her soccer team. Eventually she became the leading scorer on the team.

Hamm's talent got her placed on an Olympic development team and also brought her to the attention of Anson Dorrance, the coach of both the U.S. national team and the dominant college women's soccer team at the time, the University of North Carolina Tar Heels. Seeing Hamm play for the first time, Dorrance was immediately struck by the 14-year-old's talents. "Mia was playing right half-back," Dorrance told *People* (November 1, 1993). "I watched her take a seven-yard run at the ball. And I said, 'Oh my gosh!' I'd never seen speed like that in the women's game. She had unlimited potential." In 1987, at the age of 15, she became the youngest player ever to compete on the U.S. national team, and three years later she scored her first goal in international play.

After graduating, in 1989, from Lake Braddock High School, in Burke, Virginia, Hamm went to the University of North Carolina to play for Dorrance and the Tar Heels. In her first two years, she scored 45 goals and made 23 assists. She sat out the 1991 season to play for the U.S. national team, coached by Dorrance, in the first Women's World Cup. The youngest member of the team, she started in five out of six games and scored two goals; the U.S. ended up winning the tournament after defeating Norway, 2–1, in the finals. Returning to college play, Hamm had an outstanding 1992 season, scoring 32 goals and making 33 assists. In her senior year she added 26 more goals and 16 assists, bringing her collegiate total to 103 goals and 72 assists, a National Collegiate Athletic Association (NCAA) record. By the time she graduated, in 1994, with a degree in political science, she had helped her team win four NCAA championships and had been named first-team All American, Atlantic Coast Conference Player of the Year, and National Player of the Year three times each. Upon her departure from the team, her jersey, number 19, was retired.

Since then Hamm has played as number nine on the U.S. national team, and she has continued to terrorize her soccer opponents. She had 19 goals and 18 assists in 1995, nine goals and 18 assists in 1996, and 18 goals and six assists in 1997. In 1998 she had the best year of her post-collegiate career in terms of scoring, with 20 goals and 20 assists. The U.S. Soccer Federation named her female athlete of the year an unprecedented five consecutive times, from 1994 through 1998.

In the second Women's World Cup, in 1995, the U.S. lost in the semifinals to Norway, 1–0. Norway went on to win the tournament while the U.S. defeated China, 2–0, to capture third place. Hamm played in all five games, scored two goals, and even showed that she could play goalie. On June 8, during the game against Denmark, the U.S. goalkeeper Briana Scurry was ejected in the 84th minute. No substitutions could be made because the U.S. had already used their allotted three, so Hamm was chosen to protect the goal because of her athleticism. Despite some anxiety upon having her role reversed, she managed to block a shot on goal and thus help lead her team to victory.

The U.S. team got revenge the next year at the 1996 Summer Olympics, the first time women's soccer was included as a medal sport. In the semifinal match, the U.S. women defeated Norway, 2–1, and then beat China in the final, 2–1, to get the gold medal. Hamm, who had missed an earlier game

against China due to a sprained ankle, scored one goal in the five games the U.S. played.

Hamm did not have much time to celebrate her gold medal. Her brother Garrett, who at age 16 had been diagnosed with the blood disease aplastic anemia, was getting sicker. Hamm helped raise money for his treatment and for bone-marrow research through a benefit soccer game—called the Garrett Game—held on February 19, 1997. That same month Garrett underwent bone-marrow transplant surgery, after which he developed an infection; he died two months later, at the age of 28. Hamm subsequently received approval from Nike to include her brother's initials, GJH, on the bottom of her signature Nike M9 shoes (the M stands for Mia, the nine for her jersey number). She also joined the board of the Marrow Foundation and sponsored a second Garrett Game, in 1998.

Losing her brother did not outwardly affect Hamm's play. In 1998, one of her best years on the soccer field, five of her goals came during the Goodwill Games, including the only goals scored in the U.S.'s 2–0 victory against China in the finals. The following year Hamm set the world record for goals scored in international play with her 108th goal, in a pre–World Cup game against Brazil on May 22, 1999. The Italian Elisabetta Vignotto, who played in the 1970s and 1980s, held the record previously. Only two other women—Carolina Morace from Italy and Michelle Akers from the U.S.—have scored more than 100 goals in international play.

At the 1999 Women's World Cup, the largest sporting event ever held for women, expectations for Hamm's performance were high. The U.S. made it to the final after dispatching Denmark, Nigeria, North Korea, Germany, and Brazil; Hamm's two goals in the tournament came against Denmark and Nigeria. With more than 90,000 people watching the final against China at the Rose Bowl, Hamm and her teammates battled the Chinese for two scoreless hours; the game was decided on a penalty kick-off, which the U.S. won, 5–4.

The Women's World Cup, tickets to which were scalped for up to 10 times their purchase price, caused a media frenzy. *Mademoiselle* and other glossy magazines, and televison shows as diverse as *The Late Show with David Letterman* and *Hard Copy*, sought interviews with Hamm and her teammates. Commentators enthusiastically pointed out that for the first time, women athletes were enjoying the same attention as their male counterparts. (Few broadcasters or journalists, however, noted the pay disparity that still exists between top-rated male athletes and female athletes of even Hamm's high caliber.)

Despite all the acclaim she has received, Hamm believes that much in her game could be improved. "A great finisher can analyze in a split second what the goalie is doing, what surface of the foot to use, and then put the ball in exactly the right spot," she told Mark Starr for *Newsweek*. "It's an ability to slow down time. You don't actually shoot any faster than other players do, but you process a lot more information in the same time. I'm still working on all that." Statements like these, which seem to typify Hamm's attitude, have led some people to wonder if she is too intense about her sport. "There's a fine line between setting standards that keep you getting better and being hypercritical to the point that it undermines your confidence," the current coach of the U.S. national team, Tony Di-Cicco, told Jere Longman for the *New York Times*. "She's always flirted with that line."

Hamm, who is five feet four inches tall and weighs about 125 pounds, met Christian Corry in a political-science class, and they were married in about 1994. He has since become a marine pilot. In her spare time Hamm likes to play golf, read, and spend time with her husband. With Aaron Heifetz, she wrote the autobiographical book *Go for the*

Goal (1999), and she recently founded the Mia Hamm Foundation, which provides funding for education and research on bone-marrow disease and also supports endeavors aimed at encouraging female athletes. — W.G.

Suggested Reading: *New York Times* VIII p6 Apr. 25, 1999, with photo; *New York Times* (on-line) June 11, 1999, June 14, 1999; *Newsweek* p60+ June 21, 1999, with photos; *People* p63+ Nov. 1, 1993, with photos, p90 May 12, 1997, with photo; *Seventeen* p42+ June 1994, with photos; *Southern Living* p42+ Apr. 1996, with photos; *USA Today* C p7 Sep. 2, 1993, with photo, C p12 July 15, 1996, with photo; *Washington Post* E p1 May 23, 1995, with photo, D p4 June 8, 1997, with photos

---

Shonna Valeska

Harris, Judith Rich

Feb. 10, 1938– Theorist in psychology; nonfiction writer. Address: 54 Crawford Rd., Middletown, NJ 07748

Kicked out of graduate school in the 1960s and almost totally confined to her suburban home for many years because of an autoimmune disorder, Judith Rich Harris has spent most of her career on academia's intellectual sidelines, as a writer of textbooks rather than an active participant in innovative research. Nevertheless, she has produced what some experts consider an original theory of child development. With one article, "Where Is the Child's Environment?," which appeared in 1995 in

the prestigious journal *Psychological Review*, and one book, *The Nurture Assumption* (1998), she has ignited a controversy that is threatening to overturn longstanding assumptions about how children's personalities develop.

Based primarily on her familiarity with the literature of developmental psychology, evolutionary psychology, and behavioral genetics, Harris's theory is that, in the long term, peers have a more lasting impact on one's personality and character than do one's parents. Whether parents hug, hit, or read to their children matters less over time, she argues, than the children's experiences within the peer groups to which they attach themselves. Harris's theory contradicts a long-held tenet of mainstream contemporary developmental psychology: the "nurture assumption," according to which the way parents behave with their children influences their offspring's psychological, social, and emotional development more powerfully than any other external factor.

Harris's theory has been both praised and condemned. The linguist Steven Pinker, who wrote the introduction to *The Nurture Assumption*, has called the book a "turning point in the history of psychology." Other experts in the field have contended that Harris has placed an exaggerated emphasis on the importance of the peer group in childhood and that her book is sending a potentially dangerous message about parental responsibility. Thanks in part to the vigorous debate that has developed over Harris's ideas, as well as the media blitz that accompanied the publication of her book, it now seems likely that her ideas will be included in future child-psychology textbooks, and *The Nurture Assumption* will be cited as a primary source. "It's as if the gods were making up to me all that they had done to me previously," Harris told Malcolm Gladwell for the *New Yorker* (August 17, 1998). "It was the best gift I could have ever gotten: an idea. It wasn't something that I could have known in advance. But, as it turned out, it was what I wanted most in the world—an idea that would give a direction and a purpose to my life."

Harris was born Judith Rich on February 10, 1938. Her family moved frequently when she was young, and she attended eight different nursery and primary schools. Looking back on her early years, she later realized how much her peers had influenced her—in particular, her peers at a school in Westchester County, New York. When she arrived in Westchester, she had been an extroverted tomboy; then, shunned by her classmates, she became an introverted bookworm. "The kids in the snooty suburb had accomplished what my parents could not," she once wrote, as quoted by Bo Emerson in the *Atlanta Journal-Constitution* (October 1, 1998, on-line). "They had changed my personality."

Harris's family eventually settled in Tucson, Arizona, because the climate there was ideal for her father, Sam, who suffered from ankylosing spondylitis, an autoimmune disorder. Harris attended Tucson High School and then entered the University of Arizona. Later, she transferred to Brandeis University, in Waltham, Massachusetts, where she won the Lila Pearlman Prize in psychology and from which she graduated, magna cum laude, in 1959. She then entered a doctoral program in psychology at Harvard University, in Cambridge, Massachusetts, where she had a hard time getting her professors to take her seriously. Harris noted to Bo Emerson that at that time, "I was small, I was cute. People had a tendency to pat me on the head. I did not look like someone who would accomplish something." (Five feet tall and currently weighing about 98 pounds, she still cuts a slight figure.)

In 1960 Harris received a letter from the chairman of Harvard's Department of Psychology informing her that she was being ousted from the program. The letter, as quoted by Gladwell, stated, "I hesitate to say that you lack originality and independence, because in many areas of life you obviously possess both of those traits in abundance. But for some reason you have not been able to bring them to bear on the kind of problems in psychology to which this department is dedicated. . . . We are in considerable doubt that you will develop into our professional stereotype of what an experimental psychologist should be."

After receiving a master's degree, in 1961, and marrying Charles S. Harris, a fellow graduate student, Harris worked as a teaching assistant in psychology at the Massachusetts Institute of Technology (1961–62) and then as a research assistant at the research-and-development firm Bolt Beranek and Newman (1962–63) and the University of Pennsylvania (1963–65). In 1966 she gave birth to her daughter Nomi and became a full-time homemaker. About four years later she and her husband adopted an infant girl, Elaine. "For 10 years I did nothing but be a housewife and mother," Harris told Paula Span for the *Washington Post* (October 28, 1998).

Harris was restarting her career, in the mid-1970s, when she experienced the first symptoms of what was diagnosed as a combination of lupus and systemic sclerosis. "It started with my joints, went on to my digestive system, damaged the nervous system—I have no sense of smell," she told Paula Span. From about 1977 on she was plagued with a variety of medical problems, including pneumonia, heart murmurs, pulmonary hypertension, shingles, chronic hives, and a minor stroke. She tried to resume her studies in psychology—she brought a cot to class so that she could lie down while taking lecture notes—but the strain of commuting to school proved to be too much for her. Largely confined to her home, Harris worked, in collaboration with several others, on mathematical models of processing of visual information. In the 1980s she began writing developmental-psychology textbooks, and she continued that pursuit for about a dozen years. With R. M. Liebert, she co-authored three editions of *The Child* (1984, 1987, 1991) and a single edition of *Infant and Child: Development from Birth through Middle Childhood* (1992).

In 1994, while working on another edition of *The Child*, Harris began to have doubts about some of the information she was presenting as truths in the book. Indeed, she now feels embarrassed by the contents of *The Child*. "I don't want people to go and buy it," she told Paula Span. "I wrote it before the scales fell from my eyes."

According to Harris, the "scales fell" on January 20, 1994. On that day she read a psychology paper on juvenile delinquency that suggested that teenagers became delinquent because they want to be like adults—for example, that kids smoke because only adults are allowed to smoke, so by smoking, kids think they appear more mature. Harris sensed that something was wrong with this thesis. Teenagers want to *contrast* themselves with adults, she thought, not be *like* them. Kids want to be like other kids. After she came to that realization, it occurred to her that her idea could drastically change accepted wisdom about the importance of parenting.

Her own child-rearing experiences seemed to confirm the hypothesis that no matter how hard parents try to shape their children, their kids may not turn out the way they want. This was the case with Harris's daughter Elaine, who, at age 11, started getting into all sorts of trouble. "As the girls got older, Nomi became a brain and Elaine became a dropout," Harris explained to Malcolm Gladwell. "Nomi was a member of a very small clique of intellectual kids, and Elaine was a member of the delinquent subgroup. They went in opposite directions." Although she and her husband felt that, in Harris's words, they "had followed all the rules" in raising Elaine, their efforts in parenting seemed to have had no effect, and they were powerless to change her behavior outside the home or influence her choice of companions. (Harris is quick to point out that Elaine is now happily married, has two children and a career as a licensed nurse, and enjoys good relations with her parents.)

Harris knew that she needed more systematic evidence to support her hunch. She immediately stopped work on the textbook she was writing and began an exhaustive investigation into the topic, delving into social psychology and cultural anthropology. Since the closest university to her home, Rutgers, was too far for her to commute to regularly, she relied on her local public library and interlibrary loans.

Gradually, Harris fleshed out her theory. Her hypothesis, for example, seemed to explain why children of immigrants don't retain the accents of their parents and why children of deaf parents learn to speak as well as children of parents who can hear. If parents are more important than peers, then presumably children would speak like their parents; if peers are more important, that would explain the accent-free English of the children of immigrants. Harris's theory also seemed to explain why two adopted children raised in the same home aren't more similar to each other than two randomly picked strangers, and why identical twins raised in the same household are no more alike than identical twins raised in separate households. She also noted that prior to the 1950s, many developmental psychologists didn't consider parenting the most crucial factor in shaping a child's personality.

In August and September 1994, Harris outlined her theory in an article entitled "Where Is the Child's Environment? A Group Socialization Theory of Development." She sent it to *Psychological Review*, a leading psychology journal that, like other distinguished journals, rarely publishes articles submitted by individuals not associated with any academic institution. Nevertheless, the article was accepted after a process of blind review (meaning that Harris's identity was not revealed to the reviewers), and it was published in 1995. Immediately, Harris was flooded with E-mail from psychologists interested in her hypothesis. Buoyed by the encouragement of many of them, over the next three years she expanded her article into a book, *The Nurture Assumption: Why Children Turn Out the Way They Do*. It was published by the Free Press in 1998.

Much of the article and the book is devoted to rebutting studies that claim to show the power of parental influence. Harris believes that many of those studies are flawed by epistemological problems—that is, basic problems connected with the ways developmental psychologists carry out their research and interpret their results. Thus, the tendency for "good" parents to have "good" children may appear to be an effect of nurture, but it may actually be the result of genetics. Harris has also pointed out that it is often difficult to separate cause and effect in child development. A researcher might find, for instance, that there is a correlation between hugging a child and the congeniality of that child, namely, that children who get hugged a lot are more pleasant and sociable than children

who do not. One interpretation of that finding is that a lot of hugging causes a child to be more congenial. But it may also be true that a child who is by nature congenial elicits more hugs from the parent than a child who isn't.

Other studies have shown that kids with single parents are more likely to drop out of school than children from two-parent homes. That finding might also seem to contradict Harris's thesis. She has argued, however, that the lack of two parents has a bearing on a child's peer relations. A single parent is likely to have less income than two parents, and thus the single parent's child is more likely to live in a worse neighborhood and be exposed to more "negative" peer behavior than a child from a two-parent home. Also, single-parent families typically relocate more often than two-parent families, causing disruption in children's connections to peers.

While parents' influence on the behavior of their children may appear strong within the home, Harris has argued that children often behave differently outside the home—a phenomenon she has termed the "Cinderella effect." In the fairy tale, Cinderella behaved in a humble, self-effacing manner at home; she behaved so differently at the king's ball that her stepmother and stepsisters did not recognize her. Similarly, children who are honest at home may cheat or lie in the outside world; those who fight with siblings may be very warm to their friends. "When children go out, they leave behind the behavior they acquired at home," Harris was quoted as saying in the *American Psychological Association Monitor* (October 1998). "They cast it off like the dorky sweater their mothers made them wear."

Linking her theory to other fields of scientific inquiry, Harris has speculated that, from an evolutionary perspective, it may make sense that kids are more influenced by their peers than their parents, because as adults—that is, for the largest portion of their lives—they will have to work with their peers, not their parents, and their partner in marriage will most likely come from among their peers.

A majority of psychologists have not accepted all aspects of Harris's theory. Some psychologists, among them Jerome Kagan, believe that Harris has ignored evidence showing that how parents behave with their children can be very effective. Others feel that Harris has purposely offered an extreme argument in hopes of promoting her book. According to Paula Span, "*The Nurture Assumption* isn't full of possiblys and maybes—it makes predictions like 'children would develop into the same sort of adults if we left their lives outside the home unchanged—left them in their schools and their neighborhoods—but switched all the parents around.'" Still, most of Harris's critics agree that she has drawn attention to an under-researched field of child psychology.

Harris believes that if her theory is correct, parents should feel less anxiety and pressure about parenting; after all, a mistake will not make or break a child's future character. "I want to tell parents that it's all right," she told Malcolm Gladwell. "A lot of people who should be contributing children to our society, who could be contributing very useful and fine children, are reluctant to do it, or are waiting very long to have children, because they feel that it requires such a huge commitment. If they knew that it was O.K. to have a child and let it be reared by a nanny or put it in a day-care center, or even to send it to a boarding school, maybe they'd believe that it would be O.K. to have a kid. You can have a kid without having to devote your entire life—your entire emotional expenditure—to this child for the next 20 years." Others, however, see Harris's theory as potentially dangerous, because it seems to excuse parents whose parenting is poor.

Harris has acknowledged that parenting does matter to some extent. For example, she has suggested that parents try to find housing in good neighborhoods, so that their children will have a better chance of associating with acceptable peers. She has also advised parents to provide clothing that conforms to the prevailing standards of fashion and to pay for orthodontics and plastic surgery, if needed, so that their kids do not look too different from their peers. "I do think there is something to the possibility that parents determine their child's peer group," she told Sharon Begley for Newsweek (September 7, 1998). Moreover, Harris has acknowledged the possibility that peer groups don't necessarily affect everything that determines

personality. "If the group doesn't care about plans for the future, then the child can retain those ideas from home," Harris told Begley. "And if things like an interior life aren't discussed by peers, then that wouldn't be affected by the group either." And parents can provide comfort—something that can benefit children substantially in the here and now, even if it doesn't shape personality.

Despite her limited mobility, Harris traveled to the American Psychological Association's annual meeting in California in 1998 to receive the George A. Miller Award, for her distinguished work in integrating various fields of psychology. (Ironically, it was George Miller who wrote Harris the letter that suggested she leave the Harvard graduate program.) Harris is continuing to write about her theory of development and to criticize the research methods used by academic psychologists. "I feel like I'm involved in teaching the next generation," she told Paula Span, "even if 90 percent of current psychologists reject what I'm saying." — W.G.

Suggested Reading: Atlanta Journal-Constitution (on-line) Oct. 1, 1998, with photo; New York Times B p9 May 8, 1999, with photo; New Yorker p54+ Aug. 17, 1998; Newsweek p53+ Nov. 7, 1998, with photo; USA Today (on-line) Aug. 4, 1999, with photo; Washington Post D p1+ Oct. 28, 1998, with photo

Selected Books: The Nurture Assumption, 1998; with Liebert, R. M.—The Child 1984, 1987, 1991; Infant and Child: Development from Birth through Middle Childhood, 1992

Hartwell, Leland H.

Oct. 30, 1939– Geneticist. Address: c/o Fred Hutchinson Cancer Research Center, LA-205, 1100 Fairview Ave. N., Seattle, WA 98109-1024

"Science is a very social thing," Leland H. Hartwell, a professor of genetics at the University of Washington and head of the Fred Hutchinson Center for Cancer Research, both in Seattle, told Susan Luce for the Seattle Times (August 8, 1995). "Ideas don't come to you in the dead of night." Rather, as he explained to Luce, he views scientific ideas as akin to clay in the hands of many artists collaborating on a sculpture. At the Hutchinson Center, sometimes referred to as the Hutch, where he has served as president and director since 1997, he has continued an initiative he spearheaded upon his arrival there, as a senior adviser, in 1996: namely, that of fostering multidisciplinary approaches to research on cancer.

Hartwell is well known for his pioneering work with yeast. In what has proved to be one of the most significant genetic discoveries of the past 30

years, he showed that yeast's cell-division cycle—the process by which one cell becomes two, thus enabling an organism to grow—is controlled genetically. He has also demonstrated the existence of "checkpoint" genes, which, in normal cells, recognize genetic errors and make it possible for them to be corrected before each stage of cell division. Hartwell went on to apply his research on checkpoint genes to the study of cancer in humans; he and others theorize that in many instances cancer may occur because of mutations in the checkpoint genes that impair their ability to recognize genetic errors; thus the mistakes multiply, creating genetic instability. While Hartwell has been described as a "scientist's scientist," he has long recognized the value of collaboration, which can lead to a sort of cross-pollination of ideas. He accepted the job as director of the Hutch largely because he had begun "to realize that people, and them trying to accomplish things and working together is more interesting than science," as he explained to Shelly Esposito, a professor of molecular genetics and cell biology at the University of Chicago, during an October 1998 interview transcribed for the Albert and Mary

Courtesy of Fred Hutchinson Cancer Research Center
Leland H. Hartwell

Lasker Foundation Web site. "I like the aspect of being more involved with dealing with people in an institution and people's careers . . . [people who] are trying to accomplish something with their lives and interact. I just find the human element, I think, of playing the game of science more fun than the science."

Leland H. Hartwell was born on October 30, 1939 in Los Angeles. "I came from a family that was very nonacademic, so I didn't recognize at an early stage the clear interest that I had in science as a child," he told Esposito. "Looking back, it's easy to see now. I always collected bugs and took things apart and spent time at the library trying to learn things about radios and astronomy and various stuff like that without noticing that my peers weren't spending their time the same way." Hartwell also occupied his free hours by working for his father, who made neon signs, and for a time electricity was his chief interest. Despite his wide-ranging natural curiosity about science-related subjects, Hartwell has acknowledged that upon entering high school, he had little direction and a less-than-impressive academic record. He became a member of a Los Angeles gang called the Sinbads, who sported black wool jackets emblazoned with an image of a dragon, and spent his nights drinking and cruising city streets.

By midway through his junior year in high school, Hartwell had lost interest in the gang, and after graduation he enrolled at Glendale Junior College, where he took science courses and received encouragement from his teachers. A counselor there got Hartwell an interview with a visiting professor from the California Institute of Technology (Cal Tech), in Pasadena, and he was admitted to that prestigious school as a second-year student "only because the recruiter had to fill in the sophomore class which was depleted by the drop-outs after freshman year," Hartwell was quoted as saying in a profile of him in the *American Society of Cell Biology (ASCB) Newsletter* (February 1999). At Cal Tech, Hartwell told Esposito, "I discovered a whole fabulous world of science that I really didn't even know existed." He added that the school "was just an unbelievable sort of fairy tale place for me. You were spending your time thinking about really interesting scientific issues, and the faculty there treated the undergraduates like they were colleagues rather than students. It just gave me a sense of involvement and the possibility of participating in science, sort of an invitation, I guess I would say, that I look back on and just cherish those years." He initially chose to study physics, but a class on DNA prompted him to join the ranks of the six biology majors in his graduating class. (Biology was an unpopular major because of students' belief that there were few available jobs in the field.) Cal Tech gave undergraduates the opportunity to do research that would have been delegated to graduate students at other institutions, and Hartwell worked in a number of professors' labs during the academic year and summers.

Upon completion of his B.S. degree, in 1961, Hartwell entered the Massachusetts Institute of Technology, in Cambridge, where he studied gene regulation under the microbiologist Boris Magasanik. "He would come by every afternoon and ask you how your experiments were going," Hartwell told Esposito, "so it sort of kept you at a feverish pace for having results every day, but he never told you what to do. . . . He made it very clear that you were plotting your own course. . . . I think it . . . really helped me develop that sense of: I was the master of my research, and I had to find my own way." After receiving his Ph.D., in 1964, Hartwell did postdoctoral work at the Salk Institute of Biological Studies, in La Jolla, California, where he studied cell division under Renato Dulbecco, a leader in that area of research. The Salk Institute was just getting off the ground, and its facilities were, in Hartwell's words, "a series of trailers." Despite the lack of amenities, he enjoyed a period of concentrated learning there, during which he studied cell division in mammals and became interested in the timing of the steps in cell division and abnormal cell growth.

In 1965 Hartwell took a position as an assistant professor at the University of California at Irvine. By the end of his year at the Salk Institute, he had grown frustrated with the research methods available, because he felt they were inadequate for the study of physiologically complex organisms. So during the several months before his lab equipment arrived in Irvine, he searched for an organism simpler than mammals that was nonetheless relatively genetically advanced. He settled on baker's yeast, a one-celled fungus, and became one of very few scientists using yeast cells to research cell division. At that time few people recognized that yeast, like the fruit fly and the mouse, is an excellent "model organism," in that in many respects its systems are analogous to those in humans. As a young scientist embarking on a career, Hartwell was therefore taking a big risk by studying yeast. He now considers this leap of the imagination—which enabled him to see "that a study of cell division, even though it was motivated by an interest in human cells and medical problems like cancer, needed to be explored in a much simpler system using genetics as a powerful tool," as he explained to Esposito—to be his most significant contribution to science. Since the late 1980s yeast has been a popular experimental subject in research involving genetics and basic cellular processes, among other fields.

In his work with yeast, Hartwell attempted to identify genes that might control the cell-division cycle. By studying mutations in the genes and looking at the primary defect each caused, he succeeded in determining the function of individual genes, including ones that guided protein synthesis and other cellular processes involved in cell division. Although all the ramifications of his research would not become clear until decades later, his findings—regarded as the defining discoveries of his scientific career—provided invaluable insights into cell division and spurred the emergence of cell biology as an important specialty. Hartwell's first published work on yeast appeared in the *Journal of Bacteriology*, in 1967, and what is considered his groundbreaking article was published in the *Proceedings of the National Academy of Sciences*, in 1970. Hartwell is currently credited with the discovery of more than 50 genes that control the cell cycle in yeast. "For over 30 years, a majority of the key insights into the cell cycle have been made by him," Mark Groudine, who directs the basic sciences division at the Hutch, told Jim Kling for *Current Biology* (1997).

In 1968 Hartwell became an associate professor at the University of Washington, largely because "it was the premier genetics department, and I had not received any formal genetic training," as he was quoted as saying in the *ASCB Newsletter* (February 1997). He set up a lab at the university, where, at any given time, he oversaw an average of eight researchers, supported mainly by a single grant (renewed periodically) from the National Institutes of Health. In 1969 Brian Reid, an undergraduate working in Hartwell's lab who later joined him as professor at the University of Washington, began taking photographs of his research subjects through a microscope. Reid's work involved genes whose mutations became apparent only at certain temperatures, and in his photomicrographs he captured images of cells at stages when they were unable to divide. This work gave Hartwell much new information about the cell-division cycle, and he and his co-workers spent the next five years studying cell-cycle mutants. Questions and ideas that arose during this period, including those which gave rise to Hartwell's work on cell-division checkpoints, fueled his research for many years.

In 1974 Hartwell theorized that the cell cycles of yeast and human cells had specific similarities, and that the cells had "originated in a common past," as Susan Luce put it. In 1987 Hartwell's idea was corroborated by the work of Paul Nurse, who found that a particular human gene that performs a specific function in the cell-division cycle can perform that same function when placed in a yeast cell that lacks the gene normally responsible for that function. That human gene and the gene it replaced in the yeast cell are called homologues; they perform the same function in different species. Homologues from different species sometimes have almost identical DNA. Scientists theorized that where there was one pair of homologue genes—the one consisting of that particular human gene and that particular yeast gene—there might be many more, and this idea proved to be correct. Hartwell and other scientists have since identified human counterparts to some of the genes that Hartwell isolated in yeast, and it is believed that many of the genes he discovered are found in both plants and animals. Thus Hartwell's research on how genes control cell division in yeast became directly applicable to the understanding of cell division in humans, and that knowledge is shedding new light on many diseases, including cancer.

In 1983 Hartwell took a sabbatical to do research at Stanford University, in California, funded by a Guggenheim Fellowship he was awarded that same year. He spent the following year, again on sabbatical, at the Fred Hutchinson Cancer Research Center. The Hutchinson Center, one of 35 comprehensive cancer research centers designated and funded by the National Cancer Institute, is one of the few such institutions that have strong faculties in four distinct research divisions: basic sciences, which involves research in cellular and molecular biology; clinical research, which involves observations of patients and includes the center's bone-marrow transplant program, the largest in the world; public-health sciences, which encompasses research in biostatistics, cancer prevention, and epidemiology; and human biology, in which techniques drawn from molecular biology, cellular biology, and genetics are used along with those of other disciplines to achieve a greater understanding of human biology and diseases. Hartwell had briefly done research on cancer biology early in his career, and he had always been interested in the implications his work on cell division held for the understanding of cancer.

At about the time of his sabbaticals, Hartwell and Ted Weinert, a postdoctoral fellow working in his lab, began identifying genes that ensured that events in the cell cycle happened according to plan. These genes, which they dubbed "checkpoints," made sure that each stage of cell division was complete before the next began. Checkpoint genes also recognize defects in cells, caused by, for example, radiation or exposure to chemicals, and will prompt pauses in the cell-division cycle that allow DNA-repair mechanisms to fix the defects before the cell divides. When the checkpoint genes themselves have mutations that cause them to malfunction, cancer may result. Thus, a greater understanding of the checkpoint genes may provide important clues for the treatment of the disease.

By the mid-1990s Hartwell believed that strides in molecular biology had created a potential for major advances in the study of many diseases. "The entire yeast genome has been sequenced," he stated for an article on the Fred Hutchinson Cancer Research Center Web site (April 4, 1996). "There are 7,000 genes in yeast and 70,000 genes in humans. We will know the identity of most of those genes by the end of the century. While it will still be a long time before we understand their functions, we are now in a position to look at the impact of genetic factors in disease." This conviction was among the many reasons behind Hartwell's decision, in 1996, to become senior scientific adviser at the Hutch. In that position, which was created specifically for him by the center's director, Robert Day, Hartwell led a project dubbed the Interdivisional Research and Training Initiative, which was intended to promote interdisciplinary education, training, and research among the center's four divisions. According to Hartwell, while the need to increase such cooperation was widely recognized among the biomedical research community at large, no other institutions—medicals schools, universities, and cancer centers—were making large-scale efforts to do so. "When we've really got it right, it will be natural for the students to look at the full dimensions of whatever they work on," Hartwell was quoted as saying on the center's Web site (April 4, 1996). "That is, they will think about the basic, the clinical, and epidemiological dimensions of their problem, and they will find it easy to talk to people in each discipline. The cross-cultural exchange will be easy for students. That clearly is not there now."

While reactions to the initiative among scientists at the Hutch ranged from approval to skepticism, many were impressed by Hartwell's interest in tackling such a problem. "It was refreshing to me that a senior person with a very substantial reputation as a basic biological scientist was willing to move his base to [the Hutch] and commit half his time to interdisciplinary research program development . . . ," Ross Prentice, the director of the center's public-health division, told Jim Kling. "As scientists we tend to have the knee-jerk reaction that whatever we don't know about can't be important, so it takes somebody with confidence to step out and endorse the groups and areas that they are not a part of." Hartwell's interest in stimulating collaboration stems from his belief that such interdisciplinary work, by helping scientists to see "the big picture," as Kling put it, will speed the discovery of effective cancer treatments. In 1997 Day retired from his post as the Hutchinson center's pres-

ident and director and, in a vote of confidence in the direction in which Hartwell's initiative was leading the center, he was named Day's replacement. Although as head administrator of an institution with 2,300 employees, Hartwell has less time to conduct his own research, he still maintains a lab at the Hutch. He has expressed wholehearted optimism about the future of cancer treatment.

Hartwell, who has made his home in Seattle for more than 30 years, told the *ASCB Newsletter* (February 1999) that when he speaks of his adopted city, "I sound like the Chamber of Commerce." He is particularly enamored of the Pacific Northwest's spectacular natural scenery, and he steals time to enjoy the outdoors by riding his bicycle to work almost every day. He is a member of numerous professional societies, including the National Academy of Sciences and the American Society for Cell Biology, and he is an American Cancer Society Research Professor of Genetics. Among his many professional honors are the Eli Lilly Award in Microbiology and Immunology, in 1973; a National Institutes of Health Merit Award, in 1990; a Gairdner Foundation International Award for Achievements in Science, in 1992; the Sloan-Kettering Cancer Center Katherine Berkan Judd Award and the Genetics Society of America Medal, in 1994; and the Albert Lasker Basic Medical Research Award and the Susan G. Komen Breast Cancer Foundation-Brinker International Award, in 1998. Hartwell's sons, Todd and Gregg, live near him in Washington State, and his daughter, Sherie, lives on the East Coast with her husband, a molecular biologist at the University of Connecticut. Hartwell's wife, Theresa Naujack, works as photographer at the Hutchinson Center. — M.B.

Suggested Reading: Albert and Mary Lasker Foundation Web site; *American Society for Cell Biology Newsletter* p2+ Feb. 1999, with photos; *Current Biology* (1997); Fred Hutchinson Cancer Research Center Web site; *Quest* p1+ Winter 1997, with photos; *Seattle Times* A p6+ Aug. 8, 1995, with photos

---

Hastert, Dennis

Jan. 2, 1942– Speaker of the U.S. House of Representatives. Address: 2263 Rayburn House Office Bldg., Washington, DC 20515-1314

In the wake of the November 1998 elections, in which a former professional wrestler, Jesse Ventura, was elected governor of Minnesota, it should have come as no surprise when, two months later, a former high-school wrestling coach, Dennis Hastert, was elected to the highest position in the United States House of Representatives. On January 6, 1999 Hastert, a Republican representative from the

Courtesy of U.S. House of Representatives

Dennis Hastert

14th Congressional District in Illinois, took the gavel from his highly controversial predecessor Newt Gingrich and formally became the 59th Speaker of the House. In a speech on the floor of Congress following his acceptance of the Speakership, Hastert pledged to forge bipartisan compromise between House Democrats and Republicans, who had been bitterly divided over the historic impeachment of President Bill Clinton. That pledge has proven easier to make than to fulfill. With a style much more laid-back than that of Gingrich—and with mixed results—Hastert has attempted to work successfully with Democrats and unite the moderate and conservative factions within his own party in addressing such issues as taxes and the military.

To hear Hastert tell it, officiating in the House of Representatives does not differ much from preparing for a wrestling tournament. Comparing the House to a large athletic team and his role as Speaker to that of a coach, he said in his speech in Congress, "A good coach knows when to step back and let others shine in the spotlight. . . . A good coach doesn't rely on only a few star players. Everyone on the squad has something to offer. You never get to the finals without a well-rounded team. Above all, a coach worth his salt will instill in his team a sense of fair play, camaraderie, respect for the game and for the opposition. Without those, victory is hollow and defeat represents opportunities lost."

The oldest of the three sons of Jack and Naomi Hastert, John Dennis Hastert was born on January 2, 1942 in Aurora, Illinois. With his younger brothers, David and Chris, he grew up on a farm in Yorkville (about 15 miles southwest of Aurora and 45

miles southwest of Chicago) in a house surrounded by corn and soybean fields. His father, who had acquired the farm in 1940, after working as an embalmer, ran a feed-supply business. By the time Hastert was a teenager, his father had entered the restaurant business as well, operating the Clock Tower restaurant in Plainfield and establishments in Naperville and Aurora. Dennis helped keep the feed-supply operations running by hauling 100-pound bags of feed to local farms. "That's where he got his football shoulders," his brother David told Alex Rodriguez for the *Chicago Sun Times* (February 1999, on-line).

Hastert attended Oswego High School (a few miles from Yorkville), where he played football, wrestled, ran track, participated in activities of the Future Farmers of America, sang in the operetta club chorus, and acted in a play called *Terror in the Suburbs*, in which he was cast as the villain. After graduating, in 1960, he entered North Central College, in Naperville, then transferred to Wheaton College, an evangelical Christian school in Wheaton, Illinois. During summers he supported himself by delivering milk, waking up before dawn to do the job.

After earning an A.B. degree from Wheaton, in 1964, Hastert returned to Yorkville to teach government and history at Yorkville High School. He also coached the wrestling team and helped coach the football team. As Alex Rodriguez reported, "His [wrestling] teams won consistently, largely because of the amount of time Hastert devoted to them. It wasn't uncommon for him to pack his team into his white Dodge van, which lacked air-conditioning, and trek them to wrestling camps in other states. Once he piled them in the van and drove to a Virginia camp to learn a single wrestling maneuver he had heard about, a move called the Gramby Roll." The Yorkville wrestling team won a state championship in 1976. Hastert also served as president of the Illinois Wrestling Coaches Association and was a member of the U.S. Wrestling Foundation.

Earlier, in 1967, Hastert earned a master's degree from Northern Illinois University, in DeKalb. In 1973 he married Jean Kahl, a physical-education teacher at Yorkville High School. Because of a shoulder injury, he was not drafted during the Vietnam War. During his summer vacations he often went abroad—to Japan, Colombia, Venezuela, Europe, and the Soviet Union—to teach for the YMCA and other groups.

Hastert has traced his interest in politics to a 1978 visit to Washington, D.C. After seeing politicians close up, he realized, as he recalled to Alex Rodriguez, "These guys are like anybody else. They don't have an aura around their heads or anything." After returning to Illinois, he began working in his spare time as an aide for then–State Senator John Grotberg, a Republican. In 1980 he ran for a seat in the Illinois Assembly, recruiting some of his ex-wrestlers and their parents to help in his campaign. He was eliminated from the race in the primary, having come in third behind Suzanne Deuchler and the incumbent, Allan Schoberlein. Then, because of illness, Schoberlein quit in the middle of the general-election campaign. Hastert took his place on the ballot and went on to win the Assembly seat. Reelected twice, he served a total of six years, from 1981 through 1986. One of his mentors in the Assembly was Thomas Ewing, who would later join him in the U.S. House of Representatives.

In 1986 ill health forced John Grotberg, who by then represented Illinois's 14th Congressional District in the House, to retire, and Hastert threw his hat into the ring. He won the Republican primary in June 1986. Meanwhile, his Democratic opponent, Mary Lou Kearns, the coroner of Kane County, had been campaigning since the summer of 1985. What had once seemed like a safe Republican seat was suddenly up for grabs. On Election Day, November 4, Hastert defeated Kearns by just 7,000 votes, or a margin of only 4 percent.

Since he arrived in the House, Hastert has never faced a serious challenger in any electoral contest. In each of his reelection bids, he has beaten his Democratic opponent in a landslide. In 1988, running against Stephen Youhanaie, he got 74 percent of the vote; in 1990, against Donald J. Westphal, 67 percent; in 1992, against Jonathan Abram Reich, 67 percent; in 1994, against Steve Denari, 76 percent; in 1996, against Doug Mains, 64 percent; and in 1998, against Robert Cozzi, 70 percent of the vote.

Early on, Hastert became a protégé of Republican Robert Michel, the House minority leader then. As a junior representative, he served on the Government Operations, Public Works, and Transportation Committee and the Select Children, Youth, and Families Committee. In 1990 he switched to the Energy and Commerce Committee. Later, he became chairman of the National Security, International Affairs, and Criminal Justice Subcommittee of the House Government Reform and Oversight Committee.

In the 103d Congress (1993–94), Hastert served as a deputy whip, a position in which he helped his party's whip line up support for various policies. After Republicans recaptured a majority of the House, in 1994, and Newt Gingrich became Speaker, Hastert was elevated to deputy chief majority whip to Tom DeLay, the newly elected majority whip.

Health-care reform is one of the issues with which Hastert became most closely associated. He served as the only House Republican on Hillary Rodham Clinton's Health Care Task Force in 1993 and helped write the health-care reform bill that President Bill Clinton signed into law in 1996. Hastert's growing prominence among Republicans became evident in 1998, when he chaired a 15-member Republican group that drafted a Republican alternative to Democratic patient-protection bills. (The Republicans' bill passed in the House but not in the Senate.) That year he also led Republican efforts to block Democratic attempts to permit the use of sampling in the next national census.

The sequence of events that paved the way for Hastert to become Speaker of the House began with the November 1998 elections. Many pundits had predicted that the Democratic Party would suffer at the polls because of the troubles of President Bill Clinton, who was facing impeachment for charges related to his affair with a former White House intern, Monica Lewinsky. But the pundits were wrong: Republicans lost five seats in the House, reducing their majority to just six. As a result of the party's unexpectedly poor showing, the Republican House leadership was thrown into turmoil. Their agitation increased when Gingrich resigned as Speaker (and gave up his House seat). In the ensuing leadership struggle, Republicans Thomas Ewing of Illinois and Michael Castle of Delaware nominated Hastert to replace Congressman Dick Armey as House majority leader. But Hastert refused to campaign for the position, explaining that he had already promised Armey his continued support. In the first round of voting for majority leader, Hastert received only 18 votes and came in a distant last behind the other three candidates—Armey, Steve Largent, and Jennifer Dunn. In runoff balloting, Armey prevailed.

In the battle for Speaker, Representative Robert Livingston of Louisiana had emerged by mid-November as the front-running candidate. Then, in mid-December, the impending publication of a *Hustler* magazine exposé prompted Livingston to admit to having had an extramarital affair, and within days, he withdrew his candidacy for Speaker and submitted his resignation from Congress. Once again Republicans approached Hastert, this time to ask him to become Speaker. With the support of Armey, Tom DeLay (who had kept his position as majority whip), and Gingrich, Hastert was elected to the position, on January 6, 1999.

Hastert assumed his seat as the presiding officer of the House three weeks after the members of the House, in an atmosphere of fierce divisiveness and almost uniformly along party lines, impeached President Clinton on charges of perjury and obstruction of justice. (The next month the Senate acquitted the President.) In his first speech as Speaker, Hastert promised to return the focus of Congress to everyday issues. To get legislation passed on these issues, he promised to make bipartisanship a reality. He outlined four priorities for the House: fixing the Social Security and Medicare systems; improving schools; providing tax relief for individuals and businesses; and increasing the preparedness of the military. "To my Democratic colleagues, I say: I will meet you halfway, maybe more so on occasion, but cooperation is a two-way street, and I expect you to meet me halfway, too," he said. Some members of Congress wondered how bipartisan Hastert could be, given his connections to DeLay, who was instrumental in drumming up support for Hastert and who is not a moderate.

Since he became Speaker, Hastert has fulfilled predictions by taking a low-key approach to leadership that contrasts sharply with Gingrich's combativeness. That approach has drawn praise from some and criticism from others. Many feel that Hastert's low profile and disinclination to take risks are exactly what is needed in the wake of the Clinton scandal and the atmosphere of divisiveness that characterized Gingrich's tenure. Others, suggesting that Hastert is perhaps not forceful enough, point to such episodes as the April 1999 House vote on the Democratic initiative to support NATO air strikes against Serbia; while DeLay worked to organize opposition to the measure, Hastert waited until the last minute to weigh in, casting his vote in favor of the military action. After the measure failed to pass, with a vote of 213 to 213, Hastert himself expressed regret that he had not asserted his views earlier. Also, in late May, House members left early for vacation after having failed to reach agreement on budget bills. (As of mid-October 1999, the Republican congressional leadership was scrambling for funds to cover its spending bills.) On the other hand, under Hastert's guidance, the House took steps toward the tax relief he had cited as one of his priorities, passing a $792 billion tax cut in late July. (After passing in the Senate, the bill was vetoed in late September by President Clinton, who nonetheless expressed a desire to reach a compromise.) "There's a general feeling in the Republican conference that the Denny Hastert style is working," Congressman Peter T. King of New York told Alison Mitchell for the *New York Times* (May 12, 1999). "Not trying to be showboating, not trying to be dramatic, just being solid."

Regarding other issues he had identified as important, Hastert continued to embrace some while putting others on hold—for example, in June he announced his intention to protect health and education programs by shifting money previously earmarked for the military. On the subject of Hastert's being independent of his former boss DeLay, a House member told Alison Mitchell that the Speaker "has gone his own way."

Hastert and his wife have two sons: Ethan, who is studying business at the University of Illinois-Champaign, and Joshua, who owns a music store called Seven Dead Arsonists in DeKalb. The Hasterts' home is just outside Yorkville and overlooks the Fox River. The Speaker also owns a building that once housed his father's restaurant, a townhouse in Washington, D.C., and a 270-acre farm in Macoupin County, in Illinois, that formerly belonged to his wife's family. He has often been seen driving around Yorkville with his Labrador retriever, Max, sitting next to him. "You get in his car and you get out, you got dog hairs all over your suit," Illinois state representative Tom Cross told the *New York Times* (January 7, 1999, on-line). An avid collector of old cars, Hastert has driven his 1953 fire truck during local Yorkville parades. — W.G.

Suggested Reading: *Chicago Sun Times* (on-line) Feb. 1999; *Los Angeles Times* (on-line) Dec. 20, 1998, Dec. 21, 1998, Dec. 22, 1998, Jan. 3, 1999; *New York Times* (on-line) Dec. 20, 1998, Jan. 7, 1999; *Roll Call* (on-line) Feb. 1, 1999; *Washington Post* (on-line) A p1 Dec. 21, 1998, with photo; *Politics in America*, various editions

---

Heckerling, Amy

May 7, 1954– Film and television director, writer, and producer. Address: c/o Paramount Pictures Group, 5555 Melrose Ave., Los Angeles, CA 90038-3197

Amy Heckerling has admitted to eavesdropping on teenagers. "It's not like I'm like Humbert Humbert spying on people," she explained to *Rolling Stone* (September 7, 1995), referring to the narrator of Vladimir Nabokov's novel *Lolita*, "but you're in a restaurant, you hear interesting conversation." As the director of such successful teen flicks as *Fast Times at Ridgemont High* (1982) and *Clueless* (1995), both of which became sleeper hits, Heckerling has attracted a reputation as an adult who understands the incomprehensible—American teenagers. "These kids aren't some race that came from another planet," she told *Rolling Stone*. "During the past I've worked with teenage actors and have maintained those relationships, and my tastes, unfortunately or fortunately, tend toward the adolescent. So it wasn't sitting in a room going, 'What do kids want nowadays?' I was expressing what *I* wanted."

The daughter of a certified public accountant and a bookkeeper, Amy Heckerling was born on May 7, 1954 in the New York City borough of the Bronx. She grew up there and in Queens, another of the city's boroughs, and has recalled disliking both her neighborhoods and her schools. "I used to draw and watch movies and daydream," she said on September 14, 1995, during the Harold Lloyd master class held at the American Film Institute (AFI), as transcribed on the AFI Web site. "The idea of going to high school with these characters I had known my whole life was just beyond awful so I wanted to go . . . get out. I wanted to get out of the neighborhood, I wanted to get away from the people I knew, and I went to art school in Manhattan." At the High School of Art and Design, Heckerling's interest in directing was sparked by a classmate's essay about his career aspirations. "I was just like, wait a minute," Heckerling told the master class. "Movie director is like for big shots, people in Hollywood. Who told you you could be a movie director? I was just so jealous, and I guess it

Elliott Marks/Archive Photos

Amy Heckerling

started to dawn on me that that was what I wanted to do."

Heckerling attended New York University, in Manhattan, where she studied film and TV. In 1975 she won a prize for her short student film *High Finance*, starring Joel Silver. After graduating, in about 1976, she enrolled in the master's degree directing program at AFI, in California. To pay her way and to finance her student film at AFI, she got a job as a sound editor through one of the school's directing fellows, who had a second job working for a producer. By the time she graduated from AFI, she was working as an assistant editor and had completed the film *Getting It Over With*, which AFI submitted for consideration for an Academy Award. Heckerling has named Martin Scorsese, Sydney Lumet, Sydney Pollack, Lina Wertmuller, and Federico Fellini among her major influences.

The producers of the film *Fast Times at Ridgemont High*, a series of interconnected sketches depicting the lives of a group of high schoolers, saw *Getting It Over With*, and they hired Heckerling to direct *Fast Times*. With actors who were still virtual unknowns then—Sean Penn, Jennifer Jason Leigh, Anthony Edwards, Eric Stoltz, Judge Reinhold, Phoebe Cates, Nicolas Coppola (now Nicolas Cage), and Forest Whitaker—and a first-time director, *Fast Times* was not expected to do well, so its release date was changed from the summer, when the presumable blockbusters come out, to the fall, when its target audience was back in school. To the surprise of many, the movie became the sleeper hit of 1982, and it gave many in the cast a big boost toward stardom. Seventeen years later, the film is still considered a quintessential teen movie and the defining one of the 1980s.

Heckerling's next film, *Johnny Dangerously* (1984), a gangster spoof starring Michael Keaton, flopped miserably with critics and audiences. Heckerling accepted responsibility for its failings. "I don't understand people—unless something horrible happened to them—who look at a film that they formerly worked real hard at and liked and then turn around and say, 'I had nothing to do with that,'" she told Tom Hinckley for *Cable Guide* (August 1986). "That isn't me." She regrouped for her next movie, *National Lampoon's European Vacation* (1985), in which Chevy Chase reprised his role (in the 1983 film *National Lampoon's Vacation*) as the accident-prone head of the globe-trotting Griswald family. Panned by critics, the film was embraced by audiences nonetheless.

Because the three films she had made were considered "guy" movies, curiosity arose about Heckerling's experiences as a female director. In a conversation with Tom Hinckley, Matty Simmons, the producer of *European Vacation*, said, "I'm not a sexist. It's just that so much of our humor is male-oriented. But when I saw *Fast Times at Ridgemont High* . . . I hired her." Heckerling herself has claimed an ignorance of being affected by gender bias. "I go project to project struggling to make whatever that project is go," she told *Rolling Stone*. "Sometimes it happens, sometimes it doesn't. And I assume that's a reflection on how worthy the thing is at that time. I don't factor gender in."

Heckerling spent much of the second half of the 1980s directing shows for television series, such as the *Twilight Zone*. She also produced the short-lived TV series *Fast Times*, based on her first feature film, and directed some episodes.

The filmmaker has claimed that the birth of her daughter, Mollie, in 1985 inspired her to write the screenplay for her next film, *Look Who's Talking* (1989). Starring Kirstie Alley as a 30-something, first-time, unwed mother and John Travolta as a taxi driver/babysitter, the movie also features the voice of Bruce Willis, who utters the thoughts of the newborn boy as he comments on the Alley character's attempts to find the perfect father for her child. The film did extremely well both in the U.S. and abroad.

Soon after the premiere of *Look Who's Talking*, Heckerling found herself enmeshed in personal troubles. While dealing with proceedings for a divorce from her second husband, Neal Israel, Heckerling was also grappling with a $20 million copyright lawsuit brought by Jeanne Meyers and Rita Stern, who maintained that Heckerling had agreed to help them adapt Meyers's short film *Special Delivery* into a feature-length movie. Like *Look Who's Talking*, *Special Delivery* features the commentary of a baby during its first year, though this baby is cared for by married parents. Four months after Heckerling had seen the short, the women contended, she abandoned the project, so they optioned the short to Tri-Star Pictures, the studio that later produced Heckerling's *Look Who's Talking*. Heckerling agreed to direct *Look Who's Talking*

Too (1990), a sequel to Look Who's Talking, even though she felt the material did not warrant a second film. She has said that she did it only to keep herself busy at that stressful time in her life. Written by Heckerling and Israel, Look Who's Talking Too was trashed by critics. In 1991 Heckerling's divorce became final and the lawsuit was settled out of court. That same year her book, The No-Sex Handbook, which she wrote with Pamela Pettler, was published.

In 1994 Heckerling began writing the screenplay for her next film project, Clueless, using Jane Austen's 19th-century novel Emma as a framework for the lives of the modern characters Heckerling had created. The movie follows the antics of Cher Hamilton, played by Alicia Silverstone, who stands in for Austen's Emma as the privileged young woman who tries to improve others while blind to her own faults. Released in 1995, the movie was not universally applauded—in the Toronto Globe and Mail (July 20, 1995), for instance, Elizabeth Benzetti complained that it was "mushy where it should have been mouthy, predictable where it could have been jolting, and, worst, not very satirical." But many reviewers enjoyed it: the New York Times (July 24, 1995) critic Bernard Weinraub called it a "wickedly funny farce," and Brian Lowry, in Variety (July 17, 1995), described it as "a fresh, disarmingly bright and at times explosively funny comedy." A sleeper hit, it earned Heckerling a National Society of Film Critics Award for best screenplay.

Heckerling's next film, A Night at the Roxbury (1998), is an expansion of a Saturday Night Live skit in which two hopelessly uncool brothers in their 20s attempt to score in L.A.'s club scene. Content to limit herself to the role of producer, Heckerling concentrated on ensuring that the movie would appeal to its target audience and on obtaining a rating that would allow the audience to see it. "There's something inherent in the story that's very adolescent, and we didn't want to rule out all the under-17s," she told Steve Tilley for the Edmonton (Canada) Sun, as reprinted on the Canoe Web site. She also said, "When you aim directly at them, and you say you can't come in but go figure out a way to get in, there's something fishy about it."

Amy Heckerling has identified herself as a liberal and an environmentalist. She told a reporter for People (Spring 1991), "What I hate about making movies is getting up early. You may say you like a script, but then you have to ask yourself, 'Do I really want to get up at 6 A.M. to make it?' That's the bottom line in moviemaking." — K.S.

Suggested Reading: Cable Guide p18+ Aug. 1986, with photos; Harold Lloyd Master Seminar: Amy Heckerling (on-line) Sep. 14, 1995, with photos; Premiere p104 Aug. 1995, with photos; Rolling Stone p53 Sep. 7, 1995, with photo

Selected Movies: as director—Fast Times at Ridgemont High, 1982; Johnny Dangerously, 1984; National Lampoon's European Vacation, 1985; as writer and director—Look Who's Talking, 1989; Look Who's Talking Too, 1990; Clueless, 1995; as producer—A Night at the Roxbury, 1998

Selected Television Shows: as producer—Fast Times, 1986; Clueless, 1996

Frank Capri/Archive Photos

Henner, Marilu

Apr. 6, 1952– Actress; writer. Address: c/o ReganBooks, 1211 Ave. of the Americas, New York, NY 10036

"Things have come easily to me because I haven't looked to make them difficult," Marilu Henner told Sid Smith for the Chicago Tribune (January 4, 1985). "Somebody asked me, 'How did you ever believe you could be so successful?' Because nobody ever told me I couldn't be." Henner's career took off in 1970, when she was about 18, with her role in the original production of the hit musical Grease. At age 26 she landed a part on the comedy series Taxi, which is widely considered to be among television's best-ever sitcoms. In the last half-dozen years, she has given birth to two sons; made a fitness video, Dancerobics (1993); appeared on Broadway in the hit revival of the musical Chicago; and written a best-selling book on health and fitness, Marilu Henner's Total Health Makeover (1998). "Since the '90s, I've been pretty fearless," Henner told Jim Jerome for Redbook

(April 1993). "I love my life. These days I feel I'm bursting forth."

The third of six children in a Polish-Greek family, Marilu Henner was born Mari Lucy Denise Pudlowski on April 6, 1952 in Chicago. The family shared their home, in the Logan Square area of northwest Chicago, with a relative who taught art, studied astrology, and kept a menagerie of "10 cats, two dogs, two birds, a skunk, and 150 fish," as Henner recalled to the *Chicago Tribune* (August 23, 1992). Henner's father, Joseph, managed car dealerships. Her mother, Loretta, ran a dance school out of the family's backyard; during inclement weather, she would move her classes into the garage. The presence of the studio made the Henner residence a community gathering place, with students of all ages coming and going during much of each day. Henner began studying with her mother at age two and a half, and by age 12, she was mastering the jitterbug and the cha-cha at Friday night boy–girl social dances held at the studio. At 14 she began instructing other students.

Henner attended Madonna High School, an all-girls Catholic school. In her teens she began performing in community theater, in such productions as that of the musical *The Boy Friend* at the Hull House theater. She graduated third in her high-school class and won an Outstanding Americans Youth Foundation scholarship as the "outstanding teenager in Illinois for 1970." The scholarship enabled her to attend the University of Chicago. The university did not offer a theater major, so Henner—who had long known that she wanted to pursue a career as a performer—studied political science. While she was in college, Jim Jacobs, whom she had met at Hull House, invited her to audition for a Chicago production of a new musical he had co-written. The musical was *Grease*, and Henner was cast in the role of Marty, one of the Pink Ladies. She performed in the show three days a week and saw the musical, which originally had 27 song-and-dance numbers, developed into a tightened and polished final version. In 1971, about a year after the opening of the Chicago production, Jacobs told Henner that *Grease* was going to New York and that he wanted her to reprise her role in the new production. Henner, who had continued to attend her college classes during the Chicago run of the show, opted to stay in school. (*Grease* went on to become an enormous hit; at one point it set a record as the longest-running musical up until that time.)

In 1972 Jacobs asked Henner to audition for the national touring company of *Grease*. She flew to New York the very day he contacted her and ended up with the role of Marty again. It was thus that she made her entrée into performing professionally. One of her fellow actors in the company was the 18-year-old John Travolta, and over the following months, they became close. For the next 15 years or so, they pursued an on-and-off romance. Meanwhile, after their stint on the tour, Henner and Travolta both appeared in *Grease* on Broadway,

and later, in 1974, they performed together in *Over Here*, a musical about the 1940s singing group the Andrews Sisters. In 1976 Henner appeared on Broadway in the musical *Pal Joey*. Also in the mid-1970s, Henner made 28 commercials, "including four for bras, two for pantyhose, and one for ring-around-the-collar, which included a trip to Venice," as she recalled to *TV Guide* (January 6, 1979). In 1977 she moved to Los Angeles and made her film debut, in *Between the Lines*. She appeared in *Bloodbrothers*, with Richard Gere, in 1978.

That same year Henner got an audition for the role of Elaine Nardo on *Taxi*, a new ensemble comedy series for the ABC network about a group of New York cabdrivers. Henner, who was then 26, won the part despite the fact that Elaine had originally been envisioned as an Italian-American woman in her 30s. One of the more down-to-earth characters in the show, Elaine was an aspiring art dealer who worked in a gallery by day and drove a taxi at night. Over the course of *Taxi*'s run, the cast also included Judd Hirsch as Alex, a career cabdriver; Tony Danza as Tony, a boxer; Danny De-Vito as Louie, the mean-spirited dispatcher; Christopher Lloyd as "Reverend" Jim, a burned-out relic of the 1960s; Jeff Conaway as Bobby, a struggling actor; Andy Kaufman as Latka, a mechanic and recent immigrant; and Carol Kane as Latka's wife, Simka. The zany but plausible characters, excellent scripts, and good chemistry among the cast members propelled the show to a top-10 spot in the Nielsen ratings during its premiere season, in 1978–79. The show was also a hit with critics, and that season and the following two, it won an Emmy Award for outstanding comedy series. But the show's ratings slid after the first year, and ABC canceled it after four seasons. At that point NBC picked up *Taxi*, but its ratings failed to improve, and it was discontinued in July 1983. Despite the show's failure to attract a large audience after its first year, it still retains a strong following. Reruns of the show have been aired nearly every year by various channels. *Taxi* is considered a classic TV sitcom, and Elaine Nardo remains the role with which Henner is most closely identified.

Meanwhile, as *Taxi* wound down and during her time off from the series, Henner was developing a film career. In 1980, during her screen test for the Wim Wenders and Francis Ford Coppola film *Hammett* (1983), Henner "fell instantly, madly in love at first sight—like forget it," she told Jim Jerome. The object of her affection was the actor Frederic Forrest, whom Henner had to kiss as part of the audition. They were both cast in the film, and were married six months after they met. Their union ended after two years, in part because of Forrest's alcoholism. *Hammett* did poorly at the box office, and Henner's other films from this period did not fare much better. She starred opposite Burt Reynolds in *The Man Who Loved Women* (1983) and *Cannonball Run II* (1984); played a 1930s moll opposite Michael Keaton in the gangster spoof *Johnny Dangerously* (1984); and portrayed a barmaid and prostitute in *Rustler's Rhapsody* (1985), a comic western that also starred Tom Berenger. In *Perfect* (1985), Henner played a woman who attends a Los Angeles health club-cum-pickup haunt, where she meets an East Coast journalist who has come to research a story about the club. Henner's romantic involvement with John Travolta, who played the journalist, ended at about that time.

During the latter half of the 1980s, Henner worked on fewer projects. In addition to several made-for-television movies, she appeared in the film *Grand Larceny* (1987) and, that same year, was seen on Broadway in the play *Social Security*, in a role originated by Marlo Thomas. Presumably, Henner was focusing much of her attention on her personal relationship with the director Robert Lieberman. The two met in 1984 and began dating about a year later. They were married in 1990 and have two young sons—Nicholas, born in 1994, and Joey, born in 1995. Lieberman, who directed Henner's fitness video *Dancerobics*, also has a grown son and daughter from a previous marriage.

In 1990 Henner took a role on a new CBS sitcom called *Evening Shade*. The show, which has the distinction of being the first network series set in Arkansas, revolved around events in a small town, particularly those involving one family, the Newtons. Burt Reynolds played Wood Newton, the coach of the town's pathetic high-school football team, and Henner portrayed his wife, Ava, a lawyer and candidate for local prosecuting attorney. The characters Ava and Wood had three children, and early in the series, Ava gave birth to a fourth. Also figuring prominently in the town goings-on were Ava's father (played by Hal Holbrook); the owner of a local eatery (Ossie Davis); and the town doctor (Charles Durning).

During her between-season breaks from *Evening Shade*, Henner acted in several films, most notably *L.A. Story* (1991), in which she played Steve Martin's "girlfriend from hell," as she has described her role. She also appeared in a film version of the play *Noises Off* (1992) and in the movie *Chasers* (1994). In 1994–95 she hosted her own daytime talk show, called *Marilu*, on the CBS television network. Her autobiography, *By All Means Keep Moving*, was published in 1994 and became a best-seller. Henner's autobiography contains frank accounts of her many relationships with men. (According to Jim Jerome, a longtime female friend of hers once described Henner as "the only adult woman I know who is still boy crazy.") "I thought about calling my book *Boys and My Weight*," Henner joked to the *Chicago Tribune* (November 13, 1994). "Every woman knows who she was dating and what she weighed for every single event in her life."

Henner's most recent projects include the television film *Titanic* (1996), in which she played "the unsinkable Molly Brown," a real-life figure who earned that moniker by surviving the sinking of the *Titanic* on its maiden voyage, in 1912. In 1997 she joined the cast of the hit Broadway revival of the musical *Chicago*, replacing Ann Reinking in the role of Roxie Hart. (Reinking and Henner had appeared together in *Over Here*.) Henner will portray herself in the film *Man on the Moon*, about the life of the talented comedian Andy Kaufman, who died in 1984 of lung cancer at age 36. That film is scheduled for release in 1999.

Henner's book on health and fitness, *Marilu Henner's Total Health Makeover: 10 Steps to Your B.E.S.T. Body: Balance, Energy, Stamina, Toxin-Free*, which she wrote with Laura Morton, came out in 1998. Henner was inspired to develop a passing expertise on fitness and health by the untimely deaths of both her parents. Henner's father died in 1969, at age 52, of a massive heart attack that occurred during a large family Christmas party. Her mother died at 58, in 1978, of a type of arthritis that damaged her spinal cord and caused circulatory problems and partial paralysis. Henner returned to Chicago to take care of her mother, and she remained there until her mother died, four months later. She has said that those months and the ones that followed were the most difficult period of her life. "I watched her suffering in the hospital," she recalled to Sid Smith, "this strong, vital person who had been teaching dance only a few months before, dying from arthritis. And I thought, 'This shouldn't happen.' . . . So I started reading everything I could. In the end, I'd read 400 books, and shifted to a macrobiotic diet." In her book Henner advocates a strict vegetarian diet with no dairy products, and she offers advice on exercise, sleep habits, and alternative medicine, among other health-related topics.

Henner has been a client of a New York City–based psychotherapist for more than 15 years. She told Jerome, "I expected after the first appointment, she'd say, 'You're sane. Let's go have lunch.' When that didn't happen, I was so shocked. So now, instead of having an eighth-grade education on myself, I have a doctorate." With her therapist, Henner organizes a conference-call group-therapy session with her five siblings every other week. She remains extremely close to her two brothers and three sisters, and returns home to Chicago nearly every holiday season for a family reunion.

According to Jim Jerome, Marilu Henner is "a nonstop talker who's almost obsessively introspective." She is known for being relentlessly energetic, positive, and upbeat and for having an uncanny memory for details. — O.J.S.

Suggested Reading: *Chicago Tribune* II p3 Jan. 4, 1985, with photo, V p3 Feb. 14, 1991, with photo, VI p12 Aug. 23, 1992, with photo, VI p6 Nov. 13, 1994, with photo; *Cosmopolitan* p244+ Mar. 1995, with photos; *New York Daily News Magazine* p14 Dec. 25, 1983, with photo, p23 Nov. 24, 1985, with photos, p1 Feb. 9, 1987, with photo; *Parade* p19 Mar. 17, 1991, with photo; *Redbook* p32+ Apr. 1993, with photos; *TV Guide* p25+ Jan. 6, 1979, with photo; *Village Voice* p39+ Nov. 29, 1994, with photo

Selected Plays: *Grease*, 1971, 1972; *Over Here*; *Pal Joey*, 1976; *Social Security*, 1987; *Chicago*, 1997

Selected Films: *Between the Lines*, 1977; *Bloodbrothers*, 1978; *The Man Who Loved Women*, 1983; *Hammett*, 1983; *Johnny Dangerously*, 1984; *Cannonball Run II*, 1984; *Rustlers' Rhapsody*, 1985; *Perfect*, 1985; *L.A. Story*, 1991; *Noises Off*, 1992; *Chasers*, 1994

Selected Television Shows: *Taxi*, 1978–82; *Evening Shade* 1990–94; *Marilu*, 1994–95

Selected Books: as co-author—*By All Means Keep Moving*, 1994; *Marilu Henner's Total Health Makeover*, 1998

Courtesy of Verso Books

Hitchens, Christopher

Apr. 13, 1949– Columnist; journalist; nonfiction writer. Address: 2022 Columbia Road N.W., Washington, DC 20009

Through his biweekly column for the *Nation* and monthly column for *Vanity Fair*, radical journalist Christopher Hitchens has gained notoriety as a critic of government policy and popular culture. His "trademark savage wit," which has targeted, among others, Mother Teresa, has been simultaneously lauded as independent thinking and derided for profaning the sacred. Reactions to his commentaries are anything but ambiguous. "To his admirers, he is someone who tells it how it is— beholden to nobody, frightened of no one and with

a fine instinct for the jugular, especially when it is contained in a fleshily prosperous neck," Anthony Howard wrote about Hitchens in the *Spectator* (June 5, 1993). "His critics, on the other hand, claim to detect a *poseur*—a man who is far more at home with cafe society than any left-winger ought to be, a writer who aspires, above all, to be the glass of fashion, a pundit who, while strong on all questions of opinion, has always been curiously weak on matters of fact." A prolific writer, Hitchens is also a frequent contributor to over a half-dozen periodicals and has penned eight books.

Christopher Eric Hitchens was born on April 13, 1949 in Portsmouth, England, the son of Eric Ernest and Yvonne Jean (Hickman) Hitchens. His father was a career officer in the British navy. The contrarian mind-set for which Hitchens would become famous was in place during his boyhood; although he grew up in a conservative household dominated by a military culture, he developed a decidedly nontraditionalist attitude toward public affairs. "I was precocious enough to watch the news and read the papers, and I can remember October 1956, the simultaneous crisis in Hungary and Suez, very well. And getting a sense that the world was dangerous, a sense that the game was up, that The Empire was over," Hitchens told Sasha Abramsky in an interview for *Progressive* magazine (February 1997).

Through his father's navy post, Hitchens's family enjoyed material advantages unavailable to its earlier generations. Christopher became the first member of the family to attend private school—at the Leys School in Cambridge—and the first to enroll in a university. Despite his rapid turn toward liberal politics, which crystallized when he was 15 and was defined mostly by his objection to the Vietnam War, Hitchens attended Balliol, possibly Oxford University's most patrician college. He graduated in 1970 with a degree in philosophy, politics, and economics, the preferred course of study among future barristers and journalists. While at Balliol, Hitchens cultivated his leftist political tendencies by studying the writings of his intellectual heroine, the German revolutionary and socialist Rosa Luxemburg; he also started writing book reviews for the *New Statesman*, publishing his first in 1969. He told Abramsky, "It wasn't very often that they asked me, but it was a start, and it gave me a huge advantage to be writing for them at that age."

After a period spent in the United States on a scholarship from Balliol, followed by a stint as the social-sciences correspondent for the *Times Higher Education Supplement* in London, Hitchens, in the late 1970s, took a job as a staff writer and editor with the *New Statesman*. Among his colleagues were such literary talents as the novelist Martin Amis and the poet James Fenton. Hitchens's association with writers of their caliber influenced his work in two ways. As Hitchens explained to Sasha Abramsky, it pushed him to focus his talent. "I realized these guys were better at that kind of writing than I was. It was rather intimidating that they were so good. It made me specialize more in the generalist-type political essay." And second, it led him to pay attention to craft. "They persuaded me it wasn't enough just to make the point; that style was substance, and that there was something in language itself. I learned by osmosis."

A decade after touring the United States on his travel scholarship, Hitchens was offered a job by the *Nation*, America's oldest weekly political magazine. During his visit to the U.S., Hitchens had not wanted to leave, but with little money left once the scholarship ran out, he had been forced to do so. He jumped at the opportunity to write for the *Nation* and has worked and lived in the United States ever since, though he maintains his British citizenship.

In his biweekly column for the *Nation*, "Minority Report," Hitchens takes aim at a wide range of targets, particularly religious fundamentalism and political hypocrisy. He criticized the recent U.S. air strikes on Iraq, noting the U.S. government's hesitance to intervene with military force in other regions of the world, including Bosnia. He was also very critical of the *fatwah*, or call for execution, that former Iranian leader Ayatollah Khomeini placed on author Salman Rushdie for alleged blasphemy against Islam in his novel *The Satanic Verses*. Hitchens criticized John Cardinal O'Connor of New York, the archbishop of Canterbury, and the Ashkenazi chief rabbi of Israel for condemning blasphemy rather than speaking out against the murderous implications of the *fatwah*. (Hitchens quipped in his column that the lifting of the *fatwah* in 1998 left "only the hysterical denunciation of [Rushdie's] novel to stand, as the mother of all bad reviews.")

Hitchens's status as internationalist is reflected in some of his books. His first pieces to appear in a book were the preface and introduction to a 1971 edition of Karl Marx's *The Paris Commune*. Next, he co-wrote, with Peter Kellner, *Callaghan: The Road to Number Ten* (1976), a well-, if not widely, received political biography of the former British prime minister James Callaghan.

The moral outrage for which Hitchens has become notorious did not show itself in a book-length study until the publication of *Cyprus* (1984), which Hitchens wrote to commemorate the anniversary of the 1974 Turkish invasion of Cyprus. His objective was to shed light on the injustices suffered by the people of Cyprus at the hands of various occupying forces, including the Turks and the British. *Cyprus* was reissued in slightly expanded form in 1989 as *Hostage to History: Cyprus from the Ottomans to Kissinger*.

For his next project, Hitchens focused on the controversy surrounding the Elgin marbles— marble figures and friezes that were originally part of the Parthenon, in Athens, Greece, and have been in the permanent collection of the British Museum, in London, for almost two centuries. In 1801 Lord

Elgin, England's ambassador to Turkey, received permission from the Turkish government, which then ruled Greece, to remove the friezes and other marble sculptures from the Parthenon. Elgin's intention was to use these works of art to decorate his estate in Scotland, but in 1816 he was forced to sell them to the British government. Four years after Greece made a formal request to England to return the marbles, Hitchens published his book on the subject, *Imperial Spoils: The Curious Case of the Elgin Marbles* (1988). Hitchens presented arguments for and against Greece's claim, ultimately coming down on the side of Greek reclamation. He argued that the Elgin marbles are a part of Greek heritage and, as they are integral to one of the ancient world's greatest architectural achievements, should be seen in their original context.

James Gardner, in his assessment of the book for the *National Review* (October 27, 1989), countered Hitchens's argument first by citing the intention of the Greek government to house the marbles away from the Parthenon. Athenian air is corrosive, and preservationists have been removing artifacts from Athens to save them from further damage; thus, argued Gardner, the marbles would never be returned to their original context. Also, Gardner stated, aside from the fact that the marbles were purchased legally, England has a legitimate claim to them as part of *its* heritage. With the passage of almost two centuries and eight generations, "the British have come to feel so great an affinity and affection for Lord Elgin's marbles . . . that they could no longer be wrested from the British without disrupting and dislocating some part of that people's very selves."

Using his perspective as a Britisher living and working in the United States, Hitchens chose as his next topic the "special relationship" that has developed between the U.S. and Britain. In *Blood, Class and Nostalgia: Anglo-American Ironies* (1990), Hitchens posited that as England's empire collapsed and America burgeoned as a world power, England began to depend on the U.S. as an ally on the world political stage, and the U.S. looked to England for culture. The results, as he explained to Sasha Abramsky, are the "Americanization of British politics" and Anglophilia in the U.S., characterized by "the whole *Masterpiece Theatre* conception of Britain as a theme park of feudalism and charm."

Considering the great deal of attention it received, *Blood, Class and Nostalgia* appears to have touched on a topic at the forefront of political thought; however, the book fared poorly at the hands of critics, who found that it lacked a definite theme and the precision of historical scholarship. Many suggested Hitchens, out of his depth, had oversimplified a complex political relationship. As Alexander Chancellor specified in his review for the *Spectator* (July 14, 1990), "The main defects of the book . . . are its relentless pursuit of irony at all costs, its excessive obliquity in dealing with episodes in American history, . . . and a failure to notice those things which are positive or merely harmless and engaging about the long Anglo-American love affair." Even less forgivingly, Hugh Brogan wrote for the *New Statesman* (July 20, 1990), "There is the endlessly troubling matter of [Hitchens's] slapdash writing, his glib inaccuracy, which amounts to a negation of scholarship. He has not taken the trouble to master the craft of history."

Out of curiosity, Hitchens visited Mother Teresa and her mission while in Calcutta, India, in 1980. She gave him a tour of the mission, through which, as she told him, she fought abortion and contraception in Calcutta. Hitchens was disturbed by Mother Teresa's admission. He told Brian Lamb in an interview for C-SPAN's *Booknotes* (October 17, 1993), "It rather, to me, spoiled the effect of her charitable work. She was saying, actually, this is not charity; it's really just propaganda." Hitchens started a file on Mother Teresa's activities, and his work led to articles in the *Nation* and *Vanity Fair*; a television program, shown in the United Kingdom, called *Hell's Angel*; and his book *The Missionary Position: Mother Teresa in Theory and Practice* (1995).

In *The Missionary Position*, Hitchens examined the theory of Mother Teresa's mission and her means of realizing its goals. By her own admission, Hitchens wrote, Mother Teresa's motive for charity was the preaching of the most extreme fundamentalist interpretations of Catholic doctrine. Hitchens viewed the Vatican's position on birth control and abortion as adding to Calcutta's problems of overpopulation and poverty, which, as far as he could determine, Mother Teresa's facilities did not help to alleviate. Furthermore, Hitchens found questionable some of Mother Teresa's associations. He documented funding she had received from, among others, Charles H. Keating Jr., former head of Lincoln Savings and Loan, who was convicted of financial fraud for embezzling millions of dollars in deposits. Hitchens told Paul Kilduff for the *Berkeley Monthly* (May 1998), "Paul Turley, the deputy district attorney in Los Angeles when Charles Keating was about to be sentenced, . . . had received a letter from Mother Teresa asking him to let Keating off. Turley wrote back telling her that Keating was not a friend of the poor. He's actually a thief of the poor. He also asked back the money that Keating had given her, $1.25 million. She never replied." "I am prepared to say that we would be better off without [Mother Teresa] altogether," Hitchens told Stephen Capen in an interview for *worldmind.com* (December 24, 1995, online). "In other words, I think her efforts amount to a net minus."

As might be expected, *Missionary Position* created a storm of criticism. Cristina Odone in the *Financial Times* (October 28–29, 1995) called Hitchens "a religious illiterate." Colman McCarthy, writing for the *Washington Post* (February 28, 1995), accused Hitchens of beating a dead horse. "Artful debunkers know how to make their case, and then move on. Hitchens's pseudo-Left artlessness is in

not letting go: He's got the goods on Mother Teresa and if the rest of the media are too fawning to nail her, he will. Again, and again and again. Until we get it, and until Hitchens is satisfied that enough people know he's a tiger." *The Missionary Position* also received positive notices. In the *New York Review of Books* (July 11, 1996), the influential journalist Murray Kempton lauded Hitchens's "stirrings" as "so far from blasphemous as almost to resonate with the severities of orthodoxy." He continued, "The compelling impulse in *The Missionary Position*'s heartbeat is not to make fun of a holy woman . . . but to chastise a heretic."

At the age of 38, Hitchens, an atheist and a supporter of an independent Palestinian state, was informed by his maternal grandmother that he is half Jewish. In order to fit better into British society, his mother had kept her heritage a secret from everyone, including her husband. Hitchens reflected on the revelation in the piece "On Not Knowing the Half of It," which closes his collection of essays *Prepared for the Worse* (1989). In a review of the collection for the *Spectator* (May 6, 1989), John Grigg noted that "an editor said to [Hitchens] when told the news of his part-Jewishness: 'That should make your life easier. Jewish people are *allowed* to criticize Israel.'"

In addition to his writing, Christopher Hitchens has begun accepting visiting professorships across the U.S., including posts at the University of Pittsburgh, the University of California at Berkeley, and the New School for Social Research, in New York City. When he is not traveling, Hitchens lives in Washington, D.C., with his second wife, Carol Blue, and their daughter, Antonia; he has two other children, a son and a daughter, from his first marriage, to Eleni Meleagrou. When not working, Hitchens enjoys reading, traveling, smoking, and drinking. In his writing he prefers a multidisciplinary approach. "I try when I'm writing about literature not to leave the political dimension out," he told Brian Lamb. "When I'm writing about politics I try and recall that politics isn't all there is to life and try and import what you might call cultural or literary or aesthetic points to it." Hitchens's latest book, *No One Left to Lie to: The Triangulations of William Jefferson Clinton*, a vitriolic condemnation of Bill Clinton's presidency, was published in April 1999. — T.J.F.

Suggested Reading: *Berkeley Monthly* May 1998; *Booknotes* Oct. 17, 1993; *Financial Times* p17 Oct. 28/29, 1995; *National Review* p53+ Oct. 27, 1989; *New Statesman* p41+ July 20, 1990; *New York Review of Books* p4+ July 11, 1996; *Progressive* p32+ Feb. 1997; *Spectator* p27+ May 6, 1989, p26 July 14, 1990, p35 June 5, 1993; *Washington Post* p20 Feb. 28, 1995; *worldmind.com* (on-line) Dec. 28, 1995; *Who's Who 1999*

Selected Books: *Cyprus*, 1984; *Imperial Spoils: The Curious Case of the Elgin Marbles*, 1988; *Prepared for the Worse*, 1989; *Blood, Class and Nostalgia: Anglo-American Ironies*, 1990; *For the Sake of Argument: Essays and Minority Reports*, 1993; *The Missionary Position: Mother Teresa in Theory and Practice*, 1995; *No One Left to Lie to: The Triangulations of William Jefferson Clinton*, 1999

Courtesy of Caseroc Productions

Hoch, Danny
(hok)

1970– Actor; spoken-word performer. Address: c/o Washington Square Arts, 12 E. 10th St., New York, NY 10003-5927

When Danny Hoch turned down a role in Quentin Tarantino's film *From Dusk Till Dawn* because the screenplay contained a racial epithet, many people thought he was principled. When he rejected the part of Ramone, a disgruntled Latino pool attendant, in the hit television series *Seinfeld*, because it represented an ethnic stereotype, some thought he was above reproach. But when Hoch laughed at a chance to earn seven figures starring in a series of Sprite commercials because it might compromise his artistic vision, many people assumed he was downright crazy. "I'm not in a rush to be a movie star," he told Nell Casey for *Mirabella* (September/October 1997). "I want to do stuff on my own terms. If I can make a living and pay my rent, what the hell do I need three million dollars for?" When not turning down offers most young performers would give their eyeteeth for, Danny Hoch

develops street-savvy one-man shows that entertain audiences with equal measures of humor and empathy—and that point up the need for understanding across racial and ethnic lines.

Hoch, who is white and Jewish, has a firm grasp of the fragmented cadences and accents of New York City patois and a rubbery visage that allows him to assume the forms of a variety of characters with dead-on accuracy. His repertoire, as taken from his show *Some People*, includes identities as culturally diverse as a West Indian radio deejay; a Polish handyman who has a hard time speaking English; and a Puerto Rican woman who talks with misplaced confidence about her risky sex life. Such characters have made Hoch a much sought-after, if reluctant, commodity in the entertainment industry. "I'm becoming what the white entertainment people see as someone who has his feet in both worlds," Hoch explained to Mary Talbot for the New York *Daily News* (October 12, 1994). "I'm a white candy coating for a lot of stuff that white people find threatening. A lot of what I say in the show *is* threatening." Refreshingly, Hoch has resisted the allure of fame and commercial success in order to remain true to his artistic message. "I'm trying to bring traditionally peripheral characters center stage," he said to Nell Casey. "Those are the ones that are important to me."

Born in 1970, Danny Hoch was raised in Lefrak City, a development in the New York City borough of Queens. Nestled among the Forest Hills, Rego Park, Corona, and Flushing sections of Queens, Lefrak City—rather than being dominated by a single culture—represented the global diaspora of, among others, Greeks, Koreans, Russian Jews, West Indians, and Middle Easterners. Hoch's neighborhood was thus the source of many of his insights into other worldviews, which inform and give context to his chameleon-like performances. One result of growing up in this setting was that Hoch had little sense of his own racial and ethnic identity. "I used to break-dance with this Indian kid named Prashant and this Puerto Rican kid named Jesus and this black kid named Kenny," Hoch told Richard Goldstein for the *Village Voice* (April 14, 1998). "I didn't know I was white until I went away to college."

Early on Hoch showed a gift for mimicry, particularly after his mother, a speech pathologist, began teaching him when he was four years old about different speech patterns. It was also through his mother that Hoch learned the value of language and verbal communication. "I spent some of my childhood . . . watching her teach people how to reclaim language," Hoch wrote in his program for *Jails, Hospitals & Hip Hop*, his third solo show. "People that were in car accidents. People that were quadriplegics from police gunshot wounds. There was one kid who was sitting on a school bus on his way home, while the landlords were burning the Bronx for tax write-offs. He got hit in the head with a brick while people were looting and protesting. Every word is now a jewel more precious than a thousand diamonds."

Danny Hoch also experimented with the seedier side of the street culture in which he had immersed himself. By the age of 14, he had been arrested six times. "I grew up a graffiti writer, break dancer, drug-doer-dealer, staying in the park until three in the morning drinking lots of Old English 800 [malt liquor] and smoking lots of marijuana," he confessed to Tad Simons for the *Chicago Tribune* (June 11, 1995). He earned money by break-dancing for passersby on the street, then used his earnings to buy drugs—some of which he would sell to others, so that he could afford to buy stage makeup and magic-show supplies. "So even with the whole homeboy thing I was into, there was always a creative aspect to it," he told Bruce Weber for the *New York Times* (November 2, 1993). Recognizing her son's talent and interest in performance, and hoping to get him off the street, Danny's mother persuaded him to audition for the New York School of Performing Arts, in Manhattan. "And my life has never been the same," he said to Weber. After high school he trained for a year at the prestigious North Carolina School of the Arts, then spent the following year in London, at the British American Drama Academy.

While in school, Hoch became increasingly aware that he was not cut out to perform in traditional ensemble casts. He therefore lobbied for a job with the New York University Gallatin Division's Creative Arts Team, a troupe of actors who conduct workshops on problem solving and conflict resolution for adolescents in high schools and prisons. He won a position, which made him, at the age of 19, the youngest instructor ever hired by the university. Hoch has since toured with the group, performing improvisations that stretch the boundaries of his talent for mimicking the accents of people who are not native English speakers. As Chris Vine, creative director of the team, told Mary Talbot, "Danny's ability to create a range of characters from observation that students can identify with, and do it quickly, is invaluable." The troupe's method of teaching was to use improvised skits to introduce such topics as racial stereotyping, then turn the roles over to members of their adolescent audience. Such exercises drove home the troupe's message of tolerance and understanding. In one of the more popular skits performed by the troupe, Hoch portrayed Hassan, a Yemeni immigrant who owns a grocery in a predominantly black neighborhood, opposite a partner who portrayed Latoya, a neighborhood resident. The performed conflict would begin with Latoya's expression of resentment of a foreigner owning the only grocery in the vicinity, countered by Hassan's strong reactions to any sign of disrespect in his store. Just before tempers would erupt into violence, usually after a heated exchange of racial epithets, the actors would freeze the action and open the floor for discussion.

Meanwhile, Hoch began working on his debut solo show, *Pot Melting*, which played to rave reviews in 1993. In the same year Hoch avoided the sophomore jinx, and expanded his range of impressions, with his follow-up solo show, *Some People*. An 11-character monologue, *Some People* showed the full range of Hoch's ability. "With a sociologist's specificity, Mr. Hoch locates the cadences and locutions that allow his often dispossessed-feeling characters to find a protective, insulating verbal pattern—even, in the case of his inner-city rappers, a poetry—that brings an illusion of order to the confusion in their lives," Ben Brantley wrote in his review of the show for the *New York Times* (October 13, 1993). "In *Some People*, language and world view are inextricably fused." Directed by Jo Bonney—whose husband, Eric Bogosian, is generally regarded as the premier monologuist exploring urban themes and represents the benchmark against which Hoch's performances are judged—the show ran Off-Broadway at the Joseph Papp Public Theater, in Manhattan. *Some People* won a 1994 Obie Award; toured to more than 20 American cities, including a run at the Kennedy Center in Washington, D.C.; and was staged in Cuba, Austria, and Scotland, where it captured a Fringe First Award at the Edinburgh Festival. HBO also filmed Hoch's performance for a special, which was nominated for a 1996 CableACE Award.

It was primarily due to the buzz created by *Some People* that Hollywood came knocking on Hoch's door. In addition to turning down the offers from Tarantino, Seinfeld, and the executives at Sprite, Hoch also had to explain to MTV why their offer of a veejay slot was unappealing. "Being in jail during the day, and sharing jovial laughs over $100 bottles of wine at night heightens your awareness about the imbalances in the country, and in your life," Hoch told Mary Talbot. "It makes you very cynical. They had an admiration for what I do but they want to capitalize on the idea that I'm the next hip thing."

In the autumn of 1997 Hoch premiered his third multicharacter, one-man show, *Jails, Hospitals & Hip-Hop*, at California's Berkeley Repertory Theatre. His edgiest and most complex project to date, *Jails* features a new array of disenfranchised personalities whose statements are as disturbing as they are funny. One character, Andy, an inmate infected by HIV, declares, "When I was on the outside, I was eatin' all organic food, everything organic. I was shootin' heroin, but I was eatin' organic." Just as disconcerting is Flip Dog, a white teenager who works in a Montana fast-food joint and fantasizes about being a famous rap artist; he insists that his brown birthmark represents his true color and that his real birthmark is his white skin. "It is part of the show's point that these characters can't be reduced to single adjectives," Ben Brantley noted in his overwhelmingly positive review of the show for the *New York Times* (March 31, 1998). "Mr. Hoch knows that identity, and even ethnicity, is often a tangle of clashing elements. . . . Ethnicity, in other words, becomes an increasingly confused and relative proposition." In 1998 *Jails* was nominated for a Drama Desk Award and was widely acknowledged as the first Off-Broadway production to use its advertising budget to fund hip-hop street teams and youth ticket subsidies, which enabled students to see the show at reduced prices or free of charge. *Jails* was made into a spoken-word audio recording and was also published, along with *Some People*, by Villard Books. The show will tour to more than 40 cities through the year 2000. The movie *Whiteboys*, based on the Flip Dog character and written by and starring Hoch, was released in 1999.

Often lauded as a much-needed voice for society's disaffected, Danny Hoch has also had to deal with his share of criticism. Inevitably, he is confronted by proponents of political correctness who question his right, as a white Jewish male, to portray a West Indian black man or a Puerto Rican woman. But Hoch feels that anyone who would deem his performances offensive either does not know his background or has simply dismissed him as a descendent of the vaudeville minstrels who wore blackface for comedic effect. Others, however, wanting Hoch to play the minstrel, accuse him of self-righteousness when he refuses. For example, as Hoch explained during a monologue from his most recent one-man show, *Evolution of a Homeboy*, which was reprinted in *Harper's* (March 1998), his refusal to do a Spanish accent for the role of Ramone, the pool attendant, led to a brief confrontation with Jerry Seinfeld. Hoch's trouble with the part began in earnest once he "started to realize that they didn't want the real thing—they wanted somebody who could do the real thing but still be one of them." The part was quickly and unceremoniously recast. "People get frustrated because they want me to be the '90s minstrel or the '90s apologetic liberal actor—and I'm neither," he told Tad Simons. "These characters are all facets of me, and I create them out of love rather than sympathy, mockery, or satire. The difference is that I'm really coming from a place I know."

As an actor who teaches, Hoch believes he has valuable lessons to impart to young performers. "I want to teach them they don't have to work for Disney to be a success," he told Stuart Miller for *Esquire* (January 1999). Despite his refusal to compromise his ethics, Danny Hoch has been working virtually nonstop for the last decade. He appeared in a small role in Terence Malick's film *The Thin Red Line*, which opened in December 1998 to acclaim and was nominated for several Oscars. "The urban griot," as he calls himself (a griot is a West African term for someone who relates tribal history through storytelling and music), Hoch has also received funding from a number of sources, including a Solo Theatre Fellowship from the National Endowment of the Arts, a 1996 Sundance Writer's Fellowship, a 1998 CalArts/Alpert Award in Theatre, and a 1999 Tennessee Williams Fellowship, to pursue his independent projects. — T.J.F.

Suggested Reading: *Chicago Tribune* XIII p10+ June 11, 1995, with photos; *Details* p112+ Sep. 1999, with photos; New York *Daily News* p32 Oct. 12, 1994, with photos; *New York Times* C p15 Nov. 2, 1993, with photo; *Village Voice* p57 Apr. 14, 1998, with photo

---

Hoffa, James P.

May 19, 1941– President of the International Brotherhood of Teamsters. Address: c/o International Brotherhood of Teamsters, 25 Louisiana Ave. NW, Washington, DC 20001

In December 1998 James Phillip Hoffa was elected president of the International Brotherhood of Teamsters, thus becoming the second member of his family to take the helm of the largest private-sector trade union in the United States. His father, James Riddle Hoffa, a ninth-grade dropout who became a truck driver, led the union in its greatest period of growth and power, in the late 1950s and early 1960s, and negotiated landmark labor contracts that pushed the Teamsters' rank-and-file membership into the United States' economic middle class. In stark contrast, James P. Hoffa is a college and law-school graduate with limited experience on loading docks, and when he took over the Teamsters, the union was laden with problems. A dearth of funds, a drop in membership to less than half what it was in the late 1970s, the increasing diversity and lack of cohesion among members, and the passage of anti-union legislation had reduced the Teamsters Union to a weakened shell of its former self. Invoking his father's name and the union's past glory, James P. Hoffa has promised to make the International Brotherhood of Teamsters powerful once again and to secure his father's legacy. "I think he'd be happy that I won," Hoffa said of his father, as quoted on CNN's Web site (December 7, 1998). "I think he'd be excited about it and I think he would be saying that the members have spoken."

Despite its recent decline, the Teamsters—officially, the International Brotherhood of Teamsters, Chauffeurs, Warehousemen, and Helpers of America—remains one of the most influential groups in labor, largely because of the work of the elder Hoffa. After assuming the union's presidency, in 1958, James R. Hoffa immediately set about centralizing union control. Convinced of the power of numbers and the importance of presenting a unified national bargaining front to industry management, he encouraged local council leaders to call on him to negotiate regional contracts. Indus-

Courtesy of the International Brotherhood of Teamsters
James P. Hoffa

an additional five-year sentence, for fraud and conspiracy in the handling of a union benefits fund. In 1967, after all his appeals were exhausted, he was sent to the Lewisburg Federal Penitentiary, in Pennsylvania, to begin serving his 13-year combined sentence. His incarceration notwithstanding, Hoffa continued to run the Teamsters for the next four years, using his son as a go-between. In 1971 President Richard Nixon commuted Hoffa's sentence, on condition that he not participate in ui.ion business (except for attendance at meetings of his Detroit local) until 1980, when his full sentence would have run its course. Hoffa proceeded to try to overturn the limitations of his parole. He was still attempting to do so when, on July 30, 1975, he vanished. He was last seen in the parking lot of a Detroit restaurant. On December 8, 1982 he was officially declared "presumed dead"; his body has never been found. Hoffa was notorious for his suspected involvement with organized crime, and it is widely believed that he was the victim of a mob hit.

James P. Hoffa "has spent a lifetime trying to move out of his father's shadow, yet he seems most comfortable within its famous outline," Rod Stodghill II wrote in *Time* (October 20, 1997, on-line). One of the two children of James R. Hoffa and his wife, Josephine, a one-time laundry worker, James Phillip Hoffa was born on May 19, 1941 in Detroit, Michigan. Along with his sister, Barbara (now Barbara Crancer, an attorney and circuit judge in St. Louis, Missouri), James P. was raised on Detroit's West Side. While in the outside world his father was known for his single-mindedness and gritty determination, James P. remembers him fondly as a family man. "He was an old-fashioned father, who didn't show affection very much," Hoffa recalled for David Grogan and Julie Greenwalt. "But he had a ready smile." The younger Hoffa has been quick to point out that any success he may enjoy as the Teamsters' leader is more a reflection of the values his parents instilled in him in his early years than of his bloodline. "As a child I stood by the fire barrel with my father during Detroit winters, standing with Teamsters who were on strike," he noted to Steven Greenhouse for the *New York Times* (October 21, 1997). "I attended union meetings my whole life. On weekends, my father took me down to the union hall. I had a great love affair with the members of this union."

try executives resisted Hoffa's efforts in vain, and truck drivers came to exert enormous control over virtually every aspect of the U.S. economy. Among James R.'s finest triumphs was the negotiation of the National Master Freight Agreement; considered by many to be one of the greatest labor contracts in history, the agreement nearly tripled wages for truckers, and it revolutionized the freight industry by standardizing the cost of labor, effectively removing that cost as a factor in competitive pricing.

The influence of the Teamsters Union—and Hoffa—did not go unnoticed by the federal government. In the late 1950s a Senate committee, known as the McClellan Committee, began looking into allegations of racketeering among Teamsters administrators. Robert F. Kennedy served as chief counsel to the McClellan Committee, and in 1961, after he became attorney general in the administration of President John F. Kennedy, his brother, the investigation of the Teamsters Union—and Hoffa in particular—was stepped up. For a while Hoffa successfully sidestepped most of Kennedy's charges, including a 1962 accusation of bribery. One of James P.'s most cherished memories of his father is connected with the outcome of the Justice Department's investigation of the bribery charge. "Kennedy made the comment, 'If Hoffa is acquitted, I'll jump off the top of the Capitol dome,'" the younger Hoffa recalled to David Grogan and Julie Greenwalt for *People* (February 1, 1993). "So when my father was cleared, he sent Kennedy a parachute."

In the end, Kennedy prevailed: in 1964 James R. Hoffa was convicted of malfeasance and sentenced to eight years in prison. Later that year he received

Though in his teens he spent summers driving trucks to earn money, James P. enjoyed amenities of a middle-class upbringing unknown to his father at that age. At Cooley High School, in Detroit, he was an honor-roll student and an all-state football star. His father never attended any of his games. "I wish he could have found the time," Hoffa said to the *People* interviewers. "For him, football wasn't important." James P. went on to attend Michigan State University, where he played football and earned a bachelor's degree in economics. After graduating, in 1963, he entered the University of Michigan Law School, where one of his classmates was Richard Gephardt, currently the minority leader of the U.S. House of Representatives. Hoffa was granted his law degree in 1966. In 1967, running as a Democrat, he made an unsuccessful bid for a seat in Michigan's House of Representatives. After that he settled into a modest labor-law practice, which he maintained for the next 25 years. During that time Hoffa often represented friends of his father's and local and regional unions and joint councils, and he remained a dues-paying member of the Teamsters. Among colleagues and associates, Hoffa was looked upon as a talented litigator and champion of labor in the courts.

In the years since James R. Hoffa's presumed death, the International Brotherhood of Teamsters has suffered a steady decline, due to corruption, poor leadership, and failure to adjust to a changing global economy. Three of the union's last six presidents have served time in prison for racketeering, and a fourth, Ron Carey, the last to hold office before Hoffa's installation, is under investigation for his role in a campaign-finance scandal. Corruption became so prevalent that in 1989 the union agreed to allow the federal government to monitor its elections and oversee all union business until an unspecified future date. As part of the agreement, the union also changed its national elections from a convention method, in which union locals sent delegates to represent them, to a more democratic, rank-and-file vote, in which each union member is allowed one vote by a secret mail-in ballot. To date, the federal government still monitors union activities.

The trend away from a protectionist economy and toward a more global economy has considerably altered labor's playing field since the heyday of the Teamsters. Trucking-industry deregulation has increased nonunion competition, and recent labor legislation permits companies to hire nonunion labor, also known as "scabs," to replace striking workers. Furthermore, economic treaties such as the North Atlantic Free Trade Agreement (NAFTA) have knocked down trade barriers between the U.S. and Canada and, more significantly, the U.S. and Mexico. As a result, American manufacturers have turned to foreign laborers, whose hourly wages are markedly less than those of unionized American workers. These factors, and a consequent drop in union membership, have combined over the past decade to diminish the Teamsters' influence over the American economy, and that reduction has led to a further decline in membership. From a peak of 2,300,000 in the late 1970s, the membership rolls have dropped by nearly 40 percent, to 1,400,000. Furthermore, the former backbone and muscle of the union, freight workers, now account for less than 10 percent of total membership. To combat the fall in numbers, the union welcomed workers from a wide array of industries, including flight attendants, custodians, and nurses. The increased diversity has weakened the organization, because many members, failing to be galvanized by the concerns of a single industry, are relatively uninvolved. The union's last national general election, held in December 1998, showed just how uninvolved: although a ballot was mailed to each member's home, fewer than 35 percent responded.

Certain that he could restore the Teamsters as a force in American labor, in 1991 James P. Hoffa decided to run for the union presidency, but he was ruled ineligible because he had not worked in one of the union's trades or councils for 24 consecutive months, as required by the union's constitution. To gain eligibility, in 1993 Hoffa gave up his legal practice and accepted a $50,000-per-year post as executive assistant to the Michigan Joint Council president Larry Brennan. In 1996 he won approval to run against the incumbent union president, Ron Carey.

Carey had won the 1991 election on a reform platform. He had been hailed as a savior of the Teamsters, someone who would root out internal corruption and improve the union's public image. In his first term he quickly gained the trust of the federal oversight committee by cutting his salary and selling off the union's private jets, and he bolstered his image as a leader by means of highly successful contract negotiations on behalf of United Parcel Service drivers. But despite his cost-cutting measures, the union's general funds fell dramatically, to near bankruptcy levels, and he lost the support of a large portion of his constituency.

Given those problems and the strength of the Hoffa name, Carey's reelection in 1996 was far from a sure thing. While promising during his campaign to restore the unity that had characterized the union under his father, Hoffa did not hesitate to remind people of his lineage, using his family name to stir feelings of nostalgia and memories of the Teamsters' former power. Fighting fire with fire, Carey reminded the rank and file of the corruption that had tainted the union during the elder Hoffa's tenure. In addition, he raised doubts about the rectitude of James P. himself. In the late 1960s, Carey campaigners noted, James P. Hoffa had invested in a partnership with a well-known organized-crime figure, Allen Dorfman, who had reportedly siphoned Teamster pension funds to the Mafia. Hoffa claimed that when he entered into the partnership, he had not known that Dorfman, who was murdered in 1983, was a criminal, and he asserted that he had backed out when he had discovered the truth. On another front, Carey pointed to allegations in the book *Mob Lawyer*, by Frank Ragano and Selwyn Raab, that when he married, in 1969, the younger Hoffa and his wife, Virginia, had received substantial sums of cash as wedding gifts from the noted mob figures Carlos Marcello and Santo Traficante, who knew his father. Hoffa denied these allegations, too. The campaign became expensive and bitter and further divided the factions within the union. The election was held in December 1996; Hoffa narrowly lost the race, with 48 percent of the vote to Carey's 52 percent.

After the election, in a strange twist of events, Hoffa was shown to be the relatively clean candidate and Carey, the reformer, was placed under investigation. The investigation was triggered after John Murphy, a South Boston Teamster leader and Hoffa campaign aide, did some digging into Carey campaign finances and found something that appeared improper. Specifically, the Carey administration had paid $110,000 from the union's general fund to a Boston public-relations consultant for services rendered to the union. Concurrently, the consultant's wife gave donations totaling $95,000—the largest single contribution to either campaign—toward Carey's reelection. On the basis of those transactions, the federally appointed election monitor overturned Carey's victory and launched a full investigation into his campaign finances. The investigation uncovered evidence that more than $800,000 of Carey's campaign funds were similarly diverted from rank-and-file dues. Carey was subsequently disqualified from running for reelection. The federal election monitor also investigated Hoffa's finances, and, as Alexander Cockburn reported in the Nation (May 8, 1998), although he uncovered violations of the law serious enough to warrant fining Hoffa's campaign almost $17,000, he ruled that the infractions were not sufficiently grave to disqualify Hoffa from the race. "I've led an exemplary life," Hoffa said to Ron Stodghill, before the investigation ended. "I don't even have points on my driving record."

In his next bid for the presidency, Hoffa ran against Thomas Leedham, the head of the Teamsters' 400,000-member warehouse division, and Ken Hall, the leader of the small-package division. In December 1998, with his opposition in disarray and his approval rating among Teamsters at an all-time high, Hoffa won the election handily. He had to wait another four months before taking office, because of numerous challenges to the election, none of which was successful.

After his swearing in, on March 22, 1999, Hoffa called his first executive meeting to order and addressed some of the union's most pressing needs. He commissioned a team of auditors to examine the union's plummeting finances and make recommendations. He revealed his plans to balance the Teamsters' budget within the first year and generate income by initiating interest-bearing union insurance accounts and credit cards. Also, the board voted to create an ethics panel independent of the government's oversight committee. The panel's sole mission would be to destroy every vestige of corruption within the union, with the goal of spurring the federal government to lift its oversight and return to the union complete control of its activities. In July 1999 Hoffa appointed former New Jersey federal and state prosecutor Edwin H. Stier to head an in-house anti-corruption program. Hoffa's selection of Stier, who gained fame as the trustee of Teamsters Local 560, in New Jersey, has been widely acclaimed as an important first step toward eradicating corruption within the Teamsters and

ending federal oversight. (Local 560, once notorious as the nation's most mob-driven Teamster outpost, was restored to probity under Stier's 12-year watch.)

"The Hoffa mystique still counts for something, yes," Arch Puddington wrote for the National Review (December 31, 1998). "But insofar as it contributes to unrealistic expectations for a revival of Teamster power, it could prove an albatross around James P.'s neck. Jimmy Hoffa [the father] was a smart, dedicated, and ruthless labor leader who was lucky enough to have risen to the top in a golden era for the unionized working man. An industrial-union leader under current conditions is viewed as a success merely if he negotiates a contract whose major feature is a no-layoff clause." Though he frequently referred to the "Hoffa mystique" throughout his campaigns, James P. is eager to identify himself as separate from his father, who characterized his own fight with America's industrial management as "war." He believes himself to be capable of handling the current climate in American labor. "I'm my own person. My father was born in 1913. He lived through the Depression. He came up through the school of hard knocks," he explained to Jeffrey Goldberg for the New York Times Magazine (February 8, 1998). "I'm not going to war with anyone."

Hoffa's agenda includes trying to effect labor-friendly "fair trade," as he has called it. With globalized free trade, he told Margaret Warner in a NewsHour interview reprinted on PBS's Web site (December 7, 1998, on-line), "we're destroying our own economy, even though it's robust, because we're buying everything else. We're buying in the world economy but no one's buying our product." To further labor issues and regain clout in the globalized marketplace, Hoffa has committed himself to breaking Teamster political tradition. Rather than backing a single political party—the Democratic Party—which has been Teamster policy for decades, the union will support individual politicians, regardless of affiliation, who side with the labor movement. In a sign of Hoffa's and the Teamsters' resurgent political influence, in October 1999 President Bill Clinton spoke at a New York dinner honoring Hoffa, thus becoming the first occupant of the White House to speak at a Teamster gathering since Franklin D. Roosevelt, who was president from 1933 to 1945. According to many observers, Clinton's appearance was prompted by both Hoffa's refusal to align the union with one political party and the Teamsters' pending endorsement of a candidate in the 2000 presidential campaign.

James P. Hoffa passed the first major test of his mettle as a negotiator in June 1999, in contract talks involving some 12,800 truckers who haul new cars from factories to dealerships. Using tactics reminiscent of those of his father, who had a famous talent for knowing exactly how and what to leverage against management, Hoffa secured a four-year deal within 25 hours of the expiration of the truckers' old contract. His leverage hinged on the realization by management that a trucking strike during a spurt in national economic growth would severely hurt the auto industry. In 1999 American auto sales were at an all-time high, and the failure to deliver cars to dealers in a timely fashion would have stalled sales. Since factories rely on truckers to remove autos from their lots, they keep little on-site space for storage; a backlog of inventory could result in manufacturing slow-downs and even, in the event of an extended strike, layoffs. Furthermore, the low national unemployment rate would make it more difficult for management to replace striking drivers, forcing manufacturers to turn increasingly to railroads to move inventory. As part of their new contract, the car haulers received a boost in earnings and pension payments and an increase in health-care coverage for retirees under the age of 65.

Although a promotional poster from the 1993 movie *Hoffa*, which stars Jack Nicholson as his father, hangs in James P. Hoffa's office, the union head did not like the film. "The ending was too graphic," he told David Grogan and Julie Greenwalt. "And it didn't depict the way [my father] was." Specifically, he did not agree with the portrayal of his father as a perpetually dour individual. By contrast, he had kind words for Disney's 1995 big-screen animated epic *The Lion King*, in which he has detected parallels with his own life. "[*The Lion King* is] about the Teamsters Union," Hoffa told Lynn Rosellini for *U.S. News & World Report* (December 22, 1997). "It's about the son coming back and in this case making the union right again."

Hoffa and his wife, Virginia—known as Ginger—have two sons, Geoffrey and David. — T.J.F.

Suggested Reading: *National Review* p21+ Dec. 31, 1998; *New York Times* A p11 May 1, 1999, with photo, A p18 June 3, 1999, with photo, A p16 July 7, 1999, A p1+ Aug. 14, 1999, with photo; *New York Times Magazine* p38+ Feb. 8, 1998, with photos; *Online NewsHour* Dec. 7, 1998, with photos; *U.S. News & World Report* p50+ Dec. 22, 1997, with photos

Thomas John Gibbons/Courtesy of EUR/PPA

Hormel, James
(hor-MEL)

Jan. 1, 1933– U.S. ambassador to Luxembourg. Address: c/o Equidex Inc., 19 Sutter St., San Francisco, CA 94104

On June 29, 1999 James Hormel, a lawyer, philanthropist, human-rights advocate, and heir to the Hormel Foods Corp. fortune, was sworn in as the United States ambassador to Luxembourg, thereby becoming the first openly gay person to represent the United States on foreign soil. Hormel's appointment followed nearly two years of controversy, during which a small group of Republicans in the Senate took issue with Hormel's avowed homosexuality and blocked a Senate vote on his confirmation. In the course of that protracted ideological battle, Hormel emerged as a symbolic champion of homosexual rights.

The youngest of three sons, James Catherwood Hormel was born on January 1, 1933 in Austin, Minnesota, to Jay Catherwood Hormel, the head of the Hormel Food Co.—later made a corporation—and Germaine (Dubois) Hormel. His grandfather George C. Hormel founded Hormel Foods in 1891, after immigrating to the United States from Germany. A Minnesota-based food-processing and meatpacking empire, Hormel Foods is best known for its creation, in 1937, of Spam, an inexpensive canned meat made from pork shoulders and ham (which comes from hogs' hind legs). The first canned meat product that did not require refrigeration, Spam was a staple of the military diet during World War II.

With his brothers, George and Thomas, James Hormel grew up in Austin on his family's estate; the 18-room family house has since become incorporated as the Hormel Historic Home and offers tours to the public. He received a B.A. degree in history, in 1955, from Swarthmore College, a prestigious liberal-arts school in Swarthmore, Pennsylvania. In 1958 he earned a J.D. degree from the University of Chicago Law School. He later served there as an assistant dean and then dean of students. In 1986 he established the James C. Hormel

Public Service Program at the school, to encourage law students to pursue careers in public service. For some time Hormel served as the director of a Chicago community-service center.

In the 1950s Hormel married, and with his wife, Alice, a psychologist, he had four daughters— Alison, Anne, Elizabeth, and Sarah—and one son, James Jr. After 10 years of marriage, the couple divorced, largely because of Hormel's homosexuality. Alice Hormel later remarried, but she and her former husband have remained friends. In the early 1970s Hormel revealed his homosexuality to his children, with whom he still enjoys a close relationship.

Meanwhile, freed from the constraints of having to masquerade as a heterosexual patriarch, Hormel chose to live as an openly gay man. Commenting on that decision, he told David W. Dunlap for the *New York Times* (January 1, 1995), "First of all, I feel an obligation to myself." He added, "If we are not public, others define who we are." In 1976 he settled in San Francisco, where he soon became a prominent member of the community. As the founder and chairman of Equidex Inc., which manages the Hormel family's investments and charitable contributions, he gained renown for the generosity with which he helped fund many cultural and educational organizations, among them the San Francisco Symphony. In 1996 he donated $500,000 to help create what is now known as the James C. Hormel Gay and Lesbian Center at the main branch of the San Francisco Public Library. The first of its kind in a public facility, the center contains the world's largest collection of gay and lesbian literature. Other Equidex beneficiaries include Swarthmore College, to which Hormel donated $1.5 million to help create a professorship in social justice; Project Open Hand, which provides meals for thousands of senior citizens and people with AIDS and symptomatic HIV in San Francisco and Alameda counties; the San Francisco AIDS Foundation; the American Foundation for AIDS Research; the United Negro College Fund; the Catholic Youth Organization; the National Holocaust Museum; and the Breast Cancer Action Network. In 1981 he helped found the Washington, D.C.–based Human Rights Campaign, the largest political advocacy group for gay and lesbian rights in the United States. He also emerged as a major Democratic Party supporter. He was a member of the host committee for the 1984 Democratic National Convention, in San Francisco, and served as a member of the Democratic Platform Committee in 1992 and as a delegate at the 1992 and 1996 Democratic National Conventions.

Ambassadorial posts have long been granted to major supporters of political parties. In 1994 reports began circulating that President Bill Clinton was considering nominating Hormel to the post of ambassador to Fiji, a republic in the South Pacific that is composed of about 320 islands. But the stories of Hormel's expected nomination came to nought. It was widely perceived that the nomina-

tion was squashed because of both Republican opposition to Hormel and the concern that Hormel's sexual orientation would prove controversial in Fiji, where a homosexual act is a crime punishable by up to 14 years in prison (and an "attempted" homosexual act by up to seven years). Despite this disappointing development, Hormel praised the Clinton administration for its record of appointments of known homosexuals. "There have been at least two dozen significant appointments," he told Dunlap, referring to, among others, those of Roberta Achtenberg, an assistant secretary in the Department of Housing and Urban Development; Deborah A. Batts, a federal judge in New York City; and Bruce A. Lehman, an assistant secretary of commerce and the commissioner of patents and trademarks. "That's two dozen more than any administration up to now. Someone like me could not even have been considered for a position in the State Department before this Administration."

In 1995 Hormel served as a member of the United States delegation to the United Nations Human Rights Commission, which met in Geneva, Switzerland. Two years later he represented the U.S. as an alternate delegate to the 51st United Nations General Assembly. His appointment to that post was confirmed unanimously by the Republican-dominated Senate. In 1995 he took part in President Clinton's Conference on the Pacific Rim, and the following year he participated in the economic summit convened by Mayor Willie Brown of San Francisco.

In October 1997 President Clinton nominated Hormel to fill the position of ambassador to Luxembourg. Bordered by France, Germany, and Belgium, Luxembourg covers 998 square miles, making it 16 percent smaller than Rhode Island, the smallest U.S. state. Given the minor significance of Luxembourg in world affairs, the post was viewed as largely ceremonial, and confirmation of the nomination by the Senate would normally have been a routine matter. In Hormel's case, however, the confirmation process was lengthy and controversial.

In the Senate Foreign Relations Committee, which is chaired by Republican senator Jesse Helms of North Carolina, a staunch conservative who is unequivocally antigay, Hormel's nomination was approved by a vote of 16 to two in November 1997. The next step in the confirmation process should have been a vote by the full Senate, but Hormel's nomination never reached the Senate floor for consideration. Three Republican senators— James M. Inhofe of Oklahoma, Tim Hutchinson of Arkansas, and Robert Smith of New Hampshire— objected to Hormel's sexual orientation and his advocacy of homosexual-rights causes, and they accused him of being antireligion and pro-pornography. They cited, for example, his failure to condemn material dealing with incest that is shelved in the San Francisco Public Library. In addition, they maintained that Hormel would take advantage of his post as ambassador to advance a "gay agenda." "Our concern is about this nominee's political views," a spokesman for Senator Inhofe explained, as quoted by Alison Mitchell in the *New York Times* (November 18, 1997). "He's been an outspoken promoter of things like same-sex marriages, things we don't agree with." Hutchinson, Inhofe, and Smith, pressured by members of such conservative religious organizations as the Family Research Council and the Traditional Values Coalition, which fiercely opposed Hormel's appointment, proceeded to exercise the traditional Senate privilege of placing a hold on a nomination, which prevents it from coming to a vote on the Senate floor. According to Senate regulations, a hold can be overridden only with the approval of 60 senators. Reportedly, about 60 of the Senate's 100 members supported Hormel, but Trent Lott of Mississippi, the Senate majority leader, did not take steps to force a removal of the hold. Indeed, in a television interview held in June 1998, according to the *New York Times* (June 22, 1998), Lott likened homosexuality to alcoholism, kleptomania, and what he termed "sex addiction."

Responding to his opponents, Hormel insisted that his sexual orientation would not affect his performance as an ambassador. In a 1998 letter to Senator Gordon H. Smith, a Republican from Oregon and a member of the Senate Foreign Relations Committee, Hormel wrote, as quoted by Philip Shenon in the *New York Times* (January 13, 1999), "I will not use, nor do I think it appropriate to use, the office of the ambassador to advocate any personal views that I may hold on any issue." Hormel's supporters decried the actions of the Senate Republicans. Senator Dianne Feinstein, a Democrat from California, told Philip Shenon for the *New York Times* (March 8, 1998), "I think it's a travesty that a handful of Senators are blocking this body from voting for a qualified nominee." "This shows that anti-gay bias continues in the United States Senate," Winnie Stachelberg, a lobbyist for the Human Rights Campaign, told Philip Shenon for the *Times* (October 20, 1998). "A small minority of Senators have taken away the opportunity for an up-or-down vote on Jim Hormel, which is all that people were asking for." Meanwhile, government officials in Luxembourg, which—like all the members of the European Community—has outlawed antigay discrimination, had made it known that it had no reservations about Hormel as ambassador to their nation.

On January 6, 1999 Clinton again nominated Hormel to the post of ambassador to Luxembourg, but the impasse persisted. As the stalemate dragged on and Hormel was exposed to increasingly personal attacks, public opinion shifted in his favor; many people came to view the conflict over his appointment as being unnecessarily fierce and, in light of Luxembourg's negligible power on the world stage, unnecessary. The public was also influenced by Hormel's bipartisan support, which came from such prominent political figures as the Democratic senator Edward M. Kennedy of Massa-

chusetts, Republican senator Orrin Hatch of Utah, and former Republican secretary of state George P. Shultz, who served under President Ronald Reagan. Perhaps even more instrumental in swaying public opinion were the public remarks of members of Hormel's family. "I have known Jim for 46 years," his former wife, Alice Turner, wrote Senator Lott, as quoted by Frank Rich in the *New York Times* (April 18, 1998), "and for 10 of those years I was married to him. During those 10 years we had five children. So for many years he tried his hardest to live what was a lie. Of course, you might say I was the injured party, but I grew to understand the terrible prejudice and hatred that he knew he would have to face . . . and is facing as he goes through the difficult process this nomination and its opponents have put him through. . . . I share with you these personal things because I gather his personal ethics have been questioned. If anyone on this earth could come close to judging that, it would be me. He is a wonderful father, grandfather, and friend. We have a very powerful, close family. My present husband considers James Hormel one of his closest friends. Jim Hormel has given enormously to his family, his community, and to this country. He is just asking to be allowed to give one more time. This is a good man. Give him a chance." Hormel's son, James C. Hormel Jr., praised his father in an essay, distributed by the Pacific News Service, that was published in several newspapers. "When I was 11 years old, my father . . . told me that he was gay," James Jr. wrote, as quoted in a Swarthmore College bulletin (June 1998, on-line). "I didn't find this an easy bit of information to digest, but I heard my father's great concern for how this disclosure would affect his son. This was not a lifestyle choice. Being gay was part of his personal makeup, something he had struggled with greatly his whole life. . . . Those who oppose my father's nomination on the premise that sexual orientation affects 'family values' are not familiar with the strength of our family. While I was growing up, my father never tried to influence my sexuality in any way. What he did teach me was kindness, acceptance of others, honesty, self-esteem, and standing up for what you believe."

During the Senate's 1999 Memorial Day recess, President Clinton broke the Senate impasse, by taking advantage of a constitutional provision that allows a president to appoint certain federal officials when the Senate is not in session. Clinton made such a recess appointment, and on June 29, 1999 Hormel was sworn in as the U.S. ambassador to Luxembourg. His partner, Timothy Wu, a gay-rights activist and former trustee of Princeton University, held the Bible at the swearing-in ceremony, which was administered by Secretary of State Madeleine K. Albright. After administering the oath of office to Hormel, Albright said, as quoted by the *San Francisco Chronicle* (June 30, 1999, on-line), "Today, we send a message that neither race nor creed nor gender nor sexual orientation should be relevant to the selection of ambassadors for the United States."

As of early June 1999 Clinton had made 57 recess appointments, fewer than President George Bush, who made 78 such appointments during his single term, and far fewer than President Ronald Reagan, who made 239 during his eight years in office. In the wake of Hormel's appointment, Senator Inhofe warned that he would thwart other presidential nominations as a protest against President Clinton's circumvention of the Senate. Barry Toiv, a White House spokesman, professed to have no worries on that score. "It's hard to imagine that the Senate would allow itself to be prevented from carrying out its constitutional responsibilities over one senator's unhappiness with a particular appointment," he remarked, as quoted by Joe Carroll in the *Irish Times* (June 10, 1999, on-line). Hormel will represent the U.S. in Luxembourg at least until the end of the Clinton administration.

Hormel is a founding member of the City Club of San Francisco, which was created to bring together community leaders of diverse backgrounds. He has served on the board of managers of Swarthmore College since 1988. He is also on the boards of directors of the American Foundation for AIDS Research, the Human Rights Campaign Foundation, the San Francisco Chamber of Commerce, and the San Francisco Symphony, among other organizations. In 1999 he was elected to the board of trustees of the World Affairs Council of Northern California. He recently established, as a function of Equidex, a charitable entity called Small Change, which will support educational projects.

Hormel's previous companion, with whom he lived for at least 18 years, was Larry Soule, an artist. The ambassador has more than 10 grandchildren. — Y.P.

Suggested Reading: *New York Times* p18 Jan. 1, 1995, with photo, A p20 Nov. 18, 1997, with photo, I p11 Mar. 8, 1998, A p12 Oct. 20, 1998; *New York Times* (on-line) June 13, 1999; *USA Today* A p8 July 14, 1998, with photo

---

Retna Ltd.

Hou Hsiao-hsien

(ho shau-shen)

Sep. 8, 1947– Film director. Address: c/o Motion Picture Development Foundation, 2 Tien-tsin St., Taipei, Taiwan

"When I conceive my films, I always pay close attention to the state of things in everyday life—the common activities such as cooking and eating," the Taiwanese film director Hou Hsiao-hsien told David Sterritt for the *Christian Science Monitor* (November 16, 1989). In an interview two months earlier, with Dave Kehr for the *Chicago Tribune* (September 13, 1989), he said, "My work as a director is to bring out the flow of undercurrents in everyday behavior, to develop a continuous tension." Hou's unconventional approach to filmmaking may explain why, despite his unmistakable talent and the critical acclaim he has received for his films—he has directed 14 so far—he does not enjoy the recognition that mainstream non-Taiwanese audiences accord directors who are far less accomplished. And although Hou has been among the most prominent figures in Taiwan's film industry since the mid-1980s and is among the world's most respected filmmakers, few of his films have been released commercially outside Taiwan, and none has come to theaters in the United States. Their absence is due in part to the reluctance of the American commercial-film industry to distribute foreign films judged to be overly intellectually challenging. Another reason is the obsessiveness that distinguishes Hou's work, a quality that manifests itself both in the subject matter and the style of his films. Unlike many other current movies, which center on unusual and often catastrophic events, Hou's films focus on the lives of seemingly ordinary Taiwanese citizens. Through such characters and their struggles, Hou has explored and commented on Taiwanese identity and modern Taiwanese history. Because many foreign audiences are unfamiliar with the history of Taiwan, they have found his films difficult to digest. But even among those knowledgeable about Taiwan's past, many have been put off by the way in which

Hou has presented his stories. In contrast to most modern filmmakers, who favor a fast pace and extremely varied camera angles, Hou relies on lengthy scenes shot from a distance with a stationary camera. Most of Hou's films are anomalies with few or no counterparts in contemporary cinema. "In conventional terms, you might describe [Hou's] vast representations of modern Taiwanese history as 'epic canvasses,'" Johnathan Romney wrote for *New Statesman & Society* (May 13, 1994), "but they don't afford the easy satisfactions of epics. Rather, with an austere style that makes no concession to audience-pleasing, they're a kind of amplified chamber-cinema, huge but intimate." Romney added, "Hou is certainly one of the most serious directors on the world scene."

Born on September 8, 1947 (according to some accounts, the year was 1946) in the city of Mei-hsien, in Canton Province, China, Hou Hsiao-hsien was just a year old when his family moved to Taiwan. (Formerly known as Formosa, Taiwan is a 14,000-square-mile island that lies 100 miles east of the southeastern coast of China. Along with some nearby islets, it comprises the Republic of China.) Hou grew up in the town of Hualien, in southern Taiwan, and is said to have been a mischievous youngster. After completing his mandatory military service, he studied film and drama at the Taipei National Academy of Arts, in Taiwan's capital, from which he graduated in 1972. The following year he gained an entry-level position in film production. "I began as an assistant and screenplay writer," Hou has recalled, as quoted by Dave Kehr in the *Chicago Tribune*, "and in those days it was just a job. If anything, I was known as a smart-aleck character. Movies were another world to me, until after a time I started to understand films more. Now when I see a film, I have the feeling that I can see directly through the screen straight into the disposition of the director."

After a decade in which he worked his way up in the film industry, Hou directed his first picture, *Cute Girl* (1981). His next directorial efforts were *Cheerful Wind* (1982), *The Green, Green Grass of Home* (1982), and *The Sandwich Man* (1983). Although the first three attracted large audiences—Hou has referred to them as "commercial blockbusters"—and *The Green, Green Grass of Home* won a nomination for a Golden Horse Award (Taiwan's equivalent of an Oscar), critics considered them formulaic undertakings that capitalized on adolescent appeal. In his conversation with David Sterritt for the *Christian Science Monitor*, Hou described his first three pictures, which starred popular singers, as "very lightweight comedies and love stories." "When it came to my third film," he said, "I started to have critical acclaim, too. And I started thinking I could really make some *good* films. So I started to become my own boss."

Hou's fifth directorial effort was *The Boys from Fengkuei* (1983), a story about poor rural teenagers who make their way to the city in search of work only to become mired in the harsh realities of ur-

ban existence. *The Boys from Fengkuei* was named best film at the 1984 Nantes Festival of Three Continents, in France. It was followed by *A Summer at Grandpa's* (1984), which portrayed the turmoil of the adult world from the perspective of two children, a brother and sister, who are forced to stay with their grandfather in the country after their mother falls ill. That film was screened at the New Directors/New Films series at the Museum of Modern Art in New York City in 1986.

Hou's distinctive style and cinematic vision emerged more pronouncedly in the mid-1980s. Increasingly, his films focused on the lives of ordinary people in Taiwan's recent past and the tensions that arose with rapid economic growth and the ensuing loss of cultural traditions and moral direction. Those "ordinary people" included his own family; in his early 20s, he told David Sterritt, he had developed a great interest in the memories of members of his family.

Also in the mid-1980s, Hou opted to photograph most of his scenes in long takes with a stationary camera. His reason for doing so was connected with his decision to cast nonprofessionals who had no training in acting. Such amateur actors "became very stiff if you asked them to act according to the camera," he told Sterritt. "I came to find that by using long takes, and keeping the camera at a distance, it was easy to get these non-actors involved in their characters. . . . That's why I became more and more attracted to this style. And it may also have something to do with my own personality. I don't want to *disturb* people." According to Sterritt, "The special feeling of a Hou film comes from its restrained acting and from technical elements: The distance of the camera prevents the movie from seeming too emotional or sentimental, yet the duration of the shots allows us to become deeply involved with the characters and prevents the film from being detached or clinical."

Hou's distinct vision came to full flower in *A Time to Live and a Time to Die* (1985), a semiautobiographical film that he both wrote and directed. It opens with a narrator confiding, "This film is some memories of my childhood, particularly impressions of my father," and proceeds to tell a poignant and troubling story about a boy growing up in Taiwan during the late 1950s and 1960s, when the government's Cold War anti-Communist propaganda colored many aspects of life on the island. The film offers a haunting view of the demise of tradition and family stability that accompanied modern Taiwan's political and economic development. Godfrey Cheshire, writing about Hou's output in *Film Comment* (November 1993), described *A Time to Live and a Time to Die* as "one of the great works of childhood and memory in the Chinese or any other cinema."

Hou then directed *Dust in the Wind* (1986), about a teenage boy and his girlfriend who leave their small town for Taipei. In a review of *Dust in the Wind* for the *Christian Science Monitor* (January 24, 1989), David Sterritt wrote, "The images are so quiet and still they seem radically different from Hollywood's hectic movies, and they're as bitter-sweet and atmospheric as they are beautiful to look at." Next came *Daughter of the Nile* (1987), which also focuses on contemporary Taiwanese urban life. Although these films received critical thumbs-up, they did not fare well at the box office. To continue making motion pictures, Hou was forced to borrow substantial sums of money.

All that changed after the run of the family epic *A City of Sadness* (1989), which centers on four sons of a middle-class Taiwanese family during the politically sensitive period between 1945, when the 50-year Japanese occupation of Taiwan ended, and 1949, when the Nationalist leader Generalissimo Chiang Kai-shek came to power on the island. The film includes a re-creation of a 1947 event in Taipei, known as the February 28 Incident, in which Nationalist forces gunned down many people who had gathered to protest a police officer's fatal beating of a cigarette peddler (the widowed mother of two young children) suspected of selling smuggled goods. The killings sparked massive demonstrations against the government of Taiwan, whose inefficiency, corruption, and authoritarianism had long angered many Taiwanese. Though by all accounts the demonstrators were unarmed, in the following weeks Nationalist forces massacred thousands of innocent adults and children. For many years the right-wing political climate in Taiwan had discouraged filmmakers from depicting the February 28 Incident; Hou was among the first to defy the taboo. Thanks to the daring subject matter and a shift in political climate that allowed for more openness in the arts, *A City of Sadness* broke box-office records in Taiwan; it has been estimated that nearly half of Taiwan's population (estimated to be about 20.5 million in 1990) saw it. At the 1989 Venice Film Festival, the movie won the Golden Lion Award, and in Taiwan Hou won the Golden Horse Award for best director. Having come to be seen as one of his nation's most respected and influential filmmakers, Hou used his newfound clout to establish informal workshops to help nurture the work of other filmmakers.

Hou's 11th directorial credit, *The Puppetmaster* (1993), dramatizes the early life of Li Tien-lu, Taiwan's premier puppeteer, who had acted in two of Hou's earlier films (*Dust in the Wind* and *Daughter of the Nile*, in both of which he played the role of a grandfather). *The Puppetmaster* depicted Li's adventures during the Japanese occupation of Taiwan. Through Li's story, Hou explored notions of Taiwan's identity, history, and complex relationship to China and Japan. Reviewing the film for the *Village Voice* (October 12, 1993), J. Hoberman wrote that it amounted to nothing less than "a rebirth of cinema itself." The film won the Jury Prize at the 1993 Cannes Film Festival and the FIPRESCI International Critics Prize at the 1994 Istanbul International Film Festival.

In *Good Men, Good Women* (1995), Hou again examined Taiwan's colonial past, this time through the story of an actress in contemporary Taiwan. While playing the part of an actual historical figure—a woman who fought the Japanese in the 1940s—the actress becomes obsessed with the character. That film was followed by *Goodbye South, Goodbye* (1996), a contemporary drama about a small-time criminal and his misfit friends, who wander Taiwan's countryside trying to make a living through one ill-conceived scheme after another. *Goodbye South, Goodbye* got a showing at the 1996 New York Film Festival.

Hou's most recent film is *Flowers of Shanghai* (1998), a drama that takes place at the end of the 19th century and is set in brothels located in Shanghai's foreign concessions—zones that foreign powers occupied until the mid-20th century. As a testament to Hou's venerated status in international cinema, *Flowers of Shanghai* and its two immediate predecessors were honored with nominations for the prestigious Golden Palm Award at the Cannes Film Festival.

Hou Hsiao-hsien has served as the executive producer of six films, among them Zhang Yimou's celebrated *Raise the Red Lantern* (1991), Wu Nien-Jen's *A Borrowed Life* (1994), and Hsu Hsiao-Ming's *Heartbreak Island* (1995). Hou wrote the script for the last-named film; his screenwriting credits also include *Six Is Company* (1982), *Growing Up* (1983), and *A Time to Live and a Time to Die*. In addition, he acted in the films *Taipei Story* (1985) and *Soul* (1986) and appeared in *Gender in Chinese Cinema* (1996) and, as himself, in both *Sunless Days* (1990) and the documentary *HHH: A Portrait of Hou Hsiao-Hsien* (1997).

Writing in 1989, David Sterritt described Hou Hsiao-hsien as "a thoughtful and friendly man who thinks before he speaks, but is rarely at a loss for something to say—and never hesitates to demystify his unusual [cinematic] style by explaining its roots and purposes." — Y.P.

Suggested Reading: *Chicago Tribune* V p7 Sep. 13, 1989; *Film Comment* p56+ Nov. 1993, with photos; *Variety* p62 Feb. 17, 1992, with photo

Selected Films: as director—*Cute Girl*, 1981; *Cheerful Wind*, 1982; *The Green, Green Grass of Home*, 1982; *The Sandwich Man*, 1983; *The Boys from Fengkuei*, 1983; *A Summer at Grandpa's*, 1984; *Dust in the Wind*, 1986; *Daughter of the Nile*, 1987; *A City of Sadness*, 1989; *The Puppetmaster*, 1993; *Good Men, Good Women*, 1995; *Goodbye South, Goodbye*, 1996; *The Flowers of Shanghai*, 1998; as director and screenwriter—*Six Is Company, 1982; Growing Up*, 1983; *A Time to Live and a Time to Die*, 1985; as producer—*Raise the Red Lantern*, 1991; *A Borrowed Life*, 1994; *Heartbreak Island*, 1995

Courtesy of AUSPIC

Howard, John

July 26, 1939– Prime Minister of Australia.
Address: c/o Liberal Party of Australia, 19 Milner
Crescent, Wollstonecraft, N.S.W. 2065, Australia

John Howard, the bespectacled prime minister of
Australia, who was described by Ean Higgins for
Maclean's (March 4, 1996) as "the ultimate
square," has led the conservative Liberal Party to
power after more than a decade of watching the
ruling faction from the sidelines. In 1996 he ended
13 years of the more left-leaning Labor Party's
dominance in Australian politics by unseating
Prime Minister Paul Keating, and in October 1998
he was reelected to a second term when the longstanding coalition formed by the Liberal Party and
the smaller National Party won a close race against
Labor, led by Kim Beazley. His reelection cemented Howard's position as his nation's leading conservative.

Howard joined the Liberal Party in the early
1960s and won a seat in Australia's House of Representatives, the lower house of Parliament, in
1974; he has since emerged as one of his party's
staunchest supporters of measures to deregulate
Australia's economy and improve conditions for
Australia's businesses. He has also successfully
supported large companies in breaking up Australia's historically strong unions and taken measures
to protect white Australian farmers' property rights
to large tracts of land against competing claims of
Australia's Aborigines.

The roots of Howard's fiscal and social conservatism may be traced to his youth. John Winston
Howard was born on July 26, 1939 in Sydney, Australia. Raised in a middle-class family, he learned

the value of hard work and entrepreneurship from
his father, who ran a gas station in Sydney. "The
last thing you ever did was work for the government: you started your own business or you
worked for a firm. You looked after your family,"
Howard once said, as quoted by Higgins. Howard's
conservative views translated into political action
at the University of Sydney, from which he graduated with a bachelor of laws degree in 1961. Unlike
his contemporaries, many of whom protested the
conservatism of their parents during the tumultuous 1960s, he spent much of that decade working
for the Young Liberal Movement, an organization
affiliated with the conservative, right-wing Liberal
Party, and campaigned in support of Australia's
military involvement in the Vietnam War.

After college Howard served as a staff member
of the New South Wales Supreme Court, then as a
partner in a Sydney law firm. Concurrently he was
a member of the state executive committee of the
New South Wales Liberal Party. In 1974 he won a
seat in Australia's House of Representatives as a
Liberal Party representative of Bennelong, a northwestern suburb of Sydney, and was reelected to
that seat repeatedly over the next two decades.

In 1975 Howard joined Prime Minister Malcolm
Fraser's conservative Liberal–National coalition
government, which had replaced Prime Minister E.
Gough Whitlam's Labor government. Howard
served Fraser's government—which was in power
from 1975 to 1983—in several capacities: as minister for business and consumer affairs, from 1975 to
1977; as minister for special trade negotiations,
from July to December 1977; and as treasurer of the
Commonwealth (finance minister), from 1977 to
1983.

Meanwhile, Howard rose within the hierarchy
of his party. He was elected deputy leader of the
Liberal Party in April 1982, then chosen by his colleagues in September 1985 to replace Andrew Peacock as the leader of the Liberal Party, the major
opposition to the ruling Labor government that had
come to power in 1983.

During his tenure Howard led his party to adopt
a rightist stance on economic issues. He championed a smaller government payroll, called for fewer governmental regulations, and advocated a
greater role for market forces in the economy.
Moreover, he sounded a clarion call to change Australia's immigration policy to curtail the influx of
Asians, who had come to Australia in increasing
numbers during the 1980s. According to figures
supplied by *New Statesman & Society* (August 26,
1988), 2.6 percent of those living in Australia at
that time had been born in Asia; despite that relatively small figure and the general consensus
among economic analysts that closer ties to Asia
would greatly benefit Australia's economy, Howard stated in 1988, as quoted by William McGurn
for the *National Review* (September 15, 1989), that
"it would be in our immediate-term interest and
supportive of social cohesion if [Asian immigra-
tion] were slowed down a little." Indeed, in August

1988 he supported legislation that sought to end Australia's non-race-based immigration policy, which had received bipartisan support for more than 20 years. Earlier in the century, Australia had followed a policy, termed "White Australia," that had imposed a language test to discourage immigration from non-European countries. That discriminatory practice ended in 1966. As of March 1996, according to Higgins, Australia's Asian population had reached about 5 percent.

In national elections in 1987, Howard unsuccessfully challenged the Labor Party prime minister, Bob Hawke, for control of the government. Setting the tone for the next decade, the Labor Party retained its majority in both the House of Representatives, which has 148 seats, and the Senate, which consists of 76 members. In 1990 Prime Minister Hawke won an unprecedented fourth term; then, in 1991, the Labor Party ousted Hawke and named Keating prime minister and party leader. In the 1993 national elections, Keating won a second term as prime minister.

Meanwhile, in May 1989 Howard lost the leadership of his party to Andrew Peacock. For the next six years, Howard watched from the sidelines as his party came in behind the Liberal Party in national elections. In January 1995 he regained the leadership of his party, in part by adopting a more moderate position on many economic and social issues. He used the same strategy when he challenged Keating in 1996, campaigning on a platform of centrist views on economic issues, similar to those espoused by his opponent. For example, he pledged to retain Medicare, the government-funded national health-insurance policy, which had been established by a Labor government, and he pledged $760 million to establish a trust to address environmental issues. However, whereas Keating recommended forging a stronger alliance with Asia and supported looser ties with Great Britain (he felt that the Queen should be replaced as head of state by an elected president), Howard defended Australia's historic ties to Europe and supported the continuation of Australia as a constitutional monarchy.

In national elections in March 1996, Howard beat Keating in a surprising landslide. Howard's coalition won 94 seats in the House of Representatives, and Howard thus ended the Labor Party's 13-year reign. Although the election had taken place while Australia was enjoying a period of relative economic stability—according to Higgins, as of March 1996 Australia's per capita income was $23,000, annual economic growth was 3.3 percent, inflation was 3.3 percent, and overall unemployment was at 8.6 percent—most analysts concurred that concern over the creation of jobs had played a key role in influencing the outcome of the election. In some areas of Australia, unemployment, particularly among young people, was nearly 30 percent.

Sworn in as prime minister of Australia on March 11, 1996, Howard became Australia's 25th prime minister since 1901, when the former British colonies of New South Wales, Queensland, South Australia, Tasmania, Victoria, and Western Australia were joined to form a federation. He faced many challenges, among the most pressing of which was the issue of land rights for Australia's Aborigines, who made up between 1 percent and 1.5 percent of the population. For years, Aborigines had contested claims of white farmers to large tracts of land—in total, nearly 40 percent of Australia's land mass. Aborigines' claims on the territories in dispute had been upheld by two Supreme Court decisions: one, in 1992, ruled that Aborigines had the right to use or occupy land as long as they could prove an unbroken connection with it, and the other, in 1996, upheld the Aborigines' native title to land, which, according to the decision, could co-exist with the rights of farmers and ranchers. To clear up the ambiguities resulting from these decisions, Howard supported legislation that would limit the rights of Aborigines to make claims over ancestral land now occupied by white farmers. The legislation passed Australia's House of Representatives but was rejected by the Senate, the upper house of Parliament. (The Labor government had generally been viewed as more supportive of Aborigines.)

Another issue in the forefront of Australia's political debate was that of Australia's unions. In April 1998 Australia's second-largest cargo-handling company, Patrick, fired all 1,400 of its dock workers, who belonged to the Maritime Union of Australia. During a bitter dispute, Patrick replaced the union workforce with scabs. Howard had long maintained that "uncooperative" unions were detrimental to Australia's economy because of their insistence on what he considered to be unreasonably high wages. Thus he supported Patrick, and he ordered police officers to maintain order at the dockyards. Although Howard and Patrick were successful in breaking the union, the ensuing clash between picketing union workers and security guards and the police was televised widely, and Howard's popularity shrank as a result.

Faced with declining support, Howard called early elections for October 1998. His coalition won a six-seat majority in the House of Representatives, narrowly beating the opposition Labor Party. (The coalition had previously held a 44-seat majority.) During the campaign Howard had proposed a 10 percent tax on all goods and services as part of an effort to reform Australia's tax structure. He had also called for a cut in personal income taxes, to offset the extra financial burden stemming from the goods-and-services levy. He faces the task of implementing his tax reform in his second term.

John Howard enjoys playing tennis and golf. He and his wife, Janette, a former secondary-school teacher of English, have been married since 1971. The couple have three children—Melanie, Tim, and Richard—and currently live in Sydney in Kirribilli House, the official residence of the Australian prime minister. — Y.P.

Suggested Reading: *Economist* p29+ Mar. 7, 1987, with photos, p31+ Mar. 9, 1996, with photo, p44 Dec. 6, 1997, with photo, p36 Apr. 18, 1998, with photo, p37+ Oct. 10, 1998, with photo; *Maclean's* p46+ Mar. 4, 1996, with photos; *New York Times* I p4 Mar. 3, 1996, I p4 Mar. 15, 1997, with photo

Courtesy of Reginald Hudlin
Reginald (left) and Warrington Hudlin

Hudlin, Warrington

1953(?)– Film and television producer; president of the Black Film Makers Foundation. Address: c/o Black Film Makers Foundation, 670 Broadway, Suite 304, New York, NY 10012

Hudlin, Reginald

1961(?)– Film and television producer, director, and writer. Address: c/o Black Film Makers Foundation, 670 Broadway, Suite 304, New York, NY 10012

The filmmakers Warrington and Reginald Hudlin first made a name for themselves with *House Party*, a small-budget 1990 hit that demonstrated audiences' willingness to pay to see middle-class teen comedies starring not lily-white brat packs (the sorts featured in such John Hughes movies as *Pretty in Pink* and *Ferris Bueller's Day Off*) but black rappers—even one with a weird, eraserhead haircut. Since then the Hudlin brothers have contin-

ued to contribute to the swelling stream of African-American–made films and television programs, and they have pushed black culture into such previously little-explored territory as animation (with their film *Bebe's Children*) and science fiction (with *Cosmic Slop*). Their aim is to appeal to audiences of all backgrounds, by combining light entertainment with satire and by employing what Reginald has labeled the "dense-pack theory of comedy": "Pack a scene with enough different types of humor and you can't help but get a laugh," as Patrick Pacheco put it in the *New York Times* (July 26, 1992). "Make [the comedy] highbrow, lowbrow, political, raunchy, or smooth," Reginald Hudlin explained to Pacheco, "and then you can sneak in anything else you want. . . . If you're funny enough and real enough, you can reach out to anybody."

Hailing from East St. Louis, Illinois (directly across the Mississippi River from St. Louis, Missouri), Warrington Hudlin was born in about 1953 and Reginald Alan Hudlin in about 1961. Their mother was a schoolteacher; their father, Warrington Hudlin Sr., was a schoolteacher turned insurance executive. Their brother, Christopher, who is between them in age, also works in the insurance business. Growing up in what the brothers like to call "the blackest city in America," Reggie and Warrington were influenced by East St. Louis's rich African-American history and traditions. "If you have any kind of storytelling impulse, East St. Louis is just such a mother lode of black folk culture," Reginald told David Mills for the *Washington Post* (March 9, 1990). It is the place, he noted, where Ike Turner met the future Tina Turner, where Chuck Berry played in his formative years, and where Miles Davis grew up.

Singled out early on for their artistic talents, both Warrington and Reginald attended a special high school for the arts. Both brothers also participated in a program set up in East St. Louis by the renowned African-American dancer and choreographer Katharine Dunham. Dunham, Reginald explained to David Mills, "would bring in master drummers from Senegal, and of course instructors from her own dance company, and martial-arts masters, and all this *culture*."

Warrington attended Yale University, in New Haven, Connecticut, on a scholarship, in the early 1970s. He planned to become a lawyer or a doctor but changed his mind after being impressed by such 1970s African-American films as Melvin Van Peebles's *Sweet Sweetback's Baadasssss Song* and *Shaft*, the latter directed by Gordon Parks. These films taught Warrington Hudlin that African-Americans could not only make films but subvert the conventions of American cinema. While at Yale he made two documentaries—*Black at Yale* and *Street Corner Stories*, the latter about black men who hung out on New Haven stoops and swapped tales.

After graduating from college Warrington Hudlin moved to New York City, where he found that support for African-American filmmakers, especially documentary filmmakers, was minimal; indeed, he has said that a "wall of institutional disenfranchisement" blocked the progress of people like himself. To change that state of affairs, he began (while continuing to make films) to set up institutional mechanisms from which future filmmakers could benefit. In particular, in 1978, with a grant from the National Endowment for the Arts, he helped found the Black Film Makers Foundation; for some time he has served as the organization's president. With support from members' dues and Warrington's Ivy League and film connections, the group has sponsored workshops, operated a job-referral service, programmed local and national film festivals, and held screenings for black filmmakers; in 1982, for instance, the organization sponsored a screening of Spike Lee's student film *Sarah*. Currently, the group has some 3,300 members.

Encouraging aspiring filmmakers was nothing new for Warrington; for years he had prodded his brother Reginald toward a film career. "I wasn't even in high school yet, and I kept telling Warrington my film ideas," Reginald recalled to Patrick Pacheco for the *New York Times*. "Then one Christmas, he gave me a book with blank pages and said, 'Here, write your stories down in this.'" In an interview with Marlaine Glicksman for *Film Comment* (May 1990), Reginald said that he "was very fortunate growing up having a brother who was a successful filmmaker, and particularly, successful outside of Hollywood." "It really opened up my head to be exposed to alternate ways of making movies—people who turned financial disadvantages into aesthetic innovations," he told Glicksman.

Like Warrington, Reginald attended an Ivy League school—Harvard College, in Cambridge, Massachusetts. As an undergraduate he made a handful of films, including *The Kold Waves*, about a white drummer trying to join a black band, and *Reggie's World of Soul*. After hearing the Luther Vandross song "Bad Boy Having a Party" in the summer before his senior year (1982–83), Reginald remembered a promise he had once made to himself. "When I was a kid," he told Marlaine Glicksman, "I went to parties . . . and I swore, 'One day, man, I'm going to make a movie about this.' So when it came time to do my thesis film at Harvard, I kept that promise." The 20-minute film he put together later served as the basis for *House Party*, his and Warrington's first feature film. After graduating from Harvard, Reginald became a partner, along with Warrington, in a company that created music videos for such acts as Uptown Crew, Heavy D, the Boyz, and the Nu Romance Crew.

In 1986 Spike Lee came out with *She's Gotta Have It*, which has been widely credited with opening the door for other black filmmakers. In 1989, for instance, the year Lee's acclaimed picture

Do the Right Thing premiered, four other films directed by African-Americans were also released. Studios began to realize that African-American films could be hot commodities: as Karen Grigsby Bates wrote in the *New York Times Magazine* (July 14, 1991), "Black film properties may be to the '90's what the car phone was to the '80s: every studio executive has to have one." New Line Cinema, the studio responsible for the highly successful *Nightmare on Elm Street* films, came knocking on the Hudlins' door. "It's a very atypical story," Warrington told *New York Newsday* (March 12, 1990). "Usually you have to chase the money. The money . doesn't chase you."

New Line Cinema gave the Hudlins a budget of $2.5 million to develop Reginald's thesis project into a full-length film. The brothers divided responsibilities—Warrington produced, while Reginald wrote and directed. The crew they hired to work on *House Party*, as they called their film, was 65 percent black (the industry average was only 5 percent at the time). They cast the rap duo Kid'n'Play (a.k.a. Christopher Reid and Christopher Martin) in the roles of the main characters: two middle-class African-American teenagers—nicknamed Kid and Play—who are growing up somewhere in the Midwest.

House Party can be described as a typical teenage comedy: Kid, who sports an outlandish haircut, is grounded by his father (portrayed by the actor and comic Robin Harris), but he sneaks out to attend a house party hosted by Play, his best friend. All sorts of hilarities ensue, including a "crisis" in which the characters try to decide whether to have sex. For all the silly humor, however, the Hudlins made sure that *House Party* contained a serious message as well. "I wanted to make a movie that had social messages, but was also entertaining, nonstop fun . . . ," Reginald told Marlaine Glicksman. "I wanted to make a film about the transference of values between fathers and sons—how that happens even though the sons don't want it to and the fathers may try too hard. A film about taking responsibility for your actions. But do that in a fun way." *House Party* proved to be extremely successful. The film won the Filmmakers' Trophy and Cinematography Award at the 1990 Sundance Film Festival and did well at the box office, netting about $27 million, or a profit of nearly 1,000 percent. New Line later produced two sequels to *House Party*. (The Hudlins were associated with neither.)

In the wake of *House Party*'s success, Paramount Pictures gave the Hudlins a far larger budget—$40 million—to make the comedy *Boomerang* (1992), starring the comedian Eddie Murphy. Supported by a nearly all-black cast, Murphy portrayed not his usual fast-talking cutup but a suave New York marketing executive who treats women as little more than sexual playthings. In the course of the film, Murphy's character experiences a reversal of fortune after meeting a female executive who is even more predatory than he. Directed by Reginald and co-produced by Warrington and Brian Grazer, the film grossed about $120 million worldwide.

For their next project, *Bebe's Children*, the Hudlins returned to their idea of making a film based on the stand-up routine of Robin Harris. They had planned to have Harris star in it, but Harris had died, in 1990, after suffering a heart attack. Unwilling to replace the inimitable Harris with another actor, the Hudlins decided to turn the story into an animated film. Written by Reginald, directed by Bruce Smith, and executive produced by both Hudlin brothers, *Bebe's Children* was released in 1992. Replete with saucy language, the film revolves around Robin, who, to go on a date with the woman he loves, must take along her child and three other children she happens to be baby-sitting. The three kids turn out to be rebellious and violent little tykes, as demonstrated when they turn a trip to the amusement park into a disaster.

The Hudlins took another creative leap with their next project, *Cosmic Slop*, which aired on HBO in 1994. They envisioned the three-part series as a multicultural variation of the hit science-fiction TV show *The Twilight Zone*. "During the 50's and 60's, *The Twilight Zone* was very provocative," Reginald told the *New York Times* (November 7, 1994). "[Rod] Serling [the creator of the *Twilight Zone*] dealt with prejudice, he dealt with social issues of all stripes. What you see missing in a lot of the clones of *Twilight Zone* made since then is that same sense of true provocativeness. And that's what we're trying to bring back." They recruited the funk musician George Clinton, the leader of Parliament-Funkadelic, to host *Cosmic Slop* (the title was taken from a Parliament album); indeed, Clinton's contribution was probably another reason that the Hudlin brothers were so eager about the project. "If I was going to name a primary aesthetic influence of any medium, it would have to be George Clinton and that whole Parliament-Funkadelic point of view and aesthetic style," Reginald told Marlaine Glicksman. "They were just so black and so cosmic at the same time. There's a kind of gleeful anarchy with very complex musical arrangements. It's driving and entertaining and never takes itself too seriously, but there's some really innovative things going on." He added that *House Party* had been "just the first tiny step towards making movies like George Clinton makes records."

Directed by Reginald Hudlin, "Space Traders," the first episode of *Cosmic Slop*, was based on a story included in the law professor Derrick Bell's collection of fables *Faces at the Bottom of the Well: The Permanence of Racism* (1992). In "Space Traders," aliens offer Americans gold, unlimited energy, and an end to pollution in exchange for every single African-American. A national debate ensues, followed by a referendum conducted by telephone. Warrington wrote the screenplay for and directed the second episode of the show, "The First Commandment," about a Puerto Rican priest who is struggling with his parishioners' belief in Santeria (a religion in which deities of the Yoruba people of Africa are associated with Catholic saints) and his own questions about the Catholic Church's hierarchy. The final episode, "Tang," based on a short story by Chester Himes, follows a couple who receive a rifle along with a message telling them to "wait for the revolution."

In a rare instance of noncollaboration, Reginald worked without Warrington to make *The Great White Hype* (1996), a satire of boxing and race relations that was described as "happily outrageous" by Janet Maslin in the *New York Times* (May 3, 1996) and also hailed by such other reviewers as Peter Travers, who, in *Rolling Stone* (May 30, 1996), reported that it "provides plenty of profane laughs." Directed by Reginald, *The Great White Hype* stars Samuel L. Jackson as a Don King–like promoter who arranges a fight between the black heavyweight title holder, James "The Grim Reaper" Roper (played by Damon Wayans), and a white boxer, "Irish" Terry Conklin (Peter Berg, from the TV series *Chicago Hope*), with the aim of using racial hostilities to boost pay-per-view sales. More recently, the Hudlins co-produced *Ride* (1998), a road movie about an aspiring director (Melissa De Sousa) who must baby-sit an emerging rap group as they travel to a video shoot. *Ride* also stars Malik Yoba, as a charismatic inner-city activist who accompanies the director and the rappers on the trip.

The Hudlins have insisted that as partners in filmmaking, they have never been troubled by sibling rivalry. Rather, they maintain that being brothers has helped them in their continuing creative collaboration. "There's so much we can know from just a raised eyebrow," Reginald told an interviewer for *Premiere* (January 1990). — W.G.

Suggested Reading: *American Film* p37+ Apr. 1988; *Film Comment* p65+ May 1990, with photos; *New York Newsday* II p3+ Mar. 12, 1990, with photo; *New York Times* C p20 June 7, 1989, II p9 July 26, 1992, with photo, C p11 Nov. 7, 1994, D p1 Nov. 9, 1995, with photo; *Variety* p6 Nov. 27–Dec. 3, 1995, with photo; *Washington Post* D p1+ Mar. 9, 1990, with photo, G p1 July 21, 1991

Selected Films: Reginald Hudlin and Warrington Hudlin—*House Party*, 1990; *Boomerang*, 1992; *Bebe's Kids*, 1992; *Ride*, 1998; Reginald Hudlin—*The Great White Hype*, 1996

Selected Television Shows: *Cosmic Slop*, 1994

Jeff Slocomb/Outline Press

Iglesias, Enrique

(ee-GLAY-see-yahs, on-REE-kay)

May 8, 1975– Pop singer; songwriter. Address: c/o Fonovisa Records, 7710 Haskell Ave., Van Nuys, CA 91406

"My dream is for my music to be heard in every corner of the world," the pop singer Enrique Iglesias told an interviewer for the *New York Times Magazine* (January 21, 1996). "I'd like to be in an elevator in Hong Kong and hear my songs." Iglesias made those remarks at age 20, a few months after the release of his first album, and in the three years since then, his dream has very nearly become a reality: as of early 1999, worldwide sales of his albums totaled well over 12 million.

Enrique Iglesias is a son of the Latin pop-music icon Julio Iglesias, and while he has acknowledged that his father's name has, in his words, "open[ed] doors," he has also pointed out that his father "didn't even know about my [debut] album until it was finished." According to Tony Campos, an executive at the Miami radio station WAMR, Enrique Iglesias "has the same appeal his father has, but to a younger audience." "He stands on stage, and the girls go crazy," Campos told a reporter for *People* (May 11, 1998), for an issue in which Iglesias was listed as one of the "50 most beautiful people in the world." Iglesias, who has thus far recorded in Spanish, Italian, Portuguese, and, in 1999 for the first time, English, wrote the music and lyrics of 16 of the 30 songs on his three albums. His many honors include a 1996 Grammy and more than 20 other awards. "Please do not introduce me as the son of Julio Iglesias," he said to Peter Castro for *People* (April 22, 1996). "I'm very proud of my father, but

when you read *Billboard* now, you see *Enrique Iglesias*."

Enrique Iglesias Preysler was born on May 8, 1975 in Madrid, Spain. His father may be the best-known Latin recording artist in history: by 1983 Julio Iglesias had sold more than 100 million albums, and that year the *Guinness Book of World Records* declared him the world's best-selling recording artist. According to his official Web page in early March 1999, his total sales have reached 220 million albums.

When Enrique was four, his parents divorced. For the next five years, he lived in Spain with his mother, Isabel Preysler, a Philippine-born journalist, and his older sister, Chabeli, and older brother, Julio José. When he was nine, his mother sent him and his two siblings to live with their father in Miami, Florida, because she was afraid they might be kidnapped. "It broke my heart to send them away," Preysler told *People* (April 22, 1996, on-line). "But we had to for security reasons. If I had known that their father wasn't around"—Julio's hectic touring and recording schedule kept him away from home most of the time—"it might have been different." In Miami Enrique and his siblings were raised primarily by their nanny, Elvira Alvares. (Iglesias dedicated his debut album to Alvares.) "I did miss [my parents], but you get used to seeing your dad maybe once a month," Iglesias told Peter Castro. "There was always a lot of communication between us, which helped a lot."

At around the time he came to the United States, Enrique began singing, an activity he tried to keep a secret from virtually everyone but his nanny. "When I was seven, I'd kneel in bed and pray I'd be a singer," he has recalled. "But I'd never have made it if I'd told my parents. If I'd heard anything negative, I wouldn't have been able to stand it." Iglesias told John Lannert for *Billboard* (July 19, 1997), "Maybe I never told my dad because he was not a big influence [in the music world] as a singer, but I never listened to his music."

In his mid-teens Iglesias began writing songs, and he resolved to make an album someday. He enrolled at the University of Miami as a business major, but in 1994, in his sophomore year, he dropped out to pursue a career in music. He had been working with a band in a friend's garage, jamming on Latino standards to hone his act, but he worried that he was not good enough. So, soon after quitting school, he invited Fernán Martínez, an acquaintance from the music industry, to appraise his musical skills. Martínez was impressed by his voice (which has been described as a "raspy baritone"), and following Martínez's suggestion, Iglesias made a demo tape. For the next few months, Martínez pushed the tape to various labels, but there were no takers.

Martínez was on the verge of giving up when he got a call from Guillermo Santiso, the president and CEO of Fonovisa Records. Santiso, too, reacted favorably to the tape—"The voice was very masculine and different," he recalled to Lannert; indeed, he has claimed that, even though he did not know Enrique's last name, he was ready to sign him to a $1 million contract for three albums. He got even bigger ideas after learning the identity of Enrique's father. According to Santiso, he urged Alejandro Quintero, vice president of new business and development for the Mexican media powerhouse Televisa, which owns Fonovisa, to approve a multimillion-dollar advance to promote Iglesias throughout South America. "I told Quintero the whole story about Enrique and he said, 'Go ahead.' He fell in love with the project," Santiso told Lannert. When Julio Iglesias learned that his son had chosen music as his profession and had no intention of returning to school, "he was shocked," Enrique recalled to Peter Campos. "I told him I was sorry. I said, 'Look, this is exactly what I've always wanted to do. Just let me do it my way, please.'"

Iglesias was 20 years old when he cut his first, self-named album, with the help of Martínez and the producer Rafael Perez Botija. In promoting the record—which they did on a grand scale—Martínez and Santiso did not mention Enrique's last name, to avoid having him come across, in Lannert's words, as "an opportunistic flash-in-the-pan" who people might think was simply trying to cash in on his father's fame. The strategy worked. Enrique's first single, "Si Tú Te Vas" ("If You Go"), released in mid-1995, soon became a hit on regional Mexican radio stations—an unusual feat for a non-Mexican artist. In the U.S., where the Latino record business had long been stagnant, Iglesias submitted to some 400 interviews in the 40 days after "Si Tú Te Vas" went on sale. In Portugal *Enrique Iglesias* went gold after just three weeks; worldwide, one million copies sold within three months. To date, sales of the album have exceeded 5.8 million. Four other singles from the disc—"Por Amarte," "No Llores por Mi," "Experiencia Religiosa," and "Trapecista"—also became huge hits.

Before his debut album appeared, Iglesias recalled to Lannert, "everyone used to laugh at me. Sony didn't want me, neither did [the Latin divisions of] EMI or Polygram. What is great about the second record is that suddenly all those people who laughed at me came back and said it is going to be a great hit." That prediction proved to be correct: In the two years since its release, in January 1997, *Vivir* ("Living") has sold close to five million copies. In March 1997 Iglesias embarked on a worldwide tour, performing 78 concerts in 13 countries in the United States, Latin America, and Europe, in venues ranging in size from 12,000 seats to 65,000. According to an Internet biography of him, a total of more than 720,000 people attended the concerts. Iglesias used so much equipment (altogether it weighed more than 150,000 pounds), and so many support people (65, including an eight-person band), that he had to charter a jumbo cargo jet to transport everything and everybody.

Iglesias's most recent album, *Cosas del Amor* ("Things of Love"), reached stores in September 1998. The music and lyrics of the title song and five others—"Esperanza," "Dicen por Ahi," "Ruleta Rusa," "Desnudo," and "Sirena"—were written by Iglesias himself. (The four other cuts are credited to Botija.) "Writing songs is very difficult for me," Iglesias acknowledged in a promotional release on *enriqueig.com*. "I am not a professional songwriter. I cannot write about a given subject, nor at any time I wish. It has to be something that has happened to me or which comes to me perhaps in a strange manner, and then I spend many hours revising what I have written, changing it until I arrive at the final result. There are many songs that die in the attempt."

Iglesias's first English single, "Bailamos," is on the soundtrack of the film *Wild Wild West* (1999), which was directed by Barry Sonnenfeld and stars Will Smith. The song was a hit on both MTV and American radio stations during the summer of 1999. Iglesias planned to release his first all-English album, *Enrique Iglesias*, later that year. But, as he told Gabrielle Schafer for *Rolling Stone.com* (on-line), he does not intend to abandon his roots: "I gotta remember something—what got me here was Spanish."

According to John Lannert, "Iglesias counters the icy, if not arrogant, aloofness of most Latino pop greats with an embraceable eagerness to get close to fans." Iglesias, whose performance attire usually consists of jeans and a T-shirt, regularly arouses among teenagers the sort of adulation associated with the young Frank Sinatra, Elvis Presley, and the Beatles. Once, while in a hotel room in Argentina, he threw his pants and shirt out the window, and scores of his fans made a frenzied attempt to catch them. "People got hurt and trampled," Iglesias recalled to *usaweekend.com* (June 1, 1997). "It was crazy. I'll never do that again." At the same time, he apparently thrives on adulation. He told Tammy D. Fonce for the *El Paso Herald-Post* (April 3, 1997, on-line), "The day nothing happens to me, that I'm not approached at a restaurant for an autograph or woken up at 4 a.m. to have my picture taken, is the day that I'm finished." — M.B.

Suggested Reading: *Billboard* p1+ July 19, 1997, with photo; *El Paso Herald-Post* (on-line) Apr. 3, 1997, with photo; *enriqueig.com* (on-line); *People* p144+ Apr. 22, 1996, with photo

Selected Recordings: *Enrique Iglesias*, 1995; *Vivir*, 1997; *Cosas Del Amor*, 1998

Courtesy of U.S. Nuclear Regulatory Commission

Jackson, Shirley Ann

Aug. 5, 1946– Physicist; university president. Address: c/o Office of the President, Rensselaer Polytechnic Institute, 110 8th St., Troy, New York 12181

One of the most prominent black scientists in the country, Shirley Ann Jackson has achieved numerous "firsts" in her nearly 30-year career. She is the first African-American woman in the United States to earn a doctoral degree in physics, and she has since published more than 100 scientific articles in her field. She is also the first woman and the first African-American to head the Nuclear Regulatory Commission, a federal government agency that was created in 1974. And on July 1, 1999 she became the first African-American woman to head a major American research university—Rensselaer Polytechnic Institute.

Jackson did not start out wanting to collect "firsts." Rather, what motivated her—ever since she was a little girl studying live bees in bottles—was her zest for scientific knowledge. "My goal was always to pursue the physics opportunities and however great or non-great I might turn out to be, I thought it was important to be in an exciting place, to work on exciting problems," she told Rushworth Kidder for the *Christian Science Monitor* (November 20, 1989). She added, "What science gives you is the chance to be the one who uncovers the unknown, who creates the new paradigm. And all along the way there are all the little thrills having to do with the little discoveries you make—and there's a lot of satisfaction."

The second of four children, Shirley Ann Jackson was born on August 5, 1946 in Washington, D.C. Her father, George Jackson, was a postal employee, and her mother, Beatrice Jackson, was a social worker. Jackson's interest in science and engineering became evident early on. As a youngster she played mathematical games in her head, built soapbox go-carts with her younger sister Gloria, and educated herself in science by reading extensively in the library. She was also an avid collector of insects. "I abhorred the typical collection with dead insects," she told Rushworth Kidder. "I thought it was more interesting to observe the insect in his environment. . . . So I used to collect bumblebees, do little experiments on them, change their nutritional situation, put different kinds together. I used to keep the jars under the back porch—we had a crawl space—so you would come out onto the porch and you'd hear all the buzzing from 20 or 30 jars."

Two historical developments—as well as the support of her family and her natural talent—helped propel Jackson into a career in science. One was the launch of the Sputnik satellite by the Soviet Union in 1957, which caused great handwringing among American politicians and led to an increased emphasis on science in U.S. schools. As a result, Jackson was able to take courses in an accelerated science track. At about the same time, civil-rights protests and government desegregation efforts in education were opening doors for African-American students in previously segregated institutions. When Jackson was a child, she had not been permitted to attend an elementary school just three blocks from where she lived and had to be driven to a black school across town. But by the time she graduated from her primarily black high school, Roosevelt High, in 1964 (as the valedictorian of her class), many formerly all-white schools had begun to welcome African-American students. So Jackson applied to the elite Massachusetts Institute of Technology (MIT), in Cambridge, Massachusetts, and she was accepted.

In her freshmen class of about 900 at MIT, Jackson was one of only 43 women and only one of about 10 black students. Attitudes toward her presence in the school were often reactionary. "When I would get on an elevator, people would sometimes mistake me for the elevator operator," she told Rushworth Kidder. "I've been shot at, I've been spit on, I've been chased—I've had all of those things." One professor even told her, "Colored girls should learn a trade." Ignoring that advice, she won respect from her professors and her peers through her outstanding performance in class. Initially interested in biology, she became more attracted to the study of physics. She also tutored in the nearby Roxbury neighborhood, volunteered at a local hospital, helped found MIT's Black Student Union, which she co-chaired for two years, and successfully lobbied the college's administration to increase the number of black students. After one year of her efforts, the number of black students entering MIT increased to 57.

Jackson graduated from MIT in 1968. Courted by numerous elite physics programs, she decided to stay at MIT for her graduate studies. Her research was directed by James Young, the first African-American tenured full professor in the school's physics department. She completed her dissertation, entitled "The Study of a Multiperipheral Model with Continued Cross-Channel Unitarity," in 1973 and became the first black woman in the United States to earn a Ph.D. in physics, as well as the first black woman to earn a Ph.D. in any subject at MIT.

Over the next few years, Jackson did research at the Fermi National Accelerator Laboratory, outside Chicago, Illinois (1973–74); the European Center for Nuclear Research, near Geneva, Switzerland (1974–75); the Stanford Linear Accelerator Center, in Menlo Park, California (1976); and the Aspen Center for Physics, in Aspen, Colorado (1976–77). In 1976 she began work for Bell Laboratories, where she did research on condensed matter and optical physics for the next 15 years. While there, she met her husband, Morris Washington, who is also a physicist. In 1991 Jackson became a professor of physics at Rutgers University in Piscataway, New Jersey, while remaining a consultant in semiconductor theory to AT&T Bell Laboratories.

Though very involved in basic research—she has published more then 100 scientific papers in various journals—Jackson has always felt it important "to contribute in ways beyond my discipline," as she told Rushworth Kidder. To that end, she has served on the boards of directors of several companies, including Public Service Enterprise Group and its subsidiary Public Service Electric and Gas Co.; the Sealed Air Corp.; CoreStates Financial Corp.; CoreStates New Jersey National Bank; and New Jersey Resources Corp. She has also served on a panel that advised the U.S. secretary of energy on the future of the Department of Energy National Laboratories; on research councils of the National Academy of Sciences; and on the Advisory Council of the Nuclear Power Operations. She was president of the National Society of Black Physicists from 1980 to 1982, and in 1989 she was appointed by New Jersey governor Thomas Kean to serve on the New Jersey Commission on Science and Technology, the aim of which was to promote collaboration between universities and the private sector. She served on that commission until 1995. In addition, she is a lifetime trustee of MIT and has served on the boards of trustees of Rutgers University and ·Lincoln University. She is a fellow of the American Academy of Arts and Sciences and a fellow of the American Physical Society, as well as a member of several other professional organizations.

On the strength of her technical expertise and her familiarity with administrative decision making, Jackson was nominated in 1995 by President Bill Clinton to chair the Nuclear Regulatory Commission (NRC), an agency with about 3,000 employees and a budget of about $473 million. Based in Rockville, Maryland, the NRC is led by the chair and five commissioners, whose duty is to ensure that the peaceful use of nuclear energy does not jeopardize the health and safety of the public. The agency's duties include issuing and renewing licenses for the operation of nuclear power plants, regulating the use of radiation in medicine and scientific research, and developing standards for the disposal of nuclear waste. Unlike many other Clinton nominees, Jackson was speedily confirmed by the Senate, in March 1995. She was sworn in on May 2, 1995 and assumed the chairmanship two months later. Her appointment made her the first woman and the first African-American to head the NRC.

Describing Jackson's tenure at the NRC in *Black Issues in Higher Education* (March 4, 1999), Michele Collison wrote, "Jackson has won considerable praise for restoring credibility to a troubled agency and increasing the agency's oversight over several nuclear power plants." In an article entitled "The 25 Most Influential Working Mothers" that appeared on-line in *Working Mother Magazine* in 1998, Michaele Weissman wrote that Jackson's "tough-but-fair approach has earned the respect both of environmentalists and the nuclear power industry." In 1997 Jackson was elected the first chairman of the International Nuclear Regulators Association, which was formed that year. The group is made of regulatory officials from Canada, France, Germany, Japan, Spain, Sweden, the United Kingdom, and the U.S.

Most recently, Jackson was unanimously chosen by the board of trustees of Rensselaer Polytechnic Institute, in Troy, New York, to become the university's 18th president, starting on July 1, 1999. (Her term at the NRC ended on June 30.) Currently, according to Michele Collison in *Black Issues in Higher Education*, of the presidents of the four-year colleges and universities in the country (of which there were some 2,244 as of 1995), only 24 (or 1 percent) are black women. Among colleges and universities with a Carnegie classification of Research I or II, the statistics are even worse. Jackson is the first black woman to head a major research university. (Only three such institutions are headed by black men.)

One of Jackson's many goals is to help increase the enrollment of black and female students in the sciences at Rensselaer. (In 1996 black students earned only 2 percent of doctorates in science at Rensselaer.) "As president of a major university, I will have a platform to speak out broadly about the need to prepare more women and minorities for math and science careers," she told Michele Collison. Jackson also hopes to attract more African-Americans to Rensselaer's faculty. The university currently has only four black professors.

Jackson has one teenage son, Alan. In 1998 she was inducted into the National Women's Hall of Fame for her contributions as a distinguished scientist and advocate for education, science, and public policy. Among many other honors, she received the New Jersey Governor's Award in Science in 1993. — W.G.

Suggested Reading: *Black Issues in Higher Education* p26+ Mar. 4, 1999, with photo; *Christian Science Monitor* p14 Nov. 20, 1989; *Ebony* p114+ Nov. 1974, with photo; *New York Times* (on-line) Aug. 21, 1999; *Washington Post* B p10+ May 4, 1995, with photos

Courtesy of the *New York Times*

Jefferson, Margo L.

Oct. 17, 1947– Cultural critic for the New York Times. *Address: c/o* New York Times, *229 W. 43d St., New York, NY 10036-3959*

In 1995 Margo Jefferson, cultural critic for the *New York Times*, was awarded the Pulitzer Prize for distinguished criticism. In its award citation, the Pulitzer committee praised Jefferson for reviewing books "forcefully and originally without ever muscling out the author in question." Though she had been with the paper for under two years, Jefferson had built a considerable reputation as a sensitive and eloquent book critic and attracted a large *Times* readership. Prior to joining the *Times*, Jefferson had distinguished herself with a body of work that attracted considerable attention. She began her career with *Newsweek*, eventually becoming an editor before going on to teach courses in journalism at New York University. Next she took on concurrent posts as a contributing editor with *Vogue* and *7 Days*. Currently entering her sixth year with the *Times*, Jefferson has expanded her role at the paper and is tackling a wider range of cultural subjects, as befits a critic of her stature. Using several areas of cultural endeavor—including books, theater, television, and film—as jumping-off points, Jefferson crafts insightful articles that address such diverse social issues as race relations, fashion and self-image in the media age, and the effects of the Internet on language.

The daughter of Irma and Ron Jefferson, Margo Jefferson was born in Chicago on October 17, 1947 and raised in the city's Hyde Park section. She went to high school at the University of Chicago's Laboratory School before attending Brandeis University, in Waltham, Massachusetts, from which she graduated in 1968. She was granted a master's degree in journalism by Columbia University, in New York City, in 1971, then pursued her dual careers in teaching and freelance journalism.

According to Edwin Diamond in his book *Behind the Times* (1993), when the *Times* book critic John Gross left the paper in 1989, the management began to woo Jefferson. "Three senior editors took turns calling her, offering counsel, describing the part she could play at the *Times* and, by extension, in the cultural life of the country," Diamond wrote. Despite the hard sell, Jefferson wavered. Though a *Times* post offered prestige, she would have to give up her successful career as a freelance journalist, since the *New York Times* forbids its writers from contributing freelance pieces elsewhere, even to periodicals not viewed as competitors. Moreover, she was reluctant to stop teaching classes for New York University's school of journalism, which allowed her ample freedom to pursue freelance work while providing a stable base income. "I was unsure that I wanted to surrender to the institution," she told Diamond. Jefferson decided in 1991 to accept a full-time teaching post as lecturer in American literature, performing arts, and criticism at Columbia University. But the *Times* persisted, making increasingly better offers with, in Diamond's words, "more money, prime display, and choice assignments," until, in 1993, Jefferson succumbed.

The *Times* knew what they were after. As a critical form, newspaper book reviews have historically had a limited appeal. Generally, more readers gravitate to theater and film reviews, which lead those forms to carry more weight at newspapers, as evinced by their greater numbers and prime placement within most papers' sections. Consequently, book reviews are usually relegated to the rear pages and tend to encompass little more than a book summary and encapsulated judgment by the reviewer. Jefferson's method helped to change this model. With concise and eloquent prose, she drew from her store of cultural knowledge to add breadth to the form. For example, when she reviewed Andrew Motion's biography of the poet Philip Larkin in the *New York Times* (August 23, 1993), she succinctly contextualized Larkin's oeuvre—which, with gritty, plain-spoken verse, broke from the erudition of his predecessors T. S. Eliot and W. H. Auden—within the panoply of poetry. "Poetry demands talent and extends fair and equal opportunity to all temperaments," she wrote. "If you need deprivation, not daffodils, to spur you into song, so be it. . . . You will be Philip Larkin then, not Wordsworth, Keats, George Herbert, or Thomas Hardy, and you will have won your laurel as a fine, exacting poet who left his mark on British and American poetry between the end of the Second World War and the close of the Vietnam War." Beyond simple summary and judgment, Jefferson placed her critical subject in a context, in the process exposing her reader to the critical faculties she used to assess the book.

She applied this approach as much to books by pop-culture icons as she did to books by literary heavyweights. Again framing her topic with historical analysis, she compared two autobiographical works, by the popular shock-jock Howard Stern and by Paul Krassner, the activist-comedian and former publisher of the defunct satiric magazine the *Realist*, respectively, for the *Times* (November 24, 1993). "Did Paul Krassner take more risks than Howard Stern takes?" Jefferson wrote. "He did, but few comics are better or worse than their times, and here Krassner had the advantage. He palled around with Lenny Bruce and Abbie Hoffman; Howard Stern got Sam Kinison and Andrew Dice Clay. Mr. Krassner could make fun of G. Gordon Liddy and the Vietnam War. Mr. Stern must make do with Regis Philbin and the Federal Communications Commission."

Jefferson's Pulitzer, awarded in 1995 for consistent output of such fine criticism, reportedly was a cause for distraction in the highly politicized climate in the *New York Times* offices. First of all, the *Times* routinely receives multiple nominations each year for the Pulitzer, but Jefferson was the paper's sole representative that year. Second, Jefferson had been nominated and won after a relatively short stint with the *Times*, which apparently did not sit well with the paper's more tenured staff. "Insiders say that long-time book reviewer Michiko Kakutani—who has been nominated in previous years but never won—was aggrieved that her work was not promoted this year by the *Times*," Pat Wechsler and Roger D. Friedman reported in *New York* (May 1, 1995). "Sources say that Frank Rich, who also never won a Pulitzer, complained to [*Times* executive editor Joseph] Lelyveld on behalf of Kakutani—another act of the intra-office congeniality for which the *Times* has become well-known." (Kakutani finally won a Pulitzer for her criticism in 1998.) Jefferson herself remained tight-lipped about the whole affair. "All I can tell you is that my employer treated me very well," the writer said to Si Liberman for *Editor & Publisher* (November 4, 1995).

Despite the grumblings her prize reportedly caused, Jefferson's stock rose at the paper, and she was reassigned as the *New York Times* Sunday drama critic in 1995. A year later she expressed a desire to pursue a wider range of cultural topics and was granted greater freedom to do so. The result has been some of her most thought-provoking cultural commentary to date. She has offered insights into a broad range of subjects, such as the cultural

resonance of politics, gender issues in fashion and the arts, and the homogenization of language caused by the proliferation of media and the Internet. But most cogently, she has engaged issues of race in the cultural milieu. Jefferson sees culture, because of its ability to cross the lines of class and social status, as an excellent vehicle for intelligent dialogue about race relations in the United States. She has weighed in on a number of volatile racial issues that have bubbled to the surface in the cultural arena, most notably the place of ebonics in American language.

On December 18, 1996 the school board of Oakland, California, unanimously voted to recognize "black English" as an independent language rather than as slang or as a dialect of standard American English. They called the language "ebonics," arriving at the name by combining the words "ebony" and "phonics." Board members argued that ebonics contained sufficient characteristics of African languages to differentiate it from standardized English and to warrant a separate linguistic classification. They also argued that the academic performance of black students would improve if the language were adopted and used more in the classroom. The Oakland vote created a storm of public criticism from politicians and civil-rights leaders. Commenting on the fracas, Margo Jefferson wrote in the *New York Times* (January 7, 1997), "Do let's remember, as the debate over ebonics lurches and struggles along generating polemical fervor and resentment at every turn, that black English plays a complicated, quite fascinating role in the culture, one that Americans of all races are much affected by, possibly even obsessed by." Placing the debate in perspective, she explained that Americans, who as a people have a limited history of their own from which to draw, have since the colonial period called on or created links to their ethnic ancestry, or the "Old World." According to Jefferson, "Afrocentric rites and claims are the latest manifestation of this national need." That said, she concluded that the struggle over the place of black English in public-school systems has more to do with class and social status than race. "So long as it's a fad, a pose, or a clearly calculated style, black English can earn its practitioners money, power, and respect as artistic innovators or popularizers," Jefferson surmised, noting that many performers and writers appropriate black English for various artistic purposes. "But the stakes change when the speakers are working class, lower class, or just poor black students who need to acquire standardized English skills and conventions to achieve what everybody in America wants: social mobility and respect."

Ultimately, Jefferson views conflicts of culture as resulting first and foremost from human insecurity, the need for familiarity, and fear of change. "Isn't it that far too many of us—and by 'us' I mean Americans in a heterogeneous society—are still most at ease when work we consider important is done well by people exactly, or almost exactly, like ourselves?" she asked in the *Times* (February 8, 1999), applying her oft-used Socratic device of question and answer. "This impulse to be happiest when our own kind excel is clearly at the heart of all culture wars going on now." Having accepted this aspect of human nature, Jefferson offered compromise. "As long as we're stuck fighting these wars, let's try for a clear sense of history, a clean use of language, and as honest a sense of our own biases and grievances as possible," since "none of us gets to be at the center of every story every time. Coming to terms with this can go against one's deepest instincts and traditions. It can take a lifetime. But it's the way we have to live now."

Roots of Time: A Portrait of African Life and Culture, a children's book that Jefferson wrote with the anthropologist Elliott P. Skinner, was published in 1990. — T.J.F.

Suggested Reading: *Jet* p22+ May 8, 1995, with photo; Diamond, Edwin. *Behind the Times*, 1993; *Who's Who in America, 1999*

David Leeds/Allsport U.S.A.

Johnson, Davey

Jan. 30, 1943– Manager of the Los Angeles Dodgers. Address: c/o Los Angeles Dodgers, 1000 Elysian Park Ave., Los Angeles, CA 90074

Davey Johnson is one of the most successful baseball managers of all time. Over the past quarter-century, he has witnessed firsthand, as either a player or a manager, some of baseball's greatest moments. A career .261 hitter, he garnered many accolades and awards as a player, among them

three Gold Gloves, four All-Star Game appearances, and the most home runs ever for a second baseman (42) in a single season (1973), tying the great Rogers Hornsby. A member of the dynastic Baltimore Orioles in the late 1960s and early 1970s, Johnson appeared—with teammates including Hall of Famers Frank Robinson and Brooks Robinson—in four World Series in six years, winning the contests in both 1966 and 1970. But it is Johnson's prowess at managing ball clubs for which he is best known. Since he began coaching in the major leagues, in 1984, he has led three different teams to the postseason. As manager of the Cincinnati Reds from 1993 to 1995 and the Orioles for the 1996 and 1997 seasons, he won a total of four division titles; he had his most successful season, however, as the skipper of the 1986 World Series champion New York Mets. His highly publicized clashes with the upper management of those teams has not dimmed his record on the field. Currently leading the Los Angeles Dodgers, Johnson, who boasted a .575 winning percentage (985–727) going into the 1999 season, enjoys a reputation as a great motivator of ballplayers.

Davey Johnson was born on January 30, 1943 in Orlando, Florida. His father was a career army officer, and Johnson's family relocated often during his childhood. An above-average ballplayer at an early age, Johnson knew that he had what it took to be a major leaguer, but he was plagued by worries about his life *after* baseball. "I spent the summer after I graduated high school getting my real-estate license," he told Joe Klein for *New York* (March 19, 1984). "I knew I'd eventually need something to fall back on." He attended Texas A&M University for two years on a baseball and basketball scholarship and then was signed by the Baltimore Orioles to a minor-league scholarship. While working his way up the Orioles' farm system over the next few years, Johnson attended Trinity University in San Antonio studying mathematics. (He would complete his degree over the course of 11 off-seasons.) During this time he also focused on his real estate career; having purchased property with his signing bonus from the Orioles, he began buying, selling, and leasing shopping centers throughout Florida. "I was in my early 20s, having lunch with billionaires at their private clubs," he told Klein. "That's when I learned to fly a plane, so I could take them up and show properties. . . . I've always liked challenges." Indeed, these years also found Johnson working as a scuba-diving instructor and trying his hand at professional golf.

On April 13, 1965 Johnson—whom the media often referred to as Dave as well as Davey early in his career—made his major-league debut, with the young and talented Baltimore Orioles, then managed by Hank Bauer. He played in only 20 games that year, most of them at third base; but in 1966 he became the team's regular second baseman, batting .257 with 56 RBIs in 131 games. The Orioles had a fantastic season that year, winning 97 games and losing only 63 to capture the American League pennant. In the World Series, Baltimore faced the formidable Los Angeles Dodgers, led by future Hall of Fame pitcher Sandy Koufax. The defending World Series champions that year, the Dodgers were overwhelming favorites, but Johnson and his teammates swept the team in four straight games, with Johnson hitting a respectable .286 in the Series. Although Johnson's batting skills were only average even at the height of his power, he was a remarkably solid second baseman, anchoring with third baseman Brooks Robinson an infield that, for the next five years, was arguably the best in baseball. During that period the Orioles would go to the World Series three more times. In 1969 the Orioles—the team with the best record in baseball that year—were heavily favored to beat the upstart New York Mets, who had been in existence only since 1962. But in a remarkable turn of events, the Mets, who had never finished better than ninth place in the American League prior to that season, upset the Orioles in five games. The loss was a tremendous letdown for the Orioles, and the defeat has gone down in history as one of baseball's greatest upsets.

The Orioles rebounded the following year, returning to the Series to defeat the formidable Cincinnati Reds in five games. This Series is remembered primarily for Brooks Robinson's remarkable play at both third base and the plate. Johnson, however, also gave a stellar performance, batting a solid .313 in 16 at bats. After two more years with Baltimore—including another trip to the World Series in 1971, the same year he won his third consecutive Gold Glove as a second baseman—Johnson began playing for the Atlanta Braves. By 1973 many observers felt that Johnson's career as a major-league player was on the decline, but the 30-year-old slugger hit a career-high 42 home runs that year, tying him with one of baseball's all-time greatest hitters, Rogers Hornsby. Actually, in total, Johnson smacked 43 home runs; one isn't included in the official statistic because it came when he was pinch hitting. He played the entire 1974 season with the Braves, but his numbers fell considerably the next year (he hit only 15 home runs and batted a below-average .251), as he took over duties at first base. Shortly into the 1975 season, with his abilities diminishing but his desire to play ball still strong, Johnson packed his bags and headed for Japan.

Arriving in a country as fervent about baseball as the one he had just left, Johnson immersed himself in Japanese culture and made concerted efforts to learn the language. It was in Asia, while playing for the Yomiuri Giants, Johnson has said, that he began to look at the game from a coach's perspective, watching and learning the Japanese style of managing. (The Japanese approach emphasizes, among other strategies, base hits over home runs—which is also Johnson's style.) After two years he returned to the U.S. to become an effective utility man for the Philadelphia Phillies. Although he stepped up to the plate a mere 156 times in 1977, Johnson hit a career-high .321. His final year

in a major-league uniform saw him traded to the Chicago Cubs, for whom he hit an outstanding .306 in 49 at bats. When the season concluded, Johnson became a player/manager with the Miami Amigos of the Inter-American League, whom he led to the league title in 1979. When the league folded, later that year, Johnson returned to Orlando and worked full-time in real estate. "I made about $200,000 the year I devoted completely to business," he told Klein. "But then, Lou Gorman [of the Mets] called and offered me $18,000 to be a minor league manager, and I jumped at it. I guess I just missed chewing tobacco and watching athletes run around." In 1981 he coached the Jackson, Mississippi, franchise of the double-A Texas League, a Mets farm team, to a 68–66 record and a Texas League championship berth. Two years later, after a promotion to the Mets' triple-A franchise in Tidewater, Virginia, Johnson led the Tides to a 71–68 record and a victory in the triple-A World Series. That October, Mets general manager Frank Cashen announced that Johnson had been hired to coach the hapless, basement-dwelling major-league New York Mets for the upcoming season.

In an interview with Marty Noble for *Newsday* (October 14, 1983), Johnson said, "I felt qualified to manage in the major leagues. . . . I feel that I have an intelligent mind, and I've played for and learned from some great managers. I feel very fortunate to come to a city where I think you make normal human beings and less-than-average ballplayers into superstars. And [with] somebody as intelligent as me and as good a ballplayer as I was . . . you ought to be able to make into a great manager." Within a few years Johnson proved to be just that, as the autumn of 1986 found the New York Mets playing in the World Series. With the remarkable talents of pitcher Dwight Gooden (who won the Cy Young Award in 1985), slugger Darryl Strawberry, lead-off hitter Lenny Dykstra, and catcher Gary Carter, the Mets were pitted against the Boston Red Sox. Fighting for their first championship since 1918, when Babe Ruth pitched a victory over the Chicago Cubs, the Red Sox had one of their best teams in years; after the fifth game of the Series, the Sox were leading the Mets three games to two in the best-of-seven contest. With only one more win, the Red Sox would be world champs.

In the 10th inning of game six, the Red Sox managed to score two runs to take a 5–3 lead. In the bottom of the 10th, the Sox inched ever closer to victory, as Mets sluggers Wally Backman and Keith Hernandez both hit pop flies to the outfield. With two outs, the aging Gary Carter slapped a single. Then Kevin Mitchell hit another weak single, resulting in two men on base for Ray Knight, who also got a base hit, sending Carter home and moving Mitchell to third base. With the score now 5–4 in Boston's favor, the Red Sox still needed only one out to win the Series. But then came one of the most famous moments in recent baseball history: Mookie Wilson, the venerable Mets outfielder, stepped to the plate and trickled a weak grounder to Sox first baseman Bill Buckner, who somehow lost sight of the ball and let it dribble between his legs. Ray Knight scored, and the Mets won the game. With the will of the Red Sox crushed, the Mets went on to defeat Boston in game seven and capture the championship. Johnson thus won his first World Series ring as a manager.

The Mets returned in 1987 with virtually the same lineup, but the team did not perform up to expectations, finishing three games behind the St. Louis Cardinals in the National League East Division. The season was also hampered by the loss of Dwight Gooden for three months due to a drug problem. The following year, though, Johnson managed to rally his troops to win a remarkable 100 games in the regular season, and it looked as though the Mets were poised to capture their second World Series crown in three years. Their quest was cut short, however, by a resurgent Los Angeles Dodgers team, who had won considerably fewer games than New York, in the National League championship series. During the off-season, rumors circulated that Johnson might be fired; such speculation had to do with reported clashes between him and Frank Cashen, the Mets' general manager. Instead, Johnson received a three-year contract, with an option for a fourth year, said to be worth around half a million dollars. Johnson went into 1989 with high hopes, only to be disappointed once again, when the Mets failed to capture the division, finishing six games behind the Chicago Cubs. Management was not happy with the Mets' performance, and the following May 29, only a few weeks into the 1990 season, Cashen relieved Johnson of his managerial duties.

To the surprise of many, for nearly three years Johnson—who at the time ranked fifth on the list of managers with the highest winning percentages of all time—did not receive a single offer from another major-league team. It was said by some that Cashen and his assistant, Joe McIlvaine, had spread the word that Johnson had difficulty getting along with baseball brass. "All I know is there were three different Davey Johnsons when I was with the Mets," McIlvaine told Bill Madden for Sport (June 1993). "The Davey who Frank hired was a five-star manager. He did a great job of handling our young pitchers in 1984, '85, and '86. But then he began to change a little as some of the veterans like [Keith] Hernandez, [Gary] Carter and [Ray] Knight took charge of the clubhouse for him. In the middle years of Davey's term, the players policed themselves. Then the policemen left, and Davey's personal problems [a divorce] began to engulf him. It was a sad end. He seemed to have retreated." During his hiatus from baseball, Johnson returned to his native Florida and worked on his real estate career and his golf game. "When I first got fired, I didn't think I'd miss managing," Johnson told Madden. "But then the longer I was out, and the more jobs that came and went, the more I wanted to get back in." On the subject of his being difficult to work with, Johnson said, "Sure, Frank and I had

differences. I definitely wasn't a 'yes' man, and if that's a control freak then I guess I plead guilty. I'm definitely opinionated when it comes to evaluating talent, but I think it was proven with the Mets that my opinions bore some good fruit."

On May 24, 1993, nearly three years to the day that Johnson was released by the Mets, he was given a shot at managing the Cincinnati Reds. Although the Reds did not fare well in Johnson's initial season, Cincinnati remained in first place in the National League Central Division in 1994, until a strike shortened the season. In 1995 Johnson and his squad took the Central Division title and soundly defeated the Los Angeles Dodgers in the first round of the play-offs, only to fall to the Atlanta Braves in the National League championship series. Although the Reds did not make it to the World Series, Johnson had again proven himself a capable manager. Despite that achievement, Johnson was soon out of work again, since the controversial Reds owner, Marge Schott, had set as a condition for his being rehired in 1995 his departure at the end of the season so that Ray Knight could replace him. "Part of me said no to it, but there was also a part of me that said I hadn't finished here," Johnson told Tom Verducci for Sports Illustrated (September 18, 1995). "Yeah, your pride stands up and says, No possibility when you hear that. But your loyalty and your consideration for the players comes into play too." After the Reds' 1995 postseason loss to the Braves, Johnson left the team.

Before long the Baltimore Orioles, the team with which Johnson had enjoyed his best years as a player, hired him as manager in time for the start of the 1996 season. Peter Angelos, the team's owner, had had an opportunity to hire Johnson for the 1995 season, but instead chose to give Phil Regan a chance to take the helm. (Angelos would later admit that he had picked Regan because of Johnson's reputation for contentiousness.) After a dismal year in 1995, the Orioles' front office overcame their reservations about Johnson and signed him to a three-year, $2.25 million contract. In his first year with the club, the Orioles finished with a respectable 88–74 record and earned the wild-card play-off spot.

Johnson's feud with Angelos began during the division series against the Cleveland Indians, when All-Star Oriole second baseman Roberto Alomar, after a disputed call by umpire Rod Hirschbeck, spat in the umpire's face. While Angelos came to Alomar's defense, Johnson declined to do so, "arguing that a public stance against an umpire in such an unsavory episode might set up his team for a season's worth of retribution in 1997," as Peter Schmuck wrote for the Sporting News (December 8, 1997). (The Orioles beat the favored Indians but ultimately lost to the Yankees in the American League championship series.) The following season, when Alomar missed an exhibition game on July 10, 1997, Johnson fined the second baseman $10,500 and ordered him to pay the money directly to a charity that employed Johnson's wife, Susan, as a fund-raiser. When news of the potential conflict of interest was discovered by the Baltimore press, and it was revealed that Johnson had committed a similar act while coaching the Reds, Angelos's patience began to wear thin. Alomar, who had not gotten along with Johnson since the spitting incident, turned to the Major League Players Association for protection, and the situation soon made national headlines. (In the end, rather than paying the fine, Alomar was penalized with a five-game suspension.)

In the midst of all the controversy, the Orioles found themselves in the American League championship series for a second straight year. The Indians, though, were soon ahead in the series three games to one, partly as a result of two debatable calls by umpires—the first after a strange bunt, laid down in game three by Cleveland's Omar Vizquel, that scored the winning run in the 12th inning, the second following a wild pitch in game four that scored Indian David Justice despite calls of interference on the outfielder's part by Orioles players and coaches. In game six of the series, the two clubs battled into the 11th inning with no score, until Indians second baseman Tony Fernandez—a last-minute replacement for the injured Bip Roberts—stroked a sweeping home run to win the game and the pennant. Johnson, dejected, confessed to the press that he was not sure if Angelos would bring him back for the final year of his contract. This statement caused the owner to see red. "When I said on October 24 [1997] that he was coming back, that was the end of it," Angelos told Schmuck. "When I said I would abide by his contract, I meant it. I wasn't going to fire him. What really made me unhappy was that he had gone public with it. He released [his thoughts] to the press. That clearly was insubordination of the worst order." Only 12 days later—on November 5, after it became clear that Angelos was going to ask for a public apology from Johnson for his handling of the Alomar charity incident—Johnson gave Angelos his letter of resignation. On the same day, Johnson was voted the American League manager of the year.

"A lot of the problem [Johnson had] with the Mets concerned the public airing of his contract difficulties," McIlvaine told Schmuck. "And in Baltimore, it seemed like the public airing of his contract situation got him in trouble. It happened in New York, constantly, and it could have been handled easily behind closed doors." Although he was interviewed by several teams, most notably the Toronto Blue Jays, Johnson, once again, found himself without a major-league affiliation for an entire baseball season. Then, after their negotiations with Montreal Expos manager Felipe Alou fell through in October 1998, the Los Angeles Dodgers set their sights on Johnson. On October 23, 1998, after only a few weeks of negotiations, Johnson was announced as the Dodgers' new manager. The Dodgers, who had recently been bought by Rupert Murdoch's Fox Corp., had been busy in the off-season acquiring high-priced playing talent, most notably signing All-Star pitcher Kevin Brown to a record $105 million contract.

At the beginning of the 1999 season, Johnson told Murray Chass for the New York Times (March 1, 1999), "At times I have been envious of guys like [former Dodgers managers] Walter Alston and Tommy Lasorda, who made their careers in one spot. But I've been blessed in that I've had the opportunity to manage some great Mets teams and great athletes in Cincinnati and Baltimore. Now I've got a fine club here." He added, "The stress of the job can age you. I've been very fortunate that I've been healthy. And I had a year off from being second-guessed."

The Dodgers, however, have not lived up to the high expectations top brass placed upon the team at the beginning of the season; despite being favored to contend for the National League West Division title in 1999, the Dodgers found themselves in last place by the All-Star break. Not all the blame has been placed on Johnson, though—many of his high-priced players, most notably Kevin Brown and slugger Raul Mondesi, have had lackluster seasons, and the Dodgers, despite many sports pundits' preseason predictions for a run at a World Series title, have already started to look toward the 2000 season.

Johnson and his wife, Susan, live in Winter Park, Florida. — M.B.

Suggested Reading: New York p52+ Mar. 19, 1984, with photos; New York Times A p19 Oct. 28, 1988, with photo, D p49+ Oct. 29, 1988, with photo, D p2+ Mar. 1, 1999, with photos; New York Times (on-line) Oct. 14, 1997, with photo; Newsday p140 Oct. 14, 1983, with photo, p12+ Apr. 1, 1984, with photos; Sport p63+ June 1993, with photos; Sporting News p83+ Dec. 8, 1997, with photos; Sports Illustrated p28+ June 7, 1993, with photos, p46+ Sep. 18, 1995, with photos; Washington Post (on-line) Nov. 5, 1997, Nov. 17, 1997

Johnson, Keyshawn

July 22, 1972– Football player. Address: c/o New York Jets, 1000 Fulton Ave., Hempstead, NY 11550-1099; c/o Keyshawn Inc., 3049 Las Vegas Blvd. S., Suite 528, Las Vegas, NV 89109

Part Jerry Rice, part Michael Irvin: that's how New York Jets wide receiver Keyshawn Johnson likes to think of himself. Indeed, his statistics stack up well against those of the veteran star football players. Comparing Johnson's first 41 professional games with those of Rice, for instance, one discovers that Johnson actually has one catch more than the legendary San Francisco 49er had. Yet the undeniably talented Johnson has often gotten more attention

Keyshawn Johnson

Ezra Shaw/Allsport

der the burden of being the Jets' "go-to" guy. In 1997 and 1998, when the Jets surfaced as one of the best teams in the American Football Conference (AFC) East, he was the team's leading receiver, even though he usually drew the opposing team's best defensive cornerback, if not an outright double team. He has also surprised many with his ability to block against defensive backs on run plays. Seemingly proving the adage that nothing succeeds like success, even some of his critics have had to admit that Johnson is emerging as one of the premier wide receivers in the National Football League (NFL).

The youngest of the six children of Vivian Jessie, Johnson was born on July 22, 1972 in Los Angeles. His sisters (Sandra, Kim, and Denise) and brothers (Dennis and Michael) all share the same father. After the father of his siblings left the family, Vivian became involved with Johnson's father, who lived in Iowa most of the time. Vivian opted not to return there with him, and he and Johnson have never met. As a single parent, Johnson's mother sometimes had to rely on welfare to support the family. She and her children often stayed with relatives, with as many as 17 people jammed into one household, and they sometimes sought refuge in homeless shelters. When times were especially bad, the family camped out in Vivian's blue Chevy, provided they could find a safe parking spot. "Most often it was in the parking lot of the mortuary," Johnson explained in his book. "It was safe there. . . . Nobody shoots up a mortuary parking lot."

As a youth, Johnson enjoyed hanging out with the University of Southern California (USC) football team. The team's coach at the time, John Robinson, made it a policy to let neighborhood kids fetch helmets and balls and watch the team practice. Johnson met such future professional football players as Marcus Allen and Ronnie Lott and often ate with them in the USC dining hall. "Most times that was the only meal I'd eat all day," Johnson wrote in his book. "I'd always grab a little extra and ask them to wrap it up so that I could take it to my mom."

Johnson has said that he never belonged to either of the two gangs—the Crips and the Bloods—that dominated the neighborhoods where he lived, but he did resort to crime in order to make some quick cash. Mainly, he would scalp tickets to sports events with his brother Mike; sometimes, he would organize daring burglaries. "I'd target the store for the break-in and then send the troops out," he recalled in his book. "I'd tell them to wait until the store closed, then smash the windows, back a truck in, and take as much as possible as quickly as possible. I was never directly involved in the actual stealing, but they'd bring me stuff to fence." When Johnson was 14, he began selling drugs—mostly marijuana and occasionally crack.

Johnson's criminal activities soon caught up with him. Before he turned 15 he was arrested for selling stolen tickets and sent to Camp Miraloma, a juvenile correctional facility. Johnson was let out

for what he has said off the field than for his accomplishments on it. After his rookie year, 1996, in which the Jets finished with a rancid 1–15 win-loss record, Johnson lashed out at some of his coaches and teammates in the book he co-wrote with Shelley Smith, *Just Give Me the Damn Ball! The Fast Times and Hard Knocks of an NFL Rookie* (1997). Dedicating the book to himself "for not giving a damn what people think," Johnson argued that if he had been thrown the ball more often, the Jets would have performed much better. That display of brazen outspokenness turned off some fans and sports commentators, who considered him just another football loudmouth. "Perception says he is all 'I,' not a fiber of being a team player in him," Thomas George wrote for the *New York Times* (November 27, 1998). "Totally interested in getting the ball, catching passes, setting records at wide receiver, setting more records after that, winning adulation, endorsements, movie roles, Hollywood and on and on and on."

To some extent the perception is true. According to Johnson, when it comes right down to it, there is nothing he wants more than to haul in game-winning touchdowns. "I am a team player—but I am an individual first," he told Thomas George. "I am going to shine. I know that I have electricity. My electricity can make everyone soar. I want the football. I want to block. I want to win. I want to do it all and I can. And I have to be the No. 1 guy with the football. Not No. 2 or No. 3. It's like a company, a business; I can't be a vice-president. I've got to be the president. If I'm not the No. 1 guy, I'm no good to you. That's who I am." But to his credit, the six-foot three-inch, 210- to 220-pound Johnson has shown that he can shoul-

on probation, but after breaking its terms and skipping school, he served another stint, at Camp Barley Flats. By then Johnson wanted seriously to reform his life. "I gave up for good the lifestyle of a hood, gave up robbing people, selling drugs . . . ," he wrote in his book. "I took a huge pay-cut, but I had had enough of playing dodge ball with the police and the people with guns."

The way out, Johnson hoped, would be through football. After attending Canoga Park High School as a sophomore and Pacific Palisades High School as a junior, he transferred to the school of his choice, Dorsey High School, in his senior year. Dorsey was a powerhouse in high-school football in Los Angeles. *Sports Illustrated* had even published a profile of the school. The NFL running back Karim Abdul Jabbar was an alumnus, and Johnson played there with Lamont Warren, who later became a tailback for the Indianapolis Colts.

Many college scouts expressed interest in Johnson, but after he failed to get the minimum score on the SAT required for eligibility to play in top-ranked football colleges, their attention cooled. To qualify for transfer to a Division I school, he attended West Los Angeles Community College for two years. During that time, in April 1993, his college football plans were nearly derailed when he was shot in the leg by an unknown assailant, but the wound was not serious and he recovered fully. Deciding which college to attend was easy for him. After working for a time in the NFL, John Robinson had returned to USC, and Johnson was eager to play for the coach who had been so generous to him in his youth.

After he became a receiver for the USC Trojans, Johnson's talent quickly became apparent. In 12 consecutive games in the 1994 season, he gained 100 or more yards receiving, despite its being his first year playing Division I football. The team won a berth in the Cotton Bowl, in which they trounced Texas Tech, 55–14; Johnson had eight catches for 222 yards and three touchdowns, a Cotton Bowl record. He finished the year with a total of 66 catches for 1,362 yards and nine touchdowns. In his senior year Johnson performed even better. Though he had only eight games in which he caught for over 100 yards, he made a total of 102 catches for 1,434 yards and seven touchdowns. USC made it to the Rose Bowl that year and defeated Northwestern University, 41–32. Johnson had 12 catches for 216 yards in that game, which set a Rose Bowl record and made Johnson the first NCAA player to get more than 200 receiving yards in back-to-back bowl games.

Given his success at USC, Johnson had high expectations when he entered the 1996 NFL draft. He had already donated his USC jersey to the Official All Star Cafe, in New York City, and landed an endorsement contract with Adidas and a book deal with Warner Books. True to Johnson's predictions, the New York Jets selected him as the number-one pick overall, making it the first time a wide receiver was selected first in the draft since Irving Fryar

was snapped up by the New England Patriots in 1984. After drawn-out negotiations Johnson settled on a contract with the Jets guaranteeing him $15 million over six years, with up to $2 million in bonuses if he met certain targets, such as being selected to the Pro Bowl, gaining more than 1,000 yards, making 85 receptions, or scoring 12 touchdowns in a season. At the time the contract gave him the highest average annual salary ever awarded to a rookie player.

After finishing his studies and graduating with a degree in history from USC, in 1996, Johnson arrived at the Jets' camp brimming with optimism about the team's future. The season before, the Jets had finished with a 3–13 win–loss record. The 1996 season looked a little more promising. The Jets had spent a lot of money to acquire the quarterback Neil O'Donnell and the offensive lineman Jumbo Elliott in addition to Johnson, who had told the *New York Times* (February 12, 1996) that he could "take the team on my back and help win a championship." As it turned out, Johnson's debut season was even more dismal for the Jets than the previous year; the team averted a 0–16 season with a single victory over a poor team, the Arizona Cardinals. Johnson—who had missed two games after colliding with his teammate Aaron Glenn in practice and undergoing surgery on his right knee on October 3, 1996—had played most games as a starter. With O'Donnell, Glenn Foley, and Frank Reich rotating at the quarterback position, Johnson had 63 catches for 844 yards (an average of 13.4 yards per catch) and eight touchdowns.

Johnson had intended the book he was working on to be a chronicle of his rookie year; instead, he turned it into a dissection of the problems of the league's worst team. In *Just Give Me the Damn Ball! The Fast Times and Hard Knocks of an NFL Rookie*, he named names, aired dirty laundry, and lashed out at the Jets' head coach, Rich Kotite, their offensive coordinator, Ron Erhardt, and quarterback O'Donnell, whom he called a "stiff puppet." The Jets could have won more games, Johnson insisted, if the ball had been thrown more often to him and not as often to Wayne Chrebet, the team's leading pass receiver that year, who had 84 catches for 909 yards. Johnson called Chrebet a "mascot" and declared that he was not even good enough to be a number-three receiver. Johnson suspected that Chrebet was thrown so many passes because Kotite, Erhardt, and O'Donnell favored him, possibly because he was white. While agreeing that Kotite's coaching and Erhardt's play calling left much to be desired, many readers felt that Johnson had overstepped his bounds in the book. Johnson maintained that he was only telling the truth. "I shoot from the hip," he told Thomas George. "A lot of people live in a fictitious world. I speak reality."

In the wake of the Jets' performance that year, major changes were implemented for the 1997 season. Kotite left, and Bill Parcells was brought in to take his place. Parcells downplayed the controversy created by Johnson's book and asserted that what mattered was Johnson's performance, not his words. "I've been asked about Keyshawn every day and I always say that I'm not worried about it," Parcells told the *Washington Post* (July 27, 1997). "It will sort itself out because it's very simple—if a guy makes plays everyone will like him, if he doesn't they won't." Parcells also pointed out that for all of Johnson's boisterous outbursts, he was no football prima donna. Parcells found that Johnson was an easy player to coach and that he did what he was told—whether it was working on his catching technique, trimming his weight, running hard in practice, or blocking defensive backs who were bigger than him. "He's a young, maturing player," Parcells told the *New York Times* (November 26, 1997). "He needs coaching, but to his credit, he's coachable. He's not sensitive to criticism."

In the 1997 season the Jets surprised everybody by compiling a 9–7 win–loss record. They barely missed making the play-offs after losing their last game, in Detroit, in which Johnson dropped two passes during the final quarter. Despite his gaffs in that clutch situation, it was still a good year for Johnson. He had his first 100-yard receiving game in a victory over the Minnesota Vikings, and he started all 16 games and hauled in 70 passes for 963 yards (a 13.8 yards-per-catch average) and five touchdowns.

In the 1998 season the Jets performed even better, finishing with a 12–4 record and winning the AFC East division title for the first time since 1969. Key to the Jets' performance that year was a much-improved passing game. O'Donnell was traded to Cincinnati, and the newly acquired backup quarterback, Vinny Testaverde, won the starting job. On the receiving end, Johnson and Chrebet (who was promoted to a starter and given a contract almost equivalent to Johnson's) became the "most prolific receiving tandem in the National Football League," as Gerald Eskenazi wrote for the *New York Times* (January 10, 1999). Johnson had 83 receptions for 1,131 yards and 10 touchdowns, statistics that helped him make the Pro Bowl for the first time. Meanwhile, Chrebet had 75 catches for 1,083 yards and eight touchdowns. Thus, despite whatever bad feelings might have arisen because of what Johnson had said in his book, both receivers managed to be productive. "This is not the odd couple," Eskenazi wrote. "It is the oddest couple."

Having made the play-offs, the Jets proceeded to beat the Jacksonville Jaguars, 34–24, in the first round. Johnson put on a show that was perhaps the most dazzling prime-time performance in his NFL career thus far, with nine receptions, 121 receiving yards, and two touchdowns, one on a 10-yard reverse running play. He also displayed hustle on a play in which the Jets' running back, Curtis Martin, fumbled. The fumble was recovered by a Jaguar player who ran to midfield and lost the ball while attempting a lateral pass to a teammate. Johnson, who had run all the way from the end zone, dove to the field and recovered the ball. To top off his multifaceted performance, Johnson was brought in

on defense on the game's last play and intercepted a Hail Mary pass. The Jets next faced the Denver Broncos in the conference championship. Had the Jets not collapsed in the third quarter, after leading the Broncos 10–0 in the first half, they might have won a berth in the Super Bowl.

At the beginning of the 1999 season, Johnson confidently told a *New York Times* (September 10, 1999) reporter, "I think Bill Parcells knows he has a receiver who is destined to redefine the position." Johnson may have to wait until after the year to fulfill that destiny, however. Injuries to many key starters, including Testaverde, who was out for the season with a ruptured Achilles tendon, hampered the Jets' offense. With inexperienced quarterback Rick Mirer leading the offense, the Jets reverted to their losing ways, with a 1–4 record as of this writing. In five games Johnson had a total of 30 receptions for 460 yards and two touchdowns.

Johnson and his wife, the former Shikiri Hightower, live in Nevada with their daughter, Maia, and son, Keyshawn Jr. Johnson is the founder of Keyshawn Inc., which he formed with the goal of providing disadvantaged youths with the opportunity to attend New York Jets home games. The organization also awards scholarships to USC. Along with some partners, Johnson recently opened Reign, an upscale restaurant in the Beverly Hills neighborhood of Los Angeles. He has also invested in a project to turn a run-down, 23-acre site in the South Central section of Los Angeles (near where he grew up) into a $53 million shopping complex. "There's more to me than just football," he told the *New York Times* (July 21, 1999). He added: "This community is desperate for this type of center. We have a chance to bring jobs here." — W.G.

Suggested Reading: *New York Times* C p1+ Feb. 12, 1996, with photos, B p7 Aug. 7, 1996, with photo, VIII p9 Oct. 19, 1997, with photo, C p7 Nov. 26, 1997, with photo, D p2 Oct. 19, 1998, with photo, D p1 Nov. 27, 1998, with photos, VIII p1 Jan. 10, 1999, with photo, D p5 July 21, 1999, with photo; *Washington Post* C p6 Dec. 29, 1995, with photo, D p1 July 27, 1997, with photo, B p4 Sep. 29, 1998, with photo, D p5 July 21, 1999, with photo; Johnson, Keyshawn, with Shelley Smith. *Just Give Me the Damn Ball! The Fast Times and Hard Knocks of an NFL Rookie,* 1997

Mary Anne Russell/Courtesy of HBO

Jones, Roy Jr.

Jan. 16, 1969– Boxer. Address: c/o Square Ring, 200 W. La Rue St., Pensacola, FL 32501-3938

To sports journalists, Roy Jones Jr. may be the current holder of the slippery, intangible—some might even say mythical—title "best boxer, pound for pound." To the average person, however, the mention of Jones's name is likely to provoke the response "Roy Jones who?" When people do remember him, they usually identify him as the boxer who got robbed of a gold medal at the 1988 Olympics. If you press them about any of Jones's subsequent fights—a total of 40, 33 of which he won by knockout—most respond with blank stares.

Jones's lack of name recognition isn't due to any lack of effort on his part. He has engaged in various attempts at flash—grandstanding in the ring, playing basketball games right before boxing matches, delivering Muhammad Ali–like boasts. Still, he has been overshadowed by heavyweight fighters and even some smaller boxers, such as Oscar De La Hoya. Part of the problem may be that Jones is, as one journalist put it, "too good for his own good." "Fifteen years ago the super-middleweight ranks bristled with immortals: Ray Leonard, Marvin Hagler, Thomas Hearns, Roberto Duran," Charles Leerhsen wrote for the *New York Times Magazine* (August 3, 1997). "But today there are no great personalities on a collision course, no scores to settle, nothing to write home or to call your local cable operator about. Simply put, Jones lacks a foil."

In search of stiffer competition, Jones has repeatedly increased his weight and thereby moved from the middleweight to the super-middleweight to the light-heavyweight division. He has also contem-plated fighting such heavyweights as Mike Tyson and Evander Holyfield. While it may seem suicidal for a 175-pound light heavyweight to go up against heavyweights who weigh in at more than 190, such challenges are nothing new to Jones. Ever since his father started training him, when he was five, Jones has been pushed to test the limit of his abilities.

Roy Jones Jr. was born on January 16, 1969 in Pensacola, Florida. Unlike many other boxers, whose skills were honed in inner-city ghettoes, Jones grew up on a hog farm in a hamlet called Barth, outside Pensacola. He has a younger brother, Corey, and three younger sisters, Tiffany, Lakesha, and Catandrea. Jones's mother is Carol Jones; his father is Roy Jones Sr., a former aircraft electrician at Pensacola Naval Air Station and a Vietnam veteran who received a bronze star for val-or after he rescued another soldier.

Roy Sr. is also a former middleweight boxer who competed in about 18 professional fights; his highest purse was $1,500, which he earned in a bout in Mexico. By his own account, he sparked his son's interest in boxing by play-sparring with him when the boy was around five years old. "I'd get on my knees . . . ," Roy Sr. told Phil Berger for the *New York Times* (March 1, 1989). "I'd let him punch me in the head. When I punched him, he'd get mad. He'd run off and cry. Then he'd come back and want to do more. When we'd finish, I'd let him get the best of me."

Gradually the stakes increased. Roy Sr. is a fiercely independent man who demands a lot of himself and those around him. One of his mottos is, "You're only hurt if you think you're hurt." He continually challenged his son to go beyond what he thought he could do. He once threw Roy Jr. into the Gulf of Mexico, telling him to learn to swim. Later, he set his son atop a horse and then a bull and told him to learn to ride. With boxing it was no different. When Roy Jr. was 10, his father matched him up against a 14-year-old boy who was 16 pounds heavier than him.

There wasn't much that passed for decent training facilities in rural Florida, so Roy Sr. constructed his own ring in a pasture and fashioned punching bags out of the barest of materials. Local kids would hang around to watch the father teach the son the fundamentals of boxing; after they, too, entered the ring, a boxing club was formed. During the day Roy Sr. worked his shift as an aircraft electrician; at night he trained the kids. He spent his own money to buy boxing equipment and at one point sold the family's tractors to finance the boxing club. When he didn't have enough of his own money, he swallowed his enormous pride and asked for donations from everyone he knew. With what he collected, he took the kids to tournaments in neighboring states; in their rickety van, wires held the doors closed.

The training was tough for all the kids, but Roy Sr. was especially tough on his son. Exercises verged on torture. To develop his son's strength, Roy Sr. made him hold bricks at arm's length; to develop his son's speed and mental acuity, he made the boy dodge boards studded with nails. To simulate the wooziness of getting hit, the father spun the son like a top and then forced him to spar. His father kept trying to pound into Roy Jr. a guiding principle: no matter how much it hurts, keep fighting. When Roy Jr. didn't live up to it, his father would revive his flagging spirit by hitting him with a switch or a pipe.

"Wasn't the ideal way to raise a kid," Roy Jr.'s mother admitted to Gary Smith for *Sports Illustrated* (June 26, 1995). "But I can't say it was bad." Roy Jr. remembers the experience differently. "After a while I didn't care about gettin' hurt or dyin' anymore," he told Smith. "I was in pain all day, every day. I was so scared of my father. He'd pull up in his truck and start lookin' for something I'd done wrong. There was no escape, no excuse, no way out of nothin'. Every day it was the same: school, homework, farmwork, trainin'. Gettin' hurt or dyin' might've been better than the life I was livin'. So I turned into a daredevil. I'd do anything. Didn't make much difference. Used to think about killin' myself anyway."

Eventually the farm was sold, and the family moved to Pensacola, where Roy Sr. took over the Escambia County Boys Club boxing program. Meanwhile, Roy Sr. continued to stoke his son's desire to win. "I prayed to God, just don't let me be average," Roy Jr. recalled to Gary Smith. "Let me be great at something. Because I knew if I was average, [my father would] dominate me all my life."

Whatever else might be said about Roy Sr.'s training methods, his son was turning into a ferocious boxing opponent. By age 19, he had racked up an amateur record of 106–4 and become the youngest member of the 1988 U.S. Olympic boxing team. In public his teammates chided him about his youth; in private they turned to him for advice. They saw how he devastated his opponents from afar and put together creative combinations, which he launched from many different angles. Jones seemed destined to win the gold medal in the 156-pound weight class.

Living up to his reputation, Jones reached the final round at the Games. His opponent was the South Korean boxer Park Si Hun. At the final bell Park's face looked battered, while Jones's appeared untouched. Journalists at ringside unofficially scored the fight 86 points to 32 in favor of Jones, who had scored two standing-eight counts. But inexplicably, three of the five judges—the ones from Uganda, Uruguay, and Morocco—gave the fight to Park. When the referee raised Park's arm, virtually everyone felt that Jones had been robbed. Even Park was stunned; he later admitted that Jones had bested him. To partially make up for the gross injustice, the International Boxing Association awarded Jones the Val Barker Cup, for being the outstanding boxer of the Olympic Games. Later, an investigation revealed that two of the three judges had been wined and dined by their South Korean hosts; those two judges were subsequently banned

from the Games for life. But because allegations of bribery could not be proved against the third judge, who remained adamant in his decision, Jones was left with the silver medal.

Ironically, the incident may have brought Jones much more media attention than might otherwise have come his way. Offers to manage him poured in from the best-known promoters and managers in the business, among them Sugar Ray Leonard and his lawyer (Mike Trainer), Lou Duva, and Don King. Jones, however, was unsure about his commitment to boxing; the loss to Park had left him feeling disillusioned. In addition, he harbored dreams of becoming a professional basketball player, even though he is only five feet, 10 and a half inches tall. He was attending Pensacola Junior College at the time, and he played on the school's basketball team.

Finally, his father took control of the situation. After listening to all the supplicants, Roy Sr. decided to become his son's manager himself, and he formed Square Ring Inc. The lawyer Stanley Levin—who had helped finance Roy Sr.'s boxing club—and his brother Fred Levin were brought in to help manage the legal and financial aspects of Roy Jr.'s boxing career. Since neither Roy Sr. nor the Levins had any experience in boxing promotion, they hired a consultant—the former boxing promoter Harold Smith, who had just completed a five-year prison term for embezzling $21.3 million from Wells Fargo Bank. Sports journalists and the spurned promoters grumbled, questioning whether the father knew what he was doing. Roy Sr. fired back: "Hey, who made all these guys authorities on boxing?" he asked Clive Gammon for *Sports Illustrated* (May 15, 1989). "Mike Trainer, them guys, ventured into it as a speculation, a money thing. Don't people who've been in boxing all their lives have better credentials in the sport?"

Jones's first professional fight occurred in May 1989. (He was the last of his Olympic teammates to turn pro.) As is customary for a boxer making his debut as a professional, he did not face a tough opponent. The relatively unknown boxer Ricky Randall was the first sacrificial lamb, and Jones demolished him in two rounds. Then came another weak opponent, and then another. Of Jones's 11 fights from the fall of 1989 to the summer of 1991 (10 of which were held in small-time Pensacola), all were against little-known opponents. One of them, Derwin Richards, even turned out to be an impostor; his real name was Tony Waddles. Roy Jr. dispatched all of them easily—the fights lasted an average of two and a half rounds. Boxing commentators began muttering about the waste of Jones's talent. Even Fred Levin was having doubts about Roy Sr.'s choices. "Roy [Jr.] was still fighting bums at the local fairgrounds," Levin told Charles Leerhsen for the *New York Times Magazine*. Roy Sr., on the other hand, asserted that his son wasn't quite ready for more formidable opponents. He pointed to boxers who had been spoiled early by fame and wealth.

By 1992 Jones had begun facing opponents with greater name recognition, such as Jorge Vaca, and was moving toward a middleweight title shot. But by then he was chafing under his father's control. A two-year deal with NBC to broadcast Jones's fights had lapsed without renewal; meanwhile, Roy Sr. was still hitting his son for mistakes. "It was like I was still a child," Roy Jr. told Charles Leerhsen. The breaking point came in June 1992, in an incident that in Jones's mind amounted to a confrontation over power and respect. A friend's pet Rottweiler, which Jones had borrowed for breeding, bit eight-year-old Catandrea on the arm, something that Roy Sr. had feared might happen. He proceeded to kill the dog—firing three shotgun blasts and two shots from a Glock 9mm pistol—even though the dog had been tied up and restrained. To Roy Jr. that was too much to bear. In August, at age 23, he moved out of his parents' trailer and took his career into his own hands. The break had lasting repercussions: To this day father and son rarely communicate. Roy Sr., who trains other fighters, refuses to attend any of his son's fights. "I bought my mother a house and my dad won't go in it," Roy Jr. told Michael Kaplan for De-tails (January 1999). "Boxing has given me a lot, but it's taken a lot from me. Basically it's taken my family."

Soon after Jones's break with his father, he recruited Alton Merkerson, the assistant coach on the 1988 U.S. Olympic boxing team, as his trainer. Again, boxing promoters flocked to Jones, hoping to sign him up, but he decided to manage himself. In 1992, in his first match without his father, Jones scored a technical knockout (TKO) against Glenn Thomas in the eighth round. Two fights later, on May 22, 1993, he faced Bernard Hopkins for the vacant International Boxing Federation (IBF) world middleweight title. Jones won in a unanimous decision.

Then Jones began putting on weight, to move up to the super-middleweight division (168 pounds maximum). On November 18, 1994, three fights after winning the IBF middleweight title, he faced probably his most talented opponent to that date: James Toney, the IBF super-middleweight champion, who had been undefeated in 46 bouts. Toney, a fighter from Detroit, was the two-to-one favorite, but Jones dominated him and won in a unanimous decision. Suddenly boxing commentators had some proof of what they had always suspected: that Jones was pound for pound one of the best fighters in the world.

Perhaps he was too good—he was outboxing his opponents far too easily. In June 1995, for instance, Jones faced Vinny Pazienza (also known as the Paz-manian Devil). The referee ended the fight in the sixth round, after it became apparent that Jones was mauling Pazienza. "I cried after the Pazienza fight," Jones told Charles Leerhsen. "It tore me up inside. It really made me wonder about what I do automatically, just because my father taught me. My father is the kind of man who kills a fly with an ax handle. That's how he wanted me to be in the ring. Don't hesitate. No mercy. But I don't have that kind of attitude."

Jones began to feel bored with boxing. He fought against the boredom by creating artificial challenges for himself. To make fighting interesting—and also to confuse his opponents—he sometimes switched to a southpaw stance. Other times, he eschewed the jab altogether and led with hooks—something he could get away with only because of his lightning-fast hands. And in 1996 he signed up to play as a point guard for the Jacksonville Barracudas, a U.S. Basketball League (USBL) team, for a little over $100 dollars a week. On June 15, 1996 he probably accomplished a boxing first, by playing in a USBL game during the day and boxing seven hours later. In the basketball game, which the Barracudas won, he scored a meager five points and had three turnovers in 14 minutes of play. In the boxing match he did much better: he scored a TKO in the 11th round against Eric Lucas, a Canadian. In interviews Jones shrugged off his accomplishment. "I played basketball the day before I fought James Toney for the title, only I wasn't playing in an organized league," he told the New York Times (June 16, 1996). "Basketball relaxes me." He signed up again to play for the Barracudas in the 1997 season, and began dreaming of fighting two boxing matches in a day. (That has yet to happen.)

From time to time Jones suggested that he could even take on the heavyweight fighter Mike Tyson, who was soon to be released from prison. He never did; instead, he stepped into the next-higher weight class, the light-heavyweight division (175 pounds maximum). In his first light-heavyweight fight, on November 22, 1996, Jones won a unanimous decision over Mike McCallum and captured the World Boxing Council (WBC) light-heavyweight belt.

Jones's sole defeat came against Montell Griffin on March 21, 1997, in the middle of the ninth round of the match. Jones was ahead on the scorecards of two judges and behind on that of the third judge. Then he delivered a right to Griffin's face, forcing Griffin to drop to one knee. Within approximately two seconds, Jones hit Griffin's head with two more blows, both of which were illegal since Griffin was on his knee. Jones, who up to that point had been undefeated in 35 fights, was disqualified, and he lost the WBC belt.

Jones complained that the decision was unfair because the referee didn't move in quickly enough to stop him from hitting Griffin. Otherwise, he maintained, he would have won the fight. To prove that contention Jones faced Griffin again on August 7, 1997. He knocked Griffin out in the first round and regained his WBC belt.

In 1998 Jones continued to dominate the light-heavyweight field, with victories over Virgil Hill, Lou DelValle, and Otis Grant. DelValle, who had worked for Jones as a sparring partner three years earlier, probably provided Jones with his greatest challenge that year. In their match in July, DelValle knocked Jones down in the eighth round. That knockdown, Jones has claimed, was the first time he has been sent to the canvas since he was 12 years old, and he attributed the blow to DelValle's familiarity with his style. Except for the knockdown, Jones dominated the fight; he won a unanimous decision and unified the WBC and World Boxing Association (WBA) light-heavyweight titles.

Many have wondered whether the lack of tougher competition is causing Jones to lose his will to fight. In the past two years, he has faced only five opponents, and once inside the ring, he has not always been sufficiently aggressive. For instance, he knocked down Otis Grant in the sixth round of their match, but he didn't go for the kill in the seventh round. The audience booed him, and the referee had to admonish him to fight. Jones has even said that he may retire soon, though he still has a three-year, nine-fight, $3 million per fight deal with HBO that he signed prior to his match with Hill. "They can call me the reluctant warrior and all that," Jones told the New York Times (November 14, 1998, on-line). "I'm not going out like that," he continued, referring to the legendary boxer Sugar Ray Robinson, who ended his career broke and in poor health. "I'm looking to be happy and enjoy a long life after boxing."

Jones is reportedly considering moving up into the cruiserweight division. He has also talked about facing the WBA and IBF heavyweight champion, Evander Holyfield. In a rare moment, Jones's father broke the silence between his son and himself and advised Roy not to become a heavyweight, because in that category he would have to wait too long to get a title shot. So far, Jones has heeded that advice.

During the first 10 months of 1999, Jones remained on top of the light-heavyweight field. On January 9 he successfully defended his WBA and WBC belts by knocking out Rick Frazier in two rounds. Five months later, on June 5, he unified the WBA, WBC, and IBF light-heavyweight belts by winning a decision against Reggie Johnson. He was scheduled to fight Graciano Rocchigiani in November.

Jones, who is unmarried and has two children, devotes a lot of his free time to charity events in Pensacola. He has used some of his boxing earnings to build a first-rate boxing gym, run by Square Ring, for kids in the area. He also owns an 81-acre homestead in Pensacola. In addition to fishing and hunting, Jones likes to raise animals, especially chickens. He has claimed that his roosters, which he enters in cockfights, have taught him a few boxing moves. They have also provided him with a metaphor for thinking about his life. "Look how this rooster walks in his cage," he told Gary Smith for Sports Illustrated. "See that? It's his cage. He owns it. It's his world. Every other male has to respect that. I spent all my life in my dad's cage. I could never be 100 percent of who I am until I left it. But because of him, nothing bothers me. I'll nev-

er face anything stronger and harder than what I already have." — W.G.

Suggested Reading: Details p83+ Jan. 1999, with photos; New York Times B p9+ Mar. 1, 1989, with photo; New York Times Magazine p23+ Aug. 3, 1997, with photo; Sports Illustrated p62+ Nov. 14, 1988, with photos, p42+ May 15, 1989, with photos, p78+ June 26, 1995, with photos, p34+ June 24, 1996, with photo

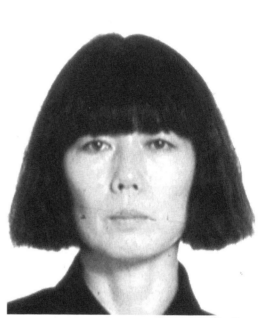

Outline Press

Kawakubo, Rei
(ka-wa-koo-boh, ray)

1942– Fashion designer. Address: c/o Comme des Garçons Ltd., 5-11-5 Minamiaoyama, Minato-ku, Tokyo 107, Japan

"To make a form in which a woman looks pretty in the conventional way is not interesting to me at all . . . ," the fashion designer Rei Kawakubo told Lynn Yaeger for the Village Voice (April 1, 1997). "Today there are so many trends, yet everything looks the same. It's our job to question convention. If we don't take risks, then who will?" Since the early 1980s, Rei Kawakubo has created commercially successful collections of women's and men's clothing that have also been praised as art. "She has an integrity and a conviction we don't often associate with the commercial world," Richard Martin, the curator of the Metropolitan Museum of Art's Costume Institute, told Yaeger. "She's a revolutionary for the end of the century, like [the French couturier Paul] Poiret was at the beginning. She has a deliberate sense of looking beyond beauty." The name of Kawakubo's label, Comme des Garçons, means "like the boys" in French, and in the opinion of the fashion critic Bernadine Morris, among others, the name suits Kawakubo's work: "[Her designs] are simple in the sense that the best men's clothes are simple," Morris wrote for the *New York Times* (March 20, 1987). "Some details startle, but the clothes are not frivolous. They are for women, not Barbie dolls." In addition to being simpler than those of most women's clothing, Kawakubo's designs never inhibit movement, and they tend to hide or distort, rather than exhibit, the parts of the body that traditionally have been eroticized by clothing.

Kawakubo is extremely reticent about her past, and little is known about her youth. She was born in Tokyo, Japan, in 1942. According to a staff writer for *People* (December 26, 1983), when asked what her parents did for a living, Kawakubo has often replied, "Nothing special." Similarly, when asked what kinds of clothes she liked as a youth, she claims not to remember. Reportedly, at least one of her parents was an educator. Rei studied fine arts and literature at Tokyo's prestigious Keio University. After graduating, in 1964, she worked for a short time in the advertising department of the Asahi textile company. She left that job in the late 1960s to become a freelance stylist.

In about 1969 Kawakubo began designing women's clothing, and in 1973 she formally established her company, Comme des Garçons Ltd., of which she remains the sole owner and operator. Her designs became popular in Japan almost immediately, and in 1978 she began designing men's clothing as well. In 1981 she began showing her seasonal collections during fashion week in Paris, an event considered at that time far more prestigious than the one in Tokyo. She also opened a boutique in Paris, and—to overcome the dramatic fluctuations of the Japanese yen and to better compete with European designers—she began manufacturing much of her clothing in France. In comparison with other collections shown in Europe in the early 1980s, Kawakubo's work seemed dark, disproportionate, and genderless. Some of the trademark features of her early Paris collections were frayed edges and such unusual materials as paper and boiled wool, which Kawakubo chose as a means of making her garments look distorted. Outfits often consisted of unusual layerings, such as pants worn under dresses. Recalling for *Vanity Fair* (August 1988) Kawakubo's first Parisian show, Ben Brantley wrote that "her all black, radically asymmetrical clothes seemed in determined defiance of every convention of tailoring. The avant-gardists adopted her as patron saint; traditionalists said her clothes were simply ugly; many retailers weren't quite sure what to think."

Because of trends at that time toward brightly colored, "body-conscious" clothing, Kawakubo's new look was not immediately accepted, particularly in the U.S., where clothing design has traditionally focused more on retail sales than on innovation. When Bernadine Morris of the *New York Times* (December 14, 1982) asked Kawakubo who she thought might wear her designs, the designer replied, "One who is independent. One who is not swayed by what her husband thinks. One who can stand by herself." A few years later her new style of clothing finally caught on, and women seemed to derive a special enjoyment from "wearing Kawakubo." In her March 5, 1983 *New York Times* article, Morris quoted the noted fashion editor Polly Mellen as saying, "[Kawakubo] gives us another option. We've had Japanese things before, but they've never been so authoritative." Pinky Black, an editor at *Rolling Stone*, told Morris, "I've been wearing the torn-up and layered look for a long time. I always wear pants under my dresses. People think I'm crazy, so it's nice to see the look become accepted." And a salesperson at Henri Bendel, the first store to sell Comme des Garçons in the U.S., recalled to Morris (March 5, 1983), "I sold a [Kawakubo] dress to a woman who is a size 14. She knew just how to wear it and she looked wonderful." "Women wanted something normal that expressed their own feelings and freedom," Kawakubo explained to Amy M. Spindler for the *New York Times* (November 8, 1994). "I feel the responsibility that I have to do that."

The 1980s were a period of tremendous growth for Comme des Garçons. By 1990 more than 300 stores had opened worldwide, including one in New York City's fashionable Soho district, and the company's earnings surpassed $100 million. Much of Kawakubo's new work—which came to include a second men's line, called Homme Deux, a line of loungewear called Robe de Chambre, and a line of knits called Tricot—was designed and marketed for sale in Japan, where she was doing more than 75 percent of her business. Because the shirts from her men's collection proved to be exceedingly popular, Kawakubo also began designing a separate line of lower-priced shirts: 50 different styles of men's shirts were produced in 20 different fabrics and sold at prices that ranged from $125 to $200— about half the price of a shirt from the Comme des Garçons Homme collection. Kawakubo's men's shirts were conventional, in the sense that they could be worn with traditional suits, but many had special touches, such as mismatched buttons, asymmetrical collars, or parts made of different fabrics. In the U.S. Kawakubo's shirts were sold in a second Soho boutique, the decor of which has shirt-like elements, including a collar and a row of metal buttons on the ceiling. All of Kawakubo's boutiques were designed by the interior designer Takao Kawasaki and are said to look more like art galleries than clothing stores.

By the late 1980s Kawakubo's dark, oversize designs had given way to simpler shapes and styles. Her knee-length pants, worn with tight jersey tops or sweaters, were popular for summer. Kawakubo began to show more of the body, albeit in ways that were different from what other designers were doing at that time. For example, her garments had big, loopy armholes and open backs. She also raised some of her hemlines above knee level, and for dressier clothes she created elaborate gathers that produced unusual drapery effects. The reaction to Kawakubo's simpler designs was mostly positive, and sales increased considerably.

Kawakubo began the 1990s by infusing more color into her work, which up to then she had confined almost entirely to black, veering only occasionally into navy blue, dark burgundy, brown, and gray. This more colorful phase, in which she used accents of fluorescent orange, pink, and yellow, culminated in Kawakubo's fall 1995 women's collection, entitled "Beyond Sweet." It included cocoon-like coats and jackets decorated with what resembled marshmallows or cotton candy, ruffled dresses, and other garments with dainty, colorful accents. In the *New York Times* (March 17, 1995), Amy M. Spindler described this collection as combining "codified trappings for women's dress—candy colors, lace, gingham, embroidery, ankle socks, tulle, and saddle shoes—in a way that purged their cloying attributes. . . . It was a collection that said 'sweet' without a hint of irony but with affection for modern women who are wary of the word." In the same article, Kawakubo was quoted as saying that in creating this unusual collection she found that "the energy from something sweet is good for the body, mind, and spirit."

At about the same time, one of Kawakubo's 1995 men's shows caused a stir in Paris. The collection, which the designer called "Sleep," featured pajama-type pants and tops. A number of these pieces were striped, and others were made of fabric onto which were stamped footprints and scattered numbers. Some observers found the clothing reminiscent of that worn by people imprisoned in Nazi concentration camps during the Holocaust and asserted that the show should not have taken place in the city-owned space where Kawakubo usually held her show. The mayor of Paris's Third Arrondissement gave in to the complaints and refused to host the next year's show, reportedly for fear of losing the Jewish vote in the next election. When questioned about the inspiration for the collection, Kawakubo said that she had been interested in loungewear from the early part of the 20th century, when such clothing had been a more important part of men's wardrobes. In the *New York Times Magazine* (April 2, 1995), Holly Brubach wrote, "For those of us in the audience that evening, . . . the Holocaust connection was one of many possible interpretations and a highly subjective one, at that. Some spectators saw the show as a late-night get together at a boy's dormitory. Others were dismayed by the overtones of emergency, as if the models had been wakened in the middle of the night. . . . Some of the most irate objections have been lodged by people who have never seen the clothes. Suspicious of fashion, they've been quick to charge it with crimes they're sure it must be capable of committing." Since Kawakubo's show, pajama-type pants and tops have become very popular, and versions exist under many other labels.

Another Kawakubo-inspired trend is the use of bold floral prints for winter clothing. Her fall 1996 women's collection featured a number of flower-patterned dresses worn with coats and scarves of contrasting prints. In the *New York Times* (March 14, 1996), Amy M. Spindler wrote, "More than any of her clothes ever did, these ached to be worn." Spindler quoted the designer as saying that she enjoyed designing with floral-print fabrics because "flowers are happy and positive. Flowers, when blooming, are in their peak of energy and strength."

Kawakubo's insertion of large, bulbous pads between layers of clothing in her spring 1997 collection was less well received. According to Lynn Yaeger's 1997 *Village Voice* article, a publicist for Comme des Garçons explained that "the theme of this collection is body meets dress, body becomes dress, dress becomes body." Yaeger described the clothes as having a "special strangeness," and wrote that "in an age of liposuction, Kawakubo overthrows the tyranny of symmetrical slenderness, gleefully depositing globs of fat where others are desperate to nip and tuck." "I don't remember how or when I got the inspiration," Kawakubo told Yaeger. "It was as if anesthesia suddenly wore off, or I had recovered from amnesia." Although much of the clothing from the collection sold well only when the pads were removed, several pieces were included in a show entitled "The Four Seasons," at the Costume Institute of the Metropolitan Museum of Art, in New York City. Curator Richard Martin felt that, as odd as it may have seemed at that moment in fashion, Kawakubo's padded look would eventually become mainstream, as so many of her earlier innovations had. The choreographer Merce Cunningham used pieces from the collection to costume members of his ensemble for the dance piece *Scenario*.

Kawakubo currently works closely with the designer Junyo Watanabe, who has been her assistant since the mid-1990s and who creates the Comme des Garçons Tricot line. Watanabe also produces his own line, with Kawakubo's financial backing. Kawakubo and the Belgian designer Martin Margiela, one of several designers who have cited Kawakubo as being inspirational to them, frequently show their collections together, because they feel that their work is similar in theme and creative focus. "For me, the reason for presenting our collections one after the other is because I hope that our belief in the importance of creation will be more strongly felt," Kawakubo told Spindler. "It provides a kind of added tension and risk which is crucial to the creative process."

Kawakubo's recent work has been described as "deconstructionist." For example, she has taken apart an ordinary coat or dress and then sewn it back together in an unusual manner. "My idea was to start with something perfect and go backward," she told Sarah Mower for *Harper's Bazaar* (September 1997). For the spring of the year 2000, Kawakubo designed clothes in vibrant hues of red, pink, purple, and green, many of which featured "elaborate ruffles resembling the crepe paper flowers schoolchildren make," Ginia Bellafante reported for the *New York Times* (October 8, 1999, online). Kawakubo also continued to use innovative tailoring, "lining jackets and coats with fabric cut larger than the exteriors and scrunching it underneath," Bellafante wrote, so that "the resulting garments almost appeared to be blossoming."

In addition to having her clothing exhibited at the Metropolitan Museum of Art and several other museums and galleries around the world, Kawakubo was honored by New York's Fashion Institute of Technology in 1987 as one of the leading women in 20th-century design. She won Tokyo's Mainichi Newspaper Award in 1983 and 1987. Unlike designers who license their names to a variety of products for large sums of money, Kawakubo has only one fragrance—Comme des Garçons. Kawakubo has also designed furniture, some of which is produced by the Italian furniture maker Palluco.

The petite Kawakubo wears her black hair in an asymmetrical bob with bangs. Nicola Jeal of the London *Observer* (October 22, 1989) described her as an "almost reclusive workaholic." When asked how she unwinds after work, she told Jeal, "[I like] playing with my five cats and one dog. This makes me smile." Although she spends a great deal of time in Paris, Kawakubo and her husband, Adrian Joffe, call Tokyo their home, and they like to vacation at spas in small Japanese villages. Her few close friends include the fashion designer Yohji Yamamoto, to whose work Kawakubo's is often compared. — C.P.

Suggested Reading: *Architectural Record* p92+ Jan. 1989, with photo; *Harper's Bazaar* p448+ Sep. 1997, with photo; *New York Times* C p10 Dec. 14, 1982, with photos, p11 Mar. 5, 1983, with photos, B p18 Nov. 23, 1984, with photos, B p8 Feb. 23, 1988, B p9 Nov. 8, 1994, B p7 Mar. 17, 1995, with photos, C p12 Mar. 14, 1996, with photo, B p8 Oct. 16, 1997, with photos; *New York Times Magazine* p67 Apr. 2, 1995, with photo, p79 Oct. 5, 1997, with photo; (London) *Observer* p36 Oct. 22, 1989, with photos; *People* p74 Dec. 26, 1983; *Vanity Fair* p91 Aug. 1988, with photos; *Village Voice* p16 Apr. 1, 1997, with photos; *Washington Post* F p3 Oct. 19, 1997, with photos

Kelly, R.

1967(?)– Singer; songwriter; record producer.
Address: c/o Interscope Records, 10900 Wilshire
Blvd., Suite 1230, Los Angeles, CA 90024

Although mainstream audiences probably know the singer and songwriter R. Kelly best for his inspirational hit song of 1996, "I Believe I Can Fly," Kelly, who has often been described as "the reigning King of Rhythm and Blues," has been a fixture of R&B for much of the 1990s. Early in the decade he exploded onto the music scene with such highly suggestive songs as "Bump 'N Grind" and "Sex Me." He has since written and produced songs for numerous other recording artists and has created a recording label, Rockland Records, to sign and promote new talent. In less than 10 years he has established himself as a masterful singer who draws from the soul, blues, rhythm-and-blues, and gospel traditions, creating an impressive body of work that attests to his prodigious musical ability and his business acumen.

The performer, songwriter, and producer was born Robert Kelly in about 1967 in Illinois and was raised by his mother, Joann Kelly, in the housing projects of Chicago's South Side. From an early age, he attended a Baptist church and sang in the choir. His singing talent helped him to stay out of trouble in his impoverished, crime-ridden neighborhood. "I got shot in the arm when I was 13 and had my bike stolen. I could have been dead. So I realized . . . I wanted to go on and do something and not be in gangs," he has said, as quoted by

Brad Talbutt/Archive Photos

T. Shawn Taylor for the *Chicago Tribune* (October 2, 1992).

While attending Kenwood Academy, a high school in Chicago, Kelly met Reverend Lena McLin. With McLin serving as his mentor both artistically and spiritually, Kelly honed his musical abilities and strove to succeed as a singer and songwriter. Meanwhile, he also taught himself to play the keyboard and began performing locally at talent shows and other small venues in and around Chicago; he often sang for money in train stations. Eventually, he was signed by Jive Records, a Chicago-based record label.

Under Jive Records, Kelly released his debut album, *Born into the 90s* (1992), which he recorded with the accompaniment of a backup troupe called Public Announcement. (The group has since released albums of its own.) Audiences were immediately drawn to Kelly's smooth voice and the suggestive lyrics in the hit singles "Honey Love" and "Slow Dance (Hey Mr. DJ)." In those songs, Kelly explicitly and unapologetically described the amorous adventures of a lothario. *Born into the 90s* sold a million copies and reached number three on the R&B album chart.

Kelly continued to sing about sex in *12 Play* (1993), his debut album as a solo artist. Indeed, the album, which featured the singles "Bump 'N Grind," "Sex Me," and "Your Body's Callin'," was deemed so racy and controversial that it was banned in several foreign countries and denounced by some social conservatives. Partly as a result of these developments, Kelly cemented his reputation for writing and singing provocative love ballads. "Sex is a reality. I love what I do. I try to write love ballads in a way no one else does. You hear some [ballads], and they all sound the same. Sometimes you have to go to the edge to be different, adventurous, and open-minded. I say things other people are afraid to say. Marvin Gaye did too," Kelly later commented, as quoted by Anita M. Samuels for *Billboard* (September 19, 1998). Offering a different assessment of Kelly's contribution to popular music, Richard Harrington, writing for the *Washington Post* (November 18, 1988), credited the album for "[melding] hip-hop's worst misogynist tendencies with the shimmering romanticism of R&B. "Despite—or because of—the controversy concerning the content of Kelly's songs, the album sold 2.8 million copies, and Kelly was embraced by a core audience of young women.

Kelly's third album was *R. Kelly* (1995), which quickly went platinum, selling over a million records. Ken Tucker, reviewing the disc for *Entertainment Weekly* (November 24, 1995), described it as "an album that moves [Kelly] into a new realm of pop ambitiousness." The following year saw the release of "I Believe I Can Fly," which had been recorded for the film *Space Jam* (1996) and was featured on the film's soundtrack. "I Believe I Can Fly" proved to be Kelly's ticket to international stardom; a hit with mainstream audiences, it earned Kelly three Grammy Awards in 1998—for best R&B song of the year, best song written for a motion picture, and best male R&B vocalist.

Meanwhile, Kelly also gained success as a songwriter and producer for other recording artists. In 1995 he won two Grammy Award nominations for writing and producing the song "You Are Not Alone" for Michael Jackson's album *History* (1995). Kelly also wrote songs for the R&B singer

Aaliyah and produced her debut album *Age Ain't Nothin' But a Number* (1994). Although some controversy greeted the news that Kelly and the teenage Aaliyah had married, in the summer of 1994, the situation did not seriously hamper the career of either singer.

Kelly's fourth album, *R.* (1998), was a commercial and critical hit. Some of the highlights of the double album, which featured 29 songs, were "Home Alone" and "I Am Your Angel," a dreamy duet that Kelly sang with Celine Dion. Although Kelly continued to sing about sex, most music critics noted that he had toned down the content of his lyrics. Observers attributed this change to personal experiences Kelly had undergone since the release of his last album. Most significant of these was his newfound desire for a closer relationship with God. While performing as a special guest singer in a concert with the gospel star Kirk Franklin in March 1997, Kelly announced, as quoted by Greg Kot for the *Chicago Tribune* (November 15, 1998), "It amazes me when I look back eight months ago—cars, women, money, the media. I had everyone's attention." He then added, "Some may think it's a gimmick, but I tell you, here stands a broken man. Every day I seem to be falling in love with the Lord. I've come to find out that whatever it is you want, it's in the Lord. I used to be flying in sin—now I'm flying in Jesus."

Following that proclamation, it was revealed that Kelly had long been struggling with the conflict between his religion and the trappings of his success. The struggle was brought to a head by the death of his mother, from cancer, in 1993. "When you're successful, especially if you went into it without really having God or church in your life, it's hard," he said, as quoted by Kevin Chappell for *Ebony* (September 1998). "But I'm at the point now where I'm saying, 'I know I got famous from doing these sex songs, but I know there is a God; I believe there is a God.'" Although these developments did not lead Kelly to focus exclusively on gospel music, they have fueled speculation that he may turn more of his energy in that direction.

Regardless of which genre Kelly embraces in the future, it is very likely that he will be involved in all aspects of his music. In addition to writing nearly all of his own songs and writing and producing for such superstars as Whitney Houston, Janet Jackson, and Toni Braxton, in 1998 he formed Rockland Records, a Chicago-based record label, and became that company's CEO. Rockland, which has a distribution deal with Interscope Records, has signed numerous recording artists and groups, among them Sparkle, Vegas Cats, Talent, and Lady.

Kelly was the recipient of the Sammy Davis Jr. Award for Entertainer of the Year at the 13th Annual Soul Train Music Awards ceremony, in 1999. He lives in a palatial house in Chicago. He and Aaliyah have a daughter, Joann. When not absorbed in making music, Kelly enjoys playing basketball. — Y.P.

Suggested Reading: *Billboard* p41+ Sep. 19, 1998, with photo; *Chicago Tribune* V p3 Oct. 2, 1992, with photo, V p1+ Nov. 14, 1995, with photos; *Ebony* p40+ Sep. 1998, with photos; *Washington Post* D p1 Nov. 18, 1998, with photo

Selected Recordings: *Born into the 90s*, 1992; *12 Play*, 1993; *R. Kelly*, 1995; *R.*, 1998

Archive Photos

Khan, Chaka

Mar. 23, 1953– Singer. Address: c/o Warner Bros. and Reprise Records, 75 Rockefeller Plaza, New York, NY 10019

"To me [singing is] like a religious experience," Chaka Khan told Isabel Wilkerson for *Essence* (October 1995). "It's almost like getting lost. You don't know what happened, and then, you know, the hour's up." The career of Chaka Khan, among the most exuberant and naturally talented of the pop singers to be called "diva," has spanned more than 20 years and produced numerous R&B hits, many with the group Rufus. Although she has not achieved the level of stardom attained by Madonna or Whitney Houston, critics agree that once heard, her unique voice is unforgettable. In the *Washington Post* (June 31, 1992), Joe Brown wrote, "That earthy, extraordinary, often-imitated voice—a sexy, sensual, shiver-inducing siren wail—can turn the most banal lyric into something stirring." And in the *New York Times* (August 20, 1992), Jon Pareles noted, "Khan can coo with a girlish sweetness, cut to the bone with a nasal Dinah Washington turn, whisper a breathy invitation. Her sense of

pitch is so confident that she leaps wide intervals in a syncopated instant. . . . She'll hang back behind the beat, swoop suddenly up or down, scatsing up to the next phrase. She uses her vocal power adeptly, saving her high notes for a song's climax."

Chaka Khan was born Yvette Marie Stevens on March 23, 1953 near Chicago, Illinois. She spent most of her childhood on a U.S. Air Force base near Chicago, where her father, who later became a freelance photographer, was stationed. Her mother, who currently manages her fan club, was a researcher at the University of Chicago. According to Isabel Wilkerson, Khan had a Catholic upbringing. "I sang Ave Maria, okay?" the singer confessed. "I wanted to be a nun and all that." She began singing in nightclubs when she was just 11 years old. "My mother used to escort me to the clubs and then take me home when things closed down," she told Larry Rohter for the *Washington Post* (March 17, 1975).

Khan began having personal problems when she was about 13 years old. During the same year that her parents got a divorce, she was expelled from her Catholic school, according to David Sheff of *People* (April 21, 1980), for asking a priest in a suggestive way "what he did with the nuns." She switched schools, but academics became secondary to her singing career, which kept her at a number of Chicago's North Side nightclubs until the early morning hours on school days. "I was doing four shows a night before I was grown up," she told Sheff. She also began drinking and experimenting with drugs, which were easy to get at the clubs where she performed. "I did uppers before the shows, downers to sleep, then [drank] peppermint schnapps till I'd pass out," she said. She continued attending classes as long as she could, becoming involved with the Black Student Union, which helped earn black studies a place in the curriculum at her high school. After dropping out of school, she joined the Black Panthers and for a time carried a gun she had stolen from a movie-theater security guard. She eventually threw the gun, unused, into a lake: "When I did think about killing people with it, I developed ulcers," she said. Khan has recently spoken to youth groups about the importance of staying in school. "I'm not the one who should be standing up there saying 'Stay in school,'" she admitted to Alison Powell for *Interview* (November 1996). "On the other hand, I am the one, because I did want to attend college. But I was driven by another force that was stronger than my will to stay in school, and it turned out lucky for me, but that's not the norm."

When she was about 17, an African holy man whom Khan met through a youth group baptized the young singer and gave her an authentic African name. According to Sheff, Khan's name became Chaka Adunne Aduffe Hodarhi Karifi, which means "red, fire, and war." Khan used the stage name Chaka Karifi until, while she was still in her teens, she married the East Indian bass player Hassan Khan. She has said that her first marriage was an arrangement of convenience rather than love: "We had an understanding," she told Wilkerson. "I think he really liked me and wanted to marry me. One half of my brain was always like, 'I like you too, but . . . '" In 1969, after singing with the Chicago-based bands Lyfe, Lock and Chains and Baby Huey and the Babysitters, Chaka Khan, as she was known by then, joined the funk band Ask Rufus. "I don't even remember the first time I sang with them," she told Lynn Van Matre for the *Chicago Tribune* (April 13, 1980). "I just remember that I needed some money and they offered me a job and I took it. I remember it being very hard at first—all those people having to come together and mold as one. That's like a hard thing to do, and it took us a long time to get to the point where we'd accomplished it." In about 1972 Khan moved with the band, which had shortened its name to Rufus, to Los Angeles.

After achieving moderate success with their first album, *Rufus* (1973), the band enlisted the help of the pop star Stevie Wonder. Impressed with Khan's voice after hearing her on the group's first album, Wonder contributed some of the music for their second recording, *Rags to Rufus* (1974). "I remember the day Stevie came by," Khan told Rohter. "I was eight and a half months pregnant at the time, and I thought I was going to have the baby on the spot." When Wonder played a song that he had written for Khan, however, the young singer was disappointed, and said so. "He wasn't too happy about that," Khan recalled to Rohter. "But he sat down at the clavinette and said he'd write me another song right then and there." The tune he came up with that day eventually became Rufus's first hit single, "Tell Me Something Good," which won a Grammy in 1974 for best R&B performance by a duo or group. The album *Rags to Rufus* sold more than one million copies, and another track, "You Got the Love," also became a hit. Khan has said that being pregnant improved her voice and contributed to the album's quality.

It was during the 1970s, while she was working with Rufus, that Khan developed the unique style of singing and performing that came to be widely imitated by other pop artists. "We were all Chaka clones then," the singer Anita Baker was quoted as saying by Chris Heim in the *Chicago Tribune* (February 12, 1989). "I mean, vocal cords were getting ripped up all over America by girls trying to imitate her voice." For performances and photographs, Khan flaunted her voluptuous figure and exotic facial features by wearing revealing clothing and dramatic makeup; these, too, were copied by her admirers. The 1970s, however, were also tumultuous years for Khan, whose drug and alcohol habits were no secret to her fans. Although she felt that having a child had been one of the few stabilizing influences in her life, her daughter, Milini, whose father was Rahsaan Morris, a stagehand at the Chicago opera, lived in Chicago with Khan's grandmother while the singer toured and made the

albums *Rufusized* (1974), *Rufus Featuring Chaka Khan* (1975), and *Ask Rufus* (1977). In 1976 Khan married Richard Holland, a white real-estate agent. When she became pregnant for the second time, she toured until she was more than eight months pregnant. "I toured pregnant with both kids," she told Lynn Van Matre for the *Chicago Tribune* (April 13, 1980). "I was out there both times until the very end, when it was time to have them. Then I went home for the births. Pregnancy is as old as time, you know. I felt better and had more energy than I do now." Shortly after the birth of her son, Demien, she divorced Holland. Part of the couple's reason for divorcing was that they had received hate letters regarding their interracial union.

According to Russell Gersten in the *Village Voice* (May 27, 1981), in 1976, following the hit song "Sweet Thing" from the album *Rufus Featuring Chaka Khan*, Rufus's popularity with white audiences declined significantly, while their popularity among African-Americans increased. Overall record sales were down, and Khan, obviously the driving force behind the band's success, became frustrated. "It bothers me," she told Wayne Robins for *Newsday* (May 29, 1981). "I hate to be categorized. I'm being denied something that I feel I've earned, which is white pop recognition. . . . Maybe I could find a scientist to create some balm to turn me white. I could build an obvious Olivia Newton John–type image. But that's so pointless." In 1978 Khan began her solo career. Her first album, *Chaka* (1978), featured the infectious song "I'm Every Woman," which became a number-one hit on the U.S. R&B charts. In the *New York Times* (August 30, 1981), Stephen Holden called the perennially popular song "a proud affirmation of erotic and musical self confidence."

For the next several years, Khan continued to appear both as a solo act and with Rufus. She worked with the band on the albums *Street Player* (1979), *Masterjam* (1979), and *Camouflage* (1981). Her second solo album, *Naughty* (1980), saw little success, but the title track from her 1981 release *What Cha' Gonna Do for Me* became a hit song, and the album fared somewhat better overall. Reviewing it in the *Toronto Globe and Mail* (June 24, 1981), Paul McGrath wrote that while "things [were] looking up for the only truly novel female vocalist to come out of rhythm and blues in the past decade . . . she still [could not] find as comfortable a musical situation as [she] enjoyed with Rufus." At about this time Khan began working with the producer Arif Mardin, who also worked with such stars as Aretha Franklin, Rod Stewart, and the Bee Gees. The arrangement seemed to work for Khan, whose next album had a new, jazzy feel and included several ballads—a medium she had not previously explored. "I want to be a jazz singer," Khan told Chris Heim. "I don't feel comfortable [singing jazz] and that is the attraction for me. Singing comes so easy for me. It's the easiest thing for me to do. You can anticipate pretty much what's going to happen in most rock songs or R&B

songs or whatever. But jazz is freestyle music. Anything can happen. Your choices are unlimited."

In addition to taking on a new style of music, in the early 1980s Khan worked at cleaning up her lifestyle. Among other things, she stopped using drugs, which she said had provided her with an escape for many years. She was quoted by Dennis Hunt in *Newsday* (March 6, 1983) as explaining, "If I had continued the way I was going I'd probably be dead now. All that wildness was a cover-up for the insecurity I've felt most of my life. I couldn't cope with it. . . . I was scared of myself, scared to be by myself. Can you imagine that? . . . It was always one insecurity or another. I was a slave to insecurities." Khan said that having been in the music business for so long had contributed to her problems because the industry was "built on insecure people." "How can you be secure in a business that feeds insecurity and feeds on insecurity?" she asked. "There are a lot of awful people in this business." Khan told Heim that part of her rehabilitation included distancing herself from friends who were "leeches" and who were "helping to drag [her] down." She began spending a great deal of her free time reading.

In 1983 Khan reunited once again with Rufus to produce the album *Rufus and Chaka Khan Live: Stompin' at the Savoy*. Like "I'm Every Woman," the single "Ain't Nobody" from that album became not only an R&B hit but one of the songs for which Khan remains well known, and it won two R&B Grammy Awards that year. "I've got to say, 'Ain't Nobody' is one of my favorite songs," the singer told *Micrografx.com*. "It's a song I'll be singing probably for the rest of my life."

Khan had another success in 1984, with her album *I Feel for You*. Written by The Artist Formerly Known as Prince, the title song began with the rapper Melle Mel chanting the name Chaka Khan and rapping about her. "It was not my doing," Khan told Joe Brown for the *Washington Post* (June 31, 1992). "I was very embarrassed by it, really—some guy saying my name over and over again. But it only proves that sometimes I'm wrong. It still haunts me. I'll never live that down." Stevie Wonder also played harmonica for the track, which reached number two on the U.S. pop charts and number one in Great Britain. A second song from the album, the ballad "Through the Fire," became an adult contemporary hit in the U.S., and the songs "This Is My Night" and "Eye to Eye" made the British charts. *I Feel for You* went platinum, and Khan won that year's Grammy for best female R&B performance.

Khan's next notable album was *CK* (1988), which Chris Heim described as having a style "that harkens back to Khan's earliest efforts with her old band, Rufus, and perhaps even to earlier influences as well." Khan has said that the album, which produced a top-five hit in "It's My Party," has "a kind of 60s energy. In the 60s, there was a quality to music, a quality that is missing today. It's a basic, not over-produced thing. And this album

to me is one of the most under-produced albums I've ever done." The album included covers of such 1960s songs as "Signed, Sealed, Delivered" and featured a variety of musicians and singers, among them Bobby McFerrin, Cecil Womack, Miles Davis, and George Benson.

The 1989 album *Life Is a Dance* featured remixed versions of Khan's most popular songs. Although the album was a money-maker, it was a project of which Khan did not entirely approve. "I just think some things are better left alone," she told Brown. "I am aware that [an album of remixed dance music] appeals to a whole genre right now. I don't like it, but I have to comply with certain things." Khan was also called upon to make several music videos for this project. "I don't enjoy shooting videos at all," she said. "I'm not an actress, I'm a singer, and I don't care for that camera trip and being seen. So I just do it and get it over with." In 1992 Khan made the album *The Woman I Am*, the first since her years with Rufus for which she wrote a significant amount of her own material. "I had to do it," she explained to Brown. "I'd had enough of other people telling me when and what to sing."

With the exception of a few more remixed and "greatest hits" albums, Chaka's most notable recent releases can be heard on the album *Come 2 My House* (1998). After working with Warner Brothers Records for over 20 years, Khan teamed up with The Artist Formerly Known as Prince, who had also been unhappy with the Warner Brothers label and formed his own company, NPG records. When asked why she had left Warner Brothers, Khan told the World African Network (on-line), "Your cut, for one, is relatively small. That right there was enough for me. That was not a very good business move on their part. You'd be surprised at all the bureaucracy that steps in there. It's taken me a year to record an album because they would say 'this song isn't radio friendly and this song is radio friendly?' It was really more like a meat market and it was not artistically friendly." One of the songs from this album, for which Khan wrote all but three tracks, is "Don't Talk 2 Strangers." The song recounts a mother's feelings of sadness as she says goodbye to a child. "I felt compelled to do this song because I remember my babies climbing into my suitcase when I had to pack to go on tour," she told Karen R. Good for *Interview* (November 1998). "That used to break my heart." The song was included on the soundtrack of the film *Down in the Delta*, the directorial debut of the poet Maya Angelou.

Chaka Khan currently owns homes in London, England, and New Jersey. She told Wilkerson that she enjoys living abroad because "[Americans] are very fickle. . . . If you don't have an album out in two years, they think you're dead and they forget about you. See, I can't have that. I didn't make an album for a year or two, but I'm still a recording artist. I just chose to make an album two years later than every [expletive] year. . . . It's nice to be in a place where they let you do what you can. . . .

I'm more free to pursue my life in all scales." The singer also told Wilkerson that she would prefer that her son, Demien, complete his schooling in Europe. "Right now in America there's a bounty on young black boys and I want him to get some kind of quality education, to speak other languages and live until he's 20 at least." Khan recently founded the Chaka Khan Foundation, through which she helps to raise money for AIDS awareness and the treatment and prevention of substance abuse. In addition, she produces a line of chocolates called Chakaletes, to help her support these causes. She is at work on an autobiography that details her involvement with drugs and alcohol.

Wilkerson described Khan, who is five feet two inches tall, as having "hieroglyphic eyes lined thick like an Egyptian deity." The singer is said to dye her ample hair auburn, to dress in black, and, as Wilkerson put it, to use "profanity like the garlic she heaps on her homemade pasta." She has at least one grandchild, a girl named Raeven. Her spare-time activities include growing herbs. — C.P.

Suggested Reading: *Chicago Tribune* VI p12 Apr. 13, 1980, with photos, XIII p20 Feb. 12, 1989, with photos; *Essence* p84+ Oct. 1995, with photos; *Interview* p109 Nov. 1996, with photo,

p70+ Nov. 1998, with photos; *Micrografx.com* (on-line); *New York Post* p42 Apr. 2, 1977, with photo; *New York Times* p56 Aug. 30, 1981, C p15 Aug 10, 1992, with photo; *Newsday* II p27 May 29, 1981, with photo, II p30 Mar. 6, 1983, with photo; *People* p113+ Apr. 21, 1980, with photo; *Toronto Globe and Mail* p12 June 24, 1981; *Vibe* p76 Sep. 1998, with photo, p177 Nov. 1998, with photo; *Washington Post* B p1 Mar. 17, 1975, with photo, G p1 Dec. 1, 1978, with photo, p18 July 31, 1992, with photo

Selected Recordings: *Rufus*, 1973; *Rags to Rufus*, 1974; *Rufusized*, 1974; *Rufus Featuring Chaka Khan*, 1975; *Ask Rufus*, 1977; *Street Player*, 1979; *Masterjam*, 1979; *Chaka*, 1978; *Naughty*, 1980; *Camouflage*, 1981; *What Cha' Gonna Do For Me*, 1981; *Chaka Khan*, 1982; *Rufus and Chaka Khan Live: Stompin' at the Savoy*, 1983; *I Feel for You*, 1984; *Destiny*, 1986; *Perfect Fit*, 1986; *C.K.*, 1988; *Life Is a Dance*, 1989; *The Woman I Am*, 1992; *The Very Best of Rufus Featuring Chaka Khan*, 1996; *Epiphany: The Best of Chaka Khan*, 1996; *Chaka Khan Greatest Hits: The Remix Project*, 1997; *Deeper Chaka: The Remix Collection*, 1997; *Come 2 My House*, 1998

Kim Jong Il

Feb. 16, 1942– Leader of North Korea. Address: c/o Central Committee of the Workers' Party of Korea, Pyongyang, Democratic People's Republic of Korea

"Depending on who is doing the talking, Kim Jong Il is a depraved movie fan who abuses women and alcohol, a terrorist who masterminded the 1983 murders of South Korean Cabinet members and the 1987 midair bombing of a South Korean airliner, a shy, awkward misunderstood technocrat who longs to be a statesman, or all, some, or none of the above," Elaine Sciolino wrote for the *New York Times* (July 17, 1994). Were Kim Jong Il the leader of a powerless country that barely registers a blip on the radar screen of U.S. foreign policy, the confusion surrounding the fundamental aspects of his personal history would not provoke much worry in intelligence and military circles. North Korea, however, presents a bona fide nuclear threat and boasts a huge conventional army that perpetually glares across the narrow demilitarized zone that has separated it from South Korea since 1953. Moreover, it has an unstable and probably oppressed populace of more than 23 million, large numbers of whom are given to demonstrations of fierce anti-Western sentiment and to a profound hatred of the economically thriving democracy that rests just to the south. North Korea tightly controls its borders, restricting access by foreign jour-

AP Photo

nalists, forbidding entry by most outsiders, and limiting travel by its citizens. Operating under this dark shroud of mystery, the Communist state controls the fuse to the powder keg that is the Korean peninsula, and with it the stability of the entire Pacific Rim.

It is therefore no comfort to Westerners that so little is known about North Korea's leader. Since the death of his father, Kim Il Sung (known as the "Great Leader"), in 1994, Kim Jong Il, who is known to his people as "Dear Leader," has been the de facto ruler of North Korea. The title of president is believed to have been retired after the death of the elder Kim; Kim Jong Il holds the title of chairman of the National Defense Commission. A career technocrat, Kim was groomed from an early age to succeed his father and rose quickly through the governmental ranks. But for a significant world leader, Kim is decidedly uncosmopolitan: he has seldom traveled outside his country, though he is believed to have studied at an East German aviation school in the 1960s and to have made a trip to China in 1983. To the knowledge of Westerners, his voice has been recorded only once, and he rarely makes public addresses. Nevertheless, he has been viewed by Western analysts as less of an ideological hard-liner than his father and as more likely both to inaugurate market reform in the country's rigidly controlled economy and to improve North Korea's abysmal human rights record. While there have been indications of such reform in recent years, millions of Koreans are believed to be on the verge of starvation; in the *New York Times* (August 20, 1999), Barbara Crossette reported that between two million and three million North Koreans may have starved to death between 1995 and 1998. In 1997 Kim wrote an essay that encouraged a thawing of relations with the United States, but then he undermined this move toward friendship by initiating submarine commando raids on South Korea, and his government later threatened to test a missile that could reach as far as Hawaii or Alaska. Despite the hopes of the West, Kim Jong Il has so far exhibited little in the way of concrete efforts toward liberalization. To many foreign-relations experts, North Korea presents a greater threat to peace and stability in the Far East and even beyond Asia's borders than any other nation on Earth.

Representative of the mystery surrounding Kim Jong Il, two competing versions of his birth exist. Western scholars hold that Kim was born on February 16, 1942 in a camp in Siberia, where his father was being trained in guerrilla tactics by members of the Soviet military in an effort to help overthrow the Japanese, who at the time occupied Korea. North Korea's official version of its leader's origins is far more fanciful: that his birthplace was in Korea, on Mount Paektu, a site of symbolic importance to the Korean people—and that his birth was foretold by an old man who had scaled Paektu and was told by a swallow, speaking with a human voice, that "on the 16th of April, a mighty general will be born who will one day rule the whole world." After this, the legend goes, a bright star shone throughout the day and night, flowers sprouted from the snow-covered land, and a rainbow appeared in the sky. The official biography adds that for all these mystical beginnings, Kim learned to hate the Japanese early on and once, as

a child, threw an inkwell against a map of Japan. Western sources are certain that Kim Jong Il's mother, Kim Jung Sook, died when he was seven years of age and that his father remarried and had two more sons.

After graduating from Namsan Senior High School, in 1960, Kim enrolled in Kim Il Sung University, where he took courses in politics and economics. He then rose quickly through the Communist hierarchy, becoming head of the Propaganda and Agitation Department by 1973. The following year he was officially designated his father's heir when his younger brother Kim Yong Ju mysteriously fell from grace. In 1980 Kim Jong Il was made a member of the Central Committee.

In the succeeding years Kim was suspected of having ordered two terrorists attacks. The first occurred in 1983, when a bomb in Rangoon, Burma, killed several visiting South Korean Cabinet members. The other was the 1987 destruction of a civilian airliner, which killed 115 people above the Indian Ocean. He has also been tied to the axing deaths of two U.S. soldiers in 1976 in the demilitarized zone that lies between North and South Korea. By 1991 he had become the leader of the Korean Worker's Party and was supreme commander of North Korea's armed forces. The following year rumors of Kim's instigation of brutal acts recurred, when he was accused of having ordered the execution of 10 military officials who were believed to have been plotting against him.

On July 8, 1994 Kim Il Sung died suddenly, prompting widespread fears that a power struggle would ensue within North Korea. Despite the fact that Kim Jong Il was acting as the head of the armed forces when his father died, many of the nation's top military leaders reportedly held him in low esteem, regarding him as less competent and intelligent than his father. But on July 13, 1994, according to *Facts on File* (July 14, 1994), the state-run radio confirmed the younger Kim's position by broadcasting the statement, "Our dear leader and comrade Kim Jong Il, the sole successor to our great leader, now holds the revered positions at the top of the party, the government, and the revolutionary forces."

The death of Kim Il Sung came during a time when North Korea was still adjusting to a post–Cold War world, which had seen the demise of its Communist trading partners. To redefine itself in the new world order, North Korea began to encourage foreign investment, but with every move away from the isolationism that was wreaking havoc on it, the country subverted the trend toward openness with belligerent acts. Though the elder Kim's unwillingness to disclose information about North Korea's nuclear potential had embroiled the country in an international controversy, he had initiated a detente between North Korea and its nemesis in the south by agreeing to a summit with the South Korean president. After Kim died the meeting was postponed indefinitely. (However, North Korean diplomats did meet with their South Korean counterparts in March 1997 to discuss a peace plan.)

The death of Kim Il Sung also interrupted high-level talks in Switzerland between North Korean and U.S. officials over North Korea's nuclear-development program. One of Kim Jong Il's first moves as leader was to resume those talks. On October 21, 1994 the two countries reached an agreement according to which the U.S. was to provide incentives to induce North Korea to halt activities linked to the development of nuclear weapons and power. The highly detailed accord called for the Communist nation to stop all activity at its Yongbyon reactor and to discontinue construction of other planned reactors. North Korea also promised to dismantle a reprocessing facility at Yongbyon that converted nuclear fuel into weapons-grade plutonium. In addition, it agreed to permit impartial inspectors to have full access to all its nuclear facilities. The U.S. and Japan were to assist in the building of two light-water nuclear reactors, and the U.S. was to provide enough crude oil to meet North Korea's energy needs during the construction. Furthermore, both North Korea and the U.S. promised to remove trade and investment barriers aimed at each other and to establish diplomatic offices in their respective capital cities. Known informally as the Agreed Framework and described in the *U.S. Department of State Dispatch* dated November 14, 1994, among other government news releases, the accord provoked mixed reactions from American government officials and analysts. Some considered it a major step on the road to global disarmament; others felt that the U.S. had made too many concessions and was leaving itself open to similar demands from Iran and other nations whose relations with the U.S. had long been tense.

In August 1998, in a demonstration of its military strength—and of its insistence on expending some of its dwindling resources on developing weapons—North Korea launched a new, long-range, multistage ballistic missile over Japan. The action prompted Japan to halt aid to North Korea. In July 1999 North Korea announced that it planned to test-fire another guided missile, known as the Taepodong-2, which experts believe has the capacity to travel up to 3,750 miles and could thus reach as far as Alaska or Australia. "Just testing that kind of missile—and then putting it up for sale on the international arms market—is enough to make huge swaths of the world very nervous," Tim Larimer reported in *Time* (August 23, 1999). "It's a perfect setup for high-priced extortion. . . . On the brink of collapse and with its people racked by starvation, North Korea's most successful business is one that involves pulling cash and aid out of South Korea, the U.S. and Japan in exchange for abandoning an arms buildup. Nobody knows just what 'Dear Leader' Kim Jong Il and his comrades would do to save themselves and their regime. And nobody wants to find out." On September 14, 1999 North Korea announced that it would temporarily halt its missile tests. In response, President Clinton ordered the lifting of various economic sanctions that had been in place for half a century.

Kim has been described as a portly, bespectacled man who wears a bouffant hairstyle. He is reportedly a fan of American cinema, especially the films of Elizabeth Taylor and the *Friday the 13th* slasher-movie series. He is also said to be fond of Western cigarettes and liquor. He is believed to have fathered two children and to own about 15 residences. — M.C.

Suggested Reading: *Maclean's* p20+ July 25, 1994, with photo; *New York Times* A p10 Mar. 25, 1993, I p16 Sep. 6, 1998; *Washington Post* A p1+ July 10, 1994, with photo; *Wilson Quarterly* p72+ Summer 1999; *World Press Review* p16+ Sep. 1994

Kiss

Criss, Peter. Dec. 20, 1947– Drummer.
Frehley, Ace. Apr. 27, 1951– Guitarist.
Simmons, Gene. Aug. 25, 1949– Singer; bassist.
Stanley, Paul. Jan. 20, 1952– Guitarist.
Address: c/o Mercury Records, 825 Eighth Ave., New York, NY 10019

"Kiss is truly the first bionic rock group, created, manipulated, and packaged with the same obsessive care that Baron von Frankenstein put into his monster . . . ," Wayne Robins wrote for *Newsday* (December 16, 1977) during the 1970s heyday of the supergroup Kiss. "It's not surprising that Kiss have become superheroes in their own Marvel comic book, or that they are as popular in Japan as they are here. . . . If only they were a *little* bit better musically, I would feel more comfortable with the flash, the costumes, and the media manipulation." The sentiment expressed by Robins is one with which Kiss has had to contend since its formation, in 1972. Indeed, many would say that it is not the group's music but their stage act—incorporating the members' Kabuki-style, black-and-white grease-painted faces and self-styled, larger-than-life personas—that has made them one of the most successful rock acts of all time.

Kiss released three relatively unnoticed albums in the early-to-mid-1970s and then shot to superstardom with their double live album, *Alive!* (1975), which has since gone multiplatinum. *Alive!* was the first in a string of million-selling albums that have earned Kiss a place in rock lore. Led by its co-founders, Gene Simmons, who in his devil-like attire took to calling himself the "Demon Lizard," and Paul Stanley, also known as the "Star Lover," the band has sold close to 80 million albums in its 25-year career.

In the early 1980s, Kiss's two other original members, Ace Frehley ("Space Man") and Peter Criss ("Cat Man")—who would always remain closely associated with the band's legend and mystique—departed from the group, leaving Simmons

Kiss (l. to r.): Ace Frehley, Peter Criss,
Gene Simmons, and Paul Stanley

Michael Sexton/Mercury Records

and Stanley with sagging record sales and a dwindling fan base. In response, the two remaining members added drummer Eric Carr, known for a time as "The Fox," and guitarist Vinnie Vincent, known briefly as "The Egyptian." Still, from 1980 to 1983 the Kiss Army, as the band's followers came to be known, continued to dwindle. Determined to build it up again, Simmons and Stanley, masters of the publicity stunt, pulled off one of the finest in their careers: they took their world-famous makeup *off*. Their next album, *Lick It Up* (1983), with its heavy sexual overtones and sleek, pop-metal style, returned the now makeup-less Kiss to platinum-record success. The band, with only slight variations in its lineup, maintained that level of success for the rest of the decade and well into the 1990s.

Then, in 1996, Simmons and Stanley suddenly fired Kiss's newer members, rehired Criss and Frehley, put their makeup back on, and embarked on a worldwide tour—the highest-grossing of 1996–97. The tour's success prompted the reunited Kiss to record their first studio album together in nearly 20 years. *Psycho Circus*, which reached stores in the fall of 1998, went gold within its first week of release.

As long ago as 1984, Gene Simmons made peace with Kiss's career-long dismissal by critics. "Even when we were selling more records than practically anybody—three million to five million with each album—radio wouldn't play us," he said in an interview with Lynn Van Matre for the *Chicago Tribune* (March 25, 1984). "It was as if they were saying, 'We don't care how popular you are, we don't like you and we won't play you.' But the fact that the band has never been totally accepted has helped us. Sure, it would be great if we got great reviews, but it doesn't bother me so much anymore if we don't. We've been around long enough that the success of the band speaks for itself; we don't feel we have to prove anything anymore."

Gene Simmons was born Chaim Witz on August 25, 1949 in Haifa, Israel. When he was nine years old, his Hungarian-Jewish parents separated, and he and his mother moved to the New York City borough of the Bronx, where Chaim began calling himself Gene Klein, and his mother, Florence, became a seamstress in a local dress factory. Florence, a Nazi concentration-camp survivor and a devoutly religious Jew, took young Gene to synagogue regularly.

Gene had a knack for languages, and by the time he entered high school, he could speak English, Hebrew, Hungarian, and German fluently. His main interests were not academic, however. And despite his mother's religious orthodoxy, when it came to things that appealed to him, nothing could "win out over the pull of 1960's American pop culture," as Geraldine Fabrikant wrote for the *New York Times* (February 23, 1997). "Once I saw Superman and the Vikings on TV having fun, getting the money and getting the girls," Simmons recalled to Fabrikant, "I thought I was on the wrong team. There was not a single person running around who had a beard [as many orthodox Jewish men do]. They [the men with beards] all looked miserable and never got the broads." In his sophomore year of high school, along with some friends, he published a science-fiction magazine.

After graduating from Richmond College on Staten Island and teaching sixth graders for a short time—"No matter how good the lessons were, the kids never applauded," he told *People* (August 18, 1980)—Gene changed his last name to Simmons, after the actress Jean Simmons, and set his sights on a career in rock-'n'-roll. He befriended fellow Bronx rock musician Stanley Eisen and formed a band while continuing to teach.

Eisen, later—and better—known as Paul Stanley, was born in Queens, another New York City borough, on January 20, 1952. He is the son of a furniture-store manager who moved his family to the Bronx when Stanley was very young. By the time Stanley was 20 years old, he had already taken his stage name and begun sharing vocals with Simmons in the band Wicked Lester, which was originally fashioned after the softer, medieval-style rock group Jethro Tull. Although Simmons, who played bass, and Stanley, who handled rhythm-guitar duties, worked comfortably together, the two felt they did not have enough talent to create a successful rock act. They made a habit of reading ads in rock magazines in hopes of hooking up with other musicians. At the time that they were doing this, Peter Criss placed an ad in *Rolling Stone* that read, "Drummer with 11 years experience will do anything to make it," according to Colette Dowling in the *New York Times Magazine* (June 19, 1977). Stanley and Simmons were the first to respond.

Before long, Criss, who was born in the New York City borough of Brooklyn as Peter Crisscoula on December 20, 1947, had joined Wicked Lester. The son of Loretta and Joseph Crisscoula, who owned and ran an antique shop, Criss was a solid Golden Gloves boxer in high school. That violent pursuit notwithstanding, in his late teens he did all he could to avoid getting drafted into the army, because he didn't want to fight in the Vietnam War. "I couldn't walk, I couldn't see, I acted gay," he told Fred Bernstein for *People* (October 20, 1980). "I just didn't believe in going to Vietnam." When Simmons called him, he was available to work with Wicked Lester.

Not long afterward, in late 1972, the band changed its name to Kiss and began experimenting with the hard rock made famous by, among others, Alice Cooper and Black Sabbath, two extremely popular acts at the time. The trio were also intrigued by the New York Dolls, then one of America's more popular bands, who in turn had been inspired by the English glitter rocker David Bowie. Simmons, Stanley, and Criss moved into a loft in Lower Manhattan and began auditioning guitarists. On January 17, 1973 Ace Frehley (born Paul Frehley in the Bronx on April 27, 1951) responded to an ad Simmons had placed in the *Village Voice*. Frehley became the "61st person to audition for Kiss," according to *acefrehley.com* (on-line), which went on to describe the event in the present tense: "He wanders into [the] loft wearing one red and one orange sneaker. He is invited to audition a second time [22 Jan.] and is subsequently hired."

On January 30, 1973 the band played its first gig at the Popcorn, a New York club, before a very small audience. That night Frehley created the now-famous Kiss logo, in which the two esses resemble bolts of lightning. "The face paint evolved as the[y] played nightly gigs at the local New York club the Diplomat Hotel," according to *rocknworld.com* (on-line). "Each night the members would do different characters until they evolved into what would be the most recognized faces in Rock n Roll."

Kiss's future manager, Bill Aucoin, first watched the band play at the Crystal Room of the Diplomat, not far from Times Square. "Figuring them to be both weird and aggressive enough to appropriate the old Alice Cooper audience, Aucoin thought he'd like to invest in them and persuaded Neil Bogart, the president of Casablanca [Records], to join him," Colette Dowling wrote. Aucoin had spent time at the New York station WNET as a cameraman and, briefly, as a director and had developed a syndicated rock show called *Flipside*. Through it, he had met many high-powered people in the music industry. He told Dowling, "I decided that rock had room for me in management. . . . When Kiss first went out, it cost us $8,000 a week just to keep them on the road. In 1975, the year royalties were held up, I had to put the entire tour on my American Express card." And, to both Aucoin and Casablanca's chagrin, Kiss's first three albums—*Kiss* (1974), *Hotter than Hell* (1974), and *Dressed to Kill* (1975)—did not sell well. On the brighter side, Kiss developed a substantial, mostly teenage male fan base while on the road. Encouraged in large part by the success of their ever-evolving stage show—which now included moments in which Simmons "breathed" fire by blowing kerosene from his mouth into a burning torch—the band decided to release a live album. *Alive!*, which came out in late 1975, became their first million-selling LP. Thanks to the success of *Alive!*, the single "Rock n Roll All Nite" from the band's previous effort, *Dressed to Kill*, became a hit, going all the way to number 12 on the *Billboard* charts.

Kiss's popularity continued with the release of *Destroyer*, in 1976, which included the Peter Criss–penned Top-10 soft-rock hit "Beth." With help from Bob Ezrin, formerly Alice Cooper's producer, the album featured heavily orchestrated songs with a pop feel.

Soon, Casablanca's PR department went into overdrive at the behest of Simmons and Aucoin, both of whom insisted that promotion was the key to the band's success. For example, to attract fans in Cadillac, Michigan, Kiss staged a free concert in the town's high-school football stadium, had all 2,000 students wear Kiss makeup, and solicited pro-Kiss statements from the mayor and the high-school principal. Next, as Colette Dowling reported, the band "jumped into an airplane and dumped out 2,000 fliers saying, 'Cadillac High, Kiss loves you.'" The strategy appeared to pay off. As Stephen Thomas Erlewine wrote for the *All-Music Guide* Web site, "Kiss mania was in full swing" during this period, as "thousands of pieces of [Kiss-related] merchandise hit the marketplace." In 1977 a Gallup poll found Kiss to be the most popular band in the United States; the group inspired pinball-machine games, board games, two Marvel comic books, and a live-action TV movie, *Kiss Meet the Phantom of the Park*. With the back-to-back platinum successes of *Rock and Roll Over* (1976) and *Love Gun* (1977), Kiss's name alone assured monetary success. In 1978 the band decided on one of the most ambitious promotional gimmicks of their careers—a self-titled solo album by each member, released on the same day. Although the albums each sold over a million copies before shipping, they did not sell as well as Kiss, Casablanca, and Aucoin had hoped.

Along with Kiss's popularity came trouble. As Bob Weiner reported for *People* (May 3, 1977), Ralph Lowery, a 17-year-old fan, inhaled a fatal dose of butane fumes, apparently inspired by Simmons's fire-breathing on stage. Simmons told Weiner, "I'm truly sorry, but we do not assume responsibility for something like that. Every time somebody's asked me how I do fire-breathing, I've said, 'I won't tell you,' because I don't want anybody else to take that risk—I've burned myself." In addition to that controversy, rumors began to circulate that the name Kiss was an acronym for Knights in Satan's Service. (Some believed that Kiss themselves spread the rumor, but members of the group have never admitted as much.) Bill Aucoin and Peter Criss reportedly had substance-abuse problems, while Ace Frehley, who had acknowledged that he had developed into a full-blown alcoholic after years on the road, often contributed nothing to the band's studio tracks. On *Destroyer*, according to *acefrehley.com* (on-line), the solo on the song "Sweet Pain" is played by session guitarist Dick Wagner. On the double live album *Alive II*, only "Rocket Ride" featured Ace Frehley's guitar playing. Rick Derringer, of "Rock n Roll Hoochie Koo" fame, and Bruce Kulick, who would become a member of Kiss in the 1980s, played on

most of the album's new songs. In later interviews, in self-defense, Frehley would point out that of the bandmembers' solo albums, only his was able to produce a hit single—"New York Groove." Propelled by "New York Groove," which reached number 13 on the *Billboard* singles chart, *Ace Frehley* went on to sell more than the three other Kiss solo albums combined.

Dynasty (1979), Kiss's next group effort, went platinum, but even so, the band's momentum seemed to be decreasing; by the turn of the decade, it looked as though the Kiss craze had run its course. *Unmasked* was released in 1980, and the disco-flavored "I Was Made for Loving You," co-written by up-and-coming songwriter Desmond Child, became a huge hit in continental Europe. But the album itself, in comparison with its predecessors, sold dismally, becoming the first Kiss disc since *Dressed to Kill* to fail to go platinum within a few months of its release. Critics attributed the record's disappointing sales in part to the departure of Peter Criss, who had been replaced, midway through the album's recording session, by drummer Eric Carr. The reason Criss left has always been a point of contention among the members. Stanley and Simmons have claimed that they fired Criss because of his drug addiction; Criss has insisted that he left of his own accord. Months after his departure, he recorded a solo album, *Out of Control* (1980), which had much of the soft-rock flavor of his hit single "Beth" and his first solo album, *Peter Criss*. He told Fred Bernstein that he was working toward "a more sophisticated following. I don't want to duck bottles anymore. I've had it with fire and bombs on stage. I see myself in a tux in Las Vegas." The album, despite decent initial sales, slowly sank into the discount bin. Criss would not be heard from for another 11 years.

Ace Frehley was the next to leave, shortly after the recording of *Creatures of the Night*, in 1982. The band's previous effort, *Music from "The Elder"* (1981), planned as the soundtrack for a never-completed film starring the band, had been a commercial failure (though it was one of the few Kiss albums to win critical praise). Legend has it that Frehley pleaded with his bandmates not to release the album after he heard the final cut. Then, after barely being heard on the recording of *Creatures*, Frehley left Kiss once the band had finished filming the video *I Love It Loud*. For years Frehley and the remaining original members of Kiss gave conflicting explanations of why the guitarist left; it wasn't until the early 1990s that Stanley and Simmons admitted to the press that Frehley had made the decision himself. Within a few months of his departure, Ace started his own band, Frehley's Comet, which, for more than 15 years, had moderate record sales and consistent touring success. Vinnie Vincent joined Kiss after Frehley's departure.

At that point the band was experiencing some of the lowest record sales in its history, and its members decided to try a drastic maneuver. "The group, weary of its carnival-like routine, wanted to remove their makeup and go in a new direction, and Mr. Aucoin was opposed," Fabrikant reported. After months of debate, Stanley and Simmons fired their longtime manager, removed their makeup, and released their most commercially successful album in three years, *Lick It Up* (1983). "Some of our business people thought we were out of our minds," Simmons told Lynn Van Matre. "The band had become huge in some parts of the world, like South America and the Far East. . . . But once you've created something and done everything to do in that format, if you don't move on, you wind up being a copy of yourself. I'm not sorry we took the makeup off. I'm thrilled." Simmons and Stanley made more money from *Lick It Up* than from any previous Kiss album, in large part because of the departure of Aucoin, who had collected a substantial portion of the band's profits throughout their 1970s glory days. The band subsequently hired Howard Marks, one of Aucoin's associates, as manager.

Animalyze, released in 1984, became Kiss's biggest-selling post-makeup album. During the album's recording, Vinnie Vincent, who had always been at odds with Simmons and Stanley, left the band and was replaced by Californian Mark St. John. (Vincent went on to form the Vinnie Vincent Invasion, who would release two minor pop-metal hits in the late 1980s.) During the *Animalyze* tour, St. John fell ill with Reiter's syndrome, an arthritic condition, and was replaced by Bruce Kulick, who would remain with the band for over a decade.

The mid-to-late 1980s proved to be a commercially rewarding, if artistically unremarkable, period for Kiss. With heavy metal's resurgence in the latter half of the decade, the members of Kiss were looked upon as elder statesmen of the genre, their stature comparable to Ozzy Osbourne's and Alice Cooper's. This perception boosted Kiss's record sales. *Asylum* (1985) and *Crazy Nights* (1987) both sold well, and the group had its first hit in some years with "Reason to Live," from *Crazy Nights*. The song became one of the most heavily requested hits of the year on MTV. In 1988 the band released a retrospective album, with two new tracks, entitled *Smashes, Thrashes, and Hits*. Peter Criss was reportedly angered by, and critics voiced their disdain for, Eric Carr's cover version of "Beth." The controversy, as usual, only increased sales, a trend that carried over into the band's next release, *Hot in the Shade* (1989). That album spawned another hit, "Forever," a song similar to many of the pop-tinged metal ballads very popular around this time, and the song became Kiss's biggest seller since "Beth."

As the band toured and then returned to the studio to record another album, a strange story surfaced, first reported in the tabloid the *Star*. "The story was dramatic—and pathetic," Cynthia Sanz and three other journalists wrote for *People* (January 21, 1991). "'Kiss Star Hits the Skids' trumpeted the headline . . . followed by the wrenching de-

tails of how Peter Criss, a former drummer for the once widely popular glam-rock band, had become a homeless alcoholic, panhandling nickels and sleeping on the floor of the men's room at the Santa Monica Pier." Soon it was discovered that a man named Christopher Dickinson, originally from Evanston, Illinois, had been impersonating Criss for years and was responsible for the confusion. The real Criss heard about the story while living in his Redondo Beach, California, home with his wife, Debra, whom he had married while still with the band. During this episode, Criss's mother died. "In the midst of the funeral and the burial, people would come up and ask if it was true that I was a bum," Criss told *People*. "And I couldn't do anything about this because my first concern was my mother. It was a frigging nightmare." Dickinson eventually confessed to the hoax.

Also in 1991, while Kiss was recording its next album, Eric Carr died of cancer. The band released *Revenge* (1992) and dedicated both the album and the upcoming tour to Carr, who had been with the band longer than any other Kiss drummer. Eric Singer, who had played for a short time with the group Badlands, stepped in to finish the record. The songs "Domino" and "I Just Wanna" charted well, and critics gave the album decent reviews—a rare occurrence for a Kiss record. The band released *Alive III* in 1993.

Kiss was now back in vogue, as demonstrated by two tribute albums recorded by various artists. The first, *Hard to Believe* (1993), was done by top alternative acts of the day, including Nirvana, who sang the track "Do You Love Me," originally from the *Destroyer* LP. The second, a more pop-oriented effort entitled *Kiss My Ass* (1994), featured such acts as Toad the Wet Sprocket, Lenny Kravitz, and Garth Brooks. Around the same time, the popular alternative band Stone Temple Pilots played a gig decked out in Kiss makeup and costumes. The time seemed ripe for a Kiss reunion, especially considering the revival of 1970s fashion around the country. In 1995 Paul Stanley and Gene Simmons invited Ace Frehley and Peter Criss to join them in playing an acoustic set on the popular MTV concert program *MTV Unplugged*. The program won high ratings, and the band decided to capitalize on their revived popularity by embarking on the 1996 Alive Worldwide Tour. It has been projected that Kiss earned over $130 million on the tour, which, according to Pollstar, was the highest-grossing tour of 1996–97.

Todd McFarlane, a highly successful comic-book artist, publisher, and toy manufacturer, struck a deal with Kiss in late 1997 involving the manufacture of a new line of Kiss action figures. Then, eager to capitalize on the group's swelling popularity, the comic-book publisher Image Comics, which puts out McFarlane's popular superhero title *Spawn*, printed a new set of comic books based on Kiss's new studio album, *Psycho Circus*. The album, released in the fall of 1998, sold beyond predictions, shooting into the *Billboard* Top

10 in its first week of release. "As culturally irrelevant and hopelessly wack as they might be . . . ," Lorraine Ali wrote for the *Rolling Stone Network* (on-line), "Kiss still have a place in rock, even if it is one created and occupied only by them."

Around the time of *Psycho Circus*'s release, the music publisher Bizarre Music, which represents Alice Cooper, the rocker whom Kiss has credited with greatly influencing their act and music, filed a lawsuit against the band, in which it charged that "Dreamin'," a cut from *Psycho Circus*, copied Cooper's 1971 hit "Eighteen." (Cooper himself reportedly had nothing to do with the lawsuit.) Despite the suit, the group embarked on another world tour—this time using a giant screen on which fans could watch the group and themselves in 3-D. While playing to a sold-out crowd at Madison Square Garden in New York City, Kiss was presented with its 30th gold record.

Although all four members of the reunited Kiss are expected to make millions of dollars from the current album and tour, the process of recording the new album did not go smoothly. While in the studio, Frehley reportedly clashed with returning producer Bob Ezrin and threatened to leave the band once again if some of his songs, which had been significantly reworked, overdubbed, and rewritten without his consent, were not released the way he wanted them. After an intense feud, a compromise was reached, and the track "Into the Void" was rerecorded, with Frehley on guitar.

In August 1999 Kiss's first feature-length film, *Detroit Rock City*, arrived in U.S. theaters. Named after a hit song from their album *Destroyer* and co-starring Edward Furlong and Sam Huntington, *Detroit Rock City* is about four Kiss fans who travel to a 1978 Kiss concert. The film proved to be a commercial and critical disaster. In a representative review, Janet Maslin wrote for the *New York Times* (August 13, 1999), "Apparently there are no bigger Kiss fans than the band members themselves, who are helpfully involved in a feature-length valentine to their enduring greatness. . . . The idea [for the film] might have promise if it had even a trace of self-mockery, but no such luck. . . . [The cast] never has much chance to shine." A few weeks after the release of *Detroit Rock City*, at a September World Championship Wrestling event, Kiss introduced a professional wrestler called the Demon, who wore make-up similar to that of Gene Simmons. The audience's reaction to the Demon during his initial outing was so lackluster that Kiss scrapped their plans for him, and he never wrestled in an official match.

"We have a meat-and-potatoes rock group," Simmons told Geraldine Fabrikant during the group's 1997 interview with her. "That's the image of who we are." "The audience doesn't care that we're not kids," Stanley declared to the *New York Times* reporter. "It makes us bigger than life." — M.B.

Suggested Reading: *Forbes* (on-line) Sep. 23, 1996, with photo; *New York Times* C p3+ Feb. 23, 1997, with photo; *New York Times Magazine* p18+ June 19, 1977, with photos; *People* p45 May 3, 1977, with photos, p100+ Aug. 18, 1980, with photos, p71+ Oct. 20, 1980, with photos, p101+ Jan. 21, 1991, with photos; *rocknworld.com* (on-line); *rollingstonenetwork.com* (on-line)

Selected Recordings: *Hotter Than Hell*, 1974; *Kiss*, 1974; *Alive!*, 1975; *Dressed to Kill*, 1975; *The Originals*, 1976; *Destroyer*, 1976; *Rock and Roll Over*, 1976; *Alive II*, 1977; *Love Gun*, 1977; *Peter Criss*, 1978; *Ace Frehley*, 1978; *Gene Simmons*, 1978; *Paul Stanley*, 1978; *Dynasty*, 1979; *Unmasked*, 1980; *Music from "The Elder,"* 1981; *Creatures of the Night*, 1982; *Lick It Up*, 1983; *Animalize*, 1984; *Asylum*, 1985; *Crazy Nights*, 1987; *Hot in the Shade*, 1989; *Revenge*, 1992; *Alive III*, 1993; *Unplugged*, 1996; *Carnival of Souls: The Final Sessions*, 1997; *Psycho Circus*, 1998

Selected Films: *Kiss Meet the Phantom in the Park*, 1979; *Detroit Rock City*, 1999

Klass, Perri

1958– Pediatrician; writer. Address: c/o Boston Medical Center, 1 Boston Medical Center Plaza, Boston, MA 02218

Writing for *New York* (October 14, 1985), Dinitia Smith described Perri Klass as a "second-generation feminist," because "in her fiction and in her life, the questions that torment so many older women seem not to trouble her at all." Klass, a well-known writer and pediatrician, first attracted attention when, while studying medicine at Harvard University in the 1980s, she wrote articles for such high-profile publications as the *New York Times* and *Discover*. She managed all that while caring for her infant son and working on the follow-up to her first novel, *Recombinations*; she has since published several other fiction and nonfiction books. While she is often portrayed in the media as a superwoman who can accomplish anything, Klass is modest about her achievements, the sacrifices she has made, and the opportunities she has had throughout her life. "I'm privileged," she told Smith. "I have it easy financially and emotionally. In many ways I'm being a very good girl, doing what I was raised to do. . . . I have chosen this way of life. There are lots of women all over . . . with children and maybe two jobs, who have no money and no encouragement. What about the women cleaning floors in the hospital who are raising their children on their own—they didn't have the luxury of deciding to do it."

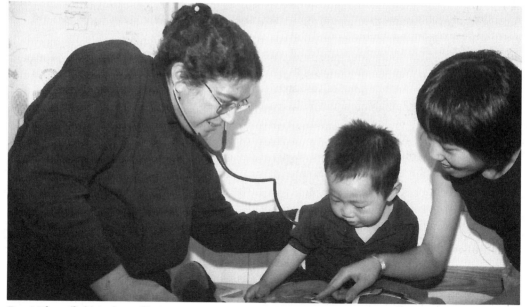

Perri Klass (left) in her office

Perri Klass was born in 1958 in Trinidad, where her father, Morton Klass, an anthropologist who also wrote science fiction, was working. According to Judith Rosen, writing in *Publishers Weekly* (June 1, 1992), on the day Perri was born, her mother—Sheila Solomon Klass—wrote the final pages of her first novel, *Come Back on Monday.* Sheila Solomon Klass went on to write eight more books and taught English at the City University of New York. Perri Klass wrote her first story—an account of her family's move from Vermont to New York City—when she was only four years old. As a child she also loved reading. "I was very eclectic," she told Cable Neuhaus for *People* (November 18, 1985). "I went happily from the classics to the backs of cereal boxes to Nancy Drew." Klass has two younger siblings, David and Judy, who are also writers. "In my family it's taken for granted that everyone writes," Klass explained to Neuhaus. "It's respected as something worthwhile to do."

When she was in the sixth grade, Klass's family moved from New York City to Leonia, New Jersey, and Klass was transferred from the Agnes Russell School, which was run by the Teachers College of Columbia University, to one of Leonia's public elementary schools. Because the student body and the teaching methods at her new school were very different from those in her school in New York, Klass had a difficult time adjusting. "At school in New York it was considered a worthwhile thing to read a book," she told Dinitia Smith. "In this school reading a book under your desk was considered a capital offense. Reading and writing were only allowed at a certain time. It became axiomatic that kids should be *made* to read and write." When she was in junior high school, her teachers often pointed ed to Klass's work to demonstrate to other students

how their own work should be done, and her classmates began to resent her. Klass told Smith that because she was unpopular, she would often spend "months at a time in a fantasy world." The isolation and awkwardness she felt during her adolescence later served as subject matter for her short story "Trivia," in which a young girl repeatedly beats her camp counselor at a trivia game. The heroine cannot, however, answer correctly any of the questions about movie stars. The counselor in the story tells the girl, "I guess you better work on being smart, because you sure are never going to be anything else. . . . Maybe an ugly little girl who's going to grow up an ugly woman just isn't too interested in watching the pretty ones." When she was a little older, Klass enrolled at the Leonia Alternative High School, where she excelled, especially in writing. Two pieces that Klass wrote in high school were published in *Seventeen* as runners-up in the magazine's annual short-story contest.

After graduating from high school, in 1974, Klass entered Radcliffe College (now Harvard-Radcliffe), in Cambridge, Massachusetts. She initially chose pre-med as a major, but after she got a number of C's in her classes, she switched to biology. Klass also continued to write, but for some time she was unsuccessful in getting any of her stories published; she estimates that during her years of undergraduate study, she received about 300 letters of rejection for her work. After graduating, with honors, Klass furthered her education at the University of California at Berkeley, where she studied the evolutionary biology of parasitic organisms. She then went to Rome, Italy, where her boyfriend, Larry Wolff, had begun a fellowship. While she was living abroad, the U.S. magazine *Mademoiselle* published one of her stories—her first published work as an adult. Shortly after that, Tom Jenks, an editor at *Esquire*, also discovered her talent; although he was unsuccessful in publishing her work in *Esquire*, he introduced Klass to Maxine Groffsky, who became her agent.

In about 1981 Klass and Wolff returned to the U.S. and took up residence in Cambridge, where Klass studied medicine at Harvard and Wolff got a job as a lecturer. In 1983 Klass's short story "The Secret Lives of Dieters" won the prestigious O. Henry Award. That exposure was followed by an article about Klass in *Mademoiselle* that described her hectic existence—while attending medical school, she was also writing articles for the science magazine *Discover*, teaching a freshman English class, and tutoring undergraduate students. Moreover, she had recently given birth to a son, Benjamin, who was given her surname.

At about this time Maxine Groffsky encouraged Klass to write about her experiences as a young mother in medical school. Klass took her suggestion, and thus became the youngest writer ever to be published in the "Hers" column of the *New York Times*. ("Hers" and another column, "About Men," later appeared on alternate Sundays in the *New York Times Magazine*; the magazine now publishes similar columns under the title "Lives.") "Mothers everywhere sent it to their daughters," Klass told Neuhaus about one among the series of articles she wrote, in which she described how it felt to work 120 hours a week while writing from midnight to 4:00 a.m., and how she had planned for her first child to be born during her second year of medical school, before she would have to start interning. In 1984 Klass won her second O. Henry Award, for "Not a Good Girl," and in 1985 her first novel, *Recombinations*, was published. A collection of Klass's short stories, entitled *I Am Having an Adventure*, was published in 1986.

Most of Klass's early fictional works were about women in the process of being liberated from traditional roles and attitudes. The heroine of "Not a Good Girl" is a scientist who feels no remorse after having sexual relations with a man she dislikes. In another story, "A Romance in Brief," a woman is similarly unruffled when her lover tells her that he fantasizes about men. And in "The Almond Torte Equilibrium," two lesbian lovers are forced to deal with the consequences of infidelity, when one of them becomes pregnant by a former boyfriend; they eventually work things out and decide to have the child. For *Recombinations*, Klass created Anne Montgomery, a career woman who seems able to balance a demanding position at a bioengineering company in New York City with what might be described as an overly active social schedule and a scintillating love life. Assessing the novel for the *New York Times Book Review* (September 29, 1985), Caroline Seebohm felt "frustrated" by *Recombinations*: "[Klass] is the person who, as many readers of this newspaper will recall, wrote a memorable series of 'Hers' columns that described life as a Harvard University medical student who was

also married and newly delivered of a baby," she wrote. (Actually, Klass and Wolff have never married.) "She evoked the conflicting pressures of husband, baby, and studies with verve and passion. The urgent and poignant prose of those articles is sorely needed here to give *Recombinations* one of the life-giving injections she knows how to give so competently to her patients." Still, a reviewer for *Library Journal* (October 1, 1985) felt that Klass had created "a gentle social satire in a manner similar to that of Margaret Drabble. But Klass's voice is her own—upbeat, unaffected, and wisely funny." Dinitia Smith described Klass's writing style as "minimal and unadorned." "There are few descriptive passages, and she often writes in the present tense. There is a certain detachment in Klass's writing, as there is about Perri Klass herself."

When asked how she managed to be so productive as a writer while meeting the high demands of medical school and motherhood, Klass told Paula Span for the *Washington Post* (April 1, 1987), "You sort of fit it in around the edges. . . . The best metaphor is with someone who has musical talent . . . to whom life would be incomplete without playing the piano. You do it because you do it. For yourself." Because Klass was so consumed by her work, however, much of the writing that she managed to do during her medical internship was about the experience of becoming a doctor. The resulting book, titled *A Not Entirely Benign Procedure*, was published in 1987. In the *New York Times Book Review* (May 10, 1987), Robert Grant wrote that in this book Klass "makes us privy to her tears of frustration, her wish to trade places with a sick patient merely for the luxury of getting a decent night's sleep, and her ambivalence during her pregnancy, about being both patient and budding doctor." According to Klass's book, doctors often see pregnancy as a "perilous if not pathological condition. None of my medical school classmates . . . would have been capable of answering even the most basic questions asked by the people in my childbirth classes." She also noted that the relationship between doctor and patient sometimes becomes antagonistic, in many cases because patients blame doctors when they are not getting better. And, as Klass wrote, "[Doctors] don't say, or think, 'Mrs. Hawthorne's cancer is making her sicker.' We say, 'Mrs. Hawthorne's crumping on me.'" *A Not Entirely Benign Procedure* was generally admired for its honesty on a subject rarely addressed by authors or doctors.

Klass's next two books, published in 1990 and 1992, respectively, were the popular novel *Other Women's Children* and a collection of essays, *Baby Doctor*. Each book is a product of Klass's experiences as a pediatrician. In the *New York Times Book Review* (September 9, 1990), Michael Dorris called *Other Women's Children* "superb" and wrote, "If there were space for but one novel in a time capsule labeled 'American Career Woman: 1990,' this novel would be a prime candidate. Rarely has the tightrope act of taking on competing and equally pressing responsibilities been as well or as honestly delineated." Unlike the heroine of *Recombinations*, the protagonist of this book, Amelia Stern, "never manages to get everything fully under control for more than a few minutes at a time, and she is castigated, professionally or domestically, at her every slip," Dorris wrote. The same struggles are addressed in a different format in *Baby Doctor*, which includes a controversial article originally published in the *New York Times Magazine*, "Are Women Better Doctors?" One of the drawbacks of *Baby Doctor*, according to Melissa Fay Greene's review for the *Chicago Tribune* (July 5, 1992), is that in spite of her honesty, Klass indeed comes across as "a not particularly appetizing person," as she described herself in *Baby Doctor*. "She works a hundred hours a week as a pediatric intern," Greene wrote, "has at home a three-year-old son whom she sees on alternate days and an accommodating husband toward whom she feels almost permanently apologetic, gets an average of four hours sleep a night while on duty, has trouble finding the time for her writing, . . . reports herself resented by other women as a modern superwoman, . . . and believes male interns are permitted to juggle home and work under less critical scrutiny. Because Dr. Klass clearly has organized her life as it suits her, it is hard to avoid thinking, 'Who asked her to take all that on?'"

Greene has not been the only person to express a dislike for Klass, and envy has at times been a serious problem in her life. According to Paula Span, the playwright Wendy Wasserstein placed Klass on a list of "unbearable women" that was published in *New York Woman*, and Klass has several times been accused of plagiarism and medical incompetence. She was also once sent a gift-wrapped package filled with human excrement. "It was horrible," Klass told Span of the incident. "Whoever was doing it really and truly hated me." Asked why she thought someone would be so intensely jealous of her, Klass said, "I've generated the fascination myself, in a way. I made my own life public. . . . I made myself a character . . . a sort of obnoxious character. . . . I sometimes wonder—am I being that obnoxious person? Or failing to live up to her?" Klass told Judith Rosen that the incident had left her "much more paranoid than [she] otherwise would have been," and that she often worried that the harassment might continue or extend to her family.

Klass has frequently been asked why she has chosen to pursue the demanding work of a pediatrician while she has achieved ample success as a writer. "One of the things I like about pediatrics in particular is that it's useful," Klass explained to Rosen. "Children get sick all the time. It's not good for children to be sick. You don't have to argue about this. . . . [Pediatrics] is a useful, practical skill with which I will be able to support myself whether or not people buy my novels." Klass also feels that being a doctor is more suitable to her temperament than writing. "I'm not someone who would be happy shut up with myself and my word processor all day every day. I like colleagues, and gossip, and going out of the house, another life besides my own room and my Microsoft Word program," she said.

Perri Klass currently lives in Boston, Massachusetts, with Wolff, her longtime companion, and their two children, Benjamin and Josephine, who was born in 1990. According to Neuhaus, Wolff, who has written three books and is now a professor at Boston College, has been an integral part of Klass's success by helping with childcare and housework. He and Klass have, however, made many sacrifices for their careers. Klass has said that her schedule rarely allows her to read the fiction she used to enjoy and that she is hardly ever able to read newspapers, go to the movies, or even have time to herself. "If you lived alone, you'd stare at the walls and decompress," she told Span. "Those of us with families have to be reasonably cheerful. I'm not entitled to come home and whine and behave like a brat. . . . If you have a family, you owe them what time you have out of the hospital." When asked if she regrets not spending more time with her young children, she told Span, "When people make predictions about how your child will grow up, well, it was always clear in my family how much happier my mother was working. She stopped for a while when my brother and I were little, and she's never pretended they were the happiest years of her life."

Klass currently works at Dorchester House, a medical facility in one of Boston's less privileged neighborhoods, and at the Boston Medical Center, where she is an assistant professor of pediatrics. She is also the director of the Reach Out and Read program, which counsels pediatricians on how to integrate books and literacy into pediatric care. "What happens in the years between birth and kindergarten is absolutely essential," Daniel A. Heller, writing in *English Journal* (March 1997), quoted her as saying. "Children either start school liking books and understanding what they are or they start school way behind, set up for failure." Klass also continues to write both fiction and nonfiction. She has won a total of five O. Henry Awards for her short stories—the most recent for "City Sidewalks," in 1995.

In her 1992 *Publishers Weekly* article, Judith Rosen described Klass as having a good sense of humor and as being "modest about her achievements." In the same article, Klass was quoted as calling herself "overweight" and "grouchy." Klass enjoys sewing, crocheting, and cooking Italian and Indian food. She also collects religious shell art and romantic medical fiction. Klass told Rosen that she often finds fault with the way journalists write about her. "It seems forced, something that is done particularly to women or felt about women. You don't read articles about men that start out, 'Hey guys, you won't hate him even though he's got a pretty good body and he's a CEO.' There's no assumption that every word that is written about [a man's] achievements is a knife in the heart of all his brothers. I don't really understand why that should be an assumption made about women." — C.P.

Suggested Reading: *Chicago Tribune* XIV p6 July 5, 1992, with photo; *New York* p56+ Oct. 14, 1985, with photos; *New York Times Book Review* p11+ Sep. 29, 1985, with photo, p7 Sep. 9, 1996; *People* p167+ Nov. 18, 1985, with photos; *Publishers Weekly* p41+ June 1, 1992, with photo; *English Journal* p109 Mar. 1997

Selected Books: *Recombinations*, 1985; *I Am Having an Adventure: Stories*, 1986; *A Not Entirely Benign Procedure: Four Years as a Medical Student*, 1987; *Other Women's Children*, 1990; *Baby Doctor*, 1992

Rocky Thies/Saba

Koch, Bill
(koke)

May 3, 1940– Oil-industry executive; yacht racer. Address: c/o Oxbow Corp., 1601 Forum Pl., West Palm Beach, FL 33401

A self-proclaimed contrarian, the oil-industry executive and yacht racer Bill Koch professes to be driven by three desires. "One is success," he told Bob Fisher for the London *Observer* (March 19, 1995); "one is doing it my way, according to my style; and I guess the third thing is doing that completely differently from anyone else." The second and third of those motivations go far in explaining Koch's decision to sponsor an all-female crew in

the 1995 America's Cup, yachting's most prestigious competition; the team, assembled under the aegis of Koch's *America³* racing syndicate, was the first in the 147-year history of the contest to exclude men. Although success eluded them—the women lost to the crew of "Mr. America's Cup," Dennis Conner, in the defender's trial series—both the team and Koch made a big splash, one that captured attention internationally.

Compared with his long-held passions for wine (by the mid-1990s he had collected upwards of 28,000 bottles) and art (his private collection includes works by such masters as Monet, Renoir, Cézanne, and Picasso), yacht racing is a relatively new interest for Bill Koch. A sometime sailor in his youth, he was about 44 years old when he took up the sport in earnest. His earliest experiences in competitive sailing were with maxis, vessels approximately 80 feet long that race with up to 30 crew members. He staffed his first maxi, *Matador*, with former Olympic medalists and America's Cup winners; in their first competition, they came in last. One reason for their dismal performance, Koch surmised, was lack of teamwork, which he traced to personality clashes among the stellar crew, many of whom had super-large egos. Another reason, he concluded, was deficiencies in the design of his boat.

Koch, who earned his bachelor's, master's, and Ph.D. degrees in chemical engineering at the Massachusetts Institute of Technology (MIT), in Cambridge, Massachusetts, already had an above-average knowledge of design. Spurred by his newfound interest in sailing to investigate the scientific theories employed in boat design, he discovered, to his dismay, that nautical architecture entailed more art than science. He told John Garrity for *Sports Illustrated* (April 20, 1992), "I'd ask each [boat designer] what made a boat go fast, and he'd give me mystical explanations, not scientific ones." By selecting what seemed to be the best features of several boats, Koch came up with a new maxi, *Matador²* (called "Matador squared"). Koch entered the boat, which he furnished with a new, more cooperative crew, in the 1990 and 1991 Maxi World Championships, and he won both. Koch then turned his focus on winning sailing's most coveted prize, the America's Cup.

In the years since Dennis Conner had lost the America's Cup, in 1983 (it was the first time ever that a country other than the U.S. had captured the prize), the consensus among competitive yachting's prognosticators was that the America's Cup would be increasingly difficult to keep in the States. Dennis Conner had succeeded in winning it back in 1987, but the emergence of a broad international field of racing talent and the availability of ample financial backing presented a serious challenge to the United States' domination of yacht racing. By launching a campaign to defend the America's Cup, Koch was acting against convention: it was almost unknown for a virtual novice to enter yachting's most competitive event, and particularly startling in what was arguably the most competitive era in its history.

Koch founded the *America³* (pronounced "America cubed") racing syndicate, with the idea of financing his campaign partly with his personal funds and partly with corporate donations. In addition, he resolved to become the first skipper-owner to race since Ted Turner, who won the America's Cup in 1977. Unlike Turner, a three-time winner of the title yachtsman of the year, Koch did not have much sailing experience to fall back on. In light of that deficiency, Koch's supreme self-confidence galled many sailing veterans. One of them, the New Zealander Chris Dickson, pointedly said to Angus Phillips for the *Washington Post* (May 6, 1991), "I think I can drive a car pretty well, but I wouldn't try to go out and race a Formula One car." As the only nonprofessional skipper entered in the regatta, Koch expected criticism. As he explained to Phillips, "You come on board and some of the crew have that look that says, 'Oh, no, not the owner again.' They want you to just sign the checks and let them run the boat."

The "cubed" symbol in the name of Koch's syndicate stands for "Talent, Teamwork, Technology" (and led to jocular references to the *America³*'s sailors as the "cubens"). Regarding talent and teamwork, Koch, remaining true to his philosophy and reputation for flying in the face of convention, hired a crew of what were considered second-tier sailors, with not a single star among them. The other crews had more talent overall: team Dennis Conner had their namesake; the Italian team, taking advantage of a Cup rule allowing two-year residents of a country to be considered nationals, hired the San Franciscan Paul Cayard; and the Japanese team, under the same rule, was skippered by Chris Dickson.

Koch believed that the state-of-the-art technology that he would be bringing to the race would overcome his competitors' advantage in experience. At a cost of $5 million each, he financed the construction of four carbon-fiber yachts, which were manufactured at Hercules Aerospace Inc.'s plant in Magna, Utah. Designed by physicists, they incorporated breakthroughs in hull and keel design. In addition, he helped develop a sail made from carbon fibers that were imbedded in a liquid polymer and then baked between layers of clear plastic. The process produced a sail just as strong as traditional sails (which are made of woven fibers) but weighing only two-thirds as much.

When the dust, or, rather, sea spray cleared at the finish line of the 1992 America's Cup, Koch had proved himself right. He defeated Conner in the best-of-13 defender's trial series seven races to four, and he successfully defended the Cup against the Cayard-led Italians four races to one in the best-of-seven finals. Though on paper the Italians were formidable in financing, technology, and experience, *America³* had faced a greater challenge from the under-financed Conner, whom Bill Koch later praised as "probably the greatest sailor that's ever, ever been."

In his next campaign for the America's Cup, in 1995, Koch functioned strictly as organizer and financial backer of the sport's first all-female crew. "What was attractive to me about the all-woman team was that it fits in with my philosophy that you don't have to be a superstar to win," he told Bob Fisher. "You have to have the right attitude, the right dedication, the right discipline, and a fast boat. If you have that, you can win with teamwork." Koch commissioned the building of a new technologically advanced racer, named *Mighty Mary* after his mother. While many observers questioned the ability of women to compete with men, especially during multiple physically demanding tacks, clearly the crew's biggest obstacle was its relative inexperience. Koch, whom some people had lauded for his support of the all-women's team, was later criticized by many of the same people for signing off on a decision to replace the starting helmsman and tactician, J.J. Isler (a woman), with a man—his 1992 starting helmsman, David Dellenbaugh. Koch had made the switch as a last-ditch effort to snatch the *Mighty Mary* from the jaws of defeat, and his detractors charged that he had sold out for the sake of winning. His team did not win, however; his second attempt at the Cup ended in defeat to Dennis Conner in the defender's trials. In the end, the Cup went to New Zealand. Koch announced his intention to recapture it in Auckland in 1999–2000, but he later sold all his assets from his 1995 syndicate to the Italian Prada Challenge crew.

The tenacity Bill Koch has exhibited in his sailing career is very much a family trait. Born on May 3, 1940 in Wichita, Kansas, William I. Koch is one of the four sons of Fred Chase Koch and his wife, Mary Clementine (Robinson) Koch. He has a twin brother, David, and two older brothers, Charles and Fred R. His father, who graduated in the 1920s from MIT with a degree in chemical engineering, developed a process for extracting gasoline from crude oil that significantly improved upon the method then in use, and he established a business, the Rock Island Oil & Refining Co., that capitalized on his invention. According to John Garrity, in the 1920s Fred C. Koch profited handsomely from one of his biggest jobs—upgrading 15 oil refineries in the Soviet Union, during the early years of the dictatorship of Joseph Stalin. In the 1940s, according to Garrity, about 40 of Fred C. Koch's American competitors, whose oil-extraction methods were similar to but less efficient than his, sued Koch for patent infringement. (In another version of events, Brian O'Reilly reported in *Fortune* [February 17, 1997] that Koch's competitors took him to court in the 1920s and that he took on the project in the Soviet Union because he was unable to carry on his business in the U.S.) In 1952 the judge presiding over the trial was found to be taking bribes from the competing oil companies, and Koch was awarded a settlement of $1.5 million.

Apparently fearful that his sons would become spoiled by wealth, Fred C. Koch made the boys do menial jobs on the family ranch, in Wichita, Kansas, and pushed them to adopt an outdoorsman's lifestyle. "We had a silver spoon, but he threw us out to the wolves," Bill Koch once said, as quoted by Barbara Lloyd in the *New York Times* (May 6, 1992). When the eldest son, Fred R., was 33, he was accused of stealing money from another man. Although he denied the charges, the incident led Fred C. to partially disinherit Fred R. and to groom his next son, Charles, to take over his company. After Charles became chairman, in 1967, he expanded the firm (renamed Koch Industries) into the second-largest privately owned corporation in the United States (the first is Cargill, which deals in grain). Koch Industries refines approximately 4 percent of the gasoline produced in the U.S. and is involved in almost every aspect of the oil industry; its subsidiaries include Purina Mills, which produces animal feed.

Beginning in 1975 Bill Koch held a series of high-ranking positions in Koch Industries, culminating with the presidency of a Boston-based subsidiary, Koch Carbon Inc. Under his stewardship Koch Carbon reportedly became a drain on the principal company's resources. While with Koch Industries, Bill expressed unhappiness with both Charles's management style and what he considered the unnecessarily low dividends paid to stockholders. With his brother Fred and some others, Bill reportedly controlled a majority of Koch Industries' stock. In 1980, backed by Fred and the other controlling stockholders, he called a meeting to elect new board members and increase dividends—in effect, to weaken Charles's control. Just before the meeting, David Koch persuaded one of Bill's followers to make an about-face. That was enough to thwart Bill's plan, and soon after, the board voted to fire him. In 1983 Bill Koch sold his shares of Koch Industries to Charles and David (who now jointly own 80 percent of the company) for $470 million; simultaneously, Fred sold his 14 percent interest.

Bill Koch used a portion of the money to start his own business, Oxbow Corp., a privately held alternative-energy company that, among other things, sells electricity from thermal plants in Nevada to utilities in southern California. Bill has cited Oxbow's excellent fiscal health to silence his detractors in the business world. "Look at my business record now," he told Bob Cox for the *Wichita Eagle* (March 7, 1998, on-line). "I've got a company that's doing $500 million in sales, and we're making $50 million to $60 million a year." Koch's forays into venture capitalism have not worked out as well. In 1993 he made an unsuccessful bid for the faltering Hollywood studio Metro Goldwyn Mayer. He also ran into difficulties in connection with Kendall Square Research Corp., a supercomputer manufacturer in Waltham, Massachusetts, for which he had provided backing in 1986. In December 1993, after auditors discovered serious discrep-

ancies in reports of revenues (primarily due to alleged sales of supercomputers that were never paid for), Koch took over as CEO. In 1994 Kendall Square's stock value plummeted, and the audit triggered a Securities and Exchange commission investigation and several shareholder lawsuits.

Bill Koch is no stranger to lawsuits. Since selling out of Koch Industries, he has filed more than 10 actions against his brothers Charles and David, his mother, Mary, and Koch Industries. Three suits in particular drew a lot of public attention. In 1987 Bill and Fred sued Mary, Charles, and David over the management of the family's charitable trust, the Fred C. Koch Foundation. Bill and Fred contended that there was an oral agreement among family members that the trust's shareholders, each according to the percentage of his or her ownership, would make decisions regarding donations; Charles, David, and Mary, they charged, had shifted that authority to the board, of which they comprised a majority. After Mary's death, in 1990, Bill and Fred contested a provision in her will that denied a portion of her $10 million estate to any son engaged in an active court action against a family member. In 1998 Bill and Fred sued Koch Industries, alleging that full disclosure of assets had been withheld from them when they sold their shares in 1983. They claimed the price of the stock had been undervalued and that they had been cheated out of $1 billion, including interest. To date Bill has not won any of his actions against his family or Koch Industries.

Reactions to the lawsuits have varied. Bill told Bob Cox, "To me, the family feud was buried a long time ago. Now it's just straight business." Also speaking to Cox, David, who has maintained that he still harbors filial affection for Bill, characterized the lawsuit over Koch Industries' assets as "90 percent business, maybe 10 percent sibling rivalry." Charles, who refused to shake Bill's hand at their mother's funeral, believed it to be more personal. Referring to Bill's actions, he said, "I cannot imagine dedicating my life for 18 years to getting somebody, hurting a company, a family, a person." George Ablah, a Wichita businessman and friend of Charles's, told John Garrity, "I think it's a one-sided vendetta. Billy is a kind of troublemaker, and he has a problem with not being the boss." By contrast, Mary Koch's younger brother, William I. Robinson, told Garrity, "I don't think any of the descriptions you read in the paper—obsessive, unstable—characterize Billy in the least. Except maybe in the minds of those who dislike him so much. Billy is a compassionate guy, unlike the rest of the family."

An oft-cited complaint about Bill Koch has been that he does not play fairly, either in business or in sporting events. In March 1992, for example, Koch Industries placed a restraining order on him after a private investigator was found going through the trash of company lawyers. The restraining order was lifted after Bill admitted to hiring the detective. During the 1992 America's Cup campaign, reports that the *America³* syndicate was using high-tech equipment to spy on the competition were confirmed by Koch's camp. They were said to be using the *Guzzini*, their 28-foot tender (a boat that helps other boats in various ways), and the Global Positioning System, a military satellite system now available to the public for navigation, in an elaborate monitoring system that determined exactly how their competitors' boats were performing. Cayard and the Italian crew were particularly outspoken against Koch's tactics.

The monitoring system turned out to be a hoax. After the stir created by the presence of the dark-windowed *Guzzini*, which had been commissioned to gather data on weather, wind, and water currents, *America³* decided to exploit the publicity. The crew affixed fake antennae, painted black, to its deck. "When the Italians began to get so spooked, they made it into something it wasn't," Bob Campbell, head of *America³*'s data-gathering, told Barbara Lloyd for the *New York Times* (May 18, 1992). "We had basic antennae on the boat, but we took the ball and ran with it." The only true espionage Koch admitted to was that he had hired divers to report on the shape of his competitors' hulls and keels, a guarded secret during Cup racing. After making that admission, Koch criticized the secrecy associated with the America's Cup; he pointed out that security is expensive and hinders public interest in yacht racing. Koch's syndicate reportedly spent $64 million on the 1992 America's Cup campaign.

With his second wife, Angela, Bill Koch now divides his time among West Palm Beach, Cape Cod, and New York City. Koch has five children: Charlotte, Lane, William Frederick, Angeline, and Wyatt. In 1993, while showing John Garrity some of the paintings he owns, he said, with reference to a photo of Wyatt, "Here's the best work of all. I love him more than I've loved anything in my entire life." A confirmed individualist, Koch described his managerial strength to John Garrity as "bringing all the pieces together, putting the right people in the right spots, and letting them do their thing." Sterling Varner, former president of Koch Industries, described Bill Koch to Garrity as "a lot better at ideas than at getting the job done." But those who have worked for him, among them Mike Toppa, Koch's 1992 America's Cup headsail trimmer, are convinced of the value of his methods. "He showed that there are new ways to do things," Toppa told Angus Phillips for the *Washington Post* (May 16, 1992), "and it didn't just work out, it worked better." — T.J.F.

Suggested Reading: *Fortune* p78+ Feb. 17, 1997, with photos; (London) *Observer* p9 Mar. 19, 1995, with photo; *New York Times* B p23 May 6, 1992, with photo, C p9 May 18, 1992, with photo; *Sports Illustrated* p62+ Apr. 20, 1992, with photos; *Washington Post* C p6 May 6, 1991, with photo, B p2 May 9, 1991, with photo, H p1 May 16, 1992, with photo; *Wichita Eagle* (on-line) Mar. 7, 1998

Courtesy of Kroll-O'Gara Co.

Kroll, Jules B.

May 18, 1941– Chairman and CEO of Kroll-O'Gara Co. Address: c/o Kroll Associates Inc., 900 3d Ave, New York, NY 10022

When people think of private detectives, they tend to think of gruff fictional characters like Phillip Marlowe or Easy Rawlins. Or they think of people who photograph cheating spouses and track down people who don't want to be found. But in the past few decades, a new class of private eye has emerged alongside the traditional gumshoe: the corporate investigator. In recent years corporations have become the biggest clients of independent investigators. Most often, corporate investigators are called on to sift through reams of accounting statements, analyze complex financial transactions, and track down money hidden in shell companies and banks all around the world, so they draw on skills that are very different from those of their street-savvy counterparts. In short, today's corporate private eyes are more likely to resemble investment bankers than characters from a Dashiell Hammett novel.

One of the best representatives of this new breed of private eye is Jules Kroll. For more than 20 years, Kroll has run what is widely considered to be the leading corporate investigative agency in the world. As the *New York Times Magazine* (August 30, 1992) put it, his company, Kroll Associates, is virtually "a CIA for hire." Some of the employees on his payroll actually are former intelligence officials. Others are former prosecutors, police chiefs, FBI agents, and even economists from formerly Communist countries. Drawing upon their diverse talents, Kroll—a lawyer by training—has excelled at doing what detectives do best: finding information that others want kept secret. By digging up financial dirt, Kroll has often saved his corporate clients from hostile takeovers, damaging lawsuits, bad business relationships, and white-collar crime.

So successful has his company been that governments, too, have sought his expertise. Some of Kroll's highest-profile cases have involved investigating the assets of such dictators as Ferdinand Marcos of the Philippines, Jean-Claude Duvalier of Haiti, and Saddam Hussein of Iraq. Kroll's success can also be measured by his company's rapid growth. Known as the Kroll-O'Gara Co. since its merger with the O'Gara Co. in December 1997, it has greatly expanded its services to include those that fall under the category "risk mitigation." In addition to corporate intelligence, this includes advising on issues of computer security and providing armored cars. As CEO and chairman of Kroll-O'Gara, Kroll aims to make his company the leading provider of such services, in a market that, one business journalist has estimated, involves billions of dollars.

The eldest of four children, Jules Barry Kroll was born on May 18, 1941 in the New York City borough of Brooklyn. He grew up in the neighboring borough of Queens, where his father operated a printing business. At Bayside High School, Kroll was a guard on the basketball team; he was also the baseball team's catcher and captain. The attorney Paul A. Goldberger, who was a teammate of Kroll's on the basketball team, remembers Kroll as a particularly feisty player. He told Larry Light for *Business Week* (November 9, 1998), "He was like one of those bulldogs that bites you and never lets go."

Kroll attended Cornell University, in Ithaca, New York, and received a bachelor's degree in government in 1963. He then entered Georgetown University, in Washington, D.C., to study law. In 1965 he interned in the office of Robert F. Kennedy, who was then the junior senator from New York. After graduating from Georgetown, in 1966, Kroll moved back to New York City and worked as an assistant prosecutor in the district attorney's office in the borough of Manhattan. He left that job to take over the family printing business after his father became ill. Kroll managed the business for three years before selling it.

In 1971 Kroll ran unsuccessfully for a seat on the New York City Council. The campaign left Kroll, who had married three years earlier, $20,000 in debt and in desperate straits. As Christopher Byron wrote for *New York* (May 13, 1991), "There he was, with an infant, a house with a mortgage, a car repossessed by the bank, no job, and no money. Every Saturday morning, a young kid from up the block . . . would come around to mow the lawn and rake the leaves. . . . Suddenly Jules had to scrape and scrounge for the money to pay the kid."

A woman who had volunteered for Kroll's election campaign steered him toward his next career. Her husband worked for Cadence Publishing, which produced Marvel Comics, and the company was looking for someone to track down cheap sources of paper. Kroll, with his knowledge of the printing business, proved helpful, and in time Cadence gave him additional tasks. With the business from Cadence, Kroll formed his own company, Kroll Associates, in 1972. "I never thought in a million years I'd ever be going into business," he told Christopher Byron. "I always figured I'd wind up either a senator or a baseball player." Kroll soon expanded into special audits and investigations of employee fraud. A corporate investigator was born.

For several years Kroll Associates toiled in relative anonymity. Then, in 1979, Kroll's company was hired by a wine and pharmaceutical company, Foremost-McKesson (now the McKesson Corp.), to investigate Victor Posner, a corporate raider from Miami, Florida, who was attempting a hostile takeover of the company. Among other tactics, Kroll and his agents used an aerial surveillance camera to determine that Posner had inflated the value of his assets at a particular steel company. This information was handed over to the Internal Revenue Service, which proceeded to investigate Posner, and in so doing, forestalled his attempt to take over Kroll's client. Thanks to the successful outcome of the Posner case, Kroll's reputation became established on Wall Street, and his company found itself in an excellent position to profit from the booming market for corporate intelligence that emerged in the 1980s.

In the heady financial atmosphere of that decade, a frenzy of mergers and acquisitions occurred. As a result, the value of a bit of legal snooping increased exponentially. In the *New York Times Magazine* (August 30, 1992), L. J. Davis wrote, "As Michael R. Milken, the junk bond wizard, created financial titans out of thin air, the entrenched powers of Wall Street came to a startling realization. They had no idea who these new guys were, and they didn't know where the sudden torrent of money was coming from—important points when one was attempting to judge the legitimacy and soundness of a transaction." As one of the few reputable corporate investigative units around, Kroll Associates experienced a boom in business. By 1984 takeover-related business constituted over three quarters of the company's work.

Questions of ethics—and even legality—were sometimes raised about Kroll's investigative methods. In 1990, for example, his agents were accused of impersonating reporters and policemen. A Delaware Superior Court judge subsequently forbade Kroll operatives from concealing their identities. The judge also ordered Kroll's agents to read a prepared script to identify themselves and their purposes before interviewing anybody. This judge's decision, however, was later reversed. Kroll has always maintained that his employees' work-related activities have been strictly legal. In fact, during an ABC News probe of various corporate investigation units that was cited in an article in *Fortune* (April 14, 1997, on-line), Kroll Associates was the only company that declined a request to illegally bug a room.

Prior to 1991 Kroll kept his work relatively hush-hush outside of Wall Street circles. That changed in 1991, when he agreed to appear on the CBS news program *60 Minutes*. On the show Kroll announced that he had been working on behalf of the Kuwaiti government to investigate the assets of Saddam Hussein, the president of Iraq. Kroll claimed that he had tracked down approximately $10 billion to $11 billion in assets either skimmed off by Hussein from the Iraqi national treasury or extorted from companies seeking to do business in Iraq. The money had been placed in bank accounts and shell companies around the world. Among the latter was a company that at the time owned 8 percent of the stock of Hatchette Publishing, which produced the magazines *Car and Driver* and *Elle*. (Kuwait later tried to freeze many of the assets identified by Kroll, as compensation for damages sustained when Iraq invaded the country in 1990.)

With much attention focused on Kroll and the relatively new phenomenon of the corporate investigator, the media revealed to the public that this was not the first time that Kroll Associates had been employed by a government. In 1987 the government of Haiti had hired Kroll to track down funds that had disappeared during the regime of the dictator Jean-Claude Duvalier. The information provided by Kroll agents led to the seizure of bank accounts in New York, London, Luxembourg, Paris, and Geneva. At the request of the United States House Foreign Affairs Committee, and at no charge, the company had also dug up evidence of the millions of dollars' worth of assets that the former president of the Philippines, Ferdinand Marcos, and his wife, Imelda, acquired during Marcos's rule. The Republic of Russia, another of Kroll's clients, hired Kroll in 1991 to find billions of dollars' worth of funds they believed had been stolen by former directors of state enterprises shortly before those industries were privatized.

The success of Kroll's company and the growing market for corporate intelligence have attracted numerous competitors to the corporate-investigation business. These include companies such as the Investigations Group Inc. and Business Risk International. Many of the so-called "big six" accounting firms have set up their own investigative divisions. Meanwhile, Kroll has continued to expand the types of services his business will provide. The company has branched out into such areas as investigating toxic-waste disposal and dealing with urban terrorism. In September 1991, for example, Laidlaw Transit hired Kroll to investigate whether bombs had been planted in fuel tanks of school buses. In 1993 Kroll Associates advised the Port Authority of New York and New Jersey on how to improve security at the World Trade Center buildings, which had been bombed earlier that year.

In December 1997 Kroll Associates completed a merger with the O'Gara Co., a manufacturer of armored cars and a provider of other security services. Kroll had long sought a partner; he originally planned to merge with Choicepoint, a company that was going to be spun off from the insurance data-collection agency Equifax. Kroll Associates would have become one of five divisions of Choicepoint, with Kroll as president of the division and a member of the board. But before that merger was consummated, Thomas O'Gara, the chairman of the O'Gara Co., aggressively courted Kroll and made him an offer he felt he couldn't refuse. The merged company would be named the Kroll-O'Gara Co. and Kroll would become the chairman and CEO; Thomas O'Gara would be vice chairman of the board, and his brother Bill O'Gara would be president and chief operating officer. As reported by Larry Light in *Business Week*, the O'Gara family bought Kroll Associates for $81 million in stock. Kroll, with approximately 17 percent of the shares, remained the company's largest shareholder; the O'Gara family holds about 16 percent.

Long before the merger, Kroll had cut down on the number of investigations in which he directly participated, involving himself only in high-profile cases, such as the Iraq and Russian investigations. Since becoming the CEO and chairman of a greatly expanded company, he has taken part in virtually none. Instead, he devotes most of his time to managing his company's global expansion. The company is striving to become a full-service "risk mitigation" provider with comprehensive expertise in such areas as corporate intelligence, computer-systems protection, and personal protection. The company's recent acquisitions include a drug-testing service, a surveillance-camera company, and an accounting firm specializing in fraud detection. In late 1998 Larry Light estimated that the market for corporate security was in the range of $4.6 billion; in fiscal year 1997 Kroll-O'Gara's combined revenues were approximately $190 million.

Kroll is married to the former Lynn Korda. The couple, who live on beachfront property in Rye, New York, have four children. The eldest, Jeremy, is one of Kroll's employees. The Kroll household also includes three dogs—Tonka, Twyla, and Thorgis. — W.G.

Suggested Reading: *Business Week* p90+ Nov. 9, 1998, with photo; *Fortune* (on-line) Apr. 14, 1997, with photo; *New York* p68+ May 31, 1991, with photos; *New York Times* III p3 Feb. 15, 1987, with photo, D p1+ Sep. 1, 1994, with photo, D p1+ Aug. 24, 1997, with photo; *New York Times Magazine* p46+ Aug. 30, 1992, with photo; *Newsweek* p40+ Apr. 8, 1991, with photo; *Time* p53 Apr. 8, 1991, with photo

Courtesy of Emeril Lagasse

Lagasse, Emeril

1958(?)– Chef; restaurant owner. Address: c/o Food Network, 177 Ave. of the Americas, 31st Fl., New York, NY 10036

"You should have fun in the kitchen," the television chef and restaurateur Emeril Lagasse has often told his fans. "Hey! It ain't rocket science, it's just cooking!" As the founder and owner of two of New Orleans's most talked-about restaurants and with a signature style of cooking to his credit, Lagasse had reached what most chefs would consider to be the pinnacle of their profession when he decided to try cooking on television. Thanks to his exposure on his shows *The Essence of Emeril* and *Emeril Live!*, which are broadcast daily on the Food Network, he has become one of the most popular chefs in the United States. According to a reporter for the *New York Times* (October 25, 1998), his "blunt, cabbylike style—not to mention his exuberant use of all things buttery and fattening—has won him adulation more familiar to a rock star than a gourmet." A specialist in the Creole cuisine of New Orleans, he has also gained fame by making mundane food like meat and potatoes more exciting, by "kicking it up a notch," as he has put it, with his special blend of spices. By all accounts, Lagasse's popularity rests on far more than his recipes and knowledge of food; according to Andrew Essex in *Entertainment Weekly* (November 13, 1998), his attraction also lies in his "larger than life, regular guy persona and strange mix of I-don't-need-no-measuring-cup confidence and spice-obsessed sex appeal."

Emeril Lagasse was born in about 1958 in Fall River, Massachusetts. He has an older sister, Delores, and a younger brother, Mark. His father, whom Lagasse calls Mr. John, is of French-Canadian descent, and his mother, Hilda, is Portuguese. (According to Molly O'Neill in the *New York Times Magazine* [February 21, 1993], however, both of his parents are Portuguese.) John Lagasse worked as a garment dyer at one of Fall River's many textile mills; he often held a second job as well, driving a cab, for example, or serving as a security guard. In an interview with John Grossmann for *Cigar Aficionado* (January/February 1998, on-line), Lagasse said that at an early age he had taken to heart his father's "tremendous respect for the work ethic." The lesson he absorbed, he explained, is that "the only way you're going to get ahead is to push and work hard. If you do it from your heart and don't screw anybody over along the way, eventually you're going to get ahead, because it all comes back to you." Lagasse has traced his love of food to his mother. Some of his earliest memories are of helping his mother make soups and a special Portuguese stuffing at Christmas, when she would cook for as many as 40 people.

In his early teens, Lagasse played drums in a 45-member Portuguese band that toured the northeastern U.S. and parts of Canada on summer weekends. He also played in a trio that performed at weddings and other local events. Starting at age 13 he worked at a local Portuguese bakery after school, often into the night, and although the hours were grueling, he enjoyed the job and learned a lot about baking. "I remember sitting on stainless steel flour bins," he recalled to John Grossmann. "Mom would have sent over my dinner with my dad, and when the Portuguese men would take their dinner break, I'd heat my supper in a brick oven. They took a liking to me and they'd teach me about bread and the Portuguese specialties. If you understand people and understand their culture, then you can easily understand their food."

During his high-school years, Lagasse won a scholarship to the New England Conservatory of Music to study percussion, but recognizing that he favored cooking over music, he turned it down. "I would just see how happy people were when they came into the bakery," Lagasse told Molly O'Neill. "Music is more distant than cooking and baking." After high school he attended the culinary school at Johnson & Wales University, in Providence, Rhode Island. While studying there he worked at a banquet-style restaurant called Venus de Milo, in Swansea, Massachusetts (not far from Providence); he started out as a waiter and was eventually promoted to chef de cuisine—head of the kitchen.

After graduating from Johnson & Wales, in 1978, Lagasse moved to Philadelphia, where he worked as a cook at a Sheraton Hotel. A few months later, eager to learn more about fine dining, he accepted a three-month apprenticeship at a restaurant in France. When he returned to the United States, he took a job with the chef Wolfgang Puck at the Berkshire Place Hotel, in New York City, where he learned, in his words, "how to work on a high-pressure [cooking] line." He next went to work at the Parker House, in Boston. Whenever he could he dined at New York and Boston's finest restaurants, taking detailed notes on their food and operations. He also taught himself about wine. "Every week on Friday, or whenever my 'Friday' was, I would go buy a bottle of wine for $10 or less," he told John Grossmann. "[I would] smell it, taste it, make notes, read about it."

In the summer of 1983, the 25-year-old Lagasse worked in a restaurant on Cape Cod, Massachusetts. While vacationing on Cape Cod, a headhunter for the New Orleans restaurateur Ella Brennan tasted Lagasse's cooking. At that time Brennan was looking for someone to replace the chef Paul Prudhomme at her famous restaurant, the Commander's Palace. On the recommendation of the headhunter, Brennan proceeded to appraise Lagasse's potential as a successor to Prudhomme, by means of a steady stream of phone calls. "Every week we would talk," Lagasse recalled to Grossmann. "She would say, 'Today I want to talk about what inspires you. Is bread inspiring you? Is a book inspiring you?' . . . We would talk for a half hour, 40 minutes. The next Wednesday, the phone would ring: 'Today I want to talk about your philosophies about people. How do you motivate people?'" After about four months Brennan began calling him every day. Finally, she arranged to fly Lagasse to New Orleans for a final interview at the restaurant. "The enthusiasm, the integrity, the energy, it was all evident," Brennan told Grossmann, recalling her impression of Lagasse during the five days he spent with her for that "interview." According to Grossmann, Lagasse had immediately won her over by telling her that the Commander's Palace "smells just like my mom's kitchen."

Lagasse worked at the Commander's Palace for seven and a half years. By his own account, Brennan became his mentor, helping him to hone his style and curb his temper. "She really sort of turned the world around for me," he told Grossmann. "You don't need to be an asshole to people. If you respect people and treat them the way you want to be treated and do it with intelligence and finesse, you could walk into the room wearing a T-shirt and they'll know you're the chef." Molly O'Neill reported that in New Orleans Lagasse learned to "translate the soul of his mother's Portuguese kitchen into Creole and Cajun" cuisines, in which elements of French, Acadian, African, and Native American cooking are combined. "Cajun is the rustic, country version of Louisiana food, where Creole is the city food of Louisiana," Lagasse explained to Christina Nifong of the *Christian Science Monitor* (March 31, 1994). With Brennan's help, Lagasse further "Creolized" the food he prepared, by integrating elements of Vietnamese, Italian, contemporary French, and many other styles of cooking into typical Louisiana fare. Chili powders, cayenne pepper, sweet paprika, thyme, and dried oregano became his favorite spices.

In 1990 Lagasse struck out on his own and opened a new, 225-seat restaurant, called Emeril's, in the then-unfashionable warehouse district of New Orleans. "There wasn't even a street light back then," he recalled to Grossmann. "Bums sleeping out. One art gallery. You could shoot a cannon down Tchoupitoulas Street and not hit anybody. [People wondered,] 'Why is he trading in his Porsche and giving up one of the top-five paying [chef's] jobs in America? Is he out of his [expletive] mind?'" *Esquire* named Emeril's the best new restaurant of 1990, and soon the success of the restaurant attracted other businesses to the neighborhood. The warehouse quarter now boasts several galleries and night spots as well as renovated loft spaces, and by 1996 an annual arts festival was drawing some 10,000 visitors.

"All I do is cook fresh using the best of what's available . . . ," Lagasse told Larry Novick for the *Standard-Times* (on-line) in 1996. "The people who eat at my restaurant should feel a little better when they leave than when they come in. I tell my staff that we are craftsmen and that is the philosophy of our craft." A few popular dishes distinguish Emeril's, not only as a hot spot for New Orleans diners but as a nationally acclaimed restaurant. Perhaps the best example is Lagasse's double-cut pork chops with a tamarind glaze, green mole sauce, and caramelized sweet potatoes. Lagasse's version of green mole (pronounced "MOH-lay") sauce, which is an ingredient in many Mexican recipes, includes nuts in addition to the traditional hot chilies and sweet chocolate. Two other noteworthy dishes are Lagasse's barbecued shrimp with homemade rosemary biscuits and his "study of duck," which consists of a marinated breast of duck, confit of duck with seared foie gras, and wild-mushroom bread pudding. Emeril's is also known for its exotic fowl and meats, such as partridge and antelope, and for a dessert—banana cream pie with caramel drizzles.

In 1992 Lagasse opened a second, more casual restaurant, called Nola—an acronym for New Orleans, Louisiana (LA)—in the city's renowned French Quarter. Since then he has taken his popular New Orleans cooking beyond the borders of the Big Easy: in 1995 he opened Emeril's New Orleans Fish House, at the MGM Grand Hotel in Las Vegas, and in early 1999 another Emeril's restaurant, at Universal Studios in Orlando, Florida. Later in the year a steak house bearing his name is scheduled to open in Las Vegas. In 1998 Lagasse bought and revamped New Orleans's classic restaurant Delmonico's.

In the mid-1990s Emeril branched into television. The first show in which he appeared was the Food Network's *How to Boil Water*, which was designed for people who knew next to nothing about the preparation of food. After the first set of installments, Lagasse told Phillip Silverstone for *Restaurant Report* (on-line), the people in charge of casting at the Food Network told him that they had "a little problem": "You are a little over-qualified for the job," they explained to him. "Maybe you should consider your own show." What emerged out of their discussions, *Emeril and Friends*, did not please Lagasse, because, he told Andrew Essex, it was "too scripted." "Then, just when I was ready to crawl back to my restaurant, [the Food Network] let me be me," he recalled to Andrew Essex. For his next show, *The Essence of Emeril*, he was given much freer rein, which made it easier for him to show off to greater advantage both his engaging personality and his enthusiasm for food. *The Essence of Emeril* drew a much larger audience than its predecessors. Still, Lagasse admitted to Essex, "the first season was very rough. I'd hunch over, hide from the camera, and swear at people under my breath."

Lagasse's most recent show, *Emeril Live!*, a daily, hour-long show that was launched about a year after *The Essence of Emeril* debuted, has become the most successful cooking show on television. In an opening reminiscent of that of Fred Rogers, the host of the famous children's program *Mr. Rogers' Neighborhood*, Lagasse changes from a sport coat to his chef's jacket and apron as he arrives on the set. A guest musician helps to liven the atmosphere. Unlike the studio audiences of most other cooking shows, a large percentage of Lagasse's audience are young people and men. (The food that Lagasse prepares on the show—predominately spicy meat and potato dishes—apparently appeals to more men than do other TV menus.) The cry "Bam!," which accompanies his liberal additions of spices to his dishes and other actions, punctuates his patter, and his audiences have learned to yell "Bam!" along with him. An often-repeated statement that almost always elicits laughter is "Pork fat rules." Another of Lagasse's signature remarks is "Happy, happy, happy." In late 1998 *The Essence of Emeril*—reruns of which are broadcast every day—and *Emeril Live!* were reportedly being viewed by close to 300,000 households.

The approach to cooking that Lagasse espouses on his television shows is not universally admired. Amanda Hesser, for example, complained in the *New York Times* (November 4, 1998, on-line) that Lagasse "rarely starts and finishes a recipe in a linear or comprehensive fashion. He uses no measurements, skips crucial steps, and is vague in his instructions. . . . His [show] has become like a prime-time sitcom filled with gags and lots of action." Hesser quoted Michael Batterberry, the founder of *Food Arts* magazine, as saying, "A lot of professional foodies are a bit dismayed at the tone of the program. It really smacks a little bit of the wrestling ring or the roller derby." In addition, after tasting a turkey-and-cheese sandwich that he had fried and then baked in the studio, she rated it "very bad." Hesser also warned that the fat content of many of Lagasse's recipes is unhealthy. "His recipe for 'smashing smashed potatoes' in [his cookbook] *Louisiana Real and Rustic* [1996] is downright suicidal," she wrote.

In his own defense, Lagasse said to Hesser, "Culinarily, I try to be correct. It's not like I'm bastardizing my craft. That's what my backbone is. I'm a chef and restaurateur. What I'm trying to do with the people is connect. . . . For me the more options and the more flexibility you give to people to get the end result, then the more interested they are about watching. I don't want to get up there and say: 'Hi, I'm Emeril Lagasse and today we're making cake batter. You add two cups flour to the bowl. Make sure you sift it. Stir in two tablespoons of butter.' I mean, after a while who wants to watch that stuff? Who's going to be inspired by that?"

Currently, Lagasse makes weekly appearances as a food correspondent on ABC's *Good Morning America*. Balancing all of his television work with the management of his restaurants leaves him little time for relaxation. "I'll bag four or five shows [on Saturday], crash on Sunday, get up exhausted, do eight shows on Monday, another eight on Tuesday, then fly back to the restaurant," he explained to Essex. His jovial on-camera manner notwithstanding, "when it comes to his food and restaurants he's extremely serious . . . ," Lagasse's business manager, Tony Cruz, told John Grossmann. "He's absolutely on top of profit and loss." "I'm not doing what I'm doing for a paycheck or to beat Martha Stewart's ratings," Lagasse told Essex. "I'm influencing a lot of people, particularly kids, which I love, and guys who have been in the cooking closet for years. So why should I quit? I get to cook every day and make people happy. I'm having a blast." Perhaps the best evidence of Lagasse's love for his work is that when he has a day off, he spends it cooking. "For me it's a way to express myself about the joy of friendship," he told Christina Nifong. He also enjoys fishing and listening to music.

In 1993 Lagasse moved his parents from Massachusetts to New Orleans, and they now help out in his restaurants. He has two daughters, Jillian and Jessica, from his first marriage. He was divorced for the second time in 1996; his second wife, Tari Hohn, has attempted to sue him for part of his business.

Lagasse's honors include the James Beard Foundation's award for Best Southeast Regional Chef in 1991 and for Outstanding Chef in 1997, *Time* magazine's award for Best Television of 1996, and the 1997 CableAce Award for Best Informational Television Series. *Food and Wine* magazine named him one of the top 25 new chefs of 1991, and he has been inducted into the American Express Fine Dining Hall of Fame. Lagasse is the author of four cookbooks: *Emeril's New Orleans Cooking* (1993), written with Jessie Tirsch; *Louisiana Real and Rustic* (1996) and *Emeril's Creole Christmas* (1997), both written with Marcelle Bienvenu; and *Emeril's TV Dinners* (1998), written with Marcelle Bienvenu and Felicia Willett. — C.P.

Suggested Reading: *Christian Science Monitor* p12 Mar. 31, 1994, with photo; *Cigaraficionado.com* (on-line), with photo;

Entertainment Weekly p43+ Nov. 13, 1998, with photos; *New York Times* F p1 Nov. 4, 1998, with photo; *New York Times Magazine* p65+ Feb. 21, 1993; *People* p97+ Dec. 22, 1997; *Restaurant Report* (on-line), with photo; *StarChefs* (on-line)

Selected Television Shows: *How to Boil Water*; *Emeril and Friends*; *The Essence of Emeril*; *Emeril Live!*

Selected Books: *Emeril's New Orleans Cooking*, 1993; *Louisiana: Real and Rustic*, 1996; *Emeril's Creole Christmas*, 1997; *Emeril's TV Dinners*, 1998

Courtesy of Steve Largent

Largent, Steve

Sep. 28, 1954– U.S. Representative from Oklahoma. Address: 426 Cannon Bldg., United States House of Representatives, Washington, DC 20515

Once best known for his stellar 14-year career in the National Football League (NFL) as a wide receiver for the Seattle Seahawks, Steve Largent has since forged a career as a young Republican leader in the U.S. House of Representatives, to which he was first elected in November 1994. Although a significant part of his political cachet may be attributed to his mediagenic appearance and his football fame, he has also won approval from some quarters as a spokesperson for Christian values and an opponent of gun control, abortion rights, and legal recognition of same-sex marriages.

In November 1998 Largent took on the reigning House majority leader, Dick Armey, in a bid for Armey's post, the second most powerful in the House Republican hierarchy. Although he failed to unseat Armey in intraparty balloting, he continues to enjoy strong name recognition and the support of Christian conservatives, an influential and well-organized segment of the Republican Party.

Steve Largent was born on September 28, 1954 in Tulsa, Oklahoma, the oldest of the three sons of Jim Largent, a salesman, and Sue Largent. His father abandoned the family when Steve was six. Soon afterward Steve and his brothers moved to Oklahoma City with their mother, who married John Cargill, an electrician with the Federal Aviation Administration. The marriage was not happy, in large part due to Cargill's alcohol abuse. "With three kids you either marry somebody you don't love or you go on welfare," Largent's mother told Melinda Henneberger for the *New York Times* (November 6, 1997). "If I had it to do over again, I'd go on welfare." Largent felt the full brunt of his stepfather's liquor-fueled rage. "Any kid who grew up with an alcoholic parent will tell you how nauseating it feels never to know what it will be like when you come home," he told Jack Friedman and Nick Gallo for *People* (November 28, 1988). Largent found himself forced to play peacemaker in the household. "I can remember a ham being thrown across the kitchen," he recalled to Jill Lieber for *Sports Illustrated* (October 20, 1986). "My mom would come to me crying and say, 'What should I do?' And I'd think, I don't know. I'm only in 10th grade."

Largent found solace from his tumultuous family life in sports. His mother encouraged him to try out for the Putnam City High School football team. "I was new to the high school and intimidated by the size of it," Largent told Leonard Shapiro for the *Washington Post* (January 29, 1995). "They had 160 guys out for football and I hadn't hit puberty. I didn't think I was big enough or fast enough. My mother sat me down at the breakfast table and said I ought to stick it out. I'm glad I did." He excelled in baseball and football at Putnam City, then attended the University of Tulsa on a football scholarship.

Although Largent, who was five feet, 11 inches tall and weighed 190 pounds, had been considered too small and slow to be a star wide receiver at the college level, he became a standout. In both his junior and senior years, he led the National Collegiate Athletic Association in touchdown receptions, with 14. "I was pushing myself out of fear of failure," Largent told Friedman and Gallo. "If I didn't do well, I didn't feel good about myself." He earned a B.S. degree in biology from the university in 1976 and finished his college football career with 126 receptions and 32 touchdowns, for a total of 2,385 yards.

Although he had not been considered a strong prospect for the NFL, Largent was selected by the Houston Oilers in the fourth round of the 1976 NFL draft. However, he was cut by the team during the preseason after spending just a few weeks at the Oilers' training camp. Then, when it seemed that his NFL career had ended before it had begun, the Seattle Seahawks—an expansion team starting out that year—acquired him from the Oilers by trading a future eighth-round draft-pick. The Seahawks had been urged to acquire Largent by Jerry Rhome, an assistant coach who had worked with Largent at the University of Tulsa. Rhome helped the Seahawks implement an offense that was familiar to Largent, and Largent quickly became a star. During his 14-year career with the Seahawks, he played in seven Pro Bowls. When he retired, in 1989, he held records for most receptions (819), most receiving yards (13,089), most touchdowns (100), and most consecutive games with a reception (177). (Those records have since been broken.) Reflecting on Largent's success, Chuck Knox, who coached Largent at Seattle, told Paul Kuharsky for the New York Times (January 28, 1995), "Steve's a very dedicated, highly motivated individual who has excellent athletic talent that he maximized by his work ethic and attention to detail." Largent was inducted into the NFL Hall of Fame in 1995.

Meanwhile, after retiring from the NFL, Largent returned to Oklahoma and started an advertising and marketing consulting firm. Then, in 1994, when the Oklahoma Republican James Inhofe left the U.S. House of Representatives for the Senate, Largent was encouraged by Oklahoma's Republican Party to run for Inhofe's old seat, in the state's First Congressional District. The opportunity was unexpected for Largent, who had not previously been very concerned about politics. "I didn't even know what GOP stood for until after I was elected," he told Lois Romano for the Washington Post (September 2, 1997). (GOP is the acronym for Grand Old Party.)

Despite his lack of political experience, Largent beat a former Tulsa mayor and the GOP's state chair in the Republican primary. He went on to win 63 percent of the vote in the general election, soundly defeating Democrat Stuart Price. On November 29, 1994, he was sworn in as a member of the 103d Congress and took over the remainder of Inhofe's term.

On January 4, 1995 Largent was sworn in to the 104th Congress, along with the freshman Republicans who had helped their party gain a majority in the U.S. House of Representatives for the first time in four decades. Many of his Republican colleagues felt that Largent's name recognition from his football days would be an asset to the party, and mainly for that reason, he was immediately given a seat on the influential House Budget Committee. He helped his party raise funds and quickly emerged as a young star in the House. As if to signal his coming-of-age, he was scheduled to speak at the GOP National Convention in August 1996 in San Diego, California, alongside the leaders of his party; delayed by traffic, however, he missed his opportunity to address the convention.

A devout Christian, Largent has attributed most of his political views to his religious beliefs. "My No. 1 foundation," he told People (June 24, 1996), "is as a believer in Christ." In accordance with his faith, he has firmly opposed abortion under any circumstances, most forms of gun control, and special legal recognition and protection for homosexuals. "It's just logical," he told Romano, discussing the last-named subject. "No culture can embrace homosexuality and remain viable because homosexuals don't procreate. . . . I am not intolerant of homosexuals. I am intolerant of the homosexual agenda." In 1996 he was one of the leading sponsors of the Defense of Marriage Act, which was passed by Congress and signed by President Clinton in September of that year. That legislation barred federal and state recognition of same-sex marriages. He was also a leading sponsor of the Parental Rights and Responsibilities Act, which sought to grant parents more control of their children's school curriculum.

As for fiscal policy, he quickly proved himself to be in agreement with most fiscal conservatives. "The most important issue to me is trying to neck-rein the Federal government in terms of how big it is and how much it costs," he told Kuharsky. "We have to try to bring the budget into some semblance of balance. I think that more than anything else threatens our families." With that in mind, he opposed federal funding for the National Endowment for the Arts. He also came out in favor of cutting the capital gains tax in April 1995, voted to relax standards for toxic-waste treatment in May 1995, and voted against the minimum-wage increase in May 1996.

Largent handily won reelection in 1996, with 68 percent of the vote. He then became a member of the Commerce Committee and also served on the Energy and Power Subcommittee, the Telecommunications, Trade, and Consumer Protection Subcommittee, and on the Finance and Hazardous Materials Subcommittee.

Meanwhile, even as he gained more experience as a politician and emerged as a champion of Christian conservatives, he found himself increasingly at odds with the entrenched Republican leadership. During his first full term, he voted against the budget proposed by House Speaker Newt Gingrich and often voiced discontent at his party's compromises with Democrats concerning social and fiscal issues. Asked about his relationship with Gingrich, Largent told Romano, "He said he didn't think I was a team player. Which I thought was a curious statement for him to make about me. I just didn't want to play on the team he had built."

Largent got a chance to challenge his party's leadership head-on in November 1998. In midterm elections held earlier that month, the Republican Party had lost five House seats. The setback was widely seen as a loss of mandate for Gingrich. Under pressure, Gingrich resigned as House Speaker. In the ensuing battle for key leadership posts, Dennis Hastert of Illinois ultimately emerged as the successor to Gingrich. Meanwhile, Largent challenged Dick Armey for the post of House majority leader. After three rounds of balloting, Largent finished with 95 votes to Armey's 127. Following his loss, Largent said, as quoted by Katherine Q. Seelye for the *New York Times*, "Steve Largent has been too slow and too small his whole life, and this is just one more occasion," then added, "But I will tell you that I'm not accustomed to losing, and I don't like to lose." Some political observers attributed Largent's failure in part to the widely held perception that he was too dogmatic and conservative. Although Largent has been mentioned as a possible candidate for national office, it is thought that his strongly right-wing positions on social issues may be an obstacle in any bid for widespread support.

Largent and his wife, Terry Bullock, have one daughter, Casie, and three sons, Kyle, Kelly, and Kramer. Their youngest child, Kramer, was born with spina bifida—a cleft vertebral column and ex-posed spinal cord—which leads to physical problems and increases chances of paralysis and mental retardation. "He's been a great blessing to us," Largent told Bart Wright for the *Sporting News* (December 18, 1989) about his son, who is now a teenager. "He has taught us what it means to be compassionate and how much we all need to help each other. He's a great kid." Largent divides his time between Washington, D.C., and Tulsa, where his family lives. He has served on the advisory board of the Salvation Army in Tulsa and on the board of trustees of Tulsa University. — Y.P.

Suggested Reading: *New York Times* A p33 Nov. 6, 1997, with photo, A p25 Nov. 11, 1998, with photos, A p1+ Nov. 19, 1998, with photos; *Newsweek* p39 Nov. 23, 1998, with photos; *Sports Illustrated* p46+ Oct. 20, 1986, with photos; *Wall Street Journal* A p1+ Oct. 28, 1996; *Washington Post* A p5 Sep. 2, 1997, with photos

---

Armando Gallo/Retna Ltd.

Lawrence, Martin

Apr. 16, 1965– Actor. Address: c/o Fox Broadcasting Co., 10201 W. Pico Blvd., Los Angeles, CA 90064-2606

When the final episode of the Fox television series *Martin* aired in the spring of 1997, it did so in the midst of a controversy swirling around its star, Martin Lawrence. In the year or so leading up to the hit sitcom's finale, several incidents, including a few run-ins with the law; the breakup of his mar-riage; and, perhaps most devastating to the show, accusations of sexual harassment brought against Lawrence by his *Martin* co-star, Tisha Campbell, marked the descent of a star who not long before had been considered one of Hollywood's brightest lights. A television personality with enormous appeal, especially to young people, Lawrence was in the process of parlaying his popularity into a film career when the damaging events occurred. The brisk box-office business done by *Bad Boys* and by *A Thin Line Between Love and Hate*, the latter of which was written and directed by Lawrence, suggested that there was a large audience eager to see the performer's act on the big screen. Working out of the blue-comic tradition of Eddie Murphy and, before him, Richard Pryor, Lawrence laced his wit with profane irreverence that often verged on the obscene. But he was out to do more than just shock his audiences, à la Andrew Dice Clay: Lawrence attempted to make relevant commentary on relationships, the differences between men and women, and life as an underprivileged African-American. His catch-phrases—"Wass up" and "You go, girl"—pervaded the culture, as he developed a persona that was brash and confident and yet softened and made palatable by his tender relationship with his on-screen girlfriend in *Martin*. Though all this appeared to be in jeopardy, and Lawrence's career seemed destined to play itself out on the covers of tabloids, his recent feature *Life*, in which he starred with Eddie Murphy, signaled his return and quieted the cynics who pronounced him another premature Hollywood wash-up. Lawrence's newest movie is *Blue Streak*.

Martin Lawrence was born on April 16, 1965 in Frankfurt, Germany, where his father, John, an officer in the United States Air Force, was stationed. Still a toddler when his family moved back to the

U.S., Lawrence lived a peripatetic life, moving from the New York City borough of Queens to various other places. When he was eight his parents, John and Chlora Lawrence, divorced, and Martin remained with his mother and five siblings, who eventually settled in Landover, Maryland. Although Lawrence was a diminutive child, he enjoyed boxing and wrestling in school. He was also a hyperactive student and something of a troublemaker, and as a result he flunked second grade. At the same time, through his constant wisecracking, he developed the comedic abilities that would make him famous. At night, when his mother would return from a hard day's work at one of her many cashier jobs, her son would relax her with his antics. "If Moms came home from a stress-filled day and I was being silly and brought a smile to her face, it made me feel good. And it became contagious," Lawrence recalled to David A. Keeps for *Details* (April 1999). Lawrence's teachers, on the other hand, weren't so amused by the constant disruptions of their classes caused by his clowning. One art teacher allowed Lawrence five minutes at the end of every class period to tell jokes in exchange for his promise to keep quiet during the rest of the lecture. This was Lawrence's first shot at stand-up comedy, and it inspired him to pursue it as a career upon graduating high school, in 1984.

Lawrence started out by giving evening performances in Washington, D.C., comedy clubs, delivering routines heavy with sexual jokes, while toiling as a janitor by day. He was often told that his material was too racy, but he refused to sanitize it. Another comic, Ritch Snyder, saw Lawrence's act one night and suggested that he call a few of Snyder's connections in New York City. Moving there, Lawrence struggled, taking work wherever he could find it. He performed in Washington Square Park and at the Improv on open-mike nights. He also held down a variety of odd jobs, including stints at a Sears department store in Queens and at a gas station, where he was once held up in broad daylight. Barely six months after he left for the Big Apple, Lawrence returned to Maryland.

Back at the D.C. clubs, Lawrence worked his experiences in New York into his act, and he eventually got a chance to compete on *Star Search*, the TV show dedicated to discovering new talent. He won in the early rounds but lost later on and returned to his job as a janitor at K-Mart. "One day, I was walking around in my drawers, totally depressed, thinking, 'Now I ain't nothin'.' Then I got a call from Columbia Pictures asking me if I was interested in television," he told Jay Martel for *Rolling Stone* (April 21, 1994). This opportunity turned out to be for a small, recurring role on *What's Happening Now!!*, a series based on the popular 1970s sitcom. Confident, Lawrence moved to Los Angeles, but the show was canceled after only 14 episodes, and he found himself once again working the comedy-club circuit. Before long, though, he got key bit parts in two popular movies, Spike Lee's *Do the Right Thing* (1989) and Reginald

Hudlin's *House Party* (1990). "When I auditioned [Lawrence] for *House Party*," Hudlin told Martel, "I just had this gut feeling that he was the guy. He was more than a stand-up—he was a comic actor." *House Party* became a big hit, and Lawrence appeared in its sequel, *House Party 2* (1991), as well as in *Talkin' Dirty After Dark* (1991) and the Eddie Murphy vehicle *Boomerang* (1992). Even in these relatively small roles, he created memorable moments. Hudlin, who also directed *Boomerang*, told Martel of one scene, involving Lawrence, that had to be left on the cutting-room floor: "There was this amazing 20-second tracking shot of him going through the crowded dance floor that was completely hilarious, no dialogue, all just physical comedy as Martin reacts happily to each of the women. I hated to lose that one."

Impressed with these performances, HBO approached Lawrence with the intent to develop a series that dealt with relationships. The network decided to promote the concept by first installing Lawrence as the host of *Def Comedy Jam*, a new series that showcased the work of young comics. Lawrence's involvement with the controversial series—whose acts often involved obscene language and misogynist subject matter—got him some negative press when Bill Cosby publicly condemned *Def Comedy Jam* as a "minstrel show" that debased African-American culture. "I respect Cosby for the road he's laid for the rest of us to be here," Lawrence later said to Martel, "but I'd rather see someone on a TV using words than taking a gun and shooting someone in the head. Comedy's an outlet—it's a way to voice our opinions, to voice our frustrations. HBO gave black people a cable show and said, 'You could say whatever you want.' So we're gonna get on there and say whatever we want. Because this is the land of the free—or so y'all tell us."

While *Def Comedy Jam* suggested the edgier side of Lawrence's repertoire, his television show, *Martin*, represented a less threatening comedic mode. The show, which was eventually sold to Fox, at that time an upstart network trying to capture young viewers, debuted in 1992. Lawrence played Martin Payne, a deejay at WZUP, who was constantly at odds with his irascible boss (Garrett Morris) and involved in an on-and-off romance with a woman named Gina (Tisha Campbell). The relationship between Martin and Gina evolved over the show's five seasons from a burgeoning love to marriage, during which the pair would spar verbally in classic "battle of the sexes" fashion. Martin would exhibit a typically masculine swagger in front of his buddies, Cole (Carl Anthony Payne II) and Tommy (Thomas Mikal Ford), while Gina would display sensitivity in the company of her friend Pam (Tichina Arnold). The clash in outlook between the two characters generally provided the show's conflict, and a compromise between their extreme positions the resolution. Over its run the show found a youthful and racially diverse fan base, a phenomenon that most critics attributed to

Lawrence's charm. "The attraction isn't the show's format, which is routine," Mark Stuart Gill wrote for the *New York Times* (August 1, 1993). "[M]ost of the show's appeal emanates from Mr. Lawrence himself," Gill concluded. "With his tiny face, jug ears and eyes that protrude slightly, he resembles a teddy bear on caffeine. His performances are loud, physical cartoons. 'I will do anything for a laugh,' he says." Despite the fact that the series and a few of its cast members had been nominated for or won NAACP Image Awards, which recognize positive images of the African-American community, Lawrence was among those criticized when Bill Cosby again complained about the state of African-American humor, particularly on sitcoms. Contrasting the realm of experience represented by Cosby in his long-running *The Cosby Show* and that shown in *Martin*, Lawrence defended his show. "*The Cosby Show* portrayed a specific type of experience—an upper-middle-class family," Gill quoted him as saying. "I'm portraying me, my personal experience. Young black men struggling to be the head of their households. Not always doing it right."

In 1994 Lawrence released *You So Crazy*, a concert film of his stand-up act. In the film he tackled such contentious topics as pervasive poverty and the Rodney King beating as well as his usual fare of relationships and racism. A controversy arose when *You So Crazy* was saddled with an NC-17 rating by the Motion Picture Association of America (MPAA) for its obscene language. Often precluding commercial success, the NC-17 tag forbids children younger than 17 to see a film in the theater, and some video chains, such as Blockbuster, refuse to carry films with the rating. Lawrence complained loudly about the MPAA's action to Jay Martel of *Rolling Stone*: "They rate my movie NC-17 for *language*, while a movie like *Basic Instinct* gets rated R. *Basic Instinct*! I mean, *Basic Instinct* has *[expletive] and killing* in the first *scene*!" Despite Lawrence's appeals, the rating stuck. It was not the first time that the comic had been sanctioned for his language. A February 19, 1994 monologue on *Saturday Night Live*, in which Lawrence encouraged young women in the audience to improve their hygiene by placing a breath mint in an extremely private orifice, prompted hundreds of irate viewers to flood NBC with complaints. This in turn led the network to cancel Lawrence's scheduled appearance on the *Tonight Show*. Unfazed, Lawrence reiterated his complaints that society was too fixated on language. "Hey, Jay [Leno] called me up and explained it wasn't him," Martel quoted Lawrence as saying. "It was the network. It happens. Hey, none of it really bothers me, because I haven't done anything wrong. I just wish there weren't such a double standard." *You So Crazy* was eventually dropped by its original distributor, Miramax, and released without a rating by the Samuel Goldwyn Co. The film received some tepid reviews, of which Caryn James's in the *New York Times* (April 27, 1994) is representative. "Anyone

older than Mr. Lawrence, who is 28, is likely to find him tiresome. His stories, after all, are about going to clubs, hanging out with friends, or casually masturbating while watching old sitcoms. Even an appreciative audience is likely to find that these stories go on too long. It may be that Mr. Lawrence is a better comic actor than comedy writer." Still, James felt that one "good omen for his future is that despite its rawness, there is nothing mean-spirited about his act." Despite these criticisms, *You So Crazy* is one of the top three highest-grossing concert films of all time. In addition to this film, Lawrence has released a comedy album, *Talkin' Sh*t*, which cracked *Billboard*'s Top 10.

Lawrence capitalized on his growing popularity by taking a co-starring role opposite Will Smith in *Bad Boys*, a cop-buddy movie in which Lawrence played a harried family man and Smith a smooth lady-killer. The two must track down the person who stole a large amount of heroin that had been confiscated by the police and also protect a prostitute (Tea Leoni) who is to serve as a witness to the crime. The film, though a commercial success, was panned by critics. "[E]ven by the low-low standards of cheap actions flicks, this one's bad, boys," Desson Howe sneered in the *Washington Post* (April 7, 1995). "As they quip through an eternity of explosions, gun battles, and hair-raising driving . . . Lawrence treats every moment as a cue for an unsuccessful improv routine, Smith plays the (inevitably shirtless) straight man, and Leoni basically shows off her legs." Lawrence's next project, *A Thin Line Between Love and Hate* (1996), with which he added directing and producing credits to his résumé, was also savaged by reviewers. Lawrence played Darnell Wright, a womanizing club owner. Darnell beds and abandons a beautiful real-estate agent (Lynn Whitfield), who then begins to stalk him. "The movie, in which Lawrence fancies himself a Casanova, just plain stinks from its lewd, witless beginning to its mean-spirited misogynistic end," Rita Kempley wrote for the *Washington Post* (April 3, 1996). She added, "Designed to fit the Fox TV star's broad, bawdy humor, the script is not the cautionary tale it pretends to be, but a vanity production of enormous insincerity. Sluggishly paced and largely uneventful, the film and its madly mugging star work overtime—if futilely—to establish the romantic credentials of the coarse self-promoter Darnell Wright."

In the spring of 1996, while filming his next movie, *Nothing to Lose*, Lawrence began to run into personal problems. On May 7 he was found wandering on Ventura Boulevard in Los Angeles, screaming "Fight the Power!" When the police subdued him, they found a gun in his pocket. After an overnight hospitalization, during which he was diagnosed with exhaustion and dehydration, he was allowed to return to his home. A few months later, he set off the metal detector in an airport with his concealed handgun. For that offense he received two years' probation. In October his wife, who had filed for divorce, placed a restraining order against Lawrence, who was deemed a danger to her and their daughter. To make matters worse, Tisha Campbell, the actress who played his girl-friend on *Martin*, filed a sexual-harassment suit against the performer, alleging that Lawrence had routinely fondled and groped her during the show's run. The suit was eventually settled out of court with the stipulation that neither side would discuss the subject in public. In a final incident, Lawrence was arrested and sentenced to perform community service for an assault in a Los Angeles nightclub. Although *People* magazine snagged a snapshot of Lawrence being led away on a gurney after the incident on Ventura Boulevard, the actor was largely able to keep the media out of his per-sonal business, so that reports about the nature of his problems are mainly speculation. It is known that he checked into a drug-rehabilitation facility in Tucson, leaving after only a day, when he decid-ed that he did not have a substance-abuse problem. Lawrence has repeatedly denied that he uses drugs but has acknowledged that he took antidepressants for a time.

When *Nothing to Lose* finally appeared in the-aters, the film was obscured by the waves of gossip about Lawrence's behavior. Short of its inspired casting, which paired Lawrence with Tim Robbins, *Nothing to Lose* (1997) failed to impress its review-ers. The film follows the actions of an unemployed man (Lawrence) who tries to car-jack a cuckolded advertising executive (Robbins). The two men bond, hold up a gas station, and then conspire to rob Robbins's boss, who has slept with his wife. Leah Rozen of *People* (July 28, 1997) called *Noth-ing to Lose* "a broad, mechanical comedy" but add-ed that "in the meager-plus column are an appeal-ing performance by Robbins, an energetic one from Lawrence, and a couple of inspired comic scenes."

Lawrence's next film, released more than a year later, marked something of a comeback for the ac-tor, who in many people's minds had been relegat-ed to the dustbin of promising entertainers de-railed by disastrous private lives. In *Life* (1999), Lawrence and Eddie Murphy teamed up as a cou-ple of convicts framed for murder. The movie's sto-ry line spans more than half a century, from the 1930s to the 1990s, tracking the ups and downs of the duo's friendship as they serve out their life sen-tences. "Murphy and Lawrence are a well-matched team for such a long haul," Tom Gliatto and Leah Rozen wrote in *People* (April 26, 1999). "Murphy, as usual, is astonishingly agile, shifting gears from gag to gag so quickly he practically sends out sparks. Lawrence plays tortoise to Murphy's hare: lower to the ground, slower with the double takes, still getting his laughs." Lawrence's most recent film is *Blue Streak*, in which he plays a newly re-leased convict who must impersonate a cop in or-der to retrieve a diamond he stashed in a police sta-tion before his imprisonment. While *Blue Streak* fared dismally with critics, it was popular with au-diences, whose patronage made it the top-grossing movie in its first week in theaters, in October 1999,

and kept its box-office receipts strong in the fol-lowing weeks.

Lawrence is divorced from Patricia Southall, a former Miss Virginia, whom he married in 1995 and with whom he has a daughter, Jasmin Paige. — M.C.

Suggested Reading: *Details* p98+ Apr. 1999, with photo; *Entertainment Weekly* p18+ Feb. 4, 1994, with photos; *People* p53+ Apr. 12, 1993, with photos; *Rolling Stone* p20 Nov. 3, 1993, with photo, p68+ Apr. 21, 1994, with photos; *Time* p68 July 21, 1997, with photos; *Washington Post* Y p7 Aug. 23, 1992

Selected Films: *House Party*, 1990; *You So Crazy*, 1994; *Bad Boys*, 1995; *A Thin Line Between Love and Hate*, 1996; *Nothing to Lose*, 1997; *Life*, 1999

Selected Television Shows: *Martin*, 1992–97

Laybourne, Geraldine

1947– Chair and CEO of Oxygen Media. Address: c/o Oxygen Media, 1370 Ave. of the Americas, 22d Fl., New York, NY 10019

"I like the impossible. It's a realm I feel truly com-fortable in," the multimedia executive Geraldine Laybourne told Disney/ABC higher-ups in 1996, a few months after her appointment as president of the company's cable division, as quoted by Sallie Hofmeister for the *Los Angeles Times Magazine* (September 8, 1996). "To motivate me," she re-marked, in another quote reported by Hofmeister, "all you have to say is 'That can't be done.'"

Laybourne's achievements, while perhaps not beyond belief, are certainly extraordinary. During the 16 years that she worked at the cable-television channel Nickelodeon, which is aimed at prepubes-cent and young teenage audiences, she developed it into the most widely watched children's station in the United States and turned it into the most profitable channel owned by Viacom, which also owns MTV and VH1. During the two years that she chaired Disney/ABC's cable networks, she guided ABC's Saturday-morning lineup to the number-one position in that time slot. In May 1998 Lay-bourne started her own company, Oxygen Media, which intends to produce quality material for women for cable television, the Internet, and print publications.

"The first time I heard the term 'glass ceiling,' I worried," Laybourne said recently in a speech. "It was such a strong image. It evoked so much. I knew it was no woman's friend. And by our repeating it, and hearing it repeated, we created a triple-ply thermopane glass—we imagined the hopelessness of having a seat at the table. We let it live in our

Joe Vericker/Courtesy of Oxygen Media

Geraldine Laybourne

brains and in our language. I longed for a time when women would come up with their own language to describe where they were going." Laybourne herself has gone very far indeed. The *Hollywood Reporter* once ranked her number one among the 50 most influential women in the entertainment industry, and in 1995 she was inducted into the Broadcasting and Cable Hall of Fame.

One of three children, Geraldine Laybourne was born Geraldine Bond in 1947 and grew up in Martinsville, New Jersey, about an hour west of New York City. Her father was a businessman; her mother worked as an actress, producer, and writer for radio soap operas before becoming a full-time homemaker. For Mrs. Bond, homemaking included using her artistic talents for the benefit of her children. "My mother routinely turned off television shows and made us write the endings," Laybourne told Kathleen Murray for the *New York Times* (March 14, 1993). "We were also the only house in the neighborhood where the kids could stay up till 3 a.m. doing things." For his part, Laybourne's father nurtured young Gerry's apparently inborn business acumen by explaining company balance sheets to her, and during the summers when she was 16 and 17, he put her in charge of the day-to-day operations of his brokerage office.

Laybourne earned a B.A. degree in art history from Vassar College, in Poughkeepsie, New York, in 1969. She intended to pursue a higher degree in architecture, but after realizing that her sense of spatial relations was limited, she abandoned that career path. In 1970 she met Kit Laybourne, who was teaching media-education courses at a high school in Philadelphia. "I didn't really connect with kids until I met my husband," Laybourne told

Murray. "That's when I saw how much influence the media could have over them." Less than six months after meeting Kit, she married him, and their first child was born within a year of their wedding. At about that time, Laybourne earned a master's degree in elementary education at the University of Pennsylvania. Soon afterward she and her husband moved to New Hampshire, where they both taught at the Concord Academy, a prep school. The academy "offered 40 media courses," she told Valerie Gladstone for *Savvy* (April 1988). "While I was there I began to get a foundation in what kids were like and how they related to media."

In 1974 the Laybournes moved to the New York City borough of Manhattan, where Kit resumed his former career as an animator and independent television producer and Gerry co-founded a consulting firm—the Media Center for Children, which recorded children's opinions, mainly for libraries and media producers. Not long afterward she co-founded another company, Early Bird Specials, along with her husband and the animator Eli Noyes. Funded by Thomas Watson, of IBM's founding family, Early Bird Specials marketed independently made programming to television networks. One of its clients was Nickelodeon; launched in 1979 and targeted at children, the network hired Early Bird Specials to develop pilots. In 1980 Laybourne, who by then had become the mother of two children—a daughter, Emmy, and a son, Sam—agreed to work for Nickelodeon full-time as a program manager.

In the late 1970s and early 1980s, what was labeled children's programming consisted solely of educational fare (such as what PBS and Nickelodeon offered) or "everything else"—mainly, Saturday morning cartoons. Whereas PBS's audience was steadily growing, Nickelodeon was less than successful then; indeed, its early years were later dubbed the "green vegetable days," because watching the channel was thought to be about as much fun as eating spinach or brussels sprouts. One example of Nickelodeon's turn-off programming was *Going Great*, which profiled whiz kids—concert pianists, prima ballerinas, and math geniuses; most children didn't want to watch it, reportedly because they felt worse about themselves after seeing the extraordinary accomplishments of other youngsters.

To determine how to improve Nickelodeon's ratings, Laybourne began doing research, and she recruited her own children among her subjects. As she recalled to Wayne Walley for *Advertising Age* (October 23, 1989), "I would bring home stacks of 50 tapes, and these poor kids would go in the back room, pull out the couch, and I'd make them watch Czechoslovakian animation. Finally it got to a point where it was, 'Please, Mom. Don't make us watch TV.'" Laybourne also set up focus groups around the country to test shows in development and to get a general feel for kids' concerns.

In 1984, thanks to Viacom's restructuring of management, Laybourne became the de facto chief of Nickelodeon. In a controversial move, she started to accept commercial advertising—a first for a network aimed at a young audience. The fees paid by the advertisers enabled Nickelodeon to invest in the production of its own programs, which it did amid dire predictions of disaster. As Laybourne told *Variety* (December 2, 1993), "We were told never to do live action, but we successfully developed game shows like *Double Dare*. We were told never to program just to girls, but we created *Clarissa Explains It All*. We were told never to do variety, but we succeeded with *Roundhouse*. And we were told in animation that you could only do pre-sold characters, but we went the way animation used to be, where the creators, not the toymakers, are in the driver's seat, which results in a much more original cartoon." In 1991 Laybourne persuaded Viacom to invest $40 million in the creation of several new animated series, and the results—*Rugrats, The Ren & Stimpy Show*, and *Doug*—soon attracted new audiences to Nickelodeon.

Meanwhile, in 1985 Arts & Entertainment (A&E), the network that had held the evening and night airtime on Nickelodeon's transponder, vacated its spot. To take advantage of that huge block of time with the little extra money available, Laybourne created the inexpensively produced *Nick at Nite*. Consisting of reruns of such classic TV shows as *Mr. Ed, Get Smart*, and *The Dick Van Dyke Show*, the evening programming became extremely popular, with whole families becoming regular viewers.

In 1989 Laybourne was promoted to president of Nickelodeon. She resolved to make Nickelodeon a brand name that signified quality children's entertainment. In 1990 she set up a studio that kids could tour at Universal Studios' theme park in Florida. Nickelodeon also collaborated with Mattel to develop new toys and other products. Laybourne established new divisions at Nickelodeon that were responsible for producing magazines, home videos, and records, and staff members continued to develop new programming. Heeding kids' complaints that televised news was too negative, Laybourne launched a news show, hosted by the broadcast journalist Linda Ellerbee, that emphasized positive stories and offered helpful advice, such as what to do in case of fire.

In 1993 Laybourne was promoted to vice chair of MTV Networks, and she took seats on Viacom's operating and executive committees. In that same year, in the first step toward realizing her dream of globalization, she struck a deal in which British Sky Broadcasting Ltd. agreed to broadcast Nickelodeon programs in Great Britain. In 1994 Nickelodeon issued a challenge to PBS, by introducing programming for toddlers. "We recognize that if we start getting kids to watch us at this age, we have them for life," Laybourne told Bill Carter for the *New York Times* (March 21, 1994). "That's ex-

actly the reason why we're doing it." Laybourne limited the advertising during shows for toddlers to half of what was allowed for programs aimed at older children.

Much to the shock of many of her co-workers, in mid-December 1995 Laybourne called off negotiations for her new contract with Nickelodeon and announced that she was leaving the network to take a job at Disney/ABC. "We were consciously doing things the way Disney was not," Herb Scannell, a Nickelodeon executive, told Eric Schmuckler for *Working Woman* (October 1996). "It was part of what was inspirational to us. Then you wake up one day and Gerry's going to Disney and your head's shaking a little bit." Laybourne defended her decision, claiming that she needed a fresh challenge. "The appeal is that it's a broad palette," she explained to the *New York Times* (December 16, 1995). "I'll get to talk to different audiences. We did important things for kids at Nick, and I look at finding the same sort of challenges for women, for news, and so on. I'll do [the] same thing I did here: roll up my sleeves, talk to consumers, and figure it out."

Laybourne joined Disney/ABC, in February 1996, as president of cable programming (excluding ESPN, an enormous network devoted to sports, which was deemed large enough to merit having its own president). Her new duties included improving the dismal fortunes of the Disney Channel and sitting on the board of cable stations in which Disney held a share—A&E, Lifetime, the History Channel, E! Entertainment Television—and their spin-offs.

Soon after she arrived at Disney/ABC, a sizable chunk of Laybourne's responsibilities evaporated, when a 24-hour all-news station was dropped, reportedly because of the enormous costs it entailed and the stiff competition presented by the well-established CNN and the new but well-funded MSNBC. Friends of hers speculated that Laybourne was disappointed by the loss of the news show and the shrinking of her power, but outwardly, she showed no signs of discontent.

Meanwhile, Disney asked Laybourne to revamp the Saturday-morning programming on the ABC network. Federal legislation mandated that all stations set aside at least three hours per week for educational programming for children. Since ABC aired only four hours of kids' television each week—the Saturday-morning shows—Laybourne had to devise a way to package the "green vegetable" shows so that kids would tune in. By the 1997–98 television season, Laybourne had succeeded in doing just that, with a four-hour block of programming entitled *One Saturday Morning*, which included cartoon series, live-action shorts, and segments of *Schoolhouse Rock* (short, animated songs that taught grammar and history). Thanks to *One Saturday Morning*, ABC soon toppled Fox as the highest-ranked Saturday-morning network, and it helped ABC climb to the number-two position (behind cable's Nickelodeon) among all stations in terms of numbers of young viewers.

In early 1998 Laybourne resigned from Disney/ABC to start up, in collaboration with her husband, a media-consulting business. Called Oxygen Media—because it "giv[es] room for the consumer to breathe," in Laybourne's words—the company, according to one of its publicity pieces, produces and distributes to television stations, the Internet, and other media "branded content" that "targets the women's and children's markets"; later, Oxygen Media decided to focus solely on women. Laybourne had long known that the most highly rated shows on cable catered to children or (in the case of sports broadcasts) men; women were largely ignored, even though, according to one statistic that Laybourne has cited, women make between 70 and 85 percent of all purchases in the U.S. "The traditional media have missed the boat with modern women," she told Saul Hansell for the *New York Times* (September 16, 1998). "There is nothing that serves women the way ESPN serves men or Nickelodeon serves kids. We want to create a brand on both television and the Internet that brings humor and playfulness and a voice that makes a woman say, 'You really understand me.'"

As chair and CEO of Oxygen Media, Laybourne secured partners among the many contacts she had made in her previous jobs. ABC Inc., for example, immediately made an investment in Oxygen, and in September 1998 America Online (AOL) agreed to share with Oxygen the rights to three content sites aimed specifically at women (Electra, Thrive, and Moms Online); in return for a 10 percent interest in Oxygen, AOL also agreed to feature the sites on a women's channel (which would provide links to various Web sites for women). In addition, with the goal of launching a cable network that would begin airing on February 1, 2000, Laybourne formed partnerships with Oprah Winfrey and Winfrey's Harpo Entertainment Group and with Carsey Werner Mandabach, a firm that has produced such hit comedies as *Roseanne, The Cosby Show,* and *Third Rock from the Sun.* Both of her new partners plan eventually to contribute shows from their extensive libraries as well as to create new ones. Laybourne has also started talks with cable operators to persuade them to carry her channel before the system switches over from analog stations (almost filled to capacity already) to digital (which will allow for a large number of new stations).

Laybourne has sat on many boards and advisory committees, among them the National Council for Families and Television, New York Women in Film and Television, and the Children Affected by AIDS Foundation. Her many honors include the Annenberg Public Policy Center's Award for Distinguished Lifetime Contribution to Children and Television, in 1997, and both the American Women in Radio and Television Genii Award and a Women in Cable Award, in 1992. — K.S.

Suggested Reading: *Los Angeles Times Magazine* p10+ Sep. 8, 1996, with photos; *New York Times* p8 Mar. 14, 1993; *Working Woman* p30+ Oct. 1996, with photos

Courtesy of Main Event

Lewis, Lennox

Sep. 2, 1965– Boxer. Address: c/o International Boxing Hall of Fame Museum, P.O. Box 425, Canastota, NY 13032

On March 13, 1999 in New York City's Madison Square Garden, the World Boxing Council (WBC) heavyweight champion Lennox Lewis faced the International Boxing Federation (IBF) and World Boxing Association (WBA) heavyweight champion Evander Holyfield in a match that promised to be one of the biggest and most thrilling heavyweight contests in two decades. But the fight did not live up to its billing. Although most boxing experts, among them the referee at the match and former heavyweight champion Muhammad Ali, agreed that Lewis had controlled the fight through much of its 12 rounds, the contest was ruled a draw. For Lewis, whose professional record currently stands at 34 wins (27 of them resulting from knockouts), one loss, and one draw, the controversial decision was particularly disappointing. Had he been declared the victor, he might finally have gained the respect of doubting boxing aficionados who have long questioned his ability, desire, and focus. Indeed, although Lewis has been one of the world's top heavyweights since he turned professional, in 1989, most fans have continued to associate the best of heavyweight boxing with the likes of Mike Tyson, Evander Holyfield, Riddick Bowe, and even George Foreman.

Lewis's relative anonymity may be attributed to several factors. First, although he cuts a formidable figure (he is six feet, five inches and 245 pounds and has a reach of 82 inches), Lewis has often been described as introverted, and he keeps a relatively low profile in a sport where fighters routinely pull outrageous antics to gain publicity and promote fights. Lewis, who was born in England to his Jamaican-born mother, Violet, and raised in Canada, may also have been hampered by his Englishness: in the latter half of the 20th century, the heavyweight division of professional boxing has been dominated by Americans. Furthermore, unlike most boxers, Lewis has often criticized the state of boxing. The top fighters earn enormous purses, and their large paychecks, as well as the high cost of promoting fights, borne by the sponsors, result in fewer fights. Boxers with large followings, won with mediagenic personalities as much as with their skills in the ring, draw the most viewers and thus the most revenue, and this, coupled with the small number of matches, makes it extremely difficult for lesser-knowns to get opportunities to face the biggest names. "I should be the undisputed heavyweight champion, that's my goal," Lewis told Ira Berkow for the New York Times (September 3, 1994). "But this is a business, not really a sport, as I've come to learn, and you can get blocked at certain points, like I've been." Another reason for Lewis's low profile is that the trials and tribulations of Mike Tyson during the 1990s have overshadowed the careers of other heavyweights.

However, what has really thwarted Lewis from attaining the respect and adulation of many fight fans has been and continues to be his untested status. For the most part, in his nearly 10 years as a professional, Lewis has not proven his mettle against the sport's top heavyweights. Perhaps the aforementioned business-sports complexities have gotten in the way; perhaps some boxers have simply avoided fighting him. Although he has been impressive at times, demonstrating an awe-inspiring right hand that has sent numerous opponents to the canvas, as well as the fortitude to go the distance by winning 12-round decisions over the likes of Tony Tucker, in 1993, and Ray Mercer, in 1996, Lewis's legitimacy has never quite been cemented in the eyes of the public.

Questions concerning Lewis's ability have plagued him throughout his career. When he began boxing professionally in England, in 1989, some viewed Lewis as the long-sought hero who would fill the country's century-long void in heavyweight boxing. (The last British heavyweight champion had been Bob Fitzsimmons, who won the crown in 1897.) However, many argued that Lewis was really Canadian, since he had lived in Canada from the age of 12 and had fought for that country in two Olympic Games. Some even went so far as to criticize Lewis and his handlers for what they perceived to be carpetbagging. Although Lewis became the first Brit to hold any world heavyweight title in nearly a century, when he first won the WBC title, in December 1992, the moment was hardly triumphant. Riddick Bowe, who had won the WBC, IBF, and WBA titles by beating Evander Holyfield in November 1992, was stripped of the first-named title when he refused to meet Lewis in

a mandatory title defense. At a news conference, Bowe renounced the WBC title, demonstrating his unhappiness with the WBC by throwing the belt in a garbage can. As deserving as Lewis may have been—he was the top contender for the unified heavyweight title—his title was earned without his ever throwing a punch in a championship fight, and his title belt was retrieved from the trash. Thus, many boxing fans questioned Lewis's legitimacy.

Lewis seemed to prove his detractors right when, in September 1994, he lost the WBC title to Oliver McCall, whose previous claim to fame was that he had been Mike Tyson's sparring partner. Such inconsistency prompted many, including Tom Friend of the New York Times (July 12, 1997), to label Lewis "the classic underachiever." However, the loss to McCall sparked a change in Lewis. He has since hired the trainer who coached McCall, and he has launched a serious and ferocious campaign to become a great heavyweight champion. In 1997 he regained the WBC title which he had so embarrassingly lost.

Lennox Claudius Lewis was born on September 2, 1965, in London's East End. His mother, Violet, separated from his father soon after their son's birth, and Lennox grew up in a tough working-class neighborhood. When he was nine, he moved from England to Canada with his mother for a year, then returned to England, where he lived with an aunt. Violet then brought Lennox back to Canada to stay with her in Kitchener, Ontario, when he was 12. She told William Nack for Sports Illustrated (February 1, 1993), "I brought him back to Canada because I thought someone would abuse him or ill-treat him. He was very stubborn and hyperactive." Lennox began boxing at age 12, soon after his arrival in Kitchener, after he walked into Arnie Boehm's gym in the Kitchener police headquarters. As he recalled to Nack, he felt an immediate attraction to the sport: "I liked it. It was ego against ego. Both looking at each other all the time. A chess game. The one-on-one is what appealed to me about boxing."

Lewis also proved to be a fierce competitor outside the ring. He was a star athlete in football, basketball, and track and field at the Cameron Heights Collegiate High School, but he eventually stopped playing other sports and focused on boxing. In 1983 he won the world junior title in boxing, then captured his first of five consecutive all-Canadian super-heavyweight titles. He represented Canada at the 1984 Olympic Games in Los Angeles, California, but lost in his quarterfinal bout to Tyrell Biggs of the U.S. Four years later, at the 1988 Olympic Games in Seoul, South Korea, he won the super-heavyweight gold medal by pummeling Riddick Bowe. After two standing-eight counts, the referee ended the fight in the second round.

In 1989 Lewis met his present manager, Frank Maloney, who assisted in bringing Lewis to England and helped him attain a lucrative contract from the Levitt Group, a business run by a group of financiers. "I saw [England] as a good place to start," Lewis told Nack. "I didn't see it as an economic thing." Others did, feeling that his rediscovery of his British identity was opportunistic, but such sentiments were quickly forgotten when Lewis, who trained with John Davenport, knocked out Al Malcolm in just two rounds in his professional debut on June 27, 1989. In October 1990, after a string of victories, Lewis became the European champion by stopping Jean Chanet in the sixth round. He then began gaining attention as "the great Brit Hope," as some fans called him.

Lewis continued to record victories in the ring, often knocking his opponent to the canvas with his powerful right. His climb through the ranks of heavyweight boxing was haunted by questions about the caliber of his competition. One of Lewis's first real tests came in October 1992, when he faced Donovan "Razor" Ruddock in London. Seven months earlier, Lewis had replaced trainer Davenport with Pepe Correa, who had trained Sugar Ray Leonard. Although Ruddock was not a champion, he had fought well against Tyson twice and he was considered by many boxing aficionados to be a skilled and formidable fighter. Thus it came as somewhat of a shock when Lewis floored Ruddock with a right in the first round, then finished Ruddock off by KO in the second. With the win, Lewis became the leading contender for the WBC heavyweight title, which was then held by Riddick Bowe. Boxing fans eagerly waited to see Lewis and Bowe go head-to-head, especially since the two had fought before as amateurs and seemed to dislike each other. However, the match and the rivalry between Lewis and Bowe never became anything more than a battle of words. Bowe refused to fight Lewis in the WBC mandatory title defense, and he discarded the WBC title.

After being denied the opportunity to prove himself a champion in the ring, Lewis moved to dispel his image as a champion by default by signing a deal with Main Events, an American boxing promotion company. Main Events helped arrange a title defense against Tony Tucker in Las Vegas, Nevada, in May 1993. Lewis won the 12-round decision over Tucker and earned $9 million for his efforts, but many boxing aficionados continued to point out that prior to his defeats of Ruddick and Tucker, Lewis had won rather empty victories. For example, Pat Putnam, writing for *Sports Illustrated* (May 17, 1993), described Lewis as having "yet to prove his heart, chin, and stamina" after having "fought a lineup of guys named Journeyman and Tomatocan."

Lewis underwent surgery on his right hand in May 1993, then defended his title for the second time in October 1993 against a fellow Brit, Frank Bruno, who had conformed to many Americans' low opinion of British heavyweights by losing badly to Mike Tyson. Although Bruno was considered to be the far inferior fighter, he took Lewis to seven rounds before losing by TKO. Most in attendance did not speak favorably about the fight or Lewis.

Pat Putnam, writing for *Sports Illustrated* (October 3, 1993), commented that "Lewis's credentials as a champion were shaky at best in Britain, and nearly nonexistent in the rest of the world," and he described Lewis's performance thusly: "While Bruno's crushing jab gradually turned the left side of Lewis's face swollen and bloody, the champion operated in retreat behind his pushing jabs and occasional overhand rights, most of which followed a Western Union message announcing their arrival."

In May 1994 Lewis defended his title for the third time, against Phil Jackson, a fighter from the U.S. Most boxing observers didn't consider Jackson to be a serious contender. In fairness to Lewis, by this time he was having difficulty setting up fights. Most top heavyweights did not actively seek him out as an opponent. Proposed fights against Holyfield and Bowe never materialized. Lewis's attempts to arrange fights with the sport's best were also hindered by the complicated regulations of boxing's three separate ruling bodies and by promoters. In the meantime, Holyfield regained the WBA and IBF heavyweight titles by beating Bowe, then lost them to underdog Michael Moorer. It was a tumultuous period in the heavyweight world, but Lewis could only watch from the sidelines and keep hoping for a chance to fight a respected opponent and perhaps unite the three titles.

Then, in what should have been an easy victory for Lewis, he was KOed by McCall just 31 seconds into the second round of their bout at Wembley Stadium in London. Lewis's handlers protested the loss by insisting that the referee, Lupe Garcia, had ended the fight too soon by counting too quickly, but the result was upheld. The loss seemed to confirm all the lingering doubts about Lewis, but it had a positive effect as well. For Lewis, the loss seemed to be a wake-up call. He fired Correa and hired his present trainer, Emmanuel Steward, who had helped train McCall. With Steward in his corner, Lewis added more effective combinations and a stronger jab to his arsenal. He also became more aggressive and focused in the ring. "From the very first moment I was learning, especially on balance or punch combinations," Lewis told the *Electronic Telegraph* (October 2, 1995). "[Steward and I] have a chemistry and good communication."

Under Steward's guidance, Lewis launched his campaign to regain the WBC title. After making quick work of Lionel Butler, Justin Fortune, and Tommy Morrison in May, July, and October 1995, respectively, Lewis won a 12-round majority decision against former heavyweight champion Ray Mercer at New York's Madison Square Garden in May 1996. Because Mercer was a former heavyweight champion and was considered a formidable fighter, Lewis's victory was viewed as a major triumph in some boxing circles. Lewis continued to seek fights against big names. To make a run at the unified title, Lewis needed not just wins but respectable wins, yet the field of choice opponents was looking exceptionally lean. Many, like Holyfield and Foreman, were phasing out of competition due to age. Others, like Bowe, had begun fading from the sport. Still, Lewis made quick work of McCall in their rematch on February 7, 1997, and won back the WBC belt. (As if to highlight the dearth of real competition for Lewis in the heavyweight division, McCall started crying and appeared to suffer a nervous breakdown during the match.) In July 1997 Lewis defended his title against Henry Akinwande of Nigeria in yet another debacle, in which the Nigerian was disqualified for excessive holding. Commenting on these less-than-stellar outings, Lewis told Timothy W. Smith for the *New York Times* (October 1, 1997), "I've been appointed to get rid of all the misfit heavyweights out there."

Lewis then beat the Polish boxer Andrew Golota, yet another misfit heavyweight, in October 1997. It was telling that although Golota, who had a reputation as a dirty fighter, was the challenger and was widely considered to lack courage in the ring, many odds-makers favored him to beat Lewis. After finishing off Golota by a technical knockout (TKO) in the first round, Lewis said, as quoted by *Boxing Times* (October 4, 1997), "I wanted to prove I'm the best heavyweight on the planet. I want to consolidate all the belts together and keep them for myself." On March 28, 1998, in Atlantic City, Lewis defeated Shannon Briggs by TKO is the fifth round. In September 1998 Lewis successfully defended his WBC title against the WBC's top-ranked challenger, Zeljok Mavrovic of Croatia, winning a unanimous decision in 12 rounds. He thereby retained his WBC title for the fourth time since capturing it from Oliver McCall in February 1997. Then came the March 1999 bout against Holyfield, in which Lewis landed 348 of 613 punches, and Holyfield 130 of 385 thrown. Despite that glaring disparity, one judge awarded the fight to Holyfield, another judge awarded the fight to Lewis, and a third ruled the fight a draw. Some boxing aficionados attributed the judges' failure to declare Lewis the winner to Lewis's insufficient aggressiveness in the later rounds, when, they claimed, he could have ended the fight with a knockout. In any event, according to Timothy W. Smith in the *New York Times* (March 15, 1999), the ruling was "one of the most controversial decisions in a big-time fight in recent history." The ensuing public furor prompted several state and federal investigations as well as cries for reform from boxing fans and officials. A rematch between Lewis and Holyfield was set for November 1999 in Las Vegas, Nevada. "In this second fight I'm going to be taking more chances," Lewis said, as quoted by Timothy W. Smith for the *New York Times* (September 30, 1999). "When [Holyfield is] hurt, this time he's going to be asking himself if he wants to go on."

Lewis has been described as very reclusive. From his 35 professional fights, he has earned more than $55 million in purses, some of which he used to open a private secondary school for disadvantaged children called Lennox Lewis College, in east London, in 1995. Until 1998, when the school

received £100,000 of public funding, it was funded mainly by personal contributions from Lewis and his financial backer, Panos Eliades. Lewis reportedly avoids the boxing scene between fights, preferring instead to travel between his homes in England, Canada, and Jamaica. He also enjoys playing chess. — Y.P.

Suggested Reading: *Electronic Telegraph* Oct. 2, 1995; *Guardian* Weekend p1+ Sep. 18, 1993, with photos; *New York Times* I p27 Sep. 3, 1994, with photo, I p31 July 12, 1997, C p5 Oct. 1, 1997, D p1+ Mar. 15, 1999, with photos; *Sports Illustrated* p38+ Feb. 1, 1993, with photos, p36+ Oct. 3, 1993, with photos

---

Courtesy of Elizabeth F. Loftus

Loftus, Elizabeth F.

Oct. 16, 1944– Experimental psychologist.
Address: c/o Dept. of Psychology, University of
Washington, Box 351525, Seattle, WA 98195

Can you remember the words that are engraved on the penny? Or the letters on the number-five key on a Touch-Tone telephone? Is memory like a videotape that records everything, or are some memories lost forever? Such questions have occupied Elizabeth Loftus, a professor of psychology and an adjunct professor of law at the University of Washington, in Seattle, for most of her career, and the answers that she has come up with have led her into some highly contentious debates concerning human memory. In the "memory wars" of the 1980s and the 1990s, in which victims claimed to have "recovered" deeply repressed memories of sexual abuse, parents and day-care workers protested their innocence, and experts battled one another in the pages of the *Times Literary Supplement*, Loftus emerged as one of the conflict's central figures. She is, as the subtitle of one of her books puts it, "the expert who puts memory on trial."

Over the course of nearly three decades, Loftus and her students have performed experiments involving more than 20,000 subjects. Her findings, which may surprise many, indicate that memory is fragile and fallible. Not only can memories be affected by leading questions; some people can even be induced to have "memories" of events that never happened. Such findings have thrown into question the reliability of eyewitness testimony and the verdicts in cases in which defendants have been sent to jail solely on the strength of such testimony. Loftus's findings also cast doubt on the claim, made by supporters of the recovered-memory movements, that traumatic cases of abuse during childhood can be deeply repressed and then brought back to consciousness years or even decades later by psychotherapeutic techniques.

Loftus's research has led her from the classroom to the courtroom. An expert much sought out by criminal-defense attorneys, she has participated in more than 200 lawsuits. These include the trials of Ted Bundy (in a rape case prior to his trial for murder), the Hillside Strangler, Oliver North, the Menendez brothers, Steve Titus, the officers involved in the Rodney King beating, and workers at the McMartin Preschool in Manhattan Beach, California. They also include such famous "recovered memory" cases as that of George Franklin, whose daughter accused him of a child's murder that she said she suddenly remembered 20 years after he committed it. Franklin was convicted in 1990 and was released five years later on appeal.

Not surprisingly, Loftus has been accused of helping murderers, rapists, child abusers, and pedophiles. Prosecutors have called her a "whore," and recovered-memory supporters claim that her findings on "ordinary" memory do not apply to cases of "traumatic" memory. At times the accusations against Loftus have been vicious. She once received a letter that compared her to the revisionist historians who deny that the Holocaust ever happened. On the other hand, to those who think that false accusations have destroyed their lives, she comes across as an Oscar Schindler figure—a comparison she herself made in a conversation with Jill Neimark for *Psychology Today* (January 1996): while watching the movie *Schindler's List*, she said, she identified with Schindler when he wished aloud that he could have saved "one more person."

"If I had known what my life would be like now—the frantic phone calls, the tearful confessions, the gruesome stories of sadistic sexual abuse, torture, even murder—would I have beaten a retreat back to the safety and security of my laboratory?" Loftus asked herself in *The Myth of Repressed Memory* (1994), one of the books she co-

wrote with Katherine Ketcham. "No. Never. For I am privileged to be at the center of an unfolding drama, a modern tale filled with such passion and anguish that it rivals an ancient Greek tragedy."

The only daughter among the three children of Sidney Fishman, a physician, and Rebecca Fishman, a librarian, Loftus was born Elizabeth Fishman on October 16, 1944 in Los Angeles. On July 10, 1959, one of the most traumatic incidents of her childhood occurred: her mother was found drowned in a swimming pool. The grief this caused Loftus is evident even today, as the very mention of her mother's death can bring her to tears. Loftus told Jill Neimark, "I miss the idea of having a mother, so I've gone around being a mother." Two years after her mother's death, Loftus's father married a woman with three children of her own.

As a teenager, Loftus planned to become a high-school math teacher, "because math was the one thing my father and I could talk about," she told Neimark. At the University of California, Los Angeles, she began studying mathematics, but an interest in psychology intervened, and she graduated, in 1966, with a degree in both math and psychology. She went on to study mathematical psychology at Stanford University, where she met and married a fellow graduate student, Geoffrey Loftus, in 1968. She earned a doctorate in psychology in 1970. (Although she would later teach law-related courses, she does not have a degree in law.) For the next several years, career moves prevented her from being in the same city with her husband. In 1973 an opportunity to work with him presented itself: Geoffrey landed a job in the psychology department of the University of Washington, and Elizabeth received offers from the University of Washington and Harvard. In 1973—after Geoffrey told her that if she decided on Harvard, they should divorce—Loftus followed her husband to Washington.

Loftus had become interested in research in long-term memory when she was a graduate student. At Washington she pursued that interest and published articles with such titles as "Memory for intentions: The effect of presence of a cue and interpolated activity." Concerned that her research had seemingly little practical value, Loftus began to ask herself how she could make her work more relevant to real life. That question led her to the topic of eyewitness testimony, which had been studied very little up to that time.

In her experiments Loftus showed her subjects films of accidents and crimes and asked them questions about what they remembered. She found that what her subjects thought they had seen could easily be influenced by the phrasing of a question. For instance, asking a subject, "How fast were the two cars going when they smashed each other?" yielded higher speed estimates than asking, "How fast were the two cars going when they hit each other?" Just by carefully controlling what she asked her subjects, she could make them "remember" nonexistent barns in fields or believe they had seen an image of Minnie Mouse when in actuality they had seen Mickey Mouse. The implications of her work were disturbing and potentially revolutionary. Juries tend to take eyewitness testimony very seriously and to weigh it more heavily than other evidence. The results of Loftus's studies seemed to indicate that eyewitness testimony could not always be trusted.

As she explored the question further, Loftus found many explanations for the fallibility of eyewitness reports. Many of these explanations are found in her books *Eyewitness Testimony* (1979), which won a National Media Award from the American Psychological Foundation, and *Memory: Surprising New Insights into How We Remember and Why We Forget* (1980). Stress during the occurrence of a crime, a tendency to focus on the weapon rather than the criminal's face, problems identifying members of other races, and an overeagerness to help the police can all contribute to inaccuracy in identifications. Police officers, in the way they present lineups or photos, may also influence eyewitnesses' identifications of suspects. "Eyewitnesses who point their finger at innocent defendants are not liars, for they genuinely believe in the truth of their testimony . . . ," Loftus told Jill Neimark. "That's the frightening part—the truly horrifying idea that what we think we know, what we believe with all our hearts, is not necessarily the truth."

Loftus's work in eyewitness memory marked the beginning of her involvement as an expert witness in nearly 200 court cases. Naturally, some prosecutors see her as an annoying hindrance. Since she receives fees of several hundred dollars per hour for her work, she is always open to the criticism that she in effect sells her science. For her part, Loftus is driven by a desire to help the accused, particularly in those cases for which eyewitness testimony is the primary or sole evidence. She has been approached for help in many such cases, and has turned down only one—when, in 1987, she was asked to work on the legal team defending John Demjanjuk, the naturalized American citizen who was accused of being Ivan the Terrible, the infamous Nazi guard who sent thousands of Jews to the gas chambers at the Treblinka concentration camp in Poland during World War II. Demjanjuk was extradited to Israel and convicted in 1988, but the conviction was reversed in 1992 by Israel's supreme court, and Demjanjuk was returned to the United States. Loftus has said that she refused to work on the case out of consideration for her family, since they are Jewish and the case would have caused them a lot of pain.

Loftus's later work on memory expanded on her earlier studies, with one difference: instead of focusing on how the details of real-life events get misconstrued, she investigated whether an entire false memory could be implanted in her subjects. This led to what she has called her "Lost in the Shopping Mall" experiments. With the help of her subjects' parents, she created false stories about her subjects' being lost in a shopping mall at about five years of age. When confronted with this story, most subjects claimed not to remember the incident. However, about 10 percent said they recalled being lost and added details to the story. Another 15 percent said that they remembered the incident vaguely. Thus, Loftus had succeeded in convincing about a quarter of her subjects of the reality of an event that had never taken place. Other researchers have since reported that they too have succeeded in planting false memories in their subjects.

These studies threw into question the central claims of the recovered-memory movement, which in the 1980s was getting national attention. A first wave of cases involved preschool children who "remembered" being sexually abused by their daycare providers. Another wave followed, with adults claiming to have recovered memories of being abused as children by their parents or other authority figures. According to Neimark, more than 800 lawsuits based on recovered-memory claims have been filed. The comedienne Roseanne and other celebrities have claimed to have recovered memories of abuse, and recovered memory has even become a central theme in the popular television show *The X-Files*.

Loftus suspected that the truth of recovered memories lay not in the past but in the techniques psychotherapists used to "recover" these supposed memories. Some psychotherapists sympathetic to the notion of repressed memories either use hypnosis or ask their subjects to give free rein to their imaginations in attempting to recover repressed memories. Loftus believed that such suggestiveness could easily lead patients to believe that what they were imagining was true. In one study designed to address this specific question, she asked her subjects to imagine that they had done certain things, such as breaking windows with their hands, when they were children. When these subjects were later asked if they had actually done those things, a significant number of those who had participated in the imagination exercise answered in the affirmative. Loftus calls this form of mistake "source confusion."

Loftus's own experience dramatically confirmed her research on false memories. On her 44th birthday, approximately 30 years after her mother's death, an uncle told Loftus that she had been the one to find her mother's body. Suddenly, Loftus began recalling the event vividly. Days later, however, she learned that her uncle had made a mistake and had confirmed with other relatives that her aunt, not Loftus, had found the body. Sheerly by accident, Loftus had succeeded in planting a false memory in her own mind.

Supporters of the repressed-memory movement have maintained that there is a crucial difference between the memory of everyday incidents, like getting lost in a mall, and the memory of traumatic incidents, like sexual abuse. They therefore question the applicability of Loftus's research in the lat-

LUZHKOV

ter category. Loftus is skeptical about these claims, and she has doubts about the "trauma" that abuse can supposedly cause. In a book with Katherine Ketcham, *Witness for the Defense: The Accused, the Eyewitness, and the Expert Who Puts Memory on Trial* (1991), she revealed that when a prosecutor accused her of knowing nothing about sexual abuse, she replied that in fact she had been sexually molested by a baby-sitter when she was six. The abuse, she has said, did not become a defining factor in her life. "It's not that big a deal," she told Jill Neimark.

Loftus has often been asked whether she feels uncomfortable about defending people who could potentially be sexual molesters or pedophiles. Such a question misconstrues the nature of her advocacy. Despite her own reservations, and despite the fiery rhetoric that makes it seem as if there are two starkly opposed camps in memory research, Loftus has admitted that she cannot claim that the theory of repressed memories is baseless. "When working on legal cases, in the end I can't say the abuse didn't happen," she told Jill Neimark. "I can only say if these memories are false, here's how they may have developed."

Elizabeth Loftus and Geoffrey Loftus were divorced in about 1991. Work, she has admitted, contributed to their breakup. "I did not realize what a workaholic I was going to become," she told Jill Neimark. Currently, she is unmarried and lives near Lake Washington in the Seattle, Washington, area.

In the course of her career, Loftus has published 20 books and textbooks, as well as more than 300 academic articles. She has received many awards, among them the Distinguished Contribution Award from the American Academy of Forensic Psychology, in 1995, and the Distinguished Contribution to Basic and Applied Scientific Psychology Award, from the American Association of Applied and Preventive Psychology, in 1996. In 1997, she became a James McKeen Cattell Fellow in the American Psychological Society, in recognition of "a career of significant intellectual contributions to the science of psychology in the area of applied psychological research." — W.G.

Suggested Reading: *Chronicle of Higher Education* A p9+ Sep. 23, 1992, with photo; *Psychology Today* p48+ Jan. 1996; *Time* p89 Jan. 5, 1981, with photo

Selected Books: *Eyewitness Testimony*, 1979; *Memory: Surprising New Insights into How We Remember and Why We Forget*, 1980; with S. A. Mednick and R. H. Pollio—*Learning*, 1973; with Geoffrey Loftus: *Human Memory: The Processing of Information*, 1976; *Essence of Statistics*, 1982; *Statistics*, 1988; with L. E. Bourne and R. L. Dominowski—*Cognitive Processes*, 1979; with C. B. Wortman—*Psychology*, 1981; with R. Bootzin and R. Zajonc—*Psychology Today* (5th edition), 1983; as editor, with G. Wells—*Eyewitness*

Testimony—Psychological Perspectives, 1984; with James Doyle—*Eyewitness Testimony: Civil and Criminal*, 1987; with Katherine Ketcham—*Witness for the Defense: The Accused, the Eyewitness, and the Expert Who Puts Memory on Trial*, 1991; *The Myth of Repressed Memory*, 1994

Archive Photos

Luzhkov, Yuri

Sep. 21, 1936– Mayor of Moscow. Address: c/o Government of Moscow, Tverskaya str. 13, 103032 Moscow, Russia

Since the dissolution of the Soviet Union, in 1991, and the ensuing end of the Cold War, Russia has suffered serious setbacks in its effort to transform its command economy into a capitalist, free-market system. Crime and corruption have run rampant, unemployment has soared, inflation has destroyed the value of countless people's earnings and savings, and the standard of living of the majority of Russians has dropped significantly. In this bleak landscape, Moscow's mayor, Yuri Luzhkov, who was described by Alessandra Stanley in the *New York Times Magazine* (August 31, 1997) as "the embodiment of capitalism with a Slavic face," has won popularity with his mix of capitalist fervor, Soviet-style social spending, and autocratic whim.

Much of Luzhkov's political mandate and appeal stems from the fact that Moscow has until recently been spared the economic devastation that has plagued the rest of Russia for most of the 1990s. After he took office, in 1992, the 11 million occupants of Russia's political and commercial capital enjoyed several years of a relatively stable standard of living, thanks to the city's consistently high revenues from taxes and its many commercial holdings. With these funds Luzhkov has initiated and carefully overseen numerous real-estate development and public-works projects, which have alleviated the city's housing shortage and helped turn Moscow into a thriving metropolis. Moscow's high revenues have also enabled Luzhkov to maintain pensions, subsidies, price controls on milk and bread, and other social safety nets for Muscovites and ailing industries. Only in the last year has Luzhkov seen signs in his own city of the economic problems that have long plagued the rest of Russia.

At a time when much of Russia's electorate has lashed out against both the economic reforms based on a Western capitalist model and the highly nationalistic, state-controlled model espoused by hard-line Communists, Luzhkov has emerged as a centrist who compares his approach to that of Prime Minister Tony Blair of Great Britain. "We think New Labor is akin to what we do in Moscow," he was quoted as saying by Janet Guyon in *Fortune* (November 23, 1998). "We distribute the fruits of capitalism in a socialist, democratic sharing."

With a firm power base in Russia's most prominent and biggest city, a reputation for getting results, strong nationalist credentials, and control of a formidable media and financial empire based in Moscow, Luzhkov is a strong contender to succeed Russian president Boris Yeltsin, whose mandate and influence have been fading for several years. Although Luzhkov has yet to formally declare his candidacy for the next presidential election—which is scheduled for the summer of 2000, but may very well take place sooner, depending on Yeltsin's health and mandate—he has laid the necessary groundwork. In November 1998 he created the broad-based, centrist Fatherland Party. He has also won the endorsement of prominent business figures, regional governors, and such notable Russian political figures as Viktor Chernomyrdin, the ex–prime minister who had once been widely expected to succeed Yeltsin.

Yuri Mikhailovich Luzhkov was born on September 21, 1936 in Moscow, at a time when that city was the capital of both Russia and the Soviet Union. His father was a carpenter; his mother worked at a state-run factory. Luzhkov graduated from the Moscow Institute of the Oil and Gas Industry, with a degree in mechanical engineering, in 1958. From 1958 to 1964 he worked at the Research Institute of Plastics Materials. He was chosen to head a division of the Ministry of Chemical Industry in 1964 and served in that post until 1987. During that time he was a lower-ranking member of the Communist Party.

In 1987 Luzhkov joined Moscow's city government as the head of its Executive Committee and was selected by Boris Yeltsin, who headed Moscow's Communist Party, to oversee the city's food distribution system. Soon afterward Luzhkov took charge of Moscow's efforts to develop business ventures, which were undertaken as a result of perestroika, the policy of economic and governmental reforms instituted by Mikhail Gorbachev, the leader of the Soviet Union. These new businesses operated neither as wholly free enterprises nor as entirely state-owned concerns.

In August 1991 Luzhkov entered electoral politics and was elected Moscow's deputy mayor. He served as the second-in-command under Mayor Gavriil Popov, a Yeltsin ally, and gained experience in running the city. Meanwhile, in 1991, he earned his democratic credentials when he sided with President Yeltsin, who faced down a coup attempt by hard-line Communists reacting against Gorbachev's reforms. When Popov retired, in June 1992, Luzhkov was appointed to the post of Moscow mayor by Yeltsin, who continued to preside over Russia after the collapse of the Soviet Union.

In his new post Luzhkov initiated and oversaw a public works and construction boom in Moscow, which resulted in numerous new apartments and office towers. Some of the construction projects held great symbolic significance for Russians and Muscovites: for example, Luzhkov led efforts for the completion of a large World War II memorial and the expensive reconstruction of the Cathedral of Christ the Savior, which was built in the 19th century and was torn down by the Soviet dictator Josef Stalin in 1931. Such gestures helped Luzhkov gain the support of Moscow's many veterans and increasingly powerful nationalists.

Much of this development was funded by Moscow's relatively high revenues, which stemmed from the city's vast holdings in real estate and businesses. As of late 1998 Moscow's government reportedly held stakes in about 400 businesses (referred to collectively as Moscow Inc.), including auto plants, an oil company, television stations, newspapers, and even a chain of fast-food restaurants. These holdings and Moscow's resulting wealth grew out of Luzhkov's decision to resist the federal government's nationwide privatization efforts, initiated in 1993 by Yeltsin's top reformer at the time, Deputy Prime Minister Anatoli Chubais. Although that program, which used a voucher system to privatize state property, resulted in one of the largest transfers of state assets to private hands in history, Moscow was not a participant; instead, Luzhkov was able to persuade Yeltsin's government in 1994 to let Moscow conduct its own privatization scheme. Luzhkov has proceeded with that plan at a slower pace than the rest of Russia; this has consistently allowed Moscow to earn more money from those assets it has sold or rented to the private sector. According to figures cited by David Hoffman in the *Washington Post* (February 24, 1997), Moscow gained $1 billion from selling or renting state property in 1996; this amount was greater than that raised by the federal government in its efforts at privatization. "We say that privatization is necessary to create new owners who will manage the factories better than the old, but that is possible only if the factories are sold for real money, so the new owner has to work to make a return on his investment," Luzhkov told Paul Klebnikov for *Forbes* (November 16, 1998).

Luzhkov's government has also benefitted from favorable tax laws for much of his two terms. These laws, which were amended in 1997, required companies to pay taxes where their headquarters were located. Thus, even companies that transacted most of their business in far-flung regions had to pay their taxes to Moscow. Moreover, as the center of commerce in Russia, Moscow received the lion's share of direct foreign investment; according to Janet Guyon's *Fortune* article, in 1997 Moscow received $8 billion in such funds, accounting for nearly 80 percent of Russia's total.

In addition to these funds, Luzhkov's government has reportedly benefitted from unofficial sources of money, such as kickbacks, graft, and coerced contributions from businesses. Such gray revenue may stem from the unusually close ties Luzhkov has forged with private businesses and from Luzhkov's firm control of property allocation. For instance, a high number of businesses in Moscow, having profited greatly from the mayor's policies, have contributed their goods and services to public-works projects initiated by Luzhkov's government. Although some have labeled this arrangement cronyism and have criticized as anticompetitive the way business is done under Luzhkov, the mayor's supporters have widely defended him for allowing some of the profits gained by Moscow's business community to return to the city. Luzhkov has also been criticized by human rights organizations for his autocratic tendencies. For example, he has repeatedly expelled homeless people from Moscow before large city events. He is also alleged to have pressured dissenting press to leave Moscow through his control of rents and taxes. In addition, he has kept up the Soviet-originated system of residence permits, without which non-Muscovites are not permitted to live in Moscow—even though that system was ruled unconstitutional by Russia's Constitutional Court in 1996.

Despite those controversial actions, Luzhkov has consistently enjoyed strong popular support in Moscow. He won reelection in 1996 with about 90 percent of the vote. His mandate stems largely from his effectiveness on the economic front, and that mandate has allowed him to address issues of national scope. In 1996 he traveled to the Crimean port of Sevastopol and spoke at a rally for ethnic Russians. In his address he urged that Sevastopol, which had been conceded to Ukraine by Prime Minister Nikita Khrushchev in 1954, be returned to Russia. Such acts announced his nationalism, which had emerged as a driving force in Russian politics in the backlash against failed free-market economic reforms. He was also prominent in September 1997 during Moscow's 850th anniversary celebration.

Luzhkov has tended to side with Yeltsin against Communist and nationalist opponents. In 1993 he supported Yeltsin in his conflict with the state Duma, Russia's lower house of Parliament; during that episode Yeltsin stationed tanks at the Parliament building to subdue a rebellion. Luzhkov also campaigned for Yeltsin during the 1996 presidential election. However, he has also maintained his independence from Yeltsin on several occasions and has increasingly distanced himself from the unpopular president. For instance, in 1997 he successfully lobbied to be exempted from the federal government's highly unpopular plan to reform public housing, which cost almost $17 billion, or nearly 30 percent of the national budget. "Everything the Russian government plans for the reform of housing and public utilities is unattainable and a fraud," he was quoted as saying by Alessandra Stanley in the *New York Times* (June 10, 1997, online). "People won't be able to pay and won't do it. We do not need such reforms."

Although Luzhkov won the right to conduct Moscow's housing reform on the local level, he faces great challenges. After over six years of forestalling economic disaster, in 1998 Moscow finally succumbed to the devastating repercussions of Russia's recession. Because of the devaluation of the ruble in August of that year, scores of businesses closed even in Moscow. As a result, Moscow's tax revenues fell drastically. Moreover, Moscow has wrestled with increasing debt obligations. Due to the loss of revenues, Luzhkov must find ways to implement drastic cuts in government subsidies for rent and utilities. Those unpopular actions are expected take place shortly after the beginning of 2000.

Despite these setbacks, Luzhkov remains a strong potential candidate in Russia's next presidential election, especially with the formation of the Fatherland Party in November 1998. At a founding meeting of that party, he said, as reported by Celestine Bohlen for the *New York Times* (November 23, 1998), that his party would "absorb everything that's logical from the left, and everything that is logical from the right." It is generally felt that one of Luzhkov's main challenges in a national election would be to overcome regionalism, since Russia's heartland has long viewed Moscow with suspicion and envy. In one probable scenario, his adversaries might include Gennady Zyuganov, the leader of the Communist Party; Aleksandr Lebed, the popular former general and current governor of Siberia's Krasnoyarsk region; Grigory A. Yavlinsky, the young liberal economist and politician who has been dissatisfied with Russia's cautious approach to free-market reform; Boris Nemtsov, the chief economic reformer in Yeltsin's government; and Yevgeny Primakov, who served as prime minister of Russia for eight months before Yeltsin fired him, in May 1999.

Luzhkov lives in Moscow with his second wife, Yelena Baturina, an economist, and their two daughters. He also has two grown sons from a previous marriage. He is the author of *We Are Your Children, Moscow* (1996), an autobiography, and more than 200 technical papers. His recreational activities include beekeeping and playing soccer and tennis. — Y.P.

Suggested Reading: *Forbes* p152+ Nov. 6, 1998, with photos; *Fortune* p234 Nov. 23, 1998, with photo; *New York Times* A p3 Nov. 23, 1998, with photo; *New York Times Magazine* p44+ Aug. 31, 1997, with photos; *U.S. News & World Report* p38+ May 19, 1997, with photos; *Wall Street Journal* A p1+ Feb. 13, 1995; *Washington Post* A p22 June 17, 1994, with photo, A p1+ Feb. 24, 1997, with photos, A p19 Mar. 13, 1998

Selected Books: *We Are Your Children, Moscow*, 1996

Michele Gregolin/Archive Photos

MacDowell, Andie

Apr. 21, 1958– Actress. Address: c/o International Creative Management, 8942 Wilshire Blvd., Beverly Hills, CA 90211

For many Hollywood actors, making a motion-picture debut is a thrilling experience, filled with fanfare and a frenzied round of promotional activity. Andie MacDowell's case was somewhat different. After being spotted by film director Hugh Hudson in a British edition of *Vogue*, MacDowell, who was a prominent fashion model, made the transition to film acting in the role of Lady Jane in *Greystoke: The Legend of Tarzan, Lord of the Apes* (1984), Hudson's adaptation of the famous Edgar

Rice Burroughs tale. After wrapping up the shooting, MacDowell was all set to begin promoting the film, which starred Christopher Lambert. She then learned that Hudson, unhappy with MacDowell's southern-tinged accent, had deleted her lines from the film and had them dubbed by Glenn Close. When news of this rather humiliating development spread through the media, MacDowell became the butt of jokes; people who had already had doubts about the acting ability of models quickly cited the episode as evidence that MacDowell, as a performer, possessed little of worth beyond a pretty face.

She was to prove her detractors wrong. Apparently viewing the experience as a challenge rather than a defeat, she worked hard to develop her acting skills, eventually turning in strong performances in such critical and commercial blockbusters as *Sex, Lies and Videotape* (1989) and *Four Weddings and a Funeral* (1994). Harold Ramis, a director who has worked with MacDowell, said to Skip Hollandsworth for *New Woman* (July 1996), "Many beautiful women just aren't very real in movies, because they tend to pose for the camera rather than emote. But Andie has this ability to forget that she is beautiful. The more I watch her, the more I'm stunned at how she can project these very complicated emotions that we all have, but that we do not know exactly how to express."

The youngest of four daughters, Andie MacDowell was born Rosalie Anderson MacDowell on April 21, 1958 in Gaffney, South Carolina. Her father was a lumber broker, and her mother was a music teacher. Her parents divorced when she was six years old. After that, her mother succumbed to alcoholism, which soon cost her her job, and MacDowell and her sisters—who had stayed with their mother—suffered financial and emotional turmoil as well as the stigma that came with being a dysfunctional family in a small southern town. "My mother was brilliant," MacDowell later recalled to Skip Hollandsworth. "She wrote poetry, she played the piano. She made cards for me on Valentine's Day. She was a wonderful gardener who would give me fresh-cut flowers to take to church. But she was trapped in a true disease that everyone pretended to ignore."

When her sisters grew up and moved away, MacDowell, then an adolescent, was left to take care of her mother, Paula. For a while the two of them worked at a local McDonald's. MacDowell showed a rebellious streak in those years: "I was wild looking. I had this wild hair and these big old lips. I was the first person to double pierce my ears, and I had friends in both races, which wasn't usual there. When people objected, I said [expletive] 'em. I just made it worse. I'd wear T-shirts with no bra and hiphuggers with small halter tops. I guess I liked being sexy," she told *People* (July 29, 1985). During this period she began modeling for a local department store. Then, in 1980, after having spent about two years at Winthrop College, in Rock Hill, South Carolina, MacDowell moved to New York City to pursue a modeling career.

Captivated by MacDowell's exotic looks and her southern charm, modeling agents promoted her as "Andie," a shortened version of her middle name. "It's a strange job," MacDowell said of modeling, during an interview with Richard Woodward for *Harper's Bazaar* (September 1990). "I did it because I didn't have any motivation and people would ask me to try on clothes when I walked into stores. And because I couldn't make a living as an actress." Despite such reservations about her occupation, she quickly proved to be an unqualified success as a model, working in Paris and New York and appearing on the cover of nearly every prestigious fashion magazine. She also starred in television advertisements for Calvin Klein jeans and became a spokesmodel for L'Oréal.

At the same time, MacDowell harbored a desire to challenge herself in new ways and to pursue a career in acting. "I was frustrated [in college] because something was missing in my life and I didn't know what it was," she explained to Lisa Liebman for *New Woman* (March 1991). "I needed to get out in the world and see something so that I could figure out what it was I truly wanted. And that's what modeling gave me the opportunity to do. I traveled. I met so many different kinds of people. I went all over the world. And *then* I was at a place where I could actually dream about what I wanted to do. And that's actually how the acting all came about. Before I was a model, I couldn't even dream of *being* an actress."

Greystoke: The Legend of Tarzan, Lord of the Apes seemed to be the perfect vehicle to launch MacDowell's acting career. To accommodate MacDowell's distinctly non-British accent, the character Lady Jane had been reimagined as a native of Baltimore, and the tale of romance between a civilized woman and a man raised in the jungle seemed to offer potential for dramatic tension. However, the film fared poorly at the box office, and MacDowell had the dubious distinction of making her film debut in image only. "I was in a very weak position at that point," she told Ellen Welty for *Redbook* (October 1995). "Embarrassed beyond belief, and hurt, I was good for laughs for a lot of people, I'm sure. But the thing that's so great is that it didn't stop me."

Indeed, the experience served largely to galvanize her resolve. In the wake of the *Greystoke* fiasco, she immersed herself in acting and voice lessons for several years. Meanwhile, she acted in a small role in *St. Elmo's Fire* (1985), alongside so-called "brat-pack" actors of the 1980s, among them Rob Lowe, Demi Moore, Judd Nelson, Ally Sheedy, and Emilio Estevez, and she starred in a miniseries for Italian television.

Then, just when she had been all but dismissed by the movie industry, MacDowell amazed the film world with her performance in the small-budget critical and commercial hit *Sex, Lies and Videotape*. Made by Steven Soderbergh, a first-time director and screenwriter, the film addressed the topic of sexuality by focusing on four characters: a sex-

ually repressed Louisiana housewife, played by MacDowell; her philandering lawyer husband (Peter Gallagher), who is having an affair with her sister (Laura San Giacomo); and a decidedly eccentric visitor (James Spader). Soderbergh had originally envisioned MacDowell's role for Elizabeth McGovern, and MacDowell had had to persuade him that she could tackle the part. At the 1989 Cannes Film Festival, *Sex, Lies and Videotape* won the Palme d'Or, the festival's most prestigious award. The film erased all doubts about MacDowell's ability as an actress; indeed, much of its appeal and emotional impact was attributed to MacDowell's carefully nuanced performance, for which she won a Los Angeles Film Critics Award and a Golden Globe Award nomination for best actress in a drama. In 1990 MacDowell was named by *Harper's Bazaar* as one of the 10 most beautiful women in the world. The accolades and critical acclaim came as something of a surprise to MacDowell. "When I did that movie," she told Liebman, "I thought at least it would show off my capabilities to casting directors. I had no idea what was going to happen with that movie. That was a gift. So you see, something horrible happens to you and then you get a gift."

In the wake of *Sex, Lies and Videotape*'s success, MacDowell won roles in a series of films. Opposite Gerard Depardieu, she starred in *Green Card* (1990), playing a New York City horticulturist who marries a French musician in order to acquire a highly sought-after apartment. "I love that character," she told Woodward. "She's strong. She's intelligent. But like some overeducated people, she's lost touch with herself. She falls in love and doesn't know it." For her work in *Green Card*, she was nominated for a Golden Globe Award for best performance by an actress in a motion-picture comedy or musical. She then starred in *Hudson Hawk* (1991), with Bruce Willis, and *The Object of Beauty* (1991), opposite John Malkovich. Both films received mixed reviews, and neither fared well at the box office.

A number of unmemorable films followed, including *Deception* (1993), which is also known as *Ruby Cairo*; *Unstrung Heroes* (1995), in which she played a Jewish mother dying of cancer; *Multiplicity* (1996), which paired her with Michael Keaton; and *Michael* (1996), starring John Travolta. These films, generally featuring MacDowell in the role of a demure wife, failed to catch on with fans or critics.

One standout during this period was Harold Ramis's *Groundhog Day* (1993), starring MacDowell as the romantic interest of a TV weatherman (Bill Murray) living through endless variations of the same 24 hours. *Groundhog Day* was a hit with reviewers and moviegoers.

Another exception was Mike Newell's *Four Weddings and a Funeral* (1994), a romantic comedy about two people (MacDowell and Hugh Grant) who meet at a wedding, have a fling, and thereafter see each other only at large gatherings—when one or the other of them is engaged to be married. The film was enormously popular, and MacDowell won praise for her performance, netting a third Golden Globe Award nomination.

Since these triumphs MacDowell has been a constant presence on the big screen. In 1997 she starred in Wim Wenders's *The End of Violence.* She then appeared in the low-budget film *Shadrach* (1998), in which she played a poor woman in 1935 Virginia. She was the unhappy girlfriend of the Andy Garcia character in *Just The Ticket* (1999; also known as *The Scalper*), a comedy about a scrappy New York City ticket scalper; she also served as an executive producer of that film. In *Muppets from Space* (1999), she played opposite Miss Piggy. Her most recent film is Albert Brooks's *The Muse* (1999), in which she was cast as the wife of a successful but fading screenwriter (Brooks) who enlists the aid of Zeus's daughter (Sharon Stone).

Commenting on the possibility that she may be offered fewer roles in the future, as a result of having entered her 40s in an industry long known for its lack of substantive roles for women past their 20s, she told *People* (September 13, 1999), "I would stand next to any 41-year-old male actor, naked, and say, 'I look just as good, if not better, than you do. So wake up and smell the coffee.'"

MacDowell married Paul Qualley, a contractor and former model, in 1986. They have a son, Justin, and two daughters, Rainey and Sarah Margaret. The couple separated in July 1999. MacDowell now lives in Asheville, North Carolina, where she enjoys hiking, horseback riding, and gardening. — Y.P.

Suggested Reading: *Chicago Tribune* VII p21+ Aug. 23, 1989, with photo; *Entertainment Weekly* p12+ Jan. 18, 1991, with photos; *New Woman* p19+ Mar. 1993, with photos, p70+ July 1996, with photo; *People* p41+ July 29, 1985, with photos; *Redbook* p92+ Oct. 1995, with photos

Selected Films: *Greystoke: The Legend of Tarzan, Lord of the Apes,* 1984; *St. Elmo's Fire,* 1985; *Sex, Lies and Videotape,* 1989; *Green Card,* 1990; *The Object of Beauty,* 1991; *Hudson Hawk,* 1991; *Deception,* 1993; *Short Cuts,* 1993; *Groundhog Day,* 1993; *Four Weddings and a Funeral,* 1994; *Bad Girls,* 1994; *Unstrung Heroes;* 1995; *Multiplicity,* 1996; *Michael,* 1996; *The End of Violence,* 1997; *Shadrach,* 1998; *Muppets from Space,* 1999; *The Muse,* 1999; as actor and executive producer—*Just the Ticket,* 1999

Mahoney, John

June 20, 1940– Actor. Address: c/o Steppenwolf Theatre Company, 1650 N. Halsted St., Chicago, IL 60614-5530

Proving that second starts in life are possible, at the age of 35 John Mahoney left a comfortable editing job that bored him for an unpredictable life in acting. The gamble paid off: he has worked almost without letup in theater, television, and film ever since. Rarely cast in a starring role, he has had a busy and fulfilling career as a character actor—a member of that often-anonymous species who play the fathers, brothers, employers, best friends, or teachers of the usually younger, sexier star. "I've had a lot of interesting roles," Mahoney told Richard Christiansen for the *Chicago Tribune* (February 26, 1989), "but people don't remember me from role to role."

The fact that very few people outside of casting directors recognize him has made it easier for Mahoney to slip into an unusually large variety of parts. But many of those parts are slim, and winning them has often seemed like getting worn hand-me-downs from elder siblings. "I remember one time [the filmmaker] Barry Levinson talking to me and saying, 'Well, we'll cast everybody else and what we can't find anybody for we'll give to you,'" he told Carla Hall for the *Washington Post* (February 26, 1991). He added, "And that's both the joy and the liability of being a character actor." Cur-

EJ Camp/Outline Press

rently, Mahoney is probably best known for a role he has been playing for the past six years: that of the father of Frasier Crane on the NBC hit comedy *Frasier.*

The seventh of eight children, John Mahoney was born on June 20, 1940 in Manchester, England. His father was a baker who loved to play the piano;

his mother was a homemaker who loved to read. "My parents had a terrible marriage," he admitted to Tom Seligson for *Parade* (April 9, 1989). "I don't remember them ever saying a kind word to each other. We were relatively poor. My dad was able to support us, but there was never a lot of money."

When he was about 11, Mahoney became interested in theater. He performed in Gilbert and Sullivan operettas in drama festivals around England and took a break from school to spend a season with the Birmingham Repertory Theatre. He nearly quit school altogether to become an actor full-time, but his parents persuaded him to get his high-school diploma. For reasons unclear to Mahoney, by the time he finished his secondary-school education, his interest in theater had fallen by the wayside. Instead, he became caught up in the idea of immigrating to the United States. He had been there once, to visit a sister who had married an American soldier and moved to rural Illinois. "My sister . . . sent back photos of her children dressed in these beautiful clothes that we had never seen growing up," Mahoney recalled to Tom Seligson. "I remember thinking that if she could do that, so could I. I could become a decent, well-dressed, well-thought-of person. Whereas once I had wanted to stand out, suddenly I became absolutely bound and determined to blend in and be no different from the people around me." Mahoney moved to the U.S. in 1959, and to him the move felt "like the moment in *The Wizard of Oz* where it goes from black and white to color," as he told a reporter for the *New York Times* (April 28, 1998).

After his arrival in the U.S., Mahoney promptly joined the army and served in Europe. He next attended Quincy College, in Quincy, Illinois. After earning a bachelor's degree, in 1966, he pursued a master's degree in English at Western Illinois University, in Macomb, where he worked as a teaching assistant. After teaching his first class, however, he decided that academia was not for him. Upon graduating he went back to Quincy and became a hospital orderly at St. Mary's Hospital, a job he had held as an undergraduate. "I was the only orderly with a master's degree in English, minor in French, wiping old men's bottoms," he told Seligson. "But I loved it. I loved taking care of those people and felt very comfortable in that little town. I decided to stay there. However people started telling me how ridiculous it was to be making $1.10 an hour, or whatever it was, after having gone to school. Eventually, I realized they were right."

In 1970 Mahoney moved to Chicago and started editing a small-circulation medical journal. With that job, he achieved the dream of middle-class comfort that had led him to the United States: he had a private office, a good income, and a home with an excellent view. Yet he felt unsatisfied. By 1975, the year he turned 35, he had tired of his daily diet of articles about hemorrhoids, cataracts, and other health problems. He began to drink more heavily, and he might have followed an even more self-destructive path had he not seen a production

of *Jumpers*, by Tom Stoppard, in London, during a trip to England to visit his family. The play "rekindled every single dead ember of acting enjoyment I had ever had," he told Seligson. "I was boiling over with excitement and then, back in Chicago, I saw a production of [Arthur Miller's] *A View from the Bridge*. I suddenly thought, 'My God, *this* is what I should be doing. *This* is what I want.'"

Mahoney quit his editorial job and began training with the St. Nicholas Theater in Chicago. His savings ran out quickly, and he was forced to sell his books and records and move to a cheaper neighborhood. He made his professional debut in 1977 in *The Water Engine*, a play by David Mamet staged at the St. Nicholas Theater. In 1979, after appearing in several other plays, he met the actor John Malkovich, who invited him to join Chicago's famed Steppenwolf Ensemble. Steppenwolf became Mahoney's theatrical home; he has appeared in more than 30 productions with the group, among them *Waiting for Lefty*, *Death of a Salesman*, *Hothouse*, and *Taking Steps*.

Beginning in the 1980s, Mahoney began supplementing his income with bit parts in such films as *Mission Hill* (1982), *Code of Silence* (1985), *Streets of Gold* (1986), and *The Manhattan Project* (1986). His name recognition received a boost when the Steppenwolf production of *Orphans* (1985) was produced in New York City. In that drama Mahoney played a mobster who is kidnapped by two orphans in a get-rich-quick scheme. The following year he appeared in a New York mounting of *The House of Blue Leaves*. For his performance as Artie Shaughnessy, a zookeeper dreaming of Hollywood success, he won a Tony Award. "I dangle that Tony over [John Malkovich's] head all the time," he told Richard Christiansen for the *Chicago Tribune*. Since then, Mahoney has appeared in many other plays, including *The Subject Was Roses* (1991), *Death and the Maiden* (1993), and *The Man Who Came to Dinner* (1998).

In the late 1980s Mahoney's skills as a character actor began to win him many roles in cinema. He appeared as an amorous communications teacher in *Moonstruck* (1987); an aluminum-siding salesman in *Tin Men* (1987); a judge in *Suspect* (1987); the manager of the 1919 Chicago White Sox—eight of whose players conspired to throw the World Series that year—in *Eight Men Out* (1988); a U.S. consul in *Frantic* (1988); a tender-hearted man, who also happens to be a white supremacist, in *Betrayed* (1988); a doting father who engages in tax fraud in *Say Anything . . .* (1989); the head of the CIA in both *The Russia House* (1990) and *In the Line of Fire* (1993); an alcoholic, William Faulkner–like writer in *Barton Fink* (1991); a villainous hospital director in *Article 99* (1992); a chief of police who is murdered in *Striking Distance* (1993); a newspaper editor in *The Hudsucker Proxy* (1994); and a dim-witted talk-show host in *Reality Bites* (1994). Other roles include parts in *The American President* (1995), *Mariette in Ecstasy* (1996), *Primal Fear* (1996), and *She's the One*

(1996). In animated films he provided the voice of an unnamed drunken scout in *Antz* (1998) and the voice of General Rogard in *The Iron Giant* (1999).

In television Mahoney has appeared in the movies *Chicago Story* (1981), *Listen to Your Heart* (1983), *Dance of the Phoenix* (1983), *The Killing Floor* (1984), *First Steps* (1985), *Trapped in Silence* (1986), *Favorite Son* (1988), *Dinner at Eight* (1989), *The Image* (1990), *The 10 Million Dollar Getaway* (1991), and *The Secret Passion of Robert Clayton* (1992). The television series in which he has acted include *Lady Blue* (1985–86), about a tough female cop; *H.E.L.P* (1990), in which he played the fire captain of the Harlem Eastside Lifesaving Program; and *The Human Factor* (1992), in which he played Alec McMurtry, a sage doctor who teaches medical students and interns about the art of caring.

Frasier, a spinoff of the popular comedy *Cheers*, premiered in 1993 and has since become one of NBC's most popular situation comedies. On this show Mahoney plays an ex-cop, Martin Crane, who, after getting shot in the line of duty, is forced to live with his son, Frasier Crane (played by Kelsey Grammer), and a live-in home-care provider, Daphne Moon (Jane Leeves). The tension that arises because of Martin's blue-collar background and Frasier's blue-blood aspirations is just one of the many running jokes in the sitcom. Since Mahoney's character is based partly on the father of one of the show's producers, Peter Casey, the actor has had to be somewhat restrained in his performance so that he doesn't embarrass Casey's father. Nevertheless, Mahoney was nominated for a Golden Globe Award for best supporting actor in 1994 and for an Emmy Award for best supporting actor in a comedy series in 1999.

John Mahoney has never been married and has no children. He once attributed his reluctance to get married to the difficulties of his parents' union. His zest for acting may be another contributing factor. "To develop some sort of relationship or raise a family—I couldn't do it," he told Carla Hall in 1991. "I just couldn't give up the work long enough to do it. And yet at the same time one craves that." — W.G.

Suggested Reading: *Chicago Tribune* XIII p8+ Feb. 26, 1989, with photos; (New York) *Daily News* p45+ June 4, 1991, with photos; *New York Times* E p1 Apr. 28, 1998, with photo; *Parade* p8+ Apr. 9, 1989, with photo; *Washington Post* B p1+ Feb. 26, 1991, with photo

Selected Plays: *The Water Engine*, 1977; *Waiting for Lefty*; *Death of a Salesman*; *Hothouse*; *Taking Steps*; *Orphans*, 1985; *The House of Blue Leaves*, 1986; *The Subject Was Roses*, 1991; *Death and the Maiden*, 1993; *The Man Who Came to Dinner*, 1998

Selected Films: *Mission Hill*, 1982; *Code of Silence*, 1985; *Streets of Gold*, 1986; *The Manhattan Project*, 1986; *Moonstruck*, 1987; *Tin Men*, 1987; *Suspect*, 1987; *Eight Men Out*, 1988; *Frantic*, 1988; *Betrayed*, 1988; *Say Anything*, 1989; *The Russia House*, 1990; *Love Hurts*, 1991; *Barton Fink*, 1991; *Article 99*, 1992; *Striking Distance*, 1993; *In the Line of Fire*, 1993; *The Hudsucker Proxy*, 1994; *Reality Bites*, 1994; *The American President*, 1995; *Mariette in Ecstasy*, 1996; *Primal Fear*, 1996; *She's the One*, 1996; *Antz*, 1998; *The Iron Giant*, 1999

Selected Television Shows: *Chicago Story*, 1981; *Listen to Your Heart*, 1983; *Dance of the Phoenix*, 1983; *The Killing Floor*, 1984; *First Steps*, 1985; *Lady Blue*, 1985–86; *Trapped in Silence*, 1986; *Favorite Son*, 1988; *Dinner at Eight*, 1989; *The Image*, 1990; *H.E.L.P*, 1990; *The 10 Million Dollar Getaway*, 1991; *The Secret Passion of Robert Clayton*, 1992; *The Human Factor*, 1992; *Frasier*, 1993–

Archive Photos

Malick, Terrence

Nov. 30, 1943– Film director; screenwriter.
Address: c/o Twentieth Century Fox, 1440 Sepulveda Blvd., Los Angeles, CA 90025

When *The Thin Red Line* opened in movie theaters on December 15, 1998, it marked a momentous occasion in American cinema: the return of director Terrence Malick, after a 20-year absence from filmmaking. With his critically acclaimed movies *Badlands* (1974) and *Days of Heaven* (1978), Malick established himself as an auteur on a par with his contemporaries Martin Scorsese, Francis Ford Coppola, and Steven Spielberg—and then seemed to fall suddenly off the face of the earth. There were many rumors about his whereabouts, and his reported activities ranged from the everyday to the exotic. Some said he was on a religious quest, practicing Buddhism with Himalayan monks. Others placed him on long trips to the Mediterranean and elsewhere. The accounts of more eccentric behavior, the ones Hollywood and the media gleefully latched onto, had Malick taking birdwatching walks through Texas and Oklahoma, resting only to call producers from roadside phone booths. But his friends said that Malick was spending time in the library, catching up on the classics and pursuing his interests in everything from ornithology to entomology—leading, in other words, an ordinary life away from the pressures of filmmaking.

"I always liked the movies in a kind of naïve way," Malick once told an interviewer. "They seemed no less improbable a career than anything else." Indeed, film was for Malick just one vocation among many—he also worked as a journalist, a philosophy teacher, and a manual laborer. His casual attitude toward the medium might explain his absence from the world of movies, but it still baffles many that a preternatural talent whose first two outings are widely viewed as classics, if not full-fledged masterpieces, would spurn an industry that was so eager to embrace him. His earlier films charted a distinct path in the cinematic landscape of the day. While Scorsese was blazing trails in gritty urban realism, Coppola was romanticizing gangsters, and Spielberg was developing the art of the special-effects epic, Malick was making in *Badlands* a detached treatment of random, amoral rural violence and in *Days of Heaven* a laconic, naturalistic montage that some saw as being evocative of silent film.

With his third film, *The Thin Red Line*, Malick took on his most ambitious project yet. Standing in stark contrast to his early, minimalist efforts, *The Thin Red Line*, with its $50 million budget and large cast (the movie included more than 60 speaking parts), represented Malick's attempt to bring his thematic obsession with nature into the realm of warfare. In doing so, he broke the long-existing war-film dichotomy of either dogged, gutwrenching realism or hyperpatriotic, glorifying fluff. Called an "austerely hallucinated battlefield vision [that] is an exercise in 19th century transcendentalism" by J. Hoberman in the *Village Voice* (December 30, 1998), the film is a philosophical war epic that strives to bring an introspective, meditative mood to the chaos of the battlefield. It marks not only Malick's resurfacing but also a solidification of his film legend and a refutation of the nattering that, during his time away, portrayed him as an ephemeral talent who couldn't hack it in Hollywood.

The oldest of three brothers, Terrence Malick was born on November 30, 1943 in Ottawa, Illinois, to Emil and Irene Malick. Growing up in Waco and Austin, Texas, he displayed a variety of talents, excelling in the classroom as well as on the football field. In the summers Malick would follow the wheat harvest north, drive cement mixers, or work on oil wells, a job obtained for him by his father, an oil geologist at Phillips Petroleum. In 1961 Malick entered Harvard University, in Cambridge, Massachusetts, as a philosophy major and quickly distinguished himself. Following his junior year, he traveled to Germany, where he met Martin Heidegger and worked on a translation of the philosopher's *Essence of Reason* at night while toiling as a log jammer by day. Back in Cambridge, Malick graduated Phi Beta Kappa in 1966 and was awarded a Rhodes Scholarship, which took him to Oxford University, where he took up Latin American studies. While at Oxford he began to ponder a career in film. He did not receive a degree from the university.

Upon returning to the United States, Malick found work as a journalist at *Newsweek*, the *New Yorker*, for which he wrote an unpublished profile of Che Guevara, and the Miami bureau of *Life*. He spent 1968 as a philosophy lecturer at the Massachusetts Institute of Technology, in Cambridge. There, he made a short film and won admission to the inaugural class of the American Film Institute (AFI).

At AFI Malick made many connections, including one with Mike Medavoy, who would become his first agent, and George Stevens Jr., then head of the institute, who would later produce *The Thin Red Line*. After graduation Malick took scriptdoctoring jobs for movies, including *Dirty Harry* and *Drive, He Said*, Jack Nicholson's directorial debut. He also sold an original screenplay called *Deadhead Miles*, the quirky story of a longdistance truck driver that was turned into an unreleasably bad film, and an adapted screenplay titled *Pocket Money*. Dejected over the slow pace of his career, Malick turned to his brother Chris, who was working as an oil executive, for help in financing a film project. Chris Malick promptly raised $350,000, which Terrence used to pay for his directorial debut.

Shot in Colorado from August to October 1972, *Badlands* was loosely based on the real-life 1950s murder spree of Charles Starkweather and Caril Ann Fugate; the film starred Martin Sheen and Sissy Spacek as a fictionalized version of the homicidal couple. Sheen, evoking James Dean, and Spacek, as the 15-year-old ingenue whose narration adds an eerily innocent layer, engage in a pointless and vicious rampage and bloody flight through South Dakota's badlands. The movie made sparing but effective use of dialogue and featured sharp visuals, including a now-famous shot of Spacek lazily twirling a baton, a lulling prelude to the impending violence. The film opened at the 1973 New York film festival to acclaim—Geoff Andrew, quoted in the Seattle Times (March 8, 1998, on-line), called it "one of the most impressive directorial debuts ever." Warner Brothers promptly picked up the movie for $1 million, but despite studio backing and the critical buzz, *Badlands* didn't fare well at the box office. Following this, Malick, using the pseudonym David Whitney, sold a B-movie script called *The Gravy Train*.

For his second directorial effort, Malick secured a budget of $3 million and, in 1976, went to Alberta, Canada, to shoot *Days of Heaven*, based on his own script. A simple, almost archetypal story, *Days of Heaven* depicts a love triangle on a farm in the Texas panhandle before World War I. Richard Gere and Brooke Adams portray a young, poor couple who flee south after the Gere character accidentally kills his boss at a Chicago mill. Accompanied by the Gere character's younger sister (Linda Manz, in a much-noted performance), the trio end up working for a lonely, terminally ill farmer (Sam Shepard), who falls in love with and marries the character played by Adams. The tensions among the characters leads to a tragic conclusion. The film, which took two years to edit, involved a difficult shoot, during which Malick earned a reputation as a perfectionist whose strict adherence to his vision caused friction with his cast and crew.

Unlike those of most movies, the simple, straightforward plot of *Days of Heaven* (1978) accounts for little of the film's power; it is the imagistic focus, rather than the story or its scant dialogue, that drives the work. As many critics noted, what drama there is often results from the way the characters' moods seem to echo events in the natural world. For instance, the farmer's wheatfields ignite in an apocalyptic blaze as Gere's character and the farmer clash over Adams. Foreshadowing the fight, locusts swarm, suggesting a biblical retribution for the sins of the characters. "There is a familiar Dreiserian moral to all of this, yet it is not so much the story itself as the way it is told—primarily through images—that makes *Days of Heaven* so memorable. In that sense it perhaps qualifies as 'pure cinema,'" Andrew Ross wrote in an appreciation for *Salon* (March 1997). Indeed, the film is so quiet, so pure in its devotion to its natural vistas (which are infrequently yet starkly interrupted, by an ominous-looking mill, a haunting Victorian house, and a hulking steam-driven machine, for instance) that Malick had to add the Manz character's precociously wise voice-over to make the narrative more accessible.

Reactions to *Days of Heaven* differed sharply. Many filmgoers were enraptured by its visual beauty, to the extent that they could overlook the flat, stock characters and lack of dramatic action. For these critics, *Days of Heaven* was comparable to silent films—especially F. W. Murnau's rural drama *Sunrise*—which relied primarily on visuals for expression. Yet *Days of Heaven* avoided the sentimentality endemic in homages to outmoded art forms and even moved its viewers—an unusual occurrence for an ambitiously experimental film. "Though the film is pervaded by an unusual prickly intelligence, its impact is visceral," one critic noted. Likewise, Andrew Ross enthused, "It is the closest to poetry in motion that I have ever seen." The movie's detractors, on the other hand, were generally unmoved by *Days of Heaven* and unwilling to accept what Judith Martin, in the *Washington Post* (October 6, 1978), called "the right of the film to make its statement of mood and beauty by other methods." For some, the already slight story line was dwarfed by the majestic cinematography. "Rather than enriching its materials, the grandiose visual texture of *Days of Heaven* has a way of impoverishing them or at least revealing their inherently simplistic quality," Joy Gould Boyum wrote for the *Wall Street Journal* (September 8, 1978). "Rendered in such spectacular scale, his characters seem less mythic than mannered, their deterministic little tale less portentous than pretentious, with the final effect of it all something like hearing 'Frankie and Johnny' played by a symphony orchestra."

Days of Heaven won many honors, bringing Malick best-director awards from the Cannes Film Festival, the New York Film Critics Circle, and the National Society of Film Critics. And despite its commercial failings, the film won Malick some influential admirers. The head of Paramount, Charlie Bluhdorn, was so enamored of the movie that he gave Malick $1 million in exchange for the rights to his next script, whatever that might be. Initially Malick planned to make his next project a version of the life of John Merrick, the "Elephant Man," but David Lynch beat him to it. Instead, in the summer of 1978, Malick went to Paris, where he was to begin work on *Q*, a World War I–era drama set in the Middle East but with a prologue set in prehistory. For this movie Malick was bent on capturing images that had never before been seen on film. Cameramen were dispatched to capture natural phenomena all over the globe—from volcanic eruptions to the behavior of jellyfish. A special-effects consultant, Richard Taylor, was hired. "Imagine this surrealistic reptilian world," Taylor told *Los Angeles* magazine (December 1995). "There is this creature, a Minotaur, sleeping in the water, and he dreams about the evolution of the universe, seeing the earth change from a sea of magma to the earliest vegetation, to the dinosaurs, and then to man. It would be this metaphorical story that moves you through time." The project never came to fruition. Paramount became increasingly frustrated with the mounting costs needed to prepare a movie whose concept was changing on a daily basis—eventually the prologue, heavy on poetry, light on dialogue, took over the story, and the Middle East part was discarded. By the summer of 1979, work on the project had ceased, a result of the studio's anxiety over the ballooning budget and the director's apparently increasing boredom with the daily grind of movie-making.

Throughout the 1980s Malick worked on several projects that never panned out, traveled extensively, and generally led a quiet, intellectual life. In the early years of the decade, he married Michele Gleason, his second wife. A year or two later, the couple, along with Gleason's daughter from another marriage, moved to Austin, Texas. In 1983 Bluhdorn, the Paramount chief, died, and the studio's patronage of Malick ended. To support himself and his family, Malick turned to scriptwriting, authoring a project for the director Louis Malle and a rewrite of a movie called *Countryman*. By then his increasingly odd behavior had begun to generate gossip. "I couldn't communicate with him directly," Robert Cortes, a producer for *Countryman*, told Peter Biskind for *Vanity Fair* (December 1998). "I would make a phone call to a certain number, leave a message, and then his brother would call me back." Malick, according to Cortes, was also hesitant about revealing where he lived: he would have the producer drop him off at a random corner, then make him drive away before walking home. Despite his resistance to socializing with Hollywood types, Malick worked hard on various film projects. He penned a dark script for a Jerry Lee Lewis biopic, which was ultimately rejected by producers who wanted a much lighter tone. He also adapted a Larry McMurtry novel, *The Desert Rose*, and did a rewrite of a script based on the Walker Percy novel *The Moviegoer*.

In 1988 Bobby Geisler and John Roberdeau, two maverick producers interested in luring Malick out of his shell, approached him to write and direct a film version of D. M. Thomas's novel *The White Hotel*. Malick declined, instead offering to adapt for the screen either Molière's *Tartuffe* or James Jones's novel *The Thin Red Line*. Geisler and Roberdeau chose the latter. But before any substantial work was done on *The Thin Red Line*, the producers persuaded Malick to write a play, which would serve the dual purpose of warming Malick up and providing contact with him as he worked on the *Line* script. For the play, Malick chose to adapt the 1954 Japanese film *Sansho the Bailiff*, for which he would receive $200,000 plus a $50,000 bonus once it opened on Broadway. This turned out to be no mean feat. The producers had to have the film, for which there was no existing script, transcribed, and they performed a mountain of additional research on 10th-century Japanese literature. Malick's first draft was sent to the top-tier directors Ingmar Bergman and Peter Brook, both of whom turned it down. Eventually, the Polish director Andrzej Wajda signed on, but his uneasy collaboration with Malick culminated in a tense, disappointing six-week workshop at the Brooklyn Academy of Music in 1993. The play never made it to Broadway, but the process, painful as it was, evidently sparked Malick to step behind the camera to direct again.

The novel *The Thin Red Line* (1962), a follow-up to Jones's Pearl Harbor drama *From Here to Eternity*, is a fictional account of the American invasion of Guadalcanal during 1942–43. The book's oft-quoted dedication, which begins, "This book is cheerfully dedicated to those greatest and most heroic of all human endeavors, WAR and WARFARE," sets a sardonic tone for a novel that, while far from pacifistic, takes an ironic view of its subject, depicting frightened, jaded soldiers, some

verging on the nihilistic, engaging more in desperate self-preservation than in a struggle for any higher ideal. But just as Jones's book offered an alternative to the popular-culture glorification of World War II, Malick's vision departed from the realism spawned by the book and its ilk in favor of a high-minded film in the spirit of *Days of Heaven*. "The notion that we discussed endlessly," Bobby Geisler told Peter Biskind, "was that Malick's Guadalcanal would be a Paradise Lost, an Eden, raped by the green poison, as [Malick] used to call it, of war. Much of the violence was to be portrayed indirectly." Malick's first draft of the screenplay, rumored to be more than 300 pages, corresponded to those aims while differing from the novel in at least three crucial areas. First, the script disposed of Jones's indictment of anti-Semitism in the military by changing the ethnicity of the company's commanding officer to Greek; second, Malick elided a homoerotic episode that, while peripheral to the main plot, provided an intimate look into the psychology of the soldier at war. Finally, Malick contrived metaphysical musings that were to be heard as voice-overs—interior monologues—as the soldiers stormed the verdant paradise.

Word about the project leaked out to the industry, and in the spring of 1995, Malick arranged a reading of the script at Michael Medavoy's house. On hand were prominent male actors, among them Kevin Costner, Will Patton, Dermot Mulroney, Peter Berg, and Malick alum Martin Sheen—all eager to work with the legendary director. A few months later a five-day workshop grabbed the attention of younger stars including Johnny Depp and Brad Pitt, who began to court the wary director who had once again become Hollywood's hottest commodity. Nevertheless, the film, one of the themes of which is the dehumanizing effect of war on its participants, was intended to be peopled with unestablished actors or even novices culled from casting calls. On the eve of the shoot, with the cast largely in place, Sony pulled its funding from the production. Fox 2000 took up the project with the condition that some stars with marquee value be given cameo roles. The producers agreed, and principal photography took place from June to November 1997 in Queensland, Australia, and the Solomon Islands. Malick then took the more than one million feet of footage into the editing room and emerged 10 months later with a finished product. (For Malick, the process of making *The Thin Red Line* was perhaps tainted by much-publicized sniping between the producers, Geisler and Roberdeau, and the director over production credit, a drawn-out conflict well documented in *Entertainment Weekly* and *Vanity Fair*.)

The Thin Red Line opened on December 15, 1998 to sold-out theaters in New York and Los Angeles. Its national run, however, wasn't nearly as successful, perhaps because the public had already had their fill of World War II movies in a year that gave them *Saving Private Ryan* and *Life Is Beautiful*. Mixed reviews from prominent critics didn't help, either. Although most reviewers were appreciative of the film's visual power, they complained about its length as well as its overbearing thematic content. "*The Thin Red Line* is one more film that could have been helped by excising repetition and focusing performances," Janet Maslin wrote for the *New York Times* (December 23, 1998), "but it wanders almost randomly instead. The heart-piercing moments that punctuate its rambling are glimpses of what a tighter film might have been." In the *Los Angeles Times* (December 23, 1998), Kenneth Turan complained about what he considered the film's esoteric nature: "Though there are moments to cherish throughout, *The Thin Red Line* remains a stubbornly personal film, an artwork that only one person will understand and appreciate completely. No one need ask who that person might be." Despite this underwhelming critical reaction, *The Thin Red Line* still garnered Oscar nominations for best director, best film, best adapted screenplay, and four other categories. Though he was ultimately shut out at the Oscars, Malick did take home the 1998 New York Film Critics Circle Award for best director.

Malick, who lives in Austin, was described by Bruce Handy for *Time* (October 13, 1997) as "tall, bald, possessed of a hawkish, handsome nose and a striking snow-white beard." He and his second wife divorced prior to the filming of *The Thin Red Line*. His next projects are an adaptation of Walker Percy's novel *The Moviegoer* and the *English-Speaker*, an original script based on the case study of Anna O., a patient of both Joseph Breuer's and Sigmund Freud's. Malick will also produce the forthcoming *Endurance*. — M.C.

Suggested Reading: *Entertainment Weekly* p42+ Sep. 5, 1997, with photo, p29+ Jan. 15, 1999, with photo; *Los Angeles* p60+ Dec. 1995; *New York Times* II p15+ Oct. 5, 1997; *Time* p92+ Oct. 13, 1997, with photo; *Vanity Fair* p202+ Dec. 1998, with photos

Selected Films: *Badlands*, 1974; *Days of Heaven*, 1978; *The Thin Red Line*, 1998

Steve Azzara/Sygma

Manson, Marilyn

Jan. 5, 1969– Singer; songwriter. Address: c/o Interscope Records, 40 W. 57th St., 22d Fl., New York, NY 10019

Marilyn Manson is one of the most controversial rock acts of the 1990s. When its breakthrough album, *Antichrist Superstar*, reached number three on the *Billboard* charts in the fall of 1996, just be-hind records by industry mainstays Celine Dion and Kenny G, the mainstream press began swarming around the quintet, focusing on its demonesque stage show and heavy metal–influenced music. Led by their lanky, six-foot-three lead singer, the band's namesake and co-founder, the group—infamous for Bible ripping, bloodletting, and, rumor had it, sacrificing animals in concert—has since been banned from playing in more cities than any other rock group of the decade. "When people sometimes misconceive us as being like Kiss or like Alice Cooper, or being a persona, I don't think they understand how deeply Marilyn Manson goes into my existence," front man Marilyn Manson told Neil Strauss for *Rolling Stone* (January 23, 1997). A certified minister of the Church of Satan, Manson claims that he has never actually worshiped the devil but that he instead thrives on dichotomies, bringing together opposites in the creation of his performance, musical, and lyrical art. His stage name, he has explained, is an example of this: the fusion of the names of Marilyn Monroe, the nation's most recognizable sex symbol, and Charles Manson, its most notorious serial killer. Manson told Neil Strauss for *Rolling Stone* (June 26, 1997), "I consider myself as much a member of the Church of Satan as [a member of the church] where I was baptized as a kid: St. Paul's Episcopal in Canton, Ohio—or as much as I'm a member of Blockbuster Video or the library. If I had to describe my beliefs, God and Satan are like your left and right hand, just like Marilyn and Manson. It's two words to describe the two sides of what you are."

In the fall of 1998, the band made a departure from its occult-metal roots, with the release of its second album, *Mechanical Animals*, which had a lighter, more pop-oriented sound. The record proved to be another platinum success, spending four months among the *Rolling Stone* Readers Top 20 and debuting at number one on the *Billboard* album chart. Manson appeared on the cover of *Rolling Stone* a month later, dressed in a manner that both echoed rock's past and harkened to its future, his eye makeup evoking the glam rock of David Bowie and Iggy Pop while his spaceman's outfit hinted at styles of music to come. Ever controversial and often dismissed as a sideshow act, Marilyn Manson is also seen by many as a progressive force in rock.

Marilyn Manson was born Brian Warner in Canton, Ohio, on January 5, 1969, the son of Hugh Warner, a furniture salesman, and Barbara Warner. By his own account, he was raised primarily by his mother. "At the time, I kind of resented it, because I felt like I was a mama's boy," he told Chris Heath for *Rolling Stone* (October 15, 1998). "I think mothers are always afraid to let go of their sons, their only child, so sometimes they create reasons for them not to go off on their own. Hypochondria. I was always a sickly kid, and I think my mother encouraged that to try and keep me under wraps." Despite this, as Manson told Neil Strauss for *Rolling Stone* (January 23, 1997), his parents gave him a lot of freedom to pursue his creative endeavors. "They took me to my first Kiss concert. . . . From an early age, I wanted so much to see and experience something that wasn't normal. My mom used to tell me when I was a kid, 'If you curse at nighttime, the devil's going to come to you when you're sleeping.' I used to get excited because I really wanted it to happen. I was never afraid of what was under the bed. I wanted it. I wanted it more than anything. And I never got it. I just became it." In 1974 Brian began attending a fundamentalist Christian grade school where the faculty would give lectures dictating which types of music were appropriate for the students to hear. "They had all these seminars where they'd tell you about the music you weren't supposed to listen to," he told Strauss. "And they would play heavy-metal songs backward. And they'd show you pictures of the bands, and I was like, 'I like this. This is what I want.'"

At about this time, Manson began to show a rebellious streak, producing tapes—which he would hand out to friends—that contained songs about sexual fantasy, flatulence, and masturbation. Sprinkled between the tracks were various comedy skits and jokes—all of which eventually found their way into the humor magazine, based on *Mad*, that he developed in the early 1980s, while still in middle school. During this period he became violent toward his mother. He told Heath, "I think it was something I got from my father, both emotionally and physically, because they were having problems and I thought they were going to get a divorce and I was blaming it all on her because he

thought she was having an affair of some nature and I believed it and acted violently. It's probably one of the only things I regret in my life. I have very few moments of remorse, but that's one thing I wish I could take back." When Brian finished high school, in 1987, his family relocated to Fort Lauderdale, Florida, where the young man became immersed in the fertile South Florida music scene. Responsible for spawning the controversial rap group 2 Live Crew, South Florida was also credited as the cradle of three sub-genres of heavy metal—industrial rock, death metal, and goth (short for "gothic") music.

After only a few months in Fort Lauderdale, Brian began creating fictional occult figures in short stories and novellas. It was in this way that he came up with the idea for the character Marilyn Manson. He wrote in his autobiography, *The Long Road Out of Hell* (1998), as quoted by James Hunter for *Rolling Stone* (March 19, 1998): "Marilyn Manson . . . would have been in a longish short story, about 60 pages, and it would have been rejected by 17 magazines. . . . But it was too good an idea to rot." When Brian met Scott Mitchell, the two hit it off from the start because of their mutual love for the local music scene, and soon they made plans to form a band. For their stage act, Brian decided to assume the persona of Marilyn Manson, through which he would indulge his love of heavy metal, glam rock, and the fledgling sub-genre industrial rock. He persuaded Mitchell to develop his own alter ego, and soon Mitchell began calling himself Daisy Berkowitz, a name evoking both the character Daisy Duke from the TV show *The Dukes of Hazzard* and the real-life David Berkowitz, better known as the killer Son of Sam. Once the two friends rounded up some cheap equipment and wrote their first songs, numerous band members began floating in and out of the lineup, each coming up with his or her own pseudonym—early examples being Olivia Newton-Bundy and Zsa Zsa Speck. Manson and Mitchell decided to call the group Marilyn Manson and the Spooky Kids. Soon the duo found two steady band members—Gidget Gein on bass and Madonna Wayne Gacy on keyboards; Berkowitz played guitar and wrote much of the band's music, while Manson sang and concentrated on writing lyrics. For the first few years of its existence, the band used a drum machine programmed by Berkowitz.

Following the tradition of countless punk and metal bands throughout the history of rock, the group began passing out at their concerts hundreds of self-produced tapes, which are now collectors' items among death-metal/goth enthusiasts. In 1992 the band dropped the drum machine and added drummer Sara Lee Lucas to the roster; meanwhile, their live shows became legend up and down the Florida panhandle. As Paula O'Keefe wrote for her Web page, *The Unofficial Chronology and History of Marilyn Manson*, "Anything might turn up [in the live show] from a Lite-Brite[TM] toy arranged to read 'Kill God' or 'Anal Fun' and peanut butter and jelly sandwiches tossed from the stage, to caged or crucified girls, skinned goats' heads, nudity, and arson." The band, feeling their name was too long, shortened it to Marilyn Manson, in the tradition of their hard-rock influence, Alice Cooper.

In 1993 Sara Lee Lucas was replaced by Ginger Fish, and Gidget Gein by Twiggy Ramirez. Manson had begun to hang out with Nine Inch Nails (NIN) founder Trent Reznor, who later signed him to a deal with his newly formed label, Nothing. With an agreement to play on Reznor's "Self-Destruct '94" summer tour, the Mansons, as they took to calling themselves, headed into the studio to record what became *Portrait of an American Family*. The album hit some snags in the recording process, resulting in producer Roli Mossiman's removal from the project, as Reznor and Manson took over production duties. In June 1994 the first single, "Get Your Gunn," was released, as was a corresponding video, which saw little airplay on MTV. Manson and NIN hit the road in August.

Controversy on a national scale first hit Marilyn Manson in 1994, the year that Anton Szandor La Vey, founder of the Church of Satan, designated Manson as a priest of the church. In a meeting in the summer of 1994, La Vey "shared with me a lot of very important things that I've taken into effect in my life," Manson told *Seconds* magazine, according to O'Keefe. "He also expressed that he felt Marilyn Manson was one of the more Satanic bands to come around in our time." In mid-October 1994 in Salt Lake City, Utah, Manson was asked to adhere to strict conditions set forth by the Delta Center, the venue in which their concert was to take place. The rules specified that the group say nothing between songs, alter certain lyrics, and agree not to sell any merchandise at the complex. The band, to many people's surprise, agreed to the stipulations, but when Reznor, during his set, called Manson to the stage, the latter carried with him a copy of the Book of Mormon and proceeded to tear up the holy text page by page. Later that year, after completing the tour with NIN, Manson was arrested for stripping at a gig in Jacksonville, Florida. In addition, he became the subject of rumors of animal sacrifice when a chicken was let loose in a mosh pit during a concert in South Carolina. Other stories also began to circulate about the lead singer, among them that he had cut off his own testicles, and it was alleged that rapes commonly occurred at the band's concerts. Although Manson denied all the allegations, the media exposure caused sales of the band's new EP, *Smells Like Children*, released in October 1995, to soar. The record spawned the band's biggest hit to date, a cover of the 1980s Eurythmics song "Sweet Dreams (Are Made of This)." As the video grabbed airplay on MTV, a rumor spread that Manson was planning to kill himself at a concert that Halloween.

The band toured for five months before returning to the studio to record what became their breakthrough album, *Antichrist Superstar*. The title was a reference to the 1970s hit musical by Andrew Lloyd Webber and Tim Rice, *Jesus Christ Superstar*. (Before the album was recorded, Berkowitz left the band and was replaced by a man known only as Zim Zum. Zim Zum left the group in mid-1999.) By the time of the disc's release, in late summer 1996, the video for the single "The Beautiful People" had begun to get heavy airplay on MTV. By October the album was at number three on the *Billboard* chart. Lorraine Ali wrote for *Rolling Stone* (November 28, 1996), "The rise of Marilyn Manson marks the end of the reign of punk realism in rock & roll. This ill-behaved Florida-based quintet, a visual and aural shake 'n' bake of mutilation theatrics, Alice Cooper-esque camp and metal-scraping-metal tonality, is a volatile reaction to five years of earnest, post-Nirvana rock." In January 1997 Manson appeared on the cover of *Rolling Stone*, his famous mismatched contact lenses making it appear that his eyes were those of an otherworldly corpse.

Antichrist Superstar quickly went platinum. The follow-up tour became so popular that Ozzy Osbourne asked the group to join him on his Ozzfest '97 summer tour. As the sold-out tour progressed toward a major date at Giants Stadium, in East Rutherford, New Jersey, stadium officials announced that Manson would not be permitted to take the stage, citing instances of Bible ripping and satanic imagery used in the band's live shows. (Local officials had blocked the band's performances in South Carolina and Utah.) In the end a federal judge, citing the First Amendment, permitted Marilyn Manson to take the stage. Osbourne, in support of the group, issued a statement, quoted by Roy Waddell for *Billboard* (May 3, 1997): "Nobody has the right to tell me who I can perform with. . . . This is not an issue of taste. It is an issue of civil liberty and freedom." The controversy helped Manson sell more albums, and *Antichrist Superstar* remained on the record charts throughout the summer.

When the tour wound down, Manson faded from the headlines and returned to the studio. There were only brief public glimpses of the front man during the final months of 1997 and the beginning of 1998. (One was a cameo appearance in David Lynch's 1997 movie *Lost Highway*.) Then, in 1998, he published his autobiography, *The Long Road Out of Hell*. According to Hunter, the last line of the book reads, "I can see already that America, Nothing Records, our friends and the media have perceived this to be the peak of our career. Unfortunately for them, this is just the beginning." The book coincided with a new look for the band's lead singer and a modified sound for the band. Just days before the release of Marilyn Manson's new album, *Mechanical Animals*, Lorraine Ali wrote for *Rolling Stone* (September 17, 1998), "In his latest incarnation, Manson has traded in his customary rotting-corpse chic for a glam look . . . [and] on the album, shimmering, flamboyant guitar grooves and strong melodic hooks replace the post-industrial grind of previous records." Manson also chose to go with another producer, Michael Beinhorn, who produced the high-profile album *Celebrity Skin*, by Courtney Love's band, Hole. "People probably expect us not to be able to function without the heavy hand of Trent [Reznor]," Manson told Ali. "Not that I have a chip on my shoulder or need to prove something, but I think this record establishes that we have our own musical identity without someone telling us what to do." When asked why he had adopted an androgenous appearance, complete with cherry-red hair, in place of his now-infamous corpse-like image, Manson told Ali, "I'm bored with that."

Mechanical Animals, released in late September 1998, met with rave reviews by critics who recognized Manson's desire to change direction as an artist. "[In] 'I Don't Like the Drugs (but the Drugs Like Me)' . . . ," John Pareles wrote for the *New York Times* (September 20, 1998), "he sings that the drugs are numbing and dehumanizing, one more consumer product to distract him and dull the only feeling he knows is real: pain. This time around, Manson is Holden Caulfield with face paint and lipstick, bitterly denouncing the phoniness he feels himself being pulled into." The album debuted at number one on the *Billboard* album chart. In *Details* (October 1998), Pat Blashill wrote, "*Mechanical Animals* marks the first time Manson's songs are as entertaining as his sideshow stomping antics. Manson isn't indulging in glam nostalgia; he's using the genre's decadent grind as a strategic vantage point." Ann Powers observed in *Rolling Stone* (October 1, 1998), "*Antichrist Superstar* was an excellent album, with lots of personality and sound scape that stretched the limits of hard rock. But Manson's ability to stand up for his sources made it a cultural event. . . . Glam lends Manson some important vocal props and outfits, but *Mechanical Animals* does not adhere to that era's playful mood. Its ultimate sources are the goths: Bauhaus, Love and Rockets, and early Cure. . . . He and his band approach [Glam's] terrain the way 1960s rocker Eric Clapton approaches the blues, with respect and a sense of entitlement."

Manson again became the subject of public debate in April 1999, when two students at Columbine High School in Littleton, Colorado, shot and killed 12 other students, a teacher, and then themselves. In the wake of the tragedy, the media disclosed that the killers—Dylan Klebold and Eric Harris—had been Manson fans. Expressing his sympathy for the victims and their families, Manson announced that he was canceling the final five dates of his summer tour with Monster Magnet, which had been scheduled to take place in western states. "People are trying to sort out what happened and to deal with their losses," Manson said in a press release, as quoted by Jaan Uhelszki in *Rolling Stone* (April 28, 1999, on-line). "It's not a great atmosphere to be out playing rock & roll shows, for us or the fans. The media has unfairly scapegoated the music industry and so-called Goth

kids and has speculated—with no basis in truth— that artists like myself are to blame."

A month later *Rolling Stone* (May 28, 1999, online) published an opinion piece by Manson, in which he wrote, "I remember hearing the initial reports from Littleton, that Harris and Klebold were wearing makeup and were dressed like Marilyn Manson, whom they obviously must worship, since they were dressed in black. Of course, speculation snowballed into making me the poster boy for everything that's bad in the world. . . . In my work I examine the America we live in, and I've always tried to show people that the devil we blame our atrocities on is really just each one of us. So don't expect the end of the world to come one day out of the blue—it's been happening every day for a long time."

In mid-September 1999 Manson released the video for his track "Coma White." He had completed it nearly six months before and, by his own account, had postponed its distribution because of the events at Columbine High School. The video features Manson and his girlfriend, the actress Rose McGowan—best known for her roles in Wes Craven's film *Scream* and Darren Stein's *Jawbreaker*—reenacting the assassination of President John F. Kennedy, in 1963, and it immediately went into heavy rotation on MTV. "This is a pageant where I used the assassination of JFK as a metaphor for America's obsession and worship of violence . . . ," Manson explained on his Web site, as quoted by Jenny Eliscu in *Rolling Stone* (September 13, 1999, on-line). " Little did I know that the tragedy at Columbine and the accidental death of JFK, Jr. [in July 1999] would follow. . . . This short film clip . . . is in no way a mockery. In fact, it is a tribute to men like Jesus Christ and JFK who have died at the hands of mankind's unquenchable thirst for violence."

When asked to comment on his vision for Marilyn Manson in the future, Manson told *Rolling Stone* (May 28, 1998), "In fusing oppositions, you create things that are stronger than the two ideas you started with. But a lot of times, you also learn by seeing things from both perspectives. I've never been into the idea of picking a side. Whatever the argument might be, it always seems more valid to take the best parts of each side and make them into something else. So Marilyn Manson is a criticism of gimmickry while being itself a gimmick. And it's a commentary on exploitation while at the same time it exploits it. I find that exploiting something is exploring it. My art is not just about the album. It's also about people's reactions—positive and negative. And how that affects me." Marilyn Manson and opening band Monster Magnet plan to embark on a tour in the U.S. in the summer of 1999. Recently Manson fired guitarist Zim Zum from the band, bought a house in Los Angeles, and began dating the actress Rose McGowan, best known for her roles in Wes Craven's *Scream* and Darren Stein's *Jawbreaker*. — M.B.

Suggested Reading: *celebsite.com* (on-line); *Details* p61 Oct. 1998, with photo; *National Review* p53+ June 30, 1997; *New York Times* B p36+ Sep. 20, 1998, with photos; *Rolling Stone* p129+ Nov. 28, 1996, with photos, p48+ Jan. 23, 1997, with photos; p19+ June 26, 1997, with photo, p19+ Mar. 19, 1998, with photos, p106 May 28, 1998, p23+ Sep. 17, 1998, with photos, p65+ Oct. 1, 1998, with photo, p15+ Oct. 15, 1998, with photos; *Time* p68 Feb. 24, 1997, with photos; *Village Voice* p75 Sep. 22, 1998, with photo

Selected Books: *The Long Road Out of Hell*, 1998

Selected Films: *Alleys and Motorways*, 1997; *Lost Highway*, 1997; *Dead to the World*, 1998; *Closure*, 1998; *Jawbreaker*, 1999

Selected Recordings: *Portrait of an American Family*, 1994; *Smells Like Children*, 1995; *Antichrist Superstar*, 1996; *Mechanical Animals*, 1998

Bernd Bodtlander/Courtesy of Henry Holt and Co.

Marcus, Greil
(greel)

June 19, 1945– Music critic; nonfiction writer.
Address: c/o Harvard University Press, 79 Garden St., Cambridge, MA 02138-1423

The task of the music critic, Greil Marcus explained to Michael Goldberg for *Addicted to Noise* (August 1, 1997, on-line), is to make a person "realize that he or she knows more than he or she thinks he or she knows. It's not to tell people what to listen to." Ever since the late 1960s, Marcus has been doing just that in magazine columns and several influential books on rock criticism, including *Mystery Train: Images of America in Rock 'n' Roll Music* and *Lipstick Traces: A Secret History of the 20th Century*. In his writings he has straddled the boundary between high and low culture and woven analyses of such bands as the Sex Pistols, Sonic Youth, and Sleater Kinney into narratives about national identity and contemporary social history. Such large concerns have led him to move beyond reviewing albums and to consider rock music's relation to everything from the beliefs of heretical 14th-century monks to 19th-century American literature. As he wrote in *Mystery Train*, "I am no more capable of mulling over Elvis without thinking about Herman Melville than I am of reading Jonathan Edwards . . . without putting on Robert Johnson's records as background music." In words that serve equally well as a summary of much of his work, he described *Mystery Train* as "no attempt at synthesis, but a recognition of unities in the American imagination that already exist." Regarded by many readers as one of the foremost critics of rock, Marcus has been called by New York's *Village Voice* "the undisputed king of taking pop (too) seriously." Charles Taylor wrote in the *Boston Phoenix* (February 1996, on-line), "After reading Marcus, you're ready to seek out the meanings lurking in newspaper reports, pop songs, the language of politicians, movies so familiar their content seems exhausted. And ordinary life no longer seems ordinary. It seems like an adventure."

Greil Gerstley Marcus was born on June 19, 1945 in San Francisco to Gerald Dodd Marcus, a lawyer, and Eleanore (Hyman) Marcus, a homemaker. As a boy he was an early fan of the music of Elvis Presley. He attended the University of California (U.C.) at Berkeley, where he earned both a B.A. degree in American studies, in 1967, and a master's degree in political science, in 1968. While pursuing a Ph.D. there, he began his career in music criticism. On a lark, he had submitted to the then-new magazine *Rolling Stone* a scathing review of an album by the Who, and to his surprise, his critique was published. In 1969 *Rolling Stone* hired him as its first records editor.

About a year later Marcus left that job to become the music critic for the rock magazine *Creem*, where he remained from 1970 to 1975. From 1971 to 1972 he also taught in U.C.-Berkeley's American studies department. Before finishing his Ph.D., he decided to give up academia for good and concentrate on writing about music. In 1975 he returned to *Rolling Stone*, where, until 1980, he wrote the book-review column "Undercover." He also wrote the column "Real Life Rock" for *New West Magazine* (later renamed *California*), from 1978 to 1982; the pop-music column for *Music Magazine* (published in Tokyo, Japan), from 1978 to 1994; and the "Real Life Rock Top Ten," for the *Village Voice*, from 1986 to 1989. Other magazines and newspapers in which his writing has appeared include *Express Times*, *RAW*, *Threepenny Review*, *New Formations*, the *New Yorker*, and *New Musical Express*. Since 1992 he has written the "Days Between Stations" column for *Interview*, and since 1990, the "Speaker to Speaker" column for *Artforum* (he also wrote for *Artforum* from 1983 to 1987). Since 1998 he has also been a contributing editor for *Esquire*.

Marcus co-wrote his first book, *Woodstock* (1969), with Jan Hodenfield and Andrew Kopkind, and his second, *Double Feature: Movies & Politics* (1972), with Michael Goodwin. His next book was *Mystery Train: Images of America in Rock 'n' Roll Music* (1975), which immediately established him as one of the leading critics in rock. In his introduction to *Mystery Train*, Marcus wrote that he was attempting "to deal with rock 'n' roll not as youth culture or counterculture, but as American culture." One of the book's most prominent themes is taken from American literature: the duality of the national character, as represented by Captain Ahab from Herman Melville's novel *Moby Dick* on one side and by the eponymous hero of Mark Twain's *Huckleberry Finn* on the other. *Mystery Train* was nominated for the National Book Critics Circle Award for criticism.

Marcus has said that his second solo book, *Lipstick Traces: A Secret History of the 20th Century* (1989), emerged out of his disgust with American politics in the 1980s. "After Ronald Reagan was elected president, I was pitched into such a violent sense of anger and despair over the course of this country which only got worse as the years went on. . . . I simply couldn't engage with American subjects as a writer," he recalled to Ann Douglas for the *Village Voice Literary Supplement* (Summer 1997). "That's why I wrote *Lipstick Traces*, which is about Europe and about the avant-garde and un-American traditions. The whole notion of the avant-garde and its elitism is so contrary to the ethos that this country is about or pretends to be about that it was hard for me to understand, and I got caught up in it. In a way, *Lipstick Traces* is an exile's book. Even though I didn't leave." As he recalled to William Brisick for *Publishers Weekly* (November 15, 1991), Marcus chose the punk group the Sex Pistols and their 1976 hit "Anarchy in the U.K." as his starting point in the book, asking himself, "Why was this song so powerful?" "That's what I wanted to know. And why couldn't I stop playing it? I didn't understand where the power came from." To answer this question and the related question of the Sex Pistols' place in history, he compared the British punk phenomenon with other acts of political and cultural rebellion, including those of the Lollards, a group of 14th-century religious reformists; the Dadaists and Surrealists of the 1920s; and the 1950s European avant-garde artists who called themselves the Situationist International.

Two years later Marcus published *Dead Elvis: A Chronicle of Cultural Obsession* (1991), which examines Presley's seminal place in American culture, not just as an appropriator of black popular music but as an original artist. "Until Elvis, the symbols in our society were primarily dualistic: black and white—black meaning evil, white meaning good," Marcus told William Brisick. "In Elvis's first record you couldn't tell whether he was black or white, and in many ways he sounded androgynous, exuding a sexuality you couldn't hear anywhere else. On some level, even the crudest symbols in our society didn't work anymore. He stopped people in their tracks." Marcus's interest in Elvis was revealed as far back as *Mystery Train*, in which he included a highly regarded essay on the musician. After Elvis died, in 1977, Marcus became even more fascinated by the continuing attention paid to him, as manifested in everything from essays to art tributes to reported Elvis "sightings." In *Dead Elvis* he discussed some of these phenomena. "It's not meant to be a definitive statement about anything," Marcus told Brisick. "It was written out of amazement, not as an argument."

Marcus's next book, *The Dustbin of History* (1995), is a collection of his reviews and essays spanning 20 years. His theme, he explained, is "about the way history is cheapened and restricted; about those people, acts, and events that are casually left out of history or forcefully excluded from it, and about the way much of history finds its voice or bides its time in art works." Marcus included the stories of largely unknown people who nevertheless made their marks on culture. One such unheralded figure is Deborah Chessler, a young, white, Jewish woman who wrote songs for and managed doo-wop groups.

Marcus's most recent full-length study, *Invisible Republic: Bob Dylan's Basement Tapes* (1997), analyzes Dylan's 1967 private recording sessions with the Band, which took place shortly after the musician's controversial conversion from folk to rock-'n'-roll. In an attempt to determine why so many people were able to "connect" with Dylan's music, Marcus examined how Dylan himself connected with an earlier generation of folk musicians—particularly those represented on Harry Smith's seminal compilation *Anthology of American Folk Music* (1952).

Another collection of Marcus's writings, *Ranters and Crowd Pleasers: Punk in Pop Music, 1977–1992* (published as *In the Fascist Bath Room* in Great Britain), appeared in 1999. Marcus has also contributed pieces to *The Rolling Stone Illustrated History of Rock and Roll* (1976), *Mid-Life Confidential* (1994), *Designing Disney's Theme Parks: The Architecture of Reassurance* (1997), *What'd I Say: The Atlantic History of Music* (1998), and *Democracy and the Arts* (1999). In addition, Marcus has edited several books, among them *Rock & Roll Will Stand* (1969); *Stranded: Rock and Roll for a Desert Island* (1979), a collection of essays written by musicians about what single album each would like to have if stranded far from civilization; and *Psychotic Reactions and Carburetor Dung* (1987), a collection of writings of the 1970s rock critic Lester Bang.

Marcus and Jenelle Bernstein, whom he married on June 26, 1966, have two children, Emily and Cecily. In addition to his career in music criticism, he is the director of Pagnol & Cie, which operates the famous Chez Panisse restaurant in Berkeley. From 1983 to 1988 he was director of the National Book Critics Circle. His rock-'n'-roll song "I Can't Get No Nookie" was recorded in 1970 by the Masked Marauders. — W.G.

Suggested Reading: *Esquire* p74 June 1996; *Gentlemen's Quarterly* p36+ July 1993, with photo; *Publishers Weekly* p53+ Nov. 15, 1991, with photo; *Village Voice Literary Supplement* p10+ Summer 1997

Selected Books: *Mystery Train: Images of America in Rock 'n' Roll Music*, 1975; *Lipstick Traces: A Secret History of the 20th Century*, 1989; *Dead Elvis*, 1991; *Ranters and Crowd Pleasers* (also published as *In the Fascist Bathroom*), 1993; *Invisible Republic: Bob Dylan's Basement Tapes*, 1997; with Goodwin, Michael: *Double Feature: Movies & Politics*, 1972; as editor: *Rock & Roll Will Stand*, 1969; *Stranded: Rock and Roll for a Desert Island*, 1979; *Psychotic Reactions and Carburetor Dung*, 1987

Grant Delin/Courtesy of Mary Ellen Mark Library

Mark, Mary Ellen

1940– Documentary photographer. Address: c/o Mary Ellen Mark Library, 134 Spring St., Suite 502, New York, NY 10012

"What you look for in a picture is a metaphor, something that means something more, that makes you think about things you've seen or thought about," Mary Ellen Mark, one of the greatest documentary photographers of our time, told Vicki Goldberg for the *New York Times Magazine* (July 12, 1987). Mark's compelling depictions of homelessness, poverty, and mental illness, which have been published in such magazines as *Time* and *Life* and exhibited in museums around the world, are far more recognizable than the photographer herself. Although her career has spanned more than 30 years and numerous publishing trends, Mark has said that she is "still interested in photography." "I am constantly finding new ways to construct an image—to better understand that visual language," she told Melissa Harris for *Aperture* (Winter 1997). "I am always trying to discover which photographs work, why they work, what is necessary to include in a photograph, and what you can leave out."

Mary Ellen Mark was born in 1940 in Philadelphia, Pennsylvania, and was raised in a nearby suburb. She told Larry Frascella for *Communication Arts* (March/April 1997) that her father, who was an architect, was "very sick," so she "never really knew him in his best years." Mark described herself to Goldberg as having been a "willful child" who became a teenager "with two major ambitions: to become the lead cheerleader and be popular with boys." According to Goldberg, Mark achieved both those goals while she was in high school.

After earning a bachelor's degree in painting and art history from the University of Pennsylvania, in 1962, Mark won a scholarship to the graduate division of the university's Annenberg School of Communications. She told Frascella that she chose to study photography because "it just felt right. I remember the first time I went out on the street to shoot pictures. I was in downtown Philadelphia . . . and I just took a walk and started making contact with people and photographing them, and I thought, 'I love this. This is what I want to do forever.' There was never another question." Her experience at the Annenberg school was a positive one. "They gave us the best equipment, all the paper, all the film we wanted, and I spent a year just shooting pictures." During her student years Mark came to admire the work of the photographers Henri Cartier-Bresson, Robert Frank, W. Eugene Smith, Irving Penn, Helmut Newton, and Diane Arbus. But no one particular style, she told Frascella, has shaped her work. "I hate when photographers are too derivative of other people's work. There's too much of that going on today. But I do look at other pictures. You look because you learn. You are inspired by them." After completing her master of arts degree in photojournalism, in 1964, Mark traveled to Turkey, Mexico, and Europe as a Fulbright scholar. Some of the pictures she took while traveling were included in her first book, *Passport* (1974).

Later in the 1960s Mark moved to New York City, where one of her first important jobs was to photograph, for *Look* magazine, the director Federico Fellini as he filmed his 1969 version of Petronius's *Satyricon*. After completing that project Mark went to London, where she took pictures at a clinic for heroin addicts. Through these two projects, both of which resulted in feature stories in *Look*, Mark established herself as a magazine photojournalist, and for the next three decades, her work appeared regularly in such publications as *Life*, *Time*, the London *Sunday Times*, the *New York Times*, *Rolling Stone*, *Paris-Match*, and the German magazine *Stern*. "I feel very lucky," Mark told Frascella. "I had some great years of magazine work. Of course magazines were very different then. They were much more about social documentary work than they are today."

Mark's first important exhibition was in 1976, at Castelli Graphics, a gallery in New York City. The show, entitled "Ward 81," was based on her six-week visit to a women's maximum-security ward at Oregon State Hospital, a facility for the mentally ill. Mark had gotten permission from both the staff and the patients to live in an unused part of the hospital building and to take pictures of the women in the ward. "For years I'd planned to go live in a mental hospital," Mark told Goldberg. "I wanted to see if I could feel something of what it was like to be set aside from society." After spending time with the patients, Mark realized that there was "not that much difference between the women's behavior and mine and my friends'." She made this observation the center of her work and attempted to capture on film the humanity of the patients she came to know. Her task was not easy. "If you're someone who photographs people, you're always an intruder," she explained to Robert Hughes for *Time* (January 23, 1978). "It took a while to get a rapport—the stronger photos didn't come till we got to know the women and they got involved in the project. They felt they were making some kind of contact with the outside world." Hughes noted that Mark's photos contained little of the grotesqueness and mystification often associated with depictions of the mentally ill, and he called the exhibit "a lamentation: one of the most delicately shaded studies of vulnerability ever set on film. . . . After seeing the show, it is hard to think about madness and confinement in the same way again." Following the exhibit Mark signed with the prestigious Magnum photo agency, and in 1979 the images from "Ward 81" were published in book form.

During the 1970s Mark traveled a great deal for her work. Bombay, India, became one of her favorite destinations. She took a special interest in the prostitutes who worked in that city's red-light district, and the people she encountered there became the subject of her next book, *Falkland Road: Prostitutes of Bombay* (1981). "People see India as poverty and death, but these woman are survivors and they have incredible spirit," Mark told Guy Trebay for the *Village Voice* (May 6, 1981). "I didn't shoot this story because it's exotic. Ten years ago that's what I might have gone for. But now I've gone to India so much that I see different things. The spirit and the sense of community and the dignity of the survivor." Regarding the process of gaining access to her subjects, Mark told Val Williams for the London *Guardian* (October 29, 1991), "Every day I had to brace myself for the street as if I were about to jump into freezing water. I started out by just walking the street. It was the same as always, crowds of men, women alternately hurling insults and garbage at me. . . . As the days passed, people began to get curious. Some of the women thought I was crazy but a few were surprised by my interest and acceptance of them. Very slowly, I began to make friends." Like her compassionate portrayal of the patients at Oregon State Hospital, *Falkland Road* presented images to which a broad audience was able to relate. Mark told Goldberg that the book "was meant almost as a metaphor for entrapment, for how difficult it is to be a woman." Goldberg described a picture showing "three Indian prostitutes uncomfortably awaiting a man's decision" as being "a poignant, harsher version of young girls at a dance." Although most of Mark's photos are black and white, she chose to shoot *Falkland Road* in color, perhaps because of the brilliant clothing that her subjects wore. An exhibit of the photos was shown in New York City, London, and Los Angeles.

While traveling in India Mark also took photos of people at the missions set up by Mother Teresa in Calcutta; some of those pictures were published in *Life* alongside an article about Mother Teresa, who began working in the slums of Calcutta in 1948. Throughout the mid-1980s an exhibit of the photos toured the U.S. Some of the pictures appear in Mark's fourth book, *Photographs of Mother Teresa's Missions of Charity in Calcutta* (1985). Mark has said that taking these pictures was more difficult emotionally than almost any other project she has pursued. "You have to be careful if you're involved [with people you're photographing] and it breaks you up," she told Williams. "If their tragedy is so great that it makes you cry, how does that make them feel? You have to be strong."

Mark began taking pictures of homeless teenagers in Seattle, Washington, in the early 1980s, while on an assignment for *Life*. After completing the job she continued working there, and she befriended a young homeless girl named Tiny, who became the focus of Mark's book *Streetwise* (1988). "Teenagers are very unpredictable. That fascinates me," Mark told Melissa Harris. "In my pictures I like to get a sense of oddness or edginess. I think that children and teenagers are much more about that. They're growing, they're changing—especially teenagers. It's such a powerful time. There's so much rawness at that time of life, and it's really interesting to me to be able to catch that. Children and teenagers aren't so formed. Their bodies are developing, their voices are changing. They are going thorough so much physically during this period of time that they exhibit a real vulnerability yet, at the same time, defiance." Mark also collaborated with her husband, the filmmaker Martin Bell, on a film version of *Streetwise*, which was nominated for the Academy Award for best documentary in 1984.

Mark's next important book was *Indian Circus* (1993). She had become interested in circuses because she feels that, like many of her other subjects, they are full of symbols of human concerns. She told Frascella that in photographing circuses she finds "fantasy and humor and irony and tragedy—and theater! The circus is all of those things, and yet it's real, it's a way of life. It can be a tough way of life but people love it. It gets in their blood." One of her most famous photos from this series is of four dogs wearing costumes and practicing their tricks. "I wanted it to be anthropomorphic," she told Frascella. "Each of [the dogs] has such a personality. And yes, the picture is about dogs in dresses—but it's also about striving. Each dog is trying so hard to succeed."

A change in magazine publishing trends in the mid-1990s led Mark, who up until that time had worked exclusively as a documentary photographer, to take her career in a different direction. She explained to Frascella that previously, "advertisers used to need magazines. Now magazines need advertising. . . . No one wants to put an ad next to a picture of a homeless family. They would rather put an ad next to a movie star." Because of the decreased demand for Mark's kind of documentary photographs, she began to take studio portraits of celebrities and to do fashion photography. "It is very different from just going out alone into the world with a camera, but you get something different from it, something with a different value," the photographer told Frascella. "Fashion is very collaborative. The editor makes the picture as much as the photographer, along with the hair and make-up people." She continued, "I think [working in fashion] has made me a better photographer. I've learned to consider certain things. Like graphics, and directing people. It made me better at portraiture. It showed me why some gestures work and some don't. Why is someone looking up better than someone looking down? . . . Fashion has taught me more about clues, all those clues that come together to make one picture better than another." Moreover, she continued, "when you're on assignment, you do have to consider the point of view of the magazine. Not that I would ever give a client something I thought was a weak picture, that it would embarrass me to have my name on. You've got to be professional. You're doing the job. You've got to consider who the client is and what they want. They're spending all this money and sending you off."

Mark still spends a great deal of time pursuing documentary photography. Her projects include photographing autistic children at a school in Connecticut and taking photos at the home of Norma Claypool, a blind woman who has adopted 15 multiply handicapped children. Her most recent books are *Mary Ellen Mark Portraits* (1995), a collection of images of both famous and ordinary people taken since the beginning of her career; *A Cry for Help: Stories of Homelessness and Hope* (1996), which shows homeless families living in shelters in New York State; and *American Odyssey*, which became available in October 1999 and contains portraits (shot between 1963 and 1999) of Americans from all walks of life. A solo exhibition of photos included in the book will be shown at the Philadelphia Museum of Art in the spring and summer of 2000.

Mark still considers documentary photography to be the most difficult genre in her field. "What [other photographers] can't do is go out with a camera to an isolated place with no plan in mind and bring back a picture," she explained to Frascella. "That is what documentary photographers do. And it's hard." She said that after years of documentary work, she has developed a "sense of being almost psychic about things. You find yourself thinking: I have to be here at this time, something is going to happen. Should I turn this corner or that corner? You try to anticipate what your subjects are going to do while analyzing who they are. This comes out of years of being very focused." She also feels that being a woman has influenced what kinds of pictures she has been able to take: "[It] allows me a different kind of access to people than a man might have," she told Williams. "I think they are less threatened. If I'm walking in a marginal neighborhood and I knock on a door, they're more likely to let me in."

Mary Ellen Mark lives with her husband in New York City, in "a sunny loft populated by a large gathering of the gods, potentates, and animals of India in paint and wood," Goldberg reported in 1987. Goldberg described the photographer as having "a soft voice, an eager smile, and long black hair, often worn in a single braid. Her eyes are so dark and narrow that from a distance they appear totally black, as if they were nothing but apertures for light."

A retrospective exhibit of Mark's work, entitled "Mary Ellen Mark: Twenty Five Years," opened in 1992 at the International Center of Photography in New York City, and it subsequently toured nationally and internationally to more than 15 museums. Among the awards and honors that Mark has won are the 1980 Page One Award for Excellence in Journalism from the *New York Times Magazine*; the 1986 Phillipe Halsman Award for Photojournalism from the American Society of Magazine

Photographers; the 1988 World Press Award for Outstanding Body of Work; the 1988 George W. Polk Award for Photojournalism; the 1989 World Hunger Media Award for Best Photojournalism; the 1992 Victor Hasselblad Cover Award; the 1994 Professional Photographer of the Year Award from the Photographic Manufacturers and Distributors Association; the 1994 Matrix Award for Photography; and the 1997 Infinity Award from the International Center of Photography. Mark won a Missouri School of Journalism Pictures of the Year award in both 1981 and 1984, and she earned the Robert F. Kennedy Journalism Award for photojournalism in 1981, 1983, and 1985. She has also received grants and fellowships from the National Endowment for the Arts, the New York State Council for the Arts, the Bell System Photography Project, the John Simon Guggenheim Foundation, and the Erna and Victor Hasselblad Foundation. In 1992 she was awarded an honorary Ph.D. from the University of Pennsylvania. In a recent poll of readers of the magazine American Photography, she was voted the favorite woman photographer of all time. — C.P.

Suggested Reading: Aperture p42+ Winter 1997, with photos; Communication Arts p52+ Mar./Apr. 1997, with photos; (London) Guardian p33 Oct. 29, 1991, with photo; New York Times Magazine p13+ July 12, 1987, with photos; Time p91 Jan. 23, 1978, with photos; Village Voice p67 May 6, 1981, with photo

Selected Books: Passport, 1974; Ward 81, 1979; Falkland Road: Prostitutes of Bombay, 1981; Photographs of Mother Teresa's Missions of Charity in Calcutta, 1985; Streetwise, 1988; The Photo Essay: Photography by Mary Ellen Mark, 1990; Mary Ellen Mark: 25 Years, 1991; Mary Ellen Mark: Indian Circus, 1993; Mary Ellen Mark Portraits, 1995; A Cry For Help: Stories of Homelessness and Hope, 1996; American Odyssey, 1999

Brett Coomer/AP Photo

Mark, Rebecca

1955(?)– Chair and CEO of Enron International. Address: c/o Enron International, 1400 Smith St., Houston, TX 77002

In the summer of 1995, newly elected local officials in Maharashtra, the wealthiest state in India, called a halt to the construction of an enormous power plant in their state because they objected to the terms of the agreement reached between their predecessors and the contractor, the United States–based corporation Enron International. In the following months, Rebecca Mark, who had been named chair of the Enron Development Corp. in 1991, when that division of Enron was established, renegotiated the contract, which involves the largest investment of foreign capital ever made in the Indian subcontinent in a single project. "I was amazed," a representative for one of the other two corporate investors in the multibillion-dollar project told Patricia Sellers for Fortune (August 5, 1996). "The more things that went against her, the more determined she seemed to be."

Enron International is the emerging-markets branch of the Enron Corp., one of the world's largest energy conglomerates. Mark, who was named Enron International's chair and CEO in 1996, has overseen the building of power plants and power supply systems in China, the Philippines, Guatemala, Colombia, Brazil, and the Dominican Republic as well as India and other countries. She is one of very few women who have attained management positions in her field. In a 1997 interview with an Associated Press reporter, published in the Lubbock [Texas] Avalanche-Journal (November 23, 1997, on-line), she said that she and her colleagues "have to put tremendous hours" into their work, "sometimes without knowing whether it will be successful or not. In order to do that you have to believe very strongly that what you're doing adds a great deal of value to the people in the countries where we're working and to the world at large." Mark told Patricia Sellers that she considers herself "a world-class problem solver." "I'm constantly asking, 'How far can I go? How much can I do?'" she said. In 1998 Mark was named vice chair of Enron Corp. as well as chair and CEO of

Azurix, the Enron subsidiary developed to explore the global water business.

Rebecca Mark was born in about 1955 in northeastern Missouri, where her family owned a farm. According to Sellers, her parents were "land rich and cash poor," so she worked to pay her way through school. After two years at William Jewell College, in Liberty, Missouri, she transferred to Baylor University, in Waco, Texas, where she earned a B.A. in psychology. Because she did not agree with many of the theories of psychology that were prevalent at that time, she found the practice of clinical psychology "depressing," as she has put it. "[It was] the antithesis of everything I learned growing up—that you can control your own destiny," she told Sellers. At some point she completed a master's degree in international management at Baylor.

In 1978 Mark moved to Houston, Texas, and entered a training program at First City National Bank. She specialized in helping companies fund some of their riskier projects. When asked how she became interested in that area of banking, Mark observed to Sellers, "Opportunities and challenges define your career. You just have to follow your instincts. Do what excites you and you don't see the path until you get there."

In 1982 Mark joined a natural-gas company called Continental Resources. Four years later Continental Resources was absorbed by the Enron Power Corp., a newly founded subsidiary of Enron Corp. Mark became part of an executive management team that was headed by John Wing, who was a graduate of the United States Military Academy, at West Point, New York, a Vietnam veteran, and a former manager at General Electric. According to Sellers, Mark had a stormy relationship with Wing; sometimes he would speak harshly to her in front of other Enron personnel, calling her a failure, and occasionally he would even fire her "for a few hours or a few days." "There's good and bad in every situation," Mark told Sellers. "John gave me my fearlessness. He taught me not to be afraid to make decisions in intense, difficult, and emotionally charged situations."

Because she seemed to be—despite her volatile relationship with Wing—on a promising career track at Enron, many of her co-workers were surprised when, in the late 1980s, Mark left her full-time managerial position to pursue an M.B.A. degree at Harvard University's Graduate School in Business Administration, in Cambridge, Massachusetts. She did not sever her ties with Enron, though; while living in Cambridge, she juggled schoolwork, child care, and various assignments from Enron. Kenneth Lay, the CEO of the Enron Corp., recalled to Sellers that Mark and her husband had separated shortly before her move to Massachusetts. "She had her small twin boys [born in about 1985] to take care of," he told Sellers, "and she still worked almost full time for us while she went to business school. It was her choice." Among her Harvard classmates, Mark's extraordinary ambition and energy earned her the nickname Mark the Shark. "She could read a case study and boil it down quickly," one of her fellow business students told Sellers. "We learned a whole lot from her." Mark graduated from the Harvard Business School, with distinction, in 1990.

The following year Mark returned to Houston, where she became more deeply involved in Enron's emerging-markets projects and took on the responsibilities of her former boss, John Wing, who had recently left the company. Eager to capitalize on the decision made by many developing countries to privatize their government-run power-producing enterprises, Mark persuaded Lay to establish Enron Development Corp., as a subsidiary of Enron Corp. that would concentrate on pursuing new international markets and obtaining lucrative overseas contracts. As CEO of Enron Development, which was formed in 1991, Mark successfully secured contracts for the building of power plants in Central America, South America, and Asia.

In December 1993 Mark secured a contract for what was perhaps her most difficult project to date: the construction of a gigantic plant in the city of Dabhol that would supply power to Maharashtra. According to the agreement, which was negotiated with the Maharashtra State Electricity Board, Enron, which was to own 80 percent of the project, would operate the plant, in collaboration with the Dabhol Power Co., and would serve as fuel manager; the G.E. Capital Corp. and Bechtel Enterprises were each to own 10 percent.

Work on the Dabhol power project, as it was dubbed, began in March 1995. The following August, the project was scrapped by newly elected Maharashtra state officials in the newly installed Hindu-nationalist government, who declared that the contract that their predecessors had negotiated with Enron was unacceptable; among other things, they charged, bids from other companies had not been accepted—the officials "implied that bribes had been paid by Enron in securing the $2.5 billion project," as Jonathan Karp and Kathryn Kranhold wrote in the *Wall Street Journal* (February 5, 1999). The state officials also maintained that the cost of construction was too high and that Enron would be setting inflated prices for power. In January 1996, after some five months of talks between Mark and Indian officials, the Maharashtra Cabinet approved the renegotiated contract. The new agreement specified that for each kilowatt hour of electricity provided, Enron would charge the equivalent of 1.5 U.S. cents less than the amount originally agreed to, thus enabling consumers to save a total of about $7 billion over the next 20 years. In addition, the capacity of the power plant was increased from 2,015 to 2,450 megawatts, and the overall cost of the project was reduced to $2 billion. The completed regasification facility (a plant that would convert liquid fuel to a gas) was scheduled to be dedicated on April 17, 1999.

While Enron had been forced to "make major concessions at the bargaining table," as Karp and Kranhold reported, and the resulting contract was more modest than the original, the outcome was certainly preferable to terminating the entire project. The new arrangement, Mark told Hillary Durgin for the *Houston Chronicle* (January 8, 1996, on-line), was "doable." "It requires us to make a little bit more aggressive assumptions [on equipment costs]," she explained. According to Karp and Kranhold, "The Dabhol Power Co. project came back from disaster because the U.S. company and nationalist Indian politicians both learned from their mistakes and actually came to champion one another, with Enron forging a consensus in the nation that economic reform must continue." Mark told Nancy Rotenier for *Forbes* (June 17, 1996) that the Maharashtra experience had made her "a lot more seasoned in how to deal with crises as they occur."

Construction of the Dabhol power plant resumed in December 1996, after various Indian state and federal government departments gave the revised contract their stamp of approval. According to a publicity piece that appeared on the official Enron Web site in January 1998, the first phase of the project was at that point "well ahead of schedule," the second phase was expected to begin in the third quarter of 1998, and plans for the regasification plant had been revived. The Dabhol plant began operating in February 1999. Meanwhile, in 1998, Mark was named vice chair of Enron Corp. and chair and CEO of Enron's Azurix division.

Patricia Sellers described the professional persona of the five-foot-seven, blond Mark as "tough" and "self-confident." Mark, she reported, "never displays the modesty that holds women back." "It's startling to people when you're attractive and also really smart or extraordinarily good at what you do," Mark told Sellers. "You have greater impact. People want to meet you. They remember you." In an interview with Sellers, the historian and world-energy specialist David Yergin described Mark as "tops in her business." Then, referring to personal resources rather than fossil fuels, he said, "She has some unfathomable source of energy that allows her to crisscross time zones and operate with acuity and focus."

Among Mark's recent projects are an oil gasification plant in Sardinia, Italy; a natural-gas combined-cycle power plant in Marmara Ereglisi, Turkey; a natural-gas distribution system in South Korea; and a 1,875-mile natural-gas pipeline from Bolivia to Brazil. In addition to her work at Enron, Mark serves on the board of Thermatrix Inc. and the Brunswick Corp. She is a member of the Council on Foreign Relations and the Private Sector Advisory Council of the Inter-American Development Bank.

Mark, who is divorced, lives in Houston with her sons and their live-in nanny. The boys attend a private school whose flexible curriculum allows them to accompany their mother on some of her trips abroad. When Sellers interviewed Mark, in 1996, she habitually ran about 15 miles a week at what Sellers called "a very human nine-minute-per-mile pace," and in what little spare time she had, she enjoyed riding horses with her sons and skiing near her vacation home in Taos, New Mexico.

When asked what type of work she might like to do in the future, Mark told Sellers, "Maybe I'm going to run the World Bank, or CARE. I think of my job as one step in a life's work. It'll lead to bigger and different things." — C.P.

Suggested Reading: *Forbes* p100 June 17, 1996; *Fortune* p42+ Aug. 5, 1996, with photos; *Houston Chronicle* (on-line) Jan. 8, 1996; *Wall Street Journal* A p1+ Feb. 5, 1999

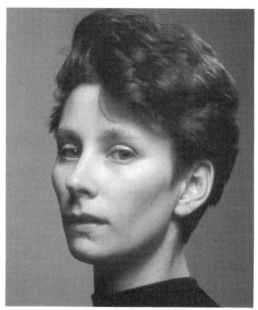

Johan Elbers, 1986

Marshall, Susan

1958– Choreographer. Address: c/o Susan Marshall & Company, Dance Continuum Inc., Box 707 Cooper Station, New York, NY 10276-0707

"My dances are about people," Susan Marshall, the internationally renowned modern-dance choreographer, has often said. "They're not about dancers." Marshall's contemporaries, among them Stephen Petronio and Mark Morris, and predecessors, who include Trisha Brown, Merce Cunningham, and Paul Taylor, have tended to create abstract dances, often based either on formal preoccupations or a piece of music. Their works are, first and foremost, about dancers moving in space. Marshall, by contrast, is known for using movement to evoke the intricacies and contradictions of human feelings and relationships. While the pioneering modern-dance choreographer Martha Graham also dealt with these topics, the emotions displayed in Graham's dances are on a mythic scale, whereas Marshall's more intimate, and no less intriguing, dances touch on feelings and experiences that are common to many people. Marshall reveals people's inner lives through simple, economical movement and the clean, elegant structures of her dances, and her work is admired as much for its form as for its humanistic content. Dance critic Deborah Jowitt wrote in the *Village Voice* (September 17, 1996) that Marshall "is famous for simplicity. Her best works have been plain, beautiful structures in which nothing seems extraneous, and every movement looks integral."

Since founding her ensemble, Susan Marshall & Company, in about 1983, Marshall has steadily risen in prominence within the dance world. The venue that served as the main launching pad for her career was New York City's Dance Theater Workshop (DTW). It was through performances of her dances at DTW's Bessie Schönberg Theater that Marshall first established a reputation as a promising young choreographer, with short dance pieces, many of them duets, such as *Arms* (1984) and *Kiss* (1987), the former of which Jowitt described as an "unforgettable" dance in which "two people reveal the essence of a relationship without ever moving from where they stand pressed together, side by side." As Marshall achieved greater recognition, she gradually began creating longer and more elaborate dances, and her company began performing at larger venues, most notably the Brooklyn Academy of Music (BAM), in New York City. Marshall's first evening-length work, *Interior with Seven Figures* (1988), was performed as part of BAM's Next Wave Festival, and since then four more of Marshall's dances have been included in that series, most recently *The Most Dangerous Room in the House* (1998). Also performed at BAM was *Les Enfants Terribles* (1996), a multi-media spectacle based on a Jean Cocteau novel, which fused dance and opera and was a collaboration with the composer Philip Glass. Marshall has also received numerous commissions to choreograph works for other dance companies in the United States and abroad. Her honors include two Bessies—formally known as New York Dance and Performance Awards—for outstanding choreographic achievement and fellowships from the National Endowment for the Arts (NEA) for at least six consecutive years, starting in 1991.

Little is known about Marshall's life before she became a choreographer. She was born in 1958 in Hershey, Pennsylvania. Her father, a behavioral scientist, and mother, a co-founder of the Pennsylvania chapter of the National Organization for Women, encouraged her pursuit of dance and gymnastics. Marshall studied modern dance for two years in the undergraduate program of the presti-

gious Juilliard School, in New York City. In the early 1980s she began choreographing dance pieces. At about that time (in 1982 or 1983, according to different accounts), she formed Susan Marshall & Company. The group has consisted of about eight members for most of its existence.

Otis Stuart, writing in *Dance* (December 1988), called Marshall's career "a classic success story" and described the early years of her company as "an almost idealized scenario for the successful contemporary dance choreographer." Her ensemble performed three seasons at the Bessie Schönberg Theater, from 1985 to 1987, and Marshall won her first Bessie in 1985. In the wake of that success, her company toured the United States and Europe, and Marshall won commissions from the Boston and Dallas ballets as well as from GRCOP, the Paris Opéra Ballet's modern-dance division.

Even that early in her career, Marshall's work carried strongly identifiable signature elements, including portrayals of the complexity and ambiguity of human relationships. In a review for the *New York Times* (December 7, 1987) of *Arms*, *Arena* (1986), *The Aerialist* (1987), *Companion Pieces* (1987), and *Kiss*, Anna Kisselgoff wrote, "The dancers are in variations of street dress and seen in recognizable situations of human intimacy and personal relationships. Yet none of these are ordinary vignettes. Miss Marshall knows how to cut deep into a small part of an emotional dilemma. She offers a cross-section, slicing into the heart of a problem. Her single image deepens as she probes further into it." Marshall conveyed emotional information through very simple movements that were often repeated with different intentions. In *Arms*, Kisselgoff wrote, the two performers, Marshall herself and Arthur Armijo, "stand, face the audience, occasionally bend from the torso but mainly rotate the arms. He hooks an arm around her neck; the embrace, according to its dynamics, can look occasionally brutal rather than tender. She rejects with a shoulder but also submits. The duet ends in a standoff."

Arena was inspired by the work of Marshall's brother, a teacher at a Fred Astaire ballroom dance studio. The piece was set in the world of ballroom dance, with twirling couples and appropriate music. "Yet," as Jack Anderson wrote in the *New York Times* (January 28, 1986), "sequences occasionally resembled athletic or even gladiatorial events. For Miss Marshall, a ballroom was an arena in which people were on display." He continued, "At times, the dancers moved smoothly. But they could also preen, engage in rivalries and mope when they felt they were being ignored."

Kiss, which premiered at the Bessie Schönberg Theater in 1987, is a short duet that features a couple who struggle to make contact with each other. Jack Anderson, in a review for the *New York Times* (August 22, 1993), wrote, "Ropes hanging from above the stage are attached to harnesses on the dancers' bodies; these contraptions permit them to sway and float with apparent weightlessness." He added, in a reference to the works of the 20th-century Russian-Jewish artist Marc Chagall, "The dancers suggest those levitating lovers who soar over rooftops in some fantastical Chagall paintings." To many, the piece and its climactic ending, in which the couple find each other in an aerial embrace, resonated with the struggles and rewards of making a relationship work.

Also in 1987, Marshall and her company served as artists-in-residence at Jacob's Pillow, a dance festival in Lee, Massachusetts. There, they were provided with room, board, rehearsal space, and stipends. Marshall took advantage of having her dancers at her disposal every day—in New York, they juggled other commitments as well—by rehearsing four pieces at once. At a public lecture-demonstration Marshall and her company gave at the festival, the choreographer told the audience, as reported in *New York Newsday* (August 23, 1987), "I work with an emotional contour, characters, narrative, and a sequence of events." She went on to explain how a gesture could be used to express "a certain intent that we can understand," and as an example, one of her dancers showed the audience how he could push someone "in a warm way" or "in a not nice way." In 1988 Marshall was an inaugural recipient of the American Choreographer Awards, given by the National Corporate Fund for Dance, and she also won a Brandeis University Creative Arts Award, placing her in a group that included such preeminent choreographers as Merce Cunningham and Paul Taylor.

Interior with Seven Figures, Marshall's first evening-length work, was presented at the Brooklyn Academy of Music's Next Wave Festival in December 1988. It was divided into 10 sections and set to music by Luis Resto. The dance revolves around a young man and his family—mother, father, and a brother who is clearly the weaker and more vulnerable of the two siblings. In a review for *New York* (January 2, 1989), Tobi Tobias described the family's life as "a quiet chamber of horrors. Theirs is a no-exit situation of desperate dependency in which nurturing and antagonism are one and the same. Life-sustaining measures are indistinguishable from violent assault; every embrace is a trap of sorts, each kiss a wound." Tobias added, "Marshall is rigorous to the point of obsession about tight, bare-bones structure and a vocabulary limited to pedestrian moves. If anything so gaudy as a dance step were to sneak into one of her rehearsals, I'll bet she'd coolly stomp it to death." The critic pointed out that Marshall's spartan movement style was used to express "a message . . . that is in its own way as bloody as the more lurid Greek myths" and suggested that Marshall might eventually feel constrained by a choreographic formula in which the tautness of the form butted up against the explosive emotions it contained. Marshall later added more-lyrical movements to her dances, beginning, notably, with *Fields of View* (1994). Speaking about that piece to Richard B. Woodward for the *New York Times* (November 6, 1994), she

said, "I never liked dance steps. I didn't know how to incorporate a ballet vocabulary. I guess it's something that I finally figured out how to do."

Marshall's work *Contenders*, performed at BAM's Next Wave Festival in 1990, featured eight dancers divided into four couples who used movements from such sports as swimming, running, wrestling, tennis, and gymnastics. Tobi Tobias, in a review for *New York* (December 17, 1990), wrote, "As with all of Marshall's work, its greatest beauty lies in the transmuting of realistic movement into a semiabstract form—Marshall has an uncanny gift for this—which is very much in tune with contemporary taste." The piece initially examines athletic competition and then addresses competition against one's self and finally the power struggles that occur between lovers. Tobias wrote that the dance also touched on "the selling of the body beautiful to an audience of voyeurs; the self-doubt that dogs accomplishment; the heartbreak of failure; the moment in which mind and spirit can no longer recall why the body is pushing itself to such extremes, and the confused physical and emotional stasis that results."

Marshall presented her dances *Spectators at an Event* (1994) and *Fields of View* at BAM's Next Wave Festival in 1994. *Spectators at an Event*, set to music by Henryk Gorecki, was one of Marshall's first works to prominently incorporate other artistic media—in this case, photographs by Weegee (the professional name of Arthur Fellig), a tabloid photographer who took pictures of horrific New York City crime scenes in the 1940s and 1950s. Marshall cropped Weegee's images, zeroing in on the faces of passersby who had stopped to gawk at some grisly spectacle. "It wasn't until I saw the number of people in his photographs who were watching the event that I became hooked on his work," Marshall told Woodward. "There's so much to be said about people watching. Why are we so morbidly drawn to tragedy? What are we looking at? I think it's interesting that we watch each other so much to gain information. But what does death look like? Maybe it's something that no matter how much you look at it, it doesn't make sense." In the dance, closeups culled from Weegee's photos were projected onto moveable screens, which the dancers rearranged during the performance. The piece also featured 38 people from the community surrounding BAM whom Marshall choreographed into the performance as onstage observers and who, according to one critic, blended so well with Marshall's dancers that it was sometimes hard to tell the two groups apart.

Spectators at an Event examined voyeurism and people's fascination with the tragedies of others while also blurring the line between participant and spectator. The performers portrayed spectators who continually gathered to stare at sights that were kept out of the audience's view. If the audience experienced a desire to see what the performers were looking at, they might also have become aware of the voyeurism involved in their act of looking at the performance. "Leaving a mystery at the heart of the event was ultimately more interesting than providing victims and restaging accidents," Marshall told Woodward. Marshall increased the complexity of her work by having lights and cameras periodically pointed toward the audience and having images of audience members projected onto the screens onstage.

Despite her use of the Weegee photos in *Spectators at an Event*, Marshall maintained to Woodward, "I don't relate to violent crime. No one in my circle of loved ones has ever been touched by that. Unfortunately I do know something about illness. It's a slower-acting violence but similar in its randomness. People are caught in its wake and don't understand what's happening. Fate steps in, and we're left to pick up the pieces." Both *Spectators at an Event* and *Fields of View* were interpreted by some dance critics as Marshall's rumination on loss in the age of AIDS; indeed, the dances gained added resonance in light of the untimely death of Arthur Armijo, a mainstay of her company who had died from that disease in 1993. *Fields of View*, which was accompanied by a string quartet by Philip Glass, seemed to address Armijo's death more directly than its companion piece. The set for *Fields of View*, created by the sculptor Judith Shea, featured snow (actually confetti), which fell continuously on a small area on the right side of the stage; the snow accumulated and then periodically got swept offstage by a gust of wind, "erasing the footsteps the dancers have left and creating a newly—cruelly—virgin terrain," Tobi Tobias wrote in a review for *New York* (November 28, 1994). The snow suggested a window between life and death; dancers would repeatedly leave the rest of the ensemble and vanish through the snow, only to reappear later. One of Marshall's most abstract dances to date, *Fields of View* conveyed the idea of the inevitability of death and renewal.

Like *Spectators at an Event* and *Fields of View*, Marshall's work *Central Figure* (1994) was generally perceived to be about the loss of a loved one. The dance, which Marshall dedicated to Armijo, was commissioned by the Lyons National Opera Ballet, a contemporary ballet troupe based in France, and it has been performed by that company extensively in Europe and the U.S. According to Anna Kisselgoff in the *New York Times* (July 28, 1997), it revolves around a central figure (danced by Stanislas Wisniewski in the performance she saw), "who repeatedly looms up with magical resonance and disappears from view." She continued, "Repeatedly, the 12 dancers regroup into lines and patterns from which Mr. Wisniewski is absent or into which he steps." The piece, she wrote, reflected "how a community reacts to a loved one's absence and presence."

Marshall, whose dances Otis called "inherently dramatic," has also tried her hand at conventional theater. In 1993 she wrote and directed *Walter's Finest Hours*, a play about a stroke victim named Walter who is visited daily by his daughter, Helen.

It played at the Downtown Art Company in the East Village neighborhood of Manhattan. Jennifer Dunning, reviewing it for the *New York Times* (May 17, 1993), wrote, "*Walter's Finest Hours* is [Marshall's] first purely theatrical effort but it has the confidence and sensitivity of long practice."

In 1996 Marshall, in one of her several collaborations with Philip Glass, directed Glass's new opera *Les Enfants Terribles: Children of the Game*, based on Jean Cocteau's novel *Les Enfants Terribles*. The opera is the final work in Glass's Jean Cocteau trilogy, each portion of which was presented at BAM's Next Wave Festival; the previous installments were *Orpheé* (1993) and *La Belle et la Bête* (1994). The main characters of the opera are Paul and Lise, possessive siblings who live together in a fantasy world and draw others into their manipulative and self-destructive games. Glass's and Marshall's rendition was billed as a "dance opera spectacle," and Paul and Lise were each played by one singer and three dancers. The audience's attention bounces back and forth among the singers, the dancers, a narrator who speaks in English, and English supertitles for the French libretto projected onto the set, which suggested alternately a street scene and a second-story apartment and incorporated falling snow. Anna Kisselgoff, reviewing the work for the *New York Times* (November 22, 1996), described it as a "groundbreaking model of integrated mixed forms." She continued, "The whole, directed with fast-paced confidence by Ms. Marshall, succeeds sensationally on its own terms." Commenting on the relationship between directing the opera and her usual process as a choreographer, Marshall told Jennifer Dunning for the *New York Times* (November 20, 1996), "Choreographers have the ability to move people through space, about the stage. And movement is one of the most powerful ways of communicating. It is so direct. We don't translate. It just hits us." Marshall won her second Bessie in 1996 for *Les Enfants Terribles*.

The Most Dangerous Room in the House, Marshall's fifth work to be presented at the Next Wave Festival, in 1998, was co-commissioned by the Jacob's Pillow Dance Festival and was partially developed there during another residency granted to Marshall and her troupe. The dance's central theme is that of a mother's recurring fear that her child will be harmed, or perhaps killed, by some domestic threat, such as choking, drowning, falling, or being cut with a kitchen knife. Marshall began creating the piece while pregnant with her son, Nicholas, who turned two in 1999, and its title, according to Marshall, came from an evaluation of potential dangers in bathrooms. "It hints at the unsettling notion that the home, the place we're all supposed to feel most secure, might not be such a safe haven after all," Marshall told Christopher Reardon for the *New York Times* (December 13, 1998). The central character in the dance is a maternal figure, played at BAM by the 60-year-old actress Norma Fire. She speaks snippets, and sometimes longer sections, of text, penned by Christo-

MARTIN

pher Renino, a novelist and Marshall's husband. "Free association and wordplay turn an account about splitting a melon in half into one about splitting a person in two," Anna Kisselgoff wrote in the *New York Times* (December 18, 1998). In the opening sequence, Fire and Marshall's dancers, all seemingly members of a family, throw themselves against a wall and climb onto or under a lone chair in an attempt to claim space and seek refuge. A group of wildly energetic dancers periodically sweep in and surge through the domestic environment Marshall has set up. A later section depicts a rescue, with bodies being dragged across the stage and, in some cases, revived. Other parts of the dance create the impression of safety and even bliss, as when a man and a woman take turns perching on each other, shifting positions and resting on each other on the floor of the stage; they could be on a bed, or on a shady patch of lawn. The text refers to a child, Jean—a play on the word "gene," according to Marshall—and in the dance's closing tableau, the audience sees Jean, in the form of a dancer, standing safely and serenely on a ramp, as if looking down at the mother figure from an upstairs window. "The flip side to all these fears is that there are completely fulfilling moments in our lives that are just as random," Marshall told Reardon. "They can happen to you at any moment."

Marshall and Christopher Renino have a house in Dutchess County, New York, and an apartment on Manhattan's Upper West Side. Marshall received a *Dance Magazine* Award in 1995, in recognition of her significant contributions to dance. — Y.P.

Suggested Reading: *Art in America* p57+ Feb. 1991, with photos; *Dance Magazine* p36+ Dec. 1988, with photos; *New York* p80+ Dec. 17, 1990, with photo; *New York Times* II p23 Aug. 22, 1993, with photo, II p23 Nov. 6, 1994, with photo, C p21 Nov. 20, 1996, with photo, II p10+ Dec. 13, 1998, with photos

Selected Works: as choreographer—*Trio in Four Parts*, 1983; *Arms*, 1984; *Opening Gambits*; *Ward*; *Fault Line*; *Routine and Variations*; *Kin*, 1985; *Arena*, 1986; *Companion Pieces*, 1987; *The Aerialist*, 1987; *Kiss*, 1987; *Interior with Seven Figures*, 1988; *Articles of Faith*, 1990; *Contenders*, 1991; *Standing Duet*, 1992; *Untitled (Detail)*, 1992; *Entr'acte 1*, 1993; *Entr'acte 2*, 1993; *Spectators at an Event*, 1994; *Fields of View*, 1994; *Central Figure*, 1994; *Les Enfants Terribles*, 1996; *Lines from Memory*, 1997; *The Most Dangerous Room in the House*, 1998; as director—*Les Enfants Terribles*, 1996; as writer and director—*Walter's Finest Hours*, 1993

Martin, Ricky

Dec. 24, 1971– Pop singer; actor. Address: c/o Sony Music Entertainment Inc., 550 Madison Ave., New York, NY 10022-3211

Thousands of screaming young women lining up for autographs. Paparazzi following his every move. Record-breaking album sales throughout the world. It's all routine for Ricky Martin, the Puerto Rican singer whose hit single, "Livin' La Vida Loca" ("Livin' the Crazy Life"), caused a sensation in the United States in the summer of 1999 and placed him among the world's most popular Latino stars. While his rise to household-name status in the U.S. happened seemingly overnight, Martin is no stranger to the spotlight or to ecstatic fans. A former child actor and member of Menudo, a pop-singing quintet of Puerto Rican youths that captured the hearts of millions of young people in the 1980s, Martin later acted in theater and television soap operas—among them *General Hospital*—in the United States and Latin America. In 1991 he launched a solo recording career as well, and in the latter half of the decade he became an international pop-music celebrity, with sensuality and personal magnetism prominent in his image. After making four Spanish-language albums that combined pop and Latin musical styles and sold a total of more than 13 million copies worldwide, Martin

Steve Granitz/Retna Ltd.

launched the aforementioned single—his first U.S. hit—from *Ricky Martin* (1999), his debut English-language record. His success in the United States has made Martin Puerto Rico's most famous cultural ambassador and one of Latin music's biggest crossover stars.

The singer and actor was born Enrique Martin on December 24, 1971 in San Juan, Puerto Rico, to Enrique Martin III, a psychologist who worked in prisons, and Nereida Morales, an accountant for banks. He has been in show business for much of his life. At age seven he told his father that he wanted to become an entertainer. The senior Martin then took his son to a casting call for models and actors held by a talent agency at a local shopping center. Agency representatives were favorably impressed, and during the next three years, Ricky, nicknamed Kiki during his childhood, appeared in 30 television commercials. He also attended a Catholic school, served as an altar boy, performed in school plays, and sang in the school choir. Ironically, as a youth he was not fond of Latin music; he preferred such American rock groups as Boston and Cheap Trick. "I'm gonna be honest," Martin said, as quoted by Elysa Gardner for *USA Today* (May 7, 1999, on-line). "Growing up, I listened to rock. I think the first album I bought was a David Bowie album, and the second was from the band Journey. In those days, Latin sounds were not hip for my generation." Nevertheless, his mother would insist that he come with her to see Tito Puente, Celia Cruz, and other Latin music icons in concert, and thanks to her efforts, he began to develop an appreciation for the music of his culture.

As a preteen Martin auditioned for Menudo, a pop group that had been created by the impresario Edgardo Diaz and was made up of five boys ages 12 to 17; periodically, members retired and replacements were sought. "I'd see Menudo and I'd get this sparkle, like I couldn't live without being in the band," Martin told Nancy Collins for *Rolling Stone* (August 5, 1999). Menudo rejected him three times, because, he was told, he was too short and looked too young. Then, in 1984, when he was 12, the group invited him to join them. He made his debut with Menudo at Radio City Music Hall, in New York City. For the next five years, he was caught up in the demands of performing with the group, which rehearsed as many as 16 hours a day and spent much of the year touring throughout the world. Although some former members later raised allegations of exploitation and abuse, Martin has maintained that his experience with Menudo was a positive one and helped prepare him for the future. "What I remember of Menudo was respect, a lot of work, discipline, and a family atmosphere . . . ," he told Collins. "When you leave the group, you have the tools to do whatever you want—if it's school, you have money; if it's to stay in the business, you've done everything, which helps a lot." However, in an earlier interview, with Peter Castro for *People* (May 15, 1995), Martin complained about Menudo's management. "Our creativity was stifled," he said to Castro. "We were told [the songs we wrote] were no good. We began to question the need for rehearsing the same routines over and over."

After leaving Menudo in 1989, when he was 17, Martin got his high school degree in Puerto Rico. He then moved to New York City, where he lived for 10 months in an apartment in Long Island City, in the borough of Queens. "I needed some anonymity," he told Collins, "to get to know myself, because, for the last five years, it had been about, 'You wear *these* clothes, get *this* haircut, sing *this* song.' I needed to get my personality back, to find out what I liked and hated." During this period Martin seriously questioned whether he should continue in the entertainment business, and he considered embarking on a career in computers or fashion.

In late 1989, less than one week into a visit to a friend in Mexico City, the capital of Mexico, Martin was offered a role in a play called *Mama Ama el Rock'n'Roll* ("Mom Loves Rock-'n'-Roll"), which starred Angelica Vale, a renowned Latina actress. Later, he auditioned successfully for a part in the most popular Mexican television soap opera at that time, *Alcanzar Una Estrella II* ("To Reach a Star II"). He made his big-screen debut in a motion picture based on the soap, and his performance earned him a Heraldo, the Mexican equivalent of an Oscar. Meanwhile, he had been singing with the pop group Munecos de Papel (Paper Puppets) and had contributed to their eponymous album. Sometime later he was offered the chance to record a solo album, and in 1991 he released *Ricky Martin*, all of which is sung in Spanish. (The songs on the album are different from those on the English-language *Ricky Martin*, released in 1999.) Martin has categorized the album as pop. "I was finding myself—who am I when it comes to music?" he told Collins. "I did ballads, because they're the shortcut. Everybody falls in love, everybody likes ballads. . . . I was building, and it was a smart move." The album was a hit, and after it came out Martin toured extensively in Latin America. He followed up his debut with *Me Amaras* ("You'll Love Me," 1993). By this time he had developed a large following, and his second tour included South America; he even recorded songs in Portuguese for Brazilian audiences.

Later in 1993 Martin moved to Los Angeles, where he began to make a name for himself in the American entertainment industry. That same year he had a role on the short-lived television series *Getting By*. Then, during the 1993–94 television season, he appeared on the highly popular daytime soap opera *General Hospital*, as Miguel Morez, a former pop star who had left Puerto Rico to put a soured relationship behind him—a character whose life had much in common with Martin's. The role gave him the chance to display his acting ability for the show's dedicated American audience. Moreover, the story line of the soap, which followed Miguel's return to a career in music, allowed Martin to showcase his singing, and he earned a legion of devout fans. Also in 1994 Martin reconciled with his father; Martin's parents had divorced when he was two years old, and he and his father had become estranged when, during his teens, Martin chose to live with his mother during the brief periods when he was not on tour with Menudo. In the summer of 1996, in a temporary assignment, Martin stepped into the role of Marius, a principal character in the Broadway production of the hit musical *Les Miserables*, in New York City. He also provided the voice of the title character in Disney's Spanish-language version of the hit animated film *Hercules* (1997).

Earlier, in 1995, Martin had released *A Medio Vivir* ("To Live by Halves"), which was co-produced by K. C. Porter and the former Menudo member Robi Rosa. It was with this record, Martin told Collins, that he began musically "having fun with my background, with the Latin sounds, with the percussive," by creating "a mix of sounds—salsa, a little *cuema* and samba." The incorporation of Latin musical elements into Martin's pop style made his record company fearful that *A Medio Vivir* would not do as well as his previous albums. However, within six months of its release, sales of the disk had reached 600,000 copies worldwide; eventually, the figure exceeded one million. *A Medio Vivir* proved popular even in such countries as China and Japan, where there were few Spanish-speaking fans. In addition, according to Martin, it boosted his popularity in Europe. The album featured the song "Maria," which was the second-best-selling single in the world in 1997.

Martin told Collins that, impressed by "Maria," representatives for the 1998 World Cup soccer tournament asked him to compose an anthem for the event, which was to be held in France that summer. He performed the song, called "La Copa de la Vida" ("The Cup of Life"), at the opening ceremony, which was viewed by a television audience of an estimated two billion people. The song, featured on Martin's all-Spanish album *Vuelve* (1998), won a 1999 Grammy Award for best Latin pop performance, and thanks to its exposure at the World Cup, it sold over six million copies worldwide. In a review for *Rolling Stone* (April 15, 1999), Barry Walters described *Vuelve* as "a rich stew of pounding percussion, deeply emotional melodicism, and ethereal, symphonic sonics." He added, "You don't need to know a word of [Martin's native] tongue to appreciate the poetry of his performance." The album sold 1.7 million copies in the U.S.; it reached the number-one spot on album sales charts in Australia, Japan, and France and won the *Billboard* Latin Music Award for best album of the year by a male artist. The song "Vuelve" won the *Billboard* Latin Music Award for hot Latin track of the year, and Martin was named favorite Latino artist at the 1999 Blockbuster Entertainment Awards.

Despite the success of his albums throughout the world, superstardom eluded Martin in the U.S. until February 1999, when he gave a rousing performance of "La Copa de la Vida" at the Grammy Awards ceremony. Martin's stage presence and dance moves, which often involve adroit hip-swiveling and have inspired comparisons to Elvis Presley, have made him a sex symbol in the U.S. as well as in countries where he has long enjoyed fame. At public appearances he is often mobbed by thousands of adoring fans in scenes reminiscent of the frenzy and hysteria provoked by such music sensations as Presley and the Beatles. "I used to freak out every time people would mention the word 'sex symbol,'" Martin told Elysa Gardner. "But I was talking to [the Latina pop singer] Gloria Estefan recently, and she said, 'You know what, buddy? If you have it, take advantage of it, 'cause it's not gonna be there forever!' . . . Gloria basically said, look, it's part of you—don't be ashamed of it." When Nancy Collins asked Martin why people respond so strongly to him, he spoke of the intensity of his performances and the energy of his music. "When I'm out there, I'm giving it my all," he told Collins. "I'm not wearing a mask. I'm having a good time, I'm dancing, I'm interpreting from my gut. At the same time, there are so many things happening on this planet—we just went through a war [in the Balkans], the earthquake in Mexico [in June 1999]. People are afraid. My music is like freedom. It hits the nail on the head. I do this kind of music because I know what I need to go through life. But I try not to analyze this too much. I just say, 'Go for it, buddy. Enjoy it. Go out there and have a blast.'"

Martin gained additional exposure in the U.S. by appearing in television commercials to promote tourism in Puerto Rico, which is a self-governing United States commonwealth. He views himself as a cultural ambassador for the island, and he has expressed a desire to promote Puerto Rican culture to the world. "It's all about breaking stereotypes. For me, the fact that people think Puerto Rico is *Scarface*, that we ride donkeys to school—that has to change," he told Andrew Essex for *Entertainment Weekly* (April 23, 1999). Martin quickly capitalized on his newfound success in the U.S. In April 1999 he performed at Carnegie Hall, in New York City, alongside such stars as Sting, Elton John, and James Taylor at a benefit concert for the Rainforest Foundation, which works to preserve the rainforests of Amazonia, in South America. Martin also made appearances on a slew of television programs, among them *The Today Show*, *Saturday Night Live*, and *The Rosie O'Donnell Show*. In May 1999 *Ricky Martin* was released on Sony Music's Columbia label. In one duet, "Be Careful" ("Cuidado con Mi Corazon"), Martin sang in English and Madonna sang in Spanish. "It's all about exchanging cultures," Martin told Gardner. The English-language *Ricky Martin*, which also contains a duet with the Swedish singer Meja, set a record for first-week sales in 1999; one song, "Livin' La Vida Loca," rose to the top of *Billboard*'s Hot 100 singles chart.

Martin's phenomenal success is another milestone in the establishment of Latin pop as part of mainstream American culture. Currently, Martin is sharing the limelight with such other Latino stars as the singers Glorida Estefan, Enrique Iglesias, and Marc Anthony and the actress turned singer Jennifer Lopez. Latin pop's increased presence on American airwaves coincides with the emergence of Hispanics as the fastest-growing minority in the U.S.; according to estimates by the U.S. Census Bureau, Hispanics will become the largest minority group in the nation by 2005.

Martin plans to launch a major concert tour of the U.S. in the fall of 1999. In addition to his music career, he hopes to do more acting in both film and theater. Martin co-owns Casa Salsa, a restaurant that offers Puerto Rican fare, in South Beach, Florida. Paparazzi often attempt to photograph him from boats when they spot him in his backyard, in Miami Beach, Florida, playing with his golden retriever, Icara, and Chihuahua, Titan. Since a trip to India in 1998, he has practiced meditation daily. — Y.P.

Suggested Reading: *Entertainment Weekly* p33+ Apr. 23, 1999, with photos, p72+ May 14, 1999, with photo; *New York* p42+ June 28–July 5, 1999, with photos; *People* p109+ May 15, 1995, with photos; *Rolling Stone* p105+ Apr. 15, 1999, p48+ Aug. 5, 1999, with photos; *Time* p84 May 10, 1999, with photo, p74+ May 24, 1999, with photos; *USA Today* (on-line) May 7, 1999, with photo

Selected Albums: in Spanish—*Ricky Martin*, 1991; *Me Amaras*, 1993; *A Medio Vivir*, 1995; *Vuelve*, 1997; in English—*Ricky Martin*, 1999

Selected Television Shows: *General Hospital*, 1993–94

P. Reitzfeld/Courtesy of Picador USA

Maynard, Joyce

1953– Writer. Address: c/o Picador USA, 175 5th Ave., New York, NY 10010

"The moment I finally got all I wanted—success, achievement, recognition—was the moment I fell in love with someone who regarded all that as dangerous," the writer Joyce Maynard commented to an interviewer in 1992. The "moment" she was referring to was the spring of 1972, when the *New York Times Magazine* published as its cover story Maynard's autobiographical essay "An 18-Year Old Looks Back on Life," and she immediately became a national celebrity who some people regard-

ed as the voice of her generation. The "someone" with whom she fell in love was the famous, and famously reclusive, fiction writer J. D. Salinger. She soon embarked on an affair with Salinger that lasted for nine months. For the next quarter-century, she revealed virtually nothing about it in public. Then, in 1998, she broke her silence, with the publication of her memoir *At Home in the World*.

The details of her relationship with Salinger were apparently among the few aspects of her life that Maynard had *not* previously described in print. "I'm really quite comfortable being in the position of somebody who talks about the dirty little secrets that a lot of people don't," she told Alison Roberts for the *Sacramento Bee* (November 6, 1997). Maynard, Roberts wrote, "is a longtime chronicler of the quotidian" who "has made a career of self-revelation." "The only difference between her life and millions of others is that she has written about it—and written about it and written about it," Roberts declared.

In some respects, Maynard's life does indeed resemble those of countless others: she dropped out of college, married at 23, gave birth to three children, and went through a bitter divorce. But she is hardly typical: she has also published three novels (one of which was made into a critically acclaimed feature film), two memoirs, a children's book, dozens of articles for national magazines, a monthly column, called "A Mother's Days," that appeared in *Parenting Magazine* for more than eight years, and a newspaper column, called "Domestic Affairs," that reached some four million readers every week, also for about eight years. Currently, she is on tour promoting *At Home in the World*, a book that has made a big stir in the literary world—and provoked a slew of criticism of Maynard herself.

Daphne Joyce Maynard was born in 1953 in Exeter, New Hampshire. Her father, Max Maynard, was an English professor at the University of New Hampshire and an avocational artist. Her mother,

Fredelle, a homemaker and freelance writer, had a doctorate from Harvard University; according to Joyce Maynard, the chauvinistic climate that prevailed in academia in the 1950s prevented her mother from finding full-time employment at any nearby university. In a review of *At Home in the World* for the *New York Times* (September 13, 1998, on-line), the poet Katha Pollitt summarized Maynard's description of her family life. "From the outside," Pollitt wrote, "the childhood of Joyce and her older sister, Rona, looked ideal: safe, warm, child-centered. But Max . . . who as a Daytime Daddy quotes poetry and teaches Joyce to draw, is also a Nighttime Daddy, who drinks and rants and blames his family for his stalled career as a painter. And Mummy, who would have loved nothing more than to teach English . . . covers her thwarted ambitions with manic housekeeping while she ekes out the family budget writing chirpy pieces for women's magazines." "A psychiatrist's nightmare," Pollitt continued, Fredelle Maynard "cuddle[d] suggestively with young Joyce" and, in addition, "nudge[d] her rail-thin daughter . . . into years of anorexia."

As a child, Maynard told Paula Chin for *People* (March 2, 1992), "I had an intense obligation to make my parents happy and redeem their disappointments." Early on, she disclosed in *At Home in the World*, her mother and father both pressed her to write. In 1960, they gave her a mimeograph machine for her birthday, and before long, she began publishing her own newspaper and pedaling it door-to-door in her neighborhood. By age 10, she had entered many writing competitions. Routinely, she would read aloud to her parents what she had written for those contests and also whatever she wrote for school assignments, and during her recitations, her mother and father would take notes and then make suggestions for improvements. Young Joyce "escaped whenever she could to the TV room," as Pollitt put it. She became a self-professed television addict and memorized not only the dialogue from reruns of such shows as *Father Knows Best* and *Make Room for Daddy* but the production credits as well. She developed a strong desire to be an actress, and wrote letters to the producers of several TV shows to suggest that they add her to their casts. She also acted in school plays. (Her closest brush with movie stardom occurred in the early 1970s, when she auditioned unsuccessfully for a starring role in the film *The Exorcist*.)

As a high-school student in 1968, Maynard handed out bumper stickers as a volunteer in the ultimately unsuccessful presidential campaign of Senator Eugene McCarthy. After her junior year, she transferred to the Phillips Exeter Academy, a prestigious private school, where she became a member of the first co-ed class. "Like the Exeter blacks, the Exeter girls moved in a gang across the campus, ate together at all-girl tables and fled, after classes, to the isolated study areas allotted to them," she wrote in her *New York Times Magazine* remembrance. She also recalled becoming "a com-pulsive overachiever, joining clubs and falling asleep at the typewriter in the hope of battering down doors I was used to having open, at my old school, where they knew me." At a New Year's Eve party that she attended in her hometown, she felt cut off from the conversation of her former schoolmates, which focused on events that did not involve her. "The school had gone on without me," she commented in her *New York Times Magazine* article. In February 1970, an essay by Maynard, who was then 16 or 17, appeared in *Seventeen*, on the magazine's "In My Opinion" page.

In 1971 Maynard enrolled at Yale University, in New Haven, Connecticut, on a partial scholarship. During her freshman year, *Seventeen* (January 1972) published another of her pieces, a short story called "Country Music." That story, which she sent to the *New York Times* once it was published, landed her a commission to write "Looking Back" for the *New York Times Magazine*. According to Maynard, she wrote "Looking Back" in a single weekend. The article met with a mixed response. It caused jealousy in many of her contemporaries; it proved distasteful to people who, as Paula Chin wrote, "found this tale of little Joyce at sea in the bewildering culture of sex and drugs and politics cloying and disingenuous." And it inspired admiration, in the case, for example, of a former vice president of the United States, Senator Hubert H. Humphrey, who wrote to Maynard to tell her that she was—in Maynard's words—"a credit to [her] generation."

Within 24 hours of the publication of "Looking Back," Maynard was deluged with calls from magazine editors who evidently viewed her as a spokesperson for her contemporaries. Before the end of the year, Maynard's by-line had appeared seven times in national periodicals, among them *Mademoiselle* and *McCall's*, for which she wrote first-person accounts called, respectively, "The Embarrassment of Virginity" and "My Parents Are My Friends." In July 1972 her "exclusive interview" of Julie Nixon Eisenhower, the younger daughter of then-President Richard Nixon, appeared in *Seventeen*, and an essay called "Searching for Sages" came out in *Newsweek*'s December 25, 1972 issue.

Meanwhile, Maynard had received a huge number of letters from people responding to her "Looking Back" article. One was from J. D. Salinger, the author of the modern classic *The Catcher in the Rye*, who advised her, Maynard recalled in *At Home in the World*, "to be careful before signing up for any of the stuff" editors offered her. "My talent should be allowed to develop without haste, he says, rather than being plastered over the pages of a bunch of magazines." Maynard and Salinger began to correspond, and they met in person during the summer of 1972, when Maynard was working as an apprentice editorial writer at the *New York Times* and housesitting for a wealthy couple. During the 1972–73 academic year, she dropped out of Yale and—with her parents' blessing—moved in with the 53-year-old Salinger, who lived in virtual seclusion in rural New Hampshire. According to Maynard, before long he displayed increasing impatience with her, and one summer day in 1973, he abruptly told her to pack up and leave. The next day, she returned to Exeter.

Meanwhile, the previous April, Maynard's first book, *Looking Back: A Chronicle of Growing Up Old in the Sixties*, had been published. An expansion of her *New York Times Magazine* piece, it struck various reviewers as both praiseworthy—for its insights and distinctive vignettes—and flawed, because of excessive generalizing and strained attempts to assume what one critic called the "Voice of Youth." Speaking of *Looking Back* with Alison Roberts, Maynard said, "I was published before I had something to say. It was this rather glib book about my generation."

With her earnings from *Looking Back*, Maynard bought a house in Hillsboro, New Hampshire, in 1973. For four years beginning that same year, she wrote news reports and reviews for the *New York Times*, gave commentaries on cultural matters on CBS radio, and, according to her home page on the Web, wrote "jillions" of magazine articles. Sometime during that period, she moved to New York City. In 1977, she married Steve Bethel, an artist, quit her *New York Times* and CBS jobs, and resumed living in Hillsboro. Her first child, a daughter named Audrey, was born in 1978; her first son, Charlie, was born in 1981.

Also in 1981, Maynard's first novel, *Baby Love*, was published. "There's much in [*Baby Love*] that recalls *Looking Back*," the novelist Anne Tyler reported in the *New York Times Book Review* (August 16, 1981). "The tone is the same: right on target, cued to the rangy, slangy rhythms of modern life, though lacking the embarrassing archness that characterized the earlier piece. There is the same acute awareness of the present moment, or at least, of the present moment as perceived by the public." Tyler also wrote, "Unfortunately, . . . Maynard takes her plot beyond its natural boundaries. . . . Things go too far, in other words. Zaniness intrudes; wacky comedy makes its clanging entrance. . . . It's a pity, because the heart of *Baby Love* is a very fine book indeed. When . . . Maynard talks about ordinary life . . . she shows herself to be a writer of uncommon promise. She has an unswerving eye, a sharply perked ear, and the ability to keep her readers hanging on her words."

Maynard talked about "ordinary life"—specifically, her own experiences as a homemaker and freelance writer, activities that she pursued with the help of a full-time baby-sitter—in her weekly syndicated newspaper column "Domestic Affairs," which debuted in 1984, the year her second son, Willy, was born. Her other pursuits included organizing, in collaboration with other Hillsboro residents, community resistance to a U.S. Department of Energy proposal to locate in the town a permanent repository for nuclear waste. An article by Maynard about the community's efforts appeared in the *New York Times Magazine* on May 11, 1986. On December 24, 1986, some of Maynard's memories of Christmases past appeared in the *New York Times*, along with recollections by the writers Eudora Welty, Reynolds Price, Garrison Keillor, Mary Lee Settle, and Samuel R. Delany.

Domestic Affairs: Enduring the Pleasures of Motherhood and the Family, a collection of Maynard's newspaper columns, came out in 1987. After describing the book as "delightful" in a review for the *Washington Post Book World* (July 5, 1987), Elizabeth Ward noted that Maynard had not offered advice in her columns; "rather," Ward wrote, "she is offering herself, in an unusually personal way, as a companion in experiences that we all go through." Maynard had not disclosed to her readers, however, the serious difficulties she had been experiencing in her marriage (or the fact that she had been the main breadwinner). "There were years there where I was running around in frantic circles trying to make everything look perfect," she admitted to Alison Roberts. "'We are going to be a happy family if it kills me' was my motto." She added, "I know I've been a woman that a lot of women loved to hate. I feel some regret that for a lot of years in my efforts to be a perfect mother I was probably leaving some women feeling really bad." In 1989 Maynard began writing about her separation from her husband and the beginning of what she has called the couple's "long hard divorce"—subject matter that led some two dozen newspapers to drop her column. *No Longer Married*, a collection of 23 of Maynard's articles about marriage, divorce, single-parenting, and romantic relationships, is listed for sale on the *Joyce Maynard Online Catalogue*, as is *Day In, Day Out*, a collection of 15 of her pieces about family life and child-raising. Maynard also sells audiocassettes and CDs through her on-line catalog.

For a year or so in 1990 or 1991, Maynard's three children lived with their father. During that time, having grown "sick of writing about my life," as she put it to Alison Roberts, Maynard completed *To Die For* (1992), which is based on a real-life murder. An adaptation of *To Die For*, directed by Gus Van Sant and with a screenplay by Buck Henry, premiered in movie theaters in 1995. The film starred Nicole Kidman, who won plaudits for her portrayal of Suzanne Stone, a ferociously ambitious TV personality who, with the goal of furthering her career, recruits three high-school students to kill her husband. Maynard, too, was cast in the film, in the role of Suzanne's lawyer.

Also in 1992, prompted by her desire to protect the privacy of her children, Maynard abandoned her newspaper column. Soon afterward, she launched the *Domestic Affairs Newsletter*. Sold by subscription, it contained stories from its readers as well as pieces by Maynard. In that same year, she made her debut as a public speaker, giving talks on "issues of women, motherhood, and family relationships," as she put it on her Web site. Since discontinuing the newsletter, she has issued on-line, about once a week, her "Letter from Joyce." Her letter of December 1, 1998 described her "second annual pie-party," at which 21 people—most of whom she was meeting in person for the first time—baked pies in her kitchen. It also directed readers to check out her on-line catalog, "to help you out with all your Christmas shopping needs."

Earlier, in 1994, at the invitation of National Public Radio (NPR), Maynard began recording first-person accounts for airing on the NPR program *All Things Considered*. Her third novel, *Where Love Goes*, was published in 1995, in conjunction with a compact disc that contained songs about love that were selected by Maynard and rendered by such performers as Emmylou Harris and Lucinda Williams. The CD, according to *Publishers Weekly* (June 12, 1995), was "meant to serve as a soundtrack for the book," which, at the end, includes a long list of the songs Maynard listened to while working on it.

In a 1998 self-interview for her Web page, Maynard said that she was prompted to write *At Home in the World* when her daughter turned 18. "I did not set out to write a book about J.D. Salinger," she explained. "I wanted only to write an honest book about my experiences and my growth from young womanhood to adulthood. . . . I believed that to do so would be helpful to a great many women my age, who have known the experience of giving up crucial parts of themselves to please the man they love. And I believed my story would be helpful, above all, to young women my daughter's age, who are still in the process of forming themselves as women, and in need of encouragement to remain true to themselves."

As Maynard had anticipated, *At Home in the World* (1998) elicited a flood of exceedingly harsh reviews. In the *Nation* (November 16, 1998), Chris Kraus wrote that "the majority" of the dozen reviews that she had read were "written with astonishing contempt and even hatred," and all of them, to a greater or lesser degree, according to Kraus, amounted to critiques of Maynard the person. Various reviewers, for example, faulted Maynard for her "shameless betrayal" of Salinger's "privacy" (a betrayal motivated, they contended, by her greedy desire to earn a lot of money from a book) and for what they viewed as her boundless self-centeredness and her lack of introspection—her apparent inability to "understand her own story," as Katha Pollitt put it in the *New York Times*.

Had those reviewers been judging a book written by a man, Kraus charged, their approach to *At Home in the World* would have been very different; they would not have questioned the author's efforts to understand himself and to come to grips with his experiences. In Kraus's view, that is precisely what Maynard tried to do. "Like a great many serious young women of her generation, Maynard had to raise herself," Kraus wrote. "No one helped her reconcile ambition ('male') with the alien state of 'femininity.' *At Home in the*

World reads like a companion piece to Mary Pipher's penetrating *Reviving Ophelia*, a study of the painful and crosswired contradictions that still plague ambitious girls."

In June 1999 Maynard announced that she had consigned Salinger's letters to her to Sotheby's, in New York City, to auction off. "I'd rather put my children through college than own a box full of Salinger's letters," she told Peter Applebome for the *New York Times* (May 12, 1999, on-line). "They were a piece of my past that I've finished with, and I'd rather use them to support my family." The letters, which Sotheby's expected would fetch between $60,000 and $80,000, were sold to the entrepreneur and art collector Peter Norton for $156,000, of which Maynard received $140,000. (Norton said that he intended to return the letters to Salinger.)

Since 1996 Joyce Maynard has lived with her children in Mill Valley, in northern California. "My next novel I'm sure will be much more invention," she told Alison Roberts. "My life has been an open book for a long time." — M.B.

Suggested Reading: *Christian Science Monitor* p23+ Sep. 14, 1987, with photo; *Irish Times* (on-line) Sep. 30, 1998; *joycemaynard.com* (various issues); *New York Times Magazine* p11+ Apr. 23, 1972, with photos, p32+ Sep. 6, 1998, with photos; *People* p65+ Mar. 2, 1992, with photos; *Sacramento Bee* (on-line) Nov. 6, 1997; *Vanity Fair* p302+ Sep. 1998, with photos; *Contemporary Authors* new rev series vol 64, 1998; Maynard, Joyce. *Looking Back: A Chronicle of Growing Up Old in the Sixties*, 1973, *At Home in the World*, 1998

Selected Books: *Looking Back: A Chronicle of Growing Up Old in the Sixties*, 1973; *Baby Love*, 1981; *Domestic Affairs: Enduring the Pleasures of Motherhood and Family Life*, 1987; *New House*, 1987; *To Die For*, 1992; *Where Love Goes*, 1995; *At Home in the World*, 1998

McDonald, Audra

1970– Singer; actress. Address: c/o Bill Butler, Gersh Agency, 130 W. 42nd St., New York, NY 10036

According to Terry Teachout in *Time.com* (October 5, 1998, on-line), the singer and actress Audra McDonald "could make a toothpaste jingle sound poignant." "There is no finer singer on Broadway," Teachout wrote. "She has a tangy, beautifully focused soprano voice and an intensely evocative way with words." McDonald made her Broadway debut in *The Secret Garden*, a 1991 musical based on Frances Hodgson Burnett's beloved 1911 children's book. She has since won Tony Awards for

Mike Segar/Archive Photos

Audra McDonald

her work in the high-profile shows *Carousel, Master Class*, and *Ragtime*. Most recently McDonald has released a successful album of songs written by contemporary composers of musicals.

Audra Ann McDonald was born in 1970 in Berlin, Germany, where her father was stationed with the U.S. Army. After returning to the United States, her family settled in Fresno, California. Her father, who had majored in music in college, became a high-school principal; her mother, an accomplished pianist, works as an administrator at California Polytechnic State University, in San Luis Obispo. Several of McDonald's aunts are gospel singers.

McDonald appeared on stage for the first time when, at the age of nine, she was cast as one of the royal children in a production of *The King and I* at Roger Rocka's Music Hall, a local dinner theater. During the next three years, she acted in a series of other Roger Rocka productions. After joining the theater's resident acting company, when she was 12, she performed in such musicals as *Hello Dolly!, A Chorus Line, Grease,* and *The Wiz*, in the last of which she played Dorothy, the main character. "I think the dinner theater just gave me a chance to be on stage every night, to really experience what that's all about," McDonald told Chris Haines for *Tony Awards Online.*

As her graduation from high school approached, McDonald decided that, more than anything else, she wanted to continue performing. "I wanted to move to New York," she told Haines. "And my parents basically said, you know, 'We're not going to let you go unless you are in school somewhere.' And so I auditioned for Juilliard on a whim, and I got in. I thought, 'Well, I better go.'" At the Juilliard

School, in New York City—perhaps the most prestigious performing arts school in the U.S.—she enrolled in a vocal-training program that relied on classical techniques. While McDonald's teachers were more concerned with classical music and opera than with Broadway-style musicals, McDonald chose not to pursue a career in opera, because, as she told Haines, in musicals "the emphasis certainly is a bit more on the acting and the whole character, whereas in opera, the main focus is the singing." Nevertheless, by her own account, the classical training she received at Juilliard has been invaluable to her. "Juilliard was able to offer me . . . the discipline and the technique, too," she explained to Haines. "A vocal technique was something that I was kind of lacking. I was just singing on sheer instinct before. I was able to—and I still am in the process of—working on a technique that can help me get through the eight-show grind."

McDonald was still at Juilliard when, in the early 1990s, she made her Broadway debut in *The Secret Garden*, as a replacement for one of the original cast members. As an undergraduate she also did summer stock at regional theaters, partly with the aim of making connections in the theater world, something that her school, with its aesthetic rather than business-oriented approach to the arts, did not facilitate directly. McDonald told Haines that she "never really had acting lessons" and that she developed her own way of fleshing out a character. "The way I basically approach a character is to find as many things in common with the character that I have. Then [I] just . . . try and go through telling their story, without getting too wrapped up in showing their story. I'm more interested in experiencing, and telling the character's story instead of making the audience think that I am presenting it to them."

Immediately after earning a bachelor's degree from Juilliard, in 1993, McDonald began auditioning for Broadway shows. Being a Juilliard graduate, she told Haines, "certainly help[ed] to get the door opened a little bit." One of her first auditions was for a revival of the Rodgers and Hammerstein classic *Carousel*, which was to be staged at the Vivian Beaumont Theater, at the Lincoln Center for the Performing Arts, in New York City, under the direction of Nicholas Hytner. In the middle of her audition, while singing "Mr. Snow," McDonald fainted. Moments later she got up and began the song again. Her singing and her reading of lines from the libretto won her the role of Carrie Pipperedge, a mill worker who is the best friend of the show's romantic heroine, Julie Jordan.

McDonald's portrayal of Pipperedge differed significantly from those of her predecessors in two ways. Traditionally, only Caucasian actresses had played the role. While there was some speculation before the revival opened that an African-American Carrie would alter the overall feeling of the show, critical response to the casting proved to be enthusiastic. McDonald believes that she was effective in the role because *Carousel* is, in her words, "a universal story, with universal music and lyrics." "You don't have to be black or white to be a wife beater," she pointed out, referring to Billy Bigelow, the character with whom Julie Jordan falls in love. "If . . . people are concentrating on the fact that I'm black in the scene when Billy is dying, well, there's nothing I can do about that." McDonald also earned praise for her novel interpretation of her role. Previously, actresses had portrayed Carrie as "ditsy and dumb, for comic relief," McDonald told Glenn Collins for the *New York Times* (May 15, 1994). "Nick [Hytner] allowed me to be solid and sensible and smart." In a *New York Times* (March 25, 1994) review of *Carousel* (quoted by Collins), David Richards wrote that McDonald, with her "vigorous" voice and "ready sense of comedy," was "the real find" of the production. McDonald, who until then had rarely performed comic roles, was particularly pleased with Richards's review. "Comedy is difficult for me," she told Collins. "I'm good at suffering and dying."

For her portrayal of Carrie, McDonald won a Tony for best supporting actress in a musical. She also won Drama Desk, Theatre World, and Outer Critics Circle Awards. According to McDonald, being so honored didn't make her professional life easier. "People kind of want to talk to you, but you still have to get out there and compete for the best roles," she told Kara Swisher of the *Washington Post* (October 7, 1995). "And with the audience there is some pressure because they think, 'They gave you a Tony, let's see why.'"

McDonald next appeared on Broadway in Terrence McNally's drama *Master Class* (1995), which Matthew Gurewitsch, writing in the *Atlantic Monthly* (October 1997), described as "an intensely personal, extremely perceptive meditation on the wellsprings and consequences of supremacy in art." The play is loosely based on a series of classes that the legendary opera singer Maria Callas gave at the Juilliard School in 1971. Callas, as depicted in a much-heralded performance by Zoe Caldwell, is seen working with three aspiring young singers, one of whom was played by McDonald. Caldwell was "amazing to work with," McDonald told Swisher. "I learn[ed] so much about the craft of acting and being on stage. No two performances are alike." For her performance in *Master Class*, McDonald won a second Tony, for best actress in a featured role in a play.

In 1998 McDonald played the role of Sarah in the $10 million Broadway production of *Ragtime*, a musical based on E. L. Doctorow's 1975 novel of the same name. In the story, which takes place around the turn of the 20th century, Sarah is in love with a jazz pianist and has given birth to his child. She and her baby are given shelter in the home of a white family, whose members are also central to the plot. McDonald found her role difficult in some ways. "I think the challenge with Sarah is that she's so innocent," she told Haines. "She's so young in her thinking, and in her way of

viewing the world. I try to wipe off the grittiness of the way I view the world and look at it through a crystalline point of view like Sarah's. She just thinks that everybody is good, and everybody should act good. If you don't then it just makes no sense to her. . . . That's why [later in the show] she does the impulsive, horrible things that she does, because of all these bad things that have happened to her, and she can't handle it." Like most other critics, the *New York Times* (January 19, 1998) reviewer Ben Brantley thought *Ragtime* was mediocre—it reminded Brantley of "an instructional diorama in a pavilion at a world's fair"—but he made special note of McDonald's performance. "McDonald finds more humanity than would have seemed possible in her sketchbook part, and as always, she sings gloriously," he wrote. McDonald won her third Tony for her work in *Ragtime*.

In 1998 McDonald participated in a celebration of the 100th anniversary of the birth of the composer George Gershwin, held at Carnegie Hall, in New York City. Accompanied by the San Francisco Orchestra, McDonald sang selections from Gershwin's opera *Porgy and Bess*. The event, which was later broadcast nationally by PBS, won rave reviews. Also in 1998 McDonald recorded her first album, *Way Back to Paradise*, which features songs written by young and theretofore unknown composers of musicals. The singer told Haines that she thought an album of music by such songwriters would be better than a collection of overly familiar Broadway standards. *Way Back to Paradise* greatly impressed Terry Teachout; he found all the songs "highly listenable" and a few "downright remarkable," and he declared that the album "points to smarter times ahead for the Great White Way."

In March 1999 the singer participated in a Drama League benefit to honor the entertainer Rosie O'Donnell. After her performance she bowed and then suddenly fainted, falling several feet off the stage. She has since recuperated from the fainting spell, the cause of which was never determined. Her upcoming appearances include the title role in *Marie Christine*, an adaptation of the Medea legend, with music and lyrics by Michael John LaChuisa, that has been described as a "Creole-flavored musical play." *Marie Christine* was scheduled to open at the Vivian Beaumont Theatre in December 1999.

Glenn Collins described the five-foot-seven McDonald as having "a big voice, big gestures, big hair, big enthusiasms, and a big laugh." Describing herself to Haines, the actress said, "I've always been hyperactive and the only place I've ever been able to really focus my hyperactive energy has been on stage. I just adore being there. And I adore exploring characters and being in front of an audience."

Audra McDonald collaborated with the Walt Disney Co. and the singer Elton John on a workshop production of a musical based on the Giuseppe Verdi opera *Aïda*. She played a voice student in the film *Seven Servants* (1996) and a singer at a wedding in *The Object of My Affection* (1998). — C.P.

Suggested Reading: *New York Times* II p5 May 15, 1994, with photo; *New York Times* (on-line) Nov. 6, 1995, Jan. 19, 1998, Oct. 2, 1998; *Time.com* (on-line) Oct. 5, 1998; *Tony Awards Online*, with photos; *Washington Post* C p2 Oct. 7, 1995, with photo

Selected Musicals: *The Secret Garden*, 1992(?); *Carousel*, 1994; *Master Class*, 1995; *Ragtime*, 1998

Selected Recordings: *Way Back to Paradise*, 1998

Courtesy of Erroll McDonald

McDonald, Erroll

1954(?)– Vice president and executive editor of Pantheon Books. Address: c/o Pantheon Books, 201 E. 50th St., New York, NY 10022

One of the few African-American executives in the publishing industry, Erroll McDonald has risen through the ranks of Random House, perhaps the most prominent of American publishers, to head one of its most prestigious imprints—Pantheon Books. Discussing the process of working in a corporate, bottom-line-oriented environment while championing the books that interest him, McDonald told Mel Watkins for *American Visions* (February 1991), "I understand that you're going to have to battle some forces that are not interested in the kind of things that you're doing. But you have to be willing to join the fray; to say, 'I know you peo-

ple are not interested in this kind of book or that you don't think this book will sell in sufficient quantities, but I'm going to do my damnedest to see that it reaches as wide a readership as possible.' My fate is linked to that commitment."

Erroll McDonald was born in the village of Limon, in Costa Rica, in about 1954. His mother was a seamstress, and according to Roger Cohen in the *New York Times* (September 25, 1990), his father left the family before taking his own life. When McDonald was about 10 years old, he moved with his mother to the United States, where she took a job in New York City's garment-manufacturing district. Mother and son rented an apartment in the Bedford Stuyvesant section of the borough of Brooklyn, which McDonald described to Cohen as "an area generally referred to by white reporters as a ghetto. But to me, it was just home, as much a ghetto as Park Avenue. I did not, as a child, live in the imagination of white liberal reporters!" According to Vince Passaro in *Esquire* (January 1991), McDonald learned about the culture of the U.S. by watching television shows starring Andy Griffith and Bob Cummings. McDonald told Passaro that "the racial history of this country is not a part of me": because blacks were not discriminated against in Costa Rica, and because he lived in a mostly black neighborhood in Brooklyn, McDonald never felt as though his race was a disadvantage during his youth.

McDonald attended New York City's prestigious Bronx High School of Science (a public school in which enrollment is determined by means of an entrance exam), where he particularly enjoyed reading the works of Homer and Shakespeare. "I was amazed at reading this English I didn't understand, this English that didn't have anything to do with the English I knew," he told Passaro. "It made me feel challenged in an aggressive way." After graduating from high school, he attended Yale University, in New Haven, Connecticut, where he studied English and comparative literature on both the undergraduate and graduate levels. The black-studies scholar Henry Louis Gates Jr., who was studying at Yale during the same years, told Passaro that McDonald was "one of the smartest students we had. He had an extraordinary memory and feel for literary nuance, and he was one of the best close readers and interpreters of text."

In 1977, while he was completing his master's degree at Yale, McDonald met Toni Morrison, who was then a senior editor at Random House and would later win both the Pulitzer Prize for fiction and the Nobel Prize for literature. Morrison recommended McDonald as an intern at the publishing house, and later that year he began working as a gofer for the subsidiary rights department. According to Watkins, McDonald at first "considered the job a temporary step on his way to becoming a lawyer." ("The fact is, black parents who have kids who go to college don't want them to go into publishing," he told Roger Cohen. "They want them to go out there and be somebody—a doctor or a lawyer—and make some money.") But when he was hired as the assistant to a junior editor, he became serious about a career in publishing. After a short time in that job, McDonald was named editorial assistant to Morrison. "[Morrison] was really my godmother and looked after me in all kinds of ways," McDonald told Watkins. "She kept my head straight because the introduction to corporate culture was an awakening for me. One of the things that startled me when I came [to Random House] . . . was that I couldn't understand these older white guys telling me what to do. I'd never had older black people telling me what to do, much less those people, who seemed like Martians to me. She taught me how to deal."

McDonald's first media exposure came in 1981, when he oversaw the publication of a book called *In the Belly of the Beast*, a collection of letters written by the convicted murderer Jack Henry Abbott while he was serving a prison sentence. Passaro described the book as "a mesmerizing description of life in prison and the mysterious consciousness of violence." The evening before an exceptionally positive review of the book was published in the *New York Times*, Abbott, who was out of jail on parole, killed an employee of a New York City restaurant after being refused access to the employees' bathroom. McDonald was subsequently approached by the police, and he and the writer Norman Mailer, who was also involved with the publication of *In the Belly of the Beast*, were criticized by the media for, as Passaro put it, "pandering to a homicidal maniac for the sake of literary fashion." The novelist Jay McInerney, who was working as a reader at Random House at that time, told Passaro, "Erroll was one of the few people involved with the Abbott book who predicted it would be the misadventure it turned out to be. . . . I was sitting in his office one day when Abbott stormed in, in a rage because he wanted to buy some toothpaste and he'd been in prison for so much of his life he didn't know where to go. He'd gone into a hardware store or something and asked for toothpaste and everybody had laughed at him. If that had happened to him in prison he would have punched them out or stabbed them. After he left, we were sitting there, and Erroll looked at me and said, 'He's not going to make it, man.' Erroll was the only person I knew in this enterprise who had the street smarts to understand what Abbott was going through."

Two years later, in 1983, McDonald was named head of a Random House book series called Aventura. The series consisted largely of contemporary fiction by Third World authors, and as Watkins noted, McDonald's being fluent in Spanish, German, Russian, and French made him the perfect candidate for the job. Some of McDonald's favorite Aventura titles were Manuel Puig's *Pubis Angelical*, Salman Rushdie's *Shame*, Thomas Bernhard's *Correction*, and Edward Limonov's *It's Me, Eddie*. McDonald considers his greatest success at Aventura, however, to be the publication of the Nobel Prize–winning Nigerian author Wole Soyinka's au-

tobiography *Aké: The Years of Childhood*. "When I tried to publish Soyinka in the '80s, I was told by people in positions of power here that you couldn't pronounce his name, reviewers wouldn't review it, and the title was unpronounceable," McDonald told Watkins. "It gave me severe pleasure early on to believe in something and see it confirmed out there in a very public way." Recalling "the social high point" of his career, McDonald described for Watkins the experience of attending the celebration in honor of Soyinka's winning the Nobel Prize, in 1986: "I dressed up in a rented tuxedo and went to the Nobel ball and danced and had a good time with those Nigerians. That gave me an infusion of strength . . . a sense that maybe what I wanted to do in publishing was not so off-the-wall after all." Probably the nadir of his career thus far came when Random House was forced to cancel the publication of the actor Klaus Kinski's memoir *All I Need Is Love*, after it was discovered that McDonald had neglected to show the manuscript to the publisher's legal department for review—and that the rights to the book were already owned by a German publisher. McDonald stayed with Aventura until the division folded, in 1987; he later became an executive editor at the Random House imprint Vintage.

In early 1990 McDonald became executive editor and vice president of Pantheon Books; his new post put him second in command after Fred Jordan, the imprint's new publisher. Perhaps the most prestigious of Random House's several publishing divisions, Pantheon Books was begun by refugees from Nazi Germany in 1942, and it rapidly developed a reputation for publishing works of great intellectual merit by leftist writers. In 1961 Pantheon was purchased by Random House but maintained its own distinct identity. The publisher Andre Schiffrin came to the helm of Pantheon in the mid-1960s and remained its head until March 1990, when he was reportedly pressured to resign because of Pantheon's financial problems—a move driven by Random House's efforts to increase profits across the board. Schiffrin's resignation was accompanied by those of most his senior editors, which triggered a demonstration outside Random House's New York headquarters by Pantheon authors, among them Kurt Vonnegut Jr., E. L. Doctorow, and Studs Terkel, as well as many others protesting what they saw as a triumph of greed over literary integrity.

It was in this setting that McDonald wrote an op-ed article for the *New York Times* that called the protest over Schiffrin's resignation an example of the pervasive "welfare mentality" that led writers to feel that they should have "their own cultural and political passions . . . subsidized by philanthropy." McDonald wrote that the goal of a publishing company "is to make money by publishing books that have value—to make money for the authors and for Pantheon." He later told Roger Cohen that the protesters "seemed to be saying they deserved money by virtue of their sheer brilliance regardless of their accomplishment. Well, we all of us would want a piece of that action."

McDonald's new editorial staff included Dan Frank, the former editorial director of Viking Press, and Shelley Wanger, once the editor in chief of the magazine *Interview.* Since 1990 Pantheon has also taken on many additional writers, including Soyinka, the African-American cultural critic and novelist Albert Murray, and Henry Louis Gates Jr. McDonald told Watkins that his decisions at Pantheon have represented "my preferences and the people I know. We won't be specializing in any kind of books . . . although it may be perceived that way by others—you know, 'Erroll is bringing in a body of black writing to the list.' As far as I'm concerned, it's a matter of publishing particular writers that I have tremendous admiration for." During his first year at Pantheon, the roster of books published included a biography of the Italian author and film director Pier Paolo Pasolini called *Pasolini Requiem*; Pasolini's novel *A Violent Life*; and a biography of the Italian writer Giuseppe di Lampedusa called *The Last Leopard*, by David Gilmour. Passaro remarked that McDonald's appointment to this position was logical, since McDonald had built his reputation at Aventura, where he had published exactly "the kinds of books Pantheon was renowned for, books of international scope, books of literary value and social awareness."

Discussing one of the pitfalls of being among a very small number of black editors, McDonald told Cohen, "There are some agents I'd rather not talk to, and they know who they are. All they do, these agents, is try to sell the terrible, terrible books writ-ten by some blacks, as if I am here to promote that kind of thing. Things they would never send to a white editor, and I wonder why." While such comments have helped to give McDonald a reputation for arrogance, he feels that that perception is an inevitable outgrowth of his "somewhat anomalous" position. "People bring concepts to bear that, however well intended, are often objectionable," he told Mel Watkins. "They just assume all kinds of things, and one has to deal with those presumptions in a direct way. It's not that I'm trying to define myself for others. It's just that you don't want to hear distortions. You have to put an end to it and, finally, you don't care how they see it."

Passaro described McDonald as "a handsome figure, tall, graceful, and deliberate. The first thing you notice about him are his eyes. The right eye, misaligned, tends to drift, so you're never quite sure he's looking at you. The effect is to make him hard to read." McDonald is married to the Polish-born Klara Glowczewska, who, though rumored to have been a European socialite, met McDonald while working in a Yale dining hall. "I had a part time job as a scholarship student," Glowczewska told Passaro. "I served him his food. That's how glamorous I was." The couple reside in a sparsely furnished apartment on New York City's Upper West Side, where they enjoy entertaining. — C.P.

Suggested Reading: *American Visions* p22+ Feb. 1991, with photo; *Esquire* p64+ Jan. 1991, with photos; *New York Times* C p13 Sep. 25, 1990, with photo

---

McFarlane, Todd

Mar. 16, 1961– Comic-book illustrator; entrepreneur. Address: c/o Todd McFarlane Productions, Inc., 40 W. Baseline Rd., Suite E-105, Tempe, AZ 85283

"He's the comic-book equivalent of a Robert Redford or a Madonna," Don Thompson, editor of the *Comics Buyer's Guide*, told *People* (May 6, 1991) about comic-artist and entertainment entrepreneur Todd McFarlane. "People will buy the comic book simply because Todd McFarlane has a piece of art in it." McFarlane, easily the most famous and influential comic-book artist of the 1990s, has used his artistic ability to create a multimillion-dollar corporation in just a few years. He started his career in the early 1980s with Marvel Comics, then worked for various other comic-book houses, including the industry giant, DC Comics (publisher of both Batman and Superman). He gained wide recognition in the late 1980s when his innovative drawings graced the pages of Marvel's *Amazing Spider Man.* When McFarlane expressed his desire to both draw *and* write the comic, Marvel gave him his own book in 1990, called simply *Spider Man.* After debuting in September of that year, it became the top-selling comic book of all time, soon selling nearly 2.5 million issues. Since that time McFarlane has left Marvel and started his own comic-book company. His own creation, Spawn, is now one of the most famous comic-book characters in the world, and *Spawn* is an annual best-seller. McFarlane's artistic prowess is matched by his ambition to make Spawn a household name. Action figures, cartoons, live-action movies, board games, video games, and Halloween costumes are just a few of the products on which the Spawn logo appears. "The things that interest me about Spawn are not the kind of comic book elements but more the kind of tragic hero, and the meaning of life kind of questions that he deals with instead of who he punches in the face . . . ," McFarlane told America Online subscribers in an interview, according to the *spawn.com* Web site (May 5, 1998). "I draw from my own experiences, which is why you'll see dozens of characters in the comic, TV, and movie named after people I work with, live by, or are family members. In terms of if I thought it would be a big success, I never set out to fail. I assumed that

Courtesy of Todd McFarlane Productions
Todd McFarlane

when I was going to try and make him big, he would be big. . . . In terms of success it depends on how you measure that. . . . Making Spawn a word known around the world has just begun."

Todd McFarlane was born on March 16, 1961 in Calgary, Alberta, Canada. When he was 18 months old, his parents moved the family to California, where they lived until Todd was 14. During his childhood Todd developed a deep affection for baseball, a sport in which he showed unusual promise. By the time McFarlane and his family returned to their native Calgary, Todd had his sights set on becoming a professional ballplayer. While attending William Aberhart High School, he began collecting comic books, in particular those featuring the work of the more notable comic artists of the time, such as John Byrne (who created the famed Marvel title *Alpha Flight*), George Perez (who revamped such sagging DC titles as *Wonder Woman* and *Teen Titans*), and Walter Simonson (who did noted work on Marvel's *Thor* comic book). Over the course of his high-school years, his love for comic books grew considerably, and he began creating and drawing his own superheroes. By his senior year, Todd considered himself an able comic-book artist, but his baseball skills had also begun to flourish, and as a center-fielder who could run and hit well, he drew attention from both collegiate and professional recruiters. After graduating from high school, Todd briefly attended Spokane Falls Community College, in Washington State, before accepting a baseball scholarship, in 1981, to Eastern Washington State University, in Cheney, Washington. McFarlane has said that if he had been able to continue on this course, he would have eventually played in the majors, but during a

game against a Pac-10 rival team, he broke his ankle while sliding into home plate. Todd was never the same ballplayer again. He therefore focused his attention on drawing comic books.

Within a few months, feeling that his drawing technique had improved considerably, McFarlane began sending samples of his work to major comic-book houses. After he had collected more than 700 rejection letters during the last months before he completed his senior year, the 22-year-old artist decided it would be wise to begin looking for other avenues of employment. Then, in March 1984, just one week before his graduation from Eastern, Marvel Comics offered him a job. A minor title called *Scorpio Rose*, a spin-off of the moderately successful title *Coyote*, needed a penciller to provide the initial drawings of the characters. Ecstatic, McFarlane began work within the month. The series lasted only three months. Then, armed with industry connections, McFarlane jumped ship and joined Marvel's chief rival, Detective Comics (DC). Beginning as a substitute penciller for the DC title *Infinity, Inc.*, he did his first three issues on an interim basis, while also pencilling another DC title, *All Star Squadron*. He was eventually hired as the full-time penciller for *Infinity, Inc.*, and in October 1984, with a steady job at last, he asked his college girlfriend, Wanda, to marry him. He stayed with *Infinity, Inc.* until early April 1987, pencilling a total of 19 issues.

McFarlane got married on July 27, 1985 in Calgary, and immediately after the wedding, he and his wife returned to Cheney, Washington, so that she could complete her degree. After she graduated they moved to New Westminster, a suburb of Vancouver, British Columbia. In late April 1987, McFarlane landed his biggest job up to that time—pencilling duties on the strong-selling Marvel title *The Incredible Hulk*. Over the course of the next few years, he did short stints for various Marvel titles such as *Daredevil* (Number 241) and *GI Joe* (Number 60). The company allowed him to do some freelance work with DC, and he provided all the art work for three covers of *Detective Comics* (numbers 576–578). Marvel and DC, two companies that rarely had contact with each other, also agreed to put out a crossover title called *Invasion*, which combined the characters of both companies in one comic book. McFarlane, for the first time, was allowed to pencil some of DC's most famous characters, among them Superman, Wonder Woman, Green Lantern, and the Flash. After the run of *Invasion*, Todd drew a one-shot book called *True North*, a work published to protest censorship in Canada. In August 1988 he left the *Incredible Hulk* to draw the DC book *Batman* (Number 423), the independent book *Flaming Carrot* (Number 27), and the Marvel titles *Wolverine* (Number 6), *Spitfire* (Number 4), *What the - ?!* (Number 3), and *Marvel Tales* (223–238). In March 1989 Marvel brass commissioned McFarlane to pencil the covers for the company's most famous title, the long running *Amazing Spider Man*.

Beginning with issue 298, McFarlane, with the help of the writer David Michilinie, created one of the most famous comic-book villains of the decade, Venom. Designed to be Spider Man's arch-nemesis, Venom had first appeared in the late 1980s in the form of Spider Man's new black costume. As the story line went, the costume, actually an alien, began controlling Spider Man telekinetically and forced the usually well-meaning superhero to perform evil deeds. McFarlane and Michilinie came up with idea of making the suit a separate character. Venom, with his huge teeth and monster-like dimensions, became a sensation, and the *Amazing Spider Man*'s sales began to soar even higher. During his early tenure with the book (issues 298–323), McFarlane's originality as an illustrator became well known, and he gave Spider Man, a superhero who had not changed significantly since the early 1960s, a new, surreal look that would become McFarlane's signature. With the character's eyes as disproportionally large as an arachnid's, his extremities more spider-like, and the story lines more psychologically oriented and dark, *Amazing Spider Man* quickly became the hottest title of all comics, going from the ninth-biggest-selling comic-book in the U.S. to number one.

With the title's success, McFarlane asked the Marvel brass to allow him to begin writing the story line for the book as well, but the higher-ups were reluctant to break up the proven writing team then in place. To keep McFarlane aboard, they gave him his own title, which he would both write and draw. When the book, called simply *Spider Man*, was released in September 1990, it became the best-selling comic book of all time, eventually reaching sales of over 2.5 million copies. McFarlane wrote and illustrated *Spider Man* through issue 13, published in August 1991, and then took a six-month break when his first daughter, Cyan, was born.

"Todd was aware," according to a promotional piece from McFarlane's *spawn.com* Web site, "that many creators, including the legendary Jack Kirby, who himself created nearly half of the comic book characters in existence today, were not only denied the respect they deserved, but [were] literally ignored creatively and financially by the large publishing companies [such as Marvel and DC Comics]. . . . Even though Todd had become the hottest [comic-book] artist of the decade, he was fully aware that he, too, could easily fall among the ranks of those once famous artists." In early 1992—after talking for many months with such prominent Marvel artists as Jim Lee, Rob Leifeld, Jim Valentin, Marc Silvestri, and Erik Larsen—McFarlane helped to form Image Comics. Designed to be a haven for creative artists who wanted control over their own characters, the company allowed each artist to maintain the rights to his or her creations—a benefit not given to such famous artists as Jerry Seigal and Joe Schuster, who created Superman, and Bob Kane, who created Batman. "Instead of the traditional comic book companies be-ing able to both release artists from books containing their own creations and making millions off the licensing products of those creations without beneficial compensation for the creator, Image Comics allowed each artist to publish together, but reap rewards individually," *spawn.com* explained. When recalling his years with Marvel Comics, McFarlane told Chris Galdieri for the *mgz.com* Web site, "[Marvel] would have board meetings and they would have conferences and they would have gatherings and all the executives . . . would kind of set the plan of attack for the year for the company. And the creative community was never represented. That's what really drove me out, was the lack of respect." With his own company, McFarlane felt free to bring to life a character he had created 10 years earlier in his college dorm room at Eastern. It was thus that in May 1992, the world was introduced to Spawn.

"In a nutshell, [Spawn] is a man [a.k.a. Al Simmons] who was a good government assassin—so he's not a [traditional] good guy," McFarlane said, as quoted on the *hbo.com* Web site. "He's not Clark Kent by any stretch. And he died. And the one element that he had in him, and I think each one of us has, is that he had somebody he dearly loved. So he made a deal [with Satan], and in a heartbeat he came back from the grave, but he didn't quite read the fine print to whatever the deal was. He came back to see his wife." Al Simmons, as the McFarlane tale goes, comes back to Earth not as a man but as a creature of mangled flesh with incredible super-powers. His wife no longer recognizes him, and Satan has given him only a limited amount of energy; every time Spawn uses his powers, he comes closer to returning to Hell. "He has the right [military] wiring [for an officer in Satan's army], and that wiring makes him more like Genghis Khan," McFarlane told *hbo.com*. "He was a decent sort of guy. He just happened to be good at being an assassin. So it's more that if [Satan's minions] can plug into [Al Simmons's] wiring, he would actually become a good general for the army of Armageddon. The whole concept of Spawns is that they exist every 400 years, but they're put back on earth to train. If they succeed, they become generals in the army, and if they fail, it doesn't matter, they just become grunts. . . . I put him in a situation he really can't win." In short, with the *Spawn* story line, McFarlane created an entire universe of characters based on a twisted interpretation of the biblical ideas of heaven and hell. "Your hero is only as good as your villain," McFarlane told Galdieri. "And the best villain I could come up with is the big fatty downstairs [Satan]. If he's the biggest fatty, then Spawn is the greatest hero if he can beat him. Superman never beat the guy downstairs. My guy has a chance to beat him. He may trip and fall, but he has a chance." When the first issue of *Spawn* was released, in May 1992, it sold 1.7 million copies, making it the highest-selling independent comic ever.

Other Image titles, however, have not fared as well as *Spawn*. Seven years after the company's creation, only one other original Image title has survived—Erik Larsen's *Savage Dragon*. The rest, including *Youngblood*, *Wild C.A.T.S.*, and *The Maxx*, have all ceased production. But *Spawn*, with its often graphic story lines and adult themes, is one of the best-selling comic books of the 1990s. Numerous mini-series have been developed out of the title, including the highly successful *Violator* book, based on Spawn's arch-enemy, a soldier of the devil who masquerades as a clown, and *Angela*, an angel bounty hunter out to kill demons and other minions of Satan (including Spawn). Spawn and the supporting characters became so popular that McFarlane decided to make them into action figures. In typical McFarlane style, he started his own company—McFarlane Toys. The highly detailed toys became an immediate hit. Costing more than most action figures at the time, McFarlane's toys were also larger and better made. Since its inception the Spawn line of figures has gone through 12 redesigns, and the company has released numerous other lines of figures, including those based on the rock band Kiss, and the horror-film characters Jason (from *Friday the 13th*), Freddy Krueger (from *A Nightmare on Elm Street*), and Leatherface (from *The Texas Chain Saw Massacre*). "The goal is to have people so talented around you that they actually do all the work and I just sit there and collect the awards," McFarlane jokingly told Galdieri. "When I have meetings about the toys, I have sculptors there, I have my toy designers there, I've got myself there, I've got my sales people there, I've got my marketing people there, I've got everybody." McFarlane Toys is now the fifth-largest action-figure manufacturer in the country.

For a short time in 1995, Image edged out DC comics as the number-two comic-book company in the country in sales, before settling in comfortably at number three. Soon afterward, *Spawn* the board game, *Spawn* the video game, and *Spawn* trading cards hit the stores. In 1996 McFarlane began pre-production on *Spawn* the movie with George Lucas's company Industrial Light and Magic, and *Spawn* the animated series was commissioned by HBO. The comic book *Spawn/Batman* became the best-selling crossover book of the year. In 1997 it was estimated that Todd McFarlane was worth $100 million. That summer *Spawn* the motion picture was released to lukewarm reviews but strong box-office sales. Starring Martin Sheen, Michael Jai White, and John Leguizamo, the movie remained in the top 10 for several weeks, becoming one of the surprise hits of the year. At about the same time, HBO premiered *Todd McFarlane's Spawn*, a six-part animated program that became one of the most critically acclaimed animated series of the decade to that date. McFarlane, as executive producer and chief animator on the project, won an Emmy Award for animation, and HBO ordered another six episodes to be made for 1998 and 1999. When the first six episodes were released on video, they became the top-selling original HBO program of all time. New episodes of the animated series are currently in the works, and the sequel to the film *Spawn*, entitled *Spawn II: Dark Justice*, is set for a 2000 release.

McFarlane has reiterated in interviews that his creation's fame is only in the beginning stages—and that he plans to make Spawn one of the most famous characters of all time. Thus far he has only "one small piece in a big puzzle," according to Joe Chidley in *Macleans* (August 11, 1997). "McFarlane—who likens himself to Walt Disney, in his paternal relationship to his characters, and to Michael Jordan, in his talents—is bent on building an empire. 'This is war and if you go to war, then it's kill or be killed,' he says. 'Maybe that's where I come in: I got no fear of dying. I will die for my causes, and I got a lot of them.'"

McFarlane is a big Cleveland Indians fan and generally enjoys rooting for underdogs. "I'm the opposite of those who jump on the bandwagon," he told an interviewer for his *spawn.com* Web site. "When the team gets good, I jump off." He claims that his favorite food is made by Taco Bell. He and his family live in Portland, Oregon. — M.B.

Suggested Reading: *Advertising Age* p41 Feb. 16, 1998, with photos; *CNN.com* (on-line) Aug. 1, 1997, with photos; *Macleans* p52+ Aug. 11, 1997, with photos; *People* p100 May 6, 1991, with photo; *Roughcut.com* (on-line); *Spawn.com* (on-line)

Selected Comic Books: *All Star Squadron* DC #47, July 1985; *The Amazing Spider-Man* Marvel nos. 298–323, 320–325, Dec. 1989–May 1990; *Batman* DC no. 423, Sep. 1988; *Coyote/Scorpio Rose* Marvel nos. 11–14, May–July 1985; *Daredevil* Marvel no. 241, Apr. 1987; *Detective Comics* DC nos. 576–578, July–Sep.1987; *G.I. Joe* Marvel no. 60, June 1987; *The Incredible Hulk* Marvel nos. 330–334, 336–346, Apr. 1987–Aug. 1988; *Infinity, Inc.* DC nos. 14–37, May 1985–Apr. 1987; *Marvel Tales* Marvel no. 223, July 1990; *Spawn* Image nos. 1–15, 20–37, 39–49 (odd-numbered issues), 50, May 1992–; *Spider-Man* Marvel nos. 1–14, 16, Sep. 1990–Aug. 1991; *Wolverine* Marvel no. 6 Apr. 1989

Selected Films: *Spawn*, 1997

Rich Freeda/Courtesy of TitanSports

McMahon, Vince
(mc-MAN)

Aug. 24, 1945– Chairman of TitanSports Inc. and World Wrestling Federation promoter. Address: c/o TitanSports, 1241 E. Main St., P.O. Box 3857, Stamford, CT 06902

Professional wrestling is not to be confused with the Greco-Roman variety that returns to the public consciousness every four years through the Olympic Games; rather, it is the domain of large participants with theatrical personas and colorful names. Throughout much of its existence in the United States, professional wrestling was associated with dark, modified boxing gyms and cigar-smoking promoters who often conducted themselves like impresarios presenting sideshows at a carnival. More often than not, sports purists looked down on it as something less than a serious sport, and entertainment-industry insiders viewed it as a third-class spectacle not fit for mainstream consumption. That situation has largely changed, however; although some people still look askance at professional wrestling, whose outsized competitors still toss each other around inside modified boxing rings, the contests are no longer relegated to seedy gyms. Rather, they constitute a multimillion-dollar industry, a "sport entertainment" that fills arenas throughout the world and is viewed by millions of fans through broadcasts on network, cable, and pay-per-view television.

Professional wrestling's metamorphosis into a sophisticated multimedia business may be attributed in large measure to Vince McMahon. McMahon is the chairman of TitanSports Inc., a privately held international marketing and communi-

cation company and, since its founding in 1980, the parent company of the World Wrestling Federation (WWF), arguably the most popular wrestling league in the world. A third-generation wrestling promoter who described himself to Larry King on the television program *Home Team Sportbeat* (June 30, 1986) as "the Walt Disney of wrestling," McMahon has transformed the WWF into an international television and marketing empire. Headquartered in a $10 million corporate compound in Stamford, Connecticut, complete with a television studio and post-production facility, TitanSports Inc. promotes live wrestling events throughout the world, partly through its unofficial network of television shows. It also has extensive merchandising interests and oversees the sale of WWF products, among them breakfast cereal, video games, and action figures. The company's publications include *WWF Magazine* and *WWF Program*. Although, as a private company, it is not required to reveal publicly its exact earnings (and has not done so), Nancy Jo Sales reported in *New York* (October 26, 1998) that its total annual revenues have been estimated at $500 million.

Vincent Kennedy McMahon was born on August 24, 1945 in Pinehurst, North Carolina. Early in his life his parents divorced, and he met his father, Vincent James McMahon, for the first time when he was 12 years old. His reunion with his father altered his life, for it introduced him to professional wrestling, which had been something of a family business for the McMahons. McMahon's grandfather, Jess McMahon, was a boxing and wrestling promoter in the early 1900s, and McMahon's father owned and promoted Capital Wrestling, whose territory encompassed the northeastern U.S. during the 1940s and 1950s. At the time, professional wrestling was controlled by some 30 promoters who presided over strictly defined territories throughout the country. Although Capital Wrestling matches appeared on the newly introduced venue of television, professional wrestling was not considered a mainstream sport. With some people viewing it as legitimate athletic competition and others regarding it as a fringe form of entertainment, it suffered from its ambiguous identity.

Still, soon after meeting his father, Vince Kennedy McMahon became hooked on professional wrestling, and in his teens he expressed an interest in becoming a wrestler himself. He told Kenneth R. Clark for the *Chicago Tribune* (March 13, 1994), "My dad threatened me with everything he could possibly threaten me with not to do it. I've always wanted to taste the physicality of being a professional wrestler, but my dad absolutely did not want me to get in the ring."

In 1968 McMahon, who was by then married, earned a bachelor of science degree in business administration from East Carolina State University, in Greenville, North Carolina. In 1971 his father agreed to help him enter the family business. McMahon was sent to oversee Capital Wrestling's operations in Bangor, Maine, the outermost point of the firm's territory. He also worked as a television announcer for Capital.

In the ensuing years McMahon turned the operations at Bangor into a big success and proceeded to oversee Capital Wrestling's operations in New England. "And it was really good," he told Jo Sales. "It was making more money than it had ever made, and so my dad was thinking it just can't get any better than this—and he was looking to get out."

In 1982 McMahon bought Capital Wrestling's entire operation from his father and became the company's chairman. He quickly began expanding his territory. He recruited talent from rival leagues and bought up much of his competition throughout the country. With his new acquisitions he formed the World Wrestling Federation, a national professional wrestling conglomerate. McMahon began leading the WWF into the mainstream by working aggressively to put his fledgling national league on television. He also began emphasizing the entertainment aspect of professional wrestling by introducing a colorful cast of wrestlers and incorporating elaborate story lines that heightened the rivalries between opponents. "We're storytellers," McMahon told James Collins for *Time.com* (June 29, 1998). "You can't just throw wrestlers out there to wrestle. That's not what an audience wants to see." McMahon began describing wrestling as "sport entertainment," and he openly admitted that since outcomes of WWF matches were known in advance, professional wrestling was not a true sport. Although this admission came as a surprise to some fans, in effect it released the WWF from costly licensing fees, drug testing, and other regulatory measures required by state athletic commissions. More important, it gave the WWF free rein to stage even more elaborate and highly theatrical shows. Although pro-wrestling purists took issue with the direction in which McMahon was pushing his league, other fans, many of them young and male, embraced the new face of wrestling and the excitement that McMahon's innovations generated.

By 1985 WWF matches were regularly televised on the major networks, and by 1987 they were filling arenas and attracting record numbers of audience members for special broadcasts on pay-per-view closed-circuit television. One of these extravaganzas occurred in 1987, when McMahon pitted Hulk Hogan, the WWF's top star, against Andre the Giant, whose fame was fading, at an event called Wrestlemania III. The event won a huge pay-per-view audience and drew 93,173 people into the Pontiac Silverdome, in Pontiac, Michigan, thereby setting the world record for indoor-audience attendance. McMahon was also credited with skillfully using rock-'n'-roll celebrities in the WWF's live shows. For example, he enlisted the rock star Cyndi Lauper to manage the WWF's champion female wrestler Wendy Richter, and he hired Aretha Franklin to sing at a WWF event in 1987.

Aided by McMahon's innovative marketing, the WWF became immensely successful. According to *Forbes* (October 17, 1988), the WWF sold $80 million worth of tickets to live wrestling shows in 1987. Thus, in less than a decade, McMahon had turned a practice widely disparaged as mere spectacle into a very lucrative form of entertainment. In an article he wrote for the *New York Times* (July 14, 1991), McMahon offered his explanation for the remarkable change in the WWF's fortunes: "Unlike my trailblazing family predecessors, I began to promote the WWF not as sport but as family-oriented sports entertainment. With this new positioning came an avalanche of popularity. We began to distribute our television programming on a national, and then international basis. We began to attract more charismatic performers. We began to license their likenesses on products the world over. More and more, we began to earn the respect, trust, and admiration of legions of fans."

In addition to McMahon's astute marketing, a significant part of the WWF's popularity in the 1980s has been attributed to the timely emergence of the charismatic Hulk Hogan (born Terry Gene Bollea). Hogan's rise to national celebrity coincided with professional wrestling's own transformation. During the nearly 10 years that Hogan wrestled for the WWF (he left the federation in 1993), McMahon expanded the WWF and turned his company into a remarkably efficient business entity that drew revenues from several merchandising ventures, which included such products as shirts, lunch boxes, a popular children's animated program for TV, and even a series of bodybuilding competitions, all of which benefited from the marketability of Hogan and other prominent wrestlers. TitanSports also began to expand internationally, staging live WWF events and broadcasting its WWF shows in Australia, France, Germany, India, and Japan. Commenting on this international expansion, McMahon told Clark, "One of America's greatest exports is her entertainment industry, and professional wrestling has been a cornerstone of the entertainment industry for years. The WWF is highly exportable."

Then, during the late 1980s and early 1990s, the WWF experienced several setbacks and a decline in popularity. In 1991 a jury in Harrisburg, Pennsylvania, convicted George T. Zahorian III, a physician who had supplied anabolic steroids to Hulk Hogan and other professional wrestling stars, in a test case of a 1988 federal law that prohibited the distribution of such drugs for nontherapeutic purposes. McMahon and the WWF received additional negative publicity in 1993, when the U.S. attorney in the New York City borough of Brooklyn charged McMahon and TitanSports Inc. with conspiring to provide WWF wrestlers with anabolic steroids from 1985 to 1991. (McMahon, who was an amateur bodybuilder, had admitted to using steroids before they were declared illegal, in 1988.)

In a highly publicized trial that took place in 1994, several ex-WWF wrestlers, including Hulk Hogan, testified that the WWF had encouraged rampant abuse of steroids. Perhaps most damaging to the reputation of the WWF was the admission by Hogan, who had championed wholesome values during his reign as the WWF's top wrestler and had long denied using steroids, that he had indeed done so for years in the WWF.

McMahon pleaded innocent to the government's six charges, and the jury found him guilty on a single count—conspiracy to defraud the U.S. Food and Drug Administration. Although the trial heaped negative publicity on Hogan, McMahon, and most of the WWF, the verdict was seen as a victory for McMahon, who would have faced a heavy fine and up to five years in prison had he been found guilty of the additional charges.

During the 1990s McMahon also faced allegations that employees of TitanSports had been subjected to sexual harassment. Although no criminal charges were filed against him or his company, those allegations did little to help the reputation of TitanSports.

Meanwhile, McMahon was grappling with a major threat to the WWF's longtime dominance of professional wrestling. For much of the 1980s, his only substantial competitor had been the National Wrestling Association (NWA), which had routinely placed a distant second to the WWF in popularity. Then, in 1988, the media mogul Ted Turner acquired a major stake in the National Wrestling Association and used that platform to launch his own wrestling league, World Championship Wrestling (WCW).

WCW quickly proved to be fierce competition for the WWF. Thanks to Turner's successful cable-television networks (TNT and TBS) and his deep pockets, the WCW received instant media coverage. The WCW also lured away several of the WWF's top wrestlers, including Hulk Hogan (whom, in 1994, WCW signed to a deal reportedly worth $4 million a year) and "Macho Man" Randy Savage. The WCW also competed against the WWF for television advertising dollars. In response to the threat posed by Turner's entry into the pro-wrestling market, McMahon repeatedly accused Turner of unfair business practices and incorporated an effigy named Billionaire Ted into WWF shows. Not surprisingly, fans were encouraged to boo Billionaire Ted. "I am a fighter," McMahon told Broadcasting & Cable (August 25, 1997). "Whether it's the U.S. government or the collective forces of Ted Turner. [The rivalry with the WCW] is not going to kill me. It will make me stronger."

The rivalry between the WWF and WCW intensified in the mid-1990s. In October 1995 Turner introduced Monday Nitro Live, a wrestling showcase on the TNT network that went head-to-head against the WWF's already popular Monday Night Raw program. Despite the competition, for much of the 1990s the WWF fared well and routinely finished ahead of the WCW in television ratings and

revenues. For example, according to figures cited by Alan Farnham for Fortune (October 16, 1995, on-line), in 1995 the WWF grossed an estimated $84 million while the WCW grossed under $50 million.

Thanks to the competition between the two well-marketed leagues, professional wrestling experienced a resurgence in popularity in the mid-1990s. As of June 1998 professional wrestling was among the top-rated types of programming on cable television. In October 1998 the WWF's Monday Night Raw became the most-watched program on cable TV. Collins reported that "taking all telecasts into account, about 34 million people watch wrestling each week." Moreover, since 1997, pay-per-view WWF and WCW broadcasts have consistently ranked among the top 10 in weekly ratings for cable television shows.

Wrestling's success in the mid-1990s has been attributed in large measure to a change in the story lines and personas of its top wrestlers. Whereas popular wrestlers of the 1980s, including Hulk Hogan, had projected patriotism and wholesome values such as good sportsmanship and hard work, the personas assumed by popular wrestlers in the mid-1990s became increasingly flawed, arrogant, and rebellious. For instance, by 1998 the most popular wrestler in the WWF was Stone Cold Steve Austin, who had modeled his image on a composite of serial killers. "I came up with the basic idea for the character," Collins quoted Austin as saying. "You know, someone who really didn't give a damn about what was going on. Not that I'm endorsing a serial killer—it was an attitude thing."

McMahon himself took on a ring persona to help promote his entertainment empire: he assumed the role of a greedy business mogul out to destroy those wrestlers who did not follow his decrees. Not surprisingly, the most maverick of the wrestlers turned out to be Stone Cold Steve Austin. During several WWF events Stone Cold Steve Austin physically attacked McMahon. Such shenanigans helped boost the WWF's television ratings and ticket sales. Commenting on the elaborate story lines that inflame rivalries, McMahon told Nancy Jo Sales, "This is a soap opera, performed by the greatest actors and athletes in the world. I'd like to say that it's the highest form of entertainment."

In September 1998 TitanSports, in conjunction with the Cleveland-based Parkview Group, purchased the Debbie Reynolds hotel and casino in Las Vegas, Nevada. McMahon has expressed a desire to open a chain of theme parks and resorts based on WWF characters and concepts. In August 1999 McMahon began broadcasting WWF Smackdown!, a two-hour prime-time wrestling show, on the UPN television network. Also that month McMahon started taking steps to sell to the public a minority stake in his company. The initial public offering, scheduled for late 1999, was expected to raise up to $172 million. McMahon will still hold a controlling stake in the company after the sale. As part of the process of setting up the public offering, in mid-1999 McMahon disclosed to the Securities and Exchange Commission that World Wrestling Federation Entertainment Inc. had recorded revenues of $251 million and a pretax profit of $56 million in the 12-month period ending in April 1999.

McMahon's family plays a large part in overseeing TitanSports' operations. His wife, Linda, serves as the company's president, and their daughter, Stephanie, also works for the company. Their son, Shane, the company's president of new media, is reportedly being groomed to succeed McMahon, to carry into the fourth generation the family's professional wrestling empire. — Y.P.

Suggested Reading: *Broadcasting & Cable* p76 Aug. 25, 1997, with photo; *Chicago Tribune* V p1+ Mar. 13, 1994, with photo; *Forbes* p133+ Oct. 17, 1988, with photo; *New York* p38+ Oct. 26, 1998, with photos; *New York Times* VIII p10 July 7, 1991, with photo, VIII p10 July 14, 1991, with photo, XIII (Connecticut edition) p25 May 23, 1993, with photo, B p2 Aug. 6, 1999, with photo; *Time* p104+ Apr. 15, 1985, with photos; *Time* (on-line) June 29, 1998

Louis Psihoyos/Matrix International

Meeker, Mary

1960(?)– Financial analyst. Address: c/o Morgan Stanley, Dean Witter, Discover & Co., 1585 Broadway, New York, NY 10036

In the *New Yorker* (May 3, 1999), John Cassidy called the new era of trade in Internet company stock "the most dramatic and concentrated period of wealth creation ever." A number of companies that offer inventive on-line services, such as America Online and Priceline.com, came to be worth more than a billion dollars within months of their debuts on the stock exchange. As the financial industry's leading Internet analyst, Mary Meeker has paved the way for some of the greatest Internet success stories. Meeker not only advises investors about which companies will become most profitable, but works with the corporate finance department at the investment firm Morgan Stanley in de-

ciding which companies' stocks should be traded publicly. Thanks to Meeker's keen insights, Morgan Stanley, which in 1997 merged with Dean Witter to become the largest securities broker in the world, has become the most successful underwriter of Internet initial public offerings (IPOs).

Mary Meeker was born in about 1960 in Portland, Indiana, a small farming town in the northeastern part of the state. According to John Cassidy, Meeker's father, who worked at Portland Forge, a metalworking company, had risen to the number-two spot in the firm when it was sold to a larger corporation. Meeker's father made a substantial sum of money at the time of the sale and invested it in stocks. He began explaining his investment strategies to his daughter, who became interested in finance and eventually majored in business and psychology at DePauw University, in Greencastle, Indiana. While in college she began to read the *Wall Street Journal*.

After graduating from college, Meeker moved to Chicago, where she spent two years working for Merrill Lynch. She then resumed her studies, at Cornell University, in Ithaca, New York, and earned an M.B.A. degree. Her next job was in New York City, at the Wall Street firm Cowen and Co., where she began researching the profitability of various personal computer manufacturers. In 1991 she was hired by Morgan Stanley, an investment company that was just beginning to build what would become the financial industry's most effective Internet-related investment department. At Morgan Stanley, Meeker studied the rapid growth of computer companies such as Dell, Compaq, and Microsoft—an experience she has credited with preparing her for her future work with Internet companies. "If you looked at Microsoft and believed [Microsoft CEO] Bill Gates when he said, 'A personal computer on every desktop. A personal computer in every home,' it was easy to extrapolate, and see that Microsoft was going to be a big company someday," she told Cassidy. "The lesson I learned was to apply the same reasoning to America Online. Simple as it sounds, I believed in 1993 that everyone would use E-mail someday." Meeker told Cassidy that she considers her official recommendation to investors to buy stock in America Online, in 1993, "a defining event in my career."

In 1994 Meeker happened to read an article about a small new company called Mosaic Communications, which had developed a user-friendly way of navigating the World Wide Web. "I read the article and a light bulb went on," she told Cassidy. Meeker then flew to California and met with Mosaic's staff. According to Cassidy, Mosaic met what Meeker believes to be the three most important criteria for success for an Internet company: a large potential market of customers or subscribers; cleverly designed technology; and an experienced management team. The fact that the company was losing money did not worry Meeker, because the lack of cash that characterized Mosaic as well as most other developing Internet companies usually plays an important part in the company's IPO, as well as in Meeker's success as an analyst. As Joe Perella, the head of Morgan's corporate finance department, explained to Cassidy, a developing Internet company is "not like Ford or Microsoft sitting there with 20 billion dollars in its bank account." Fledgling companies need to raise money in order to expand, and therefore, "Mary can make or break them with her pen." After meeting with Mosaic's officials, Meeker persuaded three leading media companies—Times Mirror, Knight Ridder, and Hearst—to invest in Mosaic, which soon changed its name to Netscape. Morgan Stanley then financed Netscape's IPO, the first of its kind on Wall Street. "With the Netscape IPO we really helped create a new business model. We helped create a new way of financing companies," Meeker told Cassidy.

An initial public offering takes place when stock in a company that has been privately owned is offered for sale to the public and traded on the stock exchange. What is remarkable about the recent IPOs of Internet companies, or of any companies presenting new technology that can be used by a large segment of the population, is that the stock's value can increase dramatically in a short time—usually the amount of time it takes for the public to purchase the technology and incorporate it into their lives. Since Netscape's IPO in 1993, Internet-related companies such as Amazon.com, @Home, CNET, eBay, Intuit, Cisco Systems, and Ascend Communications, all of which were recommended by Meeker, have followed patterns similar to that of Netscape, creating wealth in short periods of time. Meeker proved herself the most adept Internet analyst in the financial industry by pinpointing the companies that would be most successful, and her savvy has made Morgan Stanley, Dean Witter the most successful financial firm in the highly competitive Internet IPO arena. "Nothing like this has happened before," Meeker told Craig Bicknell for the on-line publication Wired (December 21, 1998). "TV and radio took years to develop. This has taken virtually months."

In 1995, with her research assistant Chris DePuy, Meeker wrote her 300-page The Internet Report (1996). In it she made the bold prediction that, although fewer than 10 million people were using the Internet at that time, the number of users would reach 150 million by the turn of the century—a prediction that has nigh come true. Janice Maloney of Fortune (June 10, 1996) noted that while the writings of most financial analysts are "dry as dust, . . . like Meeker herself [The Internet Report] is funny and direct." Moreover, the book interested a broad audience that included investors and PC users alike. Two more of Meeker's studies—The Internet Advertising Report and The Internet Retailing Report—were published in 1997. Meeker remains one of only a few people who have been able to examine thoroughly the Internet and its implications for the economy. "She has been the thought leader," Roger McNamee, of Integral Capital Partners, told Cassidy. "Mary has provided an intellectual framework for understanding the Internet."

The most recent IPO with which Meeker has been associated is that of Priceline.com, a Connecticut-based company that sells discounted airline tickets and offers hotel reservations and mortgages on-line. After Meeker recommended the sale of the company's stocks to the public, several leading financial firms, Morgan Stanley, Dean Witter and Goldman Sachs among them, participated in what is called a "bake out," in which the company in question chooses which firm will finance its IPO. Priceline.com chose Morgan Stanley, Dean Witter, and Richard Braddock, Priceline's chief executive, told Cassidy, "We just think Mary is the best. That was the distinguishing reason we chose Morgan. She has the credibility." Priceline.com began trading at $16 per share, the highest price any Internet stock has ever commanded at its IPO. The price of the stock more than quadrupled shortly after its debut, and it has continued to rise at a steady pace.

While Meeker has played an important part in what has been one of the most exciting eras in the history of the stock market, she admits that the rapid rate at which vast amounts of money have been made over the past several years probably cannot be maintained. "This party's got to end some day," she told Michelle Celarier for Euromoney (January 1999). Meeker told Cassidy that the executives of some Internet companies seeking IPOs have been "unbelievably arrogant about how successful they were going to be and . . . unbelievably arrogant about the valuations they wanted to achieve on the IPO. . . . The first generation was, like, 'Hey, isn't this great! I'm a billionaire! Well, that's kind of embarrassing. What am I going to do with all this stuff?' The next generation is saying, 'Well, if he's a billionaire, then I've gotta be a billionaire.' With every IPO, the envelope is pushed a little further. At some point, you have to scream uncle."

When discussing the future profitability of Internet companies, Meeker has used the term "digital Darwinism" to explain that not every Internet company is destined to be valued at billions of dollars. "I think there will be only a couple of handfuls of companies that really succeed," she told Cassidy. She believes that investors should stay with well-known names, and she likens smaller, unknown Internet companies to "corner stores" that go out of business when large chain stores open nearby. "The Internet is a kind of small town," she told Cassidy. "Everybody will go to *www.something.*" While Meeker also warns that companies competing directly with those that work through the Internet—such as retailers and travel agencies—will most likely lose money in the near future, she does not believe that the Internet will take over all other forms of commerce. "Things rarely happen as quickly as one thinks, so there's rarely displacement as quickly as one thinks," she told Cassidy. "Television didn't kill radio. The Internet is not going to kill television, radio, or publishing." Regarding the current high prices of most Internet stocks, she told Cassidy, "I think many of these valuations are built on air, but I don't think all of them are. Some of these companies have extraordinarily powerful business models, and they are just at the point of figuring out how to monetize them."

John Cassidy described Mary Meeker as being of average height and as having "a pinkish, round face, straight brown hair, and lively blue eyes." At her office, in New York City, she receives an average of 50 phone calls and 100 E-mail messages per day. She works with a personal assistant, two administrative assistants, and three research assistants. Meeker is known to be down-to-earth and also to lose her temper occasionally. She lives in what Cassidy described as an "unremarkable" apartment on Manhattan's Upper West Side, and she owns a vacation home in Amagansett, a town on Long Island, in New York, where she enjoys biking and in-line skating. While Meeker is rumored to have an annual salary of several million dollars, Cassidy remarked that this sum "is a pittance compared with the amounts being raked in by successful Internet entrepreneurs." "It isn't all about money," the renowned analyst said. "I'm having fun, and I think I'm doing what I do best." — C.P.

Suggested Reading: *Euromoney* p92+ Jan. 1999, with photos; *Fortune* p104+ June 10, 1996, with photos; *New Yorker* p48+ May 3, 1999, with photo; *Wired* (on-line) Dec. 21, 1998

Selected Books: *The Internet Report*, 1996; *The Internet Advertising Report*, 1997; *The Internet Retailing Report*, 1997

Meriwether, John

1947– Investment manager; founder of Long-Term Capital Management. Address: c/o Long-Term Capital Management, 600 Steamboat Rd., Greenwich, CT 06830

John Meriwether first gained attention in the late 1970s, as a bond trader for the Wall Street investment firm of Salomon Brothers, and in the following decade he led that firm to immense profits. In 1994 he founded Long-Term Capital Management, a hedge fund that produced remarkable returns for its high-profile investors and led the industry for several years. In September 1998, however, Long-Term Capital Management neared collapse. It was rescued from bankruptcy through the controversial intervention of Alan Greenspan and the U.S. Federal Reserve Board, which worked to secure the needed capital (approximately $3.5 billion) from 14 private-sector financial institutions.

John William Meriwether was born in 1947 in Chicago and grew up on the city's South Side. As a youth he earned pocket money by caddying at a nearby golf course. He graduated from Northwestern University, in Chicago, in 1969, with a degree in business, then earned a master's of business administration degree from the University of Chicago, in 1973. In the next year he began his professional life as a recruit in the prestigious management-training program of Salomon Brothers, in New York City.

James McGoon/Sygma

Meriwether experienced great success as a bond trader for Salomon Brothers and quickly moved up the ranks of the company's hierarchy. In 1980 he became a partner in the firm, and for much of that decade, even after Salomon Brothers was bought by the commodity-trading firm of Phillip Brothers, in 1982, he helped earn great profits for himself and his firm through his work in bond-arbitrage trading. This work involved putting together a team of mathematicians, computer scientists, and other academics, who used computers to develop sophisticated trading strategies; these, in turn, were used to bet on changes in interest rates on bonds of different maturities. According to figures provided by Randall Smith and Michael Siconolfi in the *Wall Street Journal* (January 12, 1993), in 1990 the bond-arbitrage group, led by Meriwether, made an estimated $400 million in profit for Salomon Brothers.

In spite of that success, Meriwether's departure from Salomon Brothers, in August 1991, was shrouded in scandal: it was discovered that the firm had failed to notify regulatory authorities of improprieties after they found out that one of Meriwether's subordinates, Paul Mozer—Salomon's top government-bond trader—had submitted improper bids at Treasury bond auctions in an attempt to influence the price for an issue of two-year U.S. Treasury notes. Meriwether, then the vice chairman in charge of all bond trading at the firm and the heir apparent to the chairman, was among three top Salomon Brothers executives who were forced out of the company. In December 1992 he and the Securities and Exchange Commission reached a settlement in which he neither admitted nor denied that he had been negligent as a supervisor; he then underwent a three-month suspension from all securities-trading activity and paid a $50,000 fine.

Although some Wall Street watchers speculated that the scandal would seriously hamper Meriwether's career, he bounced back to form Long-Term Capital Management, a hedge fund, in March 1994. Hedge funds are private investment partnerships that often use borrowed money to gamble on interest rates, stocks, and bonds. Much less regulated than other money-management funds, they can offer unusually high rates of return to those with enough money to invest. Long-Term Capital Management, headquartered in posh offices in Greenwich, Connecticut, enlisted the services of leading businessmen and academicians, including David W. Mullins Jr., a former deputy chairman of the Federal Reserve Board; the renowned economists Robert Merton and Myron Scholes, who were awarded the 1997 Nobel Prize for Economics; and several former executives from Salomon Brothers. "Academics have lots of ideas, but they don't have the skills of traders, and the two groups have very different mind sets and ways of life," Robert Merton told Saul Hansell for the *New York Times* (September 5, 1993). "What [Meriwether] was able to do was bring the best of the two together so that the communication between them is very smooth."

Bolstered by Meriwether's reputation and those of his partners, Meriwether's hedge fund drew the attention of many of the world's wealthiest investors, who provided Meriwether and his partners with access to $1.25 billion to invest in the global securities market. Even with the high cost of joining the fund—investors were required to invest a minimum of $10 million and could not withdraw their money for three years—the fund quickly became one of the premier hedge funds in the industry and remained one of the top investment choices for major financial institutions and wealthy families.

The fund performed remarkably well for much of its existence. In 1995 it earned for its investors almost 43 percent in profits. (This figure represents profit after the payment of the required 2 percent annual management fee and an additional fee of 25 percent of profits to the fund managers.) In 1996 the fund returned around 41 percent after fees. Such figures represented huge earnings for the fund and its investors, and Meriwether was hailed in financial circles as a genius.

The fund's earnings, however, had come as a result of heavily leveraged investments, which involved significant debt. For example, in the first half of 1998, Meriwether's firm used about $4 billion in capital as security to borrow $120 billion, which it invested in Treasury bonds, bonds issued by foreign governments, stocks, and other investments throughout the world. On the strength of the borrowed money, it then secured more loans and investments. When the markets took a downturn, in 1998, the fund had difficulty meeting its debt obligations. Specifically, the fund had invested heavily in emerging and European markets, and it suffered when the global financial market was stricken by anxiety in the aftermath of the Asian financial crisis, which had dampened financial markets of several Asian nations and led to Russia's defaulting on some of its foreign debt obligations in August 1998. In that same month, Meriwether announced that Long-Term Capital Management had lost $1.8 billion; by the middle of September, the firm had lost even more money and was on the verge of bankruptcy, with just $600 million in equity. In about 60 days, it had lost 90 percent of its capital. (According to Steven Mufson in the *Washington Post* [September 27, 1998, on-line], prior to August 1998 the firm hadn't lost more than $100 million of the firm's equity in any month.) Unable to secure additional loans or capital, the firm faced the task of meeting additional debt obligations while its equity continued to dwindle.

With the prodding of the Federal Reserve Board and its chairman, Alan Greenspan, who took action through the Federal Reserve Bank of New York, a 14-member consortium of private banks and financial institutions, which included Merrill Lynch, J.P. Morgan, Morgan Stanley Dean Witter, Goldman Sachs, and Chase Manhattan, pitched in with $3.5 billion of urgently needed capital and took control of about 90 percent of the fund. Meriwether and his partners' stakes in the firm were reduced drastically, and Meriwether was, in effect, removed from power.

The Federal Reserve's intervention proved to be very controversial. Many saw the action as being counter to what free-market advocates had long championed. "Why should the weight of the Federal Government be brought to bear to help out a private investor?" former Federal Reserve Board chairman Paul Volcker asked rhetorically, as quoted by John Greenwald in *Time.com* (October 5, 1998, on-line). "It's not a bank." Supporters of the intervention, however, maintained that the failure of Long-Term Capital would have had devastating repercussions for the rest of the global financial system. In other words, Long-Term Capital was deemed too large to be allowed to fail. Moreover, supporters of the intervention pointed out that the Federal Reserve had merely facilitated the deal and that the $3.5 billion in capital had come from private institutions, not taxpayers. Robert Rubin, the secretary of the U.S. Treasury Department, said, as quoted by Gretchen Morgenson for the *New York Times* (September 27, 1998, on-line), "This is not a bailout; there's no public money. It was a decision by the private sector that their economic interests lay in these arrangements."

However, critics, including Wall Street observers and some politicians, pointed out that the private banks that provided the funds for Long-Term Capital enjoyed the support of taxpayers through federal deposit insurance, which had also backed banks that had profited over the years from their dealings with Long-Term Capital Management. These critics also complained that the action hinted at cronyism, since some of those among the fund's saviors held investments in Long-Term Capital Management—David Komansky, the chairman of Merrill Lynch, was reported to hold a $22 million stake in the fund. Others also voiced concern that such a bailout would further encourage banks to make risky loans; the implication was that unwise investors would again be bailed out by the intervention of the federal government. The bailout seemed ironic since it took place around the same time that the U.S. Senate passed a bill that intended to make it more difficult for ordinary citizens to seek bankruptcy-court protection from banks and other creditors. Finally, since government officials and businessmen in the U.S. had been telling their counterparts in Japan and other financially strapped nations that inefficient or ailing businesses and banks should not be propped up by government intervention but should be allowed to collapse, the Federal Reserve Board's decision to aid Long-Term Capital Management made this advice seem hypocritical to many. "The Fed, and by extension, the entire economic policy team of the U.S. Government, will have less credibility the next time they want to preach the favored laissez-faire advice to broken-down Asian countries and Russia," David DeRosa, a finance professor at Yale University, warned, as quoted by Oliver August for the *London Times* (October 7, 1998, on-line).

The near-collapse of the once-prized hedge fund fueled concern that other hedge funds shared its financial difficulty. According to Greenwald, there are around 4,000 hedge funds in the U.S. They often are more secretive about their operations and are less regulated than some other types of money-management funds. The future of Long-Term Capital Management is perceived by most to be tenuous. As reported by *CNNfn.com* (October 9, 1998, on-line), as of October 9, 1998, the troubled hedge fund had already depleted $1.9 billion of its newly acquired capital to maintain some of its holdings and service its debt.

Meriwether, whose personal net worth was estimated by Gretchen Morgenson in the *New York Times* (October 2, 1998, on-line) to have been around $200 million at its peak, lives in Westchester County, New York. He is married to Mimi Murray, a champion equestrian and award-winning physical-education teacher. In 1991 Murray earned an Honor Award from the American Alliance for Health, Physical Education, Recreation, and Dance. — Y.P.

Suggested Reading: *Forbes* (on-line) Oct. 19, 1998; *London Times* (on-line) Oct. 7, 1998; *New York Times* D p3 Mar. 25, 1993, with photos, III p3 Sep. 5, 1993; *New York Times* (on-line) Oct. 2, 1998; *Wall Street Journal* C p1 Jan. 12, 1993, C p1 Jan. 16, 1996; *Washington Post* C p1 Aug. 31, 1991; *Washington Post* (on-line) H p1 Sep. 27, 1998

Michaels, Lorne

Nov. 17, 1944– Creator and executive producer of Saturday Night Live. *Address: c/o Broadway Video, 1619 Broadway, Ninth Fl., New York, NY 10019-7463*

Before the mid-1970s, the television industry tended to pander to the older members of its audience. Instead of mirroring contemporary culture, many shows lagged a decade or more behind the times. Then, on October 11, 1975, *Saturday Night Live* (*SNL*) debuted; by defying network censors, redefining the parameters of permissibility, and presenting fresh topical satire, the show launched a revolution in television. The brainchild of comedy writer and producer Lorne Michaels, *SNL* and its ensemble cast, known as the Not Ready for Prime Time Players, spoke to young people through live sketch comedy targeting everything from politicians to pop culture. "I wanted this show to emerge with a new sensibility when it went on the air," Michaels told Bill Barol and Jennifer Foote for *Newsweek* (September 25, 1989). "I wanted to create the impression that the network had shut down and these people had come in and taken over the studio." *SNL* is now the longest-running and

Courtesy of NBC

Lorne Michaels

highest-rated late-night program in television history; it has served as the launching pad for the careers of such comedy stars as Dan Aykroyd, Bill Murray, and Eddie Murphy and, more recently, Mike Myers and Adam Sandler. As the creative force behind *SNL* for 19 of the 24 years it has been broadcast, Lorne Michaels has seen *SNL* grow from a countercultural "tour de farce" to an American institution.

Born Lorne Lipowitz on November 17, 1944, Lorne Michaels was reared in a well-to-do section of Toronto, Canada, called Forest Hill. After the death of his father, a prosperous furrier, when Lorne was 14, he found a surrogate father in Frank Shuster, of the distinguished Canadian comedy duo Wayne and Shuster. Shuster, whose daughter Rosie was Lorne's high-school sweetheart (and, later, first wife), nurtured the teenager's dreams of one day working in show business. It was Shuster who suggested that Lorne change his last name.

After earning a bachelor's degree in English at the University of Toronto, in 1966, Michaels spent some months selling Jeeps in England (which may explain why, to many of his acquaintances, his speech sounds vaguely British). Toward the end of 1966, back in Canada, he formed a writing partnership with Hart Pomerantz. The team wrote and performed a comedy show for CBC Radio and increasingly found work in New York, doing stand-up at the Improv comedy club and writing material for such up-and-comers as Dick Cavett, Joan Rivers, and Woody Allen. Moving to the West Coast in 1968 proved even more lucrative for Michaels and Pomerantz. In Hollywood they served as fill-in writers for some of the most popular television comedy programs of the day, including *Rowan &*

Martin's Laugh-In. Although Hollywood gave Michaels and Pomerantz the opportunity to hone their craft in prominent venues, American television seemed stodgy and limiting to Michaels. "I was trying to write in other people's voices. I did whatever I was asked to do and tried to be conscientious and not make mistakes," Michaels told Rip Rense for an on-line profile written for the National Academy of Television Arts and Sciences' Hall of Fame (into which Michaels was inducted in 1999). "But by 1970, I was sort of itching to connect with what I was really interested in. The kind of comedy and work we were doing was so disconnected from what people my age were going through. You know, in the streets, universities. It was a time of turmoil, and this was very traditional television. So I had some frustration. I wanted to do the kind of comedy that was making me and my friends laugh."

Having identified a void in television, Michaels set about filling it. In 1969 he and Pomerantz returned to their native land, where they signed a deal to produce and perform in 10 variety specials for CBC television. "The CBC was the best training I could have had," Michaels told Brian D. Johnson for *Maclean's* (June 9, 1986). "I was given tremendous freedom and very little budget. What we couldn't afford, we had to make up." Returning to Canada also exposed Michaels to the British sketch comedy series *Monty Python's Flying Circus.* Not yet being aired in the U.S., *Monty Python* was bold, bizarre, irreverent, and intelligently written and made him and his generation laugh. It reinforced Michaels's ideas about television comedy's possibilities.

As early as 1973 Lorne Michaels had made a broad-based pitch to NBC for a comedy-variety show featuring a young ensemble cast, but it was not until Dick Ebersol was appointed the network's weekend late-night programming director, at the beginning of 1975, that talks became serious. At that time the Saturday-night 11:30 p.m. to 1:00 a.m. time slot was considered a television wasteland; on NBC, reruns from the previous week's *Tonight Show with Johnny Carson* filled it. Though network executives were sure that Michaels's target audience would prefer partying on a Saturday night to sitting at home in front of the television, they approved Michaels's proposal. On April 1, 1975 he signed a contract to produce the show.

With only six months to prepare for a fall debut, Michaels immediately assembled a cast of young performers who had been seasoned on theater repertory and club circuits throughout the U.S. and Canada: John Belushi, Dan Aykroyd, Gilda Radner, Laraine Newman, Jane Curtin, and Garrett Morris. He also corralled a stable of talented, off-beat writers, among them Michael O'Donoghue, a caustic, scathingly satiric writer from *National Lampoon* magazine; Chevy Chase, whom Michaels had met while waiting in line to see the film *Monty Python and the Holy Grail*; and Al Franken, a politically minded recent Harvard grad. On October 11, 1975, after increasingly frenetic preparations, the show premiered, and in an opening that instantly became part of television lore, Chevy Chase walked out on stage in studio 8H at Rockefeller Center and declared, "Live from New York, it's *Saturday Night!*"

Though many people romanticize the magic created by the groundbreaking *SNL* that first season, Michaels has told interviewers that he and his colleagues experienced as many writing and performance valleys in those months as they did peaks. "I think I knew all the ingredients of the show, but I didn't have the recipe," Michaels told Rip Rense. "And you can see, if you look at the first shows, we kind of lurched towards success." Chevy Chase left the show at the end of the first season to pursue career opportunities in Hollywood and was replaced by the future comedic star Bill Murray, and the cast and writers settled into the exhausting routine of producing comedy skits on a weekly basis. By then, Michaels has said, the show had found its footing; in its third year, he believes, it hit its stride. During its fourth season *SNL* drew its highest ratings ever, but behind the scenes, dissension arising from clashes of egos and the pressures of the work had become the order of the day. John Belushi and Dan Aykroyd, buoyed by the popularity of their characters the Blues Brothers, left after the fourth season, and the remaining cast and writers were feeling drained by the constant call to be funny week in and week out.

Michaels, too, was feeling the strain of success, and after the breakdown of negotiations with NBC to gain more autonomy for *SNL*, he announced that he was leaving the series. "I feel there is a natural life to a show of this kind. Having done 106 shows, I wanted something totally different, and I didn't feel I could create that, by September [1980], on *Saturday Night*," Michaels told Tony Schwartz for the *New York Times* (June 17, 1980). "As everyone became more and more successful, and got other offers, it was harder to do. The show was purer in the first three years. I don't think it became decadent, I just think it became successful." Michaels's departure prompted a mass exodus of *SNL*'s remaining original cast members, and many observers shared Michaels's belief that the show would fold. But *SNL* managed to survive its next five years, thanks to the talents of such rising stars as Eddie Murphy, Joe Piscopo, Billy Crystal, and Martin Short.

Earlier, Michaels had served as a writer and producer for Lily Tomlin's television specials (1972–75). After leaving *SNL* Michaels established his own audio and video production studios, named Broadway Video, and produced a number of other successful single-event performances, including Simon and Garfunkel's reunion concert in New York City's Central Park. Still under contract to NBC, he agreed to produce another comedy variety series, called the *New Show*; it aired Fridays during prime time in 1984 but was canceled after only nine weeks. In 1985 NBC asked Michaels to return

to *SNL*; if he refused, network executives told him, they intended to cancel the show. Not wanting to see it die, Michaels assented, and he has remained with *SNL* ever since.

Since Michaels's return to *Saturday Night Live*, his show has sometimes suffered from unfavorable comparisons with its original incarnation, not least because after 24 years on the air, *SNL* is now an ingrained part of the mainstream culture it once mocked, and thus its satiric edge has dulled. Another problem is that, because of *SNL*'s example, parodies of cultural phenomena appear in the media almost as soon as the phenomena emerge. Furthermore, as *SNL* approaches its silver anniversary, finding ways to keep the show fresh while maintaining continuity has become increasingly difficult for Michaels. And *SNL* must go head-to-head with copycat shows and contend with competition from the Fox network's *Mad TV*, based on the popular humor magazine *Mad*, and CBS's *Howard Stern Radio Show*, which shows video clips from shock-jock Stern's morning radio program. Notwithstanding recurring predictions by media pundits that *SNL*'s end is near, Michaels's creation remains the highest-rated late-night show on television, and its market share is nearly twice that of *Mad TV* and *Howard Stern Radio Show* combined. Michaels appears relatively unaffected by criticism of *SNL*. Displaying his trademark cutting, wry wit, he told Chris Smith, as reported in Smith's lacerating profile of *SNL* for *New York* (March 13, 1995), "If your angle is going to be that the show is decadent and out of touch, we have that reduced to a press release to save time."

When David Letterman changed networks in 1993, NBC turned to Lorne Michaels to develop a new version of the popular late-night talk-show host's program. To host the replacement, Michaels recruited Conan O'Brien, a writer for both *SNL* and the animated-cartoon series *The Simpsons*. *Late Night with Conan O'Brien* premiered on September 14, 1993. After a rocky start, the show recaptured the bulk of Letterman's audience, and it has been credited with helping Jay Leno, who took over the *Tonight Show* from Johnny Carson, fend off direct competition from Letterman's new show on CBS.

The actor and writer Steve Martin told Rip Rense that Michaels's "people skills are unbelievable." "To be dealing with mostly young people who are very headstrong and way demanding—to be able to coordinate all that, and deal with the egos of talent, I mean, it's an amazing skill. And he's a calm guy. Kind of non-confrontational. . . . He's also very wise. I don't know how to say it any other way than that. He's a wise guy!" Bernie Brillstein, Michaels's longtime manager, told Rense, "The brilliance of Lorne is between dress rehearsal and air, when he has over a hundred people in his office on the ninth floor, and he's changing the running order, changing the camera shots, changing the logos, shortening the sketches, lengthening sketches—and it's all done in 40 minutes. During this hour, Lorne, being the gentleman he is, is also remembering whose sketch he cancelled the week before. He doesn't want to hurt an actor or writer who was hurt the week before because their sketch was cancelled. And remember, he also has to take care of the host, who's a visitor that week and often new to the whole thing. So it's amazing. I've never seen anything like that in all my days of show business. That's as arduous as it can get. He's amazing, amazing, amazing." Michaels's honors include eight Emmy Awards, four Writers Guild of America Awards, and a George Foster Peabody Award, in 1991. In 1992 Michaels was named Broadcaster of the Year by the International Radio and Television Society.

Lorne Michaels lives in New York City with his third wife, Alice, a former assistant of his, and their three young children: Henry, Edward, and Sophie. — T.J.F.

Suggested Reading: *Esquire* p78+ Feb. 1986, with photo; *Maclean's* p38+ June 9, 1986, with photo; *New York* p30+ Mar. 13, 1995, with photo; *New York Times* II p1+ Sep. 19, 1999, with photo; *Newsweek* p40+ Sep. 25, 1989, with photo; *Motion Picture Almanac, 1999*; *Who's Who in America, 1999*

Miller, Bebe

(BEE-bee)

1950– Choreographer; dancer. Address: c/o Bebe Miller Company, 54 W. 21st St., Suite 502, New York, NY 10010

"I have these parallel tracks in my work," the dancer and choreographer Bebe Miller told Jann Parry for the (London) *Observer* (November 8, 1992). "One is a real curiosity about movement and what it feels like; the other is the rest of my life." In the *Village Voice* (January 6, 1987), Deborah Jowitt described Miller as "one of the most luscious and intelligent dancers around—now deft, now powerful, now yielding, always complex." Miller began creating innovative, humanistic dance pieces in the early 1980s, and she has since worked with many modern-dance companies in the United States and Europe. According to Jowitt, "[Miller] seems to be interested in making frankly difficult dancing that wears its difficulty casually, and in revealing emotion and social behavior without recourse to linear narrative or role-playing." "Since she has never been hyped as the representative of any hot new trend of any given moment," Susan Reiter wrote for *New York Newsday* (November 26, 1989), "Miller has developed a subtle, personal approach that incorporates suggestions of character and hints of relationships with her own flair for intricate, juicy movement." Miller told Reiter, "When I go to concerts I want to know what the choreographer is trying to say. . . . I want to know who they really are." Miller has tried to offer her audiences the same degree of intimacy; as she explained to Reiter, "I want them to feel me, emotionally and intellectually."

Bebe Miller was born in the New York City borough of Brooklyn in 1950, and she was raised in a public housing project in the Red Hook neighborhood. Her mother was a schoolteacher, and her father was a steward on a ship. When Miller was five years old, her mother, who suffered from arthritis, began taking exercise classes at the Henry Street Settlement, a century-old community center in Lower Manhattan that provides social services and arts programs to adults and children. Miller usually went along, and she eventually joined a children's modern-dance class there. One of Miller's first teachers was Murray Louis, who would later collaborate with Alwin Nicolais in founding the celebrated Nicolais and Louis Dance Theater. Louis used nontraditional methods in teaching his children's classes. "I learned improvisation and composition before I knew how to plié," Miller told Elizabeth Zimmer for *Dancemagazine* (December 1989). (A plié, which involves bending the knees, is a basic warmup movement in classical dance. Most complex steps in classical dance begin and end in a plié.) As a youngster Miller enjoyed art projects as well as dancing and dreamed of becoming an actress.

When she was 13 years old, Miller took some ballet classes at a studio in Carnegie Hall, in Manhattan. "All those little bunheads and me from the projects," she reminisced to Zimmer. "I was intimidated." Feeling as though, in her words, she didn't "fit in" with the other students, she stopped going to the classes. "Thank God I couldn't do a decent plié, so I could make up one."

After graduating from high school, Miller attended Earlham College, in Richmond, Indiana, where she majored in art. "I wasn't very good," she told Zimmer. "But the sense of design and making something up was always there." After earning a bachelor's degree, in about 1972, Miller moved back to New York City. She got a job as a waitress and continued taking dance classes with Murray Louis; she also studied with his partner, Alwin Nikolais. "I was 22 and living with my boyfriend for the first time," she recalled to Zimmer. "I got a loft for $350 a month. . . . The kind of economic commitment you have to have now is totally different from what it was [then]."

While in her early 20s, Miller began performing and choreographing with small, experimental modern-dance groups. She also mounted dance performances of her own, financing her productions with her own money and coming away with little or no profit. Then she won a fellowship from

Bebe Miller

Courtesy of Bebe Miller Dance Company

Ohio State University. "They thought, 'Hey, she can make something,'" she told Zimmer. "My syntheses of ideas was particular, and I did have a flair for dancing. I knew I'd end up doing my own work, because it fit my body." At Ohio State Miller studied with Nina Wiener, an alumna of the Twyla Tharp Dance Company who was then the resident choreographer at Ohio State's dance department. "Nina made me see how much fun it could be," Miller told Zimmer. "She gave me an appetite for making steps. There's no other way to do it but your own." After completing her master's degree, in 1975, Miller danced with Wiener's professional company, Nina Wiener and Dancers, for six years.

In about 1981 Miller launched her own company. Although she was one of only a handful of African-American female choreographers working in New York City at that time, she distanced herself from other black women in the dance world by identifying herself as a "female choreographer who happens to be black." Miller later reconsidered her stance. "I realize that I was a little naïve," she admitted to Jann Parry. "Color is the first thing that people notice, the world being what it is, even before gender. I want people to recognize that my work is that of a black choreographer who makes dances about a range of subjects and ideas." Miller also said that she has resisted the pressure, placed on black artists by many people in the black community, to produce works that focus on racial issues, because she doesn't want to be limited by such constraints. "The whole point, surely, is to increase your possibilities, to find ways of presenting yourselves differently on stage," she said to Parry.

In December 1981 several works by Miller were presented at the Bessie Schonberg Theater, in New York City. One of them, *Square Business*, examines human relationships—a favorite theme of Miller's—by exploring the various ways four people can move while confined within the boundaries of a square. A second piece, *Jammin'*, features six dancers in costumes reminiscent of military uniforms stomping vigorously on the stage floor. In the *New York Times* (December 2, 1981), Jack Anderson wrote that "*Jammin'* could be called an example of military chic. But because its warriors battled only the floor and never one another, it could also be viewed as a pacification of aggressive impulses."

Miller's 1981 presentation at the Schonberg theater also included two of her solo dances—*Tune*, which has been described as ethereal, and *Solo: Task/Force*, which Anderson described as "contain[ing] clearly outlined gestures and deliberate, determined steps [that] . . . might well have been part of some imaginary task." Gestures that are realistic and familiar while remaining unidentifiable were also part of a third solo, which Miller produced the following year. Reviewing a performance of *Spending Times Doing Things*, Deborah Jowitt wrote in the *Village Voice* (January 6, 1987), "When [Miller] . . . makes a motif of head-shaking, of brushing gestures close to her ears, you stare fascinated. What is she doing? Something that's real, that's deeply felt, yet mysterious."

In 1986, in collaboration with the award-winning choreographer Ralph Lemon, Miller completed *Two*, which remains one of her most highly praised works. Set to music by C. Hyams-Hart, *Two* examines the meaning of togetherness through movements that contrast connectedness with disconnectedness. In the *New York Times* (December 22, 1986), Jennifer Dunning wrote, "Heart, mind, and acute physicality come together in what promises to be one of the most powerful dances of the year." Miller also completed a second work, *Heart, Heart*, in 1986. Although she danced alone in this piece, two chairs on the stage seemed to pull her with an almost gravitational force. "You can almost see two parents shaping her moves," Jowitt wrote in her January 6, 1987 article for the *Village Voice.*

In 1987 Miller created *Working Order* and *Habit of Attraction.* The former, choreographed to music by Hearn Gadbois, Jonathan Kane, and Johann Sebastian Bach, incorporates a text that, at the premiere of the dance, was spoken by Holly Anderson. *Working Order* features a woman who does the kind of heavy labor ordinarily reserved for men. "The steps . . . convey ideas about camaraderie, triumph, energy expended, anger, confusion," Jowitt wrote in her January 6, 1987 article. "Miller has taken physical acts and gestures suggested by the text and re-patterned the literalness out of them, so that they can function as pure dancing, yet still retain something of their emotional truth." Jowitt did not find *Working Order* entirely satisfactory. "I love the richness of Miller's movement, the tough, but loving, way the dancers deal with it and with each other, but rarely can I remember one dance as being different from any other one," she complained. "[Miller] seems to put all she knows how to do in every dance. And, although she's savvy about construction on a small scale (varying themes and so forth), I never sense an overall shape to a piece of hers. . . . Fond of her work as I am, I crave something like identifiable flavors and for-sure first courses."

In *Habit of Attraction*, which premiered at the Womanworks Festival, a New York City showcase for works by female choreographers, Miller focused on ways in which male-female relationships develop. With that piece, Anna Kisselgoff wrote for the *New York Times* (January 22, 1989), "Miller thinks up a lot for her dancers to do within a limited movement range, and in fact each couple basically spend their time solving a movement problem to an exasperating tape by C. Hyams-Hart." Also in 1987 Miller was chosen to contribute work to *Parallels in Black*, a showcase of the work of contemporary black choreographers that toured England.

Allies (1989), which is widely considered Miller's most important work to date, was co-commissioned by the Jacob's Pillow Dance Festival, New England Presenters, the New England Foundation for the Arts, and the Brooklyn Academy of Music. Mounted at a cost of $80,000, it was her "most expensive" dance to that date, Miller told Zimmer. "It wasn't so long ago that I could have a good series of nights [waitressing] at the restaurant and make enough [about $3,000] to mount

a weekend at DTW [Dance Theater Workshop]," she reminisced. Although, as with her other work, human experiences provided the thematic starting point for *Allies*, Miller took a somewhat different approach when she choreographed this dance. "I had recently done a lot of dances that dealt with relationships between people, usually about things not working out, or people getting along, but not without a cost," she told Reiter. "I started thinking that I wanted to explore something more positive. Ultimately we do figure out how to work together. I was also thinking in terms of the world situation now—we seem to be at a point where having the same old enemies in the same old ways is not working." Miller was also influenced by a book about "peacemaking among primates," Reiter reported. The book, Miller explained, "discussed, in animal terms, how social systems figure out how they're going to continue, and still have aggressive tendencies and reconciliations and peacemaking."

A visually stunning piece, *Allies* was performed to music by Fred Frith and set against a backdrop on which transparencies of medical diagrams overlay photographs of the dancers taken under water. In a review for the *New York Times* (November 30, 1989), Jack Anderson wrote, "*Allies* concerned the forming of alliances, and Ms. Miller demonstrated that all alliances may not be for admirable purposes. Dancers formed groups, eyeing one another suspiciously. They impulsively threw themselves at one another. At times when they reached toward one another, they were pulled away by still other dancers. When they did succeed in holding someone, it was unclear whether they were being helps or hindrances. And when people suddenly let go of one another, the result was not liberation, but momentary loss of balance."

In her concerts, Miller paired *Allies* with a stark solo called *Rain*, which the Brooklyn Academy of Music commissioned and which Miller choreographed to music by Hearn Gadbois and Heitor Villa-Lobos. The heroine of *Rain* is an old woman who struggles to arrive at a place to rest and get refreshed. As Reiter pointed out, the work "touches on a different kind of relationship—between the dancer and the earth—and Miller . . . emphasize[s] that focus by dancing on sod. She uses terms such as 'healing' and 'cleansing' when she talks about the solo."

In 1991 Miller choreographed a dance for *The Hidden Boy: Incidents from a Stressed Memory*, a generously financed collaboration of several visual and performing artists that told the story of the sculptor and woodcutter Jay Bolotin. Staged at the prestigious City Center Theater in New York, it was not a critical success. Later that year Miller presented a new work called *Hendrix Project*, which has music by Jimi Hendrix and Hendrix's contemporary Bob Dylan. It was performed on an ornate cloth designed by the artist Caroline Beasley-Baker. In the view of Jack Anderson, who critiqued it for the *New York Times* (May 26, 1991), *Hendrix Project* addressed the perils of drug addiction; the dancers, he reported, "hurtle about on the floor cloth, never venturing far from it and always returning to it, as if to imply that, however difficult life on this surface might be, even greater woes might fill the space beyond it." On a critical note, Anderson wrote that Miller "offered few choreographic comments on the distraught community she created." "The hard-edged movements she devised were vivid without also being revelatory," he wrote. "One longed to know more about what Ms. Miller thought about Mr. Hendrix, Mr. Dylan, the culture they represented, and the kinds of rebellion they fostered."

In 1992 Miller was commissioned to create a work for the Phoenix Dance Company, a predominately black troupe based in Leeds, England. Expectations that at long last she would delve into her African heritage for this project were left unmet. Instead, Miller based her piece, *Spartan Reels*, on folk dances from Greece. "I wanted to tackle the challenge of choreographing for people I didn't know with a common background that I'm not part of," she told Parry. "So I started with the idea of folk dance from a country not my own and not British either." Unlike many of Miller's other dances, in which men and women partner each other in nontraditional ways, *Spartan Reels* took a more conventional approach to representing gender. "In my company [men and women] work very equally with each other," Miller explained to Parry. "But here I was in this piece, with the men over there doing big-guy steps, the women over here doing small things and wearing dresses. 'My God,' I thought. 'Where does this conservatism come from?'" According to Parry, the female dancers in *Spartan Reels* "are asked to do neat, pernickety steps, sharing their secrets with each other, provoking responses from the men instead of confronting them directly."

Miller's next important work, choreographed in 1994, was *Tiny Sisters in the Enormous Land*. In the *New York Times* (April 23, 1996), Jennifer Dunning felt that "if awards were given for the most bizarrely compelling dance event of the year, [this work] would certainly be a strong contender." Danced by six women in girlish dresses, the piece was based on the real-life story of British twin sisters who communicated only with each other. Two more works—*Heaven and Earth*, a solo, and *Cantos Gordos*, a jubilant dance for the entire company—also premiered in 1994. After choreographing and teaching for the PACT Dance Company in South Africa later that year, Miller created *Yard Dance*, part of which is danced to a recording in which Miller spoke about the problems she saw in South Africa. At its premiere, in 1996, *Yard Dance* was juxtaposed with *Blessed*, another new Miller work that was set to gospel music.

Miller's most recent dances include *Going to the Wall* (1999), which, according to a company press release, is about issues of "identity and difference." "I feel a new urgency about expressing my view as a black woman in this company, this field,

and this culture," Miller was quoted as saying. Currently, Miller is working on *Map of the Body*, which is scheduled to premiere in the spring of 2000. With *Map of the Body*, the choreographer is investigating "cultural assumptions around the physical act of touch." "I am looking forward to the collision of ideas culled from my work in South Africa and the Caribbean with our own inquiries into dance and life," she said.

In addition to PACT and the Phoenix Dance Company, Miller has choreographed and staged works for the Oregon Ballet Theatre; the Boston Ballet; the Dayton Contemporary Dance Company; the Zenon Dance Company; the D9 Dance Collective; the Alvin Ailey Repertory Ensemble; the Groupe Experimental de Danse Contemporaine, in Martinique; De Nieuwe Dansgroep, in the Netherlands; and the Jazzart Dance Theatre of Cape Town, South Africa. In collaboration with the choreographer Ralph Lemon and the filmmaker Isaac Julien, she worked on *The Conservator's Dream*, a film that was scheduled to be completed in the fall of 1998. The Bebe Miller Company has conducted many forums, workshops, and other community outreach programs.

Miller's honors include the Creative Artists Public Service Fellowship for Choreography, in 1984; the New York Foundation for the Arts Choreographers Fellowship, in 1984 and 1991; the National Endowment for the Arts Choreographer's Fellowship, each year from 1985 through 1988; the Bessie Schonberg Choreography Award, in 1986; the American Choreographer Award, from the National Corporate Fund for Dance, in 1987 and 1989; a Guggenheim Memorial Fellowship, in 1987; and a Dewar's Young Artists Recognition Award, in 1990.

Miller lives in Brooklyn, New York. — C.P.

Suggested Reading: *Dancemagazine* p34+ Dec. 1989, with photos; (London) *Observer* II p54 Nov. 8, 1992, with photo; *New York Newsday* II p15 Nov. 26, 1989, with photo; *New York Times* C p23 Dec. 2, 1981, C p14 Dec. 22, 1986, I p47 Jan. 22, 1989, with photo, C p20 Nov. 30, 1989, with photo, I p60 May 26, 1991, with photo; *Village Voice* p55 Jan. 6, 1987, with photo, p108 Dec. 19, 1989, with photo

Selected Dances: *Square Business*, 1981; *Jammin'*, 1981; *Tune*, 1981; *Solo: Task/Force*, 1981; *Spending Times Doing Things*, 1982; *Two*, 1986; *Heart, Heart*, 1986; *Working Order*, 1987; *Habit of Attraction*, 1987; *Allies*, 1989; *Rain*, 1989; *The Hidden Boy: Incidents from a Stressed Memory*, 1991; *Hendrix Project*, 1991; *Spartan Reels*, 1992; *Tiny Sisters in the Enormous Land*, 1994; *Heaven and Earth*, 1994; *Cantos Gordos*, 1994; *Yard Dance*, 1996; *Blessed*, 1996; *Going to the Wall*, 1999

Courtesy of Robert Mondavi Corp.

Mondavi, Robert

(mon-DAH-vee)

June 18, 1913– Vintner; business executive.
Address: c/o Robert Mondavi Winery, 7801 St.
Helena Hwy., Oakville, CA 94562

The vintner Robert Mondavi considers wine to be much more than a beverage made from the fermented juice of crushed grapes. To him, wine is the "temperate, civilized, sacred, romantic mealtime beverage recommended in the Bible and praised for centuries by statesmen, philosophers, poets, and scholars." Similarly (though less hyperbolically), to insiders in the wine industry and others who have more than a passing interest in wine, to identify Mondavi simply as a vintner is something of an understatement. As a wine maker, Mondavi came up with many techniques still used in California wineries today, and he played a major role in lifting the American wine industry from a position of inferiority among its centuries-old counterparts in Europe to one of prominence. As *Fortune* (March 11, 1991) put it when the magazine inducted him into its National Business Hall of Fame, "Mondavi the innovator was a leader in raising the quality of U.S. wines to world-class standards; Mondavi the promoter was tireless in winning world recognition for those wines."

Robert Gerald Mondavi was born on June 18, 1913 in Virginia, Minnesota. Five and a half years after his birth, the United States ratified the 18th Amendment to the Constitution, which banned the manufacture, sale, importation, exportation, and transport of alcoholic beverages in the U.S. Prohibition, as the ban came to be called, went into effect one year later. Sometime in the early 1920s, the

Italian-American club in the Mondavi family's community asked Mondavi's father, Cesare, who had emigrated to Minnesota from the Marche region of Italy, to go to California to buy grapes for the wine that members of the club produced in their homes. Cesare liked California. In 1923 he moved with his wife, Rosa, and their four children to Lodi, in the Napa Valley, where he went into business as a shipper of grapes and other produce. Following the repeal of Prohibition, in 1933 (by means of the 21st Amendment to the Constitution), Cesare Mondavi became associated with the Sunnyhill Winery in St. Helena, a town about 60 miles north of Berkeley.

At some point, Robert Mondavi recalled to J. D. Reed and Vicki Sheff-Callan for *People* (October 12, 1998), "My father suggested I become a winemaker. It was a new industry, and I decided to grow with it." After graduating from Stanford University, in 1936, with a bachelor's degree in economics, Robert joined his father as a member of the Sunnyhill Winery's small production staff.

In 1943, taking Robert's advice, Cesare bought the historic but failing Charles Krug Winery, on condition that Robert and his younger brother, Peter, work there. Keeping their promise to come on board, Robert handled marketing and development, and Peter took charge of production.

Robert and Peter differ greatly in temperament and work philosophy (they even pronounce the family name differently: the traditional "Mon-DAH-vee" in Robert's case, the Anglicized "Mon-DAY-vee" in Peter's), and at the Krug winery, they rarely got along. "Peter and I had honest differences over the rate at which we could increase our operations," Mondavi told Tony Chiu for *People* (October 20, 1980). "I wanted to move faster than my brother. But as long as my dad was living, he settled all issues." In 1959 Cesare died, leaving his sons to resolve their own disputes. In 1965 an argument over large promotional expenditures, which Robert favored and Peter considered wasteful, erupted into a physical clash. The confrontation prompted Robert to leave Charles Krug (while retaining a 24 percent share of the company) and start his own vineyard.

With two partners and a total investment of $200,000, Robert launched the Robert Mondavi Winery, in Oakville, California. After growing quickly at first, the business reached a plateau, because of limited capacity and funds. In 1969 Mondavi's two founding partners sold their portions of the vineyard to the Seattle-based beer merchant Rainier Companies, which was controlled at the time by Canada's second-largest beer manufacturer, Molson. Rainier invested millions in the winery, kept the Mondavi name, and reportedly did not interfere with Mondavi's management. Nevertheless, Mondavi felt dissatisfied, because he held only a 25 percent share in the company that bore his name.

In 1977 Rainier sold its brewing operations, keeping as its only concrete asset Mondavi's winery. Mondavi saw Rainier's action as a chance to make an offer to Molson for its 48 percent stake in Rainier and thus gain a majority control of his winery. Mondavi had tried to liquidate the vestigial percentage he held in the Charles Krug Winery, but his brother, through multiple court actions, had prevented him. In January 1978 the brothers finally came to an agreement out of court. The settlement enabled Mondavi to finance an offer to Molson of $9.40 per share for Molson's one million shares of Rainier. Molson accepted, and Mondavi wound up controlling more than 60 percent of his winery, 1,000 acres of vineyards, and a second winery, in Woodbridge, California.

Beyond a handful of summer courses taken at the University of California at Davis and his apprenticeship to his father, Robert Mondavi has no formal training in enology (the formal name for the science that deals with wine and wine making). That gap in his professional education notwithstanding, he used scientific methods, careful observation, and experimentation to develop better ways to make wine. At the same time, Mondavi regards wine making as more an art than a science. "Anyone who can read a book can make wine," he told Tony Chiu. "But there are some 400 variables, and like children, they change all the time. When you can adjust to bring out the best in a given crop, I call it art." Mondavi believed in enhancing subtleties in flavor, which were noticeably absent in American wines when he began his career. Such subtle differences in flavor distinguish varietals. (In contrast to generic wines, a varietal wine is made up chiefly of one variety of grape.) Through his research Mondavi discovered that differences in room temperature during fermentation affect the flavor of the product. He became the first California vintner to make extensive use of the so-called cold fermentation method (which requires conducting the fermentation process with the air temperature between 55 and 60 degrees Fahrenheit).

In addition, by altering fermentation techniques traditionally used on particular varieties of grapes, Mondavi succeeded in producing new classes of wine. One example is pinot blanc (white pinot), which, before Mondavi began his experiments, was a generally unpopular wine. By changing aspects of the fermentation process, he created a sweeter wine, which he called chenin blanc. In another case Mondavi fermented the unpopular sauvignon blanc so as to produce a drier—or less sweet—wine. He then combined it with wine made from another grape, semillon, and aged the blend. He christened his new concoction fume blanc. Both chenin blanc and fume blanc became prodigious sellers.

During his first trip to Europe, in 1962, Mondavi observed that the finest wines on the continent were aged in small oak casks. He noted that the size of the casks, too, significantly affected flavor. Those discoveries proved to be key to the improvement of the quality of American wines. California wines had been aged in either steel or redwood vats or barrels normally used for brandy and bourbon, and they emerged flat and without character—"industrially uniform, like Coca-Cola," Baron Philippe de Rothschild, the owner of the renowned French winery Chateau Mouton-Rothschild, famously quipped in 1973. Mondavi acknowledged to Tony Chiu, "At the time the Baron said what he did, he wasn't too far wrong. We used the same process on every type of grape, so they did come out tasting very similar." After returning to California from his maiden voyage to Europe, Mondavi purchased more than 100 French-made oak barrels of various sizes and, by means of a series of experiments, greatly improved the flavors of his wines.

Mondavi's trips to Europe, which he devoted to touring as well as to professional investigations, are legendary among vintners, because he always left a strong impression on his companions and hosts. "A couple of days on tour with Dad and you need a vacation from the vacation," his daughter, Marcia, told Frank J. Prial for the New York Times (July 15, 1979). Commenting on one such trip, the Italian wine producer Angelo Gaja told Prial for the New York Times (December 26, 1990), "He came here to Alba [in northeast Italy] to see what I do, but I think I learned more from him than he did from me."

Shortly after Mondavi took financial control of his eponymous winery, in 1978, he and the Baron Philippe de Rothschild, who less than a decade before had denigrated American wine, became partners in the first-ever enterprise of its kind. Under the terms of their agreement, Mondavi provided land and facilities and the baron made available the expertise of his wine master, Lucien Sionneaux, to produce a premium California cabernet. The deal sent tremors throughout the wine industry. The growing quality and popularity of California wines had already been recognized internationally—even by the French, who are known for their extreme chauvinism about wine. The resulting cabernet, sold under the label Opus One (decorated with the silhouetted profiles of both the baron and Mondavi), has consistently fetched market prices comparable to those of French "first growth" wines, and it remains a favorite of connoisseurs. ("First growth" is a classification established in France for its best wine makers. Only five wineries, among them Chateau Mouton-Rothschild, hold the designation.) Mondavi has since brokered similar successful multinational deals with wine makers in Italy and Chile.

Though known as a tireless and outspoken promoter, Mondavi has avoided the image of a huckster by promoting fine wine as a lifestyle rather than a product. "Making great wine and letting people taste it is what sells fine wine," Mondavi has said, as quoted in a bio of him on his winery's Web site. He introduced tastings at which consumers as well as people in the industry could evaluate wines. At the hospitality center that he built near

Los Angeles, his staff hosts dinners, cooking classes, concerts, and poetry readings. Known to give speeches on a moment's notice about the value of wine in culture, he believes that, like art, fine food, travel, and music, the moderate consumption of wine is a crucial part of a healthful, balanced life. "By traveling and tasting, I've discovered that a good wine—like a good life—is balanced and harmonious," Mondavi wrote in *National Geographic Traveler* (March 1992). "It represents the best of everything and not too much of one thing."

Robert Mondavi became particularly vocal about wine in the late 1980s, when anti-alcohol advocacy gained strength as a movement. Widespread concerns about drunk driving and the effects of excessive drinking on health contributed to a growing neo-Prohibitionist ethic. Beginning in 1990 the federal government mandated that health warnings be printed on all wines and other alcoholic beverages sold in the United States. Mondavi countered by contending that wine should be savored for its flavor and not consumed to excess. He frequently cited a seeming paradox with regard to the French: although the diets of many French people are high in fats, heart disease is much less prevalent in France, where daily consumption of wine in modest quantities is virtually universal, than it is in the U.S. And to those who rejected the use of alcohol on religious grounds, Mondavi pointed out that for centuries, wine has been a component of religious rituals in many parts of the world.

The Robert Mondavi Winery has been a family business since its inception. Mondavi's second wife, Margrit Biever, a Swiss-born polyglot who lived in various European and Asian countries while growing up, is vice president for cultural affairs. Mondavi's three children, Michael, Tim, and Marcia (all from his first marriage), are equal shareholders in the company. Marcia is currently a member of the board and conducts public-relations events across the country on behalf of the winery. In 1990 Robert Mondavi signed his executive operations over to his two sons. At first Michael and Tim shared the CEO title and responsibilities, but that led to arguments reminiscent of the battles between Robert and Peter, who only recently made peace with each other. To avoid further conflict, Robert and his sons established a hierarchy in which Michael, the elder brother, would assume full duties as president and CEO, and Tim would be managing director and winegrower. At a date yet to be determined, Michael will retire, and Tim will gain control of the operations. The family also has brought in outside managers to introduce fresh ideas and further reduce family conflict.

Since Robert Mondavi's semiretirement, the winery has continued to reap handsome profits. With land holdings totaling 5,300 acres and an output of approximately six million cases of wine each year, the winery is the eighth largest in the country. In 1993, in an effort to generate capital, the company offered shares of its stock publicly, thus becoming only the third winery in United

States history to do so. Though wineries are generally considered a questionable investment because of the vagaries of weather and other natural phenomena, Mondavi stock has performed well on the Nasdaq Stock Market; the reason, according to various observers, is the stability of the firm's management. The family retains 70 percent ownership of the corporation.

In 1995 the Mondavi winery became the first to make extensive use of mainstream advertising. With the recent proliferation of, and domination of the market by, warehouse-like discount retailers, and with thousands of new labels to choose from, quality and word of mouth among distributors and small retailers are no longer sufficient to generate sales of premium wines. To capitalize on the family's wide name recognition, Mondavi placed ads in consumer magazines with a national reach. Their Web site, too, was launched as part of the marketing push.

Robert Mondavi has published a memoir, *Harvest of Joy: My Passion for Excellence* (1998), which he co-wrote with Paul Chutkow. He is currently setting up the American Center for Wine, Food, and the Arts. To be located in Napa, the center is designed to be an educational, culinary, and performing-arts institute and venue. For his contributions to the wine industry, Robert Mondavi has received numerous awards, among them the Medal of Honor from L'Ordre Mondial; the Merit Award from the American Society of Enology and Viticulture; and a total of nine Man of the Year honors, three from the Christermon Foundation, three from *Decanter* magazine, and three from *Wines & Vines* magazine. — T.J.F.

Suggested Reading: *Brandweek* p17 Jan. 22, 1996; *Business Week* p34 Apr. 17, 1978, with photo; *Forbes* p203+ Oct. 23, 1995, with photos; *Fortune* p99+ Mar. 11, 1991, with photo; *National Geographic Traveler* p38 Mar. 1992, with photo; *New York Times* III p7 July 15, 1979, with photo, C p1+ Apr. 16, 1980, with photo, C p14 June 29, 1988, with photo, C p1 May 19, 1993, with photo, p39+ June 18, 1994, with photo, F p8 Nov. 4, 1998; *People* p113+ Oct. 20, 1980, with photos, p151+ Oct. 12, 1998, with photos; *robertmondavi.com* (on-line)

Montenegro, Fernanda

1929– Actress. Address: Avenida Vieira Souto 408/5º Andar, CEP 22 420 000 Rio de Janeiro, RJ, Brazil; Rua Costa Carvalho No. 403, apto. 301, Pinheiros, CEP: 05429-130, São Paulo/SP, Brazil

Fernanda Montenegro, who has been called the "first lady of the Brazilian theater" and a national treasure of Brazil, has been working in theater, television, and film in her native land for more than 50

Fernanda Montenegro

Bill Davila/Retna Ltd.

years; her credits include parts in more than 50 theatrical plays, some 200 television plays, 12 soap operas, and nine films, and she has earned well over 40 awards for her acting. Nevertheless, she remained practically unknown in the United States until 1999, when her performance in the acclaimed Brazilian film *Central do Brasil*, or *Central Station*, earned her an Academy Award nomination for best actress. Because Montenegro's command of English is limited, Larry Rohter noted in the *New York Times* (March 21, 1999, on-line), Hollywood scripts "are not likely to come showering down on her." But, he pointed out, "making a career abroad has never been her top priority." "We have great actors and actresses right here [in Brazil], and wonderful stories to tell," Montenegro told him. "I wouldn't change my life experience for that of any actor in any other culture. Being an actor in Brazil is like living an adventure that never ends."

Of Italian and Portuguese descent, Fernanda Montenegro was born Arlette Pinheiro Esteves da Silva in 1929 in Jacarepaguá, a working-class suburb of Rio de Janeiro. Her father was a mechanic with Rio's public utility company. Montenegro told Rohter that the cinema made a great impression on her when she was a child. "I am from a generation that, from the time we could sit in our mothers' laps, went to the movies three or four times a week to savor the dreams we saw on the screen," she said.

When she was 15 years old, Arlette went to an open audition held by the government-owned radio station in Rio de Janeiro and was accepted into a radio-announcer training program. While working for the station, she translated literary works and adapted them for serialization as soap operas.

Concurrently, she taught Portuguese to foreigners and studied English and French at a Berlitz language school. At around this time she decided to take on a more glamorous name. According to the official Fernanda Montenegro Web site, she chose "Fernanda" because "it had . . . a sonority that reminds [one of] the characters of the romances of [the French novelists] Balzac or Proust." The surname "Montenegro" was that of a friend of her family's—a homeopathic doctor who was regarded as "capable of true 'miracles,'" according to the Montenegro Web site.

Montenegro made her theatrical debut in 1950, in the play *Alegres Canções nas Montanhas* ("Happy Songs of the Mountains"), in which a young actor and director named Fernando Torres also appeared. Montenegro and Torres were married in 1953, and her legal name became Arlette Pinheiro Monteiro Torres. Meanwhile, Montenegro had begun getting roles in television detective dramas. She much preferred to work in the theater, however, and she became one of the most popular theater actresses in both Rio de Janeiro and São Paolo.

In 1963 Montenegro and her husband established their own theater company. To raise money for productions in Rio de Janeiro, the couple went virtually door to door asking for help. "Everything we have, the theater has given us," Montenegro told Rohter. "We live in the world of theater, doing plays our entire lives." Montenegro and Torres's company has traveled throughout Brazil on at least 30 tours, bringing both Brazilian dramas and foreign plays in translation to even the smallest towns. The company has presented works by, among others, Racine, Molière, Chekhov, Strindberg, Pirandello, George Bernard Shaw, Edward Albee, Samuel Beckett, Harold Pinter, Eugene O'Neill, Arthur Miller, Noel Coward, Neil Simon, and Brazilian playwrights, prominent among them Nelson Rodriguez. In the 1960s Montenegro also worked as an actress and director for a television program called *Grande Teatro Tupi*, which brought theatrical works to the small screen. To date she has appeared in some 200 teleplays.

The theatrical play for which Montenegro has perhaps become best known is *Dona Doida* ("Miss Crazy"), a one-woman show by the Brazilian writer Adélia Prado, which, according to a Montenegro Web site, "teaches the art of being happy." Sporadically since the late 1980s, Montenegro has performed the work in many parts of Brazil and Portugal. In 1992, in her first appearance in the United States, Montenegro acted with her daughter, the actress Fernanda Torres, in the Brazilian playwright Gerald Thomas's *Flash and Crash Days*, which was featured in that year's Serious Fun Festival at Lincoln Center, in New York City. The play, a "grotesquely funny cartoon or a terrifying children's story for adults," as Montenegro described it to Robert Meyers for the *New York Times* (July 12, 1992), is about the mutually antagonistic and violent relationship between a mother and daughter. Montenegro told Meyers, "This isn't just any mother and any daughter. People outside Brazil could even ignore that, but we know it, and so for us it's also a domestic game." For her part, Fernanda Torres found it "difficult and embarrassing to play violent and erotic scenes with her mother," Myers reported. "But my mother is also a monster to me," Torres said to Myers, "and Gerald [Thomas, with whom Torres was living] understood that and used it. The play between being a monster and a real person is what the work is about."

In the late 1960s Montenegro began to perform in *telenovelas*—soap operas—which are far more respected and more widely viewed in Brazil than they are in the U.S. Among the earliest of the dozen in which she has starred are *Renascer* ("Born Again") and *Brilhante* ("Brilliant"). The actress has described her usual *telenovela* role as that of "the rich woman, the elegant, well-dressed magnate's wife who lives in a big mansion." When asked to compare working on *telenovelas* and films, she told Rohter, "We live in a different reality here [in Brazil]. Nobody can make a living just from acting for films. If I accept a role, I always do it with maximum effort and position myself honestly. I don't disparage it. I throw myself into it. Why am I going to limit myself? If I see an interesting role with a good script and a good cast, why refuse to participate? After all, in the 19th century, Balzac and [the Russian novelist] Dostoevsky wrote serials, which were the equivalent of what television is today." Jose Wilker, who has appeared with Montenegro in several soap operas, told Rohter that "working with her is a lot of fun. At the same time that she is very cultured, intelligent, and well read, she has a great sense of intuition, and as an actor it's quite enjoyable to be challenged to keep pace with that intuition and try to give something back to her."

Montenegro made her cinematic debut in 1964, in *A Falecida* ("The Deceased"), directed by Leon Hirszman from a screenplay by Nelson Rodriguez. The film depicts an unhappy suburban housewife who constantly fantasizes about her own funeral. In 1978 Montenegro appeared in the comedy *Tudo Bem* ("Everything's All Right"), which was directed by Arnaldo Jabor, and in 1981 she starred in another Leon Hirszman film—*Eles Nao Usam Black Tie* ("They Don't Wear Black Tie"). She had a small role in her next film, *A Hora da Estrela* ("Hour of the Star"), directed by Susana Amaral, which was released in the U.S. in 1987 to generally positive reviews. In 1994 Montenegro starred with her husband in *Veja Esta Cancao* ("See This Song"), which contained four separate love stories set in Rio de Janeiro. She was next featured in the Academy Award–nominated *O Que E Isso, Companheiro*, which was released in 1997 in the U.S. and in Europe as *Four Days in September*. Based on a memoir by Fernando Gabeira, the film is about a group of young people who, in the late 1960s, formed a terrorist group that opposed the dictatorship ruling Brazil. The group kidnapped the American ambassador to Brazil as a means of winning the freedom of some of their imprisoned members.

As Montenegro noted to Rohter, the films in which she starred until 1999 remained mostly unknown outside Brazil. "The only time they are likely [to] turn up is when someone is organizing a Brazilian or Latin American film festival." Moreover, in comparison with those of American-made films, the budgets for Brazilian films are generally extremely low. "The Italians showed the Third World that you didn't need a big budget to make a good movie," Montenegro told Rohter. "There was an alternative to Hollywood's way of doing things, and that esthetic infected a whole generation of film makers in Brazil. It was one of our directors from the Cinema Novo period, Glauber Rocha, who talked about needing just an idea in the head and a camera in the hand to make a movie."

Central do Brasil (1998), called *Central Station* in the U.S., was created by the director Walter Salles and the writers Marcos Bernstein and Joao Emanuel Carneiro. "From the very start, the role of Dora was written with her in mind," Salles told Rohter. "I had seen a lot of her theater work and all of the films she had done, and what struck me is that she always brings an integrity to the characters she plays, an interpretation with so many layers it is impossible not to be fascinated." The film tells the story of an irascible old woman and a motherless child who learn to love each other during a journey that takes them from Rio de Janeiro to Brazil's rural frontier. Dora is a retired schoolteacher who earns much-needed money by writing letters for illiterate people, working at a portable desk set up in Rio de Janeiro's Central Station. At the outset of the film, the character seems entirely unsympathetic; not only does she not mail the letters she writes, but she cruelly mocks their authors at the end of the day. "I knew Fernanda would feel a sense of solidarity with the character and not judge her," Salles told Rohter. "That courage to dive into the abyss is what makes her one of the best actresses not just in Brazil, but in the world." The sudden death, right outside the station, of a woman who has asked Dora to write a letter to the father of her young son leads to a change of heart in Dora. She takes the orphaned boy (played by the 10-year-old Vinicius de Oliveira, who was working as a shoeshine boy at an airport when Salles discovered him) into her home and eventually sets out on a journey to find his father. Reviewing *Central Station* in the *New York Times* (November 20, 1998), Janet Maslin wrote, "[Montenegro's] performance here is superbly modulated as Dora begins rediscovering herself in ways she could never have expected. Though eternally gruff, she finds herself regaining a long-lost faith in life and in the very humanity she scorned when those letter writers came her way." "In a performance that suggests toughmindedness and tenderheartedness are not at odds, Montenegro acts the part superbly by playing it with her eyes," an *Entertainment Weekly* critic (March 1, 1999) wrote. "She gracfully moves from the misanthropic (glaring skeptically over wirerimmed spectacles) to the sympathetic (beaming need, fear, and faith). Better yet, she imbues Dora with enough wit (slapstick squints, deadpan double takes) to rescue the movie from its sentimental journey."

In a review for *Maclean's* (January 25, 1999), Brian D. Johnson described *Central Station* as "a road movie with universal appeal" and as "a wonderful movie that mixes compassion, realism, and optimism with a magic that Hollywood continually tries, and fails, to fabricate." At the Berlin Film Festival, *Central Station* won the award for best film, and Montenegro won the Silver Bear Award for best actress. Those tributes caused a buzz in film circles, and Arthur Cohn, the producer of *Central Station*, told Montenegro that she might be considered for an Academy Award for best actress. Montenegro told Rohter that she heard Cohn's words "with disbelief" and regarded them "as simply a compliment, a warmer, nicer way of saying 'Have a pleasant day.'" When news came that she had been officially nominated for the best-actress Oscar (along with Gwyneth Paltrow, Cate Blanchett, Meryl Streep, and Emily Watson), many Brazilians showed their enthusiasm for Montenegro by shouting "We're praying for you!" as she passed them on the street. Montenegro lost the Oscar to Paltrow, but she won several other prizes for her work in *Central Station*, among them the 1999 Golden Satellite Award (given by the International Press Academy, an organization of entertainment journalists), the Los Angeles Film Critics Association Award, and the U.S. National Board of Review award for best actress. She was also nominated for a Golden Globe Award. (*Central Station*, too, won a bevy of prizes, and it was nominated for the Academy Award and the Golden Globe for best foreign-language film.)

Fernanda Montenegro and Fernando Torres live in Rio de Janeiro. Their son, Cláudio Torres, has directed and designed sets for productions mounted by his parents' theatrer company. A film director as well, Cláudio directed his mother in one section of the three-part 1997 film *Traição* ("Betrayal"). In *Sidewalk.com* (on-line), Val Moses described Montenegro, who has won more than 40 theater and film awards in Brazil, as having strawberry blond hair and expressive eyes, as dressing elegantly, and as seeming "stately without being distant." Recalling his interview of her, he wrote, "Occasionally when we find a moment of common ground, she squeezes my hand or touches my shoulder. Even though we cannot communicate directly, she is personable, approachable, soft, and welcoming." Montenegro's daughter, who has worked with her in film and theater, described her to Rohter as being "strong and wise. . . . She comes into a scene like Mike Tyson ready to bite off Evander Holyfield's ear." *O Exercício da Paixão* ("The Exercise of Passion"), a biography of Montenegro by Lucia Rito, was published in Brazil. — C.P.

Suggested Reading: *New York Times* H p5 July 12, 1992, E p10 Nov. 20, 1998, with photo; *New York Times* (on-line) Mar. 21, 1999, with photo; *Sidewalk.com* (on-line), with photo

Selected Films: *A Falecida*, 1965; *Tudo Bem*, 1978; *Eles nao Usam Black Tie*, 1981; *A Hora da Estrela*, 1985; *Fogo e Paixao*, 1988; *Veja Esta Cancao*, 1994; *O Que E Isso, Companheiro*, 1997; *Traicao*, 1997; *Central do Brasil*, 1998

Scott Harrison/Archive Photos

Morgan, Lorrie

June 27, 1959– Country singer. Address: c/o BNA Entertainment/RCA Records, 1 Music Circle N., Nashville, TN 37203

When the country-music star Lorrie Morgan sings about the loss of loved ones, relationships gone sour, loneliness, and other painful and distressing events and emotions, she brings to her interpretations a diaryful of personal knowledge and experience. Her father died when she was a teenager; the first and third of her four marriages ended in divorce; the second came to an abrupt end when her husband of four years—with whom, she has said, "I was happier than I'd ever been in my life"—died of an overdose of alcohol; she went bankrupt; her career remained in the doldrums for years; her romances made her the target of supermarket tabloids. Knowing so well whereof she sings may be an important ingredient in the success of *Leave the Light On*, *Something in Red*, "Out of Your Shoes," "Five Minutes," and others among her albums and singles. In an impressive demonstration of her popularity, she is a four-time winner (in 1994, 1996, 1997, and 1998) of the TNN (the Nashville Network) Music City News Award for female vocalist of the year, the winner of which is determined through ballots cast by fans.

Lorrie Morgan's life has been inextricably tied to country music since her birth, on June 27, 1959, in Hendersonville, Tennessee. Originally named Loretta Lynn Morgan, she is the youngest of the five children—four daughters and a son—of Anna Trainor and George Morgan. Her father was a country-music star; best remembered for his 1949 hit "Candy Kisses," he was for many years a featured performer at the Grand Ole Opry, the entertainment complex and country-music mecca in Nashville, Tennessee, from which a country-music program was broadcast weekly on radio from 1943 to 1974. As a child Morgan often spent time with the country-music stars her father knew.

Morgan began performing publicly at age 13, when, with her father's encouragement, she sang "Paper Roses" at the Grand Ole Opry's famous Ryman Auditorium. Her "knees were absolutely knocking," she recalled to Steve Dougherty for *People* (May 7, 1990). "But I saw Dad standing there just bawling, and those people gave me a standing ovation. I thought, 'This is what I'm doing the rest of my life.' I thought it was going to be that easy. Little did I know."

Off and on during the next three years, Morgan toured with her father and his band. In 1975 George Morgan died, at age 50, during heart surgery. The 16-year-old Lorrie felt overwhelmed by grief; her father, she has said, was one of "the two most important men" in her life (the other was her second husband, Keith Whitley). Nevertheless, after his death, she continued touring with her father's band for almost two years. Then she left the group, having decided to pursue a solo career.

For the next several years, Morgan performed in such unglamorous venues as county fairs, honky-tonks, and the Opryland USA amusement park. Meanwhile, in 1976, she landed a spot as the opening act for the country music star George Jones. During the nearly two years that she remained with Jones, she gained a reputation in and around Nashville as a capable singer.

In 1979 Morgan signed a recording contract with Hickory Records, a small label based in Nashville, and she released several singles. Also that year, she married the steel guitarist Ron Gaddis. Their marriage, which produced one daughter, was rocky, and it ended in divorce in 1980, in part because of Gaddis's and Morgan's excessive drinking. "I went through a wild period," Morgan told Robert K. Oermann for the *Washington Post* (March 18, 1995). "I guess I grew up real quick. I did a little too much drinking and a little too much partying." For several years following her divorce, she took a break from the music business, concentrating instead on putting her life back in order and raising her daughter.

After resuming her career, in 1984, Morgan released a single, "Don't Go Changing," on the MCA label. She also joined the regulars at the Grand Ole Opry, thereby becoming, at age 25, the youngest member of the Opry cast. Recalling her debut with the Opry, she told *People Weekly's Country Music Supplement* (Fall 1994), "That was a great night. I was teary-eyed thinking of my father, wishing he was there. He would have been so proud." For the next several years, she performed at the Opry and appeared in *Nashville Now*, the Opry's cable-television show, which aired on TNN.

Despite those achievements, national prominence—which she had long sought—eluded her. A big part of the problem stemmed from her failure to make an album, which in turn stemmed from her inability to persuade recording executives of her appeal as a musician. At the time—the mid-1980s—the trend in country music was shifting toward a more pop sound, and Morgan's style, many executives reportedly felt, too closely reflected the traditional style of Grand Ole Opry performers. Morgan has never attempted to distance herself from the Opry and its veteran stars. "I loved them all," she told Oermann, "especially Tammy Wynette. At the Opry, Jeannie Seely is a wonderful friend of mine. She was very supportive of me, as were Jean Shepard and Jeannie Pruett. I can't get next to half of the female artists who are out there right now. It's all so competitive. These people here at the Opry don't care about that." She then added, "All the ladies here are my buddies. It's like, 'We're friends in country music. Let's hang out.' The Opry is about sharing."

In November 1986 Morgan married the country-music singer Keith Whitley. After Whitley's 1988 album, *Don't Close Your Eyes*, became a hit, the couple (who now had an infant son) became the darlings of country-music fans. Meanwhile, in the late 1980s, country music had started to return to traditional styles, and in 1988 Whitley succeeded in persuading his record company, RCA, to sign Morgan to a contract. Soon afterward Morgan began recording her debut album, *Leave the Light On*.

As Morgan and friends of Whitley's knew, Whitley had a long history of alcohol abuse; he would remain sober for months at a stretch and then, apparently tormented by self-doubt, binge on such huge quantities of alcohol that he would have to be hospitalized. One day in May 1989, while Morgan was in Alaska promoting the yet-to-be-released *Leave the Light On*, Whitley "literally drank himself to death," as Ron Tannenbaum reported in *TV Guide* (August 14, 1993); an autopsy revealed that he had died of alcohol poisoning. A week later—on a date chosen before the tragedy—*Leave the Light On* was released, and thanks in part to the publicity surrounding Whitley's death, it eventually sold more than one million copies. Positive reviews also helped boost sales; in one such assessment, written for the *Chicago Tribune* (July 9, 1989), Jack Hurst described the album as "a masterful combination of vocal emotion and vocal beauty." The album, Hurst declared, "is no dyed-in-the-wool stab at traditionalism; it is one of the richer, more vocally diverse and yet utterly heartfelt-sounding LPs on the current market." "Dear Me," a song from *Leave the Light On* about a woman who recalls a lost love in a letter she writes to herself, became a Top 10 single. "Here I am in this tragedy," Morgan told Steve Dougherty, "and I had something I had wanted for so long, a hit record."

Morgan canceled few if any of her singing dates after Whitley's death. By her own account, maintaining her heavy schedule—about 16 performances per month—helped her cope with her grief and with the mental and emotional pain caused by "whispers," to use Tannenbaum's word, that suggested that because she had left Whitley to go on tour, she was somehow responsible for his death. "The audiences are my therapists," she explained to Dougherty. "The more emotional I am, the more I can release the pain." By May 1990, two of Morgan's singles—"Out of Your Shoes" and "Five Minutes"—had each reached the top spot on the country-music charts.

Morgan's second album, *Something in Red*, was released in 1991. Four of its songs became hits, and the album reached platinum status. Morgan's third album, *Watch Me*, came out in 1992; its title song turned into a hit single. Jack Hurst, writing for the *Chicago Tribune* (November 15, 1992), described *Watch Me* as "a smashing demonstration of the sophisticated traditional style that has made [Morgan] easy to listen to." Also in 1992, Country Music Television named Morgan the female vocalist of the year.

Her troubles were far from over, however. According to Tannenbaum, in 1992 or 1993 she had to deal with "a lawsuit from her management, a hysterectomy, and bankruptcy." Her falling-out with her manager led her to organize her own production team. "I'm starting to build an organization around myself where everybody involved with me cares legitimately about Lorrie," she told Jack Hurst for the *Chicago Tribune* (November 15, 1992). "When it's all over, of course, I'm going to come out looking like a bitch. If a man in this business is strong-willed, weeding out people who aren't right, he's an intelligent man. A woman who does it is a bitch." Also in 1992 she entered into a third marriage, to Brad Thompson, who drove the tour bus owned by the country-music singer Clint Black; that union ended in divorce after a year and a half. "I hope that in time I can totally erase it from my mind," Morgan told Tannenbaum.

At around that time, Morgan tried her hand at acting, something she had long wanted to do. In the cable-television movie *Proudheart* (1993), which TNN broadcast in 1993, she starred as a single mother who puts her life on hold to care for her mother after the death of her father. Morgan identified strongly with the character. "I felt hostility toward my own mother at times," she admitted to Tannenbaum. "After I divorced my first husband, I was living at home, with someone telling me how

to raise my child." Following her divorce from Thompson, she had a series of relationships with high-profile figures—among them the Dallas Cowboy quarterback Troy Aikman, the singer Kenny Rogers, and U.S. senator Fred Thompson—that attracted a lot of media attention.

In 1994 Morgan released her next album, *Warpaint*, which contains such hit singles as "My Night to Howl" and "Heart Over Mind." Then, venturing again into acting, she starred in *The Enemy Within*, a television movie that aired on the ABC network in 1995. Two compilation albums, *Reflections* and *Greatest Hits*, followed in 1996. That summer, along with such singers as Pam Tillis and Carlene Carter, Morgan took part in the Kraft Country Tour, country music's first all-female concert tour. Soon afterward she teamed up with John Randall to sing the duet "By My Side" for her album *Greater Need* (1996). Morgan and Randall, who met through their collaboration on that album, were married in November 1996. Morgan coproduced her next album, *Shakin' Things Up* (1997). That same year she published her memoir, *Forever Yours, Faithfully: My Love Story*, which was co-written by George Vecsey. An account of her marriage to Keith Whitley, it reveals the extent of Whitley's dependence on alcohol. Her aim in writing the book, Morgan told Arlene Vigoda for *USA Today* (November 25, 1998, on-line), was to "let people know you can't love someone into sobriety. It just doesn't work."

For her most recent album, *Secret Love* (1998), Morgan moved beyond the country-music genre. Accompanied by a symphony orchestra, she offered love songs by George Gershwin and pop standards from the 1940s and 1950s. She has credited her eclectic musical interests to her father, who, she has said, encouraged her to be open to good music of all genres. Commenting on the theme of *Secret Love*, she told Wendy Newcomer for *Countryweekly Online* (October 6, 1998), "Everybody—whether you're male, female, young or old—loves romance and dreams of the knight in shining armor or the princess in the tower. It represents a less stressful time. I grew up appreciating and really loving that kind of music because my dad listened to it."

Morgan lives in Hendersonville, Tennessee, with her husband, her teenage daughter, Morgan Anastasia, and her son, Jesse Keith. She enjoys swimming, golf, and board games and sits on the board of directors of the Country Music Association. — Y.P.

Suggested Reading: *Chicago Tribune* XIII p24+ July 9, 1989, with photo, XIII p20+ Nov. 15, 1992, with photo, XIII p26 June 18, 1995, with photo; *People* p177+ May 7, 1990, with photos; *TV Guide* p22+ Aug. 14, 1993, with photos; *Washington Post* D p1+ Mar. 18, 1995, with photos

Selected Recordings: *Leave the Light On*, 1989; *Something In Red*, 1991; *Watch Me*, 1992; *Warpaint*, 1994; *Reflections*, 1996; *Greatest Hits*, 1996; *Greater Need*, 1996; *Shakin' Things Up*, 1997; *Secret Love*, 1998

Selected Books: with George Vecsey—*Forever Yours, Faithfully: My Love Story*, 1997

Selected Television Movies: *Proudheart*, 1993; *The Enemy Within*, 1995

Courtesy of Judy Schoen & Associates

Morton, Joe

Oct. 18, 1947– Actor and director. Address: c/o Judy Schoen & Associates, 606 N. Larchmont Blvd., Suite 309, Los Angeles, CA 90004

During a career that spans nearly three decades, the veteran stage, television, and screen actor Joe Morton has played a wide variety of intelligent, well-rounded characters—a scientist, doctors, lawyers, a police officer, and even a wise, three-toed, mute alien from outer space. Morton, an African-American, selected many of these roles with an eye toward broadening the range of character types portrayed by African-American actors. "I try to read for roles that could be played by white people," he told Jon Silberg for *American Film* (April 1988). As Morton explained to Deborah Gregory for *Essence* (August 1990), "For a Black actor there are always problems. Years ago it was because there weren't enough roles. Nowadays it's difficult convincing a director to 'go Black' on a part that's not color-specified." Speaking of the casting niches

successful African-American film actors have carved for themselves in Hollywood, Morton told Felicia R. Lee for the *New York Times* (May 18, 1995), "My category is 'that guy who happens to be black.'" He continued, "The black community at large reacts to those roles very strongly. It gives them pride, it gives them honor. They know I'm not going to do something that will make them ashamed."

Morton made a name for himself in 1973 when he earned a Tony Award nomination for his performance in the Broadway musical *Raisin*. Over the next decade he made numerous film and television appearances. In the 1980s he formed a creative friendship with the highly regarded director John Sayles, who cast Morton in the title role in his acclaimed film *The Brother from Another Planet* (1984). A witty story with a distinctive spin on racial issues, the film became a cult classic, and Morton's role in it is arguably the one for which he is most famous. In the 1990s Morton appeared in two more critically praised John Sayles movies, *City of Hope* (1991) and *Lone Star* (1996). In 1989 Morton was cast in the television series *Equal Justice*; more recently he appeared in the Arnold Schwarzenegger vehicle *Terminator 2: Judgment Day* (1991); *Of Mice and Men* (1992); and both *Speed* (1994) and *Speed 2: Cruise Control* (1997). "All I bemoan is that there is not a lot of choice in terms of seeing different kinds of black people in the world," Morton told Christopher Kimble for *Premiere* (September 1991), "because there are."

The son of Joe T. Morton and his wife, Evelyn, Joe Morton was born on October 18, 1947 in New York City. His father was a captain in the intelligence arm of the U.S. Army, and not long after Joe's birth, Captain Morton was assigned to help integrate American army bases overseas. Until Joe was 10, the family relocated frequently. "At four, I was in Okinawa, playing in a field of bamboo, eating escargots we found in the back yard . . . ," Morton told Robert Wahls for the New York *Sunday News* (October 28, 1973.) "I learned to speak Japanese and the derivative Okinawan dialect." The Mortons lived in Hawaii and then the Azores before settling in Dachau, Germany. Morton has recalled overtly racist actions by white military families in army communities and race-related fights between him and white boys his age. As an eight-year-old, he sold Christmas cards door to door; one day a white boy responded to his ring, and Morton heard him call out matter-of-factly, "Mommy, there's a nigger at the door." Morton has said that more often than not, white officers refused to believe that his father, a proud and outspoken man, was a fellow officer. "One thing [my father] did for me was present me with a painting of a black Santa Claus," Morton told Lee. "No one had ever introduced me to the concept that Santa could be someone who looked like me."

One morning while the family was living in Dachau, Morton's mother later told him, his father woke her before he left for work and said, "If anything happened to me and I didn't say good-bye, you'd never have forgiven me." That day Morton's father was killed in a jeep accident during maneuvers. The army reported that the captain had been thrown from the car, but his injuries were inconsistent with their version of what had happened. The man who had been in the jeep with Morton's father when the accident occurred refused to speak openly about the incident. "My theory," Morton told Kimble, "is that [my father] was causing too many waves in terms of trying to put forward the ideas of black officers. He just got to be a burr under somebody's saddle, and they shot him." Morton has often said that he would like to find out the truth about how his father died, and perhaps, he told Lee, turn the story into "something artistic, in a film."

After his father's death, Morton and his mother moved to the Sugar Hill section of Harlem, in New York City, where Morton's grandmother Autherine Hoagland lived. His mother later became a medical secretary. Because of his slight German accent and unusually "proper" behavior, Morton was teased by other kids, and he was often chased home. "Race prejudice has nothing to do with color. It has to do with being the stranger," he observed to Lee. Morton's mother enrolled him at St. Joseph's Academy in Newburgh, New York, where nuns taught the academic subjects and officers from Stewarts Air Force Base (which was located across the street) administered military training. "It was a great time for me," Morton told Wahls. "We were treated like little adults. And when I left after eighth grade, I was the second-ranking student, a major, and major of the band. I'd learned discipline and how to study, and I did a little composing and mastered the steel guitar after a few raps on the knuckles."

After the eighth grade, Morton entered Andrew Jackson High School in the St. Albans section of the New York City borough of Queens. It was his first experience at a public school as well as the first school he had attended where the majority of the students (60 percent) were African-American. He told Wahls that in his estimation, the school was "way behind both the German schools and St. Joseph's, and I missed small classes and being encouraged to explore my mind. But I've always known enough to take the good in any situation."

Morton won a scholarship to Hofstra University, in Hempstead, New York. He started his freshman year (1964–65) as a psychology major but soon switched to drama. "I was the only black drama student and I found it frustrating, but I learned," he told Wahls. "At first, there were only walk-ons and bit parts. And academically, I was into Shakespeare and the Greeks. There was nothing nasty about race. It was just that the students and plays were white. I made a little noise and I was cast in *Madwoman of Chaillot*. And they gave me Leroi Jones' *The Dutchman* to cast and direct, maybe the first integrated company. I enjoyed myself."

After three years Morton dropped out of college to pursue a career in the performing arts. In 1968 he won his first major role, in an Off-Broadway production entitled *A Month of Sundays*. Since that time he has rarely been out of work as an actor. Following *A Month of Sundays* he appeared on stage in the musicals *Hair* and *Jesus Christ Superstar* and in the plays *Salvation* and *Two Gentlemen of Verona*. During that period Morton appeared on the CBS soap opera *Search for Tomorrow*.

In 1973 Morton got his big break: a featured role in *Raisin*, an original Broadway musical that showcased his musical and acting talents and earned him a Tony Award nomination. At about the time he finished his stint in *Raisin*, he felt the need to focus all his energy on his acting career. Partly for that reason, he and his wife, a schoolteacher whom he had married in 1971, divorced. In 1974 he was cast in the television series *Grady* (1975); it lasted only a season, but it led to numerous other parts on television for Morton, including ones in *Lawman Without a Gun* (1977), *Death Penalty* (1980), *We're Fighting Back* (1981), and a regular role on the daytime drama *Another World* (1983–84).

In 1984 Morton appeared in *The Brother from Another Planet*, which John Sayles wrote as well as directed and which won rave reviews. Morton didn't speak a word of dialogue in the film, but the script attracted him nevertheless. "It was, in fact, primarily a black science-fiction screenplay . . . ," he told Lawrence Van Gelder for the *New York Times* (September 14, 1984). "The analogy was to the underground railway of slave days. It took a traditional story and flipped it around in terms of science fiction." Morton told Christopher John Farley for *USA Today* (May 29, 1990), "If I'm going to be tagged with any one movie, that should be the one, because of what the film had to say and how it was done. Plus, I met my wife [Nora Chavoorshian] on that movie; she designed the sets. I have a lot of good feelings about the movie." Not long after the shooting of the film, Morton and Chavoorshian, who is also a sculptor, got married, and they moved into a converted sewing-machine factory in the New York City borough of Brooklyn with Hopi, Morton's teenage daughter from his first marriage.

In 1986 Morton played the devil's assistant in the film *Crossroads*, and in 1988 he starred as the prosecuting attorney in *The Good Mother*, with Diane Keaton in the title role. He played a victim of a racially motivated attack in *Howard Beach: Making a Case for Murder* (1989), a television film based on the true story of three young black men whose car broke down in front of a pizza parlor in a predominantly white Queens neighborhood in 1986. The tap dancer and actor Gregory Hines, who remembered him from his days on Broadway, recruited Morton to play opposite him as a psychotic thief in the moderately successful film *Tap* (1989). Morton and Chavoorshian's son, Ara, was born that same year.

In the fall of 1989, Morton was cast in the ABC crime drama *Equal Justice*. The producer-director Thomas Carter and his colleagues "wanted me to play an Al Sharpton-type role," he told Michael E. Hill for the *Washington Post* (December 3, 1989), referring to the outspoken activist minister. But Morton persuaded Carter to let him audition for the leading role, that of chief prosecutor Mike Pirelli, whom the writers had envisioned as an Italian-American. "My pitch was that you could have a black . . . with an upper middle- or upper-class background with an interest in justice," he told Hill. Overcoming the producers' reservations, he won the part. "Once they gave me the role," Morton told Farley, "we kept everything that had been in the original, the fact that he was an opera buff, a gourmet Italian cook, all of that stayed intact. Because my point is that there is a wide range of types of black people in the world." Although *Equal Justice* was critically acclaimed, its ratings were dismal, and the series was canceled after only one season. Shortly thereafter Morton joined the cast of the NBC series *A Different World*, a spin-off of the highly successful sitcom *The Cosby Show*.

In John Sayles's film *City of Hope* (1991), Morton played Wynn Himes, a college professor turned city councilman in a fictitious city in New Jersey who is "trying desperately to stay clean," as Morton told Christopher Kimble. Morton also appeared in the hugely popular film *Terminator 2: Judgment Day*. He told Kimble that he took the role because "when it comes to sci-fi films, black people usually have no presence whatsoever. . . . This character clearly has something to do with how the future will come out."

In 1993 Morton tried his hand at directing, first an Off-Broadway play, and shortly thereafter, an episode of the Fox series *Tribeca*, in which he also starred. Fox did not pick up *Tribeca* as a regular series. Later that year Morton and Chavoorshian's daughter, Seta, was born, and the family moved to Essex County, New Jersey. Over the next few years, Morton appeared in various films and television programs; of the former, the most notable are *Of Mice and Men* (1992), *The Inkwell* (1994), and the highly successful action film *Speed* (1994), which starred Keanu Reeves and Sandra Bullock.

Then a script for a television drama arrived from Thomas Carter, the producer-director who had cast Morton in *Equal Justice*. The series was entitled *Under One Roof*, and Morton accepted the role of an ex-marine who is forced by financial problems to move into the home of his recently widowed father, played by James Earl Jones. "It's a family drama," Morton told Michael E. Hill for the *Washington Post* (April 2, 1995). "It's a chance to project some different images of African-Americans. . . . There's never been an African-American drama on TV. There's never been an all-black drama." Most critics praised the show, in some cases lavishly: Lee reported that the *New York Times* television critic John O'Connor called it "the best new family drama of the season." While *Under One Roof*

earned moderately good ratings in its first weeks on the air, it later fared poorly, and CBS dropped the show. Earlier, Morton had turned down the role of Peter Benton on *ER*, a series that became the runaway hit of the 1994 season. "I felt *ER* was a great role, a great part," he told Hill (April 2, 1995), "but *Under One Roof* is a historic event, something that's never been done before. It seemed like that was what I should do." During the next three years, he was involved in three acclaimed but short-lived television series: *New York News* (1995), *Prince Street* (1997), and *Mercy Point* (1998), playing a reporter, an undercover cop, and a doctor, respectively.

Three of Morton's recent film projects have brought him considerable attention. In *Lone Star* (1996), perhaps John Sayles's best-received film to date, he played a career marine colonel who resembled Morton's father in many ways. In 1997 he appeared in the made-for-TV film *Miss Evers' Boys*, about an infamous medical study conducted in Macon County, Georgia, in 1932, in which 412 African-American men infected with syphilis were led to believe they were receiving treatment when in actuality they were getting placebos. Morton played a doctor in the film, which won several awards. In *Apt Pupil* (1998), a film inspired by a Stephen King short story, Morton played an FBI agent assigned to track down a Nazi war criminal. In the latter half of the 1990s he also appeared in *Speed 2: Cruise Control* (1997), in which he reprised the role he had played in *Speed*, that of Captain Herb MacMahon. (In the latter film he was uncredited.) He was also in the casts of three soon-forgotten films: *Trouble on the Corner* (1997), *The Pest* (1997), and *When It Clicks* (1998). In *Blues Brothers 2000* (1998), a sequel to the cult favorite *The Blues Brothers*, he portrayed police commander Cabel Chamberlain.

In the fall of 1998, winning a dramatic part on Broadway for the first time, Morton joined the cast of *Art*, by the Parisian playwright Yasmina Reza. Morton, the first black man to appear in the production, told Jesse McKinley for the *New York Times* (December 18, 1998), "I think it's refreshing that the black actor is not playing the least intelligent character on stage." Morton starred as Supreme Court Justice Thurgood Marshall in the television movie *Mutiny* (1999), and he acted in *The Astronaut's Wife* (1999). He will appear in the films *What Lies Beneath* and *Bounce*, both of which are scheduled to reach theaters in 2000.

In his conversation with Lee in 1995, Morton talked about his quarter-century-long efforts to change the images and stereotypes of African-Americans in film and television. Lee wrote, "He now aspires, he said, to make films in which African-Americans are as sophisticated, romantic, and complex—and even mundane—as they are in real life." Morton asked Lee rhetorically, "When was the last time you saw a straight black love story without any guns?" According to Lee, the office of Morton's New Jersey house is "filled with books, music, photographs, and a mini-studio of equipment on which Mr. Morton records blues songs and strums the guitar, just for his own pleasure." — M.B.

Suggested Reading: *American Film* p72 Apr. 1988; *Essence* p45 Aug. 1990, with photo; *Premiere* p53 Sep. 1991, with photo; *New York Times* C p1 May 18, 1995, with photos, C p18 June 22, 1995, with photo, C p1 June 21, 1996, with photo; *USA Today* D p3 May 29, 1990, with photo, D p3 Mar. 23, 1993, with photo; *Washington Post* E p1 Mar. 14, 1995, with photo, TV Week p7 Apr. 2, 1995, with photos

Selected Films: *Between the Lines*, 1977; . . . *And Justice for All*, 1979; *The Clairvoyant*, 1982; *Brother from Another Planet*, 1984; *Trouble in Mind*, 1985; *Crossroads*, 1986; *Stranded*, 1987; *Zelly and Me*, 1988; *Hostile Witness*, 1988, *The Good Mother*, 1988; *Tap*, 1989; *City of Hope*, 1991; *Terminator 2: Judgment Day*, 1991; *Forever Young*, 1992; *Of Mice and Men*, 1992; *The Inkwell*, 1994; *Speed*, 1994; *The Walking Dead*, 1995; *Executive Decision*, 1996; *Lone Star*, 1996;

Trouble on the Corner, 1997; *The Pest*, 1997; *Speed 2: Cruise Control*, 1997; *When It Clicks*, 1998; *Apt Pupil*, 1998; *Blues Brothers 2000*, 1998; *The Astronaut's Wife*, 1999

Selected Plays and Musicals: as actor—*A Month of Sundays*, 1968; *Hair*, 1969; *Jesus Christ Superstar*, 1970; *Two Gentleman of Verona*, 1971; *Salvation*, 1972; *Raisin*, 1973; *Art*, 1998; as director—*Crumbs from the Table of Joy*, 1995

Selected Television Shows: *Search for Tomorrow*, 1973; *Lawman without a Gun*, 1977; *Death Penalty*, 1980; *We're Fighting Back*, 1981; *Another World*, 1983–84; *The Files on Jill Hatch*, 1983; *A Good Sport*, 1984; *Terrorist on Trial: The United States vs. Salim Ajami*, 1988; *Alone in the Neon Jungle*, 1988; *Police Story: Burnout*, 1988; *Howard Beach: Making a Case for Murder*, 1989; *Equal Justice*, 1990; *Challenger*, 1990; *A Different World*, 1991–92; *Tribeca*, 1993; *American Cinema*, 1994; *In the Shadow of Evil*, 1995; *Under One Roof*, 1995; *New York News*, 1995; *Prince Street*, 1997; *Mercy Point*, 1998

Noble, Adrian

July 19, 1950– Artistic director of the Royal Shakespeare Company. Address: c/o Barbican Theater, London EC2Y 8BQ, England

"We have to defend theater," Adrian Noble, artistic director of Britain's Royal Shakespeare Company (RSC), told Suzanne Cassidy for the *New York Times* (November 12, 1990). "We have to run up the flags of theater at a time when we're actually up against the wall. We have to ask ourselves, 'What should a company like the Royal Shakespeare be addressing . . . ?' We have to give audiences really big, big experiences, mighty plays, mighty performances, poetry." Noble has been head of the RSC, widely regarded as the greatest classical theater troupe in the world, during a period in which its government funding has decreased and the cultural relevance of its work, and to some degree of theater in general, have been questioned. Noble has nonetheless taken the company in important new directions, most notably by expanding its touring schedule and thus bringing theater of the highest caliber to more parts of the United Kingdom and the world. Prior to 1990, the year he was appointed the RSC's artistic director, he made a name for himself as an astute interpreter of plays ranging from those of Shakespeare, to Greek tragedy, to the works of Henrik Ibsen, to contemporary dramas. He is known for his conception of poetic language as the essence of theatrical expression, as well as for his interest in theater that addresses the moral issues that face human beings.

Martha Swope/Time-Life

Adrian Noble was born on July 19, 1950, the son of William John Noble, an undertaker, and Violet Ena (Wells) Noble. He was raised in Chichester, south of London, England—an area that he told Michael Billington for the London *Guardian* (July 5, 1981), "has to have the most smug population in the country." Noble has described his background as working-class. He told Alasdair Palmer for the

Electronic Telegraph (September 14, 1996, on-line), "The primary thing that affected my life was the 1944 Education Act, which meant that a bloke from my background went to grammar school, and could go on to university. That was really revolutionary." He attended the Chichester High School for Boys and frequented local theaters, where he saw performances by Sir Laurence Olivier, among others. Noble went on to Bristol University, earning a B.A. degree; he also completed a two-year directing program at the Drama Centre in London.

After working in community theater in Birmingham, Noble received an IBA director's traineeship to work at Bristol's Old Vic theater under its artistic director, Richard Cottroll. As the Old Vic's associate director, a position Noble held from 1976 to 1979, he forged a reputation as a talented up-and-comer with a penchant for the classics, staging such productions as Shakespeare's *Titus Andronicus*. "Severely over-drawn at the blood bank," that 1978 production was "savage, brilliant, and stomach-turning," Michael Billington wrote in 1981. He continued, "Since then, everything I have seen from this rising 30-year-old has had a strong directorial signature." The other early productions that Billington mentioned were of Shakespeare's *Timon of Athens* (1979), at the Old Vic; John Webster's *The Duchess of Malfi* (1980), at the Royal Exchange Theater in Manchester; and *The Forest* (1981), at the Other Place, the smallest of the RSC's three theaters in Stratford. In 1980 Noble was made a resident director at the RSC, where Henrik Ibsen's *A Doll's House* was among his initial efforts, and from 1980 to 1981 he was a guest director at the Royal Exchange Theater, where he directed *Dr. Faustus*. In a remark that would prove prophetic, in terms of the difficulties he would later face as head of the RSC, Noble told Billington of this period in his career, "Running one of the big [theater] companies—though it's a bit presumptuous even to talk about it—must be like managing a city-state. Right now, I'm doing the plays I want to do with the people I want in the places I want. You can't ask for more than that."

By this time Noble's work as a director was already distinguished by his interest in seeing characters grapple with moral and political dilemmas. "My early adult life was dominated by the idealism of the Sixties," Noble told Alasdair Palmer. "I believed that we could bring about political change, directly, through theater." Still, Noble, who for a time was a member of the Workers' Revolutionary Party, chose primarily to direct classical works rather than plays with overt political messages. As he told Billington, his attributed his choice of material partly to chance and partly to his interests. "When I got to Bristol Old Vic we didn't have access to good new plays and there was a shortage of directors interested in the classics. But on top of that I love Elizabethan, Jacobean, and Caroline drama. Partly it's because of the language; partly it's because the political and social melting pot England was at that time gave rise to characters and sit-uations that speak to me directly." Furthermore, while Noble believes in theater's potential to change society, good theater, in his opinion, is—as Billington put it—"never purely . . . an arm of political change." Noble told Billington, "One always has to try to understand the intricate interplay between the fabric of society and the heart and soul of the people. Take half that equation away and you reduce a play's possibilities."

A prime example of the way Noble uses drama to explore moral and political issues was his 1984 production of *Henry V* at the RSC, where he had become an associate artistic director two years earlier. The production marked the first time that the actor and director Kenneth Branagh, who played the title role, appeared in a professional staging of a Shakespeare play, and according to some, Branagh's later film adaptation of the play borrowed amply from Noble's version. The reason Noble chose to direct the play at that time, he told Andrea Stevens for the *New York Times* (May 31, 1998), was that "we were suddenly fighting this South American state, Argentina. We were into a fully fledged war, it wasn't a little skirmish. And I witnessed my country effectively drop its moral knickers. Suddenly, rational people, rational newspapers, were becoming jingoistic. It was horrible. So I did that play to try to understand the attraction of war as well as its horror. People can be manipulated by the destructive power of the human voice as well as by its creative power. . . . Through all of Shakespeare's plays, his principal tool is language: the ability of one to persuade another through words."

Among the other memorable productions from this period in Noble's career was *The Plantagenets*, an adaptation by Charles Wood of the three parts of Shakespeare's *Henry VI* as well as of *Richard III*. *The Plantagenets* comprises three plays, entitled *Henry VI*, *The Rise of Edward IV*, and *Richard III, His Death*. Set during the period of the Wars of the Roses, the plays are fictionalized accounts of the reigns of the English rulers for which they are named, with *Richard III* chronologically following *Henry VI* and *Edward IV*. Like Sir Peter Hall and Terry Hands, both former artistic directors of the RSC who had also directed versions of the plays, Noble felt that audiences who saw one of Shakespeare's originals without the others were being robbed of the full story. However, as Noble explained to Michael Romain for the London *Observer* (October 23, 1988), performing Shakespeare's originals would take about 16 hours, and the plays were thus "impossible to stage as an all-day trilogy, because you run into all sorts of problems with meal-breaks and so on." Wood's version condensed the story without adding to or rewriting any of Shakespeare's original verse, a tactic used in previous adaptations. Noble then reworked the new scripts in rehearsals; "being on the shop floor, as it were, with the writing, gave me a practical sense of what worked and what didn't," he told Romain. Noble's production of Wood's three plays, collectively titled *The Plantagenets*, opened in Stratford in 1988, starring the young Ralph Fiennes as Henry VI, Ken Bones as Edward IV, and Anton Lesser as Richard III, and it was hailed as a major theatrical event. For Noble, the plays amount to "a powerful indictment of war: not just the futility of war, but also the cant—the words we use and the flags we fly to do our fellow creatures down," as he told Romain. "And what really captures the audience's imagination is the scale of the plays, which is essentially Greek—the epic working-out of a tragic curse."

Noble's 1989 production of Ibsen's *The Master Builder*, although smaller in scale than *The Plantagenets*, was hailed by Michael Billington of the *Guardian* (October 8, 1989) as "the theatrical event of the year." The play tells the story of an architect, Halvard Solness, who is tormented by doubts about his talent and remorse over the deaths of his children, and torn between his duty-bound wife and his idealistic young lover. Billington wrote, "Everything about this engrossing evening is harmoniously exact and Mr. Noble's specific triumph is to show that in exploring his own psyche, Ibsen states permanent truths about our own conflict between confining guilt and sky-reaching aspiration."

That same year Noble made his U.S. directing debut with a production of a contemporary play, *The Art of Success*, by the young British playwright Nick Dear. The play focused on a fictional day in the real life of the 18th-century British artist William Hogarth. Through this lens it addressed such issues as the relationship between the sexes and the self-censorship in which artists sometimes engage in order to make their work commercially appealing or politically unobjectionable. The production opened at the Manhattan Theater Club to good reviews. Earlier, in 1987, Noble directed the Cole Porter musical *Kiss Me Kate*, which is based on Shakespeare's *The Taming of the Shrew*. Although it received a mixed critical response in Britain, it moved from the RSC to a commercially successful run on the West End, London's equivalent of Broadway. (Talk of a New York run came to nought.)

The RSC was founded in 1961 by Sir Peter Hall and proceeded to grow into one of the most highly respected theater institutions in the world; it has spawned the careers of a great number of revered performers, and its productions of Shakespeare have come to be regarded as the benchmark in the genre. Hall headed the company until 1968, when Trevor Nunn took over; Nunn was sole artistic director until around 1980, when Terry Hands became co-director; after 1987, Nunn departed, and Hands was left in charge. Currently, artistic directors of the RSC are appointed to five-year terms, and it was known well in advance that Hands, who preceded Noble, would be stepping down officially in 1991. Over the years the company's reach had expanded to include musical comedy and contemporary plays, and loss of focus was one of the criticisms facing the troupe when Noble's appointment was announced, in April 1990. Another major concern was that of the company's finances; the RSC had amassed a budget deficit of close of $6.8 million, and two weeks before Noble's appointment came the news that in order to help recoup its losses, it would be closing its London home, the Barbican Center, for four months. "Some people have said I've been offered a poisoned chalice," Noble said at the news conference announcing his assignation, as quoted by the *New York Times* (February 15, 1990). "I've simply been offered to guide and run the greatest theater company in the world."

The RSC is largely dependent on funding from the British government, and Noble has little control over the amount of money the company receives. Members of the government and the press have criticized the existence of subsidized theater, arguing that the theater productions of an organization such as the RSC should have enough popular appeal to generate sufficient income to support the company. Noble, however, as he told Alasdair Palmer, "regard[s] subsidized theater in the same way I regard subsidized Health Service." He continued, "Look, you have to accept that there are certain things in life which are benign and nourishing. Education is one of them, and that is what we are involved in. . . . All great theater has been subsidized. The purse has been different, but the fact of the subsidy has been the same." For some time, increases in the company's subsidy had consistently failed to keep up with the rate of inflation, and the situation has not improved since Noble took the helm. Since 1993 the RSC's subsidy has been "falling steadily in real terms," as Alan Riding put it for the *New York Times* (May 17, 1998). As of the date of that article, the RSC received $14 million of its annual $50 million budget from the government. Annual expenses for 1998 included those of paying 750 employees and mounting 2,100 performances of 29 different plays.

One of the means of financial survival for the RSC has been the musical *Les Miserables*, which Nunn and John Caird directed in London for the RSC in 1985 and which continues to generate royalties from the production on Broadway, where it is still running, as well as from world tours. At the same time, productions such as this led many to question the RSC's focus. In addition to *Les Miserables*, prior to Noble's tenure the RSC had also produced a dismally received musical based on Stephen King's horror novel *Carrie*; the well-reviewed *Les Liaisons Dangereuses*, a new adaptation of an 18th-century French novel; a whole season of works by the experimental 20th-century French playwright Jean Genet; as well as many contemporary British plays. As Benedict Nightingale wrote in the *New York Times* (September 29, 1991), "It was, said Mr. Noble, like an upscale car company marketing so many models it no longer had a clear identity: 'Rolls-Royce or Jaguar trying to be Ford.'"

When Noble took over, he reaffirmed the company's commitment to classical repertoire. As he told Suzanne Cassidy for the *New York Times* (November 12, 1990), "Our brief, as I understand it, is to be the greatest classical ensemble in the English-speaking world. We have to be very, very careful about just being a big producing house." Thus, while the company has continued to do socially and politically relevant new plays, which Noble believes provide an important counterpoint to the company's classical work, he has more or less dispensed with musicals. He has also increased the company's emphasis on training its actors in speaking verse, to compensate for what he described in the *Washington Post* (May 1, 1994) as "a rupture in knowledge, technique, and craft" among young actors. According to Noble, as he told *New Statesman and Society* (October 26, 1990), "We do have to define what makes theater different to television, to other arts. . . . It's the great inheritance of Shakespeare, a theater of poetry. That's what we really need to be celebrating, investigating and putting up as our primary raison d'être. Poetry, verse, language. Which can inspire, which can affect us in ways other media can't." He added, "A classical ensemble is trained in the use of language, not just how to speak it, but how you connect the living word with the human emotion and with the spirit."

Noble's other major shift in the company's agenda, one for which he received much criticism in the British press, was his decision to vacate the Barbican Center in London for six months out of every year in order to tour nationally in Great Britain. In Stratford-upon-Avon, Shakespeare's birthplace and the company's center of operations, the RSC currently has three theaters: the original 1,500-seat Royal Shakespeare Theater, which is currently operating in the midst of renovations; the Swan, a 450-seat theater; and the Other Place, a 175-seat space that will also be redeveloped in the near future. In addition, since 1982, the RSC has shown its productions year-round at the two theaters in the Barbican Center, the Barbican and the smaller Pit. Noble's choice to show no plays at either theater in London from May to November in order to expand the RSC's tours to the outer reaches of England, Northern Ireland, Wales, and Scotland made the London theater community irate, because people believed it would damage the overall quality of theater in the capital. Noble's rationale for the decision was simple. As he told Alasdair Palmer, "Every taxpayer in the country contributes to our costs. There is no reason at all why only taxpayers who live in London should get the benefits. I want to redefine the RSC as a genuinely national theater company—not merely a metropolitan one." Along with that decision, he resolved to make Shakespeare accessible to audiences with little prior experience with the plays. "This has to be a wonderfully exciting and vibrant experience of the classics," Noble told Alan Riding. "So I am seeking to present what I would call popular—not populist—theater, a theater that can actually talk

quite directly to people coming in off the street. For us, that means especially the young and people who are enjoying Shakespeare for the first time."

Along with Noble's commitment to increase the RSC's presence in the United Kingdom came the hope that the company would do more touring internationally as well. In 1998 the RSC had its first full-fledged residency in the United States, at the Brooklyn Academy of Music (BAM) in New York City; the productions later traveled to Washington, D.C. During the residency the company performed five plays in repertory, recreating the experience audiences would have if they visited Stratford and saw the same actors in different roles over several days. The full program included a hip staging of *Hamlet* by the young director Matthew Warchus, who also directed *Art* on Broadway; the 16th-century morality play *Everyman*; *Henry VIII*, a rarely staged Shakespeare history play; *Krapp's Last Tape*, by the radical Irish playwright Samuel Beckett; and *Cymbeline* (directed by Noble), one of Shakespeare's late romances, also seldom produced. Of the five, *Henry VIII* met with particularly enthusiastic reviews from New York critics. Noble's *Cymbeline* was praised especially for his interpretation of the opening scene, in which the story and characters are introduced by a soothsayer around a fire; in Noble's staging, the people gathered to listen onstage stand in turn and throw off their white robes, revealing themselves to be the characters in the play before jumping into action. Joanne Pearce's performance as Imogen, the leading role, also won critical accolades. A longtime company member, Pearce also appeared in Noble's production of *The Master Builder*. Noble and Pearce married in 1991.

In London the RSC's productions had, overall, been taking a severe beating from many critics for several seasons. Charles Spencer, chief drama critic for the British newspaper the *Daily Telegraph*—or *Electronic Telegraph* (March 29, 1999), as it is known on-line—wrote, "Last year people were writing obituaries of the Royal Shakespeare Company, which often appeared to be turning out productions on a factory line, with no clear sense of identity or purpose." However, as of 1999, Spencer continued, Noble "seems to have inspired the company with a renewed sense of artistic vision." The critic praised several recent offerings, including Noble's production based on the children's story *The Lion, the Witch and the Wardrobe*, as "big and deserved" hits, and said that the new Stratford season looked to be the "strongest and most imaginative" in years. Some of the more unusual productions include that of the poet Ted Hughes's version of Ovid's *Metamorphoses* and an adaptation by the Nigerian writer Biyi Bandele of the novella *Oroonoko*, about an African prince, written by the 17th-century writer Aphra Behn, who was reportedly the first woman to make her living as a writer.

Spencer even revised his appraisal of Noble's 1998 production of Shakespeare's *The Tempest*, a play that begins with a shipwreck. Upon seeing

Noble's version for the first time, Spencer praised its "truly thrilling storm sequence. A model sailing boat bobs along on a turbulent sea of billowing silk, before we move in for a cinematic close-up of the battling mariners and the frightened, garrulous nobility. The sound and lighting effects are tremendous, the staging virtuosic. Magic has been conjured out of 'air, thin air,'" he wrote in the *Electronic Telegraph* (March 7, 1998, on-line), quoting from Shakespeare's text. However, Spencer still found the production as a whole "prosaically earthbound." When the critic viewed it again, however, he wrote (January 7, 1999, on-line), "Either I got it wrong or the production has deepened, for this now strikes me as a hauntingly beautiful and deeply felt production."

Noble told Andrea Stevens for the *New York Times* (May 31, 1998), "D. H. Lawrence said something very relevant: the essential function of art is moral. It's not pastime, it's not entertainment. Yes, in theater we have to do other things: we have to attract people, bewitch them, charm them, disturb and frighten them. But ultimately we're dealing with morality, the choice between good and evil, this political idea, that political idea, how we live our lives, the moral choices. The artist tries to find a means to show the most challenging choices facing a society." Having been reappointed in 1996, Noble is slated to remain the RSC's artistic director until at least the year 2000.

In his younger years Noble was often described as wearing slightly rumpled clothing and a white scarf around his neck. Alasdair Palmer called him "a disarmingly charming and modest individual, full of energy and enthusiasm, and totally besotted by Shakespeare." — O.J.S.

Suggested Reading: *Electronic Telegraph* (online) Sep. 14, 1996; (London) *Guardian* p20 July 5, 1981, with photos; (London) *Observer* p39 Oct. 23, 1988, with photo; *New York Times* II p5+ Jan. 7, 1990, with photo, C p11+ Nov. 12, 1990, with photo, C p13+ June 21, 1995, with photo, II p1+ May 17, 1998, with photos, II p4+ May 31, 1998, with photos; *New York Times* (online) June 5, 1998; *Washington Post* G p1+ May 1, 1994, with photos

Selected Theatrical Productions: *Ubu Rex*, 1977; *A View From a Bridge*, 1978; *Titus Andronicus*, 1978; *The Changeling*, 1978; *Timon of Athens*, 1979; *Duchess of Malfi*, 1980; *Dr Faustus*, 1981; *A Doll's House*, 1981; *King Lear*, 1982; *Antony and Cleopatra*, 1982; *Measure for Measure*, 1983; *Henry V*, 1984; *Macbeth*, 1986; *The Art of Success*, 1986; *Kiss Me Kate*, 1987; *The Plantagenets*, 1989; *The Master Builder*, 1989; *The Three Sisters*, 1990; *The Thebans*, 1991; *Hamlet*, 1992; *The Winter's Tale*, 1992; *A Midsummer Night's Dream*, 1994; *The Cherry Orchard*, 1995; *Romeo and Juliet*, 1995; *Little Eyolf*, 1998; *The Tempest*, 1998; *Cymbeline*, 1998; *The Lion, the Witch, and the Wardrobe*, 1999

Selected Films: *A Midsummer Night's Dream*, 1995

Obasanjo, Olusegun

(oh-bah-SAN-joh, oh-loo-SHEH-gun)

Mar. 5, 1937– President of Nigeria. Address: P.O. Box 2286, Abeokuta, Ogun State, Nigeria

Eight generals in succession have ruled Nigeria since the country became independent from Great Britain in 1960. Olusegun Obasanjo, a hero from the country's bloody civil war, was one of those dictators, ruling from 1976 to 1979. But unlike the others, he gave up power voluntarily. That willingness to step down—and also his imprisonment for three years, which was widely interpreted as an attempt to stifle his criticism of the leadership of General Sani Abacha, who led the country from 1993 to 1998—boosted Obasanjo's reputation in Nigeria and in the West as a defender of democracy and made him a front-runner to become president when General Abdulsalami Abubakar engineered a return to civilian government. On February 27, 1999, despite lingering suspicions about Obasanjo's ties to the military—voiced most strongly by members of his own tribe, the Yoruba, who have long felt oppressed by the country's military rule— Obasanjo became Nigeria's first democratically elected president in 16 years.

Having assumed leadership in May 1999, Obasanjo now presides over a country weakened by years of mismanagement and "kleptocracy"— wholesale theft of funds, resources, and goods by those in power. With the largest population of any country in Africa (estimates range from 100 million to 111.7 million people) and a wealth of natural resources, particularly oil, Nigeria was once thought to be a country where democratic rule and economic development would flourish. But a merry-go-round succession of coup d'états, rampant corruption, and religious and other differences that have divided the country's three main ethnic groups (the Yoruba in the south, the Ibo in the east, and the Hausa-Fulani in the north) have so far prevented the country's potential from being fully realized. Nevertheless, Obasanjo believes that his country's problems can be rectified. "At every crisis, big or small, people talk of Nigeria breaking up," he told a *New York Times* (July 15, 1998) reporter shortly after being released from prison. "The enormous challenge facing us now is to get beyond these mutual suspicions." He added, "Per-

Corinne Dufka/Archive Photos

Olusegun Obasanjo

haps I can be a stabilizing influence, a conscience for our nation."

Obasanjo was born Matthew Olusegun Fajinmi Aremu Obasanjo on March 5, 1937. (He dropped "Matthew" in high school; at that time, cultural nationalist movements led many Nigerians to purge Western influences from the country.) He was the first child of Obasanjo Bankole and Bernice Ashabi. His father later acquired a second wife, Aduke, and both wives gave birth to several children, though only one other child of Ashabi's, her daughter Oluwola Adunni, survived infancy. Obasanjo and his sister were raised as Christians in Abeokuta, a town about 60 miles north of Lagos, the nation's capital, in what is currently known as Ogun State but was then part of what was called Nigeria's western province. (The country's four provinces were reorganized into 12 states in 1967; seven more states were added in the late 1970s, then 11 more in the late 1980s.) This section of the country is dominated by ethnic Yorubans. Abeokuta is the birthplace of two other famous Yorubans, who were born within a year of Obasanjo and whose fates would become entwined with his: Moshood Abiola, the politician and billionaire publishing and shipping magnate; and Fela Anikulapo-Kuti, who created Afro-beat music.

Obasanjo's father was once a successful farmer, but in time the family's economic situation grew precarious, especially after Obasanjo Bankole left the family, right before Obasanjo was to take his high-school entrance exams. A bright youth, Obasanjo was accepted into Baptist Boys' High School, in Abeokuta, in 1952; Abiola was one of his classmates. In his fifth year he passed the London General Certificate of Education examination, then

worked briefly in a clerical job for the United African Co. Next, for about a year, he taught science and religion at African Church Modern School (similar to a junior high school) in Ibadan. At the same time, he applied to the University of Ibadan—the only university in the country then—but decided that the cost would be prohibitive. In 1958, to further his career opportunities at minimal expense, he joined the army and became a cadet at the Regular Officers' Special Training School at Teshie, Ghana, which had originally been founded to train officers for the West African Frontier Force, the colonial army of the British West African colonies of Nigeria, Gold Coast (as Ghana was known in colonial times), Sierra Leone, and Gambia. He also received military training in Britain and India.

Obasanjo rose steadily within the ranks of the Nigerian army. In 1960, the same year Nigeria gained formal independence, Obasanjo, then an infantry officer, began a seven-month stint with the Nigerian contingent of the United Nations peacekeeping force in the Congo. By 1963 he was commanding the Nigerian Army Field Engineering Squadron in Kaduna. In 1966 two bloody coups occurred—the first led by a group of primarily Ibo military men who installed Major General Johnson T. U. Aguiyi-Ironsi as head of state, the second by a group of primarily northern, Hausa officers, who made Colonel Yakubu Gowon the country's leader. In 1967 the resulting ethnic tensions sparked the Biafran Civil War, during which the Ibo in the east attempted to secede. Obasanjo became head of the Third Marine Commando in 1969 and won several key battles; those victories helped push the rebel Ibo forces to surrender, in January 1970.

After the end of the war, Obasanjo returned to commanding the Engineering Corps. In January 1975 Gowon, who had risen to the rank of general, appointed Obasanjo commissioner for works and housing. He remained in that position until July 29, 1975, when General Murtala Muhammad led a bloodless coup and became head of state. Obasanjo was appointed chief of staff of the armed forces in Muhammad's Cabinet. Muhammad, who had announced his intention of handing power to civilians in 1979, was assassinated in his car on February 13, 1976, in an attempted coup. The coup was quelled, and Obasanjo, who was then in the second most powerful position in the country, succeeded Muhammad, thus becoming Nigeria's first Yoruban head of state.

Obasanjo immediately announced that he would abide by his predecessor's timetable for scheduling democratic elections. A new constitution was adopted in 1978, and on September 21 of that year, both the state of emergency and the ban on political parties were lifted. Elections were held in the summer of 1979, and Shehu Shagari, a northerner, won. But his election aroused controversy, because under Nigeria's new constitution, a presidential candidate had to win a plurality of the popular vote *and* 25 percent of the popular vote in two-thirds (or 13) of Nigeria's 19 states to avoid a run-off election; Shagari received 25 percent or more of the votes in only 12 states. Even so, the election commission declared him the winner, and their decision was upheld by the country's Supreme Court. On October 1, 1979 Obasanjo (who had earned the rank of general earlier that year) became the first Nigerian general to hand over power to a popularly elected civilian.

In one of the ironies of Obasanjo's career, his action earned him the respect of many non-Yorubans and prodemocratic international observers. Many Yorubans, by contrast, felt that in effect they had been disenfranchised, and they blamed Obasanjo. Their anger fueled the simmering resentment they already felt toward Obasanjo for cracking down on Yoruban students who, during his rule, had protested tuition hikes. In addition, in 1977, soldiers had burned down the home of Fela Anikulapo-Kuti, a vocal critic of the military; in the process of that raid, the soldiers had thrown Fela's 77-year-old mother out of a second-story window, and she had subsequently died of her injuries. Fela later wrote a popular song about the incident, "Coffin for Head of State," in which he criticized Obasanjo and his "big fat stomach."

After giving up leadership of the country, Obasanjo took up farming, raising pigs and bananas. He also became increasingly involved in international organizations and diplomacy. He founded (in 1987) and chaired (to the current date) the African Leadership Forum; served on the board of the Ford Foundation (1988–present); directed the Better World Society in Washington, D.C. (1987–93); and became involved in various mediation efforts in Namibia, Angola, Sudan, South Africa, Mozambique, and Burundi. His interest in international affairs was a carryover from his three-year rule, during which Nigeria's international presence had grown significantly. Norimitsu Onishi wrote in the *New York Times* (March 2, 1999) that during Obasanjo's rule, "Nigeria became the leading African opponent of white-ruled regimes in South Africa—Obasanjo was one of the few prominent people to visit Nelson Mandela in jail—Namibia and the former Rhodesia, now Zimbabwe. It also became the center of liberation movements whose leaders operated out of Lagos." Obasanjo had also established close ties with President Jimmy Carter. Obasanjo visited Washington in October 1977, and half a year later Carter visited Nigeria, thus becoming the first U.S. president to visit a sub-Saharan African country. Obasanjo maintained his ties with Carter after Carter left the White House. Since 1991 he has served on Carter's International Negotiations Network.

By the late 1980s Obasanjo's international reputation had become very strong. In 1991 some considered him a candidate to succeed Javier Perez de Cuellar as the United Nations secretary general. "I don't think there is an African leader, with the possible exception of Nelson Mandela, who is better known or respected by a multiplicity of interna-

tional organizations as Obasanjo is," Jimmy Carter told Onishi. Further enhancing his image, Obasanjo wrote books about his career and about the economic and political situation in Africa. These include *My Command* (1980), *Africa in Perspective: Myths and Realities* (1987), *Nzeogwu* (1987), *Africa Embattled* (1988), *Constitution for National Integration and Development* (1989), *Not My Will* (1990), *Elements of Development* (1992), *Elements of Democracy* (1993), *Africa: Rise to Challenge* (1993), and *Hope for Africa* (1993).

Meanwhile, Nigeria's fledgling democracy quickly deteriorated. Shagari's presidency lasted until December 31, 1983, when a group of generals engineered yet another coup and installed Muhammadu Buhari as head of state. This was followed in August 1985 by a coup in which Major General Ibrahim Babangida became the country's new leader. Babangida promised an eventual restoration of democratic rule, but his progress toward achieving this was erratic. Finally, on June 12, 1993, an election was held, and Moshood Abiola apparently won a majority of the votes. However, Babangida nullified the results, sparking mass protests. Under pressure, in August 1993 Babangida resigned. Ernest Shonekan was appointed to succeed him.

In November 1993 General Sani Abacha took over the government in a coup. On June 23, 1994 Abiola was arrested on charges of treason and imprisoned. Obasanjo, who had been critical of Abacha's regime, was imprisoned on March 13, 1995 on charges that he was plotting a coup. He was convicted along with about 40 others; some were sentenced to death, while others, among them Obasanjo, were sentenced to life in prison. Obasanjo described the convictions as a blatant attempt to silence Abacha's critics. He later wrote for the *New York Review of Books* (September 24, 1998), "At my secret military trial, Colonel Bello Fadile falsely accused me of connivance in planning a coup, although I could prove during the trial that I had been in the U.S. on the days of the alleged meetings. Later, after I was imprisoned, Colonel Fadile sent me a handwritten letter of apology, passed from prison cell to prison cell. He said he had been tortured almost to death to bear false witness against me (and he was the only witness)." Many international observers also suspected that the charges of conspiracy were false; Amnesty International declared Obasanjo a prisoner of conscience. Perhaps responding to international calls for clemency, Abacha reduced the death sentences handed out to 25 years in jail, and the life prison sentences to 15 years.

Obasanjo spent the next three years in prison. According to him, attempts were made to inject him with a deadly virus. "I managed to refuse to have my blood taken when I was told the authorities wanted to give me a physical examination and take blood for tests," he later wrote for the *New York Review of Books*. He continued: "I realized very early that the people in charge of my treatment meant to break my spirit and kill me slowly if quick and direct killing by poison was not possible. I decided that three types of exercise were essential. Each day I took physical exercise for at least an hour—running or jogging indoors or outdoors. Spiritual exercise took the form of Bible study, prayers, and regular fasting in solitude; the closest companion one has is God, through faith and trust in him. The third type of exercise was mental. With no intellectual companion, hardly anyone to talk to, I wrote on whatever pieces of paper I could get my hands on. I had a small garden, and occupied myself watering, weeding, planting, or harvesting vegetables."

On June 8, 1998 Abacha unexpectedly died, and the more prodemocratic General Abdulsalami Abubakar took over. Abubakar immediately released dozens of political prisoners, including Obasanjo (but not Abiola, who died in jail on July 7, 1998). Abubakar also scheduled a relatively quick transition to civilian rule, with elections to be held in February 1999.

In November that year Obasanjo announced his intent to enter the presidential race. He won the nomination of the People's Democratic Party over his strongest challenger, Alex Ekwueme, the former vice president in Shagari's government. His main opponent in the general election was Olu Falae, a former finance minister, who represented a coalition of the All People's Party and the Alliance for Democracy. During the campaign, Obasanjo promised to crack down on corruption, abide by International Monetary Fund plans to privatize industries, increase foreign investment, restore free education, and increase employment, but he offered no details about how he thought he could accomplish all those goals. In another major theme of his campaign, he touted himself as an effective bridge from military to civilian government, since he was close to the military and could prevent them from seizing power again. And perhaps taking populist inspiration from President Ronald Reagan and his jelly beans, President George Bush and his pork rinds, and President Bill Clinton and his Big Macs, Obasanjo emphasized his love of pounded yam with egusi soup. "And you know that I enjoy it more when I eat with my fingers," he was quoted as saying by Norimitsu Onishi. "It tastes better when you're able to lick your fingers."

With deep party coffers and backing from the military, Obasanjo got 62.8 percent of the vote in February 1999, while Falae received only 37.2 percent. However, the elections were tainted by numerous improprieties. International observers, including Jimmy Carter, claimed that there were irregularities on both sides. Obasanjo admitted the existence of abuses and fraud, but called on Falae to accept the results for the sake of national unity.

Obasanjo became president on May 29, 1999. He now faces very complex problems. Three decades of kleptocratic rule has left Nigeria in a poor state. The country has recently been ranked by various organizations (including Transparency International, a group that Obasanjo helped found in Ger-

many in 1993) as one of the most corrupt in the world. For instance, during Abacha's regime, two refineries were allowed to fall into disrepair. Thus, despite the fact that their country has one of the largest crude-oil deposits in the world, Nigerians were forced to import oil through agents of Abacha, who charged highly inflated prices and made a tidy profit. Abacha's scheme resulted in fuel shortages that have not yet ended. Meanwhile, the Ogoni, the Ijaw, and other relatively small ethnic groups have demanded greater autonomy and a bigger share of oil revenue to compensate them for environmental damage caused by spills; some have threatened to engage in terrorist violence if their demands are not met.

In the *New York Times* (June 10, 1999), Norimitsu Onishi reported that immediately after Obasanjo's inauguration, violence erupted in Nigeria among various ethnic groups and within subsets of the Ibo and other large groups; dozens of people were killed, and many people's homes were destroyed. According to Onishi, the clashes were "rooted in a struggle over political dominance." "As the imminent installation of a civilian government raised Nigerians' expectations, ethnic clashes multiplied, and they risk increasing now that power has been handed over from the military," Onishi explained. He noted that although almost 90 years have passed since Nigeria's territorial boundaries were set by the British, nearly 40 years since the nation gained independence, and 38 years since it became a republic, in many areas "there is no sense . . . that as citizens of Nigeria, people can resettle anywhere in the country." "In a country with as many as 400 ethnic groups," he wrote, "where decades of colonial and military rule reinforced the belief that each group is being oppressed by another, it was perhaps inevitable that fashioning some sort of social unity in Nigeria would be one of the biggest challenges facing President Obasanjo."

Obasanjo has been married twice. He married his first wife, Oluremi Akinlawon, on June 22, 1963. Their association goes back to his high school days, when they sang together in the Owu Baptist Church choir. They had two sons and four daughters together, then separated in the late 1970s. With his second wife, the former Stella Abebe, Obasanjo has at least one child. — W.G.

Suggested Reading: *New York Review of Books* p55+ Sep. 24, 1998; *New York Times* A p1+ July 15, 1998, with photo, A p1+ Mar. 2, 1999, with photo, A p14 June 10, 1999; *Time* p39 Aug. 7, 1995, with photo; *Time Magazine International* (on-line) Mar. 15, 1999; *International Who's Who 1997–98*; Ojo, Onukaba Adinoyi. *Olusegun Obasanjo: In the Eyes of Time*, 1997

Selected Books: *My Command*, 1980; *Africa in Perspective: Myths and Realities*, 1987; *Nzeogwu*, 1987; *Africa Embattled*, 1988; *Constitution for National Integration and Development*, 1989; *Not*

My Will, 1990; *Elements of Development*, 1992; *Elements of Democracy*, 1993; *Africa: Rise to Challenge*, 1993; *Hope for Africa*, 1993

Courtesy of Japan Information Center

Obuchi, Keizo
(oh-boo-chee, kay-zoh)

June 25, 1937– Prime Minister of Japan. Address: Office of the Prime Minister, 1–6, Nagata-cho, Chiyoda-ku, Tokyo 100, Japan

On July 12, 1998 Prime Minister Ryutaro Hashimoto of Japan resigned from his post following the disastrous showing of the Liberal Democratic Party (LDP), the current governing party and the one to which Hashimoto belongs, in elections for the upper house of Parliament. The election results were perceived as an expression of the public's dissatisfaction with the LDP's, and Hashimoto's, response to Japan's financial crisis, its worst in decades. Japanese citizens were counting on the government to lead the nation out of the crisis, which threatened the country's pension funds and risked creating a rise in unemployment.

Keizo Obuchi, Japan's foreign minister and a 35-year LDP representative, quickly emerged as the front-runner to fill the post of prime minister in the wake of Hashimoto's resignation. Obuchi's candidacy was supported by many older members of the LDP, including Noburo Takeshita, a former prime minister (1987–89) and an influential figure within the party. "[Obuchi] has Takeshita behind him, and that's all he needs," John Neuffer, a political analyst, told Mark Landler for the *New York Times* (July 25, 1998). "[He] is going to be prime minister because Japan's 'shadow shogun' put him there."

With the backing of Takeshita and others, on June 30, 1998 Obuchi became Japan's 23d prime minister since the end of World War II. His victory received little public support in Japan, however, where the Parliament is responsible for electing the prime minister. Japanese citizens clamored for a stronger, more decisive leader than Obuchi, who is perceived as mild-mannered and conciliatory in the tradition of most Japanese politicians.

Obuchi was the anointed choice of senior members of the LDP, which, except for a brief fall from power in 1993, has reigned virtually unchallenged over Japan since World War II. Prior to the 1998 election, in an unprecedented move that amounted to revolt from within the party's ranks, two fellow LDP members emerged to challenge Obuchi for the presidency of the party and the job of prime minister. (Traditionally, Parliament has selected the president of the ruling party as prime minister.) One of these rival candidates, Seiroku Kajiyama, resigned in 1997 from the government of Hashimoto and has since been an outspoken critic of the government's efforts to revitalize the economy. The other, Junichiro Koizumi, a young, outspoken minister of health and welfare who has daring ideas, had been considered something of an upstart since 1995, when he ran against Hashimoto for the presidency of the LDP and lost. In vying for the leadership positions, Kajiyama and Koizumi actively lobbied other LDP members for support, flying in the face of the party's elite. Still more damaging to Obuchi and the established order of the LDP, Kajiyama and Koizumi promoted their candidacies and criticized the party leadership on television and in the press, appealing not just to LDP members but to the public.

Although the candidates espoused similar remedies for Japan's economic crisis and none emerged as the clear champion of Japan's citizens, the public debates between them fueled the perception that of the three, Obuchi displayed the least vitality and appeal. In opinion polls he lagged far behind Koizumi, especially in Tokyo and other urban centers, where the impact of the financial crisis was felt most strongly.

Despite the competition from within the party and low public support, the LDP hierarchy prevailed, and on July 24, 1998 Obuchi was elected as the new president of the LDP by a vote of 225 out of 411 votes cast by party members. However, in an indication of how much the succession process had strayed from the norm, the tallying of the votes for party president was televised for the first time in the history of Japanese politics. Furthermore, in the parliamentary election for prime minister that followed, on July 30, 1998, Obuchi prevailed in the lower house but was not the choice of Parliament's upper house, which selected Naoto Kan, leader of the Democrats, the largest opposition party. (The LDP had lost its majority in the upper house in the elections that precipitated Hashimoto's resignation.) In such a split, the candidate chosen by the more powerful lower house wins the election.

Obuchi inherited the challenge of dealing with Japan's economic woes. Japanese banks were struggling under an estimated $600 billion in bad debts, the pension system was on the verge of bankruptcy, and unemployment was on the rise, hitting a new high in the week that Obuchi took office. The sweeping economic reforms that experts believed were necessary to turn the situation around would be tough medicine for Japan's populace to swallow. For instance, many economists view higher unemployment rates as a necessary side effect of efforts to repair an ailing economy; higher rates indicate that companies are streamlining in an effort to raise profits and regain competitiveness internationally. Obuchi, however, feared that high unemployment might cause a social backlash that could drive him and the LDP from power. He therefore faced the difficult task of striking a balance between enacting the tough measures necessary to ensure the country's long-term economic health while also creating short-term results that would appease the general public.

Obuchi also had to answer to the world community, whose economic interests are linked to Japan's economy—currently, the second largest in the world. Japan's financial crisis was having devastating effects on its Asian neighbors, which for decades had depended on loans from Japanese banks to fuel their own economic growth. As Japanese banks became insolvent and were forced to call in loans made to other Asian countries, the economies of those nations began to falter as well, as governments and businesses fell short on capital. Experts believed that until Japan recovered, economies in the entire region would suffer. There was intense pressure on Japan, particularly from Western nations, to restructure and deregulate its banking system; for starters, such measures would require Japan's government to shut down some of the country's largest banks, now devoid of funds, rather than using government money to bail them out. Hashimoto had taken steps toward closing the banks by creating a bridge-bank program that would protect deposits in smaller banks. While some experts predicted that Obuchi would continue on the path toward banking reform that Hashimoto had begun, true change would mean tough times for Japan, and many doubted whether Obuchi had the resolve to push stronger reform measures through the Japanese Parliament.

In addition to Japan's banking problems and their repercussions throughout Asia, many countries, including the U.S., feared that a surge in Japanese exports spurred by Japan's weakened yen would also hurt Japan's neighbors, by cutting into their export markets. Yet another potential effect of Japan's crisis was a loss of confidence in the Japanese economic model, namely, the creation of a few large business conglomerates linked closely to banks and the government. Some analysts worried that Japan's troubles would cause countries such as South Korea and Malaysia, which had based their economic systems on Japan's, to abandon the model altogether, creating further instability in the region.

The Japanese and the world community had hoped that a dynamic leader would emerge to help Japan through such difficult times, and Obuchi's lack of public appeal stemmed in large part from his seeming inability to rise to the task. His failure to make a notable impact on his country's policies during his years in Parliament was a main topic in discussions concerning Japan's economic fate, both nationally and in the world community. Obuchi was perceived by most as quiet, cautious, and even bland. Many worried that he would back down on proposed economic reforms under pressure from members of Parliament who feared for the short-term well-being of their constituents. Others thought he simply did not possess the charisma to lead his people through what was sure to be a difficult period.

Some experts on Japanese politics, however, pointed out that throughout its history, Japan has had few strong or dynamic leaders. These experts saw Obuchi's quietness as an asset. Obuchi is considered a consensus-builder whose rise through Japan's entrenched political hierarchy serves as a testament to his skill at working within the system and gathering support from many sides. "The secret of [Obuchi's] success is to fly low," Takashi Inoguchi, a political science professor at Tokyo University, told Mark Landler. "Nobody feels threatened by him." Inoguchi added, "His talent is in aggregating support. In one sense, it's unfair to say he's had no impact. He's actually had a lot of impact simply by amassing so much support behind his own candidacy." These qualities, many felt, would prove crucial to the task of economic reform. In the *New York Times* (July 28, 1998), Landler, paraphrasing Ronald Bevacqua, an economist based in Tokyo, wrote that Obuchi has "as good a chance of success as any Japanese politician—partly because he has many friends in his party and few enemies outside it. That may enable him to steer a painful financial package through the Parliament more effectively than a more confrontational leader."

Obuchi acknowledged his lack of public appeal in a post-election victory speech, in which, as Stephanie Strom reported in the *New York Times* (July 25, 1998), he stated, "I am inferior to the other candidates in general popularity. I know well that popularity among the people and popularity in the party should match each other." Widely regarded as an extremely nice, warm, and sincere man, Obuchi accepted his image problems good-naturedly. When, during his campaign, a political analyst characterized him as having as much charisma as a cold pizza, Obuchi responded by buying pizza for the reporters who were staked out around his home, encouraging them to eat it while it was hot.

After he had been elected party president but before he assumed the post of prime minister, Obuchi, still acting as Japan's foreign minister, spoke with U.S. secretary of state Madeleine K. Albright in Manila, the capital of the Philippines, at a meeting of foreign ministers of the Association of Southeast Asian Nations and other countries with interests in the region. Attempting to dispel his weak image, he declared that he would tackle the challenge of managing Japan's financial crisis head-on. U.S. government officials were heartened by the take-charge manner Obuchi displayed and by his stated determination to stick by his campaign pledges to revitalize the Japanese economy.

Within days after taking office, Obuchi formed his Cabinet, including both senior party members and young members from smaller factions within the LDP who were pushing for change. As many had expected, he named as his finance minister Kiichi Miyazawa, a 78-year-old party elder and former prime minister, who brought years of experience in financial negotiations on the international level to his new post. Miyazawa's reputation internationally was such that his appointment dispelled to some extent the fears of those who lacked confidence in Obuchi's financial resolve. Obuchi named Seiko Noda, a woman and the youngest Cabinet member in postwar history, as head of the powerful Ministry of Posts and Telecommunications, which manages a large portion of Japan's enormous trust of private savings. Noda, who had publicly voiced concerns about the LDP's ability to win over Japanese voters, had supported the presidential campaign of Seiroku Kajiyama, and her appointment to Obuchi's Cabinet was seen as both a nod and a peace offering to younger members of Parliament.

In August 1998 Obuchi announced his plans to cut taxes by $42.4 billion in 1999 and spend $71 billion on public-works projects, with the goal of stimulating the economy. He also pledged to lower the corporate tax rate from 46.3 percent to 40 percent starting in April 1999, and in the future to reduce the highest combined local and national individual income-tax rate from 65 to 50 percent. Making reference to Japanese newspaper articles that characterized his Cabinet as teetering at the edge of a cliff, Obuchi told Parliament, as quoted by Stephanie Strom for the New York Times (August 8, 1998), "I am determined to make my utmost effort, at the risk of the Cabinet's life, to bring the Japanese economy to a recovery path within a year or two." Many experts noted that Obuchi's economic recovery plan differed from that of his predecessor, Hashimoto, only in terms of the speed with which the proposed measures would be enacted, and they suggested that Japan's economy needed something more drastic. Obuchi's long-term goal of cutting the government payroll by 20 percent and government costs by 30 percent was also not a new idea. "It seems [Obuchi] wants to engineer a soft landing of the Japanese economy," Heizo Takenaka, a professor at Keio University, told Strom, "and the basic question is, Is that possible? I personally feel that some kind of shock therapy is necessary."

Keizo Obuchi was born on June 25, 1937 in Nakanojo, Japan, the son of an affluent silk manufacturer who won a seat in Parliament but also lost many elections. As a youth Obuchi displayed a predilection for literature. He was not a top student, and he failed the entrance examination for Japan's prestigious Tokyo University three times. Eventually he enrolled in Waseda University, in Tokyo, where he studied English literature. Like many others who have studied English in Japan, he did not learn to speak the language. After the death of his father, during his freshman year, Obuchi became interested in politics, and he joined a debating group to sharpen his skills in oratory. He graduated from Waseda, with a B.A. degree in English literature, in March 1962. He then entered a graduate program in political science, but he soon grew dissatisfied with the theoretical study of politics and left school.

In January 1963 Obuchi set off by himself on a trip around the world. In nine months he visited 38 countries in Asia, the Middle East, Africa, Europe, and the Americas. A highlight of his trip occurred in Washington, D.C., when he met Robert Kennedy, whom he had heard speak at Waseda University and who was then the U.S. attorney general. Obuchi had approached his secretary with a request to meet with Kennedy, and a week later the attorney general agreed to do so. During their conversation Kennedy encouraged Obuchi's ambition to become a politician. In November 1963 the 26-year-old Obuchi was elected to Japan's House of Representatives, as the representative of his home district, Gumma Prefecture.

Obuchi's early political career was largely overshadowed by two of Japan's most powerful postwar politicians, Takeo Fukuda and Yasuhiro Nakasone, both of whom came from Gumma. As Mark Landler reported in the New York Times (July 25, 1998), Obuchi once compared himself to Fukuda and Nakasone by using the analogy of "a noodle shop between two high-rise buildings." Obuchi rose quietly through the ranks of the LDP, serving in such posts as vice minister for mail and telecommunications, in 1970; vice minister for construction, in 1972; and director general and minister of state, in 1979–80. One of the few times that he commanded national attention was in the winter of 1989, when, acting as the chief Cabinet secretary in the government of Prime Minister Noburo Takeshita, he announced the official name of Japan's new Imperial era following the death of Emperor Hirohito.

Obuchi's political climb has in large part resulted from his association with Takeshita. Obuchi was considered an acolyte of Takeshita and helped him gain control of the LDP's largest faction and ascend to the post of prime minister in 1985. In turn, with Takeshita's help, Obuchi became increasingly powerful within the LDP. In 1991 he served as the LDP's secretary general and then held the post of LDP deputy secretary general. In 1997 he was appointed to the post of foreign minister by Prime

Minister Hashimoto and served the government in that capacity until he became prime minister. Takeshita's support was considered possibly the determining factor in Obuchi's successful campaign for party president and prime minister.

Obuchi faced the obstacle of administering to the depressed economy at a time when the upper house of Parliament was no longer controlled by his party. The loss of the upper house threatened to stall the passage of measures to revamp the banking system, legislation that was sure to be controversial among Japanese politicians and their constituents. Obuchi also proposed measures to fund tax cuts through the sale of deficit bonds and to continue Japan's path toward more deregulation of, and openness in, its banking and business sectors. Obuchi's greatest challenge was to enact such measures without further losing public support for the ruling party.

Many political analysts believed that since the LDP held only a slim majority in the lower house of Parliament, a coalition of opposing parties might sweep Obuchi's party from power. But Obuchi surprised his detractors. In August 1999 he led the LDP's successful attempt to form a coalition with the New Komeito Party, a former segment of the opposition that has links to a Buddhist sect. This political marriage gave his coalition government greater clout in Parliament. In September 1999 he won reelection as the leader of the LDP, with nearly 70 percent of the 514 votes cast, and thus retained the post of prime minister. At the same time his popularity and approval rating among the public, as measured by opinion polls, also rose significantly.

Bolstered by his government's increasing power and his own greater popular support, Obuchi is expected to press for bolder steps to lead Japan out of its economic troubles. On another front, he pushed for the passage of legislation—strongly opposed by members of the opposition—that established Japan's current anthem, "Kimigayo," and flag, the Hinomaru (Rising Sun), which are remnants from the nation's imperial past, as the country's official emblems; the measure passed into law on August 9, 1999. In addition, he favors a controversial amendment to Japan's constitution that would allow that nation to become stronger militarily. Japan's constitution, which was crafted by U.S. officials and went into effect in 1947, has prevented Japan from developing its armed forces. The prospect of weakening the pacifist doctrine embodied in the constitution has dismayed many Japanese citizens, members of opposition parties within Japan, and neighboring Asian nations. On the other hand, various officials in the U.S. government and governments overseas have criticized Japan's relatively inconsequential role in international peacekeeping missions. (For example, Japan has contributed medical supplies and food but no troops to such troubled areas as the Balkans.)

Obuchi and his wife, Chizuko, have been married since 1967; the couple have two daughters and a son. In 1963 the prime minister, who was born in the Year of the Ox, the second year in the traditional, 12-year Chinese zodiac, began collecting figurines of oxen, and he reportedly now owns several thousand of them. He also enjoys reading, watching movies, listening to music, and playing golf. — Y.P.

Suggested Reading: *New York Times* A p6 July 20, 1998, A p5 July 25, 1998, with photo, A p3 July 31, 1998, D p1+ Aug. 8, 1996, with photo; *International Who's Who, 1996–97*

Courtesy of Denon Records

Oe, Hikari
(oh-eh, hee-kah-ree)

June 13, 1963– Classical-music composer. Address: c/o Denon Records, 200 W. 57th St., New York, NY 10019-3211

When Hikari Oe was a baby, his doctors thought he had no chance whatsoever of living a fruitful life. Born with a potentially fatal cranial deformity, Hikari underwent traumatic brain surgery during infancy that left him severely developmentally disabled. Oe is now 36 years old, and although his language skills are those of a small child and he is not capable of living independently, his doctors turned out to be quite mistaken: with the help of his parents, the Nobel Prize–winning writer Kenzaburo Oe and his wife, Yukari Oe, Hikari Oe has surprised everyone by becoming a recognized composer of classical music. His first two CDs, *Music* of *Hikari Oe* (1992) and *Music of Hikari Oe, 2* (1994), have been best-sellers in his native Japan; worldwide, more than 300,000 copies have been sold. That number may seem negligible when compared with sales of albums of pop groups like the Spice Girls, but in the classical-music world, it constitutes blockbuster success. And as many music critics have pointed out, the popularity of the albums cannot be chalked up merely to interest in Oe's extraordinary personal story. Many listeners have found his compositions beautiful, subtle, and expressive; in short, his music has moved them.

Historically, there are many well-documented cases of people who, although mentally disabled, have displayed prodigious abilities of a highly specialized sort. Commonly referred to as idiot savants, some such people can solve complex arithmetical problems mentally at phenomenal speed. Others, like Hikari Oe, have incredible musical gifts: they can play any piece of music after a single hearing. But Oe can do much more. "Hikari Oe is unique in several respects," Leon Miller, an expert on musical savants, told Lindsley Cameron for her book *The Music of Light: The Extraordinary Story of Hikari and Kenzaburo Oe* (1998). "There are a few other musical savants with compositional predilections—they are few and far between—but Hikari Oe is remarkable in terms of his compositional style, in a practical sense. The others make music sitting down at a keyboard; Hikari thinks it up and writes it down." While no experts have claimed that Hikari Oe is a great composer, some have noted that judged analytically, his music could be taken for work produced during the youth of some famous 19th-century composer.

In addition to his musical achievements, Hikari has had a tremendous impact on the literary career of his father. During the ceremony in Stockholm, Sweden, at which Kenzaburo Oe accepted the 1994 Nobel Prize for Literature, he said that in a sense his son Hikari, rather than he himself, had won the award. As quoted in Cameron's book, Kenzaburo Oe explained that "the central theme of my work, throughout much of my career, has been the way my family has managed to live with this handicapped child. Indeed I would have to admit that the very ideas that I hold about his society and the world at large—my thoughts, even, about whatever there might be that transcends our limited reality—are based on and learned through living with him."

The first of the three children of Kenzaburo and Yukari Oe, Hikari Oe was born on June 13, 1963 in a hospital in Tokyo, Japan. His father selected the name Hikari, which means "light," after doctors told him that his son's vision was impaired. Of far greater concern was the presence of what the doctors identified as a brain hernia: emerging from a hole in Hikari's skull was a huge growth that gave the baby the appearance of having two heads. Surgeons told Kenzaburo Oe that they could remove the growth and place a plastic plate over the hole but that such surgery would likely result in severe complications, including mental retardation and seizures. Hikari, they predicted, would probably end up a vegetable, requiring continual personal attention and financial support for as long as he lived. The other option, which the doctors recommended, was to withhold treatment and simply let Hikari die.

At the time of Hikari's birth, Kenzaburo Oe was already one of Japan's most famous writers. He was also among the more controversial, because, as Masao Miyoshi reported in the *Nation* (May 15, 1995), his work had begun to "relentlessly criticiz[e] Japan's history of war, suppression, provincialism, its political—especially imperial—system, and its bourgeois sexual hypocrisy." Two of Oe's works in particular had aroused a great deal of controversy: the novella "Seventeen" and its sequel, "Death of the Political Youth," which together constituted a thinly disguised account of the 17-year-old right-wing terrorist who, in 1961, in an action hailed as heroic by many on the political far right, had assassinated the chairman of the Japanese Socialist Party. Oe had portrayed the assassin in what right-wingers considered a bad light, and consequently, he and the publisher of the magazine in which the stories had appeared received death threats. Then Oe became the target of leftists as well, some of whom criticized him for "allowing" the publisher to print a full-page apology for whatever offense Oe's stories had caused.

How such events affected Kenzaburo Oe's consciousness is unclear, but Kenzaburo later admitted that in the years just prior to Hikari's birth he had reached a psychological low point. "By the time I reached 25 or 26," he told David Remnick for the *New Yorker* (February 6, 1995), "I lost all sense of identity, all the stability of feeling that I might have had before. For several years, suicide became a strong preoccupation." When Hikari was born, Oe thought that the baby was "the personification of my unhappiness," as he told Remnick.

While agonizing about the choices Hikari's doctors had presented to him, Kenzaburo Oe accepted an assignment to report on an international disarmament rally being held in Hiroshima. While in that city he interviewed victims of the atomic-bomb attacks on Hiroshima and Nagasaki, in 1945, and doctors who had treated them (some of whom were themselves survivors). In Oe's view, these people, many of whom had been horribly burned or otherwise hurt, had good reason to commit suicide, and seeing how passionately they continued to fight to live inspired him to rethink what it means to be human. "I felt great shame that I was doing nothing for my son—my son, who was silent and could not express his pain or do anything for himself," he told Remnick. He promptly returned to Tokyo and, with the consent of his wife, asked the doctors to operate on Hikari.

Raising Hikari, Kenzaburo Oe told Remnick, was both a burden, because of the child's serious physical and mental problems, and a boon, in that, fulfilling the promise of his given name, Hikari "illuminated the dark, deep folds of my consciousness." Lifted from his depression and abandoning thoughts of suicide, Oe devoted himself to becoming a medium of expression for his son. Over the next 30 years, Hikari-like characters figured prominently in Oe's fiction. In *A Personal Matter* (1964), one of Oe's most highly acclaimed novels, for example, a father is distraught over the birth of his deformed son; he flees to a former lover and makes plans to murder the "monster baby" before experiencing a last-minute change of heart. In subsequent novels Oe wrestled with the same themes—guilt, interdependence, and absolution; many of his stories feature either someone with a deformity or the parent of a handicapped child. In some cases a character named Hikari has a father who is a famous writer. Kenzaburo has maintained, however, that none of his novels should be interpreted as representations of actual events.

The real Hikari was found to have an I.Q. of 65, which indicates mild retardation. He could not cry, because he lacks tear ducts, and until age six, he did not express himself in words; thus his parents had great difficulty figuring out what he needed or wanted. Meanwhile, the Oe family had become the objects of their neighbors' scorn. Some writers have suggested that the Japanese have less tolerance of handicapped people than do people in most other societies. That intolerance has eased in recent years, but it was rampant in Japan when Hikari was growing up, in the 1960s and 1970s. In many cases the handicapped—and even many atom-bomb survivors—were kept in seclusion. The Oe family, however, which includes Hikari's sister, Natsumiko, and brother, Sakurao, refused to succumb to prevailing prejudices, and they tried to address Hikari's needs creatively.

Early on, the Oe family realized that, in the main, Hikari responded not to visual stimuli (even with corrective lenses his vision is poor) but to aural cues, particularly classical music and other melodious sounds, such as the songs of birds. In hope of keeping him engaged, when he was four his parents bought a record that presented and then identified the songs or chirps of dozens of birds. One day, while on a woodland walk with six-year-old Hikari, Kenzaburo Oe heard the chirping of a bird and then, immediately afterward, the words, "It's a water rail." After a moment of confusion, Oe realized that the voice was that of his son: Hikari had uttered his first words. Although Oe had no way of knowing whether the boy had merely repeated what he had heard on the record or had actually tried to communicate, the incident seemed to indicate that much more was going on inside Hikari's head than anyone had thought possible. The Oes later discovered that Hikari had memorized all 70 of the birdcalls on the record.

Gradually, more of Hikari's savant-like abilities became apparent. Yukari Oe often played works by Bach and Mozart and other classical composers for her own enjoyment at home. Hikari seemed to like the music; it was one of the things that calmed him in times of distress. (Even today, he insists on putting on music for those close to him who are unhappy or unwell.) The Oes later discovered that Hikari was memorizing everything he heard. Remarkably, he could listen to a few measures from a Mozart composition and then identify the piece by its Köchel number—one of the more than 600 numbers that the 19th-century Austrian musicologist Ludwig von Köchel assigned in his chronological catalogue of Mozart's works. The Oes also discovered that Hikari had perfect pitch, the ability to recognize a note that is played by itself or to sing a particular note correctly on demand, without any clues. (It is estimated that fewer than four out of every 100 people have perfect pitch.)

When Hikari was eight, his mother began to give him piano lessons. A professional teacher, Kumiko Tamura, took over when Hikari was 11. The boy's weak eyesight and poor physical coordination prevented him from playing with both hands with ease, so Tamura taught him how to write music, Hikari began transcribing practically every piece he heard—at least, that is what everybody thought he was doing. At some point, when Hikari was in his teens, Tamura looked through his notebook, and she found pieces that she didn't recognize. She assumed that they were obscure works that he had heard on the radio. Then she realized that they were Hikari's own, original compositions.

By that time Hikari had entered the Seicho Municipal School for the Handicapped. After he graduated, in 1981, he began working under the auspices of the Karasuyama Occupational Therapy Center, in Tokyo, which gave him such jobs as cleaning parks or assembling clothespins. Despite his progress, Hikari still needed nearly as much attention as a young child. Sometimes he would get lost in public spaces. After he started suffering seizures, at age 15, he was not permitted outdoors without a companion, to make sure that, while in the throes of a seizure, he didn't wander into traffic. His father's fame, too, presented dangers. In 1975 Hikari was abducted by a pair of kidnappers, who accused Kenzaburo Oe (insofar as their vague charge could be understood) of having no political commitments. They finally released Hikari in a crowded train station. Neither kidnapper was ever caught.

Hikari's music got its first public exposure in 1986, when Kenzaburo Oe's book *M/T and the Marvels of the Forest* came out. The book contained a copy of one of Hikari's pieces, written in his childish scrawl. It caught the attention of Hiroyuki Okano, an executive at Nippon Columbia, who took it upon himself to produce Hikari's first CD. That disc, *Music of Hikari Oe* (1992), contains 25 short pieces for solo piano or for piano and flute. Each composition is written in either the Baroque, classical, or Romantic style; Hikari has rarely shown any interest in developments in music written after the 19th century.

Kenzaburo Oe was prepared to buy 3,000 copies of his son's CD to ensure that Nippon Columbia did not take a loss on the project, but he did not have to carry out that plan. Within the first three months of its release, sales of *Music of Hikari Oe* reached 80,000; by the end of 1992, the album had become that year's best-selling classical-music record in Japan, and Hikari subsequently received a Gold Disc from the Recording Industry Association of Japan. His second album, *Music of Hikari Oe, 2*, which contains 22 pieces for solo piano, piano and flute, or piano and violin, was released in 1994. That record also sold well. By April 1997 some 300,000 copies of his two albums had been sold worldwide, for a total of $8 million. Kenzaburo Oe has said that at the time, that sum surpassed what his books had earned outside of Japan.

Describing Oe's music for the *New York Times* (March 5, 1995), Lindsley Cameron wrote, "It is entirely accessible, and while the early pieces are appealing primarily for their simplicity and charm, some of the later, darker ones are extremely moving, with haunting melodies and striking elegance and economy of development. The pieces are not long; most of them take less than three minutes. As in haiku, much of their power comes from their compression."

Whereas for much of his life Oe often drew disapproving stares when he was in public, he now has to deal with requests to sign autographs and other such burdens of celebrity. Two films have bolstered his fame. One is a Japanese documentary, released in 1994, about his relationship with his father. The other is an adaptation by the director Juzo Itami (who was Yukari Oe's brother) of Kenzaburo Oe's book *A Quiet Life*, which features a character named Hikari, who resembles the real Hikari in many ways. (*A Quiet Life* was among the last films of Itami, who committed suicide in 1997.)

Hikari Oe's accomplishments have been the source of much pride on the part of his parents. When he won the Nobel Prize, 31 years after the birth of his son, Kenzaburo announced that he would no longer attempt to write on behalf of his son. "For a long time, I felt that it was my role to express things for him," Kenzaburo told David Remnick, "but now he can do it on his own." Hikari Oe's third album, *Hikari Oe Anew*, came out in 1998. — W.G.

Suggested Reading: *New York Times* II p25+ Mar. 5, 1995, with photos; *New Yorker* p38+ Feb. 6, 1995; Cameron, Lindsley. *The Music of Light: The Extraordinary Story of Hikari and Kenzaburo Oe*, 1998

Selected Recordings: *Music of Hikari Oe*, 1992; *Music of Hikari Oe 2*, 1994; *Hikari Oe Anew*, 1998

Ormond, Julia

Jan. 4, 1965– British actress. Address: c/o Creative Artists Agency, 9830 Wilshire Blvd., Beverly Hills, CA 90212-1825; c/o Nancy Seltzer & Associates, Inc., 6220 Del Valle Dr., Los Angeles, CA 90048

"It happened very quickly. The very first interview I had was for a commercial. I got the job. It was for cottage cheese." That is how, in a conversation with David Blum for the *New York Times Magazine* (April 9, 1995), the actress Julia Ormond recalled the launching of her career, which occurred right on the heels of her graduation from acting school. Ormond swiftly moved beyond dairy ads to work in British television, theater, and film. Then, within the space of two years, she starred in three big-budgeted Hollywood pictures—*Legends of the Fall* (1994), *First Knight* (1995), and a remake by Paramount Pictures of the classic 1954 romance *Sabrina* (1995). Sherry Lansing, the chairperson of Paramount, who is a former actress, described Ormond in almost ecstatic terms when Blum interviewed her in 1994. "I thought she was the most beautiful thing I had ever seen in my life," Lansing said. "She's just breathtaking. She's magnificently beautiful. But that's not enough. What she has is that she can act. What makes her a star is she's magical on screen. And she's unique. That's what makes a movie star."

Bob Grant/Archive Photos

Ormond's physical beauty and dramatic skills had also drawn the attention of other powerful people in the entertainment industry, and at the time that Lansing uttered those words, Ormond was the focus of an intense publicity campaign in which she was being touted as the country's next great female star. But that status has thus far eluded her, in part because *Legends of the Fall, First Knight*, and *Sabrina* proved to be inadequate vehicles to propel her in that direction and in part because her performances failed to generate sufficient enthusiasm among critics or the public to overcome the shortcomings of the films. Although Hollywood no longer buzzes about her potential greatness, Ormond's skills and beauty have continued to draw respectful attention, as reviews of her latest film, *Smilla's Sense of Snow* (1997), attest.

Julia Karin Ormond was born on January 4, 1965 in Epsom, a town that is a stone's throw from London, England, and is famous for its annual horse race, the Epsom Derby. The second of five children—she has an older sister and three younger brothers—Ormond was born into wealth; her father, a stockbroker, became a millionaire by the age of 30. While attending the Cranleigh Public School, a prestigious private secondary school in Surrey, she worked as a waitress. After her graduation she entered the West Surrey College of Art and Design. A year later, following the advice of a West Surrey tutor who thought acting might suit her better than painting, she transferred to the Webber Douglas Academy, in London, where she studied dramatic acting full-time.

Almost immediately after her departure from the academy, in 1988, Ormond landed the job in the cottage-cheese ad. Many other assignments for commercials followed. With the help of her agent, Patricia Marmont, who had noticed her in a 1988 Webber Douglas Academy production of a David Hare play, she also won parts in television and on the stage, in productions of *The Crucible, Harvey, Arms and the Man, Wuthering Heights*, and *Faith, Hope, and Charity*. For her work in the last-named play, a work by Christopher Hampton, she won the 1989 London Drama Critics Award for best newcomer. Hampton, who wrote the screenplay for the film *Dangerous Liaisons*, had first seen Ormond when she appeared in Alastair Reid's multi-award-winning British television series *Traffik* (1989), and she had impressed him powerfully. "She was one of those actresses who just jumps out at you," he noted to Blum. "She was playing a drug addict, and she was wonderful, unforgettable." Ormond also had a role in the British TV series *Capital City*. She made her London West end debut at the Almeida Theatre in *The Rehearsal*, by Jean Anouilh.

Christopher Hampton recommended Ormond in glowing terms to various Hollywood producers, and after the run of *Faith, Hope, and Charity*, she won roles in several American television projects. Notable among them are the TNT miniseries *Young Catherine* (1991), in which she played Catherine the Great; for her portrayal of Catherine, the 18th-century empress of Russia, she earned a 1992 Genie award nomination from the Academy of Canadian Cinema and Television. She also appeared in the HBO movie *Stalin* (1992), as the second wife

of the 20th-century Russian dictator Joseph Stalin (played by Robert Duvall). She next starred in *The Baby of Macon* (1993), by the independent British filmmaker Peter Greenaway, and then in Angela Pope's *Captives* (1994), the latter of which, Stephen Holden wrote for the *New York Times* (May 3, 1996), "yanks Julia Ormond off the perfect-woman pedestal . . . to engage in some down-and-dirty thrashing around" with her co-star, Tim Roth.

Meanwhile, thanks to Marmont and Clifford Stevens, one of Marmont's American contacts, Ormond had attracted the notice of Edward Zwick, who directed the film *Glory* and co-created the television series *Thirtysomething*. Zwick had recently been commissioned to direct *Legends of the Fall*, a film based on a novella by Jim Harrison about a libertarian early-20th century rancher and his three sons, each of whom falls in love with the same woman. After several of his picks for the lead female role proved unavailable or unsuitable, Zwick asked Ormond to send him a video as a substitute for a screen test. Faced with the task of doing so within 24 hours, Ormond asked a friend of hers, the actor Tim Piggot-Smith, for help. "Somehow Julia had gotten the wrong information that she was supposed to do an American southern accent," Piggot-Smith told Blum. "And so there we were late at night, Julia perfecting this delightful southern accent, when we got a call to say it was a Boston, almost English accent. So we had just a few hours to make it, but I guess it worked out all right."

Ormond's performance on the tape thrilled Zwick. "Frankly, by virtue of that performance and having seen *Stalin*, if I could just meet her, I was prepared to cast her," he recalled to Blum. "But it became a question of convincing the studio." The video convinced Tri-Star executives of the wisdom of Zwick's choice, and they offered Ormond the role two weeks later. By that time she had departed for Romania, to film *Nostradamus* (1994), about the famous 16th-century French astrologer. After she completed the shooting for that movie, she flew to Calgary, in the Canadian province of Alberta, where, to prepare for her role in *Legends of the Fall*, she took lessons in horseback riding, archery, and roping calves. *Legends*, which also starred Anthony Hopkins as the father and Brad Pitt, Aidan Quinn, and Henry Thomas as his sons, did well at the box office despite critics' distinctly cool reception to Zwick's adaptation. Many reviewers nevertheless had kind words for the actors, and in the *New Republic* (January 2, 1995), Stanley Kaufmann called Ormond's performance a "standout."

Meanwhile, the director Jerry Zucker, who had seen some of the dailies for *Legends of the Fall*, had recruited Ormond for the part of Queen Guinevere in *First Knight*, his version of the King Arthur legend. Not long afterward the director Sydney Pollack cast her in his remake of Billy Wilder's Cinderella tale, *Sabrina*, which had starred Audrey Hepburn as the title character—a chauffeur's daughter who captures the affection of the two sons (played by Humphrey Bogart and William Holden) of her father's wealthy employer.

Ormond seemed to be on the fast track to stardom, and such magazines as *Vanity Fair* and *Premiere* and such high-profile gossip columnists as Michael Musto and Liz Smith hailed her as the next Julia Roberts or Meg Ryan. In March 1995, before the release of either *First Knight* or *Sabrina*, Ormond received the Sho West Award, through which the National Association of Theater Owners recognizes the "female star of tomorrow." At the awards ceremony, Blum reported, Sherry Lansing heaped praise on Ormond, "telling her how *great* the dailies have been from *Sabrina*, how *great* Julia is in them, how *great* the movie is going."

The word "great" did not appear in any reviews of *First Knight* or *Sabrina*, however. Indeed, few critics found much to applaud in either film. Janet Maslin, for example, in the *New York Times* (July 7, 1995), described *First Knight* as "a tepid romance" with "overdone special effects and too many awkward silences," but she added, "This film does have one touch of class: Julia Ormond, playing Guinevere as a regal English rose. Freshness, intelligence, and stately bearing again establish Ms. Ormond as an appealing presence, but her role isn't much of a showcase." According to Brian D. Johnson in *Macleans* (July 17, 1995), Ormond gave "the film's only spirited performance"; by contrast, in *People* (July 10, 1995), Ralph Novak wrote that Ormond "seemed distracted" and came across as "bland," and John Simon, mincing no words in his critique for the *National Review* (August 14, 1995), described her portrayal as "boring."

Sabrina, which also featured Harrison Ford as the super-serious business-executive brother and Greg Kinnear as the younger, playboy brother, did not fare any better. Nearly all reviewers complained that the remake had little to recommend it, and they labeled it far inferior to the original version; as John Simon put it in the *National Review* (January 29, 1996), it served as "a powerful argument for leaving well enough alone." Most agreed as well that Ormond lacked Audrey Hepburn's dazzle and appeal—her "movie-star glamour," as Peter Travers wrote for *Rolling Stone* (January 25, 1996)—and they detected no signs of chemistry between Harrison Ford and Ormond.

The unfavorable critical and popular reception accorded *First Knight* and *Sabrina* effectively ended Hollywood trumpetings of Ormond as the next great female star. Judging by interviews she gave at the time, Ormond had almost foreseen just such a turn of events. Speaking to Blum before the release of *Sabrina* and *First Knight*, she said, "I look back on the work and I think how much is actually coming out this year and I think: How in the world did that happen? I don't know that it's such a good thing, actually. I think it could backfire quite badly."

Ormond has been hurt to some degree by her refusal to disguise her opinions to please others. "I don't like a lot [of] what I see on the screen," she told Blum. "I can't sit there and say, 'I do, it's wonderful,' because if I don't, I don't." Hiring and then firing several agents in succession between 1993 and 1995 also contributed to Ormond's reputation for being difficult to work with. But as Blum pointed out, "difficult" is a "common label for female stars who often speak their mind (look under Streisand, Barbra)." "If you respect Julia, and her right to say what she wants, she'll treat you great in return," Jerry Zucker told Blum.

The continual references to Ormond's beauty have also frustrated her. "It becomes a distorted impression," she complained to Blum. "I treat that with a pinch of salt. A lot of talent is wasted. At the Royal Academy of Dramatic Art they'd go around and tell people what surgery they should have done. And look at the state of women and plastic surgery in Hollywood. Conform, conform. You *must* do this. And it's sad but it's understandable that people go off and do it. Because the pressure to do it, the pressure to *be* something, is enormous."

After a hiatus of nearly a year and a half, Ormond returned to the silver screen, in *Smilla's Sense of Snow*. An adaptation by Bille August of a best-seller by the Danish novelist Peter Hoeg, the film traces the efforts of Smilla, the bitter, antisocial daughter of an American doctor and an Eskimo hunter, to find the killers of a young Eskimo boy whom she had befriended. In an investigation that grows increasingly tangled and bizarre, the intrepid Smilla travels from Copenhagen, Denmark, to the Arctic. "It's quite unusual to see a woman on screen who is as complex as Smilla," Ormond told Lauren Hunter for *CNN.com* (February 29, 1997, on-line). "Somebody who was uncompromising, who was intelligent, and who was tough and aggressive at different moments, but also deeply vulnerable underneath."

"As [*Smilla's Sense of Snow*] sails off to the frozen north," Janet Maslin wrote for the *New York Times* (February 28, 1997), it "leaves credibility behind." Describing Ormond as "an elegant Smilla," Maslin reported that the actress's "remoteness works better here than it has in other roles. Ms. Ormond plays Smilla in the chic, alert, unsmiling fashion of a French film star, and she richly rewards the camera's many beautiful close-ups of Smilla cogitating on crime." In *Time* (March 10, 1997), Richard Schickel expressed a similar reaction. "What will surprise everyone is the dry iciness, the burning coldness of Ormond's Smilla," he wrote. "Up to now she has trafficked largely in vulnerability—melting in *Legends of the Fall*, perhaps a shade too winsome in *Sabrina*. Here, she is all contained fury, except for the flashes of anger and contempt that burst without warning from the darkness within. It's not exactly the diva acting such as we used to get from the great ladies of the movies' classic era. She achieves her effects with less obvious calculation. But, like a Barbara Stanwyck or a Bette Davis, she takes us into that country where strength shades into neurosis, and we fear that she can never be reclaimed for the more orderly pleasures of ordinary life."

In 1995 Ormond secured a deal with Miramax Films to produce and direct several films of her own. "It's up to women to develop their own stuff, take the responsibilities and the risks . . . ," Ormond told Paula Span for the *Washington Post* (December 15, 1995). "Take the female away from the appendix role—the wife, the girlfriend, the one who does the sex scene. I can no longer sit back and say, 'Oh, there are so few good parts for women' when I've been given this opportunity." Meryl Poster, Miramax's senior vice president for production, told Span, "Julia comes to work everyday. She's in the office; she's on the phone. . . . She seems to be someone who can do two things at once. She's a working producer." Poster also said that Ormond "gets into the thick of things. She's very opinionated, and opinions count in our company." Ormond helped to produce *Calling the Ghosts* (1996), a documentary by Mandy Jacobson and Karmen Jelincic about atrocities against women in a concentration camp in Bosnia and Herzegovina. In 1997 Ormond signed a two-year contract with Fox Searchlight Pictures to write, direct, and produce. She has reportedly been trying to secure the rights to *West with the Night*, a memoir by Beryl Markham, the first person to cross the Atlantic from east to west in a solo flight.

In 1999 Ormond appeared in *The Barber of Siberia*, directed by Nikita Mikhalkov. Set in Russia at the turn of the 20th century, the film is "a passionate and epic love story about lost love, betrayal, and the human spirit," according to a promotional piece on the World Wide Web. Although it was shown at several international film festivals, as of October 1999 *The Barber of Siberia* had reached few theaters in the U.S. Also in 1999 Ormond supplied the voice of the dog Jessie in a made-for-television movie based on George Orwell's classic political fable, *Animal Farm*.

Ormond's brief marriage to the actor Rory Edwards ended in divorce. — M.B.

Suggested Reading: *CNN.com* (on-line) Feb. 29, 1997, with photos; *New York Times* C p10 July 7, 1995, C p10 May 3, 1996, with photo; *New York Times Magazine* p49+ Apr. 9, 1995, with photos; *Time* p90 Mar. 10, 1997, with photo; *Washington Post* F p1+ Dec. 15, 1995, with photos, F p7 Dec. 15, 1995, with photo

Selected Films: *The Baby of Macon*, 1993; *Legends of the Fall*, 1994; *Captives* 1994; *Nostradamus*, 1994; *First Knight*, 1995; *Sabrina*, 1995; *Smilla's Sense of Snow*, 1997; *The Barber of Siberia*, 1999; for television—*Stalin*, 1992; *Young Catherine*, 1991; *Animal Farm*, 1999

Selected Television Shows: *Capital City*, 1990

Oz, Frank

May 25, 1944– Puppeteer; film director. Address: c/o Jim Henson Productions, 117 E. 69th St., New York, NY 10021

Jim Henson, the creator of the puppet characters known collectively as the Muppets, told Nan Robertson for the *New York Times* (July 13, 1984) that Frank Oz "is probably the person most responsible for the Muppets being funny." Indeed, some of the most beloved Muppet personalities from both the children's television program *Sesame Street* and *The Muppet Show* have been puppeteered by Oz, among them Cookie Monster, Grover, Bert, Miss Piggy, Fozzie Bear, Animal, and Sam the Eagle. The character Yoda from George Lucas's *Star Wars* films is also performed by Oz. After working exclusively as a puppeteer for many years, Oz has gained a reputation as a talented film director as well; his credits, which have accumulated since the mid-1980s, include *Little Shop of Horrors*, *Dirty Rotten Scoundrels*, *The Indian in the Cupboard*, and *In & Out*. "I'm interested in the creation of a world," Oz told Sonia Taitz for the *New York Times* (December 25, 1988), referring to his work with both puppets and live actors. "People have always condescended to the Muppets and they shouldn't.

John Spellman/Retna Ltd.

They're not puppets to me. To me, what they are are characters. And that's what it's all about."

Frank Oz, whose legal name is Frank Oznowicz, was born on May 25, 1944 in Hereford, England, to Isidore and Frances Oznowicz. He has a brother, Ronald, and a sister, Jenny. After living in Belgium until Oz was five years old, his family moved to Oakland, California, where his father worked as a window dresser for clothing stores. Oz told John Clark for *Premiere* (July 1992) that talking about how he got started in puppetry "bores" him: "It's the same stock answer I've given to everybody, which is I started puppeteering when I was about 11 years old. Did it in the San Francisco Bay Area until I was about 18. . . . It was my parents' hobby." As he told Edwin Miller for *Seventeen* (November 1980), "[Puppetry] was only a small part of my life, but it seemed a way to express myself and make some money, playing birthday parties, supermarket openings, fairs, and bazaars. I worked marionettes—string puppets—a skeleton, a roller-skating bear. Most of the kids in school thought it was really silly—they called me the 'puppet man,' although I was interested in playing ball and dating girls." While he was still a teenager, Oz performed at the National Puppetry Festival, and it was there that he first met Jim Henson. Although Henson offered him a job immediately, Oz couldn't accept because he hadn't yet finished high school. Intending to pursue a career in journalism, Oz enrolled at Oakland City College. During his freshman year, in about 1963, some two years after their initial meeting, Henson again offered Oz work as a performer, and this time Oz left school to join Henson's fledgling company in New York City. According to the official Jim Henson company Web site, one of Oz's first projects during his and Henson's nearly 25-year collaboration was operating the right hand of the Muppet character Rowlf the Dog, while Henson controlled Rowlf's head and left arm and supplied the voice.

For a while Oz and Henson's company worked in obscurity. As Oz recalled to Edwin Miller, "We made our money in commercials and industrial shows, doing television appearances on the Ed Sullivan and Perry Como shows. Gradually, we started getting bigger." This growth in the Muppets' fame and popularity was brought about by *Sesame Street*, which debuted in 1969; produced by the Children's Television Workshop, it is widely considered "the most important children's television show in the history of television," to quote *Total Television*, a guide to TV encompassing 50 years. The show, whose intended audience is inner-city preschoolers, centers on characters—some played by live actors and some who are Muppets—who live on the fictional Sesame Street. Henson's company was involved with the program from its outset. Oz's characters on the show included the small, lovable, furry blue monster named Grover, the somewhat larger and more boisterous Cookie Monster, and Bert, a tallish, whiny character who shared a home with his best friend, the shorter, round-faced, giggly Ernie, who was performed by Henson. While Oz no longer provides the voices of these characters on a regular basis, the personalities with which he imbued them have helped make them beloved by millions, and *Sesame Street* continues to be enormously popular with parents and young children alike.

In the first half of the 1970s, Oz and Henson did puppetry for episodes of the comedy show *Saturday Night Live*. Then, in 1976, Jim Henson Productions began its own weekly television series, *The Muppet Show*, which was hosted by Kermit the Frog, one of Henson's popular *Sesame Street* characters. The half-hour evening program was formatted like a variety show, with musical numbers, short comedic skits, and a guest star; celebrities who appeared over the years included Elton John, Raquel Welch, and Bernadette Peters. Oz is credited with performing several roles: the glamorous and tough-as-nails starlet Miss Piggy; the lively stand-up comedian Fozzie Bear; the wild, incomprehensible Animal, who played drums in the rock band headed by Dr. Teeth; and the moralizing, somber-voiced eagle Sam. *The Muppet Show* became the most popular first-run syndicated series in television history up until that time, and it was broadcast in more than 100 countries, in many different languages. In 1979 the Henson company produced its first full-length feature film, *The Muppet Movie*, for which Oz performed all his major *Muppet Show* characters. The movie was greeted with great acclaim. Vincent Canby, reviewing it for the *New York Times* (June 22, 1979), wrote, "I'm in particular awe of the techniques by which these hand puppets are made to walk, run, sing, and play musical instruments. As do the [non-Muppet] actors in the movie, we very quickly come to accept the Muppets as real people who just happen to be made largely of felt." Since then, several more successful feature films starring the Muppets have been made, with Oz collaborating on all of them.

In 1980, when George Lucas made *The Empire Strikes Back*, the second installment of the original *Star Wars* trilogy, Oz supplied the voice and movements of the character Yoda, the 900-year-old teacher of the Jedi knights—a "small, delightful, Muppet-like troll," as Vincent Canby described him in the *New York Times* (June 15, 1980). It took four people to operate Yoda: three puppeteers for his right hand, his eyes, and his ears, respectively, and Oz for all of Yoda's other moving parts. "With Yoda, you can't perform spontaneously, [when you're dragging] three other people along with you . . . ," Oz told a writer for the magazine *Starlog* (July 1984). "In this kind of situation, the satisfaction you get working with two or three other people occurs after you rehearse and rehearse and suddenly the role opens up to you. It's a living organism. It just happens. It unfolds like a flower, because you are so in tune with each other. It's a wonderful moment." With his distinctive voice and expressive features, Yoda has captured the imaginations of several generations of moviegoers. Yoda was also featured in the third *Star Wars* movie, *Return of the Jedi* (1983).

In the early 1980s Oz also had his first non-puppeteer acting role, playing a corrections officer in the film *The Blues Brothers* (1980), starring John Belushi and Dan Aykroyd and directed by John Landis. The second movie to feature the Muppets, *The Great Muppet Caper*, came out in 1981, and in 1982 Henson's company released *The Dark Crystal*, a fantasy with an entirely different cast of puppet characters. Oz co-directed *The Dark Crystal* with Henson and also served as a puppeteer for it.

Two years later Oz made his solo debut as a film director, with *The Muppets Take Manhattan* (1984), for which he also wrote much of the screenplay. "Jim [Henson] was the one who really was instrumental in helping me be a director," Oz told Clark. "He gave me all the opportunities." In this film the Muppets are college co-eds who decide to take their senior show to Broadway. In New York City they struggle in vain to find a producer, lose hope, and separate before being reunited in a happy ending. Before the movie's release, there was much speculation as to whether Miss Piggy would finally wed her longtime love interest, Kermit the Frog. By this time Miss Piggy had become perhaps the most popular Muppet of all, with her image appearing on pinup-style posters and other merchandise. In his review of *The Muppets Take Manhattan*, Vincent Canby, writing for the *New York Times* (July 13, 1984), called Miss Piggy "one of the great showbiz creations of our age." "It's worth the price of admission just to watch Miss Piggy demolish three male-chauvinist construction workers and a Central Park mugger," David Sterritt wrote in an assessment of the movie for the *Christian Science Monitor* (July 24, 1984). "I know she's a sore point with some feminists, who consider her an unflattering female caricature, but after this movie I feel more than ever that she's the most interesting Muppet of all, and in some ways the strongest." In an interview for the *New York Times Magazine* (June 10, 1979), Oz talked about the complexity of Miss Piggy: "the coyness hiding the aggression; the conflict of that love [for Kermit] with her desire for a career; her hunger for a glamour image; her tremendous out-and-out ego—all those things are great fun to explore in a character," he said. In an interview for the *Detroit News* (July 23, 1984), he explained that all of his Muppet characters drew on parts of his own personality for which he might not otherwise have an outlet. "Miss Piggy is the neurotic, emotional, high-strung aspect of myself. Bert is the boring aspect of myself. Animal is the insane aspect of myself."

By the early 1980s Oz was ready to do more work with live actors. As he told *Rolling Stone* (February 3, 1983), "I've been doing this for almost 20 years, and puppets have been good to me. I'm still excited about doing my characters, but puppets are limiting. For instance, doing *Sesame Street*, you're working for kids, and your sophistication has to be held in check, because your job is to do it for that audience. One reason I like Miss Piggy is because there are so many levels. . . . But

at the same time, we're still not talking Chekhov." Oz directed his first non-puppet movie in 1986, when he made a film version of the successful Off-Broadway musical comedy *Little Shop of Horrors*. The tale of a plant that eats the customers of a flower shop, the film takes place in the 1960s and starred Rick Moranis as the unlikely hero, Seymour, and Ellen Greene as Audrey, the object of his admiration. It also featured the well-known comic actors James Belushi, Bill Murray, John Candy, and Steve Martin in cameo roles. The people-eating plant, named Audrey II, starts out small; growing as she devours her victims, she becomes, by the end of the film, a 12-foot puppet requiring 50 people to operate her. At first Oz found the project daunting. "I looked at the script and said, 'No, I can't do this movie,'" he told the *New York Post* (January 2, 1987). "I didn't think I could get my hands around it. There were too many elements. It was a period piece, it was horror, it was comedy, there were 14 songs, and a puppet that was going to weigh a ton." Despite Oz's initial doubts, most critics judged the film a success. In the *Washington Post* (December 19, 1986), Rita Kempley wrote, "Virtually every number becomes a show-stopper under the direction of Muppeteer Frank Oz. The staging is at once boisterous and big . . . but still intimate enough to make the screen seem like a stage." According to John Clark, Oz himself was happy with the way the film turned out except for the ending, which was changed at the insistence of the producer, David Geffen. While in the original musical, the monster plant kills the two lead characters, Oz told Clark that "in order to make the movie releasable, we had to change the ending. I'm sure if I didn't do it, somebody else would have."

The next film that Oz directed was *Dirty Rotten Scoundrels* (1988), a remake of the 1964 big-screen comedy *Bedtime Story*. The new version starred Steve Martin and Michael Caine as competing smooth operators who take advantage of wealthy women they meet on the French Riviera. "What I liked about the script was that the actual words weren't so important," Oz told Taitz. "I saw an opportunity for the actors to have juice between the lines. The structure was good; the relationships and the characters' expectations were clear, so there was room for a lot of fun when we got to the floor, the pit, the actual cooking moment." Contrasting his work with popular comedic films like *Police Academy*, he also said, "Some of the comedy these days is one-note. There's no texture." According to Taitz, *Dirty Rotten Scoundrels* was "praised for its rare combination of gut hilarity and sophisticated snap." In the *Washington Post* (December 14, 1988), Hal Hinson wrote that Oz's direction "brought a devilish tang to the machinations" of the plot.

After that success Oz signed on to direct *Mermaids* (1990), a drama starring Cher and Winona Ryder. Early in the production, however, Oz disagreed with Cher on how to play the script's more lighthearted moments. "To me humor from character is different than going for comedy, and I had no intention of going for comedy," Oz explained to Clark, whose article implied that Cher wanted to downplay the comedy in the film altogether. "Cher and Winona really didn't trust me. You can't work with two actresses who don't trust you when there are some very emotional scenes coming up. It's not fair to the actresses. And it was a very tense time. Cher was very upset. . . . Everyone was behaving badly, including me. It was just not worth it." Oz left the film two weeks into production. "I lost my confidence for about two or three months after that," he told Clark. "It upset me very much. But the great thing was that I came home and I got all these calls, from [Disney chair Jeffrey] Katzenberg, from Orion people, that they were very supportive of me. But even so, I just felt lousy. And then slowly I got back up into it."

In addition to helping him regain his confidence, Oz's next film, the comedy *What About Bob?* (1991), helped him to overcome the grief he felt after the loss of his good friend and longtime collaborator Jim Henson, who died of pneumonia in 1990. The film features the actors Richard Dreyfus and Bill Murray as a psychiatrist and his patient, respectively. Murray's character hounds his psychiatrist while the latter is on vacation and causes many embarrassing scenes between the doctor and his family. According to Oz's interview with Clark, filming this movie was difficult because Dreyfus and Murray did not get along. "I think it had to do with everybody wanting to make the best movie their way, and that doesn't work when you should have one person guiding it," Oz told Clark. Another problem arose when, once again, Oz disagreed with the film's producers about how the story should end. "We showed the two endings in preview just before we were ready to ship it out, and whichever ending [the audiences] liked best, we were going to ship. . . . They liked [screenwriter] Laura Ziskin's ending best. And we shipped it out that way. I didn't like the ending—I still don't—but I must say that I didn't have a better idea. I wasn't smart enough to get the right ending." Most critics described the film as funny.

Oz's next film was the romantic comedy *Housesitter* (1991), which starred Goldie Hawn and Steve Martin. Hawn's character, a waitress, tells a series of outrageous lies so that she can move into the home of an architect, played by Martin, with whom she has spent just one night. "The movie to me is about creating a better reality through fiction," Oz told Clark. "The character knows her circumstances and chooses not to be depressed that she's a waitress, single, without a man, without a family, alone in the world. She's admirable in seeing the world in a better light and creating an ambience around her that seems rich. And that improved reality is achieved through fiction." The producer Brian Grazer, who worked with Oz on this film, told Clark that the director was at times uncompromising. "I clashed with him a couple of times on

a few things, and he normally won," he said. "Actually, quite frankly, he won every time." Grazer added, "He's nice about it, but he's not Socrates or something, talking it out forever. He just says no!"

In 1995 Oz directed *The Indian in the Cupboard*, a children's film about two boys who find that a small Native American doll comes to life when they put it in an old cupboard. According to Ralph Novak, writing for *People* (July 31, 1995), the film "not only drags two fifth-grade boys through the crises of responsibility, racism, and mortality but it also leads them to consider the existential problems of gods, and, indeed, to wonder whether or not they are gods." While Novak criticized the film for failing to "maintain a playful tone," Richard Alleva of *Commonweal* (September 8, 1995) praised it as an "ascetic" movie that "gives [children] something to care about. . . . What might have been an orgy of special effects obstinately remains human and humane, and proceeds to a climax determined by neither lighthearted slaughter nor multi-hued explosions but moral scruple. The grandest special effect in this film is the look of wonder in the eight-year-old hero's face."

Oz's next film was *In & Out* (1997), a comedy that featured Kevin Kline as a gay high-school English teacher. The story was inspired in part by the speech that the actor Tom Hanks gave when he won an Oscar for his performance in *Philadelphia* (1993); upon receiving the award, Hanks thanked, among others, his high-school drama teacher, who at the time of the broadcast was openly gay. In the film Kline's character is forced to "come out" after one of his former students wins a best-actor award for playing the part of a gay soldier in a Vietnam War movie and reveals the homosexuality of his teacher in his acceptance speech. To further complicate matters, Kline's character is about to be married (his fiancée is played by Joan Cusack). Short sections of the made-up war film were shown in *In & Out*, and because it seemed impractical to go to Asia to shoot them, they were filmed in a section of Orchard Beach, in New York City. Paul Rudnick, who collaborated on the screenplay for *In & Out*, wrote in *Premiere* (September 1997), "Oz loved shooting those scenes because he got to meticulously parody every important film cliché imaginable; he would giggle maniacally as he plotted swoopingly melodramatic crane shots and a soundtrack featuring a lone trumpet. 'Paul,' he once asked me, momentarily concerned about how much fun he was having, 'this is supposed to be really stupid, right?'" Oz told John Clark, "I never intended to do comedies only. It's been an accident. I never even wanted to be a movie director, as a matter of fact. I always wanted to direct theater. Still do. This is just a kind of ride I'm taking, and I'm really excited about it."

Oz returned to the role of puppeteer for the films *Star Wars Episode I: The Phantom Menace* (1999), which features Yoda, and *Muppets in Space* (1999), in which he was responsible for the performances of Miss Piggy, Fozzie Bear, Animal, and

Sam the Eagle. He will perform his *Sesame Street* character Bert in the upcoming feature *The Adventures of Elmo in Grouchland.* Oz's most recent directorial effort is the comedy *Bowfinger* (1999), which stars Steve Martin and Eddie Murphy and opened in the summer of 1999 to largely positive reviews. Oz has had a number of bit roles as an actor, mostly in films directed by his good friend John Landis; in addition to *The Blues Brothers,* Landis cast him in *An American Werewolf in London* (1981), *Trading Places* (1983), *Spies Like Us* (1985), *Innocent Blood* (1992), and *The Blues Brothers 2000* (1998). In 1995 Oz directed a series of "Energizer Bunny" battery commercials.

Nan Robertson described Oz as being "a lanky, owlish, low-key man." He resides in Connecticut with the former Robin Garsen, a painter and illustrator whom he married in 1979 and with whom he has four children. Oz is a member of the board of directors of the Jim Henson Co. According to the company's Web site, he has won four Emmy Awards, two George Foster Peabody Awards, and the American Comedy Creative Achievement Award. Of the albums he has created in conjunction with Muppet and *Sesame Street* projects, two have gone platinum and three have gone gold. After working with Oz on *In & Out,* Paul Rudnick wrote, "Frank is one of the most pathologically decent people I ever met; he made himself available

to everyone involved with the film, he actually listened to any and all suggestions, and he took enormous joy in the process." — C.P.

Suggested Reading: *Commonweal* p18+ Sep. 8, 1995; *New York Times* July 13, 1984, with photo, 2 p24 Dec. 25, 1988, with photo; *People* p19 July 31, 1995; *Premiere* p34+ July 1992, with photos, p41+ Sep. 1997, with photos; *Washington Post* (on-line) Dec. 19, 1986; *Something About the Author,* vol. 60, 1990

Selected Films: *The Muppet Movie,* 1979; *The Empire Strikes Back,* 1980; *The Great Muppet Caper,* 1981; *The Dark Crystal,* 1982; *Return of the Jedi,* 1983; *The Muppets Take Manhattan,* 1984; *Sesame Street Presents Follow That Bird,* 1985; *Little Shop of Horrors,* 1986; *Dirty Rotten Scoundrels,* 1988; *What about Bob?,* 1991; *The Muppet Christmas Carol,* 1992; *Housesitter,* 1992; *The Indian in the Cupboard,* 1995; *Muppets Treasure Island,* 1996; *Elmo Saves Christmas,* 1996; *In & Out,* 1997; *Star Wars Episode I: The Phantom Menace,* 1999; *Muppets from Space,* 1999

Selected Television Shows: *Sesame Street,* 1969–; *The Muppet Show,* 1976–81; *Muppets Tonight!,* 1996

Pak, Se Ri

(PAKH, suh-REE)

Sep. 28, 1977– Golfer. Address: c/o LPGA, 100 International Golf Dr., Daytona Beach, FL 32124

Se Ri Pak made golf history in 1998, her debut season in the U.S. Ladies Professional Golf Association (LPGA) circuit, by capturing two major championships—the McDonald's LPGA Championship in Wilmington, Delaware, in May, with a score of 11-under-par 273, and the U.S. Women's Open in July, which she won after a steely performance in a thrilling 20-hole play-off. She became the youngest person ever to win the LPGA Championship since it came into being, in 1955, and the first woman to win two major championships before age 21. Juli Inkster, who won the Dinah Shore Classic and the du Maurier Classic in her rookie year (1984), is the only other female golfer to win two major titles in her rookie season.

Pak has continued to take the LPGA by storm. She broke the record for the lowest 18-hole score in LPGA history by three strokes, with a 10-under-par 61, en route to capturing the Jamie Farr Kroger Classic in Sylvania, Ohio, in July 1998. Her score of 261 for four rounds (71, 61, 63, and 66, respectively) was the lowest ever on the LPGA tour, and her 23-under-par total tied the all-time LPGA record for 72 holes. In the same month, she won

Jeff Hornback/Courtesy of LPGA

her fourth tournament at the Giant Eagle LPGA Classic, thus establishing herself as one of the top golfers in the LPGA. In addition, she has generated a new level of excitement in, and attracted international attention to, a sport that had often been eclipsed by men's golf and had suffered from a dearth of new young stars. For that reason, she has often been compared to Tiger Woods, who brought a similar media frenzy and excitement to men's golf in 1997 when he captured the Master's title. (Woods won only one major tournament that year.) Jim Ritts, commissioner for the LPGA Tour, told *CNN/SI* (July 20, 1998), "Very simply put, there has probably not been this level of interest and attention on the LPGA tour for 20 years, since Nancy Lopez's rookie year."

Lopez's rookie year was 1977. Se Ri Pak was born on September 28 of that year, in Taejon, a city about 100 miles south of Seoul, South Korea. She is the second of the three daughters of Joon Chul Pak, a construction company CEO, and Jung Sook Kim, a homemaker. Her father, a Korean amateur golf champion in the 1980s, introduced her to golf when she was 11, during the brief period that her family lived in Hawaii. Although Pak displayed great talent right from the start, she did not begin to pursue golf seriously until she was 14. In the meantime, she excelled as a sprinter; at age 13, she ran the 100-meter dash in 13 seconds. She also performed outstandingly in hurdles and shot put.

After she turned her focus to golf, Pak trained with singular determination. Her father, who served as her coach, pushed her to follow a rigorous training regimen, which included "waking her at 5:30 in the morning to run up and down 15 flights of stairs in the apartment building where they lived," as Holly Brubach reported in the *New York Times Magazine* (October 18, 1998), and practicing her stroke late into the night. He also forced her to spend nights by herself in a neighborhood cemetery, Brubach wrote, "to steel her nerves," and took her to watch dog fights to help her recognize the difference—in this case, the brutal difference—between winning and losing. "He wanted me to win everything—not second, not third, but win," Pak told Nisid Hajari for *Time Asia* (August 17, 1998, on-line). "But people are not machines. Sometimes I miss an easy one, and he was angry, he keeps pushing, 'What are you thinking? Why did you miss?' I was really upset, and I don't have anyone to talk to, so I would cry by myself in my room."

Helped by her intense training, Pak quickly emerged as a young golf star in her native country. In 1991 she won the Korea Herald Cup Student division; the next year, she won the Presidential Cup Middle and High School League and finished 10th in the Korea Women's Open. At 17, in 1994, she won the 12th Korean Junior Competition and was a member of the Korean team that narrowly lost to the U.S. in the 1994 World Amateur Team Championship in Paris.

In 1996, after winning 30 tournaments as an amateur, Pak turned professional. That February she signed a lucrative, 10-year endorsement deal with Samsung Group, one of South Korea's largest conglomerates. During the next year she won six of the 14 Korean LPGA events in which she played and was runner-up seven times. Her only misstep was a sixth-place finish.

In January 1997 Pak moved to Orlando, Florida. To prepare herself for tackling the stiffer competition in the U.S., she trained with David Leadbetter, the renowned swing expert who coached the British golf star Nick Faldo and the Zimbabwean champion Nick Price. Leadbetter's pupils have included few women, and he coached those few only on rare occasions. Pak told Brubach that Leadbetter agreed to work with her regularly because, as she put it, she "swing[s] like a man." When Brubach asked her to explain what that meant, she said that the swing of female golfers "maybe looks better" than those of males—"really flexible, smooth, pretty. But man's game more strong, hit longer, big spin." "Pak's swing is indeed succinct and powerful," Brubach reported, "stripped of all flourishes, with a distinctive finish—the right shoulder rotated remarkably far forward toward the target." While working to improve her game, Pak also strived to learn English and adapt to American customs.

Pak earned her LPGA card on her first attempt, by tying for a first-place finish at the LPGA Qualifying Tournament in October 1997. Standing a compact five feet, six inches, she repeatedly sent her balls beyond those of her rivals. (Currently, she remains one of the top long hitters in the LPGA tour and routinely sends the ball a distance of more than 265 yards.) In the first nine U.S. LPGA events in which she played, she failed to finish in the top 10.

At the LPGA Championship in May 1998, Pak led throughout all four rounds, demonstrating her mental toughness by calmly fending off challenges by seasoned pros. In addition to becoming the youngest player to win the LPGA Championship, she became the third-youngest female player to win any major tournament. (The youngest is Betty Hicks, who won the 1937 Western Open when she was 17; next comes Patty Berg, who won the 1937 Titleholder Championship when she was 19. Both of those competitions were considered major tournaments in 1937.) With that victory, Pak surprised Samsung Group executives, who had earlier announced that they hoped Pak would capture a major tournament win by the year 2006, and she became an even greater hero in South Korea. In the U.S., Pak impressed her audience by speaking in English and fielding questions from the press without a translator.

Demonstrating that her LPGA Championship win was not a fluke, Pak captured the U.S. Women's Open title in July 1998, in Kohler, Wisconsin, after a 20-hole play-off against Jenny Chuasiriporn, a 20-year-old amateur from the U.S. It was the first such play-off ever at the U.S. Open, and Ed Sherman, writing for the *Chicago Tribune* (July 7, 1998), described the match as "a drama as compelling as any in golf history." Pak made an especially impressive play in the 18th hole, after her ball landed in a thick clump of grass just inches from a body of water. As Sherman reported, "She was faced with the choice of taking a drop and a penalty or trying to hit the ball from the hazard." After some agonizing minutes, she took off her shoes and stepped into the water, so that the ball now rested above her knees. From that awkward position, she hacked the ball out of the hazard. "Then," Sherman reported, "she hit an 8-iron to within 12 feet of the hole, and two-putted for a bogey" (one stroke more than par). "I thought I had lost already," Pak said afterward, as quoted by Sherman. "But I didn't want to give up. Last ball, last chance, last day. I wanted to try something." Chuasiriporn could have won at the 18th hole, but she missed a 15-foot putt, thus sending the game into a two-hole, sudden-death play-off. Both Pak and Chuasiriporn parred the first hole of sudden death. On the par-four second hole, each had an opportunity for a birdie (one stroke less than par). After Chuasiriporn missed a 20-foot putt, Pak calmly sank an 18-foot birdie putt, and thus captured her second consecutive major title.

According to Dave Leadbetter, Pak has "a fantastic temperament for golf." "She doesn't get flustered," he told Holly Brubach. "She doesn't get nervous at all. Most players are in their late 20s or early 30s before they find a formula for handling the pressure. Se Ri loves the pressure."

Since her success at the U.S. Open, Pak has signed a new contract with Samsung. It is reportedly worth around $2.5 million a year after taxes (the precise amount depends partly on the fluctuation of the exchange rate between the Korean *won* and the U.S. dollar) and allows her to negotiate other endorsement deals with equipment companies. According to Brubach, 10 Samsung marketing executives work full-time to promote her.

Also after her U.S. Open victory, Pak was feted by a parade in her home country, and she received the Blue Dragon Award, Korea's top sports honor, from the South Korean president, Dae Jung Kim. In August 1998, to mark the 50th anniversary of the establishment of South Korea as an independent state, an international edition of *Time* magazine carried her image on the cover.

Prior to the 1999 season, Pak had a falling out with her coach, David Leadbetter, and stopped working with him. She started the season with lackluster performances: in her first nine tournaments, her best finish was a tie for 18th place. Most golf experts attributed her problems to the intense pressure she felt from the media and her fans. Nevertheless, she improved her play, and in the latter part of the season, she captured three LPGA titles: the ShopRite LPGA Classic, in Atlantic City, New Jersey, in June; the Jamie Farr Classic, in Sylvania, Ohio, in July; and the Samsung World Championship of Golf, in Maple Grove, Minnesota, in September. As of October 11, 1999 Pak was ranked fourth in LPGA Tour prize-money earnings, with $730,366, behind Karrie Webb of Australia ($1,426,584), Juli Inkster of the U.S. ($1,263,703), and Annika Sorenstam of Sweden ($840,406).

Pak told Brubach that her efforts to win at golf are "maybe 70 percent for Mom and Dad, 30 percent for me." "I like golf for myself," she explained. "Otherwise too difficult—no people meet, no friends, no free time. I give that up long time ago. Now is for my mom and dad. They looking at me, I see them, I make them happy. That is why I keep doing, keep working. It's not that long I can do this—maybe 10 years, 20 years. Now I have to do this really good. Then later my life, later happy." Pak told Hajari that she aspires to be like Nancy Lopez, but it is not Lopez's prowess as a golfer that she has in mind; rather, she said, it is because Lopez is "always smiling, a friendly person, like a mom."

Se Ri Pak lives in Orlando with her pet beagle, Happy. — Y.P.

Suggested Reading: *Chicago Tribune* Sports p1+ July 7, 1998, with photos; *New York Times* C p2 May 18, 1998, with photo, D p8 June 2, 1999, with photos; *New York Times Magazine* p82+ Oct. 18, 1998, with photo; *Washington Post* C p1 May 18, 1998, with photos

Stephane Kempinaire/Allsport USA

Pantani, Marco

Jan. 13, 1970– Cyclist. Address: c/o Mercatone Uno, Blocco 1/B, Galleria B No. 159–161, I-40050 Funo di Argelato (Bo), Italy

On August 2, 1998, when cyclist Marco Pantani became the first Italian in 33 years to win the Tour de France, the last Italian to do so—Felice Gimondi—told *letour.fr* (August 2, 1998, on-line), "I think this

Tour has served as a lesson, and Pantani's victory shows that you can still ride with your heart and win. Marco loves to improvise, he rides how he feels. He doesn't train with a heart-rate monitor, and he simply relies on his feeling." Pantani's victory marked a triumphant return for a cyclist whose career was marred in its early stages by two accidents. In 1995, while traveling downhill at close to 80 kilometers per hour (kph), Pantani collided with an oncoming Jeep. Two years later he was the locus of a massive bike pile-up when a cat darted in front of his wheel. Pantani's miraculous comeback in 1998 included a first-place finish not only at the Tour de France but at the Tour of Italy (Giro d'Italia), making him the winner of the two most prestigious cycling crowns in the world—and he thus became one of Europe's most celebrated athletes. (The last Italian to win both races was Fausto Coppi, in 1952.)

Pantani has been given various nicknames, and he is commonly referred to by these monikers alone. While still an amateur, he was known as "Il Elefantino" (the Elephant), because of his large, protruding ears—a situation he changed by wrapping a bandanna around his head and donning an earring. Now known as "Il Pirata" (the Pirate), Pantani is considered to be one of the best uphill cyclists in the sport today—if not the best. After winning the illustrious double victories in France and Italy in 1998, Pantani told *CNN/SI* (June 7, 1998, on-line), "I demonstrated that I am still strong despite everything that has happened to me." In June 1999 Pantani experienced another setback: nearing the completion of that year's Giro d'Italia, he failed a random blood test. Suspected of ingesting a hormone that can boost the oxygen level in blood, he was forced out of the race. Pantani, who was in the lead when he was disqualified, insisted that he had taken no banned substances; as of October 1999, an investigation of the circumstances surrounding the blood test was underway. Pantani declined to participate in the 1999 Tour de France, but according to recent reports, he intends to resume cycling competitively in 2000.

Marco Pantani was born on January 13, 1970 in Cesenatico, Cesena, a small resort town in the Emilia-Romagna region of north-central Italy. According to *velocity.sportsline* (July 7, 1997, on-line), he began to develop an interest in cycling around age 12; during this period, he often wore a T-shirt emblazoned with the face of his cycling idol, Fausto Coppi. Marco began racing in competitions as a teenager, and by the time he reached his 20s, he had become a force to be reckoned with in the annual Giro d'Italia, which Italians consider to be the most prestigious tournament in the world. Placing third in the Giro in 1990 and second in 1991, Pantani at last won the event in 1992, and his victory landed him a lucrative contract with the Italian cycling team Carrera.

It was around this time that Marco began to develop a reputation as a maverick in the cycling world. Despite his coaches' constant suggestions, the cyclist insisted upon using only his natural skill and intelligence, rather than state-of-the-art equipment and high-tech training techniques, to pace himself. Early in his career, as both an amateur and as a young professional, his overeagerness often led him to take an early lead, only to tire and eventually fall far behind the leader's pack. He was equally undisciplined between races. "I'm not like the others in the world of cycling, but I've managed to settle in. I go out, I do what young men of my age do, and that's my way to be a cyclist," he told *CNN/SI* (August 2, 1998, on-line). "[Team director Giuseppe] Martinelli has sometimes struggled to understand me, and my father gets mad because I won't go to bed early, but I need this freedom."

In 1994, in spite of these tendencies, Pantani placed third in the Tour de France behind the Spaniard Miguel Indurain and the Russian Piotr Ugrumov. In addition to being named Best Young Rider, he won two stages of the Giro that year, placing second overall. In 1995, having developed into a formidable uphill rider, he won the L'Alpe d'Huez and Guzet-Neige stages of the Tour de France—both known for their mountainous terrain and steep inclines—and he claimed the bronze medal at the World Championships. "He's a throwback, the old-fashioned kind of rider," Italian premier Romano Prodi said of him, according to the *New York Times* (August 2, 1998), referring to Pantani's aversion to high-tech training equipment.

On October 18, 1995, while in the Milan-to-Turin race, Pantani was careening down a hill when, rounding a bend, he smacked against a Jeep that was coming towards him. He suffered a double compound fracture in his leg and spent most of 1996 on crutches, learning to walk again. "I seriously thought in the first week after the accident I would retire, but the doctor encouraged me to keep going," he said later. While Pantani was recovering, the famous cyclist and boss of the respected Mercatone Uno team, Luciano Pezzi, visited him and offered him a new, three-year contract. (Pantani's contract with his old club, Carrera, expired in 1996.) At the time doctors were not even sure that Pantani would be able to ride again. But he endured a rigorous rehabilitation, staged an impressive recovery, and rejoined the circuit in 1997.

"My aim is to have the satisfaction of being able to tell myself, 'Marco, you're back where you were,'" he told *wedge.nando.net* (January 19, 1997, on-line) at the beginning of the season. "If by the end of 1997 I hadn't done anything, and had suffered for a whole season without being up to it physically, I'd be really unhappy and I wouldn't continue with this sport. Being the sort of person I am, I cannot accept compromises. If I was destined to be some sort of nobody, I'd probably stop racing—irrespective of my contracts. It would be humiliating for me to ride without being able to show what I felt inside. There are other important things in life."

While Pantani was attempting to win the Giro for the first time as a professional, a cat ran across the road in front of his bike, causing a pile-up. Pantani was forced to leave the race with a torn muscle. "I don't know if [the cat] was black," he told *velocity.sportsline* (June 19, 1997, on-line). "But, believe it or not, I'm not superstitious." The torn muscle healed quickly, and a few months later, in an unanticipated finish, Pantani came in a dramatic third in the Tour de France (the same position in which he had finished in 1994), behind the German Jan Ullrich and the Frenchman Richard Virenque. Despite suffering from a sore throat the entire race, Pantani won both the L'Alpe d'Huez and Morzine stages of the race. "I really had been feeling bad the last few days," Pantani told Samuel Abt for the *New York Times* (July 22, 1997) after winning the l'Alpe d'Huez. "I even told my team officials that if this went on and I kept losing sleep, I wasn't sure I could make it to Paris. My throat was sore again today, but I guess I was able to overcome that." He followed up his impressive showing in France with a victory in the Rominger Classic. After competing in numerous minor races later in 1997 and in early 1998, Pantani was ranked sixth in the world on the eve of the 1998 Giro d'Italia.

Alex Zuelle of Switzerland dominated the initial stages of the Giro, but as the contest wore on, Pantani emerged as the stronger cyclist. "Pantani is an amazing competitor," Zuelle told *CNN/SI* (June 7, 1998, on-line). "I didn't expect him to be so strong." Pantani fought back from deep in the pack to take the lead with six days left—with the cyclists entering the Italian Alps. Excelling at uphill racing, he never lost the lead, finishing in 95 hours, 50 minutes, 39 seconds. "I am extremely satisfied. This victory allows me to see this sport as a huge source of enjoyment . . . ," Pantani told *CNN/SI*. "I think I won because I attacked the most and refused to finish second even if sometimes the conditions did not favor me." During the Saturday celebrations after the race, Marco surprised many people by defeating Russian Pavel Tonkov, who had won the 1996 Giro and placed second in 1998, in an individual time trial—the Russian's specialty. That evening, the entire Mercatone Uno team shaved their heads to imitate and honor Pantani.

A little over a month later, on July 11, in Dublin, Ireland, the Tour de France began on an ominous note. Allegations of drug use swirled around the French team Festina, and soon riders Richard Virenque and Alex Zuelle, against whom Pantani had competed in the past, were disqualified from the race after performance-enhancing drugs were found by French police in the car of their masseur, Willy Voet. Festina's coach later admitted he had supplied many of his riders with illegal drugs. More than 20 racers, coaches, team doctors, and masseurs were questioned by the police, and several were charged. Many of the racers from the other teams, feeling that their fellow riders' civil rights were being violated, voiced their dissatisfaction with French authorities. By the Alpine stage of the

event, one of the final tests of the Tour, competitors held a protest against French police for their handling of the drug investigations, and refused to ride. The stage was eventually canceled.

Despite these distractions, Pantani tried to maintain his focus on the race, but for a while, it seemed that the bad luck of 1995 and 1997 had returned to plague him anew. In the early stages of the competition, while the pack of riders was still congested, a series of crashes caused Pantani to fall numerous times. Although he was not injured, he was slowed considerably by the accidents. About a quarter of the way through the Tour, Pantani was riding in 62d place, seven minutes behind the leader. As the uphill stages approached, he was asked if he felt ready for the mountainous section of the tournament. Pantani told *CNN/SI*, "Not ready, no, because I still am very uncertain. I'm not 100 percent. I'm dragging along the efforts I made in the Giro and the [two stages in the] Pyrenees [in which he finished third and second]. To do something big, you have to know how to concentrate, and that state is hard to maintain durably. And I'm going to have to be in great shape. There are going to be many climbs." Pantani finished a respectable fifth in the first Alp stage—and then made remarkable gains on the second day in the Alps, the Tour's 13th stage, ending the day in third place overall. Ullrich, again among the leaders, said of Pantani that day, according to Abt, "Pantani was too strong." In the second-to-last day of the Tour, Pantani finished third once again, better than anyone had predicted; his high placing secured him his first-ever victory in the Tour de France, and the final stage of the race was merely a victory ride for the Italian, who was mobbed by fans and greeted as a hero. "To win the Giro and the Tour de France is something my country has been waiting for a long time," Pantani told CNN/SI (August 3, 1998, on-line). "This day will remain one of the most important days of my life." The Italian government planned a giant celebration for the cyclist. (His victory softened the blow of the Italian soccer team's shockingly poor performance that summer in the World Cup.)

Pantani was a favorite to win the 1999 Giro, which was held in early June. On June 5, with only two stages left, he was comfortably in the lead and showing little sign of letting up. Then, a random drug test administered by the Union Cycliste Internationale (International Cycling Union, known as UCI) allegedly revealed that the level of red cells (indicated by a ratio called the hematocrit value) in Pantani's blood exceeded by 2 percent the acceptable limit (50 percent). Although a level above 50 percent may occur naturally, the UCI suspected that Pantani had taken a substance that it has ruled illegal for racers—specifically, erythropoietin (EPO), which increases the number of red cells in the blood and thus enhances the blood's ability to carry oxygen throughout the body. UCI officials promptly ejected Pantani from the race and suspended him from competitive cycling for two weeks. Described by Samuel Abt in the *New York Times* (June 6, 1999) as "devastated," Pantani maintained his innocence. "I have already undergone two tests as race leader, and I think there is something strange going on here," he told a reporter for Agence France-Presse, as quoted by Abt. "I feel all sorts of things but words would be too much. I had the pink jersey [which the race leader wears], my hematocrit level was at 46 percent, and I wake up to this surprise. I think there's certainly something not quite right." At a press conference held a few days later, Pantani declared, as reported in the *New York Times* (June 10, 1999), "I am a clean rider. My conscience is clear." The cyclist hired lawyers to press for an investigation of the blood test, and on October 14, Bruno Giardina, an Italian prosecutor, ordered that DNA tests be conducted to determine whether the blood in question was actually Pantani's and whether UCI doctors had examined the blood properly.

Pantani's ejection from the Giro led to a deluge of negative publicity for professional cycling, which intensified when 10 other competitive cyclists also failed UCI drug tests. Cycling's image worsened further with the publication of *Chain Massacre: Revelations of 30 Years of Cheating* (1999), by Willy Voet, who is awaiting trial on drug-pushing charges; in his book Voet asserted that the use of performance-enhancing drugs is almost universal among professional cyclists but that few athletes are caught, because there are ways to fool the drug testers. Meanwhile, Pantani and other prominent cyclists declined to enter the 1999 Tour de France, which was held in July; as a headline in the *New York Times* (June 20, 1999) put it, the contest was "filled with no names." Indeed, Pantani warned that he might abandon competitive cycling altogether. He has apparently had second thoughts, however; according to an Associated Press report carried in *CNN Sports Illustrated* (October 14, 1999, on-line), he "said recently [that] he planned to return to action" in 2000.

"The great thing about life is to have goals," Pantani told CNN/SI (August 2, 1998, on-line). "I have reached a physical maturity so, as from next year, I shall try something different, a world championship, a Vuelta to find new motivation." Although Pantani's left leg is eight millimeters shorter than his right, a result of the double compound fracture in 1995, the disability apparently does not hamper his performance. Before a race he usually dyes his goatee the color of the winner's shirt—yellow for the Tour de France, pink for the Giro. He weighs 132 pounds and is five feet, seven inches tall. Since his early 20s, he has been a fixture around his hometown of Cesenatico in the off-season, playing his guitar in local restaurants and bars. — M.B.

Suggested Reading: *CNN/SI* (on-line) June 2, 1998, with photo, June 7, 1998, with photo, July 26, 1998, with photo, July 27, 1998, Aug. 2, 1998, with photo, Aug. 3, 1998, with photo, Sep. 2, 1998, with photo; *letour.fr* (on-line) Aug. 2, 1998; *New York Times* H p11 July 20, 1997, with photo, B p6 July 22, 1997, with photo; *New York Times* (on-line) Aug. 2, 1998, with photos; *velocity.sportsline* (on-line) July 19, 1997, with photos; *wedge.nando.net* (on-line) Jan. 19, 1997

Parks, Suzan-Lori

1963– Playwright; screenwriter. Address: c/o International Creative Management, 40 W. 57th St., New York, NY 10019

In works of literature, art, and music by African-Americans—for example, the novels of Richard Wright, the plays of Lorraine Hansberry, the paintings of Jacob Lawrence, even some of the music of contemporary rappers—the dominant style has often been social realism. At the same time, other African-Americans have been eager to explore the surreal, the fantastic, and the just plain outrageous. Suzan-Lori Parks, the two-time Obie-winning playwright who has claimed that she is from the planet Venus, is such an artist. Indeed, given the wild flights of fancy in Parks's plays, her taste for the mothership imagery associated with the music of Parliament-Funkadelic, and her insistence that each of her plays, like the radioactive element plutonium, must be approached carefully—"If it gets inside you, it can kill you," she has said—her joking assertion that she has extraplanetary origins does not seem entirely preposterous.

Consider, for instance, her play *The Death of the Last Black Man in the Whole Entire World* (1989–92), in which the names of her two main characters echo stereotypes—Black Man With Watermelon and Black Woman With Fried Drumstick; or her work *The America Play* (1992–94), in which one of her characters, an African-American who looks like Abraham Lincoln, digs a hole in the middle of the stage—he calls it "The Great Hole of History"—and then proceeds to use it as his own bully pulpit. Many critics have detected the influence of Samuel Beckett in Parks's work. Parks has acknowledged the influence of Beckett, but has cited the southern writer William Faulkner and the experimental African-American playwright Adrienne Kennedy as her primary influences.

For some inveterate theatergoers, among them her fellow playwright Tony Kushner, Suzan-Lori Parks is one of the most important voices to emerge in American theater in the past two decades. Many others have complained that her work is extremely difficult and esoteric. In his essay "The Art of the Difficult," which appeared in the magazine *Civili-*

The second of three children, Parks was born in 1963 in Fort Knox, Kentucky. During Suzan-Lori's early years, her mother was a teacher, and her father was an army officer. Because of her father's periodic reassignments to different military bases, Parks grew up in five different states and attended junior high and high school in Germany. Her father later became an assistant professor of education at the University of Vermont, and her mother became the director of African-American programs at Syracuse University, in New York State.

As a child Parks harbored what she thought were great ambitions: she wanted to become "a go-go dancer or a geologist or ascend into heaven," as she wrote in *The America Play and Other Works*. She started writing at an early age. As an undergraduate at Mount Holyoke College, in South Hadley, Massachusetts, she majored in both English and German. Her interest in theater was sparked when she took a course in short-story writing taught by the acclaimed novelist, essayist, and playwright James Baldwin. The students "had to read [their] work out loud," she told Erika Munk for the *Washington Post* (February 28, 1993). "I got so deep into it, really acting out my stories, moving around the room, that [Baldwin] said, 'Why don't you start writing plays?'" Parks had her doubts about a career in theater—"Theater people made me nervous because they dressed funny and had this attitude, so much affect," she told Munk—but she had no intention of rejecting the advice of the famous writer. "When James Baldwin makes a suggestion, you listen," she told Monte Williams for the *New York Times* (April 17, 1996).

Early on Parks was inspired by the works of the playwright Adrienne Kennedy, whose best-known play is *Funnyhouse of a Negro*. In her senior year Parks directed a production of Ntozake Shange's *For Colored Girls Who Have Considered Suicide / When the Rainbow is Enuf*. She also wrote a play, which, despite her instructor's insistence that she write in a realistic mode, veered into the fantastic. "In my play, the house kept blowing up and the yard exploded," she told Susan Morgan for *Mirabella* in the early 1990s. "I could never write a naturalistic play."

After graduating from Mount Holyoke, in 1985, Parks went to London to study acting at the Drama Studio. She was "absolutely horrible" at acting, she told Alisa Solomon for the *Village Voice* (September 19, 1989), but she stuck with the program as a means of improving her writing. "I knew if I wanted to be a great playwright, I had to know what actors did and respect it," she explained to Solomon. After finishing her studies at the Drama Studio, she moved to New York City, where she supported herself by working as a paralegal, a building manager, and a typist; while on the job, she read James Joyce's *Ulysses* and other books on the sly. Making use of her imagination and verbal ingenuity, she also briefly worked as a phone-sex operator.

Suzan-Lori Parks

Courtesy of the Wilma Theater

zation (1997), Kushner noted that Parks "is the only American playwright I know who makes use of footnotes, which . . . present a conundrum for the production team: How do you stage a footnote? Or do you? Parks doesn't tell you." Parks's plays, he admitted, "are full of these sorts of provocations." Confused by the lack of stage directions and the presence of seeming nonsense sounds ("blubblubblub" and "do in diddly dip didded thuh drop," to quote two) and incessant wordplay in her scripts, some directors have told Parks that she is harder to read than the modernist writer James Joyce.

To help directors, actors, scholars, and readers, Parks discussed her ideas about playwrighting in introductory essays in her compilation *The America Play and Other Works* (1995). In a glossary within one essay, she explained, among other things, that "do in diddly dip didded thuh drop" is a fancy way of saying "Yes!" or can be used in place of the question, "Yeah?" In another essay she outlined her aesthetic vision. In her plays, she wrote, she tries to avoid what she called the "Theater of Schmaltz." "Theater seems mired in the interest of stating some point, or tugging some heartstring, or landing a laugh, or making a splash, or wagging a finger. In no other artform are the intentions so slim! As a playwright I try to do many things: explore the form, ask questions, make a good show, tell a good story, ask more questions, take nothing for granted." She also wrote, "Realism, like other movements in other artforms, is a specific response to a certain historical climate. I don't explode the form because I find traditional plays 'boring'—I don't really [find them boring]. It's just those structures never could accommodate the figures which take up residence inside me."

Imperceptible Mutabilities of the Third Kingdom (1986–89), Parks's first full-length play to be produced in New York, opened at BACA Downtown in 1989, under the direction of Liz Diamond. Seemingly spanning African-American history, the play is divided into four parts—"Snails," "Third Kingdom," "Open House," and "Greeks"— with "Third Kingdom" reprised between "Open House" and "Greeks." The first part takes place in the present and deals with three African-American women who are being observed by a white male naturalist via a camera attached to a cockroach. The second is set on a slave ship crossing the Atlantic—which, as the "watery crossroads," in Parks's words, between Africa and America, is the "Third Kingdom" of the title. The third section illuminates the life of an elderly former slave by means of "memories and nightmares," among them one in which her teeth are being extracted and another in which "her antebellum Master comes to visit," as Parks wrote in an essay for a publicity piece distributed by the Wilma Theater, in Philadelphia, in 1998. The final section, based partly on Parks's family history, deals with the family of a sergeant patiently awaiting his "distinction."

In each section of *Imperceptible Mutabilities*, slides are projected on the back wall of the stage, to suggest, as Parks explained to Alisa Solomon, "African-American history in the shadow of the photographic image." In an essay for the Wilma Theater publicity piece, Parks wrote that *Imperceptible Mutabilities* shows "changes that could happen over hundreds of years, enormous and subtle evolutionary changes—subtle changes that we don't notice but that influence us just the same." "The play works very much like dreaming," she explained. "'Snails' is closest to present-day reality; 'Third Kingdom' takes us into the depths; 'Open House,' with its fears and confusions, is the place of deepest REM sleep; 'Third Kingdom Reprise' brings us back to the surface, and 'Greeks' is a dream of the present day draped with the deep myth of sleep." *Imperceptible Mutabilities* won the 1990 Obie Award for best new American play.

Parks's next full-length play, *The Death of the Last Black Man in the Whole Entire World* (1989–92), premiered in 1990 at BACA Downtown under the direction of Beth Schachter. As unusual as its predecessor, the play follows a character named Black Man With Watermelon and his companion, Black Woman With Fried Drumstick, as they travel through a world of spirits inhabited by other fancifully named characters, among them Before Columbus, Queen-then-Pharaoh Hatshepsut, Lots of Grease and Lots of Pork, and Yes And Greens Black-Eyed Peas Cornbread. During the course of their adventures, Black Man With Watermelon is repeatedly killed and brought back to life. Then, "when he is good and dead," Parks wrote in an essay for the Wilma Theater, "Black Woman feeds him feathers, her homestyle taxidermy." Black Man "needs to know his origins before he can embrace his death . . . ," she explained. "The spirits, a plethora of theatrical figures drawn from history, religion and literature, come forth and tell him of his past, which helps him in his journey forward toward his final resting place." She also wrote, "The shape of *Last Black Man* patterns itself on the passion of Christ, specifically the Stations of the Cross, where we see Christ's journey to Calvary in a series of dramatic scenes."

As both *Imperceptible Mutabilities* and *The Death of the Last Black Man* showed, Parks had little interest in linear narratives that led to a climax and denouement. Instead, she structured the plays like jazz compositions, with improvisation around a single theme. "'Repetition and Revision' is a concept integral to the Jazz esthetic in which the composer or performer will write or play a musical phrase once and again and again . . . ; with each revisit the phrase is slightly revised," she wrote in *The America Play and Other Works*. "'Rep & Rev' as I call it is a central element in my work; through its use I'm working to create a dramatic text that departs from the traditional linear narrative style to look and sound more like a musical score."

The Death of the Last Black Man was followed by *The America Play* (1992–94), which opened in 1994 at the Yale Repertory Theater, in New Haven, Connecticut, with Liz Diamond directing, and was produced later that year at the Joseph Papp Public Theater, in New York City. *The America Play* is about a black man named the Foundling Father, who is said to look like Abraham Lincoln. He digs a hole in the ground—"the Great Hole of History," which represents gaps in recorded American history—and, to enable people to reenact the assassination of Lincoln, he lets them shoot him with blanks. In the second half of the play, the Foundling Father's wife and son search for his remains after they hear that he is dead; instead of finding his bones, they find such artifacts as George Washington's wooden false teeth. As in her previous plays, the script of *The America Play* is heavy with wordplay, such as in the words "hole" and "whole," or "foe-," "faux-," and "fore-" father. "Dig" can mean either "to excavate" or, as in slang, "to understand" or "to appreciate," as in "Can you dig it?" As Parks told Andrea Stevens for the *New York Times* (March 6, 1994), words are meant to "bang up against each other and do things" in her plays.

The America Play also reveals Parks's abiding concern for questions about history. "Since history is a recorded or remembered event," she wrote in *The America Play and Other Works*, "theater, for me, is the perfect place to 'make' history—that is, because so much of African-American history has been unrecorded, dismembered, washed out, one of my tasks as playwright is to—through literature and the special strange relationship between theater and real-life—locate the ancestral burial ground, dig for bones, find bones, hear the bones sing, write it down." In the Wilma Theater publicity piece, she wrote that *The America Play* is about "digging and listening. It's about piecing your history together from sound fragments and broken artifacts."

Parks often has been reluctant to explain the meanings of her plays. In fact, while writing a play, she is often not completely sure herself what it means. "I don't consciously start writing a play that involves issues," she told Monte Williams. "After it's done, I sit back like everyone else and think about what it means." The director Liz Diamond—who met Parks in a coffee shop in 1988—explained to Andrea Stevens that a Parks play can be "about family, the country, race, men and women. Her work is layered like phyllo dough."

Layered meanings notwithstanding, Parks has insisted that her plays are definitely *not* about African-American victimization or heroism—what James Baldwin once derisively called "protest literature." As she told Erika Munk, her plays are not "dramas that tell audiences, 'Oh, black people were doing all these things we don't know about, or [that show] how oppressed we are by white people and how we triumph over oppression and how, by extension, we're obsessed.' I don't want to create an audience in which the black people just feel good and the white people are just 'mea culping.'" Instead, she told Monte Williams, "My plays are for the kind of black people who relate to funk music, to Parliament-Funkadelic. When those guys get out of a spaceship—the idea that black people are from outer space, there's a poetic truth to that. We are this vast people." She has summed up her stance on race and theater in two pithy equations: "Black People + 'Whitey' = Standard Dramatic Conflict; Black People + X = New Dramatic Conflict"—"where X is the realm of situations showing African-Americans in states other than the Oppressed by/Obsessed with 'Whitey state'; where the White when present is not the oppressor," as she wrote in *The America Play and Other Works*.

Parks's disdain for works that merely depict black victimization or black heroism are evident in a film, *Girl 6*, and a play, *Venus*, both of which premiered in 1996. *Girl 6*, for which Parks collaborated on the screenplay with the filmmaker Spike Lee, is about a struggling young actress who supports herself by taking a job as a phone-sex operator. She becomes obsessed with the fantasy worlds she creates and begins to enjoy her job as much as the people who call in; she even arranges a face-to-face meeting with one of her customers.

Venus was produced at the Joseph Papp Public Theater under the direction of the avant-garde auteur Richard Foreman. The play is based on the true story of an African woman, Saartjie Baartman, who was brought to England in the 19th century and, billed as the Hottentot Venus, was displayed in a circus show, because she had what were considered unusually large buttocks. Parks depicts Baartman as playing an active role in her own humiliation. "I could have written a two-hour saga with Venus being the victim," she told Monte Williams. "But she's multi-faceted. She's vain, beautiful, intelligent and yes, complicit."

Many critical responses to *Girl 6* and *Venus* zeroed in on Parks's depiction of exploitation and agency. The mainstream critic Roger Ebert wrote in the *Detroit News* (March 22, 1996, on-line) that *Girl 6* "seems conceived from the point of view of a male caller who would like to believe that the woman he's hiring by the minute is enjoying their conversation just as much as he is." Echoing many other reviewers, he called the film "Lee's worst." Similarly, the critic Jean Young argued in *African-American Review* (Winter 1997) that Parks's depiction of Baartman's complicity in *Venus* was historically inaccurate. Other critics, however, praised *Venus* precisely because Parks had avoided portraying Baartman as a victim. The play won a 1996 Obie for playwrighting. For Parks, the inability of critics to see the female protagonists in *Girl 6* or *Venus* as complex characters represents essentialist thinking. "I never wanted to be a spokesperson for the race," she told Monte Williams.

Some of Parks's shorter works include the one-act plays *Betting on the Dust Commander* (1987) and *Devotees in the Garden of Love* (1991) and two radio plays, *Pickling* (1988–90) and *Locomotive* (1992). She has also completed some short films, including *Anemone Me*, co-written and co-directed by the poet Bruce Hainley, about a black family in Maine who meet a "merboy" (the male equivalent of a mermaid). "It's about losing your tail and finding your feet," Parks told Susan Morgan.

Parks's most recent play, *In the Blood*, is scheduled to premiere in 1999 at the Wilma Theater, where Parks is currently a resident artist. According to the playwright, *In the Blood* was inspired by Nathaniel Hawthorne's novel *The Scarlet Letter*. The play's main character is Hester La Negrita, who has given birth to five illegitimate children. Hester "realizes that her 'life is [her] own fault' but she desperately needs help," Parks wrote in a Wilma Theater essay. She also revealed, "My interest in sex and love (coupled with time and distance) runs wild" in the play.

Parks has received more than half a dozen grants, from the Rockefeller, Ford, Whiting, W. Alton Jones, and Cal Arts-Herb Alpert Foundations, the New York Foundation for the Arts, the National Endowment for the Arts (twice), and the Lila Wallace Reader's Digest Fund. With the last of those, she established the Harlem Kids Internet-Playwriting Workshop. She has taught playwriting at the Yale School of Drama and the New School University, in New York, among other schools, and is currently a regular columnist for *Grand Street*. Recently, she completed a screenplay for the actress and director Jodie Foster. — W.G.

Suggested Reading: *African-American Review* p687+ Winter 1997; *Drama Review* p56+ Fall 1995; *Essence* p74 Apr. 1996, with photo; *New York Times* II p5 Mar. 6, 1994, with photo, C p1+ Apr. 17, 1996, with photos; *Village Voice* p102+ Sep. 19, 1989, with photo; *Washington Post* G p3 Feb. 28, 1993, with photo

Selected Plays: *Imperceptible Mutabilities in the Third Kingdom*, 1986–89; *Pickling*, 1988–90; *Betting on the Dust Commander*, 1987; *The Death of the Last Black Man in the Whole Entire World*, 1989–92; *Devotees in the Garden of Love*, 1991; *Locomotive*, 1992; *The America Play*, 1992–94; *Venus*, 1996

Selected Films: *Anemone Me*; *Girl 6*, 1996

Joel Meyerowitz/Courtesy of Boneau, Bryan/Brown

Patinkin, Mandy

Nov. 30, 1952– Singer; actor. Address: c/o United Talent Agency, 9560 Wilshire Blvd., Beverly Hills, CA 90212

"All blood cells and no skin." That is how Joseph Papp, the founder of the Public Theater, in New York City, and the New York Shakespeare Festival, described the actor and singer Mandy Patinkin in a 1989 interview. "You can just look at him cross-eyed and he feels he's being whipped. That's how exposed he is when he works." "Not much known for tranquility," as Evelyn Renold put it in the *New York Daily News Magazine* (September 20, 1987), Patinkin vaulted to fame in 1980, when he won a Tony Award for his portrayal of Che Guevara in the Broadway production of the Andrew Lloyd Webber–Tim Rice musical *Evita*. Later, he earned widespread praise for other performances on stage—in, for example, the Stephen Sondheim–James Lapine musical *Sunday in the Park with George* and in his solo theater-concerts. Similar accolades came his way for his acting on such television series as *Chicago Hope* and for his work on the silver screen, in

such films as *Ragtime*, *Yentl*, *Alien Nation*, and *The Princess Bride*. Despite his many successes, he has remained, according to various reporters and colleagues of his, intense, highly emotional, unusually high-strung, and boundlessly perfectionistic. One day during the filming of *The Princess Bride*, in the late 1980s, when Patinkin was, in his own words, "agonizing over some little scene, . . . pouring my heart out to Rob [Reiner, who directed the film], telling him I was letting the movie down," Reiner blurted out to him, "Get out of your way, man!" Those words, he told John Stark for *People* (May 8, 1989), "are at the heart of my struggle: . . . I will always have to work at getting out of my own way."

The son of Doris and Lester Patinkin, Mandel Patinkin was born on November 30, 1952 in Chicago. He was named in memory of his paternal grandfather, who, in about 1900, founded the scrap-metal company where Patinkin's father later earned his living. That grandfather, a Russian-Jewish immigrant, "started out with a pushcart, eventually got a truck, then a shack, and he turned it into a major business," Patinkin told Aileen Jacobson for *Newsday* (August 31, 1981). Mandy Patinkin's parents—his mother was a homemaker—raised him in what he described to Jacobson as a "conservatively religious" Jewish atmosphere. "I went to Hebrew school five days a week, had a big bar mitzvah, did the whole thing. . . . It wasn't so much a religious background to me as family background, and a tradition, a culture. That world . . . is what I love and want to hold onto in our family."

At age nine, Patinkin began singing in the choir of the synagogue his family attended. "It's how I got attention," he told John Stark. (Years later he incorporated in his singing a cry that resembles the cry in the voice of his synagogue's cantor.) As a bar mitzvah gift, his father took him to New York City to see two shows—*Mame* and *Walking Happy*. "I remember going back to Chicago and singing all the songs around the house," he recalled to Stephen Holden for the *New York Times* (February 1, 1989). When he was 14, his mother suggested he get involved in activities at a local branch of the Young Men's Jewish Council. "At first, I didn't want to go," he recalled to Jacobson. "I thought, that's ridiculous. Then I heard a bunch of guys talking about it in the lunchroom at school, and that changed my mind. So I went, I got into a play, and I loved it." While in his teens, he appeared in a TV commercial for 7-Up.

Heeding his parents' advice that he attend a liberal-arts college rather than focus exclusively on studying drama, Patinkin enrolled at the University of Kansas. After two years, he left the university and entered the drama program at the Juilliard School, in New York City. Two years later, in 1974, he left Juilliard, reportedly because he had lost the desire to earn a degree. After traveling in Europe for a few weeks, he returned to New York to seek work as an actor. He soon landed a series of bit parts in low-budget Off-Broadway and regional

PATINKIN

productions, and within a year or so, he had built an impressive résumé. It was strengthened considerably during the years 1975 to 1981, when he was associated with Joseph Papp's New York Shakespeare Festival. He made his debut with the festival in 1975, in a small role in Arthur Pinero's play *Trelawny of the 'Wells'* at the Vivian Beaumont Theater in Lincoln Center. During the next few years, he appeared in productions of *Rebel Women*, *Hamlet*, *Savages*, and *Leave It to Beaver Is Dead*, the last of which was directed by Des McAnuff and enabled him to showcase his talents in a more substantial supporting role than his earlier ones. As a cast member of *Split*, a play by his friend Michael Weller, he met the actress Kathryn Grody, whom he married in 1980.

After *Split* closed, Patinkin's agent suggested he try out for *Evita*, a musical about Eva Perón, the first wife of the Argentine dictator Juan Perón, that was then playing to sellout audiences in London and was slated for production in New York. "I didn't even know what part I was auditioning for," Patinkin recalled to Jacobson. Having little interest in musical theater at that time, he went to the audition half-heartedly, dressed in jeans and a Mickey Mouse sweatshirt. Later that same day, the producers told him that he had gotten the part of the narrator-cum-Greek chorus, a character who, though identified only as Che, is presumably the Marxist revolutionary Che Guevara. Much to his surprise, he learned that the entire book of *Evita* is presented in song and recitative; to prepare for his role, he took lessons with a voice coach. (Reportedly, he has never learned to read music and has had little other musical training.) By the time the show opened on Broadway, in September 1979, the buzz in the theatrical world was that he would be a leading candidate for the Tony Award that year. Although many New York reviewers expressed misgivings about the musical as a whole and about Che's presence in the story (in reality, Guevara never met the Peróns), most praised Patinkin's fiery portrayal of the character, and he did indeed win a Tony, for best actor in a musical.

After *Evita* closed, Des McAnuff cast Patinkin as the hot-headed warrior Hotspur in a Joseph Papp production of Shakespeare's *Henry IV, Part I*, which was performed in Central Park, in New York City, in 1981. McAnuff declared to Aileen Jacobson that Patinkin *was* Hotspur. "He's an actor who has a lot of heat, passion, emotional power. And he is very moral, very idealistic. He sees no gray, only black and white. Mandy's more mature [than Hotspur], but sides of him are still younger. Parts of him are pretty naïve. He doesn't see dark things about people right away. He's very uncynical."

At Patinkin's request, Michael Weller introduced him to Milos Forman, who had recently directed the film *One Flew Over the Cuckoo's Nest* and whose work Patinkin had long admired. He accepted Forman's invitation to audition for his next film, *Ragtime* (1981), which is based on the novel of that name by E. L. Doctorow, and he won the

part of Tateh, a struggling Jewish immigrant who becomes a Hollywood movie mogul. "On the first day, I was terrified," Patinkin told Jacobson. "We were getting ready for this scene, and [Forman] said, so you move here, and then you do this and then this. All these people are telling me to do things, and then we do the take. And in the middle of the take, I forgot to do one of those things and I stopped and [Forman] goes, 'Mandy, Mandy, what are you doing? Listen, everybody's going to tell you 10,000 things. When we shoot it, forget it. Just forget everything. If it happens, it happens.' . . . I was afraid, and he told me not to be afraid, and there's a way that some people can tell you not to be afraid and you won't be. And he has that way." While *Ragtime* did poorly both critically and commercially, Patinkin earned positive reviews. According to McAnuff, "It's that believability, that complete conviction, that's what gives him his brilliance. You only get that very rarely in an actor."

Struck by Patinkin's performance in *Ragtime*, Barbra Streisand sent him the script for her next project, *Yentl* (1983)—a film, adapted from a short story by Isaac Bashevis Singer, that she produced, directed, and starred in—with the idea that she might cast him as Avigdor, the male lead. As Evelyn Renold reported in the *New York Daily News* (May 20, 1984), Patinkin told Streisand that he disliked the characterization of Avigdor. Streisand was open to his suggestions; she discussed the role with him repeatedly during the next year, and as Patinkin put it to Renold, the script "evolved" to reflect his requested changes "about 100 percent." "Though the movie received mixed reviews," Renold reported, "Patinkin's performance was widely praised; critics took note of his strong sexual presence and anointed him a romantic leading man." Also in 1983 Patinkin appeared in *Daniel*; directed by Sidney Lumet, the film was adapted by E. L. Doctorow from his novel *The Book of Daniel*, which was loosely based on the real-life story of Julius and Ethel Rosenberg (who were executed in 1953 on charges of spying for the Soviet Union) and their two children. In *Variety Movie Guide '96*, Patinkin's portrayal of Julius Rosenberg is called "superb."

In 1984 Patinkin returned to Broadway to star in *Sunday in the Park with George*, the inspiration for which was a painting by the 19th-century French pointillist Georges Seurat. A bearded Patinkin played the role of Seurat; clean-shaven, he portrayed Seurat's supposed great-grandson. In an assessment that reflected the general critical reaction to the musical, a *Variety* (May 9, 1984) reviewer wrote that, in a "difficult dual role," Patinkin "offers an intense, skillfully considered, low-key performance that isn't able to animate the stubbornly resistant intellectualized basis of the two parts." Nevertheless, he earned a Tony nomination less than a week after the show opened.

In about 1985, Patinkin signed on to co-star in *Heartburn*, the movie version of Nora Ephron's roman à clef about the breakup of her marriage to the journalist Carl Bernstein. During the first week of production, Patinkin and Mike Nichols, who directed *Heartburn*, began butting heads. "I took the role disagreeing with a lot of what was in the script," Patinkin explained to Renold. "I thought, how can I say no [that is, 'No, I don't want the part'] to Meryl [Streep, the female lead] and Mike? What am I, nuts? I thought I'd find a way, that it would all work out." After a month of conflict, Nichols fired Patinkin and then hired Jack Nicholson to replace him—actions that received a great deal of publicity. By his own account, while viewing *Heartburn* (1986) in a theater, Patinkin detected troublesome aspects of Nicholson's performance, of a kind that indicated to him that Nicholson had had problems with the script similar to his own. Feeling somewhat vindicated did not comfort him. He told Renold, "I said to myself, 'Okay, Mandy, you were right. But Jack did it, and did it kill him? No. Did it hurt his life? No. Did it affect his career? No. Would it have mattered, Mandy, if you'd just *done* it? No.'" He also learned from the experience, he told Renold, "to trust my feelings and to express them *before* I agree to do a part."

For one year after his ouster from *Heartburn*, Patinkin "didn't get a single call" from Hollywood, he told Renold. "So, yup, I paid the price. Did it make me mad? Hell, yes." "The price" included great emotional distress. The intense emotionality that Patinkin typically invests in his roles "has a downside," John Stark reported in his 1989 *People* article about the actor. "He is quite capable of worrying himself sick, and his constant anxiety about his career and how to portray a given role correctly has, on more than one occasion, driven employers, friends, and Patinkin himself to distraction." Patinkin has reportedly attended weekly sessions with a psychotherapist for years.

When Patinkin's phone began ringing again, he received offers for several choice roles: those of Inigo Montoya, a Spanish swordsman, in Rob Reiner's *The Princess Bride* (1987), a fairy tale based on a novel by William Goldman; a U.S. senator up to no good, in Peter Yates's political thriller *The House on Carrol Street* (1988); and the humanoid partner of a human policeman (played by James Caan) in Graham Baker's *Alien Nation* (1988). His work in all three drew enthusiastic reviews.

In *Esquire* (April 1989), Daniel Okrent wrote that people who, like Okrent, considered Patinkin "the greatest singer of theater music we have" felt frustrated, because "Patinkin's skill as an actor" had led him to "expend great chunks of time and effort on nonsinging movies." "Patinkin is like Michael Jordan—when you watch him score, it's easy to ignore how great a defensive player he is," Okrent noted. "Watch Patinkin act, and it's too easy to forget how brilliantly he sings." Okrent made those observations in a review of Patinkin's first solo album, *Mandy Patinkin* (1989), in which

he described the singer's phrasing as "impeccable," his diction as "nearly supernatural," and his "shining tenor" as "an instrument of absolute purity." In a review of the album for *Newsweek* (February 20, 1989), Cathleen McGuigan was similarly impressed: "He doesn't barge in on a song and take it over," she wrote; "instead, he treats it like an actor getting into character. . . . What's remarkable is Patinkin's straight, uncynical approach to music that went out with the rumble seat. Given his vocal firepower, he turns almost every song into a show stopper, though at moments the achingly pure delivery seems almost obsessive and over the edge." McGuigan also noted with admiration Patinkin's "intensely personal" selection of songs.

Patinkin drew rave reviews with a solo show, *Mandy Patinkin in Concert: Dress Casual*, that he presented six times at the Public Theater in early 1989 (to benefit both the New York Shakespeare Festival's Shakespeare in the Park series and victims of AIDS) and then, later in the year, on Broadway, at the Helen Hayes Theatre. Describing him in the *Christian Science Monitor* (August 8, 1989) as an "ingratiating singer-actor" and his concert as "something special," John Beaufort wrote that Patinkin had demonstrated "mastery of assorted musical styles and trends from the 1890s to the 1980s." Patinkin's album *Dress Casual* (1990) offers some songs from the concert as well as other tunes. Earlier, for two years beginning in 1994, Patinkin was seen on TV on the medical drama *Chicago Hope*, in the role of a physician named Jeffrey Geiger. In 1995 he won an Emmy Award for his portrayal. He left the series with three years left on his contract, because, as he told Barbara Isenberg for the *Los Angeles Times* (January 14, 1996), "I did not have time to spend with my family. I was there 24 hours a day, eight days a week, and I had no time for a life."

Patinkin's work in the 1990s also includes, in theater, performances in *The Secret Garden* (1991) and *Falsettos* (1993); on television, his appearance in the made-for-TV movie *The Hunchback* (1997), in which he created, in the character Quasimodo, "a gentle and quite moving creature," as John J. O'Connor wrote for the *New York Times* (March 14, 1997); on the big screen, a starring role in *The Music of Chance* (1993), based on a Paul Auster novel; and the albums *Experiment* (1994), *Oscar & Steve* (1995), and *Mamaloshen* (1998). On *Mamaloshen* (the word means "mother tongue" in Yiddish), Patinkin sings in Yiddish; he learned the language recently, not only to make the album and prepare for a series of concerts but also as a way of enriching his personal life. "I've always had these other goals in life," he explained to Howard Reich for the *Chicago Tribune* (April 13, 1998), "but they had to do with being successful, or whether I was going to make it. I remember my first goal was: Could I make a living [in the arts] by age 25, and if I couldn't, I'd get out of the business. . . . And, in the end, I look at them all as petty goals that had nothing to do with the meaning of life or any kind of a lesson that I'm interested in passing on to my children. These Yiddish songs became something more important. Like love, they came in from the back door."

In 1998 Patinkin returned to *Chicago Hope* as a regular member of the cast, reprising the Emmy-winning role of Dr. Jeffrey Geiger. Most recently he played the villainous Huxley in the Muppet movie *The Adventures of Elmo in Grouchland* (1999), and Kenneth Duberstein, a former White House aide, in *Strange Justice* (1999), a drama broadcast on the cable TV station Showtime. *Strange Justice* documents the enormous controversy surrounding the 1991 Senate Judiciary Committee hearings during which Anita Hill, a University of Oklahoma professor of law, testified that Supreme Court nominee Clarence Thomas had sexually harassed her at work some years before. In a review of *Strange Justice* for the New York Times (August 27, 1999), Caryn James wrote, "It is Mandy Patinkin who holds the film together as Kenneth Duberstein, the consultant who is assigned by the White House to help Thomas navigate through the hearings and who is just as much a player as the principals. . . . What Mr. Patinkin's subtle depiction brings to the character are decency and pragmatism in a portrayal more chilling than if Duberstein had been presented as a monster. His conservative politics are sincere, and a job is a job, even when he comes to doubt the nominee's truthfulness. Here is the scary reality of politics as usual."

Mandy Patinkin and his wife, Kathryn Grody, live on the Upper West Side of Manhattan with their two teenage sons, Isaac and Gideon. — M.B.

Selected Reading: *Chicago Tribune* C p1 Apr. 13, 1998, with photo; *Cosmopolitan* p116 Jan. 1988, with photos; *Entertainment Weekly* p28+ May 10, 1996, with photos; *Esquire* p40 Apr. 1989, with photo; *Los Angeles Times* D p7 Jan. 14, 1996, with photos; *New York Daily News* p3 May 20, 1984, with photos; *New York Daily News Magazine* p26+ Sep. 20, 1987, with photos; *Newsday* B p3+ Aug. 23, 1981, with photo; *New York Times* L p3+ Mar. 16, 1997, with photos; *People* p145+ May 8, 1989, with photos

Selected Recordings: *Mandy Patinkin*, 1989; *Dress Casual*, 1990; *Experiment*, 1994; *Oscar & Steve*, 1995; *Mamaloshen*, 1998

Selected Films: *The Big Fix*, 1978; *Last Embrace*, 1979; *French Postcards*, 1979; *Night of the Juggler*, 1980; *Ragtime*, 1981; *Yentl*, 1983; *Daniel*, 1983; *Maxie*, 1985; *The Princess Bride*, 1987; *Alien Nation*, 1988; *The House on Carrol Street*, 1988; *Dick Tracy*, 1990; *True Colors*, 1991; *The Doctor*, 1991; *Impromptu*, 1991; *Life with Mikey*, 1993; *The Music of Chance*, 1993; *Squanto: A Warrior's Tale*, 1994; *Men with Guns*, 1997; *Lulu on the Bridge*, 1998; *The Adventures of Elmo in Grouchland*, 1999; for television— *The Hunchback*, 1997; *Strange Justice*, 1999

Selected Television Shows: *Taxi*, 1978; *Charleston*, 1979; *The Simpsons*, 1989; *Picket Fences*, 1992; *The Larry Sanders Show*, 1992; *Chicago Hope*, 1994–95, 1998–; *Broken Glass*, 1996

Selected Plays: *Trelawny of the 'Wells'*, 1975; *Hamlet*, 1976; *Leave It to Beaver Is Dead*, 1977; *Savages*, 1978; *Split*, 1978; *Evita*, 1979; *The Shadow Box*, 1980; *Sunday in the Park with George*, 1984; *The Knife*, 1987; *The Winter's Tale*, 1990; *The Secret Garden*; 1991; *Falsettos*, 1993

Selected Solo Concerts: *Mandy Patinkin: Dress Casual*, 1989; *Mamaloshen*, 1998

Barron Claiborne/Courtesy of Verve Records

Payton, Nicholas

Sep. 26, 1973– Jazz trumpeter. Address: c/o Verve Records, 555 W. 57th St., 10th Fl., New York, NY 10019

Possessing the round, cherubic looks and natty style of Louis Armstrong, Nicholas Payton is often spoken of as the spitting image of the late jazz icon. For those who have heard Payton blow his horn, the comparisons do not end there. "He's the greatest of the New Orleans–style trumpet players that I've ever heard," the legendary jazz trumpeter Adolphus "Doc" Cheatham told Greg Devlin for *Creative Loafing* (September 1997, on-line). "He's pure, he's not fooling around. And every time I hear him he sounds better and better. I haven't heard anybody like him since Louis Armstrong."

Hyped by jazz aficionados as the next great musician from New Orleans while he was still a teenager, Payton was proving the pundits correct by age 20. His virtuosity and vast knowledge of his city's musical tradition mark him as a prodigy, but his gift for melodic improvisation and the expressiveness with which he molds a tune are the qualities that make him a standout among the young musicians on the resurgent jazz scene. "Nicholas is a great musician, who was very serious about learning and developing all aspects of jazz musicianship," the trumpeter and composer Wynton Marsalis has said, according to Verve Records' Internet site. "He has tremendous talent and a work ethic that matches that talent. This is a rare combination which ensures an originality fundamental to jazz expression."

Nicholas Payton was born on September 26, 1973 in New Orleans, Louisiana, and was raised in the city's Treme section, which has long been known as a hotbed of jazz brass talent. Musical talent runs in his family, as both his parents, alumni of Xavier University, are musicians: Maria Payton is a classically trained pianist and operatic singer, and Walter Payton is a renowned jazz bassist. At age four Nicholas asked for a trumpet for Christmas; his parents gave him a pocket trumpet, since his hands were too small to handle a full-sized instrument. Nicholas's skill on his horn developed rapidly. Though unable to read music, he acquired over the next four years enough of a musical ear to play with his father. "I remember one of the first gigs I did was with the Young Tuxedo Brass Band," Payton said, according to the Verve record label's Internet site. "I was about eight years old, and my dad took me along with him to do a Mardi Gras parade. At the time, I only knew about two or three tunes at best, but they let me play the whole parade anyway. After the parade, all of the guys chipped in to pay my salary of about $10, which is a lot of money to an eight-year-old. With $10 you can buy all of the bubble gum and candy bars in the world." Clyde Kerr Jr., a famed New Orleans trumpeter who would later give Payton formal music instruction, remembered the boy's preternatural ability and desire to play among adults. "We used to rehearse with his dad, and Nicholas used to come sit on the sofa next to me and try to play my part when he was 10 years old," Kerr recalled to Bill Milkowski for Down Beat (March 1995). "And he was always serious about it. I think a lot of musicians around town knew even then that he was something special." By the age of 12, Payton was playing steadily with the All-Star Jazz Band, a group of talented preteens that performed throughout New Orleans and at European jazz festivals.

At about this time Payton came under the watchful eye of the highly influential Wynton Marsalis. A prodigy himself, Marsalis is credited with the revival of traditional or "straight-ahead" jazz in the early 1980s, when he was barely out of his teens. One evening Marsalis called to speak with Walter Payton, who was a friend of his, only to be treated to an impromptu, over-the-telephone performance by the 13-year-old Nicholas. Marsalis was so impressed by the young man's nerve and, more importantly, by his ability that he took an interest in Payton's development. He began sending Payton tapes to study and introduced him to still more working jazz musicians. By the time Payton enrolled in the New Orleans Center for the Creative Arts to study under the jazz department head, Clyde Kerr Jr., he had acquired a minor reputation as an up-and-comer. In addition to his burgeoning trumpet virtuosity, Payton was becoming skilled at classical piano, the upright bass, and drums.

Payton attended the University of New Orleans for one semester to study under Wynton's father, Ellis Marsalis, who taught him valuable lessons about music that extended beyond scales and other rote exercises into theory, arranging, and composition. However, mounting offers from nationally known bandleaders proved too tempting to Payton, and he put off his studies to tour as a sideman with such celebrated musicians as trumpeter Clark Terry and pianist Marcus Roberts. Having traded in traditional formal classroom training for live performance, Payton found that his working apprenticeships taught him more about musical phrasing and expression than he had learned as a student. "When you're a sideman, you concentrate on your own musical development, just getting your chops together," Payton explained to Melba Newsome for American Visions (October/November 1996). "When I was 14 and 15, I didn't have the patience and control to play a ballad and deliver the melody without being busy." In contrast, now he "strive[s] to relax and play with more focus, which tends to make for better music."

Among his numerous mentors, Payton has singled out Elvin Jones, whose band he joined in 1992, as the one who taught him the most about professionalism. "Elvin always showed up to play at his best," Payton said, as quoted by Greg Devlin. "When it was time to hit the bandstand he was unforgiving, you either went with him, or you got washed away." Jones, a giant among jazz drummers and a former sideman of the sax great John Coltrane, appointed Payton as musical director of his group, the Jazz Machine, a little over a year after the trumpeter's arrival. Though just 20 years old, Payton was responsible for running rehearsals and composing and arranging pieces, yet he always deferred to Jones's expertise on the bandstand. Payton's stint with the Jazz Machine was his final preparation for leading his own band.

Payton's experiences on the road as a working musician brought home a lesson his father had been trying to teach him for years. "My father used to always tell me about phrasing . . . ," Payton said, according to Greg Devlin. "'Cause all I wanted to do was play a bunch of notes fast and clean, not even thinking about harmony or whatever. But he would tell me, think about phrasing and pacing yourself and leaving space for what you play to breathe—give it time to take shape." In addition to having learned practical lessons by performing for an audience, Payton gained his sense of place in the jazz tradition, playing with the music's elder statesmen, who in turn had played with the legends of an earlier era. "Music is very shallow that has no history," Payton told Laura Andrews for the *New York Amsterdam News* (September 11, 1997). "I always try to incorporate as much of the past into what I do." As a result, his technical command of the trumpet, characterized by speed, precision, and tonal intensity, was given polish and luster: individual notes became rounder and warmer, and his overall style grew increasingly expressive and evocative.

Payton released his debut album as a bandleader in 1995. *From This Moment*, a compilation of jazz standards and original tunes by Payton, showcased the young musician's maturing style and received universal critical acclaim. In his critique of the album for the *Washington Post* (March 10, 1995), Geoffrey Himes wrote, "Payton mixes superior chops with a warm, Southern sensibility that's a delight." The following year Payton released his second album, *Gumbo Nouveau*, a tribute to the New Orleans tradition of jazz. "Hearing these songs a certain way my whole life, I wanted to perform them in a different context, at the same time being respectful to the original composers," Payton told Melba Newsome. The *New York Times* (April 23, 1996) critic Peter Watrous initially found the compilation of updated renderings of New Orleans classics commercial and contrived, but he concluded that Payton's ability made the record "something out of the ordinary." "Payton's tone is magnificent and big, sounding as if it were made not from sound waves but from something more tactile," Watrous wrote. "And he quotes from much of jazz's trumpet tradition, moving effortlessly from the music of Louis Armstrong to Miles Davis and beyond."

Though myriad influences have informed his music, Payton learned the lessons that may define the rest of his career at the feet of "Doc" Cheatham. That veteran trumpeter had spent most of his career as a sideman for a long list of celebrated musicians, including Billie Holiday and Cab Calloway, and did not emerge as a noted soloist and vocalist in his own right until he was in his 70s. Payton and Cheatham met in 1989 and played together at extemporaneous jam sessions. Cheatham found the 16-year-old's style reminiscent of both Armstrong's and Joe "King" Oliver's in his technical command of crisp, bell-tone high notes and his use of bluesy, rasping lows. Eight years later the two men, born nearly seven decades apart, would team up to record *Doc Cheatham & Nicholas Payton*. The album was released just months before Cheatham's death, at the age of 92. "The thing I loved about him even at his age was that he still had the approach to music as if he was 15 years old just finding out about it," Payton said in an interview with Theresa Crushshon for *All About Jazz* (July 1, 1999, on-line). "It was still important to

him. He still had a hunger . . . a passion for it. And I think that it is important to never lose that. Otherwise, you're not very productive." Payton also said that he learned a great deal about humility from his elder. According to virtually all critics, the instinctive connection between Cheatham and Payton, which transcended generations, is tangible throughout the recording; *Doc Cheatham & Nicholas Payton* won a Grammy Award for best solo jazz performance for the duo's version of "Stardust."

For his modern renditions of jazz standards, Payton has been labeled a traditionalist, but he doesn't see it that way. "I don't look at it as old music," Payton told Michael J. Agovino for *Esquire* (May 1997). "That's a big misconception. I mean, standards are timeless to me. There's an endless amount, through improvisations, that can be done with them." Still, as if to counter his critics, in 1998 Payton released his third album as leader, *Payton's Place*. Characterized by John McDonough in *Down Beat* (July 1998) as "a good career move," *Payton's Place* is comprised predominantly of Payton's originals and features a faster and more experimental bop sound. Three of the 10 tracks include guest appearances by fellow trumpeters Wynton Marsalis and Roy Hargrove, who with Payton, in McDonough's words, "have great fun bouncing cordial and often fiery bons mots off one another." Dedicated to four influential individuals in his life whom he lost in 1997—his grandmother, Elizabeth Williams; "Doc" Cheatham; the reedman Fred Kemp; and a 22-year-old alto saxophonist, Charles Taylor—the album closes with a piece titled "The Last Goodbye," which showcases the artist's evolving musical expressiveness.

Besides his recordings as a bandleader, Nicholas Payton has appeared numerous times on recordings featuring multiple artists, most notably *Fingerpainting: The Music of Herbie Hancock*, with Christian McBride and Mark Whitfield; *Joe Henderson Big Band*; *Going Home*, with Elvin Jones; *Testimonial*, with Carl Allen; and a recording of Jazz at Lincoln Center, *They Came to Swing*. Furthermore, he portrayed the legendary trumpeter Oran "Hot Lips" Page in Robert Altman's 1996 film *Kansas City*, on whose soundtrack he is featured, and frequently appears with Wynton Marsalis's Lincoln Center Jazz Orchestra.

While he is gifted with remarkable musical talent, Nicholas Payton has always cited another factor when asked about the secret of his success. "When I am not touring I will practice up to 10 hours a day," Payton told Theresa Crushshon. "Practice means everything to a musician. When I was growing up and lived at home I practiced so much that I would drive my parents crazy, so much so that they would beg me to stop." — T.J.F.

Suggested Reading: *All about Jazz* (on-line) July 1, 1999, with photo; *American Visions* p40+ Oct./Nov. 1996, with photo; *Down Beat* p40+ Mar. 1995, with photo, p24+ Nov. 1997, with photo; *New York Amsterdam News* p28 Sep. 10, 1998, with photo

Selected Recordings: *From This Moment*, 1995; *Gumbo Nouveau*, 1996; *Payton's Place*, 1998

Charles Yen/Archive Photos

Piazza, Mike

Sep. 4, 1968– Baseball player. Address: c/o New York Mets, Shea Stadium, 123-01 Roosevelt Ave., Flushing, NY 11368-1699

Mike Piazza, the New York Mets' All-Star catcher, is the greatest hitting-catcher ever to play the game of baseball. Since he broke into the big leagues, in 1992, with the Los Angeles Dodgers, Piazza has accumulated a lifetime batting average of .328 (as of the end of the 1999 season) and has already surpassed the milestones of 200 home runs and 1,000 hits. Now entering his eighth full season in the majors, Piazza is beginning the second year of a seven-year, $91 million contract he signed in October 1998 with the Mets—a contract that made him, at the time, the highest paid baseball player ever. "I've never let other people put pressure on me," Piazza told Gordon Verrell for the *Sporting News* (February 28, 1994). "I'm intense—I can't worry about other people's expectations. What I'm concerned about is this: going out, playing hard, and winning the game. If we win, and I help as a catcher and get three hits, too, fine. If we win, and I help as a catcher and I don't get any hits, that's fine, too."

Originally a first baseman, Piazza was the final draft choice of the Los Angeles Dodgers in the 1988 free-agent draft; he was chosen as a favor to then-Dodger manager Tommy Lasorda, who is a childhood friend of Piazza's father's. Dodger brass did not expect Mike to develop into a major league–caliber ballplayer, but Lasorda, who had long been Piazza's mentor of sorts, suggested that the young slugger switch to the position of catcher—a position held by weak hitters in most major-league lineups. Piazza worked hard at developing his fielding skills and soon began to rise in the Dodger farm system. He was promoted to the majors well into the 1992 season, and by 1993 he had secured the starting catching position for the Dodgers. He went on to have a remarkable season at the plate—hitting .318 with 112 RBIs—and was unanimously voted the National League Rookie of the Year. (He did not play enough games to quality for the award in 1992.) Since his rookie season, Piazza has become one of the most consistent hitters in the game, blending the unusual combination of high batting average with home-run power. After having the greatest offensive year ever by a catcher in 1997 and then refusing a lucrative deal put forth by the Dodgers a few months later, Piazza was traded during the 1998 season to the struggling Florida Marlins in a stunning seven-player deal, the largest baseball trade ever at the time. A week later he was shipped to the New York Mets for three minor-league prospects. The catcher helped the Mets contend for a wild-card spot, missing the post-season by a single game.

Piazza and the Mets entered the 1999 season with high expectations. Although the team nearly self-destructed in the final week of the season (as they did in the final five games of 1998), they succeeded in winning four straight games, beat the Cincinnati Reds in a one-game play-off to determine the National League wild-card winner, and headed to the National League Division Series. After vanquishing the National League West champions, the Arizona Diamondbacks, four games to one, the Mets lost to their NL East Division arch-rival, the Atlanta Braves, in a hard-fought best-out-of-seven contest. In a series in which every game was decided by no more than two runs, the Braves clipped New York four games to two. Piazza had a relatively poor postseason; however, he hit a crucial home run to produce a tie in the seventh inning of game six. The Mets went on to lose, 4–3, in 11 innings and were ousted from the play-offs.

Michael Joseph Piazza was born on September 4, 1968 in Norristown, Pennsylvania. His father, Vince Piazza, is a successful used-car salesman turned entrepreneur. A distant relative of Los Angeles Dodger manager Tommy Lasorda's, Vince Piazza was good friends with Lasorda while growing up. "I was his little buddy," Vince told Kelly Whiteside for *Sports Illustrated* (July 5, 1993). "We were inseparable." By time he was 11, young Mike was busy building a batting cage in his backyard with the help of his father. "I was out there every day," Piazza told Whiteside. "I would come home from school, get a snack, watch cartoons, and then hit. Every spring I would see I was hitting the ball farther and farther." He would even hit balls in the dead of winter, heating the baseballs on the stove and wrapping pipe insulation around the bat to prevent his hands from stinging. "[The batting cage] was such an ugly thing; I can't believe the neighbors didn't complain," Vince told Whiteside. "Actually the zoning board came by once to investigate. When they asked what it was, I told them it was my son's ticket to the big leagues."

When the Dodgers came to Philadelphia to play the Phillies, Piazza, thanks to his father's friendship with Lasorda, was allowed to work as bat boy for the Los Angeles squad. In the summer of 1984, when Mike was 15 years old, the former Boston Red Sox slugger Ted Williams—a Hall of Famer and the only player currently alive who has hit over .400 for an entire season—visited the Piazza home. A friend of Vince's, Williams had some spare time while headed elsewhere and stopped by to give the teenager some batting instruction. "I couldn't talk because I was so nervous," Piazza, who had read Williams's instruction book on hitting many times, recalled to Whiteside. On a videotape that the Piazzas made during the visit, Williams is heard declaring, as Whiteside reported, "Mike hits harder than I did when I was 16. I guarantee you, this kid will hit the ball. I never saw anybody who looked better at his age."

In his last year in high school, Piazza played first base and broke the all-time Phoenixville High School home-run record, previously held by Andre Thornton, who played with the Cleveland Indians in the 1980s. Although his hitting was solid—he batted over .400 in his senior year—Piazza was a slow runner with only average skills at first base. "I have talked to a lot of scouts since then who said they didn't like anything about me," Piazza told Whiteside. By phoning a few contacts, Lasorda succeeded in getting Piazza admitted into the University of Miami, a respected college for baseball, but as a freshman Piazza played poorly, getting just one hit during nine at-bats as a backup first baseman. For his sophomore year Piazza transferred to Miami-Dade North Community College, where he rebounded and hit a solid .364.

In order to pique institutions' interest in Piazza, Lasorda asked the Dodger franchise to pick Mike as the final player chosen overall in the free-agent draft—number 1,389. "I asked the Dodgers to draft him as a favor," Lasorda told Whiteside. "Thank God, they did." Knowing that Piazza was not a top prospect, the Dodger scout assigned to Mike put off phoning him for a few months. When he finally dialed him, the scout assumed Piazza would tell him what school he would be attending during the upcoming academic year. Instead, Mike wangled a tryout with the Dodgers. "I just hammered balls into the blue seats," Piazza recalled to Whiteside of his tryout. As Whiteside reported, Lasorda remembers asking Ben Wade, the Dodger scouting director, "If he was a shortstop who could hit balls into the seats like that, would you sign him?" When Wade answered in the affirmative, Lasorda then asked, "If he was a catcher who could hit balls into the seats like that, would you sign him?"

When Wade again said yes, Lasorda announced, "Then he's a catcher." Subsequently, Wade offered Piazza a $15,000 signing bonus under the condition that he fly to the Dominican Republic to attend Campo Las Palmas—the Dodgers' training site for Hispanic prospects—to learn the catching position. Despite problems with language (Spanish was the lingua franca at the camp) and waking up to find tarantulas in his bed several times, when he returned to the United States he was thinner, stronger, and a better catcher. In 1991 he led the Dodgers' farm teams with 29 home runs, hitting .277 with their A-ball affiliate in Bakersfield.

In his 1992 season Piazza split his time between the Dodgers' Double A squad in San Antonio, where he hit .377 in 31 games, and their Triple A team in Albuquerque, where, in 94 games, he hit .341 with 16 home runs. In late September the Dodgers called him up for a brief stint in the majors. Batting 69 times in 21 games, he hit .232, enough for him to be invited to the Dodgers' spring training camp in March 1993. That off-season, the Dodgers let go of Mike Scioscia, their starting catcher from the previous season, and Piazza hit a remarkable .478 during spring training. He thus succeeded in beating out four other players for the starting position.

Piazza worked hard to live up to expectations. "He takes everything so seriously," Eric Karros, one of his former Dodger teammates, told Whiteside. In an example of his seriousness, Whiteside described an incident that occurred during the May 3, 1993 game between the Dodgers and the St. Louis Cardinals. "With Tom Candiotti on the mound for L.A., Piazza lunged for a low knuckleball and threw off balance to second, trying to catch Ozzie Smith stealing," Whiteside reported. "But the ball hit Candiotti square on the butt. Laughter broke out on the field, but Piazza was embarrassed and angry." His intensity apparently paid off: he was invited to represent the National League in the Major League All-Star Game that summer. He ended the season with a splendid .318 average and 112 RBIs and received the National League Rookie of the Year Award, which is bestowed by the Baseball Writers Association of America. With first-place votes from 28 reporters (each city with a National League team is represented by two writers), he thus became only the sixth person since 1947, when the title was established, to earn the award in a unanimous decision. Piazza's performance also earned the 25-year-old a three-year, $4.2 million contract—the most lucrative deal for a second-year player up to that time.

Failed contract negotiations between the Players Union and major-league owners in 1994 led to a strike that ended the season in the third week of August. Though he played in only 107 games (normally 162 games constitute a full season), Piazza still managed to shine, with a .319 batting average and 92 RBIs (both of which were team records that year). Recognized as a respectable power hitter capable of delivering clutch home runs with runners on base, Piazza also finished the season with 24 home runs—a remarkable number for a catcher in so few games (and another 1994 Dodger record). He had also been elected to the All-Star team, and this time he was a starter.

The players' strike ended on April 1, 1995, and in the following months Piazza's batting average reached an astounding .346, second in the league that year only to that of the future Hall of Famer Tony Gwynn, an outfielder for the San Diego Padres. Piazza also hit more home runs—32—than he ever had before, and he racked up 93 RBIs in 434 at-bats. Again, for the third consecutive year, Piazza was elected to play in the All-Star Game. But as the season wound to a close and the Dodgers began to flounder in the standings, Piazza's performance behind the plate became the subject of criticism. "Despite his offensive heroics, Piazza is being ridiculed ever so quietly for his pitch selection and defense," Bob Nightengale wrote for *Baseball* (September 4, 1995). "No one on the team says anything publicly. No one wants to hurt anyone's feelings. Besides, you're talking about the best-hitting catcher in baseball. But it is the ominous little secret that won't go away." In response, Piazza told Nightengale, "Listen, I know there are times when I'm not great behind the plate. You can't argue with that. But it's a Catch-22. It's fatiguing being behind the plate every game, but because of my bat, they can't afford to take me out of the lineup too often. That's not an apology, that's just a fact." In any event, the Dodgers made the play-offs—Piazza's first post-season appearance—but fell to the Cincinnati Reds three games to none in the National League Division Series.

Piazza entered the 1996 season as a leader on the Dodger squad. Again selected for the National League All-Star team, Piazza powered his team into the play-offs, hitting a respectable .336 with 184 hits and 105 RBIs. In the final days of the season, the San Diego Padres and the Dodgers found themselves in a peculiar situation: tied at the end of the season with identical records, the West Coast rivals were forced to battle it out in a one-game play-off. Traditionally a contest of high drama and tense play, the one-game play-off carried with it the mystique of sudden-death, make-it-or-break-it baseball. The contest between the Padres and Dodgers, however, what with the new play-off format designed to allow more teams to make it into the post-season, simply decided which team would be given home-field advantage in the upcoming best-of-five contest. In other words, the two teams would play each other in the first round of the post-season no matter what the outcome of the one-game play-off. The complaints of many baseball purists notwithstanding, the two teams battled it out, and the Padres won the game. They then went on to manhandle the Dodgers in the best-of-five Division Series, winning three straight games. Piazza, despite his stellar season, went home early once again.

Early in 1997 Piazza, now an L.A. fixture and a recognizable face in southern California, published an article in the liberal *Los Angeles Times*. "L.A.'s an extremely liberal town, and when I aired some of my conservative views I saw a lot of negative letters . . . ," Piazza told Alan Schwarz for *Inside Sports* (May 1997). "I'm very conservative when it comes to the way taxes are. . . . People shouldn't rely on the government for their existence. People think that having kids is, like, a right, but it's privilege. Anyone who's responsible will plan to have a family. Don't get me wrong, I know there are some exceptions. . . . If I had it my way, we'd provide some food and lodging and medicine and that stuff, but not just give money to people who have proved they cannot spend it effectively or build upon it."

Piazza went on to have the best offensive year ever by a major-league catcher. With a batting average of .362, he surpassed the Hall-of-Fame Brooklyn Dodger Roy Campanella—who hit .312 in 1953—as the best-hitting catcher in a single season in Dodger history. And although, with 124 RBIs and 40 home runs, he fell short of the 142 RBIs and 41 home runs that Campanella compiled in the 1953 season, he finished second only to the Colorado Rockies' slugger Larry Walker in the National League's Most Valuable Player voting and became, arguably, the best-known catcher in the majors. As for the 1997 play-off race, though, the Dodgers, who managed to pull within sight of the division-leading San Francisco Giants late in the season, went on a losing streak in the final games of the regular season and missed the play-offs.

According to conventional wisdom, as Piazza geared up for the final year of his contract with Los Angeles, he and the Dodgers would agree on a new contract by the end of the upcoming 1998 season. But Piazza did not get off to a good start that year, prompting the local sports media to suggest that perhaps he did not deserve the reported $100 million contract for which he and his agent were pushing. Criticism of Piazza by past and present Dodger teammates also began to leak out to the press—something that had never occurred before. "This year, Piazza has not only been criticized by retired teammate Brett Butler for placing himself above the team, but also by [the then–] Dodger pitcher Ramon Martinez, for the way he calls games," Jason Diamos wrote for the *New York Times* (May 23, 1998, on-line). When talks between the Piazza and Dodger representatives stalled—Piazza apparently rejected a six-year, $79 million deal early in the season—the Dodgers shipped Piazza, who was hitting a below-average .282 in 37 games, to the hapless Florida Marlins in a tremendous, seven-player deal. Piazza, once the toast of L.A., was now on a last-place Florida team committed to selling most of the high-priced talent that had helped them win the 1997 World Series. A week later Piazza, after only five games with the Marlins, was sent to the New York Mets in exchange for three minor-league prospects. On May

22, 1998 Piazza met with the press. "I know the media in New York is bigger than in Los Angeles, so it's not going to be easy," Piazza said, as quoted by Diamos. "I'm definitely not Superman, so I just want to try to get in there and help the team as much as possible and contribute and just kind of settle down a little bit."

The Mets brass, who regarded the team as playoff contenders before the Piazza deal, saw their baseball club go on a nine-game winning streak after his arrival. Piazza did not immediately pay off at the plate, but eventually he began to do very well indeed. He ended the season with a remarkable .328 average—despite having endured the stress of relocation and uncertainty—and, for the Mets, Piazza batted .348 in 109 games. The Mets, however, with the National League Wild Card spot all but locked up with five games left to play in the regular season, went on a five-game skid that resulted in their elimination from the play-offs in the season's final game. The Mets had enjoyed their most successful season in years, and, in light of their missed opportunity, many speculated that Piazza, who had been booed in the final weeks of the season because of strikeouts in clutch situations with men on base, would not remain with the club. Then, on October 26, 1998, Piazza appeared at a press conference at Shea Stadium with the Mets' owners, Fred Wilpon and Nelson Doubleday, to announce that they had come to terms on a contract. The $91 million, seven-year deal made Piazza the highest-paid ballplayer up to that time and in all probability secured Piazza's services for the Mets for the rest of his career. "When I realized what had transpired with the Dodgers, I knew that no matter where I went, it would be the same," the catcher told Jason Diamos for the New York Times (October 27, 1998, on-line), referring to the jeers fans had aimed at him in his final weeks with Los Angeles. "And I just felt I might as well get booed by the best. Going somewhere else—with no offense to any other place—would be a letdown. When you come here, you get infected by the attitude. And you always know where you stand."

In addition to Piazza, the Mets re-signed pitchers Al Leiter and Dennis Cook in the off-season, adding veteran leadership to their many free-agent acquisitions, most notably lead-off hitter Ricky Henderson and outfielder Bobby Bonilla. The club started the 1999 season well and shot immediately to the top of their division. Piazza, too, came out of the gate quickly, only to sprain his knee in the sixth game; he spent the next two weeks on the disabled list. After returning to the line-up, Piazza performed impressively during the second half of the regular season and wound up with a total of 40 home runs, 124 RBIs, and a .303 average. The Mets, meanwhile, during the last two weeks of the regular season, suffered a three-game sweep by the Atlanta Braves before pulling themselves together to win their final four games and thus force a one-game play-off with the upstart Cincinnati Reds. Al Leiter, who had not pitched well for most of the season, put in a stellar performance, and the Mets defeated Cincinnati 5–0. The victory sent the Mets to the play-offs for the first time since 1988.

In the play-offs the Mets faced the Arizona Diamondbacks of the National League West—a team, led by manager Buck Showalter and a core of veteran players, that debuted in the majors in 1998. Going into the series, the Mets were the underdogs. Nevertheless, they defeated Arizona four games to one and advanced to the National League Division Series, where they met their arch-nemesis, the Atlanta Braves. After dropping the first three games of the series, the Mets bounced back to win their next two at home. Then, in a thrilling 11-inning ball game that included a game-tying home run by Piazza in the seventh, the Mets' Kenny Rogers, with the bases loaded, walked in the Braves' winning run. Thus, after a host of seeming miracles, the Mets lost the 1999 play-offs. Piazza, who absorbed several hard hits at home plate during the play-off games and suffered a mild concussion after one impact with the ball, told reporters that he was simply looking forward to playing baseball the next season.

In his free time Mike Piazza likes to listen to heavy-metal music and play his drum set. In recent years he has played drums at concerts given by the heavy-metal bands Motorhead and Anthrax. — M.B.

Suggested Reading: Baseball p13 Sep. 4, 1995, with photo; Inside Sports p23+ May 1997, with photos; New York Times C p1+ July 12, 1993, with photos, B p17 Oct. 28, 1993, with photo; New York Times (on-line) May 23, 1998, with photos, Oct. 27, 1998, with photos; Sports Illustrated p12+ July 5, 1993, with photos; 1999 New York Mets Information Guide

---

Piëch, Ferdinand

(PEE-esh)

Apr. 17, 1937– CEO of Volkswagen; engineer. Address: c/o Volkswagen AG, Brieffach 1880, 38436 Wolfsburg, Germany

"0–60? Yes." "Less Flower. More Power." With ad messages like those, which played on people's feelings of nostalgia and alluded to high-tech advancements, the German-based auto company Volkswagen AG reintroduced the Beetle to the United States in the spring of 1998, two decades after production of the car's predecessor had ceased. The prize-winning ads and the product they plugged turned out to be big hits: Volkswagen's sales in the U.S. rose more than 60 percent in 1998, making it the firm's best year on this side of the Atlantic since 1981. Volkswagen's total sales in 1998 earned the company more than $1.2 billion—a remarkable achievement in light of the fact that in

Courtesy of Volkswagen of America, Inc.
Ferdinand Piëch

1993, the company had ended the year $1.1 billion in the red. With worldwide sales in 1998 of more than 4.7 million vehicles, Volkswagen may be poised to replace Toyota as the world's third-largest automaker (after General Motors and Ford). The person credited with this extraordinary turnaround is Ferdinand Piëch, who in 1993 became Volkswagen's chief executive officer—a position, he told Janet Guyon for *Fortune* (March 29, 1999), that he had coveted "nearly since I was born."

Volkswagen's supervisory board turned to Piëch for leadership partly because of his proven track record during his 30-year career in the automotive industry and partly because of his lineage. Born in Vienna, Austria, on April 17, 1937 to Anton Piëch and the former Louise Porsche, Ferdinand Piëch is a grandson of the legendary automotive developer Ferdinand Porsche, the founder of the Porsche sports-car company. Ferdinand Porsche also played a key role in the coming-into-being of the Volkswagen. According to various accounts, in the early 1930s the German Nazi dictator Adolph Hitler conceived the idea that all Germans deserved to have the opportunity to buy an affordable family automobile—a "Volkswagen," or "people's car"—with streamlining as efficient as that of a beetle. At Hitler's behest, Ferdinand Porsche designed a Beetle prototype, and in 1938 the first true Beetle was produced. In 1941 Anton Piëch, a lawyer, became the CEO of the state-owned Volkswagen precursor, and during World War II he directed the manufacture of a Jeep-like forerunner of today's Beetle (as well as aircraft engines, parts for tanks, and other war machines), using many slave laborers from Eastern Europe. (In 1998 Volkswagen created a $12 million fund to be distributed to the surviving

workers.) Full-scale production of the Volkswagen sedan did not begin until after the war ended and the Allies rebuilt the heavily bomb-damaged Volkswagen plant. In 1955 the one-millionth Volkswagen rolled off the assembly line.

Ferdinand Piëch grew up on an estate in Zell am See, in southwestern Austria, a short distance from both Germany, on the north, and Italy, on the south. He attended the Swiss Technical University, in Zurich, where, David Woodruff reported for *Business Week* (October 5, 1998), he "threw himself into automotive studies with single-minded intensity." In his spare time he tinkered with the engine of his Porche. He graduated from college in 1962, with a degree in engineering, and in the next year he began working as an engine tester at Porsche's Stuttgart, Germany, headquarters. In 1968 his mother and her brother, known as Ferry Porsche, who co-owned the company, named Piëch head of research and development. In that position he spent millions of dollars to create state-of-the-art race cars, among them the legendary 240-mile-per-hour Porsche 917, which won the 1970 Le Mans, a 24-hour-long competition held in France.

Piëch's hopes of someday running Porsche were shattered in 1972, when his mother and uncle, "fed up with fights among their children over management of the company," as Janet Guyon reported, barred family members from management posts. Piëch reacted by leaving Porsche to join Volkswagen's Audi subsidiary, with the title of director of special projects in the research-and-development department. At Audi he helped to develop the five-cylinder gas engine and a full-time four-wheel-drive system for passenger cars. In 1988, "despite his rottweiler reputation," as Guyon wrote, he became head of Audi. Thanks to his gifts for innovation, efficiency, and finance, Audi's profits soon increased markedly.

On January 1, 1993 Piëch became Volkswagen's chief executive officer. He took control shortly after the company had embarked on an aggressive, five-year, $51 billion, worldwide expansion campaign. Launched by his predecessor, Carl H. Hahn, the campaign was theoretically designed to enable Volkswagen, the world's fourth-largest auto maker, to compete globally with its bigger rivals, General Motors, Ford, and Toyota. But the timing of the expansion was poor; Germany was slipping into its worst economic recession since World War II.

Another huge problem was Volkswagen's production costs, which ranked among the highest in the world. The average hourly wage of German auto workers was greater than that of auto workers anywhere else; moreover, according to industry analysts, assembling a car in the Volkswagen factories took twice as long as it did in Japanese carmakers' factories, even though Volkswagen used four times as many workers as did their Japanese counterparts. "Volkswagen's main problem is too many people," Daniel T. Jones, a professor of motor-industry management at Cardiff University, in Wales, told Ferdinand Protzman for the *New York*

Times (March 15, 1993). "They have too many people on the shop floor, in engineering, in management. . . . The result is that the cars are overengineered and cost too much to build."

Furthermore, in a typical German shop, cars were tested for defects after they were completely assembled. Japanese plants, by contrast, gave workers the authority to stop the assembly line if they identified a problem, a procedure that increased both product quality and speed of manufacture. Also, rather than arranging timely delivery of parts by suppliers, Volkswagen relied on parts machined in-house—a costlier alternative. According to David Woodruff, before Piëch's arrival, Volkswagen "could make a profit only by working factories overtime."

An avid student of *kaizen*—a Japanese term, associated with Toyota's philosophy of "lean manufacturing," that means "continuous improvement" in an activity with the goal of creating added value with less waste—Piëch took over the reins of Volkswagen AG with a plan to make the company more competitive. First, he put many of Hahn's expansion initiatives on hold and cut investment spending by a third. Next, he set about shrinking Volkswagen's 13-level management pyramid. "I have always paid more to those people who did not see it as their business to build up hierarchies than to those who built up substructures in order to push themselves one step higher," he told Christopher Parkes for the *Financial Times* (April 1, 1993). He reduced the number of members on the company's board from nine to five and ousted at least 20 top-level managers and many more at lower levels.

In a search for new managers, Piëch saw a kindred spirit in José Ignacio López de Arriortúa, General Motors's head of global purchasing, whom he had met in 1992. A charismatic Spanish-born Basque, López was widely known for merciless cost-cutting; indeed, he had often been referred to as "López the Terrible" and the "Russelsheim Strangler," the latter a reference to the German city where he had overseen purchasing for GM's subsidiary Adam Opel. Piëch believed that his own experience in engineering and development paired with López's background in purchasing and production would enable Volkswagen "to make quantum leaps both in the development of new products and in cutting costs," as he told Kevin Done for the *Financial Times* (June 7, 1993).

In March 1993, hours before a scheduled press conference at which GM executives planned to announce a promotion for López, López joined the staff of Volkswagen, as Piëch's second-in-command, with the titles of chief of production and head of purchasing. In collaboration with López, Piëch set about reducing the number of platforms used in all car models produced under the aegis of Volkswagen AG, including the Audi, Seat (in Spain), and Skoda (in Czechoslovakia) subsidiaries, so as to simplify production and lower costs. (In the automotive industry, "platform" has

no set meaning; in the case of Volkswagen, it refers to such basic components as almost all of the inner body structure, the wheel wells, and the side rails; it also includes such items as door handles and cigarette lighters.) By identifying all elements then common, or potentially common, to multiple car models, Piëch decreased the number of platforms from 19 to five. By the end of 1999, Volkswagen will produce only four platforms, on which 51 different models will be fitted.

In another cost-saving measure, while Volkswagen continued to manufacture particular automotive elements, including engine blocks, gear boxes, and body parts, it began outsourcing many others. Suppliers provided standardized components, such as brake systems, already assembled. López put pressure on suppliers to lower the costs of their products. If they balked, Piëch would deploy teams of efficiency experts to consult with them. "If a supplier does not think he is able to manage, our people will go in and help," Piëch told Parkes. "We can only survive together in symbiosis." On another front, Piëch, who believed that Volkswagen's payroll included 30,000 workers too many, reached an agreement with the automotive union whereby, to avoid wholesale layoffs, workers' hours were reduced by 20 percent, to four days a week, and their pay by 16 percent. The compromise was a significant accomplishment in Germany, where unionization is far more extensive and unions far more powerful than they are in the United States. It laid a foundation of goodwill between Piëch and the union, representatives of which, by law, hold half the seats on Volkswagen's 20-member supervisory board.

Meanwhile, López's decision to leave GM had sparked what turned into a nearly four-year, widely publicized criminal investigation and series of legal battles involving López, GM, and Volkswagen. Seven of López's Opel colleagues had joined him in his move to Volkswagen, and in April 1993 Opel, fearing a hemorrhage of its top people, successfully asked for a temporary court injunction forbidding Volkswagen from further recruitment of Opel executives. Later, a court ruled that since López was known for engendering strong loyalty among his assistants, their departure from Opel was understandable and indicated nothing illegal. Then, in May 1993, in the opening chapter of what has been called "one of the most spectacular cases of industrial espionage in modern history," Adam Opel AG accused López of having brought secret GM documents with him to Volkswagen and of sharing them and other confidential GM information with Piëch and others. At Opel's request, the public prosecutor in Darmstadt, Germany, launched an investigation into the charges. Within weeks, law-enforcement officers had found boxes filled with GM documents, including copies translated into German, in a flat shared by two López aides. Nevertheless, López vehemently denied the accusations, and Piëch staunchly defended him. On July 28, 1993, according to *Facts on File* (September 16, 1993), Piëche accused GM of waging "international economic war in order to ruin" Volkswagen and of "leading a personal campaign of revenge against Dr. López and at the same time trying to misuse the state prosecutors, the media and the public in order to denigrate our company." GM, for its part, insisted, as Louis Hughes, a company representative, told Alex Taylor III for *Fortune* (August 23, 1993), "This is not GM against VW—this is a question of law." The controversy spread to include high-ranking German politicians and business leaders, among them officials of BMW and other competing German auto makers, who feared that the allegations would dampen the public's interest in all German cars both in Europe and overseas. "At its height," John Schmid reported in the *International Herald Tribune* (July 28, 1998, on-line), "the conflict between GM and VW . . . took on nationalistic and emotional overtones and nearly escalated into a boycott of U.S. cars in Germany."

In May 1994 Hamburg prosecutors declared publicly that López had lied in sworn affidavits filed with the court in 1993, but they dropped the case against López nevertheless. And while López refused to admit his guilt, he agreed to the prosecutors' demand that he contribute the equivalent of $45,000 to a charity. Elsewhere in Germany, the probe into López's actions continued. In December 1996 other German prosecutors produced evidence that López had conspired to steal secrets from GM some months before he had gone to work for Volkswagen, and he was indicted on charges of theft and espionage. Two weeks earlier, in anticipation of the indictment, López had resigned from Volkswagen. On January 9, 1997, in an out-of-court settlement of a civil suit that GM had brought against the firm, Volkswagen agreed to pay GM $100 million in damages and to purchase $1 billion worth of GM parts during the next seven years. The final chapter in the matter ended on July 27, 1998, when a Darmstadt court dropped all charges against López (but, again, required him to make a donation to a charity, this time a sum of $232,000). "A spokeswoman for the court said the case would have taken at least two years to try and raised difficult legal ambiguities over the application of German laws to a foreign-based company like GM," John Schmid reported.

Just two months later, Ferdinand Piëch, who was never personally charged in the López case, unveiled the newly designed Volkswagen Beetle. Piëch told Janet Guyon that the rounded shape of the Beetle accounted for its appeal. "Thirty-five years ago, I remember a Beetle study in which people said they felt they were inside a sphere," he explained. "It gives them a sense of security in the primordial sense." The new Beetle helped push Volkswagen's world market share up one percentage point, to 11.4 percent, in 1998. The company anticipates that sales in North America in 1999 will exceed 260,000 cars, double its 1997 totals.

Volkswagen has introduced other cars as well under Piëch's leadership. The Passat, a totally new line, debuted in 1997. Before journalists and other outsiders tested the first Passat models manufactured, David Woodruff reported, "Piëch personally drove nearly 60 cars to be sure they were in tiptop shape." (According to Woodruff, Piëch routinely test-drives prototypes of his company's products, and he requires all his top managers to do so. Normally within the automotive industry, development engineers are assigned that job.) In 1998 Volkswagen unveiled the much-less-expensive Lupo, a mini-car.

Piëch is also gambling on the continuing growth of the ultra-luxury-car market. Within the last two years Volkswagen has purchased the Italian sports-car companies Lamborghini and Bugatti and the British firm Rolls-Royce Motor Cars, which makes Bentleys as well as Rolls Royces. Volkswagen will retain rights to the Rolls Royce name only until 2003, however. That is because the trademark was owned by Rolls-Royce PLC, a jet-engine manufacturer, which split from the car maker in the 1970s, and Rolls-Royce PLC—in an action that reportedly took Piëch by surprise—has sold the trademark to BMW. Some observers have pointed to Piëch's failure to secure the trademark as evidence that, as David Woodruff wrote, he maintains a "virtual autocracy" at Volkswagen and "there are few checks and balances on his decisions." According to widespread reports, few Volkswagen higher-ups dare to disagree with Piëch, for fear that his reaction will be an icy stare and a long, angry silence; at meetings, one former Volkswagen executive told Woodruff, "critical questions aren't asked, because people know things can rapidly get uncomfortable." Guyon reported that Piëch "neither reads nor writes memos." "If something goes wrong and you want to prove you're not guilty, then you write it down," he said to her. "This is something I don't like."

"By all accounts," Guyon wrote, Piëch is "driven, intense, unpredictable, and quirky," and he can be "both brutally abrupt and charming." He has at least 13 children by four different women. Among them are five by his first wife and three by his current wife, who, in the 1980s, worked for Piëch and his then live-in companion, with whom he also fathered three children. — T.J.F.

Suggested Reading: *Automotive Industries* p50+ Apr. 1999, with photos; *Business Week* p29 Aug. 9, 1993, with photos, p82+ Oct. 5, 1998, with photos; *Financial Times* p13 Apr. 1, 1993, with photos, p28 June 7, 1993, with photo; *Fortune* p64+ Aug. 23, 1993, with photos, p96+ Mar. 29, 1999, with photos; *New York Times* D p1+ Mar. 15, 1993, with photo, D p1 Aug. 7, 1998, with photos; *Wall Street Journal* A p1 Nov. 23, 1994; *Washington Post* C p1 Aug. 10, 1993, with photo; *Who's Who 1999*

Joseph A. Rosen/Archive Photos

Pileggi, Nicholas

(pih-LEJ-ee)

Feb. 22, 1933– Nonfiction writer. Address: c/o Sterling Lord Literistic, Inc., 65 Bleecker St., New York, NY 10012

Nicholas Pileggi, a journalist and longtime chronicler of the Mafia, has attained a reputation for revealing the realities beneath glossy popularized images of the mob. "I'm not interested in how the Rigatoni family took over the Spumoni family," Pileggi told Tim Appelo and Meredith Berkman for *Entertainment Weekly* (October 12, 1990), using the names of a pasta and a kind of ice cream to comment on the many highly fictionalized and, he feels, romanticized tales of the Mafia. "I'm fascinated by the true story. It speaks to the dark side of American life." Pileggi is the author of two best-selling nonfiction books that detail the inner workings of organized crime, both drawn largely from his interviews with key players. *Wiseguy: Life in a Mafia Family* (1985) is based on Pileggi's extensive conversations with Henry Hill, an average mob criminal who worked the streets but nonetheless had extensive knowledge of those higher up the ladder. (In Mafia slang, a "wiseguy" is a low-level mobster.) *Casino: Love and Honor in Las Vegas* (1995) tells of the shriveling of the mob's involvement in Las Vegas casinos as related primarily by Frank "Lefty" Rosenthal, one of the linchpins in the Mafia's operations there in the 1970s and 1980s. Both books have been made into successful films, *Goodfellas* (1990) and *Casino* (1995) respectively, directed by Martin Scorsese, with whom Pileggi co-wrote the screenplays.

Nicholas Pileggi was born on February 22, 1933 and grew up in Brooklyn, New York, the son of Nick and Susan (Defaslo) Pileggi, immigrants from Calabria, the southern Italian province closest to Sicily. His father owned a shoestore. Among Pileggi's neighbors in the Bensonhurst and Bedford-Stuyvesant sections of Brooklyn were people involved with the Mafia, and he was acutely aware of their presence during his youth, even though no one spoke openly about them. When Pileggi was a child, a relative of his was found dead in a trash can; dressed as priest, he was riddled with bullets. "They wouldn't explain it to me," Pileggi recalled, as quoted by Appelo and Berkman. "Nobody would talk, but I knew."

Pileggi attended Long Island University, where he majored in English and intended to pursue a career teaching literature. After he got a job as a copyboy at the Associated Press (AP) during his last two years of college, however, he was drawn to journalism. He told Joseph Barbato for *Publishers Weekly* (February 7, 1986), "Once I saw what being a reporter was like, I was hooked. You were always where everyone wanted to be. You were always seeing what was happening—crossing the police lines, seeing the bodies or the fire. You were the messenger. You would go back and tell everybody what it was like. I found that fascinating as a kid. I loved the idea of doing it." After graduation, Pileggi was offered a job as a reporter for the Associated Press in New York City, where he worked from 1956 to 1968, covering police, labor, and political activities. Pileggi actually did very little writing as an AP employee; rather, he gathered information, all the while developing a strong background in subjects that he would later write about. "The city was broken into police districts then," he told Barbato. "And reporters actually covered the cops. You didn't write a story; you gave in notes." Gradually, Pileggi began writing articles during his off-hours that were published in magazines such as *Esquire*. In 1968 he left the AP to become a contributing editor of the newly formed *New York* magazine, where he specialized in reporting on New York City crime and politics. For that magazine, he has written dozens of articles on such topics as the activities of the mob boss Paul Castellano; rumors that former New York governor Mario Cuomo harbored Mafia connections; and corruption among rank-and-file city employees. "The magazine has been a terrific base, because the stories I do are not global in any sense," Pileggi told Barbato. "They're New York stories about politics, crime, and corruption."

Pileggi's first book, *Blye, Private Eye* (1976), is an account of the day-to-day work of Irwin Blye, a real-life private detective whom Pileggi spent a year observing with the intention of writing the book. In stark contrast to his fictional counterparts, Blye spent most of his time obtaining legal forms and poring over old tax returns and telephone bills. While Pileggi's objective was to document the mundanities of the private detective's job and thus give the lie to fictional images of intrigue and glamour, many critics found *Blye, Private Eye* a fascinating read.

In 1981 Pileggi became acquainted with Henry Hill, a career criminal who, confronted with a life sentence on a narcotics charge, had decided to testify against his associates and begin a new life as part of the government's Witness Protection Program. Hill's lawyer contacted the publisher Simon and Schuster about the possibility of creating a book based on Hill's experiences with the mob, and the publisher in turn contacted Pileggi's agent. Pileggi found appealing the idea of writing a book about the Mafia's version of an average workingman—as opposed to a *Godfather*-type crime boss. As Pileggi told Barbato, Hill "was a worker. And I thought by taking a look at the worker ant, so to speak, you had a better opportunity to tell how the whole colony works." After he had settled on this approach, Pileggi told Selwyn Raab for the *New York Times Book Review* (January 26, 1986), a single conversation with Hill convinced him he had found the perfect subject. "Once he realized I was not judgmental about his life, he was unbelievably open and full of details," Pileggi told Raab. "I checked him out with the FBI and prosecutors and they all agreed he was a moneymaker, not a shooter or a muscle man." Pileggi spoke with Hill by telephone almost every day for two years. As Pileggi told Raab, they also met in person at prosecutors' offices in New York and in cars, parks, hotels, and restaurants in cities in the Midwest. Because of Hill's participation in the Witness Protection Program, he had received a new identity, and Pileggi does not know Hill's new name and address.

Half Sicilian and half Irish, Hill grew up in Brooklyn, where he began working for the mob as an errand boy at age 11, in 1955. By the time he was a teenager, Hill was committing arson, using fake credit cards, working at crap games, and using counterfeit $20 bills to make small purchases and then pass the change to his superiors. He also collected loan-shark payments for Paul Vario, a boss in the Lucchese crime family, eventually becoming recognized as one of Vario's regular crew. Later, Hill was involved with bribing the Boston College basketball team to participate in a point-shaving scam, and, most notoriously, he credits himself with obtaining the information that allowed his friend James Burke—also known as Jimmy the Gent—to organize the largest cash robbery in history. That heist, which included over $6 million in cash and jewels stolen from Lufthansa Airlines at Kennedy Airport, in New York City, in 1978, resulted in 12 murders, after Burke refused to share the take with the others who helped with the job. One of those Burke threatened to kill was Hill himself.

In relating many stories of Hill's life as a criminal, the author interspersed his subject's first-person accounts with those of Hill's wife and Pileggi's own straightforward retelling. Pileggi won praise from critics for keeping his writing simple

and allowing the events Hill described to speak for themselves. In the *New York Times Book Review* (January 26, 1986), Vincent Patrick wrote, "*Wiseguy* evoked for me the quality of the best documentary films." This impression was in keeping with Pileggi's intentions. He told Barbato, "I never thought of this as a cops-and-robbers book. It's more like an anthropological study—watching wiseguys in Samoa, in a sense." After reading *Wiseguy*, Martin Scorsese called Pileggi and expressed his interest in collaborating on a screen version of the book. "I told him I had been waiting for that phone call all my life," Pileggi recalled to Patrizia DiLucchio for *People Online*. *Goodfellas* (1990), which starred Ray Liotta as Hill and featured performances by Robert De Niro and Joe Pesci, is widely considered to be one of Scorsese's best films.

The three main players in Pileggi's third book, *Casino*, are the gambling genius Frank "Lefty" Rosenthal, who moved from Chicago to Las Vegas in 1967 to look after the mob's interest in its casinos; the woman he married there, Geri McGee, formerly a high-class call girl; and Tony "the Ant" Spilotro, a mob heavy and sometime friend of Rosenthal's who came to Las Vegas to pursue his own criminal interests. *Casino* shows how the personality of each of the three and the clashes among them contributed to the curtailment of the Mafia's involvement in the Las Vegas casino industry. The narrative was culled primarily from Pileggi's conversations with Rosenthal, with supporting material drawn from court and FBI records and other sources. Pileggi told DiLucchio, "I did try something new with *Casino*: I had the cooperation of real people who had actually been there and I felt the story told by the real people in their own [words] was so compelling to me that I decided to get out of the way and let these people tell their own story. There is not one blind quote in the book. You have a man telling you what it is like to be blown up in a car, and you have a hit man complaining about how hard it is to kill one of his victims. I didn't feel I wanted to get between the reader and the original material. I guess it worked for some people and didn't work for others, but I didn't feel there was any other way for me to deal with the material I had." As with *Wiseguy*, critics were impressed by the way Pileggi created a gripping narrative from his material without reducing the impact of the raw testimony of his subjects. Robert Lacey, writing for the *New York Times* (October 8, 1995), commented that Pileggi "polishes [his raw material] with the narrative skills of a novelist or screenwriter." Lacey added that one of the book's strengths lay in "Pileggi's ability to convey that satisfying unease that is the essence of gangster drama. Something nasty, we feel certain, is waiting for us around the corner—and each character is so vivid that we are willing to follow wherever he leads."

In the case of *Casino*, Pileggi's collaboration with Scorsese began before the book was published; in fact, the film was released in 1995, about one month after the book became available to the general public. Although the names of the people in the book were changed for the film, Robert De Niro's character was based on Rosenthal; Joe Pesci played the character based on Spilotro; and in what was widely thought to be the performance of her career, Sharon Stone portrayed the character based on McGee.

Pileggi has commented that like many other Americans, he associated Mafia life to some degree with the romanticized images disseminated by films such as *The Godfather* (a movie he much admires), until he discovered that the real lives of gangsters are "grubbier" than he had expected. He told Barbato, "There are occasional pay days, but there are far more empty days. The romantic notion of that world is so far from the truth. I can't imagine anyone in his right mind reading [*Wiseguy*] and saying, 'Oh, that's what I want to be. I want to be a gangster.' It's a career filled with pain, much of it inflicted on others. . . . They're not those characters in movies. There's nothing noble about them. They're quite loathsome."

Pileggi's most recent screenplay, based on the life of the singer and film actor Dean Martin, is entitled *Dino*. (Martin's original name was Dino Crocetti.) Scorsese is expected to direct the film in 2000.

Pileggi is married to the writer and film director Nora Ephron, who has two sons from a previous marriage. When asked by DiLucchio how they manage to juggle their marriage and their creative projects, Pileggi responded, "We cope blissfully. Nora reads everything I write and may be the best editor I've ever come across in my life. And she shows me just about everything she's working on and I try to help." In 1986 Pileggi received the Peter Kihss Award for excellence in reporting on New York City government. — O.J.S.

Suggested Reading: *Chicago Tribune* XIV p10 Oct. 29, 1995, with photos; *Entertainment Weekly* p39 Oct. 12, 1990, with photo, p54+ Oct. 6, 1995, with photo; *New York Times* C p21 Jan. 16, 1986, with photo, B p10 Dec. 15, 1986, C p17 Sept. 28, 1995, with photo; *New York Times Book Review* p7 Jan. 26, 1986, with photo, p28 Oct. 8, 1995; *People Online*; *Publishers Weekly* p56+ Feb. 7, 1986; *Contemporary Authors* new revision series vol. 52, 1996

Selected Books: *Blye, Private Eye*, 1976; *Wiseguy: Life in a Mafia Family*, 1985; *Casino: Love and Honor in Las Vegas*, 1995

Selected Screenplays: with Martin Scorsese— *Goodfellas*, 1990; *Casino*, 1995

Pinsky, Robert

Oct. 20, 1940– Poet laureate of the United States. Address: c/o Dept. of English, Boston University, 236 Bay State Rd., Boston, MA 02215-1403

Robert Pinsky, the poet laureate of the United States, wants Americans to appreciate poetry "as related to the other ways we use language—as something that gives pleasure, that is an important part of life," as he put it to David Streitfeld of the *Washington Post* (March 28, 1997). Pinsky, who was named poet laureate in 1997, has compared poetry to the Internet, in that both are part of our shared culture. Like poetry through the ages, his own poems attempt to communicate the inner life of the artist and, by extension, to shed light on the human condition. At the same time, his preference for simple, direct language and his interest in both pedestrian events and broad universal themes have set him apart from many of his contemporaries. While his earlier poems were often marked by what has been called a didactic, public, and explanatory tone, his later poems are more deeply introspective and challenge the reader to discover other meanings hidden within his images.

A collection of Pinsky's poems spanning three decades was published in 1996; called *The Figured Wheel*, it was nominated for a Pulitzer Prize in po-

Sigrid Estrada/Courtesy of Steven Barclay Agency

etry. Katha Pollitt, who assessed the collection for the *New York Times Book Review* (August 18, 1996), wrote of Pinsky, "Here is a poet who, without forming a mini-movement or setting himself loudly at odds with the dominant tendencies of American poetry, has brought into it something new. . . . Call it a way of being autobiographical without being confessional, of connecting the particulars of the self—his Jewishness; his 1940s and '50s childhood in Long Branch, N[ew] J[ersey]; his adult life as 'professor or / Poet or parent or writing conference pooh-bah'—with the largest intellectual concerns of history, culture, psychology and art."

The son of Milford Simon Pinsky, an optometrist, and Sylvia (Eisenberg) Pinsky, Robert Pinsky was born on October 20, 1940 in Long Branch, New Jersey, an oceanfront resort town. One of Pinsky's grandfathers had been a bootlegger during the Prohibition era (1919–33) and had owned a local tavern, so the family was well known in the community. By the early 1940s, Long Branch had declined in popularity as a holiday destination and was becoming run-down, but young Robert nevertheless found a certain beauty in the merry-go-round and the boardwalk. There are many references to Long Branch in Pinsky's poetry.

From an early age Pinsky was interested in words, and he would browse through the dictionary to amuse himself. He did not find an outlet for this curiosity at school, and he was not an outstanding student. He attended Rutgers, the state university of New Jersey, where he became friends with a group of aspiring writers who published their work in the campus literary journal, the *Anthologist*. Pinsky and his friends generally eschewed writing courses, preferring to develop their talents independently. After graduating from Rutgers, in 1962, with a B.A. degree, Pinsky attended Stanford University, where he studied with the poet, teacher, and critic Yvor Winters. He earned a Ph.D. in 1966.

Pinsky then embarked on an academic career. From 1967 to 1968, he was an assistant professor of humanities at the University of Chicago; he then moved on to become an associate professor of English at Wellesley College, in Massachusetts, where he taught from 1968 to 1980. Then, until 1988, he was a professor of English at the University of California at Berkeley. After that he assumed his current job, as a professor of English and creative writing at Boston University, where he now teaches graduate creative-writing courses. From 1978 to 1986 he was the poetry editor of the *New Republic*, and at present he is the poetry editor of *Slate*, an Internet magazine. Pinsky has also been a guest instructor at several universities, including Harvard, in Cambridge, Massachusetts, and a contributor to *NewsHour with Jim Lehrer* on the PBS television network. When he is not traveling to fulfill speaking engagements as poet laureate, he lives in the Boston area with his wife, Ellen Bailey, a clinical psychologist. The couple married in 1961 and have three adult daughters, Nicole, Caroline, and Elizabeth.

Pinsky published his first book of poetry, *Sadness and Happiness*, in 1976. The following year saw the publication of the first of his two books of criticism, *The Situation of Poetry: Contemporary Poetry and Its Traditions*, an examination of language in works by several contemporary poets. Pinsky's second book of critical essays, *Poetry and the World* (1988), contains a wide-ranging group of essays, among them autobiographical sketches, reviews of recent books, transcripts of lectures on the origins of American poetry, and discussions of politics and the Bible. *Poetry and the World* left many readers with the impression that Pinsky was a traditionalist who held with longstanding ideas about poetry; for example, he expressed the belief that poetry should act as, in his words, "a bridge between the worldly and the spiritual."

Pinsky's poems, however, starting with those in *Sadness and Happiness*, went against the predominant grain by assuming a voice that was less personal and confessional, and more often omniscient and removed, than those of his contemporaries. His early poems already exhibited his preference for clear, direct language. Pinsky has said that he aspires to write poetry that is "discursive," which Maureen McLane, writing for the *Chicago Tribune* (May 2, 1997), interpreted to mean "inclusive in scope, measured in tone, talkative, and flexible enough to move through, expand upon, or easily change subjects." An excellent example of his discursiveness—and the poem for which *Sadness and Happiness* is perhaps most noted—is the 17-page "Essay on Psychiatrists." In the *New York Times Book Review*, Katha Pollitt wrote, "In its free and vigorous play of mind, his 'Essay on Psychiatrists' really is an essay, a witty, clear-eyed 21-part argument that moves from a group portrait of psychiatrists as a bourgeois social type (liberal politics, B'nai B'rith, 'a place on the Cape with Marimekko drapes') to a large and fully earned conclusion: 'But it is all bosh, the false / Link between genius and sickness.'"

Pinsky's book-length poem, *An Explanation of America* (1979), which was published by the Princeton University Press, was awarded the Saxifrage Prize as the year's best volume of poetry from a small or university publisher. The poem is considered his most ambitious work to date. Written for his oldest daughter as a history of the United States, it examines specific events as well as the ideological underpinnings of the nation. One period, that of the Vietnam War, was a formative era for Pinsky. He told McLane, "There's no question that the war in Vietnam—and the protests, teach-ins, and other activities I was involved in—were a watershed in my experience and in that of many poets of my generation." In *An Explanation of America*, he wrote that he will always feel "as if I lived / In a time when the country aged itself / As if we were a family, and some members / Had done an awful thing on a road at night, / And all of us had grown white hair, or tails."

Several critics consider Pinsky's collection *History of My Heart* (1984) a turning point in his work. While Pinsky had used autobiographical subject matter before, in this volume his poems are more personally revealing. As J. D. McClatchy wrote in his review for the *New Republic*, Pinsky "takes his stand on the contradictions and desires of the self." In the title poem, for example, as Stephen Corey wrote in the *Georgia Review* (Spring 1985), "across some 200 lines, [Pinsky] confronts and defeats constant threats of sentimentality as he explores the minutiae of autobiography, searching for what can only be called a theory of desire. Early in [the poem], Pinsky says that 'happiness needs a setting,' and nearly all of the poem is devoted to providing this—from his mother's early stories of life before his birth, on up through his own memories of infancy, childhood, and adolescence."

History of My Heart, which won the Poetry Society of America's William Carlos Williams Prize in 1985, marked a departure from Pinsky's previous work in his use of language and imagery as well, according to some critics. Katha Pollitt, for one, wrote that Pinsky "finds a way of writing a poem that is, well, poetical, that makes images and the connections—or gaps—between images bear a meaning whose emotional resonance derives in part from its indeterminacy." "The Figured Wheel," another of the notable poems in the collection, takes its central image from its title, but Pinsky never spells out what the image represents. Elizabeth Frank offered her interpretation in the *Nation* (April 7, 1984): "In 'The Figured Wheel,' the bizarre juggernaut of the title rolls unstoppably over the world, gathering all times, places, persons, mythologies, religions, and literatures into its gorgeous hangings and inscriptions, which add up to nothing less than the human race's whole inheritance of metaphor."

In *The Want Bone* (1990), Pinsky chose to explore in depth an aspect of human feeling he had touched on in *History of My Heart*; as McClatchy put it, "The [volume's] title calls it want. Desire, sexual appetite, romantic love, religious longing, nostalgia, imaginative poverty: it takes many forms." In the title poem Pinsky wrote of the jawbone of a shark washed up on a beach. Although it was a remnant of a creature long dead, its "welded-open shape kept mouthing O," evoking what Edward Hirsch referred to in the *New York Times Book Review* (November 18, 1990) as "the primal voice of longing": "But O I love you it sings, my little my country / My food my parent my child I want you my own / My flower my fin my life my lightness my O." Pinsky posits desire, in the words of Hirsch, as "an almost metaphysical principle of the universe that determines being, a fundamental song of appetite and need with large, complex, and ramifying consequences." Religious references, particularly to Judaism and Christianity, form an important component of Pinsky's writings, and *The Want Bone* includes several works based on religious stories. In the prose piece "Jesus and

Isolt," Pinsky imagines a meeting between Christ and the doomed lovers of an Irish fable, Tristram and Isolde. (In retellings of the fable, their names are spelled various ways.) Jesus tells Isolt of the political and religious divisions within Judea, and Isolt describes to him her experience of romantic love.

Another major vein in Pinsky's writing is a concern with everyday objects and events, including those that are seemingly mundane. Frank wrote of Pinsky's "sense that there is an impervious, bullying reality out there, defying the poet to make something out of it." In *Contemporary Authors* (1991), Pinsky is quoted as saying that his poems "try to get at the profoundly emotional, obsessive side of such supposedly ordinary activities as playing tennis or watching passers-by from a parked car." In "The Shirt," for example, which appears in *The Want Bone*, Pinsky examined the intricate history of a simple article of clothing—something that most shoppers probably take for granted. The poem moves from planters and pickers to fabric mills and sweatshops: "George Herbert, your descendent is a Black / Lady in South Carolina, her name is Irma / And she inspected my shirt. Its color and fit / And feel and its clean smell have satisfied / Both her and me." Pinsky also drew into the story of the shirt historical events and phenomena (among them the fire at the Triangle clothing factory in 1911, in which 146 workers died; the creation of tartan plaids in Great Britain hundreds of years ago; and slavery), so that, as McClatchy wrote, "by the end of the poem, the plain sportshirt has become a mythological shirt of flame, a history laid on the poet's back."

The work for which Pinsky is perhaps best known is his translation of the *Inferno*, the first of the three parts of the *Divine Comedy*, which the Italian poet Dante Alighieri wrote in the early 1300s. The *Divine Comedy*, one of the masterpieces of world literature, is considered one of the most difficult works to translate into English. This is not least because of its rhyme scheme, which Dante developed specifically to give the *Inferno* a sense of spiraling downward momentum. Called terza rima, the scheme consists of tercets in the structure a-b-a, b-c-b, c-d-c, and so on. "To write triple rhyme in English is not easy," Pinsky told Diana Jean Schemo for the *New York Times* (January 31, 1995). "English has an immense vocabulary, larger than Italian. And one of the classic mistakes you can make is to draw on that huge wealth of synonyms to supply rhymes. If you do that, you have an extremely unnatural, unidiomatic language; you end up with phrases that no one would ever say."

Although he had long been drawn to the poem, Pinsky was not an expert in Italian, and his experience as a translator was limited to his collaboration, in 1984, with the American poet Robert Hass on an English rendition of *The Separate Notebooks* by the Lithuanian-born poet Czeslaw Milosz, who won the Nobel Prize for literature in 1980. Pinsky embarked on his translation of the *Inferno* somewhat by chance. Along with other distinguished poets, he was invited by the 92nd Street YMHA in New York City to participate in a public reading of the poem's 34 cantos. Each poet was asked to do his or her own translation of one or two cantos. Once he began translating, Pinsky found the process so intriguing that he decided to do the entire poem. "It just gripped me, like a child with a new video game," he told Schemo. "I literally couldn't stop working on it." By the time the reading was held, Pinsky had completed a rough draft of all 34 cantos.

Many translators have not even tried to replicate the *Inferno*'s rhyme scheme, but Pinsky was determined to do so, while simultaneously conveying the poem's musicality. He also worked to retain the original's lack of decorum, by keeping the language informal and idiomatic. Pinsky used slant, or near, rhymes (for example, "room" and "soon"; "years" and "yours") rather than actual rhymes to avoid making the rhyming overbearing. Published in 1994, his translation won rave reviews from several prominent publications, including the *New Yorker* and the *New York Times Book Review*. Thanks to its selection by the Book of the Month Club, it became Pinsky's biggest commercial success.

Pinsky took over the post of poet laureate in October 1997, after being appointed by the librarian of Congress, James Billington, to succeed Robert Hass. The position, created in 1937, currently extends for one year (many laureates are reappointed for a second year); it comes with few official responsibilities, leaving appointees free to develop their own agendas. Pinsky has often expressed the view that "poetry is an art that's very much on an individual scale," as he told David Streitfeld. "The medium is one human body, one person—not necessarily the artist, but anyone saying the words of the poem over to him or herself." Out of this idea, as well as Pinsky's desire to gather evidence of Americans' interest in poetry at the end of the millennium, he decided to take advantage of his post to create an archive of audiocassette recordings of Americans from all walks of life reading their favorite poems aloud. "I've got a marine with a Hispanic surname who wants to read some Wallace Stevens, a black preacher with a poem by Longfellow—every age, every region of the country, every kind of profession," he told Francis X. Clines for the *New York Times* (March 17, 1998). "It's going to be fun." Pinsky hopes to collect about 1,200 recordings and has arranged to have them kept permanently in the attic of the Library of Congress, where the poet laureate's office is located. "[Walt] Whitman had this vision of poetry as holding together a country that might be fragmented . . . ," Pinsky told Clines. "We don't have a single unfolding folk culture the way a more homogeneous country might have, no traditional aristocratic class as hereditary curators. So the love of an art like poetry has no social props and is somewhat in-

visible. But it's there and the archive will demonstrate that."

Robert Pinsky's two most recent books are *The Sounds of Poetry: A Brief Guide*, and the anthology *The Handbook of Heartbreak*, both published in 1998. In 1996, he received the Shelley Memorial Award from the Poetry Society of America. — O.J.S.

Suggested Reading: *Chicago Tribune* p1+ May 2, 1997, with photo, p1 Nov. 18, 1997, with photo; *New Republic* p46+ Sep. 24, 1990; *New York Times* C p13 Jan. 31, 1995, with photo, C p3 Mar. 28, 1997, with photo, A p29 Apr. 10, 1997, with photo, A p18 Mar. 17, 1998, with photo; *New York Times Book Review* p24+ Nov. 18, 1990, p3+ Jan. 1, 1995, with photo, p9 Aug. 18, 1996, with photo; *Washington Post* C p1+ Mar. 28, 1997, with photo; *Contemporary Authors* first revision vols. 29–32, 1978; *Contemporary Authors* new revision series vol. 58, 1997; *Contemporary Literary Criticism* vol. 38, 1986, vol. 94, 1997

Selected Works: *Landor's Poetry*, 1968; *Sadness and Happiness*, 1975; *The Situation of Poetry: Contemporary Poetry and Its Traditions*, 1976; *An Explanation of America*, 1979; *History of My Heart*, 1984; *Poetry and the World*, 1988; *The Want Bone*, 1990; *The Figured Wheel: New and Collected Poems 1966–1996*, 1996; as translator—*The Inferno of Dante: A New Verse Translation*, 1994, with Robert Hass—(Czeslaw Milosz) *The Separate Notebooks*, 1984

Pipher, Mary

Oct. 21, 1947– Clinical psychologist; writer.
Address: 3201 S. 33d, Suite B, Lincoln, NE 68506

"I think it's because I'm so ordinary." According to the clinical psychologist Mary Pipher, that is why her book *Reviving Ophelia: Saving the Selves of Adolescent Girls* (1994) became a best-seller. Elaborating on that statement during an interview with Megan Rosenfeld for the *Washington Post* (May 16, 1996), Pipher said, "My ideas are probably very close to what most people are thinking. They come up to me at book signings and tell me, I'm so glad you're saying what I've been saying." Pipher's first book, *Hunger Pains: From Fad Diets to Eating Disorders: What Every Woman Needs to Know About Food, Dieting, and Self-Concept,* failed to generate interest from publishers, so Pipher published it at her own expense, in 1988. (In 1997 it was reissued in paperback by Ballantine Books with the title *Hunger Pains: The Modern Woman's Tragic Quest for Thinness.*) Her second, *Reviving Ophelia,* grew out of her ruminations about the growing number of adolescent girls among her clients and the in-

Mary Pipher

Randy Barger/Riverhead Books

creasingly disturbing problems that had brought them to her. During a subsequent lecture tour across the country, Pipher discovered how troubled many American families were. In her next book, *The Shelter of Each Other: Rebuilding Our Families* (1996), she discussed their problems and offered ways of dealing with them that avoided traditional psychotherapeutic approaches. "By focusing so much on inner psychology, we've eroded the family's faith in themselves," she told Megan Rosenfeld. "That's part of the problem with words like dysfunctional and co-dependent. We imply that if they could just get it together, everything would be okay. . . . People do not respond well to being blamed. If you want to change behavior, encourage them to believe they have the power to make change." Pipher's most recent work is *Another Country: Navigating the Emotional Terrain of Our Elders* (1999), in which she examines the potential rifts between baby boomers and their aging parents and offers advice intended to increase understanding of the aging process and draw members of these two groups closer together.

Mary Pipher was born Mary Bray on October 21, 1947 in Springfield, Missouri, the eldest of the seven children of Frank Houston Bray and Avis Ester Page Bray. She grew up in Beaver City, Nebraska, whose population in the early 1950s was about 500. Her father, a farmer, and her mother, the town physician, did not encourage Pipher's early interest in writing. "Neither of my parents could be called intellectuals," Pipher told Rosenfeld. "My father never read a book, and my mother . . . worked all the time. I don't think there was a book in the house. And when I talked to my father once about being a writer, he said, They don't make any

money." In *Reviving Ophelia*, Pipher recalled that for two decades after one of her teachers strongly criticized her early attempts at writing, she confined her literary efforts to school assignments.

Pipher attended the University of California at Berkeley, where she majored in cultural anthropology and received a B.A. degree, in 1969. During her undergraduate years she became interested in how culture affects families and individuals—or, as she put it to Liz Walker for "Tulsa Kids" on *family.com* (on-line), "What part of family business is unique to the family and what part is cultural?" Pipher continued her education at the University of Nebraska, where she earned a Ph.D. in clinical psychology in 1977. Earlier, in 1974, she had married Jim Pipher, a psychologist and jazz and bluegrass musician, and the couple settled in Lincoln, Nebraska. Their son, Zeke, and daughter, Sara, are currently in their 20s.

When her daughter entered third grade, Pipher, finding herself with some spare time and an eagerness to try her hand at writing again, enrolled in an undergraduate creative-writing course. The first short story she wrote for the class won an award, and thereafter writing became one of her serious pursuits. She set up an office in her home, and since then she has written every day from 5 a.m. until 10 a.m. In the afternoon she sees patients (who number about 30 at any given time) and makes phone calls. In addition to her nonfiction books, Pipher has continued to write short fiction; one of her short stories won the Alice P. Carter Award, and another earned her recognition in the National Feminist Writer's Competition.

In an interview for the on-line publication *Commitment*, Pipher explained that the inspiration for the title of *Reviving Ophelia* was the daughter of Polonius in Shakespeare's tragedy *Hamlet*. "Ophelia was mentally intact and happy until she fell in love with Hamlet," she said. "She was torn between her desire to please him and to please her father. She grows confused, depressed, and eventually, she kills herself. Her experience is a good metaphor for what happens to many girls in early adolescence. They become confused by others' expectations and their true selves are lost." In *Reviving Ophelia*, Pipher contended that with the onset of adolescence, girls in the U.S. begin to feel pressure to conform to the mass media's idealized images of femininity, which require physical attractiveness—in particular, thinness—popularity, sexual experience, and possibly even lack of intelligence: as Pipher pointed out, girls are often ridiculed for their academic accomplishments. According to Pipher, many girls who feel that they will never measure up to the ideal become depressed and self-loathing. Moreover, some of them ignore talents or stifle aspects of their personalities that don't conform to the ideal.

Pipher argued that although troubled girls tend to blame themselves or their parents for their unhappiness, the true culprits are elements of what she called the "girl-poisoning" American culture.

Recognizing that no one can single-handedly change society, she suggested ways of dealing with societal pressures. She advised young women to spend 15 minutes each day in a quiet place by themselves, in order to get in touch with their emotions and thoughts, a process that she called centering. She also encouraged them to express their feelings by keeping journals or writing poetry and to think positively about their talents. As an alternative to striving for popularity, she recommended spending time with one or two close friends, taking care of a pet, and getting involved in volunteer work in the community. She advised parents to talk to their daughters about the girls' lives and to recognize the peer pressures surrounding their children. In interviews, she expressed the hope that by reading *Reviving Ophelia* and thus gaining an understanding of the problems girls face, parents and daughters would be better equipped to cope with the difficulties girls encounter during adolescence.

Some critics complained that *Reviving Ophelia* is too pessimistic, mainly because it does not examine cases of girls who have coped successfully with the trials of adolescence. Others have pointed out that Pipher's theories are far from new; however, many agreed that thanks to Pipher, many more people had been exposed to those theories. Pipher told Margaret Nelson, "I deliberately set out to be accessible. Not simple ideas, but ideas simply put." Linda Grey, the president of Ballantine, which published *Reviving Ophelia* in paperback, noted that while Pipher was obviously calling for change, she had done so in a nonaggressive way. Grey told Elizabeth Gleick for *Time* (February 19, 1996), "Mary is able to convey difficult information in a very reassuring, comfortable, and positive way."

With the success of *Reviving Ophelia*, Pipher became much sought after as a speaker. "As I travel giving lectures, I have found that families all over the country are facing the same problems and blaming themselves," Pipher told Margaret Nelson for *People* (June 24, 1996). "I wanted to look at those issues and offer some ideas." Pipher made those issues the subject of her next book, *The Shelter of Each Other: Rebuilding Our Families*, the title of which comes from an Irish proverb: "It is in the shelter of each other that people live." In that book, which also became a best-seller, Pipher asserted that mainstream American culture is hurting not only young women but families. As she told Nelson, "For lots of reasons, we as a culture started thinking that other things were more important than family—careers, possessions, individual fulfillment. We let ourselves get too busy to spend time with our children." Pipher maintained that society's emphasis on consumerism and material objects as a route to happiness prompts people to work harder and for longer hours. Thus, families spend less time together; parents devote less time to transmitting their values to their children and often do not adequately monitor what their chil-

dren are consuming by way of television, movies, and video games. Parents also spend less time with neighbors and friends in their communities and with members of their extended families, many of whom often live far away. Consequently, children have fewer connections to the world outside the home. That isolation, along with a continual stream of highly publicized incidents of violence, makes the world a scarier place for children than it was years ago, and thus children feel more anxious and less secure.

As she did in *Reviving Ophelia*, in *The Shelter of Each Other*, Pipher proposed what Elizabeth Gleick referred to as "commonsensical, unthreatening solutions." Pipher encouraged families to vacation together, enjoy outdoor activities together, maintain regular contact with relatives, friends, and neighbors, and have family celebrations and rituals. She also advised families to get involved in community organizations in which people of different ages participate, so that, among other benefits, children have an opportunity to interact with older adults. On a political level, Pipher called for a national mandate for television networks to show educational programming from three to six p.m., with no advertising. She also stressed the need for more funding for public television and day care and shorter hours for employees who are normally expected to work more than 40 hours weekly.

Rosenfeld reported that *Reviving Ophelia* and *The Shelter of Each Other* both ask "two central questions": "How does culture affect mental health?" and, in Pipher's words, "How has the world changed since I was a girl?" Pipher's response to the second question was that today, the media and advertising are omnipresent; kids are exposed to drugs and alcohol at younger ages; violence is more prevalent, both in the media and in real life; and people feel more isolated from one another in their families and communities. She told Gleick, "I don't think the past was idyllic. But children felt safer."

The title of Pipher's latest book, *Another Country: Navigating the Emotional Terrain of Our Elders*, is taken from the writer May Sarton's description of old age as "a foreign country." Pipher wrote the book over a year-long period during which she was taking care of her ailing mother, and she drew on her own experiences as well as on those of her clients; transcribed material from her sessions with some patients is included in the book. Pipher pointed out the many stumbling blocks that can impede communication between older adults and their grown children, including differences in values and communication styles. Thanks to the cultural mores prevalent when baby boomers (people born right after World War II) came of age, Pipher explained, those adults are able to talk about personal problems—be they emotional or physical—more openly than their parents, who often find such discussions uncomfortable or even shameful. Guilt—suffered, for example, by adult children who are unable to spend time regularly with their aging parents—can also get in the way of healthy relationships. After elucidating such potential barriers and attempting to shed light on some of the feelings many elderly people experience as they go through this often difficult stage in life, Pipher provided examples of how lines of communication may be opened and feelings of closeness achieved. As in her earlier books, she stressed the importance of spending time together as a family, emphasizing that contact among all generations, from great-grandparents to infants, will create a healthier emotional environment for everyone. "The more we love and respect our elders," Pipher wrote, as quoted by Sara Rimer in the New York Times (March 11, 1999), "the more we teach our children to love and respect us."

Remaining "connected" to her family and community, Pipher told Rosenfeld, is among her main priorities. Although she could earn $30,000 per speaking appearance, she keeps her fees comparatively low. "How could I take that much money from a place like the Detroit Medical Center, which treats girls for free?" she remarked to Rosenfeld.

She added, "Time is the real wealth." Pipher is reported to be serious and straightforward in her demeanor. "I'm a middle-class, middle-aged woman from the middle of the country," Pipher told Nelson. "That's why people relate to me." — O.J.S.

Suggested Reading: Commitment (on-line); People p121+ June 24, 1996, with photos; New York Times (on-line) Mar. 11, 1999; Time p73 Feb. 19, 1996, with photos; Washington Post C p1+ May 16, 1996, with photos

Selected Books: Hunger Pains: From Fad Diets to Eating disorders: What Every Woman Needs to Know About Food, Dieting, and Self-Concept, 1988 (reissued as Hunger Pains: The American Woman's Tragic Quest for Thinness, 1997); Reviving Ophelia: Saving the Selves of Adolescent Girls, 1994; The Shelter of Each Other: Rebuilding Our Families, 1996; Another Country: Navigating the Emotional Terrain of Our Elders, 1999

Jan Press/Courtesy of Delacorte Press

Plain, Belva

Oct. 9, 1919– Writer. Address: c/o Delacorte Press, 1540 Broadway, New York, NY 10036

Though not a favorite among most critics, Belva Plain has been a best-selling author for more than 20 years. In the early 1960s, after having published numerous short stories in magazines, she took time off to devote herself to her family. She did not re-

turn to writing until she was in her 50s, at which point she began a successful career as a novelist. Starting with Evergreen (1978) and continuing in such novels as Random Winds (1980), The Golden Cup (1986), Tapestry (1988), Treasures (1992), and The Carousel (1995), Plain's work has focused on families—particularly women—experiencing dramatic difficulties. Her novels typically feature melodramatic plot twists and, in part for this reason, have been criticized as little more than soap operas, a label Plain adamantly rejects. Her most recent novel, Legacy of Silence, was published in 1998.

The writer was born Belva Offenberg on October 9, 1919 in New York City, the only child of a contractor, Oscar Offenberg, and his wife, Eleanor. Her interest in writing manifested itself early on, when she edited her high-school literary magazine. While attending Barnard College, in New York City, she submitted several pieces to the campus literary journal. Shortly after graduating from Barnard, in 1941, she married Irving Plain, an ophthalmologist, with whom she would eventually have three children. The Plains lived in Philadelphia for six years while Irving completed his residency, and then, in 1947, moved to South Orange, New Jersey, where they lived for many years.

Starting in the 1940s Plain published short fiction in such women's magazines as Cosmopolitan and Good Housekeeping, at the suggestion of a friend who provided illustrations for some of those periodicals. The stories were formulaic, focusing on women's romantic problems. Plain continued writing for magazines until the early 1960s, when she devoted herself full-time to her responsibilities as a homemaker. "It became difficult to do two things at once," she told Carol Horner for the *Chicago Tribune* (September 17, 1980). During her years away from writing, Plain also served as president of the local parent-teacher association and sat on the boards of various charitable organizations. All the while, she jotted down notes and fragments of fiction, which she intended to use when she resumed her career as an author. She got back into writing in the 1970s.

Plain, who is Jewish, was troubled by the representations of Jews in much of the fiction she was reading. "I was tired of the stereotyped Jewish mother whose chicken soup renders her son impotent," she told *People* (August 7, 1978). "I thought it was time to write about the kind of people I know." The result was her first novel, *Evergreen*, published when Plain was 58 years old. The book, which opens in about 1900, tells the story of a Jewish immigrant who works as a maid and falls in love with the son of her employers. *Evergreen* was a major departure from Plain's material for women's magazines, in that it recorded the trials and triumphs of three generations of a Jewish family, following them from the ghettos of Warsaw to the suburbs of America. An immediate success, the novel spent 41 weeks on the best-seller list and sold 3.5 million copies. (According to *Contemporary Authors* [1997], 11 million copies are in print, in a dozen languages.) With the novel's brisk sales, Belva Plain became, at age 59, a major name in the world of popular fiction. "I'm a younger Grandma Moses," she mused, as quoted in the *New York Times* (July 30, 1978). In 1985 NBC produced a miniseries based on *Evergreen*.

Two years after the publication of *Evergreen*, Plain's second novel, *Random Winds* (1980), appeared. The novel features a doctor married to a woman suffering from curvature of the spine. The idea for the story came to Plain after she observed a couple in which the woman suffered from the same malady.

Plain continued to publish prolifically into the 1980s. In 1982 she released *Eden Burning*, a story set on a Caribbean Island, about the fall from grace of a wealthy planter's daughter. Two years later she published the ambitious *Crescent City*, a tale of an American Jewish family during the Civil War. *The Golden Cup*'s plot unfolds in New York City at the beginning of the 20th century; its protagonist is one of *Evergreen*'s secondary characters, who is much more idealistic than the rest of her well-to-do family and seeks to help the poor. At the same time she must deal with her husband's womanizing.

In *Newsday* (October 12, 1986), Frances A. Koestler expressed her disappointment in *The Golden Cup*, a book she thought was weakened by the reappearance of the two main characters from *Evergreen*. Koestler suggested, however, that this less-than-satisfying effort should not permanently turn readers away from Plain, whom the reviewer described as an "indisputable talent."

The third novel in the trilogy begun in *Evergreen* and continued in *The Golden Cup* is *Tapestry*. Here, Plain examined the generations that followed her original characters. The book spans the years from 1920 to just before World War II; with the power of the Nazis ever growing, the characters must reassess their identities as Jews. Writing for the *New York Times Book Review* (June 19, 1988), Karen Ray expressed the view that the novel was a step down from the trilogy's previous two installments. "Despite her ambitious plotting," Ray wrote, "Belva Plain has produced a serviceable saga that lives, if at all, only in the shadow of her earlier books." Plain's first published effort of the 1990s was *Harvest* (1990). Continuing the exploits of the characters first introduced in *Evergreen*, *Harvest* takes place in the 1960s, a generation after the previous installment in the series, and centers on the illegitimate daughter of *Tapestry*'s main character. Joanne Kaufman of *People* (Aug. 27, 1990) proved even less kind to *Harvest* than Karen Ray had been to *Tapestry*. "Nothing a reviewer can say will stay Belva Plain from her appointed rounds—spinning twaddle," Kaufman wrote. The reviewer singled out the novel's "pat, platitudinous writing" for particular criticism.

With *Treasures*, Plain departed at last from the family saga begun in *Evergreen*. The novel deals with the conflict between family values and worldly values, tracing the aspirations of three siblings who make different decisions when faced with the choice between maintaining an old-fashioned lifestyle and seeking glamour and fortune in the big city. In the end, Plain suggests that life's true "treasures" come from within. While the review in *Publishers Weekly* (January 27, 1992) described this message as somewhat trite, it noted that Plain's "warm narrative nevertheless endears itself to the reader and provides a rewarding reading experience." In the *New York Times Book Review* (May 17, 1992), Katherine Ramsland found fascinating the novel's perspective on Manhattan's upper class but criticized the lack of tension and the predictable plot.

Continuing to explore the myriad relationships and emotional interconnections of the extended family, Plain published *Whispers* in 1993. The family presented in the novel maintains an elaborate façade, hiding such problems as physical abuse behind a veneer of success and comfort. The novel's main female character is in the end made to face her family's numerous difficulties. The book received many negative reviews, but a writer for *Publishers Weekly* (March 22, 1993) praised the author's effective characterizations and avoidance of melodrama.

Daybreak (1994), the story of two babies switched at birth, takes up issues of Jewish life explored in Plain's earlier novels, as one of the infants grows into an anti-Semitic adult, unaware that he is Jewish. Jean Hanff Korelitz remarked in the *New York Times Book Review* (May 8, 1994) that the novel's imagery derives from clichéd language and that the dialogue "suggests background music." Nevertheless, Korelitz felt that the book's "plot device . . . is meaty enough to compensate for these shortcomings."

Plain has continued to write prolifically, publishing novels throughout the 1990s. *Daybreak* was followed by *The Carousel* (1995), *Promises* (1996), *Homecoming* (1997), and *Secrecy* (1997). In the last-named book, Plain followed a young rape victim's struggle to overcome her fear of intimacy. The plot of Plain's most recent novel, *Legacy of Silence*, begins in Germany at the brink of World War II and concludes in present-day America, as it follows the fates of two daughters of a rich Berlin family.

To fight what she perceives as the stereotype of the "Jewish mother" that exists in much of popular American culture, Plain fills her works with female characters of exceptional strength and dignity. They deal courageously with problems that often stem from their heritage as well as their family lives. The author's tremendous success over the years has proven that her stories have a wide appeal that extends beyond a Jewish readership. "I think I show real people and a real understanding of human nature, how people function and react to their environment," Plain told the *Chicago Tribune* (October 12, 1984).

One of the overriding themes of Plain's work is forbidden love. In this respect her novels bear a resemblance to the stories she published in the earlier portion of her career. Many of her female protagonists are faced with difficult decisions regarding matters of the heart. Yet despite the frequency of love affairs in her novels, Plain has made it a point not to include gratuitous sex scenes. "I think they're vulgar," she told the *Chicago Tribune* (October 12, 1984). "People [have written] love stories, the greatest in the world, and didn't feel it necessary to include those scenes." In this regard, Plain has always considered her work to be far above the often lurid novels that make up a good deal of the romance genre.

The author has also made it clear that her material comes purely from observation and imagination, not from experience. "I had one love affair in my life and that was . . . Irving," she told the *Chicago Tribune*. Her happy and somewhat traditional family life contrasts sharply with the tumultuous events of her characters' lives.

Many book critics have labeled Plain's novels soap operas, charging that they substitute sensationalism and sap for believable plot structure and character development. During a *Chicago Tribune* (September 17, 1980) interview, Plain asked rhetorically, "What is a soap opera? An attractive young woman is married to a stodgy man. She takes a lover . . . and goes away with him. He tires of her, and she is terribly jealous. She commits suicide, and he is overcome with guilt. . . . Is that a soap opera? It's the plot of *Anna Karenina*." She went on to accuse her critics of "intellectual snobbery."

Plain's daily regimen involves writing for five hours each morning, then recording her material on tape for a secretary to type. Her husband, Irving, died in 1982.—B.S.

Suggested Reading: *Chicago Tribune* p13+ Sep. 17, 1980, with photo, p2+ Oct. 12, 1984, with photo; *New York Times Book Review* p30 July 30, 1978, with photo, p20 June 19, 1988, p35 Sep. 30, 1990, with photo, p35 May 17, 1992, p18 May 8, 1994; *Newsday* p22 Oct. 12, 1986, with photo; *People* p85 Aug. 7, 1978, with photo, p32+ Aug. 1, 1988, p30 Aug. 27, 1990, with photo; *Publishers Weekly* p89 Jan. 27, 1992; *International Authors and Writers Who's Who* 1997/98

Selected Books: *Evergreen*, 1978; *Random Winds*, 1980; *Eden Burning*, 1982; *Crescent City*, 1984; *The Golden Cup*, 1986; *Tapestry*, 1988; *Blessings*, 1989; *Harvest*, 1990; *Treasures*, 1992; *Whispers*, 1993; *Daybreak*, 1994; *The Carousel*, 1995; *Promises*, 1996; *The Homecoming*, 1997; *Secrecy*, 1997; *Legacy of Silence*, 1998

Courtesy of *Jane*

Pratt, Jane

Nov. 11, 1962– Editor of the magazine Jane.
Address: c/o Fairchild Publications, Inc., 7 W. 34th St., New York, NY 10001-8191

In some professions, credibility comes with experience and age. Jane Pratt, however, has found the opposite to be true during her career. When Pratt was hired as the founding editor in chief of the teen magazine *Sassy* in 1987, at the age of 24, she and her staff joked that because of the publication's young audience, she would have to retire at age 30. Under Pratt's leadership, *Sassy* won attention from both readers and the publishing world; speaking to teenage girls on their level and, more radically, reflecting their distinctive manner of speech, the magazine addressed subjects both serious and frivolous in a fresh and frank way. There was speculation from outside *Sassy*'s ranks as to how long a maturing Pratt would be able to stay so intimately in touch with teens' dilemmas and diction. In an interview with Susan Hovey for *Folio* (April 15, 1991), Pratt expressed little concern. "As I get closer to 30," Pratt, then 28, said, "I realize that I'm not really maturing that rapidly. I don't feel that I relate any less to the readers than when I got the job. I'm still very much 15 at heart. I mean, I have to be a mixture of really responsible and really wild in my current job and that's what I've always been. . . . I'd love to create a magazine like *Sassy* for people my own age."

Pratt's last statement turned out to be prophetic. After hosting two short-lived television talk shows aimed at teens while retaining her job at the magazine, Pratt left *Sassy* in about 1994. Then, in September 1998, Fairchild Publications launched the magazine *Jane*, with Pratt as its namesake and editor in chief. *Jane* re-created *Sassy*'s spunky, in-your-face sensibility for 18-to-34-year-old women. Although *Jane* is not groundbreaking in the way *Sassy* was, its tone clearly differs from that of most women's magazines. "We aren't stuck with some of those old ideas about how to get a husband or how to get a guy back after he has an affair or even how to lose 15 pounds in 15 days," Pratt told Robin Pogrebin for the *New York Times* (September 7, 1997). "I didn't want to create a magazine that would make women feel bad after reading it. I didn't want it to be a manual for all your flaws and all the things you need to fix."

Jane Pratt was born on November 11, 1962 and grew up in Durham, North Carolina. Her parents, both painters who taught fine arts at Duke University, separated when Jane was 13 and divorced two years later. Pratt attended the Carolina Friends School, a Quaker institution where there was little pressure to fit in or be popular and where grading was done on the pass-fail system. While Pratt later told Susan Hovey that she was "the absolute worst" at basketball, she still made the team. This atmosphere contrasted starkly with that at Phillips Exeter Academy, in Exeter, New Hampshire, the socially and academically competitive school her father and uncle had attended. Pratt transferred there for her junior year of high school, and the adjustment proved to be difficult for her. She spent the following summer changing her looks, "with way too much makeup," as she told Hovey, and training for the cross-country team, so that she could make friends with the new students when she went back to school. "When you're a teen," she told Hovey, "you do what you have to do to get by

and be happy. Those years are so hard for kids." She later shared some of her traumatic high-school experiences with *Sassy* readers.

Pratt's adolescent growing pains helped spark her love of magazines. "I fell in love with them as this potential lifeline," she told Robin Pogrebin. "I felt like, there I was, stuck in boarding school, but there were magazines that could show me other places and other ways of living." Pratt attended Oberlin College, in Oberlin, Ohio, where she majored in dance and communications, and she did summer internships at *Rolling Stone* and *Sportstyle*. After graduation she landed a job as an assistant editor at *McCall's* and moved to New York City. In 1986 she became an associate editor at *Teenage* magazine. Then, in 1987, Pratt was introduced to representatives of John Fairfax Ltd., an Australian media conglomerate. Fairfax, the publisher of *Dolly*, a hip and very successful teen magazine in Australia, was looking for an editor in chief for a new title, *Sassy*, loosely envisioned as an American version of *Dolly*. Pratt was at first unaware that she was a candidate for the top editorial position at *Sassy*; she considered herself too young for a job as editor in chief of a national publication. Furthermore, after a friend told her to "be herself" at her job interview, Pratt took that advice to the extreme—wearing "thrift-store clothes," as she recalled to Hovey, and scuffed black shoes, and telling her interviewer about a college episode in which she went off with a rock band the day before exams started.

Pratt went on to win the job, and after her training period, which included six months in Australia at *Dolly*, *Sassy* debuted, in March 1988. The magazine attracted immediate attention for its risky—some might say risqué—editorial content. The cover of the first issue alerted readers to features entitled "So You Think You're Ready for Sex? Read This First" and "Three Suicides: Stories You Won't Forget," alongside more traditional teen-magazine fare, such as "Our Beginner's Guide to Makeup" and "Justine Bateman Speaks." It was predicted that some adults would object to the fact that articles on sex, suicide, AIDS, and gay awareness were being aimed at teenagers. Pratt, however, stood by her approach, arguing that these were issues that affected teens and about which they should be better informed. "We don't leave anything out," she told Marilyn Gardner for the *Christian Science Monitor* (March 7, 1988). "We don't use euphemisms, and we don't apologize. Basically, there's nothing of interest to teens I wouldn't publish." In the same interview, Pratt cited a letter from a 13-year-old reader who reported that reading the article on sex in *Sassy*'s first issue gave her the courage to say no to her boyfriend, who had been pressuring her. "Readers are getting a lot of explicit information from us," Pratt told Gardner. "But underlying that there's a very responsible tone. We're saying, 'You don't have to rush out and do this.'" In another controversial move, Pratt made *Sassy* the first teen magazine in the U.S. to accept advertisements for condoms. "It was done very intentionally," she told Gardner. "The United States has twice as much teen-age pregnancy as countries where there is mandatory sex education in schools." On the other hand, Pratt rejected certain advertisements, found in the pages of other teen magazines, that she felt were lascivious. This group consisted mainly of perfume and clothing ads (such as one for the Calvin Klein perfume Obsession) that, Pratt told Gardner, "promote sexuality in a very general way."

Sassy was also noted for a number of less contentious innovations. The magazine's articles and editorial pages were written in "a teen slang previously uncommitted to print," as Rebecca Mead observed in *New York* (September 15, 1997). They were also written in a confiding tone that made readers feel as if they were on a first-name basis with the magazine's writers and editorial staff. Furthermore, through features such as readers polls, Pratt found ways to create an actual, rather than merely a perceived, dialogue with readers. One of the briefer polls, printed on the spine of the October 1990 issue, asked readers if Pratt should get a nose ring. Of the 199 respondents, 189 voted yes. (The 10 who voted no included Pratt's grandmother.) Accordingly, Pratt got her nose pierced, on national television, on an installment of *First Person with Maria Shriver*, a program that spotlighted the day-to-day lives of famous people. In another example of reader involvement, *Sassy's* December 1990 issue was produced entirely by readers; more than 80 teens wrote articles or made other contributions, and about 30 came to New York and worked for several days in *Sassy's* offices. Hovey wrote of Pratt's "ability to orchestrate what has become an amazingly gratifying give-and-take between *Sassy* staff and readers. . . . It's that sensitivity that allows for articles like 'Your (and our) 20 coolest women ever.' Those parentheses that may look like an afterthought really are much more. They are a device that says, 'Yeah, we pretty much agree with you; but here's some other people you should know about, too.'"

Pratt's ability to connect with a teenage audience allowed *Sassy* to explore world events and moral issues without seeming preachy or condescending. Later in her tenure, the magazine included features about the conflicts in such trouble spots as Northern Ireland and the Persian Gulf. An article that dealt with racism in the U.S. was entitled, "What's with All the Asian-bashing?" Pratt also published an article on environmental conservation written by Michael Stipe, the lead singer of the rock group R.E.M. and a friend of Pratt's since her days at Oberlin, where the two had met after the band performed there. "When I think about our role in speaking to the next generation," Pratt told Susan Hovey, "instilling values in these kids and giving them information they can use in really important ways—it's incredible. We want to keep breaking new ground. We want to give them not only what isn't in other teen magazines, but other

magazines period." As she did later with *Jane*, Pratt also strove to encourage in her readers healthy attitudes about their looks, and she thus shunned features on calorie-counting and spot-toning. As Pratt told an interviewer for *Interview* (June 1992), "We get letters from girls saying stuff like, 'Oh, I hated my freckles. And then I saw you had a model on your cover with freckles, and I thought, Oh, maybe they're okay after all.' We show models with braces and big noses and different-shaped bodies. We show models who are not six feet tall and 90 pounds. We show a lot of normal looking girls."

Pratt was largely credited with *Sassy's* success. Media-industry insiders felt that the editorial tone she was able to strike made *Sassy* a hit with readers. Circulation grew from about 250,000 in 1988 to 715,000 in 1993, in spite of stiff competition from *Sassy's* entrenched counterparts in the field, *Seventeen* and *YM*. Aside from her winning ways with her teen readership, Pratt was also a poised leader who inspired admiration from her staff. "Jane is incredibly professional, fair and honest," Mary Kaye Schilling, executive editor of *Sassy*, told Susan Hovey. "Staff meetings that should take 10 minutes end up taking two hours because everybody's opinion matters. That's how we come up with stuff that is so fresh." Schilling also credited Pratt with the magazine's success in getting readers' input. *Sassy* was temporarily hurt, however, by an advertising boycott organized by Focus on the Family, a conservative group. By 1991 the magazine's original publisher, Fairfax, had sold the title to Lang Communications.

Sassy's "cult status in media circles," as Rebecca Mead described the magazine's cachet, made Pratt herself into something of a media darling. *Jane*, the first of her two talk shows, premiered in early 1992, on the New York City affiliate of the Fox television network, airing at 5 p.m. on weekdays. It was credited with being the first talk show aimed at teenagers. "I thought it would be interesting to take the basic *Sassy* idea and do it on TV," Pratt told an interviewer for the *New York Times* (April 15, 1992). "*Sassy* gives [teens] a voice, but this gives them a literal voice. It was a way to get out there in a major way." In the latter statement, Pratt was referring to the fact that while *Sassy* had a large readership for a relatively new magazine, the number of teens it reached was tiny when compared with the potential television audience.

Pratt had limited control over the topics featured on the show. The first installment, for example, was about being jilted at the altar, a subject more appropriate, she felt, to a slightly older audience than that targeted by the show. The program's content turned out to be a point of contention between Pratt and Fox, with the latter stressing that sensationalistic topics won better ratings than the more informative, awareness-raising ones Pratt hoped the show would address. "The bottom line," Pratt told *Glamour* (October 1995), "is the show 'X-rated Ways I Worked My Way Through College' got about twice as many viewers as the one on AIDS risks for women." Pratt had reportedly become disenchanted with *Jane* when, after 13 weeks on the air, the program was canceled by Fox.

Despite the show's problems, *Jane* won respectable ratings, and many television insiders were impressed with Pratt's television persona and easy rapport with studio audiences. "It's sort of like hosting a party," Pratt told the *Chicago Tribune* (April 25, 1993) of her approach. "You work the room, you try to get people talking." The basic format of *Jane* was revived in 1993 on the Lifetime cable television network as *Jane Pratt*. The new show, however, ultimately suffered from the same types of problems with subject matter, with shows like "Cheapskate Boyfriends" winning out over more socially conscious fare. *Jane Pratt* was canceled later in 1993.

Pratt continued to act as editor in chief of *Sassy* throughout her stints as a talk-show host. Beginning in about 1991, she also served as an editorial adviser to *Dirt*, a magazine aimed at teenage boys. *Dirt* was created by *Sassy*'s publisher in response to estimates that boys made up 10 to 15 percent of *Sassy*'s readers. Pratt left *Sassy* in the mid-1990s. The magazine's competitors had copied many of *Sassy*'s innovations, and circulation had failed to meet expectations for continued growth; the magazine folded within a few years of Pratt's departure. Pratt continued to work in television. Among other projects, she interviewed celebrities on the music television cable network VH-1. She also co-authored a book with Kelli Pryor, entitled *For Real: The Uncensored Truth About America's Teenagers* (1995), and wrote another book, *Beyond Beauty: Girls Speak Out on Looks, Style, and Stereotypes* (1997).

Pratt began developing ideas for the magazine that would become *Jane* while at Time Inc. Ventures, a new division of Time-Life magazines. The project had not coalesced when the division was shut down. Fairchild Publications, which publishes *W* and *Women's Wear Daily*, became the new magazine's publisher. Pratt initially felt trepidation about naming the magazine after herself; she had wanted to call it "Girlie," but focus groups did not warm to that title. *Jane* was the final choice because, as Robin Pogrebin wrote, it "connotes a certain everywoman accessibility." To dispel Pratt's fears that readers would think her self-obsessed, she subtitled her first editor's note "Why I'm Not Quite the Biggest Egomaniac in the World Even Though the Name of This Magazine May Lead You to Believe Otherwise."

For *Jane*, Pratt borrowed many of the editorial devices she had used so successfully at *Sassy*. Virtually all articles are written by the magazine's in-house staff and are often self-referential. Many emphasize the writer's personal experience, such as an article in the debut issue that described a young man's attempt to join the Promise Keepers, an all-men's Christian group. "I want to establish unique voices in the magazine that [readers] get to know,"

Pratt told Pogrebin. As with *Sassy*, Pratt uses the magazine's spine to grab readers' attention with quirky phrases or questions, and she frequently includes reader polls. In the May 1999 issue, the results of a poll on beauty products were published under the title "Thank You, Gorgeous Readers."

The magazine projects a self-conscious, slightly ironic attitude that tells readers that *Jane* does not take itself too seriously. While other magazines aimed at young women tend to dole out beauty and fashion advice as if it were gospel, *Jane*'s monthly columns poke a little fun at these topics. Two regular features are "Fashion Blender," which focuses on affordable clothing items mixed and matched with abandon, and "The *Jane* Makeunder." For this column, a young woman sporting too much makeup is spotted on the street by *Jane* beauty editors. An expert then redoes her makeup in a more natural-looking style. "Before" and "after" photos of the woman are published in the magazine, along with an account of how her new look was accomplished. Other regular columns include one on food, entitled "Eat"; an advice section, "Deal With It"; a shopping guide, "It's Only Money"; and a political-opinion column, "Soapbox."

Media-industry experts, including Pratt, knew it would be a challenge for *Jane* to attract readers amidst the many other magazines, including *Glamour*, *Mademoiselle*, and *Cosmopolitan*, that target young women. However, as she had at *Sassy*, with *Jane* Pratt has displayed an uncanny ability to connect with readers. In November 1998, a little over a year after the magazine's debut, *Jane*'s circulation had topped 480,000.

Arguably, one of the reasons for Pratt's success is the sincerity behind her editorial approach; at *Sassy*, she aimed to inform teens, and at *Jane*, according to Pratt, she is endorsing a view of life to which she herself subscribes. "I'm living the lifestyle I'm writing about because I care passionately about it," Pratt told *USA Today* (September 9, 1997). *Jane*'s readers, Pratt told Robin Pogrebin, "don't see singlehood as a period to put behind you as quickly as possible. The 20's now are more about enjoying your independence." Pratt, currently age 36, lives in a loft overlooking the Hudson River in Manhattan's West Village, and she is still enjoying the independence to which she referred. As she told Rebecca Mead, although she wants children, she is less sure about marriage: "I think I change a lot, and I like to believe I will have completely changed in five years anyway. That is part of what I don't like about the idea of growing old with somebody: It sounds like it is already over when you say, 'Okay, this is it.' I like the feeling that I could get on a motorcycle tomorrow, drive to California, have a whole different lifestyle, move to Europe, whatever." — O.J.S.

Suggested Reading: *Chicago Tribune* VI p5 Mar. 20, 1988, with photos, VI p12 Apr. 25, 1993, with photo; *Christian Science Monitor* p23+ Mar. 7, 1988, with photo; *Folio* p30+ Apr. 15, 1991, with photos; *Glamour* p173+ Oct. 1995, with photos; *Interview* p80+ June 1992, with photo; *New York* p49+ Sep. 15, 1997, with photos; *New York Post* p45 Sep. 2, 1997, with photo; *New York Times* C p1+ Apr. 15, 1992, with photos, I p1+ Sep. 7, 1997, with photos; *Village Voice* p59+ Sep. 23, 1997, with photos

Selected Books: *Beyond Beauty: Girls Speak Out on Looks, Style, and Stereotypes*, 1997; with Kelli Pryor—*For Real: The Uncensored Truth About America's Teenagers*, 1995

Selected Television Shows: *Jane*, 1992; *Jane Pratt*, 1993

Alexander Natruskin/Archive Photos

Primakov, Yevgeny

(PRIM-ah-kov, yev-GEN-ee)

Oct. 29, 1929– Former prime minister of Russia. Address: c/o Otechestvo, Fatherland-All Russia Coalition, Government of Moscow, Tverskaya str. 13, 103032 Moscow, Russia

Throughout the long career of Russian politician Yevgeny Primakov, many political observers, especially those in the U.S., have expressed concern about his ties to the Arab world and to Russia's intelligence community. Indeed, Primakov's prestige has been inextricably bound with his knowledge in those two areas. Whether as a journalist for the Communist Party's newspaper, *Pravda*, in the 1970s, as a foreign-policy adviser for President Mikhail Gorbachev in the late 1980s, as Russia's head of foreign intelligence in the early 1990s, or

as President Boris Yeltsin's foreign minister and prime minister later in the decade, Primakov has played an integral role in the formulation of his nation's Middle East policy. This was most evident during his tenure as Russia's prime minister, from September 1998 to May 1999. Although his actions have often been at odds with the stance advocated by the U.S. and its allies, Primakov, who has been described by some as a Russian Henry Kissinger, has helped to maintain Russia's presence on the international stage at a time when it faces serious domestic problems and has seen its influence on global politics diminish. Recently, with his knack for articulating nationalist sentiments that resonate with Russia's nostalgia for its recent past, Primakov has placed himself in a strong position to succeed the ailing and increasingly unpopular President Yeltsin.

As befits a former head of Russia's foreign-intelligence operations, information about Yevgeny Maximovich Primakov's early years is murky. There has been speculation that he comes from a Jewish family by the name of Kirschenblatt or Finklestein. He has also been beset by allegations that he spied for the KGB, the Soviet Union's powerful security apparatus, in his years as a journalist in the Middle East. Primakov has denied both rumors. According to official reports, he was born on October 29, 1929 in Kiev, the capital of Ukraine, which was then a part of the Soviet Union. He was raised by his mother, a gynecologist, in Tbilisi, the capital of Georgia. He left Tbilisi for Moscow in the late 1940s to study Arabic, and in 1953 he graduated from Moscow's Institute of Oriental Studies.

In 1959 Primakov became a member of the Soviet Union's Communist Party, which was then under the leadership of Premier Nikita Khrushchev. Meanwhile, he began his career as a journalist. In the 1960s he covered the Middle East for *Pravda*, the Communist Party's newspaper, as a correspondent based in Cairo, Egypt. Through that post Primakov cultivated relationships with influential Middle Eastern leaders, including Hosni Mubarak, who would become the president of Egypt, and King Hussein of Jordan. He also developed an association with Saddam Hussein of Iraq. In an article in *Time* (March 4, 1991), Primakov recalled that relationship: "My long-standing acquaintanceship with Saddam was no secret. I first met him in 1969, when I was working as a *Pravda* correspondent in the Middle East. At that time, he was not yet the president, but he had already become one of the most influential members in the Iraqi leadership."

In the 1970s Primakov was promoted to chief editor of *Pravda*. Upon his return to Russia, he took up successive positions within the USSR's Academy of Sciences, a think tank, and he established himself as a Middle East policy expert. From 1970–77 he served as the deputy director of the Soviet Academy of Sciences' Institute for Oriental Studies, and in 1977 he became director of that institute. In 1985 he became director of the Institute for World Economy and International Relations, Russia's premier think tank.

Meanwhile, Primakov maintained his ties to leaders of the Middle East. He also rose through the ranks of the Communist Party. In 1986 he became a nonvoting member of the Communist Party's powerful Central Committee. His rise coincided with that of—and was furthered by—President Mikhail Gorbachev, who became general secretary of the Soviet Union's Communist Party, and thus the Soviet head of state, in March 1985. President Gorbachev implemented a policy of glasnost (openness) and perestroika (restructuring), which sought to reform the Soviet Union's command economy and highly centralized political system. Under this mandate for reform, in December 1988, Russia's legislature took on greater powers. That same month, Primakov was appointed chairman of the Council of the Union, the upper chamber of the Supreme Soviet, Russia's newly reconstituted Parliament. Moreover, in September 1989 he was appointed by President Gorbachev a nonvoting member of Russia's Politburo, the policy-making body of the Communist Party.

In March 1990 Gorbachev was named to the new post of union president, following constitutional amendments adopted in December 1989 and March 1990 to bring about a more democratic political system in the Soviet Union. Soon afterward Primakov was appointed a member of Gorbachev's Presidential Council, the inner circle of advisers. In that capacity, Primakov served as a foreign-policy adviser to Gorbachev.

In October 1990 Primakov came to prominence in the West for attempting to broker a diplomatic solution to the escalating hostility between Iraq and the U.S. In the months before the Persian Gulf War, which began in January 1991, tensions had risen sharply in that region after Iraq, under the leadership of President Saddam Hussein, had invaded and occupied its oil-rich neighbor Kuwait, in August 1990. The invasion was widely perceived as being unprovoked, and Iraq received the censure of the U.S. and most of the international community. The United Nations Security Council denounced the invasion and, on August 6, 1990, imposed a trade embargo against Iraq. In November 1990 the U.N. Security Council demanded Iraq's immediate withdrawal from Kuwait and set a deadline of January 15, 1991 for compliance. Even as the U.S. and a coalition U.N. force readied for a military attack to liberate Kuwait, Primakov met with President Hussein as Gorbachev's special envoy to the Middle East and, speaking out against the U.S.'s willingness to seek a military solution, took on an active role in the attempt to prevent a military confrontation. But Primakov's intervention—he made three trips to Baghdad from October 1990 to February 1991—did not prevent the war, and the U.N. coalition forces, made up mostly of Americans, began bombing Iraq and Iraqi forces in Kuwait on January 16, 1991. Even as the attack escalated into a ground invasion, in February 1991, and it was clear that Iraq would soon lose, Primakov met with Saddam Hussein in Baghdad to seek a negotiated end to the war. His efforts became superfluous when Kuwait was liberated by U.S.-led troops in late February and the war came to an end, on March 3, 1991, with Iraq's formal surrender. Primakov was perceived by many nations and especially the U.S. as having been needlessly meddlesome. Moreover, his meetings with President Hussein were seen as having been detrimental to U.S. interests.

Back in Russia, Primakov's role in Gorbachev's administration expanded. In September 1991, right after a failed attempt at a coup d'état by a group of top Soviet hard-liners, Gorbachev appointed Primakov to head the nation's foreign-intelligence service, which had previously existed under the aegis of the KGB. Primakov became the first civilian to head the large network of spies in that entity's 70-year history. "If you think that spies are people in gray coats, skulking around street corners, listening to people's conversations and wielding iron bars, then my appointment is unnatural," Primakov said at a news conference, as quoted by Michael Dobbs for the *Washington Post* (October 3, 1991). "We must use analytical methods, synthesize information. This is scientific work." In line with President Gorbachev's policy of glasnost, Primakov held news conferences for foreign journalists, admitted to a fondness for the British writer John Le Carré's spy novels, and even promised to cease sending Soviet spies abroad disguised as journalists.

Primakov retained his post as head of Russia's foreign intelligence after Russia, Belarus, and the Ukraine proclaimed their independence and thus brought about the termination of the Soviet Union, in December 1991. Primakov became one of the few officials from the Gorbachev era to survive the transition to an independent, post-Soviet Russia in the administration of President Boris Yeltsin, who came to power in 1992. Primakov continued to run the foreign-intelligence service, and he also spoke out about Russia's foreign policy. However, his influence on Russia's foreign policy was often overshadowed by that of Russia's foreign minister, Andrei Kozyrev, who, like Yeltsin at the time, espoused a pro-Western stance.

It was expected that the economic and political reforms championed by Yeltsin would lead to higher living standards and greater freedoms for most Russians. However, the reforms faltered, and greater corruption and a decline in living standards resulted. These developments fueled a backlash against reform and the West. In January 1996 Kozyrev resigned, under pressure from Communists and nationalists who criticized him for being too receptive to ideas from the West, and Primakov was appointed foreign minister by President Yeltsin. Primakov was generally viewed as being much less in line with Western thinking than Kozyrev.

The appointment of Primakov was thought to reflect Yeltsin's desire to appease rising nationalist and Communist sentiment and bolster his chance for reelection in June 1996. Yeltsin had also been under pressure from the Duma, Russia's lower house of parliament, which was dominated by Communists and nationalists, to demonstrate independence from the U.S. When Yeltsin emerged victorious in that election, Primakov displayed readiness to pursue a foreign policy that disregarded the wishes of the U.S. "Despite her current difficulties, Russia was and remains a great power. Her foreign policy must reflect that status," Primakov had said half a year earlier, in his first news conference, as quoted by Lee Hockstader for the *Washington Post* (January 13, 1996). "I consider it my main task to step up the Foreign Ministry's work in defending Russia's national interests, but I don't think that will contradict the development of ties with the United States."

As had been expected, Primakov took issue with the expansion of the North Atlantic Treaty Organization (NATO) into Eastern Europe. "I think it is counterproductive for the stabilization of the situation in Europe and would undoubtedly create a new geopolitical situation for Russia," he said at his first news conference as foreign minister, as quoted by Hockstader. Despite such rhetoric, he eventually negotiated a settlement with NATO. Russia also contributed troops to the NATO-backed peacekeeping operations in Bosnia. In May 1997 Primakov met with NATO secretary general Javier Solana in Paris and signed an accord known as the Founding Act. By signing, Russia received a pledge that the Western alliance would limit military deployment in, and refrain from positioning nuclear weapons on, the territory of the new NATO member nations—Poland, Hungary, and the Czech Republic. The accord also established the NATO-Russia Permanent Joint Council, an entity that meets twice a year to discuss security concerns between NATO and Russia.

Primakov also made attempts to improve ties between Russia and other former republics of the Soviet Union. In April 1997 Yeltsin and Belarusan president Aleksander Lukashenko signed the Russo-Belarusan Community Agreement, which forged closer economic, military, and political ties between their respective nations. Primakov had waved off the West's expressions of concern at the economic and political reintegration of some of the former Soviet states. "[The reintegration] would not lead to the revival of some anti-Western monster, critical or confrontational with the West," Primakov said three years earlier, as quoted by Fred Hiatt for the *Washington Post* (September 22, 1994).

Meanwhile, in November 1997 Primakov returned to his familiar role as mediator between Iraq and the U.S. Since the end of the 1991 Persian Gulf War, relations between the U.S. and Iraq had been strained, and the two nations had come close on numerous occasions to renewed military conflict. For instance, in June 1993 the U.S., which had stockpiled military equipment in the Persian Gulf, had launched a missile attack on Baghdad after it

was revealed that U.S. president George Bush was the target of an Iraqi assassination plot. Tension also stemmed from the U.N. Security Council–endorsed economic sanctions that had been placed on Iraq in the wake of the Persian Gulf War. Under the sanctions, Iraq was allowed little economic contact with the outside world. The U.S. and its allies in the U.N. sought to maintain the sanctions until they received assurances from the U.N. Special Commission on Iraq (UNSCOM), a special team of weapons inspectors charged with monitoring Iraq, that Iraq had ended its programs to develop weapons of mass destruction. Iraq wanted the sanctions lifted as soon as possible.

In October 1997 Iraq threatened to block all further UNSCOM inspections unless the economic sanctions were lifted and U.S. personnel were removed from the team of weapons inspectors. UNSCOM had long charged that Iraq had repeatedly deterred the inspection process and concealed weapons of mass destruction. The sanctions were not lifted, and the U.S. demanded that President Hussein completely abandon all efforts to obtain weapons of mass destruction and allow U.N. inspectors free access to all of Iraq's suspected weapons sites, as required by U.N. resolutions.

Hoping to prevent another military conflict, Primakov met with his counterpart, Iraq's Foreign Minister Tariq Aziz, in Moscow in November 1997. His intervention resulted in President Hussein's backing down and inviting U.N. weapons inspectors back to Iraq, thereby preventing a military confrontation. However, Primakov's brokered peace was only temporary, and the stalemate over weapons inspections continued. In December 1997, in the thick of the stalemate, Primakov said, as quoted by Craig R. Whitney for the *New York Times* (December 18, 1997), "We are against the use of force. I think in this regard, we have in the world an overwhelming majority with us. At the same time, we feel that Iraq must deal constructively with the special commission." By this time the U.S. and Great Britain had formed an alliance to take a strong stance against Iraq, while Russia and France as well as some Arab nations advocated a less strident approach. Those nations were eventually joined by China, which spoke out against the U.S.'s threat of force.

The year 1998 began with no agreement reached among the U.S., the U.N., and Iraq over weapons inspections. The U.S. secretary of state, Madeleine Albright, commented at a news conference, as quoted by Steven Erlanger for the *New York Times* (January 31, 1998), "Unfortunately, there is no concrete evidence that Iraq is negotiating for any reason other than diversion and delay."

In late February 1998 tensions between Iraq and the U.S. were temporarily alleviated when U.N. secretary general Kofi Annan met with Saddam Hussein and secured the Iraqi president's permission to resume inspections at all sites, including presidential palaces, which had been previously declared off-limits. However, the brokered peace proved fleeting. Tensions continued through the year, and in December 1998 the U.S. and Great Britain bombed Iraq. Primakov and the rest of Russia's government condemned the bombing and recalled Russia's ambassador to the U.S., Yuli Vorontsov, from Washington, D.C.—an act generally viewed as Russia's angriest reaction to American policy in recent years.

Western analysts have generally viewed Primakov's stance regarding Iraq as being consistent with Russia's economic interests. Strategically, Iraq allows Russia access to the resource-rich Middle East and the Persian Gulf. Moreover, Iraq owes Russia around $7 billion from the pre–Gulf War era, when Iraq was one of the Soviet Union's best customers for military equipment—according to *Business Week* (February 25, 1991), Iraq had purchased $15.4 billion worth of arms from the Soviet Union between 1984 and 1988. Iraq is reportedly willing to resume those debt obligations once the U.N.-imposed sanctions on Iraq are lifted. Iraq and Russia are also reported to have in place business agreements, concerning the development of Iraq's vast natural-gas and oil reserves, that are to be implemented once the sanctions are lifted.

In March 1998 Primakov temporarily lost his post during President Yeltsin's surprise dismissal of his entire cabinet. He was reinstated shortly thereafter. Six months later he was appointed prime minister of Russia, after President Yeltsin sacked the young Sergei Kiriyenko, whose five-month tenure had followed that of Viktor Chernomyrdin, Russia's prime minister from December 1992 to March 1998.

Although Primakov faced the seemingly insuperable task of steering Russia out of its economic crisis, he soon emerged as an influential national figure, in part due to the downturn in President Yeltsin's health and popularity. For example, when Yeltsin was too ill to attend a state visit to Austria in November 1998, Primakov took his place. Primakov's foreign-intelligence credentials and demonstrated independence from the West also placed him in a good position in his dealings with the Communist- and nationalist-dominated Duma. He quickly won popular support and became one of the most well-liked and trusted politicians in Russia. In the *New York Times* (August 18, 1999), Celestine Bohlen reported that in public-opinion polls conducted in July 1999 by the All Russian Public Opinion Center, 26 percent of Russians said that they trusted him. It is indicative of Russia's bleak political landscape that that figure represented the highest approval rating of all those named in the poll, among them other Russian politicians, including people who have been considered possible presidential candidates.

Despite those developments and the fact that he enjoyed the support of both moderates and Communists in the Duma, Primakov's tenure, too, was cut short. On May 12, 1999 President Yeltsin sacked him, after announcing that Primakov had failed to create an aggressive economic reform pro-gram. Primakov's dismissal was generally viewed as a reflection of Yeltsin's determination to demonstrate his authority and choose his own successor. In addition, it has been suggested that Yeltsin and members of his inner circle were worried that Primakov and his Communist supporters were becoming too powerful.

Primakov's successor was Sergei V. Stepashin, a former head of the domestic intelligence service and interior minister. Stepashin remained in office for an even shorter time than had Primakov. On August 9, 1999 Yeltsin removed Stepashin and appointed Vladimir V. Putin, a former KGB officer, as Russia's prime minister. This was Yeltsin's fourth government shake-up in 17 months. Putin's appointment, like Stepashin's, was confirmed by Russia's Duma in the first confirmation vote. Russia experts speculated that Yeltsin's seemingly erratic government shuffles were intended to influence the nation's upcoming presidential election, which is scheduled for July 2000, when the president's second term ends. (Russia's constitution allows a president to serve no more than two terms.)

Meanwhile, three months after his dismissal, Primakov resurfaced in Russian politics. In August 1999 he joined Mayor Yuri Luzhkov of Moscow as the co-leader of the left-center Fatherland-All Russia Coalition, the members of which also include several regional governors. This coalition is expected to be heavily influential in Russia's December 1999 parliamentary elections, in which Primakov will compete for a seat in the 450-seat Duma, and in the next presidential election.

Although Primakov has yet to officially declare himself a presidential candidate, many political observers consider him to be in a strong position to win the post. Other likely candidates include Yuri Luzhkov; Gennady Zyuganov, the leader of the Communist Party; Aleksandr Lebed, a former general and national security adviser; and Grigory A. Yavlinsky, a young liberal economist and politician who has been dissatisfied with Russia's cautious approach to free-market reform.

With his first wife, Laura, now deceased, Primakov had two children—one of them also deceased—and two grandchildren. He is currently married to Irina, a doctor. In addition to his native Russian, he speaks Arabic and English.—Y.P.

Suggested Reading: *New York Times* A p6 Jan. 10, 1996, with photo, A p1+ Aug. 18, 1999, with photo; *Time* p74+ Nov. 9, 1998, with photos; *Washington Post* A p12 Jan. 10, 1996, with photo, A p24+ Jan. 25, 1998, with photo

Courtesy of ASF

Protess, David

*Apr. 7, 1946– Journalism professor; social
activist; writer. Address: c/o Medill School of
Journalism, Northwestern University, 1845
Sheridan Rd., Evanston, IL 60208*

David Protess, a professor of journalism at Northwestern University, in Evanston, Illinois, believes that it is not enough for a reporter to reveal injustices in society. "The higher calling of journalism," he told Pam Belluck for the New York Times (March 6, 1999), "is that after you find the truth, you can in fact right the wrong." Protess's self-appointed mission is to right wrongs in the criminal-justice system—in particular, to overturn the convictions of people who have been sentenced to death for crimes that they did not commit. So far, he has been credited with securing freedom for eight innocent people, among them two men who had spent 18 years on death row and one who had remained there for 16 years and had come within two days of being executed.

(PRO-tess)

In unearthing evidence of forced confessions, false eyewitness accounts, failure of the police to act on promising leads or make available crucial evidence, systematic racism, and other phenomena that have resulted in gross miscarriages of justice, Protess has increased his effectiveness by working in collaboration with his students at Northwestern; the students, in turn, get hands-on experience in investigative journalism in real, and sometimes life-and-death, situations. "We need someone to conduct these full-blown investigations because indigent clients aren't getting them through the legal system," Protess told Kari Lyder-

sen for the New Abolitionist (February 1998), an anti–death-penalty publication. "I'm astonished to see how little preparation and legwork is done [by defendants' lawyers] for most Death Row defenses. And federal funding is gone at the same time that we're increasingly filling prisons. The problem's getting worse."

Protess strongly opposes the death penalty, without exception. In the New York Times (August 22, 1999), Caitlin Lovinger reported that "since the United States Supreme Court reinstated capital punishment in 1976, 566 people have been executed. In that same period, 82 convicts awaiting execution have been exonerated—a ratio of one freed for every seven put to death." "Capital punishment discriminates against minorities and protects the lives of white people as more valuable," Protess noted to Lydersen. "The death penalty makes politicians appear tough on crime," he added. "Instead of dealing with the causes, it deals with individual symptoms. It's a medieval system of dealing with social problems."

David Protess was born on April 7, 1946 to Sidney Protess, a businessman, and Beverly (Gordon) Protess, a full-time homemaker, in the New York City borough of Brooklyn. He grew up in Sheepshead Bay, a middle-class section of the borough. In his evolution as a seeker of justice, he has identified two historic events as especially significant. The first was the execution of Julius Rosenberg and his wife, Ethel, both of whom, in a highly publicized and bitterly controversial espionage case, had been found guilty of conspiring to transmit to the Soviet Union top-secret information on the nuclear weapons being developed by the United States during World War II. On June 19, 1953 the Rosenbergs, who were the parents of two young boys, were put to death by means of the electric chair. The day after the execution, Protess—who was then seven years old, the same age as the Rosenbergs' younger son—saw a brutal headline on a local tabloid: "Rosenbergs Fried." "It seemed so unjust, and I'm not just taking a position about whether they were guilty or not," Protess told Pam Belluck. "What was unjust was that the state orphaned two young boys."

The second event that, by his own account, was crucial in his choice of career occurred two decades later, after Protess had earned a B.A. degree from Roosevelt University, in Chicago, in 1968, and a master's degree from the University of Chicago, in 1970. This was the Watergate scandal, which followed the break-in at the Democratic National Committee headquarters by Republican operatives in 1972 and led to the resignation of President Richard Nixon two years later. The scandal came to light through the efforts of the Washington Post reporters Bob Woodward and Carl Bernstein. Their accounts of the Watergate affair, which involved skulduggery, abuses of the office of president, and an illegal cover-up, dominated the front pages during the period in which Protess was striving to complete his doctorate in public policy at the

School of Social Service Administration at the University of Chicago. The coverage of Watergate by Woodward and Bernstein and other members of the media impressed Protess deeply. "I saw journalism as having a higher calling," he recalled to Ericka Mellon for the *Daily Northwestern* (February 8, 1999, on-line), the student newspaper at Northwestern University. "I wanted to practice journalism that made a difference."

After earning his Ph.D. degree, in 1974, Protess taught political science for two years as an assistant professor at Loyola University, in Chicago. From 1976 until 1981 he served as research director of the Better Government Association (BGA), also in Chicago. Founded in 1923, the BGA is a watchdog group whose aim is to foster high standards of public service. According to an official BGA blurb, the organization "uses official documents, on-the-record interviews, undercover operations, and sophisticated techniques of investigative reporting to uncover corruption" in the government and "works closely with national and local media to expose waste, inefficiency, and corruption and to educate the public on the inner workings of the government."

In 1982 Protess joined the faculty of the Medill School of Journalism at Northwestern University as a professor of journalism and urban affairs. He was also named a faculty fellow in journalism at the university's Institute for Policy Research, which supports studies on issues connected with poverty, social welfare, race, employment, education, crime, and community development. Concurrently, from 1984 to 1989, he served as a contributing editor and staff writer at *Chicago Lawyer*, an independent investigative monthly that, in the words of Rob Warden, its editor and publisher, "was founded [in 1978] for the purpose of exposing corruption and other problems in the criminal justice system in Cook County, Illinois, and neighboring jurisdictions." In the course of pursuing a story for that magazine, Ericka Mellon reported, Protess helped to obtain a not-guilty verdict for Sandra Fabiano, a Chicago resident who had been brought to trial on charges of child molestation. During later investigations for *Chicago Lawyer*, he enlisted the help of his students, counting their case-related activities as part of their course work.

As a professor, John Tang reported in the *Daily Northwestern* (February 3, 1998, on-line), Protess views his primary mission as teaching his students the techniques of investigative journalism. These include ways to conduct difficult interviews, such as those with prisoners who have not discussed their cases with anyone outside the prison walls for years, or meetings with reluctant witnesses. Before attempting such encounters, the students practice by engaging in role play. They also get tips from private investigators. When carrying out assignments in the field that are potentially dangerous, the students are accompanied by Protess or a private investigator. "The best way of learning is by doing," Protess has observed, as quoted in the *Northwestern Observer* (February 11, 1999, on-line), the university's faculty and staff newspaper. Protess's outstanding contributions as a teacher of journalism were recognized in 1986 by the Poynter Institute, a school for "journalists, future journalists, and teachers of journalism" in St. Petersburg, Florida, which presented him with the National Teaching Award for Excellence in the Teaching of Journalism Ethics. In 1994 the Searle Center for Teaching Excellence, at Northwestern University, named him the Charles Deering McCormick Professor of Teaching Excellence, an honor associated with an endowed chair. In an on-line release, the Searle Center described Protess as a teacher "who brings his own research and investigative journalism into the classroom so as to create uniquely relevant, real-world, thought-provoking learning experiences for his students. The excitement he arouses in his many students as he engages them in the subtle confluence of investigative journalism, the law, and ethics, is legendary in the University and in the broader educational and professional communities beyond this campus."

The first case in which Protess's students served as collaborators involved David and Cynthia Dowaliby, of Midlothian, Illinois, a town near Chicago, who in 1988 were prosecuted for the murder of their seven-year-old daughter, Jaclyn. The defense argued that the child had been murdered by an intruder who had broken into a basement window of the Dowaliby house and abducted her. Toward the end of the trial, the judge dismissed the charges against Cynthia, but not David, for lack of sufficient evidence. The jury decided that David was guilty, and he was sentenced to 45 years in prison. Dowaliby spent nearly two years behind bars before his conviction was overturned on appeal. In *Gone in the Night: The Dowaliby Family's Encounter with Murder and the Law* (1993), Protess and his co-author, Rob Warden, tried to demonstrate the Dowalibys' innocence while lambasting what they regarded as the prosecution's many excesses. They also took to task the defense lawyers, members of the press who were unsympathetic to the defense, and Richard M. Daley, who was then the Cook County state's attorney and thus the county's chief prosecutor. Political considerations, Protess and Warden contended, had led Daley to approve the way the prosecution handled the case despite its lack of evidence. (In April 1989 Daley, who compiled a strong law-and-order record as state's attorney, was elected mayor of Chicago, which makes up a large part of Cook County.) In their book, Protess and Warden also attempted to illuminate the ways in which journalists, government officials, and law-enforcement agents influence decision-making in trial and appellate courts. In a review of *Gone in the Night* for *Library Journal* (May 1, 1993), Gregor A. Preston wrote, "This is a tragic story, superbly narrated, of how a normal family was victimized by the criminal justice system," and he called the book "gripping" and "moving." "Despite their obvious bias," Sue-Ellen Beauregard wrote for *Booklist* (April 15, 1993), Protess and Warden "offer an illuminating look at a curious, tragic case that remains unsolved." *Gone in the Night* was named the best book of 1993 by Investigative Reporters and Editors, an organization "dedicated to improving the quality of investigative reporting within the field of journalism."

Another case in which Protess became deeply involved was that of Girvies Davis, who was sentenced to death for the murder of an elderly man in 1978. At his trial, the prosecution entered into evidence Davis's written confession of guilt in the murder. Protess later discovered that at the time that Davis had supposedly penned his confession, he could neither read nor write; furthermore, as a result of brain damage stemming from a childhood accident, his IQ placed him just above the level of a retarded person. In addition to expressing serious doubts about the credibility of Davis's confession and questions about the conduct of the police (who had also charged him with complicity in several additional murders), Protess and his students raised issues of race and class in the handling of his case. Despite their efforts and those of other groups, in 1995 the state of Illinois executed Davis, by means of lethal injection. To help his students cope with the despair they felt when they heard of Davis's death, Protess brought a grief counselor to the class.

Before his death, Ericka Mellon reported, Davis urged Protess to take up the case of one of his fellow inmates, Dennis Williams. Davis already knew something about Williams's plight: In 1978 Williams and three other young African-American men—Verneal Jimerson, Kenneth Adams, and William Rainge, all of whom lived in Ford Heights, a poverty-stricken Chicago neighborhood—had been convicted of abducting a young man and his fiancée from a gas station where the man worked and then, after bringing them to an abandoned building in Ford Heights, repeatedly raping the woman and shooting both her and her fiancé to death. Despite having alibis, the four had been arrested, on the basis of several accounts by ostensible eyewitnesses. Brought to trial and represented by court-appointed attorneys whom Protess later described as shockingly incompetent, all had been found guilty; Adams had gotten a prison term of 75 years, Rainge, a life sentence, and Williams and Jimerson, the death sentence.

Protess began working with several lawyers who had been making intermittent, unsuccessful attempts, without pay, to help the Ford Heights Four, as the men became known. He also assigned the case to three senior journalism majors—Stacey Delo, Stephanie Goldstein, and Laura Sullivan—in his investigative-reporting class. He and the three students reviewed the transcripts of the trials and then, with the help of a private investigator, Rene Brown, who had looked into the case sporadically for years at the behest of a defense lawyer, began six months of legwork. Tracking down a witness who had placed the four men at the crime scene,

they learned that the police had coerced her into making a false statement; other eyewitness reports also proved to be bogus. They also dug up, in a police file, papers that identified other potential suspects, most notably a group of men—among them the brothers Ira and Dennis Johnson—who had been spotted near the gas station shortly before the killings. Although those men had been seen the day after the murders selling distinctive items stolen from the station, the police had never questioned them. Protess has speculated that they failed to do so because, as Kari Lydersen put it, "in a tough-on-crime push, politicians were putting pressure on police to put someone behind bars for the murder," and the police, who had already locked up the Ford Heights Four, felt that having *any* poor young black men in custody was "good enough regardless of the defendants' guilt or innocence." "There's a police attitude toward young black men that if they didn't do this they probably did something else," Protess observed to Lydersen.

With the help of Brown, the students found Ira Johnson—in prison, serving a long sentence for a 1990 murder. When asked about the 1978 killings, Johnson admitted his guilt and implicated several others. Moreover, DNA testing, which had not been available in 1978, showed that the semen found in the body of the murdered woman could not have come from any of the Ford Heights Four. After 18 years in prison—including, for Williams, years spent in a cell only about 30 feet from the electric chair—Williams, Rainge, Jimerson, and Adams were freed. Protess and Rob Warden described the four men's long ordeal in their book *A Promise of Justice: The Eighteen-Year Fight to Save Four Innocent Men* (1998). For his efforts to prove them innocent, Protess earned the 1996 Champion of Justice Award from the National Association of Criminal Defense Lawyers.

In 1999, in another case of criminal justice gone awry, Protess and five of his students—Shawn Armbrust, Erica LeBorgne, Tom McCann, Syandene Rhodes-Pitts, and Cara Rubinsky—along with Paul Ciolino, a private investigator with whom Protess has often worked, established the innocence of Anthony Porter, who had been sentenced to death in 1983 for the 1982 murder of a young couple during a nighttime robbery in a Chicago park. According to the transcripts from the trial and other court records, the gunman had used his left hand to fire the fatal shots; Porter, however, was right-handed. Moreover, the state's key witness, William Taylor, had sworn under oath that he had seen Porter shoot, but when the students went to the park to re-create the circumstances of the crime, they determined that from where Taylor testified he had been standing—about 500 feet from Porter—they could barely see the place where the couple had been slain, even in daylight. When the Northwestern sleuths talked to Taylor, he declared that the police had coerced him into making a false statement. The estranged wife of Alstory Simon, a man whom the police had identified as a witness in 1982, told the students that Simon was the killer, and a nephew of his told them that Simon had admitted his guilt to him. When Protess, Ciolino, and the students confronted Simon, he confessed. On February 5, 1999, on orders from a judge, Porter gained his freedom after 16 years of imprisonment. He was the 10th death-row inmate exonerated in Illinois since the state's reinstatement of the death penalty, in 1977. In May 1999 Illinois Attorneys for Criminal Justice (IACJ), a group composed of public defenders and private defense attorneys, presented Protess and the five students with the organization's Advocates Award, in honor of what an IACJ official described as their "extraordinary efforts" in "uncover[ing] crucial evidence resulting in the freeing of Anthony Porter from custody and death row."

For a decade beginning in about 1980, Protess directed a study in which he and six of his colleagues at the Institute for Policy Research examined the impact of investigative reporting and media exposés on public opinion, government officials, and policy makers. The results of their research appear in *The Journalism of Outrage: Investigative Reporting and Agenda Building in America* (1991), by Protess, Fay Cook, Jack Dippelt, and James Ettema. With Maxwell McCombs, Protess edited the book *Agenda Setting: Readings on Media, Public Opinion, and Policymaking* (1991). He has also conducted studies of press coverage of hate crimes and other race-related matters in Chicago and media portrayal of the violence that erupted in Los Angeles and other cities in 1992, after a jury acquitted four white Los Angeles police officers charged with beating Rodney King in 1991. (An onlooker had videotaped the police attacking King after pulling over his car, allegedly for speeding.) Protess's current projects include setting up what will be known as the Center for Wrongful Convictions and the Death Penalty, at Northwestern University.

In recent years Protess has received thousands of letters from prisoners seeking his help. "I pay attention to every case and personally answer each letter," he told John Tang. Prisoners even call him at home. "My home number is scribbled on every death row in the country," Protess said in an interview with Martha Brant for *Newsweek* (May 31, 1999). Protess lives with his second wife, Joan Perry, and their son, Benjamin; his first marriage, to Marianne Kreitman, which ended in divorce, also produced one son, Daniel. His honors include the Peter Lisagor Award for Exemplary Journalism, in 1989; the Amoco Foundation Faculty Award, from Northwestern, in 1993; and the Human Rights Award, from the National Alliance Against Racist and Political Repression, in 1996. Also in 1996, ABC Network News named him person of the week. — M.C.

Suggested Reading: *New York Times* A p7 Mar. 6, 1999; *Newsweek* p32+ May 31, 1991, with photo; *People* p44+ July 29, 1996, with photos; *Washington Post* C p1+ Feb. 17, 1999

Selected Books: *The Journalism of Outrage: Investigative Reporting and Agenda Building in America*, 1991; *Agenda Setting: Readings on Media, Public Opinion and Policy Making*, 1991; *Gone in the Night: The Dowaliby Family's Encounter with Murder and the Law*, 1994; *A Promise of Justice: The Eighteen-Year Fight to Save Four Innocent Men*, 1998

New York Times

Puryear, Martin

May 23, 1941– Sculptor. Address: c/o David McKee Gallery, 745 Fifth Ave., #400, New York, NY 10151-0499

"If you believe strongly, you can pump life into materials," the sculptor Martin Puryear told Paul Richard for the *Washington Post* (March 25, 1988). "You can, you really can, see them lifting off the ground like some hot-air balloon." Indeed, many art critics have agreed that Puryear's works have precisely that transcendent quality. Puryear has shown that he can mutate hard wood—his primary medium—and other materials, such as rawhide and wire, into supple and sinewy elegance. As Michael Kimmelman noted in the *New York Times* (March 1, 1992), "No artist today has a greater reverence for wood or can do more with it. He can turn it into monolithic forms, in a work like *Self* (1978). He can twist it into giant bracelets, like *Big and Little Same* (1981). He can, as with *Old Mole* (1985), treat it as a basket weaver treats straw."

Drawing much of his inspiration from various craft traditions, Puryear has helped challenge the distinctions between craft and art and between low and high art. His abstract shapes—and sometimes a single shape viewed from different angles—look like ordinary tools, vegetables, vessels, animals, or people. At the same time they can evoke the high abstraction of a Brancusi sculpture. His pieces seem to "quote" styles as diverse as Scandinavian furniture design, Surrealism, West African woodwork, European modernism, and Arctic carving, but, at the same time, they cannot easily be pigeonholed. "They seem happy with an identity that cannot be fixed," Michael Brenson wrote in the *New York Times* (October 29, 1989). "They have an ease and a voluptuousness that contrasts with Minimalist macho bristle."

As a sign of his stature in the art world, Puryear has won many awards, including a National Endowment for the Arts grant, a Guggenheim Fellowship, and a MacArthur "genius" award. He was also the first African-American artist to represent the United States in a major international exhibition. Nevertheless, he would be the first to insist that more attention should be paid to his work than to his race. Usually reticent about describing his sculpture, he told Alan Artner for the *Chicago Tribune* (February 1, 1987), "I'm not interested in using words to prime the world's eyes to look at my work, but without getting too literal I think that all my work has an element of escape. Call it what you want: fantasy, escape, imagination, retreat. It is an idea of otherness." In his interview with Michael Kimmelman for the *New York Times*, Puryear added, "I think my work speaks to anybody who has the capacity to slow down."

The oldest of the children—five sons and two daughters—of Reginald Puryear, a postal worker, and Martina Puryear, an elementary-school teacher, Martin Puryear was born on May 23, 1941 in Washington, D.C. His maternal grandfather fixed clocks, and his father was adept at repairing things around the house. Puryear's brother Michael became a cabinetmaker; his brother Mark became a musician; and his brother Maynard, a chef.

Puryear began drawing at a very early age and won a scholarship to attend a children's art school run by Cornelia Yuditsky. Even as a youngster, he was adept at making wooden objects. "If I became interested in archery, I made the bows and arrows; if I became interested in music, I made the guitar," he told Neal Benezra, the curator of the Department of Twentieth-Century Painting and Sculpture at the Art Institute of Chicago, who interviewed him for an essay in *Martin Puryear* (1991), the catalog prepared for an exhibition of the same title mounted at the institute in 1991. Because he was fascinated by nature, Native American traditions, and animals, especially falcons, Puryear's youthful dream was to become a wildlife illustrator. After graduating from Archbishop Carroll High School, he attended the Catholic University of America, in Washington, D.C., where he studied biology. In part due to the persuasion of the art professor Kenneth Noland, Puryear switched his major to art in his junior year. He worked primarily on paper and

canvas and also experimented a little with sculpture. Fond of the works of such artists as Pieter Brueghel and Andrew Wyeth, he painted in the realist tradition. One of his teachers, Nell Sonneman, helped push him toward greater abstraction. Puryear participated in his first group exhibition in 1962, at the Adams-Morgan Gallery, in Washington, D.C.

After graduating from Catholic University, in 1963, with a degree in fine art, Puryear joined the Peace Corps. He was assigned to teach biology, French, English, and art in a village in the West African country of Sierra Leone. During his time there, he developed an appreciation for the work of the country's indigenous carpenters, sculptors, weavers, potters, and cloth dyers, who used manual implements, not electric tools. Until that point Puryear had not considered wood carving an art; Sierra Leone's wood sculptors began to convince him otherwise.

Puryear was nudged even further toward sculpture in Sweden, where he moved in 1965 to study printmaking at the Swedish Royal Academy of Art, in Stockholm. While attending the school, with a Scandinavian-American Foundation grant, he was exposed to Scandinavian techniques of woodworking, and he met the famous furniture maker James Krenov. In 1968 Puryear had his first individual exhibition, at the Gröna Palletten Gallery.

Although Puryear's stays in Africa and Sweden were important to him, he feels that journalists have sometimes exaggerated the influence of those experiences on his work. Thus, his sojourns overseas "have become the myth behind the work," as he told Alan Artner for the *Chicago Tribune* (November 3, 1991). He added, "I find it's a little unfortunate because it eclipses the fact that I've been here working and changing for all the time since." In the same interview, he explained that his "time in Africa was very strong, if for nothing else because it happened when I was young and was my first trip out of the country, my first time seeing another culture, my first time making contact with the source of my own people. That was powerful. But I don't know that it got into my work in a way that you can say is direct. I mean, I have an enormous admiration for tribal art of all kinds and I had an incredible interest in African sculpture, although I have to say that I feel its otherness very strongly."

At the age of 27, Puryear returned to the United States. For a short time he worked as a designer for SCAN, a Scandinavian furniture company. In the fall of 1969, he entered the graduate fine-arts program at Yale University, in New Haven, Connecticut. For the next two years, he studied with such artists as the abstract painter Al Held and the sculptors Richard Serra and Robert Morris. He earned a master's degree in fine arts in 1971, a time when minimalism was one of the dominant trends in sculpture. Though some art critics have likened Puryear's abstract sculptures to minimalist works, Puryear has drawn a sharp contrast between his approach and that of the minimalists. "Minimalism celebrates stasis, absoluteness; it tries to expunge references," he explained to Paul Richard for the *Washington Post*. "I could never in a million years do that sort of art. I tasted minimalism. It had no taste. So I spat it out."

In 1971 Puryear began teaching art at Fisk University, a traditionally black college in Nashville, Tennessee. The following year he had his first exhibition of sculpture in the U.S., at the Henri 2 Gallery in Washington, D.C. In 1973 he moved to the New York City borough of Brooklyn, where he set up a studio and supported himself by commuting to teach at the University of Maryland, College Park. A fire in February 1977 at his Brooklyn studio destroyed or damaged much of his work. The surviving pieces include *Circumbent* (1976), a freestanding work made of ash and resembling a curiously curved tripod, and *Bask* (1976), which is suggestive of the hump of a whale.

"The fire was followed by a period of grieving and then by an incredible lightness, freedom, and mobility," Neal Benezra quoted Puryear as saying. Puryear set up a temporary studio in Washington, D.C., and that summer, at the invitation of curator Jane Livingston, he exhibited some of his sculpture at the Corcoran Gallery of Art, in Washington. One of the pieces shown was *Cedar Lodge* (1977), a large, sheltering, wooden structure that, in light of Puryear's recent loss of his Brooklyn studio, struck people as poignant. Another work was *Some Tales* (1975–77), a collection of long, thin, wooden objects arranged horizontally on a wall. Puryear compared the latter work to a *quipu*, a device, consisting of a cord knotted with smaller pieces of string, with which the Incas did calculations and kept accounts. In 1978 Puryear resettled in Illinois, where he became a full professor at the University of Illinois, in Chicago.

Puryear's post-fire works can be grouped according to several themes. In the late 1970s and early 1980s, the artist was preoccupied with making colorful ring-like sculptures, among them *Primavera* (1979), *Big and Little Same* (1981), and *Dream of Pairing* (1981), which appealed to him because they created a perceptual dissonance. "Interesting to me was that the rings inhabit the kind of space on a wall a painting inhabits, but they deny the center," he told Alan Artner for the *Chicago Tribune* (November 3, 1991). "They're things you stand in front of and, in a sense, there's nothing, the whole experience is peripheral." At about this time Puryear also executed several pieces named after James Pierson Beckwourth (1798–1866), who was born to a white man and a black slave. As chronicled in Beckwourth's autobiography, after gaining his freedom he served as a guide in expeditions in the American West, fought in the Mexican War (1846–48), and was made a chief by the Crow Indians. Beckwourth's mutability seemed to appeal to Puryear's own sense of mutability, which he was expressing in his creations. The Beckwourth pieces include *Some Lines for Jim*

Beckwourth (1978), consisting of pieces of twisted rawhide arranged like lines of text on a wall, and *For Beckwourth* (1980), a mound with flattened sides fashioned out of earth, pitch pine, and oak.

Structures suggesting shelter continued to be a common theme in Puryear's work. The widely spaced slats of *The Bower* (1980) form a shape reminiscent of the surface of a nautilus; *Sanctum* (1985) is an imposing hut-like structure made of pine, wire, and tar. Puryear also worked with avian images, which seem to suggest flight and travel as opposed to shelter. *Old Mole* (1985) and *Cask Cascade* (1985), for instance, both resemble stylized falcon heads; whereas *Old Mole* is a tightly wound lattice of red cedar, *Cask Cascade* is a solid, fluted, dark mass. In another piece, *Where the Heart Is (Sleeping Mews)* (1981), Puryear combined both the shelter theme and bird images. At the center of that piece stands a wooden structure that resembles a yurt (a collapsible dwelling that seminomadic peoples in Central Asia fashion out of animal skins or felt). At the fringes of *Where the Heart Is*, bird-like figures look away; their eyes hidden, they evoke a sense of longing for something distant.

Despite the strong figurative references in his work, Puryear purposely makes the associations ambiguous. "I value the referential quality of work, the fact that it has the capacity to allude to things," he told Artner for the *Chicago Tribune* (November 3, 1991). "But I don't want to have the work go back the other way, linking to some source from which I have carefully pruned the inessentials. I do not start with a particular thing and abstract from it. I have more a recombinant strategy. It's like combining from many sources into something that has clarity and unity. I like a flickering quality, when you can't say exactly what the reference is." Puryear's "recombinant strategy" is perhaps more evident in some of his later works, in which he more explicitly yoked disparate elements. *Sanctuary* (1982), for instance, features an open box that rests on tree limbs connected to the axle of a wooden wheel. The structure seems to play with notions of stability and mobility. As Michael Kimmelman put it in the *New York Times, Sanctuary* brings "to mind the image, slightly comical, of a thin-legged unicyclist. . . . It is about movement; it looks poised, arrested in its tracks, at any moment capable of rolling away." Duality is also depicted in *Night and Day* (1984), an arc—half white, half black—meant to resemble the passage of the sun. Another hybrid piece, *The Spell* (1985), is composed of two intersecting cones, one with a mostly closed surface, the other suggested by just a few steel wires attached to a truncated wooden ring.

Recently, some critics have taken to analyzing Puryear's sculpture as a commentary on race, rather than simply experiments in form and abstraction. "I won't put a value judgment on [the interpretations]," Puryear told Alan Artner for the *Chicago Tribune* (November 3, 1991). "It is just interesting. I am the same artist, but the work is increasingly written about with race as a strong element.

Probably something is there to tease apart, but I'm not going to become involved in it because I prefer to respect my own complexity."

Puryear's creations have generally been well received within the art world. "What makes his rise unusual is that he's never played the party game, or stroked the art world's egos, or sought Manhattan chic," Paul Richard wrote for the *Washington Post*. In 1977 Puryear received a National Endowment for the Arts grant and a Robert Rauschenberg Foundation grant. The following year he was included in the Guggenheim Museum's "Young American Artists" exhibition, and in 1979 some of his works were featured at the Whitney Museum's Biennial. In 1980 he was honored with a one-man show at the Museum of Contemporary Art, in Chicago, followed in 1984 by an exhibition at New York's New Museum. All four of New York City's major museums—the Museum of Modern Art, the Metropolitan Museum of Art, the Whitney, and the Guggenheim—have acquired pieces by Puryear for their permanent collections. In 1987 he held his first commercial New York show, at the David McKee Gallery. The bird-like figures in "Decoys," as the exhibit was called, reportedly sold for about $50,000 each.

In 1989 Puryear received a MacArthur Foundation "genius" grant of $295,000. (Such grants come without strings and are given in five annual installments.) That year he was also selected to represent the United States at the São Paulo Bienal, thus becoming the first black artist to represent the U.S. officially in an international art exhibition. An international five-member jury awarded Puryear, who was among the more than 140 exhibitors, the grand prize for best artist in the show. His pieces at the Bienal included *Rawhide Cone* (1980), a roughly shaped cone that is a version of a piece originally executed in 1974; *For Beckwourth*; *Maroon* (1987–88), an ovoid sculpture made of steel wire mesh, wood, and tar, which, Michael Brenson wrote in the *New York Times* (October 16, 1989), "seems to be at the same time sleepy, growing, sailing, and beached"; *Charm of Subsistence* (1989), a flattened woven-wood basket that looks like "a flask out of which a giant might drink rum," according to Brenson; *Lever No. 1* (1988–89), which resembles a slim coffin, its lid sticking straight up; *Lever No. 2* (1988–89), which features a long curving rod connected to a doweled cone-like structure; *Lever No. 4* (1989), which many reviewers likened to Constantin Brancusi's famous sculpture *The Seal*; and an untitled biomorphic figure with a looping handle (1987). Three years after the São Paulo show, a major Puryear retrospective was mounted at the Art Institute of Chicago.

In addition to indoor sculptural pieces, Puryear has created several outdoor works. His first was *Box and Pole* (1977); standing in the Artpark in Lewiston, New York, it juxtaposes a cube 54 inches on each side with a towering, 100-foot pole that seems to suggest a branchless tree. This was followed by *Equivalents* (1979), displayed at Wave Hill, in the New York City borough of the Bronx, in which a cube that is 54 inches high stands a few feet from a cone that rises to 75 inches; and *Knoll for NOAA [National Oceanic and Atmospheric Administration]* (1981–83), a slightly sloping mound 45 feet in diameter at the NOAA's Western Regional Center, in Seattle, Washington. His largest outdoor work is *Bodark Arc* (1982), located on the prairies of the Nathan Manilow Sculpture Park at Governor's State University, in University Park, Illinois. The piece consists of a long walkway that, from an aerial view, traces the curve of an Indian bow. The string of the "bow" is a wide row of ancient Osage orange trees. At the center of the line of trees is a small bronze chair, which is intended to direct the sitter's attention to the design of the walkway and its integration with the landscape. "That piece is really a kind of garden setting, like a wild garden," he told Alan Artner for the *Chicago Tribune* (February 1, 1987). "And one reason that gardens are so interesting to me is that they are retreats. To go there is to put yourself in a state of mind where you are open to, in a sense, escape."

Camera Obscura, another dramatic outdoor piece, was displayed in "Landscape as Metaphor: Visions of America in the Late Twentieth Century," mounted at the Denver Art Museum in 1994. A "camera obscura" is a dark box—sometimes big enough to stand in—with an aperture that allows inverted images of whatever is outside to be projected onto the far inner wall of the box. Playing with conceptions of inside/outside and inversion, Puryear's "camera obscura" consists of a cherry tree strung upside down from a wooden gallows-like structure. Some Denver residents immediately protested the chopping down of the tree for the sculpture. The protestors didn't object to wooden sculptures set up inside the museum, which seemed to show that they had not considered one message that Puryear seemed to be sending: throughout history, sculptors have been killing trees for art.

Puryear has also constructed two "gateway" pieces. The first, *Ampersand* (1987–88), at the Walker Art Center, in Minneapolis, Minnesota, is composed of two pieces of granite, one seeming to point downward, the other, upward. *Pylons*, at the waterfront in Battery Park City, at the southern end of the New York City borough of Manhattan, form a symbolic portal to Battery Park City's North Cove. *Pylons*, too, consists of two structures, one that is solid, angular, and appears to thrust downward; the other is made of steel mesh and looks as if it is spiraling upward.

In what Michael Van Valkenburgh, the Charles Eliot professor of landscape architecture at Harvard University, described as a "true collaboration," he and Puryear planned and directed the renovation of the 4,500-square-foot Vera List courtyard at the New School College (formerly the New School for Social Research), in the Greenwich Village section of New York City. The project, launched in 1991 and completed in 1997, "accomplished the design equivalent of a heart transplant . . . transform[ing] a poorly functioning part of the university into its vital center," Andrea Oppenheimer Dean wrote for *Landscape Architecture* (October 1998). The renovation, which was funded by the National Endowment for the Arts and Vera List, includes three sculptures that Puryear designed and built for seating; resembling round, centrally columned, Victorian-era couches and fashioned, respectively, out of stainless steel, granite, and maple, they enable sitters to face outward and in different directions. Thus, if they so desire, the sitters can remain "quite alone" despite the proximity of others, as Puryear explained to Dean. Working with the New York architectural firm Mitchell/Giurgola, Puryear eliminated the oppressiveness of an overhead walking bridge connecting two buildings by hanging from it what Dean described as "a glazed canopy resembling glass wings." Puryear thus "transformed the skywalk into a light, soaring object, a protection for pedestrians walking beneath it in rain or snow." In working on the courtyard, Van Valkenburgh told Dean, he and Puryear "were on the same wavelength." Puryear, for his part, said to Dean, "I'm not above accepting a better idea than my own."

In the April 1998 issue of *Artforum*, Massimo Carboni reviewed a recent, dual show of works by Puryear and the sculptor Nunzio di Stefano held at the American Academy in Rome. One of the three Puryear pieces displayed was *Vessel* (1997); described by Carboni as a "large, skeletal wooden structure" that "was sunk into a mound of earth, as if a ship had run aground," it reminded him of both "a mysterious animal and the remains of a vessel." "Looking closely," Carboni wrote, "one discovered that depressions and protuberances in the soil formed an image—a face or a mask reminiscent of Easter Island idols." In July 1999 the Contemporary Arts Center in Cincinnati, Ohio, mounted an exhibit of drawings and other preliminary studies that Puryear had made for some of his works. Called "Drawing into Sculpture," the two-month-long show includes a model of *Bearing Witness* (1995); the final product rises 40 feet and stands in the plaza of the Ronald Reagan Building in Washington, D.C.

In 1986 Puryear married Jeanne Gordon, a classical pianist and artist. In about 1990 he stopped teaching to devote himself to his art. He and his wife have lived in the Hudson River Valley of New York State since 1990, in a house that he designed with the help of the architect John Vinci. He also designed and built a studio on the same property. An avid traveler, Puryear has trekked in Norway, canoed (with handmade paddles) in the Noatak River, in Alaska, and lived in Japan, thanks to a 1983 Guggenheim Foundation grant. — W.G.

Suggested Reading: *African-American History Through the Arts: Martin Puryear* (on-line), with photos; *Chicago Tribune* XIII p14+ Feb. 1, 1987, with photos, XIII p12+ Oct. 1, 1989, with photos,

X p10+ Nov. 3, 1991, with photos; *Landscape Architecture* p48+ Oct. 1998, with photos; *New York Times* C p15+ Oct. 16, 1989, with photo, II p37+ Oct. 29, 1989, with photos, II p35 Mar. 1, 1992, with photo, XIII Dec. 20, 1992, with photo; *Time* p61+ Mar. 2, 1992, with photos; *Washington Post* D p1+ Mar. 25, 1988, with photos; Benezra, Neal. *Martin Puryear*, 1991

Selected Works: *Circumbent*, 1976; *Bask*, 1976; *Some Tales*, 1975–77; *Cedar Lodge*, 1977; *Box and Pole*, 1977; *Some Lines for Jim Beckwourth*, 1978; *Primavera*, 1979; *Equivalents*, 1979; *Bower*, 1980; *Rawhide Cone*, 1980; *Big and Little Same*, 1981; *Dream of Pairing*, 1981; *For Beckwourth*, 1980; *Equation for Jim Beckwourth*, 1980; *Where the Heart Is (Sleeping Mews)*, 1981; *Knoll for National Oceanic and Atmosphereic Administration*, 1981–83; *Sanctuary*, 1982; *Bodark Arc*, 1982; *Night and Day*, 1984; *The Spell*, 1985; *Sanctum*, 1985; *Old Mole*, 1985; *Cask Cascade*, 1985; *Ampersand*, 1987–88; *Lever No. 1*, 1988–89; *Lever No. 2*, 1988–89; *Lever No. 4*, 1989; *Charm of Subsistence*, 1989; *Camera Obscura*, 1994

Courtesy of Harvard University

Quine, W. V.

June 25, 1908– Philosopher; educator. Address: Room 201, Dept. of Philosophy, Emerson Hall, Harvard University, Cambridge, MA 02138

As the nation's foremost practitioner of analytic philosophy, the school of thought that has been dominant in American philosophical circles for much of this century, W. V. Quine has strived to reduce metaphysics—the branch of philosophy that is concerned with the ultimate nature of being—to questions of logic and language. An intellectual descendant of—among others—the French philosopher August Comte and the German mathematician and philosopher Gottlob Frege, both of whom worked during the 19th century; the British philosophers G. E. Moore and Bertrand Russell; the Austrian-born Ludwig Wittgenstein; and the Americans William James and John Dewey, Quine believes that weighty questions about reality and existence that are widely regarded as the proper domain of philosophy cannot be addressed unless they are phrased in terms of mathematics, logic, or science.

When asked by D. C. Denison for the *Boston Globe* (July 14, 1985) whether the public should seek the opinions of philosophers on social questions, Quine replied, "I don't see that philosophers, by virtue of their profession, have any special claim to competence on such points."August Comte (1798-1857), by contrast, was concerned mainly with social reform—that is, with creating conditions in which people and nations could exist harmoniously and in comfort. The originator of the terms "positivism" and "sociology," Comte believed that certain principles, or laws, govern social phenomena, and that they could be discovered through scientific investigation. The laws would form the basis of a new science, Comte asserted, that would be applicable to modern industrial society and could guide social planners. Wittgenstein (1889-1951), who studied with Bertrand Russell at Cambridge University, in England, was preoccupied with the connections among language, thought, and reality. In his *Tractatus Logico-Philosophicus* (1921), he wrote, "Most of the propositions and questions of philosophers arise from our failure to understand the logic of our language. (They belong to the same class as the question whether the good is more or less identical to the beautiful.) And it is not surprising that the deepest problems are in fact *not* problems at all." His assertion that rooting out linguistic confusion is the business of philosophy ushered in a new intellectual epoch in which philosophers sought to elucidate the structure of "ordinary" language. Working at roughly the same time were members of the so-called Vienna Circle; called logical positivists, these thinkers maintained that useful philosophical propositions must be verifiable through observation or experimentation and that questions of ethics and metaphysics, if not expressible in scientific terms, contribute not to enlightenment but to confusion. While the Vienna Circle disbanded after the Nazis came to power in Austria in the late 1930s, their ideas survived in their writings and in the work of other Western philosophers, prominent among them W. V. Quine. "Quine has won a world reputation for his work on logic," John Gross wrote for the *New York Times* (September 29, 1987); "those in a position to know have often described him as one of the greatest of living philosophers."

In more than 20 books and dozens of journal articles, Quine has presented subtle yet important modifications of logical positivism and analytic philosophy. Peppered with logical and mathematical symbolism, many of his writings have bewildered lay readers; even an encyclopedia article, headed "Logic, Symbolic," that Quine prepared "must surely daunt all but the cleverest of technically innocent inquirers," Anthony Quinton wrote in the *New York Review of Books* (January 12, 1967). Quinton, a former president of Oxford University's Trinity College, in England, and a specialist in the history of philosophy, wrote of Quine's work, "Quine's aim is to show the essential continuity of all forms of rational discourse. Taking science as ordinarily conceived to be the central form of rationality, he seeks to connect it with direct observation of the world on the one hand and with logic, mathematics, and ontology on the other. . . . The final upshot of Quine's philosophy is an assertion of the essential unity of science and, even more, of the ultimate identity of science with all rational thought. He emphasizes its unity in opposition to a long tradition of dualism distinguishing pure mathematics as the achievement of unaided reason from natural knowledge derived from the senses, that stretches back, through [the 18th-century Scottish philosopher David] Hume and [the 17th–18th-century German philosopher and mathematician Gottfried Wilhelm] Leibniz, to [the classical Greek philosopher] Plato's separation of knowledge and opinion. . . . Science, with its inextricably mathematical and observational aspects, as the most precise and most firmly established body of human beliefs, is the criterion by which all our convictions must be judged." Whereas Wittgenstein saw the potential for deriving philosophical insights from nonsensical statements and thus left room for metaphysics, Quine applied Wittgenstein's analysis of "ordinary language" and "common sense" to the more complex structures of math and science, which are neither common or ordinary. One outgrowth of this approach is Quine's theory of knowledge, in which, as Quinton wrote, "[Quine] identifies the mental state of a subject with the physical condition of the organism in question at the time, leaving it to neurophysiology to discover the precise details of the relevant physical states." Rejecting the Platonic mind-body duality—the theory that the mind and the body are separate entities—he proposes that mind and body must be considered a single phenomenon. In Quine's view, tackling metaphysical questions amounts to tackling scientific questions.

Quine's seminal paper "Two Dogmas of Empiricism," published in 1951 in the *Philosophical Review*, attacked epistemological assumptions central to logical positivism and established the complex relationship between Quine's philosophy and that school of thought. In his introduction to his article (which was reprinted in his 1953 book *From* a *Logical Point of View*), he wrote, "Modern empiricism has been conditioned in large part by two dogmas. One is a belief in some fundamental cleavage between truths which are *analytic*, or grounded in meanings independently of matters of fact, and truths which are *synthetic*, or grounded in fact. The other dogma is *reductionism*: the belief that each meaningful statement is equivalent to some logical construct upon terms which refer to immediate experience. Both dogmas, I shall argue, are ill founded. One effect of abandoning them is . . . a blurring of the supposed boundary between speculative metaphysics and natural science. Another effect is a shift toward pragmatism."

The first dogma that Quine considered, known as the analytic-synthetic opposition, was expounded by the 18th-century German philosopher Immanuel Kant. An analytic proposition is essentially a tautology, something that is true by definition: for example, "All bachelors are unmarried men." Other examples are mathematical and scientific axioms, which are taken as self-evident. A synthetic proposition, on the other hand, is not tautological; the concept of the subject is not included in the predicate. The statement "Golden retrievers are dogs" is analytic, whereas "Golden retrievers enjoy chasing squirrels" is synthetic. The analytic statement, furthermore, is known a priori, that is, prior to experience; its meaning is deduced by reasoning from self-evident statements. The synthetic is generally known a posteriori; its meaning is derived by reasoning from something that is observed. For Kant, the analytic and the synthetic were discrete categories; Quine, however, argued that the analyticity of any statement can be refuted if the linguistic system of which the statement is a part is altered. As he wrote in his paper, "It is obvious that truth in general depends on both language and extra-linguistic fact. The statement 'Brutus killed Caesar' would be false if the world had been different in certain ways, but it would also be false if the word 'killed' happened rather to have the sense of 'begat.'" He concluded, "A boundary between analytic and synthetic statements simply has not been drawn. That there is such a distinction to be drawn at all is an unempirical dogma of empiricists, a metaphysical article of faith." The second tenet that Quine attacked, the concept of reductionism, holds that, in his words, "Every meaningful statement is held to be translatable into a statement (true or false) about immediate experience." But Quine argued that "the two dogmas are . . . at root identical," and thus reductionism, too, does not hold up under scrutiny. In the last paragraph of his paper, he wrote, referring to the 20th-century philosophers Rudolf Carnap and C. I. Lewis, "Carnap, Lewis, and others take a pragmatic stand on the question of choosing between language forms [and] scientific frameworks; but their pragmatism leaves off at the imagined boundary between the analytic and the synthetic. In repudiating such a boundary I espouse a more thorough pragmatism. Each man is given a scientific heritage plus a continuing barrage of sensory stimulation; and the considerations which guide him in warping his scientific heritage to fit his continuing sensory promptings are, where rational, pragmatic."

Word and Object, Quine's magnum opus, appeared in 1960, and it has since become regarded as an indispensable work of 20th-century philosophy. The book expands upon the conclusions of "Two Dogmas" by presenting two famous theses. The "indeterminacy of translation" thesis maintains that translating between languages necessarily presents the possibility of numerous interpretations, without any particular translation being necessarily and absolutely correct. The related "uncertainty of reference" thesis recognizes a fundamental problem of language: the inherent indeterminacy in the process of reference between a word and the object to which it refers.

With *Word and Object* and such other works as *A System of Logistic* (1934), *Mathematical Logic* (1940), and *Set Theory and Its Logic* (1963), Quine laid out his system of logic in detail. In a passage from the 1966 Harvard yearbook, J. Randolph Moore wrote of the system, "There are various approaches to mathematic logic, including the axiomatic method advanced by [Albert North] Whitehead and Bertrand Russell in *Principia Mathematica*, but Quine's method of 'natural deduction,' with fewer axioms, is less cumbersome and more efficient. The entire concern is 'mathematical' in that his notation is comprised of a vocabulary of abstract variables (algebra is another example), and reasoning proceeds in strict accordance with rules of inference derived from the theory itself." In the *New Republic* (September 30, 1985), Anthony Quinton wrote, "[Quine] thinks that the prime task of philosophy is to understand and clarify the language of science, and that the best way to go about it is logical 'regimentation,' in which the lucid formal replacements of logical notation are offered for the problem-engendering conceptions of language and thought."

The second of two brothers, Willard van Orman Quine was born in Akron, Ohio, on June 25, 1908 to Cloyd Robert Quine and Harriet "Hattie" Ellis (van Orman) Quine. Early in life he developed a love of maps and amused himself by drawing his own. In high school he became a serious stamp collector and even turned his hobby into a business: he founded the Orchard Stamp Co. (named for his street) and published a newsletter, called *OK Stamp News*. He later sold his collection to help pay for his education. In 1926 Quine enrolled at Oberlin College, in Oberlin, Ohio, near Cleveland, where he majored in mathematics. When he was an undergraduate, his mother, knowing of his interest in science and the history of words, gave him a copy of *Principia Mathematica* and a book on the etymology of the English language by the British philologist Walter W. Skeat. Quine graduated summa cum laude from Oberlin with an A.B. degree, in 1930, and in September of that year, he married his first wife, Naomi Ann Clayton. The couple then settled in Cambridge, Massachusetts, where Quine studied philosophy at Harvard University under Whitehead. He earned an M.A. degree in 1931 and a Ph.D. a year later, thus completing his graduate work in the extraordinarily short time of two years.

For a year beginning in 1932, having won the Harvard-administered Frederick Sheldon Traveling Fellowship, Quine went with his wife to Vienna; Prague, Czechoslovakia; and Warsaw, Poland. While in Prague he studied with Rudolf Carnap, a leading exponent of logical positivism, which is concerned mainly with the logical soundness of scientific language. "That was a great year," he has recalled, as quoted in the *Beacon Hill Paper* (May 15, 1996; reprinted on the W. V. Quine Web page). "We used up our resources very accurately—I had $7 when we got back to America." Quine returned to Harvard in 1933 as a junior fellow, and he has been associated with the university ever since. In 1936 he began teaching philosophy as an instructor and tutor. His courses had such titles as "Mathematical Logic," "Set Theory," and "Logic in Philosophy." "What I enjoyed most was more the mathematical end than the philosophical, because of it being less a matter of opinion," he told the *Beacon Hill Paper* interviewer. "Clarifying, not defending. Resting on proof. . . . Harvard was good about letting me teach my own interests." He became a full professor in 1948, Edgar Pierce professor of philosophy in 1956, and Pierce professor of philosophy emeritus in 1978, the year he turned 70 and was forced to retire. (A special dispensation issued by Harvard's president enabled him to teach for five years beyond the then-mandatory retirement age of 65.)

Quine's teaching career was interrupted by World War II, during which he served in the U.S. Naval Reserve (1942–46), reaching the rank of lieutenant commander. Assigned to Atlantic Radio Intelligence, in Washington, D.C., he helped to decipher messages emanating from German submarines. "At first, I was put on harmless stuff, like direction finding," he told the *Beacon Hill Paper* (May 15, 1996). "Then we were let in on the top secret." During his wartime service he met his second wife, Marjorie Boynton, a fellow code-breaker, whom he married in 1948. (His first marriage ended in divorce.)

Quine's first book, *A System of Logistic*, which was largely a refinement of the system conceived by Whitehead and Russell, was published in 1934. It was followed by the textbooks *Mathematical Logic* (1940); *Elementary Logic* (1941); and *O Sentido da Nova Logica* ("The Meaning of the New Logic," 1944), written in Portuguese. (Quine is fluent in six languages and has studied several others, including Japanese and Chinese.) Others among his books are *Methods of Logic* (1950); *The Ways of Paradox and Other Essays* (1966); *Ontological Relativity and Other Essays* (1969); *The Web of Belief* (1970), written with J. S. Ullian; *The Philosophy of Logic* (1970); *The Roots of Reference* (1974); *Theories and Things* (1981); *Pursuit of Truth*

(1990); and *From Stimulus to Science* (1995). Quine's more casual writings include *Quiddities: An Intermittently Philosophical Dictionary* (1987). In a review for *Choice* (February 1988), W. Taschek wrote, "*Quiddities* is quintessential Quine—compact, quick-witted, quirky, and, if occasionally quibbling, always to the point. The author's taste for alliteration and puns is given full rein. . . . This collection provides considerable insight into the personality, quality of mind, and character of this very important philosopher; in this respect, it is more revealing than Quine's autobiography, *The Time of My Life* [1985]." In his review of *Quiddities* for the *New York Times* (September 29, 1987), John Gross wrote that "at almost every turn there are cheerful ripples of wordplay" and that the book "is infused with a deadpan humor that can light up even the most austere subjects."

By his own account, Quine has "little bent for soul-searching." A passionate traveler, he has visited 118 countries (though a few for only minutes, when he was en route elsewhere) and all 50 states. (During his first 90 years, he traveled to every state but North Dakota, so, as a 90th birthday present, his son, Douglas B. Quine, and Douglas's family took him there.) W. V. Quine has also kept track of the number of countries he has flown over but never landed in (19) and seen "from the side" while "passing by" (eight). Described as politically conservative, he has lived for more than 40 years in the Beacon Hill section of Boston, from which, until recently, he still commuted by subway to his office at Harvard. He is a jazz buff and a collector of maps, and he has reviewed atlases for many publications. His son told *Current Biography* that Quine's "lifelong hobbies also include walking and canoeing. He used to paddle upwind in the lake at his summer house in Harvard, Massachusetts, lie down, and read dissertations until he coasted into the shore, and then paddle upwind to the end of the lake again and repeat the cycle." Having no interest in computers (though computer theorists have made use of his work), he continues to write with the 1927 Remington typewriter on which he typed his Ph.D. dissertation.

Quine served as a consulting editor to the *Journal of Symbolic Logic* from 1936 to 1952, as a consultant to the Rand Corp. in 1949, and as a member of the Institute for Advanced Study, in Princeton, New Jersey, in 1956–57. His many honors include the prestigious Kyoto (Japan) Prize in creative arts and moral sciences (1996) and 17 honorary degrees. From his first marriage he has two daughters, Elizabeth and Norma; from his second he has a daughter, Margaret, and his son, Douglas, who maintains the Willard van Orman Quine home page (http://www.triskelion-ltd.com/drquine/wv-quine.html) on the World Wide Web. Quine has six grandchildren and one great-grandchild. His second wife, Marjorie Boynton Quine, died in 1998.
— M.C.

Suggested Reading: *Boston Globe* p58+ Oct. 12, 1987; *New Republic* p40+ Sep. 30, 1995; *New York Review of Books* p12+ Jan. 12, 1967; *New York Times* IV p1+ May 12, 1995, A p19 Aug. 15, 1998; *Who's Who in America, 1999*

Selected Books: *A System of Logic*, 1934; *Mathematical Logic*, 1940; *Elementary Logic*, 1941; *O Sentido da Nova Logica*, 1944; *Methods of Logic*, 1950; *From a Logical Point of View*, 1953; *Word and Object*, 1960; *Set Theory and Its Logic*, 1963; *The Ways of Paradox and Other Essays*, 1966; *Ontological Relativity and Other Essays*, 1969; *Philosophy of Logic*, 1970; *The Roots of Reference*, 1974; *Theories and Things*, 1981; *The Time of My Life: An Autobiography*, 1985; *Quiddities: An Intermittently Philosophical Dictionary*, 1987; *Pursuit of Truth*, 1990; *The Logic of Sequences: A Generalization of Principia Mathematica*, 1990; *From Stimulus to Science*, 1995; with J. S. Ullian—*The Web of Belief*, 1970; with Richard Creath, ed.—*Dear Carnap, Dear Van: The Quine–Carnap Correspondence and Related Work*, 1991

John Abbott Photography

Rainwater, Richard

1945– Investor. Address: c/o Crescent Real Estate Equities, 777 Main St., #2100, Fort Worth, TX 76102-5325; c/o Gainsco, Inc., P.O. Box 2933, Fort Worth, TX 76113-2933

"Richard's style has always been to buy when no one else wants to buy and sell when everybody wants to get into it. The crux of Richard is that he is one of the best value investors of all time," the Washington, D.C., investment banker and dealmaker David Bonderman has said of the Texas billionaire investor Richard Rainwater, as quoted by Stephanie Anderson Forest in *Business Week* (November 30, 1998). "Someone asked me what are the secrets of my success, and I said there are three," Rainwater told John Morthland for *Texas Monthly* (December 1996, on-line). "Timing, timing, timing." After graduating from the Stanford University Graduate School of Business in the late 1960s, Rainwater got his start at Goldman, Sachs & Co., then quickly made his way into the upper ranks of the Bass family's oil corporation in Fort Worth, Texas. In the early 1980s he persuaded the family to buy stock in the then–foundering Walt Disney Co., and he was instrumental in bringing to Disney as CEO Michael Eisner, now one of the most renowned chief executives in the world, with the result that Disney soon began experiencing a renaissance. By the time Rainwater left the Bass family, the company was worth $5 billion, up from a relatively paltry $50 million in 1970, when Rainwater had arrived. "When he is negotiating, Rainwater can be a charming, persuasive man, using the tenacious force of his personality to get his way," Morthland wrote. When he struck out on his own, in 1986, securing controlling interests in Blocker Energy and the larger, more prestigious Penrod Drilling, Rainwater suddenly became a major player in the world's oil-drilling industry. Soon afterward he began expanding into other lucrative, but at the time risky and unpopular, investments. By 1996, having added to his portfolio numerous companies that exercised clout in their respective fields, he was personally worth well over $1 billion. Currently, he controls corporations in real estate (Crescent Real Estate Equities Co.), health-care services (Columbia/HCA Healthcare Corp.), the oil-drilling industry (Ensco International), the natural-gas industry (Pioneer), and the insurance business (Mid Ocean Ltd.).

Of late, however, chinks in Rainwater's investment armor have begun to show. In *Business Week*, his good friend Henry R. Silverman, the CEO of Cendant Corp., was quoted as saying that Rainwater's investments "are all in the crapper at the same time." As of November 1998, his net worth had fallen 29 percent since the previous January—the biggest loss of his career. Many people in high finance, however, believe that Rainwater will turn things around. "With his reputation as a rainmaker at stake, Rainwater is spending more time on damage control," a reporter for *Business Week* wrote. "He's turning up the heat on managers of his companies to cut costs." "It's not money or pretense or wearing a tie that drives Richard," his wife, the investment banker Darla Moore, told Morthland. "Richard was a math major in college. His great love is to study a problem, come up with an answer before anyone else does, and be proven right. It's what I call his Master of the Universe mentality." Samuel Moore, a vice president at Goldman,

Sachs, & Co., told Morthland that Rainwater can look "several years into the future and see trends that others don't see." Throughout his career Rainwater has applied this ability to his dealings, as he told Allen R. Myerson for the *New York Times* (March 1, 1996). "If you happen to be in the right place at the right time, the capitalist system is a beautiful thing."

Richard E. Rainwater was born in 1945 in Fort Worth, Texas. His mother, a second-generation Lebanese-American, worked as a saleswoman at J.C. Penney Co. His father, also of Lebanese descent, had a Cherokee Indian ancestor—hence the family name. Rainwater's father ran a modest wholesale grocery business founded by Richard's maternal grandfather. Morton H. Myerson, a high-ranking Rainwater employee and fellow investor, told *Business Week*, "Part of Richard's success is that he has this immigrant mentality of being very driven, working very hard, and really, really wanting to be successful." Rainwater has said that his mother went to work as a saleswoman to help finance his college education, at the University of Texas at Austin, where he majored in math and physics. After graduation he packed his bags and, with only $400 and a car to his name, drove to northern California, where he attended the Stanford University Graduate School of Business. There, he met another Fort Worth native, Sid Richardson Bass, the nephew of the oil millionaire, Sid Richardson, and the two became good friends. After graduation Rainwater went to work for Goldman, Sachs & Co. as a trader, while Bass returned to the family business in Fort Worth. Two years later, in 1970, Rainwater went to work with the Basses. "For the first two years, every single deal I did with them, I lost every single penny," Rainwater told Morthland. He grew more successful by buying shares in such companies as Texaco Inc. and Disney when their stocks were inexpensive and then watching their worth grow exponentially. In this way the Bass fortune climbed from $50 million in 1970 to $5 billion 16 years later.

In 1986, having set his sights on building his own empire, Rainwater left the Basses, taking with him the $100 million he had saved, and proceeded to set up his own company. "Rainwater soon displayed his gambler's derring-do when he entered the oil business at the very moment oil prices plummeted to $9 a barrel," Morthland wrote. In the same year that he became an independent investor, Rainwater bought shares in the Houston oil-drilling company Blocker Energy, which had more than $100 million in bank-loan debts; he then assumed the debt and paid $12 million in return for 65 percent of the stock—controlling interest—in the company. Now, with Blocker under his control and world oil prices still extremely low, Rainwater parlayed his ownership of one oil-drilling company into the acquisition of a second. He obtained nearly a half-billion dollars in financing from backers, telling banks he would help relieve a fraction of the $1.5 billion in loans made to Penrod Drilling,

one of the largest offshore-drilling operations in the world. Owned by the famously daring and notoriously ruthless Hunt brothers, Penrod had had financial problems for some time, and many competing oil companies had their sights set on the huge firm; they were waiting for the brothers to declare bankruptcy so that they could take it over. By the time the brothers did so, Rainwater had traded $430 million for the Penrod debt and won control of the company, "which still had assets of nearly $1 billion," as Morthland reported. The deal, which was completed in late 1986, "was described by one energy analyst as 'easily among the slickest pick-offs in modern corporate history.'" Rainwater had created an oil empire with influence throughout the world. He named the merged conglomerate Ensco International. "If I had tried to do those deals at any other time, I would have fallen flat on my face," he told Morthland. "But the essence of good business is knowing when to step on a train and when to step off."

Soon afterward Rainwater honed in on the health-care market, hoping to reap equally astronomical profits. In October 1987, with Dallas lawyer Richard L. Scott, a specialist in health-care buyouts, Rainwater started Columbia Hospital Corp., with each man fronting $125,000. In just under four years, the new company acquired, at rock-bottom prices, 14 hospitals (mostly in Texas and southern Florida) from nine different parties. Within a decade Columbia became the world's biggest owner of hospitals. A short time later, Rainwater, taking advantage of falling real-estate prices, put together a publicly held company, Crescent Real Estate Equities, which bought distressed properties—those mired in financial troubles. Rainwater's reputation for turning ailing businesses around was such that investors quickly bought $350 million in Crescent stock. One of Crescent's acquisitions, purchased for a remarkably small sum, was the newly built Fountain Palace in downtown Dallas, which became the headquarters of Rainwater's business operations. Eventually, Crescent split into two entities—Crescent Real Estate Equities and Crescent Operating—to prevent conflicts of interests between certain types of real-estate purchases. In 1991, as Milt Freudenheim reported in the *New York Times* (July 21, 1991), "health care represented about 30 percent of [Rainwater's] wealth; oil and oil services about 20 percent; and 'cash,' 35 percent. The remaining 15 percent [was] in Texas real estate and other deals." That year *Forbes* magazine reported Rainwater's personal worth to be $350 million.

In 1991 Rainwater married the then-36-year-old South Carolina investment banker Darla Moore, and she quickly became his chief financial deputy; within a few years, she was running most of his operations. When Rainwater left the board of Columbia/HCA (HCA is a medical-video production company), in 1994, Moore took his place. In the same year she became president of Rainwater, Inc.; in that capacity she manages Rainwater's portfolio.

In 1992 Rainwater and several others invested in Mid Ocean Ltd., which was "created to take advantage of the upheaval in the catastrophic-reinsurance business after the devastation wrought by Hurricane Andrew," as Rainwater wrote for worth.com (March 1997, on-line). By 1996 all of Rainwater's ventures—in oil, health care, and insurance—were in the black, and he was believed to be worth over $1 billion. In March of that year Rainwater embarked on his most ambitious maneuver to date: he attempted to gain a controlling stake in Mesa, Inc., a once highly profitable natural-gas company run by the legendary corporate raider T. Boone Pickens Jr. The executive-compensation expert Graef S. Crystal explained to Allen R. Myerson for the New York Times (March 1, 1996) the irony of Rainwater's role as Pickens's financial savior: "In [Pickens's] raiding days, companies were trying to bring in their own white knights to save themselves from him. It's sort of poetic justice." After months of debate—and to the chagrin of other Mesa investors, whose stakes in the company were greatly diminished after Rainwater's $265 million investment—Rainwater obtained a controlling interest in Mesa, securing yet another mammoth slice of the energy industry. Shortly thereafter, he bought Parker & Parsley, another natural-gas company, and merged it with Mesa, creating what is now known as Pioneer Natural Resources Co.

While on vacation in Las Vegas in 1997, Rainwater suggested to his wife that Crescent buy into Station Casinos, Inc., a multimillion-dollar gambling operation that catered more to Las Vegas residents than to tourists. Within a few months, Crescent offered $635 million for the company, a sum many experts—and investors—thought grossly excessive. Shortly after the preliminary stages of the plan were announced, Station's stock value sank, and Crescent bailed out of the deal. That action was widely seen as the beginning of Rainwater's first-ever financial crisis. Shortly after the aborted Station agreement, a Rainwater transaction involving 90 psychiatric hospitals went sour, and Rainwater backed out of that deal as well. Commenting on those actions, Frederick S. Carr Jr. of the Penobscot Group, Inc., told Business Week, "You don't bust deals because market prices change. They could become known as a company that doesn't close deals, and that will hurt them."

For his part, Rainwater told Business Week, "People are correct in that we have made mistakes. But that happens all the time. There are some things we did at every company I've ever been associated with—Disney, Honeywell, company after company—that we wish we'd never done. . . . [But] when I sit back and look at my results, I say the collective decisions I've made, from the time I started to date, appear to be sound. They have not been flawless . . . but they've created a lot of fortunes—not only for me."

In September 1999, according to the Dallas Business Journal (June 30, 1999, on-line), Gainsco, Inc., a Fort Worth–based insurance and holding company, agreed to accept an investment of $31.6 million from Goff-Moore Strategic Partners, a firm in which Rainwater is a principal; in exchange, Goff-Moore would gain a 23 percent stake in Gainsco, with an option to buy an additional 12 percent. Gainsco stockholders approved the agreement, and the transaction was accomplished on October 4, 1999.

Darla Moore has said that she fell for Richard Rainwater when he told her, "I view you like an equity investment," as Patricia Sellers reported on the Fortune Web site (September 8, 1997). "It was the ultimate compliment," Moore said. Rainwater's wife has instilled in him a love for fine wine and healthful food, and since their marriage he has dropped nearly 50 pounds. His aides have reported that he spends much of his free time working out or playing golf. Rainwater recently bought Canyon Ranch, an exclusive, state-of-the-art spa in Arizona. A drag-racer since his youth, he owns three drag cars and a souped-up Buick. He is a former shareholder in the Texas Rangers baseball club and currently owns stock in basketball's Dallas Mavericks; when he is unable to attend Maverick games, he watches the team via satellite in the "dream house" that he and his wife own in the foothills outside Santa Barbara. His other relatively small investments include a real-estate firm that he owns jointly with ex–Dallas Cowboy quarterback Roger Staubach, a health-food chain (Fresh Choice), and a costume-jewelry manufacturer (Monet Group). He has also begun financing a school and day-care center in Fort Worth for underprivileged children. Regarding the school, Rainwater told Business Week, "Doing this, I could live the rest of my life getting up in the morning and saying, 'Boy, I've really got something worthwhile to do today.' I don't necessarily feel that way about doing another business deal." — M.B.

Suggested Reading: Business Week p113+ Nov. 30, 1998, with photos; fortune.com (on-line) Sep. 8, 1997; New York Times C p1+ July 21, 1991, with photos, D p6 Mar. 1, 1996, with photo, D p2 May 1, 1996; Texas Monthly (on-line) Dec. 1996; worth.com (on-line) Mar. 1997

Courtesy of Exxon Corp.

Raymond, Lee R.

*Aug. 13, 1938– Chairman and CEO of Exxon
Corp. Address: c/o Exxon Corp., 5959 Las
Colinas Blvd., Irving, TX 75039*

In 1911, ruling in favor of the federal government
in a famous antitrust case, the United States Supreme Court broke up the Standard Oil Co. into 34
smaller companies. Before the Court's action, Standard Oil, a corporate empire created by John D.
Rockefeller, had controlled nearly 90 percent of
the nation's oil business. Nearly nine decades later, two of the largest of the companies that came
into being in 1911, which together had comprised
more than 50 percent of Standard Oil, have sought
to undo the Court's action: On December 1, 1998
Lee R. Raymond, the CEO and chairman of Exxon
Corp., once known as Standard Oil of New Jersey,
and Lucio Noto, the CEO of Mobil Corp., once
known as Standard Oil of New York, signed an
agreement to merge. Exxon, the country's largest
oil company, formally agreed to purchase Mobil,
the second largest, for about $77 billion in stocks,
leaving Exxon shareholders in possession of 70
percent of the resulting company, which was to be
named Exxon Mobil. The proposed merger was the
largest in U.S. history, surpassing the planned
$72 billion merger of Bell Atlantic Corp. and GTE
Corp., which was announced in July 1998, and the
intended $70 billion merger of SBC Communica-
tions and Ameritech, also announced in 1998. In
its present formulation, the Exxon-Mobil merger
may not win approval from the Federal Trade Commission and state regulatory agencies—the companies would likely be required to divest some of
their holdings in the U.S. to meet antitrust regula-

tions. But if it were to become a reality, it would
be one of the world's largest and most powerful
multinational firms. According to Allen R. Myerson in the *New York Times* (December 2, 1998), the
new company would control about 13 percent of
the U.S. gasoline market and have annual sales of
some $204 billion, topping General Motors as the
U.S.'s largest company and Royal Dutch/Shell
Group as the world's largest oil and gas company
in terms of revenue. For Lee Raymond, who has
been Exxon Corp.'s chairman and CEO since 1993,
the proposed merger represented yet another accomplishment in a long and distinguished career
that began at Exxon in 1963.

Lee R. Raymond was born on August 13, 1938
in Watertown, South Dakota, to a railroad conductor and his wife. He earned a bachelor's degree in
chemical engineering from the University of Wisconsin, in 1960, and a Ph.D. degree in chemical engineering from the University of Minnesota, in
1963. He joined Exxon Corp. that year as a production research engineer in the company's Tulsa,
Oklahoma, offices. During the next decade, in addition to working in Tulsa, he assisted in Exxon's
Latin American and Caribbean operations and
helped manage the Creole Petroleum Corp., Exxon's Venezuelan affiliate, which the Venezuelan
government eventually nationalized. From 1972 to
1975 he was manager of planning at the international division of Exxon in New York City. Next,
until 1979, he served first as vice president and
then as president and director of Lago Oil, an Exxon affiliate in the Caribbean island of Aruba, in the
Netherlands Antilles. Lago Oil had been losing
$10 million a month; thanks to Raymond's efforts,
it was earning $25 million a month by the time he
left.

From 1979 to 1981 Raymond served as president
of the Exxon Nuclear Co., a division of Exxon Corp.
that had experienced serious setbacks, mainly because of the downturn in the nuclear-power industry. He soon closed several facilities, reduced the
number of employees, and took other steps to lower expenses, thereby turning a corporate liability
into an asset. In the process he earned a reputation
as an aggressive cost-cutter.

In 1981 Raymond returned to New York City, to
become executive vice president of Exxon Enterprises, a subsidiary of Exxon Corp. When he took
over, the subsidiary was in the red; in Raymond's
view, it was overextended, and in addition, as he
explained to Richard Teitelbaum for *Fortune*
(April 28, 1997), its goals were not defined. Raymond closed the operation entirely, and he was
credited with preventing a further hemorrhaging of
money. In 1983 he became president of Esso Inter-
American Inc., a subsidiary of Exxon Corp. that operated out of Coral Gables, Florida, where he was
responsible for overseeing Exxon's international
supply and transportation of crude oil and petroleum products. In the following year he was named
senior vice president and a member of the Exxon
Corp.'s board of directors.

In 1987 Lawrence Rawl, the president of Exxon, advanced to the positions of chairman and CEO, and Raymond succeeded him to the presidency. Raymond thus became one of the youngest presidents in Exxon's history. Under Rawl, Raymond helped implement various restructuring and cost-cutting strategies. These efforts, which continued into the early 1990s, involved eliminating jobs and taking steps to increase productivity.

Meanwhile, Raymond helped Exxon navigate what has generally been regarded as one of the worst environmental disasters and corporate public-relations fiascoes in American history. In March 1989 the *Exxon Valdez*, an oil tanker making its way along the coast of Alaska, crashed into a charted reef and spilled 11 million gallons of crude oil into Prince William Sound. The oil contaminated an estimated 1,500 miles of shoreline, killed countless wild creatures, and severely damaged what had been a pristine ecosystem. Although Exxon spent about $2.1 billion in clean-up activities and reimbursements to federal, state, and local governments for their attempts to clean up the congealed oil, the corporation became the object of prolonged public outrage and protests from environmental groups. Raymond helped negotiate a $900 million settlement of a civil suit brought by the governments of Alaska and the U.S. The governments earmarked the money, which was to be paid in 10 annual installments starting in December 1991, for efforts aimed at restoring the environment. In addition, in 1994, in a class-action lawsuit launched by fishermen and other Alaska residents, a federal court jury in Anchorage, Alaska, found Exxon liable for the oil-caused catastrophe and ordered the corporation to pay $5 billion in punitive damages—among the largest sums ever imposed in an environmental pollution case against a corporation. Despite widespread public approval of the punishment, Exxon appealed the decision, and as of 1999 the plaintiffs had received no money.

Earlier, in 1993, Rawl had reached Exxon's mandatory retirement age of 65, and—as had been expected by outsiders as well as Exxon insiders—Raymond was named to succeed him as the corporation's CEO and chairman. The consensus was that Raymond's relative youth as well as his reputation and long years of experience had positioned him well for the promotion.

Because of advances in technology and changes in the global economy, the oil industry has grown more competitive in recent years. Large state-owned companies, such as Saudi Aramco and Petroleos de Venezuela, as well as corporate giants, such as Royal Dutch/Shell, have been vying with Exxon for business. To increase Exxon's profits, Raymond continued shrinking the company's workforce after he took command. As of 1995 Exxon employed fewer people than it had at any time since the 1920s, and during the next two years, the payroll shrank to 79,000, the smallest number since 1911. Raymond also implemented measures to decrease corporate bureaucracy and increase flexibility. "In a bureaucracy it's never clear who decided to do something. That's a far bigger problem than paperwork," he told David Lascelles. By 1997 Exxon had increased its operating efficiency significantly: according to figures cited by Richard Teitelbaum in *Fortune*, Exxon made a profit of $4.70 on every barrel of oil it pumped outside the U.S., 33 percent more than Texaco, Chevron, and other American companies.

Finding new sources of natural gas (one of the world's fastest-growing energy sources) and oil was also high on Raymond's agenda. In 1995 Exxon signed an agreement with the Indonesian government to develop the Natuna natural-gas field in that country. On another front, Exxon engineers developed a method—patented under the name AGC-21—to convert natural gas into a liquid, thus making it much easier to transport.

With earnings in 1996 of $7.5 billion, Exxon ranked as the most profitable company in the U.S., surpassing such computer-industry behemoths as Microsoft and Intel. That same year Exxon stocks returned a profit of 26 percent to shareholders. For such achievements Raymond was compensated handsomely. In 1997 his salary and bonus totaled $3.25 million. He also owned about $25 million in Exxon shares and about $71 million in stock options and other assets.

In December 1998, when the proposed merger with Mobil was announced, Exxon was the world's second-largest oil company, behind Royal Dutch/Shell, and owned refineries, production facilities, and retail businesses in more than 100 countries. Mobil was the world's fourth-largest oil company; it extracted oil and gas in about 25 countries and had other oil- and gas-related operations in more than 140 countries. Exxon's 1997 revenues amounted to $120.3 billion, and its net income was $8.5 billion. Mobil's 1997 revenues added up to $58.4 billion, and its net income to $3.3 billion. Both Mobil and Exxon expected their merger to lead to increased productivity and profits. "This is the case of the whole being greater than the sum of the parts," Raymond noted, as quoted by Myerson. He also said, according to *CNN/FN* (December 1, 1998, on-line), "In the exploration and production area, . . . Mobil's and Exxon's respective strengths in West Africa, the Caspian region, Russia, South America, and North America line up well, with minimal overlap. Our respective deep water assets and deep water technology also complement each other well."

The announced merger reflected a trend in the oil industry toward greater consolidation. Indeed, on the same day that Exxon and Mobil announced their plans, Total SA, the second-largest oil company in France, announced its plans to purchase the Belgian company Petrofina SA, and British Petroleum PLC, the world's third-largest oil company, was in the process of finalizing its purchase of Amoco Corp. for around $58.5 billion. Consolidation had grown more attractive as oil prices had dropped in recent years. In 1998 the price of a barrel of oil averaged about $12, down from an average of $21.01 in 1996. (The price has since returned to 1996 levels.) This decline reflected an overabundance of oil on the market, the weakening influence of the Organization of Petroleum Exporting Countries (OPEC), the cartel of major oil-producing nations, and a sharp drop in demand from Asian nations, which were gripped by an economic recession. The announced merger aroused concern among some labor and consumer advocates, with regard to payroll cuts and the threat of monopolization. Indeed, much of the projected savings was expected to come at the cost of about 9,000 jobs among the companies' 123,000 employees worldwide. And as Andrew Heaney, president of a fuel-buying cooperative, told Myerson, "There's little question in my mind that if you have industry consolidation on this magnitude, you're going to see energy prices controlled by fewer people."

If Exxon Mobil becomes a reality, Raymond is expected to take the title of chairman, chief executive, and president, and Lucio Noto the title of vice chairman. Exxon Mobil will be headquartered at Exxon's present headquarters, in Irving, Texas, a suburb of Dallas. Its refining and marketing operations will most likely be situated in Mobil's present headquarters, in Fairfax, Virginia, and its exploration and chemical operations are expected to be located in Houston, Texas.

According to Myerson, Raymond is "reserved and analytical"; Teitelbaum described him as "scary smart." "That intelligence can be intimidating, current and former colleagues say, and in public he can come off as arrogant or dismissive," Teitelbaum wrote. "As Raymond himself admits: 'I'm not known to suffer fools gladly.'" Raymond has zealously guarded his private life from the media; he told Teitelbaum that he was "pleased to hear" that the reporter could find almost no published information about him. He admitted to Teitelbaum, however, that he has no close colleagues and no hobbies. He and his wife, Charlene, have triplet sons. In 1995 one of them, John, was working as a securities analyst at a New Orleans energy boutique. Lee Raymond has served on the boards of directors of J. P. Morgan, the Morgan Guaranty Trust Co., the United Negro College Fund, and the New American Schools Development Corp., and on the College Board's national task force on high achievement by members of minorities. — Y.P.

Suggested Reading: *Financial Times* p14 May 2, 1995, with photo; *Fortune* p134+ Apr. 28, 1997, with photos; *New York Times* A p1+ Dec. 2, 1998, with photos, C p1+ Dec. 2, 1998, with photos, C p1+ Dec. 4, 1998, with photo; *Wall Street Journal* p2 Aug. 28, 1986; *Who's Who in America, 1999*

Reagon, Bernice Johnson

(REE-gun)

Oct. 4, 1942– Curator emerita at the Smithsonian Institution; professor of history; founder of and performer with Sweet Honey in the Rock. Address: c/o Dept. of History, American University, 4400 Massachusetts Ave. N.W., Washington, DC 20016

"When I got out of jail in '61," Bernice Johnson Reagon, founder of the internationally acclaimed a cappella singing group Sweet Honey in the Rock, casually remarked to Michael Kernan for *Smithsonian* (February 1999), "I went to a mass meeting and I was hoarse because I sang all the time in jail. I opened my mouth to sing . . . I never heard that voice before. It was very similar to the way people describe religious conversion. . . . For the first time I really understood what was in that singing that I had heard all my life." Jailed for her participation in a freedom march and expelled from college for her active support of the civil-rights movement, Reagon embarked on a less than traditional educational journey. She traveled the country with the Student Nonviolent Coordinating Committee (SNCC) Freedom Singers, raising money and awareness for the fight for civil rights; organized folk festivals and collected old songs and oral traditions; and married and had two children.

Courtesy of Songtalk Publishing

Eventually recognizing that she needed academic legitimacy to further her goals, Reagon returned to college. She earned a Ph.D. in history, studying oral culture and the musical traditions of the civil-rights movement. Now a curator emerita at the Smithsonian Institution, a distinguished professor of history at American University, and a performer in Sweet Honey in the Rock, which specializes in politically charged songs as well as traditional African-American music, Reagon blends her backgrounds in history, music, and social activism to share her knowledge and experiences in a variety of formats. As Roger G. Kennedy, the director of the Museum of American History at the Smithsonian, told Barbara Gamarekian for the *New York Times* (June 17, 1988), "Bernice is a real scholar, a hell of a performer, and a potent force here in a lot of ways. We listen to her—she discovers new truths for us all. Her special strength is the way she ties music to the social, historical, and political context of American cultural traditions." In fact, Reagon herself feels that she is on a mission. "I don't accept the world the way it works," she explained to Mary H. J. Farrell and Rochelle Jones for *People* (December 12, 1994). "I take on the world. I want to make the world the way it should be." As her daughter, Toshi, observed to Richard Harrington for the *Washington Post* (June 25, 1987), "She sometimes gets tired *during* her mission, but I don't think she ever gets tired *of* her mission."

Reagon learned early on in life about hard work. Her parents each undertook more than one job while Reagon, who was born Bernice Johnson in Georgia on October 4, 1942, was growing up. Her mother, Beatrice, worked as a housekeeper and toiled in the cotton fields on her days off; her father, Jessie Johnson, was a carpenter and a Baptist minister. Her parents fostered her interests in activism and song. Her father was involved in voter registration drives as early as 1945, and her mother, although not involved in an organized effort, instilled the true meaning of activism in Bernice. "She could always see that we could operate in a different world with more opportunities," Bernice Reagon told Harrington. "She mortgaged her life to make sure we had a chance to do that. More than anybody, I take my sense of what a black woman is from her."

As a preacher's daughter, Reagon was introduced to music in church. "For the first 11 years, our church had no piano," she told Audreen Buffalo for *Ms.* (March/April 1993), "and I'm still an a cappella singer. I grew up singing in the 19th-century congregational tradition—a style that can be traced to Africa. I learned three major repertoires in this style: spirituals, hymns, and children's secular play songs." She had to rely on her siblings to educate her about other styles of music. "My parents called the blues 'reals,'" she explained to Jon Pareles for the *New York Times* (April 18, 1986). "You weren't supposed to sing reals. But my brother would take the radio out of my parents' room and listen to the blues station, and since the boys' room was next to the girls' room, I'd hear them in my sleep. When I got old enough to buy records, the first one was by Howlin' Wolf—he's my favorite singer in the universe."

In 1959 Reagon entered Albany State College, in her hometown of Albany, Georgia, to study Italian arias and German lieder as a contralto soloist, but her extracurricular activities put her at odds with the university administration. Fearing an onslaught of campus protests, in December 1961 school officials expelled those students, including Reagon, who were taking part in the growing civil-rights movement. "On my first march in Albany, from the college, it was all students," Reagon recalled for Michael Kernan. "By the third march—when I was arrested—there were as many adults as students. The action became broader, and the songs, too. We would do our swinging freedom songs, but we'd also do old 19th-century lined hymns. When the SNCC people came to town they found that the Albany sound was different. They'd heard students sing, but they had never heard black people of all ages sing at that power level." In 1962 Reagon joined with three other SNCC members—Cordell Hull Reagon (to whom she was briefly married), Charles Nebbett, and Rutha Mae Harris—to form the SNCC Freedom Singers. Traveling the country to raise awareness and money, the group was "the movement's singing newspaper," as Audreen Buffalo described it, "reporting and defining the actions and issues from the civil rights war zones where they were frequently arrested." Only halfway through her junior year at the time of her expulsion, Reagon had transferred to Spelman College, in Atlanta, in 1962, to continue her course of classical music studies, but she completed only one semester before she dropped out to participate in the movement full-time.

The original members of the Freedom Singers disbanded in 1963, but Reagon kept herself busy organizing folk festivals and collecting and performing material drawn from African-American culture. At around the same time that Reagon divorced her husband, in the late 1960s, she grew disenchanted with the interracial folk-music circles. "I was trying to put my music in a sociopolitical context," she told Hollie I. West of the *Washington Post* (June 8, 1975). "But many white singers didn't want to address with any level of consistency the racism in this country. They focused on their own problems, like coal mining. Some of them would stop their music with the coal mining strikes of the '40s. I'd get so mad and say to them, 'Can't you get any closer to the '60s than that?'" As an alternative outlet for her singing, she organized the Harambee Singers, an all-female quartet with a social-activist agenda. "[The Harambee Singers] were afraid of tape recorders," Reagon told Hollie I. West. "We saw ourselves as political activists. Everything had to be political. If somebody talked about love to us we'd think our politics was slipping." At around the time that the Harambee Singers were formed, Reagon tried to interest the Atlanta school board in a social-studies program for teaching oral traditions, but she was turned down. "I realized I could sing, I could produce festivals, I could work real well with audiences," she told Harrington, "but the minute I met the establishment structure, I would be turned around. . . . So I went back to school, because I felt that wherever black people are, this material [oral history] should be, and that the oral process should be allowed right along with the written process." Returning to Spelman College, this time to the history department, Reagon earned her bachelor's degree in 1970. Starting in June 1970 and continuing into the following year, with the aid of a grant provided by the Southern Education Foundation, she developed a model to test the usefulness of oral traditions in public-school social-studies curricula.

Reagon moved to Washington, D.C., in the early 1970s to begin studies for her doctoral degree in history at Howard University. Because the school did not have a program in oral history, she completed a number of interdisciplinary independent studies while simultaneously pursuing passions outside academia. Since the late 1960s Reagon had been working as a field researcher for the Smithsonian Institution on a consultant basis. In 1972 she agreed to head what she christened the African Diaspora program, a research group formed to showcase African-American culture at the Smithsonian Institution Bicentennial Festival of American Folklife, which focused on various aspects of American culture. "Old Ways in the New World," one of the central themes of that festival, allowed Reagon to send scholars of black culture to Africa, the Caribbean, and South America and then to present to the public the antecedent cultural practices—such as cooking and music—of the Old World alongside the descendant practices of the New World. The program was the first in the Smithsonian's history to attempt to present African-American culture, and it met a lot of resistance and criticism from those who felt it couldn't be done or shouldn't be done in the way in which Reagon had envisioned it. "One of the most wonderful things that happened to me as a scholar," Reagon told Marvette Pérez for the *Radical History Review* (Spring 1997, on-line), "was that one of the folklorists who had said about our festival program for the bicentennial, 'you can't do this concept and apply it to African Americans,' came to the program and said, 'I opposed this, but I was wrong, this absolutely worked.' That was really, really great. But others would bring people there to look at what we were doing to actually say it was bad so that they could justify eliminating it." Reagon, who had hired only African-American scholars, was herself accused of being racist. Although at the time she didn't respond to that charge, she later admitted to Marvette Pérez that the accusations were true: "Blacks who were coming up in university departments of folklore and ethnomusicology were not getting any of the grants to do field research. Therefore their cv's never looked right. And there were whites who were doing their field research and their dissertation research in Africa, all over the Caribbean, but Blacks in those same depart-

ments had difficulty securing support to do research outside of the United States. So as a result of our program several African American scholars were hired to conduct field research in these regions."

As if her work with the Smithsonian were not enough to keep her busy, Reagon assumed two more posts in 1972, spending the summer as a visiting lecturer in black American music at Ithaca College, in Ithaca, New York, and serving as vocal director at the D.C. Black Repertory Theater Company. In the latter position she held a singing workshop that brought together four men and four women, but the group dissolved after a couple of months. At the urging of one woman, Reagon agreed to organize another workshop. Only four women showed up. "I was disappointed," she admitted to Richard Harrington, "but I was fairly dictatorial, so I started singing and it just fell in place and it was *tight*. And we got through the first song and we looked at each other and went 'Yeah!' We went song after song after song and everything was *right*." The first song they sang was "Sweet Honey in the Rock," a song from Reagon's youth. "When I asked my father about its meaning," she told Audreen Buffalo, "he said it was a parable that referred to a land where, when rocks were cracked, honey would flow from them." Feeling that the image was an appropriate symbol of African-American womanhood, Reagon dubbed the new ensemble Sweet Honey in the Rock.

Over its more than 25-year history, Sweet Honey has comprised 22 members, though never more than five singers at a time; in 1980 a sign-language artist, Shirley Childress Johnson, was added. The group's sound is built on complex five-part harmony; the styles of doo-wop, gospel, soul, jazz, blues, folk, rap, and traditional African and Caribbean music are coupled with socially relevant subject matter. From the beginning Sweet Honey in the Rock proved very popular with audiences, even though its members—who hold down other jobs during the workweek—perform only on weekends. "The group saved my life and it made it possible for me to work at the Smithsonian," Reagon explained to Marvette Pérez. "People would say to the women in Sweet Honey: 'Why aren't you singers full-time?' And we would say, 'Why should we be? Why should we choose between areas of work that we love to do, that combined makes us whole.'"

From February 1973 to May of the following year, Reagon was a teaching fellow in the School of Music at Howard University. In 1974 she also officially joined the staff of the Smithsonian full-time, as the director of the African Diaspora Program in the Division of Performing Arts. That year, and again the next year, she traveled to Africa to do field research for the program. In 1975, after completing her dissertation—entitled "Songs of the Civil Rights Movement, 1955–1965: A Study in Culture History"—she received her Ph.D. and began working as a lecturer in the history department at the University of the District of Columbia. At a folk festival hosted by the University of Chicago that year, Sweet Honey in the Rock was offered a recording deal with Flying Fish Records after a representative of the company heard them perform. Their first album, *Sweet Honey in the Rock*, was released in 1976, the same year that Reagon became the director of the Program in African American Culture (PAAC), a permanent program that grew out of the African Diaspora project. She also worked that summer as a visiting scholar in black culture and history at the American Studies Summer Institute at Skidmore College. In 1977 Reagon finished her stints as the vocal director at the D.C. Black Repertory Theater Company and lecturer at the University of the District of Columbia. That spring, she was a visiting fellow in black American culture at the University of California at Santa Cruz, and in the summer of 1980, she was a visiting fellow in the women's studies program at Portland State University.

In 1982 the PAAC was moved to the Public Programs division of the National Museum of American History, after the Smithsonian's Division of the Performing Arts was dismantled. Reagon designed the infrastructure of the PAAC and did not immediately notice the difference between her program and others in Public Programs. Instead of acting as a producer—hiring writers and singers to present material—she and her staff conducted the research and found a way to present it to the public themselves. Part of her responsibilities included fighting to ensure that her program received every penny of the $50,000 budget allotted by Congress. "And that was the beginning of my moving in the museum in a way in which nobody was supposed to move," she told Marvette Pérez.

In 1988 Sweet Honey in the Rock won the Grammy Award for best traditional folk recording for its version of Leadbelly's "Grey Goose." Reagon decided to make a transition in her museum career that same year, leaving behind the directorship of the PAAC to become a curator in the Division of Community Life, a position that allowed her more time for research. Even though she had been studying black culture and oral traditions at the Smithsonian for almost 15 years by that point, she still met with constraints. "When I first came into the Division of Community Life as a curator," she told Marvette Pérez, "I remember the collections manager saying to me: 'Here, we are interested in collecting three-dimensional objects,' and I thought, oh, here I go again. Why can't I just go someplace and just do what everybody else is doing? I remember when I asked for a promotion. They have a peer review committee, and I talked to the chairman of the committee, and he said, 'This is interesting, I wonder how people are going to look at this.' And the whole issue was that my work did not look like anything they were used to evaluating: it did not fit the usual curatorial categories." In 1989 she received a grant from the MacArthur Foundation—

commonly called the "genius" grant—which she used in part to further her research for the museum.

In 1991 Reagon was profiled in a documentary entitled *The Songs Are Free: Bernice Johnson Reagon with Bill Moyers*. She also received a Candace Award for outstanding achievement from the National Coalition of 100 Black Women, a nonprofit organization that encourages leadership, development, and employment opportunities for black women.

In 1993 Reagon was appointed distinguished professor of history at American University, and in January 1994 she became a curator emerita at the Smithsonian. In the same month, portions of the project she had worked on at the Smithsonian for the previous 10 years, *Wade in the Water: African American Sacred Music Traditions*, began airing on the radio. Consisting of 26 one-hour segments and supplemental educational materials, *Wade in the Water* traces the development of sacred music and its reciprocal impact on black history and culture. The program, produced conjointly by the Smithsonian and National Public Radio and funded in part by a portion of Reagon's MacArthur grant, won a Peabody Award for significant and meritorious achievement in broadcasting.

The awards continued to come Reagon's way. In 1995 the National Endowment for the Humanities awarded her the Charles Frankel Prize for outstanding contribution to public understanding of the humanities, for which she was honored at the White House. In 1996 she won the Isadora Duncan Award for her score to *Rock*, a ballet directed by Alonzo King for the LINES Contemporary Ballet Company. In that same year she also completed the traveling exhibition for *Wade in the Water*, which was set to tour in 16 U.S. cities over a period of four years.

In addition to her work in theater, film, and video, Reagon has written articles for numerous journals and anthologies and has made solo recordings. During her 1997 interview with Marvette Pérez, she said, "I've had young people ask me how was I able to do so much. And I suggest that I'm not a good model, it really was over-extension. It's not a normal life to do what I did. But people who are oppressed cannot live a 'normal' life. Baby, you try to live a normal life if you're oppressed, you will never be free. . . . I think you have to over-extend yourself."

On May 30, 1996, recognizing that she could not keep up the frenetic pace required for all her activities, Reagon resigned as the sole artistic director of Sweet Honey. She agreed, however, to become one of the six members of the new artistic directorship. Two years later, in 1998, Sweet Honey celebrated its 25th anniversary with the release of its album *. . . twenty-five . . .*. On the same day Reagon also released *Africans in America*—a soundtrack that she had produced, compiled, and composed for a public-television documentary of the same name. She is currently collaborating with Souleymane

Koly on an opera to premiere in Abidjan, Ivory Coast, in 2001.

Although Reagon has not slowed her pace in recent years, she has learned to prioritize better. "As I've gotten older," she told Geoffrey Himes for the *Washington Post* (November 20, 1998), "I've felt it was important to reduce the amount of work I'm doing. I've had a very productive and intense life, but as I've gotten older, I had to find ways to keep doing this work and still keep myself going. And I've done it. I've found ways to do the work I love to do—whether it's singing or composing or doing research or teaching or working on radio and TV series—without carrying so much of the weight of the infrastructure."

Reagon's son, Kwan, is a cook; her daughter, Toshi, is a musician. — K.S.

Suggested Reading: *Dallas Morning News* C p2+ May 17, 1997, with photos; *Ms.* p24 Mar./Apr. 1993, with photo; *New York Times* B p6 June 17, 1988, with photo; *People* p149+ Dec. 12, 1994, with photos; *Radical History Review* (on-line) Spring 1997; *Smithsonian* p32+ Feb. 1999, with photos; *Washington Post* L p1+ June 8, 1975, with photo, B p1+ June 25, 1987, with photo

Selected Books: *Compositions One: The Original Compositions and Arrangements of Bernice Johnson Reagon*, 1986; *We'll Understand It Better By and By: African American Pioneering Gospel Composers*, 1992; *We Who Believe in Freedom: Sweet Honey In The Rock . . . Still on the Journey*, 1993

Selected Television Documentaries: *Eyes on the Prize*, 1986; *We Shall Overcome*, 1989

Selected Radio Series: *Wade in the Water: African American Sacred Music Traditions*

Selected Recordings: *Songs of the South*, 1964; *Give Your Hands to Struggle*, 1977, re-released in 1997; *River of Life*, 1986; with The Freedom Singers—*We Shall Overcome*, 1963; with Sweet Honey In The Rock—*Sweet Honey in the Rock*, 1976; *Live at Carnegie Hall*, 1988; *We All . . . Everyone of Us*, 1989; *Still on the Journey*, 1993; *. . . twenty-five . . .*, 1998

Reinhard, Johan

(RINE-hard, YO-han)

1943– High-altitude archaeologist; anthropologist; mountain climber. Address: c/o Field Museum of Natural History, 1200 S. Lake Shore Dr., Chicago, IL 60605; c/o Mountain Institute, Main and Dogwood Sts., Franklin, WV 26087

"I don't know if you've seen that mummy," President Bill Clinton said at a political fund-raiser in Connecticut in May 1996, as quoted by Roxanne Roberts in the *Washington Post* (May 24, 1996). "But, you know, if I were a single man, I might ask that mummy out. That's a good-looking mummy. That mummy looks better than I do on my worst days. . . . You need to go see her." The object of the president's admiration was the frozen, 500-year-old sacrificial remains of an Incan girl—christened "Juanita, the Ice Maiden"—which the anthropologist Johan Reinhard dug up near the 20,700-foot summit of the Peruvian volcano Mount Ampato. An explorer, mountaineer, archaeologist, and anthropologist, Reinhard is a pioneer in the anthropological subspecialties known as sacred geography and high-altitude archaeology, which is conducted at least 17,000 feet above sea level. He has built his career by unraveling some of the mysteries of the Incan civilization, which disappeared from South America almost half a millennium ago.

Gregarious and self-reliant, Reinhard was long viewed by his colleagues as something of a maverick. Since unearthing Juanita, in September 1995,

Courtesy of Mountain Institute

he has enjoyed celebrity status rarely accorded anthropologists or archaeologists. *Time* magazine rated Juanita one of the 10 most important scientific discoveries of 1995, and record crowds came to view Juanita when she was displayed in Washington, D.C., in 1996. Reinhard has since continued his work as an expert on the cultures of South American mountain tribes. In April 1999 he unearthed the well-preserved remains of three Incan child sacrifices at the peak of Argentina's Mount Llullaillaco, a discovery that, by all accounts, will prove to be even more significant than that of Juanita.

The son of a detective, Johan Reinhard was born in Joliet, Illinois, in 1943. As a boy, he told Roxanne Roberts, he read "every Hardy Boys book I could get my hands on," referring to the popular series about the amateur teenage sleuths Frank and Joe Hardy. At the age of 16, he ran away from home to join a railroad crew in Kansas. That motley group of workers, most of whom were southerners, fascinated Reinhard. "What astonished me was that there were people in my own country who had a whole different culture," he recalled to Roberts. His fascination with people and cultures led him to major in anthropology at the University of Arizona, where he earned a bachelor's degree. He later completed a Ph.D. in cultural anthropology at the University of Vienna, in Austria.

Reinhard's interest in mountaineering and high-altitude climbing dates to the early 1970s, and he gradually incorporated those activities into his work in his academic field. He spent the bulk of his early career in Nepal, researching shamanism and witchcraft for his doctoral dissertation and also directing a training program for the Peace Corps. He was a member of the successful 1976 American expedition that climbed the 29,028-foot Mount Everest, on the border between Nepal and Tibet in the Himalayas. Reinhard recognized that the Buddhists and Hindus from the Himalayan region shared a belief in the sacredness of the mountains. "To these people the Himalayas were not merely the homes of the gods, they *were* the gods, capable of killing by avalanche, rockfall, lightning, blizzard and wind, or blessing with rain-filled clouds, pouring life into rivers and lakes," he was quoted as saying in the *Geographical Magazine* (January 1998). By the 1980s Reinhard had begun working in the Andes mountains, which run from Panama to the southern tip of South America. His earlier observation of shared beliefs among disparate religions and cultures became the linchpin for his work relating to the Incan civilization.

For about a quarter-century, Reinhard toiled in relative obscurity. Like others among the few archaeologists who work without an affiliation with any major institution, he spent a lot of his time trying to secure grants to fund his projects. It was during a rare moment of leisure in 1995 that he happened on the find that attracted so much attention. Recent eruptions of long-dormant volcanoes in the Peruvian Andes had caused shifts in layers of ice and deposited black ash on perpetually snow-covered Mount Ampato, which stands about 60 miles from the city of Arequipa in southern Peru. Thanks to the heat of the ash, the snow had melted. "The Incas would not have been able to build on permanently snowcapped peaks, so I never paid attention to Mount Ampato before," Reinhard said to Shanti Menon for *Discover* (January 1996). "But I

had some free time, and I thought I'd take a look at the effects of the eruptions." On September 8, 1995 Reinhard and his climbing partner, Miguel Zarate, a Peruvian mountaineer, stumbled upon a colorful ceremonial doll frozen in the ice about 200 feet shy of Ampato's summit. Nearby lay Juanita. Exposure to the air had dried the skin of her face and parts of her arms, and Reinhard and Zarate feared that her body would be badly damaged. As it turned out, most of the rest of her remains were encased in permafrost—a permanently frozen layer of ice and rock—so that her internal organs were preserved in a frozen state rather than freeze-dried.

As Reinhard gazed at Juanita, he felt exhilarated, because he knew that she was the first frozen female Inca to be found intact. He also knew that he was, in his words, "in for a hell of a night," because, not having anticipated making such an extraordinary discovery, he did not have proper equipment with him. "The worst part was getting [the body] out of the crater," he told Shanti Menon. "It was really icy and full of gravel. The thing weighed about 85 pounds, and it was getting late—it was pretty unpleasant. And then I had to go down a 45-degree incline in the dark." It took Reinhard and Zarate two days to descend the mountain. Then they took the mummy on a seven-hour bus ride to the research center at Catholic University in Arequipa, worrying the whole time that the body might thaw and decompose. Later examination revealed that the mummy's body was wrapped in an elaborate and finely woven cloth made from the wool of alpacas, animals that are native to Peru, and on its head rested a colorful and ornate headdress. On a stone platform next to the girl's remains Reinhard found such items as maize and silver and gold statuettes between two and a half and six and a half inches long.

In the late 1400s and early 1500s, the Incas ruled the most powerful empire in South America—an area that encompassed much of what is now Peru, Ecuador, Bolivia, Chile, and Argentina. In the century following the Spanish conquest, which began with the arrival of Francisco Pizarro in 1532, the Incas all but disappeared, driven away or killed by Spaniards in search of gold and decimated by diseases the Europeans introduced to South America. Among the things known about the Incas is that they were highly skilled mathematicians and builders and kept records by tying knots in cords of different colors and lengths—a system that has yet to be deciphered. It is also known that the Incas performed human sacrifice—a highly controversial and little-understood practice—much less often than the Mayan, Aztec, and Toltec peoples who lived in the same regions.

Apparently the Incas preferred to use animals in their rituals, resorting to human sacrifice only when they believed an extra tribute was necessary to honor or appease their deities. "One reason the sacrifice [of Juanita] was done might have been that crops and herds were suffering," Reinhard said to Shanti Menon. "Because of the difficulty of getting to the summit [of Mount Ampati], I'd say the main reason for the sacrifice had to do with the mountain, not, say, the sun, because they could have done that lower down." The Incas revered the mountains as sources of water and feared them as sources of tremendous destructive forces, and they considered being chosen for sacrifice to the gods a great honor for the family of the person selected. "They wanted young—boy or girl—because they're more pure," Reinhard told Roxanne Roberts. The act of sacrifice, he added, brought "honor to the community." Examinations of Juanita's body revealed that the Ice Maiden was killed by a sharp blow just above her right eye.

Johan Reinhard's discovery of Juanita, which many have called a "mine of biological and anthropological information," has advanced anthropologists' and archaeologists' understanding of the Incas' culture. It has also eased Reinhard's struggle to secure grant money and other funding. The mummy was put on display in 1996 at the National Geographic Society's Explorers Hall in Washington, D.C., where record numbers of visitors came to view her. "What makes her attractive is the same thing that draws people to ancient Egyptian mummies, to the relics of saints, to bodies that have been dug up from bogs, to the bones of Holocaust victims, and to the embalmed corpse of Lenin, which has outlasted Soviet communism," Sarah Boxer posited in the New York Times (October 29, 1995). "Dead bodies are magnetic not as examples of extinct cultures, proofs of ritual sacrifice, evidence of human atrocities or emblems of political movements but as fleshly humans who chewed with these very teeth, walked on these very legs, and furrowed these very brows."

The publicity surrounding Juanita and Reinhard's archaeological excavations in the Andes also attracted the attention of looters, and some of Reinhard's research sites were picked clean after the initial dig. In addition, Reinhard has received some bothersome calls. One company approached him in the vain hope that, if the mummy's ovaries had been frozen intact, they would be permitted to harvest some of the eggs for insemination with sperm from 20th-century donors.

In April 1999, during an expedition sponsored by the National Geographic Society, Reinhard found three mummified bodies at the 22,057-foot summit of Mount Llullaillaco, in the Andes on the Argentine-Chilean border. The remains were those of youngsters, ranging in age from about eight to about 15, who had been sacrificed and buried in much the way that Juanita had. Scientists have confirmed that they, too, died approximately 500 years ago. What makes Reinhard's latest find potentially so significant is the mummies' remarkable state of preservation. Buried under ice and scree atop a mountain more than 22,000 feet high, the bodies were protected from exposure to an even greater degree than Juanita. Two of the bodies looked as if they had died merely days before; the third showed evidence of lightning damage. "The

preservation of the mummies is just fantastic," Reinhard told John Noble Wilford for the New York Times (April 7, 1999). "It's eerie looking at the arms. You can still see the light hair on their arms." Scientists plan to conduct medical examinations of the bodies in search of evidence of infections and diet and to determine genetic makeup. If the mummies' DNA has remained intact in their frozen blood, it will theoretically be possible to trace their lineage to living South Americans. Such information would offer scientists clues to the fate of the Incas following the collapse of their empire.

Reinhard has climbed mountains of at least 17,000 feet more than 100 times, and according to the American Alpine Club, he currently holds the record for most ascents of peaks at least 6,000 meters (19,680 feet) high. He has also done underwater research: he has examined Roman shipwrecks in the Mediterranean Sea; explored an early Etruscan village submerged in an Italian lake; conducted the first archaeological research in Lake Titicaca, the largest body of water in the Andes and considered by the region's inhabitants to be the most sacred; and carried out the first archeological research at a neolithic lake site in Austria. In 1987 Reinhard won the Rolex Award for Enterprise, and in 1998 he became the first Rolex laureate to serve on the selection committee for that honor. Currently, he is a senior research fellow at the Mountain Institute, in Franklin, West Virginia, a scientific and educational organization that, according to its home page on the World Wide Web, is dedicated to "preserving mountain environments and advancing mountain cultures throughout the world." Reinhard is also a research associate at the Field Museum of Natural History, in Chicago, Illinois, and an honorary professor at Catholic University in Arequipa. He has appeared as a guest lecturer on many cruises. — T.J.F.

Suggested Reading: Discover p22+ Jan. 1998; Geographical Magazine p78+ Jan. 1998; New York Times A p1+ Apr. 7, 1999; Washington Post D p1+ May 24, 1996

Rich, Frank

June 2, 1949– Columnist for the New York Times. Address: c/o New York Times, 229 W. 43d St., New York, NY 10036-3913

"The Butcher of Broadway": that is what many people called Frank Rich when, from 1980 to 1993, he served as the chief drama critic for the New York Times. Widely condemned as a hack with inordinate power to influence the fates of productions, he angered many theater insiders and, as a target of their wrath, was said to have sparked a flowering of the art of criticizing the critic. At the same time, he was widely praised as one of the best writers in

Courtesy of the *New York Times*

Frank Rich

the area of theater criticism. Whether attacked or commended, Rich fulfilled his duties with relish. In "Exit the Critic," which was published in the *New York Times Magazine* (February 13, 1994) after he left the newspaper's drama desk, he wrote, "Even the occasional contretemps were fun. . . . Critics may not be, as is generally presumed, frustrated actors or playwrights, but few of us mind playing our assigned role in the timeless sideshows of the rialto." In January 1994 he began writing a column, "Journal," for the op-ed page of the *Times*, turning his analytical eye from Broadway to the broader theaters of American politics and culture. His last twice-weekly, 700-word "Journal" piece appeared on February 13, 1999.

During a four-month leave of absence from the *Times*, which began in February 1999, Rich worked toward completing a memoir for Random House. Upon his return to the newspaper, in June, he became the first *Times* employee to hold the dual title of op-ed columnist and senior writer for the *New York Times Magazine*. In an indication of his growing prominence within the *Times*'s hierarchy, his columns are now twice as long as they were before—a change that Rich requested, because he is eager "to explore a variety of subjects at greater depth," as a New York Times Co. press release, dated February 1, 1999, put it. The expanded column runs on the op-ed page on alternate Saturdays. In addition, full-length commentaries and articles by Rich are published regularly in the *New York Times Magazine*.

Frank Hart Rich was born in Washington, D.C., on June 2, 1949. His father, Frank Hart Rich Sr., was a businessman; his mother, Helene Bernice (Aaronson) Fisher, was an educational consultant.

Rich has traced his first theater experience to his attendance at a production of the musical *The Pajama Game* at the National Theatre, when he was seven or so. About two years later, his parents divorced. His mother, sensitive to the disruptive effect of the divorce on young Frank and knowing that the theater served as a means of escape for him, would take him to New York City to see Broadway shows. When he was 10, she gave him his first "adult" book, the playwright Moss Hart's memoir, *Act One* (1959). Rich's mother died in 1991, from injuries sustained in an automobile accident.

Early on, Rich also liked journalism. As a youngster he produced his own newspaper, presciently calling it the *Times* and writing it by hand. During his teens he attended a camp, located in the Berkshire Mountains in Massachusetts, that focused on theater and music. At Indian Hill, as the camp was called, he reviewed productions for camp publications and thus combined his interests in journalism and theater for the first time.

In 1967 Rich entered Harvard University, in Cambridge, Massachusetts, where he studied American history and literature. He spent most of his time there working on the *Harvard Crimson*, the campus daily. In his junior year, he was elected editorial chair of the paper. He continued to write theater criticism for the *Crimson*, and in addition, at the suggestion of his peers, branched out into film criticism. As an undergraduate he was an honorary Harvard College scholar, won election to Phi Beta Kappa, and earned a Henry Russell Shaw traveling fellowship. He received an A.B. degree from Harvard, magna cum laude, in 1971.

In 1972, along with some of his *Crimson* friends, Rich co-founded a weekly newspaper in Virginia called the *Richmond Mercury*, and he became its editor. During the next year he moved to New York City, to accept a job as a film critic for *New Times*. He remained with *New Times* until 1975 (the magazine later folded), when he began a two-year stint as a film critic for the *New York Post*. He was only 27 or 28 when, in 1977, he joined the staff of *Time* magazine as a television and film critic, and he was only 30 when, in March 1980, the *New York Times* recruited him. In his collection *Hot Seat: Theater Criticism for The New York Times* (1998), Rich wrote that he thought he would be embarking on "a long apprenticeship as sort of a floating theater, movie, and TV critic" for the *Times*. But his apprenticeship ended before Rich had even completed his first piece: Walter Kerr, who was then the paper's chief drama critic, fell ill, and Arthur Gelb, the editor who had hired Rich, assigned Rich to cover theater full-time. In September 1980 the *Times* named Rich chief drama critic.

Rich's appointment was greeted with a great deal of suspicion within the theater community, largely because up until the *New York Times* had hired him, his professional experience had consisted of criticism of film—a medium some people consider inferior to theater. Their misgivings soon deepened, because, shortly after Rich took over at the *Times*, Broadway began to suffer the first of a series of poor seasons. Speculation had it that his reviews, which were distinguished by their sarcasm, were killing productions. Suspicion soon turned to fear. A brief survey of articles written about Rich between 1980 and 1993, when he occupied what one writer called "the most powerful post in cultural journalism," reveals that with few exceptions, people with a stake in the theater business agreed to comment on Rich only on condition of anonymity. Robert Brustein, the artistic director of the American Repertory Theatre at Harvard, observed in his theater column for the *New Republic* (March 16, 1992) that the same was true of people in the television industry. Commenting on a profile of Rich that was broadcast on the TV newsmagazine *60 Minutes* in 1991, Brustein wrote, "Only a handful of [Rich's] victims were sufficiently unintimidated to speak on record, though scores more were willing to testify off-camera."

Not surprisingly, the presence of stars and the receipt of major awards can significantly affect the fortunes of plays and musicals. But it may seem puzzling that Rich, who provided neither talent nor financial backing to theatrical productions and bestowed no prizes on them, held so much sway on Broadway. Part of the explanation for his dominance lies in the atypical relationship that has existed between Broadway and the *New York Times* since the years immediately following World War II. During the late 1940s and early 1950s, the *Times* theater critic Brooks Atkinson muscled his way to the head of the theater critics' class. Highly suggestive of the paper's status on Broadway is the fact that Atkinson and Walter Kerr are the only drama critics who have theaters named after them.

Another explanation for the power wielded by the *Times*'s critics on Broadway is linked to the state of the newspaper industry in the city. Productions mounted at another world-famous location—the West End, London's theater district—are generally covered by critics from a dozen newspapers. In New York, by contrast, where decades of attrition in the newspaper industry have led to the demise of many dailies, the *Times* is sometimes the only newspaper to review a show. Since the *Times* now boasts an international readership that looks to New York City as a center of culture as well as commerce, and since Broadway increasingly depends upon tourism as a source of theatergoers, the *Times*'s clout as a major voice in cultural reportage has also increased.

Yet another reason for Rich's power stemmed from his skill with words. In its December 1985 issue, *Esquire* declared that Rich "may be the best prose stylist the *Times* has ever assigned to the job." Chip Brown, writing in *GQ* (June 1990), noted, "Rich's sentences tumble smartly and always land on their feet." Robert Brustein, a longtime critic of Rich, charged that Rich's "literary competence has been responsible for exacerbating the problem [of the *Times*'s influence on Broadway],

since it has helped to enhance his position with his editors and his readers." "I have often thought of Rich as a competent critic in the wrong place," Brustein wrote. "Without the clout of the *Times*, he might have been a welcome, even admired, presence. As any critic would be in the powerful chair he now occupies, however, he is something of a menace." In *New York* (March 14, 1994), Mimi Kramer charged that Rich's style "implicitly rejected the voice or mask of the gentleman critic" in favor of "the mask of portentous authority." She explained that the former offers an opinion yet implicitly positions it as one among many; the latter leaves no room for discussion and carries "an air of infallibility."

One of the most outraged, and well publicized, responses to a review by Rich came from the playwright David Hare, after the New York premiere of Hare's drama *The Secret Rapture*, in 1989. Ten months earlier, Rich had written approvingly of a London production of Hare's play, directed by Howard Davies. Perhaps because he attended the New York production with raised expectations, he came down hard on it. "Mr. Hare, serving as his play's own director for its Broadway premiere at the Barrymore, is his own worst enemy," he wrote, as quoted in *Hot Seat*. "The passion and wit that reside in his script—and that are essential to engage an audience and lead it to his ideas—are left unrealized in his production. . . . The textual tinkering since London may be minor, but the wholesale changes of casting and design have flattened the play's subtleties into coarse agitprop and tossed its overall intentions into confusion. It's a measure of how poorly *The Secret Rapture* has been mounted here that a designer as gifted as Santo Loquasto has provided a dingy black-and-tan set that makes England, as much a character in the play as its people, indistinguishable from, say, metropolitan Cleveland."

Hare replied in a letter to various periodicals (he almost immediately ordered that it not be published). In the letter, Hare charged that underlying Rich's harsh words was a bitterness toward artists. Speaking to Richard Hummler for *Variety* (November 15, 1989), in an article topped by what Rich has called a "classic headline" ("Ruffled Hare Airs Rich Bitch"), Hare said, "I think Rich is totally irresponsible in the use of his power. He started out as a fresh and interesting new critic, but he seems to have gotten more bitter and to have less and less regard for the impact of what he writes." (The *New Yorker* and other popular publications also panned *The Secret Rapture*, and the play closed after only five weeks.)

Rich's review of the all-black, 1990 mounting of the musical *Oh, Kay* triggered another widely publicized incident. The musical was produced by David Merrick, the most prolific producer in Broadway history and winner of 12 Tony Awards, whose hits include *Hello, Dolly!* and *Gypsy*. Whereas most other reviewers found things to like about *Oh, Kay*, Rich trashed it. "This loose adaptation of the

Gershwins' 1926 musical is a chintzy, innocuous slab of stock that is likely to leave more than a few theatergoers shrugging their shoulders and asking, 'Didn't I doze through that a couple of summers ago in a barn?'" he wrote in his critique, which is included in *Hot Seat*. He concluded by calling the musical a "pallid entertainment to which [Merrick] has unaccountably lent his name."

Outraged, Merrick accused Rich of allowing himself to be swayed by the *New York Times* reporter Alexandra "Alex" Witchel, who had been dating Rich and had attended the performance with him. Merrick claimed in a letter to the *Times*'s publisher, Arthur Ochs Sulzberger Jr., that he had witnessed Witchel, who at that time reported theater news for the *Times*, nudging and whispering to Rich throughout the performance. Merrick also paid for a full-page advertisement in the *Times*, headlined "At last, people are holding hands in the theater again!"; an image of a heart contained quotes from Rich and Witchel, and Merrick's signature appeared above the line, "To Frank and Alex, all my love." The ad ran in one edition, and then the newspaper's management pulled it. Merrick's charges of collusion between the two reporters resurfaced in theater circles after Rich and Witchel married, on June 9, 1991.

Rich often downplayed his influence as the *Times*'s chief drama critic; as he put it in "Exit the Critic," "The power of the job was not so vast as the Butcher of Broadway jokes would have it." Early on in his tenure, he often refused to discuss the potential impact of his reviews on Broadway, contending that his obligation was to his readers and not to the theater. But eventually he acknowledged the weight that the *Times* carries. "If a review of mine could convince people to check out the work of an exciting new playwright, the *Times*'s influence seemed worthwhile," he wrote in "Exit the Critic." "If it had the opposite effect, who could take pleasure in that?" At the same time, he remained steadfast in upholding what he viewed as his responsibility to his readership. "Was the alternative to write waffling reviews, imploring readers to go to some well-meaning mediocrity for the good of the theater and those who worked in it?" If he were to do that, he argued, readers would come to distrust his evaluations, and he would consequently be doing a disservice to playwrights, producers, actors, and everyone else connected with productions he deemed praiseworthy.

Hot Seat offers, Rich estimated, "barely a quarter" of his writings as chief drama critic for the *Times*. Along with the more than 300 theatrical reviews and essays, Rich included italicized commentary on events surrounding certain productions. An appendix lists plays that he felt he had overrated or underrated, and, as evidence of the limitations of his clout, he noted the short Broadway runs of plays to which he had given rave reviews and the long runs of productions that he had panned. In his introduction, he noted that the vast majority of shows he had reviewed were neither smashes nor disasters but somewhere in between; often, he wrote, such productions "reveal the temper of the theater more accurately than do the relatively anomalous hits and bombs." Most of his reviews were written in the 1980s, a decade in which the theater world was ravaged by AIDS and that saw Broadway shift from, in his words, a "source for American theater" to a "showplace for theater that originated elsewhere." In the *New York Times Book Review* (December 6, 1998), Harlow Robinson praised *Hot Seat* as a "vibrant, eloquent, and often moving collection."

In his op-ed column "Journal," Rich greatly extended his journalistic horizons to include, among other topics, politics, the media, and other aspects of American culture. After January 1998 many of his articles addressed the scandal involving President Bill Clinton and the former White House intern Monica Lewinsky and, more recently, the impeachment of the President. He often criticized media coverage of those events. In his January 16, 1999 column, for example, Rich compared the approach of the mainstream media to the Clinton-Lewinsky sex scandal with that of Larry Flynt, the notorious publisher of *Hustler* magazine and a self-proclaimed seller of smut, who has been forthright about his interest in the scandal. "After a year in which the President repeatedly told us he didn't have sex with that woman, and his antagonists repeatedly told us that their case 'is not about sex,' and the media constantly lamented how horribly sad they were to be covering this sex-driven, albeit lucrative, story, Mr. Flynt's candor is downright refreshing," Rich declared. He concluded, "In the land of the pious hypocrite, the honest pornographer is king."

Rich's frequent "Journal" criticisms of the actions and agenda of far-right politicians and religious figures and groups angered many people. Some sent him mail attacking his Jewish heritage. "I don't take [hate mail] seriously," Rich told Howard Kurtz for the *Washington Post* (December 28, 1995). "It's crazy people, people writing in crayon." Some of Rich's targets professed not to take *him* seriously. "What Frank Rich doesn't understand is that the Christian Coalition can't be closed down with a bad review," the Christian Coalition spokesperson Mike Russell quipped to Kurtz.

Articles by Rich about culture and politics have appeared in such publications as the *New Republic*, the *Washington Monthly*, and *Esquire* as well as the *New York Times*. He is also the author of *The Theatre Art of Boris Aronson* (1987), about the work of the renowned Russian-Jewish scenic designer and painter. Co-written by Lisa Aronson, the designer's widow, the book was lavishly illustrated and earned excellent reviews.

Frank Rich has two teenage sons, Nat and Simon, from his marriage to Gail Winston, which ended in divorce. He and his second wife, Alex Witchel, live in New York City. Rich remains an avid theatergoer. "I can't imagine being a daily critic again—I enjoy having my nights back—but I can't imagine a life in which I didn't go to the theater constantly," he wrote in *Hot Seat*. "But these days I'm a little more selective in what I choose to see. Sometimes I even wait for the reviews." — T.J.F.

Suggested Reading: *Esquire* p86 Dec. 1985; *GQ* p172+ June 1990, with photos; *New Republic* p27+ Mar. 16, 1992; *New York* p46+ Mar. 14, 1994; *New York Times* A p17 Jan. 16, 1999; *New York Times Book Review* p44 Dec. 6, 1998; *Variety* p1+ Nov. 15, 1989, with photos; *Washington Post* C p1 Dec. 28, 1995, with photo; Rich, Frank. *Hot Seat: Theater Criticism for the New York Times, 1980–1993*, 1990; *Who's Who in America 1999*

Selected Books: *Hot Seat: Theater Criticism for the New York Times, 1980–1993*, 1998; with Lisa Aronson—*The Theatre Art of Boris Aronson*, 1987

Doug Pensinger/Allsport USA

Richmond, Mitch

June 30, 1965– Basketball player with the Washington Wizards. Address: c/o Washington Wizards, MCI Center, 601 F St. N.W., Washington, DC 20004

In his 11-year career, basketball player Mitch "Rock" Richmond has taken on the positive attributes of his nickname. One of the most consistently excellent players in basketball history, in 1996 Richmond joined a select group that includes Kareem Abdul-Jabbar, Rick Barry, Larry Bird, Wilt

Chamberlain, Michael Jordan, and Oscar Robinson, all players who averaged at least 21 points per game throughout each of their first seven professional seasons. In an interview with *Sports Illustrated* (December 4, 1995), veteran guard Doc Rivers summed up Richmond's impressive repertoire of skills: "Mitch can post you up, shoot the jump shot, put the ball on the floor and drive past you—and he plays defense. If you trap him he finds the open man. If you don't trap him, he scores. Pick your poison. He's a great unselfish player, and that's the worst kind."

In the few times he has occupied the spotlight, however, Richmond has performed impressively. In the vote for the 1995 National Basketball Association (NBA) All-Star Game, for example, Richmond did not place among the top-10 guards in fan balloting; he was selected to the Western Conference's team only by the coaches' vote. During the game he stunned the crowd by scoring 23 points in 22 minutes, making 10 out of 13 shots from the floor and hitting all of his three-point attempts in the West's decisive victory over the East. Although the All-Star Game typically showcases individual effort rather than team play, after winning the game's most-valuable-player (MVP) trophy, Richmond was quick to credit his teammates, a characteristic gesture that goes far in explaining his lack of stardom. "With about seven minutes left, the guys started saying, 'Go in there and wrap it up,'" he said following the game, as reported by the *Washington Post* (February 13, 1995). "Coach Westphal ran some plays for me, and the guys were setting me up. I found myself open a lot." Richmond was the first non-starter to be named MVP of an All-Star Game since Tiny Archibald won the award in 1981.

Despite such high praise, which others around the league have echoed, Richmond's public profile is lower than those of many lesser talents. That he has been called "the best basketball player you've never heard of" can be attributed to his unassuming style of play and off-court demeanor, which get lost in a game dominated by towering egos. As Phil Taylor described the six-foot five-inch, 225-pound guard in *Sports Illustrated* (December 4, 1995), "He is as consistent as a metronome and about as flashy." In addition, Richmond has suffered from a lack of exposure. To date, he has spent the bulk of his career playing for the Sacramento Kings, who, as a mediocre team in a small market, receive scant national attention; in 1998 he was traded to the similarly low-profile Washington Wizards. In August 1999 Richmond signed a four-year, $40 million contract with the Wizards, thus becoming the highest-paid shooting guard in the NBA.

Mitchell Richmond was born on June 30, 1965 in southern Florida. He was raised in Fort Lauderdale, where his circle of friends included the future National Football League (NFL) stars Michael Irvin, Benny and Brian Blades, and Brett Perriman. Richmond's association with Irvin, whose run-ins with the law during his pro-football career have been well publicized, might lead one to expect that Richmond had a wild youth. Actually, Richmond's mother, Ernell O'Neal, kept her son under tight rein. "I wouldn't let him sleep over at his friends' houses," she told Phil Taylor. "I wanted to know where he was at night." O'Neal was also a strict disciplinarian. During his senior year at Boyd Anderson High School, Richmond sprained his ankle and missed an algebra test, causing him to fail the course and leaving him short of the credits he needed to graduate. Frustrated, he announced that he was done with school, even though he knew he might lose his chance at a basketball scholarship. His mother refused to accept his decision and ordered Richmond to attend a summer session, thus enabling him to graduate.

Richmond was not heavily recruited as a high-school player. After graduation he attended Moberly Area Community College in Moberly, Missouri, where he played two seasons of basketball for the Greyhounds. Despite intense homesickness, he was able to focus his abilities, scoring an average of more than 13 points per game and leading Moberly to a two-year win–loss record of 69–9. Dana Altman, the Greyhounds' coach, improved Richmond's game by correcting his awkward shooting form and changing his position from forward to guard. In 1986 Richmond transferred to Kansas State, in Manhattan, Kansas, where as a senior he averaged 22.6 points per game and was named to the second team All-America. In the spring of 1988, Richmond graduated from Kansas State with a degree in social sciences. That summer he traveled to Seoul, South Korea, as part of the United States Olympic basketball team, which came home with a bronze medal.

In the first round of the 1988 NBA draft, Richmond was chosen fifth by the Golden State Warriors. He was an immediate sensation: in his first season, 1988–89, he scored an average of 22 points per game and led the Warriors to an improved record, up 23 wins from the previous season. They even performed well in the play-offs, upsetting the Utah Jazz before being stopped in the Western Conference semifinals by the Phoenix Suns. Following the season, Richmond was a nearly unanimous choice as NBA Rookie of the Year. As a team, the Warriors regressed in the 1989–90 season, failing to make the play-offs. As an individual player, however, Richmond succeeded in duplicating his rookie success; his scoring, field-goal shooting, and free-throw shooting all improved slightly, and his 4.6 rebound average led those of all the league's guards. The team bounced back the following season with another post-season upset, this time defeating the San Antonio Spurs, only to lose in the semifinals. While the Warriors were not a top team during these seasons, they developed a reputation as one of the league's most exciting and promising squads. Led by the triple-threat combination of point guard Tim Hardaway, two guard Richmond (also called a shooting guard or an off guard), and

small forward Chris Mullin—collectively known as Run TMC, after their first initials—the Warriors boasted an intimidating lineup that could score from anywhere on the court and still play solid defense.

Prior to the 1991–92 season, just as Richmond and the Warriors were beginning to attract national attention, Richmond was traded to the Sacramento Kings, in exchange for the draft rights to Billy Owens, a young star out of Syracuse University. Richmond was unhappy about the trade and took a long time to adjust to his new locale, despite its being only 80 miles from his home in Oakland. Nevertheless, he continued his excellent play on the court, continuing to average more than 20 points a game. Notwithstanding Richmond's efforts, after he joined the Kings, the team spent the following two seasons in the cellar of the Pacific Division. During more than half of the 1992–93 season, he was sidelined with a broken thumb. In 1993–94, the Kings harbored expectations of improvement due to the strong backcourt play of Richmond and former Duke star Bobby Hurley. These hopes were dashed when the latter was severely injured in an automobile accident 19 games into the season. The Kings got only slightly better that year, moving from last to second-to-last place in their division.

The Kings improved dramatically in 1994–95, winning 39 games and barely missing the play-offs. In March, playing against the Houston Rockets, Richmond tied his career-high of 47 points in one game and, on the same night, set a franchise record by scoring 25 points in the fourth quarter. The following season, the Kings again won 39 games and made the play-offs in a weaker conference. (The top eight teams in each conference qualify for the play-offs. Theoretically, all eight could have losing records.) Richmond played well in the post-season, averaging 21 points a game before his team lost, in the first round, to the Seattle Supersonics. Over the course of the next two seasons, the Kings became progressively worse, winning 34 games in 1996–97 and only 27 in 1997–98, in the latter of which Richmond missed 12 out of the last 14 games due to a knee injury. Despite that, he remained one of the Kings' few bright spots, averaging a career high of 25.9 points per game in 1996–97 and 23.2 points per game in 1997–98.

Despite the Kings' lack of success, Richmond continued to earn accolades. In 1998 he was selected to play in his sixth consecutive All-Star Game. He has been named to the All-NBA Second Team three times, in 1994, 1995, and 1997, and to the All-NBA Third Team twice, in 1996 and 1998. He was also a part of the "Dream Team" that took the gold medal at the 1996 Summer Olympics, in Atlanta, Georgia. Doug Collins, himself a legendary shooting guard, ranked Richmond third in the league at his position. "[Richmond] possesses an enormously strong body that enables him to post up bigger defenders. Not surprisingly, he attempts more free throws than most any other backcourt player," Collins wrote in *Inside Sports* (March 1995).

During his last few seasons in Sacramento, trade rumors swirled around Richmond. Now a veteran player, he was hungry for a championship, and many clubs saw great value in a seasoned guard of his caliber. Each year, as spring approached and teams began to examine their chances for success in the play-offs, many expressed interest in Richmond. Consequently, the Kings' road trips to cities rumored to be considering such a trade became more notable for the press's courting of Richmond than for the games themselves. Among the teams that considered Richmond were the New York Knicks, the Los Angeles Lakers, the San Antonio Spurs, and the Miami Heat, the last of which, had a deal been inked, would have reunited him with his former Warriors teammate Tim Hardaway. In the New York Times (November 10, 1997, on-line), noting the importance of the outcome of the trade, Mike Wise wrote, "Richmond's career move may tilt the NBA axis like no other deal in the past year." Unlike many great players who have been stuck in small markets, Richmond never complained loudly; rather, he quietly asked the Kings' management to trade him to a team with championship aspirations. While rumors of many proposed and even sealed deals continued to float, at the end of the 1997–98 season Richmond remained a King.

When the trade finally did materialize, shortly after the close of that season, it wasn't what anyone had expected: Richmond was sent to the mediocre Washington Wizards, in the nation's capital, a team that was neither a contender nor a safe bet to become one anytime soon. Richmond left the

Kings as the franchise's all-time leader for three-point shots made, and he ranks second in steals and third in points scored. It is expected that in Washington, Richmond and the Wizards' veteran point guard Rod Strickland will form one of the most formidable backcourts in the league. One-fifth of the way into the strike-abridged 1998–99 season, Richmond's solid play was in evidence in D.C., with his averaging about 20 points per game. (As a team, however, the Wizards were struggling near the bottom of the Atlantic division.)

Richmond has been active in many charity organizations since 1992, when he created the Solid As a Rock Foundation, a scholarship fund for Fort Lauderdale–area student-athletes. He is an honorary board member of the National Committee to Prevent Child Abuse and received that organization's Special Friend Award. He also works with Dayspring Outreach, which aids poor immigrants from Latin America, and the Pediatric AIDS Foundation.

Mitch Richmond and his wife, Juli, who have been married since Richmond's third season in the NBA, have two sons, Phillip Mitchell and Jerin Mikell. Richmond enjoys bowling and playing video games, and he has been known to entertain teammates with his uncanny impressions of other NBA players. — M.C.

Suggested Reading: Inside Sports p36+ Mar. 1995, with photo; New York Times B p11 Feb. 26, 1997; Sports Illustrated p 72+ Dec. 4, 1995, with photos, p100+ Mar. 8, 1998, with photo; Washington Post C p1 Feb. 13, 1995

Ritchie, Dennis

Sep. 9, 1941– Computer scientist. Address: c/o Lucent Technologies, 700 Mountain Ave., Murray Hill, NJ 07974

Thompson, Kenneth

Feb. 4, 1943– Computer scientist. Address: c/o Lucent Technologies, 700 Mountain Ave., Murray Hill, NJ 07974

In December 1998 President Bill Clinton awarded the coveted National Medal of Technology to Dennis Ritchie and Kenneth Thompson, citing their development of the Unix operating system and C programming language. Unix and C ushered in a new era in computing and remain vital to our current culture of personal desktop machines interconnected through vast networks. Prior to Unix, operating systems were built for individual machines, usually large mainframes, with specific processing goals. Unix became the first portable operating system, meaning that it could be installed efficiently and effectively on virtually any hardware. Though it was developed almost 30 years ago, Unix is still widely used today by Internet servers and large research-oriented institutions. C was created concurrently with Unix to program the operating system. Known for efficiency and simple elegance, C and its direct descendants, C++ and Java, remain the languages of choice among applications and Internet programmers.

Ritchie and Thompson began their collaboration at Bell Telephone Laboratories in 1968, when they were assigned to the Multics project. Multics, which stands for "multiplexed information and computing service," was a joint venture of Bell Labs, General Electric, and the Massachusetts Institute of Technology to create a time-sharing operating system for large mainframe computers. Early mainframes could accommodate only one user at a time, a wasteful and time-consuming way to use a computer, particularly when many people were competing for usage. The time-sharing system under development was intended to accommodate up to a thousand users simultaneously on a single mainframe.

Courtesy of Bell Labs

Dennis Ritchie

Courtesy of Bell Labs

Kenneth Thompson

In 1969 Bell Labs withdrew from Multics, the costs and manpower necessary to complete the project having grown unwieldy. Left without an assignment, Ritchie and Thompson were given an unusual amount of freedom by Bell Labs to explore their own ideas and research. (Because Bell Labs has traditionally placed a premium on inventiveness and creativity—always with an eye on utility—and promoted an atmosphere in which an unusual degree of intellectual freedom prevails, the company is known among researchers as a good place to be employed.) The two men, disappointed by the cancellation of the Multics project, decided to work on a small operating system that would be simple yet versatile and able to accommodate multiple users. The operating system they eventually developed was named Unix, a play on the name Multics credited to their Bell Labs colleague Brian Kernighan.

Ken Thompson was born on February 4, 1943 in New Orleans. Pursuing a longtime interest in short-wave radios, he majored in electrical engineering at the University of California at Berkeley, graduating with a bachelor's degree in 1965 and a master's, in the same discipline, in 1966. While an undergraduate, Thompson had worked part-time in a computer center; this experience altered his career plans. "I used to be an avid hacker in an electrical sense, building things. And ever since computers, I find it very similar," he told Robert Slater for the book *Portraits in Silicon* (1987). "Computing is an addiction. Electronics is a similar addiction but not as clean. Much dirtier. Things burn out." Thompson joined Bell Labs in 1966.

Dennis Ritchie was born in Bronxville, New York, on September 9, 1941. He graduated from Harvard University in 1963 with a degree in physics and stayed to pursue a Ph.D. in applied mathematics. Despite five years spent in intensive doctoral study and a completed dissertation, Ritchie never received his doctorate. "I was so bored, I never turned [my dissertation] in," he told Robert Slater. Like Thompson's, Ritchie's career choice diverged from his field of study. Following his father, who was a director of a Bell Labs engineering laboratory, Ritchie went to work for the company—two years after Thompson.

When Ritchie and Thompson approached the company's administration about their intentions of developing a new, portable operating system, Bell Labs, still gun-shy from the Multics failure, denied their request for hardware. Undeterred, Ritchie and Thompson began working on an obsolete and underpowered PDP-7 model computer, made by Digital Equipment Corp., that their office had discarded. Starting with such limited hardware made simplicity less a desire on Richie and Thompson's part than a necessity; the limited storage and processing capacity of their machine forced them to use as little valuable memory as possible. Since an operating system's primary function is as a data manipulator, Ritchie and Thompson tackled the problem of data storage first. "We wrote the code for the manipulations that would run this file system," Ritchie told Robert Slater. "In the process it became evident that you needed various commands and software to test out the file system. . . . And so we wrote a small command interpreter that would be things you typed to the keyboard, a command to copy files and delete them, do the various operations that you need to work on files." The PDP-7 contained no software, so Ritchie and Thompson had to write their programs on a large General Electric machine. They then transferred the programs to the PDP-7 by hand, using paper-tape output that the PDP-7 could read. By early 1970, they had a complete, though primitive, Unix system that could process data and support itself without the aid of another computer.

Despite the early and rapid success of Ritchie and Thompson, Bell Labs remained resistant to their work. The limitations of the PDP-7 became increasingly pronounced as Unix evolved, and the duo resorted to cunning to continue their research. Upon learning that Bell Labs' patent department was looking for a word-processing system, Thompson wrote a proposal to management suggesting that he and Ritchie provide the system. Deemed a cost-effective and practical expenditure, the proposal was approved, and a new, $100,000 PDP-11 model was purchased. Ritchie later acknowledged his and Thompson's trickery. "There was a scam going on," he was quoted as saying in *Byte* magazine (September 1995). "We'd promised a word processing system, not an operating system. But by the time the full computer had arrived in the summer of 1970, work was moving at full steam on both." Ritchie and Thompson had significantly upgraded their hardware, and now they had a subject on which to test their new operating system. In 1971 Unix had evolved sufficiently to test on the patent department, which successfully used it to enter patent applications and adopted the system for full-time use. Ritchie and Thompson had produced a functional operating system, and with backing from Bell Labs, a development group was established to further Unix.

The early development of Unix was led primarily by Thompson, who adapted a computer language called BCPL to accommodate the constraints of memory space on the PDP-7. BCPL had been used during the Multics project, during which Thompson was first exposed to it, but it had proved too cumbersome for the PDP-7 to handle. The streamlined version Thompson created, called B, operated efficiently within the confinements of the PDP-7. Spurred by the acquisition of new equipment and the need to transfer Unix to it, Ritchie derived from B a new programming language they named C. Subsequently, Unix was rewritten in C, and the operating system for the first time became portable.

C proved to be as innovative a programming language as Unix was an operating system: it was the first to fully integrate elements of a high-level language with assembly language. In computer terms, a high-level programming language is one that allows a person to write programs without a detailed understanding of the bare workings of a computer. High-level languages often use words and phrases as commands and sometimes resemble spoken or written language. Conversely, assembly languages' commands correspond directly to computers' bi-nary codes. They are generally more difficult to learn and install, but they are more efficient because they communicate more directly with the computer. According to the *Dictionary of Computer and Internet Terms* (1996), C is unique among high-level languages because, "unlike other general purpose languages, it gives the programmer complete access to the machine's internal (bit-by-bit) representation of all types of data. This makes it convenient to perform tasks that would ordinarily require assembly language, and to perform computations in the most efficient way of which the machine is capable." This access to the internal workings of the computer is the reason for C's, and thus Unix's, portability. Furthermore, the efficient use of memory and binary access make C and Unix applicable to small systems and mainframes alike.

Besides portability, C introduced "pipes" to data processing. A pipe is a mechanism that connects two programs: the output of one feeds into the next. This mechanism allows programs to run concurrently and communicate data to solve large problems. Long, intricate programs were once required to perform complex tasks; the longer the program, the greater the risk of its being riddled with mistakes. Pipes allowed multiple shorter, simpler programs to be written to take on large tasks with less risk of complication. This innovation gave computers extensive multi-tasking capabilities and introduced a new communal programming philosophy. "What we wanted to preserve was not just a good environment in which to do programming, but a system around which a fellowship could form," Robert Slater quoted Ritchie as saying. "We knew from experience that the essence of communal computing . . . is not just to type programs into a terminal instead of a keypunch, but to encourage close communication." Programmers could now divide and conquer a project by splitting the task into more manageable parts, writing the most efficient independent pieces possible, and reassembling them into a more effective whole. This communal philosophy of programming is also referred to as "toolbox" programming: each tool is designed to do a specific task efficiently and well, contributing to the success of the larger project, which no single tool can handle on its own.

Innovations aside, the timing of Unix and C played an integral role in their initial success among computer users, who were growing tired of large centralized mainframe systems and the painfully slow methods necessary to operate them; because of the limited access to mainframes, due to cost and space constraints, users were forced to sign up to use terminals for short sessions, with long intervals in between. Some institutions developed a batch-processing method in which students and researchers could submit requests for data-processing early in the day and receive the results later. Though this method proved quicker, users were even more isolated from computers. Advancements in smaller and less-expensive minicomputers led many to seek alternatives in independent, decentralized machines. As minicomputers manufactured by many different companies proliferated, Unix and C's portability became valuable. "Because they were starting afresh, and because manufacturers' software was, at best, unimaginative and often horrible, some adventuresome people were willing to take a chance on a new and intriguing, even though unsupported, operating system," Ritchie told Martin Campbell-Kelly and William Aspray for their book *Computer: A History of the Information Machine* (1996). Universities in particular were willing to adopt the new software, and as their graduates moved to the workforce, so did Unix and C.

The history of the computer industry is defined by obsolescence. Rapid technological advancements render hardware and software obsolete within years of their development. Thus the longevity and utility of Unix and C are remarkable. Though out of the mainstream home-computing public's eye, Unix continues to be a presence in major scientific and technical institutions. It affects the general public most through Internet providers, who make extensive use of Unix to operate their servers. The system's portability has led to multiple modifications and several versions based on the original operating system. Though they are similar in structure and nature, the Unix family of operating systems lacks a unifying standard. Individual versions of the operating system, consequently, often differ significantly from each other. C has taken on a life of its own. After 10 years of evolution in Bell Labs, universal standards for the language were adopted in 1983. C dominated applications programming over the next decade and spawned two programming languages, C++ and Java.

Dennis Ritchie and Ken Thompson still work for Bell Labs, which is now a subsidiary of Lucent Technologies. Thompson is part of a group of researchers, headed by Ritchie, that continues to explore operating systems and programming languages. Among the group's recent accomplishments are the release of the Plan 9 operating system in 1995 and the Inferno operating system in 1996. Inferno is particularly innovative in design because it not only can stand alone as an operating system for many different processing chips but can run as an application under other operating systems, such as Windows 98.

The science and technology community has recognized Ritchie and Thompson many times for their work with Unix and C. In addition to the National Medal of Technology, they jointly won the 1983 Turing Award and the 1983 Software Systems Award, both from the Association of Computing Machinery, and the 1990 Hamming Medal. Both men were elected to the National Academy of Engineering in 1988. — T.J.F.

Suggested Reading: *abcnews.com* (on-line), Dec. 11, 1998, with photos; *Byte* p133+ Sep. 1995, with photo; *New York Times* III p7 Oct. 3, 1993; Campbell-Kelly, Martin and William Aspray. *Computer: A History of the Information Machine*, 1996; Dowling, Douglas A., et al. *Dictionary of Computer and Internet Terms*, 1996; Slater, Robert. *Portraits in Silicon*, 1987

Courtesy of the University of Pennsylvania

Rodin, Judith

Sep. 9, 1944– President of the University of Pennsylvania. Address: c/o University of Pennsylvania, Office of the President, 3451 Walnut St., Philadelphia, PA 19104

In 1994 Judith Rodin became the seventh president and chief executive of the University of Pennsylvania, in Philadelphia, and the first woman to be named the president of an Ivy League university. Rodin, who holds a Ph.D. in psychology, is well known for her research on the relationship between psychological and biological processes in health and human behavior, particularly in regard to obesity and eating disorders in women. In nearly three decades of research, she has been awarded some 20 grants, co-authored 10 academic books, and written more than 200 academic articles and more than 60 chapters that appear in various anthologies. She has also edited three scholarly journals and has been on the editorial boards of eight others; the latter currently include *Medicine, Exercise, Nutrition and Health, Journal of Substance Abuse, Psychological Inquiry, Basic and Applied Social Psychology* and *Journal of Gerontology*. After beginning her teaching career at New York University, in the early 1970s, she moved to Yale University, where she served as a professor and administrator for nearly 23 years. In addition to her duties at the University of Pennsylvania (often referred to simply as Penn), Rodin currently serves on President Clinton's Committee of Advisors on Science and Technology.

The younger of two daughters, Judith Seitz Rodin was born on September 9, 1944 in Philadelphia, Pennsylvania. Her mother, Sally Seitz, was a homemaker; her father, Morris Seitz, worked as an insurance agent. Rodin has often recalled to interviewers that as a young student, when she brought home test scores of 97 percent, her father would ask about the whereabouts of the other 3 percent. "At the end of his life he told me he was kidding," Rodin told Molly O'Neill for the *New York Times* (October 20, 1994). "I always thought he was serious." Rodin attended the Philadelphia High School for Girls, where she was an honor student, and she was awarded a full scholarship to the University of Pennsylvania. In her first year at Penn, Rodin commuted to school from her parents' home, a little over an hour away, but often slept on friends' floors to avoid the drive home. Later in her freshman year, she was accepted as a sister at a sorority—the Nu chapter of Delta Phi Epsilon. Rodin moved into the sorority house at the beginning of her sophomore year, and quickly became a leader; over the next three years, she served as both rush chair and treasurer. She later told the *Triad* (Winter 1997) that at the sorority, she spent a lot of time "just getting to know people, making friends, hanging out. To me, Delta Phi Epsilon was a home base within which to navigate through a large university. It gave me a great comfort and a great home, and provided me with a comfort level which enabled me to cultivate my leadership abilities." Rodin was also active in athletics and student government. As president of the women's student government in her junior year, she helped to merge that organization with the men's government (they had been separate entities up until that time). Rodin received awards for her leadership skills from various campus organizations throughout her time at Penn.

When she enrolled at Penn, Rodin planned to major in foreign languages, but she soon became deeply interested in psychology. "With one psychology class and a renowned Penn professor named Henry Gleitman, my academic life took another course altogether," she told the *Triad*. "As a result of my work in that course, I was invited to assist another distinguished professor, Richard Solomon, in his research. I fell in love with the discipline." Rodin graduated cum laude from Penn in 1966, with a degree in psychology. Shortly afterward she married Bruce Rodin, who later became a city planner, and they moved to New York City, where they both entered doctoral programs at Columbia University. In her graduate courses Rodin concentrated on experimental psychology, focus-

ing her research on the interrelationship between body image and eating disorders. Her days as a sorority member apparently influenced her choice of subject. "In all my years of research on body image, I have been consistently struck by the number of women in sororities affected by eating disorders," she told the *Triad* in 1997. "It is critical for sororities to be aware of this and to do something about it." Rodin graduated from Columbia in 1970 with a Ph.D. in social psychology. She then worked for two years as an assistant professor of psychology at New York University before becoming an assistant professor at Yale, in 1972.

While at Yale, O'Neill reported, Rodin "became famous among students" for her skill at lecturing. She also became a noted expert on eating disorders. As part of her research, she headed a clinic where, as Randi Glatzer wrote for *American Health for Women* (October 1998), "some of the country's brightest women revealed that they were more interested in losing weight than saving the world." According to Glatzer, Rodin's work in this area "set the standard for treatment." In 1977 the University of California at Los Angeles offered her a teaching position, and Rodin used the offer as leverage to secure early tenure at Yale. That same year Rodin, who had gotten divorced several years earlier, wed Nicholas Neijelow, who as of the mid-1990s was the president of an optical company in Connecticut. The couple's son, Alex, was born in 1982. Rodin told O'Neill that the arrival of her son "softened my edges, made me less driven."

In 1986 a *New York Times* article featured Rodin and several other nationally prominent doctors of psychology and their research on feelings of control. These scientists reported that in general, having a sense of control over one's environment and activities is even more crucial to psychological health than was previously thought. Rodin's study involved elderly men and women living in a convalescent home. She found that her subjects were happier, more alert, and had a lower mortality rate when they were given greater control over their environments, specifically, by being allowed to decide how the furniture in their rooms was arranged, what food they would have at meals, and when they could receive phone calls. "These may seem like trivial decisions, but they are very powerful in the closed, regimented world of a convalescent home," Rodin told Daniel Goleman for the *New York Times* (October 7, 1986). "These were opportunities for the residents to be in control where there had been no chance for them to make a decision before." In Goleman's article, Rodin also cited evidence that stress caused by lack of control has a greater negative impact on the immune systems of elderly people than on those of people in their prime.

Earlier, in about 1983, Rodin had begun to see academic administration as a possible career path. "I had always thought that I must distance myself from administration if I was going to do good science," she told the *Triad*. "I had thought the two were mutually exclusive, but I learned they could be incredibly synergistic. I discovered that an effective leader could enable others, and I found it energizing and very rewarding." In 1986, when Radcliffe College offered Rodin its presidency, she instead chose to remain at Yale and become chair of the psychology department. In 1991 the president of Yale, Benno C. Schmidt Jr., appointed her dean of the Graduate School of Arts and Sciences. In that position Rodin oversaw the academic policies affecting some 2,500 students and 600 faculty members. While at the graduate school, she also developed a 10-year budget plan. Then, in 1992, only one year into her five-year appointment as dean, Rodin was appointed to the prestigious position of provost of Yale, thus becoming the highest-ranking female administrator in the Ivy League. Also in 1992 Rodin published a self-help book entitled *Body Traps: Breaking the Binds That Keep You from Feeling Good About Your Body*. According to O'Neill, the book "draws on [Rodin's] two decades of research into obesity, bulimia, and anorexia to show how distorted body images affect women's lives." "People seem to be more preoccupied and less satisfied with their bodies," Rodin wrote in *Body Traps*, as quoted by *American Health for Women* (October 1998). "The thinner and more beautiful the ideal becomes, the harder it is for most people to attain." Rodin made an appearance on *The Oprah Winfrey Show* to promote the book.

As provost of Yale, Rodin became acting president of the university upon the resignation of Benno C. Schmidt Jr., in 1993. By the spring of 1994, it had become clear that Rodin was a top candidate for the presidency. Eventually the university chose a candidate whom many perceived as more conservative. A Yale search committee member who spoke to O'Neill on the condition of anonymity said, "Yale was at wit's end with high profile presidents. Judy scared them." Rodin, however, had no shortage of other prestigious job opportunities. While being considered for the presidency of Yale, she was also a leading candidate to head the National Institutes of Health, the federal government's largest scientific and medical research agency. Shortly after she was passed over by Yale, Rodin accepted the presidency of the University of Pennsylvania, becoming the first Penn graduate to be given the top position at the school. Also at around this time, Rodin, who had divorced for a second time in 1991, married Paul Verkuil, a former president of the College of William and Mary, who shortly before had been appointed by the Supreme Court to oversee the dispute between the states of New York and New Jersey regarding ownership of Ellis Island. "Initially, I was disappointed by Yale's decision," Rodin told O'Neill. "But then I was relieved and exhilarated. At the risk of sounding revoltingly Pollyannaish, right now I have a perfect job, a perfect child, and a perfect husband. Everything worked out for the best."

Rodin's tenure at Penn did not begin smoothly, as she was faced almost immediately with two potentially divisive campus issues. First, as a result of the university's relatively low income from its $1.35 billion endowment (by contrast, Harvard's endowment is $5.8 billion), departments in the undergraduate school of arts and sciences had to be consolidated. The year before, the school had "eliminated religious studies, civilization and regional economic departments, shifted the astronomy department into physics and brought in outside administrators to overhaul the Slavic languages department," William H. Honan reported in the *New York Times* (December 7, 1993). "Many faculty members were distressed by the action." Rodin had the difficult task of making this process, which was potentially disruptive to students, as smooth as possible. In addition to these administrative problems, Penn's campus had recently been plagued by a series of racially divisive incidents, most notably one in which the Black Student League destroyed some 14,000 copies of the *Daily Pennsylvanian*, a student newspaper. The league acted to protest an article in the paper about Haitians that, Penn's Haitian student body alleged, carried a racist slant. In another incident that aroused passionate debate, a professor received a research grant from a foundation that was believed to support neo-Nazi and racist agendas. A retrospective exhibit of the work of Andres Serrano at Penn's Institute of Contemporary Art produced an even greater storm of controversy, sparked by the inclusion in the show of what Rodin later referred to as "the notorious" *Piss Christ*, in which a crucifix stood in a container filled with the artist's urine. In an address given in 1998, Rodin talked about these troubling incidents. "The common cry in each of these incidents, and in many, many others we all confront, was, 'Why doesn't the university stop this?'" Rodin said. She then explained that she did not try to do so "not because I believe in the first amendment, although I do, but because I believe so strongly that attempts to shut down the discourse, to civilize the debate, or even to control the sometimes outrageous behavior of students before the fact, will not bring about the kind of reasoned and reasonable exchange . . . that we seek."

In April 1999, in an article in the *Daily Pennsylvanian* (April 20, 1999, on-line), Catherine Lucey celebrated the approach of Rodin's fifth anniversary as president of the University of Pennsylvania. "Four years [after her appointment]," Lucey wrote, "officials point out the tangible changes made under Rodin's agenda, . . . including the development of new interdisciplinary programming, an increase in funded research projects and the creation of the college house system [which more efficiently regulates student living accommodations]. Additionally, Rodin's fundraising efforts, as a result of the plan, have pushed the endowment to a new high of over $3 billion. . . . Penn has risen to No. 6 on the *U.S. News & World Report* ranking, and the Class of 2003 accepted just 26.6 percent of applicants, an all-time low." "We do it best," Rodin told Lucey. "We're the only Ivy that has all of our schools and centers together in one campus, [and] we really can create a strategic niche for ourselves that no one else can imitate." Undergraduate dean Richard Herring added that Rodin's administration has led to a "feeling, which is luckily contagious, that this is an institution going places," as Lucey quoted him as saying.

With base pay of $529,677, benefits of $18,697, and an expense account of $12,000 in the fiscal year that ended on June 30, 1998, Rodin is one of the highest-paid college presidents in the United States. During the summer of 1999, Eric Tucker reported in the *Daily Pennsylvanian* (September 24, 1999), she signed a "letter of understanding" with the university in which she committed herself to at least five more years as head of Penn. The letter, which is not a binding agreement, served in part to quell suspicions that Rodin intended to leave the university in the near future to accept a government post in the nation's capital. "I really haven't considered the next job," Rodin told Tucker. "I came very late to administrative roles. Never did I set out early in my career to be a university president."

The same type of intensity and enthusiasm that Rodin brings to her job as Penn's president used to be evident in her tennis game. "I'm ranked," she told O'Neill. "But since I took this job I haven't had time to play." Rodin's recreational interests include attending the theater and collecting art. In 1998 the White House Project, which was set up to prompt Americans to regard women as worthy presidential candidates and to encourage qualified women to run for president, listed Rodin among the nation's top 20 female leaders. Rodin was one of four winners of the 1999 Sara Lee Frontrunner Awards, which honor "women who have defined greatness through their groundbreaking successes." — M.B.

Suggested Reading: *American Health for Women* p68+ Oct. 1998, with photos; *Daily Pennsylvanian* (on-line) Oct. 1, 1998, with photo, Apr. 29, 1999, with photos; *New York Times* C p1+ Oct. 7, 1986, B p8+ Dec. 7, 1993, C p4+ Oct. 29, 1994, with photos; *Philadelphia Business Journal* p1+ Mar. 12, 1999, with photos; *Triad* p10+ Winter 1997, with photos

Selected Books: *Body Traps*, 1992

Rodriguez, Cecilia

Sep. 15, 1952– Social activist. Address: c/o National Center for Democracy, Liberty and Justice, 601 N. Cotton St., #A10, El Paso, TX 79902

Cecilia Rodriguez was only 14 years old when she organized her own recreation program for the children of one of the poorest neighborhoods in her native El Paso, Texas. Thus it is not surprising that the same person, as an adult, would reach far across the border to the poorest indigenous citizens in Chiapas, a state in southeastern Mexico, to attempt to help the rebellious Zapatista army in their struggle against governmental and economic oppression. Perhaps because she grew up hearing her father's tales of "wading across the river to cross the border and work," she has always felt keenly the vast discrepancies in wealth and privilege that exist in Mexico, and she has made it her life's work to alert Mexico's wealthy northern neighbor of the dire realities south of the border.

Named for Emiliano Zapata, the hero of the Mexican Revolution of 1910, the Zapatista army—known formally as the Zapatista National Army of Liberation (EZLN)—was formed in the early 1990s. Its members believed that the free-market policies of the North American Free Trade Agreement (NAFTA), along with a coinciding repeal of an article in the Mexican constitution that protected the land holdings of the indigenous peoples from privatization, would further erode the living stan-

Courtesy of National Center for Democracy, Liberty and Justice

dards of the already poverty-stricken majority of citizens of the region. Chiapas has the largest indigenous population in Mexico, and although it is one of the nation's leading producers of coffee, corn, cocoa, hydroelectric power, and timber, the state's schools, hospitals, public buildings, and highways are often described as "run-down" and, in many cases, "nonfunctional." The Zapatistas blamed the national government, which has been controlled by the reputedly corrupt Revolutionary Institutional Party (PRI) for well over 60 years, for the negligence with which their communities had been treated, and also claimed that the party, under the leadership of Carlos Salinas de Gortari, who was elected president in 1988, helped the very small but immensely powerful landowning class of Mexicans to strengthen their private armies, the Guardias Blancas. In *Ms.* (November/December 1996), Jennifer Bingham Hill also credited the Zapatistas, one-third of whose army consists of female soldiers, with having created the "Revolutionary Law of Women," which—ratified by a council of Chiapan communities in 1993—"gave Indian women the right to own land, to decide how many children they will have, and to choose when and whom they marry."

On January 1, 1994 the Zapatistas descended from the Chiapan mountains and brazenly took the city of San Cristobal de las Casas and the nearby towns of Altamirano, Las Margaritas, Ocosingo, and Chantal, in what became 12 days of fighting and resulted in approximately 140 casualties. The EZLN demanded democratic rule of the land occupied by poor indigenous peoples as well as housing, food, jobs, and education. The events of New Year's Day brought Cecilia Rodriguez from New York City, where she had been serving as the executive director of a philanthropic institution called the Funding Exchange, to Chiapas, where she became part of an emergency human-rights observation team. In a 1995 presentation at the University of Oregon, Rodriguez explained her theories about why violent uprisings such as the Zapatista rebellion of 1994 occur and why she believes that the convictions of the Zapatistas are worth fighting for. "The effect of squeezing resources and people from the south up to the north is the exclusion from participating with future decisions and results in political conflicts," she said. "It's not just Chiapas. The Mexican government is desperate to believe this is a local conflict; that only one group is unhappy. This is a false hope." She explained that the Zapatistas were defending a "tradition of dignity and justice." "At this point in time," she declared, "when there's a climate of fear and people are told these problems are from too many dark people, too many gay people and that women should stay home to care for the house, that is in our tradition to say 'no.' Our tradition is not based on fear."

In July 1994, with the EZLN and the army of the Mexican government still poised for combat in Chiapas, the charismatic Zapatista leader known as Subcomandante Insurgente Marcos, who was later identified by the Mexican government as Rafael Sebastian Vicente Guillen, named Rodriguez the official U.S. spokesperson for the Zapatista cause. Rodriguez, who would travel frequently between Mexico and the U.S. for the next several years, returned to her native El Paso, where she

quickly organized the National Commission for Democracy in Mexico (currently operating as the National Center for Democracy, Liberty and Justice). Through the center, Rodriguez coordinated support for the Zapatistas, acted as the organization's U.S. media agent, and—in the most difficult portion of her job—actively opposed U.S. military sales and support to the Mexican government. Then–U.S. defense secretary William Perry was eager to maintain the "stability and security" of Mexico, contending that the security of the larger and far wealthier U.S. was "indissolubly linked" to that of its southern neighbor. According to EZLN documents, the U.S. government sold an estimated $250 million in military equipment to Mexico between the years 1991 and 1995, and the organization strongly suspected that arms were often filtered from the Mexican government down to the ruthless Guardias Blancas. According to a report by Oscar Fernandez at McGill University, the Guardias Blancas were known to terrorize and, in some cases, torture activists who attempted to alter or draw attention to the region's grievous economic situation.

Following the 1994 uprising, Chiapas saw a significant increase in the terrorizing, torture, and abduction of activists. In addition, both Amnesty International and the Women's Group of San Cristobal reported significant increases in reports of sexual harassment and rape. Rodriguez has termed the persistence of these forms of violence "implementations of a low intensity war" that the Mexican government and the wealthy landowners waged on the poor people of Chiapas in order to "disintegrate a social movement." She believes that such violence, if it is anything short of a full-scale war, is usually ignored by the media and by governments that have, more often than not, an interest in maintaining the status quo. "They're fighting for survival. They're facing hunger. They're facing extinction," Rodriguez told Jennifer Bingham Hill of the Zapatistas, whose numbers have decreased over the past several years and who are constantly in danger of both physical and moral defeat. It has become an important part of the Zapatistas' program to characterize all violent and coercive practices, including rape and other crimes against women, as mechanisms of war that have been ignored too often and for too long.

On October 26, 1995, while on a daytime excursion with a male companion to a popular tourist attraction near the border of Guatemala, Rodriguez was brutally assaulted and raped by three masked men. During the attack she heard one of her assailants shout, "You know how things are in Chiapas, right? Shut up then, shut up or you know what will happen to you." Since the uprising there had been several reports of human-rights workers and health-care volunteers, both foreign and Mexican, being harassed and accosted. In most cases, including that of Rodriguez, the assailants were said to be wearing the type of ski masks worn by the Zapatistas and "shiny army boots." The attack on Rodriguez came right after she made a public statement about the October 21st capture and subsequent imprisonment of Zapatista leader Fernando Yanez Munoz, which she believed would seriously delay negotiations between the Zapatistas and the Mexican government. Documents of an Austin, Texas, organization called Accion Zapatista cite both the arrest of Munoz and the rape of Rodriguez as being linked to Defense Secretary Perry's visit to Mexico, and they strongly imply that both events were connected to U.S. and Mexican government activities. The Accion Zapatista report goes so far as to refer to the men who attacked Rodriguez as "minions of the Mexican government." Immediately after the rape, Rodriguez was warned by human-rights workers to leave Chiapas. She made her way to Mexico City, where she was treated at a private clinic; on October 31 she filed a complaint at the U.S. Embassy. While the embassy asked Chiapan officials to investigate the rape, the prevailing attitude about such crimes could be summed up by what one American embassy official told Rodriguez: "Nobody ever prosecutes in Mexico."

Although she was initially incapacitated by the rape, a letter from Subcomandante Insurgente Marcos helped Rodriguez to recover and to use what had happened to her in a constructive way. "We want you to know," Marcos wrote her, "that we repudiate, together with all honest men and women, the criminal intent to which you were subjected. Yes, 'subjected,' because that kind of aggression consists of making a thing, an object of a human being and 'using' that human being as things are used." When she received the letter, Rodriguez has said, she felt as though the painful "shell" in which she had been living since the assault had cracked: "I was able to cry for the first time," she told Jennifer Bingham Hill. "[Marcos] was able to name something, and I was very moved by it. How could this man in the mountains, surrounded by 60,000 troops, say to me the things I needed to hear? And I realized then that this was the essence of the things that they were fighting for: that human connection, that ability to look beyond yourself and be able to put yourself in the position of someone else."

Rodriguez held press conferences in Mexico City and Los Angeles, challenging the relative silence that the U.S. media had maintained in regard to the situation in Chiapas. With only a handful of representatives of the alternative and Hispanic press in attendance in Los Angeles, Rodriguez said, "I have a question of those men who raped me. Why did you not kill me? It was a mistake to spare my life. I will not 'shut up,' I will not stop my work or travel to Chiapas or my work in the United States as a representative of the Zapatistas; this has not traumatized me to the point of paralysis. I will follow the example of the other thousands of Mexicans who continue to work for a true democracy in Mexico in spite of the danger to themselves and their loved ones, who tell the truth in spite of physical and mental suffering. You have left me my life

and from this will come the strength to continue to work."

No doubt in part because of the work Rodriguez had been doing on behalf of the Zapatistas since 1994, several prominent figures from around the world have taken an interest in the Zapatistas and their cause. In the *Chicago Tribune* (July 29, 1996), Colin McMahon reported that the filmmaker Oliver Stone and Danielle Mitterrand, the widow of the French president François Mitterrand, had recently visited Chiapas. Mitterrand was so taken with the cause that she wrote a memoir of her experiences with the Zapatistas in Chiapas entitled *These Men Are Above All Our Brothers*. McMahon described an event hosted by Zapatistas, "The Intercontinental Encounter for Humanity and Against Neoliberalism," as having drawn more than 2,000 visitors from 41 countries. "For them," McMahon wrote, "the Zapatistas serve as inspiration. They embody the world's poor standing up against neoliberalism, a catch-all term for the capitalist, free-trade economic changes sweeping the globe." While no other major American newspapers mentioned the Chiapas event and even McMahon described the Zapatistas as being "adrift" and as "not having evolved into a legitimate political party," Rodriguez's words on the meeting expressed optimism on the very same points: "It's germinating," she said. "[The Zapatistas] are not putting out any recipes and saying, 'This is the way we're going to do it.' There's an ongoing debate." In 1996 the Zapatista National Liberation Army fostered the formation of the Zapatista Front of National Liberation (FZLN), which, according to Rodriguez, would "organize local, regional and national committees of dialogue which will develop proposals and plans of action . . . and provide a way for civilians who agree with the Zapatista principle to work peacefully."

At the beginning of 1997, Rodriguez issued a statement, picked up by the A-Infos News Service (on-line), accusing President Carlos Salinas's successor—Ernesto Zedillo Ponce de Leon, who took office in 1994—of preparing for a "military strike against the Zapatistas," which would "serve as a diversionary explanation for a possible financial upheaval" in Mexico. Rodriguez condemned Zedillo's refusal to accept the agreements reached between his own negotiators and the Zapatistas over rights of indigenous people. Following the December 1997 massacre of 45 Indian men, women, and children carried out in Chiapas by masked gunmen—an act prompted by local government officials—Rodriguez prepared a communiqué that stated in part, "We are overwhelmed by pain and sorrow at what most of us knew was coming. . . . The blood of the children calls to all of us now. . . . It reminds us with poignant clarity that we will never win as long as we allow ourselves to doubt that justice exists only when people are willing to defend it. . . . *May the lesson nourish the wisdom of resistance deep within our hearts.*" In the last weeks of 1998, Zapatistas rejected peace proposals by the Mexican government (which had denied involvement in the 1997 massacre).

Cecilia Rodriguez, who was born on September 15, 1952 in El Paso, Texas, and attended the University of Texas, continues to travel to Mexico, raise support for the Zapatistas, and lobby against military aid to Mexico. While her work is difficult, she has traced people's failure to understand the needs and motives of the Zapatistas mainly to the immense geographical, cultural, and economic differences between the peoples of the United States and Mexico. In February 1995 she participated in a three-week hunger strike to protest the Mexican government's offensive against the Zapatistas, in which the organization's headquarters were captured by the army of President Zedillo.

In addition to her work with the Zapatistas and her previous directorship of the Funding Exchange, in 1981 Rodriguez helped to found La Mujer Obrera, a women's labor group in Texas. As a member of that organization, she protested unfair treatment of workers by chaining herself to a sewing machine, eventually spurring a federal investigation that forced several El Paso garment companies to pay $85,000 in delinquent wages. While studying at the University of Texas, she was active in the Chicano movement, which sought to improve health care, housing, and educational opportunities for Hispanic Americans. Rodriguez is the mother of three children and lives in El Paso. — C.P.

Suggested Reading: *Ms.* p28+ Nov./Dec. 1996; *National Catholic Reporter* p20 Dec. 8, 1995

Associated Press

Roy, Patrick
(rwah)

Oct. 5, 1965– Goaltender for the Colorado Avalanche. Address: c/o Colorado Avalanche, McNichols Sports Arena, 1635 Clay St., Denver, CO 80204

Patrick Roy accomplished in his first season as a professional hockey player what it takes others a career to do: he led his underdog team, the Montreal Canadiens, to a victory in the 1985 Stanley Cup finals while capturing the Conn Smythe trophy as the most valuable player (MVP) in the play-offs. But what has ensured Roy's legacy as one of the all-

time great goaltenders, perhaps the greatest, is his consistency—as demonstrated by the 412 victories and three league championships he has compiled over his 15-year career. Early on Roy developed a reputation for being brash, quirky, and quotable, but his aplomb never exceeded his performance. With his technique of luring shots by flashing wide-open spaces in the net and then snapping his pads shut to deny the puck, Roy almost single-handedly brought championship hockey back to Montreal—which, after a decade of dominance by the legends Guy LaFleur, Serge Savard, and Guy LaPointe, had settled into a spell of mediocrity. Roy became a celebrity, dubbed "Saint Patrick" by his adoring fans. But not long after his second championship season with the Canadiens, troubles with management sent the all-star netminder to the Colorado Avalanche, whom he promptly led to a championship. Roy, still with the Avalanche, seems to have lost nothing over the years, still winning more than 30 games a season and letting in fewer than three goals a game. Already possessing the most victories of any single player in the Stanley Cup finals, he is poised to become hockey's all-time winningest goalie.

Patrick Roy was born on October 5, 1965 in Quebec City. Michel Roy, a high-ranking official in Quebec's provincial government, and his wife, Barbara, raised Patrick and his two siblings in Sainte-Foy, an affluent suburb of Quebec. As a child Roy spoke French, the area's dominant language. From age six he devoted much of his time to playing ice hockey, especially as a goalkeeper. Athletics were apparently in his genes: his father was an avid baseball and tennis player, his mother was a nationally ranked synchronized swimmer, and his brother had a short professional hockey career. Despite his pedigree as the son of educated parents, Roy dropped out of school in 11th grade to play junior hockey in Granby, a town outside Montreal. At Granby, Roy's statistics were less than spectacular—he had a losing record and a high goals-against average—but he was nevertheless the fourth pick of the Montreal Canadiens in the 1984 National Hockey League (NHL) draft. Roy spent the next year with the Canadiens' American Hockey League (AHL) farm club in Sherbrooke. There, he formed a relationship with François Allaire, who is his goaltending coach to this day.

In 1985 the Canadiens—or the Habs, as they are known to their fans—called Roy up to share goalie duties with veteran Brian Hayward. Over the next four seasons, the pair formed an intimidating presence in the net, winning the Jennings trophy for best team goals-against average three times. It was Roy, however, who became the standout in the play-offs for the 1985–86 season. After a successful but inconsistent year in which the Canadiens finished as the seventh-best team of the league, no one picked the very young team to go very far in the postseason. The Edmonton Oilers and Philadelphia Flyers were expected to meet in a championship rematch. But Roy and the Habs bucked these predictions. Roy won 15 out of his 20 starts, holding opponents to only 1.93 goals per game. "He was our big-play man throughout the play-offs. Every time we needed him he was there," Canadien forward Mats Naslund, citing Roy's clutch play, told Jim Matheson for the Sporting News (June 2, 1986). Following the Habs' defeat of the Calgary Flames in five games in the final, Roy was awarded the Conn Smythe trophy as play-off MVP, becoming the youngest ever to win it. That honor was the subject of mild controversy, for two reasons: first, his postseason excellence was a surprise after a solid if undistinguished regular season, and second, Roy had received a lot of help, both from the legendary defensemen Larry Robinson and Rick Green in front of him and from some lucky bounces off goalposts.

If there were any vestigial doubts about Roy's game going into his sophomore season, they were quickly dispelled by his excellent play. In each of the next six seasons Roy posted a goals-against average of less than 3.00, and in three of those years he helped win more than 30 games. A stylistic innovator, Roy perfected the technique known as the "butterfly," which requires the goaltender to kneel close to the ice with his pads fanned. This perspective allows the goalie to see through opposing screens and react quickly to screaming low shots he wouldn't otherwise see. Moreover, Roy, at six feet and 192 pounds, takes up a lot of space in the crease and complements this advantage with an uncanny ability to play angles. But unfortunately for the Habs, Roy's development into one of the game's premier goalkeepers did not translate into play-off success. Though they qualified for the postseason in each of those years, they were bounced out early in every year except 1989, when they lost to the Calgary Flames in a rematch of the 1985–86 championship series. Roy played solidly throughout the spring tournament that year, allowing a mere 2.09 goals per game. He won the Vezina

trophy, which goes to the league's most effective goalie, three times in a row beginning in 1988. In those same years he was named to the NHL All-Star first team.

After three years of early exits, the Habs were back in the finals in 1993. Squaring off against Wayne Gretzky and his Los Angeles Kings, who were heavy favorites, the Canadiens started strong, with a two-games-to-one lead. But in the fourth game, with the Habs up by a goal, Kings defenseman Marty McSorley beat Roy with a deflating power-play goal, to tie the score with only five seconds left in the second period. Angered, Roy stormed into the locker room during intermission and offered neither apologies nor excuses but a bold promise. "That's it," Larry Wigge of the Sporting News (June 21, 1993) quoted him as saying, "I'm not going to give up any more goals. We don't want to go back to Montreal with this series tied 2–2." His words proved to be prophetic: Roy shut down the Kings' attack, and John LeClair won the game with an overtime goal. "I've read about Babe Ruth pointing to the stands and calling his shot and I've heard about Knute Rockne asking his Notre Dame players to win one for the Gipper, but this was the most dramatic job of leadership I've ever seen," Canadien captain Guy Carbonneau told Wigge. Even more audacious was a gesture by Roy in the same game. During a scrum in front of the goal, after Roy stoned Luc Robitaille and froze the net, the goalie gave Kings forward Tomas Sandstrom a cocky wink, caught by the television cameras and replayed time and again. Roy later told E. M. Swift for Sports Illustrated (June 21, 1993) that the gesture was meant to demonstrate "that I was in control." Two nights later the Canadiens finished off the Kings in front of a home crowd at the Montreal Forum. For his efforts, Roy won his second Conn Smythe Award, in recognition of his 10 consecutive overtime wins and a 12–0 record in one-goal games. (The series was doubly sweet for Roy because he and his wife had their first child after game one.)

Roy followed that performance with a strong 1993–94 season, winning 35 of his 68 starts and tying a personal career best with seven shutouts. The play-offs, however, were disappointing, as Roy spent part of the first-round series in the hospital with an inflamed appendix. The next season was even worse; the low-scoring Habs failed to make the play-offs despite the continued splendid play of their goaltender. This meant that a shakeup was imminent for the proud hockey franchise, which had won 23 championships in its history, paralleled in professional sports only by baseball's New York Yankees.

This came to pass the next year, as the Canadiens' management, in an effort to make over the team before they moved into their brand-new arena, traded several key players, leaving only a handful from the squad who won the 1993 championship. Tensions were reportedly already high as Roy went into his 22d game of the year and was bombed by the Detroit Red Wings with five goals in the first period and two more in the first five minutes of the second. Roy met the Montreal crowd's burst of sarcastic applause, which greeted his next save, with an equally sarcastic gesture. After the Red Wings' ninth goal, the Canadiens' coach, Mario Tremblay, pulled the angered and frustrated goaltender, who promptly walked up to the team president's box and announced that this was his last game in a Montreal uniform. The next day Roy was suspended and put on the trading block. On December 6 he was dealt, along with captain Mike Keane, to the Colorado Avalanche for three players, among them the young goalie Jocelyn Thibault. The Montreal press immediately began to float theories to explain the epoch-ending transaction. Some thought that the Canadiens were merely trying to get rid of an enormously popular local sports legend with the least amount of fuss. Others thought that Roy had planned his explosion in order to make an easy exit from the city. There were also rumors that a combative Roy had trouble with many of his teammates and was an extremely high-maintenance goalie who wanted special treatment. Whatever the reason, Roy left Montreal just 23 victories shy of breaking Jacques Plante's team record.

Starting anew in Denver, where the former Quebec Nordiques had just relocated as the Colorado Avalanche, Roy joined an already star-studded lineup that included fellow new acquisitions Claude Lemieux and Sandis Ozolinsh as well as holdover Joe Sakic. These veteran additions were widely expected to give the young and inexperienced Avalanche a good shot at contending for the Cup; the team had been knocked out of the previous year's play-offs in the preliminary round by the New York Rangers. Roy certainly did his part, going 22–15–1 and posting his best goals-against average in two years. He extended his hot play into the postseason, winning 16, including three shutouts, and losing only six. In the finals the Avalanche easily swept the Florida Panthers, and Roy won his third championship. Many hockey insiders credited Roy with being the player who put Colorado over the top. "I think [the acquisition of Roy] showed everyone in our locker room that we were serious about winning the Stanley Cup," coach Marc Crawford said, as quoted in the *Sporting News* (June 24, 1996). "With all the experience we had on this team, you could see something very special was happening with this group."

In 1996–97, his first full season in Denver, Roy had his best year statistically, discrediting any gossip that he was nearing retirement. He won a career-high 38 games, seven of which were shutouts, and had a career-low (to that point) 2.32 goals-against average. The Avalanche entered the play-offs looking for a repeat and rolled over the Chicago Blackhawks and Edmonton Oilers before losing to the Detroit Red Wings. This, however, was not due to Roy's play, as the goalie let in only 2.21 goals per game. The following year, after another strong regular season, the Avalanche disappointed

in the play-offs, being sent to an early vacation after a tough first-round loss to the Oilers. Since he went to Colorado, Roy has improved his stickhandling ability, adding yet another weapon to his arsenal, which will only lend support to his offensive, by facilitating the transition from defense to attack.

In 1998–99 the Avalanche, after winning 44 regular-season games—in which Roy improved his career-low goals-against average to 2.29—were seeded second in the Western Conference play-offs. The team advanced through the play-offs, coming one win shy of a berth in the Stanley Cup Finals after losing to the Dallas Stars in game seven of the Western Conference series. Roy underwent hip surgery during the off-season and spent the beginning of the 1999–2000 season recovering on the sidelines.

Like many goalies, Roy is famous for his numerous superstitions. His pregame regimen involves eating the same food, spaghetti and water, at the same time, 1:00 p.m., on every game day. After pregame warm-up he bounces the same puck in the same way and then leads his team through a ritual of stick-and-glove tapping. Roy, who has three children, is an avid golfer and collector of hockey trading cards, the most treasured of which is his complete set of the 1912–13 Montreal Canadiens. A member of the Canadian Olympic hockey team in 1998, Roy allowed only 1.46 goals a game, and the Canadians just missed getting a medal. — M.C.

Suggested Reading: *Saturday Night* p44+ Mar. 1995, with photos; *Sports Illustrated* p38+ Oct. 13, 1986, with photo, p26+ June 21, 1993, with photos, p42+ Dec. 18, 1995, with photos

---

Ryan, Meg

Nov. 19, 1961– Actress. Address: c/o International Creative Management, 8942 Wilshire Blvd., Beverly Hills, CA 90211

"Meg Ryan, with a radiance that neither forbids nor threatens, . . . is the modern mediator between the goddesses onscreen and the mortals in the theater seats," Richard Corliss wrote in *Time* (May 22, 1995). "She's the star you could take home to Mom." Often described with such adjectives as "cute," "fresh," "bubbly," or "perky," the actress Meg Ryan has a lightness and charm that have consistently endeared her to audiences; many of her films have grossed top dollar at the box office, and she currently commands a salary of more than $10 million per picture.

Ryan became the subject of countless conversations among moviegoers in 1989, thanks to some footage in the smash hit *When Harry Met Sally*, in which the actress and Billy Crystal co-starred as the title characters. In the now-famous scene, set in

Meg Ryan

a New York City deli, Harry makes a fatuous remark to Sally about his ability to please women sexually. In response, Sally noisily demonstrates to him how easy it is for a woman to fake an orgasm. As her astonishing monodrama reaches a crescendo, the other restaurant patrons fall silent. Then, as Sally ends her simulation and smiles triumphantly at Harry, a middle-aged woman at a neighboring table calls over a waiter, gestures toward Sally, and says, "I'll have what she's having."

Her apparently natural, girl-next-door charm notwithstanding, Ryan's knack for comedy is not effortless. "She prepares very hard for everything and comes in with her own little props that turn a scene from being mildly amusing to something more than that . . . ," Nora Ephron, who wrote the screenplay for *When Harry Met Sally* and directed two other romantic comedies in which Ryan starred—*Sleepless in Seattle* and *You've Got Mail*—explained to Rachel Abramowitz for *Premiere* (May 1996). "She really is killing herself at all times to make it work as humor."

Since launching her career, when she was barely out of her teens, Ryan has appeared in more than two dozen movies. She has often been pigeonholed as a comedian who specializes in froth, but she has played many serious roles as well, in such films as *Flesh and Bone*, *Courage Under Fire*, *Hurlyburly*, and *When a Man Loves a Woman*, for the last of which she earned a nomination for a Screen Actors Guild Award for outstanding performance by an actress in a leading role. At the 1999 ShoWest Convention, the annual trade show of the National Association of Theater Owners, Ryan was named actress of the year.

Meg Ryan was born Margaret Mary Emily Anne Hyra on November 19, 1961 in Fairfield, Connecticut. When she was 12, the family—which included her older sister, Dana; younger sister, Annie; and younger brother, Andrew—relocated to the town of Bethel, where her father, Harry, taught high-school math and coached school baseball and basketball teams. About three years later, her parents separated. Her mother, the former Susan Ryan, who had acted professionally before becoming a full-time homemaker, moved to New York to resume her career, and her father assumed full responsibility for the day-to-day care of Peggy, as Meg was then called, and his three other children. "When I was putting on the hats of mother and father, getting the dinner and doing the laundry, I found out it was pretty hard work . . . ," her father told Karen C. Schneider for *People* (August 2, 1993). "[I was] not always paying a lot of attention to the kids. I wish I'd been more caring, more affectionate. . . . Maybe Meg felt out on her own." Although Meg and her siblings visited their mother regularly, various accounts indicate that Ryan viewed her mother's action as a form of abandonment.

At Bethel High School, Ryan did well both socially and academically. Tracy Parsons, one of her longtime friends, observed to Schneider that while many girls "want to hate" a "beautiful, smart" fellow student, "there was something about [Ryan] that stood out from the day she walked in, a charisma thing. Everyone wanted to be her friend." Ryan was elected senior class secretary, voted "cutest" by her classmates, and chosen homecoming queen (though by default, after the original winner was suspended from school), and in her senior year she ranked 11th out of a class of 253 students.

By the time Ryan completed high school, in about 1979, her mother was acting in regional repertory theater and working part-time for a casting agent. After Ryan's graduation she began to take her daughter to other casting agents, introducing her as a young actress, and Ryan began to get roles in commercials. In 1978, when she received her Screen Actors Guild membership card, she took her mother's maiden name as her surname.

In 1980, also through her mother's connections, Ryan won her first part in a feature film—*Rich and Famous*. Starring Candice Bergen and Jacqueline Bisset, *Rich and Famous* is an adaptation by George Cukor of his 1943 film *Old Acquaintance*. No critics made note of Ryan's 10-line turn in the movie, as the Bergen character's troubled teenage daughter, Debby—Ryan was billed simply as "Debby at 18"—but the movie served as a sort of screen test that brought her additional work.

According to various sources, Ryan studied journalism at both the University of Connecticut and New York University. As an undergraduate she viewed acting as simply a way to earn extra money. So many small jobs came her way that she began attending night classes. In 1982 she got her first big break, landing a major role in the CBS television soap opera *As the World Turns*—that of

Betsy Stewart Montgomery Andropoulos, whose life, like those of many soap-opera characters, consisted of a series of crises: she was kidnapped, abused, impregnated, and married to a psychotic paraplegic. Ryan took a two-year break from college to work full-time on the series, then returned to school for one semester before dropping out permanently. Her next roles included that of Jane in the television series *One of the Boys* (1982) and Lisa in the film *Amityville III: The Demon* (1983; also called *Amityville 3-D*), a forgettable installment in the *Amityville Horror* series.

While in her early 20s, Ryan told Iain Blair for the *Chicago Tribune* (July 16, 1989), "I always thought I'd be going back to school. . . . It's amazing when I look back now, because I got into acting in spite of myself. I kept getting hired for jobs without even trying. I was doing commercials to help myself through school, and then they'd send me out on auditions, and I'd get them, and then I'd be hooked. . . . It's only very recently that I've discovered what acting is all about, and that it's something worthwhile doing."

In 1985 Ryan moved to Los Angeles. The next year she was cast in the blockbuster hit *Top Gun*, as the wife of the Navy fighter-pilot Goose (played by Anthony Edwards). Although her screen time was brief, her part carried weight, and her appearance in the film helped her win bigger roles. One was that of the glamorous reporter Lydia Maxwell in *Innerspace* (1987), directed by Joe Dante. *Innerspace* features Dennis Quaid as Tuck Pendleton, a hapless Navy test pilot who volunteers for a top-secret experiment in which he is miniaturized and injected into an unsuspecting, hypochondriacal supermarket clerk (Martin Short). Lydia must find the computer chip needed to restore Pendleton to normal size. "Ryan's blitheness gives the picture a lift," the film critic Pauline Kael wrote for the *New Yorker* (July 27, 1987); "she brings a quirky, resilient spirit to the scenes in which she and Short [appear]."

In the dramatic thriller *Promised Land* (1988), Ryan played Bev, whose husband, just two years out of high school, has become a drifter. Her characterization of the "raucous," "trampy," and "wacked out" Bev, as critics described her, was "show-stealing," Rita Kempley wrote in the *Washington Post* (February 6, 1988), in a representative admiring critique of Ryan's performance. Also in 1988 Ryan co-starred with Dennis Quaid in *D.O.A.*, a remake of the 1949 film of the same title. Ryan portrayed a college freshman who helps her dying professor (Quaid) find the person who slipped him a slow-acting poison. Directed by Rocky Morton and Annabel Jankel, *D.O.A.* was panned as overly contrived, but Ryan received mostly positive reviews. Discussing her performances in *D.O.A.* and *Promised Land*, David Edelstein wrote for the *Village Voice* (March 22, 1988), "Ryan has something rare in an actress—she's an ingenue with the soul of a sprite. As a reckless sociopath in *Promised Land*, she conjured up the other side of that

sprightliness. . . . An actress who can explore both the light and dark sides of her own charm has much to show and tell."

When Harry Met Sally (1989), directed by Rob Reiner, was the first smash-hit film in which Ryan had a leading role. In a variation of the boy-meets-girl theme, the movie follows Harry and Sally for about 10 years after their first meeting and addresses the question of whether the issue of physical intimacy can be avoided in a friendship between a man and a woman. Amid a barrage of violent Hollywood thrillers released around the same time, *When Harry Met Sally* captured the affections of moviegoers apparently starved for adult romantic comedies. Ryan's increasingly nuanced depiction of Sally, from chirpy undergraduate to 30-ish yuppie, earned her a 1989 Hollywood Women's Press Club's Golden Apple Award and a Golden Globe Award nomination.

In the one movie in which she appeared in 1990—*Joe Versus the Volcano*, written and directed by John Patrick Shanley, the Academy Award–winning screenwriter for *Moonstruck*—Ryan displayed her versatility by playing three very different roles: the mousy DeDe; the wealthy, silly Angelica; and the glamorous Patricia, who more closely resembled Ryan as she usually appeared onscreen. Each woman in succession becomes involved with Joe (Tom Hanks), who, after learning that he has only six months to live, accepts a billionaire's offer of a week of high living in exchange for agreeing to jump into a volcano on Hawaii to appease its god. "Anyone in doubt of [Ryan's] credentials as a character actress should relent" *Joe Versus the Volcano*, Eve MacSweeney declared in a *Harper's Bazaar* (December 1998) cover story; Ryan's depictions of DeDe and Angelica, MacSweeney predicted, will "have you squinting at the screen in disbelief that they could possibly be Ryan."

Joe Versus the Volcano, which got mostly thumbs-down reviews, "didn't work out as well as we all hoped, but I loved making it," Ryan told Joan Goodman for the *Guardian* (August 23, 1993). The film marks the first of Ryan's three cinematic pairings with Hanks, who is a close friend of hers. The second was the romantic comedy *Sleepless in Seattle*, one of the biggest box-office successes of 1993, in which Ryan played a Baltimore reporter who falls in love with a Seattle architect after hearing his tender description of his love for his deceased wife on a radio call-in show.

Nora Ephron, who directed and co-wrote *Sleepless in Seattle*, told Joan Goodman, "Meg and I go together. I write a certain kind of dialogue and there are not honestly that many people that can bring it off. First of all, the number of funny women is a very short list. And the number of smart, funny women is much shorter." After directing Ryan and Hanks in *You've Got Mail* (1998), which she co-wrote with her sister Delia Ephron, Nora Ephron told Eve MacSweeney, "I think [Ryan's] the funniest woman working. She understands that whatever's on the page, it's her job to make it funny. . . . For a physical comedian, you have to go back to Lucille Ball before you can find anybody who's on her level." In *You've Got Mail*, which is a 1990s version of Ernst Lubitsch's 1940 romance *The Shop Around the Corner*, Ryan and Hanks play professional rivals who unwittingly fall in love after meeting in a cyberspace chat room. In an assessment of the film that was more generous than those of most critics, Ryan told MacSweeney, "I saw the movie and it's extremely sweet . . . and I'm very nice in it." But she also said that films like *You've Got Mail* and *Sleepless in Seattle* sometimes strike her as "fairy tales," stories "so light that they disappear and become nothing." "I find that very nerve-racking to watch, and so I'm going to avoid doing them for a little while now."

Actually, some half-dozen of Ryan's films during the 1990s are anything but lighthearted and offer few laughs, if any. Among them are *The Doors* (1991), Oliver Stone's biopic—widely regarded as pretentious and wrongheadedly admiring—about the mythologized, self-destructive rock superstar Jim Morrison, in which Ryan played Morrison's girlfriend, Pamela Courson. In Steve Kloves's *Flesh and Bone* (1993), her role was that of a heavy drinker married to an abusive gambler; in running from her husband, she takes up with a dull, emotionally repressed loner (Dennis Quaid). Ryan again played an alcoholic, though this time one with a loving husband (Andy Garcia), in *When a Man Loves a Woman* (1994), directed by Louis Mandoki. In *Courage Under Fire* (1996), directed by Edward Zwick, she was cast as Captain Karen Walden, a medevac helicopter pilot who is killed while attempting to rescue some ground troops during the Persian Gulf War. Ryan's cameo role in *Hurlyburly* (1998), an adaptation by David Hare of his scathing 1987 drama about the dissolute moral climate in Hollywood (and by extension, the United States), was that of an exotic dancer who performs oral sex on strangers in the backs of cars while her six-year-old daughter sits in front. Another of Ryan's recent films, *Addicted to Love* (1997), Griffin Dunne's directorial debut, has been described as a screwball comedy (though one of uneven quality), but her character, Maggie, is far from bubbly; thrown over by her lover and almost unhinged by the misery of rejection, the tough-talking Maggie becomes obsessively bent on revenge.

Ryan's upcoming projects reportedly include three films scheduled for release in 1999: *Hanging Up*, described as a comedy-drama, directed by Diane Keaton and co-written by Delia and Nora Ephron, about three sisters (Ryan, Keaton, and Lisa Kudrow) grappling with the imminent death of their prickly, alcoholic father; *Higgins and Beech*, a love story set in the early 1950s, directed and written by Nora Ephron; and *Lost Souls*, a mystical tale involving a teacher at a seminary, directed by Janusz Kaminski. Ryan is also at work on a remake of the classic 1939 film *The Women*, in which she will co-star with Julia Roberts and Marisa Tomei.

Both *Lost Souls* and *The Women* are being produced by Prufrock Pictures, Ryan's own production company. According to several sources, Ryan also hopes to produce a film based on the life of the poet Sylvia Plath, who committed suicide in 1963.

Ryan married Dennis Quaid in 1991, after he made good on his promise to conquer his addiction to cocaine. Their son, Jack Henry, was born in 1992. Ryan and Quaid own homes in Los Angeles and New York City and a ranch in Montana. According to Eve MacSweeney, the couple practice yoga and meditation, "regularly visit ashrams, both in the United States and India, and follow the teachings of Gurumayi, a spiritual leader based in upstate New York." When MacSweeney asked Ryan to identify her priorities, she responded, "I want to keep my own definition of myself. I don't ever want to feel that I've evaporated into somebody else's idea of me, and I'll forget . . . how people get greedy or self-involved. And I just want to keep growing up a little bit, and growing out." — B.L.

Suggested Reading: *Chicago Tribune* XIII p4+ July 16, 1989; *Good Housekeeping* p96+ July 1998, with photos; *Harper's Bazaar* p214+ Dec. 1998, with photos; *McCall's* p40+ Aug. 1998, with photos; *People* p69+ Aug. 2, 1993, with photos, p152+ Dec. 8, 1997, with photos, p104+ Dec. 21, 1998; *Premiere* (on-line) May 1996; *Rolling Stone* p37+ Feb. 11, 1988; *Who's Who in America, 1999*

Selected Films: as actress—*Rich and Famous*, 1981; *Amityville III: The Demon*, 1983; *Top Gun*, 1986; *Innerspace*, 1987; *Promised Land*, 1988; *The Presidio*, 1988; *When Harry Met Sally*, 1989; *Joe Versus the Volcano*, 1990; *The Doors*, 1991; *Prelude to a Kiss*, 1992; *Sleepless in Seattle*, 1993; *Flesh and Bone*, 1993; *I.Q.*, 1994; *When a Man Loves a Woman*, 1994; *Restoration*, 1995; *French Kiss*, 1995; *Courage Under Fire*, 1996; *Addicted to Love*, 1997; *Anastasia* (voice), 1997; *City of Angels*, 1998; *Hurlyburly*, 1998; *You've Got Mail*, 1998; as co-producer—*French Kiss*, 1995; *Two for the Road*, 1997

Selected Television Shows: *One of the Boys*, 1982; *As the World Turns*, 1982–84; *Wildside*, 1985

Jonathan Daniel/Allsport USA

Sales, Nykesha

May 10, 1976– Basketball player. Address: c/o Orlando Miracle, Eastern Conference, Two Magic Place, 8701 Maitland Summit Blvd., Orlando, FL 32810

In the Huskies' final game of the 1998 regular season, against Villanova University, Nykesha Sales sank a basket in the opening seconds that made her the all-time scoring leader of the University of Connecticut (UConn) women's basketball program. Though few at the beginning of the season doubted that Sales would break the school's scoring record, her record-setting basket ignited a firestorm in the press that marred an otherwise exceptional season and collegiate career. The reason for the uproar was the way in which Sales set the record. In her previous game, against Notre Dame University, she had sustained an injury when she was just one point shy of making UConn history. The injury left her barely able to walk, much less run, the length of the court. Eager to help her, Geno Auriemma, the coach of the Huskies, in concert with Villanova's coach, devised a plan to get Sales in the game to score her two points for the record. The fallout from that move kept the media busy for days discussing the integrity of sports. What got lost in much of the hoopla was the reason why so many were willing to assist Sales in pursuit of the record: she was one of the most unselfish and beloved stars ever to play at UConn. Now fully recovered from her injury, "Cool Keesh," as her college teammates dubbed her, has successfully completed her rookie season with the Orlando Miracle of the Women's National Basketball Association.

Born on May 10, 1976 and raised in the town of Bloomfield, Connecticut, Nykesha Sales grew up under the attentive eyes of Kim and Ray Sales. When not working one of his two jobs, Ray Sales tutored Nykesha and her brother, Brooke, in the finer points of basketball. "'Anticipate the pass, anticipate the pass,'" Kim Sales remembered her husband repeating to Nykesha, as she told Daryl Perch for *Northeast* (January 25, 1998). "That's what he'd always say, and she got it." (Sales holds the UConn and Big East Conference records for on-court thefts: 447.) Kim Sales, too, supported Nykesha's pursuit of basketball, seeing it as a way to induce her daughter to study; she allowed Nykesha to play ball on the condition that she maintain good grades. The strategy worked: Sales learned to balance her activities and graduated from UConn on time, with a degree in business. "No getting cut any extra slack," Sales told Robin Finn for the *New York Times* (February 21, 1997). "A lot of guys who are good at ball don't think about the school part of being at college, but . . . I'm not about letting athletic ability or fame take me the wrong way."

Sales further developed her explosive style of basketball at Bloomfield's town courts, where she spent every spare moment. Her experiences there toughened her on and off the court. "I've played with guys all my life," she told Daryl Perch. "I got ranked on a lot for being a tomboy. It made me feel like garbage. But there were no girls my age in the neighborhood. So I played with the guys." Her determination to play regardless of the taunts of adolescent boys was rewarded. When Sales was a junior in high school, she was selected to participate in the United States Olympic Festival as a member of the East team. The festival is a competition that showcases the talent pool from which future U.S. Olympians will be drawn, and taking part in it is an honor for *any* amateur basketball player, much less one still in high school. Sales's team ended up with a silver medal, while the West team, coached by Geno Auriemma, went winless in the four-game tournament. As a high-school senior in 1994, Sales was heralded by *USA Today* as the national female player of the year, and she made *Parade* magazine's All-American list for the second year in a row. In addition, Sales's academic record earned her a place on her school's honor roll.

As a high-school senior, Sales was one of the country's most sought-after college recruits; *Street & Smith* ranked her among the top five scholastic recruits. She eventually narrowed her college choices to UConn and Ohio State University. Though she had publicly rejected the idea of staying in her home state to attend college, the possibility of playing with such talented players as Rebecca Lobo and Jen Rizzotti attracted her, so she signed a letter of intent to attend UConn. Her action made Auriemma, who had met her at the Olympic Festival, feel confident about the future of his program. "I knew the minute she walked on campus, by the way she reacted to the team and the way she behaved, that you could build a team around her," he told Daryl Perch. "She's not just a skilled basketball player, she's a solid person."

Sales quickly proved to be as much a part of UConn's present as its future. Despite being a newcomer on a veteran squad well stocked with talent, Sales saw playing time in every game in her freshman year and contributed significantly to the Huskies' perfect 35–0 win–loss record and national championship. In the championship game, against the University of Tennessee—a team that Pat Summit, the coach of the school's women's basketball program, has built into a perennial powerhouse—both Lobo and Rizzotti got into foul trouble, and Sales was forced to step up her role. She proceeded to contribute 10 points, in some 30 minutes of play, toward the Huskies' victory.

Throughout her next two seasons, Sales continued to grow as a player and student. On the court she assumed a full-time starting role on a championship-caliber team; off the court she adjusted to the rigors of being a student-athlete. "College athletes don't have much of an outside life," Sales told Robin Finn. "You don't even have time for a boyfriend; it's basketball and schoolwork." Sometimes her only outlet was watching television. Nevertheless, Sales made peace with her atypical lifestyle. "Some kids go on spring break; we go to the Final Four," Sales told Finn. "I mean, you can always go to Cancun; I'd rather get a [championship] ring." Toward that end Sales spent her off-seasons as a member of the USA Basketball National Teams that won gold medals in 1994 and 1996 and a bronze in 1995 in international competition. By the time she completed her junior year, Sales had evolved from a young prospect with potential into an explosive scorer and powerful presence on the hardwood. She had earned All-American honors, dominated Big East play with averages of 16.4 points and 4.2 steals per game, and was poised to eclipse all of UConn's major records in her final year.

Sidelined by mononucleosis for the early part of her senior season, Sales made a well-timed recovery. Six weeks into the 1997–98 season against the nationally ranked Stanford University team, she led the Huskies to victory with a remarkable 46-point performance. In so doing she set the mark for single-game scoring by a Big East player. Going into her final week of regular-season play before the Big East tournament, Sales had captured the team and league records for steals and was certain to surpass UConn's career point record of 2,177, set in 1991 by Kerry Bascom. But in the closing minutes of the Huskies' penultimate regular-season game, against Notre Dame University, Sales, who was just one point shy of UConn's scoring mark, ruptured one of her Achilles tendons, thus effectively ending her college career. The sequence of events that followed Sales's injury sparked a national debate that encompassed issues as diverse as sportsmanship, the nature of competition, gender politics, and the economics of sport.

In the final game of the regular season, the Huskies would play Villanova University, whose head coach, Harry Perretta, was a longtime friend of Geno Auriemma's. Auriemma conceived a plan to get Sales in the game so that she could sink the basket that would break the scoring record. According to the plan, Sales would start the game, despite being hobbled, and would position herself under the opponents' basket. Villanova would allow UConn to control the opening tip-off, and the ball would be passed to Sales for an uncontested layup. UConn would return the favor to Villanova by allowing them to score an uncontested layup to even the score, after which the game would continue on a normal, competitive course.

After Perretta agreed to the plan, he and Auriemma approached their respective teams, athletic directors, and school presidents, and all of them OKed it. Then Auriemma contacted Bascom, who held the record and was working as an assistant coach at the University of New Hampshire, and received her blessing. Finally, they presented their proposition to Big East commissioner Mike Tranghese. Tranghese sanctioned it, and everything went ahead as planned. Sales received a standing ovation as she sank her record-breaking shot.

"United Nations Secretary General Kofi Annan was not consulted," Thomas Boswell quipped in the Washington Post (February 27, 1998). "But everybody else was." Similarly, Joel Stein observed in Time (March 9, 1998), "Peace in Iraq was accomplished with fewer people." The sportswriters' sarcastic statements typified the initial response among commentators regarding Sales's choreographed basket. Recognizing the problematic nature of her coach's gesture, which he categorized as righting an unfortunate wrong for a deserving athlete who had given much to UConn and women's basketball, Sales admitted that she had felt uneasy about the plan at first. "But Coach said it was a gift from him to me," William C. Rhoden of the New York Times (February 26, 1998) quoted her as saying.

Such "gifts" are not unusual in sports. The professional basketball player A. C. Green was given token playing time in a series of games after he was injured, to enable him to hold onto his record number of consecutive games played (sometimes referred to as the "ironman" record). In another example, in April 1997 the Washington Bullets (now the Wizards) allowed Allen Iverson of the Philadelphia 76ers, a National Basketball Association team, to score 40 points in a game during his rookie season, to maintain his string of 40-point games. (Washington could afford to be generous, because they were so far ahead in the game. The team eventually won by 21 points.) And it is well known that in September 1968, Detroit pitcher Denny McLain served up a meatball to Mickey Mantle, who hit the pitch over the fence to gain his 535th career home run and thus move to third place on professional baseball's all-time home-run list.

Despite ample precedent, the way in which Sales set her record provoked uneasiness and even outrage among sports commentators. Purists saw it as an example of how the pursuit of individual records has detracted from the team aspect of sports. The event even provoked political commentator George Will to examine the nature of competition and the value of records. "Part of the beauty and much of the moral seriousness of sport derives from the severe justice of strenuous play in a circumscribed universe of rules that protect the integrity of competition," he wrote for the *Washington Post* (March 4, 1998). "Records are worth recording, and worth striving to surpass, because they serve as benchmarks of excellence achieved under the pressure of competition." In the *New York Times*, William C. Rhoden offered the view that Auriemma's tampering, despite his good intentions, was not far removed from fixing a score for gamblers. "Stretching the bounds of competition is acceptable: sending a player back in to get one more yard, complete one more pass, score two more points; it's all part of the game," Rhoden wrote. "The troubling aspect of Auriemma's 'gift' is the amount of choreography that went into delivering it. This sort of pre-arrangement for a 'good cause' is actually the flip side of pre-arrangements for a 'bad cause,' namely the manipulation of points for the spread. Each has the final effect of manipulating the competition to achieve a desired outcome."

Other commentators looked upon Auriemma's gesture as harmless. Dave Anderson of the *New York Times* (February 27, 1998) called it a "nice wrong," "like the husband who gives his wife flowers, then discovers she's allergic to them." In a letter to the editor of the *New York Times* (March 2, 1998), Christopher F. Black wrote, "To suggest that Geno Auriemma's and Harry Perretta's 'gift' to Nykesha Sales . . . somehow violates the spirit of competition or the sacred rules of the game is to proclaim that our most animal instincts are in fact our most honorable. Those who are outraged would do well to investigate what has been compromised and to justify why the integrity of the game should supersede human integrity." And Michael Wilbon, writing for the *Washington Post* (March 2, 1998), directed his attacks at those who derided the choreographed basket: "Who, exactly, did this action offend? . . . From what I can tell, it starts with a bunch of holier-than-thou columnists and radio-talk heads who would never actually cover a women's basketball game. They now want to tell you what the game is, isn't, should or shouldn't be."

"It got an awful good philosophical discussion going, didn't it?" Tara VanDerveer, who works at Stanford University and coached the 1996 U.S. Olympic women's basketball team, observed to Greg Garber and Lori Riley for the *Hartford Courant* (February 26, 1998, on-line). The discussion probably would have died down within a few days had it not been for Big East commissioner Mike Tranghese, who admitted that he would not have sanctioned a similarly choreographed scenario for a men's game. "I knew there would be a ruckus about this, but you have to understand that males are made up differently from women, and I try to be sensitive to women," Tranghese told Robert Lipsyte for the *New York Times* (February 26, 1998). "Men compete, get along, and move on with few emotions. But women break down, get emotional, get so much more out of the game. These are entirely different sports cultures." This statement, which reappeared in the press nationwide, brought the issue of gender equality to the surface and further fueled the debate. Since the three key participants in the plan—Auriemma, Perretta, and Tranghese—are all men, their gesture was seen as patronizing in light of Tranghese's words; his statement added weight to the arguments of those who did not condone the effort to help Sales break the record. "Handed the ball, the basket, and the record," Anna Huntington wrote in the *New York Times* (March 1, 1998), "Sales was treated like a child being given a huge headstart in a race against a parent, and then celebrated with paternalistic cheers for her victory." Some even concluded that Auriemma's contrivance would have far-reaching economic effects. They predicted that the surge in popularity in women's sports, which had resulted in an upswing in marketing revenues, would stall or decline because women's sports would be seen as less serious, and therefore less worthy, than men's sports.

A more-or-less final word on the issue was offered by Steve Wulf in the inaugural issue of *ESPN Magazine* (March 1998), where he reported, "All of it may have been not for two, but for naught. The well-meaning and well-orchestrated attempt to get her the record, the bittersweet celebration soon after tip-off, the subsequent furor for days after the game—that all seems pointless now." According to Wulf, an anonymous tip led him to review a videotape of UConn's January 22, 1998 game against Seton Hall University. Game officials credited Sales with scoring 25 points in that game. However, the tape shows that she actually scored only 23. Sales had deflected a pass to her teammate Kelly Hunt, who scored the bucket credited to Sales. Thus Sales actually needed more than the one orchestrated basket against Villanova to set a record. Despite Wulf's revelation, the record stands. Officials with UConn, Seton Hall, the Big East, and the NCAA were unwilling to challenge the record. Also, Wulf noted, no one had reviewed the tapes of all 137 games in which Sales played with the Huskies. "Perhaps she scored two points that she didn't get credit for. Mistakes do happen. Better yet would be the discovery that she scored four uncredited points—enough to close this can of worms."

Though her name may always be associated with a measure of controversy, Sales emerged from the fracas relatively unscathed. After withstanding the disappointment of missing the final postseason of her college career, she finished her degree and underwent rehabilitation to strengthen her mending tendon. She was also honored by the Big East Conference with their Player of the Year and Defensive Player of the Year awards. In April 1998 she was signed to play professionally for the WNBA. Although her injury prevented her from playing in 1998, she was drafted by the Orlando Miracle, one of the league's two expansion franchises. A preseason tour with a squad of WNBA players, who took on Brazil's best women's teams, marked Sales's successful return to the hardwood.

Despite her time off from basketball for recovery from her injury, Sales showed little rust in her rookie season. On June 15, 1999—less than one week after her WNBA debut—she led the Orlando Miracle to a rousing 88–86 win over the Los Angeles Sparks, with a five-assist, three-steal, and career-high 29-point performance. During the next two weeks, Sales added 23-point and 20-point performances against the Phoenix Mercury and Houston Comets, respectively, to her budding professional résumé. Thanks to such on-court pyrotechnics, she was named to the East team for the inaugural WNBA All-Star Game in July. Overall, Sales

finished her rookie season averaging 32.5 minutes and 13.7 points per game. (The Miracle ended the 1999 season in fourth place in the Eastern Conference, just beyond the conference's final play-off spot.)

Though Nykesha Sales presumably still has many years ahead of her in the WNBA, she is already thinking about life after basketball. With first-hand experience of the problems facing six-foot-tall women and with a degree in business and a love of clothes and shoes—she has been called "Miss Fashion"—Sales has thought about opening a "shoestore for women with big feet." During a live chat with fans on the WNBA Web site (December 22, 1998), she said, "Most shoes stop at [size] 10, and most basketball players start at 10 and a half. I'd like to be there for the women with big feet." — T.J.F.

Suggested Reading: *ESPN Magazine* (on-line) Mar. 1998; *Hartford Courant* (on-line) Jan. 25, 1998, Feb. 26, 1998; *New York Times* C p1 Feb. 25, 1998, with photo, A p1 Feb. 26, 1998, with photo, C p2 Feb. 26, 1998; *Time* p78 Mar. 9, 1998, with photo

---

Sandage, Allan

June 18, 1926– Astronomer. Address: c/o Carnegie Observatories, 813 Santa Barbara St., Pasadena, CA 91101

For over 40 years, the astronomer Allan Sandage has been involved in one of the most ambitious of human endeavors: determining the size and age of the entire universe by making careful observations with powerful telescopes. This branch of astronomy is called observational cosmology. Sandage's undertaking is not only ambitious but also solitary: it has required him to spend thousands of nights by himself in the cramped, often freezing observation cages of giant telescopes. Sandage's work has also been exceptionally frustrating, because for many years, he has tried without success to convince many of his colleagues that his estimate of the age of the universe—between 15 billion and 20 billion years—is correct. Other astronomers, using different methods, have produced much lower estimates—between nine billion and 12 billion years.

The key to determining the age of the universe is finding the value of the Hubble constant. The search for the Hubble constant can be traced back to 1929, when the astronomer Edwin Hubble discovered that the spectral lines in the light from distant objects in the universe were shifted toward the red end of the spectrum. Put another way, Hubble discovered that the characteristic colors in light from distant objects had longer wavelengths than the characteristic colors of light measured in a lab on Earth. This phenomenon was dubbed the redshift.

Hubble believed that the redshift was caused by the Doppler effect—a change in the frequency and lengths of waves that results when the source of the waves is moving toward or away from an observer. If the former, the frequency of the waves appears to increase and the length to decrease; if the latter, the frequency of the waves appears to decrease and their length to increase. In addition, the magnitude of the decrease or increase of the wavelengths indicates the speed with which the source of the waves is moving away from or toward the observer.

Hubble observed that the farther an object is from Earth, the greater the redshift, and therefore, the greater the speed with which the object is moving away from Earth. He therefore conjectured that the universe is expanding, and that the speed with which an object in the cosmos is receding from our planet is proportional to its distance from the Earth. This proportion is expressed as the Hubble constant. The distance of an object from Earth multiplied by the Hubble constant equals the object's speed of recession.

Once the Hubble constant is known, astronomers can use it to determine how long ago everything in the universe existed as a single mass—the moment of the putative Big Bang. A low Hubble constant would mean the universe is expanding slowly and thus is relatively old. A high Hubble constant would mean the universe is expanding quickly and is thus relatively young. Determining the exact value of the Hubble constant, however, is a tricky matter. Astronomers can easily determine an object's speed of recession by measuring its redshift. Measuring an object's distance from Earth is much more difficult. Since light gets dimmer as it moves farther away from its source, a galaxy that looks faint to an observer on Earth could be either a dim galaxy that is close to Earth or a very brilliant galaxy that is extremely far away.

To determine distance, astronomers search for what they call "standard candles," or objects whose absolute, as opposed to perceived, luminosity can be measured. Among standard candles identified so far are some stars categorized as the Cepheids, whose luminosity varies according to a precise rhythm. From the rate at which a Cepheid star goes from its dimmest magnitude to its brightest and then back to its dimmest, astronomers can measure its absolute brilliance. By comparing this figure to the star's perceived luminosity on Earth, they can then determine how far the light from the Cepheid star has traveled to reach Earth. Cepheid stars are not very bright, so at present, astronomers can establish distances only for those that are relatively close to our own galaxy, the Milky Way. Because different astronomers rely on different techniques for measuring distances of more-distant stars, their figures for the age of the universe vary greatly. Sandage and his critics have long engaged in vigorous debate about whose method is more accurate.

Discovering the actual age of the universe will help resolve deep cosmological mysteries. For instance, according to the calculations of some theoretical physicists, certain stars are about 15 billion years old. That figure, determined independently of the work of observational cosmologists, fits comfortably with Sandage's estimated age of the universe. But if the younger age of the universe is accepted, that would lead to the strange proposition that some stars are older than the universe. Since presumably the universe is older than the stars

within it, evidence of its youthfulness would mean that something is wrong either with the theoretical physicists' methods of determining the ages of stars or with conventional theories about the expansion of the universe.

Also at stake is Sandage's reputation as an observational cosmologist. At one point, he was considered one of the leading authorities in astronomy. In his book Lonely Hearts of the Cosmos (1991), the science journalist Dennis Overbye wrote, "Allan Sandage's stature in astronomy was almost beyond measurement. By the mid-seventies he had been Mr. Cosmology—'SuperHubble' some people called him—for more than 20 years." From his position at the Carnegie Observatories, in Pasadena, California, Sandage had access to the 100-inch Hooker telescope atop Mount Wilson and the 200-inch telescope atop Mount Palomar. Armed with these two powerful telescopes, Sandage made many contributions to astronomy, including discoveries concerning the evolution of stars and the first photos of quasars. This work has won him numerous awards, including the Eddington Medal of the Royal Astronomical Society, the National Medal of Science, the 1975 Bruce Medal, and the 1991 Crafoord Prize from the Royal Swedish Academy of Sciences.

But in recent years, Sandage's reputation has suffered somewhat, in part because of the controversy over the age of the universe. "Ninety percent of America's astronomers think I'm a has-been, totally out of touch, like dinosaurs," he told Frederic Golden for Astronomy (December 1997). Although Sandage stopped stargazing in 1994—after observing the cosmos 100 nights a year for more than 40 years—and retired, on September 1, 1997, he continues to publish papers, and he has stuck by his estimates of the age of the universe. Studies derived from data obtained from the Hubble Space Telescope may ultimately disprove or support his work.

An only child, Sandage was born on June 18, 1926 in Iowa City, Iowa, and was raised in Ohio. His father, who descended from a Missouri farmer, was a professor of business. Sandage's mother was the daughter of the president of a Mormon school. Sandage became interested in astronomy in his youth, after sneaking a peek through a friend's telescope. He began watching the skies both night and day, and for one four-year period in his teens, he kept a record of the number of sunspots he observed. His preferred reading at the time included such books as Hubble's The Realm of the Nebulae (1936) and the popular-science writings of the British astronomer and mathematician Arthur Stanley Eddington.

Sandage attended Miami University, in Oxford, Ohio—where his father taught—and studied physics and philosophy. After two years of study, he was drafted into the navy; he served for 18 months during World War II as an electronics specialist in Gulfport, Louisiana, and at Treasure Island, in San Francisco, California. By the time he left the navy, his father had started teaching at the University of Illinois, in Urbana, so he enrolled there. He gained practical experience in astronomy by working as a volunteer in the university's observatory. In 1948, he completed an A.B. degree in physics.

When Sandage graduated from Urbana, the grand 200-inch Hale mirror telescope—the biggest telescope in the world at the time—was being constructed, at the Palomar Observatory, in southern California. Eager to work at the observatory, he entered the newly created astronomy program at the California Institute of Technology, in Pasadena, which was then running the Palomar Observatory in collaboration with Carnegie Observatories. While there, he got an opportunity to work with some of the best-known astronomers of the day, among them Hubble and Walter Baade. After Hubble suffered a heart attack and sought a graduate student to help him, Sandage took on that duty. He began making regular trips to Palomar, which was about two hours southeast of Pasadena, to serve as Hubble's surrogate observer. "It was an opportunity that was beyond imagination—first of all, observing with the 200-inch, and, second, working on the long-range program of cosmology with Hubble," Sandage told Dennis Overbye. "And at the same time being a graduate student, trying to pass the course in physics and astronomy. So it was a very high-pressure atmosphere."

Before getting his doctoral degree, Sandage was offered a position at Mount Wilson with Carnegie Observatories. He accepted, and then delayed his appointment so that he could spend the next year at Princeton University, in New Jersey, doing postdoctoral work on the evolution of stars under the supervision of Martin Schwarzschild. While a student at the California Institute of Technology, Sandage had conducted observations of globular clusters, formations of stars that are believed to be extremely old. By analyzing Sandage's data, observing which types of stars had already expired within the globular clusters, and then making use of theoretical physics, Schwarzschild came up with a model to explain stellar evolution. This work within the realm of theoretical physics gave Sandage a tentative but independent estimate for the age of the universe of around 3.2 billion years—more than 50 percent greater than Hubble's estimate of the age of the universe.

In September 1953, shortly after Sandage returned to Pasadena, Hubble died of a heart attack. Sandage assumed responsibility for carrying on his work. "Hubble died too young and left me with a burden, an incredible burden, to carry out his program," Sandage told Dennis Overbye. Part of Hubble's project entailed a long-term series of observations that Hubble had hoped would lead to the discovery of two numbers: the Hubble constant and q-nought, a number that describes the shape of space. Theoretically q-nought will reveal whether the universe will expand indefinitely, collapse back upon itself, or remain in a steady state between expansion and collapse. Sandage has described cosmology as essentially the search for the Hubble constant and q-nought.

As data poured in and errors were discovered in Hubble's work, Sandage gradually revised Hubble's estimate of the age of the universe. By 1958, Sandage had announced that the universe was actually about seven to 13 billion years old—much older than Hubble had thought.

In the course of his everyday work, Sandage contributed to the discovery of a unique phenomenon in the universe. Tom Matthews, a California Institute of Technology radio astronomer, had given him a list of radio sources he wanted to identify. The first one Sandage photographed, 3C 48, had a spectrum unlike any he had seen before. After determining that the luminosity of the source was changing, Sandage concluded that 3C 48 was a star, not a galaxy. Never before had a star that emitted such radio signals been identified, and Sandage subsequently announced the discovery of the first "radio star," later named "quasar" (for "quasi-stellar radio source"). Another astronomer, Maarten Schmidt, revealed that the spectrum signal emitted by the source indicated a redshift of incredible magnitude, meaning that the quasar was an intensely brilliant object farther away than anything yet observed in the universe. In search of more quasars, Sandage eventually discovered radio-silent quasars, which he found were much more abundant then the radio-emitting variety.

Although quasars are remarkable, they are not "standard candles," and so are not useful in the quest to pin down the Hubble constant. To learn its value, Sandage and his long-time collaborator Gustav Tammann attempted to construct a "distance ladder" of measurements extending to the farthest galaxies. Each "rung" of the ladder depended on the distance calculated for the rung immediately below it. For the first rung, Sandage and Tammann established distances to nearby galaxies by locating Cepheids, a feat that took years of careful observation. To measure the distances of farther-away objects, they relied on the discovery that the brightness of spiral galaxies is related to the size of patches of ionized hydrogen gas on the galaxies' arms. Thus, galaxies with similarly sized gaseous regions were assumed to be of the same absolute brilliance. Figuring out the absolute distance to one (by means of the Cepheid measurements) provided a tool for determining the absolute distance to ones farther out. Additional rungs of the distance ladder were calculated by a similar method that involved making correlations between absolute luminosity and measurable physical characteristics of stars and galaxies and then calibrating the actual distances by referring to lower rungs of the distance ladder. By 1975, Sandage had revised his estimate of the age of the universe to between 15 billion and 20 billion years.

By this time, however, other astronomers had begun to challenge Sandage's methods and work. Those astronomers included Gérard de Vaucouleurs; Richard Fisher and Brent Tully, who developed the Tully-Fisher method of correlating the absolute brightness of spiral galaxies with their rotational velocity; and Marc Aaronson, John Huchra, and Jeremy Mould, who used infrared methods to measure distance. Those six astronomers have published studies in which they claimed that the Hubble constant is higher and that the universe is much younger than Sandage thought. Thus started what some science journalists have taken to calling the "Hubble wars."

In response to his critics, Sandage reconstructed his distance ladder using other methods. For instance, in the eighth of an ongoing series of papers entitled "Steps to the Hubble Constant" (1982), he used as a standard candle Type 1A supernovas of white dwarfs, which are believed to display uniform brightness. Since such supernova are extremely brilliant, they are suitable for establishing extremely far distances. With that method, Sandage still got figures for the Hubble constant of about 50.

The debate over the Hubble constant continues. Astronomers hope that observations made from the powerful Hubble Space Telescope, which was launched in 1990, will ultimately resolve the debate over the constant. So far the space telescope, too, has produced contradictory evidence. One group of astronomers, led by Wendy Freedman, who also works at Carnegie Observatories, measured Cepheids in the distant Virgo cluster and got an estimate for the age of the universe of between nine and 12 billion years. A team led by Sandage also used the space telescope to make observations of Type 1A supernovas; they came up with an age of at least 15 billion years. "The media says the data show that the two sides are coming together, but that's not true," Sandage told Frederic Golden for *Astronomy*. "We've stayed rock bottom with our numbers [that is, the value of the Hubble constant and the age of the universe] all along."

The intellectual skirmishes of the "Hubble wars" have led some journalists to describe Sandage as feisty and combative. Sandage prefers to view his strong advocacy of his position as part of the process of science. "Since science is the only self-correcting human institution I know of, you should not be frightened to take an extreme stand, if that causes the stand to be examined more thoroughly than it might be if you are circumspect," he told John Noble Wilford for the *New York Times* (March 12, 1991). "I've always been positive about the value of the Hubble constant, knowing full well that it probably isn't solved."

Contrary to the stereotype of scientists, Sandage has said that he believes in the existence of God. In 1980 he converted to Christianity. "Science cannot answer the deepest questions," he explained to Wilford. "As soon as you ask why is there something instead of nothing you have gone beyond science. I find it quite improbable that such order came out of chaos. There has to be some organizing principle. God to me is a mystery, but is the explanation for the miracle of existence, why there is

something instead of nothing." Sandage believes that his religious feelings do not in any way compromise his scientific objectivity. "In this office I have to be a rational reductionist," he told Wilford. "None of this feeds back at all into the hard-nosed business of the laboratory or the observatory. It must not."

In 1959 Sandage married the former Mary Connelly, who was at the time a teacher of astronomy at Mount Holyoke College, in Massachusetts. She later gave up her career to raise their two sons, David and John, but at times she has helped Sandage with mathematical calculations for his work. In addition to more scientific papers, Sandage intends to publish a history of Mount Wilson astronomy. — W.G.

Suggested Reading: *Astronomy* p54+ Dec. 1997, with photos; *New York Times* C p1+ Mar. 12, 1991, with photos, C p1+ Mar. 5, 1996, with photo; Overbye, Dennis. *Lonely Hearts of the Cosmos*, 1991

Courtesy of Cristina Saralegui Enterprises

Saralegui, Cristina
(sa-ra-LEG-ee)

Jan. 29, 1948– Spanish-language talk-show host. Address: c/o Cristina Saralegui Enterprises, 64 Palm Ave., Palm Island, Miami Beach, FL 33139

Often referred to as the Hispanic Oprah Winfrey, the Cuban-born talk-show host Cristina Saralegui, whose Miami-based TV program, *El Show de Cristina*, is viewed by an estimated 100 million people in 15 countries each day, feels that it is her responsibility to educate and open the minds of her viewers. Speaking of her Spanish-speaking audience, she told Gloria Nicola for *2020mag.com*, "Our people need information. We try to teach them that they should not be embarrassed to ask for help. And we try to teach people how to live together in this country, without abandoning their Latin roots. . . . I want them to succeed and thrive without forgetting who they are."

Cristina Saralegui was born on January 29, 1948 in Havana, Cuba, the eldest of the five children of Francisco and Cristina Saralegui. In Cuba, several generations of the Saralegui family had been involved in publishing; Cristina's father and grandfather published three best-selling magazines—*Vanidades*, *Bohemia*, and *Carteles*. They also owned paper mills. The family businesses were confiscated in about 1959, after Fidel Castro and his Communist government took over the country. Saralegui told Valerie Menard for *Hispanic* (April 1998) that she remembers her father waking her up late one night when she was 12 years old and telling her that they were leaving Havana. "My father only told us we were leaving, not that we were leaving forever," she said. "But somehow I knew." Although she would like to return to her homeland someday, Cristina has said that she will not do so "until Castro is overthrown or he dies, whichever comes first."

After emigrating to Miami, the Saralegui family partially rebuilt their former business. As a girl, Cristina often expressed a wish to work with her father when she grew up, but according to Alec Foege in *People* (April 13, 1998), her parents often told her that it was more appropriate for women to "work in the house." In spite of her parents' advice, when she completed high school, Saralegui enrolled at the University of Miami, where she studied mass communication and creative writing. In *Moderna* (December 1997, on-line), Valerie Menard reported that she stopped attending college one semester short of graduating because of financial difficulties and her father's "chauvinistic" belief that her brother's education was more important than hers. She then took a job as an assistant at the photo library of the Spanish-language women's magazine *Vanidades*, a new incarnation of the magazine her father had published in Cuba. "I landed the job because I was able to identify a photograph of Senator Edward Kennedy," Saralegui told Gloria Nicola.

Saralegui still had her heart set on becoming a journalist, and because she found herself working at a Spanish magazine, she retaught herself to write in her first language. (Her formal education had been predominantly in English.) In 1973 she was hired as a staff writer at the Spanish-language version of *Cosmopolitan*, and for the next several years, she worked for both *Cosmopolitan* and the Spanish-language weekly *TV y Novelas*. In 1979 she was promoted to editor in chief of the Spanish-language *Cosmopolitan*. In that position, Saralegui attempted to give the magazine a feminist edge.

She told Julie Rigby for the *Chicago Tribune* (May 31, 1992) that what she wanted to get across to her readers was that "liberation is from the neck up." "I tried to give my readers the answers to the questions that would arise after they joined the workforce," she said. "Here [in the United States], if an Anglo woman makes more money than her husband, it's a problem. But for a Hispanic woman, it destroys her whole house."

In 1989, noting Saralegui's overwhelming popularity among Hispanic Americans, the directors of Univision, a Miami-based Spanish-language television network, approached her about developing a talk show. Cristina agreed to the plan, and the production of *El Show de Cristina* was soon underway. "I was petrified, the director was petrified, and the audience was petrified," she told Nicola, recalling her first experience in front of a camera. "I didn't even know how to hold a mike." Saralegui also told Nicola that sometimes she felt that she "had to fight really hard to make people understand that a Cuban from Miami could represent Hispanics anywhere." She explained to Rigby, "People would write me hate letters. How dare I try to represent Hispanics when I was so white? I tried to make them see it was racism. I'm very, very Spanish. . . . The Cubans are just my tribe. Hispanics are my people. Cuba is my roots, but this is my country." In viewer polls conducted in the U.S. within six months of its premiere, the hour-long talk show was rated first among Spanish-language television shows. By 1992 it was being broadcast throughout the U.S. and in 15 Latin American countries.

One of the surprising things about *El Show de Cristina* was that it demonstrated that, contrary to popular expectations, many Hispanics were willing to talk about their problems on television. "It was assumed that Hispanics wouldn't talk," Saralegui told Larry Rohter for the *New York Times* (July 26, 1992). "But you know what? They are not reticent and they are not shy. There are a lot of misconceptions about them. They are dying to talk, just the same as you." She also told Rohter that her show has confirmed her belief that "whether we came 15 minutes ago or 10 generations ago, we all brought our roots with us [to the U.S.]." As a host, Saralegui tries to create an atmosphere in which people feel comfortable with their ethnicity. "Whenever we are on the *Donohue* show or whatever, we try to be very American, rather than Italian, Jewish, Irish, Hispanic, or black, [but] I want my guests to be what they really are, because diversity makes this country fun and great."

Ranging from sensational to serious, the subject matter of *El Show de Cristina* generally mirrors that of many English-language talk shows in the U.S., but it differs from its English-language counterparts in several ways. Perhaps the most obvious is that Saralegui allows children to be members of her audience and to participate in discussions, even ones on topics considered to be inappropriate for young people. "The world is not ideal, and the only weapon we can give our children is information," she explained to Rigby. "Whenever I have a sexual topic, I try not to get graphic. I don't get down and dirty. I establish the problem, and then I go straight into the consequences. There's a lot of pain involved. And I don't want to hear people complain that children are watching. I know that." Saralegui also tries to keep loud or offensive arguments to a minimum on her show. "When a fight breaks out, I stop taping," she told Rigby. "It might not be good television, but once [the fighting has] cooled down, I can communicate, educate, and inform."

In 1992 the CBS television network produced an 11-part English-language pilot of Saralegui's talk show. "My problem is to translate the feeling of the Spanish show into English," the TV host, who speaks English fluently but with an accent, told Rigby after the show debuted. "Not the words, but the feeling." She also pointed out that although, in her opinion, her show was "more refreshing, quirky, and more spontaneous" than many other talk shows, "the competition is so fierce." "Nowadays even milk of magnesia has to be flavored like mint or else people won't drink it. . . . You're teaching [the audience] a lesson, like a little schoolteacher, but it still has to look good." The ratings on the initial 11 installments of the English-language show were mixed, and because CBS did not offer Saralegui and her husband, who managed the show, as much money as they wanted, no further programs were produced in English. Saralegui has said that she would welcome another try at making an English-language show, and she feels that, since English-speaking Americans have recently become more exposed to Hispanic culture, such a program would now have a better chance of succeeding. "Americans have changed a lot in the last five years," she told Foege. "They know salsa is something that Cubans dance and Mexicans eat." Since 1992 Saralegui has begun publishing her own Spanish-language magazine, *Cristina la Revista* (Cristina: The Magazine), which has a circulation of 150,000 in the U.S. and Latin America. She also broadcasts a radio show, *Cristina Opina* (Cristina's Opinion), which airs on ABC Radio International in 90 countries around the world.

Saralegui's career is managed by her second husband, Marcos Avila, a bass player who was a founding member of Gloria Estefan's group, the Miami Sound Machine. (Saralegui counts Estefan among her close friends.) She was previously married to Tony Menendez, a Miami firefighter and real-estate salesperson, and she has two daughters—Cristina Amalia and Stephanie Ann—from that marriage. "I got married the first time because I wanted to have a family," she told Rigby. "I thought romance was for foolish ladies. I met [my second husband] when I was 35, and I thought, God sent me this to show me how wrong I was before. . . . I was 11 years older than him, I wore a suit, I was the editor in chief of a ladies' magazine, and I had a big staff. [Marcos] was a little musician

with a blond ponytail and an earring. Imagine him at an editorial cocktail party! Everybody's family had a fit! But here we are . . . very happy." She has admitted, however, that working with a loved one can be difficult. "We fight all the time," she told Rigby. "He's my boss. I'm his on-air person. I've heard people say they get home and they don't talk about it, but I can't do that. . . . When things come up, they need to come out." The couple have one son, Jon Marcos.

In 1998 Saralegui's autobiography, *Cristina! My Life as a Blonde*, was published by Warner in both English and Spanish editions. The book chronicles her rise to the top of the world of Hispanic media. Saralegui has said that she intended the title to be not an attention-getter but, rather, as Menard wrote, an expression of "the dichotomy in which she has found herself upon first arriving in the U.S." She has explained that, because she has light skin and blond hair, she was readily accepted by Anglo-Americans until they found out she was Cuban. Hispanic Americans, meanwhile, often refused to look past her coloring.

By her own account, what the celebrated talk-show host enjoys most about her job is that she is constantly learning. "I learn from everybody and everything," she told Nicola. "I learn from the good and the bad. I am on a quest. I want to know what life is all about." In addition, she said, she "love[s] thinking that [she has] helped someone." What she likes least about her job is, perhaps, her demanding schedule and having to travel so much. "Maybe I'm selfish," she told Rigby. "People say, 'What about your kids?' What about me? I miss them so much." To some extent, her children are involved in her career. "When we do a mailing we are all in the garage," she said. "The kids help out. They like to feel part of it."

Saralegui and her family live in a bay-front Mediterranean-style mansion on Palm Island, in Miami Beach, Florida, with their four dachshunds, a pet rabbit, and a large aquarium of fish. In what little spare time she has, she enjoys reading biographies and listening to Brazilian music, jazz, and salsa. Saralegui has served as a spokesperson for the American Foundation for AIDS Research. She is also the Hispanic spokesperson for AT&T and has her own line of eyewear. — C.P.

Suggested Reading: *Chicago Tribune* VI p5 May 31, 1992, with photo; *Hispanic* p30+ Apr. 1998, with photo; *Moderna* (on-line); *New York Times* II p23 July 6, 1992, with photo; *People* p71+ Apr. 13, 1998, with photos; *2020mag.com* (on-line) Feb. 1998, with photo

Selected Radio Shows: *Cristina Opina*

Selected Television Shows: *El Show de Cristina*, 1989–

Selected Books: *Cristina! My Life as a Blonde*, 1998

Archive Photos

Sassoon, Vidal
(sah-SOON, VEE-dahl)

Jan. 17, 1928– Hairstylist; entrepreneur. Address: c/o Vidal Sassoon National Press Office, General Motors Plaza, 767 Fifth Ave., New York, NY 10022

"Americans used to see hairdressers as someone who lisped slightly and did pretty things on top of the head," Vidal Sassoon told a reporter in 1973. "But now, hairdressing has come out of the boudoir." Sassoon has played a major role in the development and legitimization of the hair-care industry. In the 1960s he was the main force behind the wash-and-go philosophy of haircutting, which freed countless women from the daily time-consuming chore of styling their hair. Sassoon has also developed an extremely successful line of hair-care products and styling tools, now manufactured by the Procter and Gamble Co. Currently, there are 31 Vidal Sassoon hair salons in six countries, and Sassoon's name is recognized worldwide. "It was a natural progression," the hair stylist-turned-mogul told Leslie Tonner for the *Wall Street Journal* (October 8, 1973). "I turned toward something bigger than my personal ego standing behind a chair."

Vidal Sassoon was born on January 17, 1928 in London, England. His parents, Nathan and Betty Sassoon, were descendants of Sephardic Jews (that is, Jews from Spain and Portugal). When Vidal was five years old, his father, a carpet salesman, left the family "for another lady," as Vidal explained to James Langton for the *Electronic Telegraph* (January 24, 1998, on-line). Betty Sassoon was left in dire financial straits, and, unable to support her

two sons, she arranged for their care in a Jewish orphanage in the Maida Vale section of London. Speaking of the years he spent there, Vidal Sassoon told Langton, "I really don't remember feeling deprived or unhappy." He remained in the orphanage until his mother remarried, when he was 13.

After leaving the orphanage, Vidal entered a regular middle (or junior-high) school. Perhaps because the education he had received earlier had been inadequate, he did very poorly in school, and he dropped out before his 15th birthday. His mother, inspired by a dream in which her son was styling her hair, took Vidal to a reputable London hairdresser named Adolph Cohen, in the hope that he would teach her son the trade. At first Cohen asked for an apprenticeship fee, but Sassoon could not afford it; taken by the teenager's politeness as the interview progressed, Cohen waived the fee and hired him.

In Cohen's shop Sassoon shampooed hair, swept the floor, and cleaned combs. His thick Cockney accent prevented him from progressing to stylist. "When I was a kid, you couldn't get a job outside the East End [a low-income section of London] with a Cockney voice like mine," he was quoted as saying in a release from the Vidal Sassoon National Press Office. To alter his speech, he began buying theater tickets as soon as he could afford to, and he listened carefully to the actors' "good English." Years later he also took voice and elocution lessons.

During and after World War II, Sassoon would work at Cohen's salon by day and then attend evening meetings of antifascist groups and Zionist organizations. "I actually spent a night in jail for breaking up a fascist meeting at a pub in Kilburn [a section of London]," Sassoon told Langton. "The following day, the judge told us all to be good boys and behave ourselves." In 1948, when he was 20 years old, Sassoon volunteered to fight in Israel's War of Independence. He joined the Palmach, one of several small armies that eventually became part of the Israeli government defense force. Sassoon counts his experiences as a Palmach fighter among the most important in his life. "As manual labor strengthened my body, I began to discover a sense of pride, the dignity of achievement," he told Margaret Manson for the *Washington Post* (February 12, 1976). "I was not simply an object of hate, something to be despised." Moreover, after he returned to England, he told Sean O'Hagan for *New Statesman and Society* (December 7, 1990), he "came back to hairdressing with a commitment, a sense of purpose, and a totally different concept of who I was. I basically came back with a spirit of adventure about hair."

In 1954 Sassoon opened his first salon, at 108 Bond Street, in London. A full-fledged stylist by then, he specialized in creating precise, modern-looking shapes that required little or no daily styling. Through word-of-mouth, news of his unique haircutting method spread, and many fashion models and actresses began to patronize his shop.

In 1957 he began collaborating with the iconoclastic British designer Mary Quant, the "mother of the miniskirt." For several seasons he cut and styled models' hair for Quant's much-talked-about fashion shows. For one of her 1963 shows, Quant asked Sassoon to create a new hairstyle that would leave models' shoulders and necks bare. The result was the Sassoon bob, a cut that is short at the nape of the neck and hangs to chin- or shoulder-length in front, depending on the features of the subject. The cut was an instant hit, and to satisfy the many customers who were seeking easy-to-manage hairstyles, other salons began offering it. More than 35 years later, the Sassoon bob is still considered fashionable.

In the following years Sassoon created several other popular haircuts that required little if any styling. For the asymmetrical bob, Sassoon left a long swoop of hair that almost covered the face, and on the other side of a side part, he created a much shorter, trimmed look. The five-point cut, a style for short hair, produced a pixie look and was adopted by many actresses in the 1960s. Another of Sassoon's very short cuts, known as the Greek goddess, featured tousled, close-cropped curls. By the late 1960s, Sassoon was styling hair for several couture designers in Paris. He gained further acclaim in the U.S. after creating the pixieish cut worn by the actress Mia Farrow in the director Roman Polanski's film *Rosemary's Baby* (1968).

Earlier, in 1965, Sassoon had opened his first salon in the U.S., on Madison Avenue in New York City. Because he was already world famous, the state board of cosmetology allowed him to operate without the required license for more than one year. When the board finally insisted that he take the exam, Sassoon became infuriated, because he felt that someone of his renown should be exempted from licensing requirements. He showed up for the exam but handed in a blank test paper and therefore failed. Sometime later he took the exam again and passed. He had yielded to the board, he told Elisabeth Dunn for the London *Guardian* (October 7, 1970), because operating without a license had hurt his business. "I fought them for a year, but they just wouldn't let me do anything until I passed the test," he said.

In the late 1960s Sassoon began laying the foundation for his hair-care empire. First, to staff his growing number of salons in Europe and North America, he developed a comprehensive training program for aspiring stylists and then opened two schools, in London and New York, respectively. The popularity of the course soon spurred him to open a second London school and then one in San Francisco. A high percentage of his graduates went on to work in his salons, where their creativity was respected and encouraged. "I was the first person . . . to let my staff have credits in magazines," Sassoon told Dunn. "I feel very strongly people should get the credit they deserve."

Sassoon had begun producing shampoos and protein mixtures (forerunners of present-day hair conditioners) for different types of hair much earlier in the decade. In the late 1960s he started manufacturing his formulations in large quantities and began selling them in his salons. He also came out with a line of brushes, combs, hand-held blow dryers, and curling irons, all of which sold extremely well. In the *Detroit News* (October 30, 1997, online), Craig Wilson wrote that Sassoon is "partly responsible for a hair dryer now being in most everyone's bathroom." Profits from his products eventually exceeded those from his salons and schools. "I became a businessman to survive," he told Suzy Kalter and Thomas Levenson of *People* (May 10, 1982). "There's no money in being a hairdresser. Products are where the money is." Sassoon's product lines, which are now owned and manufactured by the Procter and Gamble Co., are sold in retail stores around the world. Until recently Sassoon was a consultant to Procter and Gamble and was actively involved in promoting the products.

In 1970 Sassoon and his wife, Beverly Adams, a model and actress, moved to New York with their children. The following year Sassoon turned over the direction of his salons to Roger Thompson, a Sassoon-trained stylist who had served as artistic director for the salons for several years. Sassoon then began to focus his energy on promoting his new salons and his products in U.S. cities and in Canada, Italy, and Germany. He also became a frequent guest on many nationally broadcast television and radio talk shows. *A Year of Beauty and Health*, which Sassoon co-authored with his wife and the former *Vogue* editor Camille Duhe, was published in 1975; it was one of the top-selling books in the U.S. that year. In their spare time Sassoon and his wife studied literature at New York University and vacationed at health farms in the western United States.

In the 1980s the combined earnings of the Sassoon salons, schools, and product lines soared to about $100 million per year. By then, perhaps because he was no longer consumed with the businesses of his salons and schools, Sassoon had begun dabbling in a number of other business projects, including the marketing of a collection of designer jeans, which became moderately successful. He also launched his own radio show, on which he offered advice on beauty and health. Despite his previous popularity on talk shows, his radio program got poor ratings, and it was canceled after a run of 26 weeks. One critic of the show said, as quoted by Kalter and Levenson, "Mr. Sassoon emerges as a thoroughly unpleasant little man spewing forth some of the most obnoxious advice imaginable." During the 1980s Sassoon appeared in TV commercials for his products. The ads featured the motto "If you don't look good, we don't look good."

In 1993 a 50-year retrospective of Sassoon's work—demonstrated through photos and videos—was mounted successively at several museums in

Europe, North America, and Asia, including the Costume Institute at the Metropolitan Museum of Art in New York City. "Sassoon is in the small coterie of creative individuals who have defined what it means to be modern," Richard Martin, a curator at the Metropolitan Museum, observed, as quoted by the *New York Times* (February 28, 1993). *Sassoon: Fifty Years Ahead*, the book that accompanied the exhibit, was published by the Italian firm Rizzoli.

Vidal Sassoon has been inducted into the U.S. Cosmetology Hall of Fame and the British Hairdressing Hall of Fame. He has earned the North American Hairstyling Award for Lifetime Achievement, the French Ministry of Culture Award, and the British Intercoiffure Award. According to his company press release, he is the subject of questions in the board-game Trivial Pursuit, and a hybrid rose bears his name. Sassoon is often a special guest at fashion shows in London and New York.

Among the charities that Sassoon supports are HairCares, an organization of salon professionals who offer help to those among their colleagues who have been diagnosed with AIDS. In cooperation with the Urban League of Los Angeles, he established a scholarship program that enables disadvantaged African-Americans to attend his schools. He has also underwritten projects for the Dance Theater of Harlem and the Los Angeles Music Center, and he produced one mounting of Athol Fugard's 1989 play *My Children, My Africa*. He is the founder of the Vidal Sassoon Centre for the Study of Anti-Semitism and Related Bigotries at the Hebrew University in Jerusalem, Israel.

Sassoon's autobiography, *Sorry I Kept You Waiting, Madam*, was published in 1968. In a representative positive assessment, Zena Sutherland wrote for the *Saturday Review* (October 19, 1968), "Much of his story consists of professional or social chit-chat, but the author's high good humor and breezy style are quite engaging." A *Times Literary Supplement* (May 23, 1968) critic, by contrast, ended the autobiography feeling cheated. "The book could . . . have been useful to the historian of fashion; but instead of giving us a picture of his times Mr. Sassoon persists in projecting the image his publicists have invented," the reviewer complained.

Vidal Sassoon has four children—Catya, Eden, Elan, and David—from his first marriage, to Beverly Adams. He is currently married to Rhonda Sassoon, an interior designer, with whom he lives in Beverly Hills, California. When Langton asked Sassoon why he chose to stay in the U.S. and become an American citizen, he replied, "It's the separation of church and state in the United States; as a Jew the established church in Britain makes me feel an outsider. The idea of an official religion is so outmoded." Sassoon works out in a gym in his large home and swims in his pool every day. His two small dogs, he told Craig Wilson in 1997, "have the best geometric cuts in all Los Angeles."

Sassoon equates success with creativity rather than wealth. "I do believe there's an enormous difference between success and rewards," he told Karen E. Klages for the *Chicago Tribune* (March 31, 1993). "The excitement of the moment when a creative idea happens—I believe that's what success is all about. . . . The rest are just rewards." — C.P.

Suggested Reading: *Chicago Tribune* p10+ Mar. 31, 1993, with photos; *Detroit News* (on-line) Oct. 30, 1997, with photo; *Electronic Telegraph* (on-line) Jan. 24, 1998; (London) *Guardian* p9 Oct. 7, 1970, with photo; *New York Post* p63 Nov. 18, 1970, with photo, p35 June 3, 1974, with photos, p31 Feb. 9, 1976; *New York Times* p42 Oct. 18, 1971, with photos; *People* p105+ May 10, 1982, with photos; *Wall Street Journal* p1+ Oct. 8, 1973; *Washington Post* D p1+ Feb. 12, 1976, with photo

Selected Books: *Sorry I Kept You Waiting, Madam*, 1968; with Beverly Sassoon and Camille Duhe—*A Year of Beauty and Health*, 1975

Allsport

Schott, Marge

1929– Car dealer; former owner of the Cincinnati Reds. Address: 100 Cinergy Field, Cincinnati, OH 45202

Until the spring of 1999, Marge Schott was the only female controlling partner in all of major-league baseball. President and chief executive officer of the Cincinnati Reds since 1984, Schott—with the help of her management staff—was able to build the small-market team in only six years into one of the most formidable in baseball. By 1990 the Reds, led by manager Lou Piniella and general manager Bob Quinn, were World Series champions and had a core of young players who many predicted would keep them in contention for years to come. But in just two years the Reds fell apart at the seams, with Quinn and Piniella having left the team and Schott having become best known for her racial slurs and other insensitive comments. Twice in the 1990s Schott has been banned from baseball, and she is still forbidden to perform day-to-day operations for the Reds. In April 1999, after more than three years of pressure from baseball officials to sell a majority of her interest in the club, Schott finally agreed to hand over most of her shares in the franchise, ending one of the sport's most embarrassing ownership tenures.

Marge Schott was born in Ohio in 1929, one of the five daughters of a proud, difficult, second-generation German-American, Edward Unnewehr, the millionaire owner of a lumber company that specialized in manufacturing plywood and veneers. According to Rick Reilly, writing in *Sports Illustrated* (May 20, 1996), Schott's father was openly unhappy that he did not have a son, and, just as disagreeably, would ring a bell when he wanted to get his wife's attention. In addition, Edward Unnewehr reportedly refused to eat dinner with any of his children until they were four years old, to avoid what he referred to as "the messy age." Marge Schott told Reilly that her father was "very *achtung*! You didn't get sick in Daddy's family, honey. We coughed into our pillows." Edward's desire to have a son was so intense that he began treating Marge as though she were a boy. "He called her Butch," Reilly wrote. "She grew up the wisecracking girl Daddy took to work whenever he could, the circle-skirted jokester who would bring cigars to slumber parties and smoke them. She was less comfortable around women than men, whom she was learning to love and hate all at once."

In 1952 Marge married Charles Schott, the son of Walter Schott, who was at the time the largest auto dealer in Ohio. Although her father wanted her to take over his lumber company, Marge Schott's efforts went into her father-in-law's business affairs. It wasn't long before Charles took over the family business full-time from his father, and Marge, with an impressive mind for business and a gift for cost-cutting, became her husband's loyal deputy. Their marriage, however, began to deteriorate as Charles's drinking increased. In 1968 Charles Schott died of a heart attack.

Upon her husband's death, Scott took control of the couple's prosperous string of General Motors car dealerships, in effect becoming the company's president. For nearly three years, however, the GM top brass refused to recognize her as the lawful "dealer," an important distinction in the automotive-sales business; many saw this refusal as gender discrimination. In 1971, after a long legal battle, General Motors backed down and acknowl-

edged Schott as the rightful head of the company. With that battle behind her, Schott was able over the course of the next decade to expand the company, in the process becoming one of the most visible and respected female executives in Ohio. By the beginning of the 1980s, the Schott-controlled GM lots were among the biggest dealership rings in the country.

Schott had never been much of a sports fan, but seeing the opportunity as a good business investment, she bought a percentage of the Cincinnati Reds, major-league baseball's oldest team. With a history going back to the 1870s, the Reds are considered an American institution by followers of the game. "I bought the team with my head and not my heart," Schott told Ira Berkow for the *New York Times* (November 29, 1992). "It was Christmas time, and you know how women are at Christmas. You buy things and you charge it." For three years Schott remained a limited partner with the team. Then, in 1984, when several of the other limited partners put their shares up for sale, Schott purchased them. Controlling six and a half of the 15 shares—or 43 percent of the club—Schott became the team's general partner. The move made her the undisputed head of the franchise, despite her scanty knowledge of baseball.

Schott's first move as the team's owner was considered a wise one. Longtime Reds infielder Pete Rose, in the twilight of his career but on his way to breaking the legendary Ty Cobb's all-time base-hit record, was brought in as a player/manager at the start of the 1985 season. A popular figure in Cincinnati, Rose had spent the finest years of his career as a vital member of the mid-1970s Reds. Known collectively by the nickname "the Big Red Machine," a team that included such other famous ballplayers as Joe Morgan, Johnny Bench, Tony Perez, Dave Concepcion, and Ken Griffey Sr., the Reds won the World Series in 1975 and 1976. Now, on the verge of breaking one of baseball's most prestigious records—it had stood since Cobb's retirement, in the late 1920s—Rose added a new vitality to the young and talented team. On September 11, 1985, in front of a roaring Riverfront Stadium crowd in downtown Cincinnati—led by a cheering Marge Schott—Rose slapped his 4,193d career hit, topping the great Cobb. With Rose as player/manager, the Reds enjoyed several relatively successful seasons, finishing second in their division every year from 1984 to 1989. Rose's career as a major-league player ended on August 23, 1989, when, after months of investigation into Rose's financial dealings, baseball commissioner A. Bartlett Giamatti announced that Rose would be banned from baseball for an unspecified time because of overwhelming evidence that he had bet on games. Schott and her general manager, Bob Quinn, decided to hire former Yankee slugger Lou Piniella to lead the team for the 1990 season. The Reds went on to beat the powerful Oakland Athletics in that year's World Series, claiming the world championship for the first time since the mid-1970s.

As Tim Kurkjian reported in *Sports Illustrated* (October 19, 1992), Schott doubled Piniella's salary after the 1990 season, but her "love affair" with her manager—to quote Kurkjian—soured during the following year, when the Reds posted 74 wins and 88 losses, the worst record ever for a defending World Series championship team. Relations between Schott and her manager became even more strained when she refused to give Piniella, one of the most coveted managers in the game at the time, an expected contract extension late in 1992, the final year of the contract. When Schott finally got around to offering him a contract, a one-year deal that called for a pay cut, Piniella left town and signed with the Seattle Mariners. Then Quinn—who had tried to make some crucial mid-season trades in 1992 but was denied permission by Schott, despite the fact that the team was fighting for a play-off spot—simply waited for his contract to expire in early October of that year. Schott, it seemed, had single-handedly dismantled the most prosperous team in baseball.

Trouble of a different sort began to brew just over a month later. Press reports revealed that in 1991 Tim Sabo, a one-time controller for the Reds, had brought a $2.5 million lawsuit against Schott for wrongful dismissal, claiming that he had been fired for disagreeing with the owner's racist statements—which included the word "nigger." As Ira Berkow put it, the controversy over Schott's remarks had "transformed her image from that of a quirky eccentric known best for parading her St. Bernard around Riverfront Stadium into a mean-spirited, insensitive woman." Shortly thereafter Hank Aaron, baseball's all-time leading home-run hitter and a top executive for the Atlanta Braves, publicly called for her suspension. The law, however, was on Schott's side, and Sabo lost the suit, with the judge citing that under an Ohio law Schott could fire whomever she wished. Remarkably, the situation blew over after only a couple of weeks. The Reds went back to business as usual; Schott and the team's top brass hired former Mets skipper Davey Johnson as manager.

But in the winter of 1993, Schott's questionable racial attitudes once again came to the forefront of baseball. During an interview with Diane Sawyer on ABC's news program *Primetime Live*, Sawyer asked Schott about her alleged racist statements. Schott, instead of apologizing, as many expected her to do, went on to elaborate on her beliefs. Among other statements, the Reds CEO said that the Nazi swastika was "not a symbol of anything evil to me." (Several of her relatives had fought for Germany in World War II.) She also said that racism was sometimes "created by the press" and "really isn't there." As a result of her inflammatory comments, on February 3 baseball officials suspended Schott for one year.

In June 1993 sportswriter Mike Bass, a one-time winner of the Associated Press Sports Editors Award for his series of articles on racism in sports, published *Marge Schott: Unleashed*, which de-

tailed his extensive investigation into allegations of Schott's racial prejudice. Among the many incidents reported in the book, Schott allegedly once called Reds outfielder Dave Parker, who played for the team from 1984 to 1997, her "million dollar nigger." Another famous tale from the book is that of former Reds marketing director Cal Levy, whom Schott called "a beady-eyed Jew," according to Reilly, and who, while looking for a dinner bell in her home at Schott's behest one day in 1987, reportedly found a Nazi armband in one of her drawers. "Figures a Jewish guy would find it, huh, honey? What's a Jewish guy looking through my drawers for anyway?" she would later say to Reilly when questioned about the matter.

As part of the suspension, Schott was forced to relinquish her role in the day-to-day activities of the team. Despite the controversy, the Reds managed a respectable record in 1994 and won the Central Division crown. After her ban ended, Schott returned to the organization to see the team top the Central Division for the second year in a row. In a highly controversial move, she then announced that Johnson, a one-time World Series–winning manager, would be relieved of his duties at the conclusion of the season. It was said that Schott wanted to give her close friend Ray Knight, then a bench coach with the Reds, a chance to head the club. Before his stint with Cincinnati, Knight had never coached a major-league franchise, and the 1996 season proved to be a disaster. Knight's inexperience in field-managing the club combined with Schott's intense cost-cutting measures that season caused the team to fall to third place in the division, with an 81–81 record. Knight was relieved of his managerial duties before the season ended.

But it was not Knight's actions that ignited the largest firestorm of protest in Cincinnati that year. While talking with an ESPN interviewer in early May 1996, Schott shared some of her opinions regarding the German dictator and Holocaust architect Adolf Hitler. "Everything you read, when he came in [to power] he was good. . . . They built tremendous highways and got all the factories going," Schott said, according to the Anti-Defamation League's official Web page. "Everybody knows he was good at the beginning but he just went too far." The comments caused outrage among baseball officials and the general public. Shortly thereafter, Schott was suspended from baseball for two years and once again was forbidden to have anything to do with the day-to-day operations of the club. Her comments marked the beginning of the end for her as principal owner of the franchise, as baseball officials began a vigorous campaign to force her to sell her controlling interest in the Reds.

Controversy followed Schott off the baseball diamond as well, when General Motors filed a complaint against the dealership owner with the Ohio Motor Vehicles Dealers Board, alleging that she had falsified 57 sales at her Chevrolet-Geo dealerships in 1995. In doing so she had used the names of actual Cincinnati Reds employees, without their knowledge or consent. In January 1997, after two months of investigation, GM dropped the suit. Major-league baseball, however, took up an investigation of its own. After a few months of research, baseball officials informed Schott that if she did not give up controlling ownership in the Reds, she would be suspended from baseball for another two years after her initial two-year suspension ended, in 1998. In April 1999, after nearly two years of wrangling, Schott agreed to sell five and a half of her six and a half shares in the club to a group headed by minority owner Carl Lindner. According to the details of the deal, which is set to be completed in February 2000, Schott will retain part ownership of the club but will not be allowed, as she initially wished, to keep an office at the stadium.

As one of her final acts as the principal Reds owner, Schott guaranteed the team a new, 45,000-seat ballpark right next to their current, outdated stadium in downtown Cincinnati. In a ceremonial passing of the torch, Schott stood on the pitcher's mound on the Astroturf of the Reds' home field as team and government officials announced the 30-year lease agreement between the team and the city. When asked if the signing was a bittersweet moment, Schott replied, according to *CNN/SI* (May 21, 1999, on-line), "Kind of, yeah. But you do things baseball wants you to do. It's a boys' club." — M.B.

Suggested Reading: *Anti-Defamation League* (on-line) May 6, 1996; *CNN/SI* (on-line) May 21, 1999; *ESPN* (on-line) Apr. 21, 1999; *New York Times* J p1+ Nov. 29, 1992, with photos; *Sports Illustrated* p28+ Oct. 19, 1992, with photos, p72+ May 20, 1996, with photos; *Washington Post* D p1 Feb. 15, 1993

AP Photo

Schrempp, Juergen
(shremp, YER-gen)

Sep. 15, 1944– Chairman and chief executive officer of the DaimlerChrysler Corp. Address: c/o DaimlerChrysler Corp., 1000 Chrysler Dr., Auburn Hills, MI 48326

A high-school dropout who started out as an apprentice mechanic and self-taught trumpeter in a wedding band, Juergen Schrempp is chairman and CEO of the largest industrial conglomerate in Germany: the DaimlerChrysler Corp., formerly the Daimler-Benz Corp., which produces, among other things, the Mercedes line of luxury cars. As might be guessed from his unconventional background, Schrempp is something of a maverick in the German corporate world. "Schrempp doesn't fit the profile of the typical CEO, much less the typical German CEO," Alex Taylor wrote for *Fortune* (November 10, 1997). "His odd rectangular glasses are the tip-off: Anybody with the courage to wear them must (1) be utterly unconventional and (2) not care what anyone thinks."

Schrempp's willingness to stand apart from German convention is as evident in his business decisions as it is in his choice of eyewear. Since he assumed control of Daimler-Benz, in May 1995, Schrempp has helped the sprawling conglomerate become a leaner, more focused company by axing businesses that were not earning enough profit. While such actions may seem ordinary from an American perspective, they are revolutionary within the context of a German business culture that, since the post–World War II period, has more typically emphasized stability and cooperative labor-management relations over the unfettered pursuit of profit and higher dividends to shareholders. "If there's a European executive whose style resembles that of a no-nonsense American CEO . . . it's Schrempp," Karen Lowry Miller and Joann Muller wrote for *Business Week* (November 16, 1998). In fact, members of the European press have nicknamed Schrempp "Neutron Juergen," a reference to the General Electric CEO, Jack Welch, who was dubbed "Neutron Jack" because, like the neutron bomb, his cutbacks at GE eliminated people while leaving buildings intact.

Yet while Schrempp has amply demonstrated his skills at corporate slash-and-burn, he has also shown qualities of a visionary builder. In a move that created waves throughout the automobile industry, he orchestrated in 1998 a merger with the Chrysler Corp. that amounted to the biggest industrial takeover in history. The merger has already established DaimlerChrysler as the fifth-largest automaker in the world; should Schrempp prove successful in harmonizing the two companies' different corporate cultures, DaimlerChrysler could make even further gains in the 21st century.

Schrempp was born on September 15, 1944 in Freiburg, a university town in southwestern Germany, where he grew up. His father, an administrator of admissions tests at the University of Freiburg, "had trouble supporting three sons who wanted to study," Schrempp told Alex Taylor. Schrempp dropped out of school when he was 15 years old and joined Daimler-Benz as an apprentice motor mechanic. "I learned to do the most with as little effort as possible—I still do," he told Karen Lowry Miller and Joann Muller. Schrempp met the woman whom he eventually married, Renate, when he was 18, and at some point he went back to school to earn an engineering degree. It was during this period that Schrempp sometimes played trumpet at weddings to help make ends meet. In 1967, after finishing his degree, he went back to Daimler-Benz and worked in the company's sales division.

Much of Schrempp's early career with Daimler-Benz was spent abroad. From 1974 to 1982 he worked in the customer-services division of the Daimler-Benz unit in South Africa. He often angered his superiors in Stuttgart, where the company was headquartered, by speaking out against apartheid. His views helped him befriend Nelson Mandela, who later made him an honorary consul general. From 1982 to 1984 Schrempp was assigned to Cleveland, Ohio, to sell off Euclid, Daimler-Benz's heavy-equipment business in the United States. In 1984 he returned to South Africa, and in the following year he became CEO of Mercedes-Benz South Africa. His connections to the country remain strong: he owns both a home and a game reserve there.

In 1987 Schrempp returned to Stuttgart, and two years later he was named head of Deutsche Aerospace (DASA). In the 1980s Daimler-Benz had acquired an assortment of aircraft, aerospace, and military-technology companies, and Schrempp's job was to integrate them into one cohesive unit. "We merged companies, we dissolved companies, we cut layers of management, we cut head office from 700–800 people down to 300, we resolved the problem of the state, local, or federal, having great influence in the company," he told Wolfgang Münchau for the Financial Times (November 7, 1995). "We had to fight with a 60 percent cut in the defense budget. . . . The job was very exciting because everything that happened then in Germany and the world was against us. And I must tell you I like that."

Schrempp served as the head of DASA for six years before he was appointed, in May 1995, to replace Edzard Reuter, who served as CEO of Daimler-Benz from 1988 to 1995. During his tenure Reuter had embarked on an ambitious program to diversify the company's holdings and create an "integrated technology concern" made up of automobile, aerospace, electronics, and software companies. But this strategy backfired. The end of the Cold War led to declining military budgets worldwide, and a recession in the U.S. caused a rise in the value of the German mark against the dollar, which in turn drove the price of German exports upward. The losses sustained at Daimler's non-auto businesses dragged the entire company down; only marginal profits were reported in 1993 and 1994, rattling the company's primary shareholder, Deutsche Bank.

Once he took over, Schrempp immediately set out to reverse the company's many-tentacled growth. Short-term profit, rather than market share or long-term strategic interests, became the company's mantra. "When I started here, I asked people what the stock price was, and they didn't know," Schrempp told the New York Times (January 26, 1996). "The tradition in German companies is that if somebody doesn't perform, you move him sideways. Now if they don't perform, they have a material problem." Shedding businesses that were underperforming, in just a few years he shrank the number of ventures in which Daimler was involved from 38 to 23. He even cut off support to the Dutch aircraft maker Fokker NV, which had been his personal "love baby." Schrempp, as head of DASA, had acquired a majority stake in the aircraft manufacturer in 1993; three years later he acknowledged that the deal had been a mistake and wrote the investment off as a loss of over a billion dollars.

As a result of the company's downsizing, about 40,000 jobs were trimmed in two years. All surviving units were given an ultimatum: earn profits of at least 12 percent of capital employed, or else. Meanwhile, Schrempp reorganized the company's hierarchy to bring all of its units under more direct control. By 1997 he had stripped Mercedes's chief executive, Helmut Werner, of autonomous power.

Schrempp's actions were considered unusual for the business culture that had evolved in Germany. "What is happening at Daimler Benz is familiar enough in corporate America these days," one journalist wrote for Business Week (February 5, 1996). "Major shareholder gets mad; shareholder boots out old CEO; new CEO gets tough. But in Germany, this scenario has until recently been a rarity. Boardroom politics are too consensual, and shareholders unaccustomed to rocking the boat." Yet for all the changes he wrought, Schrempp maintained some continuity with the policies of his predecessor. Daimler still possesses holdings in several non–automobile manufacturing fields. Moreover, Schrempp has publicly stated his commitment to try to preserve stability for workers—not least because nine members of Daimler's governing board of 20 are union leaders. "We are not the cool portfolio managers," he told Wolfgang Münchau. "We have a mission. I want our people to identify with the company. We want to give them a stable perspective. We are prepared to go through difficult times and not just say, if in the next two years things are bad, we get out."

For the fiscal year 1995, Daimler reported a loss of over $3 billion, largely because of the write-off of Fokker. Shed of underperforming units, Daimler-Benz began reporting profits again by the following year. As a sign of investors' approval of Schrempp's moves, Daimler's stock price has steadily increased to an all-time high since he became the corporation's head, although flat earnings reported for the second quarter of 1999 precipitated a 7.5 percent fall in the value of the company's shares (compared with their value when the merger was completed).

With Daimler-Benz reorganized, Schrempp began looking for a possible merger partner. In 1998 he found one in Chrysler, the number-three automaker in the U.S. and the producer of such cars as the Plymouth Neon, Dodge Durango, and Jeep Grand Cherokee. The deal—an approximately $36 billion stock swap in which Daimler-Benz effectively acquired Chrysler—was the biggest industrial takeover in history. The combined company is now known as DaimlerChrysler, and with $131 billion in combined revenues in 1997, it became the fifth-largest automaker in the world, behind General Motors, Ford, Toyota, and Volkswagen. Chrysler's CEO and chairman, Robert Eaton, who currently shares power as co-chairman with Schrempp in the new company, is expected to retire by 2001.

Both Schrempp and Eaton believed that the merger was necessary because of a current overcapacity in the production of cars. "We in the motor industry all agree that over the next 10 years, you'll see consolidation, perhaps a halving in the number of the independent manufacturers," Schrempp told *Fortune* (June 8, 1998). "The answer can't be joint venture here, joint venture there. We said to ourselves, 'We have to find a partner.' Once we did the studies of Japanese, European, and American companies, it became obvious that Chrysler was the ideal partner." The two companies complement each other nicely. There is little overlap in product lines, for instance. Chrysler sells primarily moderately priced cars and light trucks, while Daimler specializes in luxury cars and heavy trucks. The combined company can now offer a full range of vehicles. Moreover, since Chrysler's sales are primarily in the U.S. and Daimler's are primarily in Europe, each company can help the other increase its presence in a foreign market. There are also potential savings to be had by combining purchases, overhead, and research. Schrempp and Eaton have pledged to cut $1.4 billion in costs before the end of 1999.

But there are many possible problems. Mergers of this sort in the past—like the 1978 acquisition of American Motors Corp. by the French carmaker Renault—have not always been successful. One potential pitfall is in integrating what many consider different corporate cultures. Daimler is usually perceived as a conservative company that embraces engineering over marketing. Chrysler, on the other hand, is typically seen as a more gung-ho company that has fewer bureaucratic procedures and that emphasizes rapid product development. Whether Schrempp will succeed in making these different corporate styles mesh well remains to be seen. He has certainly set demanding goals for the company. "In 10 years we must be, I won't say largest though we may be, but the greatest transport and auto company in the world," he told an interviewer for the international edition of *Businessweek* (November 16, 1998, on-line). "That means in terms of profitability, in being attractive to employees around the world, in being accepted as a good corporate citizen wherever we operate, in being a company which is geographically located where the markets are, and in being accepted and loved by our shareholders."

Schrempp's current contract lasts through 2000, and he has said that he won't mind if it is not renewed, because he has plenty of other interests. These include going on safaris, playing jazz trumpet, and climbing mountains. The time he spends mountain-climbing, he explained to Karen Lowry Miller and Joann Muller, is "the only time in my life I do what others tell me to." — W.G.

Suggested Reading: *Business Week* p56+ Feb. 5, 1996, with photo, p83+ Nov. 16, 1998, with photo; *Financial Times* p15 Nov. 7, 1995, with photo; *Forbes* p165+ Apr. 22, 1996, with photo; *Fortune* p144+ Nov. 10, 1997, with photo, p138+ June 8, 1998, with photos; *German Tribune* p9 Oct. 29, 1989, with photo; *New York Times* D p1+ Jan. 26, 1996, with photo, A p1+ May 7, 1998, with photo; *Time* p66+ May 18, 1998

Selig, Bud

(SEE-lig)

July 30, 1934– Commissioner of baseball. Address: c/o Office of the Commissioner, 777 E. Wisconsin Ave., Suite 2010, Milwaukee, WI 53202

In 1964 the Milwaukee Braves moved from Wisconsin to Atlanta, Georgia. Bud Selig, a native of Milwaukee and lifelong baseball fan who had owned more stock in the Braves than any other individual, was heartbroken, and many other Milwaukeeans felt similarly upset. "I remember so starkly the last night the Braves played here," Selig told Michael Bauman for the *Milwaukee Journal*

Courtesy of Milwaukee Brewers

Bud Selig

waukee Brewers—and she fostered her son's love for baseball. Early on, he became a fan of the Chicago Cubs (Chicago was the closest city to Milwaukee that had major-league teams). Throughout his childhood, Pat Jordan reported in the *New York Times Magazine* (September 18, 1994), Selig's parents kept "a little red radio on the kitchen windowsill tuned to baseball broadcasts." As a high-school student, Selig dreamed of becoming a professional baseball player—"that is, until he faced his first curve ball and missed it by a mile," Jordan wrote. "He knew then, he says, that 'I had to figure a different course to get into baseball.'" In 1953 the Boston Braves, who had always taken a backseat to the Boston Red Sox, moved to Milwaukee, and the city began building a state-of-the-art ballpark. Happy to have a hometown team at last, Selig immediately switched his allegiance to the Braves.

Selig attended the University of Wisconsin, from which he graduated in 1956. After serving a two-year stint in the army, he returned to Milwaukee, to work at one of his father's car dealerships. Before long he became a part owner of the Braves, and by the early 1960s, he had become their largest public shareholder. (By law, major-league franchises must be at least 51 percent privately owned and operated, and they are considered autonomous corporations.) In 1964, giving only a few months' notice, Braves' executives announced that they were moving the team to Atlanta, and they refused to reconsider despite much public protest from Selig and his supporters. Selig's memories of the team's last game in Milwaukee are of ovations for the Braves' champion sluggers Hank Aaron and Eddie Mathews, of weeping spectators, and of "the trauma that night," in his words. Before the Braves moved away, Selig sold all his shares in the team at a handsome profit.

By that time Selig had developed a reputation as a wholehearted supporter of Milwaukee, and after the Braves' departure he worked hard, as he had publicly promised, to bring another major-league franchise to Wisconsin. In both 1968 and 1969, he arranged to have a few Chicago White Sox games played at County Stadium. During the latter season, it was announced that the White Sox were up for sale, and Selig, along with several other investors, mounted a bid for the franchise; at the last minute, the deal fell through. After the 1969 season, major-league baseball expanded by two teams. Much to the chagrin of Milwaukeeans, their city was awarded neither one; rather, Kansas City and Seattle won out. A few months later, the newly created Seattle club filed for bankruptcy. Selig asked baseball executives for permission to take over the ailing franchise, and on April 1, 1970 a Seattle bankruptcy court awarded the team to him. Within weeks Selig moved the team to Milwaukee.

The Miller Brewing Co., one of the country's largest producers of beer, has long dominated industry in Milwaukee, and because beer is so closely identified with the city, Selig suggested that the team be named the Brewers. After discussion with

Sentinel (August 4, 1998, on-line), "and a woman came up to me, a handicapped woman. . . . She looked at me and she had tears in her eyes and she said: 'You know how much these last 13 years have meant to me? Baseball is really all I have.' Then she said, 'I'm going to tell you something,' and she stuck her finger right in my face. She says: 'You're all we have. Don't you fail.' I never forgot that."

In 1970 Selig took over ownership of a bankrupt Seattle team, and once again Milwaukee became the host of a major-league club: the Brewers. "My guiding philosophy was, 'Always do what is the right thing for baseball, the right thing for the Brewers, and the right thing for Milwaukee,'" Selig told Bauman. "The thing that has made me happiest is that I have had more day-to-day contact with our fans than any other owner in sports." Selig spoke with Bauman a few weeks after the owners of the major-league teams elected him commissioner of baseball. For six years before that, he had served as the acting commissioner. "I have dedicated my adult life to the game of baseball and have always tried to act in the best interests of the game," Selig said when his election was announced, as quoted by *ESPN* (July 9, 1998, on-line). "I understand the public sanctity of those interests and the public trust that goes with being the caretaker of the game."

The son of Ben Selig, a successful car salesman who owned many dealerships, and Marie Selig, a schoolteacher, Bud Selig was born Allan Huber Selig in Milwaukee, Wisconsin, on July 30, 1934. His father was a busy man and was hardly ever home. It was his mother, a person of great enthusiasm, who took young Bud to his first baseball game—a minor-league contest involving the Mil-

investors and Milwaukee citizens, Selig and his colleagues bought the rights to the name, and the Seattle Pilots became the Milwaukee Brewers. On April 7, 1970, before 37,237 screaming spectators, the Brewers played their maiden game in Milwaukee County Stadium. (They lost to the California Angels, 12–0.) Four days later, the franchise got their first win, over the White Sox.

Taking steps to win the respect of the Brewers' fans and opponents, Selig brought Hank Aaron, major-league baseball's all-time home-run leader, back to Milwaukee. Robin Yount, who began his career at shortstop at the age of 18, quickly became one the Brewers' greatest ballplayers, as did the pitcher Rollie Fingers. Yount would go on to become the youngest player to reach 1,000 hits, and Rollie Fingers, to become the first relief pitcher in history to receive both the Cy Young Award and the most-valuable-player award in the same season.

Before the 1982 season, Selig hired Harvey Kuenn as manager and acquired the all-star pitcher Don Sutton. Then, with Fingers, Yount, and slugger Paul Molitor on board, the Brewers won their division and advanced all the way to the 79th World Series, where they faced the St. Louis Cardinals. Since both Milwaukee and St. Louis (where the Anheuser-Busch Brewing Co. is headquartered) are known for beer, the tough seven-game series was dubbed the "Suds Series." In the deciding game, the Cardinals edged the Brewers, 6–3. During the rest of the 1980s, the Brewers, for the most part, foundered in mediocrity, and thus Selig was seldom deemed newsworthy nationally. Locally, however, he remained a celebrity. Beginning in the 1970s he had expanded his influence throughout Wisconsin. He hobnobbed with the state's representatives in Congress, and in 1990 he was named to the board of directors of the Green Bay Packers, who play in northern Wisconsin. He also consolidated his family's car dealerships, presiding primarily over the highly profitable Selig Ford Executive Leasing Co.

In 1992 Selig was thrust into the national spotlight. At that time, the commissioner of baseball was Fay Vincent, who, throughout most of his brief tenure, had been at odds with the owners. The commissioner's office dates from 1919; it was established in the wake of the so-called Black Sox scandal, when it was discovered that eight players for the Chicago White Sox had been bribed into intentionally losing the 1919 World Series. At its founding, the office of the commissioner was charged with "protect[ing] the game from the perfidy of both owners and players," in Pat Jordan's words.

Vincent, who worked hard to realign the grossly outdated (and demographically incorrect) divisions in the majors, became extremely unpopular because, as Jordan reported, realignment "disrupted a number of longstanding rivalries," and he fell victim to a Selig-led coup in September 1992. On September 9—two days after Vincent's resigna-

tion—Selig was named chairman of baseball's executive council. In effect, he became baseball's "acting" commissioner.

From the start many owners noticed Selig's outstanding leadership abilities and skill at compromise. In one of his first actions, Selig directed the suspension of the owner of the Cincinnati Reds, Marge Schott, for using racial and ethnic slurs. Then, exactly one year after he took over from Vincent, Selig and other club owners voted in favor of Vincent's realignment and play-off restructuring plan, a move than led many observers to question the real reason for Vincent's dismissal and to speculate that the 28 owners simply wished to create an elite "old boys" club.

On August 12, 1994—in the middle of the baseball season—disaster struck. Frustrated by the deadlock in the months-long negotiations between owners and the players' union over contracts and labor agreements, the players left the stadiums and did not return for the remainder of the season. For the first time in 90 years, there was no World Series.

To help resolve the dispute and to determine whether baseball owners had abused their powers, a Senate committee called hearings. As a witness at the hearings, Selig "dodge[d] and equivocate[d]" and apparently "stymied" the senators in attendance, Ronald Blum wrote for the Associated Press (July 6, 1998). "He's missed his calling," Jerry Reinsdorf, the owner of the Chicago White Sox, said, as quoted by the Associated Press. "He should be Senate majority leader."

The players' strike ended on April 1, 1995, after 232 days. In total, 669 games had been missed in the 1994 season and 242 games in the 1995 season. According to the Associated Press, "The strike, caused by management's demand for a salary cap, led to a 20 percent drop in attendance in 1995 and $850 million in operating losses [in] 1994–96." The dispute not only inflamed ill feelings between management and players but also aroused anger among baseball fans against both the players and management; in addition, it resulted in disillusionment with baseball as a business. During the strike, for example, the public was reminded of the franchises' 72-year exemption from antitrust laws. Thanks to that exemption, "the 28-team fraternity is allowed to keep its membership exclusive," Jordan observed. "Major league baseball, the most storied sport in American history, operates in a manner that has come to be considered decidedly un-American: as a cartel."

For some time after play resumed, radio and television announcers and talk-show hosts referred to baseball as "America's former pastime," partly because of the significant drop in attendance at games. Despite the celebration when, on September 16, 1995, Cal Ripken Jr. broke Lou Gehrig's record for consecutive games played, ticket sales and merchandise revenues that season remained far below those of previous years. When the Yankees won the pennant the following year, experts—

including Bud Selig—predicted that baseball's popularity would begin to rebound. But even with baseball's winningest team (and arguably the most famous sports franchise in the world) in the championship, the 1996 World Series ratings were among the lowest in years. In 1997 owners voted to start interleague play—for the first time ever—and crosstown rivals such as the New York Yankees and Mets, the Chicago White Sox and Cubs, and the Los Angeles area Dodgers and Angels were scheduled to compete with each other. The gimmick helped boost overall attendance for those games, but the allure soon wore off, and in 1997 the number of spectators at the World Series, which pitted the Florida Marlins against the Cleveland Indians, was even lower than in 1996.

The 1998 season got off to an exciting start when Mark McGwire, the St. Louis Cardinals' phenomenal slugger, hit a home run in each of his first four games, thus lending weight to the idea that that year his home-run total might surpass Roger Maris's 61, which was perhaps the most famous record in baseball and had stood for 37 years. Interest increased when the Cubs' outfielder Sammy Sosa became a serious contender in the race later in the summer. In the final weeks of the season, McGwire and Sosa *both* broke Maris's record, and so eager were fans to witness history-in-the-making that games in stadiums throughout the league sold out. An official biography of Selig issued by major-league baseball gave him a lot of credit for the turnaround; Selig, it reported, was "in the process of guiding the game back to its pre-strike level of popularity. At its current pace, 1998 attendance at Major League Baseball's 30 ballparks will be the second highest total in history." While this is obviously a Selig-friendly interpretation of events, it is indisputable that baseball enjoyed a banner year in 1998, and, by all accounts, it seemed to have regained its lofty pop-culture status as "America's pastime." Selig, many critics agree, was responsible at least to some degree for the game's resurgence. On July 6, 1998, after he had held the office of acting commissioner for six years, the major-league owners (currently, there are 30) unanimously elected Selig the ninth full-time commissioner of baseball. His election was seen as a symbolic gesture representing the owners' desire to foster a spirit of cooperation among owners and players, one that will remain in force in 2001, when the labor agreement signed in 1995 expires.

Upon taking office as the full-time commissioner, Selig stepped down as president, CEO, trustee, and director of the Brewers. He was succeeded by one of his daughters, Wendy Selig-Prieb, who had served as the Brewers' vice president and general counsel and whom he had long been grooming for his job; indeed, the Associated Press reported, she had "been in charge of most [Brewers] operations for five years."

Earlier, at the beginning of the 1998 season, the Brewers, as part of the leagues' realignment, moved from the American League to the National League (the league to which the Braves had belonged as a Milwaukee club). Adjacent to the Milwaukee County Stadium, the team's dilapidated ballpark, a new stadium is being built, as a cooperative project of the Brewers and the Southeast Wisconsin Professional Baseball Park District, which represents the state of Wisconsin, five counties (Milwaukee, Ozaukee, Racine, Washington, and Waukesha), and the city of Milwaukee. The stadium, to be called Miller Park, will feature a retractable roof and, in line with a current trend in ballpark construction, will include features of early-20th-century stadiums. The Brewers hoped to begin playing in Miller Park in 2000, but because of a tragic construction accident at the site in which three workers were killed, the opening date has been pushed back to the spring of 2001. At the end of the 1999 season, the Brewer brass fired the team's longtime manager, Phil Garner, and hired Dean Taylor, formerly the Atlanta Braves' assistant general manager, as the team's new general manager. In 2002 Milwaukee is set to host the Major League All-Star Game, which has not been played in that city since 1975.

Bud Selig and his second wife, Suzanne Lappin Steinman, were married in 1977. According to the Brewers' press office, they have three daughters and five granddaughters. In 1978 UPI named Selig the major-league executive of the year. Among his other honors are the International B'nai B'rith Sportsman of the Year Award, in 1981; the U.S. Olympic Committee's Sportsman of the Year Award, in 1988; the August A. Busch Jr. Award, for long and meritorious service to baseball, in 1989; and the Ellis Island Congressional Medal of Honor, in 1993. Selig is a co-founder of Athletes for Youth, and he helped establish the Child Abuse Prevention Fund. He and his wife co-chaired the 1989 Cerebral Palsy Telethon. — M.B.

Suggested Reading: *Nando Sportserver* July 6, 1998 (on-line); *New York Times Magazine* p46+ Sep. 18, 1994, with photos; *Sports Illustrated* p24 May 18, 1995, with photos, p17+ Nov. 18, 1996, with photos; *Sportzone* July 7, 1998 (on-line); *USA Today* C p5 Oct. 24, 1997, with photos

Simpson, Carole

Dec. 7, 1940– Anchor and correspondent for ABC News. Address: c/o ABC News, 1717 DeSales St. N.W., Washington, DC 20036-4407

"I guess that's the hallmark of my life, making adaptations where you need to make them," Carole Simpson, a senior correspondent and anchor for ABC News, told Donita Moorhus during a series of interviews conducted for the Washington Press Club Foundation between October 6, 1992 and

Courtesy of ABC

Carole Simpson

June 17, 1994. An African-American who began her career in journalism as the civil rights movement began to take hold and well before feminism made headlines, Simpson encountered many obstacles during her rise to prominence in her profession. Faced with situations that might have discouraged many others, she persisted, by confronting problems head-on or circumventing them. She has consistently found ways to thrive in her work environments, never allowing herself to be affected by the opinions of people whose expectations of her are lower than her own.

Carole Simpson was born on December 7, 1940 in Chicago. Her father, Lytle Simpson, was a talented artist, but with opportunities for African-Americans scarce when he was growing up, he became a sign painter. Later, for 34 years, he worked as a mail carrier. Simpson's mother, Doretha (Wilbon) Simpson, was a seamstress who worked out of the family's home, in the Woodlawn area of Chicago. Simpson's sister, Jacqueline, who is nine years older, began voice lessons at age 14, and afterward Simpson's parents devoted much of their financial resources to developing her talent. Carole, an imaginative child who read avidly and listened to such radio programs as *Let's Pretend* and *Inspector Keane: Tracer of Lost Persons*, took piano lessons with the goal of becoming Jacqueline's accompanist. "I hated the piano," Simpson told Moorhus. "I took it for five years, but I hated it." After graduating from college Jacqueline got married and gave up pursuing a career. "All of a sudden I had to make [my parents] happy because my sister had disappointed them . . . ," Simpson told Moorhus. "I think that's a very strong influence on my drive, my determination, my ambition, which

now is second nature to me, but then I think that was the beginning of it: 'I can't let them down the way she did. I've got to do something to make them proud of me.'"

The public schools Simpson attended were racially diverse, and she remained unaware of the existence of racism until the age of 11, when her family drove south to visit her maternal grandfather in Georgia. During a visit to the Great Smoky Mountains National Park, which straddles North Carolina and Tennessee, a white woman rebuked Simpson harshly for drinking from a water fountain that, Simpson suddenly noticed, was marked "White." Simpson then caught sight of the "Colored" fountain, a spigot surrounded by refuse. She recalled to Moorhus, "What was so incredible about that . . . was the contrast. Here I was at the most beautiful natural sight I had ever seen in my life. . . . [As] a kid growing up in the city of Chicago, . . . to have that jarring reminder that you're less than some other people, was just incredible to me. . . . The world never looked the same after that moment. From that day on, race became an issue for me. I began to understand it. I looked for signs of [discrimination]. . . . My antenna then began to be up at all times. And it's continued to be up throughout all these years, but that day was defining—a defining moment in my understanding of what it means to be black in America today."

Simpson set herself on a course of achievement that included getting excellent grades, participating in student government, and acting in school plays. Being on stage helped her overcome shyness and develop self-confidence and a strong, clear speaking voice. During her junior year at Hyde Park High School, in Woodlawn, she worked on the school newspaper; as "the gossip columnist for all the homerooms," in her words, she enjoyed talking to people and seeing her words in print. An English teacher, noting her writing talents, suggested that she seek a career as a reporter. "I'd never heard the word 'journalism,'" Simpson told Moorhus, "and the only newspaper reporters that I had heard of were Brenda Starr and Lois Lane in the comic strips. But I thought, 'Hey, they live pretty glamorous lives.' And I began to think of myself as a colored Lois Lane or Brenda Starr." Her parents, however, advised her to become a teacher—that way, they argued, she would always be able to get a job and support herself. Simpson refused to bend, and after weeks of arguing, her parents gave her their support.

With grades that placed her among the top students in her class, there was never any doubt that Simpson would attend college. During an interview at Northwestern University's Medill School of Journalism, the best program in the Midwest, an admissions counselor told her—presumably because of her race and gender—that she would never be hired as a journalist and should become an English teacher instead. Northwestern was the only journalism school to which Simpson had applied, and being rejected was a huge blow to her.

After graduating from Hyde Park, in 1958, she enrolled at the University of Illinois at Navy Pier. After two years she transferred to the University of Michigan, from which she earned a bachelor's degree, in 1962; she was the only African-American among the 60 graduating journalism majors.

Despite having worked for the campus papers in both Illinois and Michigan and for her community newspaper in Chicago during summers, Simpson could not find a job as a reporter. "Everyplace I went, I got the same story that I had three strikes against me: I was Negro, I was a woman, and I was inexperienced," Simpson told Moorhus. "Nobody wanted to hire me." She returned to Chicago and worked full-time for the public library, where she had worked part-time for the previous five summers. Meanwhile, Wesley Maurer, a University of Michigan professor, had promised that he would find her a job. Before the end of the summer of 1962, he secured an internship for her at the Tuskegee Institute, an all-black college in Alabama. Simpson would be a journalism instructor and the editor at the school's information bureau, a job that entailed conducting interviews with notable visitors to the campus and writing press releases. The pay was excellent, so despite her reservations about returning to the South, she accepted the job. Most of her students came from impoverished rural areas, and making a difference in their lives gratified her greatly. While at Tuskegee she made her broadcasting debut: each month she would interview one of the school's African students for the Voice of America, which would broadcast a recording of the conversation in African nations. Simpson did not participate in any of the marches or freedom rides that were being held at that time to protest racial segregation, but she did make a personal stand against racism. "We'd have to go to Montgomery, Alabama, to shop, and I would use the restrooms that blacks were still afraid to use," she told Moorhus. "I would stand in the bus stations—in the areas, not the colored waiting room, but in my own little way, doing my little piece to integrate, and having it be very frightening."

In 1964 Simpson entered a master's degree program in journalism at the University of Iowa. One semester a radio-television workshop was the only course that fit into her schedule, and she worked at the campus radio station to supplement her class assignments. "I became the first woman to broadcast news on WSUI in Iowa City," Simpson told Moorhus. "The whole community heard it," she said. "And I loved it, because I got to write and I got to report, and then I had this added thing of being able to go on the air with my material, and people hearing you and hearing your name and saying your name. . . . From then on it was broadcast journalism. I just thought this was the neatest stuff in the world."

When Simpson finished her graduate work, in 1965, the civil rights movement was at its peak, and as a talented and well-qualified black reporter, she suddenly found herself in demand. "Everyone started becoming conscious of this big story, this huge national story of the civil rights revolution . . . ," she told Moorhus. "People in this business began to say, 'We probably need a black perspective on this, and there are probably stories that can be told, an access that can be gotten that a white reporter could not [get].'" Simpson was about to accept a job offer from a St. Louis newspaper when WCFL, a major Chicago radio station, invited her for an interview. As a test of her skills, the news director gave her a tape recorder and told her to return in a few hours with a story about the taxi-driver strike underway in the city. Simpson based her piece on conversations she had with commuters affected by the strike. Impressed with her story, the station immediately offered her a job. Thus Simpson became the first woman to broadcast hard news in Chicago, which was then the second largest market in the country, after New York City.

Although she got a spot as an anchor, as a reporter Simpson was relegated at first to covering feature stories—"celebrities coming to town, the child care conferences, first day of school for kindergartners . . . any baby animal that was born at the zoo," as she recalled to Moorhus. Only when a male reporter was unavailable would she be given the chance to report firsthand on a major news story.

Her situation changed in 1966, when Martin Luther King Jr. brought his civil rights campaign to Chicago. He did not reveal in advance precisely what he hoped to accomplish, and Simpson determined that she would be the first to find out. With help from co-workers, she discovered which hotel King was staying at, and after some snooping, she found his room. No one in King's entourage would speak to her, so she camped out in the hallway. Early the next morning, King saw her when he emerged from the room, and impressed by her persistence, he told her his plans. "He said, 'Well, if you stayed up all night . . . ,'" Simpson recalled to Moorhus. "I mean, Martin Luther King gave me my first scoop! And he said, 'It's fair housing. We're going to attack the housing segregation patterns in this city, and we're going to open up Chicago to fair housing.' And I had it!" Simpson's station became the first to announce King's intentions, and thereafter—during a period of turmoil in Chicago and elsewhere in the U.S.—she got to cover protest marches, riots, and other stories of the sort she craved. "It was a horrible, horrible period," Simpson told Moorhus, "but for a young reporter, it was the best experience I could possibly have gotten, because there was so much [news], and under deadline."

In early 1968 Simpson joined WBBM, a CBS-affiliate in Chicago and one of the country's first all-news radio stations. In addition to serving as an anchor, she covered the riots that shook the city following the assassination of King in April 1968 and, later that year, a demonstration in Lincoln Park during the Democratic National Convention, during which she was caught in a fracas and escaped with a sprained ankle after the police charged the crowd. What for many years Simpson considered to be, in her words, her "crowning achievement" as a journalist occurred while she was with WBBM. In 1966 she had married James Marshall, an engineer whom she had met at the University of Michigan, and she was pregnant when, in 1969, she was assigned to cover the trial of the Chicago Seven, a group charged with having crossed state lines to incite riots in Illinois. The trial attracted international attention, and more than 50 media representatives were reporting on the event. Simpson's stories were to be broadcast on CBS-affiliated radio stations nationwide. Given the importance of the assignment, Simpson kept her pregnancy a secret, continuing to work long hours and filing as many as 10 updates daily despite severe morning sickness. The trial lasted nearly six months, and by the time the jury began deliberating, in February 1970, Simpson's pregnancy had become quite obvious. To enable her to announce the verdicts on the air, live, as quickly as possible, her station rigged a special phone line down the hall from the courtroom. The security at the trial was tight, and the doors to the courtroom were locked while the verdicts were being read. "All of a sudden, the deputy marshal came to the back of the courtroom and unlocked the door," Simpson recalled to Moorhus. "To this day I do not know what made me do it, but I just got up and walked right behind him, and all of a sudden the other reporters look up, and everybody like leaps up, and the judge turns around and says 'Bolt that door!' And I was gone. . . . All the [other] reporters were locked inside. I got to that phone, scooped everybody by 10 minutes. . . . And it was so satisfying because the whole nation had been scooped by a black pregnant woman! . . . All the things that are supposed to make me not be able to do [this job]."

For several years Simpson had had a standing offer to become an on-air reporter at WMAQ-TV, the NBC-affiliated television station in Chicago. In September 1970 she accepted the offer and began her career in television. She started as a general assignment reporter, covering murders, accidents, fires, and occasionally City Hall. She learned how to work with cameramen to obtain effective footage, how to collaborate with producers on presentation and length, how to work with technicians to make sure she was lit well and could be heard properly, and how to enhance her appearance for the camera. In 1972 she began anchoring the weekend news, and she won good ratings, in part, according to her own assessment, because she was the only African-American anchoring news in Chicago at that time. Despite her success, in about 1973 the station's news director told her that a man whom the network wanted to groom was to replace her as weekend anchor. Earlier, in 1972, she had been offered a position as a correspondent with NBC network news, and in 1974, after the death of her mother, Simpson joined the staff of NBC.

Her husband was still in business school, so instead of moving directly to Washington, D.C., Simpson spent about six months working at NBC's Midwest bureau. As a correspondent reporting on several ongoing stories involving farming, she appeared regularly on NBC's national news broadcasts. After she and her family moved to Washington, in September 1974, she was assigned to cover the U.S. Department of Health, Education, and Welfare (now the Department of Health and Human Services). Although it was not her first choice—she would have preferred reporting on Congress or the White House—it was a start. However, once she began working in Washington, Simpson had trouble getting airtime. She would come up with a story idea, research it, write it up, and then learn that her piece had been given to another correspondent to be reported on the air. After nearly six months she learned from a former colleague of hers that someone had spread the rumor that she had gotten lazy and was not coming up with stories. In the spring of 1975, convinced that one of her superiors at the Washington bureau had tried to sabotage her career, Simpson confronted the top management, and a day later she went on the *NBC Nightly News* to report her first story from the capital. Soon she began doing one-minute news briefs during prime time and filling in for Jessica Savitch, who anchored the Saturday evening news.

In 1979 Simpson was assigned to cover the House of Representatives, a beat she enjoyed so much that she briefly harbored political ambitions of her own. In 1981 she was informed that her position was being given to an up-and-coming male reporter and that she was to be assigned to report on the Department of Energy. The prospect of such a major step down prompted Simpson to acquire an agent, with whose help she got a contract with ABC; she began working for that network in early 1982. Back in 1980 Simpson had covered the first, short-lived presidential campaign of George Bush, who later that year was elected vice president under Ronald Reagan. When Simpson joined ABC, Vice President Bush was considered an important figure to watch, particularly because of the attempted assassination of President Reagan in 1981. Thus one of Simpson's ongoing assignments at ABC was to travel with the vice president and report on his trips overseas, and in that capacity she visited 27 countries on five continents. Although she was one of many reporters who traveled with Bush, she developed an especially warm relationship with him and his wife, and she attended many social affairs at the vice presidential mansion. Simpson also covered a wide variety of breaking news stories, ranging from floods to political conventions. "I became what in our business is called a fireman . . . ," Simpson told Moorhus, "people you know are going to get the story, no matter what it is." She also filled in as a weekend anchor and did prime-time news briefs, as she had at NBC.

Simpson has developed and anchored three hour-long documentaries for ABC as part of the network's public-affairs programming, which FCC regulations require. Entitled *The Changing American Family*, *Public Schools in Conflict*, and *Sex and Violence in the Media*, they aired on local affiliate stations during non-prime-time hours. In 1989 Simpson helped to make *Black in White America*, a groundbreaking documentary produced for prime time by ABC, the editorial content of which was determined entirely by African-American staff members of the network. Along with the correspondent George Strait and the producer Ray Nunn, she focused on the experiences of members of the black upper middle class, the impoverished underclass, and the Tuskegee airmen, a group of World War II pilots whom the documentary presented as true American heroes. The program began with a report on a contemporary version of a famous University of Chicago study in which Simpson had participated as a child. In the original experiment, black children were given a black doll and a white doll and asked to attribute certain characteristics to each. Overwhelmingly, the children assigned positive qualities to the white doll and negative ones to the black doll. In the study depicted in *Black in White America*, the results were much the same.

Also in 1989 Simpson earned an Emmy Award nomination for a story on teenage AIDS patients in New York City, which had appeared as an "American Agenda" segment on ABC's *World News Tonight*. For two consecutive nights that same year, she filled in for Peter Jennings, the anchor of *World News Tonight*; it was the first time in the history of network television that a black woman had anchored a weeknight newscast. Another highlight in Simpson's career came in 1990, when she went to South Africa for two weeks to help cover Nelson Mandela's release from prison, after 27 years, for ABC's *Nightline*. She also reported on the problems of black South African women for *Nightline*, and she won a 1990 Emmy Award for outstanding coverage of a continuing news story for her contributions to the program.

The event that Simpson currently considers the pinnacle of her success as a journalist came in 1992, when she moderated a televised presidential debate. She had long coveted a place on one of the panels of journalists who guide the candidates' pronouncements on issues during televised debates, which—since the first one, held in 1960 between John F. Kennedy and Richard Nixon—have become a fixture of presidential campaigning. Typically, the debates are broadcast live on all three major television networks, public television stations, and cable news channels, and they are watched not only throughout the United States but also in many other countries. Unlike previous debates, the one Simpson moderated was conducted in a "town-meeting" style; the questions were posed by members of a live audience in Richmond, Virginia. Simpson's job was to make sure that no one candidate dominated the proceedings; that the candidates answered the questions posed to them (she would follow up with additional questions, if necessary); that both foreign and domestic issues were covered; and that the debate ran smoothly. Both the format and Simpson's performance were perceived among the public and media as highly successful. Following the event, members of the Bush camp accused Simpson of favoring Bill Clinton—the Democratic candidate, who went on to win the election that year—by steering the discussion away from the issue of Clinton's character. Actually, the live audience had informed Simpson before the debate that they preferred to focus on the candidates' agendas for the nation, and President Bush himself sent Simpson a note congratulating her on her performance and thanking her for her objectivity.

In 1988 Simpson had become anchor of ABC's *World News Saturday*; she is currently anchor of *World News Sunday*, and as such she has often provided live coverage on major breaking news events. "When news is breaking out, it's incredible. That's like a high," she told Moorhus. "I have been anchoring when some of the major news stories of the last 10 years have gone on. I was live with the Tiananmen Square massacre in Beijing, and I'm doing live reporting. This is just winging it. This is when TV is the most fun, when you're not scripted and when stuff is just happening, and your job there is to help collate that information, be comfortable with it, and explain it to your audience. A real challenge." Simpson also anchored breaking news on the Persian Gulf War, the downfall of Philippine president Ferdinand Marcos, and the Senate hearings into the confirmation of Supreme Court nominee Clarence Thomas, during which the testimony of Anita Hill turned the issue of sexual harassment into a national preoccupation.

Throughout her career Simpson has often publicly thanked her husband, James Marshall, for his support, without which, she acknowledges, her success in such a demanding and competitive field might not have been possible. He accompanied her when she was called on to report on news stories in Chicago in the middle of the night, for example, and encouraged her to keep her maiden name, for career purposes, at a time when it was uncommon for married women to do so. Simpson and Marshall, a vice president at a management consulting firm, live in Chevy Chase, Maryland. Their daughter, Mallika, graduated cum laude from Harvard University, in Cambridge, Massachusetts, in the early 1990s. They also have a son, Adam, whom they adopted shortly after his birth, in 1980.

Simpson taught at the Medill School of Journalism from 1971 to 1974. In 1982 and 1983 she served as the president of the Radio and Television Correspondents Association. She was instrumental in the founding, in 1987, of the ABC Women's Advisory Board, through which the concerns of the network's female employees can be brought to

ABC's top management, and she has served as its chair; she has also co-chaired ABC's Minority Advisory Board. In addition, she has set up scholarships for women and members of minorities who are pursuing careers in broadcast journalism. — O.J.S.

Suggested Reading: *ABCNews.com* (on-line); National Press Club (on-line) Oct. 6, 1992, Nov. 19, 1992, June 15, 1993, June 16, 1993, Sep. 8, 1993, Feb. 13, 1994, Feb. 27, 1994, May 3, 1994, June 17, 1994; *Washington Post* p8 Aug. 27, 1989, with photos

Kathleen Edwards/Courtesy of Hyperion Books

Sinclair, April

1955(?)– Writer. Address: c/o Hyperion Press, 114 Fifth Ave., New York, NY 10011

April Sinclair's 15 years of experience as a community activist paid off for her in the early 1990s. She had written the first 20 pages of a novel, and with no contract, no agent, and no connections in the publishing industry, she did what any activist with a dream would do—she took to the streets. First she called her favorite local bookstore in San Francisco, Old Wives Tales, and arranged for a public reading. Next she embarked on a grass-roots self-promotion campaign. She solicited her friends and colleagues at the Emergency Food Coalition in Oakland, California, which she directed, to come hear her reading, and made leaflets to post around town. "The flyers had my baby picture on them—I was awfully cute—and underneath it said, 'Come sit a spell while I read from my funny, touching,

provocative novel-in-progress,'" she told Sylvia Rubin for the *San Francisco Chronicle* (January 13, 1994). "In retrospect it sounds like I had a lot of nerve—'who the hell does she think she is?' But they came to find out."

In a remarkable turnout for an unknown and unpublished author, 125 people crammed into the shop to hear Sinclair read from her work. The crowd was not disappointed. A one-time actor, Sinclair drew from her theatrical experience to deliver an animated performance, despite a serious attack of nerves. Buoyed by her initial success, Sinclair embarked on a series of readings on the bookshop and coffeehouse circuit throughout northern California. The buzz she created brought a number of agents to her door, and by the time Sinclair had written the next 30 pages of her story, she had already sold it to a publisher. "Friends of mine had heard her read, and I was told that she literally moved audiences to tears," Leslie Wells, the executive editor of the publishing house Hyperion, told Sally Lodge for *Publishers Weekly* (August 30, 1993). "Just as I was going to try to locate her and find out about her work, I received a manuscript from agent Winifred Golden. And it was April's novel. It really grabbed me. I realized that this would be a book of interest to black as well as white readers." The finished novel, *Coffee Will Make You Black,* favorably compared in the press to the work of Terry McMillan, became a cult hit among readers and the most unlikely publishing success story of 1994. Since then, Sinclair has turned her attention to writing full-time, following up her acclaimed debut with a sequel, *Ain't Gonna Be the Same Fool Twice,* and a third novel, *I Left My Back Door Open.*

Though by all accounts an open and engaging personality, Sinclair is guarded about the specifics of her personal life. The eldest of four children—her siblings are Marcia, Byron, and Nina—April Sinclair was born in about 1955 and grew up on the South Side of Chicago. Her father was a blue-collar worker; her mother was a schoolteacher. As a teenager Sinclair became interested in Chicago's growing involvement in the civil rights movement, which was a source of misunderstanding between her and her mother. "I identified with the civil rights movement and the black power struggle," Sinclair told Sylvia Rubin. "My mother referred to me as militant because I was a member of the Afro-American club in high school and I had an Afro, but I wasn't the one setting the school on fire. I was angry, but I considered myself reasonable." In 1975 she earned a bachelor's degree in communications from Western Illinois University, in Macomb. After graduating, she moved to San Francisco, where she eventually settled into the role of community activist and took graduate-level courses at San Francisco State University.

Coffee Will Make You Black centers on the coming-of-age of a naïve black teenager, Jean "Stevie" Stevenson. The novel's main themes are the sexual awakening of an adolescent, the ambiguities of remaining loyal to both friends and family, and the adolescent need to fit in—issues played out against the backdrop of the civil rights movement in 1960s Chicago. The transition from junior high to high school proves an easy one for Stevie, who quickly ingratiates herself with a popular crowd. Her best friend, Carla, is an outspoken and popular girl, and her new boyfriend, Sean, a senior, is the object of many schoolgirls' fantasies. However, Stevie is troubled by her growing attraction to Diane Horn, the school's white nurse and Stevie's mentor and confidante. Meanwhile, at home Stevie is caught between the conflicting views of her mother and grandmother. A black teller in an otherwise all-white bank, Stevie's mother is concerned primarily with upward social mobility, at whatever cost to her sense of self. Stevie's grandmother, on the other hand, is a more progressive and independent personality, a business owner who is unashamed of her roots and carries herself in a stately manner. The title of the book comes from an old southern saying, recalled by Stevie's mother, that parents used to tell their children to keep them from drinking coffee; the saying typifies age-old prejudice by both blacks and whites against dark skin. Stevie's grandmother counters the old saw with an equally old maxim: "The blacker the berry, the sweeter the juice." Thus, gender, class, and race politics frame the story of a young girl's sexual awakening.

Providing a happy ending to the story of the novel's publication, critics received Sinclair's first book warmly. Many reviewers found Sinclair's characterizations thorough and enjoyable and her dialogue-driven narrative snappy and realistic. In the *Chicago Tribune* (February 13, 1994), Anne Whitehouse wrote, "Told with earnestness and humor, *Coffee Will Make You Black* is a realistic, entertaining examination of a girl's maturing and self-discovery as she prepares to find her place in the world." "Sexy, funny, and very smart, its power is in its unpredictability," Julie Phillips wrote about the novel in her review for the *Voice Literary Supplement* (March 1994). "Sinclair doesn't write about race, gender, and sexual politics as abstractions; they snarl together in the details."

Sinclair's writing habits improved considerably upon receipt of a six-figure advance for her second book. She quit her job to pursue writing full-time and purchased a personal computer, which helped her finish *Ain't Gonna Be the Same Fool Twice* (1996), the sequel to her first work, in half the time it took her to write *Coffee Will Make You Black*. In *Ain't Gonna Be the Same Fool Twice*, Sinclair explored Stevie's growth from an adolescent naïf into an iconoclastic young woman. Stevie graduates from a midwestern college and moves to San Francisco, the crossroads of disco and political chic in the early 1970s. Along the way she explores her sexuality, with both men and women, yet eludes any particular label; she surrounds herself with friends from the city's vibrant countercultural scene, but her days are dominated by the mundane process of finding a job; she explores her own ra-

cial identity with pride, while welcoming friendships with whites. The overriding theme is the complexity of life, which offers Stevie and the reader no tidy solutions.

Sinclair's depiction of Stevie's adventurous side has led to a minor backlash among some of the novelist's more conservative readers. "They've really taken [Stevie] to heart," Sinclair told Lynell George for the *Los Angeles Times* (February 26, 1996). "There's a woman who heckled me . . . because she's mad. She loved *Coffee* but she doesn't like the direction that Stevie took in this book. When I offered to sign it, she said she doesn't want anything to do with it. This is her Stevie. That's how they get." Conversely, as one of the relatively few writers who deal with the topic of bisexuality in an African-American character, Sinclair has been looked to as a spokesperson for the gay and lesbian community. But like her protagonist, Sinclair vehemently shuns labels. "You get it from both sides," she told Lynell George. "The politically correct on the right and the left. . . . The attitude has been: Choose a side and stick to it." Because of the apparent autobiographical nature of her novels, Sinclair must frequently fend off questions about her own sexuality, an issue she has refused to discuss. She does not want her own proclivities to overshadow the message of her work. "I wanted to create a space for people to heal and also explore," she explained to George. Sinclair argues for a life of balance, self-esteem, and individuality. (It is no coincidence that Stevie's birth sign is Libra, which is symbolized by a set of scales.)

The critical reception for *Ain't Gonna Be the Same Fool Twice* was much cooler than for its predecessor. Though many critics still admired Sinclair's dialogue, they also found her second book lacking in substance in comparison with her first. "The first person narrative reads like a series of letters written by a friend who is often too tired or too busy to labor over important events but sometimes has a moment to linger on trivia. . . . *Coffee Will Make You Black* was funny and engaging in its thoughtful creation of a young girl's emotional evolution," concluded Teresa Moore in her review for the *Washington Post* (February 22, 1996). "But throughout much of *Ain't Gonna Be the Same Fool Twice*, Stevie displays a bemused but game air that doesn't seem to suit her."

In the spring of 1999, Sinclair published her third novel, *I Left My Back Door Open*. The story's main character, Daphne "Dee Dee" Dupree, is a blues deejay for a radio station in Chicago. She has been repeatedly let down by the men in her life, most notably her ex-husband, who cheated on her during her convalescence from a hysterectomy, and a boyfriend who dumped her because she is overweight. (The latter incident nudged Dee Dee toward bulimia.) While she attempts to right her own life, Dee Dee generously offers solace and comfort to her friends, including one who is trapped in a loveless marriage to a wealthy man and another who declares herself a lesbian late in life and risks alienating her teenage daughter in the process. "The worst of it is that Dee Dee—bright and likeable, with a quick wit and a shrewd, observant eye—is trapped in a novel that is not content simply to be a snappy, entertaining romance but aspires to be a self-help primer for middle-class black women," Todd Kliman wrote in his review of the novel for the *Washington Post* (April 18, 1999). Though he praised Sinclair's characterizations, Kliman faulted her for making many of her characters "sound less like real people than like characters you'd meet on some afternoon talk show." Kliman concluded, "Sinclair's heart is in the right place; it's too bad her art isn't." On the positive side, Sarah Vowell wrote in the *New York Times Book Review* (April 18, 1999), "Many readers will respond to this novel's honesty, to its colloquial humor, and to its exacting exploration of Daphne's relationship woes."

Though writing full-time has been rewarding for April Sinclair, she has not observed any drastic transformations in her lifestyle since becoming a professional writer—except, as she has noted, that she now feels compelled to write whether or not she feels inspired. For Sinclair, writing is a job. "People think being a writer will make you happy. But it's not like all your problems go away," Sinclair remarked to Sylvia Rubin. "I'm satisfied—a sense of satisfaction and accomplishment. It's not the cake; it's the icing on the cake. The cake is your relationships, the kind of person you are. Making a difference in the world." — T.J.F.

Suggested Reading: *Los Angeles Times* p1 Feb. 26, 1996, with photos; *San Francisco Chronicle* E p9 Jan. 13, 1994, with photo; *Contemporary Authors Online*, 1999; Nelson, Emmanuel S., ed. *Contemporary African American Novelists*, 1999

Selected Books: *Coffee Will Make You Black*, 1994; *Ain't Gonna Be the Same Fool Twice*, 1996; *I Left My Back Door Open*, 1999

Courtesy of U.S. Dept. of Transportation

Slater, Rodney

Feb. 23, 1955– U.S. Secretary of Transportation. Address: c/o U.S. Dept. of Transportation, 400 7th St. S.W., Washington, DC 20590

In February 1997 Rodney Slater, who has been a close associate of President Bill Clinton since the two met in 1979 in Arkansas, succeeded Federico Peña as the U.S. secretary of transportation. Although Slater's association with Clinton has played a large role in Slater's career—Slater served as an executive assistant for then-Governor Clinton of Arkansas from 1983 to 1987 and as an adviser on Clinton's presidential campaign in 1992—he has won the respect and support of many in Congress and the Senate, and his rise from a childhood in one of the poorest regions of the U.S. to a Cabinet post has been hailed as an inspirational tale.

Rodney E. Slater was born out of wedlock on February 23, 1955 in Tutwyler, Mississippi. His mother, Velma, married Earl Brewer, a mechanic and maintenance man, not long after Slater was born, and Slater has credited his stepfather for playing a large role in his own success. "For me, my stepfather was my father," Slater told Laura B. Randolph for *Ebony* (March 1998). "He was the person who was there. He was the person who worked five and six jobs to make it possible for my brothers and sisters to enjoy the things that were important."

Slater grew up in public housing in rural Marianna, Arkansas, where segregation was still the norm and African-Americans had restricted opportunity for success. "The county I grew up in—Lee County—is one of the 10 poorest counties in America, but I did not feel poor," he told Randolph. "That's not to say I don't understand what poverty is all about. But the things that really give meaning to life—a loving family, good teachers, friends, people in the community who cared about me and believed in me—those things I had in abundance."

Slater attended Lee High School, then earned a football scholarship to attend Eastern Michigan University, in Ypsilanti, where he captained the football team as a star running-back and earned a bachelor of science degree in 1977. Three years later he earned a law degree from the University of Arkansas.

Meanwhile, in 1979, during Slater's second year at law school, his father-in-law—Henry Wilkins, an Arkansas state legislator—introduced him to Bill Clinton, who served as governor of Arkansas from 1979 to 1981 and from 1983 to 1992. Slater served from 1980 to 1982 as an assistant attorney general at the Arkansas attorney general's office before leaving to work on Clinton's successful campaign for governor of Arkansas.

From 1983 to 1987 Slater served as special assistant to Governor Clinton. Slater also served as Clinton's special assistant for community and minority affairs. "I put a lot of trust in [Slater] when he was very young because I knew—when he was first working with the Black community—that the older ministers, the older doctors, the older business people . . . , I knew they would trust him," Randolph quoted President Clinton as saying.

Slater flourished in Governor Clinton's administration. Beginning in 1987 he served as a member of the Arkansas State Highway Commission, becoming its first-ever African-American chairman in 1992. Meanwhile, from 1987 to 1993, he also served as the director of governmental relations at Arkansas State University.

In 1992 Slater became Clinton's deputy presidential campaign manager and senior traveling adviser. After Clinton's victory over the Republican incumbent, George Bush, Slater was nominated as the head of the Federal Highway Administration (FHWA), an agency of the Department of Transportation that oversees 42,500 miles of national interstate and defense highways and 800,000 miles of other federally administered roads. Slater's nomination to head the agency, which has 3,500 employees, an annual budget of $20 billion, and an office in every state, was confirmed by the Senate, and he became the first African-American administrator of the FHWA since the agency's inception in 1893 as the Office of Road Inquiry. In that post, he increased allocations to highways by 20 percent and trimmed the agency's staff by 10 percent. He also received praise from Clinton for his rapid response in the wake of the devastating 1994 Northridge earthquake: he quickly formulated a plan to rebuild freeways in southern California.

Despite these accomplishments, some consumer and safety advocates took issue with Slater's performance and what they perceived to be his overly pragmatic approach. For instance, they pointed out that Slater did not publicly oppose efforts by the trucking industry to raise the maximum allowable weight for trucks from 80,000 pounds to 175,000 pounds. Slater also faced criticism for going along with measures that abolished the national speed limit of 55 miles an hour. The consumer and safety advocate Ralph Nader told Steven A. Holmes for the New York Times (December 21, 1996), "[Slater] doesn't have any commitment to preserving and enhancing safety standards of motor vehicle, rail, and airplane systems. He's basically an accommodationist."

On February 14, 1997, shortly after President Clinton's second inauguration, Slater was sworn in as the U.S. secretary of transportation, following a Senate vote that confirmed him unanimously. Slater thus became the 13th secretary in the 30-year history of the Transportation Department and the second African-American to hold the job (the first was William T. Coleman, who served in that capacity under President Gerald Ford). The department, which manages commercial aviation and mass transportation as well as the nation's highways and the U.S. Coast Guard, has 100,000 employees and a budget of around $40 billion. In nominating Slater for the post, Clinton said, as quoted in material provided by the Department of Transportation, "He has built bridges both of steel and of goodwill to bring people closer together."

Slater immediately faced the task of meeting the needs of transportation in the face of rapid changes in communication and computer technology. In order to equip and encourage young people to update transportation capability for the next century, Slater initiated an education program designed to challenge American students to focus on math and science. The project, the Morgan Technology and Transportation Futures Program, was named after Garrett Morgan, the African-American who invented the automated traffic light and the gas mask.

Slater has maintained that safety is a key issue for him. "Safety is my No. 1 priority," he told Randolph. "Harriet Tubman, with the Underground Railroad, fought to never lose a passenger. I've said that safety is my North Star by which I will be guided and judged." In keeping with that sentiment, he urged states to implement tougher laws against drunk driving. Furthermore, in November 1997, after evidence accumulated that in collisions, air bags can harm small children and women of small stature who sit close to the steering wheel, Slater announced a new policy: upon receipt of a special Department of Transportation permit that is issued on request, a car dealer or mechanic may install a cutoff switch to override the air-bag mechanism. In an interview on the NewsHour with Jim Lehrer (November 18, 1997), Slater said, "What we've done is to identify those who are at risk. . . . We are suggesting to most people that they not take advantage of the on/off switch, but if they have to, then we've made that opportunity available."

Slater played a key role in getting Congress to pass a federal highway bill in 1998 that reserved $217 billion for the construction and maintenance of new roads. He has also played an important role in promoting President Clinton's African Initiative, announced in June 1997, to promote economic development in Africa. Addressing an international roundtable in Washington, D.C., in October 1997, he said, as quoted in Jet (October 27, 1997), "Our goal is to broaden our dialogue with African nations on aviation relations, work more closely with those who share our vision of opening markets and expanding services, and help them improve the safety of their aviation systems." In February 1998 Slater traveled to four African nations—Cape Verde, Ivory Coast, Mozambique, and South Africa—to promote transportation and economic development in those countries.

As for Slater's future after Bill Clinton's presidency, many political observers suggest that he may eventually seek public office himself. (Slater reportedly resigned as federal highway administrator in 1996 to pursue public office in Arkansas—a decision he reversed after one day.) *Ebony* named him one of the 100 most influential black Americans in 1997. He and his wife, Cassandra Wilkins, have a daughter, Bridgette Josette. — Y.P.

Suggested Reading: *Ebony* p118+ Mar. 1998, with photos; *New York Times* I p10 Dec. 21, 1996, A p22 Feb. 7, 1997

Courtesy of U.S. House of Representatives

Slaughter, Louise M.

Aug. 14, 1929– U.S. Representative from New York State. Address: 3120 Federal Bldg., 100 State St., Rochester, NY 14614; 2347 Rayburn House Office Bldg., Washington, DC 20515

A native of Kentucky who still retains traces of a southern drawl, Louise M. Slaughter has represented a section of upstate New York in Congress since 1987. Currently in her seventh term, Slaughter, a Democrat, is a tireless fighter for residents in her district, which encompasses Rochester (the third-most-populous city in the state, after New York and Buffalo) and most of the nearby suburbs in Monroe County, whose northern border lies along the shore of Lake Ontario. Her impressive record

on local concerns, particularly on matters connected with business and employment, accounts to a significant degree for her electoral success in her district, which, when she first ran for Congress, in 1986, had been a stronghold of moderate Republicanism for more than four decades. She is also recognized as a passionate advocate of so-called progressive causes, such as campaign-finance reform, women's rights, and increased funding for such endeavors as breast-cancer research, before- and after-school programs for children of working parents, educational opportunities for homeless children, and the National Endowment for the Arts.

The daughter of Oscar Lewis McIntosh and Grace (Byers) McIntosh, Slaughter was born Louise McIntosh on August 14, 1929 in Harlan County, Kentucky. She attended the University of Kentucky, where she received a B.S. degree in microbiology, in 1951, and an M.S. degree in public health, in 1953. She worked as a bacteriologist for the Kentucky Department of Health, in Louisville, in 1951–52 and then for the University of Kentucky, in 1952–53. From 1953 to 1956 she conducted market research for Procter & Gamble in Cincinnati, Ohio. In 1956 she married Robert Slaughter. When her husband got a job as an executive for a firm in Rochester, the couple moved to New York State and bought a house in Fairport, a Rochester suburb.

Slaughter began her political career in 1976, when she won election to the Monroe County legislature. During her first term, she worked as both lawmaker and regional coordinator for then–New York secretary of state Mario Cuomo. When Cuomo was elected lieutenant governor of New York, in 1978, Slaughter left the legislature to work for him full-time. Then, in 1982, when Cuomo ran for governor of New York, she resumed her own political career, winning a seat in the New York State Assembly. According to *Politics in America, 1988*, as an assemblywoman, "Slaughter concentrated on criminal justice issues, pushing an alternative sentencing program, and on the environment, pressing for funds to clean up Irondequoit Bay. Slaughter's ability to gain choice committee assignments was enhanced by Assembly Democrats' desire to help her hold a marginal seat. But her most publicized stands, including her arguments against the state's private power companies, gave an image as a populist rather than a political insider." She was reelected to the Assembly in 1984, having ruled out a race for the seat allocated to New York State's 30th congressional district in the U.S. House of Representatives. That seat was being vacated by the very popular Barber B. Conable Jr., a moderate Republican, who had announced his retirement after serving 10 consecutive terms.

Over the course of the next two years, Slaughter decided to try to unseat Conable's successor, Representative Fred J. Eckert, who planned to run for reelection. Eckert, a Republican, had proved to be far more conservative than his predecessor, and his policies did not sit comfortably even with many of his Republican constituents. At one point, when asked whether he purposely avoided meetings with residents of his district, Eckert told a reporter for a Rochester newspaper, as quoted in *Politics in America, 1988*, "I can think of better things to do on a Saturday than go down to Town Hall and listen to scores and scores of people."

Slaughter, who won the three-way Democratic primary with a whopping 81 percent of the vote, made character the focus of her campaign against Eckert. In her speeches, *Politics in America, 1988* reported, she declared that for voters, choosing between her and her opponent "c[ame] down to differences in two people and their personalities as much as anything else." Displaying her skill at grassroots fund-raising, Slaughter—with the help of Democratic strategists from Washington and her many supporters in organized labor, among others—succeeded in building a war chest of nearly $600,000. On Election Day she narrowly defeated Eckert, capturing 51 percent of the vote. She thus became the first Democrat elected to the House of Representatives from that district in 42 years.

Slaughter was a freshman member of the 100th Congress, which convened on January 6, 1987. Within her first few weeks in the Capitol, she was assigned to the House Public Works Committee. Unlike her predecessor, she diligently made herself available to her constituents. She also got high marks among voters by bringing key federally funded projects to her district. In addition, Slaughter, who is famous for her unaffected charm, ingratiated herself with the Democratic congressional leadership.

For the 1988 congressional election campaign, Slaughter raised more than $882,000. She defeated her moderate Republican opponent, John D. Bouchard, a county legislator, by more than 39,000 votes, or about 18 percent of the approximately 217,500 votes cast—a very impressive margin in a traditionally Republican district. In a move that demonstrated their faith in her potential, powerful congressional Democrats chose Slaughter to make the nominating speeches for four members of the party leadership after the 101st Congress convened.

In May 1989, a few months into Slaughter's second term, the longtime Democratic Florida congressman Claude Pepper died. Pepper had chaired the powerful, high-profile House Rules Committee, and soon after his death Slaughter got assigned to the committee. Toward the end of 1989, she attached to a homeless-assistance measure an amendment calling for federal incentives to states that enable homeless children to continue to attend school. She also added a provision to the 1988 Railway Safety Act requiring that trains with routes in the Northeast corridor be fitted with automatic safety equipment to prevent them from running through "stop" signals. "Slaughter reminded her constituents that General Railway Signal, a 30th District firm, is one of two U.S. companies producing such equipment," *Politics in America,*

1990 reported. She also pressed President George Bush to appoint a special envoy to negotiate the release of Americans who had been taken hostage in Lebanon; one of the hostages, Terry Anderson, was a registered voter in her district.

Slaughter's third congressional electoral contest, against John M. Regan Jr., a lawyer, ended with her biggest victory yet—59 percent of the vote. Upon returning to Capitol Hill, she discovered that she was the sole remaining woman on the Rules Committee. She also won appointment to the House Budget Committee. Later in the 102d Congress, she was named chair of the Committee on Organization, Study, and Review, which the Democratic Caucus had formed with the goal of increasing the efficiency of House operations. In October 1991 Slaughter and six other congresswomen marched on the floor of the Senate, to urge a delay in the vote to confirm the Supreme Court nominee Clarence Thomas, who, during his confirmation hearings, had been accused of sexual harassment by Anita Hill, a former employee of his. Although the congresswomen's action did not prevent Thomas's appointment to the Court, it helped raise awareness about attitudes and behavior toward women in the federal government.

Bowing to the wishes of many of her conservative constituents—and thus turning her back on two of her party's positions—Slaughter voted against the heavily debated budget agreement of 1990 and also fought hard for the imposition of limits on imported textiles and shoes, products that, because they are made by overseas laborers who earn very little, are sold far more cheaply than similar products produced in Rochester-area factories, whose workers must earn at least the minimum wage. On another front, Slaughter continued to press for special tax breaks for small farmers and manufacturers who wished to issue tax-free bonds through local government.

Also during the 102d Congress, Slaughter introduced a bill to support federal research and education on the health risks of exposure to diethylstilbestrol, a drug better known as DES, which, between 1947 and 1971, was prescribed to some five million pregnant women to prevent miscarriages. In about half the female offspring and many of the male offspring of women who took DES, the drug caused reproductive-system or urinary-tract abnormalities. In addition, DES has been identified as the cause of uterine and other cancers in thousands of DES women (as female victims are called). Slaughter's bill was passed and signed into law in 1992.

As a result of redistricting that year, registered Democrats in Slaughter's newly configured (and renumbered) district (it became New York State's 28th Congressional District) slightly outnumbered registered Republicans, and it looked as though Slaughter would once again cruise to victory in the November election. Emboldened by growing anticongressional sentiment among voters, her opponent, Monroe County legislator William P. Polito, ran a smear campaign that portrayed Slaughter as a supporter of wasteful spending and extravagant congressional perks. Polito ultimately lost, collecting 44 percent of the votes to Slaughter's 55 percent.

In 1993, within a few months of the inauguration of President Bill Clinton, the White House launched a massive, and ultimately unsuccessful, attempt to overhaul the U.S. health-care system. Congresswoman Slaughter challenged many elements of the President's proposal, "for fear they would jeopardize Rochester's very successful managed-competition plan," according to *Politics in America, 1996.*

In the 1994 election, Slaughter beat her opponent, the local legislator Renee Forgensi Davison, by a 17-point margin. Many other congressional Democrats did not fare nearly as well; indeed, so many incumbents failed to win reelection that the Democratic Party lost control of both houses of Congress for the first time in 40 years. As a member of the minority party, Slaughter had to give up her seat on the House Rules Committee. In the contest in early 1995 for vice chair of the Democratic caucus, she lost to Connecticut representative Barbara B. Kennelly by just three votes—her first setback in her drive to be among the House Democratic elite.

During her brief stint on the House Government Reform and Oversight Committee during the 104th Congress, Slaughter clashed with David M. McIntosh, a freshman Republican from Indiana, who had been appointed chairman of the committee's Subcommittee on National Economic Growth, Natural Resources, and Regulatory Affairs. McIntosh wanted the government to prohibit nonprofit groups that receive federal funding from lobbying federal lawmakers. In building his case for ending what he and other Republicans labeled "welfare for lobbyists," he distributed at a public hearing what looked like a press release emanating from the advocacy organization Alliance for Justice. Slaughter accused McIntosh of forging the press release, and the charge turned out to be true; McIntosh apologized publicly for his action. Slaughter then made an unsuccessful attempt, in a resolution she presented on the floor of Congress, to have McIntosh's action investigated by the Speaker of the House.

In her bid for her sixth term, in 1996, Slaughter faced a challenge by a wealthy Republican banker, Geoffrey Rosenberger. Her opponent's strategy—painting her as an old-fashioned liberal—proved fruitless; Slaughter again won reelection, with 57 percent of the vote. In December 1996, in another bid for a leadership position among congressional Democrats, Slaughter competed against Representative John M. Spratt Jr. of South Carolina for the ranking Democratic spot on the Budget Committee. After losing that contest, 106–83, she quit the Budget Committee. At about the same time, she got back her seat on the Rules Committee, replacing Representative Anthony C. Beilenson of California, who had retired.

Slaughter's initiatives in Congress include legislation requiring background checks of people who want to buy explosive chemicals and devices. Prospective buyers would have to apply for a federal permit before they could make such purchases. Slaughter is also the author of the America After School Act, which would expand and strengthen after-school programs, ranging from recreational activities in sports and the arts to academic tutoring and college preparatory work. The 1999 federal budget includes an allocation of $200 million for one such program—the 21st Century Community Learning Program, which potentially can benefit 250,000 youngsters nationwide.

Along with her fellow New York representative Amo Houghton, a Republican, Slaughter has introduced a bill designed to prevent one form of Medicare fraud: medical suppliers' provision of durable medical equipment (for example, wheelchairs or catheters) that is lower in quality than the equipment for which the suppliers have billed the government. She has also been rallying support for her bill—called the Genetic Information Nondiscrimination in Health Insurance Act—that "would prevent health insurers from denying, canceling, refusing to renew, or changing the terms, premiums, or conditions of [an insured person's] coverage based on genetic information" and "would prohibit insurers from requesting or requiring a genetic test, or the results of such a test, as a condition of coverage," as a White House statement put it, according to the *Web Administrator* (July 14, 1997, on-line).

Other legislation initiated by Congresswoman Slaughter allocated $100,000 for a Women's Rights National Historical Trail, a new project in which the National Park Service will identify notable places associated with the struggle for women's rights, propose a route to connect them, and estimate the cost of establishing such a trail. Slaughter's bill, which became law in 1998, also set aside $550,000 for renovations of the home of the 19th-century American suffragist Susan B. Anthony. In addition, Slaughter has introduced a measure to categorize sexual assaults by repeat offenders as federal crimes and to make sentences of life in prison without parole mandatory for serial rapists.

Most recently, in January 1999, Slaughter reintroduced the Airline Competition and Lower Fares bill, which would end the imposition of extraordinarily high ticket prices for flights to and from mid-sized communities like Rochester. She is also working toward passage of the Holocaust Survivors Act, which would enable Holocaust survivors to sue Germany for injuries they suffered at the hands of the Nazis; the HHS (U.S. Department of Health and Human Services) Women Scientists Employment Opportunity Act, which is designed to prevent discrimination against women with regard to promotions; and the Women's Right to Know Act, which would prohibit the imposition of gag rules, on such matters as abortion, by the federal and state governments. She is also pushing for more-effective meat-inspection laws.

In 1992 Vietnam Veterans of America named Louise Slaughter the House legislator of the year. In 1998 Slaughter, who chairs the Congressional Arts Caucus, received the Award for Outstanding Congressional Arts Leadership in the U.S. House of Representatives from the U.S. Conference of Mayors and Americans for the Arts. That same year, at a celebration of International Women's Day at the headquarters of the United Nations, in New York City, she was honored with the International Health Awareness Network Recognition Award.

Slaughter and her husband still live in the Rochester community of Fairport. The couple have three daughters—Megan Rae, Amy Louise, and Emily Robin—and several grandchildren. — M.B.

Suggested Reading: *Congressional Quarterly 1990*, 1989; *house.gov/slaughter* (on-line); *New York Times* A p18+ May 16, 1993, with photo; *New York Times* (on-line) Oct. 8, 1998; *Politics in America* (various editions)

Archive Photos

Sosa, Sammy
(SOH-sah)

Nov. 12, 1968– Baseball player. Address: c/o Chicago Cubs, Wrigley Field, 1060 W. Addison St., Chicago, IL 60613-4397

Prior to the 1998 season, Sammy Sosa was viewed by many sports commentators as a talented but raw baseball player who had yet to prove himself a star worth millions of dollars a year. Twice as a Chicago Cub he had achieved baseball's 30–30 mark (which means hitting 30 home runs and stealing 30 bases in the same season), a feat only five other players in major-league history had accomplished more than once. At the same time, he was prone to striking out, his outfielding was mediocre, and his stolen bases often did not help his team win games. Many fans criticized him for being a selfish player more interested in boosting his individual statistics than in helping his team make it to the postseason. The glittering jewelry he had crafted to celebrate his achievements only reinforced the image of him as a showy, self-obsessed player.

With his remarkable 1998 season, Sosa answered his critics in the best possible way. Shelving his jewelry and concentrating on becoming a better hitter, Sosa put together the finest season of his career in terms of batting average, hits, walks drawn, and runs batted in (RBIs). And most dramatically, his improved hitting translated into a home-run-hitting frenzy that became one of the biggest stories in the sports world in 1998. For much of August and all of September, the nation's attention was riveted on Sosa and the St. Louis Cardinals slugger Mark McGwire as they raced to break what had seemed for 37 years to be an untouchable record: the 61 home runs hit in a single season—1961—by Roger Maris.

Although McGwire eventually established the new home-run record at 70 while Sosa hit 66, Sosa will likely be remembered as more than the home-run prince to McGwire's home-run king. The gracious manner in which the two players conducted the competition helped restore high levels of interest and revenue to a sport that was still suffering from the negative publicity caused by the strike of 1994. More importantly for Chicago fans, Sosa's home runs—as well as his base running, clutch hits, and improved defensive play—helped send the Cubs to the postseason for the first time since 1989. In recognition of his contribution to his team, Sosa was voted the Most Valuable Player of the National League that season.

The fifth of seven children, Sammy Sosa was born on November 12, 1968 in San Pedro de Macoris, a city of about 125,000 in the Dominican Republic. His father, Juan Montero, died when Sammy was five. His mother, Mireya, made a living by selling food to factory workers. Sosa has two sisters and four brothers, including a younger brother, Jose Antonio, who played for the Chicago Cubs in the minor leagues. They grew up in a two-bedroom apartment that had once been part of a public hospital. To help his mother make ends meet, Sosa sold oranges, shined shoes, and washed cars in the streets of San Pedro de Macoris for the equivalent of nickels and dimes.

Initially interested in boxing—he would box with his hands wrapped in socks stuffed with rags—Sosa was introduced to baseball by his brother Luis. "He took me out to the Little League games and I knew right away I loved baseball," Sosa told Joseph Reaves for the *Chicago Tribune* (June 16, 1995). When he was 14, Sosa started playing organized baseball, hoping, like other boys from his community, that he could rise out of poverty by making it to the big leagues. The odds were not good that this would happen, but there were success stories, like those of Joaquin Andujar, Tony Fernandez, Juan Samuel, George Bell, Pedro Guerrero, and Alfredo Griffin, who had gotten rich playing professional baseball in the U.S. "I used to watch Andujar and Fernandez," Sosa told Melissa Isaacson for the *Chicago Tribune* (May 8, 1990). "They had good cars and it made me feel good thinking, maybe some day I could have a car and give my mother a good house."

When one American scout in the Dominican Republic saw Sosa play, he noted that the 150-pound, five-foot 10-inch teenager looked malnourished. (Currently, Sosa is 50 pounds heavier and two inches taller.) Nevertheless, his athletic skills were apparent. "I had an ugly swing, but I was strong," he told Reaves. "They told me all I had to do was learn how to play." At age 16, barely able to speak English, Sosa signed with the Texas Rangers and was given a bonus of $3,500, most of which he handed over to his mother; with the small sum remaining, he bought his first bicycle.

Sosa played for several years on minor-league teams and made his major-league debut with the Rangers in 1989 before being traded to the Chicago White Sox, on July 29 of that year. Before long he was a starting outfielder for the Sox. Only 20 years old, he was then the youngest Dominican to make it to the major leagues. The next year—Sosa's first full year in the majors—was not distinguished. He made 532 plate appearances and had a batting average of .233. His power was evident (he had 15 home runs), but his talent was still raw, as evidenced by 13 errors from the outfield and more strikeouts (150) than hits (124). His second year with the Sox, in 1991, was even worse: he made only 116 plate appearances and had a miserable .203 batting average. Sosa attributed the poor numbers not only to his inexperience but to the White Sox hitting coach, Walt Hriniak, who had tried to teach him a batting stance that he found awkward.

The general manager of the White Sox, Larry Himes, still had faith in Sosa, and when Himes moved across town to become the general manager of the Chicago Cubs, in the fall of 1991, he traded for Sosa again. A week before the 1992 season began, Sosa and the pitcher Ken Patterson went to the Cubs in exchange for the proven hitter George Bell. Sosa later remarked to the *Chicago Tribune* (August 17, 1993) that the trade was "like getting out of jail."

In 1992 Sosa played in a little less than half the games but improved his batting average (.260). The following year he showed why the trade for Bell, who retired at the end of the season, wasn't such a bad move after all. That year Sosa had his first 30–30 season, becoming only the 14th player to achieve this feat in major-league history. In celebration, he had a craftsman fashion a heavy gold chain with a gem-encrusted pendant that marked the achievement. In a step perhaps a little too ostentatious for some sports journalists' tastes, he also ordered a license plate for his sports car that read "SS 30–30," and he contributed a little over $1 million to help create the 30–30 Plaza in the Dominican Republic.

Despite the accomplishment, Sosa's detractors still were calling him "Sammy So-So." Their complaints went beyond the problems he had with his outfielding—such as not knowing where to position himself or when to throw to the cut-off man. The charges were much worse: his harshest critics believed that he was a selfish player who put his personal statistics ahead of the good of the team. They maintained that he always swung for the fences when a single would have sufficed and that he stole bases when it was not necessary to do so. In the last two months of 1993, to achieve his 30–30 season, he had attempted 26 stolen bases (20 of which were successful). Meanwhile, the Cubs finished 13 games back in the National League East division.

Tom Trebelhorn, the manager of the Cubs from 1993 to 1994, attributed Sosa's aggressive batting and questionable base running not to selfishness but to overeagerness. "Sammy is a reactionary player," he told Joseph Reaves for the *Chicago Tribune* (July 28, 1994). "He reacts to a situation with tremendous athletic abilities. Sometimes that reaction can result in a little more risk than we would like. But Sammy plays the game with a youthful zest." If Trebelhorn's assessment was correct, it was not the first time misunderstandings plagued Sosa. His signature gesture—he thumps his chest twice, first with his fist, then with two fingers spread in a "V"—has sometimes been mistaken for a gang symbol. Actually, he has said, the gesture symbolizes peace.

In the strike-shortened 1994 season, Sosa batted .300 with 25 home runs and 22 stolen bases. After that year he continued to put up good individual statistics. In each of the three seasons starting in 1995, he had at least 36 home runs and 100 RBIs, though his batting average hovered around .260. In 1995 he had another 30–30 season, becoming only the sixth player in major-league history to reach that mark twice. That same year the Cubs finished the season 73–71, the closest they had been in several years to the play-offs. (Five more victories would have gotten them a wild-card berth.)

Before the 1996 season Sosa signed a two-year contract for $10.25 million. He had 40 home runs by late August of that year, when he broke his right hand and was forced to miss the rest of the season. The following year, he had similarly good numbers but also a career-high 174 strikeouts. "His was probably the worst year ever by anyone with 36 dingers and 119 RBIs," Tom Verducci observed in *Sports Illustrated* (June 29, 1998). That season Sosa had a batting average of only .246 with runners in scoring position and had a worse on-base percentage than Atlanta Braves pitcher Tom Glavine (.300 to .310). Sosa stole 22 bases in 34 attempts, but one steal attempt, which he made despite an obvious sign from the Cubs' manager, Jim Riggleman, to hold his position, prompted Riggleman to lecture him in the dugout on national television. The Cubs went 68–94, their fourth losing season since Sosa joined the team, in 1992.

At the end of the 1997 season, Sosa was signed to a four-year, $42.5 million contract. Again critics openly expressed doubts about Sosa's being worth so much—this time, over $10 million a season through 2001. The Cubs' general manager, Ed Lynch, who had taken over from Larry Himes in 1994, defended the decision as an investment in a player whose skills were on the verge of maturing. "We saw a five-tool player who was coming into what are the prime years for most guys," he told Tom Verducci, "and who probably couldn't find the trainer's room because he's never [hurt]. The one important variable was Sammy's maturity as a player. We were banking that he would continue to improve."

Lynch's gamble paid off, as the 1998 season turned out to be Sosa's best. He had a career-high batting average of .308 for the season, as well as career-high 73 walks drawn and 158 RBIs, which was the highest total of RBIs in the major leagues that year. The improved results seemed to be the fruit of Sosa's efforts in the off-season to read pitches earlier, hit more balls to right field instead of pulling everything to left, and, most importantly, become a more patient batter. "I was trying to hit two home runs in every at-bat," he joked to the *New York Times* (September 1, 1998) about his mighty cuts as a young player. He explained his earlier aggressiveness as a result of his being a member of a minority from a poor country who was trying to make sure he would survive in the major leagues. "It's not easy for a Latin player to take 100 walks," he told Tom Verducci. "If I knew the stuff I know now seven years ago—taking pitches, being more relaxed—I would have put up even better numbers."

Perhaps not surprisingly, Sosa's improved patience at the plate made him a more devastating long-ball hitter. At the start of June, Sosa trailed McGwire in the home-run race, 27–13. Then Sosa went on a rampage. By the end of the month, he was behind McGwire only 37–33. Sosa had hit a record number of home runs in a single month (20); the previous record (18) had been set by Rudy York in August 1937. Sosa—who had never hit more than 40 home runs in any of his previous eight full seasons—was suddenly on pace with McGwire and the Seattle Mariner's player Ken Griffey Jr. in the race to smash Maris's record.

As the season progressed, Griffey fell behind, and the home-run derby became a two-person battle. A predictable pattern emerged. McGwire would unleash a flurry of home runs, then level off, and Sosa would catch up—on two occasions he briefly held the lead. When this happened, McGwire responded virtually immediately. On August 19, for instance, when the Cubs faced the Cardinals in St. Louis, Sosa homered in the fifth in-

ning, which put him ahead 48 homers to McGwire's 47. A scant 58 minutes later, McGwire homered in the eighth inning and again in the 10th, to retake the lead. Heading into the last month of the regular season, the sluggers were tied at 55 home runs.

As many had expected, McGwire was the first to break the Maris barrier. His 62d home run came on September 8, while, as fate would have it, he was playing against the Cubs. Sosa, in a show of the graciousness and friendliness that had marked the competition from the start, ran to home plate to congratulate McGwire. Four days later, on September 12, Sosa hit his 60th, equaling Babe Ruth's single-season home-run record. The next day—during the Cubs' 150th game—Sosa smacked his 61st and 62d home runs in an 11–10 Cub win over Milwaukee. To the confusion of many, there was little fanfare over Sosa's success at breaking Maris's record. Maris's children were not in the stands as they had been for McGwire's 62d run. The baseball commissioner wasn't even present, and the only nation to broadcast the game live was the Dominican Republic. Even Sosa's wife barely made it to the stadium in time, rushing there after having her hair done.

With more than half a month's worth of games left to play, nobody knew where the record would end up or who would hold it. Both Sosa and McGwire had their advantages. Since the Cardinals were out of the play-off race, McGwire was free to concentrate solely on hitting homers. Sosa, by contrast, had to consider his team's play-off prospects and opt for singles rather than home runs as the situation demanded. On the other hand, Sosa had more at bats than McGwire throughout the season. (In fact, at the end of the season, Sosa averaged a home run every 9.74 at bats, while McGwire averaged a home run every 7.27 at bats, though the two players had nearly the same number of home runs.)

With the media following him and McGwire everywhere, Sosa continually deflected attention from himself. "Pressure was for me . . . when I was a shoeshine boy trying to make it to America," he told Richard Jerome for *People Online* (September 28,1998). He also dismissed the notion that he was receiving less attention than McGwire because of his race, and he publicly predicted that McGwire would end up with the record at the end of the season. "I'm rooting for Mark McGwire," he told the *New York Times* (September 15, 1998). "I look up to him the way a son does to a father. I look at him, the way he hits, the way he acts, and I see the person and the player I want to be. I'm the man in the Dominican Republic. He's the man in the United States. That's the way it should be."

On September 25, just days after Hurricane Georges had wreaked havoc in the Dominican Republic, Sosa took the lead in the homer race for the second time, with 66 runs to McGwire's 65, in a game against the Houston Astros. McGwire tied him less than an hour later in a game against the Montreal Expos. In his final two games, McGwire pulled ahead for good with four home runs. Meanwhile, Sosa failed to hit any home runs in his last two games, but his hits helped push the Cubs into a tie with the San Francisco Giants for a wildcard berth in the play-offs. In a one-game tie-breaker, the Cubs beat the Giants, making it for the first time in nine years to the play-offs (where they would be swept in three games by the Atlanta Braves). In recognition of the part he played in getting his team to the play-offs, Sosa was named the Most Valuable Player of the National League. The Cubs had a miserable season in 1999, finishing last in their division, with 67 wins and 95 losses. Sosa, however, performed spectacularly, ending the year with 63 home runs. (McGwire had 65.)

Now a hero in Chicago and the rest of the United States (he became a citizen of the U.S. in 1995), Sosa is also highly esteemed in the Dominican Republic, where a National Day of Joy was proclaimed in honor of Sosa's home-run achievement. There is a statue of him in his hometown, and pesos thrown in the fountain are given to shoeshine boys in the city in recognition of Sosa's upbringing.

Sosa met his wife, Sonia, at a disco in San Pedro de Macoris in 1990; at the time she was 16 and worked as a dancer on a Dominican television show. He gave her tickets to one of his games, and she went expecting to meet him in the stands. "I didn't know he was a ballplayer," she told Richard Jerome. "I thought he was just another traveling salesman in gold chains." The couple currently have four children: Keysha, Kenia, Sammy Jr., and Michael. They live with Sosa's brother Juan in a 55-floor condominium in Chicago.

Sosa has often used his earnings to help his family members in the Dominican Republic start their own businesses. He also started the Sammy Sosa Foundation, which has donated money to several charitable causes in the Dominican Republic and the United States. Because of his generosity, he is sometimes referred to as "Sammy Claus." He has also helped found the Sammy Sosa Escuela de Beisbol in his former homeland. In recognition of both his playing ability and civic contributions, he won the Roberto Clemente Man of the Year award in 1998. And for the aid he provided during the hurricane relief effort of 1998, Sosa, seated next to Hillary Rodham Clinton, was singled out for praise during President Bill Clinton's 1999 State of the Union Address. "For far more than baseball," the president said, "Sammy Sosa, you're a hero in two countries tonight. Thank you." — W.G.

Suggested Reading: *Chicago Tribune* IV p10 May 8, 1990, with photo, IV p1+ Feb. 24, 1993, with photo, IV p1+ July 28, 1994, with photo, IV p5 Apr. 18, 1995, with photo, IV p1+ June 16, 1995, with photo; *CNN/SI* (on-line) Sep. 28, 1998, with photos; *New York Times* C p1 July 1, 1998, with photo, D p1+ Sep. 1, 1998, with photo, D p1+ Sep. 15, 1998, with photos, VIII p3 Sep. 20, 1998, with photo; *People Online* Sep. 28, 1998, with photo; *Sports Illustrated* p37+ June 29, 1998, with photos, p45+ Oct. 5, 1998, with photos, p54+ Dec. 21, 1998, with photos; *Time* p76+ Sep. 28, 1998, with photos; *USA Today* p5 June 7, 1995, with photo

---

Steadman, Ralph

May 15, 1936– Illustrator; writer. Address: c/o Sobel Weber Associates, Inc., 146 E. 19th St., New York, NY 10003

"It never leaves you, that nagging urge to comment on society's bloody nonsense and its phony moralizing and pious indignation," the illustrator and writer Ralph Steadman wrote in an autobiographical essay in the mid-1980s, as quoted by David Streitfeld in the *Washington Post* (December 30, 1997). For many years Steadman, who fiercely criticized American politics and lifestyles in his books *America* and *Scar Strangled Banger*, told interviewers that he attempted to use his art as a way to effect change. In drawings, he told Tom Zito for the *Washington Post* (October 8, 1972), "you can say things that you can't say any way else. You can call a man an absolute [expletive] and be sued for libel, but you can imply so many things in a drawing and they can't get you for it. At least I don't think they can." Since launching his career in art, in the early 1960s, Steadman has worked mostly with pen and ink and watercolors, developing a highly distinct style that Joyce Wadler, writing for the *Washington Post* (December 3, 1983), described as "a scratch, a blot, a slash on the page." Steadman's most popular works include his illustrations for a 1967 edition of Lewis Carroll's fantasy *Alice in Wonderland* and his collaborations with the journalist Hunter S. Thompson, which include *Fear and Loathing in Las Vegas*. He has also written and illustrated more than 25 books for both children and adults and illustrated many more written by others.

Ralph Steadman was born on May 15, 1936 in Wallasey, England, a town near Liverpool, to Lionel Raphael Steadman, a traveling salesman, and Gwendoline Welsh Steadman, a homemaker. "I have a gentle mother and a passive father," he told Wadler. His older sister, he has said, "looks like [the former Conservative British prime minister] Maggie Thatcher [and] *thinks* like Maggie Thatcher. I am the *antithesis* of my older sister." Steadman told Wadler that he was an exceptionally restless child. "My eternal cry was 'What can I do, What can I do?'" he recalled. During his youth he felt physically awkward; in an autobiographical sketch that was quoted by Streitfeld, he wrote, "Even as a young man I had huge ears. They didn't

Jerry Bauer/Harcourt Brace

Ralph Steadman

grow huge, they were huge from birth. It was my head that was smaller to start with so that from behind I resembled a butterfly with mumps."

When he was about 11 years old, Steadman found himself struggling to cope with a cruel headmaster at the boarding school he was attending. To escape the anxiety and unhappiness he felt, he would build and fly model airplanes for hours on end. "They gave me flight, they gave me escape," he told Wadler. "That was when I started drawing. That was also where I learned to fear authority and why my pictures come out the way they do. I get butterflies in my stomach when I draw the military or police."

Steadman dropped out of school at the age of 16. For the next few years, he took on a variety of odd jobs, apprenticing in aircraft engineering at the de Havilland Aircraft Co., in 1952; catching rats; gardening; maintaining a swimming pool; and cleaning a motor-bike track. After serving in the Royal Air Force, from 1954 to 1956, he began cartooning. "I started my drawing career more as a cause than a business," he wrote in an autobiographical statement for *Something About the Author* (1983), after noting that he is "motivated by a need to be noticed and a desire to shock." "I thought I could change the world, but now I realize that it is a hopeless dream. But, I still try. Man is still an idiot with aspiration."

For three years beginning in 1956, Steadman worked as a cartoonist for a chain of small-circulation newspapers. He took classes at the East Ham Technical College, in London, between 1957 and 1964 and at the London College of Printing and Graphic Arts, between 1958 and 1964. In the 1960s he began selling his work to the then-popular Brit-

ish magazines *Punch* and *Private Eye*. A brief stint at the even more prestigious *London Times* ended when, according to Wadler, he was fired for "sedition." He continued to produce work for *Private Eye*, and through that publication he eventually became well known in Britain.

During the early years of his career, Steadman also wrote and illustrated several children's books, among them *Ralph Steadman's Jelly Book* (1967), *The Yellow Flowers* (1968), which Fiona Saint cowrote, *The Little Red Computer* (1969), and *The Tale of Driver Grope* (1969). His illustrations for a 1967 edition of Lewis Carroll's *Alice in Wonderland* earned him the 1972 Francis Williams Memorial Award for best-illustrated book of the previous five years. He also illustrated children's books written by others, among them Frank Dickens's *Fly Away Peter* (1963) and Mischa Damjan's *The Big Squirrel and the Little Rhinoceros* (1965). An edition of Lewis Carroll's *Through the Looking Glass and What Alice Found There* with his drawings came out in 1972, and a Steadman-illustrated compilation that includes Carroll's *The Hunting of the Snark: An Agony in Eight Fits* as well as *Alice in Wonderland* and *Through the Looking Glass* was published in 1986.

In 1970 Steadman made his first trip to the United States, with the intention of spending most of his time vacationing on Long Island, New York. He also visited New York City and was none too pleased by what he saw there. "I walked down the streets, I could not believe what I was looking at," he told Wadler. He recalled asking himself, "What is so wrong with this place and why do I react so horribly against it?" He later translated his feelings of disgust into book-length critiques of the United States. In the first, *America* (1974), he presented scathing views of such places as Las Vegas, Los Angeles, Dallas, and Disneyland and of such notable episodes in U.S. history as the Watergate scandal, the Vietnam War, and the 1973 legal skirmishes regarding pornography, which culminated in the U.S. Supreme Court ruling that made the definition of obscenity a matter for localities to decide.

While Steadman was relaxing on Long Island in 1970, an editor from the magazine *Scanlan's* persuaded him to take an assignment in Kentucky. Specifically, the job called for him to set down his impressions of the Kentucky Derby; his drawings were to accompany an article about the famous horse race to be written by the rising-star journalist Hunter S. Thompson. According to Richard Rayner in *Vogue* (April 1988), Steadman and Thompson "became friends immediately, spent the weekend in a condition of drug- and alcohol-induced paranoia, and filed a very funny story about the excess they witnessed and mainly the excess in which they indulged." What he observed at the Kentucky Derby intensified Steadman's negative feelings about the United States. One incident in particular repelled him: "There was a horse with a broken leg," he told Wadler, "and they were pulling the horse on his broken leg, and the horse was pushing and screaming in pain. . . . How can you see something like that and not feel outrage; you do feel outrage and it's a reasonable thing."

The article that Thompson and Steadman produced for *Scanlan's* created a stir, and it was later included in the anthology *The New Journalism* (1973), co-edited by Tom Wolfe and E. W. Johnson. The piece marks the first of several Thompson/Steadman collaborations and paved the way for what became known as "gonzo" journalism, in which, as Richard Rayner explained, journalists "turned themselves into the story" by performing outrageous acts and becoming the catalysts for further action. For example, one year at the America's Cup, a sailing race, "Thompson convinced Steadman to swallow an illegal drug and make a nighttime raid against Australia's sailing vessel to spray paint an outrageous curse against the papacy," Steve Appleford reported in the *Washington Post* (April 28, 1988). "We were like chalk and cheese," Steadman said to Appleford. "I was the person with the feelings and compassion, and he had the wonderful, brutal disregard for another human being. . . . He provided the irresponsible initiative for doing something for the hell of it. A good combination really." In addition to articles for such publications as *Scanlan's* and *Rolling Stone*, Steadman and Thompson collaborated on the books *Fear and Loathing in Las Vegas: A Savage Journey to the Heart of the American Dream* (1972), an account of a police convention; *Fear and Loathing on the Campaign Trail* (1975), about the 1972 U.S. presidential election; and *The Curse of Lono* (1981), about Thompson and Steadman's experiences at a marathon in Hawaii.

In the 1980s Steadman began to have misgivings about the reckless lifestyle he adopted while working with Thompson. "It was great to find this wild and crazy stuff, great to do lots of it, but I knew it was destructive," he told Streitfeld. "I didn't particularly want to destroy [myself]. I haven't got Hunter's constitution." Steadman began working more seriously on his own material, and in 1983, after three years of research, he published *I, Leonardo*, about the brilliant Italian painter, sculptor, architect, and engineer Leonardo da Vinci (1452–1519). Highly innovative and quite different from what he had been doing with Thompson, the book offers "Leonardo filtered through Steadman," in Wadler's words, "written so you're never quite sure where one begins and the other leaves off." More an attempt to capture the feelings and personality of Leonardo—"to make the man human without denigration," as Steadman told *Something About the Author*—than to present a precise chronicle of his life, the book contains many historical inaccuracies "just to twit academics, whom [Steadman] loathes," Wadler reported. Steadman told Wadler that he was attracted to his subject because he felt that he understood the loneliness that that genius of the Italian Renaissance must have felt—"the way [we both] seem removed from the sort of general pattern of the way people want to live their

lives," he explained. *I, Leonardo* won a W. H. Smith Illustration Award, for best illustrated book.

In his next major book, *Scar Strangled Banger* (1988), Steadman returned to criticism of the United States, with an emphasis on politics. Among his many caustic caricatures of American political figures, he portrayed former president Richard Nixon as Godzilla-like and former president Gerald Ford as a creature resembling the monster brought to life by Dr. Frankenstein—a creature who was the puppet of an equally monstrous-looking Henry Kissinger, Ford's secretary of state. *Scar Strangled Banger* offended many reviewers and other readers in the U.S., among them the writer Gore Vidal, who, according to Rayner, declared on British television that Steadman "had no right to be saying all these rotten things about America." Responding to his critics, Steadman explained to Rayner, "I don't hate America. I love it. It's abrasive, it releases something in me that I keep bottled up at home. I can piss on their sneakers and they just smile. . . . So in my work I always do my best to be provocative. Really offensive. Like going to someone's house for dinner and being incredibly rude and getting up at the end and saying, 'Thanks for a wonderful evening.'" Steadman told Steve Appleford, "Americans are like human beings everywhere, but [they] have developed into something very high powered. They've developed sleaze into an art. They've given us the worst way of life anyone could ever imagine and made it acceptable. Hamburger joints and things of that kind are now worldwide. Their culture is imposed on the world." Its detractors notwithstanding, *Scar Strangled Banger* sold well in the U.S. According to Appleford, Steadman's attacks on "the very core of the American power structure . . . made the bemused Englishman something of a cult hero in [the U.S.]. That's because amid the disturbing violence [in the book] is a clear compassion for others—even if [Steadman is] constantly enraged and frustrated by what they are inflicting upon themselves and each other."

After the publication of *Scar Strangled Banger*, Steadman resolved to stop addressing political subjects in his cartoons, because, he had suddenly realized, "politicians have been given too much attention over the past 1,000 years," as he told Appleford. "It's time to start ignoring politicians. It's time to enter a new age, considering politicians to be the most unimportant people in society. And cartoonists could be the first to bring about the change. Those people are living on what attention you pay them; otherwise they would just wither and die." Perhaps Steadman was feeling disillusioned as well. "I thought that satire could change the world, [but] I was wrong," he told Rayner.

Early in the 1990s Steadman became the official illustrator for Oddbins, a British wine and spirits company. In this position he has created both advertisements and labels for the company's products. He has also published two books about wine and whiskey: *The Grapes of Ralph: Wine Accord-*

ing to *Ralph Steadman* (1996) and *Still Life with Bottle: Whiskey According to Ralph Steadman* (1997). Also published in 1997 was his children's story *The Book of Jones: A Tribute to a Mercurial Manic and Utterly Seductive Cat.* According to Streitfeld, who interviewed him in 1997, Steadman's recent works "wouldn't offend the most timid soul." "I'm [ticked] off at being [ticked] off with the world," Steadman told Streitfeld. "The world just doesn't get any better. . . . There is still violence in a lot of the work I do. But I've decided sometimes if I don't feel violent, what the [expletive] is the point? Why get violent?"

Steadman's books also include *Sigmund Freud* (1979); *A Leg in the Wind and Other Canine Curses* (1982); *The Big I Am* (1988), the author of which, according to Steadman, is God; and *No Room to Swing a Cat* (1989). His latest book is the autobiographical *Gonzo, the Art* (1998), which he described to *Book Page* (on-line) as "quintessential Gonzotic pictures—the first glimmer of Gonzo in some of my early work—an explanation of my birth, my mother and father, man and beast and my relation to them. The reasons for my frenetic response to the screaming lifestyle of America and my love of it through my friendship with Hunter S. Thompson and Kentucky. . . . The graffiti of my life." Steadman and Thompson served as consultants on the film version of *Fear and Loathing in Las Vegas*, directed by the former Monty Python star Terry Gilliam and co-starring Johnny Depp and Benicio Del Toro. The film opened to mixed reviews in 1998.

Writing in 1983, Joyce Wadler described Ralph Steadman as "the warmest angry man you will ever meet." Steadman lives with his second wife, Anna Deverson, a nursery-school owner and operator whom he married in 1972, and their daughter, Sadie, in a large Georgian manor house outside Maidstone, in Kent, England. From his first, 16-year marriage, to Sheila Thwaite, which ended in divorce in 1972, Steadman has four children—Suzannah, Genevieve, Theo, and Henry, each of whom helped him illustrate some of his early children's books. Steadman has contributed drawings to the charitable organizations Oxfam and Save the Children. In his spare time he enjoys making wine. "I really wanted to be an alchemist, someone who could change base metals to gold," he told Streitfeld. "I knew I couldn't do that, so [I thought] I'd change base fruit into a kind of gold, which is wine. It's not art, it's not composition, it's decomposition. . . . But it is like art—I love it when you get something juicy happening."

"All I get from my work is one little ray of personal hope—and a certain psychological reward," Steadman told Joyce Wadler. He has also gotten many honors, among them the Gold Award and the Silver Award from the British Designers and Art Directors Association, in 1977; the Illustrator of the Year award from the American Institute of Graphic Arts, in 1979; the Silver Pencil Award (Holland) for children's book illustrations, in 1982; the BBC

Design Award for Halley's Comet postage stamps, in 1987; the Critica in Erba Prize at the Children's International Book Fair in Bologna, Italy, for his children's book *That's My Dad*, in 1987; the Kent Institute of Art and Design Fellowship Award, in 1993; and an honorary doctorate from the University of Kent, in 1995. — C.P.

Suggested Reading: *Book Page* (on-line); *Vogue* p180+ Apr. 1988, with photos; *Washington Post* N p1+ Oct. 8, 1972, with photos, C p1+ Dec. 3, 1983, with photos, C p2 Apr. 28, 1989, C p1 Dec. 30, 1997, with photos; *Something About the Author* vol. 32, 1983

Selected Books: *Alice in Wonderland*, 1967; *Fear and Loathing in Las Vegas: A Savage Journey to the Heart of the American Dream*, 1972; *Through the Looking Glass and What Alice Found There*, 1972; *America*, 1974; *Fear and Loathing on the Campaign Trail*, 1975; *Sigmund Freud*, 1979; *The Curse of Lono*, 1981; *I, Leonardo*, 1983; *Scar Strangled Banger*, 1987; *The Grapes of Ralph: Wine According to Ralph Steadman*, 1992; *Still Life with Bottle*, 1994; *The Book of Jones: A Tribute to a Mercurial, Manic, and Utterly Seductive Cat*, 1997; *Gonzo, the Art*, 1998

Stiller, Ben

Nov. 30, 1965– Actor; writer; director. Address: c/o United Talent Agency, 9560 Wilshire Blvd., 5th Fl., Beverly Hills, CA 90212

"I see Ben as the conscience of his generation, and a messenger of all its excesses," Ben Stiller's father, the comic actor Jerry Stiller, told Franz Lidz for the *New York Times* (September 20, 1998). "I follow his career like I follow the path of a hurricane." Through his persona and work in film and on television, Stiller, born in 1965, has become associated with "Generation X," largely made up—according to the stereotype—of underachievers with values shaped by an overdose of TV during their formative years. He began his career as a television writer and actor before going on to star in such films as *Flirting with Disaster* (1996), *There's Something About Mary* (1998), and *Mystery Men* (1999). His credits as a director include *Reality Bites* (1994), in which he also appeared, and *The Cable Guy* (1996).

Ben Stiller was born on November 30, 1965 in New York City, the son of Jerry Stiller and Anne Meara, who performed on television and in films as a comedy team throughout the 1960s and 1970s. More recently Jerry Stiller was cast as the father of the character George Costanza on the sitcom *Seinfeld,* and currently he is playing the father of Carrie Heffernan's character on another show, *The King of Queens.* Ann Meara is a playwright who continues to act in films. Raised on New York City's Up-

Courtesy of ID Public Relations

Ben Stiller

per West Side, Ben and his older sister, Amy, would often travel with their parents to the sets of films or television shows. "I went with my parents to California when they were doing television," Stiller told Meredith Berkman for *New York* (April 3, 1989). "I got to go on the set of *The Partridge Family* and the *Brady Bunch.* I talked to Danny Partridge. Little Bobby Brady waved to me—and I never forgot it." Stiller also remembers his parents rehearsing at home, and he was sometimes confused as to whether they were really arguing or not. When the children saw their parents on television, Stiller told Lidz, Amy would sometimes "press her face to the glass and try to talk to them." Stiller was about 10 years old when he and his sister made their unofficial TV debut, on *The Mike Douglas Show*; their parents had them play a barely rehearsed violin duet. "It humiliated them," Jerry Stiller told Lidz. "They'd had three lessons and all they knew was 'Chopsticks.' I got letters asking, 'How could you bring two such untalented children in front of the camera?'" In spite of that unpleasant experience, young Ben continued to take small parts on television shows and in theatrical productions around New York during his childhood. He remembers trying, at 13, to memorize material for his bar mitzvah and the lines of a play simultaneously.

Stiller has said that the overwhelming influence from his childhood on his career was probably not his parents' work but television. "He'd watch TV for three or four hours at a time," his father told John Milward for the *New York Times* (February 13, 1994). "Now, though, I can see that he was actually studying what he was watching." Among Stiller's favorite television shows was the Canadian

comedy *SCTV*, which starred John Candy, Catherine O'Hara, Martin Short, and Rick Moranis. Although Stiller has said that television helped him to develop his sense of comedy, he told Robert Crane for *Playboy on Campus* (on-line) that he believes TV is generally "detrimental to your thinking process. Once in a while I run into somebody who doesn't watch television at all, and it's astonishing the way he or she talks about ideas and books. When you stop watching TV it's like coming off a drug. I'm not into prime-time television. I watch the late-night stuff or the fringe cable channels."

When he was a teenager, Stiller made a habit of borrowing his father's super-8 camera and making short parodies of movies that were popular at the time. One of these was his version of the 1980 film *Airplane*, for which Stiller made a paper airplane, set it on fire, and flew it into a bathtub full of water. He also made takeoffs of *Jaws*, *King Kong*, and *The Exorcist*. His interest in moviemaking led him to enroll in the film program at the University of California, Los Angeles (UCLA) in 1983, but he dropped out before completing his freshman year. At the age of 19, he moved back to his parents' home in New York City. Stiller told Desson Howe for the *Washington Post* (February 20, 1994), "It was really bad. I came back on a red-eye flight to New York. I sat on my suitcase in my house and I thought, 'Okay, what do I do now? I don't have to do homework ever again.' There's no structure. There's no nothing. That's a horrible feeling: so many options, but not in a positive way." Stiller has said that he had this period of his life in mind while he was directing his first film, the Generation X classic *Reality Bites*.

After he resettled in New York, Stiller took acting classes and found an agent. While trying to secure acting jobs, he worked for a short time as a busboy at a popular New York restaurant, Café Central. Then his mother succeeded in getting him an audition for her friend John Guare's play *The House of Blue Leaves*, which was being staged at Lincoln Center Theater. "I had rehearsed this monologue for two weeks," Stiller told Berkman. "I thought, 'These people know they're seeing me because of my mother. But you meet people any way you can.'" Stiller was cast as Ronnie Shaughnessy, a soldier who goes AWOL and dreams of assassinating the pope. *The House of Blue Leaves* won several Tony Awards. Perhaps the most important part of Stiller's experience with the production, however, was his creation of a short, comical video, made backstage with fellow cast member John Mahoney (who later became famous for his work on the sitcom *Frasier*). He showed the video to some of his parents' friends at a party and was pleasantly surprised by how entertained they were. "Just seeing people watching it and laughing, I got a sense that this was something I should keep doing," Stiller said to Howe. "And I liked doing it." Stiller told David Poland for the *Rough Cut* Web site that the video was a breakthrough for him because for many years he had been steering away from comedy: "When I was basically 10 or 11, I knew I wanted to be a director and then I thought I wanted to be a serious director for a long time," he said. "[It was] not until I was in my early 20s that I started to embrace the comedic instincts that were there." In 1987 he sold a six-minute parody of the film *The Color of Money*, which he called *The Hustler of Money*, to the long-running comedy show *Saturday Night Live*. Soon after that he was hired as a regular writer for, and cast member of, *Saturday Night Live*, becoming the youngest person ever to be featured on it. "I feel like a freshman in college," he told Berkman while he was still with the show. "I really don't know what to expect." The exposure he gained through *Saturday Night Live*, coupled with his role in a made-for-television version of *The House of Blue Leaves*, which was aired on PBS in 1987, brought Stiller supporting roles in such films as *Empire of the Sun* (1987), *Fresh Horses* (1988), which starred Andrew McCarthy and Molly Ringwald, and *Stella* (1990), with Bette Midler.

In 1990 Stiller worked with the writer Jeff Kahn and the producer Jim Jones to create his own comedy show for MTV. The show ran only briefly, but in 1992 the Fox television network decided to revive it, and Stiller moved to Los Angeles to shoot 13 new episodes. *The Ben Stiller Show* drew rave reviews but not much of an audience. Some blamed the time slot; *The Ben Stiller Show* aired on Sunday evenings opposite CBS's popular news magazine *60 Minutes*. "When you're on against *60 Minutes*, your audience is kids," Stiller told Graham. "Our show appeals to an audience that's hopefully a little older than 10 years old. We're aiming for more of the college crowd." Although the series was generally deemed funny, admiration for Stiller's efforts was not universal. Howe quoted the TV critic Tom Shales, for example, as having written, "Who is Ben Stiller, that he should have a show?" Shales called Stiller a "well-connected Hollywood brat" and described his show as "just the thing for that hard to fill 3 AM slot on the Home Shopping Channel."

Like *Saturday Night Live*, *The Ben Stiller Show* consisted of short skits, most of which parodied current movies or entertainers. Stiller did adept impressions of the rock band U2's lead singer, Bono, as well as the musician Bruce Springsteen and the actor Tom Cruise. Two memorable skits from the show were *Jazzercize with Wolves*—a spoof on the 1990 film *Dances with Wolves*—and a version of the television show *Cops* that featured a 17th-century witch hunt set in Salem, Massachusetts. Stiller also created an original character, "No, no, no man," who followed every sentence he spoke with "no, no, no." One of the regulars on the show was the comedian Janeane Garofalo, with whom Stiller would later work repeatedly. In spite of its low ratings and its cancellation after 13 episodes, *The Ben Stiller Show* won an Emmy Award for writing in 1993. "Stiller has one of the most

dexterous comic minds of his generation," Paul Tatara wrote for *CNN.com*. "His short-lived TV show is the great lost classic of the 90s. It was consistently risky, and the acting . . . was smart and effective." "The thing I feel good about was that I was able to go down with a show I was proud of," Stiller later said. "I never wanted to go through putting on a show where you lose your soul."

While Stiller was editing the pilot of *The Ben Stiller Show*, in February 1992, the producer Michael Shamberg and the actor, director, and producer Danny DeVito, of Jersey Films, sent him Helen Childress's script for *Reality Bites*, hoping that he would be interested in directing the film. "The movie's about being in your early 20s and that transitional period," Stiller explained to Howe. "This whole Generation X thing has become more of a turnoff to the people who are within it, because it has a very negative connotation—an emptiness that's associated with it." Stiller also acted in the film, playing the part of Michael Grates, the more conventional of the two men vying for the affections of a recent college graduate, Lelaina Pierce (Winona Ryder). The film also starred Ethan Hawke, Steve Zahn, Janeane Garofalo, and Swoozie Kurtz. "[I] felt like I was riding on the seat of my pants doing the love scenes," Stiller told Howe. "I kept thinking, 'What right do you have to do a love scene?' It's weird to have two people there being very intimate and you're sitting next to the camera watching it all. To direct somebody's lovemaking is, like, a responsibility." The awkwardness he may have felt notwithstanding, Stiller "fell right into the [directorial] process in a very easy way," DeVito told Howe. "It wasn't like you had to pull his coat every five minutes. . . . When you walk on a set, you can tell when things are under control, when he or she has a finger on exactly what they want. Ben did a terrific job. He was very confident."

After the success of *Reality Bites*, Stiller considered directing a film of a Rolling Stones tour. Although the project never came to fruition, Stiller said that planning the film was in itself an exciting experience. "The best part was getting into the Stones' inner sanctum," he told Jeffrey Zaslow for *USA Weekend* (August 30, 1998). "Just me, my writing partner, and the Stones. It was mind-boggling, with Mick running up and saying, 'You all right? Need a glass of water?'" When the project fell through, Stiller accepted a supporting role in the 1996 film *If Lucy Fell* and, that same year, the lead in *Flirting with Disaster*, a hit comedy about an adoptee and new father who searches for his biological parents while edging toward an extramarital affair. Stiller's next directorial project was *The Cable Guy* (1996), which starred the popular comedian Jim Carrey as a deranged cable-television repairman who lives in a TV-inspired fantasy world and develops an attachment to a customer (Matthew Broderick). The dark comedy proved to be a financial success but a critical failure. "Ben Stiller directs *The Cable Guy* with professional skill but without the blithe comic flair he brought to *Reality Bites*," Janet Maslin wrote for the *New York Times* (June 14, 1996). "Mr. Stiller fares better in staging quick, isolated gags than with finding a consistent comic tone." "Though . . . [it] came out pretty much the way I wanted, it was universally panned," Stiller told Lidz. "If I believed all the reviews, I'd think I really stink." As he explained to Claudia Puig for *USA Today* (September 15, 1998), he felt that the film was "a good experience just in terms of dealing with a studio on a picture that is that big. I really love directing. I'd like to focus on writing and directing."

Stiller was next seen opposite Cameron Diaz in the 1998 blockbuster *There's Something About Mary*. For 13 years Stiller's goofy, likable character has remained infatuated with an attractive, down-to-earth woman (Diaz) he met in high school; hoping to find her, he hires a private detective (Matt Dillon), who ends up wanting her for himself. *There's Something About Mary* was notable for pushing the limits of "gross-out" humor, and whether despite or because of that, it was a hit with audiences. "I had no idea what to expect," Stiller told Puig of the film's success. "I'd been in a few movies where you have expectations, but I'd never been in a big hit like that. So until it happened, I kind of felt, 'I'll believe it when I see it.'" Although Stiller excelled in the comic role, he told Lidz that he is "not running out to play that character again. I don't want to wind up like those *SCTV* people who were typecast by Hollywood and never allowed to exploit in films what they did so well on television. I'd enjoy being that *Something About Mary* guy if it were once every four movies, and I did three different characters in the other three. I just don't want to be him every time out. On the other hand, I realize the role has opened up opportunities for me. So that's a good thing I guess."

Stiller's other 1998 films include *Your Friends and Neighbors*, Neil LaBute's blistering examination of male-female relationships, and *Permanent Midnight*, based on the autobiography of the sitcom writer Jerry Stahl, a friend of Stiller's who battled cocaine addiction. Stahl coached Stiller for his role, which may have been his most challenging to date, by taking him to clinics and introducing him to drug addicts. "I identified with my character's alienation. I connected with his feelings of self-loathing, of being unable to embrace who he was or bond with other people," Stiller told Lidz. In 1998 Stiller also played Steve Arlo, the assistant of the private detective Daryl Zero, in the moderately successful *Zero Effect*. Stiller's 1999 movie credits are *Black and White*, *McClintock's Peach*, *The Suburbans*, and *Mystery Men*. In the last-named project, directed by Kinka Usher, he teamed up with Hank Azaria, William H. Macy, Greg Kinnear, Paul Reubens, and Janeane Garofalo to spoof the superhero genre. He will appear next in *Keeping the Faith*, scheduled for release in 2000.

With his friend Janeane Garofalo, Ben Stiller has co-authored a mock self-help manual called *Feel This Book: An Essential Guide to Self-Empowerment, Spiritual Supremacy, and Sexual Satisfaction* (1999). In addition to planning, with Jerry Stahl, the production of a film version of Budd Schulberg's 1941 novel, *What Makes Sammy Run?*, Stiller has established his own production company. "Part of [the] company's about developing movies to direct," he told David Poland. "They don't just kind of come around the corner. It really takes time. I feel like I really have to be connected to what I want to work on as a director, because it's going to be so much of my life."

Lidz described Stiller as "small and muscular. [His] face is bafflingly opaque: immobile mouth, colorless skin, gray-green eyes set deep in their sockets. On screen, he uses those eyes to cagey effect, playing ingenuous and disingenuous." Regarding Stiller's recently being placed at number 44 on *Entertainment Weekly*'s list of the 50 funniest people in show business, Jerry Stahl told Lidz, "I laughed when I saw that Ben had cracked the list of the 50 funniest people. The only list he belongs on is one of people who don't fit on any other list. He'd be the sole person on it, and his name would appear 44 times." Once engaged to the actress Jeanne Tripplehorn, Ben Stiller is single, and he spends most of his time in New York and Los Angeles. — C.P.

Suggested Reading: *CNN.com*; *Entertainment Weekly* (on-line) Sep. 18, 1998, with photo; *New York Times* H p11 Feb. 13, 1994, with photos, II p17 Sep. 20, 1998, with photo; *Playboy on Campus* (on-line); *Rough Cut* (on-line); *USA Today* D p3 Dec. 8, 1992, with photo, D p3 Aug. 6, 1998, with photo, D p9 Sep. 15, 1998, with photo; *USA Weekend* p19 Aug. 30, 1998, with photo; *Washington Post* G p6 Feb. 20, 1994, with photos

Selected Films: *The House of Blue Leaves*, 1987; *Empire of the Sun*, 1987; *Fresh Horses*, 1988; *Stella*, 1990; *Reality Bites*, 1994; *If Lucy Fell*, 1996; *Flirting with Diaster*, 1996; *The Cable Guy*, 1996, *Permanent Midnight*, 1998; *Zero Effect*, 1998, *There's Something About Mary*, 1998; *Your Friends and Neighbors*, 1998; *Mystery Man*, 1999

Selected Television Shows: *Saturday Night Live*, 1987(?); *The Ben Stiller Show*, 1990, 1992

Selected Books: with Janeane Garofalo—*Feel This Book: An Essential Guide to Self-Empowerment, Spiritual Supremacy, and Sexual Satisfaction*, 1999

AP Photo

Stine, R. L.

Oct. 8, 1943– Children's writer. Address: c/o Parachute Publishing, 156 Fifth Ave., Room 302, New York, NY 10010

In April 1994 R. L. Stine, the creator of the "Goosebumps" and "Fear Street" series for young people, suddenly realized how popular his books had become, when, while on his way to a book signing near his home town, he got caught in a traffic jam. "I thought there had been an accident," he told reporters for *People* (November 14, 1994), "until I realized the cars were all filled with kids, and they were coming to see *me*." With more than 200 published titles to his name and some 200 million of his books in print, the unassuming Stine is one of the best-selling American authors in history; according to a Web page produced by Scholastic Inc., his publisher, "'Goosebumps' is the #1, all-time best-selling book series for kids." Unlike such series as Ann M. Martin's "Baby-Sitters Club" and Francine Pascal's "Sweet Valley High," which are geared toward girls, the "Fear Street" and "Goosebumps" series attract boys and girls alike. Indeed, by writing horror novels that offer kids chills, red herrings, and cliff-hangers laced with humor, Stine, "the Stephen King of children's books," has come up with a remarkably effective way to get adolescent boys to read fiction. "I think [kids] like the books because they're like a roller coaster ride," Stine said to Kit Alderdice for *Publishers Weekly* (July 17, 1995). "They're very fast. They're very exciting. You think you're going to go in one direction—they take you off in another direction." But, he added, "no matter how scary it is, or how thrilling, or how exciting—you know that you're safe the whole time."

As he revealed in a memoir for nine-to-12-year-olds, *It Came from Ohio: My Life as a Writer* (1998), co-written by Joe Arthur, Stine—contrary to the assumption of many of his readers—had a rather ordinary childhood. The eldest of Lewis and Anne (Feinstein) Stine's three children, Robert Lawrence Stine was born on October 8, 1943 in Bexley, Ohio, a suburb of Columbus. His father earned a modest salary as a shipping manager, and the family lived in a small house near the railroad tracks. Young Robert often relied on his own imagination for entertainment. "I started writing when I was nine years old," he told Kit Alderdice. "I found an old typewriter up in the attic, dragged it down to my room and started typing little funny magazines and little joke books." Inspired by the contents of *Mad* magazine and such horror comic books as *The Vault of Horror* and *Tales from the Crypt*, he continued writing throughout grade school; to the dismay of his teachers, he would distribute what he had written to his classmates. Later, Stine wrote for his high school newspaper and edited the student humor magazine at Ohio State University.

After he graduated from college, in 1965, with a bachelor's degree in English, Stine taught social studies in a junior high school for a year—an experience he has described as "miserable." He then moved to New York City, to pursue his aspiration of writing professionally. For a while he worked as a writer and editor at a trade publication for the soft-drink industry. Growing increasingly bored with his assignments, he quit that job and took one with a phony fan magazine for a salary of $100 a week (equivalent to about $14 an hour in 1999). While writing fake interviews, he told Mary B. W. Tabor for the *New York Times* (September 7, 1995), he acquired tools he would later find useful as a writer of outlandish tales. "I learned to make stuff up and write really fast," he said. "I'd come in in the morning and [the editor would] say, 'Do an interview with the Beatles,' so I'd sit down and make it up." In 1969, the year he got married, he accepted a position as an editor for Scholastic, a major publisher of books and periodicals for children. Two years later he became the editor in chief of Scholastic's now-defunct adolescent humor magazine *Bananas*. "I actually attained my life's ambition," Stine told Kit Alderdice. "I was 28 years old and I had my own national humor magazine."

Stine lost his dream job in 1984, after sales of *Bananas* plummeted. Earlier, he had begun writing a series of books aimed at tickling kids' funny bones. Published as the work of Jovial Bob Stine, they included *How to Be Funny: An Extremely Silly Guidebook* (1978) and *The Complete Book of Nerds* (1979). Now, deprived of a steady paycheck, he accelerated his rate of production of children's books. Using the pseudonyms Eric Affabee and Zachary Blue, he wrote several a year, alternating books of humor with adventure tales and "pick-your-destiny" stories, in the latter of which the reader must make decisions that determine the outcome. At the suggestion of his former boss,

Scholastic editorial director Jean Feiwel, Stine wrote his first children's horror novel. Much to the surprise of Stine and Scholastic, *Blind Date* (1986) became an instant best-seller; currently, more than 500,000 copies have been sold. With such follow-up horror hits as *Twisted* (1986) and *The Baby-Sitter* (1989), R. L. Stine had found his niche.

With the help of his wife, Jane (Waldhorn) Stine, and her company, Parachute, Stine came up with the idea for "Fear Street," a series of creepy tales targeted at boys and girls ages nine through 14. Edited by Stine's wife and published by Archway Paperbacks, "Fear Street" debuted in 1989. The series takes place at the fictional Shadyside High School, where, as Stine has said, "there's a very high mortality rate." Relying less on monsters than on semi-realistic situations, with a hefty measure of carnage tossed in for shock value, the "Fear Street" series became the first cross-gender hit among teenage readers. Early titles include *The New Girl* (1989), *Missing* (1990), *The Sleepwalker* (1991), *Prom Queen* (1992), and *Bad Dreams* (1994). More recent ones include *The Face* (1996), in which the heroine witnesses a horrifying murder; afterward, she can't recall anything about what she has seen, but she finds herself repeatedly drawing the face of the victim. In *All Night Party* (1997), Cindy gets killed during a party held for her on Fear Island. "I work very hard to keep these books from being too real," he told Mary Tabor. "The real world is much scarier than what I write about. My books are just meant to entertain. Having written for kids for so long, I have a feeling for how far I can go and what not to do. I don't do drugs. I don't do child abuse. I don't really ever do divorce."

As "Fear Street" readership grew, Stine began to think of ways to modify his successful formula for a younger audience—kids eight to 11. Thus was born the "Goosebumps" series, which contains fewer real-life situations, more supernatural creatures, and less violence than the "Fear Street" stories. The name of the new series came from an advertisement in *TV Guide* for "Goosebumps Week," during which one of the local New York channels planned to show reruns of horror films. The new series, produced by Parachute and published by Scholastic, debuted in 1992, with *Welcome to Dead House*, a story about a brother and sister who move to a spooky old house in a strange town and make friends with people who turn out to have otherworldly links. Close on the heels of that book came *Stay Out of the Basement* (1992), in which— in a plot reminiscent of the musical *Little Shop of Horrors*—Dr. Brewer's two children notice that he is starting to grow "weedy and seedy" after experimenting with weird plants in his basement. Within two years Stine's titles dominated the juvenile best-seller lists compiled by *USA Today* and *Publishers Weekly*. To date, they have been translated into at least 18 languages.

Selling in total more than one million copies per month, the titles in "Goosebumps" and "Fear Street" have morphed their author, almost like one

of his imagined creatures, into a publishing giant. To keep up with demand, Stine contracted to write one "Fear Street" and one "Goosebumps" novel each month. When asked how he handled such a demanding schedule, he explained to Louisa Ermelino for *People* (October 9, 1995), "I'm disciplined. I don't have to be in any mood. I set a goal— 20 pages a day. I'm at the computer at nine [in the morning] and I finish by four [in the afternoon]. . . . I just love writing this stuff." For each novel, Stine starts by coming up with a title; then he creates a plot, imagining first how the book will end. In a long outline that he submits to his publisher for approval, he describes the plot in detail. It takes him about eight days to complete a "Goosebumps" book and about 12 days to finish one for the "Fear Street" series. He has maintained that he has never had to strain for new ideas and has never suffered from writer's block.

Stine's books are not universally liked. The obvious macabre appeal his novels hold for children has worried some parents, teachers, and librarians. One periodical referred to his stories as "shock schlock," and some children's libraries have categorized his books as "sub-literature" and therefore not worth acquiring. Some critics of his books take their arguments a step further, by likening Stine's tales to candy that could rot children's brains. Stine and his defenders counter that his novels are being read by many children who otherwise might never open a book. Stine does not pretend that his books are high art; rather, he has suggested that if children get into the habit of reading his books regularly, they will eventually move on to more literary fare. Encapsulating both sides of the debate neatly, Paul Gray and Elizabeth Rudolph wrote for *Time* (August 2, 1993), "Maybe the youngsters will move upward in their tastes, through Stephen King and V. C. Andrews to Hemingway, Joyce and Shakespeare. Or maybe they will boil the cat in the spaghetti." "Goosebumps" has spawned offshoots in many areas of entertainment. The Fox Children's Network, for example, produced a weekly television program based on the series, and Disney World opened a fun-house attraction called Horrorland, based on Stine's story *One Day at Horrorland* (1994). Two film adaptations of "Fear Street" stories were in production in mid-1999; for another, to be released under the "Goosebumps" banner, Tim Burton signed on as producer. In perhaps the surest indication of the cultural pervasiveness of R. L. Stine's creations, in 1995 bookstores began selling parodies of "Goosebumps"—the "Gooflumps" series, by "R. U. Slime."

In a 1995 conversation with Mary Tabor, Stine's only child, Matthew, who was then 15, said that he had read only one of his father's books, and that one only because his father patterned that story's main character after him. (The character's girlfriend turns out to be a vampire.) "I don't like to read," Matthew told Tabor. "I write music and play guitar." In a 1998 interview Stine ascribed his son's lack of interest to teenage rebelliousness. "If you're a writer, your kid will basically be a non-reader; it seems to go without saying," he told a reporter for *HomeArts* (May 1998, on-line). "Every writer I know, their kids don't read their stuff. It's like a natural way for kids to rebel."

After 25 years of writing exclusively for children, R. L. Stine received an offer from Brandon Tartikoff, formerly the programing director for NBC, to write a novel for adults. Tartikoff (who died in 1997) had recently signed on with Time's Warner Books to manage his own imprint under their aegis. His goal was to publish a handful of books each year with an eye toward selling the stories to Hollywood, and Stine was the first writer he approached. The resulting book, *Superstitious* (1995), was savaged by reviewers, who complained that it was intolerably unsophisticated in both content and style. Nevertheless, the novel sold well—sales reached about 150,000 copies—and Miramax Films gave Stine a contract for the movie rights.

Stine and his family live in New York City. His wife, Jane Stine, currently manages Parachute Publishing along with her partner, Joan Waricha. Tabor reported that during her interview with Stine, he "sprinkle[d] his conversation with self-effacing jokes about his receding hairline, unathletic physique and modestly furnished apartment." "It's amazing what has happened," he remarked to Tabor, referring to the phenomenal success of his

books. "I can hardly believe it myself." Stine has often said that he expects the popularity of his books to wane in the not-too-distant future. "Kids move on," he told Tabor. "In 10 years, they won't be buying these books anymore. They'll be into something else. I think I'll be doing some other things, too." Meanwhile, by his own account, he thoroughly enjoys his work. — T.J.F.

Suggested Reading: *HomeArts* (on-line) May 1998; *Los Angeles Times* A p3 Oct. 30, 1995; *People* p115+ Nov. 14, 1994, with photos; *Publishers Weekly* p208+ July 17, 1995, with photo; *New York Times* C p1 Sep. 7, 1995, with photos; *Contemporary Authors* new revision series vol. 53, 1997

Selected Books: *How to Be Funny: An Extremely Silly Guidebook*, 1978; *The Time Raider*, 1982; *Indiana Jones and the Curse of Horror Island*, 1984; *Jovial Bob's Computer Joke Book*, 1985; *The Seige of the Dragonriders*, 1984; *G.I. Joe-Operation: Star Raider*, 1986; *Blind Date*, 1986; *The New Girl*, 1989; *The Sleepwalker*, 1991; *Welcome to the Dead House*, 1992; *The Girl Who Cried Monster*, 1993; *My Hairiest Adventure*, 1994; *The Horror at Camp Jellyjam*, 1995; *Bad Hare Day*, 1996; *Werewolf Skin*, 1997; *Last Chance*, 1999

Tavener, John

Jan. 28, 1944– Composer. Address: c/o G. Schirmer Promotion Dept., 257 Park Ave. S., 20th Fl., New York, NY 10010

"I don't think it is an odd thing for me to be a Christian composer in the late 20th century," the British composer John Tavener told an interviewer for the *Border Television* Web site. "What I think is odd is the late 20th century [itself]." At a time when contemporary music is almost exclusively secular, Tavener has chosen to immerse himself in the musical traditions of Eastern Orthodox Christianity, many of which date back to well over a thousand years ago. As Joseph J. Feeney wrote in *America* (April 10, 1993), Tavener's intention is "to sing God's praise in a secular world and to offer busy people a rare, beautiful music of mystic stillness and simplicity." In *Cross Currents* (Spring 1992), Geoffrey Turner quoted the composer as saying, "I want to go back to the primordial roots of art, as the Orthodox icon painters do, back to worship. This is my idea of tradition and the one to which I belong—one that has essentially not changed—is unbroken." Captured on successful recordings such as *The Protecting Veil* (1992) and *Akathist of Thanksgiving* (1994), Tavener's music has achieved a level of popularity that is unusual for sacred music composed in modern times.

Michael Putland/Courtesy of Harmonia Mundi USA

John Tavener was born on January 28, 1944 in London, England. According to several sources, one of his distant ancestors was John Taverner, a 16th-century Scottish composer of sacred music who is associated with the Reformation. Tavener's immediate family was also musical; his father played the organ at a Presbyterian church, and as a child John was taught to play both the piano and the organ. By the age of 12, he was creating his own compositions for those instruments. Tavener received his formal music training at London's Royal Academy of Music.

Some of Tavener's early compositions combined the musical style of the medieval period with electronic instrumentation. In 1965 his work *Cain and Abel* won the Prince Rainier Prize for musical composition. In 1968 another biblically inspired piece, *The Whale*, a cantata about the Old Testament figure Jonah, was recorded by Apple. That record company was owned by the Beatles, and Tavener became friends with them. According to Geoffrey Turner, at about this time Tavener "wore a pink suit and drove round London in an aging Bentley."

In the 1970s Tavener turned exclusively to religious subjects. He wrote songs, choral music, and requiems that used as lyrics text from the Bible, the York mystery plays, Father Bruno de Jesus-Marie's 16th-century biography *St. John of the Cross*, and the spiritual writings of John Donne and T. S. Eliot. In 1979 his controversial opera *Thérèse* was staged at Covent Garden, in London. The piece linked the French saint Thérèse of Lisieux, who was a nun, with one of her contemporaries, the poet Rimbaud, whose work was considered blasphemous by the Catholic church in France.

By the late 1970s religion had come to play a prominent part in Tavener's life as well as in his music. In about 1977 he became a member of the Russian Orthodox Church. (In an event referred to as the Great Schism, the Orthodox and Catholic churches split in the 11th century, because of disagreements over creed and the power that the Pope held over the church and its followers. Accounts vary as to whether Tavener joined the Russian or Greek Orthodox Church.) According to the *Border Television* Web site, Anthony Bloom, the Russian metropolitan of Sourozh, was instrumental in Tavener's conversion. "I certainly had a crisis when I became Orthodox," the composer said, as quoted on the Web site. "I went to see [Anthony] week by week and he never appeared to talk about God or religion at all. He just told anecdotes about his own life, which I found incredibly helpful in moments of crisis in my life since." After Tavener's conversion, Bloom suggested that he compose music for the Orthodox mass as an expression of his faith. Tavener followed Bloom's advice. The first time one of his compositions was performed in a cathedral, however, "there was an uproar," Tavener told *Border Television*. "People started to come up to me and say, 'You don't know anything about tradition.' . . . It was a real crisis and I had to stop writing for a long time."

In order to learn the traditions that, according to the Orthodox adherents who criticized him, were not reflected in his work, Tavener went to Greece and studied sacred music that was played and sung there. "I [went] to monasteries . . . notating down little bits of chant, as [the composer Béla] Bartók did with folk music in Hungary," he told the *Border Television* reporter. According to Tavener, his study of Greek sacred music also deepened his faith. "I started to understand about this discipline which comes from within, it's a tradition which draws you so deeply. . . . First of all it happens in the mind, then by some mysterious process it goes to the heart." In an interview with Joseph McLellan for the *Washington Post* (December 25, 1994), Tavener said, "I was brought up Presbyterian, but it didn't make much impact on me. Then I turned to Rome, but I found the Catholic Church very earthly in thinking—worldly and dogmatic. I have found what I sought in the Orthodox Church, with its mystical concepts of not knowing. . . . The West wants answers; the East says, 'Well, maybe.'"

After he had immersed himself in Orthodox music, Tavener's compositions began to take on a very different style and form. Much of his work was inspired by monastic chants, and in many pieces the sounds of the cello, the oboe, the clarinet, or other instruments resembled the human voice. Tavener's music also became simpler, with single notes drawn out for many moments. In addition, Tavener had become an admirer of the age-old art of icon painting, and as he explained to Feeney, he came to think of his work as "making a lyrical icon in sound, rather than in wood." Many of Tavener's longer compositions are broken up into sections that he has chosen to call "ikons" rather than movements or songs.

In 1989 Tavener composed *The Protecting Veil*, which is perhaps the most popular and acclaimed of his compositions. The title refers to an event many Christians believe to have taken place in Constantinople in the 10th century, in which the Virgin Mary appeared and protected Christians from their persecutors with her veil. The first recording of *The Protecting Veil* was released in 1992; featuring the cellist Stephen Isserlis, it became the top-selling classical album in Great Britain that year. Praising the recording in the *New York Times* (March 28, 1993), Alex Ross wrote, "The most striking element of *The Protecting Veil* is the stratospheric cello part, shining continuously through the elegant haze of the strings. This solo, which seldom falls below middle C, is unlike any cello music ever written." "After *The Protecting Veil* came out, I had hundreds of letters," Tavener told Woods. "One in particular moved me. It said that I was trying to preserve beauty and truth. These are not fashionable concepts. But I think there's a tremendous thirst for them." In 1993 *The Protecting Veil* became the first Tavener composition to be presented in the United States; it was performed by the New England Conservatory Orchestra, in Boston. In 1998 the celebrated cellist Yo-Yo Ma released a second recording of the work.

Tavener's next major composition was *The Repentant Thief* (1991). A 20-minute rondo for clarinet and orchestra, this piece was commissioned by the London Symphony Orchestra and was first performed in London in 1991. The composition is based on the old Christian tale of the Good Thief of Golgotha, who danced his way into heaven, and the lively clarinet solos in the piece are reminiscent of rustic Greek dance music. The following year Tavener created a work called *Mary of Egypt* for the Aldeburgh Music Festival, in the county of Suffolk, in England. Although *Mary of Egypt* was billed as an opera, Tavener called it a "moving icon." Mother Thekla, an Orthodox abbess who resides in North Yorkshire and who had become a spiritual adviser to the composer, collaborated with Tavener on the libretto. *Mary of Egypt* tells the story of a prostitute who becomes a mystic and eventually a saint. According to Turner, it is one of Tavener's less successful works. "There are patches of beautiful sensuous music but this is underpinned by a pedal note F which rarely changes and which is literally and emotionally monotonous," he wrote. "While a composer with Tavener's religious intentions might aspire to represent the constancy of the divine with music that hardly moves, music in this transient life must go somewhere [and] strike a compromise between immobility and drama." A second collaboration with Mother Thekla, *We Shall See Him as He Is*, which was commissioned by the Cheshire County Cathedral for its 900th anniversary, fared better with music critics. Feeney described this work as "sumptuously scored, alternately quiet and stunning, vaguely Eastern, often ethereal, quite unlike other music."

In 1994 another successful album, *Akathist of Thanksgiving*, was released. (An akathist is a hymn of thanks or supplication.) The work was written for a chorus, vocal soloists, and an orchestra; the text, which is sung in Russian, consists of words written by an Orthodox archpriest named Gregory Petrov shortly before he died in a Serbian prison camp. "It is a prolonged song of praise to God as the source of all reality and knowledge," McLellan wrote of this work. "Through this music, one can feel the power of Tavener's cosmic vision whether or not one shares the beliefs that inspired it." Meirion Bowen of the London *Guardian Weekly* (February 6, 1994) assessed the piece differently when it was performed later that year, at a concert series sponsored by the BBC in celebration of Tavener's 50th birthday. Bowen felt that *Akathist of Thanksgiving* "sounded as lifeless as a Victorian oratorio." She also criticized the composer's technique, creativity, and choice of instruments, calling him "the Lloyd Webber of the Byzantine church." Perhaps that is precisely what the public wanted: tickets sold out for all three concerts in the BBC series.

Tavener received what may turn out to be his greatest moment of fame when his composition *Song for Athene* was played at the funeral of Princess Diana of Wales, in 1997. Immediately after the service, television and radio stations that had broadcast it were besieged with requests for the name of the composer of the somber, touching music. Tavener had a second brush with celebrity the following year, when the pop star Sting recited the lyrics to Tavener's composition *In the Month of Athyr*, as part of a performance in honor of the 25th anniversary of the Tallis Scholars at London's National Gallery.

Marking a separate 25th anniversary—that of the Academy of Ancient Music (AAM), which commissioned the work—Tavener's *Eternity's Sunrise*, released on disc in the spring of 1999, is also dedicated to Princess Diana. The title piece is performed by the soprano Patricia Rozario and the AAM, under Paul Goodwin; Bradley Bambarger, who first heard the work prior to its final edit, wrote in *Gramophone* (May 1999) that *Eternity's Sunrise* "wrung tears from my eyes." According to him, it is Tavener's favorite recording of his music to date.

In the same article, Bambarger noted that some of Tavener's best work has been "written as a balm for grief." In addition to *Eternity's Sunrise* and *Song for Athene*, such works include the cantata *Eis Thanaton*, composed after the death of Tavener's mother. *The Apocalypse*, as yet unrecorded, was written by Tavener as he awaited heart surgery.

Although traditional Orthodox music serves as the framework for Tavener's compositions and is his most obvious influence, according to Tavener he has also found inspiration in ancient Egyptian art and Hindu chants. The conductor Michael Tilson Thomas, who has performed several of Tavener's compositions, told Alex Ross that there were also subtle elements of English pastoral music, French Impressionism, and the avant-garde in Tavener's work. Tavener believes that it is imperative that his music be truly original. "It would be dangerous just to follow or to copy tradition blindly," he told Octavio Roca for *Classical Pulse* (December 1994). "We have to find our own way."

John Tavener spends most of his time composing music on the island of Aegina, in Greece, where he resides either at a monastery or in a hotel. Although he suffers from a heart condition, he continues to compose at a rapid pace, and many of his works have yet to be recorded. When questioned about the connection between his faith and his work, Tavener told the *Border Television* interviewer, "I don't know what it is like to see God. What I can say is that when I am composing I feel a connection with something divine. I feel that there is no separation between the work and prayer. In fact prayer is work and work is prayer." Tavener is the subject of a documentary film by the director Geoffrey Haydon, entitled *Glimpses of Paradise* (1994). A writer for the London *Observer* (August 14, 1994) described Tavener as "a tall impassive figure with lank, shoulder-length locks." Bambarger reported that Tavener's heart condition has left him "physically frail, contributing to the sense of otherworldliness about him." — C.P.

Suggested Reading: *America* p15+ Apr. 10, 1993; *Border Television* Web site; *Classical Pulse* p42 Dec. 1994, with photo; *Cross Currents* p54+ Spring 1995; *Gramophone* p10+ May 1999, with photo; *Guardian Weekly* p27 Feb. 6, 1994; *New York Times* II p25 Mar. 28, 1993, with photo; *Washington Post* G p12 Dec. 25, 1994

Selected Recordings: *The Whale*, 1970; *Celtic Requiem*, 1971; *Akhmatova Requiem*, 1979; *The Repentant Thief*, 1991; *The Protecting Veil*, 1992; *We Shall See Him as He Is*, 1992; *Sacred Music by John Tavener*, 1992; *Mary of Egypt*, 1993; *Ikon of Light*, 1993; *To a Child Dancing in the Wind*, 1994; *Akathist of Thanksgiving*, 1994; *Ikons*, 1994; *Thunder Entered Her*, 1994; *Innocence*, 1995; *Eis Thanaton & Theophany*, 1996; *Syvati*, 1997

Courtesy of Central Intelligence Agency

Tenet, George J.

Jan. 5, 1953– Director of the Central Intelligence Agency. Address: c/o Central Intelligence Agency, Office of Public Affairs, Washington, DC 20505

On July 11, 1997, following unanimous votes by the Senate Select Committee on Intelligence and the full United States Senate, George J. Tenet was sworn in as the 18th director of the Central Intelligence Agency (CIA). In addition to controlling all the activities of the CIA, he oversees the rest of the dozen agencies that comprise the so-called intelligence community in the United States, and he sits on the National Security Council (NSC), a presi-

dential advisory group. Before his arrival at the CIA, Tenet served the NSC as a special assistant to President Bill Clinton and as senior director for intelligence programs. Earlier, he spent more than four years as staff director of the Senate Select Committee on Intelligence, which plays a key role in congressional oversight of the CIA. Schooled in foreign service and international affairs, he launched his career in public service as a legislative assistant to the late senator John Heinz of Pennsylvania. Tenet's presence at the CIA, as both acting director (from December 1996 to July 1997) and director, has reportedly brought a much-needed measure of stability to the American intelligence community, which had bid hello and farewell to five CIA chiefs between 1991 and 1996. Said to be passionate about both his work and the mission of the CIA, he has also helped to boost morale among CIA employees, the total number of whom is a well-guarded secret.

The CIA, which celebrated its 50th anniversary in 1997, descended from the Office of Strategic Services, which was set up during World War II, and the Central Intelligence Group, which was created later during the war. It came into being at the behest of President Harry S. Truman, "as an insurance policy against the kind of surprise that caught America off guard in World War II," as Tenet, referring to the Japanese attack on American ships at Pearl Harbor, Hawaii, in 1941, said during a conference on the CIA in November 1997. Truman "was also annoyed by the confused and conflicting nature of the reports landing on his desk from various departments," Tenet explained during his speech, as transcribed for *Vital Speeches of the Day* (January 15, 1998). "He wanted someone to make sense of them, someone who had no policy axe to grind and someone whose exclusive mission was to work for him, and to ensure that he was not taken off guard by dangerous developments overseas." "As I look at the world today," Tenet continued, "it is clear to me that the potential for dangerous surprise is as great as ever."

The CIA is primarily responsible for gathering and analyzing information about foreign governments, political groups, and terrorist organizations; warning about the threats to Americans that those governments and groups pose; and, as Tenet said in his address at the conference on the CIA, "employ[ing] covert action on those occasions when [U.S.] leaders conclude that an important aim can be achieved through no other means." What the CIA does, he declared, "I do not believe can be replicated anyplace else in our government." In concluding his speech he said, "I want the American people to know that the world is safer for them because of the CIA."

The son of immigrants who came to the United States from Greece shortly before his birth, George John Tenet was born in the New York City borough of Queens on January 5, 1953. His father, John, ran the 20th Century Diner in Little Neck, New York. His mother, Evangelia, who does not speak much

English, is a homemaker. Tenet received his bachelor's degree in 1976 from the Georgetown University School of Foreign Service, in Washington, D.C. He then attended the School of International Affairs at Columbia University, in New York City, graduating in 1978. Soon after he received his master's degree in international affairs, the American Hellenic Institute (an organization, founded in 1974, whose goal is to strengthen relations between the United States and Greece and within the American-Greek community) hired him as research director. He quit that post in 1979 to take a job with the Solar Energy Industries Association.

In 1982 Tenet entered government service, becoming a legislative assistant and research director to Senator John Heinz, a moderate-to-liberal Republican from Pennsylvania. In Heinz's office Tenet focused on such matters as energy, foreign affairs, and defense. In 1985 he joined the staff of the Senate Intelligence Committee, working for about 14 months for Senator Patrick J. Leahy, a Vermont Democrat. In that position Tenet directed the committee's management of all arms-control negotiations between the Soviet Union and the United States. His report "The Ability of U.S. Intelligence to Monitor the Intermediate Nuclear Force Treaty" was presented to the Senate. "His colleagues remember him as hugely likeable—the fellow who always wants to give you the cigar in his pocket, sometimes a burning cigar," Tim Weiner wrote for the New York Times (March 20, 1997). "They said he had an ability to make many different superiors feel at ease with him, and to have confidence in him and his judgment."

In 1988 Senator David L. Boren of Oklahoma, who chaired the Senate Intelligence Committee, appointed Tenet the committee's staff director. "I'm used to dealing straight up, and he was that type of person," Boren told Congressional Quarterly (April 12, 1997). According to a CIA Web site, Tenet "was responsible for coordinating all of the Committee's oversight and legislative activities including the strengthening of covert action reporting requirements, the creation of a statutory Inspector General at CIA, and the introduction of comprehensive legislation to reorganize U.S. intelligence." Additionally, Tenet was in charge of 40 staffers who helped him set up the committee's audit unit. The controversial hearings on the appointment of Robert M. Gates as director of the CIA took place during his stint with the committee.

In early 1993 Tenet resigned his position to join the national-security transition team set up to aid President Bill Clinton, who had taken the oath of office in January of that year. Soon afterward Tenet was promoted to special assistant to the president, and then, a few months later, to senior director for intelligence programs at the National Security Council. According to the CIA's Web-site article, his responsibilities included "coordinating all interagency activities concerning covert action" and putting together "presidential decision directives" with such titles as "Intelligence Priorities,"

"Security Policy Coordination," "U.S. Counterintelligence Effectiveness," and "U.S. Policy on Remote Sensing Space Capabilities." "He did a masterful job," Nicholas Burns, a former colleague of Tenet's, told Weiner. "He's the ultimate staff guy." Tenet's outstanding performance led to his nomination for the vacant position of deputy director of the CIA—"a $30 billion secret empire of a dozen intelligence services, with the Central Intelligence Agency as the flawed jewel in the crown," in Weiner's words. Appointed in July 1995, Tenet held the position for nearly a year and a half, working under then–CIA director John Deutch. "George is a tremendously loyal and devoted public servant," Deutch told Weiner. "The time I realized how devoted a deputy he was was in an extremely important meeting with important foreign dignitaries. He cleared the room to tell me I needed to zip up my fly." According to Weiner, Tenet made significant headway in improving the CIA's "long-troubled" relations with the Federal Bureau of Investigation and the Department of Justice. "And as first mate of this huge battleship [the CIA]," Weiner wrote, "he had to steer the intelligence agency's Directorate of Operations, the house of spies, which was foundering from the betrayal of one of its own." Weiner was referring to Aldrich H. Ames, who sold CIA secrets to the Soviet Union and then, after the end of the Cold War, to Russia, in the process betraying at least a dozen Russian agents who were also working for the U.S.

When Deutch resigned, in December 1996, Tenet was named acting director of the CIA. A few months later President Clinton began lobbying for his appointment as director. Public hearings into the nomination, scheduled by the Senate Intelligence Committee, were postponed after an FBI investigation raised questions about Tenet's personal finances. In particular, as Walter Pincus reported in the Washington Post (January 13, 1998), Tenet had "technically violated government financial reporting requirements in 1993 and 1994 because he was unaware of [telephone-company] stocks and an Athens apartment his father had bought in the names of his mother, brother, and himself." Although, after his father died, he had learned about the property and had reported that he co-owned it, he and members of his family underwent months of questioning. The Department of Justice found no evidence of illegalities, and on July 11, 1997, the Senate confirmed Tenet by a unanimous vote.

As the director of the CIA, Tenet heads the entire U.S. intelligence community—that is, all federally connected intelligence agencies—and holds a seat on the National Security Council, along with Samuel R. "Sandy" Berger, President Clinton's national security adviser; Secretary of Defense William S. Cohen; and Secretary of State Madeleine K. Albright. Thus, in the sphere of foreign policy, Tenet (like his predecessors) is among the most influential people in the federal government.

Within the first few months of his swearing in, Tenet, in an action widely praised among his colleagues, recruited Jack Downing to head the Directorate of Operations. Labeled on a CIA Web page the "analytical arm" of the agency and described by Walter Pincus as "the clandestine espionage side of the CIA," the Directorate of Operations "has long defined and dominated the agency," according to a *New York Times* (May 4, 1997) editorial. Downing, a former marine and CIA station chief in Moscow and Beijing who is conversant in both Russian and Chinese, had retired in 1995 after Deutch, ignoring the expectations of Downing and others, had named someone else to head the directorate.

In testimony he has given before the Senate Foreign Relations Committee and other congressional committees that are responsible for authorizing programs of the CIA and other intelligence agencies and overseeing their activities, Tenet has talked about threats to the United States posed by Russia, North Korea, China, Iraq, and other countries. More than 16 nations, he has said, have active chemical-weapons programs, and a dozen are developing offensive biological weapons. North Korea is developing ballistic missiles capable of striking the continental United States. In an embarrassing demonstration of inadequacies in American intelligence operations, the United States was taken completely by surprise when, in May 1998, India conducted tests of nuclear weapons. In light of those dangers and deficiencies, Tenet warned Congress and the White House that additional funds—to be used for, among other purposes, the hiring of more specialists in foreign languages and cultures and experts in computer programming and other state-of-the-art technology—were needed to keep the CIA "relevant," as Tim Weiner reported in the *New York Times* (October 22, 1998). In response, in an omnibus spending bill signed by President Clinton on October 22, 1998, Congress allocated $1.8 billion in supplemental funding for the CIA and other intelligence agencies—the largest such increase in 15 years.

Tenet and a few others from the CIA played an important role in the talks, held at Wye Plantation, in Maryland, that culminated in the so-called Wye accord, which extended Palestinian self-rule in the Israeli-occupied West Bank. The agreement was signed on October 23, 1998 by Prime Minister Benjamin Netanyahu of Israel, Yasir Arafat, the president of the Palestine National Authority, and—acting as a witness—President Clinton. According to the terms of the accord, the CIA will monitor the arrests of suspected terrorists by both Israeli troops and Palestinian police officers and will arbitrate security-related disagreements that arise between the Israelis and Palestinians. A few hours before the scheduled signing of the agreement, Netanyahu demanded, as a condition of Israeli approval of the land-for-peace deal, the release of Jonathan Jay Pollard, an American citizen who was convicted of espionage on behalf of Israel and has been serving a life sentence in a U.S. prison since 1987. According to various sources, Tenet told President Clinton that if Pollard were released, he would resign as CIA director. In a last-minute compromise, Clinton promised Netanyahu that he would seriously review the Pollard case.

In 1998 and 1999 the CIA was involved in military attacks by the United States in Sudan, Afghanistan, and Yugoslavia that resulted in enormous controversy. On August 20, 1998 the U.S. bombed the Al Shifa pharmaceutical plant in Khartoum, the capital of Sudan, and a suspected terrorist training camp in Afghanistan. According to American intelligence reports, the Khartoum facility was manufacturing chemical-warfare materials that were destined for use by terrorist groups funded by Osama bin Laden, a Saudi Arabian–born multimillionaire who has vowed to wage a holy war against the United States. Widely regarded as "perhaps the pre-eminent organizer and financier of international terrorism in the world today," as President Clinton described him in an address on the day of the U.S. attack, bin Laden was believed to be associated with the August 7, 1998 bombings of the American embassies in Nairobi, Kenya, and Dar es Salaam, Tanzania, which resulted in the deaths of more than 250 people. Almost immediately after the destruction of the pharmaceutical plant, critics of the attack charged that evidence of nerve-gas production at Al Shifa had been far from "compelling," as President Clinton had described it, and that the strike—or, at least, the timing of the strike—had to some extent been a cynical attempt by the Clinton administration to draw attention from the sex scandal involving the president and Monica Lewinsky, a one-time White House intern. Moreover, they charged, by acting unilaterally, the United States had in effect thumbed its nose at international law. The American public later learned that Al Shifa had been Sudan's main producer of medicines and agricultural pesticides.

In October 1999, while giving a talk at Georgetown University, in Washington, D.C., George Tenet strongly defended the bombing of the pharmaceutical plant. He explained that the CIA had determined that a soil sample taken from near the plant contained a substance used in manufacturing the nerve gas VX, and that that information had been given to the policy makers who made the decision to attack. According to Vernon Loeb, a staff writer for the *Washington Post* (October 21, 1999, on-line), "What Tenet didn't tell policy makers in a key briefing three days before the attack was that CIA analysts had concluded in a written analysis one month earlier that additional soil sampling would be necessary for them to determine conclusively whether the plant produced, stored, or transshipped VX."

The missile strike in Yugoslavia in which the CIA played a crucial role occurred on May 7, 1999, during 11 weeks of NATO air strikes in Yugoslavia that were triggered by Serb attacks on ethnic Albanians in Kosovo, a province of Serbia, Yugoslavia's main republic. In testimony before the House Intelligence Committee on July 22, 1999, Tenet said that the CIA "nominated" only one target during the air war—a building in Belgrade that the CIA identified as the headquarters of a Yugoslav arms agency that was believed to be supplying funds to the Yugoslav military. In actuality, the structure housed the Chinese Embassy, and the bombing killed three Chinese nationals. The Chinese government accused the U.S. of destroying the embassy intentionally, and the bombing led to severe strains in the relations between the U.S. and China. Tenet explained to the House Intelligence Committee that the destruction of the embassy had resulted from a series of errors and procedural failures: the CIA's identification of the building in Belgrade had been based on maps that proved to be out of date, while two maps that correctly indicated the location of the embassy had not been consulted. Furthermore, "since this was the agency's first time developing a 'target package,' there was no procedure in place for senior officials to review the work" that had led to the misidentification, Tenet said, as paraphrased by Eric Schmitt in the New York Times (July 23, 1999). "A final backup also failed," Schmitt reported, "when several computerized databases of sites that were off-limits to bombing, including embassies, hospitals, and churches, did not have the current location of the Chinese Embassy." "Database maintenance is one of the basic elements of our intelligence effort," Tenet explained, "but it is also one that has suffered in recent years as our work force has been spread thin." As of mid-October 1999, the United States and China had not yet come to any agreement regarding compensation for the destruction of the embassy. Also under discussion was compensation by China for destruction to the American Embassy in Beijing that had occurred during protests by Chinese citizens after the Belgrade bombing.

In a cover story for the New Republic (March 22, 1999), Nurith C. Aizenman reported that Tenet habitually works to the sound of operatic arias, and he has been known to attend important meetings in surprisingly casual attire—sweatpants, for example, or jeans and "a black leather jacket emblazoned with the CIA insignia." "He is unpretentious," Aizenman wrote, "eschewing a limousine in favor of a Ford Explorer and often stopping his convoy at a McDonald's drive-in for lunch on the way to a briefing at the White House. He is informal, the kind of guy who throws an employee in a headlock when he passes him in the hall, then drags him into the cafeteria for a cup of coffee." Aizenman quoted Frederick Hitz, who served as the CIA's inspector general from 1990 to 1997, as saying that Tenet "does all the little things. He calls people up when they've done a good job." And in the main CIA cafeteria, where he often eats, he "say[s] hello to everybody from the person who he's got a relationship with to the person who's cashing him out," Kenneth Levit, special counsel to Tenet, said to Aizenman. "I love it here," Tenet

told Aizenman. "It's the perfect job. They're going to have to blow me out of here."

Tenet and his wife, A. Stephanie Glakas-Tenet, have one son, John Michael Tenet. — M.B.

Suggested Reading: *Congressional Quarterly* p857+ Apr. 12, 1997, with photo; *New Republic* p22+ Mar. 22, 1999; *New York Times* A p1+ Mar. 20, 1997, with photos, B p10 May 6, 1997, D p25 May 8 1997, B p13 May 10, 1997, with photo; *odci.gov* (on-line); *Vital Speeches of the Day* p197+ Jan. 15, 1998; *Washington Post* A p13 Jan. 13, 1998, with photos, A p4 Nov. 11, 1998

Catherine McGann/Courtesy of Girlie Action
John Linnell (left) and John Flansburgh

They Might Be Giants

Flansburgh, John. May 6, 1960– Singer; guitarist.
Linnell, John. June 12, 1959– Singer; multi-instrumentalist.
Address: c/o Girlie Action Media & Management, 270 Lafayette St., New York, NY 10012-3327

John Flansburgh and John Linnell—two acerbic, slightly geeky childhood friends from Lincoln, Massachusetts—are better known together as They Might Be Giants (TMBG), the creators of odd, dryly humorous, two-minute pop songs that often have a satiric bent. TMBG was one of several acts to benefit from a vibrant university music circuit that began flourishing in the United States in the early 1980s. Their style, which eventually came to be known as alternative rock (also referred to at the time as modern rock), incorporated the aesthetics common to such prominent rock-'n'-roll bands of the era as Blondie, Talking Heads, and the Cure—combining dance beats with off-the-wall lyrics. At their most inventive, TMBG's songs maintain a light tone while delivering insightful, sometimes poignant commentary, as in "Dead" from *Flood* (1990), in which the singer laments, "Now it's over, I'm dead and I haven't / done anything that I want / or, I'm still alive / and there's nothing I want to do."

By the time TMBG became a hit on college campuses nationwide—their first two records, *They Might Be Giants* (1986) and *Lincoln* (1989), were steady sellers—the reigning kings of the genre were R.E.M., whose five albums that decade made them mainstays on college radio play lists. With the release of *Flood*, TMBG's major-label debut, the duo became a commercial presence, rocketing to the top of the college/alternative charts and scoring a gold record within a few months. "We're serious about what we do," Linnell told Greg Kot for the *Chicago Tribune* (April 27, 1990). "We're not trying to make people laugh; we're trying to be the Beatles." After the grunge bands Nirvana, Pearl Jam, and Soundgarden began to infiltrate the airwaves and MTV in the early 1990s, TMBG retreated to their loyal cult following, touring regularly with new members Tony Maimone (bass) and Brian Doherty (drums) and releasing several records, most notably the LP *John Henry* (1994), the EP *S-E-X-X-Y* (1996), and the live recording *Severe Tire Damage* (1998). "We're constantly written off as a novelty act," Flansburgh told Michael Evans for the *Oregonian* (August 1998). "But I think this is our cross to bear. We write a lot of different kinds of songs. Some of the songs are very insignificant, which isn't necessarily that bad. There was a time when it really gnawed at my soul wanting people to understand what we were doing, but now I've just given up. But I think there are qualities to the band that are solid and musical. . . . I feel if you like the Beatles you would like They Might Be Giants." The group's 1999 release is *Long Tall Weekend*.

John Flansburgh (born May 6, 1960) and John Linnell (born June 12, 1959), who met when they were children in Lincoln, began writing songs together for fun while in high school. Although they didn't officially form a band during those days, Flansburgh and Linnell together produced a hefty catalog of short, catchy tunes. While remaining good friends, they parted ways upon graduating from high school. The college years found Linnell joining a band, a small Rhode Island New Wave group called the Mundanes. In 1981, when they were both out of college, Linnell and Flansburgh reunited and decided to move to New York City together to pursue a career in music. Avid film buffs, they settled on the name They Might Be Giants, which they took from a 1971 movie starring George C. Scott. Within a few months the group became a regular on the vibrant Manhattan alternative-music scene of the mid-1980s. With Flansburgh on guitar and Linnell playing several instruments,

among them accordion, bass clarinet, saxophone, and synthesizer, the duo shared vocal duties while using a drum machine and several tapes filled with sound effects as background support. Although they developed a cult following rather quickly, no record label was willing to give them a deal, since record executives felt that the band's eclectic, slightly nerdy image would not find a niche in the marketplace. So Linnell and Flansburgh decided to promote themselves, by setting up a telephone hotline that fans could call to hear TMBG's latest singles. The trick worked: after the line was flooded with calls, the independent label Bar/None gave TMBG a contract.

Linnell and Flansburgh released *They Might Be Giants* in 1986. The album became a cult hit, with the first single, "Don't Let's Start," gaining regular airplay on MTV, due largely to the inventive, hyperactive video conceived by the pair. A year later they released the EP *Don't Let's Start,* comprising the single and several previously unreleased tracks. With both records selling respectably for a group whose work was given little mainstream radio airplay and who had no major promotional deal, the band came out with *Lincoln* in 1989. That record became a bona fide hit on college campuses around the country. The university music circuit had been flourishing for several years by this point, with colleges around the nation developing their own radio formats based on music by underground bands popular among students. In this setting, *Lincoln*, featuring the singles "Ana Ng" and "(She Was a) Hotel Detective," reached number 89 on the *Billboard* album chart, causing large record studios to take notice.

In 1990 Flansburgh and Linnell decided to sign with Elektra Records, which released the album *Flood* later that year. Bolstered by such clever, odd singles as "Birdhouse in Your Soul" and "Istanbul (Not Constantinople)"—both of which had videos directed by Flansburgh—the record shot immediately to the top of the college/alternative charts and reached gold status within a few months. The album's 19 tracks also include "Particle Man," a quirky take on the workings of the universe; the more serious "Your Racist Friend"; and the 43-second "Minimum Wage," on which the words of the title are sung once, followed by what sounds like theme music from a movie Western. In the same year, in what was now typical TMBG promotional fashion, Elektra released several of *Flood*'s singles as EPs. Capitalizing on their former band's success, Bar/None put out a compilation of B-sides and previously unreleased TMBG tracks entitled *Misc. T* in early 1991.

The year 1992 saw the release of the group's fourth studio LP, *Apollo 18*, as well as two supporting EPs, *I Palindrome* and *The Guitar (The Lion Sleeps Tonight)*. While *Apollo 18* did not move as many copies as had *Flood*, it nonetheless sold steadily and helped to promote TMBG's upcoming nationwide tour. Up until this time the group had rarely toured, and when they had, only Flansburgh and Linnell had appeared on stage. Now, with the emergence of grunge music, spearheaded by such acts as Nirvana and Pearl Jam, whose back-to-basics rock-'n'-roll rebelled against 1980s synthesizer-based pop and rock, TMBG decided to hit the road with a full band, featuring bassist Tony Maimone (formerly of Pere Ubu) and drummer Brian Doherty. Since then TMBG has made several tours, which have drawn capacity audiences. By contrast, even after the success of *Flood* and *Apollo 18*, TMBG went largely ignored by MTV and the mainstream media for the next several years. Although *John Henry* (1994) sold respectably and the follow-up tour was highly successful, the record's receipts fell short of Elektra executives' expectations, and the label began to put pressure on the band to produce a radio-friendly pop song. TMBG, however, refused to change its ways and continued to release album-supporting EPs with never-before-heard tracks—*Why Does the Sun Shine* (1993) and *Back to Skull* (1994) being the two most notable from that period—and touring on a semi-regular basis.

Factory Showroom (1996) marked the band's return to the studio after two years; "Exquisite Dead Guy," which might be described as a macabre long song, "James K. Polk," a tongue-in-cheek ballad about the 11th U.S. president, and the 1970s-esque "S-E-X-X-Y" are three of its 14 tunes. A few months later Linnell, Flansburgh, and company released the EP *S-E-X-X-Y*. At about this time the group's two founding members also began to do side projects. Linnell, in his time away from TMBG, played saxophone on a few tracks of an eponymous 1997 compilation by the Honeymoon Killers. Flansburgh—in addition to numerous guest appearances on records by the likes of the John Spencer Blues Explosion and ex-Pixies frontman Frank Black—has released two recordings under the group name Mono Puff: *Unsupervised* (1996) and *It's Fun to Steal* (1998).

Another TMBG retrospective record, released by Restless records in 1997, featured many lost tracks from the band's early years, including never-released versions of "Don't Let's Start" and several original tracks left off either *They Might Be Giants* or *Lincoln*. *Severe Tire Damage* (1998), the band's first-ever officially sanctioned live recording, featured several reworkings of TMBG classics. Their most recent album, *Long Tall Weekend*, appeared in July 1999. "John and I have discussed on a number of occasions how drinking coffee was the big shift in our lives," Flansburgh told *Rollingstone.tunes.com* (on-line). "It created the energy . . . sad to say it, but I don't think either of us has written a song in this decade without being under the influences of coffee." — M.B.

Suggested Reading: *Chicago Tribune* E p5 Apr. 27, 1990, with photo; *New York* p52+ Feb. 6, 1989, with photo, p79+ Feb. 5, 1990; *New York Times* C p13 Oct. 29, 1994, with photo; *Rollingstone.tunes.com* (on-line); *tmbg.com* (on-line)

Selected Recordings: *They Might Be Giants*, 1986; *Don't Let's Start*, 1987; *(She Was a) Hotel Detective*, 1988; *They'll Need a Crane*, 1988; *Lincoln*, 1989; *Flood*, 1990; *Birdhouse in Your Soul*, 1990; *Istanbul (Not Constantinople*, 1990; *Misc. T*, 1991; *Apollo 18*, 1992; *I Palindrome*, 1992; *The Guitar (The Lion Sleeps Tonight)*, 1992; *John Henry*, 1994; *Why Does the Sun Shine?*, 1994; *Back to Skull*, 1994; *Factory Showroom*, 1996; *S-E-X-X-Y*, 1996; *Then: The Early Years*, 1997; *Severe Tire Damage*, 1998

James Montanus/Courtesy of Augusta Read Thomas

Thomas, Augusta Read

1964– Composer. Address: c/o A.R.T. Musings Publishing Co., 4 Strathallan Park, Rochester, NY 14607; c/o 21st Century Music Management, Inc., 459 Columbus Ave, Suite 610, New York, NY 10024

At a time when many have sought to infuse contemporary classical music with unorthodox influences like pop and rock-'n'-roll, Augusta Read Thomas has held fast to the traditions of the form as she cements her place as one of the most interesting and important American composers of her generation. "My life's goal is to work toward attempting to compose even just one excellent piece," she told Anne-Marie Seltzer for the *Radcliffe Quarterly* (March 1992). Many would contend that Thomas has already surpassed that goal, with more than 300 compositions to her credit, a number of which have been commissioned and performed by the world's leading musicians and orchestras. Thomas, a professor of music composition at the Eastman School of Music, in Rochester, New York, and the composer-in-residence with the Chicago Symphony Orchestra, has received numerous awards, prizes, and fellowships, in recognition of her prodigious output and soaring talent.

Born in 1964, in the town of Glen Cove, in Long Island, New York, Augusta Read Thomas was the youngest of the 10 children of a blended household headed by James and Susan Thomas. (Both parents brought children from previous marriages to their union.) Growing up in a household immersed in music, she studied piano and trumpet as a youth. Her playing soon led her to compose music for herself. "I took piano lessons when I was little and I remember I started to see patterns and rhythms and I just started composing. It was totally natural. Then I got very much into writing it down and then suddenly I was a composer. But I didn't ever sit there and say, 'What should I be?' It just sort of happened. Suddenly, there was this big stack of music I had written," she told Jo B. Hoffman for the *Women's Times* (September 1997).

Thomas took her interest in music to the St. Paul's School, an elite private high school in Concord, New Hampshire, and spent 1979–82 studying composition with Marilyn Ziffrin. While at St. Paul's Thomas wrote a composition for full band, a piano soloist, and two trumpet soloists. "I am a trumpet player, so I played one part and my trumpet teacher played the other part. In ninth grade this was performed, and that was a very moving and exciting event. Of course, the piece is terrible, now that I look back on it, but it was very encouraging for me at the time," she told Karin Pendle for *Contemporary Music Review* (vol. 16, 1997).

After graduating from St. Paul's, Thomas attended Northwestern University, in Chicago, Illinois, from 1983 to 1987, studying with Alan Stout and Bill Karlins and earning a bachelor's degree in music composition. She then attended Yale University, in New Haven, Connecticut, from 1987 to 1988. There, she worked with Jacob Druckman. Her development as a composer was aided by her being able to hear her compositions performed live at these institutions. She told Pendle, "I wrote an enormous amount of music—20 symphonies before I went to Yale, and eight concertos and eight string quartets—but none of that would have been as fruitful if I hadn't had the chance to hear it at a very young age. I'm the kind of composer who makes music for musicians, music to be performed. I'm someone who rolls up her sleeves and says, 'All right, I'm going to sit down and focus and create a piece that's honest and sincere and integral, with the intention of making people understand what I have to say and to collaborate with performers.' This sense of collaboration has always been important in my development."

Thomas's growth as a composer was fostered also by stints as a composition fellow at the Tanglewood Music Center in Lenox, Massachusetts, in 1987, 1988, and 1989. She also attended the Royal Academy of Music in London, England, from 1988

to 1989 and earned an advanced course diploma in music composition. After winning a Guggenheim Fellowship in 1989 (she was the youngest woman ever to win that fellowship for composing), she left Yale without earning an advanced degree and pursued composing full-time.

Success and recognition came quickly for Thomas. In 1989 she received much critical acclaim when her *Echos* premiered at the Tanglewood Music Center. A string of commissions from symphony orchestras soon followed. In 1990 Thomas's *Glass Moon* (1988), an 11-minute piece, was premiered by the Philadelphia Orchestra. Also that year another of her compositions for orchestra, the 20-minute *Wind Dance* (1989), had its debut performance, by the New York Philharmonic. Then, in 1993, Thomas's Sinfonica Concertante for Soprano Sax and Orchestra (1992) was performed for the first time, by the New Jersey Symphony Orchestra at Avery Fisher Hall in New York City, as part of a program to celebrate new American music.

From early on Thomas's musical inclinations have tended toward the traditional. John von Rhein, writing for the *Chicago Tribune* (January 4, 1998), described Thomas's work thusly: "Her musical roots extend back through the great symphonic tradition, from Stravinsky, Schoenberg and Debussy all the way to Beethoven and Bach." Thomas told von Rhein, "For me the most important thing about a work of art is that it be of extreme quality but also arise from the deepest soul of the artist. True masterpieces have a universality that invites you in but doesn't give you all the answers right away; there's an aura of mystery about them. All music of substance should convey a sense of significance, which is different from accessibility. If it has immediacy, accessibility can follow."

Meanwhile, Thomas won acclaim for her work with the renowned cellist and conductor Mstislav Rostropovich, who commissioned Thomas to compose *Air and Angels* (1992), a piece for orchestra that was performed in 1992 by the National Symphony Orchestra with Rostropovich conducting. In June 1994 *Ligeia* (1994), a 70-minute opera commissioned by the Recontre Musicale d'Evian, premiered under the baton of Rostropovich. The work, based on the life of Edgar Allan Poe and the eponymous story by Poe, and featuring the libretto of Leslie Dunton-Downer, won the International Orpheus Prize. Thomas then composed *Ancient Chimes* (1995), performed at its debut by the Moscow Conservatory Orchestra and by Rostropovich and the National Symphony Orchestra during their tour of Russia in 1995. Thomas's fruitful association with Rostropovich reached a high point in 1997, with *Chanson* (1996), which Thomas had written as a gift for Rostropovich to mark his 70th birthday. Daniel Webster described a performance of the 18-minute *Chanson* at Carnegie Hall, in New York City, for the *Philadelphia Inquirer* (April 14, 1997): "Thomas pairs the cello with solo viola in a melodic gesture, then leads the cello into shimmering orchestral areas with gradually growing sound and color. The musical narrative leads the cello gradually but steadily into its lower reaches, ending with the cello alone in a melody on its lowest string. Its message is introspective, with the cellist sounding as if he or she is exploring some inner thought to its lyrical end." (A highly acclaimed series of concerts that marked the cellist's 70th birthday also featured Rostropovich's performance of a work by Thomas's husband, Bernard Rands—Concerto no. 1, which Rostropovich had commissioned.)

Thomas maintained her feverish pace, composing music for soloists and other nonorchestral works. In 1991 she completed *Angel Chant*, a piece for a piano trio, and *Chant*, a piece for cello and piano. Describing a 1993 performance of the latter piece in Boston, Richard Buell, writing for the *Boston Globe* (March 9, 1993), praised Thomas as "a gifted young composer who will be heard from." The critical success of these works provided additional evidence of Thomas's versatility and talent; as a result, she was given the title of junior fellow in the Society of Fellows at Harvard University from 1991 to 1994. In 1993 she had a fellowship at the Bunting Institute at Radcliffe College. Then, in the following year, she joined the faculty of the Eastman School of Music, in Rochester, New York, as its first female professor of composition. She received tenure there in 1997.

In 1995 Thomas's *Manifesto* (1995) was introduced by the National Symphony Orchestra at the Kennedy Center in Washington, D.C. Also that year Thomas's theatrical oratorio, *Conquering the Fury of Oblivion* (1995), commissioned by the Eastman School of Music, was heard for the first time, in Rochester. The work, whose lyrics were written by Dunton-Downer, commemorated the 75th anniversary of the 19th Amendment to the Constitution, which gave women the right to vote, and the 175th anniversary of the birth of the suffragist Susan B. Anthony.

Thomas then composed *Words of the Sea* (1996), which was commissioned and first brought to the concert hall by the Chicago Symphony Orchestra. That collaboration eventually led Thomas to a three-year post as the Chicago Symphony Orchestra's composer-in-residence, beginning in June 1997. She has often cited the positive impact of that appointment on her career, telling von Rhein, "Other orchestras treat their composer-in-residence programs rather like window dressing; not the Chicago Symphony. In fact, I can't think of another orchestra that has such a dedicated, continuing commitment to its resident-composer program. I benefit enormously from that commitment and also from the multifaceted work Shulamit Ran and John Corigliano did here before me. The institution treats the position with respect, and that's as it should be." Her second composition for the Chicago Symphony Orchestra was *Orbital Beacons* (1998), which was featured during that orchestra's 1998 season.

In 1996 Thomas taught composition to high-school students at the Harley School, in Rochester, as part of the Commission Project, which is aimed at developing young composers. The following year she composed *Waltz in the Cave of Eros for Orchestra*. The piece was written for the Greater Twin Cities Youth Symphony Orchestra, in Minnesota. Three of Thomas's works had their maiden performances in 1998: *Brass Axis*, commissioned by the American Composers Orchestra and performed at Carnegie Hall by the Rascher Saxophone Quartet and the American Composers Orchestra; *Spirit Musings for Violin and Chamber Orchestra* (1997), played by the Boston Modern Orchestra Project as part of a series called "Women of Note," which featured works by female composers; and the ballet *Passions* (1998), written for the Saint Paul Chamber Orchestra and the James Sewell Dance Company and first performed in Minneapolis, Minnesota, in September.

Thomas has won many awards and honors for her compositions. She was the recipient of the Rockefeller Foundation Bellagio Residency in 1997 and the Charles Ives Fellowship from the American Academy and Institute of Arts and Letters in 1994. She has also won fellowships from the New York State Council for the Arts, in 1996; the National Endowment for the Arts, in 1988, 1992, and 1994; and the Tanglewood Music Center, in 1986, 1987, and 1989. In 1996 she received an honorary degree from the Royal Academy of Music and was elected an associate of the academy. In 1999 she won the Award of Merit from Northwestern University.

Thomas's husband, Bernard Rands, is a Pulitzer Prize–winning composer—he won in 1984 for *Canti del Sol*—who teaches at Harvard. The two first met in the late 1980s and were married in 1994, while Rands was a composer-in-residence with the Philadelphia Orchestra. When not teaching or engaged in musical pursuits, they live in a country house in Becket, Massachusetts. One of Thomas's upcoming works is a composition that will have its first hearing at the Berlin Staatsoper Mozart Festival, in Germany, in June 2000. In addition, she and Dunton-Downer are working on an opera entitled *Dreams in the Cave of Eros*. — Y.P.

Suggested Reading: *Contemporary Music Review* p37+ vol. 16, 1997; *Philadelphia Inquirer* C p1+ Apr. 1, 1997, with photo; *Radcliffe Quarterly* p15+ Mar. 1992, with photos; *Rochester Review* p33+ Spring–Summer 1995, with photos

Selected Works: *Glass Moon*, 1988; *Echos*, 1989; *Wind Dance*, 1989; *Angel Chant*, 1991; Sinfonica Concertante for Soprano Sax and Orchestra, 1992; *Air and Angels*, 1992; *Ligeia*, 1994; *Ancient Chimes*, 1995; *Manifesto*, 1995; *Conquering the Fury of Oblivion*, 1995; *Chanson*, 1996; *Words of the Sea*, 1996; *Waltz in the Cave of Eros for Orchestra*, 1997; *Spirit Musings for Violin and Chamber Orchestra*, 1997; *Passions*, 1998

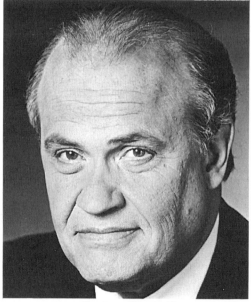

Courtesy of Senator Thompson's Office

Thompson, Fred

Aug. 19, 1942– U.S. Senator from Tennessee; former actor. Address: SD-523 Dirksen Bldg., Washington, DC 20510

On March 11, 1997 the United States Senate voted 99–0 to authorize an investigation into allegations that Democrats had engaged in illegal or improper activities in connection with the 1996 presidential election campaign. For Senator Fred Thompson, a Republican from Tennessee and the chairman of the Governmental Affairs Committee, such an inquiry was familiar territory. In 1973 he had served as the minority counsel on the Senate Select Committee on Presidential Campaign Activities, which, during its investigation of the Watergate scandal, had played a crucial role in uncovering the tape recordings that ultimately led to President Richard Nixon's resignation. Both probes helped to place Thompson in the public eye, and the latter enhanced his prominence within Republican circles. Since the mid-1980s Thompson has also been visible to the public through his numerous supporting roles in Hollywood films.

Fred Dalton Thompson was born on August 19, 1942 in Sheffield, Alabama, and grew up in Lawrenceburg, Tennessee. His father, Fletcher Thompson, became a state park inspector after working as a car salesman. Both Fletcher and his wife, Ruth, were exceptionally tall; Fred Thompson stands six feet six inches, and he played football and basketball for his high school.

On September 12, 1959, less than a month after he turned 17, Thompson married Sarah Elizabeth Lindsey, who was a year ahead of him in school. Their first child, Tony, was born in 1960. Thomp-

son spent the next several years struggling to make ends meet while completing his education and raising a family. Betsy, the couple's second child, was born while both her parents were attending what was then Florence State University, in Alabama. Thompson and his wife eventually transferred to Memphis State University (now the University of Memphis), in Tennessee, where Thompson earned a bachelor's degree in philosophy, in 1964. The couple's third child, Daniel, was born during Thompson's first year at Vanderbilt University Law School, in Nashville, Tennessee, where he earned his law degree, in 1967.

Thompson then returned to Lawrenceburg and went into law practice with his wife's uncle. Delving into politics for the first time, he co-founded the county's first Young Republicans club. Through his work with that group, he came to the attention of the state's GOP elite. Two years later the then–United States attorney general, John Mitchell, named him an assistant United States attorney in Nashville. In 1970 Thompson worked in Bill Brock's successful campaign to oust Albert Gore Sr. from his seat in the U.S. Senate. In 1972 another prominent Tennessee Republican, Lamar Alexander, recruited Thompson to run Senator Howard Baker's reelection campaign in a section of Tennessee. Thompson's connection with Baker led to his entry into Washington politics, by way of the Watergate scandal.

The scandal familiarly called Watergate was precipitated when, in 1971, Daniel Ellsberg, a disenchanted former government official, leaked to the *New York Times* an in-depth study of the U.S.'s role in the Vietnam War and the events that led up to it. The study, which became known as the Pentagon Papers, had been commissioned by Robert S. McNamara, the secretary of defense during the administration of President Lyndon B. Johnson, and its existence reportedly remained a carefully guarded secret until the day the *Times* began publishing excerpts from it. The embarrassing disclosures of government officials' deliberate distortions and the miscues that had mired the U.S. in the Vietnam quagmire fueled ongoing antiwar demonstrations. Infuriated by the protests and by the public disclosure of the government study, President Richard Nixon authorized illegal methods to discredit Ellsberg and others whose names he had placed on his so-called "enemies list." Among the many petty burglaries carried out by White House operatives was a break-in at the Democratic National Committee's headquarters at the Watergate office-apartment complex in Washington in June 1972. The five burglars and two others implicated in the crime were indicted the following September. In March 1973 John J. Sirica, the federal judge assigned to try the case, extracted fuller confessions from the burglars by threatening to impose stiff sentences. Some members of the White House staff were named as co-conspirators, and in the wake of those disclosures, the Senate created the Select Committee on Presidential Campaign Activities, to investigate the scandal. Headed by Senator Sam J. Ervin Jr. of North Carolina, it became known as the Ervin Committee.

Senator Baker, the ranking Republican on the committee, appointed the then–30-year-old Fred Thompson as the committee's minority counsel. Thanks to his key role in the high-profile Senate investigation, Thompson became a familiar figure on television, and he is widely remembered as the person who, while interrogating Nixon's former aide Alexander Butterfield, asked the famous question that produced the revelation that an extensive taping system had been installed in the White House: "Mr. Butterfield, are you aware of the installation of any listening devices in the Oval Office of the president?" The discovery of the so-called Watergate tapes and the ensuing struggle between Congress and President Nixon ultimately led to Nixon's resignation, in 1974. Relieved of his duties on the Senate committee, Thompson returned to his law practice.

Thompson's Watergate memoir, *At That Point In Time: The Inside Story of the Senate Watergate Committee*, was published in 1975. Described by various reviewers as "amiable," "chatty," "fast-moving," and "informally but well written," the book earned a bevy of complimentary assessments. "Perhaps the least enviable job on a Congressional investigatory committee is that of minority counsel, . . . [who is sometimes regarded] as a partisan obstructionist," Eric Redman wrote for the *New York Times Book Review* (February 22, 1976). "Thompson largely accepts the image in this memoir, . . . and he attempts—self-critically rather than self-servingly—merely to explain his dilemma. . . . [Thompson's] reduction of the Ervin Committee to human scale [is intriguing]." A critic for the *Virginia Quarterly Review* (Spring 1976) wrote, "Thompson reveals with wit and insight the character of the senatorial cast of the Watergate drama and, more importantly, the gradual erosion of his initial belief in Nixon's innocence. . . . The book is provocative but not sensational. . . . The result is one of the most compelling analyses yet written on the subject."

In 1977 Marie Ragghianti, who had been dismissed from her post as the chair of the Tennessee Parole Board, hired Thompson to represent her in a suit she had brought against the state for what she alleged was her illegal firing. During the trial it was revealed that Ray Blanton, Tennessee's Democratic governor, had fired Ragghianti because he believed she had been aiding an FBI probe into the selling of pardons and orders of clemency and other suspected state-government abuses. Ragghianti won the case, and in 1979 Blanton was ousted. (He later served a prison sentence for extortion.) The Ragghianti case became the subject of a best-selling book and later a film, *Marie* (1985), in which Thompson appeared as himself, alongside Sissy Spacek in the title role. In a review of the movie for *Newsweek* (October 7, 1985), David Ansen declared that Thompson's performance was superior to that of any of the others among the cast, and in *Time* (October 7, 1985), Richard Corliss wrote that in contrast to Marie, whose character the director and screenwriter had "seemingly nominated for sainthood," Thompson came across as "refreshingly human."

Thompson spent the next decade maintaining law practices in Nashville and Washington, D.C., in the latter of which he served as a lawyer-lobbyist. Meanwhile, his appearance in *Marie* had opened the door to a second career, as a character actor, and he won roles as gruff authority figures in many motion pictures, among them *Die Hard II* (1990), *The Hunt for Red October* (1990), *Days of Thunder* (1990), *Thunderheart* (1992), and *In the Line of Fire* (1993). As of mid-1999 he had appeared in 18 films. In April 1991 Thompson also joined a Washington law firm, Arent Fox Kintner Plotkin and Kahn, which lobbied on Capitol Hill for such high-profile clients as the Teamsters Union Pension Fund, Westinghouse, General Electric, and Toyota.

Thompson's next transformation, from lawyer-turned-actor to populist politician, came in the fall of 1994, when he ran for the seat in the U.S. Senate vacated by Harlan Matthews, a Tennessee Democrat who had retired after briefly filling the spot held by Al Gore before Gore became vice president. Campaigning as a populist, a Washington outsider, and a reformer, Thompson created a new image of himself by driving through Tennessee in a leased pickup truck and referring to himself in the third person, as "Ol' Fred." Rallying after a slow start, he captured 60 percent of the vote, thereby defeating his Democratic opponent, Jim Cooper, by a margin of 21 percent.

Thompson quickly emerged as a Republican star in the U.S. Senate. In December 1994 the Senate majority leader at that time, Bob Dole, selected him to come up with a response to President Clinton's television speech detailing a "Middle Class Bill of Rights." Drawing on his media savvy, Thompson addressed the American people reassuringly, saying, "Those of us who just came to town don't claim to have all the answers. I am still just unpacking my boxes. But one thing we do know, we know why you sent us here: to cut big government down to size, to turn Congress around, and to set our country in a new direction." Writing for *USA Today* (February 14, 1997), Jill Lawrence reported that on the day after Thompson's address, a photo of him appeared in the *Washington Post* with the caption, "Sen. Fred Thompson: His charismatic delivery of the GOP response was reminiscent of Ronald Reagan."

In his first year in the Senate, Thompson was elected freshman-class vice president and became a de facto Republican advocate for a range of government reform issues, foremost among them term limits. Thompson himself has pledged to serve no more than two six-year terms.

In 1996 Thompson was reelected, this time to a full term in the Senate, with 61 percent of the votes cast; his opponent, the Democrat Houston Gordon, earned just 37 percent. His victory was notable in that he won 54 percent of women's votes in Tennessee in a year in which a record number of women across the country chose to support Democrats, and also in that the Republican presidential candidate, Senator Bob Dole of Kansas, captured less than 41 percent of the votes cast and lost his bid for the nation's top elective office. Thompson's status as an emerging Republican leader was bolstered on January 7, 1997, when he was elected chairman of the Senate Committee on Governmental Affairs. It was the first time since World War II that anyone had become chairman of a major committee after having served in the Senate for only two years.

Thompson's position took on further importance in early 1997, after the Governmental Affairs Committee was assigned to investigate allegations of illegal fund-raising by the Democratic National Committee (DNC) and related improprieties connected with the 1996 election campaign. Led by Thompson, the committee looked into charges that contributors of large sums had been granted special access to the president and the White House, including overnight stays in the Lincoln Bedroom. Moreover, there were reports of political contributions from foreigners, in particular from John Huang, a fund-raiser for the DNC who was alleged to have ties to Chinese nationals. It was also alleged that through Huang and others, China had attempted to buy access to the president and members of Congress by means of campaign contributions. (U.S. law forbids foreign governments or foreign nationals to contribute to American political campaigns.) The combined charges had already prompted the DNC to return suspect donations amounting to $1.5 million. Thompson's job entailed uncovering the truth surrounding the accusations while attempting to dispel claims that his committee was merely out to discredit the Clinton administration.

From the outset, partisan conflict regarding the investigation's length, scope, and budget divided the committee. Democrats, maintaining that the inquiry amounted to little more than an attack on their party, dismissed as extravagant Thompson's request for $6.5 million to fund an official probe. Thompson predicted that the investigation would lead to campaign-finance reform, and he pressed to expand its reach to include exposing shady fundraising by members of Congress and finding ways to reform campaign financing, but he met with resistance from both parties. Some in Congress and the media noted Thompson's own questionable fund-raising practices, citing contributions he received from tobacco, pharmaceutical, and chemical interests. Others noted Thompson's relative inexperience in the Senate and faulted him for failing to establish a rapport with Senator John Glenn, who was then the ranking Democrat on the Governmental Affairs Committee, and other committee

Democrats. The extent of the senatorial schism became more evident after a campaign-finance reform bill backed by President Clinton came to the table. Thompson was one of only two Senate Republicans willing to embrace the measure, which had been sponsored by John McCain of Arizona, a Republican, and Russell D. Feingold of Wisconsin, a Democrat. In March 1997 the Senate approved the inquiry and the expenditure of $4.35 million to cover its costs.

Thompson opened the Governmental Affairs Committee's hearings, on July 8, 1997, with a statement accusing China of using campaign contributions in an attempt to influence the outcome of U.S. elections and thus further China's political interests. He said that based on U.S. intelligence reports, high-level Chinese government officials had hatched their plan after President Lee Teng-hui of Taiwan was granted a visa to visit the United States in May 1995, and that China had planned to spend $2 million on the scheme. Thompson added, as quoted in the *New York Times* (July 9, 1997), "The great majority of information about this matter can not be discussed further in open session." Democrats quickly dismissed Thompson's allegations as unfounded. Senator Glenn declared, as quoted in the *New York Times* (July 9, 1997), "I've read the same [intelligence reports], and [Thompson's] statement today goes beyond what I can say. I refuse to play around with intelligence information loosely." Others pointed out that $2 million was too paltry a sum to influence American elections.

During the opening week of the hearings, the Democratic National Committee declared, as quoted in the *New York Times* (July 13, 1997), that the Republican senators could have saved the $66,000 daily cost of the hearings and "gotten the same information seven months ago from a 60-cent [news]paper." Despite a long parade of witnesses (a few of whom invoked their Fifth Amendment right to withhold possibly self-incriminating testimony and many of whom stonewalled their questioners), and despite the introduction of many tapes and documents as evidence, the investigation ended on October 31, 1997, after 32 days of public hearings, without proof that the Chinese or anyone else had broken federal campaign-finance laws or that the political contributions of the Chinese had affected policies of the U.S. executive branch. The investigation, which had seemed initially to be a golden opportunity for Thompson to attract a lot of public notice, failed on that front as well; fewer than 10 percent of people polled said that they had followed the televised hearings "very closely."

In the current Congress Thompson is serving on the influential Senate Finance Committee, whose purview includes, among other issues, taxes, Social Security, Medicare, and welfare reform. The senator enjoys greater public recognition than most sitting senators, and some believe he may someday emerge as a presidential candidate.

Thompson, whose marriage ended in divorce in 1985, has three adult children and five grandchildren. As of October 1999, a list of his movie credits and his mother's recipes for coconut cake and coconut cream pie appeared on his government Web site. — Y.P.

Suggested Reading: *Congressional Quarterly* p776+ Apr. 5, 1997, with photos; *New York Times* A p26 Feb. 21, 1997, A p1+ July 9, 1997, with photos, A p1+ July 10, 1997, A p1+ July 11, 1997, with photo, A p14 July 13, 1997, A p16 July 15, 1997, with photos; *Wall Street Journal* A p16 Feb. 21, 1997; *Washington Post* C p1 Oct. 21, 1994, with photo, A p34 Dec. 16, 1994, A p8 Mar. 16, 1997, with photo

Selected Books: *At That Point in Time*, 1975

Selected Films: *Marie*, 1985; *Die Hard II*, 1990; *The Hunt for Red October*, 1990; *Days of Thunder*, 1990; *Thunderheart*, 1992; *In the Line of Fire*, 1993

Paul Sakuma/AP/Wide World Photos

Torvalds, Linus

1969– Computer programmer; creator of the Linux operating system. Address: c/o Transmeta, 3940 Freedom Circle, Santa Clara, CA 95054

As a 21-year-old student at the University of Helsinki, the Finnish programmer Linus Torvalds grew fed up with Microsoft operating systems, but he could not afford to buy the more powerful Unix operating system. (Operating systems such as Unix

and Microsoft Windows are the fundamental programs that tell computers what to do.) In an act of programming braggadocio, he wrote his own operating system, now known as Linux. (The name rhymes with "clinics.") Since then Linux has been maintained and updated by Torvalds and a loose-knit group of hackers who communicate over the Internet, work solely out of their love of programming, and distribute their results for free. One would not normally think that a product developed as little more than a hobby could seriously challenge another developed by armies of well-paid software programmers. Yet many people believe that Linux—which currently has about seven million users and is steadily gaining more adherents—may be the David that topples Microsoft's Goliath-like dominance of the operating-systems market. It may also herald a new era of software development that turns capitalist orthodoxy on its head. Journalists have dubbed this new model of development the "open-source movement."

Unlike those of Microsoft operating systems, the code of the Linux operating system is not kept secret. Anyone—from a teenage computer enthusiast to the most knowledgeable computer programmer—can go into Linux, tinker with its code, and suggest a change to Torvalds, who, for the past eight years, has functioned as the nerve center of this sprawling Linux community: he reads over and vets the various suggestions for improvement. Already, hackers have contributed thousands of ideas that have made the Linux better. In fact, the number of lines of code that Torvalds himself has written is now minuscule. As he explained to Amy Harmon for the *New York Times Magazine* (February 21, 1999), "The kernel [the most vital code of the operating system] is 1 percent of the entire program. Of that 1 percent, I've written between 5 and 10 percent. I think the most important part is that I got it started."

With the collective IQ of computer hackers from around the world continually nourishing Linux, many managers maintain that Linux is technically superior to Microsoft operating systems, which are notorious for their frequent crashes. Users of Microsoft's Windows NT, for example, have grown to fear the nasty surprise referred to as the "blue screen of death." By contrast, computers using Linux have been known to operate for months without requiring a single reboot. The reliability and efficiency of Linux—not to mention the fact that it can be downloaded for free from the Internet—have won it numerous converts. Linux-driven computers have done everything from generating the special effects in the movie *Titanic* to simulating atomic shock waves at the U.S. Department of Energy's Los Alamos National Laboratory, in New Mexico.

The advocacy of some Linux users resembles the fierceness of a religious crusade. To many of those adherents, Microsoft is an evil empire and Linux their savior. Torvalds doesn't share that view. "I don't mind Microsoft making money," he told

Amy Harmon. "I mind them having a bad operating system." The system is not all bad, of course. Its ease of use for computer neophytes is one of its great advantages. Another is the wide variety of applications, ranging from word processing to spreadsheet arrangements to publishing, that exist for it. But in some ways, Microsoft's advantages can become disadvantages. Revising a bug in the operating system can potentially make unusable the hundreds of programs designed for Microsoft systems. With Linux, Torvalds has argued, the process of revising the program is much simpler and more meritocratic: the best code wins.

With few graphical interfaces or program applications available for it, Linux so far remains an operating system for the technically proficient. Instead of pointing and clicking, one has to know arcane Unix-like command strings to operate Linux. Linux may never move far beyond this niche. However, many software companies have agreed to create products compatible with Linux. Moreover, graphical interfaces are in development, and their creation could ultimately spell the end of Microsoft's hegemony. "I joke a lot about Linux taking over the world and how Microsoft should be afraid," Torvalds told *Technology Review* (January/February 1999). "But with something that makes it easy for the home user—maybe it just might happen." This very real possibility has spawned worried memos within Microsoft and has transformed Torvalds into one of the most popular figures in the computing world. Indeed, Internet search engines often return more hits on Torvalds than on such film stars as Tom Cruise.

This unlikely information-age folk hero was born in Finland into a family of journalists in 1969, the very year that Unix was being developed by Dennis Ritchie and Kenneth Thompson at Bell Labs. His parents named him for both the chemist Linus Pauling and the cartoonist Charles Schultz's *Peanuts* character Linus. Torvalds got interested in programming when he was 10, after his grandfather bought a Commodore VIC-20. Young Linus used the computer to program his own games.

Torvalds attended the University of Helsinki, where he studied computer science. From what he learned, he concluded that, from a technical standpoint, Microsoft's operating systems were not the best. Unix was better, but it was designed with computer workstations, not personal computers, in mind; in any event, at the time it cost several thousand dollars, far more money than Torvalds had. Buoyed by his youthful sense that he "was the best programmer in the world," as he told a reporter for the on-line magazine *boot*, he decided to write his own operating system for his personal computer. "And a lot of people have told me that you need to be good," he added, "but you also need to be bad enough because if you knew beforehand how much work it would have been to do, nobody sane would have even started it."

After completing a bare-bones version of Linux, Torvalds thought that he would be the only person who would actually use it. But after he put it on an FTP (file transfer protocol) site to make it available to others over the Internet, several other people expressed interest in it. "What happened almost immediately was that people started commenting on the missing features that I didn't need personally," he told *Computerworld* (August 17, 1998, on-line). The Linux community began to grow, with more and more people offering their advice and help.

Originally, Torvalds placed a very restrictive license on the program; for example, because he didn't want people selling the program to others, he made it impossible to transfer the operating system to a disk. In 1992 he changed his philosophy and registered it under a General Public License (GPL) with the Free Software Foundation (FSF). Under the GPL's copyright (or, "copyleft," as the FSF calls it), anyone could charge as much as they wanted to market the Linux system without paying Torvalds a commission. But there was a catch: they would have to make any changes in the source code available to the public. Torvalds also made sure that he himself couldn't profit from Linux by taking possession of the copyright in the future. "So even if I turn to the dark side [by trying to benefit financially from Linux], nobody can take it over," he explained to Amy Harmon.

Allowing the code to be freely distributed contradicted the development model on which William Gates, the co-founder and head of Microsoft, had made his fortune. In "Open Letter to Hobbyists," a now-famous memo that he wrote in 1976, Gates contended that sharing software, which in early computer culture was common, was inhibiting product development. "One thing you do . . . is prevent good software from being written," Gates asserted in his letter. "Who can afford to do professional work for nothing?" There were alternative philosophies to draw upon as well. Richard Stallman, who founded the FSF, in 1984, was an early advocate of the open-source movement. In fact, he had developed a free operating system, called GNU, and later contributed many lines of code to Linux. The open-source model had already worked successfully: software developed on that model included several key pieces of the Internet, among them BIND (which translates machine numbers into Web-site URL names) and Sendmail (which routes about 80 percent of E-mail).

Torvalds has called his decision to get a GPL copyright and go with open source his single best decision in the development of Linux. "There are lots of advantages in a free system, the obvious one being that it allows more developers to work on it, and extend it," he told the on-line journal *First Monday*. "However, even more important than that is the fact that it in one fell swoop also gave me a lot of people who *used* it and thus both tested it for bugs and tested it for usability. The 'usability' part comes from the fact that a single person (or even a group of persons sharing some technical goal) doesn't even think of all the uses a large user community would have for a general-purpose system."

Dealing with suggestions for improvements has consumed a huge amount of Torvalds's time. "On average I almost have to read E-mail for two hours a day just to keep up," he told *Computerworld*. "On top of those two hours for just reading E-mail, [I spend an additional] two or three hours to actually do something about it." His university helped make it possible for him to devote all that time to Linux. While working toward his bachelor's and master's degrees, he worked as a teaching and a research assistant, and some of his work time was allotted to Linux development. He wrote his master's thesis on "porting" Linux, which made its use on different types of machines possible.

In explaining why he has been willing to work on Linux free of charge, Torvalds has said that, more than money, bragging rights and the sheer fun of programming motivate programmers like himself. "If you're good, it's easy to get paid," Torvalds explained to *Forbes* (August 10, 1998). "Good programmers are rare enough that people pay them well. A big part of personal satisfaction is having your work recognized by your peers. That's fundamental in any psyche." Creating Linux has led to other benefits. As the person most closely associated with Linux, Torvalds received many job offers. In 1997 he accepted one from Transmeta, a secretive Silicon Valley start-up that is partially funded by Paul Allen, who co-founded Microsoft with Gates. Transmeta is not involved with Linux development in any way. Torvalds has said that he purposely chose a job not related to Linux so that his decisions about Linux would be made from a technical perspective rather than a marketing outlook. (Torvalds blames the Microsoft system's technical problems on the company's emphasis on sales.)

The continuing growth of Linux can be measured in several ways. Some companies, among them Red Hat, Caldera, Slackware, and SuSE, market a CD version of the operating system bundled with some basic applications. Oracle, Informix, Computer Associates, Corel Computer, IBM, and other major players have announced that they will develop software compatible with Linux. Linux's success can also be gauged by the increasing momentum of the open-source movement. In a stunning move in late 1998, Netscape released the source code for its browser. Perhaps even more startling, in April 1999 Microsoft's president, Steve Ballmer, revealed that his company was "thinking with great interest" about the open-source strategy. This seemed to indicate that the company is very worried about Linux. (Some journalists have speculated that Microsoft may be exaggerating the threat Linus presents. In the U.S. Justice Department's ongoing antitrust case against Microsoft, Microsoft can point to Linux to disprove the notion that Microsoft has a monopoly.)

Fluent in Swedish (his native language), Finnish, and English, Torvalds currently lives in Santa Clara, California. He and his wife, Tove, who is a six-time karate champion of Finland, have two daughters, Patricia and Daniela, who in February 1999 were two years old and 10 months old, respectively. In *Yahoo!News* (December 8, 1998, online), Charles Babcock reported that Tove Torvalds and the two little girls attended a forum at Stanford University in which Torvalds joined a panel discussion about the open source in business. "Halfway through the proceedings, the youngest Torvalds let out a cry . . . ," Babcock wrote, "and Linus casually exited the panel to help rearrange his family in a more distant corner of the hall. No one considered this unusual, because the Torvalds treated it as part of everyday life." Babcock described Torvalds as "about five feet 10 inches tall with a square, solid build and an open face." "There is a decided normalcy to his demeanor," he noted. "He displays no aggressive instincts." Torvalds is fond of penguins, and he chose the image of a penguin as the logo for Linux. — W.G.

Suggested Reading: *Computerworld* (on-line) Aug. 17, 1998; *Forbes* Aug. 10, 1998; *New York Times* G p1+ Oct. 8, 1998; *New York Times Magazine* p34+ Feb. 21, 1999, with photo; *Technology Review* p36+ Jan./Feb. 1999, with photos; *Time Digital* (on-line) Apr. 12, 1999, with photo; *Washington Post* F p15 May 22, 1995, with photo

---

Turabi, Hassan al-

1932– Sudanese religious and political leader; jurist. Address: Manshiyah, Khartoum, Sudan

In the decade since the death of the Iranian Shi'ite Muslim leader Ayatollah Ruholla Khomeini, in 1989, a Sudanese religious and political leader, Hassan al-Turabi, has emerged as the major figure in the resurgence of Muslim fundamentalism. An ideologue, cleric, and one-time attorney general and law-school dean, the Sorbonne-educated Turabi organized the National Islamic Front (NIF), which played a key role in bringing General Omar Hassan el-Bashir to power in a coup in 1989. Afterward, the NIF assumed behind-the-scenes control of the Sudanese government. As the leader of the NIF, Turabi is the most powerful politician in Sudan, and—General Bashir's dual titles of prime minister and president notwithstanding—he is also widely acknowledged to be the nation's de facto ruler.

With 966,757 square miles, Sudan is the largest country in Africa. Strategically, it straddles black Africa and the Arab Middle East. Its northern border is Egypt's southern border, and it abuts seven other countries as well. The 70 percent of the population that is Arab-Islamic lives in the northern two-thirds of Sudan; in the south, the people are mostly black and, overwhelmingly, either Chris-

Aladin Naby/Archive Photos

Hassan al-Turabi

tian or believers in animist religions. Home to some 570 tribes, Sudan is among the poorest and most troubled nations on earth. Its difficulties stem in part from the civil war that has raged between the north and the south since the 1950s; the massive influx of refugees driven into Sudan to escape fighting in neighboring countries; a similarly large influx of refugees from southern Sudan (which has borne the brunt of the civil war) into Khartoum; and a prolonged drought. By 1994, according to various estimates, war and famine had claimed the lives of some 1.3 million people. Since then, many more Sudanese have succumbed, and at present, huge numbers of Sudanese are in danger of starving to death.

In the opinion of some longtime aid workers in Sudan and other observers, the civil war in Sudan would be more accurately described as a religious war between rebels in the Christian and animist south and the Muslim-controlled government, the capital of which is in Khartoum, in the north. The decades-long discord worsened after the 1989 coup, because the new government has transformed Sudan into a radical Islamic state—the Arab world's first such entity. "The bottom line here is that the government wants the land [in the south] without the people," Dan Eiffe, who has worked for Norwegian Peoples Aid in Sudan for nearly a dozen years, told a reporter for *Christian Century* (October 21, 1998). Moreover, the government has actively promoted the expansion of Islamic revolution to other Arab countries and the rest of Africa. By offering a safe haven to terrorists and supporting terrorist activities, the Sudanese government has compounded its troubles, since those policies have provoked the enmity of its

neighbors and of the United States and other Western countries.

On several counts, Hassan al-Turabi is a more formidable champion of the militant Muslim cause than Khomeini. Whereas Khomeini was a fanatical and xenophobic imam in Islam's minority Shi'ite sect and spoke chiefly to his Persian—non-Arab—constituency, the charismatic and urbane Turabi is a cosmopolitan Sunni cleric who not only has the ear of the entire Arab world but is also more beguiling to non-Muslims. Although the present regime in Sudan is widely accused of brutal oppression at home and complicity with Iran in sponsoring terrorism abroad, Turabi personally projects a benign public image, eschewing, for example, such inflammatory rhetoric, common among his peers, as the use of the word *jihad* ("holy struggle") to signify armed resistance to Israel and the United States and other Western purveyors of what they view as infidel cultural contamination. His people, Turabi has said, are taught that "agriculture is their *jihad*," and that "religion is a motor of development." In addition to the National Islamic Front and the presidency of the National Assembly (a post akin to Speaker of the House in the United States), Turabi exercises "guidance" through the Popular Arab and Islamic Conference, of which he is secretary general.

Hassan Abdallah al-Turabi was born to a Sunni religious leader in an eastern province of Sudan sometime between 1930 and 1933, when Sudan was ruled jointly by Egypt and Great Britain. As a student, while most of his peers were attracted to secular and often Western-influenced solutions to Sudan's political problems, he joined a then-marginal organization called the Muslim Brotherhood, which had been founded in Egypt in the 1920s with the goal of replacing colonial governments with Muslim regimes. (In the 1970s Ayatollah Ruholla Khomeini in Iran would take Islamic revolutionary doctrine a step further, becoming himself an exemplar for theocratic rule by clerics themselves, and Mohammed Hussein Fadlallah's Party of God would seize Western hostages in Beirut, Lebanon, initiating the implementation of a new theology of violence against Western influences.

After attending the Hantoul Boarding School for Boys in Khartoum, Turabi earned a bachelor of laws degree from the University of Khartoum, in 1958; a master of laws degree from the University of London, in 1961; and a doctorate in public law from the University of Paris, in 1964. "When I was a student in France, every North African student was a Marxist or an extreme socialist," Turabi recalled to Raymond Bonner for the *New Yorker* (July 13, 1992). "And before that, when I was in Britain, every student was an Arab nationalist. Now it's very different—every student is an Islamist."

For some years, Turabi was the dean of the faculty of law at the University of Khartoum. In 1965 he was elected to the Sudanese Parliament, where he was one of seven representatives of the Muslim

Brotherhood. Following a military coup headed by Gaafar Mohammed Nimeiri in 1969, he spent six years in jail or under house arrest before fleeing into a three-year exile in Libya and elsewhere. After reconciling with Nimeiri, he returned home to become attorney general in Nimeiri's Cabinet. In 1983, under Turabi's watch as attorney general, Nimeiri introduced into Sudan a penal code based on strict Islamic law—shari'a. Acting under the new code, courts dispensed thousands of floggings, amputations of limbs, and executions, and those punishments were carried out in public. Later, in an apparent attempt to disassociate himself from that regime, Turabi explained that Nimeiri "liked drama."

In April 1985 Nimeiri was deposed in a bloodless military coup headed by Abdul Rahman Suwar el-Dahab, who appointed a military council to govern pending a return to civilian rule. That December, the country officially became the Republic of Sudan, and the formation of political parties was encouraged. One that emerged was the National Islamic Front (NIF), which Turabi founded early in 1986. When he stood for Parliament in the general elections held in April 1986, the two major parties, the Umma Party and the Democratic Unionist Party, joined forces and defeated him by running one candidate between them in his district. Sadiq al-Mahdi, the leader of the Democratic Unionist Party (and, incidentally, Turabi's brother-in-law), became prime minister in the coalition government formed after the election. In a major reshuffling of his Cabinet in February 1989, Mahdi brought Turabi in as deputy prime minister. During the following weeks Mahdi alienated the NIF by negotiating a peace agreement with the Sudan People's Liberation Movement. The accord included a suspension of Islamic laws pending the drafting of a new, secular constitution at a convention scheduled to begin in September 1989.

On June 30, 1989 a group of radicalized Muslim army officers headed by Omar Hassan el-Bashir overthrew Mahdi's government and installed a junta called the Revolutionary Command Council. Soon after, Turabi was imprisoned for almost five months. His imprisonment naturally puzzled observers who believed that the NIF was behind the coup, and some of them speculated that keeping him behind bars was a ruse to hide the NIF's involvement. Others thought that resorting to such a ploy was unlikely. "Even for a man as dedicated as Turabi," Raymond Bonner wrote, "voluntary imprisonment was an extreme measure, and the most likely explanation for his imprisonment is that there was a split within the NIF over whether there should be a coup. Turabi, this analysis has it, opposed a coup, and so the more radical elements had him arrested. Whatever the explanation . . . , and whatever his views on democracy, once he was released [in December 1989] he quickly reasserted himself as the leader of the NIF."

While banning all traditional political parties, Bashir and the junta turned to Turabi for guidance. The technocrats in the National Islamic Front infiltrated the civil bureaucracy, educational and other institutions, and even the military, and they became a shadow government. In 1991 Sudan was declared an Islamic state, and an even more vigorous code of Islamic law was adopted. Afterward, according to the human-rights watchdog organization Amnesty International, such punishments as amputations, floggings (including those of women for "indecent" dress), and death by stoning (for adultery) and crucifixion became regular events in Sudan; some death sentences were imposed for apostasy from Islam. An Amnesty International report issued early in April 1992 charged that "prisoners have been shackled and suspended from their cell walls, sometimes upside down. Others have had their testicles crushed with pliers." Africa Watch also accused the Sudanese regime of torture.

In April 1992 Turabi embarked on an international speaking tour. In London, his first stop, each of his public appearances was marked by demonstrations by Sudanese political exiles holding banners with such slogans as "Turabi—the Butcher of Khartoum" and "Fundamentalism Equals Fascism." In an interview with Kathy Evans for the Guardian (April 29, 1992), Turabi said that the Arab-Israeli peace talks only helped spur the process of Islamization. "The failure of the peace talks—and they will fail—will expose the bankruptcy of the nationalists and the liberals," he said. "If America tries to stand in our way, it will only increase the momentum."

Angry protesters greeted Turabi in Washington, D.C., too, when he arrived there in early May. During his visit he justified the suppression of traditional political parties in Sudan by arguing that those parties were essentially ethnic and tribal groupings and that therefore "elections are no longer representative." Asked about the reign of terror and the stifling of dissent during the Iranian revolution, he conceded, "There were a few excesses. But the Iranian revolution compares reasonably well to the French and Russian examples." After addressing numerous gatherings of business people, scholars, journalists, and officials—including a House of Representatives foreign affairs subcommittee—in Washington, he moved on to Canada, where he was attacked at the Ottawa airport by a Sudanese political exile trained in the martial arts. Seriously injured by several karate blows to his head, he was hospitalized for three weeks before returning home.

In an interview for New Perspectives Quarterly (Summer 1992), Turabi was asked what he thought of the perception of many in the West that, with the fervor of the Iranian revolution fading, he was the "new Khomeini," the "new bearer of the flame of Islamic fundamentalism." He responded, "I merely represent a new, mature wave of the Islamic awakening taking place today from Algeria to Jordan to

Khartoum and Kuala Lumpur. At first evidenced in the Iranian revolution, this awakening is . . . a comprehensive reconstruction of society from top to bottom. This widespread Islamic revival has been given impetus by the vacuum left by a bankrupt nationalism, especially Arab nationalism, and African socialism. The post-colonial nationalist regimes had no agenda other than to throw out the imperialists. Once they achieved their goal, they had nothing to offer the people. Then they turned to socialism as an alternative to the imperial West. Now, like everyone else, the Islamic world is disillusioned with socialism."

Turabi went on to explain that the expansion of Islamic consciousness came relatively late to North Africa and even later to sub-Saharan Africa. "The Gulf War [of 1991], which brought foreigners into the vicinity of our sacred religious centers in Saudi Arabia, gave an enormous boost to the movement in North Africa, not only among the general population but also among the elites. The new and critical aspect of the recent Islamic awakening is that the elites in the army and government—the so-called modern sector—are themselves becoming Islamized. This has already happened in the Sudan and is in the process of happening in Algeria. In 1985 the Sudanese army led by defense minister General Abdul Rahman Suwar el-Dahab intervened to stop Islamization. But his efforts led to an uprising by junior officers who supported Islamization. I have no doubt the same thing will happen in Algeria. The Islamization of the modern sector is the prevalent trend throughout the region."

In his 1992 interview with New Perspectives Quarterly, Turabi tried to clarify four areas of Sudanese Islamic rule that tend to be misunderstood in the West. "First, women. It is true that a very powerful tradition developed in some Islamic countries that segregated women from men and deprived them of their rights. With the new revival of Islam, women are gaining their rights, because no one can challenge the Koran in the name of local custom or convention. . . . On the rights of minorities, under shari'a, there is a guarantee for non-Muslims of freedom of religion and cult. . . . On the penal code, . . . many in the West think that, under the rule of shari'a, every act of theft will result in such punishments as the severing of hands or even execution. That is not true. Over the past year and a half there have been only two such sentences because, under properly administered Islamic law, the degree of proof required is very high. And there are other considerations. . . . The whole idea is to associate severe punishment with major theft as a deterrent in order to morally educate the people. Petty theft is punished no more severely than in most of the world. . . . Homicide law is even more flexible under shari'a than the English law. . . . [Finally,] today in the Sudan such intellectual apostasy as [the writer Salman] Rushdie's is not punishable by death. It must involve active subversion of the constitutional order." Even so, Turabi conceded that "the case of

Sudan today," with its banning of opposition parties and detention of political enemies, is not "the ultimate model of where the Islamic awakening should end up." "The Sudan is an Islamic state-in-process and is going through many emergencies as a result of the war in the south. Security is at risk. Masses of people are streaming toward the urban centers searching for food and relief. Under such circumstances, one can't maintain the ordinary due process of law. . . . Such abnormality in time of war is, so to speak, normal. . . . But we look forward to a state where such exceptional procedures would end."

Early in 1993 President Hosni Mubarak of Egypt accused Sudan of hosting at least 17 terrorist training camps staffed by revolutionary guards from Iran. "They are farms that take outsiders, not only from Egypt but also from Saudi Arabia and North Africa," Mubarak said, as quoted by Guy Roux in the International Review. "They pose as workers, and under that cover they are taught about explosives and firearms." In August 1993 the U.S. Department of State added Sudan to its list of nations sponsoring terrorism, citing Sudan's alleged ties to the radical Muslim group Hezbollah, the Palestinian groups Islamic Jihad and Hamas, and Abu Nidal's organization. In addition, six Sudanese were charged with involvement in the 1993 bombing of the World Trade Center, in New York City.

In the New Republic (February 7, 1994), Joshua Hammer wrote about his trip to Sudan to investigate reports that the NIF was covertly sponsoring international terrorism. "I became even more intrigued by the transformation of the once-democratic Sudanese society wrought by the NIF," Hammer wrote. "[The transformation] has not only destroyed the economy and forfeited Western development aid, but has instilled fear and loathing in much of the population." Writing in the Atlantic (August 1994), William Langewiesche distinguished between the public courts and "the not-so-public plane, which consists of the military, the secret-police forces, and other groups acting with or without the knowledge of Turabi or the military leaders." Langewiesche observed that "the state-directed terror is not acknowledged by many of the Islamist intellectuals," and that "there hangs about Turabi himself an atmosphere of reflexive denial."

In December 1994 Petros Salomon, the foreign minister of Eritrea, which borders Sudan to the east, told reporters that his country had decided to sever diplomatic relations with Khartoum, because Sudan "is trying to destabilize the region." He added, "Hassan Turabi is the mastermind of this strategy." "Turabi is helping not only the Jihad in Eritrea," he asserted, "but also the Ittihad in Somalia and other organizations active among the Oromos tribesmen in Ethiopia." In an interview for the newspaper L'Humanité in 1995, the Sudanese opposition leader and feminist Fatimah Ahmad Ibrahim charged that Turabi was sending money and personnel to the militant fundamentalists in strife-torn Algeria.

In 1995, following the deaths of five political dissidents being detained in secret camps in Sudan, Sudanese opposition groups raised the volume of their appeal to the United Nations and the international community to bring pressure to bear on the Khartoum government for the release of all political prisoners in Sudan. Among those being held at undisclosed locations was al-Sadiq al-Mahdi, the former prime minister and still the leader of the opposition Umma Party, who had been arrested on May 18, 1995, following a sermon in a mosque in which he voiced his wish for "a bloodless transformation" to deliver Sudan from political oppression. (A year and a half later, he succeeded in escaping to Eritrea.) Also in 1995, President Mubarak expressed his suspicion that the NIF had conspired in the failed attempt on his life that took place in Ethiopia on June 26 of that year.

In March 1996 elections were held in Sudan for a new, 400-member National Assembly. Since the ban on political parties was still in effect, each candidate ran as an independent. In an interview with Tim Weiner for the *New York Times* (December 24, 1996), Turabi described Sudan as "a rich country. One of the richest countries on earth." But according to Weiner, "The harsh truth is that the Sudan is broke, its currency all but worthless, its treasury drained by an endless civil war between the Sudan's north and south, its government under intense pressure from the United States to change its ways." The U.S. increased that pressure in November 1997, when it imposed economic sanctions against Sudan. In addition to banning imports of Sudanese products, the U.S. government seized Sudanese assets held in the U.S.

On August 20, 1998, on orders from the administration of U.S. president Bill Clinton, American cruise missiles destroyed the Shifa Pharmaceutical Plant in Sudan. While the Sudanese government insisted that Shifa had made nothing but medications, the Clinton administration maintained that the manufacture of medicines was a cover to hide the plant's real purpose—the production of chemical-warfare material. It also charged that the funding for the plant had come from Osama bin Laden, a Saudi Arabian terrorist whom the U.S. believes was responsible for the 1995 and 1996 attacks on two American military facilities in Saudi Arabia that killed a total of 24 Americans, and who was also believed to be involved in the bombings of the American embassies in Kenya and Uganda on August 7, 1998. With the blessing of the Sudanese government, bin Laden had lived in Khartoum for two years, from 1994 until 1996, and according to U.S. intelligence reports, he had helped to train Islamic militants in camps in Sudan. Turabi dismissed those reports. "Bin Laden was not even issuing leaflets from here," he declared to Jane Perlez for the *New York Times* (August 24, 1998). "He was trying to behave."

Slight and soft-spoken, "the calculatingly charming Mr. Turabi talks nonstop, his silvery tongue and twitching fingers shaping oddly illogical arabesques," Tim Weiner wrote. "He's dangerous because he's so smooth," a Sudanese intellectual opposed to Turabi told Raymond Bonner. "Hassan Turabi will meet you as an American and convince you that he is no different from George Washington." Normally, when in Sudan, Turabi wears a thick white turban and a long, loose-fitting, white *djellabah*, but he is equally at home in a pinstriped suit when traveling in the West. He lives under heavy security in a sprawling house in the relatively well-to-do neighborhood of Manshiyah on the outskirts of Khartoum. According to Joshua Hammer, Turabi "speaks perfect idiomatic English punctuated by weirdly disarming little giggles." In addition to Arabic and English, Turabi speaks fluent French and Persian. — K.D.

Suggested Reading: *Atlantic* p26+ Aug. 1994; *Chicago Tribune* V p1+ Oct. 29, 1993, with photo; *Economist* p43 Feb. 1, 1992, with photo, p41 Apr. 18, 1992, p54 Apr. 19, 1995, with photo; (London) *Guardian* p11 Apr. 29, 1992, with photo; *New Perspectives Quarterly* p52+ Summer 1992, p42+ Summer 1993; *New Republic* p14 Feb. 7, 1994; *New York Times* A p3 Jan. 29, 1992, with photo, IV p3 May 17, 1992; *New Yorker* p70+ July 13, 1992

Turrell, James

May 6, 1943– Artist. Address: c/o Skystone Foundation, 9000 Hutton Ranch Rd., Flagstaff, AZ 86004

"My work is not about *my* seeing," the environmental artist James Turrell told James Lewis for *Connoisseur* (February 1991). "It's about *your* seeing." Turrell's media are light, space, and the world around us. Since launching his career, in the 1960s, he has specialized in manipulating projected light to create the perception of three dimensions and in using natural and artificial light to provide fresh views of urban environments. Turrell received a MacArthur Foundation "genius" grant in 1984, and his works have been exhibited in the Guggenheim Museum, the Whitney Museum of American Art, and the Museum of Modern Art, among other places in New York City, and in many other prestigious venues in the United States and Europe. According to Lewis, "Seeing a Turrell is like mainlining light, as close to pure perceptual experience as acculturated humans can get."

For the past two decades, Turrell has also devoted much of his time to a massive effort called the Roden Crater project, in which he is using earthmoving equipment to dig tunnels in and otherwise alter an extinct volcano in northern Arizona. His

Courtesy of the Mattress Factory, Pittsburgh

James Turrell

aim is to create what in effect will be a natural-light and star show that will extend in all directions as far as the eye can see. "I wanted to work with geological time as a stage set," Turrell explained to James Lewis. "And then to make spaces in that stage set that engage celestial time. So the work is powered by nature, by light from the sun, moon, and stars." According to Lewis, "As one listens to him describe his plans and the thought behind them, the crater project comes to seem less a monument to his own will than an attempt to inspire and enlighten the men and women who will come to visit it." Turrell, who originally planned to finish the project in the mid-1980s, now hopes that what he calls his "celestial theater" will be ready for visitors by the year 2000. In an interview with Tim Vanderpool for *Outside* (April 1995), he expressed his belief that experiencing the natural world at Roden Crater in the final moments of the 20th century "will be a better way to ring in the millennium than watching a ball drop in Times Square."

James Archie Turrell was born on May 6, 1943 in Los Angeles and grew up in Pasadena, California. His parents raised him in the Quaker faith. The elementary school he attended was named for the American astronomer George Ellery Hale (1868–1938), who directed the operations of several huge telescopes, among them the one at what is now called the Hale Observatory, on Mount Wilson, near Pasadena. As a child, Waldemar Januszczak reported in the *Guardian* (May 3, 1993), Turrell "was encouraged to see the night sky as a huge American planetarium." His father, an aeronautical engineer, encouraged him to take up flying, and by age 16 James had earned a pilot's license.

As a student at Pomona College, in Claremont, California, Turrell majored in psychology; his particular interests were experimental and perceptual psychology. After earning a B.A. degree, in 1965, he entered a master's program in art at the University of California at Irvine. He dropped out a year later, having decided, Calvin Tomkins reported in the *New Yorker* (December 15, 1980), that "it was time to stop 'becoming' an artist and start being one." (Turrell earned an M.A. degree in 1973, from Claremont Graduate School, now known as Claremont Graduate University.)

As an undergraduate Turrell had taken classes in art history, in which he had viewed images of American abstract paintings and other works of art projected on screens. When, at some point in his student years or soon afterward, he visited museums in New York City to see the originals, he discovered that the paintings themselves appealed to him far less than had the transparencies projected in darkened classrooms. "He realized," Adam Gopnik reported in the *New Yorker* (July 30, 1990), "that what really interested him wasn't painting but projected light, and he began to make his art out of that material."

In about 1966 Turrell rented a studio in the Mendota Hotel, in Ocean Park, a town near Santa Monica, California, and embarked on what amounted to artistic research with light. In a series of experiments, he covered the windows almost completely, allowing light to enter only through small openings in boards that he moved in particular ways. He thereby created a constantly changing interior atmosphere that was controlled both by him and by conditions outdoors. Sometime in the late 1960s, he moved his equipment from Ocean Park to a storefront in Santa Monica. Sometimes he would invite people to see his work. A reporter for *Newsweek* (October 27, 1969) who visited one evening in 1969 wrote, "A traffic light, rightly seen, can turn you on as well as slow you down. A neon sign can paint a wall as well as advertise. A car can dance while it passes. The ugliest 'facts' in the environment, in short, have surprising uses. . . . Turrell has broadened the very definition of media by making the electric environment around his storefront perform. In so doing, he tunes his audiences into their environment, making them aware . . . of the space around them."

Meanwhile, at about the time he had dropped out of the master's program at the University of California, Turrell had begun working under the mentorship of the influential perceptual artist Robert Irwin. In 1967 John Coplona, a senior editor at the magazine *Artforum* who also served as a senior curator at the Pasadena Art Museum, invited Irwin, Turrell, and two other artists who were experimenting with light—Larry Bell and Douglas Wheeler—to exhibit in solo shows at the museum. Turrell's show included *Afrum-Proto*, in which a rectangle of light projected against a corner of a room "seemed almost three dimensional," as Mark Stevens wrote for *Newsweek* (February 10, 1986).

Two other works dating from about 1969 are among Turrell's best known: *Wedge Work*, an ever-evolving piece that uses massive wedges of light, and *Aperture*, a work of low luminosity that takes on different hues and colors as the supporting light is adjusted. Works from both series have toured for years.

During the late 1960s and early 1970s, Turrell earned his living primarily through odd jobs and then, according to various accounts, through aerial photography and restoration of beat-up classic cars or airplanes. He won a grant from the National Endowment for the Arts in 1968. In 1974, after receiving a Guggenheim fellowship, he began his magnum opus, the Roden Crater project.

The first step in the project required aerial surveys: piloting his private plane over mountainous regions in the western United States, Turrell searched for a huge landform rising above a plain. One hour north of Flagstaff, at a site overlooking the Painted Desert, he found exactly what he had in mind: a dormant volcano whose bowl, about 3,000 feet in diameter, had a neat, smoothly curved rim. The land was owned by Robert Chambers, a rancher; getting Chambers to sell it to him reportedly turned into an ultimately successful three-year campaign that entailed many hours of cajolery in Arizona saloons. Much of the money to buy the land came from Count Giuseppe Panza di Biumo; a major patron and collector of modern art, he remains among the most generous supporters of the Roden Crater project, which to date has cost more than $10 million. Another major source of support was the Dia Art Foundation. Other funding has come from the National Endowment for the Arts (from which Turrell won a second grant, in 1975), private donors, who have contributed through Turrell's Skystone Foundation, and a 1984 MacArthur Foundation fellowship. To raise additional money, Turrell has also sold renderings of the project, in the form of photolithographs; in 1998 the price of a set of four photolithographs was $4,000.

Turrell met Giuseppe Panza in 1974, when the count commissioned the artist to create six light installations for his 17th-century palazzo in Varese, in northern Italy. Two of the installations, dubbed *Skyscapes*, required the creation of movable ceilings and roofs in two rooms, to enable viewers to see the sky. While constructing them, Turrell became intrigued with what Calvin Tomkins identified as "the principle of celestial vaulting—the tendency of the human eye to perceive the sky as a curved, domelike finite space." At the Roden Crater, Turrell has said, "celestial vaulting could be experienced under ideal conditions."

Turrell's other work in the 1970s includes exhibits at the Stedelijk Museum, in Amsterdam, the Netherlands, and the Arco Center for Visual Art, in Los Angeles, both in 1976. In 1980 he was honored with a one-man show at the Whitney Museum of American Art that, according to Calvin Tomkins, amounted to "an informal retrospective" of Turrell's work since the mid-1960s. Noting that the

Whitney had at the same time mounted an exhibition of the paintings of Edward Hopper, "a master of painted light," Tomkins observed, "For Turrell, light is both the subject and the medium. You look *at* a Hopper, but to see a Turrell you have to step into it. Turrell defines spaces by means of light." In one of the installations at the show, a room was "flooded with a mixture of diffused daylight and argon-gas light," Tomkins wrote—"a mixture so apparently tangible that three viewers . . . leaned up against what they took to be a wall and [fell] slap into the art." *Rayna*, a space-division installation created in 1979 and exhibited at the Art Institute of Chicago (which owns it) in 1981, provides another example of Turrell's ability to turn light into an apparent solid. In the *Chicago Tribune* (October 3, 1993), Alan G. Artner wrote about "a horizontal rectangle of one color" on one wall. "The color vibrated, as if strokes of paint applied in many directions were differently reflecting the little available light." Stealthily, Artner had tried to touch the vibrating field. "I did not feel anything. . . . My finger passed through a horizontal rectangle cut out of the wall. Behind the hole was a brownish-gray light that had no apparent source. The light did not spill into the room but seemed to have been sucked from it by a force beyond the rectangle that kept the light in movement yet mysteriously trapped. . . . The effect was indescribable. Nothing I heard or read had prepared me for the experience. Not in any way could I have predicted its power."

Waldemar Januszczak reacted similarly to the Turrell show mounted at the Hayward Gallery in Chicago in 1993. "You emerge into a room illuminated by a wall-sized rectangle of red fog . . . ," Januszczak wrote in his article for the *Guardian* (May 3, 1993). "Unless you have already encountered Turrell's work, you will not have seen foggy light of this consistency before. It is gaseous yet also very still, transparent yet opaque: there is no point wasting further adjectives on an effect that is indescribable."

At about the time he was preparing for the 1980 Whitney show, Turrell had started *Meeting*, an enormous project that was to take seven years to complete. A permanent installation at the gallery P.S. 1, a converted former elementary school in the Long Island City section of Queens, New York, *Meeting* opened to the public in 1986. *Meeting* consists of a single room—"a trapezoidal chamber with a rectangular opening cut in the ceiling," as Gary Indiana described it for the *Village Voice* (November 4, 1986). Its construction required tearing down and rebuilding parts of the school, including support beams and a section of roof. Designed to capture the drama of changes in light as day turns to night, the installation is opened to visitors late in the afternoon. "One does, of course, experience the dimensions of the room, and the skylight is framed by the ceiling," Indiana wrote. "In a literally cosmic sense the frame determines what we see and the room determines how we see it. But *Meet-*

ing essentially removes extraneous phenomena from the perceptual field so that physical matter recedes from our attention. . . . Turrell's work offers a palpable, tranquilizing, grand experience of the world minus its unpleasant sociological and physical detritus."

"To be an artist," Turrell told Pam Hait for *Omni* (September 1988), "you first have to know how to survey land and how to drive in fence posts. And it helps if you can handle heavy equipment." The Roden Crater project has involved, among other tasks, digging several tunnels in the volcano, which rises about 600 feet from the desert floor; scooping out a number of viewing chambers; smoothing the bowl into a near-perfect hemisphere; making the height of the rim the same all around; and seeding the bowl with grama grass, "to bring out the contrast with the sky," as Lewis wrote. "You'll see a moon event in one spot, then stroll several hundred feet up the tunnel to see the same event more powerfully," Turrell explained to Vanderpool. In *Newsweek*, Mark Stevens reported that "under certain conditions, visitors will see their own shadow in the light of Venus." Turrell plans to provide quarters for eating and sleeping, but only to accommodate a handful of visitors daily.

In *New York* (June 4, 1990), the art critic Kay Larson wrote that Turrell's Roden Crater project "demonstrates a stillness of the ego, a silence of mind, . . . that is submissive to the natural world in a way almost incomprehensible to the addled, urbanized, jagged consciousness of the '90s. . . . [Whereas] Turrell's gallery pieces confine themselves to slightly claustrophobic sleights of interior light, Turrell's outdoor work penetrates the cycles of day and night, sky and stars. The Roden Crater is both the grandest of the projects of Earth art and the simplest." Larson also wrote, "Turrell's work forces us to return to places we might not like to recall, to think twice about the limits we casually place on experience. It returns us to cosmic cycles we might not want to concede exist, since to invoke them would suggest that the urban jungle is not the center of the universe."

In the *New York Times Magazine* (May 13, 1979), Larson wrote that the Roden Crater project "is pervaded by a transcendentalist sense of the immanence of spirit in all things. As Ralph Waldo Emerson wrote, ' 'Tis indifferent whether you say, all is matter, or, all is spirit.'" Then Larson quoted Turrell: "Where the piece begins and the world ends just vanishes and doesn't matter anymore. It melds into where you are." — M.B.

Suggested Reading: *Connoisseur* p48+ Feb. 1991, with photos; *Guardian* G p4 May 3, 1993; *Los Angeles Times* F p5 Sep. 5, 1996; *New York* p68+ June 4, 1990; *New York Times Magazine* p22+ May 13, 1979, with photos; *New Yorker* p29+ Dec. 15, 1980, p74+ July 30, 1990; *Newsweek* p74 Oct. 27, 1969, with photo, p70+ Feb. 10, 1986, with photos; *Omni* p18 Sep. 1988,

with photo; *Outside* (on-line) Apr. 1995; *Village Voice* p93 Nov. 4, 1986, with photo; *Who's Who in American Art, 1997–1998*

Selected Works: *Afrum-Proto*, 1967; *Wedge Work*, 1969(?); *Aperture*, 1969(?); Roden Crater project, 1974–; *Skyscapes*, 1974; *Rayna*, 1979; *Meeting*, 1980–86

N. Rich Schiff/Archive Photos

Van Damme, Jean-Claude
(zhahn-klawd)

Oct. 18, 1960– Film actor. Address: c/o United Talent Agency, 9560 Wilshire Blvd., Beverly Hills, CA 90212

The star of many films with one- or two-word titles that have a punchy immediacy typical of the action-film genre (*Kickboxer, Double Impact, Universal Soldier, Sudden Death,* and *Knock Off,* to name just a few), Jean-Claude Van Damme is one of the most physically flexible action-movie idols around. Notable among Van Damme's gymnastic-like maneuvers are splits, which he executes with the ease of a pair of scissors. In one variation of the split, he suspends himself between two tall objects so far distant from each other that it seems his body must inevitably rip in two. In another variation, he jumps up with his legs apart and spins like a loose helicopter blade—a movement he has said can "kill very easily." He has performed many such feats while scantily clad, and cinematographers have often lingered on his superbly conditioned body. "If you have a decent body, why not show it?" he told the New York *Daily News* (July 5, 1992).

"I'll have something to show my grandkids . . . and then say, 'Go train! Off to the gym!'"

Despite his celebrated physique and leading-man looks, Van Damme has thus far failed to make the transition from action hero to serious actor. In part, his French accent is to blame: when he says "focus," for example, the word is likely to sound like a self-directed expletive. To explain his accent, his screenwriters have resorted to a variety of conceits: they have made his characters a French Canadian, a Cajun, a French Foreign Legionnaire, or an orphan raised by a French nun. Van Damme hopes one day to transcend both his accent and his action-hero image and be seen as more than an uncultured muscleman. "I'm a very sensitive person," he told *New York* (April 1, 1991). "Very much so. That's my luck. I love classical music, painting. I love art."

Van Damme was born Jean-Claude Van Varenberg on October 18, 1960 in Belgium to Eugene Van Varenberg, a florist and accountant, and Eliana Van Varenberg. Jean-Claude and his sister, Veronique, grew up speaking French in the Belgian town of Berchem-Sainte Agathe. He was a twiggy kid with thick glasses and little self-confidence, so when he was about 10, his father enrolled him in karate classes to toughen him up. A few years later, Van Damme started weightlifting and studying ballet. "I loved the classical music and the grace of those [ballet] movements," he told Jack Barth for *Premiere* (July 1992). Van Damme dropped out of school when he was 16, after winning some minor bodybuilding and kickboxing titles, among them the European Professional Karate Association middleweight championship. Eventually, he opened a sports club in Brussels, naming it California Gym. In 1980 he married his first wife, Maria Rodriguez; within a year or two, they divorced.

Fond of movies like *Ben Hur*, *The Cincinnati Kid*, and *Cool Hand Luke*, Van Damme dreamt of one day becoming a movie star. "Many times, I look out the window in Belgium and it is raining," he told David Richards. "The sky is gray and depressing. So I go to the cinema. And suddenly the screen is full of light and bright colors exploding. And I want to be part of that." In 1981 he sold his gym and, with approximately $8,000 in savings and little knowledge of English, moved to Los Angeles. Upon arriving in the U.S., he began to call himself Van Damme, which was the surname of a friend of his. He chose the name because it was easier to remember than "Van Varenberg" and because it lent itself to punning: he envisioned headlines reading "Hot Damme," "Damme Good," and "Wham Bam Thank You Van Damme."

Los Angeles's cult of fitness appealed to Van Damme; to him, he told John Barth, the city was "like a big gym." For his first five years there, he worked at odd jobs—limo driver, pizza delivery boy, carpet factory worker, and aerobics instructor—and also auditioned unsuccessfully for parts. In 1985 he married again; he and his second wife, Cynthia Derderian, soon divorced. Speaking of the failure of his first two marriages, he told the New York *Daily News* (August 7, 1991), "It was my fault because I was too young and only dreaming of movies. I sacrificed those marriages for my love for this career. It was a long trip, I was young, and I knew I had to do it alone."

Van Damme's film debut came in *No Retreat, No Surrender* (1986), a "karate saga" in which he played Ivan the Russian, a villainous fighter who loses to a young challenger trained by the ghost of Bruce Lee. He also landed a part as the alien in the Arnold Schwarzenegger vehicle *Predator*, but was replaced because he was a head too short to fit properly in the alien's costume.

Van Damme's big break came after he recognized Menahem Golan, a chief executive of Cannon Films, outside a Beverly Hills restaurant, and launched a surprise kick over Golan's head. Golan met with him the next day, and at their meeting Van Damme showed off other facets of his athletic ability. "I took off my shirt and did some poses, and then I took two chairs and did a split between them," he told Clifford Terry for the *Chicago Tribune* (August 27, 1993), "and [Golan] looked at me and said, 'My friend, you want to be a star. I'll make you a star.' And he called to an assistant, 'Bring me *Bloodsport*.'"

Supposedly based on the real life of the American Frank Dux and his exploits in an underground, anything-goes fight tournament held in Asia, *Bloodsport* was shot in Hong Kong for $2 million, of which Van Damme was paid $25,000. After reviewing the completed film, Golan thought it was so terrible that he felt reluctant to release it. He later changed his mind and released *Bloodsport* overseas, and to his surprise, it became a hit in Malaysia and France. In 1987 it came to theaters in the U.S., where it grossed $12 million, six times its production cost.

Suddenly Van Damme was deluged with scripts—innumerable variations of plots that resembled the *Rocky* and *Karate Kid* stories. He became very busy, appearing in *Black Eagle* (1988), in which he played a villain; *Kickboxer* (1989), in which his character learns Thai kickboxing to avenge his fallen brother; and *Cyborg* (1989), in which he played a fighter-for-hire in a 21st-century dystopia in which roving gangs of Flesh Pirates menace other people. In 1990 he appeared in *Death Warrant* and *Lionheart*, in the latter of which he played a French Foreign Legionnaire who participates in clandestine street brawls in the U.S. to earn enough money to support his search for his lost brother.

Van Damme's films made plenty of money—each was profitable—and his action shenanigans put him right behind such stars as Arnold Schwarzenegger, Sylvester Stallone, and Stephen Seagal in the American action-hero movie pantheon. Critics, however, trashed his movies, citing their formulaic plots, brain-dead action sequences, and beefcake shots. Van Damme has admitted that most of the films were mainly flimsy excuses to showcase his bulging pectoral muscles and martial-arts ability. "These are no-budget movies," he told Richards for the *New York Times*. "What else can they show? An explosion? A jet crashing? Not enough money. So they show muscles. The kids go wow. I end up being a piece of meat."

Many of Van Damme's subsequent films follow the formula established in his earlier successes. In *Double Impact* (1991), in a role considered a stretch for his acting abilities, Van Damme played twins separated as infants when their parents are murdered by a Hong Kong crime gang. One twin becomes a well-mannered fitness instructor in Los Angeles; the other, a street-savvy smuggler in Hong Kong. Van Damme also appeared in *Universal Soldier* (1992), in which he and Dolph Lundgren (nicknamed the Sulking Swede) played soldiers killed during the Vietnam War who are resurrected in a top-secret government program whose goal is to create an elite covert operations team. The film, which many critics joked was perfect for Van Damme, given what they considered his naturally robotic acting style, grossed $36 million domestically and nearly triple that worldwide. (Van Damme has claimed he faked a fight with Lundgren at the Cannes Film Festival to get more publicity for the film.) In *Hard Target* (1993), the first film directed in the United States by the Hong Kong action-film director John Woo, Van Damme starred as a Cajun merchant sailor who confronts a group of men who have taken to hunting human beings.

Some filmmakers have attempted to change Van Damme's martial-arts image. In *Nowhere to Run* (1993), a remake of the western *Shane* co-written by Joe Eszterhas, Leslie Bohem, and Randy Feldman, Van Damme played an outlaw who becomes involved with a family and their conflict with a rapacious land baron; the script was meant to show him off as a romantic lead. The film *Timecop* (1994) was also supposed to emphasize Van Damme's romantic qualities, while featuring him in traditional fight sequences as well. Van Damme appeared as Max Walker, a policeman who, in the year 2004, is sent 10 years into the past to foil criminals' attempts to profit from their knowledge of the future. The policeman is suddenly faced with an opportunity to change history and rescue his murdered wife.

So far, Van Damme's attempts to remake himself into something other than an action star have not caught on with the public. "It's upsetting because it's like when they said Sean Connery was only good for James Bond, and then he came back as one of the greatest movie stars ever," he told Terry for the *Chicago Tribune*. "When you do something good in action, you become stereotyped, and it takes time to go from action to drama, from action to love story."

Thus, Van Damme has continued to punch and kick his way through films. In *Street Fighter* (1994), an adaptation of the same-named video game, Van Damme starred as Colonel Guile, the leader of a multinational army that must bring down an evil dictator. In *Sudden Death* (1995), Van Damme appeared as a fireman who must save the vice president of the United States and 17,000 other fans at a hockey stadium targeted for immolation by terrorists. *The Quest* (1996) is Van Damme's first directorial effort. Partially inspired by Tintin comic books, the film stars Van Damme and, much like *Bloodsport* and *Kickboxer*, ends in a tournament-style fight.

More recently Van Damme has helped some Hong Kong directors break into the U.S. market. One of them, Ringo Lam, directed *Maximum Risk* (1996), in which Van Damme appeared as two brothers. (The film marks his third attempt at playing double roles; the second was in *Timecop*, in which his future self meets his past self.) Van Damme has also worked in two films with the director Tsui Hark. The first is *Double Team* (1997), in which he played a counterterrorist operative opposite Dennis Rodman. The second Hark film is *Knock Off* (1998), in which Van Damme played the executive of a jeans company who gets tangled up in a terrorist plot to implant small bombs in the pants of Americans.

Jean-Claude Van Damme has been married to four women. From his third marriage, to Gladys Portugues, a bodybuilder, he has a daughter, Bianca, and a son, Kristofer. The couple married in 1986 and split up in 1992. His fourth wife was Darcy LaPier, a model who was formerly married to the Hawaiian Tropic suntan-lotion mogul Ron Rice. He and LaPier wed in February 1994, and their marriage was a round of breakups and reconciliations. La Pier filed for divorce in November 1994 and again in June 1996. Van Damme filed for divorce in December 1996; then, in November 1997, LaPier filed for divorce a third time, accusing her husband of spousal abuse and mood swings because of a cocaine addiction. (Earlier in 1997 Van Damme had admitted to the press that he had a cocaine addiction and had gone into rehabilitation. He later claimed that he nearly died because of his addiction and that he went into treatment for cyclic manic depression.) Van Damme and LaPier, who have one son, Nicolas, eventually divorced, and on July 9, 1999, Van Damme married Gladys Portugues for the second time.

Van Damme, who turned 39 in 1999, remains a macho action star, even as Hollywood increasingly uses less-muscled actors, such as Nicolas Cage and Will Smith, in action-film roles. In 1999 he appeared in the straight-to-video film *Legionnaire* and in *Universal Soldier: The Return*, each of which has earned less than previous Van Damme vehicles. — W.G.

Suggested Reading: *Chicago Tribune* V p5+ Aug. 27, 1993, with photos; *Entertainment Weekly* p21+ Jan. 22, 1993, with photos, p44+ Sep. 4, 1998, with photos; *Interview* p94 Mar. 1991; *New York* p28+ Apr. 1, 1991, with photo; *New York Daily News* p33+ Aug. 7, 1991, with photos, p16 July 5, 1992, with photos, p41+ Sep. 15, 1994, with photos; *New York Times* II p7+ Sep. 4, 1994, with photos; *People* p83+ Aug. 3, 1992, with photos, p67 Dec. 12, 1994, with photo; *Premiere* p68+ July 1992, with photos; *Washington Post* G p1+ Aug. 11, 1991, with photos

Selected Films: *No Retreat, No Surrender*, 1985; *Bloodsport*, 1987; *Black Eagle*, 1988; *Kickboxer*, 1989; *Cyborg*, 1989; *Lionheart*, 1990; *Death Warrant*, 1990; *Double Impact*, 1991; *Universal Soldier*, 1992; *Nowhere to Run*, 1993; *Hard Target*, 1993; *Street Fighter*, 1994; *Timecop*, 1994; *Sudden Death*, 1995; *The Quest*, 1996; *Maximum Risk*, 1996; *Double Team*, 1997; *Knock Off*, 1998; *Legionnaire*, 1999; *Universal Soldier: The Return*, 1999

Courtesy of Congresswoman Velázquez's office

Velázquez, Nydia M.

(veh-LAZ-kwez, NID-ee-uh)

Mar. 22, 1953– U.S. Representative from New York. Address: 2241 Rayburn House Office Bldg., Washington, DC 20515; 15 Court St., Brooklyn, NY 11201

On November 3, 1992, the day that Bill Clinton, then the governor of Arkansas, defeated George Bush, the incumbent president of the United States, Nydia Velázquez became the first Puerto Rican woman to be elected to the United States House of Representatives. Velázquez, a Democrat and self-described liberal, represents New York State's 12th Congressional District, which encompasses the Lower East Side of the New York City

borough of Manhattan and parts of the boroughs of Queens and Brooklyn. Now serving her fourth term in Congress, she has established herself as a staunch advocate for the rights of Hispanics, immigrants, women, and the working class, which together compose the bulk of her constituency. Her voting record, which includes support for raising the minimum wage and cutting back on defense spending, has earned her 100 percent approval ratings from Americans for Democratic Action, a liberal lobbying organization, and the AFL-CIO, which has some 13 million members belonging to nearly 80 unions. In addition to voting against such culturally and politically conservative bills as the proposed ban on so-called partial-birth abortions, she is among the small number of congressional Democrats who have strenuously opposed the Clinton administration's centrist agenda on such issues as trade, immigration, and welfare. Velázquez has also become known for her long-time involvement in Puerto Rican affairs and particularly for her support for Puerto Rican statehood.

Nydia Margarita Velázquez was born into a poor family on March 22, 1953 in Yabucoa, Puerto Rico. Her eight siblings include her twin sister. Her father, Benito Velázquez, whose formal education ended with the third grade, worked as a sugar-cane cutter and a cockfight-pit operator; he was known locally for giving impassioned speeches in favor of better working conditions for sugar-cane cutters, often from the backs of pick-up trucks. Her mother, Carmen Luisa Serrano, helped out financially by making and selling *pasteles*, an island delicacy. Velázquez has recalled heated debates about politics at the family dinner table. A bright child who was eager to learn, Nydia insisted on starting school two years early, at the age of five, and in subsequent years she skipped three grades. She was the first person in her family to complete high school. By the time she was 16, she was attending the University of Puerto Rico at Rio Piedras, where she studied political science and became a vocal supporter of Puerto Rican independence. Upon graduating, with a B.A. degree, magna cum laude, in 1974, she won a scholarship for graduate study at New York University (NYU), in New York City. Initially her father was reluctant to give his daughter permission to go to the U.S., but after prodding by two of her professors, he relented. After earning an M.S. degree in political science from NYU, in 1976, Velázquez returned to Puerto Rico and joined the faculty of the University of Huracao.

In 1980 a conservative political party, the pro-statehood New Progressives, came to power in Puerto Rico. The new political climate proved less than hospitable to the young academic: members of the New Progressives who regarded Velázquez's views as far too liberal accused her of being a leftist and a Communist. These exaggerated charges led her to return to New York in 1981, and she accepted a position as an adjunct professor of Puerto Rican studies at Hunter College. Two years later she began working as a special assistant to Brooklyn congressman Edolphus Towns, dealing mostly with immigrant-related issues. In 1984 Velázquez was named to fill a vacant seat on the New York City Council, thus becoming the first Hispanic woman to serve on that body. When, in 1986, she ran for election for that seat, she lost. Following her defeat she took a Cabinet-level position with the Puerto Rican government, as head of what is now called the Department of Puerto Rican Community Affairs in the United States. In that job she served as a liaison between Puerto Rico and Puerto Rican communities on the mainland. In 1989, in one of her most influential actions, Velázquez personally called General Colin L. Powell, who was then the chairman of the Joint Chiefs of Staff, to secure a promise that federal disaster relief would be provided to the victims of Hurricane Hugo, which had ravaged the island in September of that year.

In 1992 Velázquez decided to run for the congressional seat then held by the nine-term liberal Democrat Stephen J. Solarz. The district had recently been redrawn in order to ensure that Hispanics, who composed nearly a quarter of New York City's population, would get a larger voice in Congress; at that time, only one of the city's 19 congressional representatives was Hispanic. The borders of Solarz's district had been entirely within Brooklyn, and his constituents had been mostly white and heavily Jewish. The redrawn district had been constructed block by block, and it wound through the Lower East Side of Manhattan and sections of Queens and Brooklyn, following what *Politics in America, 1998* described as a "wildly meandering path." The reconfigured district was nearly 60 percent Hispanic, thus immediately putting Solarz at a disadvantage in the Democratic primary, where he faced not only Velázquez but four other Hispanic candidates as well. Moreover, Velázquez's name recognition among Hispanic voters had increased significantly before the primary, through the exposure she gained by running a voter-registration campaign, financed by the Puerto Rican government with the goal of increasing the number of Hispanic voters. Although the initiative succeeded in registering more than 200,000 voters nationwide, Velázquez was criticized for trying to win over voters in the 12th Congressional District in particular. Meanwhile, Solarz tried to counter his opponent's increased stature by hiring Hispanic advisers and learning some phrases in Spanish. But his efforts were in vain; as a writer for *Congressional Quarterly* (January 16, 1993) put it, "Solarz, an unknown to many of his new would-be constituents, was branded as a carpetbagger and wealthy outsider." On Primary Day, Velázquez triumphed with 33 percent of the vote; Solarz captured 28 percent.

Accompanied by New York City mayor David Dinkins and a local union chief, Dennis Rivera, she celebrated her victory with a visit to Puerto Rico. The trip triggered more complaints from people who already viewed Velázquez's ties to the commonwealth as too close. "It seems to me a culmina-

tion of what was a campaign that was run out of the island of Puerto Rico," Elizabeth Colon, the former executive director of the Association of Puerto Rican Executives, who had come in third in the primary race, was quoted as saying by the *New York Times* (September 27, 1992). In defending herself, Velázquez, who at the time spoke English with a heavy accent, asserted that her heritage did not dominate her politics and in fact added another dimension to it. "I am very clear: I am not going to represent only a Puerto Rican or a Latin American viewpoint," she said, as quoted in the same *New York Times* article. "I have a very wide perspective on the needs of this district. I won through the support of a broad coalition of different groups in the district—women, African-Americans and others—and I moved immediately to try to expand that."

Despite her detractors, Velázquez was expected to trounce her opponent in the general election, because her district is overwhelmingly Democratic. But her prospects became far less certain a month before the general election, when an anonymous source stole and faxed Velázquez's medical records from the previous year to a news organization. It became public knowledge that Velázquez had attempted suicide and had struggled with excessive drinking and depression. Velázquez responded by holding a press conference, where, surrounded by family and friends, she acknowledged that during a "troublesome period," having become depressed, partly because her mother was ill, she had tried to take her own life. With the help of counseling, she said, she had emerged from the experience "stronger and more committed to public service," as Maria Newman paraphrased her in the *New York Times* (October 10, 1992). She also expressed outrage that matters of a highly personal nature had been made public. "As a public official, I understand that my actions are more open to public scrutiny than others," Newman quoted her as saying. "Yet, I am outraged and appalled that personal health records that are privileged information between a patient and his/her physician have found their way anonymously into the newsrooms of this city." Velázquez's attempt at damage control proved successful; on November 3, 1992 she defeated her Republican and Liberal challengers, taking 77 percent of the vote.

In her first term, Velázquez joined the Banking, Finance and Urban Affairs Committee and the Small Business Committee. She quickly displayed liberal leanings as well as a willingness to differ from the stand of the Clinton administration on several important issues. She opposed both the North American Free Trade Agreement (NAFTA) and the General Agreement on Tariffs and Trade (GATT), for example—legislation, pushed strenuously by the administration, that did much to remove international trade barriers. Velázquez, along with such unusual bedfellows as protectionist Republicans and labor-backed Democrats, feared that those pro-business bills would leave American workers vulnerable to replacement by cheap overseas labor. She also opposed a bill that banned federal funding for abortion except in rare cases. She voted in favor of President Clinton's budget, which raised taxes and cut spending, and approved lifting a federal ban on homosexuals in the military and imposing a mandatory five-day waiting period for handgun purchases. She supported the President's 1994 crime bill and voted against the movement to add a balanced-budget amendment to the Constitution. In April 1993 Velázquez was among 20 Latina women who met to discuss health-care reform with Hillary Rodham Clinton, who believed that computerizing medical records was a way of cutting health costs. During that meeting Velázquez stressed the importance of maintaining privacy in personal medical matters. In 1996 Velázquez introduced legislation to ensure that people receive quality care from their HMOs.

In 1994, the year in which the Republican Party won control of the House for the first time in 40 years, Velázquez easily won reelection, with some 92 percent of the vote. She spoke out against the new Republican leadership's so-called Contract with America and, in one of the more momentous votes in which she has taken part, she opposed the controversial welfare-reform bill, which is phasing out public assistance for millions of Americans. By contrast, President Clinton signed the bill into law and made it a centerpiece of his movement away from the traditional "big government" programs. Velázquez had also helped stave off GOP efforts to dispose of the Legal Services Corporation, which provides gratis legal representation to those who cannot afford it otherwise. During her second term she opposed attempts to deny public education to illegal immigrants and a move to ban late-term abortions in cases of medical necessity. She has also fought legislation that would make English the official language of the government, contending that the proposed law was a manifestation of, and would further encourage, "anti-immigrant hatred." When the Republican leadership stymied Democratic attempts to bring to the floor a bill that would increase the national minimum wage, Velázquez objected with passion. "I will say to my Republican colleagues, they have lost the battle in the court of public opinion . . . ," she said, as reported in *Politics in America, 1998*. "Instead of following the will of the American people, they are following the will of corporate America and the fat cats who have funded their campaigns. That is immoral."

In 1997, as Velázquez was preparing to run for the fourth time, a panel of federal judges ruled that the redrawing of New York's 12th Congressional District was unconstitutional because it had been done entirely along racial lines. The district, which had been nicknamed the Bullwinkle because of its resemblance to the shape of that cartoon moose, was again redrawn, so that its area in Queens was reduced and its area in Brooklyn increased. The demographic effect was that the portion of the district's population identified as Hispanic dropped from 58 percent to 48 percent and the segment

identified as Asian dropped from 19 percent to 12 percent, while the portion identified as white rose from 14 percent to 31 percent. (The number of blacks remained the same.) With that change, Velázquez's seat in Congress no longer seemed safe. In addition, she alienated several prominent Brooklyn politicians, including the head of the borough's Democratic Party, by supporting a slew of candidates whom the politicians did not favor— and who failed to win election. Sensing her weakness, two political veterans, City Councilman Martin Malave-Dilan and Assemblyman Vito J. Lopez, challenged her in the 1998 primary. But Velázquez's appeal to her existing and prospective constituents was stronger than it seemed, and she triumphod in the primary and then in the general election, where she won more than 80 percent of the vote. In one of the last legislative actions of her third term, Velázquez voted against the impeachment of President Clinton.

In February 1998 Velázquez became the ranking Democrat on the Small Business Committee, thus becoming the first Hispanic woman to achieve that position on a full committee. A year later the House approved a bill written by Velázquez that will give small businesses improved access to capital. Recently she was instrumental in procuring federal aid for victims of Hurricane Mitch, which devastated sections of Central America in late October 1998.

Nydia Velázquez, who is divorced, lives in Brooklyn when Congress is not in session. — M.C.

Suggested Reading: *New York Times* p35 Sep. 27, 1992, with photo, p25 Oct. 10, 1992, with photo, B p1+ Nov. 2, 1992, with photo, B p3 Feb. 9, 1998; *Notable Hispanic American Women*; *Notable Latino Americans*; *Politics in America, 1998*

Ventura, Jesse

July 15, 1951– Governor of Minnesota; former wrestler, sportscaster, and actor. Address: 130 State Capitol, 75 Constitution Ave., Saint Paul, MN 55155

The election of Jesse Ventura as governor of Minnesota on November 3, 1998 shocked the political world to its foundations. A straight-talking Everyman who ran on the Reform Party ticket, Ventura had criticized his Democratic and Republican opponents for catering to special-interest groups. But his victory after mounting that type of campaign was not what stunned political analysts. Rather, it was simply the idea that someone whom they had dismissed as little more than a joke could win the highest elective position in the state. The political mavens had failed to take him seriously because many people had known him only as Jesse "the

Courtesy of Minnesota governor's office

Jesse Ventura

Body" Ventura, a moniker that evoked his former career as a professional wrestler, most notably during his years with Vince McMahon's World Wrestling Federation in the late 1980s. Ventura had enjoyed even greater success as an announcer for televised wrestling matches, a job in which his charisma and colorful rhetoric had served him especially well. He has also had a modest acting career, having appeared in such films as *Predator* (1987), *The Running Man* (1987), and *Batman & Robin* (1997). In a conversation with the TV news anchor Tom Brokaw after his election as governor, Ventura joked that he wanted to be known from that point on as Jesse "the Mind" Ventura. "They said a vote for me was a wasted vote," he told reporters, as quoted in the *New York Times* (November 5, 1998). "Well guess what? Those wasted votes wasted them."

Governor Ventura was born James George Janos on July 15, 1951 in Minneapolis, Minnesota, to parents of Slovak and German extraction. His father, George Janos, was a steam fitter who worked for the city government of Minneapolis, and his mother, Bernice Janos, was a nurse anesthetist. James Janos attended Roosevelt Senior High School in Minneapolis, graduating in 1969. With war raging in Vietnam, the 18-year-old Janos enlisted in the U.S. Navy after being persuaded to do so by a friend. He soon applied for entrance into the SEALs, the navy's elite special missions force. In 1970 he completed the rigorous training program and was sent to Vietnam. To this day he has never revealed the exact nature of the missions in which he engaged, but it is known that he made many parachute jumps and deep-sea dives.

Janos remained on active duty until 1973, when he returned home from the war with an honorable discharge. While still a member of the navy reserves (until 1975), he enrolled in North Hennepin Community College, in Minneapolis. At 22, Janos was older than almost all his classmates; unable to reacclimate himself to a school environment after four years in Vietnam, he soon dropped out. For the next couple of years, he drifted from job to job and place to place, trying to find an identity for himself. Before returning to Minnesota, he spent some time in California, where he became a member of the Mongols motorcycle gang and had a short stint as a bodyguard for the Rolling Stones.

As a child, Janos had expressed interest in becoming a professional wrestler, but he had been discouraged from pursuing that goal. Once he was on his own, he began attending wrestling cards (as wrestling shows are known). One wrestler in particular caught his attention: "Superstar" Billy Graham. Sporting tie-dyed clothes and bleached-blond hair, Graham was a flamboyant, loud-mouthed "heel" (in wrestling terminology, a "bad guy"). Intrigued by this colorful character, Janos approached Graham and told him of his wish to become a wrestler. The chiseled grappler offered just the words of encouragement the young Janos needed.

Already an impressive specimen at six feet, four inches and well over 200 pounds, Janos stepped up the training regimen he had begun some time before. During one of his workout sessions at a Minnesota gym, he was spotted by Bob Geigel, one of the Midwest's major wrestling promoters. Geigel offered Janos a job wrestling for him, and Janos promptly accepted. Before he could debut, Janos and Geigel had to come up with a character, or "gimmick," to enable Janos to gain the attention of the fans. Emulating his idol "Superstar" Graham, Janos bleached his hair and took to wearing outlandishly colored tights. Geigel's idea was to portray his new protégé as a California surfer type, and in 1975 James Janos began wrestling as "Surfer" Jesse Ventura. (The surname was inspired by the southern California coastal town of that name; "Jesse" was simply a name he happened to like.)

When Ventura entered the sport, professional wrestling was a strictly regional enterprise. The territory in which Bob Geigel promoted was known as the Central States—mainly Kansas, Missouri, and Iowa—and Jesse Ventura's earliest matches took place in Wichita, Kansas. Before long he began to develop his "character"; dropping the "Surfer" from his ring name, the burly wrestler became known as Jesse "the Body" Ventura. He also began dressing far more garishly than Billy Graham had, adding to his outfits feathered boas, wrap-around sunglasses, and multiple pairs of dangling earrings.

Several months after his debut, Ventura moved from the Central States to the Pacific Northwest, an Oregon/Washington–based territory that had been run by the promoter Don Owen since the 1920s.

There he had his earliest taste of success, winning the Pacific Northwest heavyweight championship on October 17, 1975 in a bout with another up-and-coming rookie, Jimmy "Superfly" Snuka. He lost the title to a local favorite, Dutch Savage, on March 3, 1976 and then regained it on June 26. After a nine-month reign, he lost the title again, this time to Snuka. Between 1976 and 1978, he held the Pacific Northwest tag-team championship five times with a total of three different partners: Bull Ramos, "Playboy" Buddy Rose, and Jerry Oates.

In 1978, no longer a rookie, Ventura left Don Owen and returned briefly to work for his former boss, Bob Geigel, in the Central States. Ventura once again chalked up tag-team victories, joining Tank Patton to take the Central States tag-team title from Ron Starr and Tom Andrews on September 14 in Kansas City, Kansas. He and Patton held the belts for only one month before losing them to Bob Brown and Bob Sweetan in Des Moines, Iowa. Ventura left the Central States territory for good shortly thereafter.

In 1979 Ventura joined the American Wrestling Association (AWA). One of the largest wrestling companies in the nation at the time, the AWA was based in Minnesota and held shows in other states as well. Through the AWA's televised programs, which aired in many parts of the country, Ventura gained his greatest exposure yet. Because he had no formal background in wrestling fundamentals, he concentrated on something in which he excelled: talking. "He wasn't a very good wrestler, but he had charisma," Dave Meltzer, editor of the *Wrestling Observer* newsletter, recalled to a reporter for the *New York Times* (November 5, 1998). "His best move was standing on the apron yelling at the fans while his tag team partner did all the work." Ventura became known for his ability to stir up a crowd through verbal tirades, and he was especially good at shooting "promos," pseudo-interviews in which he taunted the audience and threatened his opponents. By such means, he could draw attention away from his lack of in-ring ability. "Jesse's best move was to cheat and run," his one-time opponent Hulk Hogan has recalled, as quoted in a recent press release from Ventura's office. "He'd take the tape off his wrist and choke you, he'd gouge you in the eyes, and then if you cleared your eyes or got the tape off your throat, he'd run for his life."

In the AWA Ventura achieved his greatest in-ring success. With Adrian Adonis, he formed the duo known as the East-West Connection. On July 20, 1980 Ventura and Adonis were booked to wrestle in Denver, Colorado, against the AWA world tag-team champions—Verne Gagne, who owned the AWA and was then the AWA world heavyweight champion, and Gagne's partner, Maurice "Mad Dog" Vachon, a former AWA heavyweight titlist. But Gagne was unable to appear for the match, so the belts were awarded via forfeit to Ventura and Adonis. The duo made the most of their luck, holding on to the tag-team championship of the world

for nearly 11 months before losing it to Greg Gagne (son of Verne) and Jim Brunzell in Green Bay, Wisconsin, on June 14, 1981.

Ventura made his first foray into the World Wrestling Federation (WWF) in 1981. Run by Vince McMahon Sr., the WWF was not yet the international media giant it would eventually become, but it was still just about the largest territory in the United States, running shows throughout the Northeast. With a larger platform than ever, Ventura hoped to ascend to new heights in his career. He briefly reprised his alliance with Adrian Adonis in an unsuccessful attempt to wrest the WWF world tag-team championship from the Strongbow Brothers. In 1982 he appeared in his first and only main event at Madison Square Garden, facing WWF heavyweight champion Bob Backlund. He failed to win the title, and by 1983 he had returned to the AWA.

During Ventura's second stint with the AWA, he was sent south to the Memphis territory, then affiliated with Verne Gagne's company. In the fall of 1983, Ventura engaged in a heated feud with the Memphis legend Jerry "The King" Lawler, the southern heavyweight champion. From September to November, Lawler and Ventura traded the southern title back and forth twice; Ventura was not able to hold onto it for more than a couple of weeks.

By 1984 Vince McMahon Jr. had taken over his father's company, the WWF, and had begun a national expansion that would eventually put almost all the other territories out of business and bring an end to the regional nature of the business. McMahon was recruiting talent from other organizations across the country, and one of his acquisitions was Jesse Ventura. Back in the WWF, Ventura challenged then–WWF champion Hulk Hogan, but promoters once again kept Ventura in the role of loser.

Impressed by Ventura's way with words, in 1985 McMahon made him a television color commentator and scaled down his wrestling schedule. Along with either McMahon or the legendary Gorilla Monsoon, Ventura served as a broadcaster on the WWF's various pay-per-view specials and weekly TV programs. He was even granted his own segment, called "The Body Shop," in which he conducted wrestling interviews. Up to this point, wrestling announcers had been no different from the announcers of sporting events; Ventura was the first to bring real color to the broadcast booth. Taking the side of the "heel," he became wrestling's first "bad guy" announcer. His favorite saying was, "Win if you can, lose if you must, but always cheat." Before long it became clear that Ventura was more suited to commentating than to wrestling.

Entering a new career in broadcasting proved especially fortunate for Ventura, because in 1986, a blood clot was discovered in his lung, and he was forced to retire from the ring. His announcing duties were expanded even further, and soon he caught the attention of people in Hollywood. In 1987 he appeared in his first film, acting alongside Arnold Schwarzenegger in the science-fiction thriller *Predator*. Within months he was seen in another Schwarzenegger vehicle, *The Running Man* (1987).

For the next couple of years, Ventura continued to work for Vince McMahon. In August 1988 he was the special referee for the main event of the WWF's first "SummerSlam" pay-per-view event, in which Hulk Hogan and Randy "Macho Man" Savage took on Andre the Giant and "The Million-Dollar Man" Ted DiBiase. By the summer of 1990, Ventura had departed the WWF, with the intention of focusing on his film career. The result was his first and only starring role, in the B picture *Abraxas, Guardian of the Universe* (1991). He also worked on a TV pilot, entitled *Tag Team*, in which he and his former colleague "Rowdy" Roddy Piper played retired wrestlers who form a private investigating agency. *Tag Team* was not picked up as a regular series.

In the fall of 1990, feeling frustrated by what he perceived as the ineffectiveness of local politicians, Ventura began attending city council meetings in his home town, Brooklyn Park, Minnesota (a suburb of Minneapolis). When he expressed his opinions, council members sarcastically suggested that he run for mayor. He took them up on their suggestion, and that November he was elected mayor of Brooklyn Park, unseating 18-year incumbent Jim Krautkremer. Dismayed at the election of an independent candidate, the town's Democratic and Republican council members were unwilling to cooperate with the new mayor, and he was thus unable to accomplish much during his single, four-year term in office.

In 1992, in his second year as mayor, Ventura returned to the world of professional wrestling. He went back as an employee not of the WWF, however, but of its main competitor, World Championship Wrestling (WCW), owned by Ted Turner. He debuted as a WCW announcer in February at the "SuperBrawl II" pay-per-view show. Using the slogan "The Body Is Back," WCW capitalized on Ventura's popularity, despite the fact that he had begun toning down his appearance to go along with his new role as a politician. While working for WCW, Ventura also continued his acting career, with a supporting role in the Sylvester Stallone movie *Demolition Man* (1993).

The WWF had not heard the last of Jesse Ventura, however. In early 1994 he sued his former employer for $2 million, claiming that he was being cheated out of royalties for videocassettes featuring his commentary. On April 13 a federal jury in St. Paul, Minnesota, ruled in Ventura's favor and ordered the WWF to pay him back royalties totaling nearly $810,000.

By the beginning of 1995, both Ventura's term as mayor of Brooklyn Park and his employment with WCW had ended. He moved from Brooklyn Park to the nearby town of Maple Grove, where he pur-chased a small "hobby" farm. From 1995 to 1996 he hosted a morning talk show on Minnesota AM radio station KSTP. In 1996 he appeared as a "Man in Black" in an episode of the hit sci-fi television series *The X-Files*. The following year he was reunited with Arnold Schwarzenegger, with whom he had become friends, in the film *Batman & Robin* (1997), in which Ventura had a small part as a guard in Arkham Asylum, where Schwarzenegger's character, Mr. Freeze, is imprisoned. Also in 1997 he began hosting a sports talk show on AM radio station KFAN.

In 1998, after persuasion by former Senate candidate Dean Barkley, Jesse Ventura announced that he would run for governor of the state of Minnesota. He gained the nomination of the Reform Party, which had been founded by the 1992 presidential candidate Ross Perot, and ran as the dark-horse candidate in a race that featured Republican Norm Coleman, the mayor of St. Paul, and Democrat Hubert Humphrey III, the state attorney general and the grandson of former senator and vice president Hubert H. Humphrey, who served during the administration of President Lyndon B. Johnson. At first Ventura held a distant third-place position in polls. Because of his background, his laid-back style of dress, and his lack of state-level political experience, most observers saw him as nothing more than a curiosity or fodder for stand-up comics.

Using many of the qualities that had propelled him in his wrestling career, such as showmanship, cockiness, and his charismatic way with words, Ventura began to gain the attention of voters. He emphasized that he was not a career politician and promised not to be influenced by special-interest groups, as he accused his opponents of being. He vowed to return the $4 billion state surplus to the people. His political platform defied categorization: pro-choice and pro–gay rights, but also pro-gun. Moreover, although he labeled himself a fiscal conservative, he had raised taxes each year that he was mayor of Brooklyn Park. In televised political debates, he came across as a man of the people, providing a refreshing alternative to the more conventional front-runners. His televised campaign commercials, too, were anything but run-of-the-mill; they showed him posing as Rodin's statue *The Thinker* or as what looked like an action figure battling the evil "Special Interest Man."

Ventura's no-nonsense approach and his forthright discussion of issues appealed to the citizens of Minnesota, and the tide began to change, just as it had for him during many a pro-wrestling match. On Election Day Ventura received 37 percent of the vote. Although not a majority, it exceeded what either Coleman or Humphrey had received and thus made Jesse Ventura the governor-elect of Minnesota. His victory shocked politicians and the media alike. While reporting the results on election night, a befuddled Dan Rather quipped, "The people of Washington could not be more surprised if Fidel Castro came loping across the midwestern prairie on the back of a hippopotamus." In *Time* (November 16, 1998), Garrison Keillor commented, "He glided in under the political radar." One man who was not shocked was Ventura's one-time nemesis Hulk Hogan, who told the *New York Times* (November 5, 1998), "Jesse's victory proves that people want a real man in power to lead, not a play plastic puppet like other politicians." "I simply will say that I will do the best job I am capable of doing," Ventura told a *Detroit News* (November 8, 1998) interviewer after the election. "I'm not a rebel. I'm not coming on board to create some sort of rebellion."

The bluntness that helped get him elected was displayed three weeks later, when Ventura, appearing on CNN, criticized President Bill Clinton for lying about his relationship with former White House intern Monica Lewinsky. "I frankly can't trust him again," the governor-elect told his CNN host, Wolf Blitzer. "Guess what? Keep this up and you're going to see a lot more Jesse Venturas elected around the country." His comments made front-page headlines in several newspapers nationwide.

As he had to while mayor of Brooklyn Park, Ventura as governor must grapple with partisan politics, namely a Democratic state Senate and Republican state House, neither of which have seemed eager to work with him. He must learn to work with the very "career politicians" he criticized during his campaign. "The fun is over," the political analyst Steven Schier commented in the *Detroit News* (November 8, 1998). "Now Jesse has got to lead, and . . . there is absolutely no script for him to follow." Outgoing governor Arne Carlson, who did not run for reelection, helped Ventura ease into his position, in part by allocating $50,000 for the transition and providing the governor-elect with a specially prepared transition manual. Ventura spent the weeks leading up his inauguration trying to absorb all he could about social policy and the day-to-day workings of the state government.

With his stunning victory, Ventura became the first Reform Party candidate ever elected to state or federal office, making him the party's highest-ranking member. Should Ross Perot choose not to run in the next presidential election, some supporters of Ventura's hope he will take the Reform spot on the ballot in 2000. In an appearance he made on the TV show *Lifestyles of the Rich and Famous* in 1991, when he was Brooklyn Park mayor, Ventura made the somewhat prophetic comment, "Maybe senator next. Or maybe governor. And then who knows, maybe in the year 2000 it will be Jesse Ventura for president. Now wouldn't that be something to think about?" Vince McMahon, quoted in a recent WWF press release, said, "Jesse has been talking about being president of the United States for many, many years. He was convinced he [would] be president, and maybe he will."

At the Reform Party Convention in July 1999, Ventura ruled out a run for the presidency in the year 2000. While at the convention he used his newfound political influence to propel the retired financial consultant John J. Gargan, a "noncareer politician" like Ventura, to the chairmanship of the Reform Party. Among those whom Gargan defeated in the vote for party leader was Patricia R. Benjamin, the candidate endorsed by Reform Party founder H. Ross Perot. Many observers interpreted Gargan's victory as evidence that Ventura had replaced Perot as the party's most powerful player. Ventura is also actively involved in the selection of the person who will run for president in 2000 as the Reform candidate. He has courted several possible candidates, among them former Connecticut governor Lowell P. Weicker Jr. and the billionaire real-estate developer Donald Trump.

In the summer of 1999, Ventura surprised many people when he announced that he planned to step into a wrestling ring one more time, not as a wrestler but as a referee: he had agreed to referee for the main event of the WWF's SummerSlam pay-per-view event in August. (He had served in that role during the first SummerSlam, in 1988.) The announcement was unexpected not only because of Ventura's position as an elected official but also because he had been on bad terms with Vince McMahon, the owner of WWF, since the two had parted ways in 1990. Ventura refereed a three-way match featuring "Stone Cold" Steve Austin, Hunter Hearst Helmsley, and Mankind. He donated his payment to charity but accepted copyright royalties for the use of his name. While approval ratings for the governor remained high among Minnesotans, the mainstream media criticized Ventura's involvement in SummerSlam.

The close media scrutiny to which Ventura has been subjected since his election intensified following the publication of an interview with the governor that appeared in the November 1999 issue of the popular men's magazine *Playboy*. Ventura made several controversial statements during the interview, the most incendiary of which was his assertion that "organized religion is a sham and a crutch for weak-minded people who need strength in numbers." Immediately after publication of his remarks, Ventura's approval ratings among Minnesotans dropped by 20 percent. Another consequence was that Reform Party chairman Russell J. Verney (who remained in his post until the end of 1999) called for Ventura's immediate resignation from the party. The governor has refused to comply with Verney's demand.

Ventura's autobiography, *I Ain't Got Time to Bleed: Reworking the Body Politic from the Bottom Up*, was published in mid-1999. The book (the title of which is derived from one of Ventura's lines in the movie *Predator*) includes his recollections of his wrestling career, the story of his rise to the governorship of Minnesota, and discussions of his political beliefs and objectives. It also includes such potentially scandalous disclosures as his admission of having used marijuana and having patronized (legally) a prostitute in Nevada—revelations that the media soon disseminated.

Jesse Ventura is a member of the board of advisers to the Minnesota chapter of the Make-a-Wish Foundation. He is also an active member of the Screen Actors Guild and has been a member of the American Federation of Television and Radio Announcers for more than 10 years. Since 1995 he has volunteered as the coach of the Park High School football team in Champlin, Minnesota. He and his wife, Terry, who operates a riding school at the couple's horse farm, have been married since 1976; they have one son, Tyrel, born in 1979, and one daughter, Jade, born in 1983.— B.S.

Suggested Reading: *American Journalism Review* p54+ Sep. 1999; *Detroit News* (on-line) November 8, 1998; *Internet Movie Database* Nov. 25, 1998; *KFAN* (on-line) Nov. 25, 1998; *New York Review of Books* p40+ Aug. 12, 1999; *New York Times* (on-line) Nov. 5, 1998; *Newsweek* p36+ Oct. 11, 1999; *Time* (on-line) Nov. 16, 1998; Lentz III, Harris M. *Biographical Dictionary of Professional Wrestling*, 1997; *1998 Wrestling Almanac and Book of Facts*

Selected Films: *Predator*, 1987; *The Running Man*, 1987; *No Holds Barred*, 1989; *Repossessed*, 1990; *Abraxas, Guardian of the Universe*, 1991; *Ricochet*, 1991; *Demolition Man*, 1993; *Major League II*, 1994; *Batman & Robin*, 1997

Selected Books: *I Ain't Got Time to Bleed: Reworking the Body Politic from the Bottom Up*, 1999

Courtesy of Columbia Artists Management, Inc.

Voigt, Deborah
(voyt)

1960(?)– Opera singer. Address: c/o Metropolitan Opera, Lincoln Center, New York, NY 10023

The remarkably broad repertoire of the celebrated soprano Deborah Voigt includes leading roles in operas by Verdi, Wagner, and Strauss. Of the three, she seems to have the greatest affinity for Strauss; indeed, her voice is often described as Straussian—meaning that it is as powerful, clear, and bright as the compositions of the early-20th-century German composer Richard Strauss. One of Voigt's signature roles is Ariadne in Strauss's *Ariadne auf Naxos*. A flattering review of her 1991 performance of Ariadne with the Boston Lyric Opera prompted many of the world's most prestigious opera companies to take notice of her. "It was an almost total fluke," Voigt recalled to F. Paul Driscoll for *Opera News* (March 14, 1998). The music critic "John Rockwell just happened to be in Boston and wrote a review for me in the *New York Times* that was to die for. I'd like to think I deserved it. My mother couldn't have written anything nicer." Shortly after that, the Metropolitan Opera, in New York City, cast her in the role of Chrysothemis in *Elektra*, another Strauss opera. Within two years, Voigt had debuted at several of Europe's prominent opera houses as well. "That's when things started to turn a little faster for me," she told Driscoll. But not too quickly, she added. "Twenty-two years of vocal study doesn't seem quick to me."

Deborah Voigt was born in about 1960 on the outskirts of Chicago. As a child she sang in the choir of the Baptist church to which her parents belonged. "I was one of those little girls who put on the record of *My Fair Lady* and danced around the living room," she told Anthony Tommasini for the *New York Times* (April 27, 1997). Voigt studied voice, piano, and guitar, and she starred in many theatrical productions at her high school. Often, when practicing singing in her room, she would try to drown out the sound of her brothers' rock-'n'-roll jam sessions in the garage. Her devotion to singing notwithstanding, as a girl Voigt never thought about becoming an opera singer. "I don't even think I knew what the Metropolitan Opera was until I was in my late teens," she told Driscoll. "And if I did, it was just sort of a vague notion that this thing called opera was something that other people did." She did, however, thoroughly enjoy the study of music. "[I] loved the process of learning an instrument. I guess opera was a natural road to follow, because of the intense study involved."

After graduating from high school, Voigt enrolled at Chapman College, in Orange, California, with the intention of majoring in choral conducting. She soon began to have trouble controlling her weight—a problem that persisted until recently. By her own account, she "wasn't happy" at Chapman, and after a few semesters, she left the school and took a job as a computer operator. "I worked full time at that for a couple of years, but I knew I had to sing," she told Driscoll. "I'd sit at the computer for eight hours a day and then run off and have voice lessons at night at Robert Schuller's church, the Crystal Cathedral, [where] I had a voice scholarship." Eventually, Voigt said, she realized that she "had been given a gift that [she] couldn't ignore," and she returned to college. This time, she chose California State at Fullerton, because, she told Driscoll, "it was nearby, and because I could afford it."

At Fullerton, Voigt began training with the voice coach Jane Paul, who became a great inspiration to her. During her eight years of training with Paul she also enrolled in the Merola Program at the San Francisco Opera, in which vocal students would understudy for featured artists at the opera. The students would also take smaller parts in the company's productions. Merola enrollees all lived together in a large, Victorian-style house that was nicknamed "DIT House," because its inhabitants were "divas in training."

Ariadne auf Naxos, in which Voigt sang with the Boston Lyric Opera in 1991, presents a tragic story within a comic setting. A wealthy resident of Vienna, Austria, is hosting a party at his home, and for entertainment, he decides to offer both a young composer's tragic opera, *Ariadne auf Naxos*, and a show by a comedy troupe. The two productions are staged simultaneously so that the evening's fireworks show can begin on schedule. Voigt has portrayed Ariadne several times, and each time, to greater acclaim. As Anthony Tommasini wrote for the *New York Times* (September 26, 1997), "Voigt's temperament helps out. . . . She is a down-to-earth American who doesn't take herself too seriously, a quality that comes through touchingly in her portrayal. In the great soliloquy, when Ariadne, deserted by beloved Theseus on the isle of Naxos, sings of her betrayal and death wish, Ms. Voigt fills the phrases with sumptuous sound, gleaming high notes, a consistency of delivery down to her chesty low tones, and astonishing breath control. But as the clown and dancers poke from behind the sets to see why this strange lady is so upset, Ms. Voigt, endearingly, lets herself be made fun of." "Ariadne is a magnificent role," the soprano told Tommasini. "I especially love it because it gives me a chance to be silly."

Shortly after doing her first *Ariadne auf Naxos*, in Boston, Voigt found herself in great demand. Within about two years of making her Metropolitan Opera debut, in 1991, she had performed lead roles in productions at La Scala, in Milan; the Opera de la Bastille, in Paris; Covent Garden, in London; the Vienna State Opera; and the Arena, in Verona, Italy. In 1992, in a new version of Strauss's *Elektra*, staged at New York's Metropolitan Opera, Voigt gave such a stunning performance in the role of Chrysothemis that she was said to have outshone the legendary opera singers Leonie Rysanek and Hildegard Beherens. She had yet to shed the weight she had gained years earlier, however, and—the stereotype of the overweight opera singer notwithstanding—her size prevented her from being cast in some roles to which she would otherwise have been well suited. In an interview with Walter Price for *Opera News* (February 15, 1992), Voigt said that there was "at least one company that has shown very little interest in me because of my size." "One would have thought this wonderful success would have been a catalyst to do something about myself physically," she acknowledged to Tommasini at a later date. "But I fought it for so long. It's easy to get wrapped up thinking, 'I'm a great singer, and that's what's most important.' Unfortunately, this is not the society we live in."

After subjecting herself to several fad diets, Voigt shed 80 pounds in 1996 by combining a healthy diet with exercise. She told Tommasini, "I feel vastly improved. I communicate better. I'm much freer on stage. It's great to not worry about flinging myself on the floor." Regarding the widely held notion that overweight singers have better voices, she explained, "Many of our great dramatic voices of the past have not been small people. But there is a difference between someone who is big-boned or big-statured and someone whose eating habits are out of control." Voigt also explained why losing weight seems to affect the voices of many previously overweight singers: "There is a natural support mechanism built in by carrying extra weight around your middle," she said. "If you don't know how to control those muscles, when the weight is gone, then that becomes a problem." Voigt did not have that problem, and her voice was unaffected by the loss in weight.

One of the roles for which Voigt was preparing while she was concentrating on losing weight was that of Sieglinde, the heroine of Richard Wagner's opera *Die Walküre* (a part of Wagner's *Ring Cycle*). According to Tommasini, Voigt felt that, psychologically, she had a great deal in common with Sieglinde. The daughter of the god Wotan and a mortal woman, Sieglinde is kidnapped as a child and raised by a group of bandits. When she is older, she is forced to marry a particularly vile outlaw. "She is bullied and laughed at," Voigt told Tommasini. "She is trapped in a situation where she can't express any of the specialness she feels in herself." Through a long chain of fateful events, Sieglinde comes to understand who she truly is. It would appear that Voigt's experience in overcoming her weight problem helped her to more deeply understand Seiglinde's struggle for self-discovery.

In the last few years, Voigt has appeared in a new interpretation of Wagner's *Lohengrin* at the Metropolitan Opera and a concert version of the rarely performed Strauss opera *Die Aegyptische Helena*, at both the Met and Lincoln Center for the Performing Arts, in New York City. The soprano told Driscoll that she begins preparing for roles as much as two years before she actually performs them. First, she translates into English the parts she will sing so that the story makes sense to her. Then she turns her attention to the music. "I have pretty good piano skills, so I tend to teach myself the basics—try to figure out what's going on harmonically and so forth," she said. "Then I take it to a coach—and if I am in New York, usually [the Metropolitan Opera's] Walter Taussig." Voight has been known to work with a drama coach as well. While German operas predominate on her résumé, Voight told Driscoll that she enjoys doing Italian works as well, because they help her maintain her technique. "Being able to sing the Verdi roles that are particularly high keeps my voice more youthful and more flexible than if I were to have a steady diet of just Strauss and Wagner," she said. "[Italian repertory] makes so many requirements of me vocally that I have to stay in shape if I want to continue in it." In 1997 Voight played the title role in Verdi's *Aïda*, opposite the renowned Placido Domingo, who has praised her singing highly. "The legato line is so true and lovely," he said to Tommasini. "The voice is unbelievable. When she sings a phrase . . . , it becomes part of me."

"I'm constantly amazed at how much work there is in an opera career, and how little of the work is actually singing," the singer told Driscoll. "Being on stage is the fun part, believe me. Whether it's interviews . . . or spending an hour and a half having my head molded for my *Lohengrin* wig, there are a lot of tougher things that go into it." In addition to performing, Voight spends a lot of time teaching music to children and teenagers whose schools do not offer music as part of their curricula. "These are precious little kids," she told Driscoll. "They run up and hug me—and that's because I'm the music lady, not because I'm Debbie Voigt the opera singer."

Driscoll described Voigt as "witty, articulate, and levelheaded, proud of her successes, yet free of the stuffiness that can infect prima donnas on the rise. Her conversation is self-edited with admirable political savvy." She and her husband, John Leitch, who helps manage her career, live in Jupiter, on the east coast of Florida. Among her awards and honors are the first prize at the 1988 Luciano Pavarotti Voice Competition, the gold medal at the 1990 Tchaikovsky International Competition, and the 1992 Richard Tucker Award. — C.P.

Suggested Reading: *New York Times* II p29 Apr. 27, 1997, with photo, E p6 Sep. 26, 1997, with photo; *Opera News* p34 Feb. 15, 1992, with photo, p8+ Mar. 14, 1998, with photos

Selected Recordings: *Ariadne auf Naxos*, 1991; *Elektra*, 1992; *Die Walküre*, 1996; *Aïda*, 1997; *Lohengrin*, 1998; *Die Aegyptische Helena*, 1998

Courtesy of Alonzo Washington

Washington, Alonzo

1968– Comic-book artist; writer; publisher.
Address: c/o Omega 7 Inc., P.O. Box 171046, Kansas City, KS 66117

The writer and illustrator Alonzo Washington is the founder of the most prosperous African-American comic-book company ever. His series *Omega Man* has helped transform his fledgling company, Omega 7 Inc., into a business with worldwide sales of more than one million. Recalling his reasons for creating *Omega Man*, first published in 1992, Washington told Gerda Gallop for *Black Enterprise* (November 1998), "I saw a lack of positive black role models in any fictional area in comic books and fantasy characters. [Black comic-book characters] were either side-kicks, ex-cons, or something negative. With my product, I knew I was going to break stereotypes and address social issues. I wanted to educate and enlighten African American youth." The popularity of Omega Man and of that character's ever-growing universe of cohorts, who are now the eponymous heroes of such popular magazines as *The Mighty Ace*, *Dark Queen*, and *Original Man*, are a testament to Washington's creativity, attention to current social issues and cultural trends, and knowledge of African and African-American history. "We need glorified Black images for our youth," Washington told Hilary L. Hurd for *Emerge* (July/August 1998). "My comics will always promote [the belief] that [African-Americans] will make it in the future."

Alonzo L. Washington was born in 1968 in Kansas City, Kansas. His parents divorced when he was very young, and he was raised primarily by his mother, Millie, who worked as a preschool teacher.

As a child, Alonzo was a big fan of comic books, but when he was in the fifth grade, he became fed up with them, because none of his favorite magazines included a prominent black superhero. "Even as a child I realized that the African American characters in popular culture were people I really didn't want to grow up and be like," he told Jack Mingo for the *Washington Post* (July 13, 1998). "For the most part, they were either demons or clowns, either someone to get killed, or say something stupid like 'Dyn-O-mite!'" Things were not much better in the comic-book universe. "At worst [black comic-book characters] were side-kicks or stereotypes," Washington told Mingo. "At best, they were like Superman dipped in chocolate—not really African American." During his elementary-school years, Alonzo began drawing black superhero comics, selling copies to friends and acquaintances for a quarter apiece. Sometimes he would draw his comics while in class, and then, he told Mingo, "I'd get in trouble because other kids would want to buy them." As he got older Alonzo also began to develop a strong interest in preventing crime—he and his friends took to calling themselves "anti-crime activists"—and after graduating from high school, he created and hosted his own cable TV show, with the aim of presenting positive role models for local underprivileged kids. When the show flopped, Washington was forced to find another route to reach the children.

By the early 1990s Washington had become heavily involved in community activism, spending many hours at local community centers in Kansas City. It was there, in 1991, that he launched his first fully-realized comic book, *Original Man*. Intended as a one-time-only publication to help build African-American children's self-esteem, *Original Man* turned into an overnight sensation with Kansas City youths, and soon the kids were asking Washington to produce a follow-up issue. Inspired by the reactions of his readers, in early 1992 Alonzo began talking to comic-book companies about publishing a full-fledged title with a black superhero as its star. His pitches, however, were met with lukewarm responses; publishers simply did not believe the idea would sell. Undeterred, Washington and his wife, Dana, began producing the comic book themselves. The magazine now featured a new character based on a composite sketch of heroes Washington had drawn in the past. Soon, while Dana, Washington's mother, and a few freelance artists stayed behind to produce the work, Washington hit the road to promote his yet-to-be-published comic book. After talking with various vendors and collectors, Washington, to his surprise, found himself with hundreds of advance orders for the first issue.

Orders continued to pour in as news of the book spread by word of mouth, and within a few months, advance sales had topped $1,000. Reinvesting the money in his project, Washington made a down payment on a print run of 5,000 copies of the first installment. Christened *Omega Man*,

Washington's comic book—whose hero was dressed in red, black, and yellow—became an immediate success among fans of independent comic titles. A visitor from the future, in which racism, crime, and drug abuse do not exist, Omega Man battles villains—such as an army of white-supremacist time travelers—who seek to alter history to prevent the glorious times ahead. After a whirlwind campaign of promotional book signings, sales of the book soon reached well over 5,000 copies, and Washington ordered another printing of 10,000 copies. Diamond Comics, the same company that distributes *Batman* and *Superman* comic books for DC Comics, caught wind of *Omega Man's* success and provided nationwide distribution of the title. This vote of confidence inspired Washington and his creative team to develop even more titles under the auspices of Omega 7 Inc., as he dubbed his production company, and by 1995 the firm was publishing four different titles.

"Alonzo has a good social conscience, and he puts it in his comics," Diamond Comics distributor James Eisele told *People* (April 14, 1997). "We can make money *and* do society good." After this initial success, Alonzo and Dana Washington began to tailor some of the story lines to coincide with controversial world events. In one issue of *Omega Man*, for example, the hero has the chance to save the lives of Nicole Brown Simpson and Ron Goldman, the real-life victims of the killings that sparked the racially divisive O. J. Simpson murder case. Another finds Omega Man on hand at the Million Man March.

In 1997 Omega 7 Inc. made history by becoming the first black-owned comic-book company to market an action figure. Produced in association with a Hong Kong toy manufacturer, two versions of the Omega Man figure were sold—one with light skin and one with dark skin, both with distinctly African facial features and hair. "I thought it was important to have full lips and a wide nose," Washington told Mingo. "His braid on the back of his head symbolizes African royalty." Sales of the figure were brisk, and Toys 'R' Us, the only major chain to pick up the figure, ordered an additional 100 dozen within the first few months of the toy's release. Wal-Mart and Big K-Mart, two powerful national chains—both with heavily advertised campaigns referred to as "vendor diversity programs," which are designed to promote the purchase of minority-owned companies' products—opted out of selling the toy. Washington told Mingo, "Ironically, it seems like the stores that talk the most about their vendor diversity programs have been hardest to sell." Toys 'R' Us, by contrast, flew Washington to many stores nationwide to help promote the product. During this time, in early 1998, Washington was able to observe trends among toy customers. "A lot of African Americans and some Caucasians want to present a positive, uplifting African American image to their kids," he told Mingo. "It's interesting that Hispanics and Asians often buy the lighter-colored doll for their own kids. . . . [But often white parents] almost snatch their [children's] arm out of the socket to get [the toy] away. It's almost like they'd rather their kids would be following a Satan-worshiping white rock star than a strong, moral, black image. It's the insanity of racism. Still, when white kids tell me, 'I want to be like Omega Man,' I know I've created a true hero."

By early 1999, with total company sales quickly approaching one million and the company worth over $1 million, Omega 7 Inc. boasted the production of nine separate titles—*Omega Man, The Omega 7, Dark Queen, Dark Force, Lady Ace, The Mighty Ace, Original Man, Original Boy,* and *Original Woman,* whose main character is loosely based on Dana Washington. When asked what gave him the idea to produce a comic book based on his own wife, who works as an HIV-education counselor, Washington told Wendy M. Beech for *Black Enterprise* (May 1997), "My wife responds to a community crisis like a real superhero. She dresses up as Original Woman and goes to schools, talks to kids and tells them to stay off drugs." Dana recently gave birth to the couple's sixth child, a girl; the couple's five sons, ranging in age from two to 11, remain Washington's initial test-marketing group. "If I'm working and they won't stop looking over my shoulder or stop asking questions about it, then I know I've come up with something good," he told Mingo. "When I had the prototype for the Omega

Man action figure, I knew it was going to be a good thing because they kept asking . . . to play with it."

Currently, Washington illustrates his publications with the help of staff and freelance artists. He does most of the writing, with occasional contributions from his wife and the artists. He has an array of projects in the works, among them the release of a new action figure, the Mighty Ace, early in 2000. Movie companies have contacted Washington many times about producing a film based on his characters, but he has thus far rejected all offers, because he believes that many of the ideas presented would detract from Omega Man's moral image. (One studio, for example, suggested that the character be made into an ex-convict.) "I want to see Omega Man treated seriously. Not a parody, not a campy comedy," Washington told Mingo. "We have enough black jokers already." — M.B.

Suggested Reading: *Black Enterprise* p29+ May 1997, with photo, p115+ Nov. 1998, with photos; *Emerge* p14 July/Aug. 1998, with photo; *People* p102 Apr. 14, 1997, with photo; *Washington Post* D p4 July 13, 1998, with photo

Selected Comics: *Original Man; Original Boy; Original Woman; Omega Man; The Omega 7; Dark Queen; Dark Force; Lady Ace; The Mighty Ace*

Watts, J. C. Jr.

Nov. 18, 1957– United States Representative from Oklahoma. Address: 1210 Longworth House Office Bldg., Washington, DC 20515

To many onlookers the conservatism of Republican congressman J. C. Watts Jr. seems incongruous with his having been raised in a poor, segregated small town in Oklahoma. Watts, however, feels that his values are an integral part of who he is. "To me, 'conservative' doesn't mean Republican or Democrat," he was quoted as saying by Patrick Rogers for *People* (March 24, 1997). "It means the way my mama and daddy raised me. . . . By God, you were going to work and be in church on Sunday. You were going to go to school and act civilized." Raised in a thoroughly Democratic family and once a member of the Democratic Party himself, Watts told Lois Romano for the *Washington Post* (December 2, 1994), "I didn't become a conservative just to please the Republican Party. I felt this way even when I was a Democrat." Watts is currently the only African-American member of Congress who is a Republican, and in November 1998, when he was elected to the position of Republican Conference Chair, he became the first African-American in more than 50 years to be elected to a leadership position in the Republican Party. "It is

Courtesy of U.S. House of Representatives

time to let the American people know that the Republican Party is the party of all Americans," Watts said, as quoted by Edward Walsh for the *Washing-*

ton Post (November 17, 1998) at the time of his election. "We are the party of inclusiveness. Our ideas are good for everyone."

Julius Caesar Watts Jr. was born on November 18, 1957 and was raised in Eufaula, Oklahoma, a town with a population of about 3,000, where white and black people lived in separate areas. He is the fifth of "Buddy" and Helen Watts's six children. His father, who never completed high school, raised cattle and worked as a police officer to support his family; he was also a Baptist minister. "My papa always said that the only helping hand you can rely on is at the end of your sleeve," Watts told Amy Waldman for the *Washington Monthly* (October 1996), explaining how he had learned conservative values from a politically liberal family. J. C.'s uncle Wade Watts was president of the Oklahoma chapter of the National Association for the Advancement of Colored People (NAACP) for 16 years and, as Watts told Romano, "produced more voters for the Oklahoma Democratic Party than any one single person." As president of the NAACP, Wade Watts also led the fight for the admittance of the first African-American student to the University of Oklahoma's law school.

J. C. Watts was one of only two black students to attend Eufaula's Jefferson Davis Elementary School. A few years later, he became the first African-American to play quarterback for his high school's football team, fostering a resentment that led several of the school's white players to boycott the team. Before graduating from high school, Watts fathered a child, whom Wade Watts eventually adopted and raised so that his nephew could pursue a college education. After being offered football scholarships by several colleges, Watts decided on the University of Oklahoma, in Norman. In 1980 and 1981 he led their football team, the Sooners, to victory in the Orange Bowl and was named most valuable player in both years. According to Amy Waldman, the seeds of Watts's political views were planted in 1980, when, as a journalism major, he wrote about a Senate campaign debate and found himself in agreement with the Republican, Don Nickels.

After graduating from college, Watts received an offer to play professional football with the New York Jets. He was disappointed, however, that he was not offered a quarterback position, so he decided to play pro ball in Canada instead. After six seasons in the Canadian league, Watts returned to Oklahoma, where he invested his money in real estate and petroleum businesses. Most of his investments turned out badly, and by the early 1990s, he had a number of outstanding debts on his hands, including some unpaid state and federal taxes. Around this time Watts took up preaching and public speaking, working as a youth minister at a mostly white church in Norman and taking on other public speaking engagements. He was ordained as a Baptist minister in 1993.

In 1989 Watts officially became a member of the Republican Party. Among the reasons for his decision to change affiliations, according to Waldman, was Watts's belief that public-assistance programs, which had for many years been the Democrats' chief means of dealing with poverty, fostered a dangerous level of dependence among disadvantaged minority peoples. "In the past 30 years, I do not believe the Democrats have done anything to empower the black people," he told Waldman. "There is a place for public assistance, but I believe it perpetuates a lifestyle." Attempting to explain why African-Americans are sometimes overlooked in the campaign process, Watts said, "Democrats just don't pay attention because [African-Americans] are already the most loyal voting bloc in the ranks. And the Republicans have said, 'We don't have to pay attention because they vote Democrat.'" "I want to change all that," he added. Watts's decision to become a Republican was a huge disappointment to his uncle, Wade Watts, who felt that "the ease with which J. C. Watts has made his way in the world also made it easy to turn his back on the party that helped smooth his passage," Amy Waldman reported.

In 1990 Watts was elected to one of the three seats on Oklahoma's corporation commission, which regulates the operations of utility companies in the state. He thus became the first African-American to be elected to state-wide office in Oklahoma, a highly conservative state. (In Oklahoma both Democrats and Republicans tend to be conservative on social issues; the main difference between the two major parties there is that the Democrats generally take on issues that are of concern to the working class, while the Republicans focus more on the interests of large corporations that do business there.) According to Waldman, Watts's work on the corporation commission was "particularly industry friendly."

In 1994 Watts decided to run for the seat from Oklahoma's Fourth Congressional District, and his popularity was evident in even the earliest polls. Watts based his campaign on the notion—popular among Republicans—that the welfare system, as it then existed, needed to undergo drastic change in order for people to become independent of social services. He called the system "sick" and "pathetic," saying that he preferred real "opportunity" to welfare for the underprivileged. Another important part of Watts's platform was his support for cuts in capital-gains taxes; such measures would, he said, indirectly benefit poor, working minorities by stimulating industry. According to Waldman, Watts also stood with many Republicans in repudiating abortion rights, gun control, and gay rights.

Aided by strong endorsements in the Christian Coalition's voters' guides, Watts won the November election—against the Democratic nominee, David Perryman—by a nine-point margin. He thus became one of only two African-American Republicans to be elected to Congress since the Reconstruction period in the U.S. (1865–77), which followed the Civil War. (The first, Representative Gary Franks of Connecticut, was defeated in his 1996 reelection bid. The first African-American representative in U.S. history was Joseph Hayne Rainey, a South Carolina Republican who served from late 1870 to 1879. The Republican Party attracted African-Americans during Reconstruction because it was the party of Abraham Lincoln.) Five days after being elected, Watts was asked to deliver the Republicans' response to President Clinton's post-election radio address. According to Waldman, Watts announced early on that he would not join the (solidly Democratic) Congressional Black Caucus, saying, "My father raised me to be a man, not a black man."

One of the few subjects on which Watts disagrees with the majority of Republicans in the House, and one of the major issues with which he dealt during his freshman term in Congress, is that of affirmative action. While most Republicans would like to do away in one fell swoop with what they term "quotas" for minority and female employees and students, Watts favors dismantling affirmative action gradually. He told Steven A. Holmes for the New York Times (August 6, 1995) that while he believes "affirmative action as we know it today" to be "on its last legs," he also told Kevin Merida for the Washington Post (July 29, 1995) that to end affirmative-action measures too abruptly would cause "war between men and women, black and white." As co-chair of the House minority issues task force (a position for which Newt Gingrich, then the House Speaker, had nominated him), Watts voted against a Republican-sponsored bill that sought to eliminate guarantees that female and minority-owned businesses would receive a certain percentage of federal contracts. Other actions by Watts during his first term that were considered out of step with the Republican Party were his signing of a document, drafted by TransAfrica, that protested human rights violations in Nigeria, and his support of congressional efforts to rebuild torched African-American churches in the South. He voted with the majority of his party in favor of cutting federal funding for Head Start, a program for underprivileged preschoolers; Medicaid; school lunch programs; and student loan and grant programs.

In Watts's view, one of the ways that the government can foster independence among people who rely on welfare or other forms of federal aid is to improve the communities in which they live. In 1997, the first year of his second term in Congress, Watts co-authored, with Jim Talent of Missouri, the American Community Renewal Act. According to Waldman, the idea behind the bill was to "strengthen civil society in low-income areas" by funding school-voucher programs that would enable poor kids to go to private schools and by subsidizing church-based substance-abuse programs. The proposed measures struck many representatives as too expensive, and the bill failed to pass. During the same year, Watts voted against a Repub-

lican bill that sought to end all federal aid to institutions of higher education that practiced affirmative action in admitting students.

In February 1997 Watts was chosen to deliver the Republican response to President Clinton's State of the Union Address, which, among other issues, raised the subject of the federal welfare program. While Watts's speech was generally thought to be effective and moving, it was largely overshadowed by a comment that he had made a few days earlier to the Washington Post. Referring to a number of African-American Democrats who supported welfare, he described them as "race-hustling poverty pimps." Speaking in a far more benign manner in his televised address, Watts said, "Government can't ease all pain. In fact, government sometimes rubs the wound raw and makes the healing harder." It was also during this speech that Watts first used an expression for which he has become well known: "Character is doing what's right when nobody's looking."

In 1998, after winning reelection to his seat in Congress with 66 percent of the vote, Watts made a successful bid for the newly vacant position of chair of the House Republican Conference. In doing so he became the first African-American Republican to hold a leadership position in Congress. "I'm excited about everybody working together as a team to make sure that we cut people's taxes, that we strengthen our national defense, that we strengthen Social Security, we continue working on a health-care system to make it better," he was quoted as saying by David Stout for the New York Times (November 19, 1998, on-line). Watts also said that he would like to regenerate interest in some of the ideas included in the American Community Renewal Act, such as tax breaks for companies that invest in low-income areas and church-sponsored social services.

In response to assertions that the Republican Party, which is markedly short on African-American members, has cast Watts in high-profile roles to give the appearance of diversity, Watts told Edward Walsh, "I'm surely not running as a black candidate. I'm running as a Republican. But I can assure you that if [the Republican] vision for the future doesn't include me, I'm going to be somewhat apprehensive about [their] message. That's the way many minorities feel. I've talked to them."

J. C. Watts is married to Frankie Jones, whom he met at his eighth birthday party. They have five children. Watts spends his workweek in a small apartment in Washington, D.C., and flies home to Oklahoma each weekend to be with his family. "I want to be in my church on Sundays and be in my own bed on Fridays," he told Lois Romano. Rich Galen, who is the communications director of the National Republican Congressional Committee, told Katharine Q. Seelye for the New York Times (February 5, 1997, on-line), "[Watts] represents what most Republicans want most people to think the Republican Party is—young, smart, he made his own way, he's well educated, and he works hard to help people solve their problems." Florida congressman Bill McCollum told John F. Dickerson for *CNN.com* (November 23, 1998, on-line), "He just exudes, 'I care for you.'"

Although when he was initially elected to Congress, Watts said that he would not serve more than three terms, he has recently reconsidered his promise. As he explained to Edward Walsh, there aren't "a whole lot of folks" who want him to leave. — C.P.

Suggested Reading: *CNN.com* (on-line) Nov. 23, 1998; *New York Times* p22 Aug. 6, 1995, with photo; *New York Times* (on-line) Feb. 5, 1997, Nov. 16, 1998, Nov. 19, 1998; *People* p141+ Mar. 24, 1997, with photos; *Washington Monthly* p34+ Oct. 1996; *Washington Post* F p3 Dec. 2, 1994, with photos, A p4 July 29, 1995, with photo; *Washington Post* (on-line) Nov. 17, 1998

Archive Photos

Wayans, Damon

Sep. 4, 1960– Comedian; actor; writer. Address: c/o Wife & Kid Productions, 102202 W. Washington Blvd., Culver City, CA 90232

For Damon Wayans, comedy is truth and has the power to serve as a social and personal conscience. "In olden times, only the jester could talk about the king," Wayans explained to Veronica Chambers for *Essence* (August 1992). "He could talk about how greedy the king was, how fat and ugly he was, and everybody would laugh. Comedians are one of the few groups of people who can tell the truth." Truth is, Wayans is one of the funniest and most original

comedic voices to hail from the small screen in the past decade. After working for some time as a stand-up comedian, Wayans burst into national recognition in 1990, as a cast member of the television series *In Living Color*, a controversial sketch-comedy program on the Fox Network developed by his brother Keenan Ivory Wayans. The weekly, half-hour show, which had a format similar to that of *Saturday Night Live* but featured a predominantly black cast, offered outrageous skit humor with an urban edge and scored a hit with audiences across racial lines. A gifted mimic and talented creator of characters, Wayans quickly distinguished himself among the cast with such popular personas as the mirthless Homey the Clown, whose catch-phrase was "Homey don't play that"; Anton the Bum, who gave Bob Villa–like tours of his cardboard box; and the handicapped superhero Handi-Man. Since he ended his stint on the show, in 1992, Wayans has starred in several successful films, some of which he also wrote, and he occasionally returns to his entertainment roots in stand-up comedy, which he still considers a stabilizing force in his life. "In my comedy I deal with fear; my fears and my weaknesses," Wayans told Lewis Beale for the New York *Daily News* (August 14, 1994). "I always play the underdog, because I identify. It comes down to low self-esteem, and I had that as a child."

One of 10 children, Damon Wayans was born on September 4, 1960 in the New York City borough of Manhattan. Growing up in the Fulton housing project, on 16th Street and Ninth Avenue in Manhattan's Chelsea district, was not easy; growing up with a misshapen foot harnessed in a leg brace made it even harder. An introverted child, Wayans was often targeted by neighborhood bullies because of his deformity, which was later corrected by surgery. He learned to disarm his persecutors with caustic humor. "It made me an observer, an observer with a running commentary," he told Beale. "I learned at a very young age, because this [brace] was so real to me, I would have to find something that another person found sacred to them, like their mother being the biggest whore in the neighborhood, and bring it up. . . . And everybody knew it and wouldn't say it. So I was respected." Though Wayans grew up in a loving home, life with his family was in some ways just as difficult. His mother, Elvira, who earned a college degree in social services after raising her 10 children, and his father, Howell, a supermarket manager and novelty salesman, were strict disciplinarians, particularly since Howell Wayans was a devout Jehovah's Witness. "Tough love" begot tough humor among the siblings, as Damon Wayans explained to Veronica Chambers: "We used to play a game called Make Me Laugh or Die."

As he gained the respect of his peers, Wayans began to hang out with some of the toughs who had once picked on him. He also started to get into trouble; he was expelled from school in the ninth grade, and on occasion he committed petty larceny. Despite his foray into delinquency, his home life remained strict: he always had to be back in the apartment by a certain time. "I was a criminal with a curfew," Wayans quipped to Kevin O'Sullivan for the New York *Daily News* (March 19, 1995). Wayans has admitted, from hindsight, that at the bottom of his mischief was a deep-seeded insecurity. "I put my parents through a lot because I was trying to prove I was as tough as everybody else," he told O'Sullivan. "But my parents gave me a strong sense of morality and justice and in the end my conscience wouldn't allow me to hurt them anymore."

Wayans's first job—counselor at a summer youth program—gave him a new sense of responsibility as well as pride in earning a weekly paycheck. Half of the money went directly to his parents. ("That's when I first learned what it was like to have an agent!" he joked to O'Sullivan.) That sense of responsibility carried over to other parts of his life. He earned his graduate equivalency diploma and obtained his first full-time job, at a McDonald's, where in short order he was promoted to manager. He used his newfound clout to give jobs to all his friends, but then had to fire almost half of them for stealing food from the franchise. He later worked as a mail-room supervisor at American Express.

Beginning in 1982, Wayans turned his observant eye inward, to make comedy out of the things most sacred to him; thus comedy became a vehicle to his self-discovery. Wayans started performing stand-up at the Good Times comedy club in New York City. At first his routines resonated with personal themes. For instance, according to Allan Johnson for the *Chicago Tribune* (October 27, 1989), the opening joke for his first sets was, "I'm from a poor family. We were so poor that my father drove a 1974 Big Wheel." But as his career progressed and he worked gigs in clubs throughout the country, Wayans learned to add a street-wise edge to his humor: "I like to see white bums, but I only give them money if they denounce their race." His first film break came in 1984, with a bit part in Eddie Murphy's hit comedy *Beverly Hills Cop*. In the following year Wayans parlayed his stage and film experience into a job in television, as a cast member of NBC's perennial hit *Saturday Night Live*. His tenure with the program ended after about a year, when he was fired for changing characters in mid-broadcast. For his next project he hooked up with actor and filmmaker Robert Townsend, landing a role in the movie *Hollywood Shuffle* (1987), which Townsend directed and co-wrote with Keenan Ivory Wayans. The film, a comedic look at the troubles faced by black actors trying to succeed in Hollywood, received positive critical attention and was almost guaranteed to make a profit, given that it had to earn a mere $100,000 at the box office to break even. Over the next two years, Townsend cast Damon Wayans in two of his television specials, *Take No Prisoners* and *The Mutiny Has Just Begun*. Meanwhile, Wayans's mainstream film ca-

reer began to build, with speaking parts in such films as *Roxanne* (1987), starring Steve Martin, *Colors* (1988), which featured Sean Penn and Robert Duvall, and *Punchline* (1989), with Tom Hanks and Sally Field. He also received larger supporting roles, in *I'm Gonna Git You Sucka* (1988), written by and starring Keenan Ivory Wayans, and as the voice of Eddie in *Look Who's Talking Too* (1990). In his first featured role, Wayans appeared as a sex-starved alien in *Earth Girls Are Easy* (1989), which co-starred Jeff Goldblum, Geena Davis, and Jim Carrey. (Struck by Carrey's talent, Wayans later recommended him to his older brother for *In Living Color*.)

Fox Broadcasting executives were so impressed by *I'm Gonna Git You Sucka* that they offered Keenan his own television show. The result, *In Living Color*, which debuted in April 1990, was a true family affair. In addition to Keenan, who was the show's creator and executive producer, and Damon, who performed in many skits and co-wrote much of the material with his older brother, the show employed the talents of the eldest Wayans brother, Dwayne, who served as production assistant; Shawn, who was the show's disc jockey; sister Kim, an actress; and the youngest sibling, Marlon, who joined the cast later. However, it was Damon who attracted the most attention, for his frenetic and brazen characters. Not all of the attention amounted to praise; he drew attacks from those who perceived his humor as offensive. In particular, many found abhorrent his portrayal of Blaine Edwards, a member of the flamboyantly homosexual film-reviewing duo Men on Film. (In those sketches he played opposite David Alan Grier.) "You can't care what the critics say," Wayans told Veronica Chambers in response to the objections. "First of all, it's not the gay community complaining; it's some special-interest group that sees itself as the defender of them all." That controversy notwithstanding, *In Living Color* walked away with an Emmy Award for outstanding variety, music, or comedy program after its first season. In 1991 and 1992 Wayans shared Emmys with Keenan for outstanding writing in a variety, music, or comedy series.

The success of *In Living Color*, which launched the careers of Jim Carrey and Rosie Perez, and Wayans's growing celebrity inspired HBO to offer him one of their coveted comedy specials. That show led to another the following year, whose title, *Damon Wayans: The Last Stand?*, indicated the possible end of his stand-up career. At about the same time, he also decided to leave television. Disenchanted with network executives who wanted to tape the show rather than air it live, presumably to increase their censorship control, and sensing that the program had outlived its creative potential, Damon Wayans left *In Living Color* in 1992 to become a full-time film actor. In 1991 he had co-starred opposite Bruce Willis in *The Last Boy Scout*, a big-budget action movie, and though the film had limited success and was generally panned by critics,

Wayans's decision to leave television was bolstered by the positive notices for his performance.

Seeking the same level of control over his career that he had enjoyed as a stand-up comedian, Wayans penned the screenplay for *Mo' Money* (1992). The movie featured Wayans and his brother Marlon as a pair of petty con artists. When Damon Wayans's character becomes smitten by a pretty credit-card company executive, he and his brother try to go legit by getting jobs as mail-room clerks in her company. Still, they concoct a scheme to use the preapproved credit cards that travel through their department on the way to customers. Wayans has admitted that the idea for his script came from his having attempted a similar scam when he worked in the mail room at American Express. "I wasn't being a criminal, just greedy," Wayans told *Jet* (July 27, 1992) of his actions, which resulted in his being fired and taken to court. (He served no jail time.) The film derived from the experience was a commercial hit.

Despite having abandoned stand-up two years earlier, Wayans returned to the stage in 1993. He found that stand-up filled his need for self-expression in a way that movies did not. "I love it, man," he told Allan Johnson for the *Chicago Tribune* (February 19, 1993). "It's something I really missed, and I didn't realize how much I missed it. . . . With comedy, I can go act like a fool and not care, and people laugh with me. . . . And the funny thing is, even if I stop doing standup, I still think the thoughts I think. So I might as well let 'em go."

Wayans continued to make films, writing and starring in *Blankman* (1994). That movie, which he described to Johnson as "Batman & Robin if they didn't have money," is about an inventor who fashions himself into a superhero—dubbed "Blankman" by the media—when the crime in his neighborhood becomes intolerable. Slapstick humor pervades the film, which appealed mostly to younger audiences.

Most recently, Wayans produced and starred in an ill-fated television show called *Damon* (1998) for Fox Broadcasting. He is also starring in two films slated for release in 1999, *Goosed* and *Harlem Aria*. His semi-autobiographical book, *Bootleg* (1999), is a collection of his recent stand-up bits; the title refers to his childhood affliction.

Damon Wayans lives with his wife, Lisa, and their four children—Damon Jr., Michael, Cara Mia, and Kyla (nicknamed Buddy)—in Baldwin Hills, a mostly black, middle-class neighborhood that borders South Central Los Angeles. Wayans made a conscious decision to be as strict with his children as his parents were with him. "My kids go to a private school, and at one point they weren't doing well," he explained to Veronica Chambers. "I wasn't happy with their test scores. So I took them to a public school in South Central. They begged to go back to private school—and improved their work. I wanted them to understand that private school is a privilege." — T.J.F.

Suggested Reading: *Essence* p40 Aug. 1992, with photo; *Contemporary Black Biography*, 1995; New York *Daily News* p14 Aug. 14, 1994, with photos, p4+ Mar. 19, 1995, with photos

Selected Films: as actor—*Beverly Hills Cop*, 1984; *Roxanne*, 1987; *I'm Gonna Git You Sucka*, 1988; *Colors*, 1988; *Earth Girls Are Easy*, 1989; *Look Who's Talking Too*, 1990; *The Last Boy Scout*, 1991; *Major Payne*, 1995; *The Great White Hype*, 1996; as screenwriter and actor— *Mo' Money*, 1992; *Blankman*, 1994

Selected Television Shows: *Saturday Night Live*, 1985–86; *In Living Color*, 1990–92; *Damon*, 1998

Selected Books: *Bootleg*, 1999

Courtesy of Mayor Webb's Office

Webb, Wellington E.

1941– Mayor of Denver. Address: Mayor's Office, Room 350, City and County Bldg., 1437 Bannock, Denver, CO 80202

When he ran out of money during the 1991 Denver mayoral campaign, Wellington Webb turned to a humble strategy: walking door-to-door to meet city voters face-to-face. The tactic worked. Webb, at the time the city's auditor, erased a 28-point opinion-poll deficit to win a solid victory, collecting 57 percent of the vote and thus becoming the Mile High City's first black mayor. Since that time, Webb, now in his third term, has helped guide Denver, a city that had a crumbling infrastructure and serious environmental concerns at the end of the

1980s, into a structurally sound and ecologically safe model city. Denver's 41st mayor, Webb has served as the president of the United States Conference of Mayors and vice president of the National Conference of Democratic Mayors and, from 1972 to 1977, he represented his boyhood neighborhood in northeastern Denver in the state legislature. He left the Colorado House of Representatives to serve as a regional director in the United States Department of Health, Education, and Welfare during the administration of President Jimmy Carter and then, in 1981, became a member of Colorado governor Richard Lamm's Cabinet as executive director of the Colorado Department of Regulatory Agencies. Now the top official in Colorado's largest city, he has become known—among other things—for wearing a business suit with running sneakers. "Walking allows me to have constant contact with my base, the people," he told Lynn Norment for Ebony (December 1993). "I don't exercise or play much basketball these days, but I do more walking than most people. That's my style of governing. It allows me to get out of the office and deal with people in the streets and communities and neighborhoods. And whatever is on people's minds, they bring it to me."

The son of a railroad porter, Wellington Webb was born in 1941 on the South Side of Chicago. When he was seven years old, doctors informed his mother, Mardina Devereauh, that he had asthma, and he was sent to live in Denver with his grandmother, then a dressmaker, because it was believed that the altitude would help his condition. A good student as well as a gifted athlete, he was accepted at Colorado State College at Greeley, where he played an important role on the university's basketball team until he graduated, in 1964, with a B.A. in sociology. Returning to school a few years later, Webb earned a master's degree in sociology from the University of Northern Colorado at Greeley, in 1971.

In the following year Webb mounted a campaign for state representative from his old neighborhood in northeastern Denver. The 31-year-old won by an impressive margin. In 1975 he and State Senator Regis Groff led a walkout protesting then-Governor Richard D. Lamm's failure to appoint minorities, specifically African-Americans, to high office in the state. Throughout his tenure in the Colorado House, Webb was a strong advocate for welfare, health-care and other health-related legislation, and education, and he helped pen the state's first civil-rights bill for handicapped people.

In addition to his service in the state government, Webb served as Colorado campaign chairman for presidential candidate Jimmy Carter in 1976. A year later Webb's service was rewarded: President Carter appointed him principal regional officer for the U.S. Department of Health, Education, and Welfare (HEW), Region VIII (which encompassed Colorado, Montana, North and South Dakota, Utah, and Wyoming). Webb did much dur-

ing his tenure to improve the overall welfare of the 26 Native American tribes on the 23 reservations in the six states under his jurisdiction. A legislator for most of his professional life until this point, Webb found invigorating the position of administrator within the executive branch of the government. "HEW is the people's agency. Every aspect of it deals with the people," he told an interviewer for Ebony (October 1978). "To some degree, the executive branch of government can be faster because you can emphasize certain programs by just shifting resources or by just going out [and] doing it. For example, you can pass a law [as a legislator] saying you want each agency to have an affirmative action policy. But I as an administrator can tell my department heads that I want to see a strong affirmative action program, say, for women."

In 1981 Governor Lamm, the very man whose actions Webb had protested a few years earlier, appointed the 40-year-old Webb executive director of the Colorado Department of Regulatory Agencies, a prestigious post within the governor's Cabinet. Webb held the position until 1987, when he was elected city auditor of Denver. During his tenure in that office, he earned praise from city officials for adding a heightened degree of professionalism and integrity to a department that had been tainted by scandal and intrigue only a few years before.

Near the end of his term as auditor, Webb mounted a campaign for the mayorship of Denver, a longshot bid that few thought would succeed. Indeed, with three weeks to go until the 1991 mayoral primary, Webb trailed the two leading candidates, with a mere 15 percent of those polled expressing support for him; in addition, his campaign funds were low. Perhaps reasoning that he had nothing to lose, he began campaigning strictly on foot, traveling for 39 straight days and more than 300 miles without returning home or setting foot in a car, as Lynn Norment reported; accompanied by his wife, he spent nights in housing projects and homeless shelters, among other places. (He lost 25 pounds in the process.) This grass-roots strategy paid off: on May 21, Webb won 29 percent of the vote to former district attorney Norm Early's 41 percent, and then defeated Early in the June 19 runoff election, with 57 percent of the ballots cast. "We together did the impossible," Webb told supporters during his acceptance speech, according to the New York Times (June 19, 1991). "This is a victory of people over money. This is a victory of positive over negative. This is a victory of grass roots over slick media campaign. This is a victory of shoe leather over airwaves." Upon being sworn into office, Webb succeeded the city's first Latino mayor, Federico Peña, who had decided against seeking a third term.

Webb's first act as mayor was to ask federal courts to lift the 1974 decree requiring busing in the school districts to achieve racial desegregation. Webb told Dirk Johnson for the New York Times (June 20, 1991), "The city is being depopulated. . . . But today, the president of the

Board of Education is black, and the Superintendent of Schools is black. I find it intellectually difficult to understand why a court thinks these people would discriminate." Among some of his other first-term accomplishments was the erasure of the more than $30 million deficit at Denver General Hospital, which is controlled by the city, and the overseeing of the construction of Coors Field, a new stadium for the Colorado Rockies baseball team. Webb also was instrumental in the building of Denver's new airport, which is one of the largest in the world. By the time his first term was up, Webb had been given credit for almost single-handedly orchestrating the revitalization of Denver's downtown.

Running for reelection in 1995, Webb faced a formidable challenge from City Councilwoman Mary DeGroot, who accused the mayor of cronyism—specifically, of offering lucrative airport construction contracts to friends and relatives. During the campaign DeGroot distributed a booklet detailing 64 examples of alleged corruption. The primary election, held in early May, ended with DeGroot amassing 42.8 percent of the vote to Webb's 42.7. (The official count, released a few days after the election, revealed that Webb had received only 97 fewer votes that DeGroot.) Just over a month later, on June 7, results from the runoff election were tallied; Webb won decisively, with 54 percent of the vote to DeGroot's 46 percent. "Now what we want to do is bind the city together," Webb said in his acceptance speech following the grueling campaign, as reported in the New York Times (June 8, 1995). "There's no north, south, east or west. There's just one city—Denver."

In his next four years in office, Webb greatly increased his national name recognition with frequent television appearances on such programs as The Today Show, Meet the Press, Nightline, and Politically Incorrect with Bill Maher. Due in large part to Denver's booming economy, its refurbished downtown, and its hosting of such events as the 1998 Major League All-Star Game at Coors Field; the Summit of the Eight (a global economic meeting attended by President Bill Clinton and seven other world leaders); and World Youth Day, which Pope John Paul II attended, pundits predicted that the mayor would easily win his bid for reelection to a third term. As Al Knight, a Denver Post political columnist, wrote on April 15, 1999, "Webb can be forgiven, one supposes, for feeling pretty good about himself these days. He's just a few weeks away from winning his third term against token opposition and political junkies are already speculating whether he's destined one day to hold statewide office." Given Webb's popularity, many high-profile political opponents of the mayor chose not to run in 1999, deciding to wait until the end of Webb's third term—by law his last.

On April 20, 1999 two students at Columbine High School in Littleton, Colorado, opened fire and killed 12 other students and a teacher before taking their own lives in the bloodiest school massacre in the nation's history. The shootings sparked a nationwide debate over gun control. The National Rifle Association, which had planned to hold its annual gathering in nearby Denver from April 30 to May 2, announced that its meetings would be scaled down from three days to one; Mayor Webb insisted that the group cancel the event altogether. The meetings went on as planned, but the mayor had made his point. Just over two weeks after the tragedy, Webb won his third term with a resounding 80 percent of the vote. Many people predict that he will mount a bid for either the Colorado governorship or the United States Senate when his term ends, in 2003.

Mayor Webb is the vice president of the National Conference of Black Mayors, for which he also serves as the chair of the committee on Africa. He is a member of the advisory boards of the National League of Cities and the Brookings Institution's Center for Urban and Metropolitan Policy. The University of Colorado at Denver and Metropolitan State College of Denver have both awarded him honorary doctorates, and in 1996 Newsweek named him one of the top 25 mayors in the United States.

"Denver is a city that's alive," Webb told Norment. "You can feel it growing. There's excitement about it. . . . My staff, as well as my kids, say I'm 'fiscally tight.' But it works. These are difficult times for cities. Nobody is coming to our rescue." The mayor's wife, Wilma J. Webb, a six-term Colorado state representative, is currently a regional representative for the U.S. Department of Labor. The couple have four grown children—Stephanie, Keith, Troy, and Allen. — M.B.

Suggested Reading: Christian Science Monitor p3 June 5, 1995, with photo; Denver Post (on-line) Apr. 4, 1991, Apr. 15, 1999; Ebony p45+ Oct. 1978, with photos, p29+ Dec. 1993, with photos; Emerge p52+ Mar. 1994, with photos; New York Times A p22 June 19, 1991, A p16+ June 20, 1991, with photo, A p26 June 9, 1995

Weill, Sanford I.

(wile)

Mar. 16, 1933– Chairman and co-CEO of Citigroup Inc. Address: c/o Citigroup Inc., 153 E. 53d St., 4th Fl., New York, NY 10043

In a $76 billion stock swap that led analysts and journalists to call Wall Street "Weill Street," Sanford I. Weill, the chairman and CEO of Travelers Group Inc., announced on April 6, 1998 the merger of his financial-services company with the banking and credit-card giant Citicorp. The newly formed company, Citigroup Inc., is now poised to become, in effect, a decathlete of the financial-services industry: a single company through which more than

Courtesy of Citigroup Inc.

Sanford I. Weill

100 million consumers in 100 countries can buy a home, get financing for a corporate takeover, insure a car, save for retirement, or apply for a credit card, among other transactions. Should the deal steer clear of certain federal laws and Weill and his co-CEO, John Reed, prove capable of managing the sprawling conglomerate, the merger may usher in an era in which, with many other firms forced to consolidate to stay competitive, financial-service behemoths will vie for customers on a global scale.

Call it "Weillopoly": In the past few years, billion-dollar mergers and acquisitions have become a familiar activity for Weill, whose track record and deal-making abilities are approaching legendary status. Rising from messenger at a brokerage company to co-founder of a brokerage firm to major mover-and-shaker in the financial-services industry through more than 15 acquisitions, Weill became president of American Express in 1983. Many observers thought his career was over after he was unceremoniously forced to resign from American Express two years later. But in labeling him a has-been, they were greatly mistaken. Showing the resilience, brashness, foresightedness, "close-to-the-bone thrift," as Gary Weiss put it in a cover story for *Business Week* (October 6, 1997), and willingness to take risks that had marked his past achievements, Weill succeeded in assembling yet another financial giant in just under 15 years.

The son of Polish-Jewish immigrants, Sanford I. Weill was born on March 16, 1933 in the New York City borough of Brooklyn. His mother, Etta (Kalika) Weill, was a homemaker; his father, Max Weill, worked in a series of jobs, including dressmaking, steel importation, and sales. Max Weill spent the last two decades of his life working in the Miami offices of companies his son headed.

"I was sort of a sissy as a little kid," Sanford Weill admitted during a May 23, 1997 interview for the *Hall of Business* Web site. "When we used to play and fight in the streets in Brooklyn and I would get hurt or something, my mother would always come out and save me." The Weill family lived for some time in Florida, then returned to Brooklyn when Sandy, as Weill is universally known, was entering ninth grade. Unable to find housing immediately, Weill's parents enrolled him at the Peekskill Military Academy, about 40 miles north of New York City, and he spent all of his high-school years there. "All of a sudden, I went from not doing well in school, to beginning to do better . . . ," he told the *Hall of Business*. "I think the experience in the military school—where at the beginning you learn how to take the punishment before you dish it out—teaches you a lot about how to get along with people." Weill became captain of his school's tennis team and a member of the Junior Davis Cup Team in New York City. He has referred to his tennis coach, who also taught him Latin, as one of his mentors.

Weill attended Cornell University, in Ithaca, New York. When he earned a B.A. degree, in 1955, he became the first person in his family to graduate from college. A member of the Air Force ROTC at Cornell, Weill wanted to become a military pilot. However, opportunities to do so had shrunk, he has recalled, because the administration of President Dwight D. Eisenhower was cutting back on military spending. So he returned to New York City, where, attracted to the hustle and bustle of Wall Street, he took a job as a messenger for the brokerage firm Bear Stearns, at a salary of $35 a week. (The 1999 equivalent would be about $215.) Before long he worked his way up to being a broker himself. To this day the brokerage business appeals to him, he told the *Hall of Business* interviewer, because "everything that happens in the world affects the price of securities. So it's the kind of business where you can't wait to get up in the morning and read the papers, or listen to what's on the news, and you know, how the world's going to change. And if you don't like stability, and you do enjoy change, and you look at change as something that creates an opportunity, then I think it's a very, very exciting business."

In 1960, a mere five years after first entering the financial-services industry, Weill and three of his friends pooled their money (much of it borrowed) and opened their own stock brokerage firm, Carter, Berlind, Potoma, & Weill. "We started out working around the clock," Roger Berlind, now a Broadway producer, told Leslie Eaton for the *New York Times* (September 25, 1997), adding, "and Sandy's still doing that from everything I hear." By the end of their first year, they earned enough to pay themselves annual salaries of about $12,000 each (about $65,000 in 1999 dollars). Weill became known for aggressively seeking out companies—particularly ones with name recognition—and acquiring them "like a mouse swallowing an elephant," as Leslie

Eaton and Laura Holson put it in the *New York Times* (April 11, 1998). As a result of these moves, along with turnover in partners, Weill's firm underwent many name changes. At one point the company was known colloquially as "Corned Beef with Lettuce," after the first letters of the partners' surnames—Marshall S. Cogan, Berlind, Weill, and Arthur Levitt Jr. (currently, the chairman of the Securities and Exchange Commission). The company became CBWL-Hayden, Stone, Inc. in 1970; Hayden Stone, Inc., in 1972; Shearson Hayden Stone, in 1974, when it merged with Shearson Hammill & Co.; and Shearson Loeb Rhoades, in 1979, when it merged with Loeb Rhoades Hornblower & Co. With capital totaling $250 million, Shearson Loeb Rhoades trailed only Merrill Lynch as the securities industry's largest firm.

In 1981 Weill sold Shearson Loeb Rhoades to the credit-card company American Express for about $930 million in stock. (Sources differ on the precise figure.) With that deal, Weill hoped to "go beyond Wall Street to build a great American institution," as he put it to Leslie Eaton and Laura Holson for the *New York Times*. But the deal turned out to be a major miscalculation for Weill, who began serving as president of American Express Co. in 1983 and as chairman and CEO of American Express's insurance subsidiary, Fireman's Fund Insurance, in 1984. Increasingly nettled by his forced subservience to the chairman of the company, James D. Robinson 3d, whose ideas about the business conflicted sharply with his, Weill realized that he would never be named CEO. When he resigned, in August 1985, at the age of 52, many industry observers thought that his heyday was over.

Unemployed for the first time in over 20 years, the ever-optimistic Weill came to see benefits in this low point in his career. "The first thing that was important about that was it helped my relationship with my children a lot, because they always looked at me as this person that could never do anything wrong, and therefore they couldn't contribute," he told the *Hall of Business*. "And all of a sudden, they saw their father was vulnerable, and it helped create more of an equal kind of relationship with each other, where we respect each other a lot, and that was a very, very important thing that happened. The second thing was that I found out a lot of people liked me for me, and not because I was the president of American Express, or the chairman of Shearson. I was able to be very effective in philanthropic things without having a job."

Soon enough, Weill made his return to Wall Street. After a failed attempt to buy out BankAmerica Corp., he set his sights a little lower and persuaded Minneapolis-based Control Data Corp. to spin off a troubled subsidiary, Commercial Credit, a consumer loan company. In 1986, with $7 million of his own money invested in the company, Weill took over as CEO of Commercial Credit. He then resumed his old strategy of buying out ailing firms and vigorously slashing costs in the

merged company. In 1987 he acquired Gulf Insurance. The next year he paid $1.5 billion for Primerica Corp., the parent company of Smith Barney and the A. L. Williams insurance company, and renamed his expanded corporation Primerica Financial Services. In 1989 he acquired Drexel Burnham Lambert's retail brokerage outlets. Then, in 1992, he paid $722 million to buy a 27 percent share of Travelers Insurance, which had gotten into trouble because of bad real-estate investments. In 1993, in a personal triumph, he reacquired his old Shearson brokerage (now Shearson Lehman) from American Express for $1.2 billion. By the end of the year, he had completely taken over the Travelers Corp. in a $4 billion stock deal and officially began calling his corporation Travelers Group Inc. In 1996 he added to his holdings, at a cost of $4 billion, the property and casualty operations of Aetna Life & Casualty.

In September 1997 Weill acquired Salomon Inc., the parent company of the famous investment bank Salomon Brothers Inc.—legendary for the extreme competitiveness of its bond traders—for over $9 billion in stock. Involving businesses ranging from investment services to asset management, life insurance, property and casualty insurance, and consumer lending, the deal thrust Travelers in a league with such companies as Merrill Lynch, Morgan Stanley/Dean Witter, Goldman Sachs, and big financial firms in Europe and Japan. Suggesting that the transaction represented a departure from his previous acquisitions, Weill told Leslie Eaton for the *New York Times* (September 25, 1997), "The driving force here is not cutting costs. It really is growth, and the entree into markets."

Travelers Group got even bigger in April 1998, when Weill, along with John Reed, the CEO of Citicorp, announced an agreement to undertake what was then the biggest merger in corporate history. The $76 billion joining of Travelers with Citicorp—the largest supplier of credit cards and the parent company of Citibank, the second-largest bank in the U.S.—dwarfed what had previously been the largest merger, the $37.4 billion union of MCI and WorldCom, announced just five months earlier. The thinking behind the Citicorp merger, which was completed on October 8, 1998, was that by combining a bank and insurance business under one brand, Citigroup would become akin to a financial supermarket, with the capacity to offer customers an unparalleled array of financial services.

The possibility remains that the merger will run into problems connected with federal law. Ever since the Glass-Steagall Act, passed during the Great Depression of the 1930s, banking and insurance businesses have been kept separate. Weill and Reed are betting that Congress will soon pass legislation overturning those regulations, which Weill and Reed and many other businesspeople consider obsolete. (Many European countries, for instance, have already torn down the firewall between banking and insurance.) During a two-to-five-year grace period allowed by law, Citigroup can conduct business in its merged form; should that period elapse without a change in the law, Citigroup would have to spin off its insurance businesses.

Many financial observers have speculated that the merger may signal the start of a new era, in which gigantic banks, insurance companies, and brokerage houses combine and compete on a truly global basis. Other banks and financial-service firms contemplating their own mergers are likely to watch carefully whether Reed and Weill manage successfully the merger of the two corporate cultures. In an unusual move, Weill and Reed decided to become co-CEOs of the new company. On July 29, 1999 the *Wall Street Journal* reported that the two co-CEOs had split their duties: Reed became responsible for Internet technology, human resources, and legal issues, while Weill is managing the company's operating businesses and financial functions. One noteworthy casualty in the company's restructuring was Jamie Dimon, a 15-year associate of Weill's who was once thought to be his likely successor. In November 1998 Dimon was forced to resign.

A little over a year earlier, Leslie Eaton had reported in the *New York Times*, "Despite a reputation for ruthlessness, Mr. Weill is well known for his loyalty and surrounds himself with old associates from Shearson and elsewhere." In *Time* (October 6, 1997, on-line), John Greenwald wrote that Weill "is known to keep reams of business information in his head" and to pay "close attention to detail." Weill and his wife, the former Joan Mosher, who were married on June 20, 1955, live in Greenwich, Connecticut, and have two adult children and four grandchildren. Their son, Marc P. Weill, and daughter, Jessica Weill Bibliowicz, have both worked for their father's company. Marc Weill is the chief executive officer of Travelers Investment Group, Inc. Bibliowicz served as the mutual-fund marketing chief for Smith Barney, Travelers' brokerage unit, from 1994 to 1997. In April 1999 she became president and CEO of National Financial Partners, a start-up firm specializing in financial advice for wealthy people.

Sanford Weill's philanthropic activities include service since 1983 on the board of Carnegie Hall, in New York City; he was named chairman of that board in 1991. In recognition of the substantial donation he and his wife made toward the renovation of Carnegie Hall, in 1986 the Carnegie Recital Hall was renamed Weill Recital Hall. In 1997 he received the New York State Governor's Arts Award. Weill also helped found the Academy of Finance Program, through which high-school students learn about the financial-services business. He is the principal sponsor of the High School of Economics and Finance, a New York City public high school. In addition, he has been working with the Disney Co. to create, at the children's museum being constructed in Baltimore, Maryland, a game that will teach youngsters about capitalism. In 1998 he and his wife announced that they would commit $100 million to the Cornell University Medical College, in New York City; the school is now known as the Joan and Sanford I. Weill Medical College and Graduate School of Medical Sciences of Cornell University. — W.G.

Suggested Reading: *BusinessWeek* (on-line) Oct. 6, 1997; *Fortune* (on-line) May 25, 1998, with photo; *Newsweek* p46+ Oct. 6, 1997, with photo; *New York Times* D p1+ Sep. 25, 1997, with photo, A p1+ Apr. 11, 1998, with photo; *Time* (on-line) Oct. 6, 1997

Courtesy of Cleveland Mayor's Office

White, Michael R.

Aug. 13, 1951– Mayor of Cleveland. Address: Cleveland City Hall, Rm. 227, 601 Lakeside Ave., Cleveland, OH 44114-1079

Michael R. White, the mayor of Cleveland, is often counted among the most respected public officials in the country. Since he took office, in 1989, White has led Cleveland, one of the country's most depressed cities between 1970 and 1990, to an economic resurgence that has transformed the midwestern metropolis into a model of American urban renewal. Few people thought White, a former state senator and city councilman, would be an effective leader after his narrow victory in 1989, but by practicing "cross-over" politics, as many members of the nation's press have dubbed it, he has managed to involve both blacks and whites in a comprehensive plan to revitalize the nation's 25th-largest city. "We're trying to practice the art of addition, the politics of inclusion," White told Dana

Milbank for the *Wall Street Journal* (October 11, 1993). "The city won't survive with a black strategy or a white strategy. It's got to be a Cleveland strategy."

Since the beginning of White's tenure as mayor, Cleveland's downtown, once showing the decay that resulted from years of neglect, has seen a reinvestment in its infrastructure of well over $1 billion. Now, the city's landscape boasts numerous state-of-the-art complexes, including the much-lauded Rock and Roll Hall of Fame, the Gateway Sports Complex (home to both baseball's Cleveland Indians and basketball's Cleveland Cavaliers), and the newly constructed Browns Stadium, the playing field of the Cleveland Browns expansion football team. With the promise of a refurbished downtown, White was able to persuade such major corporations as British Petroleum, National City Corp., and McDonald and Co. Securities—all of which had threatened to relocate in the early 1990s—to maintain their corporate headquarters in Cleveland. White then began an ambitious housing-development plan that, by the time he ran for reelection in 1993, had blossomed into the "city's biggest housing boom in 40 years—mostly in blighted black neighborhoods and often handled by minority contractors," as Milbank wrote. Since White took over the mayoralty, 2,500 housing units have been built and nearly 8,000 new jobs have been created. In 1997 *Travel & Leisure* magazine listed Cleveland among the world's top 10 "hot spots" for travelers, and in 1998 *Forbes* named Cleveland one of North America's six best cities for business. Such developments silenced many of White's critics, most of whom hailed from the predominantly black East Side of Cleveland and who, during much of the mayor's first term, referred to him as "White Mike," in reference to what they perceived as his pandering to white businesses. "Whatever they called him then, they'd have to call him 'Right Mike' now," Otis Moss, one of Cleveland's Baptist ministers, told Milbank. White told the reporter, "I don't have to point and scream—I'm the mayor. I don't operate from a position of powerlessness. I'm on the inside, and my challenge is to use the power. I love the town—there's not much else I love more."

The son of Robert and Audrey White, a working-class couple, Michael Reed White was born on August 13, 1951 in the mostly black Glenville section of Cleveland. White watched "his wonderful neighborhood being burned to the ground" in 1968, during the riots following Martin Luther King Jr.'s assassination, as his sister, Marsha H. Hays, told Milbank. White believes that the riots contributed greatly to the downfall of former Cleveland mayor Carl Stokes, one of the first black mayors of a major U.S. city. From those events, White told Milbank, "I learned you don't make progress standing outside throwing bricks." The riots marked the end of an era for Cleveland; the city, over the next two decades, would no longer boast the distinction of being one of America's premier metropolitan areas. From 1970 to 1990, Cleveland's population fell nearly one-third.

After graduating from Glenville High School, in 1969, White attended Ohio State University, where he earned a B.A. degree in education, in 1973, and a master's degree in public administration a year later. At Ohio State, White—a member of an all-black fraternity—led civil-rights demonstrations and worked to an extent with the militant Black Panthers. In 1972, with a white running mate, he became the first African-American to be elected president of Ohio State's student government. "I wasn't a radical," White told Milbank of his college days. "I've never been a radical in my entire life about anything."

After receiving his master's degree, White decided to pursue a career in public service. For a while he worked as an aide to Tom Moody, the then-mayor of Columbus, Ohio. At about that time White befriended the longtime city councilman and one-time city council president George L. Forbes. In 1977, with Forbes's support, he ran successfully for a council seat himself. "My generation came out of a strong black-civil-rights movement, and we always went back to black issues," George Forbes told Milbank. White adopted Forbes's racially confrontational style, and at one point, according to Milbank, he even told city councilwoman Fannie Lewis, who worked for a time under a white mayor of Cleveland, "You're a white-folks nigger, and you always will be." When asked about the incident years later, White told Milbank, "I had a sharp, quick tongue and I would draw it at a moment's notice. As you grow older, you learn a broader strategy." As a councilman he served on the city's Finance Committee and as chairman of the Community Development Committee.

In 1984 White was appointed to a vacant seat in the Ohio Senate, and two years later he was elected to a full term. As a state senator he introduced legislation to increase the penalties for rape, and he wrote provisions to cover spousal rape. He also sponsored anti-drug bills that called for stringent punishment for perpetrators of drug-related crimes and pushed for a program to assist elderly people obtain needed medications. According to Milbank, he "adapted his themes to appeal to his broader electorate, which included a large suburban Jewish population. That helped him broaden his message for his 1989 mayoral run."

In the race for mayor of Cleveland, the candidates face off in a single, nonpartisan primary. The two top vote-getters then do battle in a second-round, winner-take-all vote. After the 1989 primary, the race became one of pupil versus teacher: once the votes were tallied, White found himself in a contest with his mentor, George L. Forbes. "[White] was able to go across the river [to the predominantly white West Side of Cleveland] and represent the white interest as well as black," Forbes told Milbank. "I went over to the white neighborhoods, but it was very painful." Due to his popularity among white voters, White won the general election, held nearly a month after the primary, with virtually no black support. In January 1990 he was sworn in as the 54th mayor of Cleveland.

Within his first year in office, White took out an ad in *Fortune* that read, "Cleveland—Open for Business." The reason: many national corporations considered Cleveland a city with little to offer in the way of business potential, and White wanted desperately to change the city's image. A steel-industry capital that reached its height in the 1940s and 1950s, Cleveland had been devastated by the decline of both the steel industry and the overall American economy in the 1970s. With its decrepit factories, crumbling waterfront, and abandoned steel mills and industrial plants, the city eventually earned such degrading monikers as the "Mistake on the Lake" (a reference to Lake Erie, which Cleveland borders) and the "Armpit of America."

White's first step toward revitalizing the city was to keep its longtime baseball team, the Indians, from moving to Tampa, Florida. Like the city, the ball club had fallen on hard times, having gone nearly a quarter-century without a winning season. White paved the way to build Jacob's Field, which has become one of the most popular ball fields in the country. As if energized by the opening of the stadium, in 1994, the Indians—who had long been the doormats of major-league baseball—quickly became contenders for the American League pennant. Soon afterward the Cavaliers basketball team was lured back into Cleveland proper, after having played in the suburbs for years. An arena adjacent to Jacob's Field was built for the team, and the entire structure, dubbed the Gateway Sports Complex, built for an estimated $365 million, was working at full capacity by 1995. White also obtained for Cleveland the rights to build the Rock and Roll Hall of Fame, a $92 million structure that attracted notice nationwide.

The progress made during White's first term was overshadowed somewhat by allegations of improper financial conduct concerning a real-estate investment White had made in the early 1980s. While hosting the 1991 National Conference of Black Mayors, White was issued with a subpoena. He was later acquitted of any wrongdoing. By 1993, the year of his first reelection campaign, most of his urban-renewal plans—including a housing-development ordinance that gave many African-American firms contracts to build new homes on the long-neglected East Side—were in effect. Riding on record-high popularity ratings, White sailed to an impressive reelection victory over David Lee Rock. In the process he received national attention, and the perception of Cleveland as an industrial wasteland slowly began to change. "Everyone here is realizing that for the community to grow, *all* parts of the community have to grow," Brian Hall, owner of a freight-hauling business in Cleveland, told Mark Lowery for *Black Enterprise* (May 1994). "The things that are happening here are outstanding."

Cleveland's citizens had always maintained a fierce loyalty to its football team, the Browns, and despite the relatively small market that the city offered, the northern Ohio region still boasted some of the most lucrative television contracts in the country; as of 1995, greater Cleveland was the nation's fourth most profitable television market for sports. The requests of the Browns' owner, Art Modell, for a new stadium, which began soon after Jacob's Field was built, were all but ignored by White and other public officials until December 1995, when Modell announced that he was moving the Browns to Baltimore in exchange for a new stadium and a reported $50 million. By the time White attempted to meet Modell's demands, the owner had already signed an agreement with the city of Baltimore. White campaigned hard to keep the Browns, even threatening a lawsuit against the NFL. Eventually, a settlement was reached: in exchange for White's forgoing the lawsuit, the NFL agreed to provide a new football franchise for Cleveland by 1999. The most controversial stipulation in the agreement was that Modell was forced to relinquish the Browns' name and colors (brown, orange, and white) to the city of Cleveland. (Baltimore's new team is called the Ravens.)

In the 1997 mayoral primary, councilwoman Helen Smith proved to be a formidable opponent; she won 40 percent of the vote to White's 55 percent, and thus earned, along with White, a place on the ballot in the general election. During the ensuing campaign, Smith repeatedly claimed that the city was disillusioned with White's eight-year administration, while the mayor continued to remind the city of his accomplishments. According to Evelyn Theiss and Robert J. Vickers in the *Cleveland Plain Dealer* (October 1, 1997, on-line), "The record, [White] said, was this: Crime was down, more new housing ha[d] been built in the last eight years than at any time since the Korean War, and more than $1 billion in economic development ha[d] taken place over the last seven years, helping to retain and add jobs." Despite Cleveland's return to economic stability during White's tenure, his failure to begin repairing the city's troubled and financially strapped public-school system was an issue in the campaign. "We have a broken system," White had told the *Cleveland Plain Dealer* (October 9, 1996, on-line) nearly a year earlier, regarding the public schools. "And we have to have enough guts, I think, to try some new strategies even though we may not know whether or not they'll completely work." In September 1997 the Ohio legislature officially gave White nearly complete authority over all of Cleveland's public schools. Voters apparently had faith in the new arrangement, and White was reelected, defeating Smith with 55 percent of the vote.

Soon after White's reelection, the city began using the rubble from the old Cleveland Municipal Stadium, which had been home to both the Indians and the Browns, to build an artificial reef off the coast of Lake Erie. Construction of a new football complex on the same site began in early 1998, and it was completed by the summer of 1999. Dubbed the Cleveland Browns Stadium, it has accommodated sold-out crowds for each of the new Cleveland Browns' home games during the 1999 NFL season. Many people credit White for playing a major role in orchestrating the team's return to the city.

On another front, in the summer of 1998, the mayor came to an agreement with CSX Transportation, settling a six-month-long stalemate over a $10 billion railroad merger that would greatly affect the city. "In a breakthrough, CSX, one of the two railroads seeking to purchase and divide Conrail, pledged $13.1 million to help offset noise and potential environmental and safety hazards anticipated in Cleveland due to the increased train traffic," Tom Deimer and Kevin Harter wrote for the *Cleveland Plain Dealer* (June 5, 1998, on-line). "The railroad also agreed to divert some trains away from East Side neighborhoods." The deal helped to move Cleveland toward its goal of becoming the economic center of Ohio, and the resolution of the crisis epitomized White's hard-driving tactics, which have aided the city's return to economic and cultural prosperity. As Deimer and Harter reported, "The bargaining went down to the final hours, with an agreement reached 15 minutes before White was to register his objections to the Conrail merger with the Surface Transportation Board, the powerful federal regulatory agency." Among its other concessions, CSX agreed to give Cleveland residents 40 percent of the antici-

pated 124 new jobs that would result from the deal. At the press conference following the agreement, White said, according to Deimer and Harter, "We first had to reach an understanding that this negotiation was never a pure train negotiation—that it was a negotiation about trains and people and neighborhoods."

Michael White's honors include an award for public service from the Levin College of Urban Affairs at Cleveland State University, in 1992; the Freedom Award of the Cleveland branch of the NAACP, in 1993; the Frederick Douglass Freedom Award from the National Conference of Black Mayors, in 1994; and the Public Service Award from the American Public Power Association. In 1991 the Baptist Ministers Conference named him man of the year.

White and his wife, JoAnn, live in the Glenville section on the East Side of Cleveland, where White grew up. The couple have four children: Brieanna, Joshua, Katy, and Christopher. So far, the mayor has downplayed repeated suggestions that he run for either governor or senator. — M.B.

Suggested Reading: *Black Enterprise* p50+ May 1994, with photos; *Cleveland.oh.us* (on-line); *Cleveland Plain Dealer* (on-line) Oct. 5, 1997, Oct. 6, 1997, Nov. 5, 1997, June 5, 1998, Sep. 2, 1998, Sep. 6, 1998; *New York Times* A p8 Apr. 27, 1991, with photo; *Teacher Magazine on the Web* (on-line) Oct. 9, 1996; *Wall Street Journal* A p1 Oct. 11, 1993; *Washington Post* C p1 Mar. 3, 1998, with photos

---

Williams, Anthony A.

July 28, 1951– Mayor of Washington, D.C.
Address: Office of the Mayor, One Judiciary Sq., Suite 1100S, Washington, DC 20001

Anthony A. Williams, the mayor of Washington, D.C., has been lauded by some as "Tony the Tiger," for his strict fiscal principles and cost-cutting measures, and scoffed at by others as "Mr. Bow Tie," a reference to his trademark fashion accessory. A financial technocrat for most of his career, Williams has been an agent for fiscal change on the city, state, and federal levels across the United States. When he was appointed by then–Washington, D.C., mayor Marion Barry as the District of Columbia's chief financial officer (CFO), in 1995, he set in motion an extraordinary economic recovery. In 1998 Barry decided not to run for another term, and Williams, who had always performed well from behind the scenes, stepped to the forefront of the city's political scene. Though his buttoned-down, Ivy-League style and bookish manner have led some to question his forcefulness and his ability to succeed in urban politics, Wil-

liams has proven himself a capable leader. Now ankle-deep into his first term as mayor, Williams, a political outsider steering a city crawling with political insiders, has vowed to build a stronger Washington, D.C., by maintaining continued fiscal stability and inspiring civic involvement. "This town is known for its pundits and commentators. But for the task at hand, we don't need people up in the booth doing color commentary, or in the stands cheering or booing," Williams said, using a sports metaphor for which he is well known, during his inaugural address on January 2, 1999. "We need folks down on the field, blocking and tackling, maybe getting sacked, but getting up and helping us advance the ball a yard at a time as we move toward victory. That is my message today: C'mon out of the stands, people. Suit up. Get in the game. Let's win this together."

The adopted son of Lewis and Virginia Williams, Anthony Allan Williams was born Anthony Stephen Eggleton on July 28, 1951 in Los Angeles. Williams was abandoned as an infant and reportedly was silent and reclusive for the better part of his childhood. Under the care of Lewis, a former amateur boxer and World War II combat veteran, and Virginia, once a budding opera performer who

Anthony A. Williams

gave up singing to raise a family, and amid the bustle of a house filled with seven siblings, young Anthony began to emerge from his shell. Both parents worked as Postal Service clerks (Virginia during the day and Lewis at night so the children would not be left alone), which afforded them a house in a mostly black, working-class neighborhood south of downtown Los Angeles. Virginia and Lewis placed a premium on education and managed to have all eight children educated in Catholic schools. As a result of their parents' emphasis on academics, all eight went on to graduate from college. "We have Ph.D.'s, a doctor, a CPA, and artists, from Stanford, M.I.T., Yale, U.C. Santa Clara, Northwestern and U.C.L.A.," Williams said of his siblings, as quoted by Irvin Molotsky in the *New York Times* (November 4, 1998).

In elementary and high school, Williams received good grades and distinguished himself as a leader among his peers through class elections. In 1969 he enrolled at the University of California at Santa Clara and again proved himself a leader, but he became distracted from his studies by student activities and campus protests against the Vietnam War. After completing barely an academic year's worth of work in two calendar years, Williams left Santa Clara to come home. Craving structure and direction, he enlisted in the air force as an information specialist. With the hope of fulfilling his dream of becoming a pilot, he applied to the U.S. Air Force Academy, but his admission was deferred pending his performance at the academy's preparatory school. Although his year in the school went well and he was granted entrance to the academy, he had a change of heart and sought conscientious objector status, despite the fact that

he was eligible for an early discharge. "I wanted to make a statement," Williams told Michael A. Fletcher for the *Washington Post* (September 3, 1998). In 1974, after two years and 10 months in the military, he was granted an honorable discharge.

For the next year Williams gave art lessons to children and war veterans in Los Angeles, and he considered launching a crop-dusting business. Eventually abandoning that idea, Williams decided to go back to school, and in 1975 he was accepted into Yale University, in New Haven, Connecticut. His studies there were interrupted by, among other things, an unsuccessful attempt at selling antique maps. In 1979 Williams, still an undergraduate, was elected to the board of aldermen in New Haven. He graduated from Yale in 1982, with a bachelor's degree in economics. Though it had taken him about 13 years to complete his undergraduate education, in just under five years Williams added to his résumé two graduate degrees, one in law and the other in public policy, both from Harvard University, in Cambridge, Massachusetts.

Over the next decade Williams followed a more traditional, linear path than he had theretofore pursued, winning a series of government appointments. In those posts he earned a reputation for tough fiscal principles and hard-line cost-cutting methods, which often made him an unpopular public official. As an alderman in New Haven in the early 1980s—his only elected post prior to coming to D.C.—Williams sponsored a bill to cut public funding for a minority-owned business-financing program, believing that the business owners benefitting from the program were careless with the funds made available to them. In Boston he worked to bring businesses into poor neighborhoods in order to spark economic growth, a proposal that generated considerable community resistance. Next, in 1990, Williams worked as executive director of St. Louis's Community Development Agency; his strict oversight of city contracts led to a confrontation with two angry contractors, which in turn landed Williams in a hospital emergency room. From 1991 to 1993, as deputy comptroller for Connecticut, Williams called the state's governor on his questionable fiscal practice of withholding tax refunds to cover budget deficiencies. Then, in 1993, President Bill Clinton brought Williams to D.C. to be the chief financial officer of the U.S. Department of Agriculture. In that post he was responsible for overseeing 10,000 employees.

In the *Almanac of American Politics, 1998*, Washington, D.C., was described as a "dysfunctional polity, a city with above-average incomes and a vibrant commercial property base but with a local government so bloated with employees yet so indifferent to its duties that it is destroying one marginal neighborhood after another." It is widely thought that many of the city's difficulties can be traced to its previous mayor, Marion Barry. In 1974 the federal government ceded its control over the

District of Columbia to its residents, allowing them to vote for a governing mayor and city council. Barry, a charismatic black leader seasoned by the civil rights movement in the 1950s and 1960s, was elected mayor in 1978 and dominated city politics for 16 of the next 20 years. His early years in office were marked by success. He built a coalition that galvanized the city's predominantly black population through successful social programs. But serious flaws in the city's infrastructure and administration began to surface after Barry was arrested, convicted, and imprisoned in 1990 for smoking crack cocaine in a local hotel room. (In 1994, after his release from prison, he won reelection.) It turned out that Barry had built a bureaucracy whose size—approximately 36,000 city employees—far exceeded the needs of a metropolis with a population of just under 550,000. The city's tax base could not support its infrastructure, and the District of Columbia's economy foundered under deficits that totaled $300 million by 1995. On Wall Street, D.C.'s bond rating plummeted, and the city could no longer borrow money to stay afloat. This situation had a debilitating effect on local government services and programs, which in turn led to serious social problems. At its lowest point, Washington, D.C., had one of the highest crime rates in the country and an infant mortality rate comparable to that of some Third World countries.

Washington's budget deficits alarmed the federal government, which in 1995 transferred control of the capital city's day-to-day fiscal workings from the mayor's office to a five-member congressional oversight committee. Under that arrangement the mayor could appoint a CFO to manage the city's finances. The mayor's office was left with little to manage beyond tourism, thus giving D.C.'s CFO unusual freedom to pursue fiscal reform. Though hired by the mayor, the CFO could be dismissed only by the oversight committee.

Williams was appointed CFO by Barry in 1995. As he had in each of his previous appointments, he wasted little time in assessing and gaining control of the situation in Washington. First, he demanded that an accurate and efficient filing system for income taxes be put in place. Prior to his arrival tax returns had been piled, not filed, in haphazard stacks on the floor of a basement room in the city's business-tax bureau. Many journalists have noted that the piles were a perfect metaphor for the state of D.C.'s finances. (Williams, who also recognized the symbolic import of the stacks, kept in his office as trophies two pictures of the basement room: one image was of the disordered heaps, the other of the orderly filing system that was implemented.) Williams also forced large budget cuts on the mayor's administration, which immediately put him at odds with Barry, and Williams threatened to resign if the managers he supervised did not produce a clean tax audit. However, what caused the greatest stir was Williams's mass firing of 300 employees. Trying to impose accountability among his workers and tighten control over his office, Williams

dismissed those he felt had contributed to the city's dismal financial state and brought in highly qualified contract employees to keep his office running until he could assemble a restructured full-time staff.

Williams's aggressive move aroused the ire of union officials and the consternation of many others. "The way in which they went about removing people from office was basically an ambush," David Leonard, who had worked in the budget office for over 20 years before being ousted by Williams, told David A. Vise for the *Washington Post* (October 13, 1998). "People including myself went to work, with absolutely no idea what was taking place, were called into a meeting and told you are removed immediately, pack up and get out by the close of business today." In his own defense Williams has explained that he had limited time to make drastic changes and could not afford the incompetency of the past. "We're trying to act as an agent of change in the District," Williams told Rob Gurwitt for *Governing* (June 1997). "As a normal rule, the CFO has a control role and a support role. The better your organization is performing, the more you're going to be in a support role, because the leadership has taken the reins. But where you have deficiencies in the organization, the CFO has to take more control." Despite the criticism Williams's methods generated, it is hard to argue over their results. Helped by a strong national economy and a large return on delinquent tax collections, Williams's office reported a budget surplus of $186 million for fiscal year 1997, from a projected deficit of $74 million. In that same year the capital city's once notoriously disordered financial management systems produced the first clean tax audit in recent memory—and had a faster income-tax turnaround time than even the Internal Revenue Service. For his accomplishments, Anthony Williams was honored as a public official of the year by *Governing* magazine (December 1997).

Perhaps the best gauge of Williams's effectiveness as CFO, normally a position unseen by the public, is that a citizen coalition formed to draft him to run for mayor of D.C. in 1998. Shying away from the attention at first, Williams eventually warmed to the idea of being mayor and entered the race in May of that year. Though he was a political outsider running against three longtime D.C. council members, Williams used his career as a bureaucrat and government administrator to best advantage. "The District is at a crossroads in terms of moving from the old generation of black leadership to the new generation that still inspires hope but also delivers results," Williams said, according to David A. Vise, writing for the *Washington Post* (May 31, 1998). "I'm running because I believe District politics have changed from a politics based on political considerations and ideology to a politics based on a discussion of real needs and real results." Careful not to bad-mouth the troubled but popular Barry administration, Williams nonetheles distanced himself from the business-as-usual politics that had led to the deterioration of Washington and to congressional oversight. Specifically, Williams ran on a platform of fiscal health, economic growth, and the return of home rule to District residents.

In response, his opponents in the Democratic primary—Kevin Chavous, Harold Brazil, and Jack Evans—tried to portray Williams as a Johnny-come-lately who knew little of D.C. politics, since he had been neither born nor raised in the city. Also, because of his well-pressed, conservative, intellectual image, some people suggested that though Williams is an African-American, he might not be "black enough" to represent D.C.'s racial majority. But these concerns ultimately did little harm to Williams's campaign. He gathered endorsements and support from most of Washington's key political corners, including former constituents of Marion Barry, and rolled to victory in the Democratic primary with 50 percent of the vote.

In the District of Columbia, where registered Democrats outnumber Republicans five to one, the candidate who wins the Democratic primary is usually considered a shoo-in for the mayor's job. True to form, the person Barry defeated in the 1994 general election, Carol Schwartz, ran against Williams and was defeated by more than 30 percentage points.

Two weeks into Williams's tenure, the mayor's office became embroiled in a minor controversy involving an administration official's choice of words. On January 15, 1999 David Howard, a white man and the mayoral ombudsman, while discussing his office's budget with two colleagues, said, "I will have to be niggardly with this fund because it's not going to be a lot of money." Of Scandinavian origin, the word "niggardly," a synonym for "miserly," sounds similar to but has no etymological connection to "nigger," a racial slur directed at African-Americans. Nevertheless, one of Howard's two colleagues misunderstood him to have used the racial slur and, feeling insulted, stormed away without accepting an explanation. Howard, believing he had used poor judgment in his word choice, tendered his resignation; Williams, in agreement with Howard's assessment, accepted it.

Criticism of the mayor's decision to accept Howard's resignation was overwhelming and came from many different sources. Gay and lesbian organizations ran to support Howard, who was Williams's first openly gay appointee. Right-wing conservative radio talk-show host Rush Limbaugh used the episode to proselytize about the evils of excessive political correctness. "Some poor slob loses his job over a Swedish word and Bill Clinton keeps his job for perjury and obstruction of justice. Go figure," Limbaugh said on his daily radio show, as Melinda Henneberger reported in the *New York Times* (January 29, 1999). Similarly, Richard Dooling quipped in the *Wall Street Journal* (January 29, 1999), "Expressions ranging from *a nip in the air* to *a chink in the armor* will be removed [from the

dictionary] because they might be uttered in the wrong context. What about *whopper* or *spick-and-span* or *a finger in the dike*?" Perhaps the most sensible response came from Julian Bond, chairman of the NAACP. "You hate to think you have to censor your language to meet other people's lack of understanding. This whole episode speaks loudly to where we are on issues of race. Both real and imagined slights are catapulted to the front burner," Bond said, according to Linton Weeks in the *Washington Post* (January 29, 1999). "Seems to me the mayor has been niggardly in his judgment on this issue." The upshot of the affair was that Williams asked Howard to return to work; Howard agreed to do so, on the condition that he not return to his former post.

Despite getting mired in that situation, Williams moved forward with his plans for the revitalization of Washington, D.C. In his inaugural address, he had promised to improve the efficiency and quality of services provided by the city government, such as garbage collection, street cleaning, and graffiti removal. Toward that end, he gave his cabinet members, agency heads, and senior staff members one week to write detailed reports outlining ways to improve the services their respective divisions provide to the public. Based on those reports, Williams drew up a list of goals to be met by the city on a quarterly basis, and he has said that each department head will be held personally accountable for the productivity in his or her area of responsibility. To date, the administration is on target with the goals. Furthermore, Williams has requested from Congress, and has been granted, greater responsibility for managing the city. According to the federal dictate, the full responsibility for governing D.C. will revert to locally elected officials after the District balances four consecutive annual budgets. Under Williams's guidance Washington may reclaim home rule in two years. So far his only plan to meet with serious resistance has been his proposal to move the University of the District of Columbia from its current campus, in the comparatively wealthy northeastern quarter of the city, to a poorer section, east of the Anacostia River. Williams claims that he proposed the move to give an economic boost to a depressed area, while his opponents accuse him of trying to open the desirable land, surrounded by embassies and lavish homes, to developers willing to pay top dollar for it.

Earlier, on July 17, 1998, approximately a month after he had resigned as Washington's CFO and declared his candidacy for mayor of the city, Williams had filed a financial statement showing that he had received no income outside his government salary. However, in April 1999, in a financial statement of the kind that all Washington officials are required to file annually, he reported that he had accepted a fee of $30,000 from Arthur Andersen & Co., an accounting firm, on July 31, 1998 and had signed a contract on August 6, 1998 for an additional $10,000 from Nationsbank Corp., both for consulting. Campaign law states that all candidates for public office must report any and all changes in income within 30 days of the date of their financial disclosure filings. Since both consultancy jobs fell within that 30-day limit, Williams's April 1999 disclosure prompted an inquiry by the District of Columbia's office of campaign finance and the city's board of elections and ethics. "I should have disclosed the fact of my outside employment earlier and inadvertently failed to do so," Williams said in a statement issued in response to the inquiry, according to the *New York Times* (June 14, 1999). "For this oversight, I am sorry." He reportedly complied fully with all the finance office's requests concerning the investigation, and he asserted that there was no conflict of interest between his consultancy work and his public service. Satisfied that there was no further wrongdoing, Washington's office of campaign finance fined Williams $1,000 ($500 for each offense, the maximum permissible

amount) for failing to report his outside income within the specified time.

Anthony Williams lives in the Foggy Bottom neighborhood of D.C. with his wife, Diane. The couple have a grown daughter, Asantewa Foster. Though he has gained national attention for his initiatives and his meteoric rise through Washington politics, Williams has publicly stated that he ran for mayor only in response to a draft movement and that he has no intention of seeking higher public office. — T.J.F.

Suggested Reading: *Emerge* p24 May 1999, with photos; *Governing* p88 June 1997, with photo, p25 Dec. 1997, with photo, p66 Apr. 1998, with photo; *New York Times* A p16 June 14, 1999, with photo; *Washington Post* A p1 May 31, 1998, with photo, C p1 Sep. 3, 1998, with photos, C p1 Jan. 29, 1999; *Almanac of American Politics, 1998*

Courtesy of Grambling State University

Williams, Doug

Aug. 9, 1955– Head football coach at Grambling State University. Address: c/o Grambling State University, P.O. Box 868, Grambling, LA 71245

The quarterback and coach Doug Williams is perhaps best known for his stellar performance in January 1988, when he led the Washington Redskins to victory in Super Bowl XXII. Williams, the first African-American to start at quarterback in a Super Bowl, blazed a trail for African-American quarterbacks in the National Football League (NFL) during

his nine years as an NFL player. He has since left the playing field, and in 1998 he became the head coach at Grambling State University, in Grambling, Louisiana, his alma mater and one of the U.S.'s historically African-American colleges.

Douglas Lee Williams was born on August 9, 1955 in rural Zachary, Louisiana. He is the sixth of the eight children of Robert Williams, a disabled World War II veteran, and Laura Williams, a school cook. Although he grew up in a house without indoor plumbing, he included no complaints when he described his childhood to Derek Reveron for *Ebony* (January 1979). "We never went hungry, clotheless or shoeless, and got what we needed, not everything we wanted," he said. "When Christmas came, we got paper cap pistols, air guns and football helmets." He was encouraged to participate in sports by his older brother, Robert Jr., who was a pitcher in the Cleveland Indians farm system before an injury ended his baseball career. Although Doug Williams excelled in baseball, basketball, and football, Robert Jr. steered him toward football, and Williams began playing quarterback in the seventh grade. Reflecting on his brother's influence, Williams told William Gildea for the *Washington Post* (March 27, 1994), "When my older brother coached me [during seventh and eighth grades], I wanted to be like him. He was my hero."

A powerful right-handed quarterback in high school, Williams caught the attention of Edward Robinson, the esteemed head coach of the football team at Grambling State University, Robert Jr.'s alma mater. Doug Williams entered Grambling State in 1974 and quarterbacked the Grambling State Tigers during the 1975, 1976, and 1977 seasons (he redshirted as a freshman). Robinson, who coached Grambling's football program from 1942 to 1997, notched more career victories (408) than any other college football coach, and under his mentoring, Williams honed his skills and flourished as a quarterback. He earned the moniker "Grambling Rifle" and gained a reputation for having what Rick Telander later described for *Sports Illustrated* (January 27, 1992) as "cannon for arm." In 1976 he threw for 3,286 yards (a Grambling season record) and 32 touchdowns, and he finished fifth in the 1976 Heisman Trophy balloting. He also set most of Grambling's current passing records, including most touchdown passes in a game (seven), most touchdown passes in a season (38), and most touchdown passes during a career at the school (93). As a senior he became the first football player from an historically African-American college to be named to the Associated Press's Division I All-America team. (Division I is the most competitive bracket and Division III is the least.) At the close of his college career—he graduated in 1978 with a bachelor's degree in physical education—he had completed 484 of 1,009 passes for 8,411 yards.

Although Williams played at a relatively small school and thus had not faced as much top-caliber competition as he might have had he played at a larger school, in the 1978 NFL draft he was selected as the first-round pick of the Tampa Bay Buccaneers, an expansion team that had won only two games out of 26 since its entry into the league, in 1976. As the 17th pick overall, Williams became the second African-American quarterback to be selected in the first round of the NFL draft; the first, Eldridge Dickey of Tennessee State University, had been selected by the Oakland Raiders in 1968 but was later assigned to play wide receiver. Williams also became only the third African-American quarterback to go on to enjoy a lengthy NFL career, following James Harris of Grambling, who signed with the Buffalo Bills in 1969 and played during the 1970s with the Los Angeles Rams and the San Diego Chargers, and Joe Gilliam of Tennessee State University, who signed with the Pittsburgh Steelers in 1972 and played backup for Terry Bradshaw during the 1970s. Historically, most promising African-American athletes had been discouraged from playing quarterback. Jane Leavy suggested why in the *Washington Post* (September 20, 1987): "In part, it is because many [African-American quarterbacks] come from running offenses not used in the NFL. In part, it is simply bias. Over the years NFL owners have proven distinctly reluctant to relinquish control of their teams to black quarterbacks or, for that matter, black coaches."

To the surprise of many fans and coaches in the league, the six-foot-four, 220-pound Williams quickly emerged as the starting quarterback for the Buccaneers in 1978, his rookie season, and he made an immediate impact on the team. Although he missed several games near the end of the season because of injuries, he finished the year with 18 touchdowns and helped the Buccaneers improve to a 5–11 win–loss record that season. With Williams at quarterback, the Buccaneers improved even more during the ensuing seasons. During his five seasons at Tampa Bay, Williams led the team to three play-off appearances and two Central Division championships. He thus became the first African-American quarterback to lead an NFL team for several years as a starter.

However, all was not well between Williams and the Buccaneers. When his contract with the team expired at the end of the 1982 season, he and the Buccaneers' management became embroiled in a salary dispute. Although Williams had played an integral role in leading the Buccaneers up from the bottom of the league, he earned just $125,000 in 1982, which placed him 46th in salaries for NFL quarterbacks that year. This meant that backup quarterbacks in the league had made more money than he had. Moreover, Williams felt he hadn't been treated fairly by the Buccaneers' front office. "I don't think I've been treated like a five-year starter," he said during the dispute, as quoted by Mike Tierney for the *Sporting News* (August 22, 1983). "It's not the money anymore. It's the principle." Adding to the strain placed on Williams by the dispute was the death of his wife, Janice Goss, from an aneurysm, in 1982, just three months after the birth of their daughter, Ashley Monique. Her death "put a lot of things in perspective," Williams told Jack Friedman for *People Weekly* (March 7, 1988). "No matter who you are, no matter what you do, life is not promised to you tomorrow."

When the Buccaneers failed to meet his salary demands, Williams left Tampa Bay and played for the Oklahoma Outlaws in the now-defunct United States Football League (USFL) in 1984 and 1985. His five-year contract with that team was reported to have been worth over $2 million (one account described it as a three-year deal worth $1.87 million). Reflecting on his decision to leave the NFL, Williams told Mike Tierney for the *Sporting News* (February 27, 1984), "I regret the fact that [the Bucs] didn't give me the money. I don't regret leaving under the circumstances."

Williams's career in the USFL was not stellar, in part because he was hampered by injuries to his knee. Meanwhile, the Buccaneers, without Williams, finished the 1983 season with a 2–14 win–loss record.

When the USFL folded in 1986, Williams returned home to Zachary. Although he was a proven entity, he discovered he was not sought-after by NFL teams. In fact, the only team to approach him was the Washington Redskins, who signed him to a three-year, $1.4 million deal. During the 1988 season Williams backed up starter Jay Schroeder, and thus his playing time was limited. In fact, he played in only one game for only one play (he threw an incomplete pass).

Williams gained more playing time during the 1987 season as Schroeder's play became less consistent. By the play-offs he had established himself as the Redskins' starting quarterback, and he led the team to Super Bowl XXII. On January 31, 1988, at Jack Murphy Stadium, in San Diego, California, Williams became the first African-American quarterback to start in a Super Bowl. Despite the pressure arising from his historic role and the media frenzy over the issue of race in football, Williams performed masterfully. After giving up an early 10–0 lead in the first quarter to the favored Denver Broncos, during the second quarter he led a barrage of offense that Gerald Eskenazi, writing for the *New York Times* (February 1, 1988), described as "the greatest outpouring of first-half points in Super Bowl history." In 15 minutes Williams completed four touchdown passes, thereby tying a Super Bowl record and in effect settling the outcome of the game. The Redskins beat the Broncos 42–10. Williams completed 18 passes in 29 attempts and set a Super Bowl record of 340 passing yards, surpassing the previous mark of 331 yards set by Joe Montana of the San Francisco 49ers in Super Bowl XIX. For his impressive effort, Williams received the Super Bowl Most Valuable Player Award.

Williams's stellar performance was a history-making accomplishment. Even though by the late 1980s the majority of NFL players were African-American, few African-Americans held or had held the position of quarterback, considered by many, albeit arguably, to be the most important position in the game. According to Jill Lieber, reporting for *Sports Illustrated* (January 28, 1991), Edward Robinson called Williams "the Jackie Robinson of football." Speaking in a similar vein, Rick Telander described Williams's Super Bowl performance as a "statement about capabilities of black quarterbacks that the sports world couldn't ignore."

Williams later played down the significance of his performance in the Super Bowl. He told Lieber, "What did I change? Nothing. If there were now 10 or 12 black quarterbacks in the NFL, some black backups and third-teamers, then I'd think I had changed something. The NFL would still rather draft a [white] guy from Slippery Rock than give a black quarterback a chance. Maybe I'll feel I've made a difference when an Art Shell wins the Super Bowl."

Williams's celebrity proved to be fleeting. Although he received a three-year contract worth between $3.2 million and $3.5 million from the Redskins prior to the start of the 1988 season, he was hampered by injuries for the next two seasons. He was especially burdened by a back injury that he sustained while training during the off-season in 1989. Moreover, he was eclipsed by Mark Rypien, a younger, white player from Washington State University, who emerged as the Redskins' top quarterback by the 1989 season. In March 1990, after nine years in the NFL, Williams was released by the Redskins. He later expressed regret over his dismissal and the failure of the Redskins organization to offer him an administrative position. In *Quarterblack: Shattering the NFL Myth* (1990), which he wrote with Bruce Hunter and in which he chronicled his experience as an NFL quarterback, he charged, as quoted in the *Washington Post* (September 4, 1990), "What it comes down to is black quarterbacks do not get a chance to sit

around and make money as backups in the NFL. It's part of the syndrome that has plagued the league since its inception. A lot of NFL coaches, general managers, and owners either don't want a black man in a leadership role such as quarterback or they just don't want to buck the system, which says a black man isn't capable of handling the position. As a result, the backup quarterback position in the NFL is for white players only. Blacks need not apply."

Williams put his playing career behind him and returned to Louisiana, where he became a high-school football coach. In 1993 he led his alma mater, Chaneyville (now called Northeast) High School, in Zachary, to a 13–1 win–loss record. He then worked as an assistant coach at the U.S. Naval Academy, in Annapolis, Maryland, and next with the Scottish Claymores, a team in the World League of American Football. He then spent two seasons as a scout for the Jacksonville Jaguars, an NFL expansion team.

In 1997 Williams left the Jaguars and signed a five-year contract to serve as the head football coach at Morehouse College, a traditionally African-American school in Atlanta, Georgia, whose football team, the Maroon Tigers, competes in the NCAA Division II bracket. He took over a team that had finished the previous season with two wins and nine losses, but his fame helped him recruit young players despite Morehouse's lack of a strong football tradition and limited football budget. The team finished the 1997 season with three wins and eight losses.

The next year Williams left Morehouse and returned to Grambling, where he succeeded Edward Robinson as head coach. Robinson had retired with a career record of 408 wins, 165 losses, and 15 ties. Williams inherited a team that had finished the 1997 season with three wins and seven losses. In his first season as head coach, Grambling finished with five wins and six losses.

Williams and his third wife, LaTaunya, have a son, D.J., and a daughter, Jasmine.—Y.P.

Suggested Reading: *New York Times* C p1+ Aug. 18, 1997, with photos; *Newsweek* p61 Feb. 1, 1988, with photos; *People* p91+ Mar. 7, 1988, with photos; *Sports Illustrated* p42+ Feb. 1, 1988, with photos, p82+ Jan. 28, 1991, with photos, p118+ Aug. 25, 1997, with photos; *Washington Post* C p4 Jan. 24, 1991, with photo, D p1+ Sep. 8, 1991, with photos, D p1+ Mar. 27, 1994, with photo; Williams, Doug, with Bruce Hunter. *Quarterblack: Shattering the NFL Myth*, 1990

Michael Tighe/Outline Press

Williams, Lucinda

Jan. 26, 1953– Singer; songwriter. Address: c/o Mercury Records, 825 Eighth Ave., New York, NY 10019

Although the singer and songwriter Lucinda Williams has received virtually unanimous critical acclaim in the two decades since the release of her debut album, *Ramblin' on My Mind* (1979), widespread popularity and high record sales have eluded her. Part of the problem stems from the difficulty that record companies have had in categorizing and marketing her songs, which combine elements of rock, country, and folk and have been described as rough, raw, and overflowing with emotion. On several occasions recording industry insiders have encouraged Williams to alter her renegade style, but Williams has refused to do so. "I don't care about success if I have to change artistically," she declared to Alanna Nash for *Entertainment Weekly* (May 7, 1993). "I won't cater to record companies— never have, never will." In a review of Williams's most recent album, *Car Wheels on a Gravel Road* (1998), for *Rolling Stone* (July 9–23, 1998), Robert Christgau wrote, "Without melodrama or sentimentality, Lucinda Williams is one of the rare contemporary artists who can make it real. If that makes her too good for this world, then too bad for the world."

Born on January 26, 1953 in Lake Charles, Louisiana, Lucinda Williams is the eldest of Lucille and Miller Williams's three children. She has one brother, Robert, and one sister, Karen. Her father taught college biology in the 1950s; in the 1960s he abandoned biology for poetry and, after working for a few years at miscellaneous jobs, became a pro-

fessor of English. Since 1971 he has been on the faculty of the University of Arkansas. In 1997, at the invitation of President Bill Clinton, he read his poem "Of History and Hope" at Clinton's second inauguration. Miller Williams's job changes led the family to move many times during Lucinda's childhood, mostly within Louisiana, Georgia, and Mississippi; they also lived briefly in Santiago, Chile, and Mexico City. "I love the South," Lucinda Williams told Gil Kaufman for the *Addicted to Noise* Web site. "So much of the great music that I grew up listening to came out of the South." Among the musicians whom she admired as a child and who she has said have influenced her work are Bob Dylan, Joan Baez, Pete Seeger, Woody Guthrie, the Carter Family, Hank Williams, Lightnin' Hopkins, and the trio Peter, Paul, and Mary.

In an interview with Thomas Huang for *Dallasnews.com* (December 6, 1998, on-line), Miller Williams said that Lucinda "was always interested in language." "She wrote poetry and short stories almost from the time she could hold a pencil," he recalled. "That began to take a musical turn when she was in sixth grade. She began to sing her poems. Then, when she was given a guitar at 12, she picked it up almost immediately, as if she were born to it. She started writing her own songs." In terms of writing, Lucinda Williams, whose songs have sometimes been likened to the short stories of Raymond Carver, has identified her father as her mentor.

When Williams was 11 years old, her parents separated; she and her siblings maintained residence with their father. Her parents' eventual divorce "wasn't this big traumatic thing," she told Steve Dougherty and Beverly Keel for *People* (September 21, 1998). "I never remember getting bummed out about it. I didn't grow up in a mom-and-pop, Ozzie-and-Harriet type of environment, but who did?" Living with her father afforded Williams the company of several writers who were friends of his—James Dickey, Allen Ginsberg, and Charles Bukowski, to name a few. "There might be a party and I'd pull out songs and play [the guitar] for them," Lucinda Williams told Huang. "A few writers talking and drinking into the wee hours of the night—they were an instant support group of incredible minds."

Williams attended public schools until she was expelled from a New Orleans high school for refusing to pledge allegiance to the flag, a stance she took to protest the war in Vietnam. After her expulsion her father taught her at home, with the help of some of his creative-writing students. Music became increasingly important to her, and she decided that she would pursue a career as a musician. "It was never 'I've got to be a huge star,'" she told Dougherty and Keel. "I just wanted to be able to make a living doing this." Williams got her first taste of performing when she toured Mexico with a family friend, the folk musician Clark Jones.

After passing her high-school equivalency exams, Williams enrolled at the University of Arkansas. In her freshman year she failed a music-theory class, and soon afterward she quit school. She then moved to New Orleans, where she tried to get as much performing experience as possible. "I played the Drag, where vendors would sell their wares," Williams told Huang. "I played for change. I liked the freedom of it. I was really driven. I was always out trying to get gigs, no matter how little money was involved, trying to meet people. I didn't know anything about the music business, recording, record labels." Williams's father told Jason DeParle for the *New York Times* (March 25, 1993) that he remembered his daughter playing a gig behind chicken wire so that she wouldn't get hit by flying bottles. Williams sometimes had to support herself by taking part-time jobs.

After being rejected by many record companies because her music did not fit into any specific division or style, in 1979 Williams signed with the Smithsonian/Folkways label. Her album *Ramblin' on My Mind*, a collection of folk and country standards, came out that same year. Her next disc, *Happy Woman Blues* (1980), contains original material. Williams told Huang that the songs she wrote for *Happy Woman Blues* were mainly about breaking through the stereotypes in which she, and perhaps many other women, felt trapped. "It's about not being able to be all those things," she said. "You can't win for losing. You search for independence, and intact vision, strength—and then somebody fights you and calls you a perfectionist." Although neither *Ramblin' on My Mind* nor *Happy Woman Blues* sold well, together they established a loyal following for Williams and earned her the respect of many music critics.

Williams did not make another album until, about eight years after the release of *Happy Woman Blues*, she signed with Rough Trade, a small, little-known British record label. (Rough Trade folded a few years later.) The resulting album, *Lucinda Williams* (1988), features the popular singles "The Night's Too Long" and "Passionate Kisses." Far more commercially successful than her first two albums, it sold over 100,000 copies. It also attracted the attention of RCA Records, which signed her for a follow-up album. But Williams did not like the record she made with RCA; she felt it was far too commercial, and she refused to release it. Subsequently, she left RCA for Chameleon Records, a much smaller company—an audacious move, in the opinion of many observers. "She was told nobody walks out on RCA," her father told DeParle.

Freed from RCA's constraints, Williams suffused her next album, *Sweet Old World*, which Chameleon released in 1992, with a melancholy tone. In both the title track and a single called "Pineola," she sings about suicides and the feelings of loved ones who have been left behind. Another ballad, "He Never Got Enough Love," is based on a news report about a boy from an unhappy home who grew up to become a violent criminal. While the ambiguous song "Little Angel" makes no specific references to death, it "could be taken for a eulogy," Dan Kening noted in the *Chicago Tribune* (April 1, 1993). When asked why she is drawn to such mournful material, Williams told Kening, "Early traditional folk ballads . . . were all about death. So it's not like it hasn't been done before. . . . I think that's where my songs come out of." In her interview with DeParle, Williams said, "You hear all these albums that have 12 songs on them about, you know, 'my baby left me.' And nobody says, 'Why do you have 12 love songs?' . . . I don't know that many people walking around totally, completely satisfied and fulfilled."

In 1994 Williams's song "Passionate Kisses," which the country star Mary Chapin Carpenter had recorded for her album *Come On Come On* (1992), was nominated for a Grammy. The prospect of attending the awards ceremony "intimidated the hell out of me," Williams admitted to Dougherty and Keel. "I started thinking all these people in designer clothes would be there, judging me. 'What if I don't look good enough?' I was just filled with self doubt." So she stayed home, and thus did not accept in person her Grammy Award for best country song. She has since written songs that have been recorded by the country singers Patty Loveless and Emmylou Harris and the rock singer Tom Petty.

The songs Williams wrote for her next album, *Car Wheels on a Gravel Road*, took shape slowly. She told Kaufman that she worked on the single "Lake Charles," about the town in which she was born, "over a period of several years, just chipping away at it, like a sculptor would do." She began writing the song "Drunken Angel" as early as 1990 or 1991. "It was right after this songwriter I knew out of Austin, Blaze Foley, had been shot and killed in an argument," she recalled to Kaufman. "It happened in 1989, and so I started writing the song about him a year later, but it went through several drafts before it came out and was finished."

Williams's persistence in wanting to "get the album right," as she put it, delayed its release for several years. As she told Darcy Frey for the *New York Times Magazine* (September 14, 1997), her major fear while making it was that she would sound "overproduced." "Just listen to the radio or watch MTV," she said. "All the edge is taken off. I'm trying to keep the edge on." Having selected songs that she performed in 1995 in a string of successful concerts in Texas, Williams first recorded them with her longtime guitarist Gurf Morlix. But the result did not please her; it was "flat, lifeless, not up to par," she told Frey. The following year she began working with the renowned songwriter Steve Earle and his partner Ray Kennedy, who had access to some 1950s recording equipment. Williams hoped that using old equipment would give her songs the "raw and scratchy" feel that she wanted, but again, the outcome left her dissatisfied. She next signed with American Recordings, an affiliate of Columbia Records that had been launched by the former rap producer Rick Rubin. At American she began working with the producer Roy Bittan, the long-time keyboardist for Bruce Springsteen's E Street Band. The product of their collaboration, too, failed to meet her standards, so, in 1997, Williams switched labels again, to Mercury Records. She completed *Car Wheels on a Gravel Road* in 1998.

Williams, who is perhaps her own toughest critic, told Frey, "A million people could tell me this album is great, and it won't matter if I don't feel that way in my gut." Judging by her assessment of the album and the appraisals of various critics, the pains that she took in making *Car Wheels on a Gravel Road* have paid off. She told Steve Knopper for *Billboard* (May 30, 1998), "I definitely feel, just in terms of growth as a writer and vocally, better about this [album] than . . . any other [one] before this." In *Entertainment Weekly* (August 14, 1998), the music critic Rob Brenner wrote, "Williams's weathered twang conveys more emotion in one drawn-out vowel than [the top-selling pop singer Celine] Dion does in 10 ear-piercing wails." "Lucinda Williams seems to have experienced a thousand shades of heartbreak, and her lyrics reveal both a tortured soul and a brilliant mind . . . ," Scott Byron wrote for *VH1 On-line*. "[Her] ability to draw us into settings and emotions is what makes her so extraordinary. She uses words with exactness and care, and sings with an eerie precision and passion, always getting to the heart of her poetic lyrics." *Car Wheels on a Gravel Road* made many critics' lists of best albums of the year, and it has been called Williams's best work to date.

Lucinda Williams lives in a rented house in Nashville, Tennessee, with her boyfriend, Richard Price, who plays bass guitar in her band. In her spare time she enjoys writing letters to friends and family; she does so in longhand, with a fountain pen (she does not have e-mail). Although she is sometimes described as an artist with whom it is difficult to work because of her high standards, Williams maintained to Knopper that this is not really the case. "I don't burn bridges if I can help it," she said. "I've managed to stay friends with everybody I've worked with." With regard to her age—at 46, she is older than the average recording artist—Williams told Robert Wilonsky for the *Dallas Observer* (December 3, 1998, on-line), "In the writing world where I come out of, the older you get, the better you get. It's not like in the pop, instant-gratification world, where when you're young and hungry and living on the edge, that's where you create your best work, and when you get older, it's all over with. I don't think the amount of money you have and your level of success should have anything to do with your level of creativity. That's something between you and your demons." — C.P.

Suggested Reading: *Addicted to Noise* (on-line); *Billboard* p16+ May 30, 1998, with photo; *Chicago Tribune* V p3 Apr. 1, 1993, with photo; *Dallas News* (on-line) Dec. 6, 1998; *Dallas Observer Online* Dec. 3–9, 1998, with photos;

Entertainment Weekly p32+ May 7, 1993, with photo, p80 Aug. 14, 1998, with photo; *New York Times* C p1 Mar. 25, 1993, with photo; *New York Times Magazine* p53+ Sep. 14, 1997, with photos; *People* p113+ Sep. 21, 1998, with photos; *Rolling Stone* p131+ July 9–23, 1998; *VH1 On-line*

Selected Recordings: *Ramblin' on My Mind*, 1979; *Happy Woman Blues*, 1980; *Lucinda Williams*, 1988; *Sweet Old World*, 1992; *Car Wheels on a Gravel Road*, 1998

Adrees A. Latif/Archive Photos

Williams, Ricky

May 21, 1977– Football player. Address: c/o Integrated Sports International, One Meadowlands Plaza, Suite 1501, East Rutherford, NJ 07073

During his four-year college football career with the University of Texas Longhorns, Ricky Williams racked up an array of accomplishments that place him firmly among the best college running backs ever. He is currently the holder of 12 National Collegiate Athletic Association (NCAA) Division I records and co-holder of four other records; among those in the former category is the record for career rushing yards, previously held—for 22 years—by Tony Dorsett, who cheered Williams from the stands as the younger back surpassed Dorsett's mark, ultimately rushing for a total of 6,279 yards to Dorsett's 6,082. Displaying a rare combination of power and speed, Williams is noted almost as much for his appearance as for his play. His dreadlocks, pierced tongue, and tattoos, including a colorful one of the cartoon character Mighty Mouse, have led journalists to comment that he looks more like an art student than a jock. Williams's decision to forgo a lucrative professional contract in the National Football League (NFL) after his stellar junior year and return to a college team that appeared to have little chance for success seemed to confirm reports that he is truly worthy of the role-model status conferred on so many athletes. At the close of the 1998 football season, Williams won the Heisman Trophy and was thus recognized as the best player in college football that year. In April 1999 he was chosen fifth overall in the National Football League draft, by the New Orleans Saints.

Ricky Williams was born Errick Lynne Williams Jr. on May 21, 1977. His father, Errick Williams Sr., left the family when Ricky was five years old, and his parents divorced in 1983, amid allegations that Errick Sr. had abused Ricky and his twin sister, Cassie. Following the divorce, their mother, Sandy, worked for $5.50 per hour as a government purchasing agent and attended night school, leaving Ricky to look after Cassie and their younger sister, Nisey, in their home in San Diego, California. His responsibilities included cooking dinners for his siblings. Early on, based on his high scores on standardized tests, his teachers pegged him as academically talented, and for the most part he attended special classes for gifted students. However, for a long time he lashed out violently at other children and was labeled maladjusted and troubled. Thanks to sports, which served as an outlet for his anger, and with the help of counseling, he became better able to control his emotions by the time he finished ninth grade.

Williams was a standout in four sports at San Diego's Patrick Henry High School. He excelled in track and wrestling, and during his senior year he hit .340 as a star on the baseball team. In fact, Williams was so promising in that sport that in June of his senior year, the Philadelphia Phillies selected him in the eighth round of the 1995 amateur draft. He accepted the team's offer and a $50,000 signing bonus, and for the next four summers he played in the outfield for various Phillies-affiliated minor-league farm teams, first in the Rookie League, in Martinsville, Virginia. In 1998, his last summer with the minor-league Phillies, he played with the Class A Batavia (New York) Muckdogs, where he batted a career-high .283. In December 1998, one day after the Expos purchased the rights to Williams from the Phillies, the Texas Rangers bought the rights to his baseball talent from the Expos. The Rangers placed him on their restricted list and still hold the rights to him.

Williams's greatest high-school athletic success came on the football field; during his four years at Patrick Henry High, he rushed for 4,129 yards and scored 55 touchdowns. After considering offers from numerous college football programs, he chose to attend the University of Texas at Austin. He in-

formed the university of his decision before signing with the Phillies, but because of his professional status as a baseball player, Texas denied him an athletic scholarship. As part of his baseball contract, however, the Phillies paid his college expenses in addition to his salary, the latter of which Williams used to pay his mother's bills and his sisters' college tuition. Williams has remained close to his family; his mother relocated to Austin during his sophomore year, and both his sisters attended the University of Texas at Austin. Earlier, while he was in high school, Williams had established contact with his father, who was then living in Houston and working as a minister and as the environmental director of a nursing home, and they have since begun to develop a relationship.

During his freshman season as a Longhorn, Williams rushed for 990 yards, a school record for a first-year player. His accomplishment was more remarkable in light of the position he played, that of fullback, in which his main role was to block for other offensive players rather than run the ball himself. His exceptional play helped his team win the Southwest Conference title in 1995, and he was named Southwest Conference freshman of the year. The following season Williams, still at fullback, was even more productive. He rushed for 1,272 yards and helped the Longhorns to the championship title in their new conference, the Big 12, which they had joined at the start of the 1996 season. Despite these achievements, Williams was not the focus of the Longhorns' offense; for example, in the 37–27 upset victory against Nebraska that gave Texas the 1996 conference title—according to sportswriters, the Longhorns' most impressive victory during Williams's first three seasons with the team—he rushed for only eight yards. Williams's most significant contribution to that win was as a blocker; in that capacity he helped stave off Nebraska's formidable defense, enabling James Brown, Texas's quarterback, to pass for 353 yards.

Williams emerged as a sensation during his junior year, during which his role on the team was switched from fullback to tailback and thus provided more opportunities for him to carry the ball. His combination of size, power, and speed—he is six feet tall and weighed 225 as a college player, and he can bench-press 400 pounds and run 40 yards in 4.39 seconds—proved formidable when he was put to use as a running back, enabling him to outmaneuver and overpower his opponents. Indeed, he gained many of his rushing yards after being hit—but not tackled—by defenders. Williams led the NCAA that season with 25 rushing touchdowns, 1,893 rushing yards, and an average output of 13.2 points per game. He earned the nickname "Little Earl," because his running game reminded many of that of Earl Campbell, a former University of Texas star who had set most of the school's rushing records and won the Heisman Trophy in 1977. (Until Williams, Campbell was the only player from the school to have received the coveted award.) In February 1997 Williams was honored as the nation's top running back and received the Doak Walker Award, named after the legendary college running back for Southern Methodist State who won the Heisman in 1948. Williams was also selected to the Walter Camp All-America team and finished fifth in balloting for the 1997 Heisman Trophy. His relatively low finish in the voting for that award, given his achievements on the field, was generally attributed to Texas's dismal record of four wins and seven losses during the season. Still, his team's overall performance notwithstanding, Williams was gaining a reputation as an all-time great college running back in the tradition of Jim Brown, Tony Dorsett, Herschel Walker, and Barry Sanders.

At one point during his junior year, Williams had resolved to enter the NFL draft. He changed his mind after the Longhorns' new coach, Mack Brown (who had previously coached at the University of North Carolina), pledged to make him the focus of the Longhorns' offense, and after hearing a sermon, in a San Diego church around Christmastime, "about the grass not always being greener on the other side," as he recalled to Joe Drape for the *New York Times* (August 30, 1998, on-line). "It made me think that I'm pretty happy [at Texas], why would I need to get more when I really don't need it and risk being unhappy?" Williams's decision to remain at Texas for another year endeared him to college football's most ardent fans. It was generally agreed that he would have been a top selection in the 1998 NFL draft and would have gotten a contract that, according to the *Sporting News* (August 17, 1998), would surely have been worth upwards of $20 million.

Williams's decision to stay was a public confirmation of what those who are close to him had always known: that his character is as outstanding as his athletic gifts. He is reported to be humble, generous to a fault with time and money, shy at parties, and so softhearted that he cannot openly reject women who ask him out; instead, if he's not interested in dating them, he pretends his sister Cassie is his girlfriend. His regular visits to elementary schools and hospitals display a devotion to children that many consider remarkable when compared with the token charitable gestures of many athletes. Once, Williams almost missed an awards ceremony because he was attending the birthday party of a boy he had met during a classroom visit. Williams inspired further admiration from the press when it came to light that he had struck up a friendship with Doak Walker, whom he had met when he received the award bearing Walker's name. Williams was greatly impressed by Walker's kindness and sincerity. Several weeks after they met, the elder football great was paralyzed in a skiing accident, and Williams began writing him letters. Walker died in 1998.

Williams's gamble on remaining in college proved extremely felicitous. John Mackovic, the only head coach under whom he had played at Texas, had been dismissed because of the Long-

horns' losing record, and Mack Brown was named head coach for the 1998–99 season. Thus, Williams's fourth season at Texas would be considered a "rebuilding year," which is usually marked by a rocky transition between coaching systems. However, driven by Brown's insistence that the team play well not only for themselves but also to improve Williams's Heisman chances, the Longhorns finished the 1998 season with eight wins and three losses. Williams himself turned in one of the most breathtaking individual seasons in college-football history. Aided by Coach Brown's newly implemented offense, which centered on Williams, and the emergence of rookie quarterback Major Applewhite, whose passing game prevented opposing defenses from focusing entirely on thwarting Williams, the running back finished his senior season with 27 rushing touchdowns and 2,124 rushing yards, thereby becoming only the eighth player in NCAA history to surpass 2,000 rushing yards in a season. After an upset win against Nebraska, 20–16, the losing team's fans stayed to cheer Williams, who had rushed for 150 yards and prevented a Nebraska touchdown by making a tackle on an interception, a play that was considered the turning point in the game for the Longhorns.

But the crowning achievement of the season— and of Williams's college career—came in the Longhorns' last game of the regular season, in November 1998, against Texas A&M, which was then ranked No. 2 in the nation. Late in the first quarter of that game, Williams broke several tackles and ran for a 60-yard touchdown. It was on that spectacular play that Williams surpassed Dorsett's rushing record, which had been set in 1976 during his final year at the University of Pittsburgh. Williams went on to rush for a total of 259 yards in the 26–24 victory over Texas A&M and finished his college career with 1,003 carries. In addition to that benchmark accomplishment, he had more total yards (both rushing and receiving)—7,206—than anyone in the history of NCAA Division I football. He had also set records for career touchdowns, with 75, and for most points by a player other than a field-goal kicker, with 452. In all, he had set 12 NCAA Division I records, tied four more—among them the record for most games (11) with over 200 yards rushing, which he shares with Marcus Allen—and set or tied 44 University of Texas records. In his four seasons as a Longhorn, Williams never missed a game and averaged a remarkable 136.5 rushing yards per game. Thanks in large part to Williams, the Longhorns won a berth in the postseason Cotton Bowl, where they beat Mississippi State University, 38–11, in January 1999.

On the heels of his achievements on the field, Williams won nearly every major award in college football. He was named Associated Press College Player of the Year. He won the Walter Camp Football Foundation Award, the Maxwell Award, and, for the second consecutive year, the Doak Walker Award, thereby becoming the first two-time winner of that honor. Then came the Heisman Trophy, awarded to the player whom a panel of past Heisman winners, sportswriters, and broadcasters deem to be the best in the country. Williams had acknowledged feeling snubbed when he came in fifth the previous year; in 1999, he won the award by the fourth-largest margin in its 64-year history. "I owe the greatest amount of gratitude to my teammates," Williams said at the Heisman Trophy ceremony, as quoted by the *Washington Post* (December 13, 1998). "They say that this is an individual award, but in this case it is a team award." Cade McNown, the departing UCLA quarterback and a finalist for the trophy, applauded the Heisman panel's choice, telling a *New York Times* (December 12, 1998, on-line) reporter, "While [Williams] gives credit to his teammates, they have really asked him to carry the load and he has responded. When [opposing] teams have focused on him, he has managed to shake off defenders and make some big runs. I don't think there are many guys who are as valuable to their team as he is."

In January 1999 Williams fired his agent, Woolf and Associates, and in February he signed with No Limit Sports Management, formed in 1997 by the rap artist Master P as the newest arm of his growing business empire, which also includes the No Limit record company. In the *New York Times* (April 17, 1999), William C. Rhoden wrote that "the sports establishment" warned Williams that with No Limit representing him, NFL management might be unwilling to sign him. This was not the first time Williams had been advised—and refused—to conform to others' ideas of propriety. Throughout his college career, Williams had also been admonished to cut his dreadlocks, which he had worn since his sophomore year of high school, when he developed a fondness for the music of the reggae legend Bob Marley. He had gotten his ears pierced at age 10 and his first tattoo at age 16. Prior to the 1999 draft, Rhoden had predicted in the *New York Times* that although many people believed Williams to be the best player available, he wouldn't be selected first, not because he isn't a quarterback but "largely because he is different." Rhoden called Williams the embodiment of "a new generation of young players: they are more independent, more unpredictable, more artistic and less grateful than previous generations." "In the staid, conservative world of professional football decision makers, where military order and ritual reign, Williams potentially represents a challenge," Rhoden explained.

In March 1999 Williams announced that he would forgo baseball that spring, in order to prepare for the upcoming NFL draft. He entered the draft among a slew of highly rated college quarterbacks, and due to the demand for such players, it was widely assumed that the teams with the top three picks would pass him over. The team entitled to the fourth pick, the Indianapolis Colts, had selected a quarterback, Peyton Manning, in the previous year's draft, and with Manning solidly in-

stalled as the team's starter, many expected the Colts to select Williams. Adding to the speculation, days before the draft the Colts traded their veteran star running back, Marshall Faulk, to the St. Louis Rams. Thus many sports insiders, not least of all Williams himself, were stunned when the Colts selected the running back Edgerrin James, from the University of Miami. While many concluded that the Colts had passed on Williams because they feared difficult contract negotiations with his representatives, the Colts insisted that they chose James because of his ability to catch passes as well as run the ball. Virtually no one interested in the draft would have predicted that Williams would be the second running back chosen, and while Williams described himself as "shocked" by the turn of events, he was happy to be picked fifth, immediately following James, by the New Orleans Saints. That team's management traded away all their other picks in the 1999 draft and some of their year 2000 picks—a total of eight potential players—in order to move from the 12th to the fifth spot and select Williams. "It's flattering to know the Saints made a deal like they did," Williams told *CNN/SI* (April 18, 1999, on-line). "Now, I hope I can justify that." The Saints' head coach, Mike Ditka, wore a wig of shoulder-length dreadlocks when he met with Williams to welcome him aboard, and exuberant New Orleans fans wore T-shirts proclaiming "We got Ricky!"

Williams's rookie season in the NFL did not start out as well as most fans had anticipated. In the Saints' first exhibition game, he injured his ankle after carrying the ball nine times. He recovered from that injury enough to start in the team's season opener, on September 12, 1999, against the Carolina Panthers. In that game he rushed for 40 yards on 10 attempts and helped his team achieve a 19–10 win. The Saints then lost three straight games, to the San Francisco 49ers, the Chicago Bears, and the Atlanta Falcons, respectively. In those four games Williams gained a total of 257 yards in 72 attempts, for an average of 3.6 yards per carry; he also had seven receptions for 31 yards. These unspectacular statistics were attributed to Williams's earlier ankle injury and an injury to his elbow that he suffered early on during the season.

Although he has missed spring and summer college sessions to play baseball and is thus still several semesters away from earning his degree, Williams's plans include graduation. "I'm an education major and I want to teach," he told Joe Drape. "So the plan is work hard, succeed, invest wisely, and then teach elementary school." — Y.P.

Suggested Reading: *New York Times* (on-line) Aug. 30, 1998, Dec. 12, 1998, Dec. 13, 1998; *Sporting News* p68+ Aug. 17, 1998, with photos; *Sports Illustrated* p72+ May 18, 1998, with photos, p42+ Nov. 16, 1998, with photos; *Washington Post* D p10 Dec. 13, 1998, with photo

Michael Gomez/Courtesy of Davis McLarty Agency

Willis, Kelly

Oct. 1, 1968– Country-music vocalist; songwriter.
Address: c/o Rykodisc, Shetland Park, 27
Congress St., Salem, MA 01970

Described by Neil Pond in *Country Music* (August/September 1999) as "a square peg in the round-hole world of radio, which tends to prefer its women to be either anthem blasters or teasing male bashers," the country-music singer-songwriter Kelly Willis has since the late 1980s dazzled critics and fans alike with her distinctive, soulful singing. Her style blends elements of country and rock and draws from earlier periods in both genres, eschewing the slickness of much contemporary music. Although mainstream commercial success has eluded her, Willis has established enough of a following to be dubbed "the queen of alternative country."

Kelly Willis was born on October 1, 1968 in Lawton, Oklahoma, the youngest of the three children of Deral Willis, a colonel in the U.S. Army, and his wife. She became aware of her singing ability as a child but initially did not embrace her gift. As Willis told Jack Hurst for the *Chicago Tribune* (September 19, 1993), she noticed while singing with her classmates in the first or second grade that the other children were "just kind of moving their mouths and looking at me. I think they were astounded that a kid would sing that way: loud." She then added, "You know how when you're a kid you sing in that pretty little head voice that kids use? I think I was singing differently. . . . I always used my throat more [than the other children]. I think it must have been weird to hear a kid sing like that. Anyway, it scared me, and I stopped sing-

ing after that, because I was embarrassed. Before that, I had been picked for the school chorus."

As a child, Willis experienced the hardships of having to move frequently and witnessing her parents' divorce, which occurred when she was nine. She told Karen Schoemer for *Rolling Stone* (September 2, 1993) that her mother moved away after the divorce and that afterward, "I didn't see her but maybe once a year. My father made it hard on her even to call." As a consequence, Willis withdrew from other people. "I went to my room," she recalled to Hurst. "I just hung out there. I wasn't part of anything that was going on. I was just on the outside looking in. Watching. I think a lot of people who are creative and artistic have got some strange sort of pain in their lives that sort of makes them look at things a little differently, makes them sort of be on the outside watching everybody. I think it gives them an edge they don't even know they have. It's just the way they are."

Willis, whose family had settled in Annandale, Virginia, by the time she entered her teens, found herself gravitating toward music, a pursuit that her mother had encouraged. She told Schoemer, "My mother acted in musicals when I was young, and I was actually in some of them with her, just as an extra. She played the piano and introduced music into our lives. When she moved away, that sort of stopped. I remember singing all the time. Once I said to my dad, 'I'm always singing.' He said, 'Well, that means you're happy.' And I thought, 'Well, I guess so.' But actually, I think that music and singing is a kind of *soothant*. It's more to help you if you're not happy. That's what it was for me." Still, she felt uncomfortable singing in front of her high-school classmates because, as she told David Browne for *Entertainment Weekly* (July 12, 1991), "even if I was singing along to U2, I'd do it a lot harder and louder than my friends."

In 1987, while attending Annandale High School, Willis met the drummer Mas Palermo, and she overcame her shyness sufficiently to audition for Palermo's rockabilly band, giving them a demo tape she had made at a coin-operated recording booth. (The tape contained her version of Elvis Presley's "Teddy Bear.") At around the same time, Willis made her performance debut at her high-school talent show. Singing in public, she commented to Harrington, "was incredibly terrifying for me, but it was more exciting than terrifying. I would manage to get up there and do it, even though I was shaking like crazy and could barely stand. But there was something inside me saying, 'This is really what you want to do.'" She then added, "I was so quiet, I felt like nobody ever noticed me, but I always felt there was *something* there to be noticed and this would be my opportunity to prove it." For Palermo's band, Willis sang rockabilly songs and covers of tunes by Wanda Jackson, and she quickly emerged as the group's star. The band's name soon changed to reflect that development, and Kelly and the Fireballs became a popular band in and around Washington, D.C.

After she graduated from high school, in the late 1980s, Willis and the band moved to Austin, Texas, a thriving music town. This decision was accepted, if not applauded, by Willis's father. "My dad didn't think it was all that serious," Willis told Harrington. "He thought it was something I had to get out of my system. He didn't want to get in the way, and that way I *would* get it out of my system. But I didn't." Indeed, although Kelly and the Fireballs broke up six months after moving to Texas, Willis did not give up. She and Palermo recruited guitarist David Murray, steel guitar player Michael Hardwick, and bassist Michael Foreman and formed Radio Ranch. Willis and Radio Ranch soon proved popular in Austin. In about 1989 Willis and Palermo married.

Willis learned to play the guitar, but it was her vocal abilities that caught the attention of the singer Nanci Griffith, while Radio Ranch was performing at the Continental Club. Griffith encouraged MCA Records to sign Willis to a recording contract. Willis's debut album on MCA/Nashville was *Well Traveled Love* (1990), on which she sang with the accompaniment of Radio Ranch. The album received strong reviews and won Willis comparisons to the late Patsy Cline. "For a long time, women were singing pretty and thin," Willis told Rob Tannenbaum for *Rolling Stone* (September 6, 1990), commenting on Cline's lingering influence on contemporary country-music singers. "Now there's a lot of young women who are singing more aggressively. That's what I liked about Patsy when I first heard her, that she sounded so gutsy." Despite winning critical acclaim, the album fared poorly commercially, and its songs received little airplay on radio stations.

Willis's second album with MCA/Nashville, *Bang Bang* (1991), which Ralph Novak, writing for *People* (May 27, 1991), described as "a rough-rocking, blues-oozing, romance-defying, blurb-inspiring production if ever there was one," fared somewhat better. Two songs from the album, "I Don't Want to Love You" and "Little Honey," were included in the soundtrack for the hit film *Thelma and Louise* (1991). The album also featured the song "Baby, Take a Piece of My Heart," which reached number 50 on the *Billboard* chart. Moreover, in the wake of the album's modest success, Willis made her feature-film acting debut as a folk singer named Clarissa Flan in the film *Bob Roberts* (1992). Articles about the photogenic singer began to spring up in such magazines as *Vogue*, *People*, and *Mademoiselle*.

This publicity did little to help sales of Willis's third album on the MCA/Nashville label, *Kelly Willis* (1993). The album did, however, win notice for featuring the soulful song "World Without You," which had been co-written by Willis and had been inspired by her own experiences of longing for her mother. "Once in a while, like maybe one day a year," her mother's early absence from her life "would hit me really hard," Willis told Hurst. "For some reason out of the blue I would just

be devastated that this had happened. That feeling came again the night before I went to write with Paul Kennerley, and that's the song that came out."

By this time, Willis and MCA/Nashville were disappointed that Willis had not emerged as the music star that many had predicted she would be. Part of the problem was that her songs did not fit snugly into the conventions of mainstream country music. To country purists, Willis's sound was too much like rock-'n'-roll, while to rock devotees, it had too much in common with country. As a result, she did not receive much radio play. Commenting on that situation, Willis told Harrington that her music was a branch of country that's about "attitude, youth maybe, spirit—I don't want to come across negative toward others, so I'm limited with my words—but it's about real roots, pulling from that early '50s and '60s country and rock-and-roll, that sort of vibe you don't find in rock-and-roll today." She then added, "I see the mainstream stuff as being a little slick, and us a little rough."

In addition to the difficulty of getting airplay, Willis, who was still extremely shy, found it hard to navigate the public-relations aspect of being a professional musician. "I just couldn't walk into a room and charm people," she recalled to Pond. "I couldn't even walk into a room and say *hello*. I was really awkward at it." She has since overcome her shyness, in part through media training, which was arranged for her by MCA. "But I think what helped most was just doing it," she told Hurst, "talking to people. . . . But it was a while before I could be anywhere near myself."

Because of her poor record sales, Willis was dropped by MCA/Nashville in 1993. Despite that, she won a nomination for top new female vocalist of 1994 from the Academy of Country Music. Also that year, *People* named her one of the world's 50 most beautiful people. Before long she was signed by A & M Records, another mainstream country music label with a strong presence in Nashville. Regrettably, that association did not prove fruitful, as A & M released Willis's fourth album, *Fading Fast* (1996), rather haphazardly. The album featured just four tracks and was released only in Texas. When the record—predictably—failed to sell well, Willis was dropped from the A & M label.

Willis left Nashville, where she had gone to pursue her recording career, and returned to Austin, where she had developed a large and loyal following. Indeed, some of her fans there called her "the voice of Austin." Working away from the spotlight and the pressure of a large commercial record label, Willis worked on her songwriting and began compiling material for a new album. Meanwhile, in 1997 she toured with the Lilith Fair Tour, a music festival starring female musicians, which had been created by Sarah McLaughlin. Willis also performed with country-music singer Bruce Robison on the ballads "When I Love You" and "Don't You Ever Call My Name" on Robison's album *Wrapped* (1997).

In the spring of 1999, Willis released her fifth album, *What I Deserve* (1999), on the independent Rykodisc label. The album, which Willis produced on her own, features 13 songs, six of which she wrote or co-wrote. Asked if the title of the album referred to her career, Willis told Pond, "It was more of a spiritual, all-around thing, longing for something, not knowing exactly what, but feeling like something is missing, whatever it is—just wanting someone to recognize you in some way. It wasn't necessarily about my career. But things feel really good right now. I feel happier than I have in a long time." Once again, Willis received critical acclaim for her music, but the songs on the album received little airplay, and the album sold modestly. Despite that, Willis has maintained that she is content to be able to create her unique brand of country music. "I don't need to be a huge commercial success in order to feel like I'm doing a good job, 'cause that's like setting yourself up for failure," she told Pond. "You have to find the little areas in your life that really matter and try to be successful in those, and hopefully everything else will fall into line." She has also become better at interacting with her audience. "I can converse with people now," she told Pond. "I'm like a normal person. It's a combination of not being afraid and also not worrying about whether anyone thinks I'm perfect, great, charming, attractive, funny, all that stuff. It doesn't matter as much anymore. I'm not afraid of just going ahead and being who I am."

Karen Schoemer described Willis's voice thusly: "Throaty, lonesome, and blue, with just the faintest echo of Appalachia, it has that rare balance of emotion and technique that can elevate the simplest lyric into the realm of the transcendent." Pointing out a different quality, Richard Harrington, in the *Washington Post* (August 10, 1991), wrote, "Like Anita Baker's, the big voice that emerges from Willis seems entirely out of proportion to the frame, and carries an aura of world-weary experience that belies her [young] age."

Willis lives in Austin with her second husband, Bruce Robison, whom she married in late 1996. Her marriage to Mas Palermo ended in 1991. — Y.P.

Suggested Reading: *Chicago Tribune* V p3 Aug. 1, 1991, with photo, XIII p20+ Sep. 19, 1993, with photo; *Country Music* p36+ Aug./Sep. 1999, with photos; *Rolling Stone* p25 Sep. 6, 1990, with photo, p57 Sep. 2, 1993, with photo; *Washington Post* C p1+ Aug. 10, 1991, with photo

Selected Recordings: *Well Traveled Love*, 1990; *Bang Bang*, 1991; *Kelly Willis*, 1993; *Fading Fast*, 1996; *What I Deserve*, 1999

Selected Films: *Bob Roberts*, 1992

Woo, John

1946(?)– Film and television director. Address: c/o William Morris Agency, 151 El Camino Dr., Beverly Hills, CA 90212

Take a standard action film of the early 1980s, inject it with steroids, and blow it up into a cartoonish but beautifully choreographed spectacle that somehow still radiates pathos and sentimentality. That, in essence, is what John Woo did when he made *A Better Tomorrow* (1986) and the many other films he wrote and directed while living in Hong Kong. In the process, he became one of the preeminent makers of action films in the world. Indeed, some of his images are considered so distinctive that his name has sometimes been used as an adjective. A character leaping in the air with two guns blazing can be described as "Woo-esque," as can a character who is knocked back by an explosion yet still manages to squeeze off a few more shots in mid-air. And when two characters have their guns pressed against each other's faces so tightly that they resemble an intricate M. C. Escher drawing, that's signature Woo as well.

To be sure, Woo's films contain plenty of the elements found in standard action films: guns magically reload; protagonists with unerring aim mow down bad guys incapable of shooting straight.

Fred Prouser/Archive Photos

What distinguishes Woo's work is the sheer beauty and gracefulness of the gunplay. Cops and criminals, assassins and their targets all circle, leap, and dodge in a feverish dance punctuated by what seems like thousands of bullets. "Balletic" has become the adjective most commonly used to describe his works, and if its use has become somewhat hackneyed in describing Woo's films, it's because Woo readily admits that while crafting his action scenes, he tends to think of himself as a dance choreographer rather than a special-effects maven. "When I shoot action sequences I think of great dancers, Gene Kelly, [Fred] Astaire," he told Bernard Weinraub for the *New York Times* (February 22, 1996). "In action I feel like I'm creating a ballet, a dance. That's what I like. Even though there's violence, it's a dance." As Woo has said in various interviews, to him a beretta has "a passionate rhythm," and an explosion is like "a happy drum beating."

Woo has never fired a gun in real life, and he claims to be a peace-loving man. In fact, had things worked out differently, he might have been a minister preaching the Lutheran gospel instead of a celebrated action-film director in Hong Kong and the U.S. He still claims to be religious (though not in the church-going sense), and evidence of his faith can be observed in his films. Religious icons frequently pop up as props, and more often than not, his protagonists are sinners—an assassin with a conscience, a cop with a family he has ignored—who are trying to find some sort of redemption in a violent and chaotic world.

John Woo was born with the given name Wu Yusen in around 1946 in the Guangzhou Province of mainland China. When he was three years old, he was afflicted with a serious medical problem in his back. His parents, who were both wealthy and well educated, "spent all their fortune to find a good doctor," he told Aljean Harmetz for the *New York Times* (August 15, 1993). "At last they found a young doctor educated in Germany who cut the flesh from my leg to put on my back and who saved me. But I couldn't walk right until I was eight years old, and my right leg is shorter than my left."

In 1951 the Woo family fled to Hong Kong to escape the Communists, who had taken over mainland China in 1949. In Hong Kong Woo's father contracted tuberculosis, and he was hospitalized for 10 years. Supported solely by Woo's mother, who worked as a laborer, cutting stones for a construction company, the once-prosperous Woo family lived a hardscrabble existence and, for a brief period, made their home on the streets. Woo got his first up-close look at violence in Hong Kong's slums. "I saw it every day, the crime, the gangs, the knives, the drugs, the prostitutes . . . ," he told Bernard Weinraub. "We lived in shacks. People got killed right in front of our door. I have seen so much violence, so much unfairness. I felt we were living in hell. I just wanted to fly away from hell."

If hell was their slum neighborhood, heaven was the local cinema, where the young Woo became entranced with the sheer escapist fantasy of musicals like *The Wizard of Oz* and *Seven Brides for Seven Brothers*. These movies inspired Woo to make his

own. "I got a piece of glass and put on some color or drew some image on it," he told Desson Howe for the *Washington Post* (August 20, 1993). "Then I would pull a blanket over myself, in the dark, and I would use a torch [i.e., flashlight] shining through the glass, to project the image on the wall. For example I'd draw a cowboy on the glass. Then I moved the glass a little bit, or moved the torch a little bit. The image would move . . . just like in the movies. At that time I felt that, if I could make a real movie some day, it would be terrific."

Woo's education, as well as his brother's and sister's, was financed by an American family who, through a local Lutheran church, sponsored them for six years. That act of church-related charity deeply moved Woo (and helps to explain why doves, crosses, and images of the Virgin Mary are prominent motifs in his films). At one point he seriously considered becoming a minister, but after a seminary rejected him, film became his abiding passion. He stole books on film theory, and gradually his taste expanded to include the works of such directors as Sam Peckinpah, Stanley Kubrick, Akira Kurosawa, Alfred Hitchcock, and Arthur Penn. After he finished his education at Matteo Ricci College, a Lutheran high school, Woo continued his study of filmmaking at a local film club, and he made some artsy and introspective short films. University wasn't an option for him, because his family had no money.

In 1969 Woo got his first job in the film industry, as a production assistant at Cathay Studios. Shortly thereafter he began working for Shaw Brothers Studio, where he served as an assistant director to Chang Che, who became famous for making such martial-arts films as *Five Deadly Venoms* and *One-Armed Swordsman*. In 1973 Woo got to direct a film of his own, entitled *The Young Dragons*. He then moved to Golden Harvest Studios and churned out one picture after another, much like a worker at "a match factory," as he told Desson Howe. His films from this period include *The Dragon Tamers* (1975); the Chinese opera *Princess Chang Ping* (1976); and *The Hand of Death* (also called *Shaolin Men* and *Countdown in Kung Fu*, 1976), which starred Jackie Chan and Samo Hung, who later became big names in kung-fu comedy.

Soon bored with the martial-arts genre, Woo proposed to his bosses that they produce a modern gangster film. His bosses turned him down, instead suggesting that he go into comedy, which was the trend in Hong Kong movies at the time. Despite some reluctance Woo embraced Mel Brooks–style comedy, and his first efforts, among them *The Pilferer's Progress* (also called *Money Crazy*, 1977) and *Follow the Star* (1977) did well at the box office. From then on Woo was pigeonholed as a director of comedies, and he was assigned only comedy projects, such as *Laughing Times* (1981), and, after switching to another studio, Cinema City, in 1981, *To Hell with the Devil* (1982) and *Plain Jane to the Rescue* (1982). Perhaps unconsciously Woo expressed in his comedies his unhappiness at not being given the chance to direct any other type of film. "They became bitter laugh comedies," he told Jeff Yang for *Vibe Magazine Online* (August 1997). "People were confused. They were saying, 'It looks like a comedy, but there's so much anger here. It's so depressing.'" By the mid-1980s it had become obvious that Woo was in a rut. Several of his films did not do well, and he was being labeled box-office poison. Friends advised him to retire, even though he was only in his late 30s.

Salvation came when, with the help of the director and producer Tsui Hark, Woo finally got the go-ahead to make a gangster film, *A Better Tomorrow* (1986). In doing so, Woo made use of the talent that had remained submerged while he was making schlocky martial-arts and comedy films. Although he drenched the film in the aestheticized violence that became his hallmark, Woo conceived it as more than simply a story about gangsters. "The younger generation seemed to be lost," he explained to Jeff Yang. "They had become rootless, they were rude; they only cared about imitating foreign idols. I felt the need to make a film that would send them a message, to bring out something that has been gone for a long time: true values, like honor and chivalry. I wanted to show them what my father taught me: that a man should stand up for himself and for others." As his modern "Chinese knight," Woo cast the actor Chow Yun-Fat, whose career had been in a slump. *A Better Tomorrow* broke all box-office records in Hong Kong and quickly reversed the declining careers of Woo and Chow. Young men aped the mannerisms and style of dress of Chow's character, while the film industry aped Woo by producing numerous rip-off gangster films.

Amidst the cheap facsimiles, Woo's action films remained the standard bearers. Woo followed *A Better Tomorrow* with the films for which he is now best known: *A Better Tomorrow II* (1987), *The Killer* (1988), *Bullet in the Head* (1990), *Once a Thief* (1991), and *Hard Boiled* (1992). Like *A Better Tomorrow*, the films explore questions of honor and justice among both cops and criminals. More often than not, the films end in soul-purging bloodbaths. The last 40 minutes of *Hard Boiled*, for example, are devoted entirely to a gun battle that decimates a hospital. Four of the five films star Chow Yun-Fat; the partnership between Woo and Chow has been compared to those of two other director/actor pairs: John Ford and John Wayne, and Martin Scorsese and Robert De Niro.

In 1992 Woo settled with his family in the United States. One reason for the move was his desire to escape the constraints of filmmaking in Hong Kong. "The government in Hong Kong, the police, treat filmmakers like beggars," he told Bernard Weinraub for the *New York Times* (June 30, 1997). Also, the hectic schedules and less-structured state of filmmaking there made it impossible for him to spend time with his family—his wife, Annie Woo Ngau Chun-lung, and their three children, Kimberley, Angeles, and Frank. Making films in Hong Kong also severely cut down on the time he could spend on his favorite hobby: marathon sessions of cooking for his family and friends. "I take three or four hours to make one meal," he told Aljean Harmetz. "The reason I enjoy cooking is that's the only moment I can relax without pressure. When I'm cooking, I don't worry about the movie."

Woo's decision to work in Hollywood was enthusiastically anticipated by the directors Martin Scorsese, Sam Raimi, Quentin Tarantino, and many others among his American fans. His first American film, *Hard Target* (1993), was based on the Richard Connell short story "The Most Dangerous Game." It dealt with a group of wealthy men who have taken to hunting and killing homeless Vietnam veterans. Although, at $20 million, the budget for the film was nearly five times the amount spent, on average, on his Hong Kong films, many fans were disappointed by *Hard Target*, because it seemed to them a watered-down Woo product. Woo himself admitted to *Harper's Bazaar* (October 1993), "*Hard Target* is not a 'John Woo film.'" Part of the problem lay in the very different circumstances of filmmaking in Hollywood. In Hong Kong Woo had virtually complete freedom and could script extravagant slow-motion shots and freeze frames. Moreover, plot devices that Hong Kong audiences accept—such as homoerotic tension between the male leads and sentimental scenes in which protagonists stop in the middle of gunfights to rescue babies—apparently don't play well to American audiences. In Hollywood Woo had to deal with the many groups that had control over the final cut of the film. For example, he had to tone down the violent content of *Hard Target* seven times to get an R rating from the ratings board of the Motion Picture Association of America. He also had to deal with his studio's marketing groups, who often did not like his stylistic quirks. Terence Chang, a business partner of Woo's, told Aljean Harmetz, "John's original cut was so much better but for the test screening they recruited [Jean-Claude] Van Damme fans, and they said 'We don't like this. There's too little karate stuff.'"

Still, despite the hassles of dealing with the American studio system, Woo was glad to put the Hong Kong system behind him. "I can honestly say I'm happier making *Hard Target* than I was in Hong Kong, because even though the studios make problems for you in some ways, they also support you technically," he told *Film Comment* (September 1993). "I have so many difficult shots, so many complicated ideas, and everyone has such patience, such dedication to figuring out how it can be done and then doing it. I'm still amazed by all the actors. They're so sincere, so *serious*, about what they're doing. In Hong Kong there are many good actors, but they're too busy. The most popular actors sometimes make three or four movies at the same time, so they can only give you four or five hours and then they've got to go."

Broken Arrow and Face/Off, the second and third films, respectively, that Woo made in the U.S., fared much better than Hard Target and established him as a director with clout. Broken Arrow (1996), which stars Christian Slater and John Travolta, was budgeted at $60 million. Heavy with special effects, the film did extremely well at the box office and allowed Woo to negotiate more creative freedom for Face/Off (1997). Many fans feel that Face/Off has probably come closest to achieving the sublimity of Woo's Hong Kong films. The story involves an FBI agent (John Travolta) and a criminal (Nicolas Cage) whose faces are literally cut off and exchanged.

In addition to directing, Woo has produced a handful of films, including The Replacement Killers (1998), which is the first U.S. film to star Chow Yun-Fat, and The Big Hit (1998). Woo has also directed two television pilots produced by Alliance Communications Corp. The first, John Woo's Once a Thief (1996), was based on Woo's 1991 film, Once a Thief, and had a Caucasian cast; the pilot led to a Canadian series that Woo executive-produced. The second pilot, Blackjack (1998), went straight to video; it stars Dolph Lundgren as a personal-protection expert who has a paralyzing fear of the color white. Woo hopes to cast Chow in another of his films and revisit the genre of comedy. In the meantime he is directing Mission: Impossible 2, starring Tom Cruise. He is also slated to direct Dirty 30, about two Irish-American brothers on opposite sides of the law, and Windtalkers, a World War II picture about the Navajo tribesmen who were instrumental in sending and receiving coded messages. — W.G.

Suggested Reading: Asiaweek (on-line) Aug. 29, 1997; Chicago Tribune XIII p14+ Aug. 25, 1991, with photos, XIII p16+ Feb. 7, 1993, with photos, C p8 July 10, 1997, with photo; Film Comment p46+ Sep. 1993, with photos; Film Quarterly p23+ Summer 1996; New York Times II p11 Aug. 15, 1993, with photo, C p1+ Feb. 22, 1996, with photo, C p9 June 30, 1997, with photo; Vibe Magazine Online Aug. 1997, with photos; Washington Post D p1+ Aug. 20, 1993, with photo

Selected Films: as director—The Young Dragons, 1973; The Dragon Tamers, 1975; Hand of Death (a.k.a. Shaolin Men), 1976; Countdown in Kung Fu, 1976; Princess Chang Ping, 1976; Pilferer's Progress (a.k.a. Money Crazy), 1977; Follow the Star, 1977; Last Hurrah for Chivalry, 1978; Hello, Late Homecomers, 1978; From Riches to Rags, 1979; Laughing Times, 1981; To Hell with the Devil, 1982; Plain Jane to the Rescue, 1982; The Time You Need a Friend, 1984; Run, Tiger, Run, 1985; A Better Tomorrow, 1986; Heroes Shed No Tears, 1986; A Better Tomorrow II, 1987; The Killer, 1989; Just Heroes, 1990; Bullet in the Head, 1990; Once a Thief, 1991; Hard Boiled, 1992; Hard Target, 1993; Broken Arrow, 1996; Face/Off, 1997; as producer—A Better Tomorrow III, 1989; Peace Hotel, 1995; Somebody Up There Likes Me, 1996; The Replacement Killers, 1998; The Big Hit, 1998

Selected Television Shows: John Woo's Once a Thief, 1996; Blackjack, 1998

Yamanaka, Lois-Ann

Sep. 7, 1961– Writer. Address: c/o Susan Bergholz Literary Services, 17 W. 10th St., #5, New York, NY 10011

"Now Hawaii has found a bard of sorts, the novelist Lois-Ann Yamanaka," Jamie James wrote in a comprehensive survey of her work in the Atlantic Monthly (February 1999), "but the world she sings of is anything but a paradise. . . . Her Hawaii is green but cruel, and the 'work-day world' grinds her characters down with squalor and violence." From her earliest published writings, Yamanaka's "voice" has been that of the rural working-class who speak in a pidgin known as Hawaiian Creole English, which she and other Hawaiian writers of the "Bamboo Ridge school" have sought to preserve. Yamanaka's writings are not polemical, however, nor is the general tone of her work overly sober: James described her first novel, Wild Meat and the Bully Burgers (1995), an account of a young girl's struggle to transcend her family's dysfunc-

tioning, as "an exuberant, crazily comic series of anecdotes, virtually plotless." Her next novel, Blu's Hanging (1997), excited a storm of controversy when dissidents succeeded in having the Association for Asian American Studies withdraw its literary award from the book because of what they considered its unflattering and stereotypical portrait of Filipinos. Heads by Harry (1999), Yamanaka's third novel, is narrated by a young woman torn between two worlds: the familiar, insular one she has known since childhood, and the larger world beyond the family taxidermy business, to which she is apprenticed.

Lois-Ann Yamanaka was born on September 7, 1961 in Ho'olehua, on the island of Molokai, in Hawaii, the daughter of Harry, a taxidermist, and Jean, a schoolteacher. Her Japanese-American working-class family lived above Harry's taxidermy store, a setting that inspired many of the passages in Yamanaka's fiction, notably Heads by Harry. Describing her childhood, in Hilo, for Lan N. Nguyen in People (May 26, 1997), she said, "It was real stereotypical. You have to be good, do right, cannot make shame for the family. But there I was,

Marion Ettlinger/Courtesy of Farrar, Straus & Giroux
Lois-Ann Yamanaka

this funky loudmouthed thing." Like many in her situation, she at first tried to shed the dialect because of its lower-class connotations, telling *People* that "the skies are blue and the palm trees sway, but it's a hard life, and it has been for generations of us, because of this language." Earlier, she had told Sandy M. Fernández for *Ms.* (July/August 1996): "We were raised to believe that pidgin was substandard. . . . And you believe it, yeah. You think, 'I'll never get ahead; I'll never get a job 'cause I speak Pidgin.' So then to make it literature, that was out of the question. It was something too horrid and ugly."

While she was a student at the University of Hawaii at Manoa, however, a professor told her that her once-disdained pidgin was her "voice," a verdict that led her to rediscover what she has called "the sound of one's memory." After receiving her bachelor's of education degree in 1983 and her master's of education from the same institution in 1987, she began to write in the language of her childhood, encouraged by a 1990 National Endowment for the Humanities grant, which enabled her to devote more time to fiction. The first of her published works to attract critical acclaim was *Saturday Night at the Pahala Theatre*, a collection of novellas in verse published by Honolulu's Bamboo Ridge Press in 1993. (Bamboo Ridge was a writers' collective that had grown out of an important 1978 conference for new-wave Hawaiian voices that was organized by Darrell Lum and Eric Chock.) *Saturday Night at the Pahala Theatre* won publication in the *Pushcart XVIII* anthology that year. In 1994 the book brought Yamanaka an Asian American Studies National Book Award and led to a National Endowment for the Arts creative-writing fellow-

ship. That year she also won a *Pushcart Prize XIX* award for *Yarn Wig*, another short work.

Narrated in the voice of working-class adolescents in contemporary Hawaii, *Saturday Night at the Pahala Theatre* examines sex, drugs, and relationships from the viewpoint of teenage girls within the prism of raging hormones and shifting ethnic identity. The first work in that controversial collection, "Kala Gave Me Anykine Advice Especially About Filipinos When I Moved to Pahala," offended some with the frank—some say racist—way it described stereotypes about the Filipinos in Hawaii and with its explicitly raw descriptions of sexually tinged violence. In one of the poems, a neighborhood Filipino man is cast as a sexual predator: "Then he going drag you to his house / tie you to the vinyl chair / the one he sit on outside all day, and smile at you with his yellow teeth / and cut off your bi-lot with the cane/knife. / He going to fry um in Crisco for dinner. / That's what Kala told me." Other works in this collection describe child abuse, a girl's self-mutilation with a razor, and a tryst between an older woman and a "so-sho and emo-sho handicap" boy who burn their names into each other's backs with sparklers. Reviewing this jarring collection for the *Kenyon Review* (Spring 1995), Teresa Svoboda wrote of the disjunction between the author's vision and idyllic images of Hawaii: "Yamanaka's craftmanship, narrative skill, lack of sentimentality, and the freshness of the Hawaiian pidgin make *Saturday Night at the Pahala Theatre* an accomplished debut."

Buoyed by this critical reception, Yamanaka turned her talents toward writing her first novel, *Wild Meat and Bully Burgers*. That loosely structured, semiautobiographical work focuses on a young woman, Lovey Nariyoshi, coming to terms with adolescence while growing up in the Hilo of the 1970s. Conscious of how her low social status might be elevated by consumer-catalog products, Lovey fantasizes about some day living in "a house with Dixie cup dispensers, bunk beds with ruffled sheets, bendable straws, rose-shaped soap, Lysol and Pez." In her review for the *New York Times* (December 31, 1995), Lauren Belfer declared the book to be about Lovey's search for "an identity that will encompass her family's myths of samurai Japan and the skewed America of Barbie and *Bewitched*." Though Belfer complained of the novel's unsubtleties, such as the "increasingly exasperating" dialect, she admitted that Yamanaka "delivers moments of stinging clarity, creating haunting images as she sketches Lovey's search for a spiritual home."

Yamanaka's third book and second novel, *Blu's Hanging*, assumed a more serious tone in its probing of the tensions and miscommunication within a marginalized family. The novel, also written in Hawaiian Creole English, is narrated from the point of view of 13-year-old Ivah Ogata, who, with brother Blu and sister Maisie, tries to cope with her mother's death amidst dispiritedness and disorder. The novel was described by Jamie James in the *At-*

lantic Monthly article as "a Hawaiian *Catcher in the Rye.*" Megan Harlan, in the *New York Times* (May 4, 1997), wrote that Yamanaka "cultivates a stifling, pungent, and cruelly charged atmosphere" as she "explores the brutal divide between family duty and self-preservation, between the power of love and the power of shame." Though the author populated her own, Japanese-American community with few saints, and included characters who engage in various forms of aberrant behavior, including graphically portrayed cruelty to animals, Yamanaka was roundly condemned in some circles for allowing Ivah's brother Blu to be molested by a Filipino neighbor named Uncle Paulo. The narrative's tension is drawn to a fine pitch as Ivah struggles with a past-versus-future decision about whether to remain with the family as a surrogate mother or to accept a scholarship to a prestigious boarding school. She opts for school and the future, in what Harlan calls "a redemptive conclusion that is as arresting as her characters." An unsigned review in *Publishers Weekly* (February 24, 1997) concluded, "Yamanaka gives us a textured picture of their society and of the tensions that exist beyond the borders of a troubled family. When Blu and Maisie debate the meaning of 'sweet sorrow,' the narrative finds resolution in this mixture of hope and sadness." And Luis H. Francia commended Yamanaka in his *Village Voice* (May 27, 1997) review for her fortitude in resisting "romanticizing the marginalized," adding that "Yamanaka's eloquent, unapologetic use of pidgin, with its fiercely imaginative dimensions, remains the highlight of this flawed, passionate book, indicative of a finely attuned ear and sensitive eye."

Yamanaka's warts-and-all depiction of her pidgin-speaking characters, presented for the scrutiny of the *haole*—white—world, began to irritate some, both inside and outside her ethnic community, who were becoming increasingly embarrassed that her frankness was painting them in a negative light. This situation was complicated by the fact that the ethnic makeup of Hawaii is markedly different from that of any other state, with an Asian majority that has its own class hierarchies based on ethnic differentiation—a social universe that is foreign to the situation on the mainland, where Asians, as people of color, are seen as minorities in a dominant white culture. In Hawaii, Japanese-Americans are viewed as the most privileged of the Asian groups by those who care passionately about such matters. Because the "villain" in *Blu's Hanging* was identified as a Filipino man, several critics—"many of them scholars of ethnic studies rather than of literature," as James wrote—protested loudly when the Association for Asian American Studies (AAAS) nominated the book for its literature award in the summer of 1998. According to James, the charge was led by Jonathan Okamura, a sociologist at the University of Hawaii, who complained that he was "deeply offended and outraged by the portrayal of Filipino Americans" in Yamanaka's book (though he admitted he had not

read the book in its entirety), and to a lesser extent by Candace Fujikane, a professor of English at the same university, who was concerned not so much about the novel's stereotypical portraits of Filipinos but about Yamanaka's failure to invest *Blu's Hanging* with a therapeutic purpose to help provide uplift for disempowered groups. When the AAAS persisted in giving its award to the novel (an award that was accepted on Yamanaka's behalf by three of her Filipina students), a number of association members protested by wearing black armbands and turning their backs to the stage. This prompted the resignation of the officers and executive director, a later vote to rescind the original award, and a promise from some to give Yamanaka a different prize, "in recognition of her continuing contribution to racism in Hawaii." As Jamie James explained, many in Hawaii's literary community were disappointed that Yamanaka had not become "a local voice to speak for the islands, to correct the idylls of outside writers from [Mark] Twain to [James] Michener." Instead, Yamanaka seemed to be emerging as the "funky, loudmouthed thing" she had once called her younger self. This, along with her being a "passionate advocate of the literary potential of pidgin," in James's words, was apparently too much for critics who wanted a representative in their own image and likeness. In the wake of the controversy, 82 Asian-American writers, including Amy Tan, Maxine Hong Kingston, Lawrence Fusao Inada, Frank Chin, and Shawn Wong, came to Yamanaka's defense by writing letters arguing that the vote to rescind the award was a threat to free speech and literary creativity. Among the anti-AAAS voices were 14 Filipino-American authors, including Jessica Hagedorn, who wrote, "Yamanaka's detractors seem to be demanding that only writers who create safe, reverent, comforting stories are worthy of acknowledgment."

Yamanaka's next book, *Heads by Harry* (1999), is the third novel in her coming-of-age trilogy set in semi-rural Hawaii. Again, Yamanaka trained her sights on a working-class family, this time the wacky but functional Yagyuus—Harry and Mary Alice and their three children, all of whom live above the family taxidermy shop (whose name provides the novel's title). Yamanaka recorded the family's eccentricities and peccadilloes in microscopic and hilarious detail. The novel's narrator and central character is the middle child, teenage Toni, who, like Ivah Ogata in *Blu's Hanging*, is caught between the demands of two cultures: here, a tradition-directed life of home and preserved animal heads and a future-oriented life in the wider world. The pressures on Toni are particularly intense, because her free-spirited and flamboyant older brother, Sheldon, has chosen to reject his father's profession for his own version of taxidermy—human cosmetology. Sheldon once miffed Harry by having the Yagyuus' fire-engine-red Scout repainted metallic lavender, a deed that served only to elevate Toni's claim to the spoils of primogeniture.

In a review of *Heads by Harry* for the *Atlantic Monthly* (February 1999), Jamie James wrote, "Yamanaka is a trenchant observer and one of the most original voices on the American literary scene. The unsparing candor of her fictional worlds may offend modern-day Dr. Panglosses who would wish away the unpleasant social conditions she portrays, but her novels offer readers with a literary sensibility a stimulating introduction to a world more mysterious and exotic than the illusory idylls of Hawaii painted by outsiders." — E.M.

Suggested Reading: *Atlantic Monthly* p90+ Feb. 1999; *Booklist* p611 Dec. 1, 1995; *Harper's Bazaar* p164 Apr. 1997, with photo; *Kenyon Review* p154+ Spring 1995; *Library Journal* p101 Nov. 15, 1995, p136 Mar. 1, 1996, with photo, p105 Mar. 1, 1997; *Ms.* p88+ May 1996, p85 July 1996, with photo; *Nation* p33+ July 7, 1997; *New York Times* E p1 Oct. 6, 1998; *New York Times Book Review* p11 Dec. 31, 1995, p21 May 4, 1997; *Newsweek* p63 Aug. 17, 1998, with photo; *People* p41 May 26, 1997; *Publishers Weekly* p34+ Aug. 21, 1995, with photo; p51 Oct. 2, 1995, with photo, p62 Feb. 24, 1997; *Seventeen* p106 May 1997, with photo; *Village Voice* p63+ May 27, 1997

Selected Books: *Saturday Night at the Pahala Theatre*, 1993; *Wild Meat and the Bully Burgers*, 1995; *Blu's Hanging*, 1997; *Heads by Harry*, 1999

Card Studna/Courtesy of Paradise Artists

Yankovic, "Weird Al"

Oct. 23, 1959– Parodist; musician; comedian; songwriter. Address: c/o Paradise Artists, 108 E. Matilija St., Ojai, CA 93023-2639

Hailed as the "foremost parodist of the MTV era," "Weird Al" Yankovic has achieved longevity rare for a performer of novelty music. Following in the footsteps of such satirists as Allan Sherman, who is most famous for his song "Hello Muddah, Hello Faddah," Yankovic has used his own brand of musical arcana to dominate a genre well known for spawning one-hit wonders. Indeed, his career, which spans 16 years, has outlasted many of the more serious acts he has parodied. His 11 albums include four platinum records, and he has won two Grammy Awards and earned nominations for six others.

The son of Nick and Mary Yankovic, "Weird Al" was born Alfred Matthew Yankovic on October 23, 1959 in Lynwood, California, a suburb of Los Angeles. By all accounts, his childhood was anything but weird. He was a straight-A student, and in his spare time he practiced the accordion. As his musical tastes turned toward rock-'n'-roll, he had a hard time uniting his favorite instrument and his favorite music. He found a solution in novelty music. "Eventually I figured out that if I wanted to get out of doing the typical things an accordion player does, I could start doing humorous material and that would be a way to get around the whole situation," he explained to Tom Popson for the *Chicago Tribune* (March 18, 1984).

As a teenager Al listened avidly to Dr. Demento, a nationally syndicated disc jockey based in Los Angeles who was known for spinning comedy and novelty records. At 14 Al began sending Dr. Demento recordings of songs he had taped in his bedroom, and some of them received airplay. After enrolling at California Polytechnic State University, in San Luis Obispo, he discovered that none of the local radio stations aired Demento's show, so he started his own show on the campus station, patterning it after Demento's. On the air he called himself "Weird Al." He also continued to submit material to Demento. By the time he graduated, with a bachelor's degree in architecture, he had developed a cult following.

One of the discs Yankovic made as an undergraduate was "My Bologna," a parody of the Knack's hit single "My Sharona" that he had recorded in an acoustically correct men's bathroom. The Knack's record label, Capitol, picked up "My Bologna" and issued it as a single; it was not a commercial success. Yankovic followed it with a live recording, made in Dr. Demento's studio, of his song "Another One Rides the Bus," a spoof of Queen's "Another One Bites the Dust" that became an underground favorite. Before long Scotti Bros.

Records signed Yankovic; their relationship lasted until 1998, when Scotti Bros. was purchased by Volcano Entertainment.

Yankovic's first LP, *"Weird Al" Yankovic* (1983), featured "Ricky," a parody with lyrics about the TV show *I Love Lucy* set to the music from Toni Basil's hit "Mickey." The song made *Billboard*'s Top 100, and the accompanying video became a fixture on MTV. Successfully avoiding the sophomore jinx, Yankovic followed his strong debut effort with *"Weird Al" Yankovic in 3-D* (1984). The album, which went platinum, featured "Eat It," a spoof of Michael Jackson's "Beat It" and arguably the most famous parody of a pop song ever. "Eat It" rose to 12 on the *Billboard* charts and won a Grammy for best comedy recording; the video was an unqualified hit on MTV. Yankovic continued to break new ground with his third album, *Dare to Be Stupid* (1985), which was the first comedy record to be released on compact disc. *Dare to Be Stupid*, which contains "Like a Surgeon," Yankovic's satiric take on Madonna's "Like a Virgin," also went platinum. His fourth record, *Polka Party* (1986), garnered him a third Grammy nomination but sold poorly.

After the release of *Polka Party*, Yankovic slowed his pace to a new album every two or three years. In 1988 he released *Even Worse*, in which, returning to the proven formula of food plus Michael Jackson, he offered "Fat," a parody of Jackson's "Bad." "Fat" became a hit and won him his second Grammy Award. (Ironically, "Bad" didn't win a Grammy.) His LP *Off the Deep End* came out in 1992; one cut, "Smells Like Nirvana," is a poke at the incoherent lyrics on Nirvana's "Smells Like Teen Spirit." His three latest LPs are *Alapalooza* (1993), *Bad Hair Day* (1996), and *Running with Scissors* (1999), the last two of which reached numbers 14 and 16, respectively, on the *Billboard* charts. On another front, Yankovic co-wrote, starred in, and recorded the soundtrack for the film *UHF* (1989).

"Weird Al" has acknowledged the influence of such artists as Allan Sherman, Tom Lehrer, Stan Freberg, and Spike Jones. He himself has left his mark by focusing on popular culture and using musical styles as divergent as polka, rock-'n'-roll, and rap. His popularity stems in part from his success in lampooning pop music and culture without offending. He told Wayne Robbins for *Newsday* (March 15,1984), "I don't consider myself a critic. More than criticize, I reflect American pop culture. . . . It's all in good fun. I don't want to hurt anybody's feelings. You can joke around, and have fun with somebody's music without making them mad at you." Consequently, though he has the legal right to parody without permission, Yankovic has a policy of asking permission from songwriters to parody their work. Reportedly, most artists have felt flattered by his attention; some, like the members of Nirvana, first appreciated the extent of their stardom after "Weird Al" cannibalized their songs. The only notable exceptions are the artist formerly known as Prince, who has consistently turned down Yankovic's requests, and the rap artist Coolio, who publicly announced that he had not given Yankovic permission to record "Amish Paradise," a spoof of Coolio's "Gangsta's Paradise." Yankovic told Craig Rosen for *Billboard* (July 6, 1996) that "there was a major miscommunication with Coolio." By contrast, Yankovic recalled to Brenda Herrmann for the *Chicago Tribune* (December 7, 1993), Paul McCartney, formerly a member of the Beatles, told him that "he was upset that I hadn't parodied him."

Yankovic's rise to fame coincided with the advent of the music-video industry, and many observers—like Yankovic himself—think that by taking advantage of the new medium, he boosted his success. "Creatively, videos add another level or two to the song," he told Doug Reece for *Billboard* (March 30, 1996), "and commercially, though a lot of disc jockeys will play my stuff, '90s play lists have tightened up considerably. [Video] has become a very important venue for me." Yankovic's videos have made effective use of frame-by-frame mimicry, often achieved with sets and performers from the music videos he is parodying. In recent years Yankovic has directed some of his own videos as well as those of other artists, among them "Wail," by the Jon Spencer Blues Explosion, and the "Titanic" sequences for Hanson's "River."

"A good parody requires instantly recognizable material; otherwise nobody will know what the joke is," Yankovic was quoted as saying in the *Toronto Globe and Mail* (April 21, 1984). "It works if the original is exceptionally popular, especially if it's a crossover hit—something that people hear all the time on the radio and maybe they're just a little bit tired of." Yankovic would also like to be remembered for his original songs, which comprise roughly half of his recorded work but which are known to virtually nobody except his most devoted fans. In his conversation with Craig Rosen, Yankovic explained, "That has always been a little bit of a pet peeve. I love doing the parodies, and I'm not upset when they do well, but sometimes I wish the originals received more attention."

Al Yankovic is currently a resident of Hollywood Hills, California; he has never been married. In the mid-1980s, he said that he is grateful that thanks to his profession, he "can spend a lot of time at home watching cable TV—and tell people it's job-related research," as quoted by David Hinckley in the New York *Daily News* (August 12, 1985). Despite his nickname and stage persona, he has contended that he is quite normal. "Sometimes people are offended when they meet me on the street and I'm not going crazy in front of them," he told Lynn Van Matre for the *Chicago Tribune* (May 8, 1988). "They'll say, 'You're not weird at all!'"—T.J.F.

Suggested Reading: *Billboard* p144 Mar. 30, 1996, with photo, p9+ July 6, 1996, with photo; *Chicago Tribune* XIII p5+ Mar. 18, 1984, with photos, XIII p6+ May 8, 1988, with photos, VII p7 Dec. 7, 1993, with photo; *New York Daily News* Entertainment p35 Aug. 12, 1985, with photo; *Newsday* II p35 Mar. 15, 1984, with photo; *Toronto Globe and Mail* E p1 Apr. 21, 1984, with photo

Selected Recordings: *"Weird Al" Yankovic*, 1983; *"Weird Al" Yankovic in 3-D*, 1984; *Dare to Be Stupid*, 1985; *Even Worse*, 1988; *Off the Deep End*, 1992; *Alapalooza*, 1993; *Bad Hair Day*, 1996; *Running with Scissors*, 1999

Selected Films: *UHF*, 1989; *Spy Hard*, 1996

Selected Television Shows: *The Weird Al Show*, 1997–98

Jon Chomitz/Courtesy of CERA

Yergin, Daniel

Feb. 6, 1947– Writer; energy consultant. Address: c/o Cambridge Energy Research Associates, 20 University Rd., Cambridge, MA 02138

Daniel Yergin is best known as the author of *The Prize: The Epic Quest for Oil, Money and Power* (1991), for which he won a Pulitzer Prize, and for his most recent book, *The Commanding Heights: The Battle Between Government and the Marketplace That Is Remaking the Modern World* (1998). He is also the president of an international energy-consulting firm and an adviser to the government of the United States, as well as the governments of several other countries, on issues surrounding energy-producing industries. Describing his multifaceted career to Ken Ringle for the *Washington*

Post (April 9, 1998), Yergin explained, "I suppose I'm a historian that tries to help people grapple with the way the past informs the immediate future. I just get these obsessions. And they lead to other obsessions." James R. Schlesinger, a former head of the CIA, the U.S. Department of Energy, and the Department of Defense, who has worked with Yergin on several occasions, told Ringle that the author-consultant has "a remarkable degree of insight and freshness. His approach is totally non-ideological. His only substantive agenda is analytical. He regards the free market as a tool, not as an altar."

Daniel Howard Yergin was born in Los Angeles on February 6, 1947. His father, Irving Yergin, had worked as a police reporter in Chicago in the 1920s and 1930s; after moving to Los Angeles, he became a publicist for Warner Bros. and an editor of the *Hollywood Reporter*. Yergin told Ringle that his father also "puttered around in various unsuccessful business ventures," such as the yogurt business he became involved in during the 1950s. "My father was sort of like [the Charles Dickens character] Mr. Micawber—there was always some great deal just around the corner," he said. Yergin himself had his first job—a paper route—when he was nine years old. That same year he established a political group called the Pint-Sized Democrats. As a youngster he was also interested in writing and thought that he would become a journalist, like his father. "My father never played catch with me, but he talked to me endlessly about writing," Yergin told Ringle. "Maybe it all has something to do with that."

After graduating from Beverly Hills High School, in 1964, Yergin attended Yale University, in New Haven, Connecticut. He said that he chose Yale simply because it offered him more financial aid than any other college to which he had applied. An English major whose favorite authors were Dickens and William Makepeace Thackeray, Yergin wrote for the *Yale Daily News* and started a new publication at the university called the *New Journal*, which he described to Ringle as featuring "Tom Wolfe–style magazine writing." During his junior year, when he wrote a paper about the Spanish Civil War (1936–39), Yergin became interested in history. "[My paper] convinced me I wanted to write a Ph.D. in history," he told Ringle. "But I didn't want to go to any more classes. [So] I went to Cambridge [University, in England], where it was all tutors and independent study."

While studying at Cambridge Yergin also wrote for the U.S. publications *New York* and the magazine section of the *New York Times*, as well as for a number of British periodicals. He enjoyed writing so much that when he returned to the U.S., in 1974, after completing his Ph.D., he had a difficult time deciding whether he should accept a position teaching at Harvard University or a full-time job writing for the *New York Times*. "I really anguished over whether to pursue an academic career or a journalistic one," he told Ringle. After much deliberation he chose the position at Harvard and began lecturing in the university's government department.

In 1977, when he was 30 years old, Yergin published his first book—a revised version of his doctoral thesis, entitled *Shattered Peace: The Origins of the Cold War and the National Security State.* Although the book got a positive assessment on the front page of the *New York Times Book Review* (June 12, 1977), Yergin's colleagues at Harvard did not take his book seriously. "I think they sort of disdained me as a popularizer," he explained to Ringle. "I wrote in short, declarative sentences, for example." Nor, according to Yergin, did the university look favorably on his growing interest in business and trade. "They couldn't understand how a faculty member could want to write cover stories for *New York* magazine on the business implications of some new frozen pizza," he told Ringle. Eventually, Yergin successfully applied for a position at the Harvard School of Business. "I told them I wanted to join the business school because I was interested in capitalism," he recalled. "The interviewer looked at me strangely and said, 'Oh, we don't talk about capitalism here.'"

A short time later Yergin became part of an energy research project that the Harvard Business School launched in response to the U.S.'s boycott of Arab oil in the 1970s. The project's aim was to identify future needs and possible sources of energy, and one result of the research was Yergin's second book, *Energy Future: Report of the Energy Project at the Harvard Business School,* which he co-edited with Robert B. Stobaugh, also of the Harvard Business School. Perhaps because the book appeared during the gas shortage of 1979, when long lines of automobiles became common at gas stations, it turned into a best-seller. While the book is credited with accurately predicting the conservation efforts that helped the U.S. to become 30 to 40 percent more energy efficient over the following decade, according to the author, among others, it was overly optimistic about the increased use of solar and other alternative forms of energy in the U.S. in the near future. Still, the book gained Yergin the notice of some of the energy industry's major players. "*Energy Future* changed my life," he told Ringle. "It projected me out of the academic and foreign policy world in which I was something of a junior member, and into the business world where they measure you somewhat differently."

In 1982 the Manufacturers Hanover Co. of New York hired Yergin as a consultant on their investments in energy companies. This job led him to found Cambridge Energy Research Associates (CERA) with one of his research assistants, Jamie Rosenfield. "We still argue over just how it started," Yergin told Ringle. "I say it was with a $2 file cabinet from the Salvation Army. Jamie steadfastly maintains it was a $7 cabinet. But whatever it was, we sort of made up the business as we went along." The company now has nine offices around the world and grosses about $75 million per year; its clients include banks, pension funds, airlines, au-

tomakers, oil producers, and utility companies. Yergin told Paula Span for the *Washington Post* (February 2, 1991) that because his clients are both producers and consumers of oil and often have conflicting needs, the company's greatest challenge is working in a way in which "people on both sides of the issues can read our work and find it useful."

Although his next book was originally set to be published in 1985, Yergin did not complete *The Prize*, which he describes as an "oil-centric history," until August 2, 1990—just four days before the Iraqi invasion of Kuwait, a move that led the U.S. and its allies to take military action against Iraq. As with *Energy Future*, the timing of the publication of *The Prize* proved to be a great advantage in terms of sales. Noting this coincidence, Yergin explained to Ringle, "[It is] entirely due to my inability to meet deadlines. If I had finished my books on time, they would have been too ahead of the news to attract notice." Although many other books about aspects of the Persian Gulf War hit bookstores around the same time, Yergin told Span that "no one could accuse me of writing an instant book" as a response to the Iraqi invasion. *The Prize* includes accounts of Saddam Hussein's rise to power in Iraq and even discusses the probability of an invasion of Kuwait—a small neighboring country that is extremely rich in oil. "There'd been enough signals of Iraq's changing status versus the rest of the world to predict Hussein's action," Yergin explained to Span. When asked if he felt that the Gulf War was fought primarily because of the oil interests of the U.S. and other countries, rather than to defend Kuwait, he said, "Wars don't happen for one reason. It's neater if you can say it's about one thing, but it's about an interrelated series of things—the balance of power, nuclear and chemical weapons, the post–Cold War order. But oil is certainly very central." Yergin is doubtful whether the U.S. response to the invasion will prove efficacious in the long run. "I find so many echoes of the last 30 or 40 years. It is a real pity that people don't know their history," he told Span.

Not surprisingly, *The Prize* reached the bestseller lists of both the *New York Times* and the *Washington Post* soon after its publication. In *Business Week* (January 14, 1991), Anthony Parisi wrote that Yergin's 877-page chronicle of "the lifeblood of industrial man" is "probably the best history of oil ever written. . . . Yergin put seven years into it, and it shows." Similarly, Span wrote, "For all the footnotes and its daunting 25-page bibliography, Yergin has written a surprisingly engaging [book]. . . . The 131 years since 'Colonel' Edwin Drake struck oil in Pennsylvania became a narrative drama featuring a cast of outsize players—scheming wildcatters and capitalist moguls, desert kings and serendipitous geologists, statesmen and muckrakers and OPEC ministers. A reader can almost understand why half a dozen television producers have contacted Yergin about the possibilities of a miniseries (though the saga lacks sufficient sex)." After he won a Pulitzer Prize, in 1991, Yergin's work was made into an eight-part documentary, broadcast on PBS in 1993. The book itself has been reprinted several times and translated into 13 languages.

Yergin's next book, *Russia 2010 and What It Means for the World* (1993), which he co-wrote with Georgetown University professor Thane Gustafson, was largely a result of the research he was conducting for CERA, his growing business. Because many businesses were eager to expand into the yet-untapped consumer resources of the former Soviet Union in the early 1990s, questions about the potential for investments in Russia abounded. According to Serge Schmemann of the *New York Times* (December 26, 1993), the book tried to answer some of these questions by presenting several hypothetical situations and their possible impact on Russia's future. A few of the scenarios that are included in the book are the rise of a Russian nationalist government, a military coup, the assassination of President Boris Yeltsin, and an accident at the Chernobyl nuclear power plant, parts of which have continued to operate since 1986, when the reactor core melted down and released large doses of radiation into the atmosphere. "For all of us who dabble in trying to divine whither Russia, Daniel Yergin and Thane Gustafson have performed an invaluable service," Schmemann wrote, "And they do it in a way non-Kremlinologists will have no trouble following."

Yergin told Ringle that his most recent book, *The Commanding Heights: The Battle Between Government and the Marketplace That Is Remaking the Modern World*, began as a "60,000-word essay on privatization." Written with the help of the Paris-based financial analyst Joseph Stanislaw, this book examines the recent trend in which governments around the world have loosened their trade regulations and turned many previously state-run enterprises over to private corporations. The title comes from a speech that the Russian leader Vladimir Ilyich Lenin gave at the Fourth Congress of the Communist International in St. Petersburg, Russia, in 1922. Lenin emphasized that governments needed to carefully control the "commanding heights," or the most important aspects of a state's economy. According to Yergin, Lenin's words echoed in the minds of leaders around the world, especially during the aftermath of World War II, when many countries were faced with rebuilding their economies. Since then the pendulum has swung in the opposite direction. As Yergin explained in his book, private companies are more efficient at running businesses and services, and governments profit from the taxes that private companies must pay.

Reviewing *The Commanding Heights* in the *New York Times* (February 8, 1998), Jeffrey E. Garten wrote, "In describing the U-turn from government to market dominance, *The Commanding Heights* manages its most impressive feat: to tell a real-world story in multiple dimensions and to

make it read like a novel. . . . [Yergin and Stanislaw] have struck exactly the right balance between, on the one hand, acknowledging the powerful momentum that markets may have achieved, and on the other, recognizing the weak links in the system. Their fascinating book, at once so packed with information, so clear and so nuanced, contains this warning: The free market revolution isn't over, and no one knows where it will end." In *Commonweal* (April 24, 1998), however, Charles R. Morris criticized the book. "Sadly, *Commanding Heights*' ambitions far exceed its powers," he wrote. "Instead of grand narrative, we get a dutiful compilation of potted little economic histories of almost every country in the world—or at least it feels that way. . . . Every story is essentially the same. Once all the best people were socialists or communists, or at least believed in a strong, directive, economic role for the state. Now they don't and everybody is much better off. . . . A first-rate analysis of the kind that [the authors] have attempted would make fascinating reading. Too bad that it is still sorely needed."

As many critics noted, while Yergin's opinion of the world's current economic situation is one of general approval, some warnings resound in his book. In an interview with R. C. Longworth for the *Chicago Tribune* (February 8, 1998), Yergin said, "The embrace of markets around the world is in fact not a romantic movement but a pragmatic reaction." Yergin feels that the current global market economy's having grown out of practicality gives the economy an unprecedented strength and stability. However, he says, "an unlucky conjunction" of events could cause investors to lose confidence in the economy and cause drastic changes to occur once again. "Things can come unstuck," he told Longworth. "We don't believe in the perfectibility of human institutions, governmental or the private sector. People make mistakes and things go to excess. . . . It's important that the new [commanders] retain their modesty and their sense of limitations, just as the former commanders would have done well to have remembered."

Daniel Yergin spends a great deal of time traveling overseas, where he works as a consultant to corporations and governments. When in the U.S. he lives in Washington, D.C., where he writes and works as an adviser to the U.S. government. According to Ringle, when Yergin is at home, he rises at 7:00 a.m. and writes for two hours before going to his office. He works until 7:00 p.m., goes home for dinner and a brief nap, and then does more writing—in longhand—in his favorite leather chair until about 2:00 a.m. Writing, the author has said, is what he misses most when he is abroad.

"With his steel-rim glasses, beatific smile, and weedy hairline battling hard against recession," Ken Ringle wrote, Yergin "comes across like nothing so much as the genial professor who keeps misplacing the faculty lounge. His house in Northwest Washington is modest and unremarkable, his study looks like the wreckage from a terrorist bombing, and his efforts to explain his success keep wandering off into sunny vales of academic woolgathering. . . . What sets him apart from the average author-consultant in town is his reputation for being able to see a bit further over the global horizon. In the process he glimpses meaningful, strategically useful patterns among the political events and data-blizzards of the day." Yergin is married to Angela Stent, a professor at Georgetown University, and he has two children, whom he described to Beth Belton of *USA Today* (January 12, 1993) as being "fervent environmentalists." When asked what his next book might be about, Yergin told Ringle, "My wife's forbidden me to write any more books for three years. But I have a half-finished screenplay that deals with medieval England."

Daniel Yergin is a member of the advisory boards of the U.S. Department of Energy, the Asia-Pacific Petroleum Conference, the Solar Energy Research Institute, the National Petroleum Council, the National Council of Foreign Relations, the International Association for Energy Economics, the American History Association, the Royal Institute for International Affairs, and the Nature Conservancy. He is a fellow of the Kennedy School of Government at Harvard University and the World Economic Forum. — C.P.

Suggested Reading: *Business Week* p14+ Jan. 14, 1991; *Chicago Tribune* p3 Feb. 8, 1998, with photo; *Commonweal* p26+ Apr. 24, 1998; *New York Times* VII p2 Dec. 26, 1993, with photo, VII p7 Feb. 8, 1998, with photo; *Washington Post* D p1 Feb. 2, 1991, with photos, B p1 Apr. 9, 1998, with photo; *USA Today* B p5 Jan. 12, 1993, with photo

Selected Books: *Shattered Peace: The Origins of the Cold War and the National Security State*, 1977; *Energy Future: Report of the Energy Project at the Harvard Business School*, 1979; *The Prize: The Epic Quest for Oil, Money, and Power*, 1991; *Russia 2010 And What It Means for the World*, 1993; *The Commanding Heights: The Battle Between Government and the Marketplace That Is Remaking the Modern World*, 1998

Courtesy of Boston University

Zinn, Howard

Aug. 24, 1922– Historian; social activist; educator; writer. Address: c/o Dept. of Political Science, Boston University, Boston, MA 02215

"Who controls the past controls the future. Who controls the present controls the past." This principle, expressed by the British writer and social critic George Orwell, has guided the work of the radical historian, scholar, and social activist Howard Zinn since he began his professional life, in the late 1950s, and it lies at the heart of his groundbreaking work *A People's History of the United States: 1492–Present* (1980). Free of the academic jargon and formal tone of typical history texts, *A People's History* chronicles American history from the perspectives of those people whom Zinn believes have been exploited politically and economically by the U.S. government and social structure: namely, ethnic and racial minorities, women, and workers. Lauded by some as a voice for justice and champion of the disenfranchised and derided by others as a slipshod scholar and social agitator, Zinn has awakened several generations of students to his belief in the need for social responsibility and the dangers of irresponsible authority. Firmly entrenched as a sage of the political left, Zinn retired from his post as professor of political science at Boston University in 1988 to devote himself full-time to public speaking and other forms of social activism and also to playwriting.

Zinn's keen sense of class-consciousness developed during his childhood, in the slums of the New York City borough of Brooklyn. One of the four sons of Jewish immigrants—his father, Edward Zinn, came from Austria, and his mother, the former Jenny Rabinowitz, from Siberia—Howard Zinn was born on August 24, 1922. His father struggled to support the family with whatever work he could find: washing windows, peddling ties from a pushcart, and waiting tables at social events. "We were always one step ahead of the landlord," Zinn recalled in an interview with David Barsamian for *Z Magazine Network* (November 11, 1992, on-line). Zinn's boyhood pastime of playing in the street ended when he discovered books. He has recalled vividly the first book he ever owned: a tattered copy of *Tarzan and the Jewels of Opar* that he found on the street and proceeded to wear out further over the course of many rereadings. Seeing that their son loved to read, Zinn's parents took advantage of a promotion in the *New York Post* offering individual volumes of Charles Dickens in exchange for some coupons and 25 cents. By age 10 Zinn had collected—and devoured—the entirety of Dickens's works, which articulated for him the apparent dichotomy between the power of the wealthy and the helplessness of the impoverished. Edward and Jenny Zinn further encouraged their son's intellectual development by purchasing, for $5 (the equivalent of about $60 in 1999), a rebuilt Underwood typewriter for Howard, when he was 13.

The first public protest that Zinn attended, at age 17, had a major impact on him, as he explained in his memoir, *You Can't Be Neutral on a Moving Train* (1995). Allured by the seemingly sophisticated young Communists who had invited him, as well as the chance to visit Times Square in Manhattan, Zinn agreed to go along even though he was not sure what the demonstration was about, beyond a vague sense that it was an antiwar march. As the protest reached a fever pitch, mounted police officers wielding batons arrived to break up the crowd. Zinn was knocked unconscious in the fracas and woke up later, confused, in a doorway, after Times Square had returned to its pre-protest order. "I was nursing not only a hurt head, but hurt feelings about our country," Zinn said to David Barsamian in an interview for the *Progressive* (July 1997). "All the things these radicals had been saying were true. The state is not neutral, but on the side of the powerful; there really is no freedom of speech in this country if you're a radical. That was brought home to me, because these people were engaging in a nonviolent demonstration, presumably protected by the Constitution and—zoom!—the police are there beating heads and breaking up the demonstration."

Right after he completed high school, Zinn worked for three years in a shipyard as a shipfitter. Then, in about 1943, during World War II, he enlisted in the United States Army Air Corps, the precursor to the United States Air Force. Trained as a bombardier, Zinn flew missions over Europe in a B-17 named "Belle of the Brawl," and he learned not to question authority. "I was another member of the Air Force doing my duty," he explained to Barsamian for *Z Magazine Network*, "listening to my briefings before going out on the flight and dropping the bombs where I was supposed to, without thinking, where am I dropping them?" It was not until after the war that Zinn reflected on the lives the bombs had snuffed out and the other damage they had caused, which he learned about through research and travel. "The thing about being in the Air Force and dropping bombs from 35,000 feet is that you don't see anybody, human

beings, you don't hear screams, see blood, see mangled bodies," Zinn told Barsamian for *Z Magazine Network*. "I understand very well how atrocities are committed in modern warfare, from a distance." He later condemned what he viewed as his destructive role in World War II, and his experiences left him convinced that there can be no moral justification for war.

Zinn's military service afforded him, through the G.I. Bill, the opportunity to further his education. He earned a B.A. degree from New York University, in 1951, and a master's degree and Ph.D. from Columbia University, also in New York City, in 1952 and 1958, respectively. Meanwhile, he and his wife, Roslyn (Shecter), whom he had married prior to his military service overseas, had moved into a housing project on Manhattan's Lower East Side. Their two children, Myla and Jeff, stayed at nursery school while their parents worked and Zinn attended school.

Two years before he completed his doctoral dissertation, Zinn accepted his first full-time teaching post, at Spelman College, then a school for black women, in Atlanta, Georgia. At Spelman Zinn encountered some of his most remarkable students, several of whom later became highly prominent: the novelist Alice Walker; Marian Wright Edelman, the president of the Children's Defense Fund; and former Georgia legislator and chair of the NAACP Julian Bond, who was among a cadre of male students from nearby Morehouse College who sat in on Zinn's lectures. Also while at Spelman, Zinn's class-consciousness and leftist political philosophy began to move him to action.

After spending an unhappy first year living in a white suburb of Atlanta that was dominated by members of the Ku Klux Klan, Zinn and his family moved, during the flowering of the civil rights movement, into the predominantly black community that surrounded Spelman's campus. "Probably that time at Spelman College was the most intense experience of learning in my life," Zinn told David Barsamian for the *Progressive*. "Talk about social change: I could see social change happening all around me. I was writing about it, observing it, participating in it."

Meanwhile, Zinn was finishing his dissertation, a study of former New York City mayor Fiorello LaGuardia's tenure as a representative in Congress; eventually published as a book, *LaGuardia in Congress* (1958), it won the American Historical Association's Albert J. Beveridge Prize. Zinn's dissertation research entailed reading the letters LaGuardia received from his constituents in poverty-stricken East Harlem. Though LaGuardia served in Congress during the booming economy of the 1920s, a decade commonly referred to as the Jazz Age or the Age of Prosperity, the letters show that LaGuardia's constituents did not share in the prosperity. Although this discovery was no surprise to Zinn, it altered his view of recorded history. "It suggested to me that we need to take another look at the way we label periods of American history," he explained to Shawn Setaro for *Instant* (1998, on-line), "and we need to reconsider whether we have judged the United States and the various periods of the United States—judged the well-being of democracy in the United States—on the basis of the condition of the upper classes or the middle classes, without taking into consideration those people who are left out of what seemed to be a democratic or prosperous country."

Spelman's administration took objection to Zinn's outspokenness and vigorous participation in the civil rights movement, and in 1964 he was asked to leave the school. That same year he joined the faculty of Boston University (BU), where he was named an associate professor. With the onset of the Vietnam War, Zinn found new outlets for his activism. He became a vocal member of Boston's antiwar movement and participated in a 1968 diplomatic mission to Vietnam to mark the release of the first American prisoners of war. And once again, he found himself at odds with his employers because of his extracurricular activities; indeed, his frequent, heated battles with the university's president, John R. Silber, became legendary. "To say I was a thorn in his side is to put it very, very gently," Zinn told Elizabeth Mehren for *Newsday* (December 28, 1998). In Silber's opinion, Zinn, who repeatedly made the news and was arrested many times, was breaching an unwritten code of decorum among professors. At one point Silber even accused Zinn of arson; later, he retracted the charge and apologized. Furthermore, Zinn's academic writings, colored by concern for groups Zinn saw as disenfranchised, struck Silber as distorted, unbalanced, and unscholarly. For many years Silber saw to it that Zinn earned no salary increases; when he retired in 1988, after 24 years of tenured service to BU, Zinn was earning only $41,000 annually, far less than what colleagues with equivalent experience were getting. Earlier, in 1976 and again in 1979, Zinn had spearheaded faculty drives to have Silber removed from his post. The academic staff voted three to one and two to one, respectively, for dismissal, but Silber stayed on, thanks to the support of BU's board of trustees.

Silber was not alone in his negative assessment of Zinn's academic writing. Many others, too, have criticized Zinn's view of history, which he himself has conceded is overtly biased. Extrapolating from his Orwellian principle, Zinn believes that it is impossible to write an impartial account of history. "I decided a long time ago that this notion of objective history disintegrated as soon as you understood that you were selecting out of an infinite mass of data," he explained to Charles M. Young for *Rolling Stone* (October 17, 1996). Since any set of facts compiled into a narrative history is selected by an individual whose choices are inevitably shaped by his or her perspective, it follows, in Zinn's view, that the information presented in that account will necessarily reflect what is important to the author. For Zinn, even scholarly history that claims to be objective is written with a motive,

whether the author is conscious of his or her biases or not. In Zinn's opinion, most historical scholarship is what he refers to as "safe history": namely, history that is written to pander to controlling powers in exchange for promotion, profit, or prestige (or all of those things), and is therefore devoid of a social conscience. "Take Columbus for example," Zinn noted to David Barsamian for *Z Magazine Network*. "You can frame [Columbus's legacy], and this was the way the Harvard historian Samuel Eliot Morison in effect framed it in his biography of Columbus: Columbus committed genocide, but he was a wonderful sailor. He did a remarkable and extraordinary thing in finding these islands in the Western Hemisphere. Where's the emphasis there? . . . I say, he was a good sailor, but he treated people with the most horrible cruelty. Those are two different ways of saying the same facts."

Zinn elaborated on his version of Columbus's discovery of America to great effect in the opening chapter of his seminal work, *A People's History of the United States* (1980). In writing his account of American history, Zinn hoped to shed some light on the plights of people whose perspectives he believes have been left out of most traditional historical accounts. For example, Zinn tells the story of Columbus's landing from the point of view of the Arawak Indians, who were among the first indigenous peoples Columbus met in the West Indies. According to Zinn, Columbus traded with and befriended the tribespeople in the hope that they could lead him to gold. Later, he enslaved a number of them to bring back to Spain as proof of his landing, and thus began centuries of persecution of Native Americans at the hands of Europeans. In another example of Zinn's approach, he explained the technological and economic boom of the Industrial Revolution from the standpoint of the men, women, and children who labored in unsafe factories for barely a living wage.

Not surprisingly, *A People's History* drew strong and mixed reactions from critics. James Levin wrote in the *Library Journal* (January 1, 1980), "Zinn has written a brilliant and moving [book that] . . . is an excellent antidote to establishment history." Oscar Handlin, in a review for *American Scholar* (Autumn 1980), disagreed: "[Zinn] can produce little proof that the people he names, from slaves to peons, saw matters as he does. Hence the deranged quality of his fairy tale, in which the incidents are made to fit the legend, no matter how intractable the evidence of American history." Regardless of what critics made of it, *A People's History* is clearly one of the most influential history books written in the last 25 years: it is currently in its 15th printing, with more than 500,000 copies sold, and it has sparked the growth of a revisionist school of thought, known as "New History," in American academia. Zinn recently updated the book to include chapters on George Bush's and Bill Clinton's presidencies.

Since his retirement from teaching, Zinn has continued to give public lectures regularly. But he has been focusing less on scholarship and more on creative ventures, among them writing plays. He made his debut as a playwright in 1976, with his musical drama *Emma*, based on the life of the Russian-born American anarchist Emma Goldman (1869–1940). First staged in New York, it has since been produced several more times in New York and also on stages in Boston, London, Edinburgh, and Tokyo. His latest piece for the theater is *Marx in Soho: A Play on History* (1999). In addition, Zinn is working on a 10-part miniseries for the Fox television network based on *A People's History of the United States*, to be co-produced by Matt Damon and Ben Affleck. Damon and Affleck grew up in the same Cambridge neighborhood in which Zinn and his family live, and the two writer-actors included frequent references to *A People's History* in their Oscar-winning screenplay, *Good Will Hunting*. The film ignited a new surge of interest in the book. Many people have noted the irony in the use of Zinn's leftist tract by the Fox network, which is owned by Rupert Murdoch, a multimillionaire who is widely seen as personifying conservative capitalism. — T.J.F.

Suggested Reading: *Instant* (on-line) 1998; *Progressive* p37+ July 1997; *Rolling Stone* p93+ Oct. 17, 1996, with photos; *Z Magazine Network* (on-line) Nov. 11, 1992

Selected Writings: *LaGuardia in Congress*, 1958; *Declarations of Independence: Cross-Examining American Ideology*, 1990; *You Can't Be Neutral on a Moving Train: A Personal History of Our Times*, 1994; *A People's History of the United States: 1492–Present*, 1997; *The Zinn Reader: Writings on Disobedience and Democracy*, 1997; *Marx in Soho: A Play on History*, 1999; *The Future of History*, 1999

Timothy Greenfield-Sanders

Zorn, John

Sep. 2, 1953– Saxophonist; composer. Address: P.O. Box 4292, Great Neck, NY 11034

Since the late 1970s, when he began collaborating with leading figures in New York City's hip downtown music scene, the saxophonist and composer John Zorn has created music often described as experimental, avant-garde, and eclectic, fusing traditions from around the world into his improvisational style. The result has been a sound unlike any other. Different from most popular music, which seeks to please the audience with consonant melodies and regular rhythms, Zorn's creations fly in the face of convention and are often extremely loud, very fast-paced, devoid of smooth transitions, and made up of sounds from highly unusual sources. Duck calls, human screeching, and computer-generated bleeps are among the components of his seemingly structureless music; a piece he composed for the Kronos Quartet required the members of that prominent string ensemble to set aside their instruments and bark like dogs. Zorn's irreverence has led critics to describe him with such terms as "a musical mad scientist," as Gil Griffin phrased it in the *Washington Post* (May 1, 1991). John Rockwell, writing for the *New York Times* (February 21, 1988), called him "the single most interesting, important, and influential composer to arise from the Manhattan 'downtown' avant garde since Steve Reich and Philip Glass 20 years ago." Despite such acclaim, Zorn's music has remained an enigma to most mainstream audiences, and widespread popularity has eluded him.

Born on September 2, 1953 in New York City, John Zorn grew up in the midst of ethnic and cultural diversity in the borough of Queens. As a boy he heard a wide variety of music. His mother, a professor of education, enjoyed classical music; his father, a hairstylist, was a fan of jazz, country music, and songs from France. His older brother introduced him to doo-wop and classic rock-'n'-roll. Zorn was further exposed to the cultures of the world when he attended the United Nations elementary school, whose students hailed from many different nations.

Zorn began playing guitar and flute at age 10. As an adolescent he developed a taste for the work of such modern composers as Igor Stravinsky,

Charles Ives, and Edgard Varèse, and he began composing himself. He eventually formed an appreciation for the work of contemporary experimental composers, including Karlheinz Stockhausen and Mauricio Kagel. Commenting on his eclectic tendencies, Zorn told Howard Reich for the *Chicago Tribune* (June 11, 1989), "I suppose I've developed this way, in part, because ever since I was a kid, I've been listening to all different kinds of music, and that happens to be one of the things that ties my generation of musicians together. I remember I used to buy tons of records, then take the best cut off of each and put it on a cassette, which I would listen to over and over. One cut would be a classical piece, then a hardcore band, then a jazz song, then some easy-listening. So I eventually got into the habit of putting all those influences together, and filtering them through my sick little brain."

Zorn also became interested in compositions for film. He particularly admired the work of Carl Stalling, who wrote music for Warner Brothers cartoons featuring Bugs Bunny, Daffy Duck, and the Road Runner. Zorn remarked on the "many styles a film composer has to know in order to complement the images," as quoted by Francis Davis for the *Atlantic* (January 1991). "In that sense I think the great film composers are the precursors of what my generation is doing today."

From 1971 to 1973 Zorn studied music at Webster College, in St. Louis, Missouri. There, he immersed himself in jazz and encountered avant-garde jazz musicians associated with the Black Artists Group, based in St. Louis, and AACM (Association for the Advancement of Creative Musicians),which worked out of Chicago. Around that time Zorn began playing the alto saxophone and experimenting with improvisation. Commenting on the latter development, he said, as quoted by Gene Santoro for the *Nation* (January 30, 1988), "I began incorporating improvisation into some of the structures I'd been working on, which ranged from traditionally notated stuff like Elliot Carter, and Charles Ives, and Edgard Varèse–influenced pieces to improvisational works coming more from John Cage or Earle Brown or Stockhausen."

In the late 1970s Zorn returned to New York City, a mecca for talented experimental musicians, and began exploring the city's punk and rock scene. He also began his entry into the city's experimental jazz world, collaborating with musicians in the downtown music scene. Some of his early collaborators included the pianist Wayne Horvitz, the drummer Bobby Previte, the avant-garde guitarist Eugene Chadbourne, and the multi-instrumentalists and composers Elliot Sharp and Marty Ehrlich, all of whom defied convention and espoused improvisation as a method. Working with them, Zorn, who has long maintained that the era in which composers work in isolation is ending, blurred the lines between composition and group improvisation. He also erased the distinction between popular and high-brow music by incorporating elements and themes from popular

culture into his avant-garde sounds. The uptempo pace of his music reflected changes in society brought on by technology. Commenting on that aspect of his music, Zorn said, as quoted by Peter Kobel for the *Chicago Tribune* (August 8, 1988), "You've got to realize that speed is taking over the world. Look at the kids growing up with computers and video games, which are 10 times faster than the pinball machines we used to play. There's an essential something that young musicians have, something you can lose touch with as you get older. I love bands like Husker Du, Metallica, Black Flag, thrash bands. . . . It's a whole new way of thinking, of living. And we've got to keep up with it. I'll probably die trying."

In the early 1980s Zorn continued working with groups of musicians to create loosely structured pieces that grew out of improvisational sessions. These pieces, which were organized thematically in terms of games and sports and given titles like "Rugby," "Archery," and "Soccer," have since been dubbed collectively Zorn's "game pieces."

Zorn then began composing and performing pieces influenced by popular films. His 19-minute composition "Godard," which he unveiled in 1985, utilized musical equivalents of stylistic film elements that were a mainstay of the irreverent aesthetic espoused by the French film director Jean-Luc Godard. For instance, Zorn used abrupt musical transitions to achieve an effect similar to what Godard had accomplished with disorienting jump cuts. Another Zorn recording influenced by popular films is *Big Gundown* (1987), which revisited the music of Ennio Morricone, the Italian composer of the soundtracks of such "spaghetti" westerns as *The Good, the Bad, and the Ugly* (1966) and *Once Upon a Time in the West* (1969). The album featured Zorn's collaboration with some of New York City's finest musicians, including Wayne Horvitz, Bill Frisell on guitar, Fred Frith on bass, and Joey Baron on drums; this group eventually became the Naked City band, with whom Zorn has performed regularly all over the world since the late 1980s. The album received great acclaim and helped cement Zorn's reputation as an innovative composer and musician. Gene Santoro described the album thusly: "Zorn takes the Italian's brooding, twangy atmospherics, themselves witty reworkings of Duane Eddy and the Ventures, and twists them into scorching surrealism, redistributing the voicings of the original charts over utterly different instruments and players to produce wild, apocalyptic renditions that refract the still-recognizable material."

The following year Zorn again returned to popular cinema as a springboard for musical experimentation and released *Spillane* (1988), an album that paid homage to the hardboiled detective yarns of the pulp novelist Mickey Spillane. *Big Gundown* and *Spillane* have generally been deemed Zorn's most accessible albums.

Meanwhile, Zorn also experimented with fusing music from different cultures. One result was *Ganryu Island* (1987), an album of duets with Sato Michihiro, a master of the shakuhachi, the traditional Japanese flute. He also released *New for Lulu* (1988), on which he played jazz standards with Bill Frisell and the trombonist George Lewis.

Zorn has often attributed his use of a wide array of musical traditions and genres to the material circumstances enjoyed by his generation. "In general, my generation and younger, this is how we grew up," he said, as quoted by Davis. "We had an unprecedented variety of music available to us, because of the availability of everything on LP." Not surprisingly, Zorn has long been an amasser of world music; the records in his collection reportedly number around 13,000. "[My] musical world isn't just what I write, it's what I listen to," he said, as quoted by Peter Watrous for the *New York Times* (February 24, 1989). "Listening implies a world view—that all these genres are the same. I want to break all these hierarchies: the idea that classical music is better than jazz, that jazz is better than rock. I don't think that way. Some artists are hacks and some are masters and I'd rather listen to a master of Muzak than a classical hack."

While touring widely with Naked City, Zorn has won several commissions as a composer. In 1989 the Brooklyn Philharmonic performed his "For Your Eyes Only" at New Music America, an annual festival of avant-garde music that takes place in a different city in the U.S. each year. Also that year, he formed the band Spy vs. Spy. The group, also including the alto saxophonist Tim Berne, the bassist Mark Dresser, and the drummers Joey Baron and Michael Vatcher, played hardcore interpretations of experimental jazz compositions by Ornette Coleman and released an eponymous album. Despite these developments, wide mainstream success continued to elude Zorn. "People put down my music for various reasons, but I think most of their objections amount to the same thing—they don't like the way I mix it all up," he told Reich. Zorn also faced criticism that he lacked formal musical skills. "Some people say I can't play [chord] changes, some people say I can't play in tune, and some people say I can't play the saxophone," he told Davis. "My basic response is I'm doing the best I can. You can spend your whole life, like Frisell has, learning to get inside the chords. I don't do it that way."

Despite the lack of mainstream success, Zorn has maintained his pace of high output for much of the 1990s. Among other projects, he recorded the album *Naked City* (1990) with his band of the same name. Jon Pareles, writing for the *New York Times* (April 8, 1990), likened the album to "a car radio stuck on scan mode." Around that time, Zorn began spending more time in Japan, where he had developed a large following. In 1992 several of Zorn's recordings were released on DIW, a Japanese jazz label, which also provided Zorn with his own label, Avant Records.

Zorn then made the albums *Absinthe* (1994), *Radio* (1994), and *Masada* (1995). In 1997 Zorn teamed up with Bobby Previte to record *Euclid's Nightmare*, which featured 27 one-minute-long, improvised tracks that expanded on simple rhythms and melodies. *Masada* features his then newly formed band, Masada, the name of which is that of an ancient mountaintop fortress in Israel where, during the first century A.D., 1,000 Jews (known as Zealots) committed suicide rather than be captured by Roman troops. The album incorporates Jewish folk music in interpretations of the music of Ornette Coleman. Zorn has toured with Masada and released several albums that he made with the group. The most recent is *Masada Live in Jerusalem* (1999).

In recent years Zorn, who grew up as a secular Jew, has embraced his Jewish heritage and has devoted most of his efforts to Masada. He has often appeared in concert wearing shirts decorated with Hebrew writing, to both publicize his interest in his roots and religion and to attract other young nonobservant Jews to Judaism. Zorn is featured in *Jewish Soul, American Beat* (1999), a documentary film by Barbara Pfeffer (who died in March 1999). In addition to Zorn, the film focuses on the playwright Tony Kushner, the writer Cynthia Ozick, and other Jews who have strengthened their ties to Judaism as adults.

In addition to his many other projects, Zorn served as the curator of the Radical New Jewish Culture Festival at New York City's Knitting Factory in 1993. A month-long celebration of his compositions was presented at the Knitting Factory in the same year. Zorn splits his time between Tokyo and New York City. — Y.P.

Suggested Reading: *Atlantic* p97+ Jan. 1991; *Chicago Tribune* XIII p12+ June 11, 1989, with photos; *Nation* p138+ Jan. 30, 1988; *New York Times* II p27+ Feb. 21, 1988, with photo, II p29 Apr. 8, 1990, with photo, C p4 June 7, 1991, with photo, II p1+ Oct. 3, 1999, with photos

Selected Recordings: *Cobra*, 1986; *The Big Gundown*, 1987; *Ganryu Island*, 1987; *Spillane*, 1988; *News for Lulu*, 1988; *Spy vs. Spy*, 1989; *More News for Lulu: Live in Paris and Basil*, 1989; *Naked City*, 1990; *Filmworks:1986-90*, 1992; *Heretic*, 1992; *Radio*, 1994; *Absinthe*, 1994; *Masada*, 1995; *Euclid's Nightmare*, 1997; *Masada Live in Jerusalem*, 1999

Courtesy of Smith-Gosnell-Nicholson and Associates

Zsigmond, Vilmos
(ZIG-mund)

June 16, 1930– Cinematographer; director.
Address: c/o Smith Gosnell Nicholson, 1515
Palisades Dr., #N, Pacific Palisades, CA 90272;
c/o American Society of Cinematographers, 1782
N. Orange Dr., Hollywood, CA 90028

The Hungarian-born Vilmos Zsigmond, who immigrated to the United States after the Soviet invasion
of Budapest in 1956, is one of the most influential
and successful cinematographers in motion-
picture history. A two-time Academy Award winner for best cinematographer—he won for Steven
Spielberg's *Close Encounters of the Third Kind*
(1977) and Michael Cimino's *The Deer Hunter*
(1978)—Zsigmond has been the cameraman on a
number of other highly praised and enduring
films, among them John Boorman's *Deliverance*
(1972), Mark Rydell's *The Rose* (1979), and Robert
Altman's *McCabe and Mrs. Miller* (1971). "A cinematographer can only be as good as the director,"
Zsigmond told Jean Vallely for *Rolling Stone* (February 21, 1980). "The story is the main thing, and
the director knows the story and the characters better than anyone. . . . The cameraman shouldn't
have his own style. He doesn't have the right to, because he might kill the story, kill the director's concept. Together, they should create a style for that
particular film. A good cameraman should be able
to make his films look different every time." Most
recently, Zsigmond, who has worked in film for
over 40 years, has done the cinematography for
Dick Donner's *Maverick* (1994), Sean Penn's *The
Crossing Guard* (1995), and Brian De Palma's *Mr.
Hughes*, which is set for a 2000 release. "For us

cameramen, the good painters are those who are
terrific with lighting," Zsigmond told *American
Film* (June 1979), referring to the artists Rem-
brandt, Goya, and Georges de La Tour. Their works
are useful for cinematographers, Zsigmond said,
"because by looking at them you see a certain feeling in the composition and in the lighting which
creates mood, and that's what we are doing. Cameramen should work like painters, except they
have more time to do it. Studying paintings improves your vision a lot, and when you have to do
something fast, you think like a painter."

Vilmos Zsigmond was born on June 16, 1930 in
Cegled, Hungary. William, as his English-speaking
friends would come to call him, became interested
in film early in his childhood. His father, a legendary Hungarian soccer player, encouraged his son's
interest in the art form and, although the family did
not have much money, bought him his first still
camera. In his late teens Zsigmond enrolled at the
Budapest Film School, where he learned the basics
of filmmaking and began to develop his skill as a
cinematographer. "School in Hungary is so good,
there is really no comparison," Zsigmond told
American Film (November 1990). "You study for
four years every day for 14 hours a day. It's much
more involved than UCLA [University of California at Los Angeles] or USC [University of Southern
California]. But the biggest difference was in the
teaching. The teachers were the best cinematographers in Hungary, and they shared everything they
knew. In America they keep trade secrets—
somebody knows something that they're not going
to give to anybody else. There they give it to you.
Not only that, they took you out in the field twice
a week, where they were actually shooting a movie
and you could ask questions. So you get first-hand
experience of shooting a real movie."

In 1956, when Zsigmond was 26, Soviet troops
marched into the Hungarian capital following the
anti-Communist revolt there and installed a puppet government. Zsigmond, wanting to continue
his study of film in a free nation, decided to flee his
homeland. "I had learned everything I could in
Hungary," he told *American Film*. "That's why I
came to Hollywood." Also spurring him to leave
was his having made a film about the Hungarian
uprising, in collaboration with Laszlo Kovacs, a
fellow film student and now an established cinematographer. The two men fled with the footage
they had shot, and they managed to hide it in a
cornfield just before Russian border guards captured them. "In the middle of the night, we were
released and searched through hundreds of corn
stacks to find it," Zsigmond recalled. When he and
Laszlo finally made it to freedom in Europe, they
sold the film to a Hungarian-German producer,
who incorporated it into his own documentary,
Hungary Aflame. Selected footage from Zsigmond
and Kovacs's original film was eventually bought
by CBS and featured in *Twentieth Century,* a 1961
documentary narrated by Walter Cronkite.

In Hollywood Zsigmond worked his way up from still photographer to lab technician to cinematographer in a little over seven years. His first listed credit is the 1962 film *Wild Guitar*, on which he assisted with the cinematography; his motion-picture debut as cinematographer came in the following year, in the low-budget horror movie *The Sadist*. Directed by James Landis, that film is today considered a cult classic. "Stunningly photographed by Vilmos Zsigmond . . . [the film] may well be the greatest exploitation flick ever made (and we're taking into consideration *Night of the Living Dead*)," Hal Erickson wrote for the *All Movie Guide* (on-line). Throughout the 1960s, Zsigmond continued to work the camera on low-budget "exploitation" films, in which gore, camp, and cheap special effects prevailed. Most notably during this period, he worked on *Incredibly Strange Creatures Who Stopped Living and Became Mixed-Up Zombies*, which reunited him with Laszlo Kovacs. "The low budget movies kept me in training, so to speak," Zsigmond told *American Film* in 1990. "If you don't shoot every day, you get rusty. It's like a puzzle, basically: The camera moves, the actors are moving. You have to keep it all together. If you don't do it every day, you have a hard time getting it back." Zsigmond also worked on several comedies that decade, including *Tales of the Salesman* (1965), directed by Don Russel, and *The Monitors* (1969), which featured the Second City comedy-troupe members Ed Begley, Guy Stockwell, and Avery Schreiber.

Zsigmond continued in the horror/shock vein for the early part of the 1970s, with such films as *Horror of the Blood Monsters* (1970) and *Five Bloody Graves* (1970). He got his big break in 1971, when he and the director Robert Altman collaborated on *McCabe and Mrs. Miller*. Altman and screenwriter Brian McKay adapted the film's story, about the American West at the end of the 19th century, from a novel by Edmund Naughton. The film received rave reviews, and the star power of Warren Beatty and Julie Christie, who played the title roles, helped it become a hit at the box office. The quality of the movie was enhanced by Zsigmond's soft lighting and monochromatic filming, and the cinematographer became a star in industry circles. "That's probably Altman's most watchable film," Zsigmond told Nick Roddick for *Films and Filming* (September 1982). "He really feels at home when he does a subject like that [a period piece] because he wants that kind of photography. He's basically a still photographer himself, and he likes things that are not too clear and not too sharp."

Zsigmond worked with Altman on two more pictures over the next two years. The first, *Images* (1972), was a low-budget psychodrama about a woman who is plagued by visions of her former lovers. The second, *The Long Goodbye* (1973), loosely based on Raymond Chandler's detective novel of the same name, represented a reimagining of the film-noir genre, with Elliot Gould playing the sardonic Phillip Marlowe. (The character was first portrayed on the screen by Humphrey Bogart.) Between those films, Zsigmond worked on one of his most celebrated pictures, John Boorman's *Deliverance* (1972), about a four-man canoe trip that turns hellish. "That was a really sharp picture," Zsigmond told Roddick. "We had to shoot in Georgia in the middle of the summer. . . . There is a gorgeous shot which I like very much when Jon Voight first climbs up into the rocks and stands up against the black sky. That worked out so beautifully." The film, based on a novel by James Dickey, established Voight and Burt Reynolds as bona fide movie stars. "[*Deliverance*] was like shooting a low-budget movie with a very small crew 90 percent of the time," Zsigmond told *American Film* in 1990. "We couldn't even take many crew people down the river. We had to pack and load the cameras in canoes and rubber boats and go down the river through the rapids to the next location." The film was nominated for several Academy Awards, including best picture and best director.

Sugarland Express (1974), the tale of a Texas outlaw couple striving to keep their family together, was Zsigmond's next major project; the now-established cinematographer collaborated with then up-and-coming director Steven Spielberg. "In those days, Steven was already very good in staging and working with the actors and telling the story, and he had a tremendous number of ideas," Zsigmond said in his 1990 interview with *American Film*. "Luckily, he didn't know much about lighting. I always had to tell him, 'Steven, we should shoot the Rio Grand ending around 3:00 in the afternoon. You're going to have a nice backlight.' You know, when we shot it in that light and saw the dailies, Steven was very pleased. He said, My God, how did you know that? I just told him that it was the cameraman's job to know what has to be shot at what time. That's *part* of our job, really; you want to create mood when you shoot exteriors." Next up was Brian De Palma's *Obsession* (1976)—a critical and financial disappointment about a man's fixation with his dead wife—and the equally uninspired *Sweet Revenge* (1977), starring Stockard Channing as a charming thief.

Spielberg enlisted Zsigmond's services again for his groundbreaking science-fiction movie *Close Encounters of the Third Kind*, which became one of the highest-grossing films of the decade. The two men's relationship, however, which had been friendly before the project, quickly deteriorated. "When we worked together on *Close Encounters* . . . Steven had already learned too much, and he would not listen to me because he always had the better idea . . . ," Zsigmond told *American Film*. "What do you do with a director like that? I mean, I'm getting the credit as director of photography and in many cases, the cinematographer gets an Academy Award for the cinematography the director was responsible for." Zsigmond did in fact win an Oscar for his work on the project, but the cinematographer has not collaborated with Spielberg again to this day. He has been quoted several times as saying in essence what he told Roddick: "[Spielberg] knows exactly what the audience wants to see. He's a little bit of a sell-out, for me."

Zsigmond followed up *Close Encounters* the following year with another critically acclaimed hit, *The Deer Hunter*, starring Robert De Niro. The story of several Polish-Americans in the Vietnam War, the movie won several Oscars; Zsigmond took home his second statuette, and he also won an award from the British Academy of Film and Television Arts (BAFTA). "I like to work with Michael Cimino . . . ," Zsigmond told Roddick. "As a film director, I think he's one of the best. He is striving for excellence in everything. I think that *The Deer Hunter* was the picture where Cimino probably did his best job." In stark contrast to that film, in terms of critical reception, was Cimino's *Heaven's Gate* (1980), which also featured Zsigmond's camera work. Zsigmond had continued his late-1970s streak of successes with *The Rose* (1979) and the rock documentary starring the Band, *The Last Waltz* (1979), but *Heaven's Gate*, based on the book *The Final Cut*, by Steven Bach, remains the premier symbol of Hollywood excess and incompetence, with its out-of-control cost (the then-enormous sum of $36 million) and the near incomprehensibility of the version of the film that was released to theaters.

In the early 1980s Zsigmond kept himself highly visible, with such films as the successful *Blow Out* (1981), starring John Travolta and directed by Brian De Palma; *Jinxed!* (1982), with Bette Midler; *Table for Five* (1983), featuring Jon Voight; and *No Small Affair* (1984), which showcased a young Demi Moore and an even younger Jennifer Tilly. Another Oscar nomination came his way in 1984, for his work on *The River*, which found Mel Gibson playing a down-on-his-luck farmer, opposite Sissy Spacek (who also received an Academy Award nomination) as the farmer's wife. Among the more notable films in which he served as cinematographer later in the decade were *The Witches of Eastwick* (1987)—a box-office hit starring Jack Nicholson, Cher, Michelle Pfeiffer, and Susan Sarandon—and *Fat Man and Little Boy* (1989), which chronicled the building of the first atomic bomb. In 1990 Zsigmond teamed up with Jack Nicholson on a sequel to the 1974 film *Chinatown*. The movie, *The Two Jakes* (1990), which marked Nicholson's first time in the director's chair, received lukewarm reviews and proved to be a financial disappointment. Zsigmond did not fare much better with his next turn behind the camera: *Bonfire of the Vanities* (1990), directed by Brian De Palma and based on Tom Wolfe's best-selling book, turned out be one of the biggest box-office flops of that year.

In the early 1990s, having slowed his pace as a cinematographer, Zsigmond decided to give directing a try. His debut film, *The Long Shadow* (1992)—a joint venture between a Hungarian film company and an Israeli movie studio—featured several international film stars, among them Michael York, Liv Ullmann, Oded Teomi, Ava Haddad, and Babi Neeman. Focusing on a Hungarian actor who, upon learning of his estranged father's death, goes to Israel to dig into his family's past, the film proved extremely popular in both nations. Also in 1992, Zsigmond worked as cinematographer on *Stalin*, an HBO movie about the Russian dictator starring Robert Duvall. After finishing up the camera work on the Sharon Stone/William Baldwin project *Sliver* in early 1993, Zsigmond was recruited by Richard Donner to do the cinematography on the big-budget film *Maverick*, based on the TV western and released in early 1994. Since then Zsigmond has worked on several films, including *Intersection* (1994), with Richard Gere; *Assassins* (1995), starring Sylvester Stallone; the Sean Penn–directed *The Crossing Guard*, featuring Jack Nicholson; and *The Ghost and the Darkness* (1996), with Val Kilmer and Michael Douglas. In 1998 Zsigmond worked with writer/director Willard Carrol on the film *Playing by Heart*, featuring Gillian Anderson, Jon Stewart, and Sean Connery. Next up for the acclaimed cinematographer, who will soon enter his fifth decade in film, is another Brian De Palma project, *Mr. Hughes*, slated to star Nicolas Cage and set for a 2000 release.

When asked what films in his illustrious career had proved the most gratifying to work on, Zsigmond told *Soc.org* (on-line), "I think the films I did with Robert Altman, because he gave me enough space to use my creative abilities, and to help him. We played together like a couple of jazz musicians; also directors Mark Rydell, John Boorman, Michael Cimino. I've been lucky because most of the directors I worked with wanted my help, and I felt creative. The best directors know how to make you feel important. They know how to make everyone around them feel creative." Zsigmond has received Lifetime Achievement Awards from the American Society of Cinematographers, Worldfest-Flagstaff, and Cameraimage, in Poland. — M.B.

Suggested Reading: *American Film* p35+ June 1979, with photos, p20+ Nov. 1990, with photos; *Films and Filming* p21+ Sep. 1982, with photos; *Rolling Stone* p36+ Feb. 21, 1980, with photos

Selected Films: as cinematographer—*The Sadist*, 1963; *Incredibly Strange Creatures Who Stopped Living and Became Mixed-Up Zombies*, 1963; *The Time Travelers*, 1964; *The Nasty Rabbit*, 1964; *Psycho a Go-Go*, 1965; *Deadwood '76*, 1965; *The Name of the Game Is to Kill*, 1968; *The Picasso Summer*, 1969; *The Monitors*, 1969; *Fritz!*, 1969; *Horror of the Blood Monsters*, 1970; *Five Bloody Graves*, 1970; *The Ski Bum*, 1971; *Red Sky at Morning*, 1971; *The Hired Hand*, 1971; *McCabe and Mrs. Miller*, 1971; *Images*, 1972; *Deliverance*, 1972; *Blood of Ghastly Horror*, 1972; *Cinderella Liberty*, 1973; *Scarecrow*, 1973; *The Long Goodbye*, 1973; *The Girl from Petrovka*, 1974; *Sugarland Express*, 1974; *Death Riders*, 1976; *Obsessions*, 1976;

Sweet Revenge, 1977; *Close Encounters of the Third Kind*, 1977; *The Deer Hunter*, 1978; *The Last Waltz*, 1978; *Winter Kills*, 1979; *The Rose*, 1979; *Heaven's Gate*, 1980; *Blow Out*, 1981; *Jinxed!*, 1982; *Table for Five*, 1983; *No Small Affair*, 1984; *The River*, 1984; *Real Genius*, 1985; *The Witches of Eastwick*, 1987; *Journey to Spirit Island*, 1988; *Fat Man and Little Boy*, 1989; *The Two Jakes*, 1990; *The Bonfire of the Vanities*, 1990; *Stalin*, 1992; *Sliver*, 1993; *Maverick*, 1994; *The Crossing Guard*, 1995; *Assassins*, 1995; *The Ghost and the Darkness*, 1996; *Playing by Heart*, 1998; *Illegal Music*, 1998; as director—*The Long Shadow*, 1992

OBITUARIES

Written by Kieran Dugan

ADAMS, ALICE Aug. 14, 1926–May 27, 1999 Author; wrote novels and short stories, most typically about women who survive destructive marriages and love affairs to find emotional independence and creative fulfillment in their middle years; was, in the words of former *New Yorker* magazine editor Fran Kiernan, unexcelled in writing "about the tangled relations of men and women or about the enduring romance of friendship"; for her fiction, drew on her own life experience (including the settings and local color), from her upbringing by intellectual parents at the University of North Carolina and in a farmhouse in Chapel Hill, North Carolina, to her undergraduate years at Radcliffe College, to a job in publishing in New York, a marriage (which produced one child, a son, before ending in divorce) and other ill-starred liaisons, to an enduring (albeit not officially marital) ménage with Robert McNie, a San Francisco interior designer; evoked broad landscapes with short, deft strokes; was able to condense "so much . . . into a short form," and "with so much resonance," as Victoria Wilson, her book editor for 25 years, observed; began contributing short stories (many of which were formulaic romances) to women's magazines in 1959; broke into the higher-caliber literary marketplace with "Gift of Grass" (1969), the first of her more than 20 stories to be published in the *New Yorker* and to win O. Henry Awards; meanwhile, had published her first novel, *Careless Love* (1966), to mixed reviews; established her literary reputation with her second novel, *Families and Survivors* (1975); with her first collection of short stories, *Beautiful Girl* (1979), elicited comparisons to the work of F. Scott Fitzgerald, Katherine Mansfield, and Flannery O'Connor; reached her greatest popularity with her fifth, and longest, novel, *Superior Women* (1984), in which she traced the lives of five Radcliffe women from 1943 to 1983; wrote a total of 10 novels, including *Listening to Billie* (1978), *Rewards* (1980), *Second Chances* (1988), *Caroline's Daughters* (1991), *Almost Perfect* (1993), and *After the War* (scheduled for publication in the year 2000); published five collections of short stories, including *To See You Again* (1982), *Return Trips* (1985), and *After You've Gone* (1989); died in San Francisco, California. See *Current Biography* (August) 1989.

Obituary *New York Times* B p11 May 28, 1999

AMBLER, ERIC June 28, 1909–Oct. 22, 1998 British novelist; film scenarist; an important innovator in espionage fiction, to which he brought elegance of style, realism, and subtlety in developing ordinary types of characters in sinister contexts; early on, attempted careers in electrical engineering, acting, and writing advertising copy; in the years preceding World War II, in such novels as *The Dark Frontier* (1935) and *A Coffin for Dimitrios* (1939), raised the previously lowly spy thriller genre to the level of literature; was hailed by one of his disciples, Graham

Greene, as "the greatest living writer of suspense," and by another, John le Carré, as "the well into which everyone dipped"; began working in film as an officer with British Army Cinematography during World War II; concentrated on the writing of screenplays as a civilian for five years after the war; returning to fiction, displayed in such novels of international intrigue and adventure as *Judgment on Deltchev* (1951), *The Schirmer Inheritance* (1953), and *State of Siege* (1956) less dependence on violent action than before and a keener insight into character, a finer moral sense, a more masterly use of background, and greater social and political verisimilitude; could be good-humored, as in *The Light of Day* (1962), which was adapted into the caper film *Topkapi* (1964); not counting fiction published under the pseudonym Eliot Reed, wrote some 16 novels, including *The Intercom Conspiracy* (1969), *Doctor Frigo* (1974), and *The Core of Time* (1981); for the screen, co-wrote the script for the morale-boosting wartime documentary *The Way Ahead* (1944); wrote the scenarios for *The October Man* (1947), *The Passionate Friend* (1948), *A Night to Remember* (1958), and *The Wreck of the Mary Deare* (1959), among other motion pictures; died at his home in London. See *Current Biography* (June) 1975.

Obituary *New York Times* C p16 Oct. 24, 1998

AUTRY, GENE Sep. 29, 1908–Oct. 2, 1998 Actor; singer; songwriter; producer; businessman; the silver screen's first singing cowboy; a no-nonsense western star who stressed action and downplayed romance; was born on a small Texas cattle and grain farm; while working as a railroad telegrapher in Oklahoma, was encouraged to go into show business by Will Rogers; in the late 1920s, became "Oklahoma's Singing Cowboy" on radio station KVOU in Tulsa; first made the record charts with "That Silver-Haired Daddy of Mine," which he co-wrote; in the early 1930s, reached a national audience singing on station WLS in Chicago; later hosted his own national radio show, *Melody Ranch*; began his Hollywood career with a cameo singing role in the film In *Old Santa Fe* (1934); had his first leading role in the serial *The Phantom Empire* (1935); beginning with *Tumbling Tumbleweeds* (1935), starred in dozens of westerns produced by Republic Pictures for Saturday-matinee juvenile audiences, including *Boots and Saddles* (1937), *Springtime in the Rockies* (1937), *South of the Border* (1939), and *Melody Ranch* (1940); between 1938 and 1942 was the only western star among the top 10 Hollywood moneymakers; after serving as an Air Transport co-pilot in World War II, returned to his radio show and his filmmaking; formed his own production unit at Columbia Pictures, Flying Y Productions; produced and starred in such films as *Loaded Pistols* (1949), *Apache Country* (1952), and *Winning of the West* (1955); for television, filmed 91 episodes of the *Gene*

Autry Show during the 1950s; produced the television series *Annie Oakley* and *Death Valley Days*; performed in his own touring rodeo show with Champion, his chestnut Tennessee walking horse; recorded more than 200 popular singles, including some of his own compositions, such as "Here Comes Santa Claus"; scored his greatest hits with recordings of two songs written by others: "South of the Border," which sold more than 2 million copies, and "Rudolph the Red-Nosed Reindeer," the second-best-selling single in recording history, with sales of 15 million; on his radio and television shows, sang his signature "Back in the Saddle Again"; as a multi-millionaire businessman, owned radio and television stations, a flying school, a music production company, hotels, oil wells, the Anaheim (California) Angels major-league baseball franchise, and the Autry Museum of Western Heritage in Los Angeles; died at his home in the Studio City section of Los Angeles. See *Current Biography* (December) 1947.

Obituary *New York Times* A p15 Oct. 3, 1998

BARZIN, LEON (EUGENE) Nov. 27, 1900–Apr. 29, 1999 Belgian-born, American-bred orchestra and ballet conductor; teacher; contributed to the training of several generations of symphony conductors and musicians; was, as the critic Harold C. Schonberg observed, a "choreographic conductor" who would "crouch for pianissimos," "get on tiptoe for fortes," and "dance to the music"; as a child, studied violin and viola with his father (and namesake); in 1917 became second violinist with the National Symphony Orchestra, which merged with the New York Philharmonic Symphony Orchestra the following year; was principal violinist with the Philharmonic from 1925 to 1929, when he turned to conducting; from 1930 to 1958 was principal conductor and musical director of the National Orchestral Association, which was formed to develop young musicians and conductors in ensemble technique; in that position, opened the association to increasing numbers of women and blacks; took part in projects promoting opera companies and symphony orchestras in American cities, schools, and colleges; meanwhile, had helped Lincoln Kirstein and George Balanchine to found the New York City Ballet in the late 1940s; was musical director of that ballet company periodically until 1958, when he left the U.S. for the first of two teaching and conducting sojourns in France; was awarded the French Legion of Honor in 1960; returned to France in the late 1970s; was a guest conductor of many orchestras in the U.S., a visiting teacher at workshops and festivals, and a judge at music competitions; died at his home in Naples, Florida. See *Current Biography* (May) 1951.

Obituary *New York Times* p38 May 9, 1999

BERIOSOVA, SVETLANA Sep. 24, 1932–Nov. 10, 1998 Lithuanian-born British ballerina; a natural dancer, described by critics as possessing "poise and serenity," "the true classical style," and "the assured easy carriage of the Russian school"; brought "an inborn beauty to every pose"; was trained in part by her mother, who died when Svetlana was 10; performed in children's roles with the Ballet Russe de Monte Carlo, where her father was a dancer; as a

teenager performed with the Monte Carlo troupe, the Ottawa Ballet Company, and the London Metropolitan Ballet; in 1950 joined the second company of the Royal Ballet (then known as the Sadler's Wells); graduated to the Royal Ballet's first company in 1952; during the 1950s became known for her performances as Princess Aurora in *The Sleeping Beauty* and the title characters in *Sylvia* and *Coppélia* and for her creation of the leading female roles in John Cranko's *Pastorale* and *The Shadow* and the role of Armida in *Rinaldo and Armida*, the first of many written for her by Frederick Ashton; later danced the title roles in Ashton's *Cinderella*, *Ondine*, and *Persephone*, leading roles in Ashton's *Birthday Offering* and *Enigma Variations*, the Tsarina in Kenneth MacMillan's *Anastasia*, and the bride in Bronislava Nijinska's version of *Les Noces*; also included in her repertoire such roles as Tsarevna in *The Firebird* and the title part in *Giselle*; after retiring from the Royal Ballet, in 1975, became a dance coach and teacher; died in London. See *Current Biography* (September) 1960.

Obituary *New York Times* B p15 Nov. 13, 1998

BISHOP, HAZEL (GLADYS) Aug. 17, 1906–Dec. 5, 1998 Industrial chemist; cosmetics manufacturer and marketer; financial expert; teacher; was a research assistant to the dermatologist A. Bronson Cannon from 1935 to 1942; as a senior organic chemist with the Standard Oil Development Co. during World War II, developed a special fuel for bomber aircraft; after the war, as a senior petroleum researcher with the Socony Vacuum Oil Co., privately pursued her favorite interest, experimenting with lipsticks in her kitchen laboratory; in 1949 completed the development of the "Lasting Lipstick," the world's first nonsmear lipstick; in 1950 founded Hazel Bishop Inc. to manufacture and market the lipstick; to handle the advertising ("Stays on you . . . not on him"), retained Raymond Spector, who became the major stockholder of Hazel Bishop Inc.; soon captured 25 percent of the lipstick market; inspired the development of 50 competing kiss-proof lipsticks; in a financial dispute with Raymond Spector, resigned as president of Hazel Bishop Inc. in November 1951; as minority stockholder, filed suit against Hazel Bishop Inc. and the Raymond Spector Co. for diversion of assets and mismanagement; in a settlement in 1954 (when Hazel Bishop Inc.'s annual sales exceeded $10 million), relinquished her 8 percent of stock for $250,000; continued to develop cosmetics and other personal-care products, along with household products, as head of Hazel Bishop Laboratories and Perfemme Inc., but had lost the right to sell her products under her own name; in the 1960s worked as a stockbroker with Bache & Co. and as a financial analyst with Evans & Co.; joined the Fashion Institute of Technology in Manhattan as an adjunct professor in 1978; two years later, was appointed to the Revlon chair of cosmetics marketing at the institute; died in Rye, New York. See *Current Biography* (September) 1957.

Obituary *New York Times* B p16 Dec. 10, 1998

BLACKMUN, HARRY A. Nov. 12, 1908–Mar. 4, 1999 Associate justice of the U.S. Supreme Court (1970–94); a nominal Republican who entered the court with an ambiguous conservative reputation and left it as, arguably, the high tribunal's most liberal member; championed a strict separation of church and state; while favoring victims' over criminal rights, generally voted for individual liberties vis-à-vis governmental authority; above all, was indelibly identified as the author of the court's volatile 1973 decision legalizing abortion nationwide; at the beginning of his career, specialized in tax law and will and estate planning as a partner in a Minneapolis law firm, until 1950; concurrently, taught law at St. Paul College and the University of Minnesota; was resident counsel at the Mayo Clinic from 1950 to 1959, when he was appointed a judge of the U.S. Court of Appeals, eighth circuit; when appointed to the Supreme Court by President Richard Nixon, was described by the president as "a strict constructionalist," presumably inclined to apply the Constitution without innovative interpretations; radically changed his public image in 1973, when he was assigned by Chief Justice Warren E. Burger to write the decision arrived at by the court (seven votes to two) in the case of Rowe v. Wade that there is in the Constitution "a right of personal privacy . . . broad enough to encompass a woman's decision whether or not to terminate her pregnancy"; in subsequent opinions, wrote that "the flow of such information [advertising by licensed attorneys] may not be restrained" (Bates v. Arizona State Bar, 1977) and that "the fundamental liberty interest of natural parents in the care, custody, and management of their child does not evaporate simply because they have not been model parents or have lost temporary custody of their child to the state" (Santoski v. Kramer, 1984); in a partial dissent in the University of California v. Bakke "affirmative action" case, argued that "in order to get beyond racism, we must first take account of race"; in Garcia v. San Antonio Transit Authority (1985), wrote the court's decision overturning a previous decision exempting municipal transit systems from submission to the federal Fair Labor Standards Act; dissented from the court's 1986 decision that the constitutional right to privacy does not extend to homosexual behavior; in his concurring opinion in Casey v. Planned Parenthood in 1992, "just when so many expected the darkness to fall," expressed his encouragement at the court's continuing recognition of "a woman's right to terminate her pregnancy in its early stages"; died in Washington, D.C. See *Current Biography* (October) 1970.

Obituary *New York Times* A p1+ Mar. 5, 1999

BOGARDE, DIRK Mar. 28, 1921–May 8, 1999 British actor; writer; transcended his early reputation as "the idol of the Odeons" (a reference to the J. Arthur Rank chain of cinemas in Britain) to become a master of challenging, complex roles, often of the greatest subtlety; made his stage debut with a suburban London theatrical troupe in 1939; during World War II served as an officer with British army intelligence; achieved overnight success in London's West End with his performance as Cliff in *Power without Glory* (1947); under screen contract with the Rank Organi-

zation, following one bit part, was cast as William Latch in *Esther Waters* (1948) and as the suicidal pianist in the "Alien Corn" segment of *Quartet* (1948); for Rank and its affiliates over the following 13 years, played diverse roles in pictures of varying caliber, from Cockney "spivs," criminals, and men in combat to Sydney Carton in *A Tale of Two Cities* (1958) and Louis Dubedat in *The Doctor's Dilemma* (1958); reached the height of his popularity as the bumbling intern Simon Sparrow in the hospital comedy *Doctor in the House* (1954) and its several sequels; for his first freelance role, in a choice daring for its time, played a lawyer who risks his reputation and marriage to bring to justice the blackmailers who caused the death of a young homosexual with whom he had once had a brief liaison, in Basil Dearden's *Victim* (1961); again found a role to match his talents in Hugo Barrett, the valet who insidiously corrupts his young master in *The Servant* (1963), written with him in mind by Harold Pinter and directed by Joseph Losey; won the British Academy Award for best actor for that role and for the role of the television reporter Robert Gold in John Schlesinger's *Darling* (1965); was again directed by Losey in the roles of Captain Hargreaves, the anguished defending officer in a court martial, in the antiwar film *King and Country* (1964) and the international criminal Gabriel in the spy spoof *Modesty Blaise* (1966); again collaborated with Losey and Harold Pinter in *Accident* (1966), in which he is seen in the role of Stephen, the troubled Oxford don trying to recapture his youth; was later cast effectively as the cad exploiting seven orphaned children in Jack Clayton's Gothic horror movie *Our Mother's House* (1967), as Stephen in Richard Attenborough's *Oh! What a Lovely War* (1969), and as Friedrich Bruckman in Lucino Visconti's *The Damned* (1969); turned in an exquisitely sensitive characterization of the doomed composer Gustav von Aschenbach in Visconti's screen adaptation of *Death in Venice* (1971); was subsequently cast as Max, the sadomasochistic former Nazi concentration camp officer, in Liliana Cavani's sexually bizarre *The Night Porter* (1974), as David Langham in Alan Resnais's *Providence* (1976), and as the Jewish survivor Hermann Karovich in Rainer Werner Fassbinder's *Despair* (1978); in 1969 moved to the south of France, where he lived with his companion of 40 years, Anthony Forward, until Forward's death; wrote eight well-received books of autobiography: *A Postillion Struck by Lightning* (1977), *Snakes and Ladders* (1978), *An Orderly Man* (1983), *Backcloth* (1986), *A Particular Friendship* (1989), *Great Meadow* (1992), *A Short Walk from Harrod's* (1993), and *Cleared for Takeoff* (1995); also wrote six novels, not as well received; personally, was most satisfied with the first of the novels, *A Gentle Occupation* (1980); returned to the screen as the dying father in *Daddy Nostalgia* (1990), the last of his more than 50 films; was knighted in 1992; died at his home in London. See *Current Biography* (July) 1967.

Obituary *New York Times* A p20 May 10, 1999

BRADLEY, TOM Dec. 29, 1917–Sep. 29, 1998 Democratic mayor of Los Angeles (1973–93); the first African-American mayor of a major, largely white American city; earned a law degree while working his way up to lieutenant in the Los Angeles police department; as mayor, marshaled business and government forces in a slow but steady process of rebuilding Los Angeles following the catastrophic Watts riots of 1965; was instrumental in transforming an assortment of urban and suburban neighborhoods into an international business and trading center greater than Chicago and rivaling New York City; died in West Los Angeles. See *Current Biography* (October) 1992.

Obituary *New York Times* A p1+ Sep. 30, 1998

CALDERONE, MARY S(TEICHEN) July 1, 1904–Oct. 24, 1998 Physician; public-health advocate; crusader for family planning and sex education; was the daughter of Edward Steichen, the celebrated photographer; after working as a public-school physician, became the medical director of the Parenthood Federation of America (1953–64); in that position, persuaded the American Medical Association to permit physicians to dispense birth-control information routinely; as executive director of the Sex Information and Education Council of the United States, which she co-founded in 1964, was instrumental in setting up sex-education programs in thousands of public schools throughout the U.S., along with auxiliary "parent learning centers"; co-wrote books of sex education advice for parents; died in Kennett Square, Pennsylvania. See *Current Biography* (November) 1967.

Obituary *New York Times* p52 Oct. 25, 1998

CALLAHAN, HARRY M. Oct. 22, 1912–Mar. 15, 1999 Photographer; teacher of photography; a modernist whose experiments in capturing the interplay of light, line, space, and motion made it possible to see commonplace subjects with uncommon perception; in 1938, when he was working as an accounting clerk in Detroit, Michigan, purchased his first camera, a Rolleicord, and began teaching himself the rudiments of photography; was influenced by the "beautiful tone and texture" of the work of Ansel Adams, the purism of Alfred Stieglitz, and the formal experimentalism of Laszlo Moholy-Nogy; beginning in the early 1940s, concentrated on such subjects as landscapes, cityscapes, seascapes, architecture, urban pedestrians, and members of his family, especially his wife, Eleanor; developed a repertory of modes and techniques, dominated by wide-angle shots, multiple exposures, dizzying rotations between exposures, and other means of distortion; in addition to his still photographs, shot two films, *People Walking on State Street* and *Motion*, both in 1950; became a teacher of photography at the Institute of Design in Chicago in 1946; was head of the institute's department of photography from 1949 to 1961; chaired the department of photography at the Rhode Island School of Design in Providence, Rhode Island, from 1949 to 1961; taught at the school until 1977; worked almost exclusively in black and white until 1972; mounted his first exhibition of color photographs in 1978; published several books of photographs, including *Eleanor* (1984) and *Harry Callahan: New Color* (1988); died at his home in Atlanta, Georgia. See *Current Biography* (November) 1984.

Obituary *New York Times* B p9 Mar. 18, 1999

CARMICHAEL, STOKELY June 29, 1941–Nov. 15, 1998 Trinidad-born black radical; in 1964 became field organizer with the Southern Nonviolent Coordinating Committee (SNCC), which was then sending hundreds of middle-class northerners on literacy, voter-registration, and health-clinic missions in black communities in the "Jim Crow" South; led a SNCC task force into Lowndes County, Mississippi; raised the number of black registered voters there from 70 to 2,600; bypassing the Democratic and Republican parties, organized the black Lowndes County Freedom Organization; as chairman of SNCC (1966–67), made "black power" an effective black liberation slogan; from 1967 to 1969 was prime minister of the Black Panthers, the urban-oriented, ultra-militant black self-defense organization founded in Oakland, California by Huey P. Newton and Bobby Seale; in 1969 emigrated to Guinea as a guest of Sekou Toure, then the Marxist president of that West African country; in Guinea, became a follower and close associate of Kwame Nkrumah, the Pan-African nationalist and anticolonialist who had been living in exile in Guinea since his deposition as president of Ghana in 1966; changed his name to Kwame Ture; traveled internationally, speaking in behalf of the All African Peoples Revolutionary Party; believed that "black power can only be realized when there exists a unified socialist Africa"; was dedicated to "building a movement that will smash everything that Western civilization has created"; published the books *Black Power* (1967), written with Charles Hamilton, and *Stokely Speaks* (1971), a collection of speeches and essays; was married to and divorced from the South African singer Miriam Makeba and then a Guinean physician, Marlyatou Barry; died in Conakry, Guinea. See *Current Biography* (April) 1970.

Obituary *New York Times* B p10 Nov. 16, 1998

CARNEGIE, DOROTHY (REEDER PRICE) Nov. 3, 1912–Aug. 6, 1998 Author; public speaker; motivational instructor; after divorcing her first husband, in 1944 married Dale Carnegie, author of the self-help classic *How to Win Friends and Influence People* (1936); wrote *How to Help Your Husband Get Ahead in his Social and Business Life* (1953); after Dale Carnegie's death, in 1955, took over Dale Carnegie Training, a company offering courses in self-development and public speaking; built the company into a standard training school for corporate executives in the U.S. and an international business, with offices in 70 countries, 5 million graduates, and $187 million in annual sales; married David Rivkin in 1976; while remaining chairwoman, turned over active management of Dale Carnegie Training to a son-in-law in 1978; lived in Queens, New York City. See *Current Biography* (September) 1955.

Obituary *New York Times* A p13 Aug. 8, 1998

CARTER, BETTY May 16, 1929–Sep. 26, 1998 Jazz singer; composer; arranger; a contralto with operatic range and flexibility, strikingly original diction and phrasing, and a unique sense of pitch; when leading her own trio of drums, bass, and piano, sounded to many ears like a fourth instrument, a trumpet or saxophone; controlled dramatic shifts in tempo with deceptive artlessness; wrote such songs as "Open the Door"; with ambivalence (because she felt more akin to Dizzie Gillespie), sang with Lionel Hampton's band from 1948 to 1951; during the 1950s played one-nighters and weekends in and out of New York City with such musicians as Muddy Waters, T-Bone Walker, Miles Davis, and Thelonius Monk and on bills with such comedians as Moms Mabley and Redd Foxx; on albums produced between 1953 and 1960, recorded her renditons of such standards as "You're Getting to Be a Habit," "Don't Weep for the Lady," and "My Reverie"; worked with Ray Charles from 1960 to 1963; with Charles, recorded the 1961 album *Ray Charles and Betty Carter*, which included a memorable rendition of "Baby, It's Cold Outside"; during the 1970s gave triumphal performances in such venues as the Newport Jazz Festival, Carnegie Hall, and the Village Vanguard nightclub in Greenwich Village; in 1980 issued on her own Bet-Car label the two-disc live album *The Audience with Betty Carter*, including a 25-minute version of her "Movin' On"; won a Grammy Award for the album *Look What I Got!* (1988); in 1994 recorded the album *Feed the Fire* with pianist Geri Allen and others; died at her home in the Fort Greene section of Brooklyn, New York City. See *Current Biography* (March) 1982.

Obituary *New York Times* B p8 Sep. 28, 1998

CROSS, BURTON M(ELVIN) Nov. 15, 1902–Oct. 22, 1998 Republican governor of Maine (1952–54); had previously served as a state representative (1941–45) and senator (1945–52); in senate, was successively majority floor leader and president; earlier, had been a city council member and alderman in Augusta, Maine's capital city; grew up on a family farm; became a professional florist in 1926; from 1945 on, was president of Cross Flowers, Inc. a large greenhouse enterprise; in politics, was a fiscal conservative and governmental minimalist, favoring whenever possible municipal over state government and state over federal; died in Augusta, Maine. See *Current Biography* (April) 1954.

Obituary *New York Times* p53 Oct. 25, 1998

CULLBERG, BIRGIT Aug. 3, 1908–Sep. 8, 1999 Swedish choreographer; dancer; co-director (with her son Mats Ek) of Stockholm's Cullberg Ballet Company, founded under the auspices of the Swedish government in 1967; a creator of experimental ballets, almost without exception short pieces; in some, expressed concerned but hopeful humanistic comments on the state of the world; in others, pursued with unsparing candor, theatrical intensity, and psychological insight such universal themes as love, sex, rejection, loneliness, and death; in many of the latter pieces, reflected the emotional heights and depths of her tumultuous, on-and-off relationship with her husband, the actor Anders Ek, from whom she was finally divorced; for the inventive movements in her creations, drew on the vocabularies of both classical ballet and modern dance; in the U.S. was best known for her choreographic translations of such dramatic classics as *Medea*, *Lady from the Sea*, and, above all, *Miss Julie*; was formatively influenced by the antiwar and other so-

cial-protest ballets of the German expressionist Kurt Jooss; after studying with Jooss for four years, organized a small troupe in Stockholm for which she choreographed, among other pieces, some animal-movement solos for herself; later co-founded the Swedish Dance Theater (1946–48); in the 1950s created eight ballets for the Royal Swedish Ballet, including *The Young Swain and the Six Princesses*, and several for the National Theater Center in Västeras, Sweden, including *The Stone Portal* (Bartók), based on Franz Kafka's *The Trial*; in 1957 created for the Royal Danish Ballet *Moon Reindeer*, based on a Lapp legend; beginning in 1961 created ballets and dance dramas for television, including the prize-winning *The Evil Queen*, an adaptation of "Snow White"; presented her work in the U.S. several times, beginning in 1958; in 1982 brought the Cullberg Ballet Company to the Brooklyn Academy of Music with a program that included her erotic duet *Adam and Eve*; in 1991 performed in her son Mat's television dance production *The Old Woman and the Door*; over the years, annually contributed one of two new ballets to her company's repertory, including works based on *Romeo and Juliet* and the Phaedra legend and such visionary sociopolitical statements as *War Dances*, her first full-length ballet; after the death of her former husband, created *Dreams of Love and Death*, an affecting meditation on their life together; published a number of essays in ballet criticism and the book *Baleten och vi* (1952), a translation of which ("Ballet: Flight and Reality") comprised the entire Spring 1967 issue of *Dance Perspectives*; died in Stockholm. See *Current Biography* (November) 1982.

Obituary *New York Times* A p17 Sep. 13, 1999

DALRYMPLE, JEAN Sep. 2, 1910–Nov. 15, 1998 Theatrical publicist; producer; director; talent manager; writer; began her theatrical career as a vaudeville comedienne, touring the Keith-Orpheum circuit in an act she wrote with Dan Jarrett; also ran with Jarrett, wrote the play *Salt Water*, produced in New York by John Golden; was hired by Golden as a general production assistant and publicist; from 1932 to 1937 was married to the Broadway drama critic Ward Morehouse (later married Philip de Witt Ginder); with Morehouse, wrote the story for the motion picture *It Happened One Night* (1935); opened her own publicity office in Manhattan in 1940; handled the publicity for such Broadway productions as *Mr. and Mrs. North* (1941), *One Touch of Venus* (1943), and *Anna Lucasta* (1944); acted as press representative or manager for a host of stage and concert personalities, from Lily Pons and André Kostelanetz to Mary Martin and Leopold Stokowski; while maintaining her publicity business, produced on Broadway *Hope for the Best* (1945), *Brighten the Corner* (1945), *Burlesque* (1946), and *Red Gloves* (1948); later packaged summer theater engagements for such actors as Franchot Tone and Ella Raines and organized a series of benefit shows for the American National Theater and Academy; meanwhile, helped to found the New York City Center (now part of Lincoln Center), which opened in 1943, on the site of what had been the Masonic Shriners' Mecca Temple, with the aim of presenting plays and musicals at popular prices; devoted much of her energy to developing productions for the center, which for many years were return engagements of Broadway hits or revivals of classics, sometimes starring such actors as Orson Welles, Tallulah Bankhead, and José Ferrer (who referred to the center as "this happy beehive of the arts"); with the profit from the revivals, was instrumental in financing original productions by the center and in subsidizing the center's other companies, the New York City Ballet and the New York City Opera; in addition to plays, wrote several books, including the autobiography *September Child* (1963) and the memoir *From the Last Row* (1975); died at her home in Manhattan. See *Current Biography* (September) 1953.

Obituary *New York Times* C p30 Nov. 17, 1998

DARROW, WHITNEY JR. Aug. 22, 1909–Aug. 10, 1999 Cartoonist; in the early 1930s began contributing his witty cartoons to *Judge*, *Ballyhoo*, and other magazines; soon became identified almost exclusively with the *New Yorker*; over the following five decades, created more than 1,500 *New Yorker* cartoons, many of which made gentle fun of upper-middle-class life in Manhattan and suburban Connecticut; published four collections of cartoons, including *You're Sitting on My Eyelashes* (1943) and *Please Pass the Hostess* (1949); illustrated books by Nathaniel Benchley and Jean Kerr, among others, and a number of children's books; died in Burlington, Vermont. See *Current Biography* (December) 1958.

Obituary *New York Times* C p21 Aug. 12, 1999

DELANY, SADIE Sep. 19, 1889–Jan. 25, 1999 Schoolteacher; the longest-surviving member of one of America's most storied families; was one of 10 children of Henry Beard Delany, a former slave who became the first black Anglican bishop in the U.S.; was one of the last black Americans to remember the early years of the Jim Crow era, during which racial segregation was enforceable by law, chiefly in the South; grew up on the campus of St. Augustine's School (now College), in Raleigh, North Carolina, where her father was then the vice principal; after graduating from St. Augustine's, earned bachelor's and master's degrees at Columbia University, in New York City; in her first public-school assignment in New York City, taught at P.S. 119, an elementary school in Harlem; went on to become the first colored (the adjective she preferred) teacher of home economics (then called domestic science) in the city's then predominantly white high schools; retired from teaching in 1960; with her sister Bessie (who died in 1995), and with Amy Hill Hearth as amanuensis, wrote two best-selling books, the memoir *Having Our Say: The Delany Sisters' First 100 Years* (1993) and *The Delany Sisters' Book of Everyday Wisdom* (1994); lived to see, in 1995, the Tony-winning Broadway play *Having Our Say*, inspired by the book and set in a re-creation of the parlor of the home the sisters shared in Mount Vernon, New York; died at home. See *Current Biography* (November) 1995.

Obituary *New York Times* A p20 Jan. 26, 1999

DEMIKHOV, VLADIMIR P(ETROVICH) 1916–Nov. 22, 1998 Russian experimental surgeon; a pioneer in organ transplantation; began his experimental work, on dogs, at the Vishnevsky Surgical Institute of the Academy of Medical Sciences of the U.S.S.R. in the years immediately following World War II; performed the world's first heart transplant in 1946; subsequently implanted a mechanical heart in a dog and performed the first lung transplant; attracted international attention in 1954, when he grafted the head of one dog onto the back of the neck of another, creating a two-headed dog; operating almost without exception on dogs, transplanted all of the major animal organs; lived on the outskirts of Moscow. See *Current Biography* (June) 1960.

Obituary *New York Times* B p11 Nov. 25, 1998

DENNING, ALFRED THOMPSON Jan. 23, 1899–Mar. 5, 1999 British jurist; as Lord Justice of Appeal (1948–57), won a reputation as "the people's judge," "a great innovating" reformer; was guided by what he called "good English common sense"; from modest beginnings, rose high in the British legal hierarchy, to Master of the Rolls (1962–82), without wavering in his overriding concern for justice and the rights of the individual and without compromising his stern moral principles; in 1957 received a life peerage and entered the House of Lords; in 1963 became known to the general public as the official investigator into the "national security" and "integrity of public life" ramifications of the spectacular scandal linking Secretary of State for War John Profumo to the "party girl" Christine Keeler, who had also been sharing her sexual favors with a Soviet intelligence officer; in his last years as Master of the Rolls, showed a controversial side of his populist instinct when he took the side of the police accused of frame-ups and lies in criminal cases involving the arrest and conviction of immigrants, racial minorities, student demonstrators, and suspected Irish Republican terrorists; explained that not trusting the police would "open up an appalling vista"; was forced to withdraw from publication a book in which he questioned the ability of immigrants and nonwhite Britons to maintain impartiality as jurors; retired under pressure soon thereafter; wrote 10 books, including *The Road to Justice* (1955), *The Due Process of Law* (1980), *The Family Story* (1981), *What Next in the Law* (1982), *The Closing Chapter* (1983), *Landmarks in the Law* (1984), and *Leaves from My Library* (1986); died in Winchester, England. See *Current Biography* (July) 1965.

Obituary *New York Times* A p11 Mar. 6, 1999

DiMAGGIO, JOE Nov. 25, 1914–Mar. 8, 1999 Baseball player; a legendary center fielder and power slugger with the New York Yankees (1936–42, 1946–51); with graceful, sure, and understated proficiency, contributed to the Yankees' capture of 10 American League pennants and nine world championships; set a major-league record, still unchallenged, with a 56-game hitting streak in 1941; was a brother of Vince and Dom DiMaggio, both of whom also played major-league baseball; after dropping out of high school, played in the minors with the San Francisco Seals of the Pacific Coast League; in 1933, his first full season with the Seals, batted .340 and set a league record with a 61-game hitting streak; in the following two seasons, had batting averages of .341 and .398; in 1936, his first season with the New York Yankees, led the American League in doubles (44) and co-led in triples (15); the following year, led in runs scored (151), home runs (46), and slugging average (.673); in 1939 had the league's best batting average (.381) and was voted the Most Valuable Player in the league; again led in batting (.352) in 1940; was Most Valuable Player for the second time in 1941, when he led the league in runs batted in (125) and total bases (348); batted .408 during his record hitting streak in 1941; after three years of World War II service with the U.S. Army, returned to the Yankees in 1946; received his third MVP award in 1947; led the league in home runs (39), runs batted in (155), and total bases (355) in 1948; led the league in slugging again in 1950, with a .585 average; had a major-league career average of .325 at the plate and a total of 3,948 bases; struck out only 369 times in 6,821 at-bats, an extraordinarily low percentage for a slugger; drove in 1,537 runs, a high percentage; with his strong and precise throwing arm, made 135 assists; was on 11 American League All-Star teams; was inducted into the Baseball Hall of Fame in 1955; after his retirement as a player, briefly worked as a commentator in post-game Yankees broadcasts; later was a coach and vice president with the Oakland Athletics; in the 1970s did television commercials for the Bowery Savings Bank in New York and Mr. Coffee, a coffee-making machine, nationally; was married to and divorced from Dorothy Arnold (1939–44); had an even shorter marriage to the glamorous motion-picture superstar Marilyn Monroe (January–October 1954), but remained Monroe's protector in many ways, including his taking charge of her funeral arrangements in 1962; funded the addition of a children's wing to Memorial Regional Hospital in Hollywood, Florida; died in Hollywood, Florida. See *Current Biography* (July) 1951.

Obituary *New York Times* A p1+ Mar. 9, 1999

DRAPEAU, JEAN Feb. 18, 1916–Aug. 12, 1999 Canadian lawyer; politician; as mayor of Montreal (1954–57, 1960–86), realized his goal of creating "a great, respectable, humane place"; was the person most responsible for the transformation of a declining, divided city (Canada's largest), ridden with organized crime and vice and blighted with some very poor neighborhoods, into a gem among world metropolises; during World War II ran unsuccessfully for seats in the national and provincial (Quebec) legislatures on anticonscription tickets; began practicing criminal and civil law in Montreal in 1943; specialized in commercial and corporation law; beginning in 1948 was a legal adviser to the French-Canadian newspaper *Le Devoir* in its investigative reporting on the high incidence of the lung disease silicosis, especially among asbestos workers, in some of Canada's industrial centers; defended many of the workers arrested in the turbulent asbestos strike of 1949; subsequently collaborated on a series of articles in *Le Devoir* about corruption and laxity in the Montreal police department; was co-prosecutor at the hearings of the Caron Commission, set up by the judicial branch

of the city government to investigate the newspaper's charges; addressing his first priority as mayor, sweepingly reorganized Montreal's law-enforcement agencies; at the same time, put the finishing touches on his plans for a 3,000-seat concert hall and began to address Montreal's increasingly knotty traffic problems; keeping another campaign promise, began construction of a modern subway system (with rubber-wheeled trains), Le Métro, in 1961; later brought to Montreal a World's Fair (Expo 67), an Olympics, a major-league baseball franchise, the Habitat housing complex, the Place Ville-Marie skyline, and other impressive architectural projects; also enhanced the quality of municipal life by planting trees and creating parks and swimming pools; won reelection in 1966 with a record 94.4 percent of the vote; was Canadian ambassador to UNESCO in Paris from 1987 to 1991. See *Current Biography* (December) 1967.

Obituary *New York Times* A p11 Aug. 14, 1999

ECCLES, DAVID Sep. 18, 1904–Feb. 24, 1999 British Conservative politician; former member of Parliament; government official; rare book and art collector; first chairman of the British Museum, which he had helped to create; was dubbed "Smarty Boots" by his enemies, who viewed him as arrogant as well as elegant; began buying and selling first editions while still a student at Oxford University; before entering politics and government, managed an investment house in London and chaired the Anglo-Spanish Construction Company; from 1939 to 1942 was economic adviser to the British ambassadors in Madrid and Lisbon; was assistant director-general for program and planning in the Ministry of Production (1942–43); was first elected to the House of Commons, from Chippenham, in 1943; became minister of works in 1951; subsequently served as minister of education (until 1957, and again from 1959 to 1962) and president of the Board of Trade (1957–59); concentrated on his business career from 1962 until 1970, when he became paymaster general, a position tantamount to minister of the arts; in that position, helped to draft and push through Parliament a bill creating an independent British Library incorporating the main reference library at the British Museum; in 1973 left the cabinet to chair the new library; was created a viscount in 1964 and named a Companion of Honour in 1984; wrote *Life and Politics* (1967), *On Collecting* (1968), and *By Safe Hand: Letters of Sybil and David Eccles* (1983), among other books. See *Current Biography* (January) 1952.

Obituary *New York Times* A p19 Mar. 1, 1999

EHRLICHMAN, JOHN D. Mar. 25, 1925–Feb. 14, 1999 Writer; former government official; as President Richard Nixon's domestic affairs adviser, was implicated in the coverup of Watergate, the scandal that drove Nixon from office; at the beginning of his career, practiced law in Seattle, Washington; began working as an advance man in Nixon's political campaigns in 1960; managed Nixon's national presidential campaign schedule in 1968; in the Nixon White House, was the president's second in command, after chief of staff Bob Haldeman, from January 1969 until he resigned under pressure, in April 1973; for his part in the conspiracy to cover up the political burglary that instigated the Watergate scandal, served 18 months in prison; spent many of his post-Watergate years living and writing in Santa, Fe, New Mexico; published two popular romans à clef quarried from his experiences as a White House insider: *The Company* (1976) and *The Whole Truth* (1979); in addition to those novels, wrote the nonfiction book *Witness to Power* (1982); in his last years was a senior vice president of Law Environmental, an Atlanta, Georgia, engineering company specializing in the handling of hazardous waste; died in Atlanta, at the home he shared with his third wife, Karen. See *Current Biography* (October) 1979.

Obituary *New York Times* A p1+ Feb. 16, 1999

ELION, GERTRUDE B. Jan. 23, 1918–Feb. 21, 1999 Chemist; pharmacological research scientist; Nobel laureate; a revolutionary in her field; in 1944 joined the laboratory research staff of the Burroughs Wellcome Research Company; there, assisted George H. Hitchings until 1967, when she gained a degree of autonomy as head of the company's department of experimental therapy; working with Hitchings, primarily with the nucleic acid purine, detected crucial differences between the biochemistry of normal and diseased cells and thus discovered how to leave the former unharmed while attacking the latter; developed drugs effective against acute leukemia, gout, herpes, and other diseases and disorders; also synthesized an immunosuppressant compound that made possible the successful transplantation of organs; after her nominal retirement in 1983, participated in overseeing the scientists who had worked under her in their use of her methodology to perfect AZT, the first drug approved by the U.S. Food and Drug Administration for use against AIDS; for her pioneering drug research, shared the 1988 Nobel Prize for physiology or medicine with her colleague Hitchings and the British scientist Sir James W. Black; died in Chapel Hill, North Carolina. See *Current Biography* (March) 1995.

Obituary *New York Times* A p21 Feb. 23, 1999

EWBANK, WEEB May 6, 1907–Nov. 17, 1998 Football coach; elected to the Pro Football Hall of Fame in 1978; coached high school football for 15 years at the beginning of his career; during World War II was assistant football coach at the Great Lakes Naval Training Station; after the war was backfield football coach at Brown University for one year and head football coach at Washington University for two years; began his professional career as line coach of the Cleveland Browns (1949–53); became head coach of the Baltimore Colts in 1954; using the scouting system he had developed in Cleveland, recruited to Baltimore such talent as the great quarterback Johnny Unitas; guided the Colts to National Football League titles in 1958 and 1959; in 1963 assumed the helm of the New York Jets, then the bellwether club in the fledgling, short-lived American Football League; coached the Jets, with Joe Namath as quarterback, to the AFL championship in 1968 and to victory over the Baltimore Colts, the NFL champions, in the Super Bowl following the 1968 season; retired in 1973; in 20 professional seasons, had totals of 134 wins, 130 losses, and seven ties; died at his home in Oxford, Ohio. See *Current Biography* (June) 1969.

Obituary *New York Times* B p15 Nov. 18, 1998

FADIMAN, CLIFTON (PAUL) May 15, 1904–June 20, 1999 Literary critic; best known to the general public for the easy erudition he displayed as an affable radio and television personality; was general editor of Simon & Schuster publishers from 1929 to 1935; concurrently, reviewed books for several magazines, including the *Nation* and *Harper's Bazaar*; was book editor of the *New Yorker* (1933–43); from 1938 to 1948 moderated the network radio show *Information Please!*, which offered sets of the *Encyclopedia Britannica* as prizes to listeners whose questions stumped a panel of experts; subsequently emceed the network television program *This Is Show Business*, which brought new talent before a panel of veteran entertainers; on radio, joined with the scholar Jacques Barzun in informal talks with guests on the program *Conversation*; in 1954 moderated the word-association television quiz show *What's in a Word?*; served on the editorial board of the Book-of-the-Month Club for more than half a century, beginning in 1944; edited some two dozen anthologies, including *This I Believe* (1939) and *Reading I've Liked* (1941); published the collection of essays *Party of One* (1955); assembled "treasuries" of children's literature and of selections from the successive editions of the *Encyclopedia Britannica*; wrote introductions to new editions of works by Tolstoy, Melville, Dickens, and others; died on Sanibel Island, Florida. See *Current Biography* (October) 1955.

Obituary *New York Times* B p8 June 21, 1999

FARMER, JAMES (LEONARD) Jan. 12, 1920–July 9, 1999 Civil rights leader; a principal founder and charter leader of the Congress of Racial Equality (CORE), a nonviolent direct-action organization that was in the forefront of the struggle against "Jim Crow" segregation in the mid-20th century; after earning a bachelor of divinity degree at Howard University in 1941, served as race relations secretary of the Fellowship of Reconciliation, a pacifist organization, until 1945; subsequently, in the late 1940s and through the 1950s, held a succession of positions in the labor movement, including organizer for the Upholsterers International Union, international representative of the State, County, and Municipal Employees Union, member of a five-man delegation from the International Confederation of Free Trade Unions to 15 African countries, and a radio and television commentator for the United Auto Workers in Detroit; served as a program director for the NAACP; lectured extensively; wrote for such publications as *Crisis* and *Fellowship*; meanwhile, in Chicago in 1942 co-founded CORE, a group intended, in his words, "to substitute bodies for exhortations" in applying the Ghandian techniques of nonviolence and passive resistance to the struggle for racial equality in the U.S.; was CORE's first national chairman before becoming its salaried national director in 1961; concentrated on public school desegregation projects in the South in the late 1950s; in the spring of 1961 personally led the first of CORE's Freedom Rides challenging the practice of segregation in interstate bus travel in the South; during that ride, was attacked by mobs in Alabama; in Mississippi, was arrested and jailed for 40 days; with his cohorts, eventually succeeded in desegregating 120 interstate bus terminals in the South; also directed such tactics (first tested in the North) as standing lines at segregated theaters and other places of public assembly and sit-ins at segregated lunch counters, which spread throughout the South in the early 1960s; was also active in voter registration; after resigning from the leadership of CORE, taught at Lincoln University in Pennsylvania and ran unsuccessfully for Congress from Brooklyn, New York, as a Liberal party candidate backed by liberal Republicans; served as an assistant secretary of Health, Education, and Welfare in the administration of President Richard Nixon in 1975 and 1976; in a political dispute, severed his connection with CORE in 1976; later taught at Mary Washington College in Virginia; wrote the books *Freedom—When?* (1966) and the memoir *Lay Bare the Heart* (1985); died at Mary Washington Hospital in Fredericksburg, Virginia. See *Current Biography* (February) 1964.

Obituary *New York Times* p1+ July 10, 1999

FASCELL, DANTE B(RUNO) Mar. 9, 1917–Nov. 28, 1998 Democratic U.S. congressman from Florida (1955–93); had previously served in the Florida state legislature; practiced law in Miami; became a member of the foreign affairs committee in the U.S. House of Representatives in 1957; chaired the committee from 1984 to 1992; at various times, chaired the subcommittees on Inter-American affairs, international relations, and State Department organization; promoted bipartisanship in foreign policy; staunchly supported Israel; reflecting sentiments prevalent among Hispanic refugee communities in his constituency, opposed any relaxation of the American policy of ostracism of the Castro regime in Cuba and favored the Reagan administration's backing of the Contra rebels against the Sandinista government in Nicaragua; was among the earliest supporters of President Bush's launching of military force against Iraq; in domestic affairs, was generally a liberal on social and environmental issues; died at his home in Clearwater, Florida. See *Current Biography* (April) 1960.

Obituary *New York Times* B p10 Nov. 30, 1998

FEININGER, ANDREAS Dec. 27, 1906–Feb. 18, 1999 Photographer; author; best known for his big and poetic New York cityscapes, including "Brooklyn Bridge in the Fog" and "Sunday at Coney Island Beach," which appeared over a period of two decades in *Life* magazine, often as two-page spreads; was the eldest son of the American-born modernist painter Lyonel Feininger; was born in Paris and raised in Germany; became interested in photography while apprenticing in cabinetmaking at the Bauhaus school of architecture in Weimar; subsequently studied architecture; for many years used his camera to record buildings and cities that interested him as an architect working in Germany, France, and Sweden; began concentrating on photography in 1936; with his wife and son, moved to New York City in 1939; found freelance work with

the Black Star Picture Agency, one of whose clients was *Life* magazine; became a staff photographer with *Life* in 1943; over the following 19 years, completed 346 assignments for *Life*; used experimental techniques and equipment to achieve unusual effects, including the compressed perspective in such views of Manhattan as "Traffic on Fifth Avenue," the striking bas-relief effect in some of his photographs of buildings and skylines, the etching of figures luminously in bright high lights and deep black shadows, and various night photography effects; also did portraits, closeups revealing the unfamiliar in ordinary objects, from an ear of corn to a seashell, and "shadowgrams," patterns made on sensitized paper by a leaf, a feather, or the like; remained with *Life* until 1962; was represented in photographic shows at major museums and galleries; assembled or helped to assemble traveling exhibitions of his work, including a retrospective of his black-and-white photographs that has been touring Europe since 1997; published more than 30 books, including photographic collections, textbooks, self-help manuals, and the illustrated autobiography *Andreas Feininger: Photographer* (1986); died in Manhattan. See *Current Biography* (October) 1957.

Obituary *New York Times* A p13 Feb. 20, 1999

FUNT, ALLEN Sep. 16, 1916–Sep. 5, 1999 Television producer; creator of the weekly human-interest humor show *Candid Camera*, which has been running on and off on network television and in syndication for five decades and continues to be a staple in CBS's Friday night schedule; over most of that time, was the program's host or co-host, an agent provocateur setting up unsuspecting people in contrived, bizarre situations and using hidden microphones and cameras to catch them, in his words, "in the act of being themselves"; in the end, let the duped subjects in on the joke with the statement, "Smile! You're on *Candid Camera!*"; began the program as a radio show, *Candid Microphone*, which was carried by ABC for two years beginning in 1947; moved to ABC television with the show (under the title *Candid Mike*) in 1948; changed the television title to *Candid Camera* when the series moved to NBC (May–August 1949); shuttled with the show among the three networks from September 1949 to August 1953; after a hiatus of seven years, settled into a solid run on CBS, from 1960 to 1967; in syndication, presented *The New Candid Camera* from 1974 to 1978; returned to CBS with *Candid Camera* in 1990; three years later, was forced by a stroke to turn management of the program over to his son Peter; on the *Candid Camera* template, produced a number of specials for NBC, CBS, and (in an adult mode) cable television; died at his home in Pebble Beach, California. See *Current Biography* (December) 1966.

Obituary *New York Times* B p9 Sep. 7, 1999

GADDIS, WILLIAM Dec. 29, 1922–Dec. 16, 1998 Novelist; a modernist of enormous scope, complexity, and dark wit; preceded such writers as Thomas Pynchon in pioneering the genre of the encyclopedic and satirical "mega-novel," bursting with erudition, including historical and literary allusions; wrote fiction haunted, as the critic Steven Moore observed, by "the spirit of a dead or absent father who leaves a ruinous state of affairs for his children, a situation that can be extrapolated to include Gaddis' vision of a world abandoned by God and plunged into disorder"; after his expulsion from Harvard College in 1945, spent much of his time in Greenwich Village with William S. Burroughs, Jack Kerouac, and Allen Ginsberg; traveled widely in Central America, Europe, and North Africa; became obsessed with the perception that the world was "made up of falsehood and fraud," especially in religion and art; delineated myriad instances of the counterfeit in his 956-page first novel, *The Recognitions* (1955), a labyrinthine story in which the protagonist is a forger of Flemish master paintings; with that novel, attracted a loyal cult following and, ultimately, critical recognition as an important innovator in fiction; in the 20 years following the publication of *The Recognitions*, supported himself by teaching, by freelance public-relations writing for the U.S. Army and for corporations, including Eastman Kodak, and through grants, including the MacArthur Foundation's "genius award"; won his first National Book Award with his 726-page second novel, *JR* (1975), a satire about American business and finance (personified in an amoral 11-year-old Wall Street boy prodigy), told in a torrent of cacophonous dialogue; in 1985 published his shortest novel (262 pages), *Carpenter's Gothic*, the arch-villain of which is an anti-Marxist fundamentalist evangelist; won his second National Book Award with *A Frolic of His Own* (1994), a novel concerned with intellectual property and plagiarism; before his death, finished a fifth novel, with the working title *Agape, Agape*; died at his home in East Hampton, New York. See *Current Biography* (November) 1987.

Obituary *New York Times* B p15 Dec. 17, 1998

GODDEN, RUMER Dec. 10, 1907–Nov. 8, 1998 Sussex-born British writer; an exacting craftsman of exquisitely wrought novels, many of which were set, with earthy detail, in colonial India, where she grew up and lived intermittently until 1945; created protagonists and other key characters, often vulnerable children and willful women, with psychological sensitivity and without sentimentality; pursued such themes as the contrast between Eastern and Western cultures, the meaning of time, the interrelationship of generations in family history, the moral problems of childhood, the rewards and perils of the contemplative religious life, and her love of dance; first achieved critical and popular success with her third novel, and the first to be made into a motion picture, *Black Narcissus* (1939), about the difficulties of a community of Anglican nuns trying to maintain a school and hospital in the Himalayas; among the film adaptations of her novels, collaborated on only two: *The River* (1951), adapted from her 1946 novel of the same title, and *Loss of Innocence* (1961), adapted from her 1958 novel *The Greengage Summer*; saw *An Episode of Sparrows* (1955), her novel about London street urchins, become a successful motion picture; in 1969, a year after her conversion to Roman Catholicism, published another novel that would be made into a film, *In This House of Brede*, about a London businesswoman who becomes a

Benedictine nun; wrote a score of novels, including *Thursday's Children* (1984) and *Pippa Passes* (1994); for children, wrote approximately an equal number of books of fiction, beginning with *The Dolls' House* (1949), and two book-length narrative poems; wrote three volumes of autobiography, including *A Time to Dance, No Time to Weep* (1988); published a total of 70 books, including two collections of short stories; in 1977, two years after the death of her second husband, moved to Scotland to live with her daughter Jane; was awarded the Order of the British Empire in 1993; died in Dunfrieshire, Scotland. See *Current Biography* (August) 1976.

Obituary *New York Times* B p12 Nov. 10, 1998

GORBACHEV, RAISA Jan. 5, 1932–Sep. 20, 1999 Wife of Mikhail Gorbachev, former president of the former Union of Soviet Socialist Republics; among Soviet first ladies, cut an unprecedented figure, elegant in her persona, and intellectually her husband's peer; married Gorbachev in 1953, when both were students at Moscow State University, he in law, she in philosophy; graduated from the university in 1955; worked as a schoolteacher until the birth of her daughter, Irina, in 1956; upon acceptance of her thesis (a sociological study of the daily lives of the peasantry on collective farms in the Stavropol region in the North Caucasus, where she had been reared), received an advanced degree at the Lenin Pedagogical Institute in Moscow, in 1967; became a lecturer in philosophy at Moscow State University in 1978; after seven years, left that position to be closer to her husband as he became general secretary of the Communist Party of the USSR (1985), chairman of the Soviet presidium (1988), and president of the Soviet state (1989), with fuller powers added in 1990; served as one of her husband's channels to the intelligentsia in his pursuit of *glasnost* (openness) and *perestroika* (restructuring), liberalizing reforms of the Soviet system that, among other factors, led to the dissolution of the Soviet Union on December 26, 1991, one day after Mr. Gorbachev resigned the presidency; died in Münster, Germany. See *Current Biography* (May) 1988.

Obituary *New York Times* C p25 Sep. 21, 1999

GORE, ALBERT (ARNOLD) Dec. 26, 1907–Dec. 5, 1998 Democratic U.S. senator from Tennessee (1953–71); father of Vice President Albert Gore Jr; before taking his seat in the Senate, served in the U.S. House of Representatives (1939–53); was a rare liberal among the southern Democrats of his time; in 1956 was one of only three southern senators who declined to sign a group statement against the Supreme Court's 1954 decision desegregating the public schools; died at his home in Carthage, Tennessee. See *Current Biography* (January) 1952.

Obituary *New York Times* B p9 Dec. 7, 1998

GRADE, LEW Dec. 25, 1906–Dec. 13, 1998 Russian-born British motion-picture and television impresario; with other members of his family, including his brothers Bernard and Leslie and his nephew Michael Grade, dominated show business in Britain for many years; produced such motion pictures as *On Golden Pond, Sophie's Choice, The Muppet Movie, Raise the*

Titanic, and *The Eagle Has Landed* and such popular television series as *Emergency Ward 10, Sunday Night at the Palladium, Coronation Street,* and *Space 1999;* beginning in 1927, performed on the British and Continental vaudeville circuits as the "World's Champion Charleston Dancer"; with his brother Leslie, in 1934 formed Lew and Leslie Grade Ltd., which became the largest talent agency in Europe, with such clients as the actress Vanessa Redgrave and the actor Sir Laurence Olivier; during World War II, organized traveling shows to entertain the troops; after the war, booked popular American stars, including the comedians Bob Hope, Jack Benny, and Danny Kaye, into the London Palladium; beginning in 1947, introduced such European headliners as the singer Edith Piaf to audiences in the U.S.; sold the agency to EMI in 1967; meanwhile, in 1955, co-founded Associated Television (which later became the Associated Communications Corp.), the first commercially financed company to compete with the British Broadcasting Co.; over the following years, exported to the U.S. such series as *Robin Hood, Secret Agent, The Avengers, The Saint, This Is Tom Jones,* and *Muppet Show;* after losing control of the Associated Communications Corp., in 1982, became chairman of Embassy Communications International, the London branch of Los Angeles-based Embassy Communications; left Embassy when Coca-Cola bought it; established the Grade Co. and was elected a vice president of the Loews movie-theater chain; was knighted in 1963 and made a life peer, with the title of Lord, in 1976; died in London. See *Current Biography* (August) 1979.

Obituary *New York Times* B p8 Dec. 14, 1998

GRAHAM, VIRGINIA July 4, 1912–Dec. 21, 1998 Radio and television personality; talk-show host; early in her career, did fashion reporting for radio station WBBM in Chicago and wrote commercials for radio station WMCA in New York City; served with the American Red Cross during World War II; after the war, joined with others to establish the Cerebral Palsy Foundation; later hosted or participated in scores of telethons and hundreds of other fund-raising campaigns for that foundation and for research in muscular dystrophy and cancer; contributed scripts to several radio soap operas, including *Stella Dallas* and *Our Gal Friday;* in the early 1950s, conducted interview programs on the ABC network's flagship radio and television stations in New York City; in 1956 co-hosted the omnibus NBC radio show *Weekday,* a wide-ranging three-and-a-half-hour daily magazine of the air; from 1956 to 1961 hosted the syndicated daily television program *Food for Thought;* was seen frequently as a guest on the *Jack Paar Tonight Show* and as a panelist or substitute host on network quiz shows; hosted the syndicated *Virginia Graham Show* from 1970 to 1972; later appeared on television in the situation comedy *Roseanne* and on Tom Snyder's and Rosie O'Donnell's shows; wrote the books *Life After Harry: My Adventures in Widowhood,* published in 1988, and *I Love Antiques But I Don't Want to Be One,* completed before her death; died in Manhattan. See *Current Biography* (October) 1956.

Obituary *New York Times* B p11 Dec. 25, 1998

GROSS, ERNEST A(RNOLD) Sep. 23, 1906–May 2, 1999 Lawyer; diplomat; at the beginning of his career, held legal positions with the U.S. Department of State (1931–33), the National Recovery Administration (1933–34), the printing and publishing industries (1934–36), and the National Association of Manufacturers (1936–38); was associate general counsel for enforcement with the National Labor Relations Board from 1938 to 1943; after wartime legal service with the U.S. Army, served as deputy to the U.S. assistant secretary of state for occupied areas (1946–47); as legal adviser at the Department of State (1947–48), began working with the United Nations; served as deputy U.S. delegate to the U.N. from 1949 to 1953; was a partner in the law firm of Curtis, Mallet-Prevost, Colt & Mosle from 1945 to 1975; wrote *The United Nations—Structure for Peace* (1964); died at his home in New York City. See *Current Biography* (February) 1951.

Obituary *New York Times* B p14 May 4, 1999

GROTOWSKI, JERZY Aug. 11, 1933–Jan. 14, 1999 Polish theatrical director; methodologist; teacher; author of the manifesto *Towards a Poor Theater* (1970); a major innovator in experimental theater; as no one else since Stanislawsky, investigated the nature of acting, its phenomenon, its meaning, the nature and science of its mental-physical-emotional processes "deeply and completely," as the British director Peter Brook has observed; after nine years of theatrical apprenticeship, in 1959 formed his own company, the Polish Laboratory Theater; at a time when "total theater" was trying to compete with the rich mechanical resources of motion pictures and television, proposed a "poor theater," reduced to the sine qua non—a live actor communing with a spectator; tried to return theater to its roots in sacred ritual, without making it religious; regarded his Laboratory Theater as a sort of secular monastery in which actors undergo rigorous discipline not to acquire the skills of artifice but to become purified, "holy" enough to commune spiritually, on the level of the myths "rooted in the psyche of society," using the body for visual effects and the voice for acoustical; in his first visit to the U.S., in 1969, presented a repertory of plays, including *Acropolis* and *The Constant Prince* Off-Off Broadway, before audiences limited to 100 persons each; returned to New York City to lecture in 1970; during the 1980s taught at Columbia University and at the University of California at Irvine; with a "genius award" from the MacArthur Foundation, founded a theatrical center in Pontedera, Italy; died in Pontedera. See *Current Biography* (December) 1970.

Obituary *New York Times* C p19 Jan. 15, 1999

HASSAN II, KING OF MOROCCO July 9, 1929–July 23, 1999 Seventeenth sovereign of the Alaouite dynasty; a Western-oriented Arab leader; as crown prince, was commander in chief of the Royal Moroccan Army (beginning in 1957), minister of defense (1960–61), and vice–prime minister (1960–61); succeeded to the throne upon the death of his father, King Mohammed V, in 1961; domestically, continued the social and economic reforms begun by his father; did so slowly and cautiously, so as not to alienate Morocco's elite class; in 1962 fulfilled his father's promise of a constitution providing for an elected Parliament; in 1973 initiated programs to increase Moroccan ownership and employment in foreign industrial and business enterprises in Morocco and to redistribute foreign-owned farmland to Moroccan peasants; unlike royalty in Libya, Egypt, Iran, and Iraq, outwitted and outmaneuvered socialist revolutionaries and Islamic militants; survived two major coup attempts and six assassination attempts; internationally, maintained close ties with Washington while charting a neutral course; was an effective go-between in the pursuit of peace in the Middle East; regarded Morocco's Jewish population (which his father had protected in defiance of the Axis powers during World War II and much of which had emigrated to Israel) as a bridge between Israelis and Arabs; in 1991 emerged victorious from a 16-year multinational dispute over control of the territory of Western Sahara; died in Rabat, Morocco. See *Current Biography* (September) 1964.

Obituary *New York Times* p1+ July 24, 1999

HERZBERG, GERHARD Dec. 25, 1904–Mar. 3, 1999 German-born Canadian scientist; Nobel laureate; the founding father of molecular spectroscopy; a physicist who became most appreciated for his contributions to chemistry; as a doctoral and postdoctoral student, and as a young faculty member at the Darmstadt Institute of Technology in Germany, began his pioneering work in spectroscopy, the science that measures the light emitted or absorbed by molecules for the purpose of obtaining precise information about molecular energies, rotations, vibrations, and electronic structure; in 1935 fled Nazi Germany to find refuge at the University of Saskatchewan, in Canada; there, pursued his interest in the spectral analysis of stars and comets; as professor of spectroscopy at the University of Chicago's Yerkes Observatory (1945–48), supervised the construction of new equipment and originated new infrared methods that enabled him to make formerly impossible observations and interpretations of stars, comets, and planets; was the principal research officer in the division of physics of the National Research Council in Ottawa, Canada, from 1948 to 1994; was awarded the 1971 Nobel Prize in chemistry for "his contributions to the knowledge of electronic structure and geometry of molecules, particularly free radicals"; died at his home in Ottawa. See *Current Biography* (February) 1973.

Obituary *New York Times* A p14 Mar. 20, 1999

HIRT, AL(OIS MAXWELL) Nov. 7, 1922–Apr. 27, 1999 Musician; a Dixieland jazz trumpeter with tremendous range and power, lighting technique, and a distinctive swing sound; was an interpreter rather than an improviser of Dixieland; began playing the trumpet when he was six; studied on scholarship at the Cincinnati Conservatory of Music from 1940 to 1942; served with the U.S. Army during World War II; after the war, although he had aspired to playing with a symphony orchestra, chose to play with popular dance bands to better support his young and growing family; toured with the big bands of Tommy and Jimmy Dorsey, Ray McKinley, and others; as the

winner of a talent contest in 1949, performed on Horace Heidt's network radio program and toured the U.S. and Europe with Heidt's orchestra; after the tour, returned to his native New Orleans, his base from then on; playing with Dixieland bands for the first time, memorized his parts while others improvised; with Pete Fountain as his main sideman, formed his own band in about 1956; with that band, soon attracted a local reputation; was "discovered" nationally in 1960; played at President John F. Kennedy's inaugural ball, in January 1961; released his first album, *The Greatest Horn in the World*, in the spring of 1961; later recorded *Bourbon Street* (1952), *Trumpet and Strings* (1963), *Live at Carnegie Hall* (1965), *The Best of Al Hirt* (1965), and *Al Hirt* (1984), among many other albums; on those recordings, as in his live performances, covered the standard Dixieland repertoire, from "Muskrat Ramble" and ""Struttin' with Some Barbeque" to "When the Saints Go Marching In" and "A Closer Walk with Thee"; between engagements in Las Vegas and elsewhere, remained an attraction on Bourbon Street in New Orleans; in self-defense against purist critics, claimed to be only "a pop commercial musician"; explained, "I'm not a jazz trumpet and never was a jazz trumpet. When I played in big bands . . . I played first trumpet. I led the trumpet section. I never played jazz or improvised"; died in New Orleans, Louisiana. See *Current Biography* (February) 1967.

Obituary *New York Times* C p25 Apr. 28, 1999

HOWELL, WALLACE E(GBERT) Sep. 14, 1914–June 12, 1999 Meteorologist; early in his career, organized the weather department of Mid-Continent Airlines in Kansas City and worked as a meteorologist with the Yankee [radio] Weather Service in Boston and as a regional forecaster for the U.S. Weather Bureau in East Boston; became acting director of the Mount Washington Observatory in New Hampshire in 1948; was later installed as president of that observatory; was also research meteorologist at the Blue Hills Weather station near Boston, beginning in 1949; during a drought in New York in 1950, was hired by New York City to head its rain stimulation project; in flights over the Ashokan Reservoir in the Catskill Mountains, seeded the clouds with dry-ice pellets; from the ground, sprayed the clouds with silver iodide; also on the ground, deployed mobile radar equipment to spot rain-laden clouds; succeeded in increasing rainfall by 14 percent, by his own estimate (generally considered modest); over a period of two decades, directed similar projects in Canada, Peru, the Philippines, Cuba, and other countries, triggering rainfall for agriculture and hydroelectric power; in the 1960s, created one of the first snow-making machines for ski resorts; with the Federal Bureau of Reclamation, worked for 15 years to increase the snowpack in the Rocky Mountains; died in San Diego, California. See *Current Biography* (July) 1950.

Obituary *New York Times* p15 July 6, 1999

HRUSKA, ROMAN LEE Aug. 16, 1904–Apr. 25, 1999 Conservative Republican U.S. congressman (1953–54) and senator (1954–77) from Nebraska; lawyer; practiced law in Omaha from 1929 to 1952;

in Washington, was consistently conservative on such issues as Second Amendment rights, the curbing of violence and pornography in film and on television, and the maintenance of the criminal status of marijuana; with his votes on social policy, was graded zero by the AFL-CIO; drew most attention to himself with his unsuccessful defense of President Richard Nixon's nomination of G. Harrold Carswell to the U.S. Supreme Court in 1970; died in Omaha, Nebraska. See Current Biography (February) 1967.

Obituary New York Times B p8 Apr. 27, 1999

HUGHES, TED Aug. 17, 1930–Oct. 28, 1998 British symbolic nature poet; was perhaps as well known for the suicide (in 1963) of the poet Sylvia Plath, the first of his two wives, as for his status as Britain's Poet Laureate (since 1984); from his youth, was powerfully influenced by Robert Graves's book *The White Goddess*, with its thesis that a poet's true muse is a primitive feminine moon deity, displaced in contemporary society by male rationality; drew upon his training in anthropology, his memory of wildlife in his native Yorkshire, and his experience working with animals on his farm in Devonshire for the mythic imagery of his poetry, which evokes the raw, instinctive power and beauty of nature; with that imagery, was commenting metaphorically on less obvious civilized brutality; maintained that double message in his successive collections of verse, beginning with *The Hawk in the Rain* (1957) and including *Lupercal* (1960), *Wodwo* (1967), *Crow* (1971), *Moortown* (1979), *River* (1984), and *Wolfwatching* (1989); also wrote plays, juvenile fiction and verse, and *Shakespeare and the Goddess of Complete Being* (1992), a presentation of a systematic theory of Shakespearean tragedy; for 35 years, silently bore the accusation of Sylvia Plath's sympathizers that his infidelity had contributed to her suicide; during those years, privately wrote poems, some tender, some bitter, many heartbreaking, about his love for Plath and his grief at her death; in his final illness, published a collection of those poems, *Birthday Letters* (1998), which was regarded as a vindication by his supporters; received the Order of the British Empire in 1977 and the Order of Merit 13 days before his death; died at his home in North Tawton, England. See Current Biography (June) 1979.

Obituary New York Times A p1+ Oct. 30, 1998

HUNT, SIR (HENRY CECIL) JOHN June 22, 1910–Nov. 8, 1998 British army colonel, retired; mountain climber; the leader behind the first successful climb to the top of Mount Everest, the world's highest mountain (approximately 29,000 feet above sea level), in 1953; was born into a British military family in India; in 1930 was commissioned an officer in the Royal Rifle Corps in Lucknow, India; spent his leave time climbing mountains; began taking part in major Himalayan expeditions in 1935; early in World War II was the chief British instructor in mountain and snow warfare; later won highest military honors for his heroism in combat in Europe as part of the Royal Rifle Corps; at the end of the war, organized a mountain training course for troops in Greece; in the postwar years, served as a staff officer at Supreme Headquarters, Allied Powers Europe; under the aegis of

the Royal Geographical Society and the Alpine Club, began organizing his Mount Everest team (which included 362 Nepalese porters and 32 Shirpa guides) in 1952; in the 1953 ascent, was himself forced to turn back (because his oxygen supply froze solid) while Sir Edmund Hilary and Tenzing Norgay made it to the summit; was elevated to peerage in the House of Lords in 1966; died at his home in Henley, England. See Current Biography (October) 1954.

Obituary New York Times B p11 Nov. 10, 1998

HUNTER, CATFISH Apr. 8, 1946–Sep. 9, 1999 Baseball player; a Cy Young Award–winning right-handed pitcher with pinpoint control; was signed by the Kansas City Athletics right out of high school, in 1964; because of a serious injury to his right foot from shotgun fire he suffered during a hunting accident, spent the 1964 season on the Athletics' disabled list; during three active seasons in Kansas City, won 30 games and lost 36; in 1968 moved with the Athletics to Oakland, where his win count over a seven-year period rose to 131, as against 77 losses; led the American League in winning percentage in 1972, with .750, and 1973, with .808; received the Cy Young Award in 1974, when he led the league in wins, with 25, and earned-run average, with 2.49; was undefeated as a pitcher in five games in three World Series with the Athletics; as a free agent in December 1974, signed a five-year contract with the New York Yankees for a financial package totaling $3.35 million, the most lucrative in baseball history to that time; in 1975, his first season with the Yankees, again led the league in victories, with 23; he went 17–15 in 1975, when the Yankees won their first pennant in 12 years, 9–9 in 1976, when they won the World Series, and 12–6 in 1977, when they again won the Series; when his contract expired after the 1979 season, retired with his wife and children to his farm outside Hertford, North Carolina; had a career record of 224 wins and 166 losses, a 3.26 earned-run average, 2,012 strikeouts, and a fielding average of .952; was inducted into the Baseball Hall of Fame in 1987; was diagnosed with amyotrophic lateral sclerosis (Lou Gehrig's disease) in 1998; died in his home at Hertford. See Current Biography (May) 1975.

Obituary New York Times C p19 Sep. 10, 1999

HUSSEIN, KING OF JORDAN Nov. 14, 1935–Feb. 7, 1999 Hussein I of the Hashemite kingdom of Jordan; a major force for peace and stability in the volatile Middle East; as the Bedouin ruler of a small but strategic country sharing a long border with Israel and playing host to a huge Palestinian refugee community, steered a precarious course with bravery, agility, and finesse; was at the side of his grandfather, King Abdullah I, when Abdullah was assassinated by a Palestinian nationalist at the Al Aqsa Mosque in Jerusalem, in 1951; was proclaimed king in 1952, when the Jordanian Parliament forced his father, King Talal, to abdicate, on grounds of mental incompetence; following interim rule by regency, was crowned king in May 1953, when he turned 18 by the Muslim calendar (by the Gregorian calendar, he was still 17); despite his antipathy to the left-wing pan-Arab nationalism of President Gamal Abdel Nasser of Egypt, was persuaded by Nasser to join Egypt (and Syria) in the 1967 Arab-Israeli war, in which Jordan lost the West Bank and East Jerusalem; thereafter avoided participation in Arab confrontations with Israel; domestically, was fairly successful in promoting tolerance among the diverse groups (chiefly the Bedouin tribes and the Palestinians) in Jordan; revitalized the country's economy, chiefly by cultivating powerful patrons: Great Britain in the 1950s, the U.S. in the 1960s, and the oil-rich moderate Arab states beginning in the mid-1970s; survived several coups and at least 17 assassination attempts to become the longest-ruling leader in the Middle East and a respected senior world statesman; played an increasingly vital role in the international efforts to negotiate a peaceful resolution of the Palestinian question; with Prime Minister Yitzhak Rabin of Israel, in October 1994 signed a peace treaty bringing to an end the tacit state of war that had existed between the two countries since 1948; in addition to his autobiography, *Uneasy Lies the Head* (1962), wrote *My War with Israel* (1967); was succeeded on the throne by King Abdullah II, his eldest son, from his second marriage; was survived by his American-born fourth wife, Queen Noor (the former Lisa Najeeb Halaby), the mother of Crown Prince Hamzeh; died in Amman, Jordan. See *Current Biography* (April) 1986.

Obituary *New York Times* A p1+ Feb. 8, 1999

JOHNSON, FRANK M(INIS) Oct. 30, 1919–July 23, 1999 Federal judge; a champion of civil rights; began practicing law in Jasper, Alabama, in 1945; was appointed U.S. attorney for Alabama's northern district in 1953; advanced to U.S. district judge for Alabama's middle district in 1955; participating in a two-man majority on a three-judge panel in a class-action suit brought by Rosa Parks in February 1956, ruled that bus segregation ordinances in Montgomery, Alabama, were unconstitutional; later, alone or as a majority member of a judicial panel, desegregated Montgomery's parks, libraries, museums, YMCA, bus depot, airport, and other facilities; also in furtherance of black voting rights, outlawed the poll tax, ordered the Macon County board of registrars to register any black person whose voting qualifications equalled those of the "least qualified white" (a standard, known as the "freeze doctrine," that was incorporated into the 1965 federal Voting Rights Act), and in a 1962 legislative reapportionment decision anticipated the Supreme Court's one-man, one-vote ruling; in 1963 presided over a four-judge court that desegregated every public school, trade school, and state college in Alabama; in other rulings, desegregated Alabama's state police and struck down the state law barring blacks and women from jury service; in 1965, overruling a ban declared by Governor George C. Wallace, issued the decision permitting Martin Luther King Jr. and thousands of his supporters to march the 52 miles from Selma, Alabama, to Montgomery to petition Governor Wallace for voting rights; following the march, presided over a federal trial in which three Ku Klux Klansmen (previously acquitted in a state trial of the murder of Viola Liuzzo, a white civil rights worker) were found guilty of violating Liuzzo's civil rights; outside the area of civil rights, expanded the access of the poor

to legal assistance and effected radical reforms in Alabama's prisons and mental hospitals; in 1979 was named to a seat on the U.S. court of appeals for the fifth circuit; moved to the U.S. court of appeals for the 11th circuit in 1981; retired from the bench with senior judge status in 1991 or 1992; died at his home in Montgomery, Alabama. See *Current Biography* (August) 1978.

Obituary *New York Times* A p12 July 24, 1999

KANIN, GARSON Nov. 24, 1912–Mar. 13, 1999 Theatrical and motion-picture director; playwright; screenwriter; author; early in his career, was a jazz saxophonist, an experience that would supply the grist for his play (1950) and screenplay (1960) *The Rat Race*; made his Broadway debut as an actor in 1933; beginning in 1935, was associated with the Broadway producer George Abbott as both actor and directorial assistant; for Abbott, was full-fledged director of *Hitch Your Wagon* (1936) and *Too Many Heroes* (1937); moving to Hollywood, directed seven RKO pictures between 1938 and 1941; while serving with the U.S. Army's Office of Strategic Services during World War II, was assigned to co-direct, with Carol Reed, *The True Glory*, a compilation of war footage that received the Academy Award for best documentary of 1945; drew on his observation of corrupt profiteering in wartime Washington in writing and directing the hit farce *Born Yesterday* (1946), which ran on Broadway for three years and was adapted to the screen twice; began a period of collaboration with his first wife, the actress and writer Ruth Gordon, in 1946, when he directed her play *Years Ago*; with her, wrote the scenarios for five films, including George Cukor's romantic comedy classics *Adam's Rib* (1949) and *Pat and Mike* (1952); alone, wrote and directed the films *Where It's At* (1969) and *Some Kind of a Nut* (1969); on Broadway, directed, among other productions, the hit drama *The Diary of Anne Frank* (1955) and the long-running musical *Funny Girl* (1964); wrote more than a dozen books, including the memoirs *Remembering Somerset Maugham* (1966), *Tracy and Hepburn* (1971), and *Hollywood* (1974), several novels set behind the Broadway and Hollywood scenes, including *Moviola* (1979), and a large number of short stories and essays; set forth his positive view of aging in his book *It Takes a Long Time to Become Young* (1978); died at the home in Manhattan that he shared with his second wife, the actress Marian Seldes. See *Current Biography* (October) 1952.

Obituary *New York Times* B p7 Mar. 15, 1999

KENNEDY, JOHN F., JR. Nov. 25, 1960–July 16, 1999 Lawyer; publisher; editor in chief of the slick magazine *George*, which he co-founded with a view to contributing to a renewal of interest in politics among young adults; was the son of U.S. president John F. Kennedy, who was assassinated in Dallas, Texas, on November 22, 1963, and the late Jacqueline Bouvier Kennedy Onassis and the brother of Carolyn Kennedy Schlossberg; on his third birthday, saluted his father's casket as the funeral cortege passed St. Mathew's Cathedral in Washington, D.C.—a televised image engraved in the memory of several generations of Americans; in summers during his student years at Phillips Exeter Academy and Brown University, traveled widely with his cousin Timothy Shriver; did earthquake relief work in Guatemala (1976); studied conditions in several African countries (1979 and 1980); interned at the Center for Democratic Policy in Washington (1981); after earning a B.A. degree in American history at Brown in 1983, made an abortive venture into professional acting, lived and studied in India (1983–84); fostered job development as an assistant to the New York Commissioner of Business Development (1984–86), and served as acting deputy executive director of the 42d Street Development Corp. (1986); enrolled in the New York University Law School in 1986; during summer vacations from NYU, worked as a law clerk in the U.S. Department of Justice in Washington (1987) and as an intern with the law firm of Mannat, Phelps, Rothenberg & Phillips in Los Angeles (1988); as a member of the Juvenile Rights Clinic at NYU, was a legal aide in the defense of juveniles accused of felonies in Brooklyn Family Court; introduced Senator Edward M. Kennedy, his uncle, in a speech at the Democratic National Convention in 1988; helped to develop a Mental Retardation and Developmental Disabilities Program for New York City (1988–90); with his mother and sister, launched the John F. Kennedy Profiles in Courage Award for excellence in elective political office at the John F. Kennedy School of Government at Harvard University in 1989; received his bachelor of laws degree at NYU in 1989; passed the New York State bar examination in 1990; as an assistant U.S. district attorney in Manhattan (1989–93), won all six of the cases in which he was the prosecutor of record; in 1995 co-founded *George*, a nonpartisan bimonthly named after George Washington and described by Kennedy as "a lifestyle magazine . . . illuminating the points where politics converges with business, media, entertainment, fashion, art, and science"; headed Reaching Up, a nonprofit organization devoted to supporting and improving the training of caregivers for the mentally disabled; founded the South African Group for Education; raised funds for the John F. Kennedy Library Foundation, the Special Olympics, and numerous other causes and charities; died—along with his wife, Carolyn Bessette Kennedy, a fashion publicist, whom he married on September 21, 1996, and her sister, Lauren Bessette—when the single-engine Piper Saratoga airplane he was piloting crashed into the Atlantic Ocean near Martha's Vineyard, Massachusetts; after the recovery of his body, on July 21, 1999, and its cremation, was buried at sea, on July 22. See *Current Biography* (January) 1996.

Obituary *New York Times* A p14 July 19, 1999

KILEY, RICHARD Mar. 31, 1922–Mar. 5, 1999 Actor; singer; a versatile performer with a deep, resonant voice who moved easily between musical and dramatic roles; described himself as "a character man in a leading man's body"; established his theatrical signature in the dual role of Cervantes/Don Quixote in the hit musical *Man of La Mancha*, a role he created (with a Tony Award–winning performance) in 1965, played on the New York stage for six years, took on tour, and reprised twice on Broadway in the 1970s;

began his career as a radio actor and announcer in Chicago; in 1946 made his professional stage debut in summer stock in Michiana Shores, Michigan; first appeared on the New York stage as Poseidon in an Equity Library Theater production of *The Trojan Women* in 1947; on a national tour of *A Streetcar Named Desire* from 1948 to 1950, understudied and eventually replaced Anthony Quinn as Stanley Kowalski; came to national attention as a participant in television's Golden Age of live drama, beginning with his performance in the title role in *The Champion* on *Robert Montgomery Presents* in 1950; ultimately was seen on virtually all of the major live dramatic showcases on TV, including *Studio One*, *Playhouse 90*, and *Kraft Television Theatre*; made his Broadway debut as Joey Percival in a revival of Shaw's *Misalliance* early in 1953; in December of the same year made his Broadway singing debut as the Caliph in *Kismet*; in 1956 played Major Harry Cargill in the POW drama *Time Limit!* at the Booth Theatre; won his first Tony Award as Tom Baxter in the musical *The Redhead* (1959); in the 1960–61 Broadway season, starred as Brig Anderson in the drama *Advise and Consent*; still on Broadway, sang the male lead in the musical *No Strings* in 1962 and the role of Stan the Shpieler in *I Had a Ball* three seasons later; subsequently appeared on Broadway in *Absurd Person Singular* in 1974, in *The Heiress* (as Dr. Sloper) in 1976, and in *All My Sons* in 1989; began accruing motion-picture credits in 1950; had co-starring or important supporting roles in such films as *Blackboard Jungle* (1955), *The Phenix City Story* (1955), *Spanish Affair* (1958), *Pendulum* (1969), *The Little Prince* (1974), *Looking for Mr. Goodbar* (1977), and *Endless Love* (1981); on television, won Emmy and Golden Globe Awards for his performances in the miniseries *The Thorn Birds* (1982–83) and the dramatic series *A Year in the Life* (1987–88); won another Emmy Award for his role in the episode "Buried Alive" in the drama series *Picket Fences* (1993–94); after falling ill in 1994, concentrated his energy on the narration of television documentaries, including a *Mysteries of the Bible* series available on video; died in Middletown, New York. See *Current Biography* (April) 1973.

Obituary *New York Times* A p11 Mar. 6, 1999

KILLANIN, MICHAEL MORRIS, 3d BARON July 30, 1914–Apr. 25, 1999 Anglo-Irish businessman; banker; writer; sports executive; president of the International Olympic Committee (1972–80); honorary president of the Olympic Council of Ireland (since 1981); was a reporter with the London *Daily Express* (1935) and the London *Daily Mail* (1935–39); covered the Sino-Japanese War for the *Daily Mail* in China (1937–38); wrote a political column for the London *Sunday Dispatch* (1935–39); after serving with the King's Royal Rifle Corps in World War II, pursued a multitude of interests; produced or co-produced the motion pictures *The Rising of the Moon* (1957), *Gideon's Day* (1958), and *The Playboy of the Western World* (1963); was associated with the production of a number of other films, including *The Quiet Man* (1952); was chairman of the board of the Ulster Investment Bank, Lombard & Ulster Banking Ltd., Chubb Ireland Ltd., and Bovril Ireland; was a director of a number of other firms, including Killanin Estates, Irish Shell, Northern [Ireland] Telecom, and British Petroleum Ltd.; was president of the Dublin Theatre Festival (1960–70) and the Olympic Council of Ireland (1950–73); wrote the books *Four Days: 25–29 September, 1938* (1938), *Sir Godfrey Kneller and His Times* (1948), *My Olympic Years* (1983), and *My Ireland: An Impression* (1987); was co-author of several other books about Ireland and the Olympic games; died at his home in Dublin. See *Current Biography* (April) 1973.

Obituary *New York Times* A p19 Apr. 26, 1999

KIRBY, ROBERT E. Nov. 8, 1918–Dec. 31, 1998 Chairman and chief executive officer of the Westinghouse Electric Corporation (1969–78); a "people-oriented" manager who made himself accessible to employees of all ranks for suggestions and complaints; was originally educated in chemical and electrical engineering; joined the staff of Westinghouse's industrial electronics division in 1946; after earning an M.B.A. degree at the Harvard School of Business, became general manager of the division, in 1958; 11 years later, when Westinghouse was restructured into four major units, became president of the largest and most diversified of those units, the Industry and Defense Company; was promoted to chairman and CEO of Westinghouse at a time when the corporation, then the major builder of nuclear power plants in the U.S., was hurting from many money-losing operations, declining in earnings, and lacking in a coherent strategy for the future; tightened inner financial controls; presided over a comprehensive program of retrenchment and reorganization that restored the corporation's focus on electrical and industrial operations and turned its earnings in a sustained upward direction; died in Naples, Florida. See *Current Biography* (September) 1979.

Obituary *New York Times* A p21 Jan. 6, 1999

KIRKLAND, LANE Mar. 12, 1922–Aug. 14, 1999 Labor union official; former president of the AFL-CIO; in 1948 joined the research staff of the American Federation of Labor, which merged with the Congress of Industrial Organizations in 1955; was assistant director of the AFL-CIO's Social Security department until 1958, when he became director of research and education with the International Union of Operating Engineers; in 1960 or 1961 returned to the AFL-CIO as executive assistant to George Meany, then the organization's president; as Meany's trusted right-hand man for nine years, watched over the AFL-CIO's daily operations, wrote key position papers, and represented labor's interests at the White House and on Capitol Hill; was also the organization's chief troubleshooter, mediating jurisdictional disputes between warring member unions, resolving maritime problems, and working for "accommodation" between labor and management; worked behind the scenes to settle a crippling transit strike in New York City in 1966; coordinated the AFL-CIO's campaigns against racial discrimination within and without union ranks; in addition to his union work, served as president of the Institute of Collective Bargaining in the late 1960s; as secretary-treasurer

(1969–79), played an even more active role in the formulation and promulgation of the AFL-CIO's policies, including its political agenda; opposed President Nixon's economic policies; was hawkish against communism and supported the Vietnam War and more defense spending; in the absence of a truly free world market, supported some protective tariffs; beyond the bread-and-butter issues of wages and job security, called for greater federal involvement in health care, medical research, consumer protection, and student loans; as president (1979–95) of the AFL-CIO, brought the United Auto Workers and the Teamsters back into the larger organization and persuaded the unions of longshoremen and warehousemen to join; as president, spent much of his time concentrating on international affairs, including contacts with conservative unions in foreign countries; resigned following a revolt of union presidents angry over what they perceived to be his failure to cope with changing labor conditions in the U.S.; died at his home in Washington, D.C. See *Current Biography* (May) 1980.

Obituary *New York Times* p1+ Aug. 15, 1999

KNIGHT, FRANCES G(LADYS) July 22, 1905–Sep. 11, 1999 Former director of the U.S. passport office; beginning in 1936, worked in President Franklin D. Roosevelt's administration in a succession of medium-echelon positions, usually as an information and public-relations specialist; in 1952 became assistant deputy administrator of the State Department's bureau of security and consular affairs; three years later was appointed director of the U.S. passport office, a subdivision of the bureau; in that post, earned a reputation for both efficiency as an administrator and diligence in denying passports and entrance visas to persons she regarded as subversive; drew fire from liberals in Congress and the State Department when it was disclosed that she testified in a closed meeting of the Senate internal security subcommittee that Secretary of State Dean Rusk had ordered her to approve passport applications by "dangerous undercover Communists engaged in espionage, sabotage, and sedition"; withstanding efforts to force her to resign, served until 1977, when she was 72, two years beyond mandatory retirement age; died in Bethesda, Maryland. See *Current Biography* (October) 1955.

Obituary *New York Times* A p13 Sep. 18, 1999

KOMAROVSKY, MIRRA Feb. 4, 1906–Jan. 30, 1999 Russian-born sociologist; university professor; author; broke new ground in sociological research and analysis, especially in her studies of family, education, and gender roles in society; was a research assistant in human relations at Columbia University, in New York City, while earning advanced degrees there in the 1930s; joined the faculty of Barnard College at Columbia in 1938; chaired the sociology department at Barnard (1949–62, 1965–68); retired as a professor at Barnard in 1970; returned in 1978 to chair the women's studies program; was professor emeritus and special lecturer at the college from 1979 to 1992; co-wrote *Leisure, a Suburban Study* (1934); published her doctoral dissertation as *The Unemployed Man and His Family* (1940); in 1953 published her landmark book *Women in the Modern*

World: *Their Education and Their Dilemmas*; later wrote *Blue-Collar Marriage* (1964), *Dilemmas in Masculinity* (1976), and *Women in College: Shaping New Feminine Identities* (1985); died at her home on Riverside Drive in Manhattan. See *Current Biography* (October) 1953.

Obituary *New York Times* B p8 Feb. 1, 1999

KORTH, FRED (H.) Sep. 9, 1909–Sep. 14, 1998 U.S. Secretary of the Navy (1961–63); president of the Continental National Bank of Fort Worth, Texas; lawyer; served with the Army Air Forces' Air Transport Command in World War II; began practicing law in 1935; first went to Washington, D.C., in 1951 as a deputy counsel to the Department of the Army; was assistant secretary of the army in charge of manpower and reserve forces from May 1952 to January 1953; subsequently was a consultant to the secretary of the army; was a member of the Southwestern Texas Cattle Raisers Association; served on the board of Meridian International, a foundation in Washington, D.C., concerned with international relations; died at his home in El Paso, Texas. See *Current Biography* (July) 1962.

Obituary *New York Times* B p12 Sep. 21, 1998

KRAUS, ALFREDO Nov. 24, 1927–Sep. 10, 1999 Spanish operatic singer; a lyric tenor who attracted a solid international following with his rich voice, spare and brilliant timbre, distinct phrasing, range, elegant musicianship, confidant and controlled acting style, and masterly technique, which he refined and polished as he aged; with a view to durability, confined his repertory to a score or so of bel canto roles in works by Gounod, Massenet, Bellini, Donizetti, Rossini, and Verdi; made his professional debut singing the role of the Duke of Mantua in a performance of *Rigoletto* in Cairo, Egypt, in January 1956; later in the same year, made his European debut as Alfredo in *La Traviata* in Venice and his British debut in the same role in London; in Lisbon on March 27, 1958, sang opposite Maria Callas in a legendary production of *La Traviata*, heard throughout the world by opera connoisseurs for decades afterward on pirated tapes; sang Edgardo opposite Joan Sutherland in *Lucia di Lammermoor* in July 1959; subsequently, sang Elvino in *La Somnambula* at La Scala in Milan; made his American debut at the Lyric Opera in Chicago as Nemorino in *L'Elisir d'Amore* in 1962; the following year, returned to the Lyric Opera as Count Almaviva in *Il Barbiere di Sivigla* and Ernesto in *Don Pasquale*; made his Metropolitan Opera debut as the Duke of Manuta in 1966; among other memorable American performances, sang the title role of *Werther* with the Dallas Civic Opera in 1972; later in the 1970s, toured Japan and South America as well as North America; was reaching high D even into the 1980s; in addition to opera, was a popular performer in the Spanish operetta genre known as *zarzuela*; made numerous recordings; died at his home in Madrid. See *Current Biography* (June) 1987.

Obituary *New York Times* B p7 Sep. 11, 1999

KUBRICK, STANLEY July 26, 1928–Mar. 7, 1999 Filmmaker; alone or with others, produced, wrote, and edited most of the motion pictures he directed;

began his career as a news photographer, while still in high school in the Bronx, New York; was a staff photographer with *Look* magazine (from 1946 to 1950), when he made his first film, *The Day of the Fight*, a short documentary about a prize fighter that he sold to RKO Pathé News; backed by that company, made the one-reel documentary *Flying Padre*, about an aviator priest in New Mexico; with money borrowed from his family, wrote, directed, photographed, and edited his first feature, a low-budget film called *Fear and Desire* (1953); sold his second feature, *Killer's Kiss* (1955), to United Artists; with James B. Harris, formed a production partnership, the first product of which was the racetrack heist movie *The Killing* (1956); focused incisively on duplicity and incompetence in the French high command and the pathetic plight of men in the trenches in the overpowering World War I film *Paths of Glory* (1957); in *Spartacus* (1960), brought the story of an unsuccessful slave revolt in ancient Rome to the screen spectacularly, in Super Technirama, without losing focus on the gladiator who led the rebellion; in *Lolita* (1962), translated to the screen Vladimir Nabakov's controversial novel about a middle-aged professor's obsessive love for a "nymphet"; with savage humor, in *Dr. Strangelove: or How I Learned to Stop Worrying and Love the Bomb* (1964), depicted as madmen the military commanders and political strategists who viewed nuclear devastation as an option in the Cold War; with fantastic special effects, both visual and auditory, created in *2001: A Space Odyssey* (1968) a near-psychedelic audience experience that opened new vistas for cinema's science-fiction genre; gave vent to his bleak pessimism regarding humanity's potential for evil in *A Clockwork Orange* (1971), his adaptation of Anthony Burgess's frighteningly brutal futuristic novel; failed critically and commercially with *Barry Lyndon* (1975); chillingly, adapted *The Shining* (1981) from one of Stephen King's Gothic fables; in *Full Metal Jacket* (1987), combined a harrowing first section on Marine basic training with a compelling second section on the fighting in Vietnam; at the time of his death had recently finished editing his 13th feature film, the psychosexual thriller *Eyes Wide Shut*; died at his home in England, where he had been living since the early 1960s. See *Current Biography* (February) 1963.

Obituary *New York Times* A p1+ Mar. 8, 1999

LALL, ARTHUR S(AMUEL) July 14, 1911–Sep. 13, 1998 Indian diplomat; writer; teacher; joined India's civil service in 1933; after India gained independence from Britain, in 1947, served as his country's first trade commissioner in London; subsequently was joint secretary of India's Ministry of Commerce and Industry; became consul general in New York in 1951; was appointed India's permanent representative to the United Nations, with the rank of ambassador, in 1954; in the early 1960s, represented India in international arms-control and disarmament negotiations; after leaving the diplomatic service, remained in New York City as a teacher of international relations at the Columbia University School of International and Public Affairs; died in New York City. See *Current Biography* (November) 1956.

Obituary *New York Times* B p12 Sep. 21, 1998

LEONTIEF, WASSILY Aug. 5, 1906–Feb. 5, 1999 Russian-born economist; university professor; the creator of the input-output system that revolutionized the analysis and planning of the production machinery of national economies; in 1928 took his Ph.D. degree at the University of Berlin, Germany, with a dissertation containing the germ of his revolutionary concept (inspired by the economic equilibrium theory of the 19th-century French economist Léon Walras), the basis of which is the construction of grid-like tables, similar to road-map mileage charts, giving an overall picture of the dynamic relationships among key industries and other sectors within an economy; after immigrating to the U.S., in 1931, pursued his research in the economics department of Harvard University, in Cambridge, Massachusetts, with the help of his staff and increasingly sophisticated computers; was awarded the 1973 Nobel Prize in economic sciences "for the development of the input-output method and its application to important economic problems"; in 1975 left Harvard to found the Institute for Economic Analysis at New York University; headed the institute until 1991; wrote *The Structure of the American Economy, 1919–29* (1943), *Studies in the Structure of the American Economy* (1953, 1977), *Input-Output Economics* (1966), and *The Future of the World Economy* (1977), among other books; died in New York City. See *Current Biography* (January) 1967.

Obituary *New York Times* p50 Feb. 7, 1999

LIEBERMANN, ROLF Sep. 14, 1910–Jan. 2, 1999 Swiss-born opera manager; conductor; musician; composer; a daringly innovative impresario, dedicated to *realistischesthe Musiktheater*, or the "dramatic truth of opera," to be transmitted to the audience not only musically but also theatrically, as with a play; believed he had "a moral duty to confront the audience with its own times"; as a young man, studied at the Zurich Conservatory of Music, played jazz saxophone, and gained some recognition as a composer of serious music traditional in its tonal structure; later combined tonal with 12-tone passages in such compositions as Symphony No. 1 (1949) and Concerto for Jazz Band and Orchestra (1954); for the Lausanne Exposition of 1964, was commissioned to write Symphonie des Echanges; based that work, his most experimental ever, on the sounds made by typewriters, business machines, military telephones, and electronic equipment; established his reputation in opera with the compositions *Leonore 40/45* (1952), a serio-comic French-German romance set in World War II, *Penelope* (1954), a modern interpretation of the Odysseus legend, and *School for Wives* (1955), adapted from Molière; was a member of the music department of the Swiss Radio Corp. (1945–50); conducted and composed for the Swiss Radio Beromunster orchestra (1950–57); was musical director of the North German Broadcasting System (1957–59); as general manager of the Hamburg State Opera (1959–73), vastly expanded the repertory of that company, making it the largest in the world and one of the most avant-garde; presented a large proportion of modern and contemporary works, including *Wozzeck, Lulu, Tommy, Kyldex I*, and works by Paul Hindemith, Leos Janacek, Gunther Schuller,

and Giselher Klebe; commissioned two new works a year; as general administrator of the Paris Opera (1973–80), commissioned new works from contemporary composers and hired the best directors, set designers, and choreographers to rejuvenate the 18th- and 19th-century war horses in the company's repertory; returned to the Hamburg Opera as its director (1985–88); died in Paris. See *Current Biography* (September) 1973.

Obituary *New York Times* A p17 Jan. 4 1999

LILLEHEI, C(LARENCE) WALTON Oct. 23, 1918– July 5, 1999 Surgeon; was a pioneer in the development of open-heart operating techniques and the invention of such relevant artificial devices as oxygenators, replacements for cardiac valves, and the electronic pacemaker; after army medical service in World War II, did post-M.D. study and research in physiology and the clinical science of surgery at the University of Minnesota Medical School; became a full-time clinical instructor in the department of surgery at the medical school in 1949, when direct-vision surgery within the heart was as yet unfeasible, for want of a method of heart-lung bypass to keep the blood oxygenated during the procedure; with his team of surgeons at the medical school, used a dog's lung and a mechanical pumping system in an operation in 1954; subsequently experimented with several artificial heart-lung machines; with Dr. Richard A. DeWall, introduced the helix reservoir bubble oxygenator in 1955; two years later, made the first successful replacement of a patient's defective aortic valve with a prosthetic plastic valve; in the following years, performed many operations for the partial or total replacement of damaged aortic and mitral valves; contributed to the design of four prosthetic heart valves, including the St. Jude Medical mechanical valve; in 1960 published his and his colleagues' report on their successful use of electronic pacemakers to maintain the heart's proper rhythm in cases of heart block; was a teacher to visiting specialists from around the world, including Christiaan N. Barnard, who would perform the first successful heart transplant operation in 1967; was a full professor of surgery at the University of Minnesota Medical School from 1956 until 1967, when he moved to New York City as chief of surgery at New York Hospital and chairman of the department of surgery at Cornell University Medical College; performed his first heart transplant in 1968; in 1969 presided over teams of surgeons that performed the world's largest multiple organ transplant operation and the first inter-hospital heart transplant; returned to the University of Minnesota Medical Center, as it had become known, in 1975; was a division medical director at St. Jude Medical Inc., the St. Paul medical equipment manufacturer, starting in 1979; died in St. Paul, Minnesota. See *Current Biography* (May) 1969.

Obituary *New York Times* B p9 July 8, 1999

LONG, TANIA Apr. 29, 1913–Sep. 4, 1998 Journalist; was born in Germany to a British journalist father and a Russian-born mother; became a naturalized American citizen in 1935; was a reporter with the *Newark* (New Jersey) *Ledger* from 1936 to 1938, when she returned to Germany; reported for the New

York *Herald Tribune* from Berlin until World War II broke out, in September 1939; after brief stints in Copenhagen and Paris, was assigned to the *Herald Tribune*'s London bureau; continued reporting on wartime London after moving to the *New York Times* in February 1942; as the war in Europe neared its close, followed the Allied advance across France and into Germany; remained in Germany, covering the Nuremburg trials and postwar conditions in the country; with her second husband, Raymond Daniel, ran the *Times*'s bureau in Ottawa, Canada, from 1952 to 1964; later served as the first publicist of the National Arts Center of Canada; committed suicide at her home in Ottawa. See *Current Biography* (May) 1946.

Obituary *New York Times* p42 Sep. 6, 1998

LORTEL, LUCILLE Dec. 16, 1900– Apr. 4, 1999 Theatrical producer; theater proprietor; an innovative impresario; patron of venturesome new actors, playwrights, designers, and directors and of veterans seeking new challenges; earned the sobriquet "Queen of Off-Broadway"; by creating havens for avant-garde talent, helped to provide quality noncommercial theater to the greater New York area for half a century; beginning in 1924, had a budding career as an actress, which was cut short in the 1930s by her marriage to Louis Schweitzer, a wealthy chemical engineer and cigarette-paper manufacturer and a possessive husband; in compensation, received financial support for her theatrical projects from Schweitzer; founded the White Barn Theatre (still thriving in 1999) on the Schweitzer estate in Westport, Connecticut, in 1947; there, provided sanctuary (including room and board) from the pressures of the commercial theater to Sidney Lumet, Eva Le Gallienne, Canada Lee, Zero Mostel, Eva Marie Saint, Mildred Dunnock, James Coco, Geoffrey Holder, Peter Falk, Vincent Gardenia, and the Dublin Players, among others; in 1955 acquired the Theatre de Lys (still thriving in 1999 with the name Lucille Lortel's Theatre de Lys) in New York City's Greenwich Village; began her tenure there with a revival of *The Threepenny Opera* that ran from 1955 through 1961, setting a new record in American musical theater; followed up with a production of *Brecht on Brecht*, a "living anthology" compiled by George Tabori; from 1958 to 1975 offered at the Theatre de Lys the Matinee Series, "a laboratory for innovation" providing a showcase for new playwrights (including Adrienne Kennedy and Terence McNally), for other playwrights attempting adventurous new forms, and for actors (including such seasoned performers as Siobhan McKenna and Helen Hayes) performing in experimental works of their choosing; was responsible for mounting the first American productions of plays by Mario Fratti and Athol Fugard and previously unknown or little-known plays by Sean O'Casey, Eugene Ionesco, and Jean Genet, among others; also provided a stage for the early noncommercial work of such major American playwrights as Tennessee Williams, Edward Albee, and William Inge; died in Manhattan. See *Current Biography* (February) 1985.

Obituary *New York Times* A p25 Apr. 6, 1999

LUCKMAN, CHARLES May 16, 1909–Jan. 25, 1999 Architect; business executive; received his architectural degree from the University of Illinois and a certificate to practice architecture in Illinois in 1931, in the early years of the great worldwide economic depression; faced with a dearth of opportunities in architecture, took a job as a draftsman in the Colgate-Palmolive-Peet Co.'s advertising department in Chicago; was transferred to the sales department, where he soon rose to divisional supervisor; in 1935 moved to the Pepsodent Co. (which later became a division of the Lever Brothers Co.) as sales manager; rose up the executive ranks at Pepsodent and Lever Brothers to become president of Lever Brothers in 1946; as president, commissioned the creation of Lever House, the first glass tower to rise among Manhattan's skyscrapers; left Lever Brothers to become a partner of the architect William Pereira, in 1950, and to found his own firm, the Luckman Partnership, in 1958; was perhaps best known as the designer of Penn Station in Manhattan and the U.S. pavilion at the 1964–65 New York World's Fair; was also responsible for or associated with the designing of scores of architectural projects, including Aloha Stadium in Honolulu, Hawaii, the Prudential Center in Boston, such NASA projects as the original master plan for the Kennedy Space Center in Cape Canaveral, Florida, public buildings in Phoenix, Arizona, and Madison, Wisconsin, and numerous civic centers, office buildings, hotels, banks, and airport buildings elsewhere; in Los Angeles, designed the Convention and Exhibition Center, 9200 Sunset Tower, the Luckman Fine Arts Complex, and the Luckman Child Guidance Clinic, among other buildings; was supervising architect for the University of California at Santa Barbara; centered his activities in the Luckman Management Co., founded in 1973; wrote the autobiography *Twice in a Lifetime* (1988); died at his home in Los Angeles. See *Current Biography* (October) 1947.

Obituary *New York Times* C p23 Jan. 28, 1999

MANN, THOMAS C. Nov. 11, 1912–Jan. 23, 1999 U.S. government official; career foreign-service officer; lawyer; played a leading role in revising U.S. Latin American policy in the 1960s; grew up speaking Spanish as well as English in Laredo, Texas; began practicing law in Laredo in 1934; with the U.S. Department of State during World War II, served as special assistant to the U.S. ambassador in Uruguay; after the war, relinquished his State Department civilian rank to become a foreign-service officer; between 1947 and 1955 was assigned successively to the U.S. embassies in Venezuela, Greece, and Guatemala; was U.S. ambassador to El Salvador from 1955 to 1957; as assistant secretary of state for economic affairs (1957–60), represented the U.S. in many international trade conferences and agreements; was assistant secretary of state for inter-American affairs from July 1960 until March 1961, when President John F. Kennedy named him ambassador to Mexico; under President Lyndon B. Johnson following Kennedy's assassination, in November 1963, was special assistant to the president as well as assistant secretary of state for inter-American affairs; in those positions, was instrumental in changing the direction of

U.S. Latin American policy, away from the Kennedy administration's idealistic Alliance for Progress, which had tied economic aid to the promotion of democracy; described the change as "pragmatic"; responded to critics of the change by explaining that no social and political reforms could take firm root until the economy of a country was healthy; left government in 1966; was president of the American Automobile Association from 1967 to 1971; died at his home in Austin, Texas. See *Current Biography* (April) 1964.

Obituary *New York Times* A p11 Jan. 30, 1999

MARAIS, JEAN Dec. 11, 1913–Nov. 8, 1998 French actor; was discovered by the surrealist poet, artist, and filmmaker Jean Cocteau, whose close companion he remained until Cocteau's death in 1963; in a stage career that began in the late 1930s under the tutelage of Charles Dullin, had leading roles in plays by Cocteau as well as a classical repertoire including Racine, Molière, and Shakespeare in translation; was known to French moviegoers since the release of *Le Pavillon Brûle* (*The Pavilion Burns*) in 1941; was introduced to American audiences in 1947 as the beast/prince in Cocteau's film *La Belle et la Bête* (*Beauty and the Beast*); later starred in Cocteau's *L'Aigle à Deux Têtes* and *Les Parents Terribles*, and *Orphée* and films directed by René Clément, Jean Delannoy, Luchino Visconti, Claude Lelouch, and Yves and Marc Allégret, among others; as his acting career waned in the 1970s, turned increasingly to painting and sculpture; died in Cannes, France. See *Current Biography* (April) 1962.

Obituary *New York Times* B p11 Nov. 10, 1998

MATURE, VICTOR Jan. 29, 1913(?)–Aug. 4, 1999 Actor; a movie idol who brought a strong masculine presence to his action, romantic, film noir, and other screen assignments; his formidable acting credits notwithstanding, too often found his genuine talent obscured in the focus on his handsome physique (sometimes exploited in loincloths or toga roles) and his charming smile (sometimes enlisted in the portrayal of seductive con men); began acting at the Pasadena (California) Playhouse (1936–39), where he was discovered by the filmmaker Hal Roach; first appeared on the screen in a five-minute role in *The Housekeeper's Daughter* (1939); had his first leading screen role as Tumak, the caveman, in *One Million, B.C.* (1940); subsequently had leading roles in *Captain Caution* (1940) and *No, No Nannette* (1940); enhanced his reputation with his performance on Broadway in the male lead in *Lady in the Dark* (1941); back in Hollywood, was cast as Frankie Christopher/Botticelli in *I Wake Up Screaming* (1941); was impressive as Dr. Omar in *The Shanghai Gesture* (1941), "Doc" John Holliday in *My Darling Clementine* (1946), Nick Bianco in *Kiss of Death* (1947), Lieutenant Candella in *Cry of the City* (1948), Pete Wilson in *Easy Living* (1949), Jed, the savage hero, in *The Last Frontier* (1955), and Cliff Brandon in *China Doll* (1958); was cast opposite reigning Hollywood "pinup" queens in such films as *Song of the Islands* (1942), *My Gal Sal* (1942), and *Wabash Avenue* (1950); among his many roles in biblical and historical costume epics, was at his best as Samson in

Samson and Delilah (1948); later played Captain in *Androcles and the Lion* (1952), Demetrius in *The Robe* (1953) and *Demetrius and the Gladiators* (1954), and Horemheb in *The Egyptian* (1955); had some 56 motion-picture credits, including the title roles in *Chief Crazy Horse* (1955) and *Zarak* (1956) and that of Mike Conway in *Timbuktu* (1959); died in San Diego County, California. See *Current Biography* (December) 1951.

Obituary *New York Times* C p21 Aug. 10, 1999

MAURIAC, CLAUDE Apr. 25, 1914–Mar. 22, 1996 French writer; critic; novelist; a son of the novelist François Mauriac; in much of his nonfiction, chronicled political and intellectual life in France up close, as he experienced it; was a polemicist for the "new novelists" (e.g., Alain Robbe-Grillet, Marguerite Duras, and his friend Nathalie Sarraute), whose ranks he himself joined in the late 1950s; was General Charles de Gaulle's private secretary from 1944 to 1949; with André Malraux, founded the Gaullist review *La Liberté de l'Esprit* in 1949; published the books *Malraux* (1946), *André Breton* (1949), and *Conversations avec André Gide* (1951); meanwhile, had begun writing for *Le Figaro* and *Le Figaro littéraire*; was a regular contributor of literary and film criticism to those newspapers until 1977; began writing for *Le Monde*, a more left-wing newspaper, in 1978; in his book *L'alittérature contemporaine* (1958; *The New Literature*, 1959), coined the term "alittérature" to describe fiction freed from the limits of the traditional realistic conventions; wrote in that vein in his own fiction, using stream-of-consciousness techniques and compressed time frames to examine such themes as communication, existentialist solitude, vulnerability to love and its sexual expression, differing perceptions, problems in communication, and the process of writing itself; created the fictional alter ego Bertrand Carnéjoux, the main character in the four novels comprising the tetralogy *Le dialogue interieur* (1957–63); published a second cycle of three novels under the collective title *Les infiltrations de invisible* (1979–82); in his longest, most ambitious project, used entries from the detailed diaries he had been keeping since childhood to craft the 10 volumes of *Le temps immobile* (1974–88), a cinematic, montage-like eyewitness account of 50 years of French literature and politics; carried the account forward in the three volumes of *Le temps accompli* (1991–93); in addition to his fiction and nonfiction, wrote several plays, the texts of which were published in *Théatre* (1968); died in Paris. See *Current Biography* (September) 1993.

Obituary *Contemporary Authors* vol. 152, 1997

McALARY, MIKE 1957(?)–Dec. 25, 1998 Journalist; columnist; author; at the beginning of his career, covered sports for, in quick succession, the *Boston Globe*, the *Boston Herald-American*, the *Rochester Record-American;* and the *New York Post*; in 1985 joined the staff of *New York Newsday* as a police reporter; maintained his familiarity with the crime beat after becoming a columnist, first with *Newsday*, with the New York *Daily News* beginning in 1988, and with the *New York Post* beginning in 1990; subsequently moved back and forth between the *Post* and the *Daily News* as the two newspapers vied for his services and he enjoyed ever-larger paychecks and front-page attention; as a crime reporter and columnist, gathered the grist for his nonfiction books *Buddy Boys: When Good Cops Turn Bad* (1988), about corruption in a Brooklyn police precinct; *Cop Shot: The Murder of Edward Byrne* (1990), about a police officer shot down by crack-cocaine dealers; and *Good Cop, Bad Cop: Detective Joe Trimboli's Heroic Pursuit of NYPD Officer Michael Dowd* (1994), about a five-year investigation of "the dirtiest cop ever"; won the 1997 Pulitzer Prize for commentary for his series of *Daily News* columns about the case of Abner Louima, a Haitian immigrant who accused two police officers of brutalizing and torturing him in a Brooklyn precinct house; published the novel *Sore Loser* in 1998; died in Manhattan. See *Current Biography* CD 1998.

Obituary *New York Times* C p6 Dec. 26, 1998

McDOWALL, RODDY Sep. 17, 1928–Oct. 3, 1998 British-born actor; a versatile character actor on screen, stage, and television; began acting in motion pictures in England in 1938; immigrated to the U.S. in 1940; began drawing popular and critical attention with his second Hollywood assignment, the role of a sensitive Welsh boy in *How Green Was My Valley* (1941); subsequently had starring or featured roles in such films as *Son of Fury* (1942), *My Friend Flicka* (1943), *Lassie Come Home* (1943), *The White Cliffs of Dover* (1944), *The Keys of the Kingdom* (1945), *Kidnapped* (1948), and *Big Timber* (1950); was cast as Malcolm in Orson Welles's film version of *Macbeth* (1948); having outgrown the juvenile film roles in which he was typecast, left Hollywood for the stage in 1951; after some work in stock, off-Broadway, and at the American Shakespeare Festival in Stratford, Connecticut, moved to Broadway in the role of Whitledge in *No Time for Sergeants* (1955); subsequently on Broadway played Artie Straus in *Compulsion* (1957) and Pepe in *Handful of Fire* (1958); won a 1959-60 Tony Award for best supporting actor for his performance on Broadway as the son of a French war profiteer in *The Fighting Cock*; the following season, sang the role of Mordred in the Broadway musical *Camelot*; back in Hollywood, had supporting roles in *Cleopatra* (1963) and *The Loved One* (1965); propelled by the high success of his performance as the ape leader Cornelius in *The Planet of the Apes* (1968) and Caesar or Cornelius in three of its four sequels, was cast in a succession of science-fiction, horror, and thriller films, including *The Legend of Hell House* (1973), *Fright Night* (1985), and *Dead of Winter* (1987); made a total of 130 movies, including *The Grass Harp* (1996); also had many dramatic credits on television; as a still photographer, published five volumes of photographs, beginning with *Double Exposure* (1966); owned an outstanding private collection of old motion pictures and movie memorabilia; died at his home in Los Angeles. See *Current Biography* (April) 1961.

Obituary *New York Times* p51 Oct. 4, 1998

McEWEN, TERENCE A(LEXANDER) Apr. 13, 1929–Sep. 14, 1998 Canadian-born former general director of the San Francisco Opera, America's second-ranking opera house; beginning in 1950, worked in merchandising and artist development with Decca Records in London and Paris; went on to become executive vice president of the classical-music division of London Records, Decca's U.S. branch; after an apprenticeship of more than a year under Kurt Herbert Adler, succeeded Adler as general director of the San Francisco Opera in 1982; in 1988 retired and moved to Hawaii; died at his home in Honolulu, Hawaii. See *Current Biography* (July) 1985.

Obituary *New York Times* B p12 Sep. 23, 1998

MELLON, PAUL June 11, 1907–Feb. 1, 1999 Philanthropist; art collector and patron; environmental conservationist; humanitarian; the only son of the financial titan Andrew W. Mellon (1855-1937); not sharing his father's interest in commerce, concentrated on using the family fortune to benefit mankind and promote the arts and humanities, with stress on the Anglo-American tradition; while personally maintaining a low profile, established foundations through which he spent hundreds of millions of dollars in building and housing public art collections and supporting educational and cultural institutions and individual scholarship, among other projects; grew up in the family mansion in Pittsburgh, in England (summers), and in Washington, D.C. (where his father served as U.S. secretary of the treasury from 1921 to 1932); was educated at the Choate School, in Wallingford, Connecticut, Yale University, in New Haven, Connecticut, and Cambridge University, in Great Britain (where his father was U.S. ambassador in 1932 and 1933); in 1938 became a trustee and benefactor of the Virginia Museum of Fine Arts in Richmond; in 1941 established the Old Dominion Foundation, the educational endowments of which would include amounts as high as $15 million (to Yale), for purposes ranging from new residential colleges to the psychiatric counseling of students; in 1945 established the Bollingen Foundation, the source of the prestigious biennial Bollingen Prize in poetry and the publisher of fine editions of the works of Jung and Coleridge, the *I Ching,* and other books in the fields of mythology, religion, aesthetics, and cultural and art history; oversaw the creation of the National Gallery of Art in Washington, D.C. (completed in 1941), conceived and originally endowed by his late father; was president of the gallery from 1963 to 1979 and chairman of its board of trustees from 1975 to 1985; personally commissioned and, with his sister, Alisa, underwrote the cost of building a huge addition to the gallery, the East Building (1978), designed by I. M. Pei to house contemporary art collections and the Center for Advanced Study in the Visual Arts; over the years donated 913 works to the National Gallery; in 1976 established the Yale Center for British Art and British Studies, to which he donated his collection of 18th-century British art; was a trustee of the Avalon Foundation (founded by his sister) and of the Andrew W. Mellon Foundation, which resulted from the merger of the Avalon and Old Dominion Foundations, in 1969; through his generosity, rescued for posterity many national and state seashores and park lands; helped to restore the Jefferson mansion at Monticello, in Virginia, and to save several historic monuments in Britain; raised prize-winning racehorses at his Rockeby Stables in Virginia, his adopted state; wrote the autobiography *Reflections in a Silver Spoon* (1992); died at his home in Upperville, Virginia. See *Current Biography* (April) 1966.

Obituary *New York Times* A p1+ Feb. 3, 1999

MENUHIN, YEHUDI Apr. 22, 1916–Mar. 12, 1999 Musician; violinist; orchestra conductor; festival impresario and director; educator; author; patron of numerous charities; advocate of many humanitarian causes; a virtual world citizen, with homes in several countries; while his playing of the violin was not always technically flawless, attracted and held millions of admirers throughout the world by his innate musical intelligence and sensibility, his grand and intense style, his lyricism, his subtlety of tone, and what at least one critic called his "nobility of conception"; studied under a series of teachers, including Georges Enesco, yet seemed to have mastered the violin intuitively, before paying attention to the technical fundamentals of violin playing, including the basics of fingering; in his repertoire, in addition to the Bach, Beethoven, Brahms, and Mendelssohn classics and other violin standards, revived neglected scores and introduced compositions commissioned by him or dedicated to him, including works by Bartók, Bloch, Enesco, Oedeon, Partos, and William Walton; gave his first public performance in Oakland, California, when he was seven; between 1926 and 1929 made his debuts in New York City, Paris, Berlin, and London; before pubescence, was already making appearances with such orchestras as the New York Symphony and the Berlin Philharmonic; in 1932 began performing with his sister Hephzibah, a pianist, who would be his favorite recital partner for four decades; with her, recorded Bach's sonatas and Enesco's Sonata No. 3; made his first around-the-world concert tour in 1934 and 1935; during World War II, gave more than 500 concerts for American and Allied troops; after the war, toured Western and Eastern Europe; stirred controversy in some quarters by playing with Wilhelm Furtwängler (conducting the Berlin Philharmonic), because Furtwängler had remained in Germany during the Nazi regime; with Furtwängler conducting the Philharmonia Orchestra, recorded Beethoven's Violin Concerto; in 1956 began performing and conducting a chamber orchestra at a small, informal festival of his own creation near his summer home in Gstaad, Switzerland; later established the Menuhin Academy at Gstaad; with his chamber orchestra, recorded Bach's Brandenburg Concertos, his first recording as a conductor; later conducted the Royal Philharmonic Orchestra in recordings of works by Berlioz and Elgar and the English Chamber Orchestra in recordings of works by Vaughan Williams; as a violinist, recorded Elgar's Violin Concerto with Edward Elgar himself conducting the London Symphony Orchestra; moved to England in 1959; directed the Bath Festival from 1959 to 1968; in 1963 established the school for musically gifted children that bears his name in Stoke d'Abernon, Surrey, England;

toured North America with his chamber orchestra in 1967 and 1971; founded the Windsor Festival in 1969 and directed it until 1972; became president of Trinity College of Music in London in 1971; was knighted in 1965; was able to take on the title "Sir" when he was granted honorary British citizenship 20 years later; received similar honors in Belgium, France, Germany, and Greece; made his first tour of the U.S. strictly as a conductor with the Royal Philharmonic Orchestra in 1985; at the 1996 Lincoln Center Festival conducted the Orchestra of St. Luke in a program of 14 new works composed in his honor by Lukas Foss, Philip Glass, and Karel Husa, among others; published several books, including the collection of short memoirs and other essays *Theme and Variations* (1972), the autobiography *Unfinished Journey* (1977), and two books of instruction for violin students; made a series of films under the title *Menuhin Teaches* for BBC television; in addition to music education (including appreciation of Eastern music), was active in or supportive of a host of causes, including vegetarianism, natural foods, organic gardening, animal protection, the practice of yoga, and health-promoting city planning; played benefit concerts for both Israeli organizations and Arab refugees; died in Berlin, Germany. See *Current Biography* (May) 1973.

Obituary *New York Times* A p12 Mar. 13, 1999

MOORE, ARCHIE Dec. 13, 1913–Dec. 9, 1998 Prizefighter; light-heavyweight champion (1952–62); began boxing professionally in the mid-1930s, as a middleweight; was the leading contender for the light-heavyweight championship from 1949 to 1952; took the light-heavyweight crown from Joey Maxim by unanimous decision in December 1952; successfully defended his light-heavyweight title four times; was knocked out in challenging Rocky Marciano for the heavyweight title in 1955; the following year, after Marciano's retirement, fought Floyd Patterson for Marciano's relinquished title and lost by a knockout; concentrating on the defense of his light-heavyweight title, knocked out Tony Anthony in September 1957 and Yvon Durelle in December 1958; at that point in his career, had 127 knockouts, a record; in 1959, again knocked out Durelle; in February 1962 was stripped of his title for prolonged failure to defend it; nine months later lost by a knockout to Cassius Clay, who later became the heavyweight champion Muhammad Ali; in his last fight, in 1963, was knocked out by Mike DiBiase; after his retirement from the ring, worked from time to time as a boxing trainer; was cast as Jim in the motion picture *The Adventures of Huckleberry Finn* (1960); died in San Diego. See *Current Biography* (November) 1960.

Obituary *New York Times* B p16 Dec. 10, 1998

MOORE, BRIAN Aug. 25, 1921–Jan. 11, 1999 Ulsterborn expatriate author; a novelist's novelist who possessed an impeccable, compressed style; brought even to his more fantastic fiction a "quality of realism which gives the reader a kind of absolute confidence—there will be no intrusion of the author, no character will ever put a foot wrong," as Graham Greene observed; described himself as "obsessed with memory," with the mental "garbage you can't get rid of"; in his novels, attempted to come to terms with his Northern Irish past while at the same time keeping in focus his life in exile in Canada (since 1948) and the U.S. (since 1959); during the 1950s published several novels under the name Michael Bryan; in 1956 published his first novel under his own name, *The Lonely Passion of Judith Hearne*, a bitter and sad character study of a pathetic Catholic alcoholic spinster condemned to puritan Belfast's limbo; created other self-deceived misfits as protagonists in *The Feast of Lupercal* (1957) and *The Luck of Ginger Coffey* (1960) and central characters literally haunted by ghosts from their pasts in *Fergus* (1970) and *The Mangan Inheritance* (1979); told of young women in the U.S. insecure in their sexuality in *I Am Mary Dunne* (1958) and of their counterparts in Northern Ireland in *The Doctor's Wife* (1976); dealt with religious obsession in *The Temptation of Eileen Hughes* (1981) and *Cold Heaven* (1983); in *The Statement* (1996), related the story, inspired by fact, of a French Catholic war criminal who was protected in hiding for years after World War II by right-wing clergy; in 1998 published his last novel, *The Magician's Wife*, about a French magician whom Napoleon III sends to meet Muslim clerics in Algeria, with the ulterior mission of spearheading colonization; in addition to his score of novels, wrote some short stories and several screenplays, including *The Luck of Ginger Coffey* (1964) and *Torn Curtain* (1966); adapted his novel *Catholics* (1973) for television (1973) and the stage (1980); lived in Malibu, California; had a summer home in Nova Scotia; died at his home in Malibu. See *Current Biography* (January) 1986.

Obituary *New York Times* C p26 Jan. 12, 1999

MORRIS, WILLIE Nov. 29, 1934–Aug. 2, 1999 Writer; editor; a son of the old Deep South who brought to his literary journalism (along with some fiction) the complex sensibility of a man who had fought his way through the prejudices on which he was reared and whose liberalism was informed by a long historical memory; was torn, as he said, by the "old warring impulses . . . to be both Southern and American"; used his regionalism as a vantage point from which to survey the larger issues affecting American society; was born in Jackson, Mississippi, and raised in Yazoo City, on the edge of the Mississippi Delta; after graduating from the University of Texas, studied on a Rhodes scholarship at Oxford University; was editor of the muckraking magazine *Texas Observer* from 1960 to 1962; in 1963 became an associate editor of *Harper's* magazine; as editor in chief (1967–71) of *Harper's*, revitalized that magazine, America's oldest; during the 1970s, lived and wrote in Bridgehampton, New York; was writer-in-residence at the University of Mississippi from 1980 to 1991; in *North from Home* (1967), his autobiography, wrote evocatively and unsparingly about the contradictions that shaped his awareness; later published *Yazoo: Integration in a Deep-Southern Town* (1971), several books of memoirs, including *Good Old Boy: A Delta Boyhood* (1972) and *New York Days* (1993), and the collections of essays *Terrains of the Heart* (1981) and *Always Stand in Against the Curve* (1983); wrote fic-

tion that included the novel *The Last of the Southern Girls* (1973), several children's books, and the stories collected in *After All, It's Only a Game* (1992); died in Jackson, Mississippi. See *Current Biography* (January) 1976.

Obituary *New York Times* A p13 Aug. 3, 1999

MURDOCH, IRIS July 15, 1919–Feb. 8, 1999 British novelist; philosopher; a great, idiosyncratic stylist, compared by some to Henry James; as a novelist, combined realism with symbolism, masterly storytelling with the shaping of what she called "a small compact self-contained myth about the human condition"; felt an affinity for the 19th-century novelists who portrayed, in her words, "the complexity of morality and the difficulty of being good"; like those novelists, peopled her expansive plots with large casts of characters, British middle-class types involved, as she observed, in "erotic mysteries and deep dark struggles between good and evil"; placed those mainstream characters on paths land-mined with unexpected, often bizarre, occurrences; was born to Anglo-Irish parents in Dublin, Ireland; after completing her studies at Oxford and Cambridge Universities, was a tutor in philosophy at Oxford for 15 years (1948–63); meanwhile, when she was working with displaced persons in Europe for the U.N. (1944–46), met the French existentialist Jean-Paul Sartre; was attracted by Sartre's focus on individual will (but not his solipsism) and his development of philosophical ideas in fiction as well as nonfiction; wrote the critical treatise *Sartre: Romantic Realist* (1953); in her first published novel, the picaresque, semi-ribald *Under the Net* (1954), displayed a freer spirit and sense of humor than in her later fiction, with its heavy symbolic freight; in *The Flight from the Enchanter* (1956), introduced a favorite Murdoch character, the manipulative power figure, and a common Murdoch theme, the difference between the manipulators and the ostensibly free but actually manipulated on the one hand and, on the other, those who choose to maintain a freedom linked to personal responsibility and to build their autonomous identities in resistance to various contemporary "enchantments"; in *The Sandcastle* (1957) embodied such resistance in a married middle-aged schoolmaster who falls into adulterous love but chooses not to abandon his wife and family; reached a new level of sophistication in *The Bell* (1958), a labyrinthine and multiplotted excursion into complicated love relationships; in the black farce *A Severed Head* (1961), explored the amorous involvements of three emotionally vulnerable middle-class couples who seem incapable of free choice; moved from London and Home Counties settings to Ireland in *The Unicorn* (1963), a melodramatic parable about guilt, and *The Red and the Green* (1965), about two friends who find themselves on opposing sides in the Easter week rebellion in Ireland in 1916; wrote in a Gothic mode about religion, madness, and death in *The Time of Angels* (1966) and about the various faces of love in *The Nice and the Good* (1968); used violent death by natural disaster, accident, terrorism, murder, or suicide as deus ex machina plot resolutions and promulgations of the arbitrary, contingent, and unexpected in human life in such novels as *Bruno's Dream* (1969),

A Fairly Honorable Defeat (1970), *An Accidental Man* (1971), *The Black Prince* (1973), *The Sacred and Profane Love Machine* (1974), and *A Word Child* (1975); received the Booker Prize for *The Sea, the Sea* (1978), about the self-absorption of a protagonist trying to win back his childhood love; wrote 26 novels, including *Nuns and Soldiers* (1980), *The Philosopher's Pupil* (1983), *The Good Apprentice* (1985), *The Book and the Brotherhood* (1987), *The Message to the Planet* (1989), *The Green Knight* (1994), and *Jackson's Dilemma* (1995); wrote two plays and collaborated in adapting two of her novels for the stage; published, among other books of nonfiction, the essay collection *The Sovereignty of Good* (1971), two commentaries on Plato's dialogues, and the massive tome *Metaphysics as a Guide to Morals* (1992); also published a book of verse; was made a Commander of the British Empire in 1976 and a Dame of the British Empire in 1987; suffered from Alzheimer's disease in her last years, chronicled by her husband, the critic and novelist John Bayley, in his memoir *Elegy for Iris* (1999); died in Oxford, England. See *Current Biography* (August) 1980.

Obituary *New York Times* A p1+ Feb. 9, 1999

NEWLEY, ANTHONY Sep. 34, 1931–Apr. 14, 1999 British-born stage and screen actor; musical performer; writer; composer; director; in collaboration with Leslie Bricusse, wrote the book, lyrics, and music for his best-known theatrical vehicles, *Stop the World—I Want to Get Off* and *The Roar of the Greasepaint—The Smell of the Crowd*, musical tours de force for his talents at song, dance, and pantomime; was a showman of the stripe of such music-hall entertainers as George Pescud, in whom he found a mentor in childhood; was discovered at a London acting school (where he was working his way as an office boy) by the motion-picture director Geoffrey de Barkus, who cast him in the juvenile title role in his film *The Adventures of Dusty Bates* (*Dusty Baker*, according to one source); in 1951 was cast as the Artful Dodger in *Oliver Twist* (1951); later had roles in *Cockleshell Heroes* (1956) and *Fire Down Below* (1957), among other films; meanwhile, beginning in 1946, had garnered stage experience with provincial repertory companies; during the 1955–56 season in London's West End, starred in the hit revue *Cranks*, which flopped when transplanted to Broadway in November 1956; made his singing debut on screen as a conscripted rock-'n'-roll singer in *Idle on Parade* (1959); reached the top of the British popular-music charts with his recording of a song from that film, "I've Waited So Long"; also recorded "Once in a Lifetime," among other songs; as a songwriter/singer, exerted an influence on the singer David Bowie; in addition to heading the cast (as the musical's Everyman protagonist, Littlechap), directed the production of *Stop the World* that began its popular run in London's West End in 1961; took the role of Littlechap to Broadway in the 1962–63 season, with equal popular success; directed *Roar of the Greasepaint* in its inauspicious tryout run in the British provinces in 1964 but did not star (as the anti-Establishment underdog Cocky) in the musical until the following year, when it ran on Broadway from May to December following a tryout run on the

American road; later collaborated with Bricusse in writing the theme song for the film *Goldfinger* (1964) and the score for the film *Willy Wonka and the Chocolate Factory* (1971), which included the song "The Candy Man"; on screen, played the title role of a Soho gambler in debt to bookies in *The Small World of Sammy Lee* (1968) and co-starred with Rex Harrison in the musical *Doctor Doolittle* (1967) and with Joan Collins, the second of his three wives, in the musical *Can Hieronymus Merkin Ever Forget Mercy Humppe and Find True Happiness?* (1970), which he wrote, produced, and directed; after taking up permanent residence in the U.S. in 1970, performed in nightclubs and, occasionally, on television; returned to the stage with his original musical *Chaplin* (1983), which failed in its pre-Broadway road run; died at his home in Jensen Beach, Florida. See *Current Biography* (October) 1966.

Obituary *New York Times* A p23 Apr. 16, 1999

NKOMO, JOSHUA (MQABUKO NYONGOLO) June 19, 1917–July 1, 1999 Zimbabwean politician; helped to lead his country to majority rule; was born into the Kalanga tribe in the Semokwe Reserve in Matabeland in what is now Zimbabwe, a country conquered by the British South Africa Co. under Cecil Rhodes in 1897 and known under British colonial rule as Southern Rhodesia and under the white-minority breakaway government of Prime Minister Ian Smith (1964–79) as Rhodesia; after schooling in South Africa, became a social welfare worker with Rhodesian Railways; began his rise in liberation politics as leader of the railroad's African Employees Association; was elected president of the African National Congress in 1957; fled into exile in England when the congress was banned in 1959; in 1960, returned and founded the National Democratic Party; the following year, founded the Zimbabwe African People's Union (ZAPU), whose base of strength was the Ndebele tribe; was president of ZAPU until 1987; was held in various forms of imprisonment, detention, and banishment by Ian Smith's government from 1964 until 1974; after his release, traveled throughout Africa and Europe promoting ZAPU's goal of black majority rule in Rhodesia; in 1975 and 1976 represented the African National Council in negotiations with Smith regarding Rhodesia's constitutional future; at the same time, was overshadowed as a leader of guerrilla warfare by the more radical Robert Mugabe, founder of the Zimbabwe African National Union (ZANU), whose base of support was the Shona tribe; with Mugabe, formed an uneasy coalition in the Patriotic Front, which hastened the transition to a majority-ruled Zimbabwe, in 1979 and 1980; in Prime Minister Mugabe's Cabinet, was minister of home affairs (1980–81) and minister without portfolio (1981–82); after a falling-out of six years, returned to the government of Mugabe (who had since acquired the title of president) as minister in the president's office, in 1988, and vice president, in 1990; published his autobiography, *Nkomo*, in 1984; died in Harare, the capital of Zimbabwe. See *Current Biography* (April) 1976.

Obituary *New York Times* C p17 July 2, 1999

NUTTING, ANTHONY Jan. 11, 1920–Feb. 23, 1999 Former minister of state in the British Foreign Office; author; was a rising young Conservative luminary in the mid-1950s when his career was cut short by his disagreement with the government of Prime Minister Anthony Eden (his mentor) over British Suez policy; joined the British foreign service in 1940; was an attaché at the British embassy in Paris when France fell to the Germans within the same year; subsequently was assigned as third secretary to the British embassies in Madrid and Rome; in 1945 was elected a member of Parliament from the Melton division of Leicestershire; chaired the Young Conservative and Unionist Movement (1946–47) and the National Union of Conservative and Unionist Associations (1950); became undersecretary of state for foreign affairs in 1951; in that position, promoted British membership in the European Economic Community; was appointed minister of state in October 1954; in that position, led the U.K. delegation to the U.N. General Assembly and U.N. Disarmament Commission in 1954 and 1955; held the position until October 1956, when he resigned in protest of the secret British-French collusion against Egypt in the Suez crisis; after leaving politics and government in 1956, was a special correspondent for the New York Herald Tribune; broke his silence regarding the circumstances under which he resigned in 1956 in his book *No End of a Lesson* (1967); also wrote, among other books, *I Saw for Myself* (1958), *Disarmament* (1959), *Lawrence of Arabia* (1961), *The Arabs* (1964), and *Nasser* (1972); did gentleman farming on his estate in Scotland and hunting on his estate in Shropshire; died at his home in London. See *Current Biography* (February) 1955.

Obituary *New York Times* A p19 Feb. 26, 1999

OGILVY, DAVID M(ACKENZIE) June 23, 1911–July 21, 1999 British-born advertising executive; changed the look of American advertising with his striking, often iconic creations, such as "the man [with the eyepatch] in the Hathaway shirt"; began his career in advertising with the London firm of Mather & Crowther; in 1939 joined George Gallup's Audience Research Institute in Princeton, New Jersey, as associate director; in New York in 1948 co-founded the advertising agency that became known as Ogilvy, Benson & Mather, which grew into an international corporate empire with worldwide billings of $8 billion a year; attracted such clients as Wedgwood china, Guinness stout, the British Travel Association, Good Luck margarine, Dove soap, Ban deodorant, Shell oil, Sunoco, and Sears, Roebuck; created, among other memorable advertising campaigns, those for Puerto Rican tourism (in which he pictured Puerto Rico as an island paradise), Pepperidge Farm bread (tied to the image of an Amish-style horse-drawn bakery wagon), Rolls Royce automobiles ("the loudest noise . . . comes from the electric clock"), and Schweppes club soda (the carbonation of which he called "Schweppervesence"); after relinquishing leadership of his advertising agency and settling in France in 1975, remained titular head of some Ogilvy operations; died at Chateau Touffou, his home near Bonnes in France's Loire Valley. See *Current Biography* (July) 1961.

Obituary *New York Times* A p1+ July 22, 1999

PAKULA, ALAN J(AY) Apr. 7, 1928–Nov. 19, 1998 Motion-picture director; producer; scenarist; was not so much an auteur as an actor's director, described by Harrison Ford, the co-star of his last film, *The Devil's Own* (1997), as "a natural guide" in drawing emotion from "inner realms"; was skilled at creating psychological moods and overtones, often with music or taped conversation (as in the sexy 1971 crime thriller *Klute*, one of his major popular and critical directorial successes); with an avowed "oblique" approach to filmmaking, worked "on many levels"; after his first effort as a producer, *Fear Strikes Out* (1957), collaborated as producer with the director of that film, Robert Mulligan, on six subsequent pictures, beginning with *To Kill a Mockingbird* (1962) and including *Up the Down Staircase* (1967); made his own debut as a director with *The Sterile Cuckoo* (1969), which he also produced; entered his period of greatest directorial prominence with *All the President's Men*, which was the top-grossing film of 1976 and won more Academy Awards (four) than any of his other movies; in addition to directing, wrote the screenplays for *Sophie's Choice* (1982), *See You in the Morning* (1989), *Presumed Innocent* (1990), and *The Pelican Brief* (1993); directed a total of 16 films, including *Love and Pain and the Whole Damn Thing* (1972), *The Parallax View* (1974), *Comes a Horseman* (1978), *Starting Over* (1979), *Rollover* (1981), *Dream Lover* (1986), and *Orphans* (1987); died in an unusual vehicular accident on the Long Island Expressway near Melville, New York, when a metal pipe pierced the windshield of the station wagon he was driving and struck him in the head. See *Current Biography* (June) 1980.

Obituary *New York Times* B p11 Nov. 20, 1998

PAPADOPOULOS, GEORGE May 5, 1919–June 27, 1999 Greek army officer (retired); politician; headed a military dictatorship in Greece from 1967 to 1973; as a young commissioned officer, was a platoon leader in the Greek-Italian war of 1940–41; fought in the resistance movement during the German occupation of Greece later in World War II; after the war, saw action against Communist guerrillas in Greece; later served with the army's intelligence bureau and with the Greek Central Intelligence Service; was promoted to colonel in 1960; was appointed to the third staff bureau of the army general staff in August 1966; on April 21, 1967, when Greece was in the midst of a governmental crisis and awaiting an election (which a leftist majority was expected to win), led a successful, bloodless coup d'état; headed a three-man ruling junta until December 1967, when, relinquishing military rank, he took over as prime minister and minister of defense; subsequently assumed the additional portfolios of education (1969) and foreign affairs (1970) and the title of regent (1972); was president from July 1972 until November 1973, when he was ousted by a new military clique; was arrested in 1974; the following year, was found guilty of high treason and insurrection and sentenced to death (later commuted to life imprisonment); died in a hospital in Athens, Greece. See *Current Biography* (February) 1970.

Obituary *New York Times* B p8 June 28, 1999

POWELL, J. ENOCH June 16, 1912–Feb. 8, 1998 British politician; classical scholar; linguist, author; best known for his extreme, xenophobic, right-wing political positions; following a fellowship at Cambridge University, was a professor of Greek at the University of Sydney, Australia (1937–39); in those early years, published two books of verse and several books establishing him as an authority on Heroditus, Thucidydes, and the medieval Welsh legal code; after service as a British army staff officer in World War II, became joint head of the home affairs section of the Conservative Party's parliamentary secretariat and research department (1946–49); was a Conservative member of Parliament from Wolverhampton South West in Staffordshire (1950–74); served as parliamentary secretary to the Ministry of Housing and Local Government (1955–57), financial secretary to the Treasury (1957–58), and Minister of Health (1960–63); at a Conservative Party meeting in Birmingham in 1968, gave the "rivers of blood" address for which he would ever thereafter be best known, an inflammatory speech in which he called for a stanching of the influx of nonwhite immigrants from former British colonies and a program of grants to encourage those already in Britain to return to their home countries; shortly thereafter was dismissed from the Conservative Party's shadow Cabinet by Edward Heath, the party's leader; in 1974 left the Conservative party to protest Britain's entry into the Common Market; joined Northern Ireland's Ulster Unionist Party; represented Ulster constituencies in Parliament for most of the period from 1974 to 1987; was the author, co-author, or editor of more than a score of books, including *Collected Poems* (1990), *Reflections of a Statesman* (1991), and *The Evolution of the Gospel* (1994); died in London. See *Current Biography* (November) 1964.

Obituary *New York Times* A p17 Feb. 9, 1998

POWERS, J(AMES) F(ARL) July 8, 1917–June 12, 1999 Author; a midwestern fictionist who wrote chiefly about Catholic priests, with compassion and devastating wit; was described by fellow novelist Mary Gordon as "an absolutely masterful comedian and satirist with a very gentle and delicate touch" and "precision of form"; as a conscientious objector during World War II, was imprisoned for more than a year and worked as a hospital orderly for another year; in 1943 published his first significant short story, "Lions, Harts, Leaping Does," about an old and dying Franciscan friar whose overly scrupulous sense of his own spiritual unworthiness is subtly contrasted with the real spiritual insensitivity and emptinesss of the world around him; later wrote "He Don't Plant Cotton," a story, set in a jazz night club in Chicago, that was years ahead of its time in its civil rights sensibility; included those stories in his collection *Prince of Darkness* (1947), along with two other pieces about racial tension and several dealing with spiritual anguish and the propinquity of God and mammon in ostensibly religious lives; was widely hailed, in the words of Hayden Carruth, as "a new writer—a Northern writer, a Midwestern writer—whose stories carried as much creative authority as did the Southern writing that had dominated American fiction for three decades," displaying "the same structural finesse and verbal sensitivity [and] the same concern for ultimate value, now transplanted to a milieu in which some Southern critics had contended it could never flourish"; in his second collection, *The Presence of Grace* (1956), brought together nine stories, including several about the subversion of church clergy and hierarchy by the lure of status, power, and popular success, two narrated by rectory cats, and one ("The Devil Was the Joker") about a reprobate traveling salesman who makes the rounds of Catholic parishes hawking a Catholic magazine and such items as rosaries, scapulars, and religious medals; won the 1963 National Book Award for his first novel, *Morte d'Urban*, the cautionary tale of Father Urban Roche, a well-intentioned fund-raiser for the Order of St. Clement whose zealous wheeling and dealing turns a religious center into a golf course and reduces the cleric's own perception of his priesthood to "the easiest way to stay in the best hotels, to meet the best people," as Mary Gordon observed; in 1975 published *How the Fish Live*, a collection of 10 stories, including "Farewell"; wrote a second novel, *Wheat that Springeth Green* (1988), in which he traces the uncertain spiritual journey of the self-doubting protagonist, Joe Hackett, through seminary and priesthood; between 1951 and 1975 lived with his wife and children on and off in Ireland; taught part-time at St. John's University in Collegeville, Minnesota, for many years; died at his home in Collegeville. See *Current Biography* (January) 1989.

Obituary *New York Times* C p23 June 17, 1999

PUZO, MARIO Oct. 15, 1920–July 2, 1999 Author; wrote novels about power, its social and psychological bases, and its tendency to corrupt, especially when bolstered by terror; is best known for his chivalric saga about a proud Mafia family, the Corleones, a trilogy that began with *The Godfather*, was continued in *The Last Don*, and is concluded in *Omerta*, scheduled for publication in the year 2000; was the son of immigrants from Naples, Italy; served with the U.S. Army in Germany during and immediately after World War II; in 1950 published his first piece of fiction, the short story "The Last Christmas"; five years later published his first novel, *Dark Arena*, set in occupied Germany, in which he graphically described the dehumanizing effects of war on both conquerors and conquered; in the early 1960s contributed action and adventure fiction to such men's magazines as *Stag* and *Male*; later contributed to *Redbook* and *Holiday*; in 1965 published his second novel, *The Fortunate Pilgrim*, a semiautobiographical story about first and second generation Italian-Americans in New York City in the 1920s and 1930s; the following year, published the juvenile novel *The Runaway Summer of Davie Shaw*; began the story of the immigrant Corleones and their adaptation into a U.S. subculture with its own outlaw code of honor in *The Godfather* (1969), which became one of the most commercially successful books in publishing history (with sales of more than 21 million copies internationally) and inspired the phenomenally successful motion picture *The Godfather* (1972); with director Francis Ford Coppola, won Academy Awards for the screenplays for that film and its sequel, *The Godfather Part II*; was also credited with co-writing the screenplay for *The Godfather Part III* (1990); co-wrote the screenplays for the films *Earthquake* (1974), *Superman* (1978), and *Superman II* (1981); in the novel *Fools Die* (1978), set in Las Vegas, imitated the form of an Arthurian romance in tracing connections among the motion-picture industry, publishing, and big-time gambling in the "new Camelot" of America; touched peripherally on the Corleones' background in Sicily in *The Sicilian* (1984), brought to the screen in 1987; subsequently published *The Fourth K*, about a Kennedy who becomes president of the U.S. in the next century; in 1996 published *The Last Don*, which was made into a six-hour television miniseries in 1997; collected some of his short stories, book reviews, and articles in *The Godfather Papers & Other Confessions* (1972); died at his home in Bay Shore, New York. See *Current Biography* (March) 1975.

Obituary *New York Times* B p7 July 3, 1999

QUINTERO, JOSÉ Oct. 15, 1924–Feb. 26, 1999 Panamanian-born stage director; almost single-handedly, revived popular and critical interest in playwright Eugene O'Neill with his inspired, imaginative stagings of O'Neill's work; nurtured the acting careers of Jason Robards and Geraldine Page; after training at the Goodman Theatre Dramatic School in Chicago, moved east and co-founded a troupe called the Loft Players; with members of that troupe, established the Circle in the Square, an arena stage in Greenwich Village, in 1951; along with the Circle in the Square itself, was credited with helping to accelerate a renaissance in Off Broadway theater, beginning with his acclaimed revival in 1952 of Tennessee Williams's *Summer and Smoke*, which had failed on Broadway; next, revived Truman Capote's *The Grass Harp*, again with more success than the original Broadway production had enjoyed; subsequently directed the premiere of Victor Wolfson's *American Gothic*; 10 years after the last production of an O'Neill play in the U.S., revived with éclat *The Iceman Cometh*, with Jason Robards in the role of Hickey, in a production that opened at the Circle in the Square in May 1956; traveling uptown, won plaudits for his direction of the premiere of O'Neill's *Long Day's Journey into Night* on Broadway (1956–57); by 1961 had directed 17 of the 21 plays presented at the Circle in the Square, including Brendan Behan's *The Hostage* (1954) and *The Quare Fellow* (1958) and Thornton Wilder's *Our Town* (1959); directed O'Neill's *Strange Interlude* at the Actors Studio Theater in 1963; won a Tony Award as best director for his hit 1972 Broadway production of O'Neill's *A Moon for the Misbegotten*; left New York after the failure of his production of Tennessee Williams's last play, *Clothes for a Summer House*, in 1980; between 1956 and 1996 directed 19 O'Neill productions, including stagings of *Hughie* (1964), *More Stately Mansions* (1967), *A Touch of the Poet* (1977), a touring production of *The Iceman Cometh* with Jason Robards (1985), a Broadway revival of *Long Day's Journey Into Night* (1988), and a production of the one-act plays *The Long Voyage Home* and *Ile* in Provincetown, Massachusetts, where they had been written; wrote an autobiography, *If You Don't Dance,*

They Shoot You (1972); died in Sarasota, Florida. See *Current Biography* (April) 1954.

Obituary *New York Times* A p12 Feb. 27, 1999

REESE, PEE WEE July 23, 1919–Aug. 14, 1999 Major-league baseball player; a righthanded shortstop who was an outstanding fielder and base runner during 16 years with the Brooklyn (later Los Angeles) Dodgers; contributed significantly to Brooklyn's winning of seven National League pennants, six of them between 1947 and 1956, and one world championship; made the league All-Star team nine times; was inducted into the Baseball Hall of Fame in 1984; began playing professionally with the Louisville Colonels in the minor-league American Association in 1938; moved up to the Brooklyn Dodgers in 1940; in 1941, with another young Brooklyn player, outfielder Pete Reiser, sparked the Dodgers to their first pennant in 21 years; led National League shortstops in putouts in both 1941 (346) and 1942 (337); in 1942 also led in assists (482) and double plays (104); joined the U.S. Navy after the 1942 season; played on naval teams from 1943 through 1945; returned to the Dodgers for the 1946 season, when he set a new fielding record for Brooklyn shortstops with an average of .966; in 1947, tied for most bases on balls (104) in the National League; through his conspicuous camaraderie with Brooklyn's new 1947 recruit Jackie Robinson (described in Roger Kahn's classic baseball book *The Boys of Summer*), eased the racial integration of major-league baseball; beginning in 1948, when Robinson moved from first base to second, joined with him to produce many double plays (106 in 1951); in 1949 led all league players in runs (132) and league shortstops in putouts (316) and fielding average (.977); became team captain in 1950; led the league in stolen bases (30) in 1952; after participating in five World Series defeats at the hands of the New York Yankees, made the assist (a throw to Gil Hodges for an out at first) that clinched victory over the Yankees in game seven of the 1955 World Series; moved with the Dodgers to Los Angeles after the 1957 season; played his last season in 1958; had regular-season major-league career totals including a batting average of .269 in 8,058 at-bats, a .377 slugging average, 1,338 runs, 885 runs batted in, and 232 stolen bases; in 2,166 games, had a fielding average of .962; made 4,124 putouts and 6,131 assists; was a Dodger coach in 1959; briefly did television broadcasting; later worked for Hillerich & Bradsby, manufacturers of Louisville Slugger bats; died at his home in Louisville, Kentucky. See *Current Biography* (June) 1950.

Obituary *New York Times* B p7 Aug. 16, 1999

ROBINSON, SPOTTSWOOD W[ILLIAM] 3d July 26, 1916–Oct. 11, 1998 Civil-rights lawyer; judge; educator; after graduating from Howard University's law school, in 1939, taught law at Howard and practiced law in Virginia; in 1948 became legal representative in Virginia for the legal defense and educational fund of the National Association for the Advancement of Colored People; three years later was appointed Southeast legal counsel for the NAACP fund; argued before the U.S. Supreme Court one of the five cases leading to the court's 1954 decision in

Brown v. Board of Education outlawing racial segregation in U.S. public schools; in 1960 returned to the Howard University law school as professor and dean; was a judge of the U.S. district court in the District of Columbia from 1964 to 1966; was elevated to the U.S. court of appeals for the District of Columbia in 1966; was chief judge from 1981 to 1986: retired from the court of appeals in 1989; died at his home in Richmond, Virginia. See *Current Biography* (March) 1962.

Obituary *New York Times* B p11 Oct. 13, 1998

ROUNTREE, MARTHA 1911–Aug. 23, 1999 Radio and television producer; co-creator of the weekly Washington-based NBC public-affairs interview show *Meet the Press*, the pioneer among network political talk formats and the longest-running series of any kind on television, still in NBC's Sunday lineup in 1999, half a century after its inception; early in her career was a newspaper reporter in her native Florida; after moving to New York City, wrote advertising copy and did freelance writing, some of it for *American Mercury*, then published and edited by Lawrence E. Spivak; became a roving editor of *American Mercury*; with Spivak, launched *Meet the Press* on radio in 1945 and took it to network television two years later; was the original moderator of the television program, on which a panel of reporters questioned a public figure; beginning in 1951 also moderated the television public-affairs discussion show *The Big Issue* (originally titled *Keep Posted*); independently of Spivak, produced the distaff talk show *Leave It to the Girls*, on radio beginning in 1940 and on television beginning in 1949; after parting ways with Spivak and leaving *Meet the Press*, moderated *Press Conference* (1956–57), which had a similar format; became a popular lecturer; founded Leadership, a Washington nonprofit political-research foundation, in 1965; was president of the foundation until 1988; died in Washington, D.C. See *Current Biography* (February) 1957.

Obituary *New York Times* B p7 Aug. 25, 1999

SARGENT, FRANCIS W(ILLIAMS) July 29, 1915–Oct. 22, 1998 Republican governor of Massachusetts (1969–75); early in his career, as the owner of a sporting goods store and charter-boat service for fishermen on Cape Cod, waged a crusade against commercial use of illegal nets for mass catches; was Massachusetts state director of marine fisheries from 1947 to 1957; concurrently, served as U.S. commissioner on the International Commission for the Northwest Atlantic Fisheries; over the following years, was Massachusetts state commissioner of natural resources, chairman of the water resources commission, director of the division of fisheries and game, and commissioner of public works; also directed a federal outdoor recreation resources commission; was elected lieutenant governor of Massachusetts in 1966; succeeded John A. Volpe as governor when Volpe became U.S. secretary of transportation in January 1969; won a full term as governor in his own right when he defeated Kevin White in the gubernatorial election of 1970; inheriting an overextended budget from the Volpe regime, tightened Medicaid and other "entitlement" rules and introduced a new

state corporate tax; promoted or supported the building of several housing projects, a no-fault insurance law, a "freedom of choice" school-busing plan, and a legislative statement against the Vietnam War; in his bid for reelection in 1974, was defeated by Michael Dukakis; died at his home in Dover, Massachusetts. See *Current Biography* (June) 1971.

Obituary *New York Times* C p23 Oct. 23, 1998

SAYÃO, BIDÚ May 11, 1905(?)–Mar. 12, 1999 Brazilian coloratura soprano; made her concert debut at the Teatro Municipal in Rio de Janeiro in 1925; made her operatic debut in the role of Rosina in *The Barber of Seville* at the Teatro Reale in Rome in 1936; subsequently sang at the Paris Opera, La Scala, and the Royal Opera House of Brazil; made her first appearance in the U.S. in a recital in New York City in 1935; participated in an all-Debussy concert by the New York Philharmonic Symphony Orchestra under Arturo Toscanini in 1936; made her American operatic debut as Manon at the Metropolitan Opera House in 1937; subsequently at the Metropolitan, sang Violetta in *La Traviata* and Mimi in *La Bohème;* ultimately gave more than 200 performances of 12 different roles at the Met; resigned from the Met in 1952; retired following a concert performance of Debussy's *La Demoiselle Élue* in 1957; died in Rockport, Maine. See *Current Biography* (February) 1942.

Obituary *New York Times* A p13 Mar. 13, 1999

SCOTT, GEORGE C(AMPBELL) Oct. 18, 1927–Sep. 22, 1999 Actor; an intense, granite-faced, raspy-voiced performer who crafted a range of characters with intuitive bravura; with his air of irascibility and menace, rose to fame chiefly as a chilling heavy in the late 1950s and early 1960s but went on to win recognition as one of the most powerful all-around actors in American theater (his preferred venue), film, and television; was most closely identified with his epic portrayal of General George S. Patton Jr. in the motion picture *Patton* (1970), for which he won an Academy Award for best actor; refused to accept that award because he considered the politics of the Oscar competition professionally "demeaning"; in the following year, refused to accept an Emmy awarded him for his performance in a television production of Arthur Miller's drama *The Price*; discovered his vocation as an actor when, while studying journalism at the University of Missouri, he was cast as Sir Robert Morton in *The Winslow Boy*; in his words, he "became an actor to escape [his] own personality"; between 1953 and 1956 traveled widely playing in stock productions and, between roles, supporting himself with manual work, chiefly in construction; in New York Shakespeare Festival productions, stunned critics with his interpretations of the title role in *Richard III* (1957) and Jacques in *As You Like It* (1958); later played Shylock in *The Merchant of Venice* (1962); also Off-Broadway, was Lord Wainwright in *Children of Darkness* (1958) and Ephraim Cabot in a revival of *Desire Under the Elms* (1962–63); on Broadway, made his debut as Tydings Glen in *Comes a Day* (1958), played the prosecuting judge advocate in *The Andersonville Trial* (1959–60), portrayed a heroic Warsaw Jewish resistance leader in *The Wall* (1960–61), and starred (with

Maureen Stapleton) in Neil Simon's three-play comedy *Plaza Suite* (1967–69); made his motion-picture debut as the loathsome zealot Grubb in the Western *The Hanging Tree* (1959); subsequently was cast in such screen roles as the relentless prosecuting attorney in *Anatomy of a Murder* (1959), the cunning high-stakes poolroom bookie Bert Gordon in *The Hustler* (1961), the fanatic Commie-hating and nuclear-bomb-loving General Buck Turgidson in the apocalyptic, antimilitary, black satire *Dr. Strangelove* (1964), Abraham in *The Bible* (1966), and Dr. Herbert Bock in *The Hospital* (1971); directed as well as acted in the motion pictures *Rage* (1972) and *The Savage Is Loose* (1974); returned to Broadway triumphantly as Willy Loman in a revival of *Death of a Salesman* (1975); later on Broadway, played an old curmudgeon in *On Borrowed Time* (1991) and the Clarence Darrow–based character in a revival of *Inherit the Wind* (1996); began accruing credits in television drama in the late 1950s; starred as Neil Brock, a morally indignant and angry social worker in the slums of New York City in *East Side, West Side* (1963–64), a gritty television dramatic series, filmed on location, that was ahead of its time in its realistic approach to social problems; played the fictional U.S. chief executive in the situation comedy *Mr. President* (1987–88); in later television productions, was cast in more than a dozen roles, including Fagin in *Oliver Twist* (1982), Scrooge in *A Christmas Carol* (1984), and the title role in *The Last Days of Patton* (1986); won an Emmy for his supporting role in a new television production of *Twelve Angry Men* (1997); in private life, admitted to bouts with alcoholism; was married and divorced four times (twice to and from the actress Colleen Dewhurst) before settling into his last marriage, to Trish Van Devere; had five children, including the actors Devon Scott and Campbell Scott; died in his office in Westlake Village, California. See *Current Biography* (April) 1971.

Obituary *New York Times* A p1+ Sep. 24, 1999

SEABORG, GLENN T. Apr. 19, 1912–Feb. 25, 1999 Nuclear chemist; educator; chairman, U.S. Atomic Energy Commission (1961–71); director emeritus, Lawrence Berkeley National Laboratory (formerly the Lawrence Radiation Laboratory, University of California); viewed himself as a practitioner of "nuclear alchemy," the transmutation of atomic elements; with his associates, helped usher in the age of nuclear energy by discovering plutonium and most of the other transuranium elements; for his success in producing high-energy-yielding artificial elements by bombarding natural elements with heavy ions in a giant cyclotron accelerator built by Albert Ghiorso, shared the 1951 Nobel Prize in chemistry with Edwin M. McMillan; after earning his Ph.D. degree at the University of California, Berkeley in 1937, remained there, teaching and researching the isotopes of common elements; in 1940 and 1941, with his colleagues, made discoveries, including plutonium 94 and 239 and the fissionable isotope of uranium, U-233, that opened the way for the standard production of nuclear fuel through the accelerated conversion of uranium 238 into plutonium; after the U.S. entered World War II, did his research at the metallurgical laboratory of the University of Chica-

go, where members of the secret Manhattan Project were concentrating on the creation of the atomic bomb; at Chicago, devised and put into operation a process essential to the Manhattan Project's success, an ultramicrochemical way of separating plutonium from uranium; in 1944 and 1945 participated in research that established the existence of two new elements, americium (number 95) and curium (number 96); with the rank of full professor, returned to Berkeley in May 1946 to teach and direct nuclear chemical research at the Lawrence Radiation Laboratory; proved the existence of berkelium (number 97) in 1949, californium (number 98) in 1950, einsteinium (number 99) in 1952, fermium (number 100) in 1953, mendelevium (number 101) in 1955, and nobelium (number 102) in 1958; was chancellor of the University of California, Berkeley from 1958 until 1961; returned to Berkeley after leaving the chairmanship of the U.S. Atomic Energy Commission; in 1974 was honored by the discoverers of element 106 when they named it seaborgium; died in Lafayette, California. See *Current Biography* (December) 1961.

Obituary *New York Times* A p1+ Feb. 27, 1999

SEMON, WALDO LONSBURY Sep. 10, 1898–May 26, 1999 Chemist; as head of the B. F. Goodrich Co.'s laboratory in Akron, Ohio, beginning in the late 1920s, led research resulting in several landmark advances in polymer chemistry; found ways to preserve rubber against aging and cracking; succeeded in polymerizing vinyl chloride to form PVC (polyvinyl chloride), patented in 1933 as Koroseal, an amazingly versatile plastic, used widely in building materials, medical equipment, automobile interiors, and numerous other industrial and consumer-product applications; invented the petroleum-based product marketed by Goodrich under the trade name Ameripol (1940), the first of the rubber-like synthetics produced in the U.S. that was capable of replacing natural rubber in the manufacture of tires for military and civilian vehicles, waterproof fabrics, and myriad other products; retired from his position with the B. F. Goodrich Co. in 1963; subsequently was a research professor at Kent State University, in Ohio; was inducted into the National Inventors Hall of Fame in 1995; died in Hudson, Ohio. See *Current Biography* (Yearbook) 1940.

Obituary *New York Times* B p11 May 28, 1999

SHAW, ROBERT Apr. 30, 1916–Jan. 25, 1999 Choral and orchestral conductor; music director emeritus and laureate conductor of the Atlanta Symphony Orchestra; was admired for his precision and discipline, especially in realizing his concept of the vocal ensemble as a single instrument; as a young man, matriculated at Ponoma College in Claremont, California, with the intention of becoming a Christian evangelical minister; changed his vocational aspiration to music during the course of his undergraduate studies; extracurricularly conducted the college glee club, in a way that impressed Fred Waring, the popular radio band-cum-chorus leader, when Waring visited the campus; upon obtaining his B.A. degree, in 1938, joined the Waring organization; reorganized the Fred Waring Glee Club and directed it until 1945; found opportunity for a less commercial, more classical repertory working with a racially diverse amateur group of 200 young singers at the Marble Collegiate Church in New York City; developed that group into the nonprofit Collegiate Chorale, which he directed from 1942 to 1960; in 1948 created the Robert Shaw Chorale, a professional company of singers augmented by a small orchestra; with that ensemble, toured the U.S., Europe, and South America until 1965, performing both secular and religious choral masterpieces and the best of American black spirituals and folk music; beginning in 1956 was a guest conductor and choral consultant with leading orchestras; was music director of the Atlanta Symphony Orchestra from 1967 until 1988; founded the Atlanta Symphony Chamber Orchestra in 1967 and the Atlanta Symphony Orchestra Chorus in 1970; remained close to both even after his formal retirement; made his final appearance on the podium conducting Bach's Mass in B Minor at Carnegie Hall, in New York City, in April 1998; devoted much of his energy to the recording of choral classics by Handel, Poulenc, Stravinsky, Verdi, Bartók, Barber, and Vaughn Williams, among others; between 1961 and 1989 won 14 Grammy Awards; died in New Haven, Connecticut, where he was visiting one of his sons at Yale University. See *Current Biography* (July) 1966.

Obituary *New York Times* A p21 Jan. 26, 1999

SIDNEY, SYLVIA Aug. 8, 1910–July 1, 1999 Actress; perhaps best remembered, to her dismay, for the screen roles of vulnerable and victimized working-class heroines in which she was repeatedly cast during the Depression era; began acting professionally on the stage in 1926; made her Broadway debut as Anita in *The Squall* in 1927; over the next four years, was cast in several leading roles on Broadway, most impressively as the young wife in *Bad Girl* (1930); acquired her first screen credit as the screaming courtroom witness in *Thru Different Eyes* (1929); after settling in Hollywood, was cast as Roberta Alden in *An American Tragedy* (1931), wrongly imprisoned young women in *City Streets* (1931) and *Ladies of the Big House* (1932), the unwed mother in *Confessions of a Coed* (1931), an ex-convict in *Pick Up* (1933), Rose Maurrant in *Street Scene* (1931), a struggling chorus girl in *Good Dame* (1934), and the title role in *Mary Burns, Fugitive* (1935); against type, was cast in the title role of *Madame Butterfly* (1932) and in light roles in such comedies as *Thirty-Day Princess* (1934) and *Accent on Youth* (1935); was cast as June Tolliver in the backwoods melodrama *Trail of the Lonesome Pine* (1936); gave outstanding performances in the leading female roles in Fritz Lang's passionate social-protest movies *Fury* (1936) and *You Only Live Once* (1937), William Wyler's *Dead End* (1937), and Alfred Hitchcock's *Sabotage* (1937); was cast as Helen Dennis in Lang's *You and Me* (1938); returned to Broadway to star in *To Quito and Back* in 1937; played Eliza Doolittle in *Pygmalian* in summer stock in 1938; back on Broadway, participated in a Group Theater production of *The Gentle People* in 1939 and triumphed as Bella Manningham in *Angel Street* during the 1941–42 season; later toured in *Joan of Lorraine*, *Anne of the Thousand Days*, and *Black Chiffon*, among other productions;

toured with the National Repertory Company in the 1960s; on Broadway, created Mrs. Kolowitz in comedy *Enter Laughing* (1963), played Mrs. Banks in *Barefoot in the Park* (1967), and portrayed Mrs. Wire in *Vieux Carré* (1977); was seen in numerous character roles in television dramas; played Mrs. Carlson in the TV situation comedy *WKRP in Cincinnati* (1978); returned to motion pictures only seven times between 1941 and 1956; after an absence of 19 years from the big screen, was nominated for an Oscar for her role as Mrs. Pritchett in *Summer Wishes, Winter Dreams* (1973); in a second career, did needlepoint, sold her original needlepoint designs in kits, and wrote two books on the craft; was married, in succession, to Bennett Cerf, Luther Adler, and Carlton Alsop; died in Manhattan. See *Current Biography* (October) 1981.

Obituary *New York Times* C p16 July 2, 1999

SOLDATI, MARIO Nov. 17, 1906–June 19, 1999 Italian author; motion-picture director; scenarist; poet; began his career as an art critic in Turin; published *Salmace*, a collection of short stories, in 1929; was a correspondent for a Genoa newspaper while studying and teaching in the U.S. on a fellowship (1929–31); later wrote an affectionate memoir of his experiences in the U.S., *America primo amore* (1945); began writing and collaborating on movie scenarios in 1931; wrote about that experience in his book *24 ore in uno studio cinematografico* (1936); began directing and co-directing films (many of which he co-wrote) in 1938; made his most important contribution to the Italian cinema in the early 1940s, with such intelligent films as *Piccolo mondo antico* (1940) and *Malombra* (1942); directed a total of about 30 films, including *Led misere del Signor Travel* (1945), *Danielle Corgis* (1946), *La provincials* (1952), and *La donna del fume* (1955); was the second-unit director of the American-Italian co-productions of *War and Peace* (1956) and *Ben Hur* (1959); in the book *Fuga in Italian* (1947), recounted the period in 1943 when he went into hiding from the German Nazis in wartime Italy; covered the same experience fictionally in his novella *La giacca verde* (1948), which was translated into English as *The Green Jacket* and published along with two other novellas under the titles *The Commander Comes to Dine* (1952) and *Dinner with the Commendatore* (1953); in 1954 received the Premio Strega for his novel *Led Lettere da Capri*; in the novel *La Confessione* (1955), translated as *The Confession* (1958), described the internal crisis of an adolescent boy aspiring to become a Jesuit priest; in 1970 won the Campiello Prize for *L'Attore* (The Actor), a fictional excursion into the psychology of evil; made some television documentaries and wrote television criticism; died at his home in Tellaro, near Spezia, Italy. See *Current Biography* (April) 1958.

Obituary *New York Times* C p27 June 23, 1999

STADER, MARIA 1911–Apr. 27, 1999 Hungarian-born Swiss singer; a lyric soprano known for her purity and delicacy of style and consummate mastery of technique; generally limited her performances (even of operatic roles) to the concert stage and the recording studio; won first prize at the International

Music Competition in Geneva in 1939; beginning in 1945, was in demand at the music centers and concert halls of Europe; appeared by request with conductors Wilhelm Furtwängler in Berlin and Vienna, Otto Klemperer and the Concertgebouw Orchestra in Amsterdam and London, and Sir Malcolm Sargent in London, among others; sang at the great music festivals, including Salzburg and Prades; was awarded the Lilli Lehmann Medal by the Salzburg Mozarteum in 1950; in her New York debut, in 1954, sang Mozart's "Exultate Jubilate" and Scarlatti's "Cantata a voce sola con violini e tromba" with the Little Orchestra Society; in later American appearances, sang lieder by Schumann and Mendelssohn, songs by Mozart and Othmar Schoeck, and Mozart's Mass in C Minor; in a tour of Israel with the Israeli Philharmonic Orchestra in 1956, presented 22 concert performances of Donizetti's *Lucia di Lammermoor* and Handel's *Judas Maccabaeus*; at the Berlin Festival in 1957 gave a concert performance of Gluck's *Orfeo ed Euridice*; again won the Lilli Lehmann Medal in 1965; in her farewell performance as a concert soloist in New York in 1969, sang Mozart's Requiem; compiled a large discography, which included performances of Verdi's Requiem, Brahms's *German Requiem*, and Rossini's *Stabat Mater* and her interpretations of Pamina in Mozart's *The Magic Flute* and Constanze in Mozart's *The Abduction from the Seraglio*, among other operatic roles; after her retirement as a performer, settled down to teaching in Zurich; wrote an autobiography, *Nehmt Meinen Dank* ("Accept My Thanks") and a book on Bach arias; died in Zurich, Switzerland. See *Current Biography* (July) 1958.

Obituary *New York Times* A p27 May 3, 1999

STAHR, ELVIS J(ACOB), JR. Mar. 9, 1916–Nov. 11, 1998 U.S. secretary of the army (1961–62); educator; lawyer; practiced corporate and banking law in New York City before and after his service with the U.S. Army in World War II; in 1947 joined the law faculty of the University of Kentucky, where he became dean of the college of law in 1948; on academic leave, served as special assistant for reserve forces to the secretary of the army (1951–52); was consultant to the assistant secretary of the army for manpower and reserve forces (1953) and executive director of a presidential committee studying post-secondary education (1956); meanwhile, in 1954 was named provost of the University of Kentucky and dean of that university's school of law; subsequently was vice chancellor of the University of Pittsburgh (1957–59) and president of West Virginia University (beginning in 1959); in 1968 became president of the National Audubon Society; in that position, helped to protect the Florida Everglades against excessive commercial and industrial development; participated in discussions regarding the environmental effects of dams and other water projects, and contributed to international discussions regarding international whaling agreements; oversaw a quadrupling of the Audubon Society's membership; after retiring as president of the Audubon Society in 1981, practiced private law in Connecticut; died in Greenwich, Connecticut. See *Current Biography* (September) 1961.

Obituary *New York Times* C p16 Nov. 14, 1998

STANKY, EDDIE Sep. 3, 1917–June 6, 1999 Major-league baseball player; manager; known as "the Brat"; a small, pugnacious competitor whose physical talent as a player was less extraordinary than his aggressive team spirit, his hustle, and his ability to psych his opponents; with his shrewd judgment of balls and strikes and his facility for "spoiling" pitches, set a new National League record for walks (in 1945); began playing infield positions professionally, in the minor leagues, in 1935; was voted the most valuable player in the American Association in 1942; the following year, was called up to the National League as a shortstop by the Chicago Cubs; subsequently played second base with the Brooklyn Dodgers (1944–47), the Boston Braves (1948–49), and the New York Giants (1950–51); was playing manager of the St. Louis Cardinals in 1952 and 1953; in 1945 led National League second basemen in runs (128) and all major-league second basemen in bases on balls (148); in 1946 led National League second basemen in bases on balls (137), putouts (356), and double plays (88); in 1947 again led in double plays; in 1950 led National League second basemen in putouts (407) and assists (418) and all major-league second basemen in bases on balls (144); in 11 years of regular-season major-league play, had a batting average of .268, a fielding average of .974, and career totals of 811 runs and 996 walks; in Charles F. Faber's all-time ratings, ranked 36th among National League second basemen; after retiring as a player, continued managing the Cardinals through the 1955 season; managed the Chicago White Sox in the American League from 1966 through 1968; coached baseball at the University of South Alabama from 1969 to 1983; returned to the major leagues as manager of the Texas Rangers for one day in June 1977; as a major-league manager, compiled a record of 467 wins, 435 losses, and four ties; died in Faithhope, Alabama. See *Current Biography* (June) 1951.

Obituary *New York Times* B p10 June 7, 1999

STEELMAN, JOHN R(OY) June 23, 1900–July 14, 1999 Economist; labor-management mediator; government official; was assistant to President Harry S. Truman; after army service in World War I, traveled across the U.S. hobo style, working as a migrant field worker and logger; subsequently earned several degrees, including a doctorate in sociology and economics; while teaching sociology and economics at Alabama College in Montevallo, Alabama, mediated an industrial dispute in Mobile; in 1934 joined the U.S. Conciliation Service; became director of the service in 1937; oversaw the handling of thousands of management-labor disputes, 95 percent of which were resolved without strikes; as a member of a three-man panel in one major dispute, at the U.S. Steel Corp. in December 1941, personally cast the deciding vote in favor of a union shop for the United Mine Workers; worked as a public relations consultant in New York City for several months after leaving the Conciliation Service, in November 1944; after Harry S. Truman succeeded to the presidency upon the death of Franklin D. Roosevelt, in April 1945, returned to Washington as an adviser to Secretary of Labor Lewis B. Schwellenbach; played a leading role in settling a railroad strike in May 1946; became director of the Office of War Mobilization and Reconversion in June 1946; in December 1946, when President Truman issued an executive order dissolving some wartime agencies and consolidating others, was appointed by Truman to the new post of assistant to the president, with the specific function of "coordinating federal agency programs and policies"; in Truman's absences (during the 1948 presidential election campaign, for example), had hands-on responsibility for White House operations; among many other missions as Truman's troubleshooter, helped to avert a nationwide railroad strike in 1950; as ad hoc head of the Office of Defense Mobilization in 1952, settled a United Steel Workers strike; after leaving government in 1953, was a director of the Audio-Dynamics Corp. and a trustee of the Nationwide Investing Foundation; died in Naples, Florida. See *Current Biography* (November) 1952.

Obituary *New York Times* B p7 July 22, 1999

STEINBERG, SAUL June 15, 1914–May 12, 1999 Romanian-born artist; a brooding and sardonic cultural commentator whose bizarre cartoons and comic illustrations for the *New Yorker* magazine over a period of 58 years reflected the influence of Cubism, Dada, and Surrealism; was a pen-and-ink doodler who, with thin and rococo lines (sometimes embellished with watercolor), created visual epigrams expressing his bemusement at and ridiculing of "the mask of happiness" that Americans "manufacture . . . for themselves"; as a self-described master of the semantics of style, aimed "to make a parody of bravura" and "to create a fiction of skill in the same sense that my writing is an imitation of calligraphy: fine flourishes that can't be deciphered"; as the son of a printer, had a fascination with type that was manifested in much of his art, including the rubber stamps with which he "canceled" his postcard-like landscapes; in Milan, Italy, in the 1930s, studied architecture, which gave him the conventional grounding for his skyscraper and cityscape fantasies of the late 1960s and the 1970s; in 1941 left Italy, bound for the U.S.; after a stay in the Dominican Republic, gained entry into the U.S. in 1942 with the help of friends at the *New Yorker*, to which he had begun contributing; during World War II, in 1943, became a naturalized American citizen and joined the U.S. Navy; during his tours of wartime duty (partly with the Office of Strategic Services [OSS]) in Asia, North Africa, and Italy, sent the *New Yorker* visual reports and anti-Axis cartoons; brought together 210 of the drawings in the first and most realistic of his books, *All in Line* (1945); subsequently published *The Art of Living* (1949), *The Passport* (1954), *The Labyrinth* (1960), and *The New World* (1965), collections that documented his progression to greater abstraction and philosophical reflection; filled his work with geometric forms (including endless spirals), gigantic letters, numbers, and punctuation marks (especially question marks) and such icons as the Chrysler Building, Lady Liberty, and Uncle Sam; created a gallery of dreamlike characters, including sphinxes, cats, truncated men and women on high heels, "junk-food people" wearing Mickey Mouse hats, crocodiles (his symbol for the primitive political society), and strange representations of himself; published the collection *The Inspector* in 1973 and *The Discovery of America* in 1993; in addition to hundreds of other drawings, did 86 covers for the *New Yorker*, the most famous of which (from the March 29, 1976 issue) was a myopic Manhattanite's view of the world, looking west, with Eighth and Ninth Avenues prominent in the foreground and the rest of the U.S., the Pacific, and Asia mere backdrop; was exhibited in New York City at the Museum of Modern Art, the Whitney Museum of American Art, and the Sidney Janis Gallery; died at his home in Manhattan. See *Current Biography* (March) 1957.

Obituary *New York Times* p1+ May 13, 1999

STOPH, WILLI July 8, 1914–Apr. 13, 1999 German politician; former prime minister of Communist East Germany; joined the German Communist youth movement when he was 14; became a full-fledged Communist Party member at 17; secretly organized a courier system linking German Communists with Moscow during the 1930s; when fighting as a member of Hitler's *Wehrmacht* on the Eastern front in World War II, was taken prisoner by the Soviets; as a student in a Soviet "anti-fascist school" for prisoners of war, impressed his captors; following the defeat of Germany, became an adviser in the military administration in the Soviet sector of Germany; from 1948 to 1950 was chief of the economic policy section of the Social Unity Party (SED), successor to the old German Communist Party; joined the SED's central committee in 1950 and the central committee's politburo three years later; in the German Democratic Republic (as Communist East Germany was officially called), served as minister of the interior (1952–55) and national defense (1956–60); was deputy chief of the council of ministers from 1956 to 1964 and chief of the council of ministers, or prime minister, from 1964 to 1973 and again from 1976 to 1989; following the reunification of Germany, was arrested and detained (1991–92); in 1992 was tried for manslaughter for his part, as prime minister, in issuing and implementing shoot-to-kill orders against East Germans fleeing to the West, but escaped probable conviction and imprisonment for health reasons; died in Berlin, Germany. See *Current Biography* (October) 1960.

Obituary *New York Times* C p23 Apr. 22, 1999

STRASBERG, SUSAN May 22, 1938–Jan. 21, 1999 Actress; was identified with gentle roles; achieved her greatest success early on, with the luminous sensitivity she brought to her creation of the tragic young protagonist in the Broadway hit *The Diary of Anne Frank* (1955–57); was the daughter of Lee Strasberg, the founder and director of the Actors Studio, and his wife, Paula Miller, an acting coach at the studio, but received no training there; made her stage debut in *Maya* Off-Broadway when she was 13; played Juliet in a *Kraft Television Theatre* production of *Romeo and Juliet* in 1952; also on television, played the daughter in the series *The Marriage*, co-starring Jessica Tandy and Hume Cronyn; at 16, made her motion-picture debut, in a supporting role in *The Cobweb* (1955), a melodrama set in a private psychiatric clinic; just before her Broadway debut, in *The Diary of Anne Frank*, was cast in the supporting role of Millie, the tomboyish younger sister of the Kim Novak character, in the film *Picnic* (1955); back on stage, starred with Richard Burton and Helen Hayes in *Time Remembered* in 1957; after performing in an Actors Studio revival of *Shadow of a Gunman*, in 1958, toured with Franchot Tone in *Caesar and Cleopatra*; returned to Broadway in the title role of *The Lady of the Camellias*, in 1963; on screen, was cast in the leading role of the actress aspiring to stardom on Broadway in *Stage Struck* (1958); played leading roles in *Kapo* (1960), *The Trip* (1967), and *The Manitou* (1970); had supporting roles in *The Delta Force* (1986) and *Prime Suspect* (1988), among other films; in 1980 published her autobiography, *Bittersweet*, which included accounts of her failed marriage, her daughter's congenital birth defect, her drug abuse, and her guilt feelings; later wrote the memoir *Marilyn and Me* (1992), about her friendship with Marilyn Monroe; had homes in Los Angeles and New York City; died at her residence in Manhattan. See *Current Biography* (May) 1958.

Obituary *New York Times* A p17, Jan. 23, 1999

SVEDA, MICHAEL Feb 3, 1912–Aug. 10, 1999 Chemist; a specialist in the fields of silicon and sulfur chemistry; the discoverer of cyclamates, artificial, noncaloric sweeteners; while experimenting with sulfamides as a doctoral student at the University of Illinois in the late 1930s, accidentally synthesized sodium cyclohexyl sulfamate, trademarked as Sucaryl by Abbott Laboratories in 1950 but banned from the market by the U.S. Department of Health, Education, and Welfare (now the Department of Health and Human Services) in 1969 on the ground that rats fed large quantities of the compound over their life spans developed bladder tumors; held various research, sales, and product-management positions with E. I. du Pont de Nemours & Co. from 1939 to 1954; after leaving du Pont, directed scientific projects at the National Science Foundation (1960–61) and research at the FMC Corp. (1962–64); later lectured at universities and worked as a consultant to academia, industry, and government; in addition to his patent for cyclamates, held patents for a number of inventions in polymer chemistry and chemical intermediates; synthesized a group of waxes and lubricants from silicon; invented processes for the production of pyrosulfuryl chloride and thionyl chloride and for vapor-phase sulfonation of hydrocarbons with sulfur trioxide; contributed to the development of synthetic fabrics, the pesticide DDT, and mustard gas; from 1973 on, spent much of his energy in efforts to reinstate cyclamates, the squelching of which, he speculated, might be traced to the political influence of the sugar industry; died at his home in Stamford, Connecticut. See Current Biography (December) 1954.

Obituary *New York Times* A p11 Aug. 21, 1999

TALBERT, BILLY Sep. 4, 1918–Feb. 28, 1999 Tennis champion; a right-handed player with a stylish ground stroke, a strong volley, and excellent tactics; while fighting diabetes from the age of nine won well over a score of national titles, including eight major doubles championships; in U.S. rankings, was number two in 1944 and 1945 and in the top 10 from 1941 to 1954; in world rankings, was number three in 1949 and again in the top 10 in 1950; reached the quarter finals in the boys' nationals in 1932; six years later, when he was a student at the University of Cincinnati, played in the national intercollegiate tournament; with Gardnar Mulloy, won the men's doubles championship in 1942, 1945, 1946, and 1948; also with Mulloy, won the clay-court doubles title in 1946; shared the mixed doubles crown with Margaret Osborne duPont a record four straight years, 1943–46; with Doris Hart, captured the indoor mixed doubles title in 1947 and 1948; won the men's indoor singles championship in 1948 and 1951; shared the men's indoor doubles title with Don McNeill from 1949 to 1951, with Budge Patty in 1952, and with Tony Trabert (to whom he was mentor) in 1954; won the clay-court doubles with Bill Reedy in 1942, with Pancho Segura in 1944 and 1945, and with Gardnar Mulloy in 1946; with Trabert, won the French doubles championship in 1950; the following year, won his third Eastern grass-courts singles championship; joined the U.S. Davis Cup team in 1946; rejoining the team in 1948, paired with Mulloy to win the clinching point in the Davis Cup victory over Australia in 1948; was again a Davis Cup player in 1949 and from 1951 to 1953; as a cup player, had totals of two singles and seven doubles victories; as the Davis Cup team's captain in portions of the 1952 and 1953 seasons, in 1954 (when the team retook the cup from Australia), and from 1955 to 1957, compiled a 13–4 record; was tournament director of the U.S. Open from 1971 to 1975 and again from 1978 to 1987; with Bruce Old and Pete Axthelm, wrote several books on tennis, in addition to his autobiography, *Playing for Life*; from 1964 until his death was executive vice president of the U.S. Banknote Co., a financial printing firm; died at his home in Manhattan. See *Current Biography* (May) 1957.

Obituary *New York Times* C p21 Mar. 2, 1999

TAYLOR, ROBERT LEWIS Sep. 24, 1912–Sep. 30, 1998 Author; journalist; began his career as a newspaper reporter and editor in the Midwest; was with the *New Yorker* magazine during the 1930s and 1940s; was a regular writer of profiles of personalities ranging from New York City's fire chief and the general manager of the Brooklyn Dodgers baseball team to Charles Atlas, the body builder, and Artie Shaw, the musician and band leader; also contributed to other magazines; in 1948 published *Doctor, Lawyer, Merchant, Chief*, a collection including 11 profiles from the *New Yorker*, one each from the *Saturday Evening Post*, *Life*, and *Redbook*, some travel pieces about the South Pacific, and several short stories; later published another collection of biographies and short stories, *The Running Pianist* (1950), and the collection *Center Ring: The People of the Circus* (1956); wrote *W. C. Fields: His Follies and Fortunes* (1949), originally serialized in the *Saturday Evening Post*; also on commission by the *Saturday Evening Post*, wrote *Winston Churchill: An Informal Study of Greatness* (1952); wrote several novels, including *Adrift in a Boneyard* (1947), a fantasy about six people who survive a world catastrophe, and the better-known *The Travels of Jamie McPheeters* (1958), a picaresque tale about the adventures of an adolescent boy and his father during the California gold rush of 1849; died at his home in Southbury, Connecticut. See *Current Biography* (December) 1959.

Obituary *New York Times* p49 Oct. 4, 1998

TERRELL, ST. JOHN Dec. 12, 1916–Oct. 9, 1998 Actor; theatrical impresario; in the mid-1930s was briefly heard as the title character in the network radio juvenile-adventure serial *Jack Armstrong, the All American Boy*; in 1939 co-founded the Bucks County Playhouse, which helped turn sleepy New Hope, Pennsylvania, into a bustling regional arts mecca; 10 years later, across the Delaware River from New Hope, founded the Lambertville (New Jersey) Music Circus, a tented summer theater; for 25 years beginning in 1953, played the role of George Washington in a reenactment of Washington's crossing of the Delaware in 1776, which became an annual pageant; included prominently in his stage repertoire Shakespeare's Richard III, a character whose reputation he tried to rehabilitate; died at his home in the environs of Trenton, New Jersey. See *Current Biography* (February) 1966.

Obituary *New York Times* B p9 Oct. 20, 1998

TILBERIS, LIZ Sep. 7, 1947–Apr. 21, 1999 British-born magazine editor; president of the Ovarian Cancer Research Fund since 1997; with *British Vogue*, was fashion assistant (1970–84), executive fashion editor (1984–87) and editor in chief (1987–92); in 1992 moved to the U.S. to become editor in chief of *Harper's Bazaar* with the intention of making that 132-year-old Hearst publication "the most beautiful fashion magazine in the world"; went far toward achieving that goal, but never overcame American *Vogue*'s leadership among fashion magazines in circulation and advertising revenue; chronicled her battle against ovarian cancer in the memoir *No Time to Die* (1998), written with Aimee Lee Ball; died in New York City. See *Current Biography* (November) 1998.

Obituary *New York Times* C p22 Apr. 22, 1999

TORMÉ, MEL Sep. 13, 1925–June 5, 1999 Singer; songwriter; arranger; pianist; drummer; actor; author; an exemplary exponent of the "cool jazz" approach to popular singing; early in his career, when he was a crooner of sentimental songs, acquired the epithet "the Velvet Fog," which he loathed; developed into one of the most musically of pop/jazz/swing vocal stylists; delivered his numbers with a flawless sense of pitch, a purity of tone, a smoothness of timbre, an unsurpassed elegance of phrasing, and a relaxed improvisational technique that invested melodies with harmonic intervals rarely heard in popular song; projected geniality; wrote or co-wrote (usually with the lyricist Robert Wells) scores of songs, including "Born to Be Blue" and "Country Fair"; included "Blue Moon" among his signature songs; made his professional debut as a singer in Chicago when he was four; at six, began performing on vaudeville stages in and around Chicago; beginning in 1933 played numerous juvenile dramatic roles on network radio shows (including *Jack Armstrong*) broadcast from Chicago; wrote both

the music and lyrics for "Lament for Love," his first published song, which became a jukebox hit for Harry James's big band in 1941; toured as a rhythm singer and vocal arranger with the Chico Marx orchestra in 1942 and 1943; subsequently toured and recorded for three years with his own group, the Mel-Tones; appeared with that group in the motion pictures *Pardon My Rhythm* (1944) and *Let's Go Steady* (1945); introduced his song "A Stranger in Town" in 1945; co-wrote his best-known composition, the seasonal standard "The Christmas Song" ("Chestnuts roasting on an open fire . . . "), which was recorded by Nat King Cole in 1946; made a number of recordings with the Artie Shaw orchestra, including a popular cover of "Sunny Side of the Street" (1946); reached the number-one spot on the record charts only once, with his cover of "Careless Love" in 1949; beginning in the mid-1950s, confirmed his dedication to a jazz direction with several albums recorded with the Marty Paich Dektette, including *Mel Tormé Sings Schubert Alley* (1960); increasingly, performed and recorded with such jazz musicians as Gerry Mullian, Art Pepper, Buddy Rich, Shorty Rogers, and Rob McConnell; made memorable recordings of "Mountain Greenery" (1956) and "Comin' Home, Baby" (1962); as a live performer, graduated from small jazz clubs to the big Las Vegas rooms and other large venues, including Carnegie Hall, the Hollywood Bowl, and jazz festivals; regularly headlined packaged concerts that toured the U.S. and Europe; throughout the 1950s and 1960s, was much in demand on television as a program host, guest, performer, actor, writer, producer, composer of special musical material, and arranger; returned to the motion-picture screen in straight acting parts, including heavies, in several low-budget films in 1959 and 1960; in 1983 and 1984 won the Grammy Award for best male jazz vocalist for albums recorded with George Shearing; performed until the summer of 1996, when he suffered a stroke; in February 1999 received a Grammy Award for lifetime achievement; among his albums, included tributes to Fred Astaire and Bing Crosby; as a recording artist, is collected definitively on 10 compact discs; wrote several books, including *The Other Side of the Rainbow* (1970), about his experience working as music adviser for the *Judy Garland Show* on television (1963–64), the novel *Winner* (1978), and the autobiography *It Wasn't All Velvet* (1988); died in Los Angeles, with his wife and five children (from previous marriages) at his side. See *Current Biography* (March) 1983.

Obituary *New York Times* p50 June 6, 1999

UDALL, MORRIS K. June 15, 1922–Dec. 12, 1998 Former U.S. representative from Arizona; a liberal Democrat who was kept in Washington for 30 years by a conservative political constituency that seemed to ignore much of his left-of-center agenda (including a national health-insurance program and a plan to break up the big oil companies) while identifying with his staunch advocacy of environmental protection; was born into one of Arizona's leading political families, sired by David K. Udall, a Mormon missionary from Utah who founded the town of St. Johns, Arizona, in 1880; early in his career, practiced law in Tucson and served as a county attorney; when his brother Stewart left the U.S. House of Representatives to enter the cabinet of President John F. Kennedy as secretary of the interior in 1961, was elected by the voters of Arizona's Second Congressional District to succeed Stewart in Congress; over his years in the House of Representatives, was in the forefront of efforts to stop strip-mining, to protect the Arctic National Wilderness Refuge in Alaska, to expand the national parks system, to restructure the energy industry, to require financial disclosure by federal office-holders, to curb lobbyists, to tighten campaign-financing laws, to effect postal reform, to cut the federal debt, and to reform the seniority system in Congress; finished second to Jimmy Carter in the Democratic primaries for the presidential nomination in 1976; resigned his congressional seat for reasons of health in 1991; died in Washington, D.C. See *Current Biography* (April) 1969.

Obituary *New York Times* B p9 Dec. 14, 1998

WALKER, MARGARET July 7, 1915–Nov. 30, 1998 Poet; author; university professor; an important, generally underappreciated figure in 20th-century African-American letters; regarded her parents, a Methodist minister and a music teacher in Birmingham, Alabama, as her "first sources of poetic inspiration"; drew her imagery, in her words, from "the Southern landscape of [her] childhood and adolescence" and her philosophy from "a lifetime of reading the Bible and wisdom literature of the East"; growing up in a refined, protective household, was painfully bewildered by her encounters with racial prejudice until, as she recounted, she "discovered the background of chattel slavery behind this madness"; early on, was encouraged in her poetry writing by Langston Hughes; as an undergraduate at Northwestern University in Evanston, Illinois (her father's alma mater), found another mentor in Edward Buell Hungerford, her creative-writing teacher; in *Crisis* magazine (edited by W. E. B. Du Bois), published three of her early poems: "We Have Been Believers," "The Struggle Staggers Us," and "For My People" (with such lines as "Let a new earth rise . . . / Let a people loving freedom come to growth"); after taking her B.A. degree, spent four years in Chicago, working in the Depression-era WPA (Works Progress Administration) writers program and participating with other black writers and artists in what they called the Chicago Renaissance; developed a close friendship with Richard Wright; subsequently earned M.A. and Ph.D. degrees at the University of Iowa; in 1942 won the Yale Series of Younger Poets Award with her first collection, *For My People* (1942), comprising 26 poems; subsequently published the collection *Ballad of the Free* (1966); in *Prophets for a New Day* (1970), brought together poems reflecting her close emotional involvement in the civil rights turbulence of the 1960s; in the title poem of her fourth collection, *October Journey* (1973), recalled the journey South in 1942, when she met the man to whom she was married for 37 years; in some of the other poems in the volume, presented homages to Paul Laurence Dunbar, Phillis Wheatley, Mary McLeod Bethune, and Owen Dodson; in 1989 published the definitive volume *This Is My Century: New and Collected Poems*; fictionalized the life of her maternal great-grandmother, Margaret Duggins, from slavery to Reconstruction in the best-selling novel *Jubilee* (1965); in 1977 unsuccessfully sued Alex Haley for plagiarizing *Jubilee* in his book *Roots*; engaged in a dialogue with Nikki Giovanni that was published under the title *A Poetic Equation* (1974; reprinted with a new postscript, 1983); wrote the biography *Richard Wright, Daemonic Genius* (1988); taught briefly at colleges in North Carolina and West Virginia before joining the faculty of Jackson State College (later University) in Jackson, Mississippi; at Jackson State, founded the Institute for the Study of the History, Life, and Culture of Black People (later renamed in her honor) in 1968; directed the institute for 11 years; lived in Jackson; known after her marriage as Margaret Walker Alexander; died at the home of her daughter Marion Colmon in Chicago. See *Current Biography* (November) 1943.

Obituary *New York Times* A p29 Dec. 4, 1998

WEIDMAN, JEROME Apr. 4, 1913–Oct. 6, 1998 Author; wrote fiction reflecting the American Jewish experience from his perspective; grew up in an immigrant Jewish neighborhood on Manhattan's Lower East Side; began contributing short stories to the *American Spectator* and other magazines in the mid-1930s; burst to prominence, and set the standard of excellence for his fiction, with his first novel, *I Can Get It for You Wholesale* (1937); in that book, exposed the seamy side of New York's garment industry in chronicling the rise from clerk to wealthy dress-manufacturer of Harry Bogen, a ruthlessly ambitious and unscrupulous character who stands beside Budd Schulberg's Sammy Glick as a preeminent creation emanating from what Meyer Levin has called "the self-hating period" in American Jewish writing; continued Harry Bogen's unsavory story in *What's in It for Me?* (1938); in his eleventh novel, *The Enemy Camp* (1959), wrote with sensitivity about the crisis of Jewish identity suffered by the protagonist when he marries a gentile woman from Philadelphia's old-money Main Line; with warm nostalgia, evoked memories of the Lower East Side of his childhood and adolescence in his 17th novel, *Fourth Street East* (1970), narrated by the young protagonist Benny Kramer; less felicitously, carried Kramer's life forward in two sequels, *Last Respects* (1972) and *Tiffany Street* (1974), which were representative of his more slick and sensationalistic formula fiction; wrote a total of 22 novels, including *The Temple* (1975), in which the protagonist, David Dehn, establishes a Jewish community in a Connecticut town that he perceives to be anti-Semitic and who then goes on to become a loved and respected pillar of the town; for Broadway, with George Abbott, wrote the Pulitzer Prize–winning book for the musical *Fiorello!* (1959) and the book for the musical *Tenderloin* (1960); also wrote the book for the Broadway musical adaptation of *I Can Get It for You Wholesale* (1962) and the Broadway play *The Mother Lover* (1969); published eight collections of short stories and the essay collection *Back Talk* (1963); died at his home in Manhattan. See *Current Biography* (August) 1942.

Obituary *New York Times* C p23 Oct. 7, 1998

WHITELAW, WILLIAM (STEPHEN IAN) June 28, 1918–July 1, 1999 British Conservative Party leader; was an elected member of the House of Commons from 1955 to 1983, when he was made a hereditary peer by Queen Elizabeth II and moved into the House of Lords with the title Lord Whitelaw, first Viscount Whitelaw of Penrith in Cumbria; was parliamentary private secretary to the chancellor of the Exchequer from 1956 to 1958, assistant government whip from 1959 to 1961, and lord commissioner of the Treasury from 1961 to 1962; in the mid-1960s, gradually assumed the leadership of the liberal wing of the Conservative Party; as the parliamentary secretary to the minister of labor, resisted pressure to crack down on unofficial strikes; from 1964 to 1970, was chief opposition whip; was lord president of the council and leader of the House of Commons from 1970 to 1972; was secretary of state for Northern Ireland in 1972 and 1973; under Prime Minister Margaret Thatcher, was home secretary and deputy prime minister from 1979 to 1983; served as Conservative leader in the House of Lords from 1983 to 1988. See *Current Biography* (March) 1975.

Obituary *New York Times* C p17 July 2, 1999

WHYTE, WILLIAM H. JR. Oct. 1, 1917–Jan. 12, 1999 Author; editor; urbanologist; was described by Jane Jacobs as "a wonderful thinker about cities, both humane and hardheaded"; joined the editorial staff of *Fortune* magazine in 1946; became associate editor of the magazine in 1948; was assistant managing editor from 1953 until he left *Fortune*, in 1958; with other editors of *Fortune*, wrote *Is Anybody Listening? How and Why U.S. Business Fumbles When It Talks with Human Beings* (1952); achieved personal prominence with *The Organization Man* (1956), a classic study of, and warning against, the growth of collectivization and conformity in American society, epitomized in the ethos of the corporation, and the concomitant stifling of individual greatness; after leaving *Fortune*, devoted himself to the study of urban environments (often on the spot, walking the streets, sitting in parks, and talking with people, usually with notebook or camera in hand) and how public spaces are used therein; wrote such studies as *Conservation Easements* (1959), *Cluster Development* (1964), *The Last Landscape* (1968), *The Social Life of Small Urban Spaces* (1980), and *City* (1989); decried the "fortressing" of American cities; preferred spontaneous cityscapes, vibrant with "a nice bustle" of humanity; was a consultant on city planning in New York City; influenced city planning nationally; taught at Hunter College; died in Manhattan. See *Current Biography* (January) 1959.

Obituary *New York Times* B p7 Jan. 13, 1999

WILLIAMS, JOE Dec. 12, 1918–Mar. 29, 1999 Musician; a singer with a rich and resonant bass-baritone voice and a style described by one critic as "an amalgam of uptown class and downtown sass"; "sang real soul blues on which his perfect enunciation of the words gave the blues a new dimension," as Duke Ellington observed; also applied his clean sound, precise articulation of lyrics, and sophisticated and variable phrasing to jazz; interpreted ballads with intimate authority and popular songs straightforward-ly; was strongly influenced by Joe Turner; from 1950 on, was best known for his signature song "Everyday (I Have the Blues)," which was registered in the Grammy Awards Hall of Fame in 1992; first gained wide recognition with his 1955 recording of the song with Count Basie's big band; also included prominently in his repertoire such classics as "The Comeback," "Solitude," "Ain't Misbehavin'," "In the Evening," and "All Right, Okay, You Win"; as a child growing up in Chicago, taught himself to play the piano; sang in churches with a gospel quartet during adolescence; began singing professionally in 1937; over the following decade, worked at clubs and other venues in and around Chicago with bands led by Johnny Long, Jimmy Noone, Erskine Tate, Les Hite, Coleman Hawkins, Lionel Hampton, Andy Kirk, Albert Ammons/Pete Johnson, and Red Saunders; between gigs, worked at such jobs as porter, janitor, bartender, and Fuller Brush salesman; in 1947 suffered a nervous breakdown; worked as a soloist in Chicago from 1950 to 1954, when he joined Count Basie's Orchestra; in 1955 recorded the album *Count Basie Swings & Joe Williams Sings*, which included "Everyday"; in 1955 won *DownBeat* magazine's readers poll for best male band singer and its international critics poll for best new male singer; again won *DownBeat*'s readers poll in 1956; during six years with Basie, toured top venues in the U.S. and Canada; toured England and continental Europe in 1956; with Basie, recorded *Back to Basie and the Blues* and *Joe Williams Sings Standards*, among other albums; performed in the motion pictures *Jamboree* (1957) and *Cinderfella* (1960) with Basie; after leaving Basie (in 1961), recorded with Julian "Cannonball" Adderley, Lester Young, and George Shearing, among others; worked club and concert dates backed by small ensembles, one of which was led by the trumpeter Harry "Sweets" Edison; was sometimes accompanied by such instrumentalists as the pianists Ellis Larkins and Norman Simmons; played such clubs as the Blue Angel in Chicago and Birdland and the Village Vanguard in New York City and the Newport and other jazz festivals; recorded *Joe Williams at Newport* (1963), *Presenting Joe Williams* (1966), and *Joe Williams Live* (1966); in one of many reunions with Count Basie, toured Europe in 1972; recorded *Prez and Joe* (1979); after adding popular songs to his repertoire, attracted a new, wider audience; finished first in *DownBeat* magazine's polls of international critics in five consecutive years (1974–78); appeared frequently on television variety shows, including those of Steve Allen, Mike Douglas, and Johnny Carson; with the trumpeter Clark Terry and others, toured Africa, Asia, and the Middle East in the late 1970s; saw his star placed next to that of Count Basie on the Hollywood Walk of Fame in 1983; sang "Come Sunday" at Basie's funeral in 1984; thereafter, always dedicated "You Are So Beautiful" to Basie; won the Grammy Award for best jazz vocalist of 1984 with his album *Nothin' but the Blues*; toured the U.S. and Europe with the Basie Orchestra under the direction of Thad Jones in 1985; outside of music, reached visibility with a mass audience playing the occasional character Grandpa Al in the television situation comedy *The Cosby Show* in the 1980s; recorded an album of spirituals titled *Feel the Spirit* (1995); died in Las Vegas, Nevada, where he had been living for many years with his fourth wife, Jillean. See *Current Biography* (April) 1985.

Obituary *New York Times* B p8 Mar. 31, 1999

WILSON, FLIP Dec. 8, 1933–Nov. 25, 1998 Comedian; the first African-American performer to host a popular weekly variety show on network television; was a monologist and sketch comic who mined the lode of ethnic humor in routines largely written by himself and delivered with judicious use of dialect and notable freedom from racial rancor; after service in the U.S. Air Force in the early 1950s, developed a stand-up comedy act in small clubs and at the Apollo Theater in Harlem; was introduced to a national television audience on the *Tonight Show Starring Johnny Carson* in August 1965; subsequently became a familiar guest on such network television programs as the *Ed Sullivan Show* and *Rowan and Martin's Laugh-In*; found himself in demand in the better clubs; hosted his own special on the NBC network early in the 1968–69 television season; on September 17, 1970 launched on NBC the hour-long weekly *Flip Wilson Show*, which soon claimed the number-one spot among TV variety shows and later was second only to the situation comedy *All in the Family* in overall ratings; in 1971 won an Emmy Award for outstanding writing achievement for a variety show; hosted the *Flip Wilson Show* through four regular seasons, until June 27, 1974, when it was still among the 10 most popular television programs; over the following years, starred in several NBC specials; was outstanding in the supporting comedic role of a preacher in the motion picture *Uptown Saturday Night* (1974); recorded four albums, including *Flip Wilson, You Devil You*, which won a Grammy for best comedy record in 1968; created a small but memorable gallery of comic personae, including Freddie Johnson, his Everyman, Reverend Leroy of the Church of What's Happening Now, and the sassy, street-smart vamp Geraldine Jones; through the mouth of Jones, popularized the lines "The devil made me do it," "What you see is what you get," and "When you're hot, you're hot; when you're not, you're not"; died at his home in Malibu, California. See *Current Biography* (November) 1969.

Obituary *New York Times* B p19 Nov. 27, 1998

WILSON, O(WEN) MEREDITH Sep. 21, 1909–Nov. 7, 1998 Educator; directed the Center for Advanced Study in the Behavioral Sciences in Palo Alto, California from 1967 to 1975; at the beginning of his career, had taught at Brigham Young University and the University of Utah; was secretary and treasurer of the Ford Foundation for the Advancement of Education from 1952 to 1954; returned to academic life as the president of the University of Oregon (1954–50); at the University of Minnesota, was chancellor of the university and president of the board of regents from 1960 to 1967; died in Eugene, Oregon. See *Current Biography* (July) 1967.

Obituary *New York Times* C p21 Nov. 12, 1998

WYATT, JOHN WHITLOW Sep. 27, 1908–July 16, 1999 Major-league baseball pitcher; known as Whit Wyatt; began his major-league career with the Detroit Tigers of the American League, unimpressively, in 1929; was sent back to the minors in 1931, reclaimed by the Tigers in 1932, and traded to the Chicago White Sox in 1933; moved on to the Cleveland Indians in 1937, back to the minors in 1938, and back up to the majors—this time to the National League—in 1939; helped to lead the Brooklyn Dodgers to the National League pennant in 1941; in the World Series of 1941 (which the Dodgers lost), registered Brooklyn's only victory over the New York Yankees; after six seasons with the Dodgers, pitched the 1945 season, his last, with the Philadelphia Phillies; had major-league regular-season career totals of 106 wins, 95 losses, 642 walks, 872 strikeouts, and an earned-run average of 3.78; as a relief pitcher, won 20 games, lost 19, and saved 13; at the plate, batted .219; later was a pitching coach with the Phillies, the Milwaukee Braves, and the Atlanta Braves and a manager in the minor leagues; died in Carrollton, Georgia. See *Current Biography* (November) 1941.

Obituary *New York Times* A p15 July 19, 1999

WYNDER, ERNEST L(UDWIG) Apr. 30, 1922–July 14, 1999 Physician; scientist; cancer researcher; a pioneer in providing chemical proof of the carcinogenic potential of tobacco and tobacco smoke, especially in heavy cigarette smokers; the founding president of the American Health Foundation, a foremost private research center for preventive medicine and health maintenance; began his research while studying under the chest surgeon Evarts A. Graham at the Washington University School of Medicine in St. Louis; found that 95 percent of the patients with lung cancer he surveyed in selected hospitals had long histories of cigarette smoking; in 1950 published his findings, the first statistical evidence of a link between tobacco and cancer; inspired similar, confirmatory surveys by others around the world; in 1951 became associated with the Memorial Hospital for Cancer & Allied Diseases in New York City; the following year, began working in addition at the Sloan-Kettering Institute for Cancer Research in New York City; in 1953 reported an experiment in which tobacco tar had caused epidermoid cancer on the shaved backs of mice; in 1957 collaborated in a study establishing the relatively lower incidence of certain forms of cancer in nonsmoking, teetotaling Seventh Day Adventists; in collaboration with Dietrich Hoffman at the Sloan-Kettering Institute, announced the identification of eight separate carcinogenic tobacco tar fractions in 1959; also made progress in identifying chemicals in the tar that trigger and strengthen the cancer-causing agents; subsequently linked excessive use of tobacco to cancer of the oral cavity, the larynx, the esophagus, the bladder, and the pancreas; in 1969 founded the American Health Foundation, which is located in Manhattan and on the grounds of the Westchester Medical Center in Valhalla, New York, and staffed by some 200 researchers specializing in such fields as experimental oncology, chemistry, epidemiology, nutrition sciences, molecular biology, and behavioral sciences; while considering environmental factors, stressed that "the major killers are due to lifestyle"; collaborated with Swedish scientists in highlighting the role of poor nutrition in cancers of the upper alimentary tract; co-wrote the book *Tobacco and Tobacco Smoke* (1967); co-edited *Towards a Less Harmful Cigarette* (1968); served as editor in chief of the journal *Preventive Medicine*; died at the Memorial Sloan-Kettering Cancer Center in Manhattan. See *Current Biography* (November) 1974.

Obituary *New York Times* A p17 July 16, 1999

ZUBROD, C. GORDON Jan. 22, 1914–Jan. 19, 1999 Physician; oncologist; chiefly as a director of research with the National Institutes of Health (NIH), advanced the use of chemotherapy in the treatment of cancer; began his work with chemotherapy (at that point applied to malaria) with the U.S. Army Medical Corps during World War II; subsequently was an assistant professor of medicine and pharmacology at Johns Hopkins University, in Baltimore, Maryland; joined the National Cancer Institute of the NIH as chief of the general medicine branch in 1954; became director of intramural research in 1961 and scientific director for chemotherapy in 1965; in those positions, departed from the prevailing view of drug therapy as a last resort, after surgery and radiation, based on fear of the possible toxicity of the available agents; along with meeting broad administrative responsibilities, applied his energies to the task of focusing attention on the chemotherapeutic management of cancer, particularly leukemia; helped to make chemotherapy a standard practice; improved the experimental design of clinical trials of antitumor drugs; promoted closer communication between research teams throughout the U.S. and Canada and the acceleration of the translation of successful research into effective application; in 1974 left the NIH to join the faculty of the University of Miami School of Medicine, in Florida, as professor of oncology and chairman of the department of oncology; also directed the Florida Comprehensive Cancer Center, located at the school; retired in 1990. See *Current Biography* (January) 1969.

Obituary *New York Times* A p17 Jan. 23, 1999

CLASSIFICATION BY PROFESSION—1999

ARCHAEOLOGY
Reinhard, Johan

ARCHITECTURE
Aulenti, Gae

ART
Aulenti, Gae
Casey, Bernie
dePaola, Tomie
Engelbreit, Mary
Gilchrist, Brad
Gilchrist, Guy
Mark, Mary Ellen
McFarlane, Todd
Puryear, Martin
Steadman, Ralph
Turrell, James
Washington, Alonzo

ASTRONAUTICS
Glenn, John H. Jr.

ASTRONOMY
Sandage, Allan

BUSINESS
Armstrong, C. Michael
Barrett, Craig
Bartz, Carol
Bettman, Gary B.
Buffett, Jimmy
DeLay, Tom
Engelbreit, Mary
Flynt, Larry
Hormel, James
Koch, Bill
Kroll, Jules B.
Lagasse, Emeril
Laybourne, Geraldine
Mark, Rebecca
McFarlane, Todd
McMahon, Vince
Meeker, Mary
Meriwether, John
Mondavi, Robert
Piëch, Ferdinand
Rainwater, Richard

Raymond, Lee R.
Sassoon, Vidal
Schott, Marge
Schrempp, Juergen
Washington, Alonzo
Weill, Sanford I.
Yergin, Daniel

DANCE
Corella, Angel
Marshall, Susan
Miller, Bebe

EDUCATION
Berry, Mary Frances
Bogart, Anne
Butts, Calvin O.
Cunningham, Michael
Gott, J. Richard III
Hormel, James
Jackson, Shirley Ann
Protess, David
Quine, W. V.
Reagon, Bernice Johnson
Rodin, Judith
Thomas, Augusta Read
Yergin, Daniel
Zinn, Howard

FASHION
Donovan, Carrie
Gaultier, Jean-Paul
Kawakubo, Rei
Sassoon, Vidal

FILM
Benigni, Roberto
Berry, Halle
Blanchett, Cate
Bruckheimer, Jerry
Buscemi, Steve
Byrne, Gabriel
Casey, Bernie
Cheadle, Don
Chen, Joan
Coburn, James
Dench, Judi
Dunne, Dominick

Frakes, Jonathan
Franken, Al
Heckerling, Amy
Henner, Marilu
Hoch, Danny
Hou Hsiao-hsien
Hudlin, Reginald
Hudlin, Warrington
Kiss
Lawrence, Martin
MacDowell, Andie
Mahoney, John
Malick, Terrence
Manson, Marilyn
McDonald, Audra
Michaels, Lorne
Montenegro, Fernanda
Morton, Joe
Ormond, Julia
Oz, Frank
Parks, Suzan-Lori
Patinkin, Mandy
Pileggi, Nicholas
Ryan, Meg
Stiller, Ben
Thompson, Fred
Van Damme, Jean-Claude
Ventura, Jesse
Wayans, Damon
Woo, John
Zsigmond, Vilmos

GOVERNMENT AND
  POLITICS, FOREIGN
Abbas, Mahmoud
Aliyev, Heydar
Bouchard, Lucien
Howard, John
Kim Jong Il
Luzhkov, Yuri
Obasanjo, Olusegun
Obuchi, Keizo
Primakov, Yevgeny
Turabi, Hassan al-

GOVERNMENT AND
  POLITICS, U.S.
Ashcroft, John

Bauer, Gary L.
Bellamy, Carol
Berry, Mary Frances
Bush, Jeb
Chavez, Linda
Cox, Christopher
Davis, Gray
DeLay, Tom
Dunn, Jennifer
Finkelstein, Arthur J.
Ford, Harold E. Jr.
Glenn, John H. Jr.
Hastert, Dennis
Hormel, James
Jackson, Shirley Ann
Largent, Steve
Slater, Rodney
Slaughter, Louise M.
Tenet, George J.
Thompson, Fred
Velázquez, Nydia M.
Ventura, Jesse
Watts, J. C. Jr.
Webb, Wellington E.
White, Michael R.
Williams, Anthony A.

JOURNALISM
Angier, Natalie
Collins, Gail
Donovan, Carrie
Dunne, Dominick
Garcia, Cristina
Hitchens, Christopher
Jefferson, Margo L.
Klass, Perri
Pileggi, Nicholas
Protess, David
Rich, Frank
Simpson, Carole
Yergin, Daniel

LABOR
Hoffa, James P.

LAW
Abrams, Floyd
Abramson, Leslie
Bellamy, Carol
Berry, Mary Frances
Bettman, Gary B.
Cochran, Johnnie L. Jr.
Hoffa, James P.
Hormel, James

Loftus, Elizabeth F.
Turabi, Hassan al-

LITERATURE
Berg, Elizabeth
Buffett, Jimmy
Byrne, Gabriel
Chin, Frank
Cunningham, Michael
dePaola, Tomie
Dunne, Dominick
Galassi, Jonathan
Garcia, Cristina
Gardner, Martin
Gilchrist, Brad
Gilchrist, Guy
Klass, Perri
Maynard, Joyce
Pinsky, Robert
Plain, Belva
Sinclair, April
Stine, R. L.
Yamanaka, Lois-Ann

MATHEMATICS
Borcherds, Richard
Gardner, Martin

MEDICINE
Klass, Perri

MILITARY
Clark, Wesley K.
Obasanjo, Olusegun

MUSIC
Argerich, Martha
Buffett, Jimmy
Colvin, Shawn
Evans, Faith
Gubaidulina, Sofia
Iglesias, Enrique
Kelly, R.
Khan, Chaka
Kiss
Manson, Marilyn
Marcus, Greil
Martin, Ricky
McDonald, Audra
Morgan, Lorrie
Oe, Hikari
Payton, Nicholas
Reagon, Bernice Johnson
Tavener, John

They Might Be Giants
Thomas, Augusta Read
Voigt, Deborah
Williams, Lucinda
Willis, Kelly
Yankovic, "Weird Al"
Zorn, John

NONFICTION
Angier, Natalie
Berg, Elizabeth
Berry, Mary Frances
Chin, Frank
Collins, Gail
Dunne, Dominick
Franken, Al
Gardner, Martin
Harris, Judith Rich
Henner, Marilu
Hitchens, Christopher
Klass, Perri
Lagasse, Emeril
Marcus, Greil
Maynard, Joyce
Meeker, Mary
Pileggi, Nicholas
Pipher, Mary
Protess, David
Quine, W. V.
Reinhard, Johan
Rodin, Judith
Steadman, Ralph
Wayans, Damon
Yergin, Daniel
Zinn, Howard

ORGANIZATIONS
Bauer, Gary L.
Bellamy, Carol
Chavez, Linda
Gardner, Martin
Gibbs, Lois

PHILOSOPHY
Quine, W. V.

PHOTOGRAPHY
Alvarez Bravo, Manuel
Mark, Mary Ellen

PSYCHOLOGY
Harris, Judith Rich
Pipher, Mary
Rodin, Judith

PUBLISHING
Flynt, Larry
Galassi, Jonathan
McDonald, Erroll
Pratt, Jane
Washington, Alonzo

RADIO
Maynard, Joyce
Saralegui, Cristina
Yankovic, "Weird Al"

RELIGION
Butts, Calvin O.
Turabi, Hassan al-
Watts, J. C. Jr.

SCIENCE
Barrett, Craig
Colwell, Rita R.
Gazzaniga, Michael S.
Gott, J. Richard III
Jackson, Shirley Ann
Ritchie, Dennis
Thompson, Kenneth
Yergin, Daniel

SOCIAL ACTIVISM
Barker, Bob
Bauer, Gary L.
Bellamy, Carol
Berry, Mary Frances
Butts, Calvin O.
Gibbs, Lois
Protess, David
Reagon, Bernice Johnson
Rodriguez, Cecilia
Sinclair, April
Zinn, Howard

SOCIAL SCIENCE
Harris, Judith Rich
Loftus, Elizabeth F.
Reinhard, Johan
Rodin, Judith
Zinn, Howard

SPORTS
Akebono
Alou, Felipe
Alou, Moises
Ashley, Maurice
Bettman, Gary B.
Bowman, Scotty
Casey, Bernie
Chávez, Julio César
Chaney, John
Chrebet, Wayne
Duncan, Tim
Duva, Lou
Duval, David
Gebrselassie, Haile
Hamm, Mia
Johnson, Davey
Johnson, Keyshawn
Jones, Roy Jr.
Koch, Bill
Lewis, Lennox
Pak, Se Ri
Pantani, Marco
Piazza, Mike
Richmond, Mitch
Roy, Patrick
Sales, Nykesha
Schott, Marge
Selig, Bud
Sosa, Sammy
Ventura, Jesse
Williams, Doug
Williams, Ricky

TECHNOLOGY
Armstrong, C. Michael
Barrett, Craig
Colwell, Rita R.
Ritchie, Dennis
Thompson, Kenneth
Torvalds, Linus
Yergin, Daniel

TELEVISION
Barker, Bob
Berry, Halle
Byrne, Gabriel
Cheadle, Don

Coburn, James
Collins, Gail
Fili-Krushel, Patricia
Frakes, Jonathan
Franken, Al
Heckerling, Amy
Henner, Marilu
Lagasse, Emeril
Lawrence, Martin
Laybourne, Geraldine
Mahoney, John
Martin, Ricky
Michaels, Lorne
Montenegro, Fernanda
Morton, Joe
Ormond, Julia
Oz, Frank
Patinkin, Mandy
Ryan, Meg
Saralegui, Cristina
Simpson, Carole
Stiller, Ben
Ventura, Jesse
Wayans, Damon
Woo, John
Yankovic, "Weird Al"
Zsigmond, Vilmos

THEATER
Bishop, André
Blanchett, Cate
Bogart, Anne
Breuer, Lee
Cheadle, Don
Dench, Judi
Frakes, Jonathan
Henner, Marilu
Hoch, Danny
Mahoney, John
McDonald, Audra
Montenegro, Fernanda
Morton, Joe
Noble, Adrian
Ormond, Julia
Parks, Suzan-Lori
Patinkin, Mandy
Rich, Frank
Zinn, Howard

CUMULATED INDEX 1991–1999

This is the index to the January 1991–November 1999 issues. For the index to the 1940–1995 biographies, see *Current Biography: Cumulated Index 1940–1995*.

Augér, Arleen obit Aug 93
Augustine, Norman R. Jun 98
Aulenti, Gae Sep 99
Aung San Suu Kyi Feb 92
Auster, Paul Mar 96
Autry, Gene obit Jan 99
Aykroyd, Dan Jan 92
Azikiwe, Nnamdi obit Aug 96
Azil Singh see Zail Singh
Aziz, Tariq May 91

Babyface Jul 98
Bacon, Francis obit Jun 92
Bacon, Selden D. obit Feb 93
Badu, Erykah Apr 98
Baker, Nicholson Aug 94
Baker, Richard A. see Baker, Rick
Baker, Rick Mar 97
Bakker, Robert T. Aug 95
Baldessari, John Jun 91
Baldwin, Alec Jul 92
Baldwin, Hanson W. obit Jan 92
Ball, George W. obit Jul 94
Ball, Joseph H. obit Feb 94
Ball, William obit Oct 91
Balladur, Edouard Feb 94
Ballantine, Ian obit May 95
Banda, Hastings (Kamuzu) obit Feb 98
Banderas, Antonio Mar 97
Banderas, José Antonio Domínguez see Banderas, Antonio
Banks, Dennis Jun 92
Banks, Russell Jan 92
Banville, John May 92
Bao Dai obit Oct 97
Barad, Jill E. Sep 95
Barak, Ehud Aug 97
Barber, Carl Jerome see Barber, Jerry
Barber, Jerry obit Nov 94
Barber, Red obit Jan 93
Barbour, Haley Nov 96
Barco Vargas, Virgilio obit Aug 97
Bardeen, John obit Apr 91
Bari, Joe see Bennett, Tony
Barker, Bob Nov 99
Barkley, Charles Oct 91
Barnhart, Clarence L. obit Jan 94
Baron Franks of Headington see Franks, Oliver Shewell
Baron Wilson of Rievaulx see Wilson, Harold
Barr, Joseph W. obit May 96
Barr, William P. Jun 92
Barrault, Jean-Louis obit Mar 94
Barrett, Craig Mar 99

Barrett, William obit Nov 92
Barry, Dave May 98
Barry, Lynda Nov 94
Barrymore, Drew Oct 98
Bartoli, Cecilia Jun 92
Barton, Robert B. M. obit Apr 95
Bartz, Carol Jul 99
Barzin, Leon (Eugene) obit Aug 99
Bassett, Angela May 96
Bates, Kathy Sep 91
Baudouin I, King of Belgium obit Oct 93
Baudrillard, Jean Jun 93
Bauer, Erwin A. Feb 93
Bauer, Gary L. Jan 99
Bauer, Peggy Feb 93
Baulieu, Etienne-Emile Nov 95
Baumgartner, Leona obit Mar 91
Bayh, Birch Evan, Jr. see Bayh, Evan
Bayh, Evan Nov 98
Bazelon, David L. obit Apr 93
Beam, Jacob D. obit Oct 93
Bean, Louis H. obit Oct 94
Bebey, Francis Apr 94
Beck, Dave obit Feb 94
Becker, Gary S. Sep 93
Becker, Ralph E. obit Oct 94
Beckett, Wendy Jan 98
Beech, Olive Ann obit Sep 93
Beers, Charlotte Jun 98
Begin, Menachem obit Apr 92
Bell Burnell, Jocelyn May 95
Bell, Derrick A. Feb 93
Bell, S. J. see Bell Burnell, Jocelyn
Bell, T. H. obit Sep 96
Bellamy, Carol Oct 99
Bellamy, Ralph obit Jan 92
Belli, Melvin M. obit Sep 96
Belluschi, Pietro obit Apr 94
Belushi, James Jan 95
Ben and Jerry see Cohen, Ben
Bender, James F(rederick) obit Mar 98
Benigni, Roberto Jun 99
Bennett, H. Stanley obit Oct 92
Bennett, John C. obit Jul 95
Bennett, Richard Rodney Mar 92
Bennett, Tony Jun 95
Bennett, Wallace F. obit Feb 94
Benson, Ezra Taft obit Aug 94
Bentsen, Lloyd Apr 93
Bérégovoy, Pierre Feb 93 obit Jul 93
Berendt, John Apr 98

Beresford, Bruce Mar 93
Berg, Elizabeth Nov 99
Berger, Samuel R. "Sandy" Feb 98
Bergonzi, Carlo Nov 92
Beriosova, Svetlana obit Feb 99
Berlin, Sir Isaiah obit Jan 98
Berlosconi, Silvio Aug 94
Berman, Chris Aug 98
Bernardin, Joseph L. obit Jan 97
Bernardino, Minerva obit Nov 98
Bernays, Edward L. obit May 95
Berry, Halle May 99
Berry, Mary Frances Jun 99
Berton, Pierre Oct 91
Bessmertnykh, Aleksandr A. Jun 91
Bestor, Arthur obit Feb 95
Bettman, Gary B. Mar 99
Bettmann, Otto L(udwig) obit Jul 98
Bezos, Jeff Jun 98
Bigart, Homer obit Jul 91
Bildt, Carl Jan 93
Binchy, Maeve Nov 95
Bing, Rudolf obit Nov 97
Birnbaum, Nathan see Burns, George
Bishop, André Jul 99
Bishop, Hazel (Gladys) obit Feb 99
Black, Cathleen P. Jan 98
Black, Clint Aug 94
Black, Conrad M. Aug 92
Black, Eugene R. obit Apr 92
Blackmun, Harry A(ndrew) obit May 99
Blackwell, Earl, Jr. obit May 95
Blair, Bonnie Jul 92
Blair, Tony Aug 96
Blakey, Art obit Jan 91
Blanchett, Cate Aug 99
Blatnik, John A. obit Feb 92
Bliss, Anthony A. obit Nov 91
Blitch, Iris F. obit Oct 93
Block, Joseph L. obit Feb 93
Bloodworth-Thomason, Linda Feb 93
Bloom, Allan David obit Nov 92
Bloomberg, Michael Jun 96
Blue, Zachary see Stine, R. L.
Blume, Peter obit Jan 93
Bly, Robert Mar 93
Bochco, Steven May 91
Bogarde, Dirk obit Jul 99
Bogart, Anne Feb 99
Bohrod, Aaron obit Jun 92

Bok, Sissela Jan 96
Bokassa I, Emperor *see*
  Bokassa, Jean-Bedel
Bokassa, Jean-Bedel obit Jan
  97
Bollea, Terry Gene *see* Hogan,
  Hulk
Bolling, Richard Walker obit
  Jul 91
Bolt, Robert obit Apr 95
Bolté, Charles G. obit May 94
Bolton, Michael Aug 93
Bombeck, Erma obit Jun 96
Bonds, Barry Jun 94
Bonham Carter, Helena Jan 98
Bonnell, John Sutherland obit
  Apr 92
Bono Mar 93
Bono, Sonny obit Mar 98
Bonsal, Philip Wilson obit
  Sep 95
Boosler, Elayne May 93
Booth, Shirley obit Jan 93
Borcherds, Richard Feb 99
Borge, Victor May 93
Boris III, King of Bulgaria obit
  Yrbk 91
Boros, Julius obit Aug 94
Borysenko, Joan Oct 96
Botstein, Leon Aug 96
Botvinnik, Mikhail obit Jul 95
Bouchard, Lucien Apr 99
Bouchles, Olympia Jean *see*
  Snowe, Olympia J.
Boulding, Kenneth E. obit
  May 93
Bourassa, Robert obit Jan 97
Boutros-Ghali, Boutros Apr
  92
Bovet, Daniele obit Jun 92
Bowden, Bobby Nov 96
Bowe, Riddick Jun 96
Bowie, David Nov 94
Bowles, Erskine Aug 98
Bowman, Scotty Jan 99
Boxer, Barbara Apr 94
Boyer, Ernest L. obit Feb 96
Boyle, Kay obit Feb 93
Boyle, T. Coraghessan Jan 91
Bradbury, Norris E. obit Nov
  97
Bradford, Barbara Taylor Oct
  91
Bradley, Pat Feb 94
Bradley, Tom Oct 92 obit Jan
  99
Bradshaw, John E. Apr 93
Brady, James S. Oct 91
Brady, Sarah Oct 96
Branagh, Kenneth Apr 97
Brandt, Willy obit Nov 92
Branson, Richard Feb 95
Bravo, Ellen Aug 97

Brazelton, T. Berry Oct 93
Brazzi, Rossano obit Mar 95
Brennan, Peter J. obit Jan 97
Brennan, William J. obit Oct
  97
Breuer, Lee Oct 99
Breyer, Stephen G. Jun 96
Bridges, Jeff Mar 91
Bridges, Lloyd obit May 98
Brill, Steven Nov 97
Brinkley, Christie Feb 94
Brittan, Leon Aug 94
Broad, William Michael
  Albert *see* Idol, Billy
Broder, Samuel Aug 92
Brodkey, Harold obit Apr 96
Brodsky, Joseph obit Apr 96
Bronfman, Edgar M., Jr. Oct
  95
Brooks, Albert Apr 97
Brooks, Dede *see* Brooks,
  Diana D.
Brooks, Diana D. Jun 98
Brooks, Garth Mar 92
Brooks, Jack Jun 92
Brooks, James obit May 92
Brooks, James L. Apr 98
Brosnan, Pierce Jan 97
Brown, Bobby Apr 91
Brown, Edmund G. obit Apr
  96
Brown, Helen Hayes *see*
  Hayes, Helen
Brown, James Mar 92
Brown, Jesse Nov 93
Brown, Larry Apr 96
Brown, Lester R. Jan 93
Brown, Pat *see* Brown,
  Edmund G.
Brown, Ron obit Jun 96
Brown, Tony Feb 97
Brown, Trisha Apr 97
Brown, Virginia Mae obit
  May 91
Brown, Willie Apr 97
Browne, Coral obit Jul 91
Brownell, Herbert, Jr. obit
  Aug 96
Brownell, Samuel Miller obit
  Jan 91
Browner, Carol M. May 94
Brownlow, Kevin Mar 92
Brubeck, Dave Apr 93
Bruckheimer, Jerry Mar 99
Bruton, John Nov 96
Buatta, Mario May 91
Bubka, Sergei Jul 96
Buchanan, Edna Sep 97
Buckley, Christopher Apr 97
Buffett, Jimmy Mar 99
Bukowski, Charles Apr 94
  obit May 94
Bullock, Sandra Aug 97

Bundy, McGeorge obit Jan 97
Bunting, Mary I(ngraham)
  obit Apr 98
Bunting-Smith, Mary
  Ingraham *see* Bunting,
  Mary I.
Burdett, Winston obit Jul 93
Burdick, Quentin N. obit Nov
  92
Burger, Warren E. obit Aug 95
Burgess, Anthony obit Jan 94
Burke, Arleigh A. obit Aug 96
Burnett, Charles Sep 95
Burnett, Hallie Southgate obit
  Nov 91
Burney, Leroy E(dgar) obit
  Oct 98
Burns, George obit Nov 96
Burns, John L. obit Aug 96
Burns, Ken May 92
Burr, Raymond obit Nov 93
Burroughs, William S. obit
  Nov 97
Burton, Dan Sep 98
Burton, Tim Jul 91
Buscaglia, (Felice) Leo(nardo)
  obit Aug 98
Buscemi, Steve Apr 99
Busch, Charles Jun 95
Bush, George W. Apr 97
Bush, Jeb Feb 99
Bush, John Ellis *see* Bush, Jeb
Bush, Kate Mar 95
Butcher, Susan Jun 91
Butler, John obit Nov 93
Butler, Robert N. Jan 97
Buttenwieser, Benjamin J.
  obit Mar 92
Butterfield, Roger Place obit
  Yrbk 91
Butts, Alfred M. obit Jun 93
Butts, Calvin O. Feb 99
Byatt, A. S. Sep 91
Byrne, Gabriel May 99
Byroade, Henry A. obit Mar
  94

Cabot, Thomas D. obit Aug 95
Caccia, Harold Anthony obit
  Jan 91
Cage, John obit Sep 92
Cage, Nicolas Apr 94
Cahill, William T. obit Sep 96
Cahn, Sammy obit Mar 93
Calatrava, Santiago Aug 97
Calatrava Valls, Santiago *see*
  Calatrava, Santiago
Calderone, Mary S(teichen)
  obit Jan 99
Calkins, Robert D. obit Sep 92
Callahan, Harry M. obit Jul 99
Callahan, John Sep 98

Callender, John Hancock obit Jun 95
Calloway, Cab obit Jan 95
Calvin, Melvin obit Mar 97
Cameron, James Jan 98
Campanella, Roy obit Aug 93
Campbell, Ben Nighthorse Oct 94
Campbell, Bill Jul 96
Campbell, Naomi Feb 97
Campion, Jane Apr 94
Candy, John obit May 94
Canetti, Elias obit Oct 94
Canseco, José Nov 91
Cantinflas obit Jun 93
Capra, Frank obit Oct 91
Caputo, Philip Apr 96
Caramanlis, Constantine obit Jul 98
Caramanlis, Constantinos see Caramanlis, Constantine
Cardoso, Fernando Henrique Oct 96
Carey, Drew Mar 98
Carey, George Aug 91
Carey, Mariah Jul 92
Carey, Ron May 92
Carlson, William S. obit Jul 94
Carmichael, Stokely obit Feb 99
Carnegie, Dorothy (Reeder Price) obit Jan 99
Carnovsky, Morris Jan 91
Carpenter, Mary Chapin Feb 94
Carr, William G. obit May 96
Carradine, Keith Aug 91
Carrey, Jim Feb 96
Carroll, James May 97
Carroll, Jim Oct 95
Carroll, Joseph F. obit Mar 91
Carruth, Hayden Apr 92
Carsey, Marcy Jan 97
Carson, Benjamin S., Sr. May 97
Carstens, Karl obit Aug 92
Carter, Betty obit Jan 99
Carter, James Feb 97
Carter, Stephen L. Jul 97
Carusi, Ugo obit Sep 94
Carvey, Dana Jun 92
Carville, James Mar 93
Case, Steve Oct 96
Casey, Bernie Jul 99
Cash, Rosanne Oct 91
Cassidy, Claudia obit Oct 96
Cates, Gilbert Mar 97
Catlett, Elizabeth May 98
Caulfield, Joan obit Aug 91
Cavaco Silva, Aníbal Mar 91
Cavalli-Sforza, Luigi Luca Aug 97

Cédras, Raoul Jul 95
Celebrezze, Anthony J(oseph) obit Jan 99
Cerf, Vinton G. Sep 98
Chadli, Bendjedid Apr 91
Chadwick, Florence obit May 95
Chaikin, Sol C. obit Jun 91
Chailly, Riccardo Jun 91
Chalk, O. Roy obit Feb 96
Chamberlain, John Rensselaer obit Jun 95
Champion, George obit Jan 98
Chan, Jackie Nov 97
Chan, Kong Sun see Chan, Jackie
Chancellor, John obit Sep 96
Chandler, A. B. obit Aug 91
Chandler, Dorothy Buffum obit Sep 97
Chandrasekhar, Subrahmanyan obit Oct 95
Chaney, John Mar 99
Chang, Michael Jul 97
Channing, Stockard Apr 91
Chappell, Tom May 94
Charles, Ray Jun 92
Chast, Roz Jul 97
Chavez, Cesar obit Jun 93
Chávez, Julio César Apr 99
Chavez, Linda Nov 99
Chavis, Benjamin F. Jan 94
Cheadle, Don Sep 99
Chen, Joan Sep 99
Chenault, Kenneth I. Jun 98
Cheney, Lynne V. Oct 92
Cher Jun 91
Cherkassky, Shura obit Mar 96
Chernomyrdin, Viktor Aug 98
Cheshire, Leonard obit Sep 92
Chiang Ch'ing obit Jan 92
Chih-Yuan Yang see Yang, Jerry
Chihuly, Dale Aug 95
Chiluba, Frederick May 92
Chin, Frank Mar 99
Ch'ing, Chiang see Chiang Ch'ing
Chirac, Jacques Apr 93
Chomsky, Noam Aug 95
Chopra, Deepak Oct 95
Chouinard, Yvon Jun 98
Chow Yun-Fat May 98
Chrebet, Wayne Feb 99
Christie, William Jan 92
Christison, Alexander Frank Philip see Christison, Philip
Christison, Philip obit Feb 94
Christopher, Warren M. Nov 95
Chuan Leekpai Nov 98

Chute, Marchette Gaylord obit Jul 94
Chwast, Seymour Sep 95
Çiller, Tansu Sep 94
Cisler, Walker obit Jan 95
Claiborne, Loretta Jul 96
Clampitt, Amy Feb 92 obit Nov 94
Clark, Eleanor obit Apr 96
Clark, Georgia Neese obit Feb 96
Clark, James H. Jun 97
Clark, Mary Higgins Jan 94
Clark, Wesley K. Jul 99
Clavell, James obit Nov 94
Claytor, W. Graham, Jr. obit Jul 94
Cleaver, (Leroy) Eldridge obit Jul 98
Cleveland, James obit Apr 91
Clinton, Bill Nov 94
Clinton, George Jul 93
Clinton, Hillary Rodham Nov 93
Clinton, William Jefferson see Clinton, Bill
Coburn, James Jun 99
Cochran, Johnnie L. Jr. Jun 99
Cocker, Jarvis Nov 98
Coe, Sue Aug 97
Coen, Ethan Sep 94
Coen, Joel Sep 94
Cohen, Abby Joseph Jun 98
Cohen, Ben Apr 94
Cohen, Howard William see Cosell, Howard
Cohen, William S. Jan 98
Coker, Elizabeth Boatwright obit Nov 93
Colbert, Claudette obit Oct 96
Colbert, Lester L. obit Nov 95
Colby, William E. obit Jul 96
Cole, Johnnetta B. Aug 94
Cole, Natalie Nov 91
Coleman, J. P. obit Nov 91
Coleman, James S. obit Jun 95
Collins, Cardiss Feb 97
Collins, Francis S. Jun 94
Collins, Gail Mar 99
Collins, John F. obit Feb 96
Collins, Leroy obit May 91
Colvin, Shawn Mar 99
Colwell, Rita R. May 99
Combs, Bert Thomas obit Feb 92
Combs, Sean "Puffy" Apr 98
Comer, James P. Aug 91
Commager, Henry Steele obit May 98
Condon, Richard obit Jun 96
Cone, David Feb 98
Conerly, Charles obit Apr 96

Conerly, Chuck *see* Conerly, Charles
Congdon, William (Grosvenor) obit Jul 98
Conn, Billy obit Aug 93
Connally, John B. obit Aug 93
Connery, Sean Jun 93
Conroy, Pat Jan 96
Conway, Jill Ker Jun 91
Coolio Aug 98
Cooper, Cynthia Aug 98
Cooper, John Sherman obit Apr 91
Cooper, Louise Field obit Jan 93
Coover, Robert Feb 91
Copland, Aaron obit Yrbk 91
Copperfield, David Jul 92
Coppola, Francis Ford Jul 91
Coppola, Nicholas *see* Cage, Nicholas
Corella, Angel Mar 99
Cornwell, Patricia May 97
Cosell, Howard obit Jul 95
Costas, Bob Jan 93
Cotten, Joseph obit Apr 94
Cotter, Audrey *see* Meadows, Audrey
Couples, Fred Jul 93
Couric, Katie Mar 93
Cousins, Margaret obit Oct 96
Cousins, Norman obit Jan 91
Cousteau, Jacques-Yves obit Sep 97
Covey, Stephen R. Jan 98
Cox, Bobby Feb 98
Cox, Christopher Jul 99
Craig, George N. obit Feb 93
Crandall, Robert L. Nov 92
Crane, Eva Aug 93
Crawford, Cindy Aug 93
Crawford, Frederick C. obit Feb 95
Crawford, Michael Jan 92
Cream, Arnola Raymond *see* Walcott, Joe
Cresson, Edith Sep 91
Crichton, Michael Nov 93
Criss, Peter *see* Kiss
Crisscoula, Peter *see* Kiss
Crocetti, Dino *see* Martin, Dean
Cromer, George Rowland Stanley Baring obit May 91
Cronenberg, David May 92
Cross, Amanda *see* Heilbrun, Carolyn G.
Crouch, Stanley Mar 94
Crow, Sheryl May 98
Crowe, Cameron Mar 96
Crumb, R. Apr 95
Cugat, Xavier obit Jan 91
Cullberg, Birgit obit Nov 99

Cummings, Robert obit Feb 91
Cunningham, Michael Jul 99
Cunningham, Randall Mar 91
Cuomo, Andrew M. Oct 98
Currie, Lauchlin Bernard obit Mar 94
Curry, John obit Jun 94
Curtin, Jane Jan 97
Curtis, Jamie Lee Nov 98
Curtis, Thomas B. obit Mar 93
Cusack, Joan Jul 98
Cusack, John Jun 96
Custin, Mildred obit Jun 97

Dabney, Virginius obit Mar 96
Daley, Richard M. Aug 92
Daley, William M. Mar 98
Dalrymple, Jean obit Feb 99
Daly, Chuck Apr 91
Daly, John obit May 91
Daly, Tyne Mar 92
Damon, Matt Mar 98
Danforth, John C. Jan 92
Danilova, Alexandra obit Sep 97
Danto, Arthur C. Apr 95
Darden, Christopher A. Feb 97
Darrow, Whitney, Jr. obit Oct 99
Daschle, Tom Oct 95
D'Aubuisson, Roberto obit Apr 92
Davenport, Marcia obit Mar 96
Davey, Jocelyn *see* Raphael, Chaim
David, Larry Aug 98
Davidson, Garrison Holt obit Feb 93
Davies, Dennis Russell May 93
Davies, Robertson obit Mar 96
Davies, Ronald N. obit Jun 96
Davis, Geena Oct 91
Davis, Gray Jun 99
Davis, Joseph Graham, Jr. *see* Davis, Gray
Davis, Judy Nov 93
Davis, Miles obit Nov 91
Dawkins, Richard Aug 97
Day, J. Edward obit Jan 97
Day, Pat Oct 97
Dayan, Yaël Apr 97
De Creeft, José obit Yrbk 91
De Kooning, Willem obit May 97
De La Hoya, Oscar Jan 97
De La Torre, Lillian obit Nov 93
De Mille, Agnes obit Jan 94
De Niro, Robert May 93

De Vries, Peter obit Jan 94
Dean, Patrick obit Jan 95
Debre, Michel obit Oct 96
Deconcini, Dennis Feb 92
Deer, Ada E. Sep 94
Dees, Morris S., Jr. Jan 95
Deford, Frank Aug 96
Degeneres, Ellen Apr 96
Dejong, Meindert obit Sep 91
Delacorte, George T. obit Jul 91
Delany, Annie Elizabeth *see* Delany, Bessie
Delany, Bessie Nov 95 obit Jan 96
Delany, Sadie Nov 95 obit Apr 99
DeLay, Tom May 99
Dell, Michael Jun 98
Dellums, Ronald V. Sep 93
Demikhov, Vladimir P(etrovich) obit Feb 99
Deming, W. Edwards Sep 93 obit Mar 94
Dench, Judi Jan 99
Deng Xiaoping Jun 94 obit Apr 97
Dennehy, Brian Jul 91
Denning (Alfred Thompson Denning), Baron obit Jun 99
Dennis, Sandy obit May 92
Denver, John obit Jan 98
dePaola, Tomie Feb 99
Depp, Johnny May 91
Dern, Laura Oct 92
Derrida, Jacques Jul 93
Derthick, Lawrence Gridley obit Mar 93
Derwinski, Edward J. Aug 91
Desai, Morarji obit Jun 95
Devers, Gail Jul 96
Dewhurst, Colleen obit Oct 91
Diana, Princess of Wales obit Nov 97
Dicaprio, Leonardo Mar 97
Dichter, Ernest obit Jan 92
Dickerson, Nancy Hanschman obit Jan 98
Dickey, James obit Mar 97
Dickey, John Sloan obit Apr 91
Diebenkorn, Richard obit May 93
Dietrich, Marlene obit Jun 92
Difranco, Ani Aug 97
Diggs, Charles C(ole), Jr. obit Nov 98
DiMaggio, Joe obit May 99
Disney, Anthea Jun 98
Dith Pran Oct 96
Dixon, Jeane obit Mar 97
Dixon, Willie obit Apr 92
Djilas, Milovan obit Jul 95

Dobson, James C. Aug 98
Dodd, Martha obit Jan 91
Doi, Takako Jul 92
Dolbier, Maurice obit Jan 94
Dolci, Danilo (Bruno Pietro)
   obit Mar 98
Dole, Elizabeth Hanford Jan
   97
Dominguín, Luis Miguel obit
   Jul 96
Donegan, Horace W. B. obit
   Jan 92
Donoso, José obit Feb 97
Donovan, Carrie Sep 99
Doolittle, James H. obit Jan 94
Dorris, Michael Mar 95 obit
   Jun 97
Douglas, Emily Taft obit Mar
   94
Douglas, Marjory Stoneman
   obit Jul 98
Douglas-Home, Alexander
   Frederick see Home,
   Alexander Frederick
   Douglas-Home, 14th Earl of
Dove, Rita May 94
Dowd, Maureen Sep 96
Downey, Robert Jr. Aug 98
Downs, Robert B. obit Apr 91
Doyle, Roddy Oct 97
Dr. Seuss see Geisel, Theodor
   Seuss
Drabinsky, Garth Oct 97
Drake, Alfred obit Sep 92
Drapeau, Jean obit Oct 99
Draper, Paul obit Jan 97
Drescher, Fran Apr 98
Drexler, Clyde Jan 96
Drexler, Millard S. Jan 93
Dreyfus, Pierre obit Mar 95
Druckman, Jacob obit Aug 96
Drysdale, Don obit Sep 93
Dublin, Louis Israel obit Yrbk
   91
Dubridge, L. A. obit Mar 94
Duc Tho, Le see Le Duc Tho
Duggan, Ervin S. Oct 98
Dukakis, Olympia Jul 91
Duke, Angier Biddle obit Jul
   95
Dulles, Eleanor Lansing obit
   Jan 97
Duncan, Tim Nov 99
Duncan, Todd obit May 98
Dunn, Jennifer Mar 99
Dunne, Dominick May 99
Dunnock, Mildred obit Sep
   91
Duras, Marguerite obit May
   96
Durning, Charles Sep 97
Durocher, Leo obit Nov 91
Durrell, Gerald obit Apr 95

Durrell, Lawrence obit Jan 91
Dürrenmatt, Friedrich obit
   Apr 91
Duva, Lou Nov 99
Duval, David Oct 99
Dwinell, Lane obit Jun 97
Dworkin, Andrea Oct 94
Dyer-Bennet, Richard obit Feb
   92
Dylan, Bob Oct 91
Dyson, Esther Aug 97
Dyson, Michael Eric Oct 97

Eagleburger, Lawrence S. Nov
   92
Earle, Stephen Fain see Earle,
   Steve
Earle, Steve Oct 98
Earle, Sylvia A. May 92
Early, Gerald May 95
Ebbers, Bernard J. Feb 98
Ebersol, Dick Jul 96
Ebert, Roger Mar 97
Eccles, David (McAdam) obit
   May 99
Eccles, John C. obit Jul 97
Eckstine, Billy obit Apr 93
Edberg, Stefan Jan 94
Eddington, Arthur Stanley
   obit Yrbk 91
Edel, Leon obit Nov 97
Edelman, Gerald M. Apr 95
Edelman, Marian Wright Sep
   92
Edmonds, Kenneth see
   Babyface
Edmonds, Walter D. obit May
   98
Edwards, Douglas obit Jan 91
Edwards, Teresa Mar 98
Edwards, Vincent obit May
   96
Egeberg, Roger O. obit Nov 97
Egoyan, Atom May 94
Ehrenreich, Barbara Mar 95
Ehrlichman, John D. obit Apr
   99
Einem, Gottfried Von obit Sep
   96
Eisen, Stanley see Kiss
Eisenman, Peter Oct 97
Eisenstaedt, Alfred obit Oct
   95
Eisner, Thomas Mar 93
Eisner, Will Oct 94
Eklund, John M. obit Mar 97
Elders, Joycelyn Mar 94
Elion, Gertrude B. Mar 95
   obit May 99
Eliot, Thomas H. obit Jan 92
Elizondo, Hector Jan 92
Elkin, Stanley obit Aug 95
Ellingson, Mark obit Apr 93

Ellis, Albert Jul 94
Ellis, Bret Easton Nov 94
Ellis, John Tracy obit Jan 93
Ellison, Lawrence J. Jan 98
Ellison, Ralph Jun 93 obit Jun
   94
Ellroy, James Apr 98
Ellroy, Lee Earle see Ellroy,
   James
Ellsberg, Edward obit Yrbk 91
Elson, Edward L. R. obit Nov
   93
Elytis, Odysseus obit Jun 96
Emanuel, Rahm Apr 98
Endara, Guillermo Feb 91
Engelbreit, Mary Oct 99
Engle, Paul obit May 91
English, Diane Jun 93
Enrique Tarancón, Vicente
   Cardinal obit Feb 95
Erikson, Erik H. obit Jul 94
Esiason, Boomer Nov 95
Esiason, Norman Julius see
   Esiason, Boomer
Espy, Mike Oct 93
Estefan, Gloria Oct 95
Estes, Richard Nov 95
Eszterhas, Joe Apr 98
Etheridge, Melissa May 95
Evans, Faith Feb 99
Evans, Janet Jul 96
Evans, Poncé Cruse see
   Heloise
Evers-Williams, Myrlie Aug
   95
Ewbank, Weeb obit Feb 99
Ewell, Tom obit Nov 94
Ewing, Patrick May 91
Exley, Frederick obit Aug 92
Exon, James Nov 96
Eysenck, Hans J. obit Nov 97

Fadiman, Clifton (Paul) obit
   Sep 99
Fagan, Garth Aug 98
Fairbank, John K. obit Nov 91
Faldo, Nick Sep 92
Fallows, James Nov 96
Faludi, Susan Feb 93
Farmer, James (Leonard) obit
   Sep 99
Farrakhan, Louis Apr 92
Fasanella, Ralph obit Mar 98
Fascell, Dante B(runo) obit
   Feb 99
Fassbaender, Brigitte Jun 94
Fassett, Kaffe Jun 95
Fast, Howard Apr 91
Faubus, Orval E. obit Feb 95
Favre, Brett Nov 96
Feifel, Herman Aug 94
Feingold, Russell D. Jul 98

Feininger, Andreas (Bernhard Lyonel) obit May 99
Feinstein, Dianne Aug 95
Feinstein, John Jul 98
Fellini, Federico obit Jan 94
Fenwick, Millicent obit Nov 92
Ferber, Herbert obit Oct 91
Ferlinghetti, Lawrence Jun 91
Ferré, Gianfranco Jul 91
Ferrer, José obit Mar 92
Fiennes, Ralph Sep 96
Fili-Krushel, Patricia Nov 99
Filmus, Tully obit Jun 98
Filo, David Oct 97
Finch, Robert H. obit Jan 96
Finkelstein, Arthur J. Nov 99
Finkelstein, Louis obit Jan 92
Finley, Charles O. obit Apr 96
Finley, Karen Sep 98
Fireman, Paul Mar 92
Firkušný, Rudolf obit Sep 94
Fischbacher, Siegfried see Siegfried
Fischer, Bobby May 94
Fish, Hamilton obit Mar 91
Fishburne, Larry see Fishburne, Laurence
Fishburne, Laurence Aug 96
Fisher, Carrie Feb 91
Fisher, M. F. K. obit Aug 92
Fittipaldi, Emerson Apr 92
Fitzgerald, Ella obit Aug 96
Flanagan, Tommy Apr 95
Flansburgh, John see They Might Be Giants
Fleck, Béla Nov 96
Fleming, Renée May 97
Flemming, Arthur S. obit Nov 96
Fletcher, James obit Feb 92
Flood, Daniel J. obit Aug 94
Flynn, Raymond Oct 93
Flynt, Larry Sep 99
Folkman, Judah May 98
Fonda, Bridget Jan 94
Fonda, Peter Mar 98
Fonteyn, Margot obit Apr 91
Foote, Shelby Apr 91
Forbes, Steve May 96
Ford, Harold E. Jr. Nov 99
Ford, Richard Sep 95
Ford, Tennessee Ernie obit Jan 92
Ford, Tom May 98
Foreman, George Aug 95
Fornos, Werner H. Jul 93
Foster, Jodie Aug 92
Foster, John see Furcolo, Foster
Fowler, William A. obit May 95
Foxx, Redd obit Jan 92

Frager, Malcolm obit Aug 91
Frahm, Herbert see Brandt, Willy
Frakes, Jonathan Jul 99
Francescatti, Zino obit Nov 91
Francis, Sam obit Jan 95
Frank, Anthony M. Aug 91
Frank, Barney Apr 95
Frank, Robert L. Aug 97
Frankel, Felice Apr 98
Franken, Al Jun 99
Frankl, Viktor E. Jul 97 obit Nov 97
Franklin, Aretha May 92
Franks, Oliver Shewell obit Jan 93
Franz, Dennis Jul 95
Fraser, Brad Jul 95
Frazier, Ian Aug 96
Freed, James I. Nov 94
Freeh, Louis J. May 96
Freeman, Morgan Feb 91
Frehley, Ace see Kiss
Frehley, Paul see Kiss
French, Marilyn Sep 92
Friedman, Thomas L. Oct 95
Friendly, Fred W. obit May 98
Frisch, Max obit Jun 91
Frondizi, Arturo obit Jun 95
Fry, Stephen Sep 98
Frye, Northrop obit Mar 91
Fuchs, Joseph obit May 97
Fuchs, Michael J. Feb 96
Fudge, Ann M. Jun 98
Fukuda, Takeo obit Sep 95
Fulbright, J. William obit Apr 95
Fulghum, Robert Jul 94
Fuller, Kathryn S. Jan 94
Fuller, Millard Apr 95
Fuller, Samuel Aug 92 obit Jan 98
Funston, Keith obit Jul 92
Funt, Allen obit Nov 99
Furcolo, Foster obit Sep 95
Furness, Betty obit Jun 94

G, Kenny Nov 95
Gable, Dan Aug 97
Gabor, Eva obit Sep 95
Gaddis, William obit Mar 99
Gaines, Ernest J. Mar 94
Galassi, Jonathan Sep 99
Galdikas, Biruté M. F. Mar 95
Galliano, John Oct 96
Gandhi, Rajiv obit Jul 91
Gandhi, Sonia May 98
Garcia, Cristina Aug 99
Garcia, Jerry obit Oct 95
Gardiner, John Eliot Aug 91
Gardner, Howard Oct 98

Gardner, Martin Sep 99
Garnett, Kevin Sep 98
Garrison, Lloyd K. obit Nov 91
Garson, Greer obit Jun 96
Gary, John obit Mar 98
Gary, Raymond obit Feb 94
Garzarelli, Elaine Sep 95
Gaston, Cito Apr 93
Gates, Bill May 91
Gates, Henry Louis Oct 92
Gates, Robert M. Apr 92
Gates, William H. see Gates, Bill
Gaultier, Jean-Paul Jan 99
Gautier, Felisa Rincón De obit Nov 94
Gaver, Mary Virginia obit Mar 92
Gazzaniga, Michael S. Apr 99
Gebrselassie, Haile Jul 99
Geffen, David Jan 92
Geisel, Ernesto obit Nov 96
Geisel, Theodor Seuss obit Nov 91
Geldzahler, Henry obit Oct 94
Gell-Mann, Murray Oct 98
Geller, Margaret J. Jun 97
Gellhorn, Walter obit Feb 96
Geneen, Harold S(ydney) obit Jan 98
George, Zelma W. obit Sep 94
Gergen, David Feb 94
Gergiev, Valery Jan 98
Gerstacker, Carl A. obit Jul 95
Gerstner, Louis V. Jun 91
Gerulaitis, Vitas obit Nov 94
Getz, Stan obit Aug 91
Ghezali, Salima May 98
Gibbs, Joe Apr 92
Gibbs, Lois Sep 99
Giddens, Anthony Apr 98
Gifford, Francis Newton see Gifford, Frank
Gifford, Frank Jan 95
Gifford, Kathie Lee Nov 94
Gigli, Romeo Aug 98
Gilbert, Martin Feb 91
Gilbert, Walter Nov 92
Gilchrist, Brad Jan 99
Gilchrist, Guy Jan 99
Gillespie, Dizzy Jan 93 obit Feb 93
Gillespie, John Birks see Gillespie, Dizzy
Gilligan, Carol May 97
Gilpatric, Roswell L. obit May 96
Ginsberg, Allen obit Jun 97
Ginsberg, Mitchell I. obit May 96
Ginsburg, Ruth Bader Feb 94
Ginzburg, Natalia obit Nov 91

Gish, Lillian obit Apr 93
Gjesdal, Cornelia *see* Knutson, Coya
Gleason, Thomas W. obit Mar 93
Glenn, John H. Jr. Jan 99
Glennan, T. Keith obit Jun 95
Glennie, Evelyn Jul 97
Glover, Danny Apr 92
Glover, Savion Mar 96
Gobel, George obit Apr 91
Godard, Jean-Luc Oct 93
Godden, Rumer obit Jan 99
Godunov, Alexander obit Jul 95
Godwin, Gail Oct 95
Goebbels, Joseph obit Yrbk 91
Goetz, Delia obit Sep 96
Goizueta, Roberto C. Aug 96 obit Jan 98
Goldblum, Jeff Jul 97
Goldin, Daniel S. Jun 93
Golding, William obit Aug 93
Goldman, William Jan 95
Goldsmith, Sir James obit Oct 97
Goldwater, Barry M(orris) obit Aug 98
Gong Li May 97
Gonzales, Pancho obit Sep 95
Gonzales, Richard *see* Gonzales, Pancho
Gonzalez, Henry B. Feb 93
Goodall, Jane Nov 91
Goodman, Andrew obit Jun 93
Goodrich, Marcus obit Jan 92
Goodson, Mark obit Feb 93
Goodwin, Doris Kearns Nov 97
Gorbachev, Raisa obit Nov 99
Gordon, David Jun 94
Gore, Albert (Arnold) obit Feb 99
Górecki, Henryk May 94
Gorelick, Kenny *see* G, Kenny
Goren, Charles H. obit Jul 91
Gorton, Slade Aug 93
Gossett, William T(homas) obit Oct 98
Gott, J. Richard III Oct 99
Gould, Laurence M. obit Aug 95
Gould, Morton obit May 96
Gould, Samuel B. obit Sep 97
Grace, J. Peter, Jr. obit Jun 95
Grade, Lew obit Mar 99
Grafton, Samuel obit Feb 98
Grafton, Sue Sep 95
Graham, Donald E. May 98
Graham, John obit Apr 91
Graham, Jorie May 97
Graham, Martha obit May 91

Graham, Virginia obit Mar 99
Graham, Wallace H. obit Mar 96
Grammer, Kelsey May 96
Granato, Cammi Apr 98
Granato, Catherine Michelle *see* Granato, Cammi
Grandin, Temple Jul 94
Grant, Hugh Sep 95
Grappelli, Stéphane obit Feb 98
Graves, Earl G. Aug 97
Graves, Nancy obit Jan 96
Gray, Frizzell *see* Mfume, Kweisi
Gray, Georgia Neese Clark *see* Clark, Georgia Neese
Gréco, Juliette Jan 92
Green, Al Feb 96
Green, Julian obit Oct 98
Green, Julien *see* Green, Julian
Greenaway, Peter Feb 91
Greene, Balcomb obit Jan 91
Greene, Bob Jul 95
Greene, Graham obit May 91
Greenfield, Jerry Apr 94
Gregory, J. Dennis *see* Williams, John A.
Grès, Mme. (Alix) obit Feb 95
Greuter, Helen Wright *see* Wright, Helen
Grier, Pam Feb 98
Griffey, Ken, Jr. Aug 96
Griffith, Ernest S. obit Apr 97
Griffith Joyner, Florence obit Nov 98
Griffith, Nanci Feb 98
Grimond, Jo obit Jan 94
Grisham, John Sep 93
Griswold, Erwin N. obit Jan 95
Grizodubova, Valentina S. obit Jul 93
Grodin, Charles Nov 95
Gronouski, John A. obit Mar 96
Gross, Chaim obit Jul 91
Gross, Ernest A(rnold) obit Jul 99
Gross, Hiam *see* Gross, Chaim
Grosz, Karoly obit Mar 96
Grotowski, Jerzy obit Mar 99
Grove, Andrew S. Mar 98
Gubaidulina, Sofia Oct 99
Guccione, Bob Aug 94
Guccione, Kathy Keeton *see* Keeton, Kathy
Guinan, Matthew obit May 95
Gulick, Luther Halsey obit Mar 93
Gumbel, Greg Sep 96
Guterson, David Nov 96

Guthrie, A. B., Jr. obit Jul 91
Gwynn, Tony Oct 96

Haack, Robert W. obit Aug 92
Habib, Philip Charles obit Jul 92
Habibie, B. J. *see* Habibie, Bacharuddin Jusuf
Habibie, Bacharuddin Jusuf Oct 98
Hackett, Albert obit May 95
Hadley, Jerry Nov 91
Hafstad, Lawrence R. obit Jan 94
Hahn, Emily obit Apr 97
Hair, Jay D. Nov 93
Haldeman, Bob *see* Haldeman, H. R.
Haldeman, H. R. obit Jan 94
Hale, Clara obit Feb 93
Haley, Alex obit Mar 92
Hall, Edward T. Feb 92
Hallinan, Vincent obit Nov 92
Halsey, Margaret obit Apr 97
Hamed, Naseem *see* Hamed, Prince Naseem
Hamed, Nazeem *see* Hamed, Prince Naseem
Hamed, Nazim *see* Hamed, Prince Naseem
Hamed, Prince Naseem Oct 98
Hamer, Dean H. Jun 97
Hamill, Pete Feb 98
Hamilton, Charles obit Feb 97
Hamm, Mia Sep 99
Hammer, Armand obit Feb 91
Hammer, M. C. Apr 91
Hampson, Thomas Mar 91
Hannah, John A. obit Apr 91
Hanschman, Nancy *see* Dickerson, Nancy Hanschman
Hansen, Harry obit Yrbk 91
Hansen, James E. May 96
Hanson, Duane obit Mar 96
Harberger, John Pico *see* John, John Pico
Harbison, John Feb 93
Hardaway, Tim Jul 98
Hardy, Porter, Jr. obit Jun 95
Hare, Raymond A. obit May 94
Häring, Bernard obit Sep 98
Harkin, Tom Jan 92
Harnoncourt, Nikolaus Jan 91
Harrelson, Woody Jan 97
Harrington, David Nov 98
Harris, E. Lynn Jun 96
Harris, Emmylou Oct 94
Harris, Harwell Hamilton obit Jan 91
Harris, Judith Rich Apr 99

Harrison, Jim Jul 92
Harrison, Joan obit Oct 94
Harsch, Joseph C(lose) obit Aug 98
Hart, Mickey Jan 94
Hartley, Hal Aug 95
Hartwell, Lee *see* Hartwell, Leland H.
Hartwell, Leland H.
Harvard, Beverly Sep 97
Hasek, Dominik May 98
Haseltine, William A. Nov 98
Hashimoto, Ryutaro Feb 98
Haskell, Molly Nov 98
Hassan II obit Oct 99
Hastert, Dennis Apr 99
Hastert, John Dennis *see* Hastert, Dennis
Hatcher, Harlan obit May 98
Hatta, Mohammad obit Yrbk 91
Hauser, Philip M. obit Feb 95
Havel, Václav Aug 95
Hawes, Elizabeth obit Yrbk 91
Hawke, Ethan May 98
Hawkins, Erick obit Feb 95
Hawkins, Erskine obit Jan 94
Hayakawa, S. I. obit Apr 92
Haycraft, Howard obit Jan 92
Hayek, Friedrich A. Von obit May 92
Hayes, Denis Oct 97
Hayes, Helen obit May 93
Hayes, Peter Lind obit Jul 98
Hazzard, Shirley Jan 91
Healy, Bernadine P. Nov 92
Healy, Timothy S. Jan 93 obit Feb 93
Hearst, William Randolph, Jr. obit Jul 93
Heche, Anne Sep 98
Heckerling, Amy Jul 99
Heckscher, August obit Jun 97
Heilbrun, Carolyn G. Jan 93
Heinz, John obit May 91
Helfgott, David Mar 97
Helmsley, Harry B. obit Mar 97
Heloise Jun 96
Helprin, Mark Aug 91
Hemingway, Margaux obit Sep 96
Henderson, Joe Jun 96
Henner, Marilu Feb 99
Henreid, Paul obit Jun 92
Henry, David D. obit Nov 95
Henry, Marguerite obit Feb 98
Hensel, H. Struve obit Jul 91
Hepburn, Audrey obit Mar 93
Heppner, Ben Jan 97
Herbert, Bob Oct 98

Herlihy, James Leo obit Jan 94
Herman, Alexis M. Jan 98
Hernández, Livan Mar 98
Herrera, Carolina Mar 96
Hersey, John obit May 93
Hershey, Alfred D. obit Aug 97
Herzberg, Gerhard obit Jul 99
Herzog, Chaim obit Jun 97
Heyns, Roger W. obit Nov 95
Hiaasen, Carl Apr 97
Hickey, Margaret A. obit Feb 95
Highsmith, Patricia obit Apr 95
Higinbotham, William A. obit Jan 95
Hilfiger, Tommy Apr 96
Hill, Anita Sep 95
Hill, Benny obit Jun 92
Hillerman, Tony Jan 92
Hilliard, Harriet *see* Nelson, Harriet
Hillings, Patrick J. obit Sep 94
Hillis, Danny *see* Hillis W. Daniel
Hillis, Margaret (Eleanor) obit Apr 98
Hillis, W. Daniel Feb 95
Hills, Carla A. Mar 93
Hines, John Elbridge obit Oct 97
Hingson, Robert A. obit Jan 97
Hirt, Al obit Jul 99
Hiss, Alger obit Jan 97
Hitch, Charles J. obit Nov 95
Hitchens, Christopher Mar 99
Ho, David D. Jun 97
Hoad, Lew obit Sep 94
Hobby, Oveta Culp obit Oct 95
Hoch, Danny Oct 99
Hockenberry, John Oct 96
Hodgkin, Howard May 91
Hoffa, James P. Jul 99
Hoffman, Alice Sep 92
Hoffman, Dustin Jan 96
Hofstadter, Robert obit Jan 91
Hogan, Ben obit Oct 97
Hogan, Hulk Nov 98
Hoge, James F., Jr. Apr 98
Holbrooke, Richard C. Oct 98
Holifield, Chet obit Apr 95
Holland, Agnieszka Jan 98
Hollander, John Sep 91
Holley, Robert W. obit Apr 93
Holm, Hanya obit Jan 93
Holyfield, Evander Aug 93
Home, Alexander Frederick Douglas-Home, 14th Earl of obit Jan 96

Honecker, Erich obit Jul 94
Hooker, John Lee Nov 92
Hooks, Bell Apr 95
Hopkins, Anthony Mar 97
Horgan, Paul obit May 95
Hormel, James Oct 99
Horn, Roy Uwe Ludwig *see* Roy
Horner, James Mar 97
Horner, John R. Sep 92
Horst Jun 92
Horton, Mildred McAfee *see* McAfee, Mildred H.
Hosokawa, Morihiro May 94
Hou Hsiao-hsien Jul 99
Houphouët-Boigny, Félix Jul 91 obit Feb 94
Howard, John Mar 99
Howard, Ron Aug 95
Howe, Irving obit Jul 93
Howell, Wallace E(gbert) obit Sep 99
Howorth, Lucy Somerville obit Nov 97
Hrawi, Elias Feb 92
Hruska, Roman Lee obit Jul 99
Hsiao-ping, Teng *see* Deng Xiaoping
Huddleston, (Ernest Urban) Trevor obit Jul 98
Hudlin, Reginald May 99
Hudlin, Warrington May 99
Hudson, Charles L. obit Nov 92
Hudson, Jeffery *see* Crichton, Michael
Huebner, Robert J(oseph) obit Nov 98
Huerta, Dolores Nov 97
Huffington, Arianna Stassinopoulos Jul 98
Huggins, Charles B. obit Mar 97
Hughes, Harold E. obit Jan 97
Hughes, John Sep 91
Hughes, Richard J. obit Feb 93
Hughes, Ted obit Jan 99
Huizenga, H. Wayne Jan 95
Hull, Brett Feb 92
Humphry, Derek Mar 95
Hunt, Helen Nov 96
Hunt, James B., Jr. Jun 93
Hunt, Sir (Henry Cecil) John obit Jan 99
Hunter, Catfish obit Nov 99
Hunter, Holly Jul 94
Hunter, Jim *see* Hunter, Catfish
Hunter, Ross obit May 96
Husak, Gustav obit Jan 92

Hussein, King of Jordan obit
Apr 99
Husseini, Faisal al- Jan 98
Hutchison, Kay Bailey Sep 97
Hutton, Lauren Jul 94
Hynde, Chrissie Apr 93

Ice Cube Aug 95
Ice-T Sep 94
Idei, Nobuyuki Mar 97
Idol, Billy Jan 94
Iglesias, Enrique Apr 99
Il Sung, Kim see Kim Il Sung
Iman Jun 95
Imus, Don Feb 96
Indigo Girls see Ray, Amy
Indigo Girls see Saliers, Emily
Ionesco, Eugène obit Jun 94
Ireland, Patricia Jun 92
Irvan, Ernie Jul 98
Irwin, Margaret obit Yrbk 91
Irwin, Robert Jan 93
Isaacs, Susan Oct 93
Isaak, Chris May 93
Itami, Juzo obit Mar 98
Ives, Burl obit Jun 95
Ivey, Artis see Coolio
Ivey, John E., Jr. obit Aug 92
Ivey, Judith Jun 93
Izetbegović, Alija Aug 93

Jabbar, Kareem Abdul see
Abdul-Jabbar, Kareem
Jack, Homer A. obit Oct 93
Jackson, Bo Jun 91
Jackson, Janet Jun 91
Jackson, Jesse L., Jr. May 98
Jackson, Joe Feb 96
Jackson, O'Shea see Ice Cube
Jackson, Phil Jul 92
Jackson, Samuel L. Nov 96
Jackson, Shirley Ann Jul 99
Jacobs, Amos see Thomas,
Danny
Jacobs, Marc Feb 98
Jacobson, Leon obit Feb 93
Jaffe, Harold W. Sep 92
Jaffe, Susan Sep 97
Jagan, Cheddi obit May 97
Jagr, Jaromir Apr 97
Jamali, Mohd F. obit Aug 97
Janeway, Eliot obit Apr 93
Jansen, Dan Sep 94
Jarreau, Al Oct 92
Järvi, Neeme Nov 93
Jay, Ricky May 94
Jayewardene, J. R. obit Jan 97
Jefferson, Margo L. Jun 99
Jemison, Mae C. Jul 93
Jenkins, Lew obit Yrbk 91
Jerusalem, Siegfried Sep 92
Jett, Joan Sep 93

Jiang Qing see Chiang Ch'ing
Jiang Qing obit Jan 92
Jiang Zemin May 95
Jingsheng, Wei see Wei
Jingsheng
Jobim, Antonio Carlos Jul 91
obit Feb 95
Jobs, Steven Sep 98
John, John Pico obit Sep 93
Johnson, Bernice see Reagon,
Bernice Johnson
Johnson, Betsey Jan 94
Johnson, Beverly Sep 94
Johnson, Charles Sep 91
Johnson, Clarence L. obit Mar
91
Johnson, Davey Sep 99
Johnson, Frank M(inis) obit
Oct 99
Johnson, Jimmy Jul 94
Johnson, Joseph E. obit Jan 91
Johnson, Kathie Lee see
Gifford, Kathie Lee
Johnson, Keyshawn Oct 99
Johnson, Marguerite Annie
see Angelou, Maya
Johnson, Michael Jul 96
Johnson, Paul Sep 94
Johnson, Philip C. Nov 91
Johnson, Robert L. Apr 94
Johnson, U. Alexis obit Jun
97
Johnston, Lynn Feb 98
Jones, Bill T. Jul 93
Jones, Cherry May 98
Jones, Chuck May 96
Jones, David Robert see
Bowie, David
Jones, George Feb 95
Jones, James Earl Nov 94
Jones, Jerry May 96
Jones, Marion Oct 98
Jones, Roger W. obit Aug 93
Jones, Roy Jr. Feb 99
Jones, Sam Houston obit Yrbk
91
Jones, Tommy Lee Oct 95
Jong, Erica Apr 97
Jonsson, John Erik obit Nov
95
Jordan, Barbara C. Apr 93 obit
Apr 96
Jordan, I. King Jan 91
Jordan, Michael Feb 97
Jordan, Michael H. Feb 98
Jordan, Neil Aug 93
Jordan, Vernon E., Jr. Aug 93
Joseph, Keith obit Feb 95
Joseph, Lord see Joseph,
Keith
Joxe, Louis obit Jun 91
Juan Carlos, Count of
Barcelona obit Jun 93

Judd, Walter H. obit Apr 94
Judd, Wynonna see Wynonna
Judge Judy see Sheindlin,
Judith
Judge, Mike May 97
Julia, Raul obit Jan 95
Julia y Araelay, Raul Rafael
Carlos see Julia, Raul

Kabakov, Ilya Apr 98
Kadare, Ismail Feb 92
Kaganovich, Lazar M. obit
Sep 91
Kahane, Meir obit Jan 91
Kamali, Norma Nov 98
Kamprad, Ingvar Jun 98
Kanin, Garson obit Jun 99
Kanter, Rosabeth Moss Jun 96
Kantor, Michael see Kantor,
Mickey
Kantor, Mickey Mar 94
Kaplan, Joseph obit Nov 91
Kaplan, Justin Jul 93
Kappel, Frederick R. obit Jan
95
Kapuściński, Ryszard Sep 92
Karadžić, Radovan Oct 95
Karamanlis, Constantine see
Caramanlis, Constantine
Karamanlis, Konstantine see
Caramanlis, Constantine
Karmal, Babrak obit Feb 97
Karolyi, Bela Oct 96
Kasdan, Lawrence May 92
Kasem, Casey Nov 97
Kasich, John R. Aug 98
Katsh, Abraham I(saac) obit
Oct 98
Katz, Lillian Vernon see
Vernon, Lillian
Katz, Milton obit Oct 95
Katzen, Mollie Oct 96
Katzenberg, Jeffrey May 95
Kaufman, Irving R. obit Apr
92
Kavner, Julie Oct 92
Kawakubo, Rei Aug 99
Kazin, Alfred obit Aug 98
Kearns, Doris see Goodwin,
Doris Kearns
Keating, Paul May 92
Keaton, Diane May 96
Keaton, Michael Jun 92
Keeler, Ruby obit Apr 93
Keen, Sam Feb 95
Keenan, Mike Mar 96
Keene, Christopher obit Jan
96
Keeton, Kathy Sep 93 obit Jan
98
Keitel, Harvey Mar 94
Kell, Joseph see Burgess,
Anthony

Keller, Kasey Nov 98
Kelley, Clarence M. obit Nov 97
Kelley, David E. May 98
Kelley, Kitty Apr 92
Kelly, Edna F(lannery) obit Feb 98
Kelly, Eugene Curran *see* Kelly, Gene
Kelly, Gene obit Apr 96
Kelly, Jim Nov 92
Kelly, Nancy obit Mar 95
Kelly, Petra obit Jan 93
Kelly, R. Jun 99
Kelly, Robert *see* Kelly, R.
Kelly, Sharon Pratt Nov 92
Kemeny, John G. obit Feb 93
Kemmis, Daniel Oct 96
Kempner, Robert M. W. obit Oct 93
Kempton, Murray obit Jul 97
Kendrew, John C. obit Nov 97
Kennedy, David M. obit Jul 96
Kennedy, Jacqueline *see* Onassis, Jacqueline Bouvier Kennedy
Kennedy, John F., Jr. Jan 96 obit Sep 99
Kennedy, Nigel Jul 92
Kennedy, Paul Oct 93
Kennedy, Rose obit May 95
Kenny G *see* G, Kenny
Kerkorian, Kirk Mar 96
Kerr, Steve Oct 98
Kerr, Walter obit Jan 97
Kerrey, Bob Feb 91
Kerst, Donald William obit Oct 93
Kessler, David A. Sep 91
Kevorkian, Jack Sep 94
Khan, Chaka Jul 99
Khan, Michelle *see* Yeoh, Michelle
Khatami, Mohammad Apr 98
Khatami, Seyyed Mohammad *see* Khatami, Mohammad
Kiarostami, Abbas Jul 98
Kidman, Nicole Mar 97
Kienholz, Edward obit Aug 94
Kieślowski, Krzysztof May 95 obit May 96
Kiley, Richard obit May 99
Killanin, Michael Morris, 3d Baron obit Jul 99
Kilmer, Val Jan 96
Kim Il Sung Yrbk 94 obit Sep 94
Kim Jong Il Oct 99
Kim Sung Ju *see* Kim Il Sung
Kim Young Sam Jun 95

Kimball, Lindsley F. obit Oct 92
Kincaid, Jamaica Mar 91
King, John W. obit Nov 96
King, Mary-Claire Feb 95
Kingsley, Sidney obit May 95
Kingsolver, Barbara Jul 94
Kinsley, Michael May 95
Kintner, Earl W. obit Mar 92
Kirbo, Charles H. obit Nov 96
Kirby, George obit Jan 96
Kirby, Robert E. obit Mar 99
Kiriyenko, Sergei Aug 98
Kirk, Grayson L(ouis) obit Jan 98
Kirk, Russell obit Jun 94
Kirkland, (Joseph) Lane obit Oct 99
Kirkpatrick Miles W(ells) obit Jul 98
Kirshner, Sidney *see* Kingseley, Sydney
Kirstein, Lincoln obit Mar 96
Kirsten, Dorothy obit Jan 93
Kiss Apr 99
Kissin, Evgeny Nov 97
Kissin, Yevgeny *see* Kissin, Evgeny
Kistler, Darci Oct 91
Kitano, Takeshi Jul 98
Klass, Perri May 99
Klaus, Václav Nov 97
Kleiber, Carlos Jul 91
Klopsteg, Paul E. obit Jul 91
Kluge, John Sep 93
Knight, Frances G(ladys) obit Nov 99
Knight, Philip H. Aug 97
Knopfler, Mark Apr 95
Knudsen, Semon E(mil) obit Sep 98
Knussen, Oliver Feb 94
Knutson, Coya obit Jan 97
Koch, Bill Mar 99
Koch, William I. *see* Koch, Bill
Kohler, Foy D. obit Mar 91
Kollek, Teddy Mar 93
Komarovsky, Mirra obit Apr 99
Kopal, Zdeněk obit Aug 93
Kopple, Barbara Jul 98
Korth, Fred H. obit Jan 99
Kosinski, Jerzy obit Jul 91
Kotto, Yaphet Mar 95
Kouchner, Bernard Aug 93
Kozyrev, Andrei V. Sep 92
Krainik, Ardis Nov 91 obit Mar 97
Kramer, Larry Mar 94
Kraus, Alfredo obit Nov 99
Krauss, Alison May 97
Kravchuk, Leonid M. Jan 93

Kravitz, Lenny Apr 96
Krenek, Ernst obit Feb 92
Krick, Irving P. obit Sep 96
Kristol, William May 97
Kroft, Steve Nov 96
Krol, John Cardinal obit May 96
Kroll, Jules B. Feb 99
Kruger, Barbara Jul 95
Krzyzewski, Mike Jan 97
Kubelik, Rafael obit Oct 96
Kubly, Herbert obit Oct 96
Kubrick, Stanley obit May 99
Kuchel, Thomas H. obit Feb 95
Kuchma, Leonid Oct 97
Kudelka, James Mar 95
Kuhn, Irene obit Mar 96
Kuhn, Maggie obit Jul 95
Kukoc, Toni Jul 97
Kumaratunga, Chandrika Bandaranaike Jan 96
Kumm, Henry W. obit Mar 91
Kunstler, William M. obit Nov 95
Kuok, Hock Nien *see* Kuok, Robert
Kuok, Robert Jun 98
Kuok, Robert Hock Nien *see* Kuok, Robert
Kuralt, Charles obit Sep 97
Kureishi, Hanif Feb 92
Kurosawa, Akira Jul 91 obit Nov 98
Kurtz, Efrem obit Sep 95
Kusch, Polykarp obit May 93
Kushner, Harold S. Apr 97

L.L. Cool J Nov 97
Lagardère, Jean-luc Aug 93
Lagasse, Emeril May 99
Lake, Anthony Oct 94
Lalanne, Jack Oct 94
Lall, Arthur S(amuel) obit Jan 99
Lamb, Brian Feb 95
Lamont, Corliss obit Jul 95
Lamont, Norman Aug 92
Lancaster, Burt obit Jan 95
Land, Edwin H. obit May 91
Landon, Margaret obit Feb 94
Landon, Michael obit Sep 91
Landrum, Phil M. obit Jan 91
Lane, Burton obit Mar 97
Lane, Nathan Aug 96
Lang, Helmut Apr 97
Lang, K. D. Sep 92
Lange, John *see* Crichton, Michael
Lanier, Jaron Jun 97
Lansky, Aaron Jan 97
Lanting, Frans Nov 95

Lanusse, Alejandro Agustin obit Nov 96
Lapiere, Cherilyn *see* Cher
Largent, Steve Jun 99
Larson, Arthur obit May 93
Larson, Gary Feb 91
Lasch, Christopher obit Apr 94
Lasker, Mary obit May 94
Lasseter, John Jun 97
Latifah, Queen *see* Queen Latifah
Laughlin, James obit Jan 98
Lautenberg, Frank Jan 91
Lawrence, Geoffrey obit Yrbk 91
Lawrence, Martin Oct 99
Laxness, Halldór (Kiljan) obit Apr 98
Laybourne, Geraldine Apr 99
Layton, Joe obit Jul 94
Lazarus, Rochelle *see* Lazarus, Shelly
Lazarus, Shelly May 97
Le Duc Tho obit Jan 91
Le Gallienne, Eva obit Aug 91
Leach, Penelope Aug 94
Leakey, Mary obit Feb 97
Leakey, Richard Oct 95
Lean, David obit Jun 91
Lear, Frances Apr 91 obit Jan 97
Leary, Timothy obit Aug 96
Lecompte, Elizabeth Aug 97
Lee, Ang Mar 97
Lee, Henry C. Aug 96
Lee, J. Bracken obit Jan 97
Lee Kuan Yew Jan 95
Lee, Martin Jul 97
Lee, Robert E. obit Jun 93
Lee, Stan Aug 93
Lee Teng-hui Mar 96
Leese, Oliver obit Yrbk 91
Lefebvre, Marcel obit May 91
Léger, Paul-Émile obit Jan 92
Leguizamo, John Apr 98
Lehmann-Haupt, Hellmut E. obit May 92
Leiber, Judith Sep 96
Leibovitz, Annie Oct 91
Leigh, Jennifer Jason Aug 92
Leigh, Mike Jun 94
Leigh, W. Colston obit Sep 92
Leighton, Robert B. obit May 97
Leinsdorf, Erich obit Nov 93
Lemon, Ralph Feb 97
L'Engle, Madeleine Jan 97
Lenroot, Katharine F. obit Yrbk 91
Leonard, Bill obit Feb 95
Leonard, William A. *see* Leonard, Bill

Leonid Danilovich Kuchma *see* Kuchma, Leonid
Leontief, Wassily obit Apr 99
Lepage, Robert Apr 95
Lerner, Gerda Feb 98
Lerner, Max obit Aug 92
Leslie, Lisa Jan 98
Lessing, Doris Jan 95
Levay, Simon Oct 96
Levertov, Denise Aug 91 obit Mar 98
Levin, Ira Aug 91
Levitt, William J. obit Mar 94
Lévy, Bernard-Henri Nov 93
Levy, David Mar 98
Levy, David H. Jan 95
Levy, Marv Feb 98
Lewis, Carl Yrbk 96
Lewis, Claudius *see* Lewis, Lennox
Lewis, Henry obit Apr 96
Lewis, Juliette Feb 96
Lewis, Lennox Jan 99
Lewis, Loida Nicolas Apr 97
Lewis, Ramsey Oct 96
Lewis, Richard Jul 93
Lewis, Shari obit Oct 98
Leyland, Jim Nov 98
Li, Gong *see* Gong Li
Lichtman, Joseph *see* Layton, Joe
Lieberman, Joseph I. Jul 94
Liebermann, Rolf obit Mar 99
Lillehei, C(larence) Walton obit Nov 99
Lima, Ronaldo Luiz Nazario da *see* Ronaldo
Liman, Arthur L. obit Oct 97
Limann, Hilla obit Apr 98
Limbaugh, Rush Mar 93
Lin, Maya Apr 93
Lindfors, Viveca obit Jan 96
Lindgren, Astrid Oct 96
Lindley, Ernest K. obit Yrbk 91
Lindros, Eric Apr 98
Link, O. Winston Jun 95
Linnell, John *see* They Might Be Giants
Lionni, Leo Sep 97
Liotta, Ray May 94
Lipinski, Tara Apr 98
Lipsky, Eleazar obit Apr 93
Lithgow, John Nov 96
Litton, Andrew Sep 98
Lively, Penelope Apr 94
Livingston, John W. obit Aug 97
Lleras Restrepo, Carlos obit Nov 94
Loach, Ken Jul 95
Lobo, Rebecca Sep 97
Loeb, James I. obit Mar 92

Loftus, Elizabeth F. Jan 99
Logan, Harlan obit Mar 95
Long, Richard Sep 95
Long, Tania obit Jun 99
Longbaugh, Harry *see* Goldman, William
Lopez, Barry Jul 95
Lorentz, Pare obit May 92
Lortel, Lucille obit Jul 99
Lott, Ronnie Feb 94
Lott, Trent Sep 96
Louchheim, Katie obit Apr 91
Louis-Dreyfus, Julia Oct 95
Lovano, Joe Mar 98
Love, Courtney Jun 96
Love, George H. obit Sep 91
Love, Susan M. Oct 94
Lovelock, James Nov 92
Lovett, Lyle Sep 97
Lovins, Amory B. Jun 97
Lowe, Jack obit Aug 96
Lowey, Nita M. Sep 97
Loy, Myrna obit Feb 94
Lubic, Ruth Watson Sep 96
Lubovitch, Lar Mar 92
Lucas, Craig Sep 91
Lucas, John Oct 95
Luckman, Charles obit Apr 99
Ludwig, Daniel Keith obit Oct 92
Lukas, J. Anthony obit Aug 97
Lupino, Ida obit Oct 95
Luria, S. E. obit Apr 91
Lutoslawski, Witold Aug 91 obit Apr 94
Lutz, Robert A. Jan 94
Luzhkov, Yuri Nov 99
Lydon, John Nov 96
Lynch, Peter Nov 94
Lyne, Adrian Jan 94
Lynes, Russell obit Nov 91

Maathai, Wangari Sep 93
Macapagal, Diosdado obit Jul 97
MacArthur, Douglas, 2d obit Jan 98
MacDowell, Andie Nov 99
Machel, Graça Simbine Oct 97
MacIver, Loren obit Aug 98
MacKenzie, Warren Sep 94
MacKinnon, Catharine A. Jun 94
Mackintosh, Cameron Mar 91
MacLachlan, Kyle Aug 93
MacLennan, Hugh obit Jan 91
MacMurray, Fred obit Feb 92
Maddux, Greg Feb 96
Madigan, Edward R. Nov 92 obit Feb 95
Magaziner, Ira C. Apr 95

Maglie, Sal obit Feb 93
Maher, Bill Jul 97
Mahoney, John Aug 99
Major, John Apr 97
Makins, Roger obit Jan 97
Malick, Terrence Jun 99
Malle, Louis obit Feb 96
Mallory, L. D. obit Sep 94
Malone, John C. Aug 95
Malone, Karl Jan 93
Malott, Deane W. obit Nov 96
Mamet, David Mar 98
Mancini, Henry obit Aug 94
Mandela, Nelson Nov 95
Manessier, Alfred obit Oct 93
Mangione, Jerre obit Nov 98
Mankiewicz, Joseph L. obit Apr 93
Mankowitz, (Cyril) Wolf obit Aug 98
Manley, Michael obit May 97
Mann, Erica see Jong, Erica
Mann, Michael Jan 93
Mann, Thomas C. obit Apr 99
Manning, Ernest obit May 96
Manning, Peyton Sep 98
Manson, Marilyn May 99
Mantle, Mickey obit Oct 95
Manzù, Giacomo obit Mar 91
Marais, Jean obit Jan 99
Marble, Alice obit Mar 91
Marchais, Georges (René Louis) obit Jan 98
Marcus, Greil Oct 99
Marcus, Jacob R. obit Jan 96
Margulis, Lynn Jul 92
Mark, Herman F. obit Jun 92
Mark, Mary Ellen Sep 99
Mark, Rebecca May 99
Markey, Edward J. Nov 97
Markovic, Ante Nov 91
Marland, Sidney P., Jr. obit Jul 92
Marriott, Alice Lee obit May 92
Marrow, Tracy see Ice-T
Marsalis, Branford Sep 91
Marshak, Robert E. obit Feb 93
Marshall, Barry J. Sep 96
Marshall, David obit Feb 96
Marshall, E. G. obit Nov 98
Marshall, Garry Nov 92
Marshall, Lois obit May 97
Marshall, Penny May 92
Marshall, Susan Jul 99
Marshall, Thurgood obit Mar 93
Martin, Christy Oct 97
Martin, Dean obit Mar 96
Martin, Edmund F. obit Mar 93
Martin, Mary obit Jan 91

Martin, Paul obit Nov 92
Martin, Ricky Sep 99
Martin, William McChesney, Jr. obit Oct 98
Mary Alice Nov 95
Mary Kay see Ash, Mary Kay
Masekela, Hugh Mar 93
Masina, Guilia Anna see Masina, Guilietta
Masina, Giulietta obit Jun 94
Masserman, Jules H. obit Jan 95
Massey, Walter E. Jun 97
Mastroianni, Marcello obit Feb 97
Matalin, Mary Sep 96
Mathis, Johnny Feb 93
Matlin, Marlee May 92
Matola, Sharon Jun 93
Matsui, Robert T. Oct 94
Matthews, T. S. obit Mar 91
Mature, Victor obit Oct 99
Matzinger, Polly Oct 98
Maura, Carmen Apr 92
Mauriac, Claude Sep 93 obit Jun 99
Maw, Herbert B. obit Jan 91
Maxwell, Robert obit Feb 92
Maxwell, Vera obit Mar 95
May, John L. Jan 91 obit Jun 94
May, Rollo obit Jan 95
Mayer, Jean obit Feb 93
Mayle, Peter Oct 92
Maynard, Joyce Jan 99
Maynard, Robert C. obit Oct 93
Maynor, Dorothy obit May 96
Mazen, Abu see Abbas, Mahmoud
Mbeki, Thabo Aug 98
McAfee, Mildred H. obit Jan 95
McAlary, Mike obit Mar 99
McCaffrey, Barry R. Jul 97
McCarthy, Carolyn Mar 98
McClintock, Barbara obit Nov 92
McClinton, Katharine Morrison obit Mar 93
McCone, John A. obit Apr 91
McConnell, Joseph H. obit May 97
McCormick, Edward T. obit Oct 91
McCourt, Frank Feb 98
McCoy, Charles B. obit Mar 95
McCullough, David Jan 93
McCurry, Michael D. Nov 96
McDermott, Alice Sep 92
McDonagh, Martin Aug 98
McDonald, Audra Apr 99

McDonald, David L(amar) obit Mar 98
McDonald, Erroll Oct 99
McDonnell, Mary May 97
McDormand, Frances Sep 97
McDowall, Roddy obit Jan 99
McEntire, Reba Oct 94
McEwan, Ian Jul 93
McEwen, Terence A(lexander) obit Jan 99
McFarlane, Todd Feb 99
McGee, Gale obit Jun 92
McGill, William J(ames) obit Jan 98
McGinley, Laurence J. obit Oct 92
McGrath, Earl James obit Apr 93
McGwire, Mark Jul 98
McIntyre, Thomas J. obit Oct 92
McKinney, Cynthia A. Aug 96
McKissick, Floyd B. obit Jun 91
McKneally, Martin B. obit Aug 92
McLaren, Malcolm Aug 97
McLaughlin, Leo obit Nov 96
McMahon, Vince Feb 99
McMillan, Edwin M. obit Nov 91
McMillan, Terry Feb 93
McMillen, Tom Jan 93
McMurrin, Sterling M. obit Jun 96
McNair, Sylvia Nov 97
McNealy, Scott Apr 96
McNeill, Don obit Aug 96
McNichols, Stephen L. R. obit Feb 98
McPherson, James Alan Sep 96
McRae, Carmen obit Jan 95
Meadows, Audrey obit Apr 96
Mečiar, Vladimír Jul 94
Meeker, Mary Aug 99
Meisner, Sanford Apr 91 obit Apr 97
Mellon, Paul obit Apr 99
Menchú, Rigoberta Oct 93
Mendenhall, Thomas Corwin 2nd obit Sep 98
Menuhin, Yehudi obit Jun 99
Merchant, Ismail Mar 93
Mercouri, Melina obit May 94
Meredith, Burgess obit Nov 97
Meriwether, John Mar 99
Merrick, Elliott obit Jul 97
Merrill, James obit Apr 95
Messiaen, Olivier obit Jun 92
Messier, Mark Jul 95

Metheny, Pat May 96
Meyer, Ron Mar 97
Mfume, Kweisi Jan 96
Michaels, Lorne Aug 99
Michener, Daniel Roland obit
    Nov 91
Michener, James A(lbert) obit
    Jan 98
Middlecoff, (Emmett) Cary
    obit Nov 98
Midler, Bette Nov 97
Mifune, Toshiro obit Mar 98
Mikhalkov, Nikita Oct 95
Millar, Margaret obit Jun 94
Miller, Bebe Apr 99
Miller, Glenn obit Yrbk 91
Miller, Nicole Mar 95
Miller, Reggie Mar 96
Miller, Roger obit Jan 93
Miller, Shannon Jul 96
Miller, Zell Jul 96
Millett, John D. obit Jan 94
Millett, Kate Jun 95
Mills, Wilbur D. obit Jul 92
Milstein, Nathan obit Feb 93
Minor, Halsey Oct 98
Mirabella, Grace Oct 91
Mirren, Helen Jul 95
Mitchell, Joan obit Jan 93
Mitchum, Robert obit Sep 97
Mitford, Jessica obit Oct 96
Mittermeier, Russell A. Oct
    92
Mitterrand, François obit Mar
    96
Miyake, Issey Nov 97
Miyazawa, Kiichi Feb 92
Mizrahi, Isaac Jan 91
Mnouchkine, Ariane Mar 93
Mobutu, Joseph Désiré see
    Mobutu Sese Seko
Mobutu Sese Seko May 97
Molinari, Susan Mar 96
Mollenhoff, Clark R. obit May
    91
Mondavi, Robert Apr 99
Monk, Art Apr 95
Montana, Claude Jan 92
Montand, Yves obit Jan 92
Montenegro, Fernanda Oct 99
Montgomery, Deane obit May
    92
Montoya, Carlos obit May 93
Moon, Warren Nov 91
Moore, Archie obit Feb 99
Moore, Brian obit Mar 99
Moore, Demi 1993
Moore, Garry obit Jan 94
Moore, Julianne Oct 98
Moore, Michael May 97
Moore, Michael C. Aug 97
Morfit, Thomas Garrison see
    Moore, Garry

Morgan, Edward P. obit Mar
    93
Morgan, Henry obit Jul 94
Morgan, Lorrie Apr 99
Morgan, Thomas E. obit Oct
    95
Morini, Erica obit Jan 96
Morissette, Alanis May 97
Morley, Robert obit Aug 92
Morris, Earl obit Jul 92
Morris, Willie obit Oct 99
Morris, Wright (Marion) obit
    Jul 98
Morrison, Van Sep 96
Morse, David A. obit Mar 91
Morse, True D(elbert) obit
    Sep 98
Mortier, Gérard Jul 91
Morton, Joe Feb 99
Mosbacher, Emil, Jr. obit Nov
    97
Mosconi, Willie obit Nov 93
Moscoso, Teodoro obit Aug
    92
Moseley-Braun, Carol Jun 94
Mosley, Walter Sep 94
Moss, Cynthia May 93
Moss, John E(merson) obit
    Feb 98
Motherwell, Robert obit Sep
    91
Mowrer, Lilian Thomson obit
    Jan 91
Mudd, Emily H(artshorne)
    obit Jul 98
Muggeridge, Malcolm obit Jan
    91
Mukherjee, Bharati Apr 92
Muldoon, Robert D. obit Sep
    92
Muldowney, Shirley Oct 97
Mulligan, Gerry obit Mar 96
Mullis, Kary B. Feb 96
Murakami, Haruki Sep 97
Murdoch, Iris obit Apr 99
Muren, Dennis Mar 97
Murphy, Franklin D. obit Aug
    94
Murphy, George obit Jul 92
Murphy, Thomas F. obit Jan
    96
Murphy, W. B. obit Aug 94
Murray, Albert May 94
Murray, Arthur obit May 91
Murray, Elizabeth Apr 95
Murray, Patty Aug 94
Muskie, Edmund S. obit Jun
    96
Muster, Thomas May 97
Mwinyi, Ali Hassan Jun 95
Myers, Dee Dee Aug 94
Myers, Margaret Jane see
    Myers, Dee Dee

Myers, Mike Aug 97
Myers, Norman May 93
Myhrvold, Nathan Sep 97

Nabrit, James M(adison), Jr.
    obit Mar 98
Naifeh, Steven Mar 98
Nair, Mira Nov 93
Najibullah, Mohammed obit
    Jan 97
Narasimha Rao, P. V. see Rao,
    P. V. Narasimha
Naylor, Gloria Apr 93
Ndour, Youssou Jan 96
Nederlander, James Morton
    Apr 91
Neeson, Liam Nov 94
Neiman, Leroy Jul 96
Nelson, Harriet obit Jan 95
Nelson, Mrs. Ozzie see
    Nelson, Harriet
Nemerov, Howard obit Sep 91
Netanyahu, Benjamin Jun 96
Neumeier, John Jul 91
Neuwirth, Bebe Nov 97
Newley, Anthony obit Jul 99
Newton, Christopher Feb 95
Newton, Helmut Nov 91
Niarchos, Stavros obit Jun 96
Nichols, Mike Jan 92
Nicholson, Jack Apr 95
Nickerson, Albert L. obit Nov
    94
Niederland, William G. obit
    Oct 93
Nikolais, Alwin obit Jul 93
Nixon, Patricia obit Aug 93
Nixon, Richard M. Yrbk 94
    obit Jun 94
Nizer, Louis obit Jan 95
Nkomo, Joshua (Mqabuko
    Nyongolo) obit Sep 99
Noël Hume, Ivor Nov 97
Noble, Adrian Aug 99
Noor al-Hussein, Queen of
    Jordan Apr 91
Norodom Sihanouk see
    Sihanouk, Norodom
North, Oliver L. Mar 92
Novello, Antonia May 92
Novotna, Jarmila obit Apr 94
Nu, Thakin obit Apr 95
Nu, U see Nu, Thakin
Nur el Hussein see Noor al-
    Hussein
Nureyev, Rudolf obit Feb 93
Nuridsany, Claude Jun 97
Nutting, (Harold) Anthony
    obit May 99
Nye, Bill Jul 98
Nye, Russel B. obit Nov 93

Oaksey, Geoffrey Lawrence *see* Lawrence, Geoffrey
Oates, Joyce Carol Jun 94
Obasanjo, Olusegun Jul 99
O'Brian, Patrick Jun 95
O'Brien, Conan May 96
O'Brien, Dan Jul 96
O'Brien, Tim Aug 95
Obuchi, Keizo May 99
Ochoa, Severo obit Jan 94
O'Connor, Sinéad Jun 91
O'Donnell, Rosie Aug 95
O'Dwyer, (Peter) Paul obit Sep 98
Oe, Hikari May 99
Oe, Kenzaburo May 96
Oechsner, Frederick Cable obit Jun 92
Oettinger, Katherine Brownell obit Jan 98
O'Faoláin, Séan obit Jun 91
Ogata, Sadako Oct 97
Ogilvy, David M(acKenzie) obit Oct 99
Ohga, Norio Jun 98
Olajuwon, Hakeem Nov 93
Olav V, King of Norway obit Mar 91
Oldman, Gary Jan 96
O'Leary, Hazel R. Jan 94
Oliphant, Pat Jul 91
Olmos, Edward James Aug 92
Onassis, Jacqueline Bouvier Kennedy obit Jul 94
Ondaatje, Michael Oct 93
O'Neal, Frederick obit Oct 92
O'Neal, Shaquille Jul 96
O'Neil, Thomas F(rancis) obit Jun 98
O'Neill, Francis A., Jr. obit Mar 92
O'Neill, Gerard K. obit Jun 92
O'Neill, Thomas P., Jr. obit Mar 94
O'Neill, Tip *see* O'Neill, Thomas P., Jr.
Ongania, Juan Carlos obit Aug 95
Oort, Jan Hendrik obit Jan 93
Oosterbaan, Bennie obit Jan 91
Ormond, Julia Mar 99
Ornish, Dean Apr 94
Orowitz, Eugene Maurice *see* Landon, Michael
Osborn, Robert C. obit Feb 95
Osborne, John obit Feb 95
Osborne, Tom Mar 98
Osbourne, Ozzy Nov 98
Osmond, Donny Feb 98
Osterberg, James Newell *see* Pop, Iggy
Otter, Anne Sofie Von Sep 95

Ouédraogo, Idrissa May 93
Ovitz, Michael S. Oct 95
Owens, Dana *see* Queen Latifah
Oz, Frank Oct 99
Özal, Turgut obit Jun 93
Ozawa, Seiji Jul 98
Oznowicz, Frank *see* Oz, Frank

Pacciardi, Randolfo obit Jul 91
Packard, David obit Jun 96
Packard, Vance obit Feb 97
Page, Irvine H. obit Aug 91
Page, Robert Morris obit Jul 92
Page, Ruth obit Jul 91
Pagels, Elaine Hiesey Feb 96
Paglia, Camille Aug 92
Paine, Thomas Otten obit Jul 92
Pais, Abraham Jan 94
Pak, Se Ri Jan 99
Pakula, Alan J(ay) obit Feb 99
Palance, Jack Aug 92
Paley, William S. obit Jan 91
Palmieri, Eddie Jun 92
Pandit, Vijaya Lakshmi obit Feb 91
Panetta, Leon E. Jun 93
Panic, Milan Jun 93
Pantani, Marco Feb 99
Papadopoulos, George obit Sep 99
Papandreou, Andreas obit Sep 96
Papp, Joseph obit Jan 92
Parcells, Bill Apr 91
Paretsky, Sara May 92
Parizeau, Jacques Jul 93
Park, Thomas obit Jun 92
Parker, Alan Mar 94
Parker, Frank obit Oct 97
Parker, Robert B. Nov 93
Parker, Sarah Jessica Sep 98
Parker, Trey May 98
Parkinson, C. Northcote obit May 93
Parks, Bert obit Apr 92
Parks, Gordon Oct 92
Parks, Suzan-Lori Apr 99
Parnis, Mollie obit Sep 92
Parr, Albert Eide obit Sep 91
Parrish, Mrs. Wayne William *see* Knight, Frances G.
Parry, Albert obit Jul 92
Pärt, Arvo Feb 95
Pastrana Borrero, Misael obit Nov 97
Pataki, George E. Apr 96
Paterson, Chat obit May 92
Paterson, Katherine Nov 97

Patinkin, Mandy Jan 99
Patten, Chris Jul 93
Patterson, P. J. Feb 95
Patterson, Percival J. *see* Patterson, P. J.
Pauling, Linus C. Jun 94 obit Oct 94
Payne, Roger S. Jun 95
Payton, Nicholas Sep 99
Paz, Octavio obit Jul 98
Peabody, Endicott obit Feb 98
Peale, Norman Vincent obit Feb 94
Pearl, Minnie Nov 92 obit May 96
Peck, Gregory Oct 92
Peck, M. Scott Jun 91
Peña, Federico F. Oct 93
Penn, Sean Jun 93
Pennel, John obit Jan 94
Penney, William George obit May 91
Peppard, George obit Jul 94
Perelman, Ronald Owen Jan 91
Pérennou, Marie Jun 97
Peres, Shimon Mar 95
Perez, Rosie Sep 95
Perkins, Anthony obit Nov 92
Perkins, James A(lfred) obit Nov 98
Perot, H. Ross *see* Perot, Ross
Perot, Ross Yrbk 96
Perry, Anne Aug 96
Perry, Frank obit Nov 95
Perry, Harold R. obit Sep 91
Perry, William J. Jan 95
Pesci, Joe Mar 94
Peters, Tom Oct 94
Peterson, Esther (Eggertsen) obit Mar 98
Peterson, Roger Tory obit Oct 96
Petitpierre, Max obit Jun 94
Petronio, Stephen Mar 98
Petry, Ann obit Jul 97
Petty, Tom Nov 91
Pfeiffer, Eckhard Jun 98
Phan Dinh Khai *see* Le Duc Tho
Philbin, Regis Oct 94
Philbrick, Herbert A. obit Oct 93
Phillips, Caryl Jul 94
Phillips, Kevin Sep 94
Piazza, Mike Jul 99
Pickens, Jane obit Apr 92
Picon, Molly obit Jun 92
Piëch, Ferdinand Sep 99
Piercy, Marge Nov 94
Pile, Frederick Alfred obit Yrbk 91
Pileggi, Nicholas Jan 99

Pinay, Antoine obit Feb 95
Pineau, Christian obit Jun 95
P'ing, Lan *see* Chiang Ch'ing
Pinker, Steven A. Sep 98
Pinsky, Robert Feb 99
Piper, John obit Aug 92
Pipher, Mary Aug 99
Pippen, Scottie Mar 94
Pitino, Rick Jan 98
Pitt, Brad Mar 96
Plain, Belva Feb 99
Plant, Robert Oct 98
Plavsic, Biljana Feb 98
Pleasence, Donald obit Apr 95
Pleven, René obit Mar 93
Plotkin, Mark J. Jun 97
Plowden, David Feb 96
Pogrebin, Letty Cottin Nov 97
Pol Pot obit Jun 98
Polese, Kim Jul 97
Ponnamperuma, Cyril obit Mar 95
Pop, Iggy Jan 95
Popcorn, Faith Feb 93
Popović, Koča obit Jan 93
Popper, Karl Raimund obit Nov 94
Porter, Eliot obit Jan 91
Porter, Richard William obit Jan 97
Porter, Sylvia obit Aug 91
Posner, Richard A. Jan 93
Potter, Dennis Jul 94 obit Aug 94
Pousette-Dart, Richard obit Jan 93
Powell, J. Enoch obit Jun 99
Powell, Lewis F(ranklin), Jr. obit Nov 98
Powell, Mike Oct 93
Powers, J(ames) F(arl) obit Sep 99
Praeger, Frederick A. obit Aug 94
Pratt, Jane Jun 99
Prescott, Orville obit Jul 96
Preus, Jacob A. O. obit Oct 94
Prey, Hermann obit Oct 98
Price, Don K. obit Sep 95
Price, Nick Jun 96
Price, Richard Jan 94
Price, Vincent obit Jan 94
Primakov, Yevgeny Feb 99
Primus, Pearl obit Jan 95
Pritchett, V. S. obit Jun 97
Profet, Margie Nov 98
Protess, David Oct 99
Proulx, E. Annie Apr 95
Prusiner, Stanley Jun 97
Pucci, Emilio obit Jan 93
Puck, Wolfgang Jan 98

Puff Daddy *see* Combs, Sean "Puffy"
Puffy *see* Combs, Sean "Puffy"
Purcell, Edward M. obit May 97
Puryear, Martin Aug 99
Puzo, Mario obit Sep 99

Qaddafi, Muammar Al- Mar 92
Qing, Jiang *see* Chiang Ch'ing
Quadros, Janio Da Silva obit Apr 92
Quaison-Sackey, Alex obit Feb 93
Queen Latifah Feb 97
Quennell, Peter obit Jan 94
Quesada, Elwood Richard obit Apr 93
Quindlen, Anna Apr 93
Quine, W. V. Nov 99
Quine, Willard van Orman *see* Quine, W. V.
Quintero, José (Benjamin) obit May 99

Rabin, Yitzhak Jan 95 obit Jan 96
Rackmil, Milton R. obit Jan 92
Rae, Bob Feb 91
Raedler, Dorothy obit Feb 94
Rafael, Martos *see* Raphael
Rahman, Abdul, Prince obit Mar 91
Rainey, Froelich G. obit Jan 93
Rains, Albert McKinley obit May 91
Rainwater, Richard Apr 99
Ramaphosa, Cyril Sep 95
Ramos, Fidel Mar 94
Rampersad, Arnold Sep 98
Ramphele, Mamphela Jul 97
Rampling, Anne *see* Rice, Anne
Randolph, Jennings obit Jul 98
Rankin, J. Lee obit Sep 96
Rankin, Karl Lott obit Apr 91
Rao, P. V. Narasimha Jan 92
Raphael Aug 91
Raphael, Chaim obit Jan 95
Raskin, A. H. obit Feb 94
Rauh, Joseph L., Jr. obit Nov 92
Raven, Peter H. Feb 94
Rawl, Lawrence G. Feb 92
Ray, Amy Aug 98
Ray, Dixy Lee obit Mar 94
Ray, Satyajit obit Jun 92

Raye, Martha obit Jan 95
Raymond, Lee R. Nov 99
Reagan, Ron Feb 92
Reagon, Bernice Johnson Aug 99
Reasoner, Harry obit Oct 91
Reddy, N. Sanjiva obit Aug 96
Redman, Joshua Jan 97
Redstone, Sumner Jan 96
Reed, Margie Yvonne *see* Raye, Martha
Reed, Ralph Mar 96
Rees, Mina S(piegel) obit Jan 98
Reese, Harold *see* Reese, Pee Wee
Reese, Pee Wee obit Oct 99
Reeves, Keanu May 95
Reggio, Godfrey Jul 95
Reich, Robert B. Apr 93
Reichmann, Paul Jan 91
Reichstein, Tadeus obit Oct 96
Reid, Kate obit May 93
Reinhard, Johan Aug 99
Reiser, Paul Apr 96
Remick, Lee obit Sep 91
Remnick, David Oct 98
Renaud, Madeleine obit Nov 94
Rendell, Ed Apr 98
Rendell, Ruth Apr 94
Reno, Janet Sep 93
Rentzel, Delos Wilson obit Jan 92
Reshevsky, Samuel obit Jul 92
Reston, James obit Feb 96
Revelle, Roger obit Sep 91
Rey, Fernando obit May 94
Reynolds, Albert Sep 94
Reynolds, Albert Pierce *see* Reynolds, Allie
Reynolds, Allie obit Mar 95
Reza, Yasmina Sep 98
Rhone, Sylvia Jun 98
Riad, Mahmoud obit Mar 92
Ribicoff, Abraham A. obit May 98
Rice, Anne Jul 91
Rice, Greg obit Aug 91
Rich, Frank Apr 99
Rich, Louise Dickinson obit Jul 91
Richards, Ann Feb 91
Richards, Michael Nov 97
Richardson, Bill Apr 96
Richardson, Miranda Feb 94
Richardson, Tony obit Feb 92
Richmond, Mitch Jun 99
Richter, Sviatoslav obit Oct 97

Ridgway, Matthew B. obit
  Sep 93
Rifkind, Simon H. obit Jan 96
Riggio, Leonard Jun 98
Riggs, Bobby obit Jan 96
Riggs, Robert Larimore *see*
  Riggs, Bobby
Riley, Richard W. Oct 93
Rimes, LeAnn May 98
Rincón de Gautier, Felisa *see*
  Gautier, Felisa Rincón de
Ringgold, Faith Feb 96
Ripken, Cal, Jr. Jun 92
Ripley, Alexandra Mar 92
Ritchie, Dennis Mar 99
Ritt, Martin obit Feb 91
Rivkin, Dorothy Carnegie *see*
  Carnegie, Dorothy
Rizzo, Frank L. obit Sep 91
Robbins, Harold obit Jan 98
Robbins, Jerome obit Oct 98
Robbins, Tim Jul 94
Robbins, Tom Jun 93
Roberts, Cokie May 94
Roberts, Dennis J. obit Sep 94
Roberts, Julia May 91
Roberts, Marcus Mar 94
Robeson, Eslanda Goode obit
  Yrbk 91
Robinson, Arthur H. Mar 96
Robinson, David Jul 93
Robinson, Kim Stanley Nov
  98
Robinson, Mary Apr 91
Robinson, Randall Sep 98
Robinson, Spottswood
  W(illiam), 3d obit Jan 99
Roddick, Anita Sep 92
Rodin, Judith Jun 99
Rodman, Dennis Sep 96
Rodriguez, Andrés Sep 91
  obit Jun 97
Rodriguez, Cecilia May 99
Rodriguez, Robert Aug 96
Roebling, Mary G. obit Jan 95
Roeg, Nicolas Jan 96
Roehm, Carolyne Feb 92
Rogers, Ginger obit Jul 95
Rogers, Lynn L. Oct 94
Rogers, Roy obit Sep 98
Rogers, Will, Jr. obit Sep 93
Rollin, Betty Aug 94
Rolvaag, Karl F. obit Mar 91
Rome, Harold obit Jan 94
Romney, George obit Oct 95
Ronaldo Aug 98
Roosa, Robert V. obit Mar 94
Roosevelt, Anna C. Jun 97
Roosevelt, Elliott obit Jan 91
Roosevelt, James obit Nov 91
Root, Oren obit Mar 95
Roquelaure, A. N. *see* Rice,
  Anne

Rose, Charlie Jan 95
Rosen, Benjamin M. Jun 97
Rosen, Harold A. Jun 97
Rosenberg, Steven A. Feb 91
Rosenfield, Harry N. obit Aug
  95
Rosenman, Dorothy obit Mar
  91
Ross, Leonard Q. *see* Rosten,
  Leo
Rosten, Leo obit Apr 97
Rosten, Norman obit May 95
Rotblat, Joseph Jul 97
Roth, Ann Mar 97
Roth, Henry obit Jan 96
Roth, Philip May 91
Rothschild, Miriam Oct 92
Rotten, Johnny *see* Lydon,
  John
Roudebush, Richard L. obit
  Apr 95
Roueché, Berton obit Jul 94
Rountree, Martha obit Nov 99
Rountree, William M. obit Jan
  96
Rourke, Mickey Oct 91
Rouse, James W. obit Jun 96
Rowan, Chad *see* Akebono
Rowland, John G. Oct 97
Rowley, James J. obit Jan 93
Rowse, A(lfred) L(eslie) obit
  Jan 98
Roy Jan 98
Roy, Patrick Nov 99
Royko, Mike Jun 94 obit Jul
  97
Royster, Vermont C. obit Oct
  96
Rozelle, Pete obit Feb 97
Rózsa, Miklós Feb 92 obit Oct
  95
Rubin, Robert E. Jul 97
Rudolph, Paul obit Nov 97
Rudolph, Wilma obit Jan 95
Rugambwa, Laurian, Cardinal
  obit Feb 98
Rush, Kenneth obit Feb 95
Rusk, Dean obit Feb 95
Russert, Tim Oct 97
Russo, Rene Jul 97
Ryan, Meg May 99
Ryan, Thelma Catherine *see*
  Nixon, Patricia
Ryder, Winona Jun 94
Rysanek, Leonie obit May 98

Sabatini, Gabriela Jun 92
Sabin, Albert B. obit Apr 93
Sachar, Abram Leon obit Sep
  93
Sachs, Jeffrey D. Nov 93
Sadik, Nafis Feb 96
Sagan, Carl obit Feb 97

Sager, Ruth obit Jun 97
Salam, Abdus obit Jan 97
Salant, Richard S. obit Apr 93
Sales, Nykesha Jun 99
Saliers, Emily Aug 98
Salisbury, Harrison E. obit
  Sep 93
Salk, Jonas obit Aug 95
Salk, Lee obit Jul 92
Saloth Sar *see* Pol Pot
Salter, Andrew obit Jan 97
Saltzman, Charles E. obit Aug
  94
Samaranch, Juan Antonio Feb
  94
Sammartino, Peter obit May
  92
Sampras, Pete May 94
Samuel, Sealhenry *see* Seal
Samuelson, Joan Aug 96
Sanborn, David Aug 92
Sánchez, Arantxa *see* Sánchez
  Vicario, Arantxa
Sánchez Vicario, Arantxa Aug
  98
Sandage, Allan Jan 99
Sandberg, Ryne Nov 94
Sander, Jil Oct 97
Sanders, Barry Sep 93
Sanders, Bernard Jun 91
Sanders, Deion Jan 95
Sanders, Lawrence obit May
  98
Sandler, Adam May 98
Sanford, (James) Terry obit
  Jul 98
Sanford, John Elroy *see* Foxx,
  Redd
Santolalla, Irene Silva De obit
  Sep 92
Santos, José Edwardo Dos
  May 94
Saralegui, Cristina Jan 99
Sarbanes, Paul S. Jan 97
Sargent, Francis W(illiams)
  obit Jan 99
Sarnoff, Robert W. obit May
  97
Sarton, May obit Sep 95
Sasser, James R. Jul 93
Sassoon, Vidal Apr 99
Satcher, David Feb 97
Sauer, George obit Apr 94
Sauvé, Jeanne obit Mar 93
Savalas, Aristoteles *see*
  Savalas, Telly
Savalas, Telly obit Mar 94
Sawyer, Eddie obit Jan 98
Sawyer, John E. obit Apr 95
Sayão, Bidú obit Jun 99
Scali, John obit Jan 96
Scelba, Mario obit Feb 92

Schaefer, George (Louis) obit Jan 98

Schaefer, Vincent J. obit Sep 93

Schama, Simon Nov 91

Schapiro, Meyer obit May 96

Scheck, Barry Mar 98

Scheele, Leonard A. obit Mar 93

Scheffer, Victor B. Apr 94

Schell, Jonathan Jul 92

Scherbo, Vitaly see Shcherbo, Vitaly

Schiller, Karl obit Mar 95

Schlessinger, Laura Sep 97

Schlink, Frederick John obit Mar 95

Schmoke, Kurt L. Feb 95

Schneerson, Menachem M. obit Aug 94

Schneider, Alexander obit Mar 93

Schnittke, Alfred Jul 92 obit Oct 98

Schoonmaker, Thelma Mar 97

Schoonmaker-Powell, Thelma see Schoonmaker, Thelma

Schopf, J. William May 95

Schott, Marge Aug 99

Schottland, Charles I. obit Sep 95

Schrempp, Juergen Oct 99

Schröder, Gerhard Nov 98

Schultes, Richard Evans Mar 95

Schultz, Howard M. May 97

Schultz, Richard D. Jul 96

Schuman, William obit Apr 92

Schumann, Maurice obit Apr 98

Schumer, Charles E. Jul 95

Schwartz, Felice N. May 93 obit Apr 96

Schwarzenegger, Arnold Oct 91

Schwarzkopf, H. Norman May 91

Schwarzschild, Martin obit Jun 97

Schweitzer, Pierre-Paul obit Mar 94

Schwinger, Julian obit Sep 94

Scott, George C(ampbell) obit Nov 99

Scott, Hugh obit Sep 94

Scott, Raymond obit May 94

Scott, Ridley Oct 91

Scribner, Fred C., Jr. obit Apr 94

Seaborg, Glenn T. obit May 99

Seal Feb 97

Sebrell, W. H., Jr. obit Nov 92

Sedaris, David Jul 97

Segal, Bernard G. obit Aug 97

Seibert, Florence B. obit Oct 91

Seid, Ruth see Sinclair, Jo

Seinfeld, Jerry Aug 92

Selden, David (Seeley) obit Aug 98

Seldes, George obit Sep 95

Seles, Monica Nov 92

Selig, Allan H. see Selig, Bud

Selig, Bud Jan 99

Selzer, Richard Apr 93

Sembène, Ousmane Apr 94

Semon, Waldo Lonsbury obit Aug 99

Sen, Binay Ranjan obit Aug 93

Senghor, Léopold Sédar Jul 94

Sengstacke, John H. obit Aug 97

Sereno, Paul C. Jun 97

Serkin, Rudolf obit Jul 91

Seton, Anya obit Jan 91

Sevareid, Eric obit Aug 92

Shah, Idries obit Feb 97

Shaham, Gil Apr 97

Shalala, Donna Mar 91

Shalikashvili, John Nov 95

Shamir, Yitzhak Yrbk 96

Shanker, Albert obit May 97

Shannon, James A. obit Jul 94

Shapp, Milton J. obit Feb 95

Sharif, Mian Mohammad Nawaz see Sharif, Mohammad Nawaz

Sharif, Mohammad Nawaz Sep 98

Sharif, Nawaz see Sharif, Mohammad Nawaz

Sharpton, Al, Jr. Nov 95

Shaw, Bernard Feb 95

Shaw, Robert obit Apr 99

Shcherbo, Vitaly Jul 96

Shea, William A. obit Nov 91

Sheehy, Gail Jun 93

Sheindlin, Judith Sep 98

Shelby, Carroll Nov 93

Shelepin, Aleksandr obit Jan 95

Shelton, Henry H. Aug 98

Shelton, Hugh see Shelton, Henry H.

Shepard, Alan B(artlett) obit Sep 98

Sherrod, Robert obit May 94

Shevchenko, Arkady N(ikolayevich) obit May 98

Shilts, Randy Oct 93 obit May 94

Shirer, William L. obit Feb 94

Shirley, Donna Aug 98

Shoemaker, Eugene M. obit Oct 97

Shore, Dinah obit May 94

Short, Martin Sep 92

Shorter, Wayne Apr 96

Shortz, Will Apr 96

Shriver, Eunice Kennedy Jul 96

Shriver, Maria Nov 91

Shu-meng, Luan see Chiang Ch'ing

Shulman, Irving obit Jun 95

Sidney, Sylvia obit Sep 99

Siebert, Mickie see Siebert, Muriel

Siebert, Muriel Aug 97

Siegel, Bernie S. Jun 93

Siegfried Jan 98

Sihanouk, Norodom Aug 93

Siles Zuazo, Hernán obit Oct 96

Simkin, William E. obit May 92

Simmons, Adele Smith May 91

Simmons, Gene see Kiss

Simmons, Russell Jun 98

Simmons, Ruth J. Jan 96

Simms, Hilda obit May 94

Simms, Phil Oct 94

Simon, Claude May 92

Simon, Norton obit Aug 93

Simons, Elwyn L. Jun 94

Simpson, Adele obit Oct 95

Simpson, Alan obit Jul 98

Simpson, Carole Nov 99

Simpson, Milward L. obit Aug 93

Simpson, Mona Feb 93

Simpson, Valerie Apr 97

Sin, Jaime L. Sep 95

Sinatra, Frank obit Jul 98

Sinbad Feb 97

Sinclair, April Sep 99

Sinclair, Jo obit Jun 95

Singer, Isaac Bashevis obit Sep 91

Singer, Peter Mar 91

Singh, Giani Zail see Zail Singh

Singh, Sardar Swaran see Singh, Swaran

Singh, Swaran obit Jan 95

Singletary, Mike Mar 93

Singleton, John Feb 97

Sinise, Gary Apr 97

Sinopoli, Giuseppe Mar 91

Sinyavsky, Andrei D. obit May 97

Sirica, John J. obit Oct 92

Sister Wendy see Beckett, Wendy

Skelton, Red obit Nov 97
Skolnick, Mark H. Jun 97
Skutt, V. J. obit Apr 93
Slater, Rodney Jan 99
Slaughter, Louise M. Apr 99
Slayton, Donald K. obit Aug 93
Sleeper, Ruth obit Feb 93
Slonimsky, Nicolas Feb 91 obit Mar 96
Smallwood, Joseph R. obit Mar 92
Smith, Anna Deavere Sep 94
Smith, Austin E. obit Jan 94
Smith, B. see Smith, Barbara
Smith, Barbara Jul 98
Smith, Bruce Mar 95
Smith, Carleton Sprague obit Nov 94
Smith, Cyril Stanley obit Oct 92
Smith, Dean Apr 94
Smith, Emmitt Nov 94
Smith, Gerard C. obit Sep 94
Smith, Gregory White Mar 98
Smith, Hazel Brannon obit Jul 94
Smith, Hedrick Jun 91
Smith, James Todd see L.L. Cool J
Smith, Jeff Aug 91
Smith, Kevin Feb 98
Smith, Margaret Chase obit Aug 95
Smith, Mary Alice see Mary Alice
Smith, Mary Carter Feb 96
Smith, Mary Louise obit Nov 97
Smith, Merriman obit Nov 93
Smith, Oliver obit Mar 94
Smith, Ozzie Feb 97
Smith, Page obit Nov 95
Smith, Rosamund see Oates, Joyce Carol
Smith, Will Sep 96
Smith, William French obit Jan 91
Smoot, George Apr 94
Snell, George D. obit Aug 96
Snipes, Wesley Sep 93
Snow, Clyde Collins Apr 97
Snowe, Olympia J. May 95
Snyder, Peggy Lou see Nelson, Harriet
Snyder, Solomon H. Apr 96
Sobchak, Anatoly Jul 92
Soderbergh, Steven Oct 98
Soeharto Oct 92
Soldati, Mario obit Nov 99
Solti, Georg obit Nov 97
Somers, Jane see Lessing, Doris

Somes, Michael obit Feb 95
Sonnenfeld, Barry Nov 98
Sontag, Susan Feb 92
Sorel, Edward Mar 94
Soros, George Apr 97
Sorvino, Mira Aug 98
Sosa, Sammy May 99
Soth, Lauren K(ephart) obit Jun 98
Souter, David H. Jan 91
Spacey, Kevin Apr 97
Speare, Elizabeth George obit Jan 95
Spencer, Lady Diana see Diana, Princess of Wales
Spender, Stephen obit Sep 95
Sperry, Roger W. obit Jun 94
Sperti, George Speri obit Jul 91
Spiegelman, Art Mar 94
Spielberg, Steven Feb 96
Spilhaus, Athelstan (Frederick) obit Jun 98
Spinola, Antonio De obit Nov 96
Spitzer, Lyman, Jr. obit Jun 97
Spivak, Lawrence E. obit May 94
Spivakov, Vladimir Feb 96
Spock, Benjamin (McLane) obit Jun 98
Spofford, Charles M. obit May 91
Sprague, Robert Chapman obit Nov 91
Springsteen, Bruce Aug 92
Stader, Maria obit Aug 99
Staggers, Harley O. obit Nov 91
Stahl, Lesley Jun 96
Stahr, Elvis J(acob), Jr. obit Feb 99
Stallone, Michael Sylvester see Stallone, Sylvester
Stallone, Sylvester Feb 94
Stamos, Theodoros obit Apr 97
Stanky, Eddie obit Aug 99
Stanley, Paul see Kiss
Stans, Maurice H(ubert) obit Jun 98
Starr, Kenneth W. May 98
Starzl, Thomas E. Mar 93
Stassinopoulos, Arianna see Huffington, Arianna Stassinopoulos
Stavropoulos, George obit Feb 91
Steadman, Ralph May 99
Steber, Eleanor obit Jan 91
Steele, Shelby Feb 93

Steelman, John R(oy) obit Nov 99
Stegner, Wallace obit Jun 93
Steinberg, Saul obit Jul 99
Stennis, John C. obit Jul 95
Stephanopoulos, George Jan 95
Stern, Arthur Cecil obit Jul 92
Stern, David Apr 91
Stern, Howard Jan 96
Stern, Leonard Mar 91
Stern, Martha Dodd see Dodd, Martha
Stern, Richard Jun 94
Stevens, Edmund obit Jul 92
Stevens, Roger L(acey) obit Apr 98
Stevenson, Bryan Mar 96
Stevenson, McLean obit Apr 96
Stewart, James obit Sep 97
Stewart, Martha Aug 93
Stewart, Patrick Aug 94
Stickney, Dorothy obit Aug 98
Stigler, George Joseph obit Feb 92
Stignani, Ebe obit Yrbk 91
Stiller, Ben Nov 99
Stine, Jovial Bob see Stine, R. L.
Stine, R. L. Sep 99
Stipe, Michael Apr 97
Stockton, John Jun 95
Stockwell, Dean Feb 91
Stoddard, Alexandra Jun 96
Stokes, Carl B. obit Jun 96
Stone, Matt May 98
Stone, Sharon Apr 96
Stoph, Willi obit Aug 99
Storms, Harrison A., Jr. obit Sep 92
Storr, Anthony Jun 94
Storr, Charles Anthony see Storr, Anthony
Stowe, Leland obit Mar 94
Strasberg, Susan obit Apr 99
Stratton, Julius A. obit Aug 94
Stratton, Samuel S. obit Jan 91
Strauss, Robert S. Jul 92
Streep, Meryl Mar 97
Street, Picabo Apr 98
Streeter, Ruth Cheney obit Jan 91
Strehler, Giorgio Mar 91 obit Mar 98
Streisand, Barbra Sep 92
Strossen, Nadine Oct 97
Strouse, Norman H. obit Mar 93
Stuart, Gloria Apr 98

Studer, Cheryl Apr 92
Styne, Jule obit Nov 94
Suchocka, Hanna Jan 94
Suenens, Léon Joseph,
  Cardinal obit Jul 96
Sui, Anna Jul 93
Suits, Chauncey Guy obit Oct
  91
Sukarnoputri, Megawati Sep
  97
Sullivan, Walter obit Jun 96
Sulloway, Frank J. Sep 97
Sulzberger, Arthur O., Jr. Jan
  97
Sulzberger, C. L. obit Nov 93
Sumner, Jessie obit Oct 94
Sunderland, Thomas E. obit
  May 91
Suzuki, David T. Jul 95
Sveda, Michael obit Nov 99
Swann, Donald obit May 94
Swayze, Patrick Mar 91
Sweeney, John J. Jun 96
Swidler, Joseph C. obit Jul 97
Swoopes, Sheryl Jul 96

Taft, Robert, Jr. obit Feb 94
Tagliabue, Paul Oct 92
Tagliavini, Ferruccio obit Apr
  95
Takeshi, Beat see Kitano,
  Takeshi
Talbert, Billy obit Jun 99
Tamayo, Rufino obit Aug 91
Tambo, Oliver obit Jun 93
Tan, Amy Feb 92
Tanaka, Kakuei obit Feb 94
Tandy, Jessica obit Nov 94
Tannen, Deborah Jul 94
Tarantino, Quentin Oct 95
Tartikoff, Brandon obit Nov
  97
Tata, J. R. D. obit Jan 94
Taubman, A. Alfred Jan 93
Taubman, Howard obit Mar
  96
Tavener, John Jun 99
Taylor, Charles Sep 92
Taylor, Harold obit Apr 93
Taylor, Peter obit Jan 95
Taylor, Robert Lewis obit Jan
  99
Taylor, Susan L. Feb 97
Taylor, Telford obit Aug 98
Taymor, Julie Feb 98
Telkes, Maria obit Oct 96
Tenet, George J. Aug 99
Teng Hsi-hsien see Deng
  Xiaoping
Teng Hsiao-ping see Deng
  Xiaoping
Teng Wen-pin see Deng
  Xiaoping

Tennstedt, Klaus obit Mar 98
Ter-Arutunian, Rouben obit
  Jan 93
Teresa, Mother obit Nov 97
Terra, Daniel J. obit Sep 96
Terrell, St. John obit Jan 99
Terry, Randall A. Jan 94
Tesich, Steve Aug 91 obit Sep
  96
They Might Be Giants Nov 99
Thomas, Augusta Read Nov
  99
Thomas, Clarence Apr 92
Thomas, Danny obit Apr 91
Thomas, Dave see Thomas, R.
  David
Thomas, Elizabeth Marshall
  Mar 96
Thomas, Frank Aug 94
Thomas, Helen Nov 93
Thomas, Jess obit Jan 94
Thomas, Lewis obit Feb 94
Thomas, Michael Tilson see
  Tilson Thomas, Michael
Thomas, R. David Mar 95
Thompson, Emma Mar 95
Thompson, Fred Aug 99
Thompson, Kay obit Sep 98
Thompson, Kenneth Mar 99
Thompson, Paul W. obit May
  96
Thompson, Tommy G. Jul 95
Thorneycroft, Peter obit Aug
  94
Thorp, Willard L. obit Jul 92
Thurman, Robert A. F. Sep 97
Thurman, Uma Aug 96
Thurmond, Strom Nov 92
Tilberis, Elizabeth see
  Tilberis, Liz
Tilberis, Elizabeth see
  Tilberis, Liz
Tilberis, Liz Nov 98 obit Jul
  99
Tillinghast, Charles
  C(arpenter) obit Oct 98
Tilson Thomas, Michael Jun
  96
Timmerman, George Bell, Jr.
  obit Feb 95
Tinguely, Jean obit Oct 91
Tippett, Sir Michael (Kemp)
  obit Mar 98
Tipton, Jennifer Jul 97
Tobin, Richard L. obit Nov 95
Todd, Alexander obit Mar 97
Todd, Lord see Todd,
  Alexander
Tomba, Alberto May 93
Tompkins, Ewell see Ewell,
  Tom
Topping, Norman (Hawkins)
  obit Jan 98

Tormé, Mel obit Aug 99
Torre, Joe May 97
Torrence, Gwen Jul 96
Torrey, E. Fuller Jul 98
Torvalds, Linus Jul 99
Toscani, Oliviero Sep 97
Totenberg, Nina Mar 96
Tower, John G. obit Jun 91
Townsend, Robert May 94
Townsend, Robert (Chase)
  obit Mar 98
Trampler, Walter obit Jan 98
Travell, Janet G. obit Oct 97
Travers, P. L. May 96 obit Jun
  96
Travolta, John May 96
Tree, Marietta obit Oct 91
Trilling, Diana obit Jan 97
Troyanos, Tatiana obit Oct 93
Troyat, Henri Mar 92
Trudeau, Arthur Gilbert obit
  Aug 91
Trueblood, D. Elton obit Mar
  95
Tryon, Thomas obit Nov 91
Tsongas, Paul E. obit Mar 97
Tudjman, Franjo Sep 97
Tully, Alice obit Feb 94
Turabi, Hassan al- Jan 99
Ture, Kwame see Carmichael,
  Stokely
Turkle, Sherry Aug 97
Turnbull, Colin M. obit Sep
  94
Turner, Donald F. obit Sep 94
Turner, Lana obit Sep 95
Turner, Robert Edward 3d see
  Turner, Ted
Turner, Ted Jun 98
Turow, Scott Aug 91
Turrell, James May 99
Turturro, John Oct 96
Tuttle, Charles E. obit Aug 93
Tuttle, Merlin D. Jun 92
Tyler, Richard May 97
Tyler, Steven Aug 96
Tyner, McCoy Aug 97
Tyson, Laura D'Andrea Sep
  96

Uchida, Mitsuko Sep 91
Udall, Morris obit Mar 99
Ulanova, Galina (Sergeyevna)
  obit Jun 98

Van Damme, Jean-Claude Mar
  99
Van Duyn, Mona Jan 98
Van Fleet, James A. obit Nov
  92
Van Horne, Harriet obit Mar
  98

Van Peebles, Mario Nov 93
Van Sant, Gus Mar 92
Vandross, Luther Sep 91
Varmus, Harold E. Nov 96
Varnedoe, Kirk Feb 91
Vasarely, Victor obit May 97
Vega, Suzanne Aug 94
Velázquez, Nydia M. Jul 99
Venter, J. Craig Feb 95
Ventura, Jesse May 99
Verdi-Fletcher, Mary Jan 97
Vermeij, Geerat J. Jun 95
Vernon, Lillian Mar 96
Versace, Donatella Jun 98
Versace, Gianni Apr 93 obit
    Sep 97
Vicario, Arantxa Sánchez see
    Sánchez Vicario, Arantxa
Vieira Da Silva, Maria Helena
    obit 1992
Vincent, Fay May 91
Vine, Barbara see Rendell,
    Ruth
Viola, Bill May 98
Vogel, Paula Jul 98
Vogelstein, Bert Jan 96
Voigt, Deborah Jan 99
Voinovich, George V. May 97
Volpe, John A. obit Jan 95
Von Hayek, Friederich A. see
    Hayek, Friederich A. Von
Von Otter, Anne Sofie see
    Otter, Anne Sofie Von
Vonnegut, Kurt Mar 91
Voulkos, Peter Nov 97
Vrba, Elisabeth S. Jun 97

Wachner, Linda Nov 98
Wagner, Robert F., Jr. obit
    Apr 91
Waits, Tom Oct 97
Walcott, Joe obit May 94
Wald, George obit Jun 97
Walesa, Lech May 96
Walker, Eric A. obit Apr 95
Walker, John obit Jan 96
Walker, Larry May 98
Walker, Margaret obit Jun 99
Walker, Mildred obit Aug 98
Walker, Nancy obit May 92
Wallace, George C(orley) obit
    Nov 98
Waller, Robert James May 94
Wallerstein, Judith S. Nov 96
Walsh, Chad obit Mar 91
Walsh, Lawrence E. Oct 91
Walsh, William B. obit Mar
    97
Walton, Ernest T. S. obit Sep
    95
Walton, Sam Mar 92 obit May
    92

Warne, William E. obit May
    96
Warner, H. Ty see Warner, Ty
Warner, Ty Nov 98
Warren, Fletcher obit Mar 92
Washington, Alonzo May 99
Washington, Denzel Jul 92
Wasserman, Lew R. May 91
Waters, Maxine Nov 92
Watkins, Gloria see Hooks,
    Bell
Watson, Thomas J., Jr. obit
    Mar 94
Watts, J. C. Jr. Mar 99
Watts, Julius Caesar see
    Watts, J. C. Jr.
Waxman, Henry A. Jul 92
Wayans, Damon Nov 99
Wayans, Keenen Ivory Feb 95
Wayne, David obit Apr 95
Weaver, Robert C. obit Oct 97
Webb, James E. obit May 92
Webb, Wellington E. Aug 99
Wedgwood, C. V. obit May 97
Wegman, William May 92
Wei Jingsheng Sep 97
Weicker, Lowell P., Jr. May
    93
Weider, Joe Jan 98
Weidman, Jerome obit Jan 99
Weil, Andrew Aug 96
Weill, Sanford I. Jul 99
Weinstein, Bob Mar 97
Weinstein, Harvey Mar 97
Weiss, Ted obit Nov 92
Weld, William F. Feb 93
Welensky, Roy obit Feb 92
Welitsch, Ljuba obit Nov 96
Welk, Lawrence obit Jul 92
Wells, Julia Elizabeth see
    Andrews, Julie
Wellstone, Paul D. May 93
Welsh, Irvine Nov 97
Welsh, Matthew E. obit Aug
    95
Werblin, David A. obit Feb 92
Wertheimer, Linda Nov 95
West, Cornel Oct 93
West, Dorothy Feb 97 obit
    Oct 98
Weston, Brett obit Mar 93
Westwood, Vivienne Jul 97
Wexler, Nancy S. Aug 94
Wexner, Leslie Feb 94
Whelan, Wendy Oct 98
Whitaker, Forest Feb 97
White, Edmund Jan 91
White, Michael R. Mar 99
White, Reggie Nov 95
White, William S. obit Jun 94
Whitelaw, William (Stephen
    Ian) obit Nov 99

Whitman, Christine Todd Jun
    95
Whittle, Christopher Feb 91
Whittle, Frank obit Oct 96
Whyte, William H. Jr. obit
    Mar 99
Wickens, Aryness Joy obit
    Apr 91
Wideman, John Edgar Jan 91
Widnall, Sheila E. Oct 97
Wiesner, Jerome B. obit Jan
    95
Wiest, Dianne Mar 97
Wigner, Eugene P. obit Mar
    95
Wilbur, Dwight L. obit May
    97
Wildmon, Donald Jan 92
Wiles, Andrew J. Mar 96
Wilkens, Lenny Jul 96
Wilkins, Dominique May 95
Wilkins, Roger Aug 94
Wilkinson, Bud see
    Wilkinson, Charles
Wilkinson, Charles obit May
    94
Willes, Mark H. Mar 98
Williams, Anthony A. Oct 99
Williams, Brian Jul 98
Williams, Doug Feb 99
Williams, Errick see
    Williams, Ricky
Williams, Hank, Jr. Mar 98
Williams, Jody Mar 98
Williams, Joe obit Jun 99
Williams, John A. Oct 94
Williams, Lucinda Mar 99
Williams, Myrna see Loy,
    Myrna
Williams, Ricky Aug 99
Williams, Robin Jan 97
Williamson, Marianne Feb 93
Willis, Kelly Oct 99
Wilmut, Ian Jun 97
Wilson, A. N. Aug 93
Wilson, Angus obit Aug 91
Wilson, Cassandra Mar 98
Wilson, Don obit Yrbk 91
Wilson, Edward Foss obit
    May 94
Wilson, Flip obit Feb 99
Wilson, Harold obit Jul 95
Wilson, James Harold see
    Wilson, Harold
Wilson, John Burgess see
    Burgess, Anthony
Wilson, John Tuzo obit Aug
    93
Wilson, Logan obit Jan 91
Wilson, O(wen) Meredith obit
    Feb 99
Wilson, Pete Apr 91
Wilson, William Julius Feb 97

Wilt, Fred obit Nov 94
Winpisinger, William
  W(ayne) obit Feb 98
Wirth, Conrad L. obit Sep 93
Wirth, Timothy E. Mar 91
Witten, Edward Jun 97
Witz, Chaim *see* Kiss
Wofford, Harris Apr 92
Wolf, Naomi Nov 93
Wolfe, George C. Mar 94
Wolfert, Ira obit Feb 98
Wolff, Geoffrey Jan 97
Wolff, Tobias Jan 96
Wong Kar-Wai Apr 98
Woo, John Feb 99
Woodard, Alfre Feb 95
Woods, Eldrick *see* Woods,
  Tiger
Woods, Tiger Nov 97
Woodward, Stanley obit Oct
  92
Wörner, Manfred obit Oct 94
Worsham, Lew obit Jan 91
Worthington, Leslie B(erry)
  obit Oct 98
Wozniak, Stephen Jul 97
Wright, Helen obit Feb 98
Wright, Irving S(herwood)
  obit Mar 98
Wright, Jerauld obit Jul 95
Wright, Peter obit Jul 95
Wu, Chien Shiung obit Apr
  97
Wu, Gordon Sep 96
Wu, Harry Feb 96
Wu, Peter Hongda *see* Wu,
  Harry
Wyatt, John Whitlow obit
  Nov 99

Wyatt, Wilson W. obit Aug 96
Wynder, Ernest L. obit Sep 99
Wynette, Tammy Jun 95 obit
  Jun 98
Wynonna May 96

Xenakis, Iannis Sep 94
Xiaoping, Deng *see* Deng
  Xiaoping

Yamaguchi, Kristi Jun 92
Yamanaka, Lois-Ann Jun 99
Yang, Jerry Oct 97
Yankovic, Alfred *see*
  Yankovic, "Weird Al"
Yankovic, "Weird Al" Feb 99
Yarborough, Ralph W. obit
  Apr 96
Yassin, Ahmed Jul 98
Yates, Sidney R. Aug 93
Yearwood, Patricia Lynn *see*
  Yearwood, Trisha
Yearwood, Trisha Jul 98
Yegorov, Boris obit Nov 94
Yeoh Chu-Kheng *see* Yeoh,
  Michelle
Yeoh, Michelle Jan 98
Yepes, Narciso obit Jul 97
Yerby, Frank obit Mar 92
Yergin, Daniel Nov 99
Yevtushenko, Yevgeny Mar
  94
Yimou, Zhang *see* Zhang
  Yimou
Yokich, Stephen P. Nov 98
Yorty, Sam(uel William) obit
  Aug 98

Young, Coleman (Alexander)
  obit Feb 98
Young, Neil Jan 98
Young, Robert obit Sep 98
Young, Steve Oct 93
Youngman, Henny obit May
  98
Yount, Robin Jun 93
Youskevitch, Igor obit Aug 94
Yun-ho, Li *see* Chiang Ch'ing

Zaentz, Saul Mar 97
Zail Singh obit Mar 95
Zamora, Rubén Sep 91
Zappa, Frank obit Feb 94
Zedillo Ponce De León,
  Ernesto Apr 96
Zemeckis, Robert Sep 97
Zemin, Jiang *see* Jiang Zemin
Zhang Yimou Aug 92
Zhirinovsky, Vladimir Nov 95
Zhivkov, Todor obit Oct 98
Zim, Herbert S. obit Feb 95
Zimmerman, Robert *see*
  Dylan, Bob
Zinn, Howard Aug 99
Zinnemann, Fred obit Jun 97
Ziskin, Laura Oct 97
Zolotow, Maurice obit May
  91
Zorbaugh, Geraldine B. obit
  Sep 96
Zorn, John Aug 99
Zsigmond, Vilmos Oct 99
Zubrod, C. Gordon obit Jul 99
Zuckerman, Solly obit May
  93
Zyuganov, Gennadi A. Oct 96